INQUIRY
AND
EXPRESSION

A
COLLEGE
READER

INQUIRY

HOLT, RINEHART AND WINSTON

NEW YORK—CHICAGO—SAN FRANCISCO—TORONTO

AND
A COLLEGE READER
EXPRESSION
✸ REVISED EDITION

Harold C. Martin, HARVARD UNIVERSITY

Richard M. Ohmann, WESLEYAN UNIVERSITY

❖ *Preface to the Second Edition*

ALTHOUGH THE PLAN and substance of the first edition of this book appear to have satisfied users, we welcome the opportunity for revision on two scores. First, revision makes possible correction of errors that readers have called to our attention, and, second, it gives us a chance to make some substitutions that we believe will strengthen the book. All told, we have replaced six groups with others chosen to provide sharper focus or greater interest, and we have made substitutions within six additional groups. More often than not, the selections new to this edition are of more recent writing than those they replace, though we have taken care to avoid substance that is merely topical and style that sacrifices meaning to fashion.

HAROLD C. MARTIN

RICHARD M. OHMANN

January 1963

❋ *Preface to the First Edition*

LIKE MOST ANTHOLOGIES for courses in exposition, this volume is the result
of several years of trial and error in a particular situation. Out of our
experimentation there grew, for those of us most concerned with its methods
and results, a strong conviction that the surest means of helping students to
improve their writing is to make a direct attack on the problems they meet
in dealing with the complex, and generally new, matters they encounter in
their freshman year. For many, indeed for most, the world expands at a
startling rate in the months between September and June of that first year;
but the wonder of the new horizons is somewhat dimmed by frustration. A
few, of course, can work their way alone out of confusion and into control
of their new experiences. Most need the help of carefully planned and
thoroughly disciplined instruction if they are to profit early from the new
oceans that meet their astonished gaze.

Even a cursory glance at the table of contents for this volume will show
that we have a rationale for the course from which the book derives. For the
sake both of efficiency and of economy in time, we have chosen to make the
work of the first semester (the part of the book entitled "The Processes of
Inquiry") clearly analytic in method and in content. Students are deeply
interested in ideas, even though they seldom know how to use the tools that
will give them power to treat ideas soberly. We have found in the analysis
and development of definitions, of assertions, and of proof a rigorous and
challenging means of exploiting this natural interest and, at the same time,
of giving students the apprenticeship in reflection which most of them need.
The selections in the first part of the book are grouped with an eye both to a
single focus of subject matter and to an analytic procedure. Where courses
have abundant time, the "gatherings" provide plentiful matter for discussion
of the ideas themselves; where time is limited, they provide emphasis on
a single tool of analysis sharp enough to demonstrate its various uses in
small compass.

The second part of the book (that entitled "The Means and Modes of
Expression") deals in roughly the same manner with skills in rhetoric.
Where unity of subject matter could be achieved only at considerable
expense to accuracy of demonstration, we have not hesitated in this
section to abandon the former. In most instances, however, we have been

vii

able to join the two as we did in the first section. The order of rhetorical considerations, like that of logical considerations in the first part, is dictated not by primacy of importance so much as by suitability to the needs and states of readiness of students. Necessarily, the materials of this part of the book are more "literary" than those of the first, and this we have found to be pleasing to most students. After one term's immersion in ideas, they are eager to think about the means by which they can fully express and control their experience in writing and also to find opportunity for experiment and imitation in matters of style.

If it be objected that this division of "ideas" and "style" is entirely artificial, we can only reply that it is indeed. But classroom teaching is itself an artificial affair, and the argument should be not about such terms as "organic" and "bifurcated" but about the character and quality of the artifice employed. Certainly *le style est l'homme même* but, just as certainly, one improves by piecemeal learning rather than by sudden and total transformation. To divide the various jobs connected with teaching students to write well is, then, nothing more than to do what must be done in fact, whatever theory says to the contrary.

One word may be added about the selections themselves. Although they are not all of the same quality, none—we believe—is likely to deprave the student's taste or corrupt his mind. They represent the labors of serious men working out the serious matters of their own lives in ways which they respect. To study the writing of such men is itself worth while, however diverse their opinions, however suspect their means. The danger is not that a collection of readings will be too dangerous or too difficult for students but that it will not do justice to their hunger for ideas and for rich forms of expression. That danger we have tried hard to avoid.

At any early stage in the preparation of this book we solicited criticism from teachers in colleges of varied size, character, and location, and to these teachers we are deeply indebted for suggestions which have substantially improved the text. We wish to give particular thanks for this help to Professors George Gibian, of Smith College; Edward Stone, of the University of Virginia; G. Ferris Cronkhite, of Cornell University; John E. Jordan, of the University of California at Berkeley; Martin Steinmann, Jr., of the University of Minnesota; Seymour Betsky, of Montana State University; Dolora Cunningham, of Harpur College; and Richard Bozorth, of the University of Pennsylvania.

HAROLD C. MARTIN
RICHARD M. OHMANN

Cambridge, Massachusetts
October 1957

viii

✿ Contents

PART ONE · THE PROCESSES OF INQUIRY

ix

xiii

xiv

INQUIRY
AND
EXPRESSION

A
COLLEGE
READER

THE
PROCESSES OF
INQUIRY

* PART I

* Defining

DEFINING IS CLOSELY ASSOCIATED with what we presume must have been one of the earliest uses of language: naming. To name a thing is to give it an identity, to separate it from the mass of things around it. To define a thing is to signalize and describe its identity. Definition is, therefore, fundamentally a purifier of experience and of language. Without it, man would have little control over the world he inhabits. Yet, fundamental as the process of defining is to all intellectual activity, it is far from simple or well understood, and discussion of it continues to preoccupy philosophers, metaphysicians, and epistemologists as well as logicians.

One of the questions often argued by those interested in definition is this: when we define, what is it we define—words only, or things themselves? To use the technical terminology of the argument, are definitions *nominal*, or *real*, or both? Now it is clear that for most of our defining we use symbols of some kind, usually words; and, since in designating the object-to-be-defined we designate it by words and then define it with words, it is clear that at least a part of our defining is a defining of words—is, in other words, nominal definition. It is this defining of words by other words that gives rise to the charge of circularity in definition. One good standard abridged dictionary defines "behavior" as "conduct" and "conduct" as "personal behavior." The dictionary goes on to add other more or less synonymous expressions, of course, but the circularity of the process is inevitable. Dr. Samuel Johnson, maker of the first great dictionary of the English language, commented that the only way to solve the dilemma of circularity is to leave some words undefined, treating them as though their meanings are independent propositions, like the "given" in a theorem in geometry. The kind of circularity here referred to is not, however, very serious in practice; definitions are made, more often than not, for people who already have a fair command of language and are therefore helped rather than frustrated by simple synonymy. Nonetheless, if all definitions are nominal, the theoretical problem of circularity seems to be unsolvable.

The problem of *real* definition is even more intricate because it involves the nature of the relationship between words and the objects, events, situations, concepts and so on to which they refer. Put in simple language, the problem can be stated in this way: when you ask for the meaning, let us say, of "justice," are you asking someone to state all the ways in which

3

the word "justice" is used, or are you asking him to indicate the nature of some entity, justice, which you assume to have a real existence? Even when the question does not concern an abstract word, the same problem arises: does a definition of "chair" have to do with all the possible (and perhaps nonexistent) entities which may be referred to by that word, and therefore to the nature of the word rather than to the nature of the object, or to some ideal entity to which, regardless of accidental attributes, the word "chair" always refers? In brief, is there such a thing as a *real* definition? One of the most recent examinations of the subject concludes, after one hundred and fifty pages of careful analysis, that "the notion of real definition is a confusion of at least . . . twelve activities" and then goes on to enumerate such activities as searching for essences, searching for a cause, adopting and recommending ideals, abstracting, analyzing, and so on.*

The matter is not simply one of academic hairsplitting: if there is no single entity to which "justice" or "chair" can refer, then it may be argued that attempts to define "justice" or "chair" in anything other than a nominal sense are futile and, therefore, that definitions should be taken as saying something not about reality but only about the symbols in which reference to reality is conventionally made.

It is not possible to pursue the argument here, nor is it necessary. Men have to define in order to manage the world and themselves, and by and large they do their defining with the conviction that, for their purposes, the approximations they achieve are efficient means for dealing with the realities of their own existence. They know that their definitions may never be exact, but they have to assume that the definitions point to, and describe, not simply words but things *out there,* the real "facts" of experience. At the same time, they show their suspicion of any foolproof method of defining by the variety of methods of definition they use. Few writers are concerned with achieving a strictly logical definition, anyway; what they want is a definition which, by whatever means seem necessary, will successfully fence in what is relevant and fence out what is not, or a definition which will successfully suggest the range of relevance for the term to be defined. To build those fences or to suggest those areas of relevance, they may use, in a single exercise in definition, a half-dozen different procedures, relying on one to fill the gaps left by another and trusting to the combination for a total impression sufficiently strong and clear to bring about communication between the definer and the person for whom the definition is created. Considering the energy writers spend and the ingenuity they exercise in defining, it is important to remember that in many, and perhaps in most, instances the act of defining is self-instructive; that the definer and the person for whom the definition is made are one and the same; in short that definition is a principal procedure in inquiry.

An extended definition, or attempt to inquire into the nature of some-

* Richard Robinson, *Definition* (New York, Oxford University Press, 1950).

thing, is almost sure to include an analysis of the Aristotelian kind, a classification by likenesses and differences. First, the object referred to by the word (Aristotle apparently thought of the analytic definition as "real") is associated with others of like kind ("hatred" with "love" and "fear" as examples of the class or genus "emotion") and then it is distinguished from others in the genus by noting those characteristics peculiar to it alone (differentiae). For fencing in and fencing out, this is as satisfactory a procedure as has been so far developed. Its weakness is only that common to all systems of classification, primarily the weakness of dividing an integrated world into convenient parts and thereby postulating a separatedness and separability that do not and cannot exist. To supplement this analytic definition and perhaps, in some sense, to restore vitality which analysis tends to diminish or destroy, writers commonly use examples, illustrations (verbal and other), anecdotes, and stories. Or they may define by pointing to *un*suitable equivalences. Frequently they avoid the formal pattern of definition altogether by the simple device of using the term to be defined in a number of contexts. In practice, one activity is likely to run into another, a matter of no great concern to the writer unless such fusion or duplication leads him to contradict himself or to become so ambiguous that his definitions never really define after all.

Quite as important as the procedures of definition for anyone who is concerned with thought and language are the uses of definition. The one to which most of this discussion has relevance is that of speculation or inquiry, of finding out and demonstrating the nature of something (whether of a term or a thing is not important at this juncture). Some defining—most dictionary defining, in fact—is less concerned with inquiry than with providing a survey of accepted meanings and forms of a word; depending on their length and the quality of their lexicography, dictionaries record not only the various meanings current for a word, but meanings no longer current, as well. And some defining is quite clearly used to prescribe one particular sense in which a word is to be understood. Such "stipulative" definition is of great value for efficient and rigorous work in every discipline despite its inevitable weakness: formal, rational agreement to use a word in only one limited sense does not always silence other, and perhaps more conventional or more impressive, meanings to which we are accustomed. Humpty Dumpty defined "glory" as "a nice knockdown argument," but the most docile Alice in the world would have had a hard time making it mean that and nothing else in her conversations with the stipulative Humpty.

These three uses of definition—to stipulate a restricted meaning, to describe historical and current meanings, and to speculate about the nature of a word or a thing—do not exhaust the possibilities, but they are sufficient to illustrate the complexity and importance of this activity of the rational intellect. The challenge to define is always before the writer; he may scorn it, denounce it, resist or mock it, but he cannot escape it. The entire process of coming-to-know, in so far as it makes use of language, as it generally does, depends upon initial and ultimate acts of definition. And communication is unthinkable without it.

THE MEANING OF OWNERSHIP

THE NOTION OF PROPERTY is a puzzling one, in spite of its familiarity and in spite of the central place it occupies in our economic ideology. It is simple enough to say that a man owns what he pays for, earns, or is given, and such a rule of thumb is sufficient to settle most questions of ownership. But theorists have felt a need to go further and have contested the common-sense view of property on at least two grounds. In the first place, though all may agree that Smith owns the small section of suburbia on which his house rests, the origin of his property rights is more dubious. Perhaps his great-grandfather settled the plot and thus acquired it from the government by putting labor into it. But by what devious means did the government get the land from the aborigines? And what right did the Indians have to it? This inquiry must finally lead to an a priori principle, a claim that discovery, for example, or labor, or force, or proximity is the ultimate ground for ownership of property. A second type of attack on the common-sense idea of ownership lays siege not to Smith's historical rights, but to his present status as proprietor. Does he really own his standardized home, or does ownership involve more than merely a legal title? Some have argued that psychological control, responsibility, or other intangibles are essential to real possession of property. Either sort of attack builds largely on definition: the first involves definitions of the original nature of property, and the second deals with the inadequacy of present definitions.

It will be well, then, in reading the selections below, to keep in mind the various types and uses of definition. One type of definition we have called "stipulative." A man who writes, "the term 'property' should be used to refer only to artificial goods" is trying to require people to use words in a certain fashion (and few would agree with him here). On the other hand, a writer who makes a thorough examination of what and how people own, and bases his definition on this inquiry, is engaged in "real definition"; he is primarily describing. A third approach is that used in the dictionary; it involves collecting and analyzing actual occurrences of the word "property" in an effort to find out how the word is, in fact, used. And a fourth way of defining appears in this statement: "True property is that conse-

crated to God's service." This sort of definition is sometimes called "persuasive." (Of course, all definitions are at least partly persuasive.) Its main purpose is not to describe property or uses of the word, but to persuade the reader to consecrate his property to God, if he really wishes to own it. There are many other aims which motivate definition, but these four are enough to watch for in this unit.

The authors represent varied backgrounds. John Locke (1632-1704) was one of England's greatest philosophers and political scientists. Pierre Joseph Proudhon (1809-1865) was a French revolutionary socialist and political writer. The essays of Englishman Eric Gill (1882-1940) frequently reflect his status as an important Catholic layman, as well as his profession, stone carving and wood engraving. Herman Melville (1819-1891) is familiar as the author of Moby Dick, from which our selection is taken. Richard Neutra (1892-   ) is an Austrian-born architect who has taught in a number of American universities.

OF PROPERTY | JOHN LOCKE

Whether we consider natural reason, which tells us, that men, being once born, have a right to their preservation, and consequently to meat and drink, and such other things as nature affords for their subsistence; or revelation, which gives us an account of those grants God made of the world to Adam, and to Noah, and his sons; it is very clear, that God, as king David says, Psal. cxv. 16, "has given the earth to the children of men"; given it to mankind in common. But this being supposed, it seems to some a very great difficulty how any one should ever come to have a property in any thing: I will not content myself to answer, that if it be difficult to make out property, upon a supposition that God gave the world to Adam and his posterity in common, it is impossible that any man, but one universal monarch, should have any property, upon a supposition that God gave the world to Adam, and his heirs in succession, exclusive of all the rest of his posterity. But I shall endeavor to show how men might come to have a property in several parts of that which God gave to mankind in common, and that without any express compact of all the commoners.

God, who hath given the world to men in common, hath also given them reason to make use of it to the best advantage of life and convenience. The earth, and all that is therein, is given to men for the support and comfort of their being. And though all the fruits it naturally produces, and beasts it feeds, belong to mankind in common, as they are produced

From An Essay Concerning the True Original, Extent and End of Civil Government (1690).

by the spontaneous hand of nature; and nobody has originally a private dominion, exclusive of the rest of mankind, in any of them, as they are thus in their natural state: yet being given for the use of men, there must of necessity be a means to appropriate them some way or other before they can be of any use, or at all beneficial to any particular man. The fruit, or venison, which nourishes the wild Indian, who knows no enclosure, and is still a tenant in common, must be his, and so his, i.e. a part of him, that another can no longer have any right to it, before it can do him any good for the support of his life.

Though the earth, and all inferior creatures, be common to all men, yet every man has a property in his own person: this nobody has any right to but himself. The labor of his body, and the work of his hands, we may say, are properly his. Whatsoever then he removes out of the state that nature hath provided, and left it in, he hath mixed his labor with, and joined to it something that is his own, and thereby makes it his property. It being by him removed from the common state nature hath placed it in, it hath by this labor something annexed to it that excludes the common right of other men. For this labor being the unquestionable property of the laborer, no man but he can have a right to what that is once joined to, at least where there is enough, and as good, left in common for others.

He that is nourished by the acorns he picked up under an oak, or the apples he gathered from the trees in the wood, has certainly appropriated them to himself. Nobody can deny but the nourishment is his. I ask then, when did they begin to be his? when he digested? or when he ate? or when he boiled? or when he brought them home? or when he picked them up? and it is plain, if the first gathering made them not his, nothing else could. That labor put a distinction between them and common: that added something to them more than nature, the common mother of all, had done; and so they became his private right. And will any one say, he had no right to those acorns or apples he thus appropriated, because he had not the consent of all mankind to make them his? Was it a robbery thus to assume to himself what belonged to all in common? If such a consent as that was necessary, man had starved, notwithstanding the plenty God had given him. We see in commons, which remain so by compact, that it is the taking any part of what is common, and removing it out of the state nature leaves it in, which begins the property; without which the common is of no use. And the taking of this or that part does not depend on the express consent of all the commoners. Thus the grass my horse has bit; the turfs my servant has cut; and the ore I have digged in any place, where I have a right to them in common with others; become my property, without the assignation or consent of any body. The labor that was mine, removing them out of that common state they were in, hath fixed my property in them.

By making an explicit consent of every commoner necessary to any one's appropriating to himself any part of what is given in common, children or servants could not cut the meat, which their father or master had provided for them in common, without assigning to every one his peculiar part. Though the water running in the fountain be every one's, yet who can doubt but that in the pitcher is his only who drew it out? His labor hath taken it out of the hands of nature, where it was common, and belonged equally to all her children, and hath thereby appropriated it to himself.

Thus this law of reason makes the deer that Indian's who hath killed it; it is allowed to be his goods who hath bestowed his labor upon it, though before it was the common right of every one. And amongst those who are counted the civilized part of mankind, who have made and multiplied positive laws to determine property, this original law of nature, for the beginning of property, in what was before common, still takes place; and by virtue thereof, what fish any one catches in the ocean, that great and still remaining common of mankind; or what ambergris any one takes up here, is by the labor that removes it out of that common state nature left it in made his property who takes that pains about it. And even amongst us, the hare that any one is hunting is thought his who pursues her during the chase: for being a beast that is still looked upon as common, and no man's private possession; whoever has employed so much labor about any of that kind, as to find and pursue her, has thereby removed her from the state of nature, wherein she was common, and hath begun a property.

It will perhaps be objected to this, that "if gathering the acorns, or other fruits of the earth, etc. makes a right to them, then any one may engross as much as he will." To which I answer, Not so. The same law of nature, that does by this means give us property, does also bound that property too. "God has given us all things richly," 1 Tim. vi. 17, is the voice of reason confirmed by inspiration. But how far has he given it us? To enjoy. As much as any one can make use of to any advantage of life before it spoils, so much he may by his labor fix a property in: whatever is beyond this, is more than his share, and belongs to others. Nothing was made by God for man to spoil or destroy. And thus, considering the plenty of natural provisions there was a long time in the world, and the few spenders; and to how small a part of that provision the industry of one man could extend itself, and engross it to the prejudice of others; especially keeping within the bounds, set by reason, of what might serve for his use; there could be then little room for quarrels or contentions about property so established.

But the chief matter of property being now not the fruits of the earth, and the beasts that subsist on it, but the earth itself; as that which takes in, and carries with it all the rest; I think it is plain, that property in that too is acquired as the former. As much land as a man tills, plants, improves, cultivates, and can use the product of, so much is his property.

He by his labor does, as it were, enclose it from the common. Nor will it invalidate his right, to say every body else has an equal title to it, and therefore he cannot appropriate, he cannot enclose, without the consent of all his fellow-commoners, all mankind. God, when he gave the world in common to all mankind, commanded man also to labor, and the penury of his condition required it of him. God and his reason commanded him to subdue the earth, i.e. improve it for the benefit of life, and therein lay out something upon it that was his own, his labor. He that, in obedience to this command of God, subdued, tilled, and sowed any part of it, thereby annexed to it something that was his property, which another had no title to, nor could without injury take from him.

Nor was this appropriation of any parcel of land, by improving it, any prejudice to any other man, since there was still enough, and as good left; and more than the yet unprovided could use. So that, in effect, there was never the less left for others because of his enclosure for himself: for he that leaves as much as another can make use of, does as good as take nothing at all. Nobody could think himself injured by the drinking of another man, though he took a good draught, who had a whole river of the same water left him to quench his thirst; and the case of land and water, where there is enough of both, is perfectly the same.

God gave the world to men in common; but since he gave it them for their benefit, and the greatest conveniencies of life they were capable to draw from it, it cannot be supposed he meant it should always remain common and uncultivated. He gave it to the use of the industrious and rational (and labor was to be his title to it), not to the fancy or covetousness of the quarrelsome and contentious. He that had as good left for his improvement as was already taken up, needed not complain, ought not to meddle with what was already improved by another's labor; if he did, it is plain he desired the benefit of another's pains, which he had no right to, and not the ground which God had given him in common with others to labor on, and whereof there was as good left as that already possessed, and more than he knew what to do with, or his industry could reach to.

It is true, in land that is common in England, or any other country, where there is plenty of people under government, who have money and commerce, no one can enclose or appropriate any part without the consent of all his fellow-commoners; because this is left common by compact, i.e. by the law of the land, which is not to be violated. And though it be common, in respect of some men, it is not so to all mankind, but is the joint property of this county, or this parish. Besides, the remainder, after such enclosure, would not be as good to the rest of the commoners as the whole was when they could all make use of the whole; whereas in the beginning and first peopling of the great common of the world it was quite otherwise. The law man was under was rather for appropriating. God commanded, and his wants forced him to labor. That was his property which could not be taken from him wherever he had fixed it. And hence subduing or cultivating the earth, and having dominion, we see are joined together. The one gave title to the other. So that God, by commanding to subdue, gave authority so far to appropriate: and the condition of human life, which requires labor and materials to work on, necessarily introduces private possessions.

The measure of property nature has well set by the extent of men's labor and the conveniences of life: no man's labor could subdue, or appropriate all; nor could his enjoyment consume more than a small part; so that it was impossible for any man, this way, to intrench upon the right of another, or acquire to himself a property, to the prejudice of his neighbor, who would still have room for as good and as large a possession (after the other had taken out his) as before it was appropriated. This measure did confine every man's possession to a very moderate proportion, and such as he might appropriate to himself, without injury to any body, in the first ages of the world, when men were more in danger to be lost, by wandering from their company, in the then vast wilderness of the earth, than to be straitened for want of room to plant in. And the same measure may be allowed still without prejudice to any body, as full as the world seems: for supposing a man, or family, in the state they were at first peopling of the world by the children of Adam, or Noah; let him plant in some inland, vacant places of America, we shall find that the possessions he could make himself, upon the measures we have given, would not be very large, nor, even to this day, prejudice the rest of mankind, or give them reason to complain, or think themselves injured by this man's encroachment; though the race of men have now spread themselves to all the corners of the world, and do infinitely exceed the small number was at the beginning. Nay, the extent of ground is of so little value, without labor, that I have heard it affirmed, that in Spain itself a man may be permitted to plough, sow, and reap, without being disturbed, upon land he has no other title to, but only his making use of it. But, on the contrary, the inhabitants think themselves beholden to him, who, by his industry on neglected, and consequently waste land, has increased the stock of corn, which they wanted. But be this as it will, which I lay no stress on; this I dare boldly affirm, that the same rule of propriety, viz. that every man should have as much as he could make use of, would hold still in the world, without straitening any body; since there is land enough in the world to suffice double the inhabitants, had not the invention of money, and the tacit agreement of men to put a value on it, introduced (by consent) larger possessions, and a right to them; which, how it has done, I shall by and by show more at large.

This is certain, that in the beginning, before the desire of having more than man needed had altered the intrinsic value of things, which depends only on their usefulness to the life of man; or had agreed, that a little piece of yellow metal, which would keep without wasting or decay, should be worth a great piece of flesh, or a whole heap of corn; though men had a right to appropriate, by their labor, each one to himself, as much of the things of nature as he could use: yet this could not be much, nor to the prejudice of others, where the same plenty was still left to those who would use the same industry. To which let me add, that he who appropriates land to himself by his labor, does not lessen, but increase the common stock of mankind: for the provisions serving to the support of human life, produced by one acre of enclosed and cultivated land, are (to speak much within compass) ten times more than those which are yielded by an acre of land of an equal richness lying waste in common. And therefore he that encloses land, and has a greater plenty of the conveniences of life from ten acres, than he could have from an hundred left to nature, may truly be said to give ninety acres to mankind: for his labor now supplies him with provisions out of ten acres, which were by the product of an hundred lying in common. I have here rated the improved land very low, in making its product but as ten to one, when it is much nearer an hundred to one: for I ask, whether in the wild woods and uncultivated waste of America, left to nature, without any improvement, tillage, or husbandry, a thousand acres yield the needy and wretched inhabitants as many conveniences of life as ten acres equally fertile land do in Devonshire, where they are well cultivated?

Before the appropriation of land, he who gathered as much of the wild fruit, killed, caught, or tamed, as many of the beasts, as he could; he that so employed his pains about any of the spontaneous products of nature, as any way to alter them from the state which nature put them in, by placing any of his labor on them, did thereby acquire a propriety in them: but if they perished, in his possession, without their due use; if the fruits rotted, or the venison putrefied, before he could spend it; he offended against the common law of nature, and was liable to be punished; he invaded his neighbor's share, for he had no right, farther than his use called for any of them, and they might serve to afford him conveniencies of life.

The same measures governed the possession of land too: whatsoever he tilled and reaped, laid up and made use of, before it spoiled, that was his peculiar right; whatsoever he enclosed, and could feed, and make use of, the cattle and product was also his. But if either the grass of his enclosure rotted on the ground, or the fruit of his planting perished without gathering and laying up; this part of the earth, notwithstanding his enclosure, was still to be looked on as waste, and might be the possession of any other. Thus, at the beginning, Cain might take as much ground as he could till, and make it his own land, and yet leave enough to Abel's sheep to feed on; a few acres would serve for both their possessions. But as families increased, and industry enlarged their stocks, their possessions enlarged with the need of them; but yet it was commonly without any fixed property in the ground they made use of, till they incorporated, settled themselves together, and built cities; and then, by consent, they came in time to set out the bounds of their distinct territories, and agree on limits between them and their neighbors; and by laws within themselves settled the properties of those of the same society: for we see that in that part of the world which was first inhabited, and therefore like to be best peopled, even as low down as Abraham's time, they wandered with their flocks, and their herds, which was their substance, freely up and down; and this Abraham did, in a country where he was a stranger. Whence it is plain, that at least a great part of the land lay in common; that the inhabitants valued it not, nor claimed property in any more than they made use of. But when there was not room enough in the same place for their herds to feed together, they by consent, as Abraham and Lot did, Gen. xiii. 5, separated and enlarged their pasture, where it best liked them. And for the same reason Esau went from his father, and his brother, and planted in mount Seir, Gen. xxxvi. 6.

And thus, without supposing any private dominion and property in Adam, over all the world, exclusive of all other men, which can no way be proved, nor any one's property be made out from it; but supposing the world given, as it was, to the children of men in common, we see how labor could make men distinct titles to several parcels of it, for their private uses; wherein there could be no doubt of right, no room for quarrel.

Nor is it so strange, as perhaps before consideration it may appear, that the property of labor should be able to overbalance the community of land: for it is labor indeed that put the difference of value on every thing; and let any one consider what the difference is between an acre of land planted with tobacco or sugar, sown with wheat or barley, and an acre of the same land lying in common, without any husbandry upon it, and he will find, that the improvement of labor makes the far greater part of the value. I think it will be but a very modest computation to say, that of the products of the earth useful to the life of man, nine-tenths are the effects of labor: nay, if we will rightly estimate things as they come to our use, and cast up the several expenses about them, what in them is purely owing to nature, and what to labor, we shall find, that in most of them ninety-nine hundredths are wholly to be put on the account of labor.

There cannot be a clearer demonstration of any thing, than several nations of the Americans are of this, who are rich in land, and poor in all the comforts of life; whom nature having furnished as liberally as any other people with the materials of plenty, i.e. a fruitful soil, apt to produce in abundance what might serve for food, raiment, and delight; yet, for want of improving it by labor, have not one-hundredth part of the conveniencies we enjoy: and a king of a large and fruitful territory there feeds, lodges, and is clad worse than a day-laborer in England.

And thus, I think, it is very easy to conceive, "how labor could at first

begin a title of property" in the common things of nature, and how the
spending it upon our uses bounded it. So that there could then be no reason
of quarreling about title, nor any doubt about the largeness of possession
it gave. Right and conveniency went together; for as a man had a right
to all he could employ his labor upon, so he had no temptation to labor
for more than he could make use of. This left no room for controversy
about the title, nor for encroachment on the right of others; what portion
a man carved to himself was easily seen: and it was useless, as well as dishonest, to carve himself too much, or take more than he needed.

WHAT IS PROPERTY?
P. J. PROUDHON

1) I ought not to conceal the fact that property and communism have
been considered always the only possible forms of society. This deplorable
error has been the life of property. The disadvantages of communism are
so obvious that its critics never have needed to employ much eloquence
to thoroughly disgust men with it. The irreparability of the injustice which
it causes, the violence which it does to attractions and repulsions, the yoke
of iron which it fastens upon the will, the moral torture to which it subjects the conscience, the debilitating effect which it has upon society;
and, to sum it all up, the pious and stupid uniformity which it enforces
upon the free, active, reasoning, unsubmissive personality of man, have
shocked common sense, and condemned communism by an irrevocable
decree.

The authorities and examples cited in its favor disprove it. The communistic republic of Plato involved slavery; that of Lycurgus employed
Helots, whose duty it was to produce for their masters, thus enabling the
latter to devote themselves exclusively to athletic sports and to war. Even
J. J. Rousseau—confounding communism and equality—has said somewhere
that, without slavery, he did not think equality of conditions possible. The
communities of the early Church did not last the first century out, and
soon degenerated into monasteries. In those of the Jesuits of Paraguay, the
condition of the blacks is said by all travelers to be as miserable as that
of slaves; and it is a fact that the good Fathers were obliged to surround
themselves with ditches and walls to prevent their new converts from escaping. The followers of Babœuf—guided by a lofty horror of property
rather than by any definite belief—were ruined by exaggeration of their
principles; the St. Simonians, lumping communism and inequality, passed

From *What Is Property?*, tr. Benjamin J. Tucker (1876). The original was first published in 1840.

away like a masquerade. The greatest danger to which society is exposed today is that of another shipwreck on this rock.

Singularly enough, systematic communism—the deliberate negation of property—is conceived under the direct influence of the proprietary prejudice; and property is the basis of all communistic theories.

The members of a community, it is true, have no private property; but the community is proprietor, and proprietor not only of the goods, but of the persons and wills. In consequence of this principle of absolute property, labor, which should be only a condition imposed upon man by Nature, becomes in all communities a human commandment, and therefore odious. Passive obedience, irreconcilable with a reflecting will, is strictly enforced. Fidelity to regulations, which are always defective, however wise they may be thought, allows of no complaint. Life, talent, and all the human faculties are the property of the State, which has the right to use them as it pleases for the common good. Private associations are sternly prohibited, in spite of the likes and dislikes of different natures, because to tolerate them would be to introduce small communities within the large one, and consequently private property; the strong work for the weak, although this ought to be left to benevolence, and not enforced, advised, or enjoined; the industrious work for the lazy, although this is unjust; the clever work for the foolish, although this is absurd; and, finally, man—casting aside his personality, his spontaneity, his genius, and his affections—humbly annihilates himself at the feet of the majestic and inflexible Commune!

Communism is inequality, but not as property is. Property is the exploitation of the weak by the strong. Communism is the exploitation of the strong by the weak. In property, inequality of conditions is the result of force, under whatever name it be disguised: physical and mental force; force of events, chance, *fortune;* force of accumulated property, &c. In communism, inequality springs from placing mediocrity on a level with excellence. This damaging equation is repellent to the conscience, and causes merit to complain; for, although it may be the duty of the strong to aid the weak, they prefer to do it out of generosity—they never will endure a comparison. Give them equal opportunities of labor, and equal wages, but never allow their jealousy to be awakened by mutual suspicion of unfaithfulness in the performance of the common task.

Communism is oppression and slavery. Man is very willing to obey the law of duty, serve his country, and oblige his friends; but he wishes to labor when he pleases, where he pleases, and as much as he pleases. He wishes to dispose of his own time, to be governed only by necessity, to choose his friendships, his recreation, and his discipline; to act from judgment, not by command; to sacrifice himself through selfishness, not through servile obligation. Communism is essentially opposed to the free exercise of our faculties, to our noblest desires, to our deepest feelings. Any plan which could be devised for reconciling it with the demands of the individual reason and will would end only in changing the thing while preserving the name. Now, if we are honest truth-seekers, we shall avoid disputes about words.

Thus, communism violates the sovereignty of the conscience, and equality: the first, by restricting spontaneity of mind and heart, and freedom of thought and action; the second, by placing labor and laziness, skill and stupidity, and even vice and virtue on an equality in point of comfort. For the rest, if property is impossible on account of the desire to accumulate, communism would soon become so through the desire to shirk.

2) Property, in its turn, violates equality by the rights of exclusion and increase, and freedom by despotism. The former effect of property having been sufficiently developed in the last three chapters, I will content myself here with establishing by a final comparison, its perfect identity with robbery.

The Latin words for robber are *fur* and *latro;* the former taken from the Greek φορ, from φηρω, Latin *fero,* I carry away; the latter from ληθρω, I play the part of a brigand, which is derived from ληθω, Latin *lateo,* I conceal myself. The Greeks have also κλεπτης, from κλεπτω, I filch, whose radical consonants are the same as those of καλυπτ, I cover, I conceal. Thus in these languages, the idea of a robber is that of a man who conceals, carries away, or diverts, in any manner whatever, a thing which does not belong to him.

The Hebrews expressed the same idea by the word *gannab*—robber— from the verb *ganab,* which means to put away, to turn aside: *lo thi-gnob* (*Decalogue: Eighth Commandment*), thou shalt not steal—that is, thou shalt not hold back, thou shalt not put away any thing for thyself. That is the act of a man who, on entering into a society into which he agrees to bring all that he has, secretly reserves a portion, as did the celebrated disciple Ananias.

The etymology of the French verb *voler* is still more significant. *Voler,* or *faire la vole* (from the Latin *vola,* palm of the hand), means to take all the tricks in a game of ombre; so that *le voleur,* the robber, is the capitalist who takes all, who gets the lion's share. Probably this verb *voler* had its origin in the professional slang of thieves, whence it has passed into common use, and consequently into the phraseology of the law.

Robbery is committed in a variety of ways, which have been very cleverly distinguished and classified by legislators according to their heinousness or merit, to the end that some robbers may be honored, while others are punished.

We rob,—1) By murder on the highway; 2) Alone, or in a band; 3) By breaking into buildings, or scaling walls; 4) By abstraction; 5) By fraudulent bankruptcy; 6) By forgery of the handwriting of public officials or private individuals; 7) By manufacture of counterfeit money.

This species includes all robbers who practice their profession with no other aid than force and open fraud. Bandits, brigands, pirates, rovers by land and sea—these names were gloried in by the ancient heroes, who thought their profession as noble as it was lucrative. Nimrod, Theseus, Jason and his Argonauts; Jephthah, David, Cacus, Romulus, Clovis and all his Merovingian descendants; Robert Guiscard, Tancred de Hauteville. Bohemond, and most of the Norman heroes—were brigands and robbers. The heroic character of the robber is expressed in this line from Horace, in reference to Achilles—

Jura neget sibi nata, nihil non arroget armis,

and by this sentence from the dying words of Jacob (Gen. xlviii.), which the Jews apply to David, and the Christians to their Christ: *Manus ejus contra omnes.* In our day, the robber—the warrior of the ancients—is pursued with the utmost vigor. His profession, in the language of the code, entails ignominious and corporal penalties, from imprisonment to the scaffold. A sad change in opinions here below!

We rob,—8) By cheating; 9) By swindling; 10) By abuse of trust; 11) By games and lotteries.

This second species was encouraged by the laws of Lycurgus, in order to sharpen the wits of the young. It is the kind practiced by Ulysses, Solon, and Sinon; by the ancient and modern Jews, from Jacob down to Deutz; and by the Bohemians, the Arabs, and all savage tribes. Under Louis XIII and Louis XIV, it was not considered dishonorable to cheat at play. To do so was a part of the game; and many worthy people did not scruple to correct the caprice of Fortune by dexterous jugglery. Today even, and in all countries, it is thought a mark of merit among peasants, merchants, and shopkeepers to *know how to make a bargain*—that is, deceive one's man. This is so universally accepted, that the cheated party takes no offense. It is known with what reluctance our government resolved upon the abolition of lotteries. It felt that it was dealing a stab thereby at property. The pickpocket, the blackleg, and the charlatan make especial use of their dexterity of hand, their subtlety of mind, the magic power of their eloquence, and their great fertility of invention. Sometimes they offer bait to cupidity. Therefore the penal code—which much prefers intelligence to muscular vigor—has made, of the four varieties mentioned above, a second category, liable only to correctional, not to ignominious, punishments.

Let them now accuse the law of being materialistic and atheistic.

We rob,—12) By usury.

This species of robbery, so odious and so severely punished since the publication of the Gospel, is the connecting link between forbidden and authorized robbery. Owing to its ambiguous nature, it has given rise to a multitude of contradictions in the laws and in morals—contradictions which have been very cleverly turned to account by lawyers, financiers, and merchants. Thus the usurer, who lends on mortgage at ten, twelve, and fifteen per cent, is heavily fined when detected; while the banker, who receives the same interest (not, it is true, upon a loan, but in the way of exchange or discount—that is, of sale), is protected by royal privilege. But the distinction between the banker and the usurer is a purely nominal one. Like the usurer, who lends on property, real or personal, the banker lends on business paper; like the usurer, he takes his interest in advance; like the usurer, he can recover from the borrower if the property is destroyed (that is, if the note is not redeemed)—a circumstance which makes him a money-lender, not a money-seller. But the banker lends for a short time only, while the usurer's loan may be for one, two, three, or more years. Now, a difference in the duration of the loan, or the form of the act, does not alter the nature of the transaction. As for the capitalists who invest their money, either with the State or in commercial operation, at three, four, and five per cent—that is, who lend on usury at a little lower rate than the bankers and usurers—they are the flower of society, the cream of honesty! Moderation in robbery is the height of virtue!

We rob,—13) By farm-rent, house-rent, and leases of all kinds.

The author of the "Provincial Letters" entertained the honest Christians of the seventeenth century at the expense of Escobar, the Jesuit, and the contract *Mohatra*. "The contract *Mohatra*," said Escobar, "is a contract by which goods are bought, at a high price and on credit, to be again sold at the same moment to the same person, cash down, and at a lower price." Escobar found a way to justify this kind of usury. Pascal and all the Jansenists laughed at him. But what would the satirical Pascal, the learned Nicole, and the invincible Arnaud have said, if Father Antoine Escobar de Valladolid had answered them thus: "A lease is a contract by which real estate is bought, at a high price and on credit, to be again sold, at the expiration of a certain time, to the same person, at a lower price; only, to simplify the transaction, the buyer is content to pay the difference between the first sale and second. Either deny the identity of the lease and the contract *Mohatra*, and then I will annihilate you in a moment; or, if you admit the similarity, admit also the soundness of my doctrine: otherwise you proscribe both interest and rent at one blow"?

In reply to this overwhelming argument of the Jesuit, the sire of Montalte would have sounded the tocsin, and would have shouted that society was in peril—that the Jesuits were sapping its very foundations.

We rob,—14) By commerce, when the profit of the merchant exceeds his legitimate salary.

Everybody knows the definition of commerce—*The art of buying for three francs that which is worth six, and of selling for six that which is worth three.* Between commerce thus defined and *vol à l'américaine,* the only difference is in the relative proportion of the values exchanged—in short, in the amount of the profit.

We rob,—15) By making profit on our product, by accepting sinecures, and by exacting exorbitant wages.

The farmer, who sells a certain amount of corn to the consumer, and who during the measurement thrusts his hand into the bushel and takes out a handful of grains, robs; the professor whose lectures are paid for by the State, and who through the intervention of a bookseller sells them to the public a second time, robs: the sinecurist, who receives an enormous product in exchange for his vanity, robs; the functionary, the laborer, whatever he may be, who produces only one and gets paid four, one hundred, or one thousand, robs; the publisher of this book, and I, its author—we rob, by charging for it twice as much as it is worth.

In recapitulation:

Justice, after passing through the state of negative communism, called by the ancient poets the *age of gold,* commences as the right of the strongest. In a society which is trying to organize itself, inequality of faculties calls up the idea of merit; *équité* suggests the plan of proportioning not only esteem, but also material comforts, to personal merit; and since the highest and almost the only merit then recognized is physical strength, the strongest, αριστος, and consequently the best, αριστος, is entitled to the largest share; and if it is refused him, he very naturally takes it by force. From this to the assumption of the right of property in all things, it is but one step.

Such was justice in the heroic age, preserved, at least by tradition, among the Greeks and Romans down to the last days of their republics. Plato, in the "Gorgias," introduces a character named Callicles, who spiritedly defends the right of the strongest, which Socrates, the advocate of equality, seriously refutes. It is related of the great Pompey, that he blushed easily, and, nevertheless, these words once escaped his lips: "Why should I respect laws, when I have arms in my hand?" This shows him to have been a man in whom the moral sense and ambition were struggling for the mastery, and who sought to justify his violence by the motto of the hero and the brigand.

From the right of the strongest springs the exploitation of man by man, or bondage; usury, or the tribute levied upon the conquered by the conqueror; and the whole numerous family of taxes, duties, monarchical prerogatives, house-rents, farm-rents, etc.; in one word—property.

I have accomplished my task; property is conquered, never again to arise. Wherever this work is read and discussed, there will be deposited the germ of death to property; there, sooner or later, privilege and servitude will disappear, and the despotism of will will give place to the reign of reason. What sophisms, indeed, what prejudices (however obstinate) can stand before the simplicity of the following propositions:

1) Individual *possession* is the condition of social life; five thousand years of property demonstrate it. *Property* is the suicide of society. Possession is a right; property is against right. Suppress property while maintaining possession, and by this simple modification of the principle, you will revolutionize law, government, economy, and institutions; you will drive evil from the face of the earth.

2) All having an equal right of occupancy, possession varies with the number of possessors; property cannot establish itself.

3) The effect of labor being the same for all, property is lost in the common prosperity.

4) All human labor being the result of collective force, all property becomes, in consequence, collective and unitary. To speak more exactly, labor destroys property.

5) Every capacity for labor being, like every instrument of labor, an accumulated capital, and a collective property, inequality of wages and fortunes (on the ground of inequality of capacities) is, therefore, injustice and robbery.

6) The necessary conditions of commerce are the liberty of the contracting parties and the equivalence of the products exchanged. Now, value being expressed by the amount of time and outlay which each product costs, and liberty being inviolable, the wages of laborers (like their rights and duties) should be equal.

7) Products are bought only by products. Now, the condition of all exchange being equivalence of products, profit is impossible and unjust. Observe this elementary principle of economy, and pauperism, luxury, oppression, vice, crime, and hunger will disappear from our midst.

8) Men are associated by the physical and mathematical law of production, before they are voluntarily associated by choice. Therefore, equality of conditions is demanded by justice; that is, by strict social law: esteem, friendship, gratitude, admiration, all fall within the domain of *equitable* or *proportional* law only.

9) Free association, liberty—whose sole function is to maintain equality in the means of production and equivalence in exchanges—is the only possible, the only just, the only true form of society.

10) Politics is the science of liberty. The government of man by man (under whatever name it be disguised) is oppression. Society finds its highest perfection in the union of order with anarchy.

The old civilization has run its race; a new sun is rising, and will soon renew the face of the earth. Let the present generation perish, let the old prevaricators die in the desert!

REAL AND FALSE OWNERSHIP | RICHARD NEUTRA

ONLY THAT MEAL IS "OURS" WHICH WE CAN DIGEST; *a house, a neighborhood, a huge megalopolis, all beyond our organic controls, are not our house, our neighborhood, or our city.*

"The bigger the better" seems a fallacious maxim in scaling the value of an owned object. To be owned in a physiological sense, an object must be assimilated organically. There is a limit to bigness if we want to keep it within the possible capacity of nervous and generally organic assimilation.

A dinner cannot have innumerable courses and still be digested and controlled by our gastric juices. A megalopolis may be too gigantic to be wholesome for the nervous constitution of its individual inhabitant. A vast quantity of bric-a-brac in a Victorian room is heavy, over-rich fare compared with a sparingly furnished Japanese room, making one plum twig in a simple vase its only decoration.

The capacity to assimilate, to control nervously, may of course be impaired by many factors other than that of sheer bigness. But in all such cases of indigestibility, ownership is merely *claimed*. Food is not *my* food if I am physiologically incapable of eating it. We are reminded of Balzac's mad pawnbroker whose back room contains a gruesome agglomeration of many platters and dishes with rotting fish, meat, and fowl, which he gluttonously collects but never eats.

All objects can and must be considered as food for our nervous consumption. Indigestible, unassimilable, they can never be ours in any workable way. An ownership that is not organically operational is fictitious. The safest way to achieve belonging would seem to be to design our environment with a fine sense of our ability to assimilate it with a degree of nervous comfort. At least, we must try to control design with this aim in mind.

A suit of clothes that we order from the tailor to fit our requirements and measurements exactly, and which we control during production by repeated fittings, thus becomes, in a physiological sense, our own suit of clothes. The increase of nervous comfort and effective coordination caused by well-fitting clothes and shoes is measurable and beyond doubt. Men and women engaged in sports are distinctly aware of the fuller control over their

Reprinted from *Survival Through Design*, by Richard Neutra. Copyright 1954 by the Oxford University Press. Used by permission of the Oxford University Press.

bodily properties when dressed to suit their particular sport. The articles of clothing they wear are thus owned by them in a deeper sense than merely because they bought them in the sporting-goods store and paid cash.

Ownership in architecture, home ownership, for example, is a symbol that comes down to us from earlier periods when it did mean a full-fledged control over design, layout, and specification. Louis XIV *did* own Versailles, because he actually and truly expressed in that project his will and requirements. Moreover, through the construction and through his selection of talent to execute it, he created a style and a distinct architectural school as well as the entire manufacture of glass, furniture, and tapestries to serve his purpose. He drew on no given market for any of the articles, permitted no financial agencies to tell him how or where to modify his original intentions. He went so far as to discard existing surroundings and to create new ones imperiously. In fact, he produced a region of his own every time he chose to build anything. Ownership here was indeed the last word in self-expression. The frugal American pioneer in his forest clearing owned his humble cabin in very much the same way.

In contrast to this, there is the home ownership of a person who has the limited choice of a fifty-foot lot in a standard, previously established subdivision. He has to have his house built from standardized, marketable materials, with plans approved by the building department, and an appearance dictated by the bank appraiser and loan insurance agency, all of whom are already considering a resale after the "owner's" anticipated default and eviction. Such home ownership has indeed shrunk to an almost empty verbal symbol. There is little spiritual content and no exciting nervous appeal to its dry legality, only the ever recurrent irritation of meeting financial obligations connected with it.

An owner of this sort merely acquires the privilege of carrying capital charges and amortization over twenty years, a period so long that under contemporary conditions of general insecurity, and in view of the flimsiness of the house, final possession is but a dim promise. A mere word, though cunningly adapted to minds long conditioned by this stimulus, ownership approaches downright fiction in such a new context because from the very beginning the loan is granted under the mute proviso that the owner's self-expression through this project be kept negligible, that he conform strictly to the financial guardians' idea of *standard remarketing and ready repossession.*

Any attempt at reselling Versailles at its original cost minus depreciation would be as successful as selling the moon. But the house of today is often designed from the start with the idea that the owner will make place for an unknown successor.

In the current world, home ownership has in many cases deteriorated like other symbols, ornaments, and trappings superficially borrowed from periods in which princes and pioneers could find self-expression in a building activity that they themselves truly determined from the bottom up. Ownership has now become, semantically, a confusing word and misnomer.

It connotes an idea that must be reanalyzed to be at all constructive and fruitful for physical design.

A comparatively small, ever-dwindling number of persons may remain who build with their own funds and so do not have to dread rejection from the Federal Housing Administration, the moneylenders, and intermediate mortgage peddlers. A still smaller minority try to employ an imaginative designer of their own choice who is invited to create a minute miracle on a fifty-foot lot; the execution of his plans is then entrusted to commercial contractors and subcontractors who often enough may have to bewail their loss of profit in an individualized job to which they are not geared. Such a phenomenon, such home ownership, if it ever comes to pass, remains an erratic block in the general scene. The appraiser, the realtor, the neighbors shrug their shoulders; people in passing automobiles shake their heads in amazement. And the two adjoining buildings may still go up cloaked in the shreds of standard style, English cottage, or modified French provincial, with their bathroom windows giving on the breakfast room of our homeowner. Individual ownership is pitifully pinched in such a helpless and self-contradictory situation.

Still, in spite of frustration the word "ownership" retains its magic power. It has a psychological impact dear to millions. Governmental policies reckon with this conditioning of our minds and even contribute to it. They claim it is a stable factor in the midst of an economic order of fluctuating employment markets and a shifting population. Yet contrary to all the advertisements, buying your home on the monthly installment plan is not *like* paying rent. It actually *is* paying rent, plus, however, the added responsibility of maintenance, which commonly would not be the tenant's burden.

"Full" ownership, after twenty years of payments have been endured, and even when no economic shift or accident has interfered, often proves illusory, we have already hinted. In the meantime, the structure has become obsolete long before amortization is completed, so that the chances of equitable sale will admittedly have evaporated unless some abnormal housing shortage gives fictitious value even to decrepit shacks. Self-expression, the only thing that could possibly survive vulgar obsolescence, has in the vast majority of cases been blocked from the very start, precisely in order to produce that drab commercial value of a certain date and datedness. The whole matter is ridiculously complicated by the loan agency's insistence that the speculative builder avoid repetition and achieve a sort of pseudo-individual expression by varying, from house to house, windows, doors, porches, roof configuration, and the synthetic coloration of asphalt shingles.

The number of people in the United States who in normal times have sold their jerry-built houses for a profit is microscopic, as every expert will testify. War booms and devaluation of money may falsify this picture just as they do with everything else. Those who have seen their property become burdensome and depreciated by undesirable neighborhood developments are legion. But again, men do not necessarily live by actual experience; more frequently because of early conditioning, they respond to what looks or sounds like a magic formula.

Generally such neuromental conditioning represents a greater problem to designers and planners than all the technical difficulties or resistances of physical material. It can be changed by gradual retraining, but hardly by argument.

At the speaker's table of a housing convention, years before the last war, I was seated beside a nationally known labor leader who explained that American workers cannot wholeheartedly embrace the idea of rental projects. "In their souls," this speaker concluded—and his poetic expression was profoundly justified—"they carry the nostalgic longing for a home of their own."

In my heart I wondered whether the speaker had in words of the past oversimplified the involved circumstances of the present, and when asked to express my thoughts, I answered essentially in this vein: "We do and should deeply respect this longing for a setting that gives anchorage to the soul. We must also understand and respect a love for the words, the revered symbols, and esteemed and cherished ornaments of a bygone day—which at a distance we are often inclined to interpret as a better day. But let us in fairness consider the following quite common and current example, although there may be notable and more ingenious exceptions to the rule.

"A new industrial plant is nearing completion; employees' families will be attracted in great numbers and—it is statistically plain—will find no dwelling places ready. So, several hardboiled and fiercely competitive subdividers rush site plans for row upon row of small lots for approval by the city planning commission, borrow or secure humdrum stock plans worth less than twenty-five dollars apiece, variegate them in appearance with blue, green, and maroon roof shingles, try to lower specifications to any permissible minimum—and, often without competent contractors, execute things as much below that minimum as they can, short of detection and trouble from the authorities. They obtain maximum bank loans to cover practically all construction cost, and are backed by obliging officials of a government that is supported by other taxpayers to insure this speculative scheme.

"There may be notable exceptions. But commonly everything in such an involved transaction is done for the quickest possible turnover, and, anything else lacking, the houses are actually sold like fresh doughnuts. Each small dwelling with its ridiculously detached garage is a double speck in the landscape, within a crowd of other double specks. It pretends to be an 'individual' home, owned, like a diminutive castle, by an independent man who happily looks up at *his* supply wires descending from *his* own dear power pole placed by the utility company on an easement in *his* rear yard. He hardly understands the complex legalities of the situation when he signs up for *his* down payment.

"The subdivision burdens him with the paving of over-dimensioned and

costly 50-foot wide public traffic streets paralleling each other in a heartless
grid at intervals of 250 feet to intersect obnoxiously and dangerously with
the noisy boulevard on which the sales project, for more convincing
commercial value, abuts.

"Without all these concessions to rigid routine there would be no prompt
promotion, no loan insurance, no rushed subdivision, no cheap dwellings.
This is a wonderfully scientific, systematic age, and we know things
beforehand. We know the percentage of yet unborn children who, by law
of accident averages, are doomed to die under wheels or be crippled on this
sort of street system after a brief roller skate through life, unless these
children can be conditioned to play unnaturally, each in isolation on his
father's 'own' lot, between his 'own' gas meter and his 'own' garbage can
that is waiting for the municipal collection truck.

"Commercial subdividers—even when willing—cannot easily provide
recreational area, however small, because they see no ready way to its
maintenance. And why bother about it anyhow? The developers rightly
want to be out from under when they have sold the individual parcels.
They usually cannot afford to create an unsalable patch of green, nor, if
they are wise, do they laboriously try to file a dedication to the municipality
or the county. These local governments shun like the plague the liability
of a little park crowded with tots. It would call for supervision. And the
upkeep of a somewhat isolated bit of landscaping by their staff of
maintenance crews is cumbersome. The general run of voters would be
stunned, the politicians say, by the cost of such new-fangled neighborhood
play lawns and spray pools maintained for others. Why, practically no old
established taxpayers enjoy such provision for their own children. How
could they be expected to bear the cost of such luxuries for recently
arrived families of laborers who contribute little to revenues, but mostly
burden the budget?

"No, these new houses are not built by 'owners.' If they were owners,
they would want to protect themselves more carefully against leaks in
the cheap plumbing fittings, or in the flimsy flashings of their roofs,
unnecessarily but picturesquely intersected to catch a prospect's eye, or
against the hundred and one other repair items that are bound to crop up
as time goes on. These houses are crammed down the throats of people who,
willy-nilly, are promoted to being owners on rather weak financial legs.
The devil take the hindmost, that is the fellow who, after a few repossessions,
will by chance 'own' the property, and will do so at a time when those
repairs are liable to mount up every month to a most uncomfortable outlay.
And if toward the end of amortization, the whole dilapidated subdivision
degenerates into a slum, it is the funeral of those unlucky ones who then
happen to be the owners.

"Summed up, it is ownership in quotation marks; it is as far from the
real thing as a 'Mexican ranch' in Hollywood, California, is from a real
Mexican ranch.

"In contrast to this depressing picture, let us look at the tenants of a unified project conceived and managed as a truly integrated human neighborhood. In addition to the psychological misappropriation of a word and the application of cold financial instrumentalities, other creative and more biological considerations have been at work and have yielded a lovelier product, not for turnover but for the permanence of lasting life. The homes are arranged about a central park in the core of a well-landscaped super block, kept free from rolling traffic, with recreational facilities for all age groups, with day nursery, kindergarten, pool, and picnic grounds, built through a blanket loan or other over-all scheme of financing. If, by their payments, proportional-benefit tenants acquire a share, a vote, and a say-so in the neighborhood community, they can *decide* and *keep* in mind a wider setting *beyond* their restricted four walls. Are they not more justified in flattering themselves with the idea of ownership, a true and contemporary sort of ownership, because it again spells influence on one's environment?

"To be sure, it would not be the ownership with potential speculative profit that is so often promised and so rarely realized. But it would be an ownership with natural teeth in it, so to speak; that is, with *neighborhood control*—a control and a nervous protection that even fairly wealthy owners of individual property today can no longer enjoy. We could then speak of modified, mutually insured, mutually conditioned ownership, such as seems the only possible one for the many in this age of pronounced interdependence.

"Leaving aside economic terms that have ceased to describe correctly the facts of life, the natural, physiological terms of symbiosis (or living together for wholesome survival) can apply to such a scheme and such a design for a well-fused neighborhood. Biologically studied and restudied, this design will probably grow to be more assimilable and digestible for human beings and their nervous equipment than what we now try to swallow and absorb of surroundings that are often very hard to take."

PROPERTY | ERIC GILL

The exercise of art or work is the formal reason of individual appropriation; but only because it presupposes the rational nature and personality of the artist or workman.

In the case of the bee ... there is no exercise of art or of work in the strict sense (since there is no reason in operation); neither is there any individual ownership.

MARITAN, *Freedom in the Modern World*

From *Essays* by Eric Gill, published 1942, 1947 by Jonathan Cape Ltd., London; and *It All Goes Together: Selected Essays,* by Eric Gill, published 1944 by the Devin-Adair Company, New York.

> *Every man has by nature the right to possess private property as his own.*
>
> *As many as possible of the people should be induced to become owners.*
>
> *That which is required to preserve life is produced from the soil, but not until man has brought it into cultivation and expended upon it his solicitude and skill. By such act he makes his own that portion of nature's field which he cultivates ... on which he leaves the imprint of his individuality.*
>
> *How must one's possessions be used? Man should not consider his material possessions as his own but as common to all, so as to share them without hesitation when others are in need.*
>
> LEO XIII, *Rerum Novarum*

At the very root of all our arguments for the institution of property is the fact that man is a person, and he requires, therefore, not merely food, clothing, and shelter as such, but that particular food, clothing, and shelter which is conformed to his unique personality. And parallel, as it were, with that fact is the fact that the material world into which he is born is such that only by his personal deliberate manipulation can material be made comfortable to his needs.

There is only one necessary thing which is obtainable without deliberate labor, the air we breathe; all other necessities are in one degree or another the product of labor. If men were not persons, possessing proprietary right over themselves, mastery over themselves and over their acts, it would be possible to feed, clothe, and house them in herds and regiments and hives, and the claim to personal and private ownership of the means of production would have no rational ground. The present inclination to live in large conglomerations of identical apartments and the mass-production of food, clothing, furniture, building materials, and even houses indicates a widespread degradation of personality. The communist and other political systems which postulate the abolition of private property are products of the same degradation, and all alike are the consequence of the decay of personal ownership which industrialism has caused. For though the owners of industrial enterprises are given to boasting their close attachment to the institution of property, the effect of their politics has been the proletarianization of the masses of workers, and in the minds of the majority of persons today the idea of property is not ownership of the means of production, but simply ownership of a share of the money profits of industry and of the mass-produced furniture and pleasure-things (cars, wireless set, etc.) which money can buy.

Now, physical and mental labor upon the earth and upon raw materials is the primary necessity for the preservation of human life. We may now go farther and we may say that as the object of human life is man's sanctification, labor, being the means of life, is the appointed means to holiness and thus to beatitude. It should be clear, therefore, that of all kinds of ownership, that of the means of production is the most important, and so important is it that, as Pope Leo XIII says, it is a natural right, natural, that is to say, in accord with the will of God; it is God's will for man. We have, therefore, two things to bear in mind: the necessity of labor, and the consequent natural right to property. The one follows from the other; for it is man, a person, who must labor and "the very essence of this activity is to imprint on matter the mark of rational being." (Maritain, *loc. cit.*)

The root principles of private property being thus understood, we have next to consider the conditions of ownership in our society, and then we should consider possible remedies for the ills we discover. It is, of course, true that there are many ways in which property is held today in England, and it is held by many different classes of persons; but it is also true to say that the thing we call proletarianism is the special and peculiar mark of our time. A proletarian is one who owns nothing but his power to labor and that of his children; children are his only "real property." At all times and in all countries there have been proletarians, but in no previous society has the propertyless man been politically free! The Roman or American slave was by law *incapable* of owning anything; the industrial slave is only debarred by the economic circumstances in which the owners of industrial property have deliberately contrived to place him; for it was to the great advantage of industrialists that there should be large numbers of men economically powerless. Cheap labor was essential to them, and no labor is so cheap as that of men who own nothing but their bodily strength.

But as man has a natural right to property, so he has a natural necessity to live in social collaboration with his fellow men. "The State is bound to protect natural rights. ... If it forbids its citizens to form associations it contradicts the very principle of its own existence...." (Leo XIII, *loc. cit.*) Therefore, in spite of the desperate opposition of owners of land and factories, the Trades Unions, after much bloody and cruel proscription, established themselves and were able to force upon the owners better conditions of labor and better pay. But the result was that a very great impetus was given to the development of machinery. The inventive ingenuity of men has always been available, but never before was it thus used for the exclusive service of men whose main concern was not the improvement of things made, still less the convenience of the workers, but primarily the monetary aggrandizement of themselves. The rising cost of human labor which Trades Unionism brought about made it necessary, from the point of view of those whose main concern was (and is) profits, to seek every possible means of substitution. Thus, first of all men were enslaved by proletarianization, then they were degraded by factory employment ("for from the factory dead matter goes out improved whereas men there are corrupted and degraded" [Pius XI, *Quad. Anno*] and, as the present Pope has said: "in this age of mechanization the human person becomes merely a more perfect tool in industrial production and a perfected tool for mechanized warfare"); and lastly, they are, as far as possible, deprived of occupation altogether. That is the logical culmination of the mechanization of industry, whether under capitalism or any other form of society, for the main object of machinery is the elimination of human labor.

Now it is clear that no remedy is possible unless, in the first place, we desire it, and, particularly, unless those who use and mind machines desire it; and in the second place, unless those who desire a remedy have the necessary power to effect it. As to the first thing, in order to inculcate a desire for a remedy we must, impossible though it sounds, difficult though it be, regain in ourselves a true conception of the nature of man and of the nature of human work, and we must succeed in converting our fellow men and women. In this endeavor we should be assisted by the growing misery of our times and the palpable breakdown of the materialist society in which we live. But this misery and that breakdown will not be sufficient in themselves; for there are other diagnoses of our disease besides the christian one, and unless we are prepared and active a fascist or communist remedy will be applied, and neither the subordination of man to the States which is essential to the fascist theory nor the materialist interpretation of history which is essential to modern communism is compatible with christian doctrine.

That is the first thing, the reconversion of England to Christianity and to Christ. But in respect of the matter with which we are specially concerned in this article, the conversion of England will not suffice unless we understand that this implies much more than Sunday attendance and obedience to the Commandments of the Church. It implies also a clear knowledge of the essentials of a christian society and a determination to recreate it.

In addition to desiring a remedy we must know what the remedy is and understand its nature. The ill from which we are suffering is the decay of personality. The remedy is the revival of personal property. Under industrialism the majority of the people are deprived of personal control of their work, and such control is impossible without ownership. What you do not own you cannot control. What you do not control you are not responsible for. If you are not responsible you cannot be either praised or blamed. Christian doctrine lays it down as a first principle that man has free will and is, therefore, a responsible person—master of his acts and the intended consequences of his acts. This doctrine is flouted and denied in our society. In all but name England is a servile state.

The irresponsibility of the workman is the first and simplest way in which to see our evil condition. It is the first because the exercise of work is the formal reason of individual appropriation. It is the simplest because the exercise of work is within the experience of all but a small class of persons. But though it is the first reason, the exercise of work is not the only reason of personal and private ownership. The second, and depending on the first, is the security and dignity of the family. The proletarian is insecure, that is his first misery. He lives in perpetual fear. Thus, all decency and dignity in human life is destroyed. "They do not know that they have renounced normal and natural responsibilities which even savages enjoy, they do not own their homes, their tools or the choice of trade; the power to bring up children, and the means to keep their aged and infirm have been surrendered to a malignant bureaucracy ... from revolution they hope to gain not more responsibility, but (simply) a greater hold on the pipe line supposed to exist between ourselves and plenty." Therefore it is that Pope Leo says: "The right to property must belong to a man in his capacity of head of a family." Thus and thus alone can the principle of responsibility be brought to bear not merely upon the works of our hands (which, in any case, will be "as straw" on the last day) but upon the fruit of our loins.

But ultimately the most important fruit of individual appropriation, of private property, is the exercise of charity. We are responsible persons, responsible for what we do and for what we make. To what end is this doing and making? The greatest happiness of the greatest number, says the politician (forgetting for the moment that he lives under the shadow of the Whip); my own greatest happiness and enjoyment, says the individual (forgetting altogether that he is "standing in a perpetual queue waiting for a dole which is dependent for its coming on distant workers and an elaborate system of transport"); "that he may have something to give to him that suffers need," says the apostle; "to share them without hesitation," adds the Pope.

"Something to give"—that is the primary thought and the last word. In the word "give" we have the key to the whole problem. Whether it be the workman who must give himself for the good of the work to be done, or the parents who must provide for their children, or all of us who must live in love and charity with our neighbors, in every case economic freedom is necessary to support and make materially effective the precepts of the Gospel. Only upon this basis can a christian society be built—a christian society, that is to say, a society of free men united in and by the love of Christ—free men, that is to say, men who enjoy the ownership of land and workshops, who own not merely themselves but the means of production. For you cannot give what is another's. You cannot give yourself if you are a slave. A proletarian cannot even provide for the *proles* from whom he derives his name. Organized state "charity" is no substitute for the love of our neighbors. "Faith without works is dead," but our works cannot be good works unless they are our own.

The discussion of the political means which must be employed to give effect to the demand for property and responsibility (should we succeed in reviving it) is not within the scope of this article. In any case, the revival of workers' ownership, if it is to be a real, personal ownership and not a mere state capitalism, or bureaucratic socialism, must be gradual, as gradual, indeed, as the spread of a desire for it. At the present time there is hardly any desire for responsibility and, at the most, the only desire for ownership is a desire for an equitable share of industrial profits, for more money, shorter hours, more amusement, and fewer babies. Among all classes, among the poor no less than the rich, the quantitative advantages of industrialism are held to outweigh all its evils, and they cling desperately to the hope that the evils can be removed without loss of the pleasures and conveniences. In these circumstances ownership is still the first necessity. It is futile to preach the christian doctrine of responsibility to people who, by the nature and conditions of their work, can have none. "As many as possible of the people should be induced to become owners," that is all that can be said at present—induced, persuaded, encouraged, helped—with this qualification: that it be understood that ownership means control and responsibility and not merely a share of the profits. An immediate return to small workshops is impossible; the first step must be that the workers gain, in whole or in part, a real ownership of existing industrial enterprises —the workers, they who do the work, of whatever grade, and not the anonymous and irresponsible investors of money.

LOOSE-FISH AND FAST-FISH | *HERMAN MELVILLE*

The allusion to the waifs and waif-poles in the last chapter but one, necessitates some account of the laws and regulations of the whale fishery, of which the waif may be deemed the grand symbol and badge.

It frequently happens that when several ships are cruising in company, a whale may be struck by one vessel, then escape, and be finally killed and captured by another vessel; and herein are indirectly comprised many minor contingencies, all partaking of this one grand feature. For example, after a weary and perilous chase and capture of a whale, the body may get loose from the ship by reason of a violent storm; and drifting far away to leeward, be retaken by a second whaler, who, in a calm, snugly tows it alongside, without risk of life or line. Thus the most vexatious and violent

From *Moby Dick*, Chap. 89 (1851).

disputes would often arise between the fishermen, were there not some
written or unwritten, universal, undisputed law applicable to all cases.

Perhaps the only formal whaling code authorized by legislative enactment, was that of Holland. It was decreed by the States-General in A.D.
1695. But though no other nation has ever had any written whaling law,
yet the American fishermen have been their own legislators and lawyers in
this matter. They have provided a system which for terse comprehensiveness
surpasses Justinian's Pandects and the By-laws of the Chinese Society for
the Suppression of Meddling with other People's Business. Yes; these laws
might be engraven on a Queen Anne's farthing, or the barb of a harpoon,
and worn round the neck, so small are they.

1) A Fast-Fish belongs to the party fast to it.

2) A Loose-Fish is fair game for anybody who can soonest catch it.

But what plays the mischief with this masterly code is the admirable
brevity of it, which necessitates a vast volume of commentaries to expound
it.

First: What is a Fast-Fish? Alive or dead a fish is technically fast, when
it is connected with an occupied ship or boat, by any medium at all
controllable by the occupant or occupants—a mast, an oar, a nine-inch
cable, a telegraph wire, or a strand of cobweb, it is all the same. Likewise
a fish is technically fast when it bears a waif, or any other recognized
symbol of possession; so long as the party waifing it plainly evince their
ability at any time to take it alongside, as well as their intention so to do.

These are scientific commentaries; but the commentaries of the whalemen themselves sometimes consist in hard words and harder knocks—the
Coke-upon-Littleton of the fist. True, among the more upright and honorable whalemen allowances are always made for peculiar cases, where it
would be an outrageous moral injustice for one party to claim possession
of a whale previously chased or killed by another party. But others are by
no means so scrupulous.

Some fifty years ago there was a curious case of whale-trover litigated
in England, wherein the plaintiffs set forth that after a hard chase of a
whale in the Northern seas; and when indeed they (the plaintiffs) had succeeded in harpooning the fish; they were at last, through peril of their lives,
obliged to forsake not only their lines, but their boat itself. Ultimately the
defendants (the crew of another ship) came up with the whale, struck,
killed, seized, and finally appropriated it before the very eyes of the
plaintiffs. And when those defendants were remonstrated with, their captain snapped his fingers in the plaintiffs' teeth, and assured them that by
way of doxology to the deed he had done, he would now retain their line,
harpoons, and boat, which had remained attached to the whale at the time
of the seizure. Wherefore the plaintiffs now sued for the recovery of the
value of their whale, line, harpoons, and boat.

Mr. Erskine was counsel for the defendants; Lord Ellenborough was the judge. In the course of the defense, the witty Erskine went on to illustrate his position, by alluding to a recent crim. con. case, wherein a gentleman, after in vain trying to bridle his wife's viciousness, had at last abandoned her upon the seas of life; but in the course of years, repenting of that step, he instituted an action to recover possession of her. Erskine was on the other side; and he then supported it by saying, that though the gentleman had originally harpooned the lady, and had once had her fast, and only by reason of the great stress of her plunging viciousness, had at last abandoned her; yet abandon her he did, so that she became a loose-fish; and therefore when a subsequent gentleman re-harpooned her, the lady then became that subsequent gentleman's property, along with whatever harpoon might have been found sticking in her.

Now in the present case Erskine contended that the examples of the whale and the lady were reciprocally illustrative of each other.

These pleadings, and the counter pleadings, being duly heard, the very learned judge in set terms decided, to wit—That as for the boat, he awarded it to the plaintiffs, because they had merely abandoned it to save their lives; but that with regard to the controverted whale, harpoons, and line, they belonged to the defendants; the whale, because it was a Loose-Fish at the time of the final capture; and the harpoons and line because when the fish made off with them, it (the fish) acquired a property in those articles; and hence anybody who afterwards took the fish had a right to them. Now the defendants afterwards took the fish; ergo, the aforesaid articles were theirs.

A common man looking at this decision of the very learned Judge, might possibly object to it. But ploughed up to the primary rock of the matter, the two great principles laid down in the twin whaling laws previously quoted, and applied and elucidated by Lord Ellenborough in the above cited case; these two laws touching Fast-Fish and Loose-Fish, I say, will, on reflection, be found the fundamentals of all human jurisprudence; for notwithstanding its complicated tracery of sculpture, the Temple of the Law, like the Temple of the Philistines, has but two props to stand on.

Is it not a saying in every one's mouth, Possession is half of the law: that is, regardless of how the thing came into possession? But often possession is the whole of the law. What are the sinews and souls of Russian serfs and Republican slaves but Fast-Fish, whereof possession is the whole of the law? What to the rapacious landlord is the widow's last mite but a Fast-Fish? What is yonder undetected villian's marble mansion with a doorplate for a waif; what is that but a Fast-Fish? What is the ruinous discount which Mordecai, the broker, gets from poor Woebegone, the bankrupt, on a loan to keep Woebegone's family from starvation; what is that ruinous discount but a Fast-Fish? What is the Archbishop of Savesoul's income of £100,000 seized from the scant bread and cheese of hundreds of thousands of broken-backed laborers (all sure of heaven without any of

Savesoul's help) what is that globular 100,000 but a Fast-Fish? What are
the Duke of Dunder's hereditary towns and hamlets but Fast-Fish? What
to that redoubted harpooner, John Bull, is poor Ireland, but a Fast-Fish?
What to that apostolic lancer, Brother Jonathan, is Texas but a Fast-Fish?
And concerning all these, is not Possession the whole of the law?

But if the doctrine of Fast-Fish be pretty generally applicable, the
kindred doctrine of Loose-Fish is still more widely so. That is internation-
ally and universally applicable.

What was America in 1492 but a Loose-Fish, in which Columbus struck
the Spanish standard by way of waifing it for his royal master and mistress?
What was Poland to the Czar? What Greece to the Turk? What India to
England? What at last will Mexico be to the United States? All Loose-Fish.

What are the Rights of Man and the Liberties of the World but Loose-
Fish? What all men's minds and opinions but Loose-Fish? What is the
principle of religious belief in them but a Loose-Fish? What to the ostenta-
tious smuggling verbalists are the thoughts of thinkers but Loose-Fish? What
is the great globe itself but a Loose-Fish? And what are you, reader, but a
Loose-Fish and a Fast-Fish, too?

HEROES AND GREAT MEN

*IN ONE OF SHAKESPEARE'S liveliest comedies Malvolio, a presump-
tuous steward, remarks complacently that some men are born great, some
achieve greatness, and some have greatness thrust upon them. His observation scans the possibilities well enough though it does little to indicate
what greatness is. Most men—good-wishers as well as bad-wishers—aspire
to some kind of greatness, but few have more than a passing notion of
what attributes they believe are characteristic of it. Since the term "greatness" (like its companion term "heroism") is utterly ambiguous, definitions
of it are certain to resolve themselves into arguments, explicit or implicit,
for this or that concept of the term. And since "greatness" is a value word,
arguments about its meaning are bound to involve what we have called
"persuasive definition," or the advocacy through definition of certain ways
of acting. A man who says, for instance, "True greatness is humility" is
saying, in part, "We should all be humble."*

*Of the descriptions provided here one is by Friedrich Nietzsche (1844-
1900), a German historian, critic, and philosopher who markedly affected
the thinking of a generation of Europeans, and another is by William
Bolitho (William B. Ryall, 1890-1930), an English iconoclast now remembered primarily for the book of which this selection is the preface. Both
argue the virtue of a certain notion of greatness by distinguishing the*

characteristics that set it off from the pedestrian and the commonplace. *Philosopher Sidney Hook (1902-   ), a professor at New York University, tries to narrow the usual loose concept of greatness by distinguishing two kinds which might seem, to the unpracticed eye, quite the same. The two concluding essays in the group are departures from the general pattern set by the others. That by Fitz Roy Richard Somerset, Lord Raglan (1885-   ), in a sense depersonalizes the concept of the heroic by showing how, in its literary embodiments, it is remarkably formulaic. The implication is that heroes are made, not born; their greatness is thrust upon them. Finally, as Ihab Hassan (1925-   ), professor of English at Wesleyan University, makes clear, the characteristic hero of a particular culture may be one who refuses the role, who is an anti-hero by choice rather than by necessity or failure of will.*

> For, as I take it, Universal History, the history of what man has accomplished in this world, is at bottom the History of the Great Men who have worked here. They were the leaders of men, these great ones; the modelers, patterns, and in a wide sense creators, of whatsoever the general mass of men contrived to do or to attain; all things that we see standing accomplished in the world are properly the outer material result, the practical realization and embodiment, of Thoughts that dwelt in the Great Men sent into the world: the soul of the whole world's history, it may justly be considered, were the history of these.
>
> THOMAS CARLYLE

THE GREAT MAN | FRIEDRICH NIETZSCHE

A great man—a man whom Nature has built up and invented in a grand style—What is such a man? *First,* in his general course of action his consistency is so broad that owing to its very breadth it can be surveyed only with difficulty, and consequently misleads; he possesses the capacity of extending his will over great stretches of his life, and the despising and rejecting all small things, whatever most beautiful and "divine" things of the world there may be among them. *Secondly,* he is *colder, harder, less cautious and more free from the fear of "public opinion";* he does not possess the virtues which are compatible with respectability and with being respected, nor any of those things which are counted among the "virtues of the herd." If he is unable to *lead,* he walks alone; he may then perchance grunt at many things which he meets on his way. *Thirdly,* he asks for no "compassionate" heart, but servants, instruments; in his dealings with men

From Friedrich Nietzsche, *The Will to Power,* trans. by Anthony M. Ludovici (London, George Allen & Unwin Ltd., 1924; New York, The Macmillan Company, 1925).

his one aim is *to make something* out of them. He knows that he cannot reveal himself to anybody; he thinks it bad taste to become familiar; and as a rule he is not familiar when people think he is. When he is not talking to his soul, he wears a mask. He would rather lie than tell the truth, because lying requires more spirit and *will*. There is a loneliness within his heart which neither praise nor blame can reach, because he is his own judge from whom is no appeal.

The great man is necessarily a skeptic (I do not mean to say by this that he must appear to be one), provided that greatness consists in this: to *will* something great, together with the means thereto. Freedom from any kind of conviction is a factor in his *strength of will*. And thus it is in keeping with that "enlightened form of despotism" which every great passion exercises. Such a passion enlists intellect in its service; it even has the courage for unholy means; it creates without hesitation; it allows itself convictions, it even *uses* them, but it never submits to them. The need of faith and of anything unconditionally negative or affirmative is a proof of weakness; all weakness is weakness of will. The man of faith, the believer, is necessarily an inferior species of man. From this it follows that "all freedom of spirit," *i.e.* instinctive skepticism, is the prerequisite of greatness.

The great man is conscious of his power over a people, and of the fact that he coincides temporarily with a people or with a century—this magnifying of his self-consciousness as *causa* and *voluntas* is *misunderstood* as "altruism": he feels driven to *means* of communication: all great men are *inventive* in such means. They want to form great communities in their own image; they would fain give multiformity and disorder definite shape; it stimulates them to behold chaos.

The misunderstanding of Love. There is a *slavish* love which subordinates itself and gives itself away—which idealizes and deceives itself; there is a *divine* species of love which despises and loves at the same time, and which *remodels* and *elevates* the thing it loves.

The object is to attain that enormous *energy of greatness* which can model the man of the future by means of discipline and also by means of the annihilation of millions of the bungled and botched, and which can yet avoid *going to ruin* at the sight of the suffering *created* thereby, the like of which has never been seen before.

The revolution, confusion, and distress of whole peoples is in my opinion of less importance than *the misfortunes which attend great individuals in their development*. We must not allow ourselves to be deceived: the many misfortunes of all these small folk do not together constitute a sum-total, except in the felling of *mighty* men. To think of one's self in moments of great danger, and to draw one's own advantage from the calamities of thousands—in the case of the man who differs very much from the common ruck—may be a sign of a great character which is able to master its feelings of pity and justice.

In contradistinction to the animal, man has developed such a host of *antagonistic* instincts and impulses in himself, that he has become master of the earth by means of this synthesis. Moralities are only the expression of local and limited *orders of rank* in this multifarious world of instincts which prevent man from perishing through their antagonism. Thus a masterful instinct so weakens and subtilizes the instinct which opposes it that it becomes an impulse which provides the *stimulus* for the activity of the principal instinct.

The highest man would have the greatest multifariousness in his instincts, and he would possess these in the relatively strongest degree in which he is able to endure them. As a matter of fact, wherever the plant, man, is found strong, mighty instincts are to be found opposing each other (*e.g.* Shakespeare), but they are subdued.

Would one not be justified in reckoning all great men among the *wicked?* This is not so easy to demonstrate in the case of individuals. They are so frequently capable of masterly dissimulation that they very often assume the airs and forms of great virtues. Often, too, they seriously reverence virtues, and in such a way as to be passionately hard towards themselves; but as the result of cruelty. Seen from a distance such things are liable to deceive. Many, on the other hand, misunderstand themselves; not infrequently, too, a great mission will call forth great qualities, *e.g.* justice, The essential fact is: the greatest men may also perhaps have great virtues, but then they also have the opposites of these virtues. I believe that it is precisely out of the presence of these opposites and of the feelings they suscitate, that the great man arises—for the great man is the broad arch which spans two banks lying far apart.

In *great men* we find the specific qualities of life in their highest manifestation: injustice, falsehood, exploitation. But inasmuch as their effect has always been *overwhelming,* their essential nature has been most thoroughly misunderstood, and interpreted as goodness. The type of such an interpreter would be Carlyle.

Generally speaking, everything *is worth no more and no less than one has paid for it.* This of course does not hold good in the case of an isolated individual; the great capacities of the individual have no relation whatsoever to that which he has done, sacrificed, and suffered for them. But if one should examine the previous history of his race one would be sure to find the record of an extraordinary storing up and capitalizing of power by means of all kinds of abstinence, struggle, industry, and determination. It is because the great man has cost so much, and not because he stands there as a miracle, as a gift from heaven, or as an accident, that he became great: "Heredity" is a false notion. A man's ancestors have always paid the price of what he is.

The danger of modesty. To adapt ourselves too early to duties, societies, and daily schemes of work in which accident may have placed us, at a time when neither our powers nor our aim in life has stepped peremptorily into our consciousness; the premature certainty of conscience and feeling of relief and of sociability which is acquired by this precocious, modest attitude, and which appears to our minds as a deliverance from those inner and outer disturbances of our feelings—all this pampers and keeps a man down in the most dangerous fashion imaginable. To learn to respect things which people about us respect, as if we had no standard or right of our own to determine values; the strain of appraising things as others appraise them *counter* to the whisperings of our inner taste, which also has a conscience of its own, becomes a terribly subtle kind of constraint: and if in the end no explosion takes place which bursts all the bonds of love and morality at once, then such a spirit becomes withered, dwarfed, feminine, and objective. The reverse of this is bad enough, but still it is better than the foregoing: to suffer from one's environment, from its praise just as much as from its blame; to be wounded by it and to fester inwardly without betraying the fact; to defend one's self involuntarily and suspiciously against its love; to learn to be silent, and perchance to conceal this by talking; to create nooks and safe, lonely hiding-places where one can go and take breath for a moment, or shed tears of sublime comfort—until at last one has grown strong enough to say: "What on earth have I to do with you?" and to go *one's way alone*.

Those men who are in themselves destinies, and whose advent is the advent of fate, the whole race of *heroic* bearers of burdens: oh! how heartily and how gladly would they have respite from themselves for once in a while! how they crave after stout hearts and shoulders, that they might free themselves, were it but for an hour or two, from that which oppresses them! And how fruitlessly they crave! . . . They wait; they observe all that passes before their eyes: no man even cometh nigh to them with a thousandth part of their suffering and passion; no man guesseth to what end they have waited. . . . At last, at last, they learn the first lesson of their life: to wait no longer; and forthwith they learn their second lesson: to be affable, to be modest; and from that time onwards to endure everybody and every kind of thing—in short, to endure still a little more than they had endured theretofore.

THE EVENTFUL MAN AND THE EVENT-MAKING MAN | SIDNEY HOOK

Throughout this book we have been using the word "hero" in the rather large and vague sense given to it in common usage. It is now necessary to make the term sufficiently precise to permit some check upon the position that will be subsequently developed.

Before proceeding to the main distinction upon which our thesis hangs,

From Sidney Hook, *The Hero in History* (New York, The John Day Company, Inc., 1943). Reprinted by permission of the author.

it will be helpful to introduce a few secondary distinctions that have been alluded to in earlier chapters. First of all, we must distinguish between the hero of historical action and the hero of thought. Popular estimates of "great" or "eminent" men rarely differentiate between the two. Thus in the well-known survey made by J. McKeen Cattell on the outstanding figures in western history, the ten who headed the list of a thousand names were: Napoleon, Shakespeare, Mohammed, Voltaire, Bacon, Aristotle, Goethe, Caesar, Luther, and Plato.[1] But as far as the records of historical events go, only four out of this group can be considered as candidates for the role of historical hero. No one can plausibly maintain that Shakespeare had any influence on the occurrence or nonoccurrence of decisive historical events. It is not precluded that heroes of thought might also be great men of action or that the consequences of their ideas, as in the case of inventors, religious leaders, and social philosophers, might have impressive historical effects. But it is to the record of events that we must turn to evaluate their claims. In the history of the ancient world, it is Alexander, whose name does not appear on the list, who emerges as a historical hero rather than Aristotle. Only if it could be shown that it was Aristotle's ideas that inspired Alexander in his march toward empire could the former be considered in this connection.

A second distinction must be recognized between historical figures who are famous, who can get themselves believed in, and individuals who have influenced events without achieving great popular fame. There is no reliable correlation between historical significance, measured by the effect of action on events, and historical fame, measured by acclaim or volume of eulogy. That is why the judgment of the scientific historian, who investigates specific causal connection, on the historical work of individuals, is always to be preferred to results of polls, comparative space allotments in standard works, and frequency of citation. The latter show enormous variation influenced by fashion, picturesqueness, *parti pris,* and very little by scientific findings. Particularly today, any "front" man can be built up into a "hero." From 1916 to 1933, Hindenburg was undoubtedly the most popular figure in Germany but one could mention half a dozen individuals who had greater influence on German history including military history during that period.

Finally, we must rule out as irrelevant the conception of the hero as a morally worthy man, not because ethical judgments are illegitimate in history, but because so much of it has been made by the wicked. Only the making of history concerns us here, not whether it has been made well or disastrously.

The hero in history is the individual to whom we can justifiably attribute preponderant influence in determining an issue or event whose consequences

[1] *Popular Science Monthly,* Vol. 62 (1903), p. 359. This study was based on the comparative space allotted to a thousand pre-eminent men in standard biographical dictionaries and encyclopedias.

would have been profoundly different if he had not acted as he did. It is sometimes objected that there is no universal agreement about the "importance" of any issue, event, or consequences. Some individuals profess that it is not "important" to them whether India remains free or not, whether the war is lost or won, or whether the future world state is democratic or Fascist in form. All this is immaterial to the problem. No matter what *you* regard as important, the problem is inescapable. Would that which *you* regard as important have taken place anyhow no matter what individual figured in the events leading up to it? Or is it ever true to say that an individual was chiefly responsible for the occurrence or nonoccurrence of that important issue or event?

This brings us to the key distinction. This is the distinction between the hero as the *eventful man*[2] in history and the hero as the *event-making man* in history. The *eventful* man in history is any man whose actions influenced subsequent developments along a quite different course than would have been followed if these actions had not been taken. The *event-making* man is an eventful man whose actions are the consequences of outstanding capacities of intelligence, will, and character rather than of accidents of position. This distinction tries to do justice to the general belief that a hero is great not merely in virtue of what he does but in virtue of what he is. From this point on, unless otherwise specified, when we speak of the hero or great man in history we shall mean the event-making man.

The merely eventful men in history play a role that may be compared to that of the little Dutch boy who kept his finger in the hole of the dikes and saved the town. Without meaning to strip the legend of its glamor, we can point out that almost anybody in the situation could have done it. All that was required was a boy, a finger, and the lucky chance of passing by. The event itself in the life of the community was of tremendous significance. It saved the town just as a little Dutch boy at Pearl Harbor might have saved the fleet if his alarm had been acted upon in time. But the qualities required to cope with the situation were of a fairly common distribution. Here, so to speak, one stumbles upon greatness just as one might stumble on a treasure that will ransom a town. Greatness, however, is something that must involve extraordinary talent of some kind and not merely the compounded luck of being born and of being present at the right place at a happy moment.

In the year 313, the Emperor Constantine, in the words of Gibbon, changed his status from that of "protector" to that of "proselyte" of the Church.[3] Few events have been more important in the development of western Europe than the reversal of previous Roman policy toward

2 I owe the expression "eventful man" to Mr. Charles Haer, who is, however, in no way responsible for the position here developed.

3 Edward Gibbon, *History of the Decline and Fall of the Roman Empire,* Modern Library edition, Vol. I, p. 636.

Christianity and its adoption by the official head of the Roman Empire. But not a single one of the qualities of Constantine's character, which enter into the disputed question of the reasons for his conversion, indicate that he was much more than a politician with an eye on the main chance. Whatever religious piety he had was not strong enough to prevent him from murdering his own son on a trumped-up charge. Constantine was an eventful man independently of whether Christianity would have become the official religion several centuries later, under quite different conditions and with different consequences, or whether, without him, the Roman Empire would never have been called Holy. But as decisive as Constantine's act was for his era, *he* was not a hero. The appellation of "great" was bestowed upon him in thanks by the grateful Christian minority. His later interference in church affairs gave them second thoughts about his greatness.

Although there is no evidence that any other Roman Emperor would have eased Christianity into its new status, it could have been done readily. The growth of Christianity, the position of the Emperor in Roman society, the decay in traditional belief manifested by the absence of a strong, fanatical opposition, made the adoption of Christianity an objective possibility, but neither a social nor political necessity. Constantine proselytized for Christianity for imperial reasons.[4] But there was no greater justification for believing that he could strengthen the state by using the church primarily as an instrument of public policy than by playing off Paganism and Christianity against each other. *After* Constantine and his work, and *because* of it, the effort to restore the pagan religion was doomed to fail. It is extremely unlikely that the Emperor Julian, despite his superior gifts, would have succeeded in depriving Christianity of its privileged status even if he had lived to a ripe age. But what he failed to do as a successor of Constantine—reduce Christianity to a religious sect contending on equal terms against other sects—he could easily have done in Constantine's stead. Constantine, therefore, must be regarded as an eventful rather than an event-making historical figure.

Both the eventful man and the event-making man appear at the forking points of history. The possibility of their action has already been prepared for by the direction of antecedent events. The difference is this. In the case of the eventful man, the preparation is at a very advanced stage. It requires a relatively simple act—a decree, a command, a common-sense decision— to make the decisive choice. He may "muff" his role or let someone steal it from him. But even if he doesn't, this does not prove him an exceptional creature. His virtue or vice is inferred from the happy or unhappy consequence of what he has done, not from the qualities he has displayed in the doing of it.

The event-making man, on the other hand, finds a fork in the historical

---

[4] Cf. C. N. Cochrane, *Christianity and Classical Culture*, p. 211, Oxford, 1940.

road, but he also helps, so to speak, to create it. He increases the odds
of success for the alternative he chooses by virtue of the extraordinary
qualities he brings to bear to realize it. At the very least, like Caesar and
Cromwell and Napoleon, he must free the path he has taken from
opposition and, in so doing, display exceptional qualities of leadership.
It is the hero as event-making man who leaves the positive imprint of his
personality upon history—an imprint that is still observable after he has
disappeared from the scene. The merely eventful man whose finger plugs
a dike or fires the shot that starts a war is rarely aware of the nature of the
alternative he faces and of the train of events his act sets off.

It is easy to make a sharp distinction in analysis between the eventful
man and the event-making man, but there are few historical figures that will
fit snugly into either classification. We must leave to historians the delicate
task of ascertaining whether any particular "hero" of human history is, in
respect to some significant happening, an event-making character—or merely
lucky. That the classes defined by the distinction are not empty of members
has been made apparent for eventful men and will be established for
event-making men. Whether it is possible to treat these classes in terms of
gradations or combinations of qualities common to both is doubtful. Yet
the same historical personage may be eventful in one respect, event-making
in another, and neither in a third.

It is not suggested that this approach is the only one that can be taken
in evaluating the historical significance of individuals in history. For the
nature of their influence may be expressed in ways so manifold that they
sum up to a torrent, and yet at the same time in ways so indirect that it
is difficult to trace their path.

The influence of Thomas Jefferson and Abraham Lincoln on American
life, on the ways Americans have thought and acted, has been enormous.
Yet it would be difficult, and perhaps irrelevant, to classify them either as
eventful or event-making. Jefferson wished to be remembered after he
was gone as "the author of the Declaration of Independence, the statute of
Virginia for religious liberty, and father of the University of Virginia." Yet
separately or together these achievements do not indicate that he was an
eventful or event-making man. There is much in the contemporary rhetoric
of democracy which would now be different had Jefferson not composed
the Declaration of Independence, but the vision and faith to which he gave
such felicitous phrasing were common to the distinguished company of
whom he was one. The Statute on Religious Freedom gave formal expression
to a movement of religious tolerance already making its way through the
states. The future of higher education in America, which already had a
distinguished past before Jefferson, could hardly be said to have been
profoundly influenced by him.

Oddly enough, from the point of view of narrow historical action, it is
to something by which Jefferson himself set much less store that we must

turn to find evidence for his event-making status. This is the Louisiana Purchase, in which he was the moving figure. He carried it through in the teeth of an opposition strong enough to have daunted a weaker man. And yet had this territory not been acquired from Napoleon when it was, England would probably have fallen heir to it at the Congress of Vienna if not sooner. Without the Louisiana territory—and the west to which it furnished access—the United States might have remained an Atlantic seaboard power. Its political history as well as its economic history might have been very different. There is no assurance that another incumbent of the presidency than Jefferson would have had the foresight and energy required to seize this golden opportunity to remove a foreign power and potential enemy from our borders, and at the same time to double the area under the American flag. But however we evaluate Jefferson's part in the territorial expansion of the United States, his stature as a man and thinker and his role as a historical force on American culture do not depend upon it. There is room for others besides those whom we call historical "heroes" in a democracy. . . .

At this point it is necessary to consider the relation between the hero and social interests. For one way of losing sight of the problem is to show that heroic action fits into the needs of a class already in power or of a class that comes into power after his work is done. Such an analysis, even when it is true, does not rule out the possibility that the class that remains in power and the class that comes to power do so in virtue of the unique qualities of the hero who serves their interests. But very often it is assumed that this possibility has been ruled out when all that has been established is that the hero must take note of social interests and find support among them.

The event-making figure in history obviously can achieve nothing by himself alone. He is dependent upon a narrow group of lieutenants or assistants who constitute a "machine," and upon a much broader group in the population whom we may call a social class. Both groups are tied to him by bonds of interest, but the nature of the interests is different. An oversimplified conception of the role of interests often presents the event-making figure as their servant, selected because of his capacity to further them and replaceable when he fails. The event-making figure is thus reduced once more to an instrument of a historical or class Purpose, that is, the purposes of other men. The effect of his own purpose is regarded as a minor detail. That many, if not most, of the political personalities who stride the boards of history for a brief moment are instruments of other people's purposes may be granted. But it cannot be granted for those whom we have called event-making figures. We shall consider the relation of the hero, first to the social class that supports him, and then turn to his machine.

The dependence of the eventful figure on the support of a social class is much more in evidence before he accedes to power than when he is in possession of power and commands the state forces of coercion and education. A powerful social class which sees its vested position threatened, or which desires to use political power to break the vested position of another class, can usually arrange to give a candidate for the role of hero the *chance* to make good. But he may not be able to carry out all the tasks entrusted to him. His role may be that of a Bruening, a Schleicher, a von Papen, a Hoover, a Kerensky, or even a Leon Blum. But when he does make good, his very success, if he is skillful enough, makes him independent of the class chiefly responsible for his selection. He may still serve its interests, but the decision to do so is his now and not theirs.

The independence of the event-making man, over and against the class whose interest he actually or presumably has been selected to serve, is achieved in various ways. First, he can build up other social interests in opposition to the class that has sponsored him. This is not difficult because in the demagogic preparation for power he has already promised much to other classes, except the national scapegoat. Since he always speaks in the name of the nation or people, he can justify his independence of the class that has originally supported him in terms of the very myths this class has helped to propagate. Secondly, the event-making man comes into control of the armed forces of the state. Not infrequently he already enjoys some military prestige and power before his advent to power. Third, he brings his machine into play to take over and administer social functions, pulverize opposition, and consolidate military influence. As far as possible the machine reduces all potential centers of resistance and draws into its periphery all independent institutions. In fact, it is the machine that makes possible the pursuit of the first two methods by which the event-making figure emancipates himself from dependence upon the class whose social need gave him his original opportunity.

It is to the machine then and not to the social class that we must look to uncover the chief dependence of the hero. Whether it be a political party, a Jesuit religious order, a military camarilla, the hero must bind it to himself with hoops stronger than steel. If he is to play the man of the hour and pay his debts to the social class that supported him, the machine is a convenient instrument. If he decides to take a course independent from the one he was expected to follow, its iron loyalty is all the more necessary. In either case the machine must become *his* machine if he is to triumph. How is this accomplished? In the main by giving its members certain material and psychological privileges that are sufficiently distinctive to mark them off as a separate social grouping. As a group they must be convinced that they are the senior partner in any political alliance with other social groups. They either supplant the existing bureaucracy or fuse with it in such a way that they occupy all the strategic posts.

The historical hero, however, cannot become merely the instrument of his machine and enjoy power long. For all his reliance upon it, he must remain its master. This he accomplishes by making it evident that he is indispensable to the continuation of its privileges, that his downfall is their downfall, but not necessarily that its downfall is his. Just as he uses the machine to bring other social groups in line, the hero uses these social groups, tamed but resentful over the privileges lost to the machine, to keep the latter in tow. The event-making figure in history wins the opportunity to move freely by skillfully playing off against each other the groups upon whom he is dependent. That is why he is more than an instrument of a social class and more than a captain of a robber band. That is why he can be ruthless, if necessary, to the social class whose interests he claims to represent. That is why he can whirl his machine around into an abrupt spin in an opposite direction without consulting them or fearing defection. It goes without saying that he always strives to keep his machine in order, free of the grit and sand of dissidence and with an ample supply of spare parts at hand for necessary replacements.

Our conclusion then is that without meeting some social and group interests—economic, national, psychological—the hero cannot influence historical events; but he meets them in such a way that he always retains a considerable degree of freedom in choosing which interests to further and which to suppress or weaken. The behavior of most historical figures in relation to political and social issues can be explained in terms of the interests that speak through them. But there are individuals in history who not only talk back but react in such a way as to modify the original relations of social interest in a radical way.

The particular role that any historical character plays in relation to social interests may not be apparent from what he says about himself. He may claim to be serving the interests of a class when he is actually doing something quite different, or he may regard himself as completely independent of all social pressures when in fact he is merely a servant, sometimes even a contemptible tool, of special privilege.

This raises the question of individual consciousness and historical action.

Many leading historical figures have little consciousness, or a false consciousness, of the eventful place they hold in history. What they do seems to them to be exacted by the necessities of the situation, working through them to a foreordained result, rather than achieved by voluntary action and intelligent planning in whose absence affairs would turn out quite differently. Even genuine event-making men, like Cromwell and Lenin, regarded themselves respectively as instruments of divine and dialectical necessity.

On the other hand, there are historical characters, borne along on the tide of events, who feel that they are controlling the direction of the wave. Or they make claims of having influenced events in one field whereas their real influence is in another. A particularly instructive example of this was the pathetic illusion of Neville Chamberlain that it was he alone who was settling the destiny of our century.

Immediately after the Munich Pact in 1938, Chamberlain was widely regarded as an event-making man, admired by those who approved of his policy and condemned by those who did not. The former agreed with his conviction that he had snatched "peace for our time" from the very jaws of the Moloch of war. The latter were convinced that after Munich no western power would or could dispute Hitler's march to the East. A few made a more sober estimate of the situation.

Although we know that the Munich Pact did not bring peace in our time, its actual historical significance is still shrouded in obscurity. It depends upon the answer to the following questions. What would have happened if Chamberlain and Daladier, who dragged after him in reluctant tow, had presented an ultimatum of war to Hitler instead of flying to Munich and coming to terms with him? Would Hitler have marched into the Sudetenland as he later marched into Poland, despite the fact that Russia had not yet assured him that he would have no second front? If he had, would the English and French have been able in the ensuing war to put up a better defense than they did when war came a year later? Was the Czech military strength of greater value than a year won for additional armament—inadequate as the latter was even in 1939? Would a war begun in 1938 have resulted in the overrunning of England before the United States, still largely peace-minded, could enter it? Had war broken out, would the large pacifist and isolationist groups in England and America have seen through the hypocrisy of Hitler's claims in behalf of the "poor Sudetens" who indisputably were more German than Czech?

Without more data at our command we cannot answer these questions. But we can answer the question whether or not Chamberlain's capitulation was merely a strategic postponement, forced by lack of preparedness, of the inescapable showdown. This is a matter that is not shrouded in obscurity. If it were true, as some of his defenders have urged, that this is what determined Chamberlain's historic decision, Chamberlain's stature as a statesman would be enormously increased. If it were true, and if the Axis goes down to defeat, historians might very well regard him as among the greatest event-making men of his generation. But it is not true. By his unwearied insistence that the peace had been saved, Chamberlain himself provides the evidence that his decision was not motivated by the desire to gain time for preparation. Even if it turns out that the year won by Munich was necessary to eventual victory, Chamberlain did not organize or plan it that way. In the light of the most favorable outcome, he was not the contriver of good fortune but, duped by his fears and made foolish by his self-righteousness, he was at best a happy accident in that good fortune. His judgment was a thousand times wrong even if historians of a later day, writing in a free world, might congratulate themselves on the lucky fact that by gaining a year's grace in 1938, England was able to stave off France's fate in 1940. At best, then, Chamberlain may be considered an eventful man, certainly not event-making.

How fantastically false was Chamberlain's consciousness of his own historical role may be plainly seen in his memorable address to the House of Commons on October 6, 1938. He unequivocally declared that whether there should be war or not depended upon him, and on him alone, and that his decision had banished its shadows for our time.

> *Anyone who had been through what I have had to go through, day after day and face to face, with the thought that in the last resort it would be I, I alone, who would have to say that "yes" or "no" which would decide the fate of millions of my countrymen and their wives and families—anyone who has been through that, would not readily forget. . . . A man who gets to my age in my position tends to feel that he may disregard any abuse that is leveled at him if his conscience approves what he has done. Looking back on those events I feel convinced . . . that my action was only what one in my position would do. I say that by my action I did avert war.*

It is a sobering thought that a statesman in a democracy can believe and openly proclaim that on his single word the destiny of his nation depends. But far more significant here is Chamberlain's political innocence in seriously entertaining the notion that he could stop a war that had been in the making from the very moment Hitler assumed power.

Once Fascism had consolidated its internal position, it was beyond the effort of a host of peace-loving statesmen to block the dynamic force to war that was generated by a peculiar combination of economic need, fanatical ideology, and intense chauvinism. Hitler made no secret of his intentions before he came to power, and every step he took after he came to power showed that German society was being geared to total war. The sole effect of negotiation with him could be at most a calendar victory—an enforced change in his timetable. This might have tremendous importance, but only in relation to the striking power of the armies when war broke out. A statesman who imagined that, by a pact or memorandum, or by any concession short of total capitulation, he could immobilize the tensions straining toward release betrayed the perspectives of a small-town politician.

There are situations in the world no hero can master. They break with such fury that neither the potentially event-making man nor his pedestrian camp follower can withstand it, although they may ride them out differently. These situations are commonly found at the end of prolonged periods of distress and oppression, as in the great revolutionary upheavals. They are also found when two powerful nations are so organized that one or both cannot feel safe so long as the main trade routes, the markets reached by them, and the sources of raw materials and supply are straddled by the other —conditions antecedent to many wars from the days when Rome faced Carthage to the days when Imperial Germany challenged British sea power and Japan strove for the hegemony of the entire Pacific. In general, whenever opposing sets of interests are conceived in an absolute way so that the fulfillment of one set demands the liquidation of the other, without compromise or pity or reference to other interests that are common, we have the makings of social catastrophes. They burst on society with the elemental force of natural phenomena and overwhelm alike the just and the unjust, the wise and the foolish.

But there are other situations in which a gifted man of good or evil genius can so profoundly affect men and events that he becames an event-making man. That there are such situations and such men is something difficult to establish. In the next chapter we shall examine a great historical event as a crucial test of the theoretical position already sketched. We will show that there has been at least one event-making man[5] in our time who has redetermined the course of history and, in so doing, has influenced the life of the great majority of men, women, and children on the face of the globe.

THE ADVENTURER | WILLIAM BOLITHO

Adventure is the vitaminizing element in histories, both individual and social. But its story is unsuitable for a Sabbath School prize book. Its adepts are rarely chaste, or merciful, or even law-abiding at all, and any moral peptonizing, or sugaring, takes out the interest, with the truth, of their lives.

It is so with all great characters. Their faults are not mud spots, but structural outcroppings, of an indivisible piece with their personality. But there is a special reason for the inveterate illegality, or if you prefer, wickedness, of your true adventurer, which is inherent in the concept of Adventure itself. Adventure is the irreconcilable enemy of law; the adventurer must be unsocial, if not in the deepest sense anti-social, because he is essentially a free individualist.

This is what boys—those natural judges of the matter—have been trying to mutter for centuries, when fobbed off with lives of missionaries, or generals, where varied incident in vain ornaments an essentially un-adventurous character. A feat, a danger, a surprise, these are bonbons adventure showers on those who follow her cult with a single mind. Their occurrence even repeated does not constitute a life of adventure.

5 Lenin.

From William Bolitho, *Twelve Against the Gods.* Copyright, 1929, by Simon and Schuster, Inc., and Copyright, 1957, by Cybil Bolitho Fearnley. Reprinted by permission of Simon and Schuster, Inc.

Here also we renounce utterly the comfort of Mr. Kipling, who believes commuting, and soldiering in the British Army, and buying English country houses, adventurous; and Mr. Chesterton, who is certain that a long walk on Sunday and a glass of beer set one spiritually in the company of Alexander, and Captain Kidd and Cagliostro. All this amiable misconception is as touching as the children's wish for a good pirate, for bloodshed in which no one gets hurt, and roulette with haricot beans. Tom Sawyer knew better. The adventurer is an outlaw. Adventure must start with running away from home.

But in the mere fact that the essentially socially-minded, the good, the kind, and the respectable long to adopt the adventurer, it is clear that the opposition set between adventure and order, between the adventurer and society, is not exterior to humanity, but an inner antithesis, which divides our will.

The adventurer is within us, and he contests for our favor with the social man we are obliged to be. These two sorts of life are incompatibles; one we hanker after, the other we are obliged to. There is no other conflict so deep and bitter as this, whatever the pious say, for it derives from the very constitutions of human life, which so painfully separate us from all other beings. We, like the eagles, were born to be free. Yet we are obliged, in order to live at all, to make a cage of laws for ourselves and to stand on the perch. We are born as wasteful and unremorseful as tigers; we are obliged to be thrifty or starve, or freeze. We are born to wander, and cursed to stay and dig.

And so, the adventurous life is our first choice. Any baby that can walk is a splendid and typical adventurer; if they had the power as they have the will, what exploits and crimes would they not commit! We are born adventurers, and the love of adventures never leaves us till we are very old; old, timid men, in whose interest it is that adventure should quite die out. This is why all the poets are on one side, and all the laws on the other; for laws are made by, and usually for, old men.

It is this doublemindness of humanity that prevents a clear social excommunication of the adventurer. When he appears in the flesh indeed, he can hope for no mercy. Adventure is a hard life, as these twelve cases will remind you. The moment one of these truants breaks loose, he has to fight the whole weight of things as they are; the laws, and that indefinite smothering aura that surrounds the laws that we call morals; the family, that is the microcosm and whip lash of society; and the dead weight of all the possessors, across whose interwoven rights the road to freedom lies. If he fails, he is a mere criminal. One-third of all criminals are nothing but failed adventurers; they usually get a stiffer sentence than the rest, the imbeciles and the hungry. It is when he imposes himself and gets out of reach of the police that society's reaction is most curious. No one cares to say that Napoleon, or Alexander, or Caesar, were worse men, before any fair court, than Deadwood Dick and Jesse James; we try to digest them. The consequences of their actions are turned into motives; boys are urged to imitate some version of their lives from which all their disgraceful, but practicable and necessary, stepping-stones have been carefully removed.

To these perjuries and frauds, the respectable can plead "crime passionnel." It is violently unpleasant to send a Napoleon to prison— though when they had to, they did it. But in another aspect of the social problem of adventure, the deliberate trickery of the adventurous into lawfulness, the altered signpost and the camouflaged cage, "we of the virtue" are harder to defend. These booby traps are always set; the recruiting sergeant is always waiting at the first corner for the runaway to sell him a uniform or a flag, but in unsettled times, when the drive to adventure becomes too general and fierce for any ordinary method of society to contain, law and order do not hesitate to descend to special ruses. So the wild riders of the Middle Ages were embrigaded into that flattest of enterprises, knight errantry, shipped off to the dull and most legitimate wars of the Crusades, or bamboozled into being a sort of blue police of the great highroad.

No, the adventurer is an individualist and an egotist, a truant from obligations. His road is solitary, there is no room for company on it. What he does, he does for himself. His motive may be simple greed. It most often is, or that form of greed we call vanity; or greed of life, which is no more admirable, after all. But beware of underestimating this motive. Greed has been loaded with almost as many stupid insults as that other fundamental, sexual instinct; yet it would be gratitude for us at least, the adventurous race by definition, the insatiable Europeans, the conquistadores, to think of it as a virtue, a manorial virtue, out of which our difference from and supremacy over the contented breeds has demonstrably proceeded. God help the ungreedy . . . that is, the Australian blacks, the poor Bushmen of South Africa, those angelic and virtuous Caribs, whom Columbus massacred in the earthly paradise of Haiti, and all other good primitives who, because they had no appetite, never grew.

At the beginning of most careers stands an adventure, and so with states, institutions, civilizations. The progress of humanity, whatever its mysterious direction, is not motored by mere momentum. Let ethics make what it can of it. There is therefore a sociological role of adventure; necessarily an accidental one, since it is in itself nonsocial. History is jolted along with great breaches of law and order, by adventurers and adventures. From the flint-jabber age to standing room in the subway, from a cave at Les Eyzies to the plumbing of New York, we have come by two forces of effort, not one; the guard and the search, made by the home-stayer on the one hand, and by the bold affronter of the New on the other. That is, by the adventurer as well as by the citizen. By law, but also by those who leaped outside its protecting palisade, caring nothing if they damaged it in the action, and augmented the treasures of the race by courage and not thrift.

The first adventurer was a nuisance; he left the tribal barricade open to the risk of the community when he left to find out what made that noise in the night. I am sure he acted against his mother's, his wife's, and the counsel of old men's strict orders, when he did it. But it was he that found where the mammoths die and where after a thousand years of use there was still enough ivory to equip the whole tribe with weapons. Such is the ultimate outline of the adventurer; Society's benefactor as well as pest.

On the strength of this sociological role, then, the adventurer may depart on his high and lonely quest with some of our sympathy restored to him. He, our alternative self, has need of it, for the odds are against him. His first enemy we know, the mechanical, interlocking weight of law, social and moral. The second is the Unknown itself. In so far as the nature of all living things is conditioned by their enemies, the adventurer is defined by his fight with Order, and his fight with Chance. The first he may win —if he does not, he will go to prison. The second he cannot beat, for it is a manifestation of the universal. This book contains no invitation to the life of adventure: that has the same end as all the rest. I do not mean that in our material categories an adventurer cannot be successful. Some, though not the greatest, have died of old age, on heaps of that they set out to get. There is a more subtle tragedy that waits for adventurers than ruin, penurious old age, rags, contempt. It is that he is doomed to cease to be an adventurer. The law of his morphology is that, setting out a butterfly, he is condemned when his development is ripe to become a caterpillar. The vocation of adventure is as tragic as that of Youth; its course is parabolic, not straight; so that at a certain point it leads back to the cage again. The greatest adventurer that ever lived ended as a nervous, banal millionaire.

The secret of this ultimate tragedy of adventure is psychological; it hides in the nature of the adventurer's motive, swinish and god-like. It is interwoven in his personality. For this greed they have in all their five senses, for gold, for power, for vainglory, for curiosity, even at their highest moments, the greed for life itself, is dual. It contains the urge to keep, as well as to grab. It is retentive as well as prehensile. One of the fascinations of watching these lives is to follow the beautiful interplay of static and active greed in them, the slow advantage of conservation creeping upon acquisition, the sudden incursion of fear, the fear to which even Alexander sacrificed in his tent, when he knew he had won too much and the adventure was over, which is the sign of conservation's progress within him, and the inevitable deadening of its complement that follows.

For these are men betrayed by contradiction inside themselves. Their mixture differs from ours only in its proportions; in them too is a social man at war with a free man, miser as well as spendthrift, stay-at-home as well as rolling stone, hoarder and gambler, shepherd and hunter. It is his own social self that trips up the adventurer, and strangles him.

Above these closely related sociological and psychological struggles of the adventurer there is another, sublimely interesting, transcendent to both: the fight, which is like a wooing of the unknown, whose names are also chance, danger, inexhaustible container of everything that is new. It is with desire of her, herself inseparable from her gifts, that he is greedy. It is her perfidy—here is her majesty and cruelty—that loads him with prizes, that muffles him with the veils of her benevolence, to chain him with gold and victories so that he dares not go on, to change him from a lover into a slave. It is when the pirates count their booty that they become mere thieves.

So much for the main outline, sociological, psychological and in a sense mystical, of adventurer and adventure, which I hope these twelve practical researches that follow will fill in with many curious and interesting variations. Among them there will be found two or three women, out of the few that so far have clearly merited to be in the sublime company by the size and originality of their fate. During the interminable age (which however seems just ending), in which marriage was the career of women, it might be defended that every woman's life contained an adventure; and that every woman of marriageable age was an adventuress, just as married women are society's irreducible bodyguard. This is the old novelists' thesis —the stereotype of that adventure and its banality puts it outside our scope. But now that times are changing, the once purely speculative question as to whether women, outside the simple limits of their economic dependence on man, could feel and follow adventure has become important, and any light the study of undoubted woman-adventurers (adventuresses is a question-begging epithet) of the past can throw on this, and any evidence for or against a different morphology of the sexes in adventure will be interesting.

It is evident that the varying resistances of the three formative elements, that is, the social complex, the field, and the psychology of the adventurer, alter not only adventure's features—since every age produces its peculiar type, conquerors in antiquity, discoverers in the Middle Ages, prospectors in the nineteenth century—but its quantity and incidence, at any rate from the point of view of the historian. Of these we must neglect the third, supposing it constant since we cannot estimate it. But it is obvious enough that the influence of the other two can be expresed in a simple law: that adventure is harder, rarer, and less important, according to the strength of the social tie, and to the narrowing of the field of the unknown. Both these adverse conditions are in operation today. We are far from an international government, but we already have an international police, with cables, posts, aeroplanes and a general similarity of codes and understanding at its service, which would make short work today of the adventurous lives of a Cellini, a Casanova, a Cagliostro. This ecumenical civilization, as Keyserling calls it, allows less and less space for the individual. Concurrently the field has cramped with the mapping of the world. The geographical unknown, the easiest of access and the most naively alluring, has gone. There is a telephone wire to Lhassa, flags on each Pole, and though from time to time a few indomitable ladies try to convince us that the Sahara is not commonplace, and romantic Travels to places in Asia—to which the tourist agencies will sell you a ticket—still dribble from the press, in the gloomy schoolboy commonplace, "exploration is worked out." Is adventure, with these handicaps, a thing of the past?

I have already discarded the comfort of those writers and poets, who in the difficulty try to palm off as adventure what is only "interesting" and often only mildly interesting at that. Without descending to the adulteration of good notions, adventure does still exist, and even the adventurer, in his fortunate and aesthetic form, with a fate out of contact with sordidness, is no rarer than he has always been. There have been lean seasons for adventurers before, the eighteenth century notably, when everything seemed owned, done, mapped. In such times the new is to be sought inwards, not in immutable Nature, but in the ever renewed flux of human life. Geography has become banal, but topography is inexhaustibly original.

It is there that immortal adventure has taken refuge in our days, in the deserts of high finance, the jungles of business among the innumerable savage tribes that our great cities have disguised and not exterminated, in the human world, where there are greater spaces than between the stars. In the titanic works and events of our day there is the same hostile cooperation of runaway and stay-at-home, the same cult-struggle with the same enigmatic goddess, who asks all and gives all. History has always treasured a catalogue of adventurers—she has not changed her ways, though she may not, for business reasons, be allowed to publish it.

THE ARTIFACT | *FITZ ROY RICHARD SOMERSET, LORD RAGLAN*

In the earlier chapters of this book I took a succession of well-known heroes of tradition, and attempted to show that there is no justification for believing that any of these heroes were real persons, or that any of the stories of their exploits had any historical foundation. In the course of the discussion I had frequent occasion to suggest that these heroes, if they were genuinely heroes of tradition, were originally not men but gods, and that the stories were accounts not of fact but of ritual—that is, myths. As my chief object in those chapters was, however, to show that the heroes had no claim to historicity, I made no attempt to link them, or the beliefs connected with them, to any general ritual scheme. Before so doing, it

From *The Hero*, by Lord Raglan. Reprinted by permission of Random House, Inc.

seemed desirable to demonstrate, both theoretically and by examples, the intimate association of myth with ritual, an association that has been recognized by many leading students of these subjects, and upon which depends the validity of the conclusions I have reached.

Some years ago I had occasion to study the myth of Œdipus, and to try to analyze it,[1] and I was struck by the similarity of many of the incidents in it to incidents in the stories of Theseus and Romulus. I then examined the stories of a number of other traditional heroes of Greece, and found that when these stories were split up into separate incidents, there were certain types of incident which ran through all the stories.

Whether these parallels have any significance, or whether they are merely coincidences, the sort of thing that might happen to or be readily invented about any hero, are questions to which we shall come later. My first task is to show that the parallels exist, and for that purpose it is necessary to tabulate and number them. What I have done is to take a dozen heroes whose stories are narrated in sufficient detail, to tabulate the incidents in their careers, and to regard as typical such incidents as occur in the majority of the stories. By tabulating these typical incidents, I have arrived at what appears to be a pattern, in which I include all incidents, whether they are miraculous or whether they seem insignificant, which occur with sufficient regularity. I have then fitted the pattern back on to my dozen heroes and, finding that it fits, have extended it to a number of heroes from outside the classical area, with what have been to me surprising results.

I should like it to be quite clear that in the potted biographies which follow there is no intention of giving a complete account of the heroes. Irrelevant incidents and alternative versions are omitted, and no attempt is made to distinguish between genuine mythology—that is, mythology connected with ritual—and the imitation mythology which probably forms a large part of the stories of Arthur and of Romulus. The wearing of an imitation sword may be just as significant as the wearing of a real one, and it is with the uniform of the heroes and not with their outfitters that I am at present concerned.

The pattern, then, is as follows:

(1) The hero's mother is a royal virgin;

(2) His father is a king, and

(3) Often a near relative of his mother, but

(4) The circumstances of his conception are unusual, and

(5) He is also reputed to be the son of a god.

(6) At birth an attempt is made, usually by his father or his maternal grandfather, to kill him, but

(7) He is spirited away, and

---

[1] *Vide* my *Jocasta's Crime.*

   (8)   Reared by foster-parents in a far country
   (9)   We are told nothing of his childhood, but
  (10) On reaching manhood he returns or goes to his future kingdom.
  (11) After a victory over the king and/or a giant, dragon, or wild beast,
  (12) He marries a princess, often the daughter of his predecessor, and
  (13) Becomes king
  (14) For a time he reigns uneventfully, and
  (15) Prescribes laws, but
  (16) Later he loses favor with the gods and/or his subjects, and
  (17) Is driven from the throne and city, after which
  (18) He meets with a mysterious death,
  (19) Often at the top of a hill.
  (20) His children, if any, do not succeed him.
  (21) His body is not buried, but nevertheless
  (22) He has one or more holy sepulchers.

Let us now apply this pattern to our heroes, and we will start with

ŒDIPUS

His mother, Jocasta, is (1) a princess, and his father is (2) King Laius, who, like her, is (3) of the line of Cadmus. He has sworn to have no connection with her, but (4) does so when drunk, probably (5) in the character of Dionysos. Laius (6) tries to kill Œdipus at birth, but (7) he is spirited away, and (8) reared by the King of Corinth. (9) We hear nothing of his childhood, but (10) on reaching manhood he returns to Thebes, after (11) gaining victories over his father and the Sphinx. He (12) marries Jocasta, and (13) becomes king. For some years he (14) reigns uneventfully, but (16) later comes to be regarded as the cause of a plague, and (17) is deposed and driven into exile. He meets with (18) a mysterious death at (19) a place near Athens, called the Steep Pavement. He is succeeded by (20) Creon, through whom he was deposed, and though (21) the place of his burial is uncertain, he has (22) several holy sepulchers.

He does not seem to have been regarded as a legislator; apart from that we may award him full marks....

The lives of the Old Testament heroes have been heavily edited, but the same pattern is nevertheless apparent. Let us take three examples:

JOSEPH

His mother, Rachel, is (1) the daughter of a patriarch, and his father, Jacob, is (2) a patriarch, and (3) her first cousin. His mother conceives him (4) by eating mandrakes. In his childhood his brothers (6) attempt to kill him, but he is (7) saved by a stratagem, and (8) reared in Egypt. On reaching manhood he is (11) the victor in a contest in dream-interpretation and weather-forecasting, is (12) married to a lady of high rank, and (13) becomes ruler of Egypt. He (14) reigns prosperously, and (15) prescribes laws. We hear nothing of his later years, but the mention of a king who "knew not Joseph" suggests that he fell into disfavor.

Anyhow, we can give him twelve points.

MOSES

His parents (1 and 2) were of the principal family of the Levites, and (3) near relatives; he is (5) also reputed to be the son of Pharaoh's daughter. Pharaoh (6) attempts to kill him at birth, but (7) he is wafted away, and (8) reared secretly. We are told (9) nothing of his childhood, but on reaching manhood he (11) kills a man, and (10) goes to Midian, where (12) he marries the ruler's daughter. Returning (10) to Egypt, he (11) gains a series of magical victories over Pharaoh, and (13) becomes a ruler. His rule lasts a long time, and (15) he prescribes laws, but later he (16) loses the favor of Jehovah, is (17) removed from his leadership, and (18) disappears mysteriously from (19) the top of a mountain. His children (20) do not succeed him. His body (21) is not buried, but (22) he has a holy sepulcher near Jerusalem.

He scores twenty points, several of them twice, or, if we include Josephus's account, even three times. . . .

We find the same pattern in the life of a Javanese hero.

WATU GUNUNG

His mother, Sinta, appears (1) to be a princess, and his father is (2) a holy man. Since his mother sees his father only in a dream, the circumstances of his conception are (4) unusual. When quite young, he incurs his mother's wrath, and she (6) gives him a wound on the head. He (7) flees into the woods and does not return. We are told (9) nothing of his childhood, except that he is brought up by a holy man in (8) a far country. On reaching manhood he (10) journeys to a kingdom where (11) he kills the King, and (13) becomes king in his stead. After this he (12) marries his own mother and sister, who do not recognize him. For a long time he (14) reigns uneventfully, and has a large family, but eventually his mother recognizes the scar she gave him when a child, and is overcome with grief. The gods having (16) refused his request for another wife, he (17) invades heaven, but the gods, having learned by a stratagem the answer to his riddle and the secret of his invulnerability, put him to death (19) there by (18) separating his arms. His sons do not (20) succeed him, and (21) there is no mention of his burial.

His story, as given by Sir Stamford Raffles,[2] is obviously incomplete, yet

2 *History of Java*, Vol. i, pp. 421-4.

its resemblance to the Œdipus myth is striking, and we can give the hero eighteen points. . . .

The next two examples I shall give are Celtic and are interesting as showing how variations of the same theme can exist in the same culture area. The story of Llew Llawgyffes is given by Professor W. J. Gruffydd.[3]

LLEW LLAWGYFFES

His mother, Arianrhod, is (1) a royal virgin, and his father is apparently Gwydion, who is (2) a prince, and (3) her brother. The circumstances of his conception are (4) unusual, since his mother believes herself to be a virgin at the time of his birth. As soon as he is born he is (7) spirited away by his father, and (8) nursed by a foster-mother. When less than two years old he is (9) a "big lad," and (10) returns to the court. With his father's help he (11) wins magical victories, (12) marries a supernatural being, and (13) becomes a ruler. For a time he rules uneventfully, but later (16) loses favor with his wife, who (17) induces him to leave his court. He is (18) speared, but flies off in the form of an eagle, from (19) a curious elevated position. He has (20) no children and (21) no real death or burial.

He scores seventeen points.

ARTHUR

His mother, Igraine, is (1) a princess, and his father is (2) the Duke of Cornwall. He is, however, (5) reputed to be the son of Uther Pendragon, who (4) visits Igraine in the Duke's likeness. At birth he is apparently in no danger, yet is (7) spirited away and (8) reared in a distant part of the country. We hear (9) nothing of his childhood, but on reaching manhood he (10) travels to London, (11) wins a magical victory, and (13) is chosen king. After other victories he (12) marries Guinevere, heiress of the Round Table. After this he (14) reigns uneventfully, and (15) prescribes the laws of chivalry, but later there is (16) a successful conspiracy against him, while (17) he is abroad. He meets with (18) a mysterious death, and his children do not (20) succeed him. His body is (21) not buried, but nevertheless he has (22) a holy sepulcher at Glastonbury.

He scores nineteen points.

Traces of the pattern are also to be found in the story of

ROBIN HOOD

His father is a Saxon yeoman, but he is also (5) reputed to be the son of a great noble. We (9) hear nothing of his youth, but on reaching manhood he leads a life of debauchery until compelled to fly (10) to Sherwood, where

[3] *Math vab Mathonwy*, pp. 17 ff.

he (11) gains victories over the Sheriff of Nottingham, (12) marries Maid Marian, the Queen of May, and (13) becomes King of May and ruler of the forest. For a long time he reigns, and (15) prescribes the laws of archery, but eventually illness overtakes him, and he (17) has to leave the forest and meets (18) a mysterious death in (19) an upper room. He (20) has no children. The place of his death and burial are (21) variously given, but (22) miracles were performed at his tomb at Kirkley, in Yorkshire.

We can give him thirteen points.

Cuchulainn also scores a good number of points, and it is interesting to compare these heroes of myth with Hengist, who makes a journey, wins a victory, and becomes a king, but otherwise is not alleged to have done anything which brings him within the pattern. But the story of Hengist, as I have tried to show, is not myth but pseudo-history. It may be added that although several of the incidents are such as have happened to many historical heroes, yet I have not found an undoubtedly historical hero to whom more than six points can be awarded, or perhaps seven in the case of Alexander the Great. The differences between the hero of myth and the hero of history will emerge from our discussion of the significance of the pattern, which had better be left to another chapter.

The fact that the life of a hero of tradition can be divided up into a series of well-marked features and incidents—I have taken twenty-two, but it would be easy to take more—strongly suggests a ritual pattern. I doubt whether even the most fervent euhemerist would maintain that all these resemblances are mere coincidences; and if not, then three possibilities remain. The first is that all, or some, of the heroes were real persons whose stories were altered to make them conform to a ritual pattern; the second is that all, or some, of them were real persons in whose lives ritual played a predominant part; and the third is that they were all purely mythical. A discussion of this question will be attempted in the next chapter; in the present one I shall review the incidents of the hero's career, as they appear in the foregoing stories, and make some suggestions as to their significance.

The first point to be noted is that the incidents fall definitely into three groups: those connected with the hero's birth, those connected with his accession to the throne, and those connected with his death. They thus correspond to the three principal *rites de passage*—that is to say, the rites at birth, at initiation, and at death. I shall have more to say on this when we reach point number nine; let us now start at the beginning.

In connection with the first two points, we note that whenever there are royalties available, the hero is the son of royal parents; that he is nearly always the first child of his mother and, except where his father is a god, of his father, and that with very few exceptions his father does not marry twice. There is, of course, nothing marvellous in all this—some historical heroes have been the eldest child of monogamous royal parents, but I have laid stress upon it because it seems to be typical of the traditional hero, and is definitely not typical of the historical hero.

There is, it is true, a type of folk-tale in which the hero (or heroine), though of obscure origin, obtains a royal spouse and a throne, but this type of tale is probably derived from romances based on the central part of the myth, in which, as we have seen, the hero, though really of royal birth, appears, so to speak, out of the blue. In these tales we are never told of the hero's death, but merely that he "lived happily ever afterwards," which seems to suggest a desire to omit, rather than falsify, the latter part of the myth.

The fact that the hero's parents are often near relatives brings to mind the widespread custom by which kings marry their sisters, with which I have dealt elsewhere.

The circumstances in which our hero is begotten are very puzzling. When, as in the case of Heracles, a god takes the form of the hero's father, we are reminded that the Pharaoh, on particular occasions, approached his queen in the guise of a god.[4] In our stories, however, the circumstances, though almost always unusual, are extremely various, as are the guises in which the god appears. He may take the form of a thunderstorm, a bull, a swan, or a shower of gold. We may suspect, however, that the attribution of divine birth to a hero is not the result of his heroism, but is derived from the ritual union of a princess to her own husband, disguised as a god. It is comparatively easy for a man to disguise himself as a bull or swan, but while the thunderstorm and the shower of gold present greater difficulties and require further investigation, they clearly suggest a ritual rather than a historical origin for the stories.

We now come to the attempt on the hero's life at birth, which happens in almost every case and is one of the most striking features of the pattern. We are all familiar with such rites as that of the Phœnicians, by which the eldest son was burnt as a sacrifice to Moloch; in our stories, it would seem, a pretense is made of sacrificing the child, and sometimes an animal is sacrificed instead. It is often the father who tries to kill the infant hero, and this brings the stories into line with that of Abraham and Isaac. The attempt on the life of Moses, like that of nearly all the other heroes, was made at birth, but the story of Abraham and Isaac suggests that at one period the Hebrews performed this rite at puberty. We may note that while a ram was sacrificed in place of Isaac, Jacob appeared before his father wearing the skin of a kid, and Joseph wore a special garment which was soaked in goat's blood. We may perhaps suppose that a pretense was made of killing the child, which was wrapped in the skin of a sacrificed goat, and soaked in its blood. Such a rite accounts for some of our stories, such as that of Pelops, and also the widespread story of the Faithful Hound. Sometimes, it would seem the child itself was wounded in the leg; hence

[4] J. G. Frazer, op. cit., Vol. ii, p. 133.

perhaps the name "Œdipus," "swell-foot," and the many heroes who are lame, or who have scars on their legs. Many of the infant heroes, however, are set afloat in baskets or boxes, and these stories are found not merely in Greece and western Asia, but as far east as Japan.[5] I shall discuss them no further, except to say that while the story of the attempt on the infant hero's life can be explained as ritual, it is, though not miraculous, absent or at any rate extremely rare in the case of genuinely historical heroes.

Having escaped death, our heroes are all removed to a distance, and are usually brought up by a foreign king, though Jason and Asclepios are brought up by Cheiron. The latter is easy to understand if we suppose that Cheiron was the title given to a prince's official tutor, but nearly all our heroes are brought up by kings. This suggests several possibilities. The first is that it was actually the practice for kings to send their sons to be brought up by other kings, as we read of in the story of Hakon Adalstein's fostri. The second, which I have put forward elsewhere,[6] but which I am by no means confident about, is that princes succeeded their fathers-in-law, but became their sons by formal adoption. This might lead to a belief, or a pretense, that they were their real sons who had been removed at birth. The third is the opposite of the second. It is that it was part of the ritual that the prince, though a native, should pretend to be a foreigner. The question needs much more investigation than I have been able to give it.

We next come to point number nine: that we are told nothing of the hero's childhood. This may seem unimportant, since there are, of course, many great men of whose childhood we know nothing. In such cases, however, we equally know nothing of the circumstances of their birth. We may know the place and date, but that is all. With our heroes it is quite different; their birth is the central feature in a series of highly dramatic incidents—incidents that are related in considerable detail, and such as seldom, if ever, occur in the lives of real people. The most exciting things happen to our hero at birth, and the most exciting things happen to him as soon as he reaches manhood, but in the meantime nothing happens to him at all. If, as I suppose, our hero is a figure not of history but of ritual, this is just what one would expect, since as a general rule children take no part in ritual between the rites at birth and those at initiation. The story of the hero of tradition, if I understand it aright, is the story of his ritual progress, and it is therefore appropriate that those parts of his career in which he makes no ritual progress should be left blank. I would compare the blank that occurs during childhood with the blank that occurs after his installation as king has been completed.

The fact that on reaching manhood the hero forthwith sets out on a

5 B. H. Chamberlain: *The Kojiki*, p. 21. Frazer collects a number of these stories: *Folklore in the Old Testament*, Vol. ii, pp. 437 ff.

6 *Jocasta's Crime*, p. 195.

journey from the land of his upbringing to the land where he will reign is, of course, involved in the problem I have discussed under point number eight—that is, his being reared in a far country. It is a remarkable fact, however, that his victories almost always take place either on the journey or immediately after arrival at his destination. He makes a definite progress from a far country to the throne, and all his feats and victories are connected with that progress. Another remarkable fact is that the hero of tradition never wins a battle. It is very rarely that he is represented as having any companions at all, and when he has, he never trains them or leads them. The warrior kings of history, whether civilized or barbarian, have won their renown as leaders. When we think of them we think of serried ranks, of the Argyraspides, of the Tenth Legion, of the Guard which dies but does not surrender, and the impis which think it better to go forward and die than to go back and die. But there is nothing like that in the stories of the heroes of tradition. Our hero's followers, if any, are out of the way or killed off when his crucial fight takes place. All his victories, when they are actual fights and not magical contests, are single combats against other kings, or against giants, dragons, or celebrated animals. He never fights with ordinary men, or even with ordinary animals. And the king whom he fights is the king whom he will succeed, and who is often his own father. It is also possible that the monster with which the hero fights is merely the reigning king in disguise, or, in other words, that the reigning king had to wear an animal costume or mask in which to defend his title and his life. I will return to that later, but will first touch on the magical contest, which seems sometimes to be more important than the actual fight. Œdipus wins his throne by guessing a riddle, Theseus his by finding the way out of a maze. The magical victories of the three Jewish heroes are all connected with rain-making: Joseph successfully prognosticates the weather; Moses is successful in a series of magical contests in which rain-making is included; and Elijah defeats the prophets of Baal in a rain-making contest. Power over the elements is the most unvarying characteristic of the divine king, and it would seem that sometimes at least the candidate for the throne had to pass in a rain-making test.[7]

Our hero, then, has to qualify for the throne in two ways: he must pass a test in some such subject as rain-making or riddle-guessing, and he must win a victory over the reigning king. Whether this was a real fight or a mock contest in which the conclusion was foregone we cannot be certain. There have undoubtedly been many cases in which the king was put to death at the end of a fixed term, or when his powers began to wane. There may have been cases in which there was a fair fight with equal weapons between the king and his challenger, but the evidence for them is rather uncertain. What several of the stories suggest is that the old king was ritually killed,

[7] Some interesting suggestions on this point are made by Dr. C. B. Lewis: *Classical Mythology and Arthurian Romance*, pp. 41-5.

and that his successor had to kill an animal—wolf, boar, or snake—into which his spirit was supposed to have entered. I shall refer to this again when we come to point number eighteen.

After passing his tests and winning his victories, the hero marries the daughter, or widow, of his predecessor, and becomes king. It has often been assumed from this that the throne always went in the female line, and that the reigning queen or heiress could confer the title to it upon her husband simply by marrying him; in other words that any man who managed to marry the queen became king automatically, whatever his antecedents, and that the only way in which any man could lawfully become king was by marrying the queen. Such an assumption is going a great deal beyond the evidence of the stories, which suggest that the new king established his title to the throne by his birth, his upbringing, and his victories. There were, it would seem, recognized qualifications for the kingship, just as there were recognized qualifications for the queenship. We do not know for certain that the new queen was really the old queen's daughter, any more than we know for certain that the new king was really the old king's son. There may have been a ceremony of adoption in both cases, and in many tales of the Cinderella and Catskin types the future queen has to achieve her journey, her tests, and her victory. There is evidence, too, that at Olympia the winner of the girls' race became Hera, just as the winner of the men's race became Zeus.[8]

Anyhow, the fact that our hero marries a princess and at the same time ascends the throne is far from proving that he ascends the throne by virtue of his marriage. It may merely indicate what we know from other sources to be a fact: namely, that a *hieros gamos* or sacred marriage normally formed an essential and highly important feature of the coronation or installation ceremony. I know of no case, in any age or country, in which a man has become king simply by marrying the queen; he must first, so far as I can learn, have qualified for the throne, either by birth or by performing some feat or passing some test, and our heroes seem all to have qualified in all these ways. Even in modern Europe marriage never confers the right to a throne; princes and princesses who marry unqualified persons, who contract, that is to say, what are called morganatic marriages, not merely fail to raise the partners to the throne, but lose their own title to it. It is difficult to believe that the rules were less strict in ages when the ritual functions of a king and queen were far more important than they are today. The chief qualification for the throne has always been the possession of power, the power that is conferred by divine descent and the absorption of divine wisdom, and that is demonstrated by victory over the elements and over man. The conqueror may become king, since by his conquests he proves his possession of power, but that it has ever been believed that such power is conferred by a simple marriage ceremony is unproved and improbable.

[8] J. G. Frazer: *The Golden Bough*, Vol. iv, p. 91.

Our hero has now become king, and what does he do? It might be supposed that, having shown himself so brave and enterprising before coming to the throne, he would forthwith embark upon a career of conquest; found an empire and a dynasty; build cities, temples, and palaces; patronize the arts; possess a large harem; and behave generally as the conquering heroes of history have behaved, or tried to behave. The hero of tradition, however, in this as in most other respects, is totally unlike the hero of history. He does none of these things, and his story, from the time of his accession to the time of his fall, is as a rule a complete blank. The only memorial of his reign, apart from the events that begin and end it, is the traditional code of laws that is often attributed to him. As a fact, however, a code of laws is always the product of hundreds, if not thousands, of years of gradual evolution, and is never in any sense the work of one man. One man, a Justinian or a Napoleon, may cause laws to be codified, or may alter their incidence, but it has never been suggested that all, or even any, of the laws in their codes were devised by these monarchs. It is well known, in fact, that they were not. On the other hand it has been clearly shown by Sir James Frazer[9] that the Ten Commandments, in their familiar form, could have had nothing to do with Moses, since the original Ten Commandments, whoever first composed them, were entirely different. It seems clear, then, that the attribution of laws to a hero of tradition is merely a way of saying that they are very old and very sacred.

Our next point is that the hero of tradition, unlike most heroes of history, normally ends his career by being driven from his kingdom and put to death in mysterious circumstances. Sigurd is the only one of those whom we have considered of whose death we have a clear and non-miraculous account; even of Joseph we are told nothing of what happened between his father's death and his own. We may conclude that deposition and a mysterious death are a part of the pattern, but a puzzling feature is that there is nothing to suggest that the hero suffers a defeat. As he has gained the throne by a victory, one would expect him to lose it by a defeat, but this he never does.

Œdipus kills his father and marries his mother; one might expect that one of his sons, or some other prince would kill him and marry Jocasta, or, if she were too old, Antigone, and become king. Creon, however, who succeeds him, does so by turning the oracle against him, and several others among our heroes fall out with a god and, of course, get the worst of it. Others become unpopular with their subjects. In either case the hero's fall from favor is not gradual but sudden; at one moment he is apparently in full favor both with gods and men, and the next he has no friends, either human or divine.

The hero's death is mysterious, but one thing clear about it is that it never takes place within the city. Usually he is driven out, but sometimes he has

9 *Folklore in the Old Testament,* Vol. iii, p. 115.

left the city on some sacred mission. Then there is the hilltop, which appears in the stories of Œdipus, Theseus, Heracles, Bellerophon, and Moses, and which is suggested in several of the others. Taken in conjunction with the chariot of fire in which Romulus and Elijah disappear, and the lightning flash that kills Asclepios, it seems justifiable to conclude that in the most usual form of the rite the divine king was burned, either alive or dead, on a pyre erected on a hilltop, and that he was believed to ascend to the sky, in some form or other, in the smoke and flame. It is possible that, before being burnt, he was compelled to fight with and be defeated by his successor, but in the majority of stories there is nothing to suggest this.

The fact that the hero is never succeeded by his son—Nyikang seems to be the sole exception—might suggest that the inheritance went in the female line, but then no hero is succeeded by his son-in-law. If the king reigned for eight years only, and married at his coronation, his children could not succeed him, since they would be too young, but they might succeed his successor, and there is some evidence that this is what happened The succession at Thebes is not easy to make out, but Creon seems to have preceded and succeeded Œdipus, and also to have succeeded his sons. Perseus is said to have killed and succeeded Proetus, and to have been killed and succeeded by the latter's son. Ægisthus kills and succeeds Agamemnon, and eight years later is killed and succeeded by the latter's son Orestes. There were two royal families at Sparta, and it is possible that originally they reigned alternately.

The last point to be considered in the hero's career is that although he is usually supposed to have disappeared, yet nevertheless he has a holy sepulcher, if not several. I have attempted to explain his disappearance by suggesting that he was cremated, but if kings were cremated they could hardly have a sepulcher in the usual sense of the term, since we know that in all forms of religion the essential feature of a sepulcher, or a shrine, is that it is supposed to contain the bones, or at any rate some of the bones, of the holy person to whom it is dedicated. A great deal has, of course, been written on the customs of the Greeks with regard to the disposal of the dead, and their beliefs about the Otherworld, but I am here concerned merely to consider the rites which are suggested by the hero stories, and what they suggest to me is that, while ordinary people were buried, the bodies of kings were burnt, but not burnt thoroughly, so that the bones were left and could be buried. I understand that this view was put forward by Dörpfeld, though on different grounds, some thirty years ago, but I have not been able to see what he wrote. At any rate, similar customs are found in many parts of the world.

In conclusion, I should like to make it quite clear that I do not claim to have produced final solutions for any of the problems I have discussed in this chapter. What I have tried to show is that they are problems of custom and ritual, and not problems of history.

THE ANTI-HERO
IHAB HASSAN

"In its essence literature is concerned with the self," Lionel Trilling writes in *Freud and the Crisis of Our Culture,* "and the particular concern of the literature of the last two centuries has been with the self in its standing quarrel with culture."[1] The image of the self in its standing, and recently embittered, quarrel with culture—indeed in its quarrel with itself, as Mr. Trilling neglects to say—comes to focus in the figure of the anti-hero.

In fiction, the unnerving rubric "anti-hero" refers to a ragged assembly of victims: the fool, the clown, the hipster, the criminal, the poor sod, the freak, the outsider, the scapegoat, the scrubby opportunist, the rebel without a cause, the "hero" in the ashcan and "hero" on the leash. If the anti-hero seems nowadays to hold us in his spell, it is because the deep and disquieting insights revealed to us by modern literature often require that we project ourselves into the predicament of victims.

The gradual process of atrophy of the hero may have begun with Don Quixote, or perhaps even Job, Orestes, and Christ. It enters the critical phase, however, only late in the eighteenth century. Goethe's Werther introduces the "tragic" Romantic hero who, in his inordinate conception of himself, severs the traditional bond between the hero and his society, and points the way to such extreme stances of alienation as were to find expression in the Byronic and Sadist hero, in the gothic and demonic protagonist, in werewolf, ghoul, and vampire. But as the new bourgeois order, which the Romantic hero rejected, became a powerful social reality, the strategy of opposition changed. The characters of Stendhal, Balzac, and Flaubert often seem, as Raymond Giraud has recognized, "heroes of ironies" whose "ideals, desires, and feelings are in disharmony" with their "adult conception of reality."[2] Similarly, the subtitle for *Vanity Fair: A Novel Without a Hero,* suggests that Victorian fiction was quietly disposing of the heroic protagonist. The ambivalences of a bourgeois hero in an overwhelmingly middle-class society raise for him problems of estrangement and communion, sincerity and simulation, ambition and acquiescence, which we recognize as the patent themes of the great novels of the last century. The wretched fate of the lower-class hero, caught between malignant Heredity and crushing Environment in the *roman experimental* of Zola, and in the less experimental but more benign novels of the brothers Goncourt, reflects the familiar bias of Naturalism and marks a further stage in the disintegration of heroism.

From *Radical Innocence: Studies in the Contemporary American Novel* (Princeton, Princeton University Press, 1961).

[1] Lionel Trilling, *Freud and the Crisis of Our Culture* (Boston, 1955), pp. 58 ff.

[2] Raymond Giraud, *The Unheroic Hero* (New Brunswick, 1957), p. 189. See also Harry Levin, "From Priam to Birotteau," *Yale French Studies,* vi (1950), p. 76.

Victim to immitigable "cosmic laws," with little or no control over his fate in the world, man turns inward again. The next development is predictable. "The way was open from the realist to the intimist novel," Mario Praz concludes in *The Hero in Eclipse in Victorian Fiction.* "Disillusioned observation of life as it really was, led to the eclipse of the hero and the disclosure of man's swarming interior world, made up of disparate and contradictory things."[3]

With the retrenchment of the individual, the drama of good and evil which the hero and villain once objectified in society becomes blurred. The traditional forms of moral conflict are so internalized that no victory or defeat, where self is divided against itself, can claim to be more than pyrrhic. Cunningly introspective, the modern novel redefines the identity of its central character and redirects his energies toward the virtues of love or self-discovery, virtues that are a good deal more personal than social. To become someone, to know who or what one is, to reach finally another human being with love, and to do so in terms that society may censure, this is the passionate, bitter concern of the modern anti-hero. But the modern identity proved an elusive thing to capture. "You mustn't look in my novel for the old stable *ego* of the character," D. H. Lawrence wrote to Edward Garnett. "There is another *ego,* according to whose action the individual is unrecognizable, and passes through, as it were, allotropic states. . . ."[4] A new shifty ego, a new concept of man. The sad history of the anti-hero is nothing more than the history of man's changing awareness of himself. It is the record of his recoil.

The encounter between the new ego and the destructive element of experience, we have insisted, lies at the dramatic center of the modern novel in Europe and America. The encounter is further illumined by some striking European images which define the modern idea of the self and clarify its responses. We shall view some concrete instances of the anti-hero—whom in hope and charity we may simply call "hero." These instances are taken from writers of very different age and background, yet they add to a remarkably persistent theme.

To consider Dostoyevsky's *Notes from Underground,* 1864, modern is perhaps to stretch the idea of modernity to its permissible limit. The document so shrill and anxious, so full of spite and spleen, reveals, in any case, what the modern soul likes most to gnaw upon: itself. The dagger is turned inward, the most refined tortures are reserved for the self. Whom else are we really interested in? Listening for forty years from the crack under his floor, Dostoyevsky's hero looks at existence with a cringe and a snarl. He knows the intense pleasure of degradation and of despair and knows, while gnashing his teeth, that "there is no one even for you to feel vindictive

[3] Mario Praz, *The Hero in Eclipse in Victorian Fiction* (New York, 1956), p. 383.
[4] Aldous Huxley, ed., *The Letters of D. H. Lawrence* (London, 1956), p. 198.

against, that you have not, and perhaps never will have, an object for your spite. . . ."[5] Precisely the condition which Albert Camus calls, in *The Rebel,* metaphysical rebellion, and which our hero understands as a revolt against "the whole legal system of Nature."[6] But no one is to blame; "consequently there is only the same outlet left again—that is, to beat the wall as hard as you can."[7] This frenzy is not only meant to be a protest against the whole order of Nature, the terrible fact that "every sort of consciousness . . . is a disease," or merely a protest against the historical enemies of Dostoyevsky— rationalism, meliorism, and science, the coxcomb fact that two plus two equals four.[8] The frenzy, in the form of caprice, is also directed against our individuality. That Dostoyevsky's "insect" can establish his identity only by forcing himself to collide ignominiously with an arrogant officer who does not even recognize his existence is of no importance. The important thing is that it is *he* who *forces* the recognition. This is freedom.

The grotesque image of this strange creature haunts modern literature and remains at the center of our dread. Its cracked reflections in some way or other penetrate the works of most European novelists. And its perverse truths, almost insupportable, infiltrate recent American fiction which does not stem only, as Hemingway claimed, from a book by Mark Twain called *Huckleberry Finn* but also from another, it may be argued with equal perti- nence, by Dostoyevsky called *Notes from Underground.* The image, taken up, modified, and recreated by later novelists deserves further attention.

Conrad, we know, shared with Dostoyevsky more than the dubious heri- tage of a Slavic temper. His metaphysical romances of the seven seas subject the idea of heroism to an ironic rhetoric which is peculiarly modern, and his abiding interest in the theme of the double—his *Secret Sharer* and Dos- toyevsky's *The Double* come to mind—probes the distempers of the modern self in a way that seems now familiar. While no character of his strictly reminds us of the hero of the *Notes,* the state of immersion, the desperation felt in the heart of darkness or in the underground habitations of conscious- ness, the surrender to the "destructive element," compel our terrified assent in the novels of both authors. Kurtz, in *Heart of Darkness,* had perhaps immersed himself too deeply, there where victim and victimizer become one, till he could distinguish only the horror. But Kurtz creeping on all fours in the night-time jungle and Lord Jim erect and dazzling in spotless white are still two sides of the same image, two sides separated really by the enor- mous distance between action and heroic intention. Conrad does not repu- diate human striving. In a celebrated passage from *Lord Jim* he simply points to the way of fulfillment. "A man that is born falls into a dream like a man who falls into the sea," Conrad writes. "If he tries to climb out into the air as inexperienced people endeavor to do, he drowns. . . . The way is to

[5] *The Short Novels of Dostoyevsky,* Introduction by Thomas Mann (New York, 1945), p. 137.
[6] *Ibid.,* p. 137. [7] *Ibid.,* p. 140. [8] *Ibid.,* p. 132.

the destructive element submit yourself. . . ."[9] The unintelligent brutality of existence leaves man no other choice.

It is, of course, the unintelligent brutality of existence that dominates the Dublin of Joyce's *Ulysses;* the city becomes a focus, in Eliot's famous words, to "the immense panorama of futility and anarchy which is contemporary history."[10] The proportions of the hero are further shrunken, his self pushed further underground in the world of memory and fantasy. The element to which Bloom submits himself, in humor and humility, is the ignominious element. Insult and pathos, loneliness and failure, are his familiars. Leopold Bloom, wandering Jew, mock Odysseus, and lowly Christ, finally appears to us, above all, as "Everyman or Noman."[11] He stands between Stephen Dedalus and Molly Bloom, between intelligence and nature, as a pathetic monument to the generosity of suffering. For intelligence, in the person of Stephen—he is Lucifer and Hamlet and Dedalus—can only cry: *Non serviam!* And Nature, in the person of Molly—Ceres, Hera, eternal Mother Earth—must endlessly murmur: Yes I will Yes. Man, meanwhile, goes clowning his sentimental way into eternity, unable to reconcile himself completely to one or the other.

The two heroes of Joyce and of Dostoyevsky show that humility lies on the other side of spite. But the clown in man has many disguises. He is Bloom, "one lonely last sardine of summer."[12] He is also, as we shall see, an insect, a sentient tubercle, at best a shaggy wolf. The self in recoil cannot afford to be choosy.

Dostoyevsky's metaphor of man as an insect inevitably calls to mind Kafka's story, "Metamorphosis," in which the narrator is transformed into a huge, hideous, and pathetic vermin. This, too, is self-degradation, a form of the self in recoil. This, too, is protest. The theme is everywhere in Kafka, in *The Castle,* in *The Trial,* in "The Penal Colony" or "The Judgment." Man is always judged, and found invariably guilty. He is the victim of an unappeasable power, a horrible and recurrent outrage, and even in his most serene moments he can only exclaim, like the Hunter Gracchus: "I am here, more than that I do not know, further than that I cannot go. My ship has no rudder, and it is driven by the wind that blows in the undermost regions of death."[13] The vision of man is as grotesque as that of Dostoyevsky; but it goes farther, denying man freedom, the sheer horror of choice, and denying him grace. Indeed, of man Kafka can only say, "He found the Archimedean point, but he used it against himself; it seems that he was permitted to find it only under this condition."[14] The lever which gives man mastery over his

---

[9] Joseph Conrad, *Lord Jim* (New York, 1931), p. 214.

[10] T. S. Eliot, "Ulysses, Order and Myth," in John W. Aldridge, ed., *Critiques and Essays on Modern Fiction* (New York, 1952), p. 426.

[11] James Joyce, *Ulysses* (New York, 1946), p. 712. [12] *Ibid.,* p. 284.

[13] *Selected Stories of Franz Kafka,* Introduction by Philip Rahv (New York, 1952), p. 187.

[14] Franz Kafka, *Dearest Father* (New York, 1954), p. 378.

universe, moving worlds at the touch of a finger tip, is still the inbred dagger of the soul. In Kafka as in Dostoyevsky, the sense of compounded guilt and absurdity defines the point at which victimization and rebellion meet.[15]

This view of the human predicament will no doubt seem to many both exigent and extreme. It borders, people argue, on disease. Exactly. In the panoramic view of Thomas Mann, whose sane vision did not prevent him from cultivating a lifelong interest in Kafka and Dostoyevsky, disease and even death become an ultimate response to life. The idea informs at least two of his masterpieces, *The Magic Mountain* and *Death in Venice,* and it hovers about his latest work, *The Confessions of Felix Krull.* Hans Castorp reflects, as if prompted by the hero of Dostoyevsky's *Notes,* "Disease was a perverse, a dissolute form of life. And life? Life itself? Was it perhaps only an infection, a sickening of matter? . . . The first step toward evil, toward desire and death, was taken precisely then, when there took place that first increase in the density of the spiritual, that pathologically luxuriant morbid growth. . . ."[16] But the radical disease of consciousness, which the hero of Dostoyevsky resented to the end of his spite, and to which the Kafka hero finally submits in a lucid nightmare, is transmuted by Thomas Mann into a condition of spiritual refulgence. It is thus that Mann is able to claim, with Nietzsche and Dostoyevsky in mind, that "certain attainments of the soul and the intellect are impossible *without disease, without insanity, without spiritual crime, and* the *great invalids* are *crucified victims,* sacrificed to humanity and its advancement, to the broadening of its feeling and knowledge—in short, to its more *sublime health* [italics mine]."[17] Man, we see, pitches himself at the terrible limit of experience, as Lucifer did.

Mann's statement reminds us that grace, if it is to be found at all, lies deep in the soft core of violence. The saint and the criminal stand back to back on either side of the demonic. Both are protestants, both victims. But pure violence, like the demonic, has no reality in the public realm, the domain of action. Pure violence, as we shall repeatedly observe in modern fiction, seems almost the ultimate form of introspection. That the saint and the criminal, the suppliant and psychopath—they are conjoined in the recent literature of hipsterism and in such enduring figures as Greene's Pinkie and Faulkner's Christmas—partake of violence compulsively is no surprise. For untrammelled violence is not an act, it is merely a state; it is the experience of world negation. As Miss Arendt saw, the saint and the criminal are both lonely figures: ". . . . the one being for, the other against, all men; they, therefore, remain outside the pale of human intercourse and are, politically, marginal figures who usually enter the historical scene in times of corruption, disintegration, and political bankruptcy. Because of its

---

[15] Parallels between the two novelists are well elaborated by Renato Poggioli, "Kafka and Dostoyevsky," in Angel Flores ed., *The Kafka Problem* (New York, 1946), pp. 97-107.

[16] Thomas Mann, *The Magic Mountain* (New York, 1927), pp. 285 ff.

[17] "Introduction," *The Short Novels of Dostoyevsky,* p. xv.

inherent tendency to disclose the agent together with the act, action needs for its full appearance the shining brightness we once called glory, and which is possible only in the public realm."[18]

It is perhaps unnecessary to recover for our age the Corneillian idea of glory, but when the focus of moral energy moves so far from the center of human effort in the world, losing itself in the domain of holy silence or demonic violence, then it is time to give vent to our anxiety. The dissociation of action from intelligence, we remember, is manifest in Dostoyevsky's *Notes* whose hero openly contemns the active life. The consequences of this attitude are not limited to the cult of inactivity, living in a hole, like the man from underground, or in a jar like the hero of Beckett's *The Unnamable*, living, if you will, in the "packing-box shanty on the city dump" thoughtfully reserved by the editors of *Life* for our most promising novelists. The consequences also involve the alienation of the moral and artistic imagination from things of this world, often leading to a criminal state of autonomy.

The rebel-victim, we see, is also the outsider in search of truth.[19] Harry Haller, in Hermann Hesse's *Steppenwolf,* is still an isolate genius of suffering "whose fate it is to live the whole riddle of human destiny heightened to the pitch of a personal torture, a personal hell."[20] He is still grappling with the radical multiplicities of the human ego, oscillating not merely between the wolf and the man, not merely between two poles, such as the body and the spirit, the saint and the sinner, but between "thousands and thousands."[21] In the "Treatise on the Steppenwolf," however, the outsider is finally made to reckon with the fact that man may be nothing more than a temporary agreement between warring opposites, nothing more, in fact, than "a bourgeois compromise"—such as Bloom!

The idea of man as a transient compromise in the universe entails the acceptance of permanent outrage. Harry Haller could find some redemption of that condition in love or art, or even in humor which reconciles all opposites, and in whose "imaginary realm the intricate and many-faceted ideal of all Steppenwolves finds its realization."[22] Other writers—Mauriac, Bernanos, Graham Greene—sought for their characters a solution more commensurate with their religious faith; for, as Colin Wilson has loudly noted, the problems of modern man, rebel, victim, or outsider, lend themselves to an intense religious apprehension which need not be specifically Christian.[23] Yet even the Christian novelists, so Jansenist they seem in their insistence

18 Hannah Arendt, *The Human Condition* (Chicago, 1958), p. 180.

19 See Colin Wilson, *The Outsider* (Boston, 1956), for an extended documentary more valuable for its recognition of the general problem and for its range of significant reference than for its particular insights into the crucial documents it uses.

20 Hermann Hesse, *Steppenwolf* (New York, 1929), p. 28.

21 *Ibid.,* p. 77. 22 *Ibid.,* p. 73.

23 *The Outsider,* p. 261. Also Colin Wilson, *Religion and the Rebel* (Boston, 1957).

on human depravity, manage to convey only the terrible intricacies of damnation. Thus, for instance, is the pursuit of damnation conceived in *Brighton Rock* as an appalling manifestation of the mercy of God. The modern Christian martyr, it seems, can aspire only to perdition.

To the religious and the humanist solutions of man's plight in the universe must be added the Existentialist. The basic question here is still one of freedom, the search for identity under the aspects of violence or alienation. Freedom, we recall, is known to the hero of the *Notes* only as caprice; he understands that men, himself included, must seek freedom and must be repelled and horrified by it. The same ambivalence haunts the quest of Kafka's characters. Beginning with Gide, however, the ambivalence is seemingly resolved in favor of positive action. Man asserts his liberty in a gratuitous act of murder, as in Lafcadio's case, in acts of social repudiation, or ruthless heroism, as in the case of Michel and Theseus. Freedom consists of revolt, against morality, against the social order, against history. But the blood-curdling price is one that only heroes and supermen can afford. In this direction, the Existentialist novelists go farther than Gide was willing to go, and their view is correspondingly more special. Victory, in their novels, depends on the certainty of defeat, *is* the process of defeat. But unlike the heroes of classical tragedy, their protagonists act in full foreknowledge of their fatality, act *only* in *despite* of that fatality. And there is never any reconciliation.

It is thus that Sartre understands man—a creature *condemned* to be free. Antoine Roquentin, in *The Nausea,* suffers from metaphysical disgust. His consciousness is like a decayed trap door through which the sordid impressions of his world endlessly sift. Nothing happens in his life, nothing begins or ends; Phenomena merely change, and Things, grotesque, obdurate, and unnamable, simply exist. Roquentin thinks: "I have only my body: a man entirely alone, with his lonely body, cannot indulge in memories; they pass through him. I shouldn't complain: all I wanted was to be free."[24] Thinking is his game, the famous Cartesian proof of existence his plaything. In Kafka's work, as Erich Heller perceived, a cursed Intelligence asserts its omnipresence; the Cartesian formula becomes: "I think, and therefore I am not."[25] Such negation of being is inadmissible to Sartre; the proper formula should read: "My thought is *me.* . . . At this very moment—it's frightful—if I exist, it is because I am horrified at existing."[26] The change is less of an improvement than it may seem. For as Roquentin comes to believe, existence is nothing if not superfluous. Everything is *de trop,* everything is rooted in the Absurd, the irreducible condition of all reality. Man, we see, is not only a clown or a transient compromise, he is a contingency of existence. The way to true being, seldom realized, lies through Nausea.

24 Jean-Paul Sartre, *Nausea* (Norfolk, Conn., n.d.,), p. 91.
25 Erich Heller, *The Disinherited Mind* (New York, 1957), p. 202.
26 *Nausea*, pp. 135 ff.

Sartre's doctrine that existence precedes essence, carried to its atheistic conclusion, defines no limit to the idea of freedom and gives no value to the concept of being. Camus, a far more accomplished artist if not a more systematic thinker, starts with his "absurdist" philosophy of man and reaches, in *The Rebel* and *The Fall,* a more complex awareness of freedom. In his early novel, *The Stranger,* Meursault surrenders to the absurd, the destructive element, and loses his life, it seems, without ever finding it. In the following novel, *The Plague,* a small light of hope, even of redemption, flickers through the night of human victimization. Doctor Rieux says: "All I maintain is that on this earth there are pestilences and there are victims, and it's up to us, as far as possible, not to join forces with the pestilences. . . . I decided to take, in every predicament, the victim's side, so as to reduce the damage done. Among them, I can at least try to understand how one attains to the third category: in other words, to peace."[27] To join the victims is an act of rebellion against and alienation from the prevalent norm. But such an act is never purely nugatory. "Rebellion," Camus wrote, "though apparently negative, since it creates nothing, is profoundly positive in that it reveals the part of man which must always be defended."[28] Rebellion is therefore an aspiration to order, a means of lifting pain and evil from personal to collective experience. For the rebel-victim, the Cartesian argument par excellence is: "I rebel—therefore *we* exist [italics mine]."[29]

The problem of the anti-hero is essentially one of identity. His search is for existential fulfillment, that is, for freedom and self-definition. What he hopes to find is a position he can take within himself. Society may modulate his awareness of his situation, but only existence determines his stand. The recoil of the modern self is its way of taking a stand. The retreat weakens its involvement in the living world. It leads it in the ways of violence and alienation, augments its sense of guilt and absurdity, and affords it no objective standard for evaluating the worth of human action. But living in the world exclusively, living in what Ortega Y Gasset has called the Other, is also brutish and deadening. Complete immersion in the otherness of things is a ghastlier form of alienation: it is alienation from the self. "Without a strategic retreat into the self," Ortega rightly notes, "without vigilant thought, human life is impossible."[30] It is precisely in fear of the Other— total loss of selfhood—that the modern conscience has fallen back on its internal resources. The schizophrenic goes too far in that direction, the rebel-victim remains in the field of our vision.

Camus' statement, "I rebel—therefore we exist," brings to surface a dialectic that has been implicit in all the works we have viewed. In its naked form, the dialectic can be seen as an interplay between the essential Yes and the radical No, two piercing utterances beyond which the human voice can-

27 Albert Camus, *The Plague* (Paris, 1948), p. 229.
28 *The Rebel,* p. 19.   29 *Ibid.,* p. 22.
30 Ortega Y Gasset, *The Dehumanization of Art* (New York, 1956), p. 185.

THE CONCEPT OF VIRTUE

not rise. Such utterances may sometimes blend. It is only silence they equally abhor. In the modern novel, man seems to overcome the contradictions of his experience, its destructive or demonic element, by assuming the role of the anti-hero, the rebel-victim. The rebel denies without saying No to life, the victim succumbs without saying Yes to oppression. Both acts are, in a sense, identical: they affirm the human against the nonhuman. The figure of modern man, when he chooses to assert his full manhood, always bears the brave indissoluble aspects of Prometheus and Sisyphus—the eternal rebel and the eternal victim. The paradox is resolved when man cries, in the ringing words of Jaspers, "Although I am an anvil, as a hammer I can consummate what I must suffer."[31] Sparks from the same anvil were struck when Christ said to his disciples, "For whosoever will save his life shall lose it; and whosoever will lose his life for my sake shall find it."[32]

The condition of modern life may not be more desperate, as relativists sapiently remind us, than those which prevailed in any earlier age. Men, as usual, like to exaggerate their predicament to convince themselves, if nothing else, that they are still alive. All this is beside the point. It is certainly not the wretchedness of modern existence that we have sought to illustrate in this chapter, but rather man's peculiar awareness of his own situation. This awareness is both critical and adverse. The spirit of recoil in modern literature continues to affirm itself despite all our bounties.

THE CONCEPT OF VIRTUE

VERY LITTLE WRITING is formal definition. Yet much writing which has other ostensible aims resolves itself into problems of defining. A political theorist, for example, who sets out to argue that the United States is not a democracy will concern himself, in all likelihood, with what he considers to be the real meaning of the term "democracy." Once his definition is clear he can attempt, by describing the American government, to prove his point. Say that he defines "democracy" as "a society in which all men have equal political and economic powers." This idea of democracy may not be the usual one, but once it is granted, the writer can easily show that hoboes have very little economic power, and thus that the United States is, in one respect at least, undemocratic.

In similar ways, many arguments break down into matters of definition, either overtly or indirectly, as the selections in this unit make clear. Of the five pieces, only that by Aristotle is a strictly formal definition, placing virtue

31 Karl Jaspers, *Man in the Modern Age* (New York, 1957), p. 205.
32 Matthew 16:25.

in its genus *and listing its* differentiae. *The other four suggest how many different roads lead to definition, and also what an elusive thing the idea or virtue is, how it not only seems to defy precise defining, but also eludes any single methodological approach. Plato, for instance, assumes that virtue is a real entity and attempts to decide what its source is. This procedure leads him back to its nature. The essay by Lord Russell is far distant from a formal definition of virtue, for, at bottom, he is trying to decide whether questions of ethical behavior are within the realm of possible knowledge at all! The other two selections, those by Samuel Clemens and William James, deal with the relationships between moral ideas and the facts of experience. James theorizes about the relationship; Clemens epitomizes it in the spiritual conflict of a boy torn between the laws and principles of society and an intuition born of living. All of the procedures in these selections lead, directly or indirectly, toward definition, a fact which serves to emphasize the importance of defining in nearly all inquiry.*

Plato (427?-347 B.C.*) and Aristotle (384-322* B.C.*) were the two giants of ancient Greek philosophy. William James (1842-1910), American philosopher and psychologist, was the first to formalize the ethic of "pragmatism." Bertrand Russell (1872-   ) is the patriarch of contemporary English philosophy and a well-known mathematician and essayist as well. Samuel L. Clemens, (1835-1910; pseudonym, Mark Twain) is famous as a novelist, humorist and journalist.*

THE SOURCE OF VIRTUE | PLATO

SOCRATES. . . . shall you and I make an effort to inquire together into the nature of virtue?

MENO. By all means, Socrates. And yet I would much rather return to my original question, Whether in seeking to acquire virtue we should regard it as a thing to be taught, or as a gift of nature, or as coming to men in some other way?

SOCRATES. Had I the command of you as well as of myself, Meno, I would not have inquired whether virtue is given by instruction or not, until we had first ascertained "what it is." But as you think only of controlling me who am your slave, and never of controlling yourself—such being your notion of freedom—I must yield to you, for you are irresistible. And therefore I have now to inquire into the qualities of a thing of which I do not as yet know the nature. At any rate, will you condescend a little and allow the question "Whether virtue is given by instruction, or in any other way," to be argued upon hypothesis? . . . Let the first hypothesis be that

From *Meno*, trans. by Benjamin Jowett (1871).

virtue is or is not knowledge—in that case will it be taught or not, or, as we were just now saying, "remembered"? For there is no use in disputing about the name. But is virtue taught or not, or rather, does not everyone see that knowledge alone is taught?

MENO. I agree.

SOCRATES. Then if virtue is knowledge, virtue will be taught?

MENO. Certainly.

SOCRATES. Then now we have made a quick end of this question: If virtue is of such a nature, it will be taught; and if not, not?

MENO. Certainly.

SOCRATES. The next question is, whether virtue is knowledge or of another species?

MENO. Yes, that appears to be the question which comes next in order.

SOCRATES. Do we not say that virtue is a good? This is a hypothesis which is not set aside.

MENO. Certainly.

SOCRATES. Now, if there be any sort of good which is distinct from knowledge, virtue may be that good; but if knowledge embraces all good, then we shall be right in thinking that virtue is knowledge?

MENO. True.

SOCRATES. And virtue makes us good?

MENO. Yes.

SOCRATES. And if we are good, then we are profitable; for all good things are profitable?

MENO. Yes.

SOCRATES. Then virtue is profitable?

MENO. That is the only inference.

SOCRATES. Then now let us see what are the things which severally profit us. Health and strength, and beauty and wealth—these, and the like of these, we call profitable?

MENO. True.

SOCRATES. And yet these things may also sometimes do us harm, would you not think so?

MENO. Yes.

SOCRATES. And what is the guiding principle which makes them profitable or the reverse? Are they not profitable when they are rightly used, and hurtful when they are not rightly used?

MENO. Certainly.

SOCRATES. Next, let us consider the goods of the soul: they are temperance, justice, courage, quickness of apprehension, memory, magnanimity, and the like?

MENO. Surely.

SOCRATES. And such of these as are not knowledge, but of another sort, are sometimes profitable and sometimes hurtful; as, for example, courage wanting prudence, which is only a sort of confidence? When a man has no sense he is harmed by courage, but when he has sense he is profited?

MENO. True.

SOCRATES. And the same may be said of temperance and quickness of apprehension; whatever things are learned or done with sense are profitable, but when done without sense they are hurtful?

MENO. Very true.

SOCRATES. And in general, all that the soul attempts or endures, when under the guidance of wisdom, ends in happiness; but when she is under the guidance of folly, in the opposite?

MENO. That appears to be true.

SOCRATES. If then virtue is a quality of the soul, and is admitted to be profitable, it must be wisdom or prudence, since none of the things of the soul are either profitable or hurtful in themselves, but they are all made profitable or hurtful by the addition of wisdom or of folly; and therefore if virtue is profitable, virtue must be a sort of wisdom or prudence?

MENO. I quite agree.

SOCRATES. And the other goods, such as wealth and the like, of which we were just now saying that they are sometimes good and sometimes evil, do not they also become profitable or hurtful, accordingly as the soul guides and uses them rightly or wrongly; just as the things of the soul herself are benefited when under the guidance of wisdom and harmed by folly?

MENO. True.

SOCRATES. And the wise soul guides them rightly, and the foolish soul wrongly?

MENO. Yes.

SOCRATES. And is not this universally true of human nature? All other things hang upon the soul, and the things of the soul herself hang upon wisdom, if they are to be good; and so wisdom is inferred to be that which profits—and virtue, as we say, is profitable?

MENO. Certainly.

SOCRATES. And thus we arrive at the conclusion that virtue is either wholly or partly wisdom?

MENO. I think that what you are saying, Socrates, is very true.

SOCRATES. But if this is true, then the good are not by nature good?

MENO. I think not.

SOCRATES. If they had been, there would assuredly have been discerners of characters among us who would have known our future great men; and on their showing we should have adopted them, and when we had got them, we should have kept them in the citadel out of the way of harm, and set a stamp upon them far rather than upon a piece of gold, in order that no one might tamper with them; and when they grew up they would have been useful to the state?

MENO. Yes, Socrates, that would have been the right way.

SOCRATES. But if the good are not by nature good, are they made good by instruction?

MENO. There appears to be no other alternative, Socrates. On the supposition that virtue is knowledge, there can be no doubt that virtue is taught.

SOCRATES. Yes, indeed; but what if the supposition is erroneous? ...

[*Socrates proceeds, by the same method, to show that virtue cannot be taught, and that there cannot, therefore, be any teachers of virtue, not even among those, like the sophists, who especially profess that skill.*]

SOCRATES. But if neither the Sophists nor the gentlemen are teachers, clearly there can be no other teachers?

MENO. No.

SOCRATES. And if there are no teachers, neither are there disciples?

MENO. Agreed.

SOCRATES. And we have admitted that a thing cannot be taught of which there are neither teachers nor disciples?

MENO. We have.

SOCRATES. And there are no teachers of virtue to be found anywhere?

MENO. There are not.

SOCRATES. And if there are no teachers, neither are there scholars?

MENO. That, I think, is true.

SOCRATES. Then virtue cannot be taught?

MENO. Not if we are right in our view. But I cannot believe, Socrates, that there are no good men; and if there are, how did they come into existence?

SOCRATES. I am afraid, Meno, that you and I are not good for much, and that Gorgias has been as poor an educator of you as Prodicus has been of me. Certainly we shall have to look to ourselves, and try to find someone who will help in some way or other to improve us. This I say, because I observe that in the previous discussion none of us remarked that right and good action is possible to man under other guidance than that of knowledge—and indeed if this be denied, there is no seeing how there can be any good men at all.

MENO. How do you mean, Socrates?

SOCRATES. I mean that good men are necessarily useful or profitable. Were we not right in admitting this? It must be so.

MENO. Yes.

SOCRATES. And in supposing that they will be useful only if they are true guides to us of action—there we were also right?

MENO. Yes.

SOCRATES. But when we said that a man cannot be a good guide unless he have knowledge, in this we were wrong.

MENO.   What do you mean by the word "right"?

SOCRATES.   I will explain. If a man knew the way to Larisa, or any-where else, and went to the place and led others thither, would he not be a right and good guide?

MENO.   Certainly.

SOCRATES.   And a person who had a right opinion about the way, but had never been and did not know, might be a good guide also, might he not?

MENO.   Certainly.

SOCRATES.   And while he has true opinion about that which the other knows, he will be just as good a guide if he thinks the truth, as he who knows the truth?

MENO.   Exactly.

SOCRATES.   Then true opinion is as good a guide to correct action as knowledge; and that was the point which we omitted in our speculation about the nature of virtue, when we said that knowledge only is the guide of right action; whereas there is also right opinion.

MENO.   True.

SOCRATES.   Then right opinion is not less useful than knowledge?

MENO.   The difference, Socrates, is only that he who has knowledge will always be right; but he who has right opinion will sometimes be right, and sometimes not.

SOCRATES.   What do you mean? Can he be wrong who has right opin-ion, so long as he has right opinion?

MENO.   I admit the cogency of your argument, and therefore, Socrates, I wonder that knowledge should be perferred to right opinion—or why they should ever differ.

SOCRATES.   And shall I explain this wonder to you?

MENO.   Do tell me.

SOCRATES.   You would not wonder if you had ever observed the images of Daedalus; but perhaps you have not got them in your country?

MENO.   What have they to do with the question?

SOCRATES.   Because they require to be fastened in order to keep them, and if they are not fastened they will play truant and run away.

MENO.   Well, what of that?

SOCRATES.   I mean to say that they are not very valuable possessions if they are at liberty, for they will walk off like runaway slaves; but when fastened, they are of great value, for they are really beautiful works of art. Now this is an illustration of the nature of true opinions: while they abide with us they are beautiful and fruitful, but they run away out of the human soul, and do not remain long, and therefore they are not of much value until they are fastened by the tie of the cause; and this fastening of them, friend Meno, is recollection, as you and I have agreed to call it. But when they are bound, in the first place, they have the nature of knowledge; and, in the second place, they are abiding. And this is why knowledge is more honorable and excellent than true opinion, because fastened by a chain.

MENO.   What you are saying, Socrates, seems to be very like the truth.

SOCRATES.   I too speak rather in ignorance; I only conjecture. And yet that knowledge differs from true opinion is no matter of conjecture with me. There are not many things which I profess to know, but this is most certainly one of them.

MENO.   Yes, Socrates; and you are quite right in saying so.

SOCRATES.   And am I not also right in saying that true opinion leading the way perfects action quite as well as knowledge?

MENO.   There again, Socrates, I think you are right.

SOCRATES.   Then right opinion is not a whit inferior to knowledge, or less useful in action; nor is the man who has right opinion inferior to him who has knowledge?

MENO.   True.

SOCRATES.   And surely the good man has been acknowledged by us to be useful?

MENO.   Yes.

SOCRATES.   Seeing then that men become good and useful to states, not only because they have knowledge, but because they have right opinion, and that neither knowledge nor right opinion is given to man by nature or acquired by him—(do you imagine either of them to be given by nature?

MENO.   Not I.)

SOCRATES.   Then if they are not given by nature, neither are the good by nature good?

MENO.   Certainly not.

SOCRATES.   And nature being excluded, then came the question whether virtue is acquired by teaching?

MENO.   Yes.

SOCRATES.   If virtue was wisdom, then, as we thought, it was taught?

MENO.   Yes.

SOCRATES.   And if it was taught it was wisdom?

MENO.   Certainly.

SOCRATES.   And if there were teachers, it might be taught; and if there were no teachers, not?

MENO.   True.

SOCRATES.   But surely we acknowledged that there were no teachers of virtue?

MENO.   Yes.

SOCRATES.   Then we acknowledged that it was not taught, and was not wisdom.

MENO.   Certainly.

SOCRATES.   And yet we admitted that it was a good?

MENO.   Yes.

SOCRATES.   And the right guide is useful and good?

MENO.   Certainly.

SOCRATES.   And the only right guides are knowledge and true opinion—these are the guides of man; for things which happen by chance are not under the guidance of man; but the guides of man are true opinion and knowledge.

MENO.   I think so, too.

SOCRATES.   But if virtue is not taught, neither is virtue knowledge.

MENO.   Clearly not.

SOCRATES.   Then of two good and useful things, one, which is knowledge, has been set aside and cannot be supposed to be our guide in political life.

MENO.   I think not.

SOCRATES.   And therefore not by any wisdom, and not because they were wise, did Themistocles and those others of whom Anytus spoke govern states. This was the reason why they were unable to make others like themselves—because their virtue was not grounded on knowledge.

MENO.   That is probably true, Socrates.

SOCRATES.   But if not by knowledge, the only alternative which remains is that statesmen must have guided states by right opinion, which is in politics what divination is in religion; for diviners and also prophets say many things truly, but they know not what they say.

MENO.   So I believe.

SOCRATES.   And may we not, Meno, truly call those men "divine" who, having no understanding, yet succeed in many a grand deed and word?

MENO.   Certainly.

SOCRATES.   Then we shall also be right in calling divine those whom we were just now speaking of as diviners and prophets, including the whole tribe of poets. Yes, and statesmen above all may be said to be divine and illumined, being inspired and possessed of God, in which condition they say many good things, not knowing what they say.

MENO.   Yes.

SOCRATES.   And the women too, Meno, call good men divine—do they not? and the Spartans, when they praise a good man, say "that he is a divine man."

MENO.   And I think, Socrates, that they are right, although very likely our friend Anytus may take offense at the word.

SOCRATES.   I do not care; as for Anytus, there will be another opportunity of talking with him. To sum up our inquiry—the result seems to be, if we are at all right in our view, that virtue is neither natural nor acquired, but an instinct given by God to the virtuous. Nor is the instinct accompanied by reason, unless there may be supposed to be among statesmen someone who is capable of educating statesmen. And if there be such an one, he may be said to be among the living what Homer says that Tiresias was among the dead, "he alone has understanding; but the rest are flitting shades"; and he and his virtue in like manner will be a reality among shadows.

MENO. That is excellent, Socrates.

SOCRATES. Then, Meno, the conclusion is that virtue comes to the virtuous by the gift of God. But we shall never know the certain truth until, before asking how virtue is given, we inquire into the actual nature of virtue. I fear that I must go away, but do you, now that you are persuaded yourself, persuade our friend Anytus. And do not let him be so exasperated; if you can conciliate him, you will have done good service to the Athenian people.

A DEFINITION OF VIRTUE | *ARISTOTLE*

We now come to the formal definition of virtue. Note first, however, that the human soul is conditioned in three ways. It may have (1) feelings, (2) capacities, (3) dispositions; so virtue must be one of these three. By "feelings" I mean desire, anger, fear, daring, envy, gratification, friendliness, hatred, longing, jealousy, pity and in general all states of mind that are attended by pleasure or pain. By "capacities" I mean those faculties in virtue of which we may be described as capable of the feelings in question—anger, for instance, or pain, or pity. By "dispositions" I mean states of mind in virtue of which we are well or ill disposed in respect of the feelings concerned. We have, for instance, a bad disposition where angry feelings are concerned if we are disposed to become excessively or insufficiently angry, and a good disposition in this respect if we consistently feel the due amount of anger, which comes between these extremes. So with the other feelings.

Now, neither the virtues nor the vices are feelings. We are not spoken of as good or bad in respect of our feelings but of our virtues and vices. Neither are we praised or blamed for the way we feel. A man is not praised for being frightened or angry, nor is he blamed just for being angry; it is for being angry in a particular way. But we *are* praised and blamed for our virtues and vices. Again, feeling angry or frightened is something we can't help, but our virtues are in a manner expressions of our will; at any rate there is an element of will in their formation. Finally, we are said to be "moved" when our feelings are affected, but when it is a question of moral goodness or badness we are not said to be "moved" but to be "disposed" in a particular way. A similar line of reasoning will prove that the virtues and vices are not capacities either. We are not spoken of as good or

From Aristotle, *Ethics,* trans. by J. A. K. Thomson (London, George Allen & Unwin Ltd., 1953) Bk. II, Chaps. 4-8.

bad, nor are we praised or blamed, merely because we are *capable* of feeling. Again, what capacities we have, we have by nature; but it is not nature that makes us good or bad. . . . So, if the virtues are neither feelings nor capacities, it remains that they must be dispositions. . . .

It is not, however, enough to give this account of the *genus* of virtue—that it is a disposition; we must describe its *species*. Let us begin, then, with this proposition. Excellence of whatever kind affects that of which it is the excellence in two ways. (1) It produces a good state in it. (2) It enables it to perform its function well. Take eyesight. The goodness of your eye is not only that which makes your eye good, it is also that which makes it function well. Or take the case of a horse. The goodness of a horse makes him a good horse, but it also makes him good at running, carrying a rider, and facing the enemy. Our proposition, then, seems to be true, and it enables us to say that virtue in a man will be the disposition which *(a)* makes him a good man, *(b)* enables him to perform his function well. We have already touched on this point, but more light will be thrown upon it if we consider what is the specific nature of virtue.

In anything continuous and divisible it is possible to take the half, or more than the half, or less than the half. Now these parts may be larger, smaller, and equal either in relation to the thing divided or in relation to us. The equal part may be described as a mean between too much and too little. By the mean of the thing I understand a point equidistant from the extremes; and this is one and the same for everybody. Let me give an illustration. Ten, let us say, is "many" and two is "few" of something. We get the mean of the thing if we take six; that is, six exceeds and is exceeded by an equal number. This is the rule which gives us the arithmetical mean. But such a method will not give us the mean in relation to ourselves. Let ten pounds of food be a large, and two pounds a small, allowance for an athlete. It does not follow that the trainer will prescribe six pounds. That might be a large or it might be a small allowance for the particular athlete who is to get it. It would be little for Milo but a lot for a man who has just begun his training. It is the same in all walks of life. The man who knows his business avoids both too much and too little. It is the mean he seeks and adopts—not the mean of the thing but the relative mean.

Every form, then, of applied knowledge, when it performs its function well, looks to the mean and works to the standard set by that. It is because people feel this that they apply the *cliché*, "You couldn't add anything to it or take anything from it" to an artistic masterpiece, the implication being that too much and too little alike destroy perfection, while the mean preserves it. Now if this be so, and if it be true, as we say, that good craftsmen work to the standard of the mean, then, since goodness like Nature is more exact and of a higher character than any art, it follows that goodness is the quality that hits the mean. By "goodness" I mean goodness of moral character, since it is moral goodness that deals with feelings and actions, and it is in them that we find excess, deficiency, and a mean. It is possible, for example, to experience fear, boldness, desire, anger, pity, and pleasures and pains generally, too much or too little or to the right amount. If we feel them too much or too little, we are wrong. But to have these feelings at the right times on the right occasions towards the right people for the right motive and in the right way is to have them in the right measure, that is, somewhere between the extremes; and this is what characterizes goodness. The same may be said of the mean and extremes in actions. Now it is in the field of actions and feelings that goodness operates; in them we find excess, deficiency, and, between them, the mean, the first two being wrong, the mean right and praised as such. Goodness, then, is a mean condition in the sense that it aims at and hits the mean.

Consider, too, that it is possible to go wrong in more ways than one. (In Pythagorean terminology evil is a form of the Unlimited, good of the Limited.) But there is only one way of being right. That is why going wrong is easy, and going right difficult; it is easy to miss the bull's-eye and difficult to hit it. Here, then, is another explanation of why the too much and the too little are connected with evil and the mean with good. As the poet says,

Goodness is one, evil is multiform.

We may now define virtue as a disposition of the soul in which, when it has to choose among actions and feelings, it observes the mean relative to us, this being determined by such a rule or principle as would take shape in the mind of a man of sense or practical wisdom. We call it a mean condition as lying between two forms of badness, one being excess and the other deficiency; and also for this reason, that, whereas badness either falls short of or exceeds the right measure in feelings and actions, virtue discovers the mean and deliberately chooses it. Thus, looked at from the point of view of its essence as embodied in its definition, virtue no doubt is a mean; judged by the standard of what is right and best, it is an extreme.

But choice of a mean is not possible in every action or every feeling. The very names of some have an immediate connotation of evil. Such are malice, shamelessness, envy among feelings, and among actions adultery, theft, murder. All these and more like them have a bad name as being evil in themselves; it is not merely the excess or deficiency of them that we censure. In their case, then, it is impossible to act rightly; whatever we do is wrong. Nor do circumstances make any difference in the rightness or wrongness of them. When a man commits adultery there is no point in asking whether it is with the right woman or at the right time or in the right way, for to do anything like that is simply wrong. It would amount to claiming that there is a mean and excess and defect in unjust or cowardly or intemperate actions. If such a thing were possible, we should find ourselves with a mean quantity of excess, a mean of deficiency, an excess of excess and a deficiency of deficiency. But just as in temperance and justice there can be no mean or excess or deficiency, because the mean in a sense *is* an extreme, so there can be no mean or excess or deficiency in those vicious actions—however done, they are wrong. Putting the matter into general language, we may say that there is no mean in the extremes, and no extreme in the mean, to be observed by anybody.

THE MORAL PHILOSOPHER AND THE MORAL LIFE | WILLIAM JAMES

The last fundamental question in Ethics [is] the *casuistic* question. Here we are, in a world where the existence of a divine thinker has been and perhaps always will be doubted by some of the lookers-on, and where, in spite of the presence of a large number of ideals in which human beings agree, there are a mass of others about which no general consensus obtains. It is hardly necessary to present a literary picture of this, for the facts are too well known. The wars of the flesh and the spirit in each man, the concupiscences of different individuals pursuing the same unshareable material or social prizes, the ideals which contrast so according to races, circumstances, temperaments, philosophical beliefs, etc.—all form a maze of apparently inextricable confusion with no obvious Ariadne's thread to lead one out. Yet the philosopher, just because he is a philosopher, adds his own peculiar ideal to the confusion (with which if he were willing to be a skeptic he would be passably content), and insists that over all these individual opinions there is a *system of truth* which he can discover if he only takes sufficient pains.

We stand ourselves at present in the place of that philosopher, and must not fail to realize all the features that the situation comports. In the first place we will not be skeptics; we hold to it that there is a truth to be ascertained. But in the second place we have just gained the insight that that truth cannot be a self-proclaiming set of laws, or an abstract "moral reason," but can only exist in act, or in the shape of an opinion held by some thinker really to be found. There is, however, no visible thinker invested with authority. Shall we then simply proclaim our own ideals as the lawgiving ones? No; for if we are true philosophers we must throw our own spontaneous ideals, even the dearest, impartially in with that total mass of ideals which are fairly to be judged. But how then can we as philosophers ever find a test; how avoid complete moral skepticism on the one hand, and on the other escape bringing a wayward personal standard of our own along with us, on which we simply pin our faith?

The dilemma is a hard one, nor does it grow a bit more easy as we

From *The Moral Philosopher and the Moral Life* (1891).

revolve it in our minds. The entire undertaking of the philosopher obliges him to seek an impartial test. That test, however, must be incarnated in the demand of some actually existent person; and how can he pick out the person save by an act in which his own sympathies and prepossessions are implied?

One method indeed presents itself, and has as a matter of history been taken by the more serious ethical schools. If the heap of things demanded proved on inspection less chaotic than at first they seemed, if they furnished their own relative test and measure, then the casuistic problem would be solved. If it were found that all goods *quâ* goods contained a common essence, then the amount of this essence involved in any one good would show its rank in the scale of goodness, and order could be quickly made; for this essence would be *the* good upon which all thinkers were agreed, the relatively objective and universal good that the philosopher seeks. Even his own private ideals would be measured by their share of it, and find their rightful place among the rest.

Various essences of good have thus been found and proposed as bases of the ethical system. Thus, to be a mean between two extremes; to be recognized by a special intuitive faculty; to make the agent happy for the moment; to make others as well as him happy in the long run; to add to his perfection or dignity; to harm no one; to follow from reason or flow from universal law; to be in accordance with the will of God; to promote the survival of the human species on this planet—are so many tests, each of which has been maintained by somebody to constitute the essence of all good things or actions so far as they are good.

No one of the measures that have been actually proposed has, however, given general satisfaction. Some are obviously not universally present in all cases—e.g., the character of harming no one, or that of following a universal law; for the best course is often cruel; and many acts are reckoned good on the sole condition that they be exceptions, and serve not as examples of a universal law. Other characters, such as following the will of God, are unascertainable and vague. Others again, like survival, are quite indeterminate in their consequences, and leave us in the lurch where we most need their help; a philosopher of the Sioux Nation, for example, will be certain to use the survival-criterion in a very different way from ourselves. The best, on the whole, of these marks and measures of goodness seems to be the capacity to bring happiness. But in order not to break down fatally, this test must be taken to cover innumerable acts and impulses that never *aim* at happiness; so that, after all, in seeking for a universal principle we inevitably are carried onward to the *most* universal principle—that *the essence of good is simply to satisfy demand.* The demand may be for anything under the sun. There is really no more ground for supposing that all our demands can be accounted for by one universal underlying kind of motive than there is ground for supposing that all physical phenomena are cases of a single law. The elementary forces in ethics are probably as plural as those of physics are. The various ideals have no common character apart from the fact that they are ideals. No single abstract principle can be so used as to yield to the philosopher anything like a scientifically accurate and genuinely useful casuistic scale.

A look at another peculiarity of the ethical universe, as we find it, will still further show us the philosopher's perplexities. As a purely theoretic problem, namely, the casuistic question would hardly ever come up at all. If the ethical philosopher were only asking after the best *imaginable* system of goods he would indeed have an easy task; for all demands as such are *prima facie* respectable, and the best simply imaginary world would be one in which *every* demand was gratified as soon as made. Such a world would, however, have to have a physical constitution entirely different from that of the one which we inhabit. It would need not only a space, but a time, of *n*-dimensions, to include all the acts and experiences incompatible with one another here below, which would then go on in conjunction—such as spending our money, yet growing rich; taking our holiday, yet getting ahead with our work; shooting and fishing, yet doing no hurt to the beasts; gaining no end of experience, yet keeping our youthful freshness of heart; and the like. There can be no question that such a system of things, however brought about, would be the absolutely ideal system; and that if a philosopher could create universes *a priori,* and provide all the mechanical conditions, that is the sort of universe which he should unhesitatingly create.

But this world of ours is made on an entirely different pattern, and the casuistic question here is most tragically practical. The actually possible in this world is vastly narrower than all that is demanded; and there is always a *pinch* between the ideal and the actual which can only be got through by leaving part of the ideal behind. There is hardly a good which we can imagine except as competing for the possession of the same bit of space and time with some other imagined good. Every end of desire that presents itself appears exclusive of some other end of desire. Shall a man drink and smoke, *or* keep his nerves in condition?—he cannot do both. Shall he follow his fancy for Amelia, *or* for Henrietta?—both cannot be the choice of his heart. Shall he have the dear old Republican party, *or* a spirit of unsophistication in public affairs?—he cannot have both, etc. So that the ethical philosopher's demand for the right scale of subordination in ideals is the fruit of an altogether practical need. Some part of the ideal must be butchered, and he needs to know which part. It is a tragic situation, and no mere speculative conundrum, with which he has to deal.

Now we are blinded to the real difficulty of the philosopher's task by the fact that we are born into a society whose ideals are largely ordered already. If we follow the ideal which is conventionally highest, the others which we butcher either die and do not return to haunt us; or if they come back and accuse us of murder, every one applauds us for turning to them a deaf ear. In other words, our environment encourages us not to be philosophers but partisans. The philosopher, however, cannot, so long as he clings to his own ideal of objectivity, rule out any ideal from being heard. He is confident, and rightly confident, that the simple taking counsel of his own intuitive preferences would be certain to end in a mutilation of the fullness of the truth. The poet Heine is said to have written "Bunsen" in the place of *"Gott"* in his copy of that author's work entitled *God in History,* so as to make it read "Bunsen in der Geschichte." Now, with no disrespect to the good and learned Baron, is it not safe to say that any single philosopher, however wide his sympathies, must be just such a *Bunsen in der Geschichte* of the moral world, so soon as he attempts to put his own ideas of order into that howling mob of desires, each struggling to get breathing-room for the ideal to which it clings? The very best of men must not only be insensible, but ludicrously and peculiarly insensible, to many goods. As a militant, fighting free-handed that the goods to which he *is* sensible may not be submerged and lost from out of life, the philosopher, like every other human being, is in a natural position. But think of Zeno and of Epicurus, think of Calvin and of Paley, think of Kant and Schopenhauer, of Herbert Spencer and John Henry Newman, no longer as one-sided champions of special ideals, but as schoolmasters deciding what all must think—and what more grotesque topic could a satirist wish for on which to exercise his pen? The fabled attempt of Mrs. Partington to arrest the rising tide of the North Atlantic with her broom was a reasonable spectacle compared with their effort to substitute the content of their clean-shaven systems for that exuberant mass of goods with which all human nature is in travail, and groaning to bring to the light of day. Think, furthermore, of such individual moralists, no longer as mere schoolmasters, but as pontiffs armed with the temporal power, and having authority in every concrete case of conflict to order which good shall be butchered and which shall be suffered to survive—and the notion really turns one pale. All one's slumbering revolutionary instincts waken at the thought of any single moralist wielding such powers of life and death. Better chaos forever than an order based on any closet-philosopher's rule, even though he were the most enlightened possible member of his tribe. No! if the philosopher is to keep his judicial position, he must never become one of the parties to the fray.

What can he do, then, it will now be asked, except to fall back on skepticism and give up the notion of being a philosopher at all?

But do we not already see a perfectly definite path of escape which is open to him just because he is a philosopher, and not the champion of one particular ideal? Since everything which is demanded is by that fact a good, must not the guiding principle for ethical philosophy (since all demands conjointly cannot be satisfied in this poor world) be simply to satisfy at all times *as many demands as we can?* That act must be the best act, accordingly, which makes for the *best whole,* in the sense of awakening the least sum of dissatisfactions. In the casuistic scale, therefore, those ideals must be written highest which *prevail at the least cost,* or by whose realization the least possible number of other ideals are destroyed. Since victory and defeat there must be, the victory to be philosophically prayed for is that of the more inclusive side—of the side which even in the hour of triumph will to some degree do justice to the ideals in which the vanquished party's interests lay. The course of history is nothing but the story of men's struggles from generation to generation to find the more and more inclusive order. *Invent some manner* of realizing your own ideals which will also satisfy the alien demands—that and that only is the path of peace! Following this path, society has shaken itself into one sort of relative equilibrium after another by a series of social discoveries quite analogous to those of science. Polyandry and polygamy and slavery, private warfare and liberty to kill, judicial torture and arbitrary royal power have slowly succumbed to actually aroused complaints; and though someone's ideals are unquestionably the worse off for each improvement, yet a vastly greater total number of them find shelter in our civilized society than in the older savage ways. So far then, and up to date, the casuistic scale is made for the philosopher already far better than he can ever make it for himself. An experiment of the most searching kind has proved that the laws and usages of the land are what yield the maximum of satisfaction to the thinkers taken all together. The presumption in cases of conflict must always be in favor of the conventionally recognized good. The philosopher must be a conservative, and in the construction of his casuistic scale must put the things most in accordance with the customs of the community on top.

And yet if he be a true philosopher he must see that there is nothing final in any actually given equilibrium of human ideals, but that, as our present laws and customs have fought and conquered other past ones, so they will in their turn be overthrown by any newly discovered order which will hush up the complaints that they still give rise to, without producing others louder still. "Rules are made for man, not man for rules"—that one sentence is enough to immortalize Green's *Prolegomena to Ethics.* And although a man always risks much when he breaks away from established rules and strives to realize a larger ideal whole than they permit, yet the philosopher must allow that it is at all times open to anyone to make the experiment, provided he fear not to stake his life and character upon the throw. The pinch is always here. Pent in under every system of moral rules are innumerable persons whom it weighs upon, and goods which it represses; and these are always rumbling and grumbling in the background, and ready for any issue by which they may get free. See the abuses which the institution of private property covers, so that even today it is shamelessly asserted among us that one of the prime functions of the national government is to help the adroiter citizens to grow rich. See the unnamed and unnamable sorrows which the tyranny, on the whole so beneficent, of the marriage-institution brings to so many, both of the married and the unwed. See the wholesale loss of opportunity under our *régime* of so-called equality and industrialism, with the drummer and the counter-jumper in the saddle, for so many faculties and graces which could flourish in the feudal world. See our kindliness for the humble and the outcast, how it wars with that stern weeding-out which until now has been the condition of every perfection in the breed. See everywhere the struggle and the squeeze; and everlastingly the problem how to make them less. The anarchists, nihilists, and free-lovers; the free-silverites, socialists, and single-tax men; the free-traders and civil-service reformers; the prohibitionists and anti-vivisectionists; the radical Darwinians with their idea of the suppression of the weak—these and all the conservative sentiments of society arrayed against them, are simply deciding through actual experiment by what sort of conduct the maximum amount of good can be gained and kept in this world. These experiments are to be judged, not *a priori,* but by actual finding, after the fact of their making, how much more outcry or how much appeasement comes about. What closet-solutions can possibly anticipate the result of trials made on such a scale? Or what can any superficial theorist's judgment be worth, in a world where every one of hundreds of ideals has its special champion already provided in the shape of some genius expressly born to feel it, and to fight to death in its behalf? The pure philosopher can only follow the windings of the spectacle, confident that the line of least resistance will always be towards the richer and the more inclusive arrangement, and that by one tack after another some approach to the kingdom of heaven is incessantly made.

All this amounts to saying that, so far as the casuistic question goes, ethical science is just like physical science, and instead of being deducible all at once from abstract principles, must simply bide its time, and be ready to revise its conclusions from day to day. The presumption of course, in both sciences, always is that the vulgarly accepted opinions are true, and the right casuistic order that which public opinion believes in; and surely it would be folly quite as great, in most of us, to strike out independently and to aim at originality in ethics as in physics. Every now and then, however, someone is born with the right to be original, and his revolutionary thought or action may bear prosperous fruit. He may replace old "laws of nature" by better ones; he may, by breaking old moral rules in a certain place, bring in a total condition of things more ideal than would have followed had the rules been kept.

On the whole, then, we must conclude that no philosophy of ethics is possible in the old-fashioned absolute sense of the term. Everywhere the ethical philosopher must wait on facts. The thinkers who create the ideals come he knows not whence, their sensibilities are evolved he knows not how; and the question as to which of two conflicting ideals will give the best universe then and there, can be answered by him only through the aid of the experience of other men. I said some time ago, in treating of the "first" question, that the intuitional moralists deserve credit for keeping most clearly to the psychological facts. They do much to spoil this merit on the whole, however, by mixing with it that dogmatic temper which, by absolute distinctions and unconditional "thou shalt nots," changes a growing, elastic, and continuous life into a superstitious system of relics and dead bones. In point of fact, there are no absolute evils, and there are no non-moral goods; and the *highest* ethical life—however few may be called to bear its burdens—consists at all times in the breaking of rules which have grown too narrow for the actual case. There is but one unconditional commandment, which is that we should seek incessantly, with fear and trembling, so to vote and to act as to bring about the very largest total universe of good which we can see. Abstract rules indeed can help; but they help the less in proportion as our intuitions are more piercing, and our vocation is the stronger for the moral life. For every real dilemma is in literal strictness a unique situation; and the exact combination of ideals realized and ideals disappointed which each decision creates is always a universe without a precedent, and for which no adequate previous rule exists. The philosopher, then, *quâ* philosopher, is no better able to determine the best universe in the concrete emergency than other men. He sees, indeed, somewhat better than most men what the question always is—not a question of this good or that good simply taken, but of the two total universes with which these goods respectively belong. He knows that he must vote always for the richer universe, for the good which seems most organizable, most fit to enter into complex combinations, most apt to be a member of a more inclusive whole. But which particular universe this is he cannot know for certain in advance; he only knows that if he makes a bad mistake the cries of the wounded will soon inform him of the fact. In all this the philosopher is just like the rest of us non-philosophers, so far as we are just and sympathetic instinctively, and so far as we are open to the voice of complaint. His function is in fact indistinguishable from that of the best kind of statesman at the present day. His books upon ethics, therefore, so far as they truly touch the moral life, must more and more ally themselves with a literature which is confessedly tentative and suggestive rather than dogmatic—I mean with novels and dramas of the deeper sort, with sermons, with books on statecraft and philanthropy and social and economical reform. Treated in this way ethical treatises may be voluminous and luminous as well; but they never can be *final,* except in their abstractest and vaguest features; and they must more and more abandon the old-fashioned, clear-cut, and would-be "scientific" form.

SCIENCE AND ETHICS | *BERTRAND RUSSELL*

Those who maintain the insufficiency of science...appeal to the fact that science has nothing to say about "values." This I admit; but when it is inferred that ethics contains truths which cannot be proved or disproved by science, I disagree. The matter is one on which it is not altogether easy to think clearly, and my own views on it are quite different from what they were thirty years ago. But it is necessary to be clear about it if we are to appraise such arguments as those in support of Cosmic Purpose. As there is no consensus of opinion about ethics, it must be understood that what follows is my personal belief, not the dictum of science.

The study of ethics, traditionally, consists of two parts, one concerned with moral rules, the other with what is good on its own account. Rules of conduct, many of which have a ritual origin, play a great part in the lives of savages and primitive peoples. It is forbidden to eat out of the chief's dish, or to seethe the kid in its mother's milk; it is commanded to offer sacrifices to the gods, which, at a certain stage of development, are thought most acceptable if they are human beings. Other moral rules, such as the prohibition of murder and theft, have a more obvious social utility, and survive the decay of the primitive theological systems with which they were originally associated. But as men grow more reflective there is a tendency to lay less stress on rules and more on states of mind. This comes from two sources—philosophy and mystical religion. We are all familiar with passages in the prophets and the gospels, in which purity of heart is set above meticulous observance of the Law; and St. Paul's famous praise of charity, or love, teaches the same principle. The same thing will be found in all great mystics, Christian and non-Christian: what they value is a state of mind, out of which, as they hold, right conduct must ensue; rules seem to them external, and insufficiently adaptable to circumstances.

One of the ways in which the need of appealing to external rules of conduct has been avoided has been the belief in "conscience," which has been especially important in Protestant ethics. It has been supposed that God reveals to each human heart what is right and what is wrong, so that, in order to avoid sin, we have only to listen to the inner voice. There are, however, two difficulties in this theory: first, that conscience says different things to different people; secondly, that the study of the unconscious has given us an understanding of the mundane causes of conscientious feelings.

As to the different deliverances of conscience: George III's conscience told him that he must not grant Catholic Emancipation, as, if he did, he would have committed perjury in taking the Coronation Oath, but later

From Bertrand Russell, *Religion and Science* (London. Oxford University Press. 1935).

monarchs have had no such scruples. Conscience leads some to condemn the spoliation of the rich by the poor, as advocated by communists; and others to condemn exploitation of the poor by the rich, as practiced by capitalists. It tells one man that he ought to defend his country in case of invasion, while it tells another that all participation in warfare is wicked. During the War, the authorities, few of whom had studied ethics, found conscience very puzzling, and were led to some curious decisions, such as that a man might have conscientious scruples against fighting himself, but not against working on the fields so as to make possible the conscription of another man. They held also that, while conscience might disapprove of all war, it could not, failing that extreme position, disapprove of the war then in progress. Those who, for whatever reason, thought it wrong to fight, were compelled to state their position in terms of this somewhat primitive and unscientific conception of "conscience."

The diversity in the deliverances of conscience is what is to be expected when its origin is understood. In early youth, certain classes of acts meet with approval, and others with disapproval; and by the normal process of association, pleasure and discomfort gradually attach themselves to the acts, and not merely to the approval and disapproval respectively produced by them. As time goes on, we may forget all about our early moral training, but we shall still feel uncomfortable about certain kinds of actions, while others will give us a glow of virtue. To introspection, these feelings are mysterious, since we no longer remember the circumstances which originally caused them; and therefore it is natural to attribute them to the voice of God in the heart. But in fact conscience is a product of education, and can be trained to approve or disapprove, in the great majority of mankind, as educators may see fit. While, therefore, it is right to wish to liberate ethics from external moral rules, this can hardly be satisfactorily achieved by means of the notion of "conscience."

Philosophers, by a different road, have arrived at a different position in which, also, moral rules of conduct have a subordinate place. They have framed the concept of the Good, by which they mean (roughly speaking) that which, in itself and apart from its consequences, we should wish to see existing—or, if they are theists, that which is pleasing to God. Most people would agree that happiness is preferable to unhappiness, friendliness to unfriendliness, and so on. Moral rules, according to this view, are justified if they promote the existence of what is good on its own account, but not otherwise. The prohibition of murder, in the vast majority of cases, can be justified by its effects, but the practice of burning widows on their husbands' funeral pyre cannot. The former rule, therefore, should be retained, but not the latter. Even the best moral rules, however, will have *some* exceptions, since no class of actions *always* has bad results. We have thus three different senses in which an act may be ethically commendable: (1) it may be in accordance with the received moral code; (2) it may be sincerely intended to have good effects; (3) it may in fact have good effects. The third sense, however, is generally considered inadmissible in morals. According to orthodox theology, Judas Iscariot's act of betrayal had good consequences, since it was necessary for the Atonement; but it was not on this account laudable.

Different philosophers have formed different conceptions of the Good. Some hold that it consists in the knowledge and love of God; others in universal love; others in the enjoyment of beauty; and yet others in pleasure. The Good once defined, the rest of ethics follows: we ought to act in the way we believe most likely to create as much good as possible, and as little as possible of its correlative evil. The framing of moral rules, so long as the ultimate Good is supposed known, is matter for science. For example: should capital punishment be inflicted for theft, or only for murder, or not at all? Jeremy Bentham, who considered pleasure to be the Good, devoted himself to working out what criminal code would most promote pleasure, and concluded that it ought to be much less severe than that prevailing in his day. All this, except the proposition that pleasure is the Good, comes within the sphere of science.

But when we try to be definite as to what we mean when we say that this or that is "the Good," we find ourselves involved in very great difficulties. Bentham's creed that pleasure is the Good roused furious opposition, and was said to be a pig's philosophy. Neither he nor his opponents could advance any argument. In a scientific question, evidence can be adduced on both sides, and in the end one side is seen to have the better case—or, if this does not happen, the question is left undecided. But in a question as to whether this or that is the ultimate Good, there is no evidence either way; each disputant can only appeal to his own emotions, and employ such rhetorical devices as shall rouse similar emotions in others.

Take, for example, a question which has come to be important in practical politics. Bentham held that one man's pleasure has the same ethical importance as another man's, provided the quantities are equal; and on this ground he was led to advocate democracy. Nietzsche, on the contrary, held that only the great man can be regarded as important on his own account, and that the bulk of mankind are only means to his well-being. He viewed ordinary men as many people view animals: he thought it justifiable to make use of them, not for their own good, but for that of the superman, and this view has since been adopted to justify the abandonment of democracy. We have here a sharp disagreement of great practical importance, but we have absolutely no means, of a scientific or intellectual kind, by which to persuade either party that the other is in the right. There are, it is true, ways of altering men's opinions on such subjects, but they are all emotional, not intellectual.

Questions as to "values"—that is to say, as to what is good or bad on its own account, independently of its effects—lie outside the domain of science, as the defenders of religion emphatically assert. I think that in this they are right, but I draw the further conclusion, which they do not draw, that questions as to "values" lie wholly outside the domain of knowledge. That is to say, when we assert that this or that has "value," we are giving expression to our own emotions, not to a fact which would still be true if our personal feelings were different. To make this clear, we must try to analyze the conception of the Good.

It is obvious, to begin with, that the whole idea of good and bad has some connection with *desire*. *Prima facie*, anything that we all desire is "good," and anything that we all dread is "bad." If we all agreed in our desires, the matter could be left there, but unfortunately our desires conflict. If I say "what I want is good," my neighbor will say "No, what *I* want." Ethics is an attempt—though not, I think, a successful one—to escape from this subjectivity. I shall naturally try to show, in my dispute with my neighbor, that my desires have some quality which makes them more worthy of respect than his. If I want to preserve a right of way, I shall appeal to the landless inhabitants of the district; but he, on his side, will appeal to the landowners. I shall say: "What use is the beauty of the countryside if no one sees it?" He will retort: "What beauty will be left if trippers are allowed to spread devastation?" Each tries to enlist allies by showing that his own desires harmonize with those of other people. When this is obviously impossible, as in the case of a burglar, the man is condemned by public opinion, and his ethical status is that of a sinner.

Ethics is thus closely related to politics: it is an attempt to bring the collective desires of a group to bear upon individuals; or, conversely, it is an attempt by an individual to cause his desires to become those of his group. This latter is, of course, only possible if his desires are not too obviously opposed to the general interest: the burglar will hardly attempt to persuade people that he is doing them good, though plutocrats make similar attempts, and often succeed. When our desires are for things which all can enjoy in common, it seems not unreasonable to hope that others may concur; thus the philosopher who values Truth, Goodness and Beauty seems, to himself, to be not merely expressing his own desires, but pointing the way to the welfare of all mankind. Unlike the burglar, he is able to believe that his desires are for something that has value in an impersonal sense.

Ethics is an attempt to give universal, and not merely personal, importance to certain of our desires. I say "certain" of our desires, because in regard to some of them this is obviously impossible, as we saw in the case of the burglar. The man who makes money on the Stock Exchange by means of some secret knowledge does not wish others to be equally well informed: Truth (in so far as he values it) is for him a private possession, not the general human good that it is for the philosopher. The philosopher may, it is true, sink to the level of the stock-jobber, as when he claims priority for a discovery. But this is a lapse: in his purely philosophic capacity, he wants only to enjoy the contemplation of Truth, in doing which he in no way interferes with others who wish to do likewise.

To seem to give universal importance to our desires—which is the business of ethics—may be attempted from two points of view, that of the legislator, and that of the preacher. Let us take the legislator first.

I will assume, for the sake of argument, that the legislator is personally disinterested. That is to say, when he recognizes one of his desires as being concerned only with his own welfare, he does not let it influence him in framing the laws; for example, his code is not designed to increase his personal fortune. But he has other desires which seem to him impersonal. He may believe in an ordered hierarchy from king to peasant, or from mine-owner to black indentured laborer. He may believe that women should be submissive to men. He may hold that the spread of knowledge in the lower classes is dangerous. And so on and so on. He will then, if he can, so construct his code that conduct promoting the ends which he values shall, as far as possible, be in accordance with individual self-interest; and he will establish a system of moral instruction which will, where it succeeds, make men feel wicked if they pursue other purposes than his.[1] Thus "virtue" will come to be in fact, though not in subjective estimation, subservience to the desires of the legislator, in so far as he himself considers these desires worthy to be universalized.

The standpoint and method of the preacher are necessarily somewhat different, because he does not control the machinery of the State, and therefore cannot produce an artificial harmony between his desires and those of others. His only method is to try to rouse in others the same desires that he feels himself, and for this purpose his appeal must be to the emotions. Thus Ruskin caused people to like Gothic architecture, not by argument, but by the moving effect of rhythmical prose. *Uncle Tom's Cabin* helped to make people think slavery an evil by causing them to imagine themselves as slaves. Every attempt to persuade people that something is good (or bad) in itself, and not merely in its effects, depends upon the art of rousing feelings, not upon an appeal to evidence. In every case the preacher's skill consists in creating in others emotions similar to his own—or dissimilar, if he is a hypocrite. I am not saying this as a criticism of the preacher, but as an analysis of the essential character of his activity.

When a man says "this is good in itself," he *seems* to be making a statement, just as much as if he said "this is square" or "this is sweet." I believe

---

[1] Compare the following advice by a contemporary of Aristotle (Chinese, not Greek): "A ruler should not listen to those who believe in people having opinions of their own and in the importance of the individual. Such teachings cause men to withdraw to quiet places and hide away in caves or on mountains, there to rail at the prevailing government, sneer at those in authority, belittle the importance of rank and emoluments, and despise all who hold official posts." Waley, *The Way and its Power*, p. 37.

this to be a mistake. I think that what the man really means is: "I wish everybody to desire this," or rather "Would that everybody desired this." If what he says is interpreted as a statement, it is merely an affirmation of his own personal wish; if, on the other hand, it is interpreted in a general way, it states nothing, but merely desires something. The wish, as an occurrence, is personal, but what it desires is universal. It is, I think, this curious interlocking of the particular and the universal which has caused so much confusion in ethics.

The matter may perhaps become clearer by contrasting an ethical sentence with one which makes a statement. If I say "all Chinese are Buddhists," I can be refuted by the production of a Chinese Christian or Mohammedan. If I say "I believe that all Chinese are Buddhists," I cannot be refuted by any evidence from China, but only by evidence that I do not believe what I say; for what I am asserting is only something about my own state of mind. If, now, a philosopher says "Beauty is good," I may interpret him as meaning either "Would that everybody loved the beautiful" (which corresponds to "all Chinese are Buddhists") or "I wish that everybody loved the beautiful" (which corresponds to "I believe that all Chinese are Buddhists"). The first of these makes no assertion, but expresses a wish; since it affirms nothing, it is logically impossible that there should be evidence for or against it, or for it to possess either truth or falsehood. The second sentence, instead of being merely optative, does make a statement, but it is one about the philosopher's state of mind, and it could only be refuted by evidence that he does not have the wish that he says he has. This second sentence does not belong to ethics, but to psychology or biography. The first sentence, which does belong to ethics, expresses a desire for something, but asserts nothing.

Ethics, if the above analysis is correct, contains no statements, whether true or false, but consists of desires of a certain general kind, namely such as are concerned with the desires of mankind in general—and of gods, angels, and devils, if they exist. Science can discuss the causes of desires, and the means for realizing them, but it cannot contain any genuinely ethical sentences, because it is concerned with what is true or false.

The theory which I have been advocating is a form of the doctrine which is called the "subjectivity" of values. This doctrine consists in maintaining that, if two men differ about values, there is not a disagreement as to any kind of truth, but a difference of taste. If one man says "oysters are good" and another says "I think they are bad," we recognize that there is nothing to argue about. The theory in question holds that all differences as to values are of this sort, although we do not naturally think them so when we are dealing with matters that seem to us more exalted than oysters. The chief ground for adopting this view is the complete impossibility of finding any arguments to prove that this or that has intrinsic value. If we all agreed, we might hold that we know values by intuition. We cannot *prove,* to a color-blind man, that grass is green and not red. But there are various ways of proving to him that he lacks a power of discrimination which most men possess, whereas in the case of values there are no such ways, and disagreements are much more frequent than in the case of colors. Since no way can be even imagined for deciding a difference as to values, the conclusion is forced upon us that the difference is one of tastes, not one as to any objective truth.

The consequences of this doctrine are considerable. In the first place, there can be no such thing as "sin" in any absolute sense; what one man calls "sin" another may call "virtue," and though they may dislike each other on account of this difference, neither can convict the other of intellectual error. Punishment cannot be justified on the ground that the criminal is "wicked" but only on the ground that he has behaved in a way which others wish to discourage. Hell, as a place of punishment for sinners, becomes quite irrational.

In the second place, it is impossible to uphold the way of speaking about values which is common among those who believe in Cosmic Purpose. Their argument is that certain things which have been evolved are "good," and therefore the world must have had a purpose which was ethically admirable. In the language of subjective values, this argument becomes: "Some things in the world are to our liking, and therefore they must have been created by a Being with our tastes, Whom, therefore, we also like, and Who, consequently, is good." Now it seems fairly evident that, if creatures having likes and dislikes were to exist at all, they were pretty sure to like *some* things in their environment, since otherwise they would find life intolerable. Our values have been evolved along with the rest of our constitution, and nothing as to any original purpose can be inferred from the fact that they are what they are.

Those who believe in "objective" values often contend that the view which I have been advocating has immoral consequences. This seems to me to be due to faulty reasoning. There are, as has already been said, certain ethical consequences of the doctrine of subjective values, of which the most important is the rejection of vindictive punishment and the notion of "sin." But the more general consequences which are feared, such as the decay of all sense of moral obligation, are not to be logically deduced. Moral obligation, if it is to influence conduct, must consist not merely of a belief, but of a desire. The desire, I may be told, is the desire to be "good" in a sense which I no longer allow. But when we analyze the desire to be "good" it generally resolves itself into a desire to be approved, or, alternatively, to act so as to bring about certain general consequences which we desire. We have wishes which are not purely personal, and, if we had not, no amount of ethical teaching would influence our conduct except through fear of disapproval. The sort of life that most of us admire is one which is guided by large impersonal desires; now such desires can, no doubt, be encouraged by example, education, and knowledge, but they can hardly be created by the mere abstract belief that they are good, nor discouraged by an analysis of what is meant by the word "good."

When we contemplate the human race, we may desire that it should be happy, or healthy, or intelligent, or warlike, and so on. Any one of these desires, if it is strong, will produce its own morality; but if we have no such general desires, our conduct, whatever our ethic may be, will only serve social purposes in so far as self-interest and the interests of society are in harmony. It is the business of wise institutions to create such harmony as far as possible, and for the rest, whatever may be our theoretical definition of value, we must depend upon the existence of impersonal desires. When you meet a man with whom you have a fundamental ethical disagreement— for example, if you think that all men count equally, while he selects a class as alone important—you will find yourself no better able to cope with him if you believe in objective values than if you do not. In either case, you can only influence his conduct through influencing his desires: if you succeed in that, his ethic will change, and if not, not.

Some people feel that if a general desire, say for the happiness of mankind, has not the sanction of absolute good, it is in some way irrational. This is due to a lingering belief in objective values. A desire cannot, in itself, be either rational or irrational. It may conflict with other desires, and therefore lead to unhappiness; it may rouse opposition in others, and therefore be incapable of gratification. But it cannot be considered "irrational" merely because no reason can be given for feeling it. We may desire A because it is a means to B, but in the end, when we have done with mere means, we must come to something which we desire for no reason, but not on that account "irrationally." All systems of ethics embody the desires of those who advocate them, but this fact is concealed in a mist of words. Our desires are, in fact, more general and less purely selfish than many moralists imagine; if it were not so, no theory of ethics would make moral improvement possible. It is, in fact, not by ethical theory, but by the cultivation of large and generous desires through intelligence, happiness and freedom from fear, that men can be brought to act more than they do at present in a manner that is consistent with the general happiness of mankind. Whatever our definition of the "Good," and whether we believe it to be subjective or objective, those who do not desire the happiness of mankind will not endeavor to further it, while those who do desire it will do what they can to bring it about.

I conclude that, while it is true that science cannot decide questions of value, that is because they cannot be intellectually decided at all, and lie outside the realm of truth and falsehood. Whatever knowledge is attainable must be attained by scientific methods; and what science cannot discover, mankind cannot know.

I SPARE MISS WATSON'S JIM | SAMUEL L. CLEMENS

[*Admirers of Mark Twain will need no introduction to Huck and Jim, the two main characters of Twain's wise and moving novel about the outcast in a "virtuous" society. For those who have not yet read* Huckleberry Finn, *a brief note of introduction is necessary. The story is told by Huck, motherless son of the village drunkard and homeless resident of a Mississippi river-town, a boy born outside the conventions of the world he lives in and reared with as little regard to those conventions as though he were a creature of another species. Yet, impelled by the need to know what it is that separates him from the world, Huck roams the fringes of society, puzzling out its actions and gradually coming to understand it and himself. The selections reprinted below are crucial in the novel, for they concern Huck's most important decision and its consequences and they include the other outcast of the novel—Jim, a Negro, and, at this point in the story, a runaway slave, hence a fugitive from the law.*

The first excerpt is merely a prologue to the chapters which follow. The scene is an island where Huck has taken temporary refuge and where he has discovered Jim also in hiding. From this point the two take to the river, making their way downstream and, they hope, out of danger.]

When breakfast was ready we lolled on the grass and eat it smoking hot. Jim laid it in with all his might, for he was most about starved. Then when we had got pretty well stuffed, we laid off and lazied.

By and by Jim says:

"But looky here, Huck, who wuz it dat 'uz killed in dat shanty ef it wasn't you?"

Then I told him the whole thing, and he said it was smart. He said Tom Sawyer couldn't get up no better plan than what I had. Then I says:

"How do you come to be here, Jim, and how'd you get here?"

He looked pretty uneasy, and didn't say nothing for a minute. Then he says:

"Maybe I better not tell."

"Why, Jim?"

"Well, dey's reasons. But you wouldn't tell on me ef I 'uz to tell you, would you, Huck?"

"Blamed if I would, Jim."

"Well, I b'lieve you, Huck I—I *run off.*"

"Jim!"

"But mind, you said you wouldn' tell—you know you said you wouldn' tell, Huck."

"Well, I did. I said I wouldn't, and I'll stick to it. Honest *injun,* I will.

From *Adventures of Huckleberry Finn* (1885).

People would call me a low-down Abolitionist and despise me for keeping mum—but that don't make no difference. I ain't a-going to tell, and I ain't a-going back there, anyways. So, now, le's know all about it." . . .

THE RATTLESNAKE-SKIN DOES ITS WORK

We slept most all day, and started out at night, a little ways behind a monstrous long raft that was as long going by as a procession. She had four long sweeps at each end, so we judged she carried as many as thirty men, likely. She had five big wigwams aboard, wide apart, and an open campfire in the middle, and a tall flag-pole at each end. There was a power of style about her. It *amounted* to something being a raftsman on such a craft as that.

We went drifting down into a big bend, and the night clouded up and got hot. The river was very wide, and was walled with solid timber on both sides; you couldn't see a break in it hardly ever, or a light. We talked about Cairo, and wondered whether we would know it when we got to it. I said likely we wouldn't, because I had heard say there warn't but about a dozen houses there, and if they didn't happen to have them lit up, how was we going to know we was passing a town? Jim said if the two big rivers joined together there, that would show. But I said maybe we might think we was passing the foot of an island and coming into the same old river again. That disturbed Jim—and me too. So the question was, what to do? I said, paddle ashore the first time a light showed, and tell them pap was behind, coming along with a trading-scow, and was a green hand at the business, and wanted to know how far it was to Cairo. Jim thought it was a good idea, so we took a smoke on it and waited.

There warn't nothing to do now but to look out sharp for the town, and not pass it without seeing it. He said he'd be mighty sure to see it, because he'd be a free man the minute he seen it, but if he missed it he'd be in a slave country again and no more show for freedom. Every little while he jumps up and says:

"Dah she is?"

But it warn't. It was Jack-o'-lanterns, or lightning-bugs; so he set down again, and went to watching, same as before. Jim said it made him all over trembly and feverish to be so close to freedom. Well, I can tell you it made me all over trembly and feverish, too, to hear him, because I begun to get it through my head that he *was* most free—and who was to blame for it? Why, *me*. I couldn't get that out of my conscience, no how nor no way. It got to troubling me so I couldn't rest; I couldn't stay still in one place. It hadn't ever come home to me before, what this thing was that I was doing. But now it did; and it stayed with me, and scorched me more and more. I tried to make out to myself that *I* warn't to blame, because *I* didn't run Jim off from his rightful owner; but it warn't no use, conscience up and says, every time, "But you knowed he was running for his freedom, and you could 'a' paddled ashore and told somebody." That was so—I couldn't get around that no way. That was where it pinched. Conscience says to me, "What had poor Miss Watson done to you that you could see her nigger go off right under your eyes and never say one single word? What did that poor old woman do to you that you could treat her so mean? Why, she tried to learn you your book, she tried to learn you your manners, she tried to be good to you every way she knowed how. *That's* what she done."

I got to feeling so mean and so miserable I most wished I was dead. I fidgeted up and down the raft, abusing myself to myself, and Jim was fidgeting up and down past me. We neither of us could keep still. Every time he danced around and says, "Dah's Cairo!" it went through me like a shot, and I thought if it *was* Cairo I reckoned I would die of miserableness.

Jim talked out loud all the time while I was talking to myself. He was saying how the first thing he would do when he got to a free state he would go to saving up money and never spend a single cent, and when he got enough he would buy his wife, which was owned on a farm close to where Miss Watson lived; and then they would both work to buy the two children, and if their master wouldn't sell them, they'd get an Ab'litionist to go and steal them.

It most froze me to hear such talk. He wouldn't ever dared to talk such talk in his life before. Just see what a difference it made in him the minute he judged he was about free. It was according to the old saying, "Give a nigger an inch and he'll take an ell." Thinks I, this is what comes of my not thinking. Here was this nigger, which I had as good as helped to run away, coming right out flat-footed and saying he would steal his children— children that belonged to a man I didn't even know; a man that hadn't ever done me no harm.

I was sorry to hear Jim say that, it was such a lowering of him. My conscience got to stirring me up hotter than ever, until at last I says to it, "Let up on me—it ain't too late yet—I'll paddle ashore at the first light and tell." I felt easy and happy and light as a feather right off. All my troubles was gone. I went to looking out sharp for a light, and sort of singing to myself. By and by one showed. Jim sings out:

"We's safe, Huck, we's safe! Jump up and crack yo' heels! Dat's de good ole Cairo at las', I jis knows it!"

I says:

"I'll take the canoe and go and see, Jim. It mightn't be, you know."

He jumped and got the canoe ready, and put his old coat in the bottom for me to set on, and give me the paddle; and as I shoved off, he says:

"Pooty soon I'll be a-shout'n' for joy, en I'll say, it's all on accounts o' Huck; I's a free man, en I couldn't ever ben free ef it hadn't ben for Huck; Huck done it. Jim won't ever forgit you, Huck; you's de bes' fren' Jim's ever had; en you's de *only* fren' ole Jim's got now."

I was paddling off, all in a sweat to tell on him; but when he says this, it seemed to kind of take the tuck all out of me. I went along slow then, and I warn't right down certain whether I was glad I started or whether I warn't. When I was fifty yards off, Jim says:

"Dah you goes, de ole true Huck; de on'y white genlman dat ever kep' his promise to ole Jim."

Well, I just felt sick. But I says, I *got* to do it—I can't get out of it. Right then along comes a skiff with two men in it with guns, and they stopped and I stopped. One of them says:

"What's that yonder?"

"A piece of raft," I says.

"Do you belong on it?"

"Yes, sir."

"Any men on it?"

"Only one, sir."

"Well, there's five niggers run off to-night up yonder, above the head of the bend. Is your man white or black?"

I didn't answer up promptly. I tried to, but the words wouldn't come. I tried for a second or two to brace up and out with it, but I wan't man enough—hadn't the spunk of a rabbit. I see I was weakening; so I just give up trying, and up and says:

"He's white."

"I reckon we'll go and see for ourselves."

"I wish you would," says I, "because it's pap that's there, and maybe you'd help me tow the raft ashore where the light is. He's sick—and so is mam and Mary Ann."

"Oh, the devil! we're in a hurry, boy. But I s'pose we've got to. Come buckle to your paddle, and let's get along."

I buckled to my paddle and they laid to their oars. When we had made a stroke or two, I says:

"Pap'll be mighty much obleeged to you, I can tell you. Everybody goes away when I want them to help me tow the raft ashore, and I can't do it by myself.

"Well, that's infernal mean. Odd, too. Say, boy, what's the matter with your father?"

"It's the—a—the—well, it ain't anything much."

They stopped pulling. It warn't but a mighty little ways to the raft now. One says:

"Boy, that's a lie. What *is* the matter with your pap? Answer up square now, and it'll be the better for you."

"I will, sir, I will, honest—but don't leave us, please. It's the—the— Gentlemen, if you'll only pull ahead, and let me heave you the headline, you won't have to come a-near the raft—please do."

"Set her back, John, set her back!" says one. They backed water. "Keep away, boy—keep to looard. Confound it, I just expect the wind has blowed it to us. Your pap's got the smallpox, and you know it precious well. Why didn't you come out and say so? Do you want to spread it all over?"

"Well," says I, a-blubbering, "I've told everybody before, and they just went away and left us."

"Poor devil, there's something in that. We are right down sorry for you, but we—well, hang it, we don't want the smallpox, you see. Look here, I'll tell you what to do. Don't you try to land by yourself, or you'll smash every-thing to pieces. You float along down about twenty miles, and you'll come to a town on the left-hand side of the river. It will be long after sun-up then, and when you ask for help you tell them your folks are all down with chills and fever. Don't be a fool again, and let people guess what is the matter. Now we're trying to do you a kindness; so you just put twenty miles between us, that's a good boy. It wouldn't do any good to land yonder where the light is—it's only a wood-yard. Say, I reckon your father's poor, and I'm bound to say he's in pretty hard luck. Here, I'll put a twenty-dollar gold piece on this board, and you get it when it floats by. I feel mighty mean to leave you; but my kingdom! it won't do to fool with smallpox, don't you see?"

"Hold on, Parker," says the man, "here's a twenty to put on the board for me. Good-by, boy; you do as Mr. Parker told you, and you'll be all right."

"That's so, my boy—good-by, good-by. If you see any runaway niggers you get help and nab them, and you can make some money by it."

"Good-by, sir," says I; "I won't let no runaway niggers get by me if I can help it."

They went off and I got aboard the raft, feeling bad and low, because I knowed very well I had done wrong, and I see it warn't no use for me to try to learn to do right; a body that don't get *started* right when he's little ain't got no show—when the pinch comes there ain' nothing to back him up and keep him to his work, and so he gets beat. Then I thought a minute, and says to myself, hold on; s'pose you'd 'a' done right and give Jim up, would you felt better than what you do now? No, says I, I'd feel bad—I'd feel just the same way I do now. Well, then, says I, what's the use you learn-ing to do right when it's troublesome to do right and ain't no trouble to do wrong, and the wages is just the same? I was stuck. I couldn't answer that. So I reckoned I wouldn't bother no more about it, but after this always do whichever come handiest at the time.

I went into the wigwam; Jim warn't there. I looked all around; he warn't anywhere. I says:

"Jim!"

"Here I is, Huck. Is dey out o' sight yit? Don't talk loud."

He was in the river under the stern oar, with just his nose out. I told him they were out of sight, so he come aboard. He says:

"I was a-listenin' to all de talk, en I slips into de river en was gwyne to shove for sho' if dey came aboard. Den I was gwyne to swim to de raf' agin when day was gone. But lawsy, how you did fool 'em, Huck! Dat *wuz* de smartes' dodge! I tell you, chile, I 'spec it save' old Jim—ole Jim ain't going to forgit you for dat, honey."

Then we talked about the money. It was a pretty good raise—twenty dollars apiece. Jim said we could take deck passage on a steamboat now, and the money would last us as far as we wanted to go in the free states. He said twenty mile more warn't far for the raft to go, but he wished we was already there.

Towards daybreak we tied up, and Jim was mighty particular about hiding the raft good. Then he worked all day fixing things in bundles, and getting all ready to quit rafting.

That night about ten we hove in sight of the lights of a town away down in a left-hand bend.

I went off in the canoe to task about it. Pretty soon I found a man out in the river with a skiff, setting a trot-line. I ranged up and says:

"Mister, is that town Cairo?"

"Cairo? no. You must be a blame' fool."

"What town is it, mister?"

"If you want to know, go and find out. If you stay here botherin' around me for about a half a minute longer you'll get something you won't want."

I paddled to the raft. Jim was awful disappointed, but I said never mind, Cairo would be the next place, I reckoned.

We passed another town before daylight, and I was going out again; but it was high ground, so I didn't go. No high ground about Cairo, Jim said. I had forgot it. We laid up for the day on a towhead tolerable close to the left-hand bank. I begun to suspicion something. So did Jim. I says:

"Maybe we went to Cairo in the fog that night."

He says:

"Doan' le's talk about it, Huck. Po' niggers can't have no luck. I alwuz 'spected dat rattlesnake-skin warn't done wid its work."

"I wish I'd never seen that snake-skin, Jim—I do wish I'd never laid eyes on it."

"It ain't yo' fault, Huck; you didn't know. Don't you blame yo'self 'bout it."

When it was daylight, here was the clear Ohio water inshore, sure enough, and outside was the old regular Muddy! So it was all up with Cairo.

We talked it all over. It wouldn't do to take to the shore; we couldn't take the raft up the stream, of course. There warn't no way but to wait for dark, and start back in the canoe and take the chances. So we slept all day amongst the cottonwood thicket, so as to be fresh for the work, and when we went back to the raft about dark the canoe was gone!

We didn't say a word for a good while. There warn't anything to say. We both knowed well enough it was some more work of the rattlesnake-skin; so what was the use to talk about it? It would only look like we was finding fault, and that would be bound to fetch more bad luck—and keep on fetching it, too, till we knowed enough to keep still.

By and by we talked about what we better do, and found there warn't no way but just to go along down with the raft till we got a chance to buy a canoe to go back in. We warn't going to borrow it when there warn't anybody around, the way pap would do, for that might set people after us.

So we shoved out after dark on the raft.

Anybody that don't believe yet that it's foolishness to handle a snake-skin, after all that that snake-skin done for us, will believe it now if they read on and see what more it done for us.

The place to buy canoes is off of rafts laying up at shore. But we didn't see no rafts laying up; so we went along during three hours and more. Well, the night got gray and ruther thick, which is the next meanest thing to fog. You can't tell the shape of the river, and you can't see no distance. It got to be very late and still, and then along comes a steamboat up the river. We lit the lantern, and judged she would see it. Upstream boats didn't generly come close to us; they go out and follow the bars and hunt for easy water under the reefs; but nights like this they bull right up the channel against the whole river.

We could hear her pounding along, but we didn't see her good till she was close. She aimed right for us. Often they do that and try to see how close they can come without touching; sometimes the wheel bites off a sweep, and then the pilot sticks his head out and laughs, and thinks he's mighty smart. Well, here she comes, and we said she going to try and shave us; but she didn't seem to be sheering off a bit. She was a big one, and she was coming in a hurry, too, looking like a black cloud with rows of glow-worms around it; but all of a sudden she bulged out, big and scary, with a long row of wide-open furnace doors shining like red-hot teeth, and her monstrous bows and guards hanging right over us. There was a yell at us, and a jingling of bells to stop the engines, a pow-wow of cussing, and whistling of steam—and as Jim went overboard on one side and I on the other, she come smashing straight through the raft.

I dived—and I aimed to find the bottom, too, for a thirty-foot wheel had got to go over me, and I wanted it to have plenty of room. I could always stay under water a minute; this time I reckoned I stayed under a minute and a half. Then I bounced for the top in a hurry, for I was nearly busting. I popped out to my arm pits and blowed the water out of my nose, and puffed a bit. Of course there was a booming current; and of course that boat started her engines again ten seconds after she stopped them, for they never cared much for raftsmen; so now she was churning along up the river, out of sight in the thick weather, though I could hear her.

I sung out for Jim about a dozen times, but I didn't get any answer; so I grabbed a plank that touched me while I was "treading water," and struck out for shore, shoving it ahead of me. But I made out to see that the drift of the current was towards the left-hand shore, which meant that I was in a crossing; so I changed off and went that way.

It was one of these long, slanting, two-mile crossings; so I was a good long time in getting over. I made a safe landing, and clumb up the bank. I couldn't see but a little ways, but I went poking along over rough ground for a quarter of a mile or more, and then I run across a big old-fashioned double log house before I noticed it. I was going to rush by and get away, but a lot of dogs jumped out and went to howling and barking at me, and I knowed better than to move another peg.

[Reunited, Huck and Jim fall in with two scoundrels who befriend them in order to exploit them. Duped at first by the pretentious language and claims of this pair of rascals, Huck and Jim soon come to know them for what they really are. Even when they know, however, they cannot cut themselves off from their companions, for—good and bad together—all are people living outside the law: the duke and the king, for frauds and larcenies too numerous to recount; Jim, for running away from his legal owner; Huck, for aiding and abetting him. The final test of Huck's new-found principle of human equality comes near the end of the novel, a test which he meets with the cunning he has learned as one to whom the world gave only as much as could be forcibly taken from it.]

YOU CAN'T PRAY A LIE

We dasn't stop again at any town for days and days; kept right along down the river. We was down south in the warm weather now, and a mighty long ways from home. We begun to come to trees with Spanish moss on them, hanging down from the limbs like long, gray beards. It was the first I ever see it growing, and it made the woods look solemn and dismal. So now the frauds reckoned they was out of danger, and they begun to work the villages again.

First they done a lecture on temperance; but they didn't make enough for them both to get drunk on. Then in another village they started a dancing school; but they didn't know no more how to dance than a kangaroo does; so the first prance they made the general public jumped in and pranced them out of down. Another time they tried to go at yellocution; but they didn't yellocute long till the audience got up and give them a solid good cussing, and made them skip out. They tackled missionarying, and mesmerizing, and doctoring, and telling fortunes, and a little of everything; but they couldn't seem to have no luck. So at last they got just about dead broke, and laid around the raft as she floated along, thinking and thinking, and never saying nothing, by the half a day at a time, and dreadful blue and desperate.

And at last they took a change and begun to lay their heads together in the wigwam and talk low and confidential two or three hours at a time. Jim

and me got uneasy. We didn't like the look of it. We judge they was studying up some kind of worse deviltry than ever. We turned it over and over,
and at last we made up our minds they was going to break into somebody's
house or store, or was going into the counterfeit-money business, or something. So then we was pretty scared, and made up an agreement that we
wouldn't have nothing in the world to do with such actions, and if we ever
got the least show we would give them the cold shake and clear out and
leave them behind. Well, early one morning we hid the raft in a good, safe
place about two mile below a little bit of a shabby village named Pikesville,
and the king he went ashore and told us all to stay hid whilst he went up to
town and smelt around to see if anybody had got any wind of the "Royal
Nonesuch" there yet. ("House to rob, you *mean*," says I to myself; "and
when you get through robbin it you'll come back here and wonder what
has become of me and Jim and the raft—and you'll have to take it out in
wondering.") And he said if he warn't back by midday the duke and me
would know it was all right, and we was to come along.

So we stayed where we was. The duke he fretted and sweated around,
and was in a mighty sour way. He scolded us for everything, and we couldn't
seem to do nothing right; he found fault with every little thing. Something
was a-brewing, sure. I was good and glad when midday come and no king;
we could have a change, anyway—and maybe a chance for *the* chance on
top of it. So me and the duke went up to the village, and hunted around
there for the king, and by and by we found him in the back room of a little
low doggery, very tight, and a lot of loafers bully-ragging him for sport, and
he a-cussing and a-threatening with all his might, and so tight he couldn't
walk, and couldn't do nothing to them. The duke he begun to abuse him
for an old fool, and the king begun to sass back, and the minute they was
fairly at it I lit out and shook the reefs out of my hind legs, and spun down
the river road like a deer, for I see our chance; and I made up my mind
that it would be a long day before they ever see me and Jim again. I got
down there all out of breath but loaded up with joy, and sung out:

"Set her loose, Jim; we're all right now!"

But there warn't no answer, and nobody come out of the wigwam. Jim
was gone! I set up a shout—and then another—and then another one; and
run this way and that in the woods, whooping and screeching; but it warn't
no use—old Jim was gone. Then I set down and cried; I couldn't help it.
But I couldn't set still long. Pretty soon I went out on the road, trying to
think what I better do, and I run across a boy walking, and asked him if
he'd seen a strange nigger dressed so and so, and he says:

"Yes."

"Whereabouts?" says I.

"Down to Silas Phelps's place, two mile below here. He's a runaway
nigger, and they've got him. Was you looking for him?"

"You bet I ain't! I run across him in the woods about an hour or two ago, and he said if I hollered he'd cut my livers out—and told me to lay down and stay where I was; and I done it. Been there ever since; afeared to come out."

"Well," he says, "you needn't be afeared no more, becuz they've got him. He run off f'm down South, som'ers."

"It's a good job they got him."

"Well, I *reckon!* There's two hundred dollars' reward on him. It's like picking up money out'n the road."

"Yes, it is—and *I* could 'a' had it if I'd been big enough; I see him *first*. Who nailed him?"

"It was an old fellow—a stranger—and he sold out his chance in him for forty dollars, becuz he's got to go up the river and can't wait. Think o' that, now! You bet *I'd* wait, if it was seven year."

"That's me, every time," says I. "But maybe his chance ain't worth no more than that, if he'll sell it so cheap. Maybe there's something ain't straight about it."

"But it *is,* though—straight as a string. I see the handbill myself. It tells all about him, to a dot—paints him like a picture, and tells the plantation he's frum, below Newr*leans*. No-sirree-*bob,* they ain't no trouble 'bout *that* speculation, you bet you. Say, gimme a chaw tobacker, won't ye?"

I didn't have none, so he left. I went to the raft, and set down in the wigwam to think. But I couldn't come to nothing. I thought till I wore my head sore, but I couldn't see no way out of the trouble. After all this long journey, and after all we'd done for them scoundrels, here it was all come to nothing, everything all busted up and ruined, because they could have the heart to serve Jim such a trick as that, and make him a slave again all his life, and amongst strangers, too, for forty dirty dollars.

Once I said to myself it would be a thousand times better for Jim to be a slave at home where his family was, as long as he'd *got* to be a slave, and so I'd better write a letter to Tom Sawyer and tell him to tell Miss Watson where he was. But I soon give up that notion for two things: she'd be mad and disgusted at his rascality and ungratefulness for leaving her, and so she'd sell him straight down the river again; and if she didn't, everybody naturally despises an ungrateful nigger, and they'd make Jim feel it all the time, and so he'd feel ornery and disgraced. And then think of *me!* It would get all around that Huck Finn helped a nigger to get his freedom; and if I was ever to see anybody from that town again I'd be ready to get down and lick his boots for shame. That's just the way: a person does a low-down thing, and then he don't want to take no consequences of it. Thinks as long as he can hide, it ain't no disgrace. That was my fix exactly. The more I studied about this the more my conscience went to grinding me, and the more wicked and low-down and ornery I got to feeling. And at last, when it hit me all of a sudden that here was the plain hand of Providence slapping me in the face and letting me know my wickedness was being watched all the time from up there in heaven, whilst I was stealing a poor old woman's nigger that hadn't ever done me no harm, and now was showing me there's One that's always on the lookout, and ain't a-going to allow no such miserable doings to go only just so fur and no further, I most dropped in my tracks I was so scared. Well, I tried the best I could to kinder soften it up somehow for myself by saying I was brung up wicked, and so I warn't so much to blame; but something inside of me kept saying, "There was the Sunday-school, you could 'a' gone to it; and if you'd 'a' done it they'd 'a' learnt you there that people that acts as I'd been acting about that nigger goes to everlasting fire."

It made me shiver. And I about made up my mind to pray, and see if I couldn't try to quit being the kind of a boy I was and be better. So I kneeled down. But the words wouldn't come. Why wouldn't they? It warn't no use to try and hide it from Him. Nor from *me*, neither. I knowed very well why they wouldn't come. It was because my heart warn't right; it was because I warn't square; it was because I was playing double. I was letting *on* to give up sin, but away inside of me I was holding on to the biggest one of all. I was trying to make my mouth *say* I would do the right thing and the clean thing, and go and write to that nigger's owner and tell where he was; but deep down in me I knowed it was a lie, and He knowed it. You can't pray a lie—I found that out.

So I was full of trouble, full as I could be; and didn't know what to do. At last I had an idea; and I says, I'll go and write the letter—and *then* see if I can pray. Why, it was astonishing, the way I felt as light as a feather right straight off, and my troubles all gone. So I got a piece of paper and a pencil, all glad and excited, and set down and wrote:

Miss Watson, your runaway nigger Jim is down here two mile below Pikesville, and Mr. Phelps has got him and he will give him up for the reward if you send.

HUCK FINN

I felt good and all washed clean of sin for the first time I had ever felt so in my life, and I knowed I could pray now. But I didn't do it straight off, but laid the paper down and set there thinking—thinking how good it was all this happened so, and how near I come to being lost and going to hell. And went on thinking. And got to thinking over our trip down the river; and I see Jim before me all the time: in the day and in the night-time, sometimes moonlight, sometimes storms, and we a-floating along, talking and singing and laughing. But somehow I couldn't seem to strike no places to harden me against him, but only the other kind. I'd see him standing my watch on top of his'n, 'stead of calling me, so I could go on sleeping; and see him how glad he was when I come back out of the fog; and when I come to him again in the swamp, up there where the feud was; and suchlike times; and would always call me honey, and pet me, and do everything he could think of for me, and how good he always was; and at last I struck the time I saved him by telling the men we had smallpox aboard, and he was so grateful, and said I was the best friend old Jim ever had in the world, and the *only* one he's got now; and then I happened to look around and see that paper.

It was a close place. I took it up, and held it in my hand. I was a-trembling, because I'd got to decide, forever, betwixt two things, and I knowed it. I studied a minute, sort of holding my breath, and then says to myself:

"All right, then, I'll *go* to hell"—and tore it up.

It was awful thoughts and awful words, but they was said. And I let them stay said; and never thought no more about reforming. I shoved the whole thing out of my head, and said I would take up wickedness again, which was in my line, being brung up to it, and the other warn't. And for a starter I would go to work and steal Jim out of slavery again; and if I could think up anything worse, I would do that, too; because as long as I was in, and in for good, I might as well go the whole hog.

Then I set to thinking over how to get at it, and turned over some considerable many ways in my mind; and at last fixed up a plan that suited me. So then I took the bearings of a woody island that was down the river a piece, and as soon as it was fairly dark I crept out with my raft and went for it, and hid it there, and then turned in. I slept the night through, and got up before it was light, and had my breakfast, and put on my store clothes, and tied up some others and one thing or another in a bundle, and took the canoe and cleared for shore. I landed below where I judged was Phelps's place, and hid my bundle in the woods, and then filled up the canoe with water, and loaded rocks into her and sunk her where I could find her again when I wanted her, about a quarter of a mile below a little steam-sawmill that was on the bank.

Then I struck up the road, and when I passed the mill I see a sign on it, "Phelps's Sawmill," and when I come to the farm-houses, two or three hundred yards further along, I kept my eyes peeled, but didn't see nobody around, though it was good day-light now. But I didn't mind, because I didn't want to see nobody just yet—I only wanted to get the lay of the land. According to my plan, I was going to turn up there from the village, not from below. So I just took a look, and shoved along, straight for town. Well, the very first man I see when I got there was the duke. He was sticking up a bill for the "Royal Nonesuch"—three-night performance—like that other time. *They* had the cheek, them frauds! I was right on him before I could shirk. He looked astonished, and says:

"Hel-*lo!* where'd *you* come from?" Then he says, kind of glad and eager, "Where's the raft?—got her in a good place?"

I says:

"Why, that's just what I was going to ask your grace."

Then he didn't look so joyful, and says:

"What was your idea for asking *me?*" he says.

"Well," I says, "when I see the king in that doggery yesterday I says to myself, we can't get him home for hours, till he's soberer; so I went a-loafing around town to put in the time and wait. A man up and offered me ten cents to help him pull a skiff over the river and back to fetch a sheep, and so I went along; but when we was dragging him to the boat, and the man left me a-holt of the rope and went behind him to shove him along, he was too strong for me and jerked loose and run, and we after him. We didn't have no dog, and so had to chase him all over the country till we tired him out. We never got him till dark; then we fetched him over, and I started down for the raft. When I got there and see it was gone, I says to myself, 'They've got into trouble and had to leave; and they've took my nigger, which is the only nigger I've got in the world, and now I'm in a strange country, and ain't got no property no more, nor nothing, and no way to make my living'; so I set down and cried. I slept in the woods all night. But what *did* become of the raft, then?—and Jim—poor Jim!"

"Blamed if *I* know—that is, what's become of the raft. That old fool had made a trade and got forty dollars, and when we found him in the doggery the loafers had matched half-dollars with him and got every cent but what he'd spent for whisky; and when I got him home late last night and found the raft gone, we said, 'That little rascal has stole our raft and shook us. and run off down the river.'"

"I wouldn't shake my *nigger,* would I?—the only nigger I had in the world, and the only property."

"We never thought of that. Fact is, I reckon we'd come to consider him *our* nigger; yes, we did consider him so—goodness knows we had trouble enough for him. So when we see the raft was gone and we flat broke, there warn't anything for it but to try the 'Royal Nonesuch' another shake. And I've pegged along ever since, dry as a powder-horn. Where's that ten cents? Give it here."

I had considerable money, so I give him ten cents, but begged him to spend it for something to eat, and give me some, because it was all the money I had, and I hadn't had nothing to eat since yesterday. He never said nothing. The next minute he whirls on me and says:

"Do you reckon that nigger would blow on us? We'd skin him if he done that!"

"How can he blow? Hain't he run off?"

"No! That old fool sold him, and never divided with me, and the money's gone."

"*Sold* him?" I says, and begun to cry; "why, he was *my* nigger, and that was my money. Where is he?—I want my nigger."

"Well, you can't *get* your nigger, that's all—so dry up your blubbering.

Looky here—do you think *you'd* venture to blow on us? Blamed if I think I'd trust you. Why, if you *was* to blow on us—"

He stopped, but I never seen the duke look so ugly out of his eyes before. I went on a-whimpering, and says:

"I don't want to blow on nobody; and I ain't got no time to blow, nohow; I got to turn out and find my nigger."

He looked kinder bothered, and stood there with his bills fluttering on his arm, thinking, and wrinkling up his forehead. At last he says:

"I'll tell you something. We got to be here three days. If you'll promise you won't blow, and won't let the nigger blow, I'll tell you where to find him."

So I promised, and he says:

"A farmer by the name of Silas Ph—" and then he stopped. You see, he started to tell me the truth; but when he stopped that way, and begun to study and think again, I reckoned he was changing his mind. And so he was. He wouldn't trust me; he wanted to make sure of having me out of the way the whole three days. So pretty soon he says:

"The man that bought him is named Abram Foster—Abram G. Foster— and he lives forty mile back here in the country, on the road to Lafayette."

"All right," I says, "I can walk it in three days. And I'll start this very afternoon."

"No you won't, you'll start *now;* and don't you lose any time about it, neither, nor do any gabbling by the way. Just keep a tight tongue in your head and move right along, and then you won't get into trouble with *us,* d'ye hear?"

That was the order I wanted, and that was the one I played for. I wanted to be left free to work my plans.

"So clear out," he says; "and you can tell Mr. Foster whatever you want to. Maybe you can get him to believe that Jim *is* your nigger—some idiots don't require documents—leastways I've heard there's such down South here. And when you tell him the handbill and the reward's bogus, maybe he'll believe you when you explain to him what the idea was for getting 'em out. Go 'long now, and tell him anything you want to; but mind you don't work your jaw any *between* here and there."

So I left, and struck for the back country. I didn't look around, but I kinder felt like he was watching me. But I knowed I could tire him out at that. I went straight out in the country as much as a mile before I stopped; then I doubled back through the woods towards Phelps's. I reckoned I better start in on my plan straight off without fooling around, because I wanted to stop Jim's mouth till these fellows could get away. I didn't want no trouble with their kind. I'd seen all I wanted to of them, and wanted to get entirely shut of them.

PATTERNS OF DEFINITION

BECAUSE DEFINITIONS are implicit in language, it might seem reasonable for writers to assume that their discourses with others would proceed without interruption for the purpose of getting terms straight. But if the writer is alert, if he has a lively sense of the difficulties he has himself overcome but which may still impede his reader, he will not make that comfortable assumption. He will, rather, be intent on making sure that nowhere in the course of his presentation does his reader lose contact with him for having encountered a baffling term or concept. Between reader and writer there is an unstated agreement that makes such contact possible. For his part, the reader promises to think as he reads and to be ready for any term or concept in general circulation among those for whom the writing is intended. And, for his part, the writer promises to give warn-ing whenever he departs from conventional usage and to provide explana-tion whenever he makes choices among several common possibilities, attempts to develop a new distinction, or departs significantly from the meanings current for the audience he assumes.

From time to time, and very often in academic discourse, definition becomes something more than casual. It may, indeed, become the central preoccupation of a writer, since it is one of the traditional duties of academic people to clarify their language by preserving the distinctness of meanings. The ultimate aim of such exercises in definition may, however, be more—or other—than clarification. Even when they give their total energies to the single act of defining, men are likely to be acting from motives that transcend the scholarly. The terms they choose to define may, by themselves, give some indication of intentions larger than elucidation, or the strategy of the definition may do so. Of the essays in definition that follow, only the one by Arthur Lovejoy (1873-1962), a student of the history of ideas and former professor of English at The Johns Hopkins Uni-versity, is really unmarked by ulterior intent. Though the essay by J. B. S. Haldane has the air of no-nonsense exactitude we expect to find in the sciences, it is slyly an admonition and a defense as well. As one of the leading scientist-philosophers of our century, Haldane (1892-   ), never loses sight of the fact that the welfare of his profession depends in no small way on the sympathy and comprehension of those outside it. This essay, one of his many efforts to make the point of view and knowledge of science apparent to laymen, sets out to deal with a word "in its ordinary sense," a disarming but entirely honest aim. The reader suddenly finds himself committed to a restriction for a word he undoubtedly felt confident about before he began to read. The restriction is imposed with complete matter-

*of-factness; but the ending of the definition shows that Haldane had some-
thing more than definition in mind all along. The definition of language
developed in the essay by Edward Sapir (1884-1939), foremost of scholars
in the application of anthropological learning to the study of language, is
clearly the work of a man well aware that his readers need to be taken, step
by step, into the subtle region where language is being used to discuss
language. From an original distinction between walking and speaking,
Sapir moves to definition by exclusion (what language is not) and then by
comparison (what language is more than), and finally to the hardest discrimination of all, that between language and thought. His purpose ("the
way is now cleared for a serviceable definition") is explicitly to develop
a working concept of language as the basis for further study, and he is at
great pains to make sure that no potential disciple is misled or confused
at the outset of his indoctrination. After the specificity of Haldane, the
explicit delimitation in time and content of Lovejoy, and the patient re-
hearsal of elementary matters of Sapir, it may be something of a shock to
come upon the assertion, in the next essay, that a definition of myth "must
be both broad and loose." Mark Schorer (1908-   ), professor of English
at the University of California at Berkeley, qualifies the assertion, to be
sure, but the qualification is not an evasion. Not only for his purposes, but
for very general purposes, it may be argued that a definition is most useful
in measure as it is most comprehensive. Certainly in this essay the breadth
is well exploited but at the same time carefully controlled: definition is
constantly at the service of statement, and statement itself moves steadily
from general to particular. The final essay in this series, by C. S. Lewis,
(1898-   ), professor of English literature at Cambridge University, is at
bottom an argument and an uncompromising one. Though he frequently
turns to ordinary language as a source for his meanings of the word "pain,"
Mr. Lewis is bent on something more than semantic distinctions. From
the initial division into physiological and psychological meanings and the
subordination of the first to the second, he is engaged in building on
definition a persuasive argument for the value of pain and the reasonableness of its existence in a God-governed world.*

*Taken together, these essays not only demonstrate the usefulness of defi-
nition in all areas of human knowledge but also exemplify conscious patterns and deployments of a high order.*

WHAT "HARD" MEANS | *J. B. S. HALDANE*

In the last article I wrote about the way in which ordinary words change their meaning as they are used in science and technology, taking as an example the word "hot." All adjectives start as descriptions of qualities. They end up as descriptions of quantities, if they are taken over by science. A word like "big" or "long" is entirely relative. A mile is a long swim but a short walk, because an ordinary man often walks a mile, but seldom swims a mile. A man is large compared to a cat, and small compared to an elephant, and so on. This sort of contradiction does not trouble anyone but philosophers, because we are accustomed to measure lengths, and we all know what a foot or a mile means.

But we are in much greater difficulties with some other common adjectives such as "hard." Of course we use the word metaphorically, as when we talk of a hard question, meaning one which is difficult to answer, or hard X-rays, meaning rays which penetrate easily through matter. But I want to deal with the word in its ordinary sense, as when we say that iron is harder than butter. Everyone will agree that this is true. But it is not so easy to decide which of two pieces of iron is harder, and as a matter of fact there may be no definite answer to the question. When we come to accurate measurement, we find that the word "hard" has dozens of slightly different meanings.

The most usual test of hardness in steels is that of Brinell. A very hard steel ball of 10 millimetres diameter is pressed onto a steel plate for 30 seconds with a load of 3 tons. The hardness number decreases with the depth of the indentation.

Another test of hardness which generally agrees pretty well with the Brinell test is the weight which must be put on a diamond point in order that it should just produce a visible scratch when pulled sideways. But as soon as we use moving bodies to measure hardness things become very complicated. For example at a relative speed of 30 feet per second a disc of "soft" iron was cut by a steel tool; at 100 feet per second the disc cut the tool itself, and at 300 feet per second the disc cut quartz. In the same way hardness varies with temperature.

If we compare an ordinary hardened carbon tool steel and a high-speed tool steel at ordinary temperatures, the former is probably a little harder by the Brinell test. But at a dull red heat the high-speed steel is still hard, while the ordinary tool steel is about as soft as is copper at room temperature. . . .

Hardness is also used as a measure of the amount of wear which a

From *A Banned Broadcast and Other Essays* (London, Chatto & Windus, 1946).

material will stand. But here again the details are very important. We may want to test how a metal stands up to rolling friction without lubricant. This is essential in tests of rails, and wheels of railway vehicles. Or we may want to know how a metal stands up to sliding abrasion, either with or without a film of oil. One steel may stand up better to rolling friction, and another to sliding friction. Here their differences in hardness probably depend on the fact that metals sliding over one another actually melt at the point of contact, so their properties at high temperatures become important.

Within a century or less we shall probably be able to calculate the various kinds of hardness with great exactitude from a knowledge of the forces between atoms. At present we can only do so very roughly. Probably the physicists of the future will be able to specify the different kinds of hardness very completely in terms of a few numbers.

It would be possible to deal in the same way with the meanings of various words such as toughness, elasticity, and brittleness, which are applied to solids. None of these can be expressed by a single number.

The properties of liquids are a good deal simpler than those of solids, and the properties of gases are simpler still, though anyone concerned with the design of aeroplanes finds even gases quite complicated enough. And when we come to such a property of material systems as life, the complications are of course vastly greater. Scientists are reproached because they cannot say in simple terms what life is. It is easy enough to point out differences between a dog or a cabbage and a stone or a machine. It is much harder to draw the line when we get down to the agents of smallpox and other diseases, which behave in some ways as if alive and in others as if dead. But if anyone reproaches science because it cannot yet give a complete account of life, it is a fair reply to ask him what he means by hardness, and how he would tell if one thing is harder than another.

"PRIDE" IN EIGHTEENTH-CENTURY THOUGHT | *ARTHUR O. LOVEJOY*

It has doubtless been noted by most students of modern literature that satirists and moralizing writers in the late seventeenth and the eighteenth centuries were much preoccupied with a vice which they called "pride," and were usually given to denouncing it with peculiar vehemence. It has not always been noted that two different—though not unrelated—conceptions, or rather, groups of conceptions, were expressed by the word.

From *Essays in The History of Ideas* (Baltimore, The Johns Hopkins Press, 1948).

On the one hand, it designated a "passion," or set of passions, which was recognized by many, not to say most, of the more acute literary psychologists of the period as the most powerful and pervasive motive of men's behavior, the "spring of action" which differentiates *homo sapiens* from all the other animals, and by which all his most distinctive human propensities and performances, good or bad, are to be explained. There is a long series of passages, in prose and verse, which dilate upon the diversity of the manifestations of this motive in the conduct of various types of individuals and upon its innumerable disguises, discuss the question—then deemed a highly important question—whether its consequences for society in general are preponderantly harmful or benign, and deduce conclusions pertinent to social ethics, politics and education from the assumption of its ubiquity and singular potency in the affective constitution of man. The term, even as the name for a determinant of men's behavior in their social relations, was equivocal; for it was often used to designate two distinct, though kindred, types of feeling or desire: self-esteem, or the craving to think well of oneself, in its many degrees and forms, especially its emulative form; and the desire for, and pleasure in, the esteem, admiration or applause of others, especially the craving for "distinction," the *fureur de se distinguer*. But in one or the other, or both, of these senses, "pride" was one of the most frequent and pregnant themes of what may be called the social psychology of the period.[1]

But the pride to which such a typical writer as Pope, in the *Essay on Man*, most frequently refers is not primarily the pride of the individual human creature comparing himself with others of his species, but the generic pride of man as such. The featherless biped, it was observed, has a strange tendency to put himself in the center of the creation, to suppose himself separated by a vast gap from all other and "irrational" creatures, to credit himself with the possession of virtues of which he is inherently incapable, and to attempt tasks, especially intellectual tasks, which he has in reality no power to accomplish. A sense of the dignity and importance of the *genus homo* had been fostered by the medieval Christian view of man's place in the universe. Though the Church had bidden the individual man walk humbly with his God, and had dwelt upon the inner corruption of unregenerate human nature, it had nevertheless given its sanction to certain conceptions flattering to men's racial self-esteem. Upon his own planet, at least, man reigned supreme over the brute creation, infinitely removed in dignity from even the highest animals by his sole participation in the intellectual light of the divine Reason; all other terrestrial creatures existed

[1] The material for the history of this phase of seventeenth and eighteenth-century thought is both rich and complicated. The author has attempted a survey and analysis of it in a course of lectures on the Cooper Foundation given at Swarthmore College in 1942, now (1947) being amplified and revised for publication. Most of what follows in the present essay, dealing with another aspect of the idea of "pride," was published in *Modern Language Notes*, 1921, pp. 31ff.

solely for his use and benefit; upon the acts of will of individual men inex-
pressibly momentous issues depended; and the good which man was capable
of attaining immeasurably transcended all that could be experienced in this
temporal world of matter and sense. But there were certain ideas especially
current in (though not original with) the eighteenth century which forbade
mankind to hold any such flattering opinion of itself; and it was these
ideas which underlay many of the recurrent invectives against "pride."

1) The first of these, which I need only briefly recall here,[2] was among
the most characteristic and influential of all eighteenth-century ideas: the
so-called "principle of continuity," *lex continui,* one of the components of
the conception of the Great Chain of Being. According to this conception,
the world is necessarily a *plenum formarum,* a system

> *Where all must full or not coherent be,*
> *And all that rises, rise in due degree.*

In other words, every logically possible kind of being, through all the
infinite graded scale of conceivable "natures" between Deity and nonentity,
must necessarily exist; and between any two adjacent links in the chain
there can be only infinitesimal differences. One of the principal events in
European thought in the eighteenth century was the rapid growth of a
tendency towards a deliquescence of all sharp distinctions, resulting from
the introduction of this assumption that all things must be regarded as
parts of a qualitative continuum—the assumption embodied in the maxim
Natura non facit saltus. Since all gaps thus disappeared from nature, there
could be none between man and the other animals. He could differ from
them only in degree, and from the higher animals in an almost insensible
degree, and only with respect to certain attributes.[3] No link in the Chain
of Being, moreover, is more essential than another, or exists merely for
the sake of another. The lower creatures are no more means to the convenience of man than he is a means to their convenience.[4] Thus, so long
as man remained normal, *i.e.,* in the state of nature, he assumed no grand
airs of superiority to the creatures of the field and wood:

> *Pride then was not, nor arts that pride to aid;*
> *Man walked with beast joint-tenant of the shade.*[5]

In its most significant aspect, then, "pride" gets its meaning for eighteenth-
century thought from this group of conceptions. It is, in Pope's words,

[2] The topic has been dealt with at greater length in the writer's *The Great Chain of
Being,* (1936), pp. 186-203.

[3] *Essay on Man,* I, 173ff.

[4] *Id.,* III, 22-70, I, 53-68; *cf.* Voltaire, *Discours sur l'homme,* VI.

[5] *Essay on Man,* III, 151-2. Pope's lines are the probable source of Rousseau's remark,
in his second *Discours,* that man's emergence from the pure state of nature began with
his invention of certain practical arts, which was followed by "le premier mouvement
d'orgueil," in the form of a feeling of superiority to the other animals.

the "sin against the laws of order," *i.e.*, of gradation; it is the vice which causes man to set up pretensions to a place higher in the Scale of Being than belongs to him.

> *Pride still is aiming at the blest abodes,*
> *Men would be angels, angels would be gods.*

The virtue which is its opposite lies in a contented recognition of the limitations of the human lot and the littleness of man's powers;

> *The bliss of man (could pride that blessing find)*
> *Is not to act or think beyond mankind.*[6]

   Thus the eighteenth-century denunciations of pride are often, at bottom, expressions of a certain disillusionment of man about himself—a phase of that long and deepening disillusionment which is the tragedy of a great part of modern thought. True, the conception of the Chain of Being owed its vogue largely to its use in the argument for (so-called) optimism; and it had its cheerful aspects. But it clearly implied the dethronement of man from his former exalted position. In the bitter spirit of Swift this disillusionment, though for other reasons, already touched its extreme; the Yahoo is not merely brought nearer to the other animals, he is placed below them. The most detestable and irrational of beings, he crowns his fatuity by imagining himself the aim and climax of the whole creation. Yet Swift had been anticipated in his opinion of the Yahoo by Robert Gould:

> *What beast beside can we so slavish call*
> *As* Man? *Who yet pretends he's Lord of all.*
> *Whoever saw (and all their classes cull)*
> *A dog so snarlish, or a swine so full,*
> *A wolf so rav'nous, or an ass so dull?*
> *Slave to his passions, ev'ry several lust*
> *Whisks him about, as whirlwinds do the dust;*
> *And dust he is, indeed, a senseless clod*
> *That swells, and yet would be believ'd a God.*[7]

   Two further aspects of the eighteenth-century notion of "pride" are in part special applications of the principle of continuity, in part consequences of the vogue of certain other conceptions.

   2)   It was upon his rational faculty and his intellectual achievements that modern man had been wont most to plume himself. But the conception of the graded scale of being tended to fix attention especially upon the limitations of man's mental powers. Moreover, the primitivism which

---

[6] *Essay on Man*, I, 189, 190.
[7] Gould's "Satire against Man" (*ca.* 1708), *Works*, II, 149 f. It should be added that, as an orthodox churchman, Gould elsewhere, not too consistently, insists upon man's superiority, as evidenced by his possession of a conscience and an immortal soul. The poem is one of a number of imitations of Boileau's Eighth Satire (1667).

had long been associated with the cult of the sacred word 'nature' had
expressed itself, among other ways, in the disparagement of intellectual
pursuits and the depreciation of man's intellectual capacity. In the sixteenth
century both Erasmus and Montaigne had dilated upon the vanity of speculation and the corrupting influence of science.

*"In the first golden age of the world," wrote Erasmus, "there was no sort of learn-
ing but what was naturally collected from every man's common sense improved
by an easy experience. They were not so presumptuous as to dive into the depths
of Nature, to labor for the solving all phenomena in astronomy, or to wreak their
brains in the splitting of entities and unfolding the nicest speculations, judging it
to be a crime for any man to aim at what is put beyond the reach of his shallow
comprehension.*[8]

This strain, less in evidence in the seventeenth century, the age of great
systems in philosophy and science, became in the eighteenth one of the
most popular of commonplaces. Finally, the reigning philosophy of the
period, in England and France, that of Locke, had as its characteristic aim
to fix the boundaries of human knowledge; and it ostensibly found those
boundaries to be very narrow.[9] In consequence, chiefly, of the convergence
of these three lines of influence, it became customary to berate and satirize
all forms of intellectual ambition, and to ascribe to it a great part in the
corruption of the natural innocence of mankind. So Pope exhorts:

Trace science, then, with modesty thy guide,
First strip off all her equipage of pride, etc.[10]

The condemnation of "pride," then, is frequently, in the eighteenth
century, one of the ways of expressing a primitivistic anti-intellectualism.
Rousseau was but repeating a current commonplace when he wrote in the
Premier Discours that "toutes les sciences, et la morale même, sont nées
de l'orgueil humain," and that " le luxe, la dissolution et l'esclavage ont
été de tout temps, le châtiment des efforts orgueilleux que nous avons faits
pour sortir de l'heureuse ignorance où la sagesse éternelle nous avait placés."

[8] *Moriae Encomium.* For the equation of "pride" with the spirit of science in Montaigne,
cf. the following: "Le soing de s'augmenter en sagesse et en science, ce feut la premiere
ruyne du genre humain; ...l'orgueil est sa perte et sa corruption" (*Apologie de Raimond
Sebond*). Note also how closely much of Swift's contrast of the Yahoos and the Houyhnhnms
follows Montaigne's comparison of man with the other animals, in the same essay.

[9] *Essay Concerning Human Understanding,* I, chap. i, §§ 5-7.

[10] *Essay on Man,* II, 43 ff.; *cf.* Robert Gould's satirical picture of the scholar's life
("Satire against Man," 167-9) and his praise of the ignorance of the state of nature
(170 ff.). In the mid-eighteenth century it is, of course, true that this sort of anti-intellectualism co-existed—sometimes even in the same minds—with that enthusiasm for the "study
of nature," *i.e.*, of empirical physical science, of which M. Mornet has admirably written
the history in his *Les sciences de la nature en France au 18ᵉ siècle.*

3) In ethical as in intellectual endeavor, typical moralists of the early eighteenth century believed in a program of limited objectives. Here, again, the tradition of ethical naturalism which had been handed down especially through Erasmus and Montaigne readily combined with the idea of the graded scale of being. Man must not attempt to transcend the limitations of his "nature"; and his nature, though not the same as that of the animals below him in the scale, is close to it. "Reason" has a part in the conduct of human life, but it is an ancillary part. Pope devotes many lines of versified argumentation to showing that the motive-power and the principal directive force in man's life is—and should be—not reason, but the complex of instincts and passions which make up our "natural" constitution.[11] "Pride," then, in an especially important sense, means a sort of moral overstrain, the attempt to be unnaturally good and immoderately virtuous, to live by reason alone. Erasmus and Montaigne had come to have an antipathy to this lofty and strenuous moral temper through a direct revulsion against the revived Stoicism in fashion in the late Renaissance; and the Stoics passed in the eighteenth century for the proverbial embodiments of "pride" in this sense. Thus Pope describes man as a being "with too much weakness for the Stoic pride"; and Wieland in his *Theages* (1760) remarks that the Stoic pride and self-sufficiency "departs very widely from nature" and "can be possible only in God." "Eben so wenig," he adds, "konnte ich die Unterdrückung des sinnlichen Teils unsers Wesens mit der Natur reimen."

I have dwelt upon this and the preceding aspect of the conception of pride especially because it has become customary seriously to exaggerate the rationalism of the period, its "extravagant claims to reason," its confidence in "the dry light of reason." Unless "reason" is carefully and somewhat peculiarly defined, such expressions are misleading. The authors who were perhaps the most influential and the most representative in the early and mid-eighteenth century made a great point of reducing man's claims to "reason" to a minimum, and of belittling the importance of that faculty in human existence; and the vice of "pride" which they so delighted to castigate was exemplified for them in any high estimate of the capacity of the human species for intellectual achievement, or in any of the more ambitious enterprises of science and philosophy, or in any moral ideal which would make pure reason (as distinguished from natural "passions") the supreme power in human life. "Pride" was, indeed, exemplified, for some such writers, in everything "artificial"; and in the homilies against it the whole gospel of the Return to Nature was sometimes implicit.

11 *Essay on Man*, II, 59-202.

LANGUAGE DEFINED | EDWARD SAPIR

Speech is so familiar a feature of daily life that we rarely pause to define it. It seems as natural to man as walking, and only less so than breathing. Yet it needs but a moment's reflection to convince us that this naturalness of speech is but an illusory feeling. The process of acquiring speech is, in sober fact, an utterly different sort of thing from the process of learning to walk. In the case of the latter function, culture, in other words, the traditional body of social usage, is not seriously brought into play. The child is individually equipped, by the complex set of factors that we term biological heredity, to make all the needed muscular and nervous adjustments that result in walking. Indeed, the very conformation of these muscles and of the appropriate parts of the nervous system may be said to be primarily adapted to the movements made in walking and in similar activities. In a very real sense the normal human being is predestined to walk, not because his elders will assist him to learn the art, but because his organism is prepared from birth, or even from the moment of conception, to take on all those expenditures of nervous energy and all those muscular adaptations that result in walking. To put it concisely, walking is an inherent, biological function of man.

Not so language. It is of course true that in a certain sense the individual is predestined to talk, but that is due entirely to the circumstance that he is born not merely in nature, but in the lap of a society that is certain, reasonably certain, to lead him to its traditions. Eliminate society and there is every reason to believe that he will learn to walk, if, indeed, he survives at all. But it is just as certain that he will never learn to talk, that is, to communicate ideas according to the traditional system of a particular society. Or, again, remove the new-born individual from the social environment into which he has come and transplant him to an utterly alien one. He will develop the art of walking in his new environment very much as he would have developed it in the old. But his speech will be completely at variance with the speech of his native environment. Walking, then, is a general human activity that varies only within circumscribed limits as we pass from individual to individual. Its variability is involuntary and purposeless. Speech is a human activity that varies without assignable limit as we pass from social group to social group, because it is a purely historical heritage of the group, the product of long-continued social usage. It varies as all creative effort varies—not as consciously, perhaps, but none the less as truly as do the religions, the beliefs, the customs, and the arts of different peoples.

Walking is an organic, an instinctive, function (not, of course, itself an instinct); speech is a non-instinctive, acquired, "cultural" function.

There is one fact that has frequently tended to prevent the recognition of language as a merely conventional system of sound symbols, that has seduced the popular mind into attributing to it an instinctive basis that it does not really possess. This is the well-known observation that under the stress of emotion, say of a sudden twinge of pain or of unbridled joy, we do involuntarily give utterance to sounds that the hearer interprets as indicative of the emotion itself. But there is all the difference in the world between such involuntary expression of feeling and the normal type of communication of ideas that is speech. The former kind of utterance is indeed instinctive, but it is nonsymbolic; in other words, the sound of pain or the sound of joy does not, as such, indicate the emotion, it does not stand aloof, as it were, and announce that such and such an emotion is being felt. What it does is to serve as a more or less automatic overflow of the emotional energy; in a sense, it is part and parcel of the emotion itself. Moreover, such instinctive cries hardly constitute communication in any strict sense. They are not addressed to any one, they are merely overheard, if heard at all, as the bark of a dog, the sound of approaching footsteps, or the rustling of the wind is heard. If they convey certain ideas to the hearer, it is only in the very general sense in which any and every sound or even any phenomenon in our environment may be said to convey an idea to the perceiving mind. If the involuntary cry of pain which is conventionally represented by "Oh!" be looked upon as a true speech symbol equivalent to some such idea as "I am in great pain," it is just as allowable to interpret the appearance of clouds as an equivalent symbol that carries the definite message "It is likely to rain." A definition of language, however, that is so extended as to cover every type of inference becomes utterly meaningless.

The mistake must not be made of identifying our conventional interjections (our oh! and ah! and sh!) with the instinctive cries themselves. These interjections are merely conventional fixations of the natural sounds. They therefore differ widely in various languages in accordance with the specific phonetic genius of each of these. As such they may be considered an integral portion of speech, in the properly cultural sense of the term, being no more identical with the instinctive cries themselves than such words as "cuckoo" and "killdeer" are identical with the cries of the birds they denote or than Rossini's treatment of a storm in the overture to "William Tell" is in fact a storm. In other words, the interjections and sound-imitative words of normal speech are related to their natural prototypes as is art, a purely social or cultural thing, to nature. It may be objected that, though the interjections differ somewhat as we pass from language to language, they do nevertheless offer striking family resemblances and may therefore be looked upon as having grown up out of a common instinctive base. But their case is nowise different from that, say, of the varying national modes of pictorial representation. A Japanese picture of a hill both differs from and resembles a typical modern European painting of the same kind of hill. Both are suggested by and both "imitate" the same natural feature. Neither the one nor the other is the same thing as, or, in any intelligible sense, a direct outgrowth of, this natural feature. The two modes of representation are not identical because they proceed from differing historical traditions, are executed with differing pictorial techniques. The interjections of Japanese and English are, just so, suggested by a common natural prototype, the instinctive cries, and are thus unavoidably suggestive of each other. They differ, now greatly, now but little, because they are builded out of historically diverse materials or techniques, the respective linguistic traditions, phonetic systems, speech habits of the two peoples. Yet the instinctive cries as such are practically identical for all humanity, just as the human skeleton or nervous system is to all intents and purposes a "fixed," that is, an only slightly and "accidentally" variable, feature of man's organism.

Interjections are among the least important of speech elements. Their discussion is valuable mainly because it can be shown that even they, avowedly the nearest of all language sounds to instinctive utterance, are only superficially of an instinctive nature. Were it therefore possible to demonstrate that the whole of language is traceable, in its ultimate historical and psychological foundations, to the interjections, it would still not follow that language is an instinctive activity. But, as a matter of fact, all attempts so to explain the origin of speech have been fruitless. There is no tangible evidence, historical or otherwise, tending to show that the mass of speech elements and speech processes has evolved out of the interjections. These are a very small and functionally insignificant proportion of the vocabulary of language; at no time and in no linguistic province that we have record of do we see a noticeable tendency towards their elaboration into the primary warp and woof of language. They are never more, at best, than a decorative edging to the ample, complex fabric.

What applies to the interjections applies with even greater force to the sound-imitative words. Such words as "whippoorwill," "to mew," "to caw" are in no sense natural sounds that man has instinctively or automatically reproduced. They are just as truly creations of the human mind, flights of the human fancy, as anything else in language. They do not directly grow out of nature, they are suggested by it and play with it. Hence the onomatopoetic theory of the origin of speech, the theory that would explain all speech as a gradual evolution from sounds of an imitative character, really brings us no nearer to the instinctive level than is language as we know it to-day. As to the theory itself, it is scarcely more credible than its interjectional counterpart. It is true that a number of words which we do not now feel to have a sound-imitative value can be shown to have once had a phonetic form that strongly suggests their origin as imitations of natural sounds. Such is the English word "to laugh." For all that, it is quite impossible to show, nor does it seem intrinsically reasonable to suppose, that more than a negligible proportion of the elements of speech or anything at all of its formal apparatus is derivable from an onomatopoetic source. However much we may be disposed on general principles to assign a fundamental importance in the languages of primitive peoples to the imitation of natural sounds, the actual fact of the matter is that these languages show no particular preference for imitative words. Among the most primitive peoples of aboriginal America, the Athabaskan tribes of the Mackenzie River speak languages in which such words seem to be nearly or entirely absent, while they are used freely enough in languages as sophisticated as English and German. Such an instance shows how little the essential nature of speech is concerned with the mere imitation of things.

The way is now cleared for a serviceable definition of language. Language is a purely human and non-instinctive method of communicating ideas, emotions, and desires by means of a system of voluntarily produced symbols. These symbols are, in the first instance, auditory and they are produced by the so-called "organs of speech." There is no discernible instinctive basis in human speech as such, however much instinctive expressions and the natural environment may serve as a stimulus for the development of certain elements of speech, however much instinctive tendencies, motor and other, may give a predetermined range or mold to linguistic expression. Such human or animal communication, if "communication" it may be called, as is brought about by involuntary, instinctive cries is not, in our sense, language at all.

I have just referred to the "organs of speech," and it would seem at first blush that this is tantamount to an admission that speech itself is an instinctive, biologically predetermined activity. We must not be misled by the mere term. There are, properly speaking, no organs of speech; there are only organs that are incidentally useful in the production of speech sounds. The lungs, the larynx, the palate, the nose, the tongue, the teeth, and the lips, are all so utilized, but they are no more to be thought of as primary organs of speech than are the fingers to be considered as essentially organs of piano-playing or the knees as organs of prayer. Speech is not a simple activity that is carried on by one or more organs biologically adapted to the purpose. It is an extremely complex and ever-shifting network of adjustments—in the brain, in the nervous system, and in the articulating and auditory organs—tending towards the desired end of communication. The lungs developed, roughly speaking, in connection with the necessary biological function known as breathing; the nose, as an organ of smell; the teeth, as organs useful in breaking up food before it was ready for digestion. If, then, these and other organs are being constantly utilized in speech, it is only because any organ, once existent and in so far as it is subject to voluntary control, can be utilized by man for secondary purposes. Physiologically, speech is an overlaid function, or, to be more precise, a group of overlaid functions. It gets what service it can out of organs and functions, nervous and muscular, that have come into being and are maintained for very different ends than its own.

It is true that physiological psychologists speak of the localization of speech in the brain. This can only mean that the sounds of speech are localized in the auditory tract of the brain, or in some circumscribed portion of it, precisely as other classes of sounds are localized; and that the motor processes involved in speech (such as the movements of the glottal cords in the larynx, the movements of the tongue required to pronounce the vowels, lip movements required to articulate certain consonants, and numerous others) are localized in the motor tract precisely as are all other impulses to special motor activities. In the same way control is lodged in the visual tract of the brain over all those processes of visual recognition involved in reading. Naturally the particular points or clusters or points of localization in the several tracts that refer to any element of language are connected in the brain by paths of association, so that the outward, or psychophysical, aspect of language is of a vast network of associated localizations in the brain and lower nervous tracts, the auditory localizations being without doubt the most fundamental of all for speech. However, a speech-sound localized in the brain, even when associated with the particular movements of the "speech organs" that are required to produce it, is very far from being an element of language. It must be further associated with some element or group of elements of experience, say a visual image or a class of visual images or a feeling of relation, before it has even rudimentary linguistic significance. This "element" of experience is the content or "meaning" of the linguistic unit; the associated auditory, motor, and other cerebral processes that lie immediately back of the act of speaking and the act of hearing speech are merely a complicated symbol of or signal for these "meanings," of which more anon. We see therefore at once that language as such is not and cannot be definitely localized, for it consists of a peculiar symbolic relation—physiologically an arbitrary one—between all possible elements of consciousness on the one hand and certain selected elements localized in the auditory, motor, and other cerebral and nervous tracts on the other. If language can be said to be definitely "localized" in the brain, it is only in that general and rather useless sense in which all aspects of consciousness, all human interest and activity, may be said to be "in the brain." Hence, we have no recourse but to accept language as a fully formed functional system within man's psychic or "spiritual" constitution. We cannot define it as an entity in psycho-physical terms alone, however much the psycho-physical basis is essential to its functioning in the individual.

From the physiologist's or psychologist's point of view we may seem to be making an unwarrantable abstraction in desiring to handle the subject of speech without constant and explicit reference to that basis. However, such an abstraction is justifiable. We can profitably discuss the intention, the form, and the history of speech, precisely as we discuss the nature of any other phase of human culture—say art or religion—as an institutional or cultural entity, leaving the organic and psychological mechanisms back of it as something to be taken for granted. Accordingly, it must be clearly understood that this introduction to the study of speech is not concerned with those aspects of physiology and physiological psychology that underlie speech. Our study of language is not to be one of the genesis and operation of a concrete mechanism; it is, rather, to be an inquiry into the function and form of the arbitrary systems of symbolism that we term languages.

I have already pointed out that the essence of language consists in the assigning of conventional, voluntarily articulated, sounds, or of their equivalents, to the diverse elements of experience. The word "house" is not a linguistic fact if by it is meant merely the acoustic effect produced on the ear by its constituent consonants and vowels, pronounced in a certain order; nor the motor processes and tactile feelings which make up the articulation of the word; nor the visual perception on the part of the hearer of this articulation; nor the visual perception of the word "house" on the written or printed page; nor the motor processes and tactile feelings which enter into the writing of the word; nor the memory of any or all of these experiences. It is only when these, and possibly still other, associated experiences are automatically associated with the image of a house that they begin to take on the nature of a symbol, a word, an element of language. But the mere fact of such an association is not enough. One might have heard a particular word spoken in an individual house under such impressive circumstances that neither the word nor the image of the house ever recur in consciousness without the other becoming present at the same time. This type of association does not constitute speech. The association must be a purely symbolic one; in other words, the word must denote, tag off, the image, must have no other significance than to serve as a counter to refer to it whenever it is necessary or convenient to do so. Such an association, voluntary and, in a sense, arbitrary as it is, demands a considerable exercise of self-conscious attention. At least to begin with, for habit soon makes the association nearly as automatic as any and more rapid than most.

But we have traveled a little too fast. Were the symbol "house"— whether an auditory, motor, or visual experience or image—attached but to the single image of a particular house once seen, it might perhaps, by an indulgent criticism, be termed an element of speech, yet it is obvious at the outset that speech so constituted would have little or no value for purposes of communication. The world of our experiences must be enormously simplified and generalized before it is possible to make a symbolic inventory of all our experiences of things and relations and this inventory is imperative before we can convey ideas. The elements of language, the symbols that ticket off experience, must therefore be associated with whole groups, delimited classes, of experience rather than with the single experiences themselves. Only so is communication possible, for the single experience lodges in an individual consciousness and is, strictly speaking, incommunicable. To be communicated it needs to be referred to a class which is tacitly accepted by the community as an identity. Thus, the single impression which I have had of a particular house must be identified with all my other impressions of it. Further, my generalized memory or my "notion" of this house must be merged with the notions that all other individuals who have seen the house have formed of it. The particular experience that we started with has now been widened so as to embrace all possible impressions or images that sentient beings have formed or may form of the house in question. This first simplification of experience is at the bottom of a large number of elements of speech, the so-called proper nouns or names of single individuals or objects. It is, essentially, the type of simplification which underlies, or forms the crude subject of, history and art. But we cannot be content with this measure of reduction of the infinity of experience. We must cut to the bone of things, we must more or less arbitrarily throw whole masses of experience together as similar enough to warrant their being looked upon—mistakenly, but conveniently—as identical. This house and that house and thousands of other phenomena of like character are thought of as having enough in common, in spite of great and obvious differences of detail, to be classed under the same heading. In other words, the speech element "house" is the symbol, first and foremost, not of a single perception, nor even of the notion of a particular object, but of a "concept," in other words, of a convenient capsule of thought that embraces thousands of distinct experiences and that is ready to take in thousands more. If the single significant elements of speech are the symbols of concepts, the actual flow of speech may be interpreted as a record of the setting of these concepts into mutual relations.

The question has often been raised whether thought is possible without speech; further, if speech and thought be not but two facets of the same psychic process. The question is all the more difficult because it has been hedged about by misunderstandings. In the first place, it is well to observe that whether or not thought necessitates symbolism, that is speech, the flow of language itself is not always indicative of thought. We have seen that the typical linguistic element labels a concept. It does not follow from this that the use to which language is put is always or even mainly conceptual. We are not in ordinary life so much concerned with concepts as such as with concrete particularities and specific relations. When I say, for instance, "I had a good breakfast this morning," it is clear that I am not in the throes of laborious thought, that what I have to transmit is hardly more than a pleasurable memory symbolically rendered in the grooves of habitual expression. Each element in the sentence defines a separate concept or conceptual relation or both combined, but the sentence as a whole has no conceptual significance whatever. It is somewhat as though a dynamo capable of generating enough power to run an elevator were operated almost exclusively to feed an electric doorbell. The parallel is more suggestive than at first sight appears. Language may be looked upon as an instrument capable of running a gamut of psychic uses. Its flow not only parallels that of the inner content of consciousness, but parallels it on different levels, ranging from the state of mind that is dominated by particular images to that in which abstract concepts and their relations are alone at the focus of attention and which is ordinarily termed reasoning. Thus the outward form only of language is constant; its inner meaning, its psychic value or intensity, varies freely with attention or the selective interest of the mind, also, needless to say, with the mind's general development. From the point of view of language, thought may be defined as the highest latent or potential content of speech, the content that is obtained by interpreting each of the elements in the flow of language as possessed of its very fullest conceptual value. From this it follows at once that language and thought are not strictly coterminous. At best language can but be the outward facet of thought on the highest, most generalized, level of symbolic expression. To put our viewpoint somewhat differently, language is primarily a prerational function. It humbly works up to the thought that is latent in, that may eventually be read into, its classifications and its forms; it is not, as is generally but naïvely assumed, the final label put upon the finished thought.

Most people, asked if they can think without speech, would probably answer, "Yes, but it is not easy for me to do so. Still I know it can be done." Language is but a garment! But what if language is not so much a garment as a prepared road or groove? It is, indeed, in the highest degree likely that language is an instrument originally put to uses lower than the conceptual plane and that thought arises as a refined interpretation of its content. The product grows, in other words, with the instrument, and thought may be no more conceivable, in its genesis and daily practice, without speech than is mathematical reasoning practicable without the lever of an appropriate mathematical symbolism. No one believes that even the most difficult mathematical proposition is inherently dependent on an arbitrary set of symbols, but it is impossible to suppose that the human mind is capable of arriving at or holding such a proposition without the symbolism. The writer, for one, is strongly of the opinion that the feeling entertained by so many that they can think, or even reason, without language is an illusion. The illusion seems to be due to a number of factors. The simplest of these is the failure to distinguish between imagery and thought. As a matter of fact, no sooner do we try to put an image into conscious relation with another than we find ourselves slipping into a silent flow of words. Thought may be a natural domain apart from the artificial one of speech, but speech would seem to be the only road we know of that leads to it. A still more fruitful source of the illusive feeling that language may be dispensed with in thought is the common failure to realize that language is not identical with its auditory symbolism. The auditory symbolism may be replaced, point for point, by a motor or by a visual symbolism (many people can read, for instance, in a purely visual sense, that is, without the intermediating link of an inner flow of the auditory images that correspond to the printed or written words) or by still other, more subtle and elusive, types of transfer that are not so easy to define. Hence the contention that one thinks without language merely because he is not aware of a coexisting auditory imagery is very far indeed from being a valid one. One may go so far as to suspect that the symbolic expression of thought may in some cases run along outside the fringe of the conscious mind, so that the feeling of a free, non-linguistic stream of thought is for minds of a certain type a relatively, but only a relatively, justified one. Psycho-physically, this would mean that the auditory or equivalent visual or motor centers in the brain, together with the appropriate paths of association, that are the cerebral equivalent of speech, are touched off so lightly during the process of thought as not to rise into consciousness at all. This would be a limiting case—thought riding lightly on the submerged crests of speech, instead of jogging along with it, hand in hand. The modern psychology has shown us how powerfully symbolism is at work in the unconscious mind. It is therefore easier to understand at the present time than it would have been twenty years ago that the most rarefied thought may be but the conscious counterpart of an unconscious linguistic symbolism.

One word more as to the relation between language and thought. The point of view that we have developed does not by any means preclude the possibility of the growth of speech being in a high degree dependent on the development of thought. We may assume that language arose pre-rationally—just how and on what precise level or mental activity we do not know—but we must not imagine that a highly developed system of speech symbols worked itself out before the genesis of distinct concepts and of thinking, the handling of concepts. We must rather imagine that thought processes set in, as a kind of psychic overflow, almost at the beginning of linguistic expression; further, that the concept, once defined, necessarily reacted on the life of its linguistic symbol, encouraging further linguistic growth. We see this complex process of the interaction of language and thought actually taking place under our eyes. The instrument makes possible the product, the product refines the instrument. The birth of a new concept is invariably foreshadowed by a more or less strained or extended use of old linguistic material; the concept does not attain to individual and independent life until it has found a distinctive linguistic embodiment. In most cases the new symbol is but a thing wrought from linguistic material already in existence in ways mapped out by crushingly despotic precedents. As soon as the word is at hand, we instinctively feel, with something of a sigh of relief, that the concept is ours for the handling. Not until we own the symbol do we feel that we hold a key to the immediate knowledge or understanding of the concept. Would we be so ready to die for "liberty," to struggle for "ideals," if the words themselves were not ringing within us? And the word, as we know, is not only a key; it may also be a fetter. . . .

There is no more striking general fact about language than its universality. One may argue as to whether a particular tribe engages in activities that are worthy of the name of religion or of art, but we know of no people that is not possessed of a fully developed language. The lowliest South African Bushman speaks in the forms of a rich symbolic system that is in essence perfectly comparable to the speech of the cultivated Frenchman. It goes without saying that the more abstract concepts are not nearly so plentifully represented in the language of the savage, nor is there the rich terminology and the finer definition of nuances that reflect the higher culture. Yet the sort of linguistic development that parallels the historic growth of culture and which, in its later stages, we associate with literature is, at best, but a superficial thing. The fundamental groundwork of language —the development of a clear-cut phonetic system, the specific association of speech elements with concepts, and the delicate provision for the formal expression of all manner of relations—all this meets us rigidly perfected and systematized in every language known to us. Many primitive languages have a formal richness, a latent luxuriance of expression, that eclipses anything known to the languages of modern civilization. Even in the mere matter of the inventory of speech the layman must be prepared for strange surprises. Popular statements as to the extreme poverty of expression to which primitive languages are doomed are simply myths. Scarcely less impressive than the universality of speech is its almost incredible diversity. Those of us that have studied French or German, or, better yet, Latin or Greek, know in what varied forms a thought may run. The formal divergences between the English plan and the Latin plan, however, are comparatively slight in the perspective of what we know of more exotic linguistic patterns. The universality and the diversity of speech lead to a significant inference. We are forced to believe that language is an immensely ancient heritage of the human race, whether or not all forms of speech are the historical outgrowth of a single pristine form. It is doubtful if any other cultural asset of man, be it the art of drilling for fire or of chipping stone, may lay claim to a greater age. I am inclined to believe that it antedated even the lowliest developments of material culture, that these developments, in fact, were not strictly possible until language, the tool of significant expression, had itself taken shape.

MYTH | MARK SCHORER

The definition of mysticism, to be useful at all, must be stringent, for mysticism is in itself a highly specialized experience. But the definition of myth, if the term is to be used in the discussion of modern poets, particularly of William Blake, must be both broad and loose, for myth operates universally and diversely. The term must include such varying manifestations as the sharply formed figures of classic fable and the malformations of delusion and neurosis. Even a loose definition does not include, however, the current journalistic sense of falsehood, nor does it imply anti-intellectualism or any other such pejorative. The term denotes, in fact, neither the negation nor the contrary of ideas, but their basis and their structure, the element by which they are activated. "The doctrines which men ostensibly hold," wrote Leslie Stephen, "do not become operative upon their conduct until they have generated an imaginative symbolism."

Myths are the instruments by which we continually struggle to make our experience intelligible to ourselves. A myth is a large, controlling image that gives philosophical meaning to the facts of ordinary life; that is, which has organizing value for experience. A mythology is a more or less articulated body of such images, a pantheon. Without such images, experience is chaotic, fragmentary and merely phenomenal. It is the chaos of experience that creates them, and they are intended to rectify it. All real convictions involve a mythology, either in its usual, broad sense or in a private sense. In the first case it is embodied in literature or in ritual or in both, in which it has application to the whole of a society and tends to be religious. In the second, it remains in the realm of fantasy, in which it tends to be obsessive and fanatical. This is not to say that sound myths of general application necessarily support religions; rather that they perform the historical functions of religion—they unify experience in a way that is satisfactory to the whole culture and to the whole personality. Philip Wheelwright, from the point of view of an uncommon philosophical theism, argues understandably that "the very essence of myth" is "that haunting awareness of transcendental forces peering through the cracks of the visible universe." Durkheim pointed out that myth suggests the sacred rather than the profane; that is, the enormous area of experience into which technology cannot usefully enter rather than the relatively small area into which it does. Yet this does not make religious experience proper more than a portion of the larger area. That myth cannot be so limited is made clear by our own civilization, which seems to be struggling toward a myth that will be explicitly ethical, even political. Today, Thomas Mann has said, "the question of the human conscience ... is presented to us essentially in its political form; perhaps more than in any other epoch of history, it wears a political face." Wars may be described as the clash of mythologies; and a basically disorganized society such as ours is the result of a number of antithetical and competing mythologies that fail to adjust themselves.

Rational belief is secondary. We habitually tend to overlook the fact that as human beings we are rational creatures not first of all but last of all, and that civilization emerged only yesterday from a primitive past that is at least relatively timeless. Belief organizes experience not because it is rational but because all belief depends on a controlling imagery, and rational belief is the intellectual formalization of that imagery. As a basic set of images, Christianity has commanded the unanimous faith of millions; as a system of belief capable of a wide variety of dogmas, it has commanded the intellectual assent of hostile sectarian groups. Such a more recent mythology as socialism, which as a faith presents an international hope for the full development of democratic man, is, as political dogma, rent by schisms.

All those systems of abstractions which we call ideologies activate our behavior, when they do, only because they are themselves activated by images, however submerged. An abstraction is a generalization, and the essential antecedents of generalizations are *things*. Jung, writing of language, has made the useful observation that "Speech is a storehouse of images founded in experience, and therefore concepts which are too abstract do not easily take root in it, or quickly die out again for lack of contact with reality." Are not ideas, like language itself, supported by the "submerged metaphor"? In this sense, myth is indispensable to any form of belief. And in this sense, one may even concur with Hume's offensive remark that "there is no such passion in human minds, as the love of mankind, merely as such"; for this passion, like all others, must have an image, real or ideal, as its correlative. Myth is fundamental, the dramatic representation of our deepest instinctual life, of a primary awareness of man in the universe, capable of many configurations, upon which all particular opinions and attitudes depend. Wallace Stevens writes: ". . . we live in an intricacy of new and local mythologies, political, economic, poetic, which are asserted with an ever-enlarging incoherence." Even when, as in modern civilization, myths multiply and separate and tend to become abstract so that the images themselves recede and fade, even then they are still the essential substructure of all human activity.

Most profoundly they apply in literature. Great literature is impossible without a previous imaginative consent to a ruling mythology that makes intelligible and unitive the whole of that experience from which particular fables spring and from which they, in turn, take their meaning. Literature ceases to be perceptual and tends to degenerate into mere description without adequate myth; for, to cite Malinowski, myth, continually modified and renewed by the modifications of history, is in some form an "indispensable ingredient of all culture." Thus, for example, the prevailing and tiresome realism of modern fiction. When we feel that we are no longer in a position to say what life means, we must content ourselves with telling how it looks. Those of our novelists who have transcended realism have done so by a boot-strap miracle, by supplying the myth themselves. Mann has made a possibly artificial use of literary myth. Joyce attempted to distil their mythical essences from specifically modern developments such as psychology. Kafka disturbingly dramatized neurosis. In a disintegrating society such as this, before it can proceed with other business, literature must become the explicit agent of coherence. In the realm of the imagination, serious artists must be like Hart Crane's tramps in their cross-country freight cars: "They know a body under the wide rain." All readers are aware that the chief energies of modern poets have been expended not simply in writing poetry but in employing poetry to discover its indispensable substructure. They have been compelled to build a usable mythology, one that will account for and organize our competing and fragmentary myths. T. S. Eliot is the most familiar example; here excursions into anthropology and Orientalism preceded and enriched the final embrace of Christian orthodoxy. The example of Yeats is no less spectacular and is even more systematic: Years devoted to the exploration of magic and spiritualism and all the disreputable purlieus of mysticism were combined with the results of a late interest in politics, and the curious mixture seems to have served its purpose. Americans generally have found the material for their myths nearer at hand than have modern Europeans. Hart Crane ingeniously but unsuccessfully utilized a combination of American Indian legend and modern American industrialism in the construction of his single sustained work. Older poets and poets less given to self-questioning, like Robert Frost, were apparently quite comfortable in employing the available myth of the independent American democrat for which younger men no longer find historical sanction. Among younger men, the quest is apparent in such diverse examples as W. H. Auden, Delmore Schwartz, and Karl Shapiro, and one could multiply the instances. The hunt for the essential image goes on everywhere today—but the problem is hardly new.

HUMAN PAIN | *C. S. LEWIS*

Since the life of Christ is every way most bitter to nature and the Self and the Me (for in the true life of Christ, the Self and the Me and nature must be forsaken and lost and die altogether), therefore in each of us, nature hath a horror of it.

Theologia Germanica, xx.

I have tried to show in a previous chapter that the possibility of pain is inherent in the very existence of a world where souls can meet. When souls become wicked they will certainly use this possibility to hurt one another; and this, perhaps, accounts for four-fifths of the sufferings of men. It is men, not God, who have produced racks, whips, prisons, slavery, guns, bayonets, and bombs; it is by human avarice or human stupidity, not by the churlishness of nature, that we have poverty and overwork. But there remains, none the less, much suffering which cannot thus be traced to ourselves. Even if all suffering were man-made, we should like to know the reason for the enormous permission to torture their fellows which God gives to the worst of men.[1] To say, as was said in the last chapter, that good, for such creatures as we now are, means primarily corrective or remedial good, is an incomplete answer. Not all medicine tastes nasty: or if it did, that is itself one of the unpleasant facts for which we should like to know the reason.

Before proceeding I must pick up a point made in Chapter II. I there said that pain, below a certain level of intensity, was not resented and might even be rather liked. Perhaps you then wanted to reply "In that case I should not call it Pain," and you may have been right. But the truth is that the word Pain has two senses which must now be distinguished. *A.* A particular kind of sensation, probably conveyed by specialized nerve fibers, and recognizable by the patient as that kind of sensation whether he dislikes it or not (e.g., the faint ache in my limbs would be recognized as an ache even if I didn't object to it). *B.* Any experience, whether physical or mental, which the patient dislikes. It will be noticed that all Pains in sense A become Pains in sense B if they are raised above a certain very low

From C. S. Lewis, *The Problem of Pain* (London, Geoffrey Bles Ltd., 1940; New York, The Macmillian Company, 1944).

[1] Or perhaps it would be safer to say "of creatures." I by no means reject the view that the "efficient cause" of disease, or some disease, may be a created being other than man. . . . In Scripture Satan is specially associated with disease in Job, in Luke xiii, 16, I Cor. v, 5, and (probably) in I Tim. i., 20. It is, at the present stage of the argument, indifferent whether all the created wills to which God allows a power of tormenting other creatures are human or not.

level of intensity, but that Pains in the B sense need not be Pains in the A sense. Pain in the B sense, in fact, is synonymous with "suffering," "anguish," "tribulation," "adversity," or "trouble," and it is about it that the problem of pain arises. For the rest of this book Pain will be used in the B sense and will include all types of suffering: with the A sense we have no further concern.

Now the proper good of a creature is to surrender itself to its Creator —to enact intellectually, volitionally, and emotionally, that relationship which is given in the mere fact of its being a creature. When it does so, it is good and happy. Lest we should think this a hardship, this kind of good begins on a level far above the creatures, for God Himself, as Son, from all eternity renders back to God as Father by filial obedience the being which the Father by paternal love eternally generates in the Son. This is the pattern which man was made to imitate—which Paradisal man did imitate—and wherever the will conferred by the Creator is thus perfectly offered back in delighted and delighting obedience by the creature, there, most undoubtedly, is Heaven, and there the Holy Ghost proceeds. In the world as we now know it, the problem is how to recover this self-surrender. We are not merely imperfect creatures who must be improved: we are, as Newman said, rebels who must lay down our arms. The first answer, then, to the question why our cure should be painful, is that to render back the will which we have so long claimed for our own, is in itself, wherever and however it is done, a grievous pain. Even in Paradise I have supposed a minimal self-adherence to be overcome, though the overcoming, and the yielding, would there be rapturous. But to surrender a self-will inflamed and swollen with years of usurpation is a kind of death. We all remember this self-will as it was in childhood, the bitter, prolonged rage at every thwarting, the burst of passionate tears, the black, Satanic wish to kill or die rather than to give in. Hence the older type of nurse or parent was quite right in thinking that the first step in education is "to break the child's will." Their methods were often wrong: but not to see the necessity is, I think, to cut oneself off from all understanding of spiritual laws. And if, now that we are grown up, we do not howl and stamp quite so much, that is partly because our elders began the process of breaking or killing our self-will in the nursery, and partly because the same passions now take more subtle forms and have grown clever at avoiding death by various "compensations." Hence the necessity to die daily: however often we think we have broken the rebellious self we shall still find it alive. That this process cannot be without pain is sufficiently witnessed by the very history of the word "Mortification."

But this intrinsic pain, or death, in mortifying the usurped self, is not the whole story. Paradoxically, mortification, though itself a pain, is made easier by the presence of pain in its context. This happens, I think, principally in three ways.

The human spirit will not even begin to try to surrender self-will as long as all seems to be well with it. Now error and sin both have this property, that the deeper they are the less their victim suspects their existence; they are masked evil. Pain is unmasked, unmistakable evil; every man knows that something is wrong when he is being hurt. The Masochist is no real exception. Sadism and Masochism respectively isolate, and then exaggerate, a "moment" or "aspect" in normal sexual passion. Sadism[2] exaggerates the aspect of capture and domination to a point at which only ill-treatment of the beloved will satisfy the pervert—as though he said "I am so much master that I even torment you." Masochism exaggerates the complementary and opposite aspect, and says "I am so enthralled that I welcome even pain at your hands." Unless the pain were felt as evil—as an outrage underlining the complete mastery of the other party—it would cease, for the Masochist, to be an erotic stimulus. And pain is not only immediately recognizable evil, but evil impossible to ignore. We can rest contentedly in our sins and in our stupidities; and anyone who has watched gluttons shoveling down the most exquisite foods as if they did not know what they were eating, will admit that we can ignore even pleasure. But pain insists upon being attended to. God whispers to us in our pleasures, speaks in our conscience, but shouts in our pains: it is His megaphone to rouse a deaf world. A bad man, happy, is a man without the least inkling that his actions do not "answer," that they are not in accord with the laws of the universe.

A perception of this truth lies at the back of the universal human feeling that bad men ought to suffer. It is no use turning up our noses at this feeling, as if it were wholly base. On its mildest level it appeals to everyone's sense of justice. Once when my brother and I, as very small boys, were drawing pictures at the same table, I jerked his elbow and caused him to make an irrelevant line across the middle of his work; the matter was amicably settled by my allowing him to draw a line of equal length across mine. That is, I was "put in his place," made to see my negligence from the other end. On a sterner level the same idea appears as "retributive punishment," or "giving a man what he deserves." Some enlightened people would like to banish all conceptions of retribution or desert from their theory of punishment and place its value wholly in the deterrence of others or the reform of the criminal himself. They do not see that by so doing they render all punishment unjust. What can be more immoral than to inflict suffering on me for the sake of deterring others if I do not *deserve* it? And if I do deserve it, you are admitting the claims of "retribution." And what can be more outrageous than to catch me and submit me to a disagreeable process of moral improvement without my consent, unless (once more) I *deserve* it? On yet a third level we get vindictive passion—

[2] The modern tendency to mean by "sadistic cruelty" simply "great cruelty," or cruelty specially condemned by the writer, is not useful.

the thirst for revenge. This, of course, is evil and expressly forbidden to Christians. But it has perhaps appeared already from our discussion of Sadism and Masochism that the ugliest things in human nature are perversions of good or innocent things. The good thing of which vindictive passion is the perversion comes out with startling clarity in Hobbes's definition of Revengefulness: "desire by doing hurt to another to make him condemn some fact of his own."[3] Revenge loses sight of the end in the means, but its end is not wholly bad—it wants the evil of the bad man to be to him what it is to everyone else. This is proved by the fact that the avenger wants the guilty party not merely to suffer, but to suffer at his hands, and to know it, and to know why. Hence the impulse to taunt the guilty man with his crime at the moment of taking vengeance: hence, too, such natural expressions as "I wonder how he'd like it if the same thing were done to him" or "I'll teach him." For the same reason when we are going to abuse a man in words we say we are going to "let him know what we think of him."

When our ancestors referred to pains and sorrows as God's "vengeance" upon sin they were not necessarily attributing evil passions to God; they may have been recognizing the good element in the idea of retribution. Until the evil man finds evil unmistakably present in his existence, in the form of pain, he is enclosed in illusion. Once pain has roused him, he knows that he is in some way or other "up against" the real universe: he either rebels (with the possibility of a clearer issue and deeper repentance at some later stage) or else makes some attempt at an adjustment, which, if pursued, will lead him to religion. It is true that neither effect is so certain now as it was in ages when the existence of God (or even of the Gods) was more widely known, but even in our own days we see it operating. Even atheists rebel and express, like Hardy and Housman, their rage against God although (or because) He does not, on their view, exist: and other atheists, like Mr. Huxley, are driven by suffering to raise the whole problem of existence and to find some way of coming to terms with it which, if not Christian, is almost infinitely superior to fatuous contentment with a profane life. No doubt Pain as God's megaphone is a terrible instrument; it may lead to final and unrepented rebellion. But it gives the only opportunity the bad man can have for amendment. It removes the veil; it plants the flag of truth within the fortress of a rebel soul.

If the first and lowest operation of pain shatters the illusion that all is well, the second shatters the illusion that what we have, whether good or bad in itself, is our own and enough for us. Everyone has noticed how hard it is to turn our thoughts to God when everything is going well with us. We "have all we want" is a terrible saying when "all" does not include God. We find God an interruption. As St. Augustine says somewhere "God wants to give us something, but cannot, because our hands are full—there's no-

[3] *Leviathan,* Pt. I, Chap. 6.

where for Him to put it." Or as a friend of mine said "we regard God as an airman regards his parachute; it's there for emergencies but he hopes he'll never have to use it." Now God, who has made us, knows what we are and that our happiness lies in Him. Yet we will not seek it in Him as long as He leaves us any other resort where it can even plausibly be looked for. While what we call "our own life" remains agreeable we will not surrender it to Him. What then can God do in our interests but make "our own life" less agreeable to us, and take away the plausible sources of false happiness? It is just here, where God's providence seems at first to be most cruel, that the Divine humility, the stooping down of the Highest, most deserves praise. We are perplexed to see misfortune falling upon decent, inoffensive, worthy people—on capable, hard-working mothers of families or diligent, thrifty, little trades-people, on those who have worked so hard, and so honestly, for their modest stock of happiness and now seem to be entering on the enjoyment of it with the fullest right. How can I say with sufficient tenderness what here needs to be said? It does not matter that I know I must become, in the eyes of every hostile reader, as it were personally responsible for all the sufferings I try to explain—just as, to this day, everyone talks as if St. Augustine *wanted* unbaptized infants to go to Hell. But it matters enormously if I alienate anyone from the truth. Let me implore the reader to try to believe, if only for the moment, that God, who made these deserving people, may really be right when He thinks that their modest prosperity and the happiness of their children are not enough to make them blessed: that all this must fall from them in the end, and that if they have not learned to know Him they will be wretched. And therefore He troubles them, warning them in advance of an insufficiency that one day they will have to discover. The life to themselves and their families stands between them and the recognition of their need; He makes that life less sweet to them. I call this a Divine humility because it is a poor thing to strike our colors to God when the ship is going down under us; a poor thing to come to Him as a last resort, to offer up "our own" when it is no longer worth keeping. If God were proud He would hardly have us on such terms: but He is not proud, He stoops to conquer. He will have us even though we have shown that we prefer everything else to Him, and come to Him because there is "nothing better" now to be had. The same humility is shown by all those Divine appeals to our fears which trouble highminded readers of scripture. It is hardly complimentary to God that we should choose Him as an alternative to Hell: yet even this He accepts. The creature's illusion of self-sufficiency must, for the creature's sake, be shattered; and by trouble or fear of trouble on earth, by crude fear of the eternal flames, God shatters it "unmindful of His glory's diminution." Those who would like the God of scripture to be more purely ethical, do not know what they ask. If God were a Kantian, who would not have us till we came to Him from the purest and best motives, who could be saved? And this illusion of self-sufficiency may be at its strongest in some very honest, kindly, and temperate people, and on such people, therefore, misfortune must fall.

The dangers of apparent self-sufficiency explain why Our Lord regards the vices of the feckless and dissipated so much more leniently than the vices that lead to worldly success. Prostitutes are in no danger of finding their present life so satisfactory that they cannot turn to God: the proud, the avaricious, the self-rightous, are in that danger.

The third operation of suffering is a little harder to grasp. Everyone will admit that choice is essentially conscious; to choose involves knowing that you choose. Now Paradisal man always chose to follow God's will. In following it he also gratified his own desire, both because all the actions demanded of him were, in fact, agreeable to his blameless inclination, and also because the service of God was itself his keenest pleasure, without which as their razor edge all joys would have been insipid to him. The question "Am I doing this for God's sake or only because I happen to like it?" did not then arise, since doing things for God's sake was what he chiefly "happened to like." His God-ward will rode his happiness like a well-managed horse, whereas our will, when we are happy, is carried away in the happiness as in a ship racing down a swift stream. Pleasure was then an acceptable offering to God because offering was a pleasure. But we inherit a whole system of desires which do not necessarily contradict God's will but which, after centuries of usurped autonomy, steadfastly ignore it. If the thing we like doing is, in fact, the thing God wants us to do, yet that is not our reason for doing it; it remains a mere happy coincidence. We cannot therefore know that we are acting at all, or primarily, for God's sake, unless the material of the action is contrary to our inclinations, or (in other words) painful, and what we cannot know that we are choosing, we cannot choose. The full acting out of the self's surrender to God therefore demands pain: this action, to be perfect, must be done from the pure will to obey, in the absence, or in the teeth, of inclination. How impossible it is to enact the surrender of the self by doing what we like, I know very well from my own experience at the moment. When I undertook to write this book I hoped that the will to obey what might be a "leading" had at least some place in my motives. But now that I am thoroughly immersed in it, it has become a temptation rather than a duty. I may still hope that the writing of the book is, in fact, in conformity with God's will: but to contend that I am learning to surrender myself by doing what is so attractive to me would be ridiculous.

Here we tread on very difficult ground. Kant thought that no action had moral value unless it were done out of pure reverence for the moral law, that is, without inclination, and he has been accused of a "morbid frame of mind" which measures the value of an act by its unpleasantness. All popular opinion is, indeed, on Kant's side. The people never admire a man for doing something he likes: the very words "But he *likes* it" imply the corollary "And therefore it has no merit." Yet against Kant stands the obvious truth, noted by Aristotle, that the more virtuous a man becomes the more he enjoys virtuous actions. What an atheist ought to do about this conflict between the ethics of duty and the ethics of virtue, I do not know: but as a Christian I suggest the following solution.

It has sometimes been asked whether God commands certain things because they are right, or whether certain things are right because God commands them. With Hooker, and against Dr. Johnson, I emphatically embrace the first alternative. The second might lead to the abominable conclusion (reached, I think, by Paley) that charity is good only because God arbitrarily commanded it—that He might equally well have commanded us to hate Him and one another and that hatred would then have been right. I believe, on the contrary, that "they err who think that of the will of God to do this or that there is no reason besides His will."[4] God's will is determined by His wisdom which always perceives, and His goodness which always embraces, the intrinsically good. But when we have said that God commands things only because they are good, we must add that one of the things intrinsically good is that rational creatures should freely surrender themselves to their Creator in obedience. The content of our obedience—the thing we are commanded to do—will always be something intrinsically good, something we ought to do even if (by an impossible supposition) God had not commanded it. But in addition to the content, the mere obeying is also intrinsically good, for, in obeying, a rational creature consciously enacts its creaturely *rôle,* reverses the act by which we fell, treads Adam's dance backward, and returns.

We therefore agree with Aristotle that what is intrinsically right may well be agreeable, and that the better a man is the more he will like it; but we agree with Kant so far as to say that there is one right act—that of self-surrender—which cannot be willed to the height by fallen creatures unless it is unpleasant. And we must add that this one right act includes all other righteousness, and that the supreme canceling of Adam's fall, the movement "full speed astern" by which we retrace our long journey from Paradise, the untying of the old, hard knot, must be when the creature, with no desire to aid it, stripped naked to the bare willing of obedience, embraces what is contrary to its nature, and does that for which only one motive is possible. Such an act may be described as a "test" of the creature's return to God: hence our fathers said that troubles were "sent to try us." A familiar example is Abraham's "trial" when he was ordered to sacrifice Isaac. With the historicity or the morality of that story I am not now concerned, but with the obvious question "If God is omniscient He must have known what Abraham would do, without any experiment; why, then, this needless torture?" But as St. Augustine points out,[5] whatever God

---

[4] Hooker. *Laws of Eccl. Polity,* I, i, 5.   [5] *De Civitate Dei,* XVI, xxxii.

knew, Abraham at any rate did not know that his obedience could endure such a command until the event taught him: and the obedience which he did not know that he would choose, he cannot be said to have chosen. The reality of Abraham's obedience was the act itself; and what God knew in knowing that Abraham "would obey" was Abraham's actual obedience on that mountain top at that moment. To say that God "need not have tried the experiment" is to say that because God knows, the thing known by God need not exist.

If pain sometimes shatters the creature's false self-sufficiency, yet in supreme "Trial" or "Sacrifice" it teaches him the self-sufficiency which really ought to be his—the "strength, which, if Heaven gave it, may be called his own": for then, in the absence of all merely natural motives and supports, he acts in that strength, and that alone, which God confers upon him through his subjected will. Human will becomes truly creative and truly our own when it is wholly God's, and this is one of the many senses in which he that loses his soul shall find it. In all other acts our will is fed through nature, that is, through created things other than the self—through the desires which our physical organism and our heredity supply to us. When we act from ourselves alone—that is, from God *in* ourselves—we are collaborators in, or live instruments of, creation: and that is why such an act undoes with "backward mutters of dissevering power" the uncreative spell which Adam laid upon his species. Hence as suicide is the typical expression of the stoic spirit, and battle of the warrior spirit, martyrdom always remains the supreme enacting and perfection of Christianity. This great action has been initiated for us, done on our behalf, exemplified for our imitation, and inconceivably communicated to all believers, by Christ on Calvary. There the degree of accepted Death reaches the utmost bounds of the imaginable and perhaps goes beyond them; not only all natural supports, but the presence of the very Father to whom the sacrifice is made deserts the victim, and surrender to God does not falter though God "forsakes" it.

The doctrine of death which I describe is not peculiar to Christianity. Nature herself has written it large across the world in the repeated drama of the buried seed and the re-arising corn. From nature, perhaps, the oldest agricultural communities learned it and with animal, or human, sacrifices showed forth for centuries the truth that "without shedding of blood is no remission";[6] and though at first such conceptions may have concerned only the crops and offspring of the tribe they came later, in the Mysteries, to concern the spiritual death and resurrection of the individual. The Indian ascetic, mortifying his body on a bed of spikes, preaches the same lesson; the Greek philosopher tells us that the life of wisdom is "a practice of death."[7] The sensitive and noble heathen of modern times makes his imagined gods "die into life."[8] Mr. Huxley expounds "non-attachment." We

[6] Heb. ix, 22.   [7] Plato. *Phaed.*, 81, A (cf. 54, A).   [8] Keats. *Hyperion*, III, 130.

cannot escape the doctrine by ceasing to be Christians. It is an "eternal gospel" revealed to men wherever men have sought, or endured, the truth: it is the very nerve of redemption, which anatomizing wisdom at all times and in all places lays bare; the unescapable knowledge which the Light that lighteneth every man presses down upon the minds of all who seriously question what the universe is "about." The peculiarity of the Christian faith is not to teach this doctrine but to render it, in various ways, more tolerable. Christianity teaches us that the terrible task has already in some sense been accomplished for us—that a master's hand is holding ours as we attempt to trace the difficult letters and that our script need only be a "copy" not an original. Again, where other systems expose our total nature to death (as in Buddhist renunciation) Christianity demands only that we set right a *misdirection* of our nature, and has no quarrel, like Plato, with the body as such, nor with the psychical elements in our make-up. And sacrifice in its supreme realization is not exacted of all. Confessors as well as martyrs are saved, and some old people whose state of grace we can hardly doubt seem to have got through their seventy years surprisingly easily. The sacrifice of Christ is repeated, or re-echoed, among His followers in very varying degrees, from the cruellest martyrdom down to a self-submission of intention whose outward signs have nothing to distinguish them from the ordinary fruits of temperance and "sweet reasonableness." The causes of this distribution I do not know; but from our present point of view it ought to be clear that the real problem is not why some humble, pious, believing people suffer, but why some do *not*. Our Lord Himself, it will be remembered, explained the salvation of those who are fortunate in this world only by referring to the unsearchable omnipotence of God.[9]

All arguments in justification of suffering provoke bitter resentment against the author. You would like to know how I behave when I am experiencing pain, not writing books about it. You need not guess, for I will tell you; I am a great coward. But what is that to the purpose? When I think of pain—of anxiety that gnaws like fire and loneliness that spreads out like a desert, and the heartbreaking routine of monotonous misery, or again of dull aches that blacken our whole landscape or sudden nauseating pains that knock a man's heart out at one blow, of pains that seem already intolerable and then are suddenly increased, or infuriating scorpion-stinging pains that startle into maniacal movement a man who seemed half dead with his previous tortures—it "quite o'ercrows my spirit." If I knew any way of escape I would crawl through sewers to find it. But what is the good of telling you about my feelings? You know them already: they are the same as yours. I am not arguing that pain is not painful. Pain hurts. That is what the word means. I am only trying to show that the old Christian doctrine of being made "perfect through suffering"[10] is not incredible. To prove it palatable is beyond my design.

[9] Mark x, 27.   [10] Heb. ii. 10.

In estimating the credibility of the doctrine two principles ought to be observed. In the first place we must remember that the actual moment of present pain is only the center of what may be called the whole tribulational system which extends itself by fear and pity. Whatever good effects these experiences have are dependent upon the center; so that even if pain itself was of no spiritual value, yet if fear and pity were, pain would have to exist in order that there should be something to be feared and pitied. And that fear and pity help us in our return to obedience and charity is not to be doubted. Everyone has experienced the effect of pity in making it easier for us to love the unlovely—that is, to love men not because they are in any way naturally agreeable to us but because they are our brethren. The beneficence of fear most of us have learned during the period of "crises" that led up to the present war. My own experience is something like this. I am progressing along the path of life in my ordinary contentedly fallen and godless condition, absorbed in a merry meeting with my friends for the morrow or a bit of work that tickles my vanity today, a holiday or a new book, when suddenly a stab of abdominal pain that threatens serious disease, or a headline in the newspapers that threatens us all with destruction, sends this whole pack of cards tumbling down. At first I am overwhelmed, and all my little happinesses look like broken toys. Then, slowly and reluctantly, bit by bit, I try to bring myself into the frame of mind that I should be in at all times. I remind myself that all these toys were never intended to possess my heart, that my true good is in another world and my only real treasure is Christ. And perhaps, by God's grace, I succeed, and for a day or two become a creature consciously dependent on God and drawing its strength from the right sources. But the moment the threat is withdrawn, my whole nature leaps back to the toys: I am even anxious, God forgive me, to banish from my mind the only thing that supported me under the threat because it is now associated with the misery of those few days. Thus the terrible necessity of tribulation is only too clear. God has had me for but forty-eight hours and then only by dint of taking everything else away from me. Let Him but sheathe that sword for a moment and I behave like a puppy when the hated bath is over—I shake myself as dry as I can and race off to re-acquire my comfortable dirtiness, if not in the nearest manure heap, at least in the nearest flower bed. And that is why tribulations cannot cease until God either sees us remade or sees that our remaking is now hopeless.

In the second place, when we are considering pain itself—the center of the whole tribulational system—we must be careful to attend to what we know and not to what we imagine. That is one of the reasons why the whole central part of this book is devoted to human pain, and animal pain is relegated to a special chapter. About human pain we know, about animal pain we only speculate. But even within the human race we must draw our evidence from instances that have come under our own observation. The tendency of this or that novelist or poet may represent suffering as wholly bad in its effects, as producing, and justifying, every kind of malice and brutality in the sufferer. And, of course, pain, like pleasure, can be so received: all that is given to a creature with free will must be two-edged, not by the nature of the giver or of the gift, but by the nature of the recipient. And, again, the evil results of pain can be multiplied if sufferers are persistently taught by the bystanders that such results are the proper and manly results for them to exhibit. Indignation at other's sufferings, though a generous passion, needs to be well managed lest it steal away patience and humility from those who suffer and plant anger and cynicism in their stead. But I am not convinced that suffering, if spared such officious vicarious indignation, has any natural tendency to produce such evils. I did not find the front-line trenches or the C.C.S. more full than any other place of hatred, selfishness, rebellion, and dishonesty. I have seen great beauty of spirit in some who were great sufferers. I have seen men, for the most part, grow better not worse with advancing years, and I have seen the last illness produce treasures of fortitude and meekness from most unpromising subjects. I see in loved and revered historical figures, such as Johnson and Cowper, traits which might scarcely have been tolerable if the men had been happier. If the world is indeed a "vale of soul making" it seems on the whole to be doing its work. Of poverty—the affliction which actually or potentially includes all other afflictions—I would not dare to speak as from myself; and those who reject Christianity will not be moved by Christ's statement that poverty is blessed. But here a rather remarkable fact comes to my aid. Those who would most scornfully repudiate Christianity as a mere "opiate of the people" have a contempt for the rich, that is, for all mankind *except* the poor. They regard the poor as the only people worth preserving from "liquidation," and place in them the only hope of the human race. But this is not compatible with a belief that the effects of poverty on those who suffer it are wholly evil; it even implies that they are good. The Marxist thus finds himself in real agreement with the Christian in those two beliefs which Christianity paradoxically demands—that poverty is blessed and yet ought to be removed.

* Asserting

AN ASSERTION (or statement) may be most simply described as a group of words which say something about a subject. From that description it follows that assertions may be classified in two groups, accordingly as they are true or false: some assertions say something true about a subject; some assertions say something false about a subject. The true-false classification is not by any means the only one into which assertions may be divided, but it is in some ways the most important and useful one because it bears directly on the fundamental human experiences associated with assertions. When we make an assertion, we are conscious of some intention in making it and of our responsibility for it. When we read or hear an assertion, we are concerned with what it implies and with the means by which it can be corroborated or, at least, by which it can be fully understood as a meaningful utterance. To all of these considerations, truth and falsity are very important.

Before any analysis of assertions is made, however, it is essential to note that, although all assertions may be called sentences, not all sentences may be called assertions, at least not in their explicit form. Questions do not directly say something about a subject, nor do commands or exclamations. Indirectly, it is true, they may do so: the question "Did you open the door?" implies the assertion "The door was opened"; the command "Shut the door!" implies the assertion "The door is open"; and even the exclamation "Bang!" would seem to imply some unverbalized assertion such as "The door was slammed hard." Despite the likelihood that all sentences imply, even if they do not explicitly make, assertions, it will be useful to keep questions, commands, and exclamations separate from assertions and to say that classification as to truth or falsity is reserved to assertions alone.

Not *all* declarative sentences make true or false assertions, for that matter. Consider the so-called "performatives"—sentences like "I promise to be there," or "I object to your manners." The truth or falsity of such statements cannot reasonably be questioned, since to say "I promise" *is* to promise.

Now if truth or falsity is to be the classifying criterion for the analysis of assertions, it is at once clear that there must be some discussion of the way in which a given assertion may be recognized to be true or false. (The intricacies of demonstrating it to be so are discussed at the beginning of the section of readings entitled *Proving*.) All of us know enough about language and the world to realize that determination of the truth or falsity of an assertion is seldom simple and even more seldom final, complete, or universally acceptable. Indeed, the number of statements on which one can be *sure* of agreement is very small in comparison with the number of those about which disagreement is likely to persist. The ones about which finality is possible can be described as assertions true or false by *resolution* or by *deduction*.

"A yard is three feet long" is a statement of the first kind. This assertion we know to be true and beyond dispute because we agree to a general resolution to use the word "yard" to mean specifically "a length of three feet." The assertion is, as a matter of fact, nothing more than a concealed definition. It could have been written in this fashion: "A yard is a measurement of distance equivalent to three feet"; and we would then have recognized it as a definition at once. It is wise to note, however, that such an assertion may be true in one situation and false in another ("A gallon contains 128 ounces" is true in the United States but false in Canada), but this limitation does not in any way diminish the finality with which we can recognize the truth or falsity of such assertions within a known context or situation.

A second kind of statement is that in which truth or falsity is absolutely determinable *if the statements on which it depends are known to be true or false*. The assertion "Lincoln was ignorant because he had little formal education" implies the deduction of "Lincoln was ignorant" from the premise that ignorance is a consequence of lack of formal education and from the premise that Lincoln did not have much formal education. If those premises are true (as one is not) and if the final assertion follows logically from them, then it is also true.

A third kind of assertion derives neither from a resolution nor from prior assertions but instead purports to refer directly to the "facts" of experience. "Women are more courageous than men" is such an assertion. It claims to be nothing more than a report about "things as they are," and it makes evidence of the senses the sole warrant for its accuracy. "Formal education is wasted on half of those who receive it" is another. This kind of assertion makes up the bulk of our discourse; it is the means by which a good part of the business of the world is conducted. Since that is so, the recognition of the truth or falsity of such assertions is a vital matter to us; yet it is apparent that assertions like these are almost impossible to classify with certainty. The best that we can do with most of them is to check them as fully as we can by all relevant means of verification (personal observation, reports of others, "authority," tradition, and so on) and then to consider them as *tentatively* classifiable as true or false. Evidence may be so strong for some of these assertions (for instance, "The earth moves around the sun") that the likelihood of wrong classification is almost

zero, but it is never absolutely conclusive except when the assertion rests
on a body of evidence known to be complete and unalterable.

A fourth group of assertions, the ones about which we are likely to have
very strong feelings, raises a peculiar difficulty. These are *ethical assertions*
or assertions of obligation. One group of modern logicians contends that
such statements ("Men ought to live peaceably together" is an example)
are really compounds of assertion, resolution, command, and exclamation,
and must be sorted into their components before classification is meaningful. For the example given, these critics would make separation as follows:
"I approve of living peaceably together" (assertion, true or false—either the
speaker does or does not approve of peaceable living together, a claim
that can be tested and determined, though not finally, by observation of
his behavior); "Let us live peaceably together" (resolution); "Live peaceably together" (command); "Hurrah for living peaceably together!" (exclamation). Of the four components only the first has any truth value, and it
is a statement of personal choice; expression of approval or preference, say
these logicians, is all that ethical assertions really amount to when they are
carefully analyzed. To this critique, another group of modern logicians
objects on the grounds (1) that the components do not express the full
content of the original assertion, (2) that behind ethical assertions there
are primary assumptions about the rightness or wrongness of certain actions
in this world, and (3) that the truth or falsity of these assumptions is
intuitively known to men. To fortify their position against those who are
skeptical about intuition, they point out that the empirical evidence demanded for verification of an assertion draws *its* authority from assumptions about perception and about the nature of reality which are themselves
the result of intuition, not of empirical proof. Every ethical assertion is,
at bottom, an attempt to say something about order in the universe; some
have only short-range order in mind ("Men should be generous to their
neighbors *so that* their neighbors will be generous to them"), but many are
certainly intended, like that in the original example, to indicate an enduring and ideal order in the nature of the universe.

Obviously, the foregoing technical analysis is not the sort of thing we
commonly go through in taking an attitude toward our own statements
or toward those made by other people. Instead, we are likely to use three
loose classifications of entirely different kind: *fact, opinion,* and *preference*
(or *taste*). To oversimplify the matter slightly, in the classification "assertions (or statements) of fact" we put all those assertions which seem to us to
be true on whatever grounds; in "assertions of opinion" all those which
seem to us open to general argument and likely to provoke it and those
which, even though we think them true, we recognize to be unsusceptible
of ready proof; in "assertions of preference (or taste)" all those which we
think to be outside the range of argument because they have, or appear
to have, reference only to the asserter. Such a classification is largely

psychological. The way we feel about certain subjects undoubtedly influences the form into which we cast our thoughts, and the classification into fact, opinion, and preference, handy as it is, really provides an analysis of the asserter's intention, expectation, or attitude toward the assertion more than an analysis of the assertion itself. For that reason it is less useful than the truth-falsity classification for logical analysis. The total analysis of assertions, however, cannot dispense with the psychological context of assertion any more than literary analysis of a line of poetry can dispense with the poem in which it occurs. On the other hand, although the last limits of logic do not exhaust the resources of language, logical analysis is nonetheless one of the most effective means of realizing and exploiting these resources.

The purpose of all such analysis of assertions, as we suggested at the beginning, is to establish grounds for considering the inferences to be drawn from the assertions. These inferences are of two kinds: the *assumptions* which underlie assertions and the *implications,* or logical consequences, which may be said to follow from them. Generally speaking, implications and assumptions are not stated; they must be achieved, or worked out, by the reader or listener. Assumptions and implications are, then, simply assertions, generally unstated, which—once they are brought to light—are susceptible to the same kinds of classification as all assertions and to the same tests of validity.

In the usual procedures of reading and writing, of course, we do not separate our analysis of the nature of an assertion from our judgment of its truth or falsity, but we may not know which tests to apply to it unless we are able to classify it accurately first. To practice the analysis of assertions and to develop skill in the detection of unstated assumptions and implications is, therefore, to pave the way for the making of intelligent judgments.

ABOUT SOVIET RUSSIA (1927-1936)

OPINION IS BOTH servant and master to fact. To be sure, a writer builds his opinions from the facts. But from which facts? The world is extravagant and impartial, perhaps to a fault, in supplying facts to liberal and conservative alike, to Freudian and behaviorist, to theist and atheist. (Consider: are the facts for or against socialized medicine?) A writer describing what he sees is necessarily influenced in his choice of facts by prior opinions about which facts are relevant, significant. If, for instance, he writes of his native land, the data he selects will be those which his point of view allows him to see. No chauvinistic German is likely, in proselytizing, to dwell on Buchenwald and Dachau; Americans in the same role prefer art festivals and know-how to mob killings and Mc-Carthyism.

    The degree to which opinion rides herd over evidence will vary with intensity of involvement. A New Yorker may be relatively unbiased in reporting on the weather in Chicago. When he visits Nepal, he can free himself even more completely from preformed animosities and attachments. Yet he will be deceived if he thinks himself a perfectly objective observer, for his opinions and standards are so much a part of him that they inevitably screen his experience; but in Nepal the screen may at least be more nearly a sieve than a curtain. If no journey except the last one of all can take the traveler quite outside himself, still, the traveler's report, by ancient agreement, makes up in freshness of outlook for what it lacks in completeness of information.

    Peripatetic license was never put under a more severe strain than by those "scoundrels, duffers and liars" (Liam O'Flaherty's words)—and plain curiosity-seekers—who flocked to the Soviet Union and wrote about it in the decade we are considering. For Russia was nobody's Nepal. Probably even today, with our interest stimulated by cold curtain and iron war, we cannot recapture the extraordinary excitement that was generated in the West by the idea of the first communist state, anathema to some, source of infinite hope to others. What traveler could preserve his objectivity, faced with the Soviet assault on economic freedom, family, church, and very many of the assumptions of Western society? Yet among the duffers and scoundrels there were a few who tried, among them a surprising number of important writers. Five such are represented here. How well, or badly they insulated fact from opinion may be judged by the excerpts which follow.

    Three of the observers are American: Edmund Wilson (1895-   ), our most versatile contemporary man of letters, who later wrote a brilliant history of the events that prefaced the Russian Revolution, in To the Finland Station; *Theodore Dreiser (1871-1945), whose realistic novels documented the lives of ordinary Americans; and E. E. Cummings, (1894-1962), maverick poet, and, as the present selection shows, maverick writer of prose. André Gide (1869-1951) went to Moscow from France, where he was generally regarded as his country's greatest writer. The Irishman Liam O'Flaherty (1897-   ) is a novelist and writer of short stories.*

NOTES ON CASUAL ENCOUNTERS | EDMUND WILSON

I had expected Moscow to be old and musty, but it is modern and energetic. The people are better dressed and more prosperous-appearing, in general, than the people of Leningrad. The main business section, the "Center," is much like an American city. They have set out to rearrange the whole place, and already there are only little patches of the original Moscow of the Muscovite tsars, embedded in drab streets and crowded traffic: the jewel-box of the Kremlin with its needle-pointed gleaming gilt spires (which, as a result of the Kírov shooting, vistors are no longer allowed to see); the shabby domes of St. Basil's in their big ugly bulbous mushroom-clump. St. Basil's, inside, is a labyrinth, lined with faded saints and angels which the authorities have done nothing to freshen, and plastered with aggressively glaring texts from Marx and Engels and Lenin, which declare that religion is a fraud. In the streets, the innumerable stubby little people who have been flocking into the metropolis but who are not used to getting around in a city, are plunging about and bumping into one another. Moscow seems even to a New Yorker a terribly exhausting place. The tram-cars are usually crowded, and the people hang on to the outside and fall off and get under the cars and have their legs and arms run over. And though the pace of Russian life is in general so much slower and less effortful than ours, their new mechanical means of locomotion seem some-times to have gone to their heads. They rip around the streets in their Russian-made cars, tooting wild defiant horns, like galloping Cossacks; and the escalators in their new little subway rush the passengers up and down at a speed unknown in America. Women and children scream: a first ride is a major adventure. When the subway was opened, Comrade Stalin, who can take it, rode the escalator twice in succession.

This subway, for the foreign visitor, is worth thinking about. They are all very much excited over it, and they eagerly ask every foreigner how it compares with the subways in other countries. The truth is, of course, that, compared to most of them, it is tiny; but it is the only *pretty* subway in the world. Every station is in a different style, so that it is full of delightful surprises, like a superior sort of scenic railway: there are murals, ornamental columns, novel effects of light. Even the trains are done in pleasing com-binations of red, light tan and yellow, or red, light tan and green. What it most resembles, on its smaller scale, is the interiors of the Radio City

From *Red, Black, Blond and Olive* (New York, Oxford University Press, Inc., 1956). Reprinted by permission of the author.

theaters. The moral of the Moscow subway is that it is perfectly natural that a public utility, if built by the people for their own use, should be dignified, handsome and attractive.

I sometimes wake up in the morning with a feeling I have never had before of being obliged to adjust myself to a new set of social dimensions.

They are certainly much pleasanter with each other, for all their jostling and jamming, than New Yorkers. They have arguments on street-cars and in queues, always calling one another "Comrade"—quite different from our crowds in the subway, for example, where the people rarely speak to one another, each penned up in his particular anxieties, each with his particular schedule to make. In Moscow, if anyone behaves hoggishly, there is general remonstrance and protest. In one case I heard of, a man in a street-car was made to feel so cheap that he got off.

It is much easier to establish friendly relations with Russians than with the people of any other country I know. When you smile at them, they always smile back: it is a queer kind of childlike responsiveness. When they are frightened or suspicious, they become, not stiff, but simply shy.

Old women walking along the streets with cigarettes drooping out of their mouths. The Russians have been getting more cigarettes lately.

I was taken to a commissar's home for tea. He and his family were living in what would be for New York a very moderate-sized middle-class apartment. Lots of interesting sweet things to eat: cranberries candied in white sugar, for example. The Russians love these sweets and are only just beginning to get them again. The Commissar had the Communist seriousness, reticence, intentness, severity. Over tea in the bosom of his family, he almost never smiled—though he was evidently not unamiable and, from behind his rather heavy manner, was evidently going to be helpful in the case of some unfortunate person in whose behalf one of the visitors appealed to him.

They tried to tell me the news that Roosevelt's N.R.A. had been declared unconstitutional by the Supreme Court; but, little confidence though I had in the N.R.A., I was so unprepared for this, subconsciously no doubt so loth to admit it, that I thought they said *constitutional*. They had apparently been surprised and had expected that I should be surprised. It was only the next day, when I read about it in the paper, that I grasped it.

It is curious losing track of the days of the week. Their week consists now of six days, with a holiday called "Free Day" on the sixth. Everything is reckoned by the date; and I believe I miss the old Saturdays and Mondays. Each of the traditional days has its own special psychological atmosphere; the week is a moral cycle.

We went up to a traffic-cop, and I was astonished when she turned around and revealed a little, red-cheeked, freckled country girl, very serious, concentrated and cute in her helmet and masculine clothes.

It is unexpected and stimulating for an American, after leaving the writers at home preoccupied with what they imagine to be the Soviet point of view about literature, to find the Russians studying intently everything that reaches them from the States—rather dissatisfied now with their own post-revolutionary literature and seeming to feel that in America we have been able to do the kind of thing that they would like to do themselves. Very amusing to reflect that the three living American writers most popular in the Soviet Union—Upton Sinclair, Dos Passos and Dreiser—are all people who have recently been in wrong with the literary Communists at home.

Hemingway has just been translated and, among the intelligentzia, is attracting a great deal of attention. I come to realize that the young people in Russia are interested in the American writers for certain reasons, among others, which I hadn't been aware of before. I was told by a Russian that the hero and heroine of Dos Passos' *Manhattan Transfer,* both types of the unquiet intellectual, were as well known in Russia as characters in Pushkin; that young men would say, "I am Jimmy Herf," etc. The young Russians of the Jimmy Herf type have this in common with these characters of Dos Passos: that they are up against a social machine to which they have difficulty in adapting themselves. That the Soviet machine has a more rational base and a nobler aim than American business does not always make the situation easier—and, after all, the conditions of a democracy, with their tendency to lower cultural standards, present the same kind of problems to both. And there must be people in Moscow who would sometimes be glad of "a clean bright place," like the man in Hemingway's story—a story which, I note, is included in a Russian selection from his work. I am reminded of a young woman who tells me that she dreams about having a room to herself.

An air-meet. It took place on the outskirts of Moscow, and we reached it along a road lined with little old mud-brown log houses, which had fancy peaked cornices over the windows and fringes of wooden lace.

Some of them seemed to have sunk into the earth till their windows were almost on a level with it.

It was on this field that the crowds were trampled to death at the coronation of Nicholas II. Today there is a loud-speaker and a band playing the *International* through it. Ballet-patterns by gliders, which would sheer off symmetrically from the plane that had trailed them and wheel slowly over on their sides; a regular rocket-burst of parachute-jumpers, some of the women coming down with two parachutes. The weather was cold and wet: a little group of girls and young men had joined hands and were running around in a ring to keep warm. There were appealing boy and girl couples leaning against their bicycles and looking up at the flyers.

A small policeman in a helmet was trying to make the people get back behind a rope. They argued with him about it, calling him "Comrade." The crowd maintained that so long as there were cars parked in front of the rope, people ought to be able to stand there. The policeman, on his side, pointed out that, so far as seeing airplanes went, it didn't matter where you stood. Somebody said that it wasn't that you couldn't see: it was the psychological effect of having something in front of you. The policeman apparently felt the force of this, but he urged them to get back "a tiny bit." Presently, the cars drove away, and the policeman then returned and showed logically that, now the obstruction was removed, they ought to keep back behind the ropes. Persuaded by this argument, they finally complied.

The relations between the police and the public seem almost ideal. Lenin insisted on having the former called "militia." The role of the old police had become so hateful to him that he had not wanted to preserve even the name. The "militia," like any other militia, were supposed to represent the citizens themselves; and it is true that on an occasion like this air-meet, the Moscow militia are much more like the ushers at a college ball-game than like the police of the capitalist states. I afterwards saw a man arrested, and the same sort of parliamentary methods seemed to regulate the proceedings. Two militiamen had the man by the arms, but he kept stopping and arguing with them. They would unhand him and explain their case. Finally, they led him away.

There are, of course, the secret police, who are apparently a different matter.

I have not been troubled by espionage, as some people complain of being—though I have had one or two mysterious telephone calls which woke me up at early hours of the morning. When I answered, there would be nobody on the line; and I was told that this was the ordinary way of finding out whether you were sleeping at the address you had given. Once when I was taking a Russian lady home from the Metropole café, we were followed very closely by a man who seemed to have a special interest in us.

I always find that Americans who become bitter over espionage in Russia have never had any experience of what may happen in the United States in any industrial center. These people have never been made uncomfortable at home, because they have never been suspected of supporting the interests of labor against the interests of the employing class. So I was not made uncomfortable in Russia, because I was a visiting journalist known to be sympathetic with the Soviet regime. In America, the visiting journalist whose sympathies are not known, though he may be merely reporting strikes or even merely looking at factories, soon finds the police and the officials checking up on his lodgings and his movements; and in the ruder and more remote communities, he is likely to be confronted with gun-thugs who threaten to run him out of town. If he is known to be engaged in pro-labor work, he may be followed on the train by a detective and very likely *will* be run out.

I locked myself out of my room at the hotel. There was no one at the chambermaid's table. The elevator-boy promised to send the porter, but nothing came of this. I went downstairs and told the porter myself, and he immediately turned to a young boy who was standing across from the desk with a box of tools under his arm. I asked the porter whether he didn't have a key: they had opened it that way before. But he insisted that the boy would attend to it. I went upstairs with the boy, who produced from his kit a large wedge and started hammering it, with deafening racket, into the crack between the double doors. Presently he stopped doing this and, taking out another huge tool, began to gouge it into the keyhole. Then he tried the wedge again. He had evidently no equipment for dealing with locks. An old man with a shaved head had turned up at the chambermaid's table. I told him that they had a key there with which they had let me into my room before; but he only opened his drawer and looked at the keys and shook his head. I remonstrated with the boy, who was damaging the door but who was easily persuaded to stop. And now the old man and I, seizing two different phones simultaneously, made efforts to get the porter, but nobody even answered. The boy and I went downstairs, where we found the porter behind his desk. He immediately produced a key, with which I opened the door. His sending the boy in the first place had apparently been due merely to the accident that the latter happened to be standing by with a box of tools for breaking into things, and that it had seemed to the porter a pleasing idea to have him give a demonstration on my door. I had been trying to think that Moscow was much more efficient than Leningrad....

The Park of Culture and Rest* is neutral, enormous, bare, colorless. It is impossible to imagine till you see it a world without paints or dyes.

* It would probably be better translated "Park of Recreation and Training," but this is what everybody calls it.

There are a few indispensable red flags in the Park of Culture and Rest, but, in general, there is no more color than you find in a photograph in either clothes, posters, buildings or signs—nor in faces: the people are pale like all people who live in cities. Vast expanses of wide dirt walks, recently scraped out on the shadeless site; only meager sprigs of trees, dim grass. In the eating pavilion, where the women in sneakers, the men without neckties, the shaved-headed children, drift in by the thousand and are gradually served, there are only heads of purple hortensia among the bottles of pale yellow wine and the Soviet chocolate slabs spiral-piled on the bar. To an American, it seems like limbo—for we, in our amusement parks, have wild games and giddy music; we squeal and guffaw and shriek. But these people move very slowly; they neither laugh aloud nor sing, they seem not even to talk to one another, and in their faces there is no expression. Are they afraid of being overheard? are they afraid of being arrested for "hooliganism?—or have their hardships sobered them so terribly?—or are they still so numb and dumb from their old subhuman life of serfdom that they have not yet been able to discover how human beings enjoy themselves?

Yet at the same time—it is one of the paradoxes of Russia which make it so hard to explain to people who have not been here—one finds here a kind of freedom that one does not feel in other countries. Here nobody is socially self-conscious; nobody is disagreeable or rude. There is no class of petty officials who snap at people and keep them from doing things. If one carelessly throws anything away, one at once picks it up again: one remembers that there is an old woman standing by with a long-handled broom and a long-handled shovel, who is ready to scoop up a cigarette butt the moment that one is dropped, and one's relation to this old woman is already quite different from one's relation to the people who sweep up parks at home. Here the people in the park do own it, and they are careful of what is theirs. A new kind of public conscience has come to lodge in these crowds.

One wanders with the flaccid stream, dazed by the wanness and rawness. The amusements are mostly intended to train people for aviation—for aviation and war. The young people go in for contrivances like metronome pendulums upside down, which swing them over and back, in order to get themselves accustomed to looping the loop in the air; or, to develop their sense of equilibrium, they balance on narrow rails and try to knock each other off by slapping their right hands together; or they jump from a spiral tower in parachutes fastened to strings. Sometimes the parachutes get caught, and they remain dangling half-way down. One tries an exhibition of paintings, and it turns into a revolutionary museum, where little children who have come out for a holiday are looking at photographs of Communists having their penises strung up by Nazis and wax tableaux of women with their breasts cut off.

In the depths of the park, one finds at last a corner of natural trees and grass. To the music of a three-piece orchestra, a little group of young people in a clearing are dancing an old-fashioned Russian dance. It is simple, very quietly cheerful; they dance round and round in a ring, the same figures, the same little tune, again and again and again. A group of girls on grassy bank—an outing of some sort of girls' club—are singing an interminable and sad-sounding song, an old ballad, I was told by my Russian companion, lamenting the plight of young daughters married off against their wills.

One returns and tries a movie: *The Golden Lake,* a very poor adventure picture, with scarcely a tinge of imagination. It is almost with a shock one realizes that it is possible for a Soviet film to be mediocre and dull.

At last, one decides to leave. The entrance is decorated with flowerbeds, planted on steep banks, that make portraits in pansies of Lenin and Stalin. Outside, the toneless loud-speaker is relaying *Cielito Lindo* and *Oi Mari,* the songs of happier ages, brighter climes.

The whole world is stalled today. Capitalism runs down, ceases to function; Communism makes little progress. The nations and the classes wait. We go neither forward nor back, we hardly know which way we are facing. And in the meantime, while the capitalist New Deal goes through its unreal motions of imitating the Five-Year Plan, even in the Soviet Union the weight of the heavy old society dragging down the world outside, the old fear of the rapacity of one's neighbor, must obstruct the way to health and freedom.

THE PEOPLE AT WORK AND PLAY | *ANDRÉ GIDE*

Entering into direct contact with a people of workers in factories, workshops and yards, in gardens, homes of rest and "parks of culture," I had moments of intense joy. I felt the establishment of a sudden sympathy between these new comrades and myself; I felt my heart expand and blossom. This is why I look more smiling—more laughing even—in the photographs that were taken of me out there, than I am often able to be in France. And how often too the tears would start to my eyes—tears of overflowing joy, of tenderness and love! In that rest-home for the miners of the Don Basin, for instance, in the immediate neighbourhood of Sochi ... No, no! There was nothing artificial there, nothing that had been prepared beforehand. I arrived one evening unexpectedly, without having been announced, but there and then they won my confidence.

From *Back from the U.S.S.R.,* translated by Dorothy Bussy (London, Martin Secker & Warburg, Ltd., 1937).

And that impromptu visit I paid to the children's camp near Borzhom—
a modest, an almost humble place, but the children in it, radiant with
health and happiness, seemed as though they wanted to make me an
offering of their joy. What can I say? Words are powerless to grasp so
deep and simple an emotion. But why mention these rather than so many
others? Poets of Georgia, intellectuals, students, and above all workmen,
how many inspired me with the liveliest affection! I never ceased to
regret my ignorance of their language. And yet their smiles, their eyes
spoke so eloquently of sympathy that I began to doubt whether much
more could have been added by words. It must be said too that I was
introduced everywhere as a friend, and what all these looks expressed
as well was a kind of gratitude. I wish I could deserve it still better than
I do; and that is another motive that urges me to speak.

What they like showing you best are their greatest successes. Of course,
and quite naturally. But numberless times we came unexpectedly upon
village schools, children's playgrounds, clubs, which no one thought of
showing us and which were no doubt indistinguishable from many others.
It was those that I especially admired, precisely because nothing had been
prepared in them for show.

The children in all the pioneer camps I visited are handsome, well-fed
(five meals a day), well cared for—made much of even—and merry. Their
eyes are frank and trustful; their laughter has nothing spiteful or malicious
in it; they might well have thought us foreigners rather ridiculous; not for
a moment did I catch in any one of them the slightest trace of mockery.

This same look of open-hearted happiness is often to be seen too among
their elders, who are as handsome, as vigorous, as the children. The "parks
of culture," where they meet in the evening after the day's work is over, are
unquestionable successes; the finest of them all is the one at Moscow.

I used to go there often. It is a pleasure resort, something like a Luna-
Park on an immense scale. Once inside the gates, you feel yourself in a
foreign land. These crowds of young men and women behave with propriety, with decency; not the slightest trace of stupid or vulgar foolery, of
rowdiness, of licentiousness, or even of flirtation. The whole place is pervaded with a kind of joyous ardor. In one spot you find games being
organized; in another, dances; they are generally started, led and directed
by a man or woman captain, and are carried out in perfect order. Immense
chains are formed in which anyone may join, but there are always many
more spectators than performers. In another place, there are popular dances
and songs, accompanied usually by a simple accordion. Elsewhere, in an
enclosure to which access is free, the devotees of physical jerks exercise
their acrobatic skill in various ways; a professional trainer superintends
the more dangerous movements, advises and guides; further on are gym-
nastic apparatus, bars and ropes; everyone awaits his turn patiently with

mutual words of encouragement. A large space of ground is reserved for volley-ball; and I never tired of watching the strength, grace and skill of the players. Further on, you come upon the section of quiet amusements— chess, draughts and quantities of trifling games which demand skill or patience; some of these were unfamiliar to me and extremely ingenious, as were many other devices for exercising strength, suppleness or agility, which I had never seen and cannot attempt to describe, though certainly some of them would become popular with us. Enough occupations were here to fill hours of one's time. Some were for adults, some for children. The smallest of these latter have their own separate domain where they are supplied with little houses, little boats, little motor-cars, and quantities of little tools adapted to their size. In a broad path, following on from the quiet games (there are so many candidates for these that sometimes you have to wait a long time before finding a free table), wooden boards are set up on which are posted all sorts of riddles, puzzles and problems. All this, I repeat, without the smallest vulgarity; these immense crowds behave with perfect propriety and are manifestly inspired with good feeling, dignity and decorum—and that too without any effort and as a matter of course. The public, without counting the children, is almost entirely composed of work- ing people who come there for sports-training, amusement or instruction; for reading-rooms, lecture-rooms, cinemas, libraries, etc., are also provided, and there are bathing pools on the Moskowa. Here and there too, in the immense park, you come upon a miniature platform where an impromptu professor is haranguing—giving object-lessons, or instruction in history or geography, accompanied by blackboard illustrations—sometimes even in medicine or physiology, with copious reference to anatomical plates. Every- body listens with intense seriousness. I have already said that I never any- where caught the smallest attempt at mockery.*

But here is something better still—a little outdoor theatre, the auditorium of which is packed with some five hundred spectators, listening in religious silence to an actor who is reciting Pushkin (parts of *Eugene Onegin*). In another corner of the park, near the entrance, is the parachute ground. This is a sport which is highly appreciated in the U.S.S.R. Every two minutes or so, one of the three parachutes is launched from the top of a tower some 130 feet high and lands its occupant somewhat roughly on the ground. On with you! Who'll venture next? Volunteers press forward, wait for their turn, line up in queues. And still I haven't mentioned the great open-air theatre, where for certain performances close upon twenty thousand specta- tors assemble.

The Moscow park of culture is the largest and best, provided with various

---

* "And you think that a good thing?" cried my friend X. . . . , when I told him this. "Mockery, irony, criticism are all of a piece. The child who is incapable of making fun will turn into the credulous and submissive youth whom later on you, my dear mocker, will criticize for his conformity. Give me French banter—even if I'm the one to suffer from it."

attractions; the one in Leningrad is the most beautiful. But every town in the Soviet Union now possesses a park of culture, besides children's playgrounds and gardens.

I also visited, of course, a good many factories. I know and constantly say to myself that the prosperity and happiness of the generality depend on their good management. But I am not qualified to speak of this. It has been done by others, to whose encomiums I refer you. My domain is the psychological side of things; it is of this especially—of this almost solely—that I meant to treat. If I glance indirectly at social questions, it will still be from a psychological point of view.

With increasing years, I feel less, far less, interested in scenery, however beautiful, and more and more in men. The peoples of the Soviet Union are admirable—those of Georgia, of Kakhetia, of Abkhasia, of Ukraine (I mention only those I saw) and even more so to my mind, those of Leningrad and the Crimea.

I was present in Moscow at the Festival of Youth in the Red Square. The ugliness of the buildings opposite the Kremlin was concealed by a mask of streamers and greenery. The whole thing was splendid and—I make haste to say it here, for I shan't always be able to—in perfect taste. The admirable youth of the Soviet Union, gathered together from the North and South, from the East and West, were here on parade. The march past lasted for hours. I had never imagined so magnificent a sight. These perfect forms had evidently been trained, prepared, selected; but how can one fail to admire a country and a regime capable of producing them?

I had seen the Red Square a few days previously on the occasion of Gorki's funeral. I had seen the same people, the same and yet how different! —more like, I imagine, the Russians of the time of the Tzars. They filed past the catafalque in the great Hall of Columns, uninterruptedly, interminably. This time they did not consist of the handsomest, the strongest, the most joyful representatives of the Soviet peoples, but of an indiscriminate concourse of suffering humanity—women, children, children especially, old people sometimes, nearly all of them badly dressed and some looking in the depths of poverty. A silent, dreary, respectful and perfectly orderly procession which seemed to have come up out of the past—a procession which lasted certainly much longer than the other (and glorious) one. I too stayed there a long time watching them. What was Gorki to all these people? I can hardly imagine. A master? A comrade? A brother? At any rate someone who was dead. And on all these faces—even on those of the youngest children—was imprinted a sort of melancholy stupor, but also, and above all, a force, a radiance of sympathy. There was no question here of physical beauty, but how many of the poor people I watched passing by presented me a vision of something more admirable than beauty—how many I should have liked to press to my heart!

Nowhere, indeed, is contact with any and everyone so easily established, so immediately, so deeply, so warmly, as in the U.S.S.R. There are woven in a moment—sometimes a single look suffices—ties of passionate sympathy. Yes, I think that nowhere is the feeling of a common humanity so profoundly, so strongly felt as in the U.S.S.R. In spite of the difference of language, I had never anywhere felt myself so fully a comrade, a brother; and that is worth more to me than the finest scenery in the world. . . .

In the U.S.S.R. everybody knows beforehand, once and for all, that on any and every subject there can be only one opinion. And in fact everybody's mind has been so moulded and this conformity become to such a degree easy, natural and imperceptible, that I do not think any hypocrisy enters into it. Are these really the people who made the revolution? No; they are the people who profit by it. Every morning *Pravda* teaches them just what they should know and think and believe. And he who strays from the path had better beware! So that every time you talk to one Russian you feel as if you were talking to them all. Not exactly that everyone obeys a word of command; but everything is so arranged that nobody can differ from anybody else. Remember that this moulding of the spirit begins in earliest infancy. . . . This explains their extraordinary attitude of acceptance which sometimes amazes you if you are a foreigner, and a certain capacity for happiness which amazes you even more.

You are sorry for those people who stand in a queue for hours; but they think waiting perfectly natural. Their bread and vegetables and fruit seem to you bad; but there is nothing else. You find the stuffs and the articles which you are shown frightful; but there is no choice. If every point of comparison is removed, save with a past that no one regrets, you are delighted with what is offered you. What is important here is to persuade people that they are as well off as they can be until a better time comes; to persuade them that elsewhere people are *worse* off. The only way of achieving this is carefully to prevent any communication with the outside world (the world beyond the frontier, I mean). Thanks to this, the Russian workman, who has a standard of living equal or even noticeably inferior to that of a French workman, thinks himself well off, *is* better off, much better off, than a workman in France. Their happiness is made up of hope, confidence and ignorance.

It is extremely difficult for me to introduce any order into these reflections owing to the interweaving and overlapping of the problems. I am not a technician and what interests me in economic questions is their psychological repercussion. I perfectly understand the psychological reasons which render it necessary to operate in close isolation, to prevent any leakage at the frontiers; in present-day conditions, and so long as things have not improved, it is essential to the inhabitants of the U.S.S.R. that this happiness should be protected from outside influences.

We admire in the U.S.S.R. the extraordinary *élan* towards education and towards culture; but the only objects of this education are those which induce the mind to find satisfaction in its present circumstances and exclaim: *Oh! U.S.S.R.... Ave! Spes unica!* And culture is entirely directed along a single track. There is nothing disinterested in it; it is merely cumulative, and (in spite of Marxism) almost entirely lacks the critical faculty. Of course I know that what is called "self-criticism" is highly thought of. When at a distance, I admired this, and I still think it might have produced the most wonderful results, if only it had been seriously and sincerely applied. But I was soon obliged to realize that, apart from denunciations and complaints—("The canteen soup is badly cooked" or "the club reading-room badly swept")—criticism merely consists in asking oneself if this, that or the other is "in the right line." The line itself is never discussed. What is discussed is whether such-and-such a work, or gesture, or theory conforms to this sacrosanct line. And woe to him who seeks to cross it! As much criticism as you like—up to a point. Beyond that point criticism is not allowed. There are examples of this kind of thing in history.

And nothing is a greater danger to culture than such a frame of mind. I will go more fully into this later on.

The Soviet citizen is in an extraordinary state of ignorance concerning foreign countries.* More than this—he has been persuaded that everything abroad and in every department is far less prosperous than in the U.S.S.R. This illusion is cleverly fostered; for it is important that everyone, even those who are ill-satisfied, should be thankful for the régime which preserves them from worse ills. Hence a kind of *superiority complex,* of which I will give a few examples.

Every student is obliged to learn a foreign language. French has been completely abandoned. It is English, and especially German, that they are supposed to know. I expressed my surprise that they should speak them so badly; in our countries a fifth-form schoolboy knows more.

One of the students we questioned gave us the following explanation (in Russian and Jef Last translated it for us):—

"A few years ago Germany and the United States still had something to teach us on a few points. But now we have nothing more to learn from foreigners. So why should we speak their language?"*

As a matter of fact, though they do take some interest in what is happening in foreign parts, they are far more concerned about what the foreigner thinks of them. What really interests them is to know whether we admire them enough. What they are afraid of is that we should be ill-informed as to their merits. What they want from us is not information but praise.

---

* Or at least, he is only informed as to things which will encourage him in his own frame of mind.

* Confronted by our undisguised amazement, the student, it is true, added: "I understand—we all understand to-day—that such an argument is absurd. A foreign language, when it no longer serves for learning, may still serve for teaching."

Some charming little girls who gathered round me in a children's play ground (which I must say was entirely praiseworthy, like everything else that is done here for the young) harried me with questions. What they wanted to know was not whether we have children's playgrounds in France, but whether we know in France that they have such fine children's play grounds in the U.S.S.R.

The questions one is asked are often so staggering that I hesitate to report them. It will be thought that I have invented them. They smile sceptically when I say that Paris too has got a tube. Have we even got trams? Buses? . . . One of them asks (and these were not children but educated workmen) whether we had got schools too in France. Another, slightly better informed, shrugged his shoulders, "Oh yes, the French have got schools; but the children are beaten in them." He had this information on the best authority. Of course, all workers in our country are wretched; that goes without saying, for we have not yet "made the revolution." For them, outside the U.S.S.R. the reign of night begins. Apart from a few shameless capitalists, everybody else is groping in the dark.

Some educated and most "refined" young girls (in the Artek camp where only exceptional characters are admitted) were highly surprised when I mentioned Russian films and told them that *Chapaiev* and *We from Kronstadt,* had had a great success in Paris. Had they not been assured that all Russian films were banned in France? And, as those who told them so are their masters, I could see perfectly well that it was my word they doubted. The French are such leg-pullers!

In a circle of naval officers on board a battleship which had just been presented to our admiration ("This one is entirely made in the U.S.S.R."), when I went so far as to say that I was afraid that people in the Soviet Union were less well informed about what is being done in France, than the people in France about what is being done in the Soviet Union, a distinctly disapproving murmur arose: "*Pravda* gives us sufficient information about everything." And suddenly somebody in a lyrical outburst, stepping out from the group, exclaimed: "In order to describe all the new and splendid and great things that are being done in the Soviet Union, there would not be paper enough in the whole world."

THE CAPITAL OF BOLSHEVIA | THEODORE DREISER

I heard much concerning Moscow before I went there—and more since my return—among other things that it is not an attractive city; that it is unbelievably dull, half-starved, half-clothed. With the statement that it

From *Dreiser Looks at Russia* (New York, Liveright Publishing Corporation, 1928).

is not well-clothed and rather crowded, I will agree, but as for being dull,
do not believe it! I have never seen a city, either in Europe or America,
that I thought possessed more of that extreme essence of all attractiveness—
difference, and best of all, the difference that springs from color and variety.

Rambling, disjointed streets and squares! Numerous and agreeable surprises in the way of open spaces, trees, monuments, vistas. Drab, moth-eaten
and yet colorful palaces and once grand private homes, obviously the former
residences of capitalists, traders, social parasites, social blood-suckers! Oh,
and the churches! 384! Count em! With lovely green or gold or brown
or red or white or purple pineapply domes. And bell towers packed with
a most amazing variety of bells—bells that emit such a clatter of sweet,
tinny, somber, even ominous, sounds as never anywhere else issued out of
any belfry, I am sure. And cobblestones and general untidiness and casualness. (These were not introduced by the Bolshevists, as I understand it.)

And then cars, and busses, and droshkies, and trucks, and queer little
tatterdemalion wagons hauling practically nothing—(these casual, easy-
going Russians)—a barrel, a few fish, a dozen chairs, or a bathtub! And
one day an open hearse (not otherwise employed at the time and therefore,
of course, in Russia, available for any purpose), hauling a bale of hay!
I lie not! As God is my judge! These Russians, you know. And business is
business! And why not, pray? In Moscow? In Russia? A mere commonplace,
I assure you. And up in front, in some three hundred and eighty-four furs,
more or less, and seventeen hats, a comfortable, if somewhat rounded,
Russian, ambushed in whiskers and smoking what I am sure must have
been a pipeful of Mahorka, the most infamous tobacco that was ever grown.
A deadly weed, indeed, and one whiff of which almost did for me on the
snowy sidewalk to the right, where, spell-bound and open-mouthed, I stood,
an easy victim to its deadly fumes. (If I had gone under, he would merely
have added me to the bale of hay, I am sure. A little extra business!)

And then thousands of men and women in padded furs and skirts,
looking more like walking mattresses than anything else I can think of.
And fur hats or caps—shakos or woolen drums or muffs—only always on
the head—that in America would add glory and distinction to even a
Shriner band or a K. P. guard. And booths, where men in beards, boots and
sheepskins, sell pirojki (meat rolls), cigarettes, and fruits from the Crimea.
And women with shawls over their heads peddling everything from apples
to brassières. And against them the Byzantine glory of those monuments
to former rulers—palaces, and, above all, churches, lavish in gold, roofed
in cobalt and jade, or gilt and green, and making up for lack of grace of
form in fantastic design and daring ornamentation, looking not unlike
Oriental jewels in tarnished and shabby settings.

The new Russia, remember, contains 163, or 167 (I never *could* fix that
figure, even in Russia!), tribes, or peoples or small nations—call them what
you will—varying considerably in color, costume, language, physical design,

and other little details of temperament or emotion. Consider only the Turks, Turkomans, Armenians, Persians, Afghans, Mongolians, Kazaks, Kirghiz, Georgians, Usbeckistanese, Tadshikistanese—all roving about the mighty empire of the U.S.S.R. and free under the new rules to do so—and then consider that Moscow is the renowned and nominated head of the same, and you can imagine what an interest it holds for the live and dynamic tribes of this great world. Samples of them drift daily to Moscow, many of them to stay. Positively, I was sometimes so astounded by a quite uncalculated effect approaching along a thoroughfare that I was rendered speechless. "Does this man actually feel that he is all right?" "Can any one truthfully say to me that he does not feel a—ah, well, slightly in the public eye?" They can, and would. Except for yourself, new to this amazing world, he or she attracts no attention. In short, I do now aver that I could put a tin saucepan on my head, a pair of Dutch wooden shoes on my feet, wrap a Navajo blanket or a bed quilt or mattress around my body, strap it all on with a leather belt, and sally forth and attract not so much attention as I would should I appear in a silk hat and evening clothes. It is Russia. It is U.S.S.R. It is that amazing medley of nations or tribes that have now joined in one common bond and are on the march to a better day.

Another thing concerning Moscow—they always tell you that the over-crowding there is since the war, or, more accurately, since Moscow was once again made the seat of government by the Bolsheviks. But this is not true. The housing problem was acute in 1902 and 1907, over ten per cent of the dwelling places of the poor being underground then. The city has grown rapidly since 1870, and is growing rapidly now, and although much is made of the fact that to-day two or more persons occupy one room, in 1907 there were more than 10,000 domiciles with four occupants to each room, and representing one-fourth of the population. Yet to-day, if you speak of two or more occupants to a room, the Communists themselves apologize. They do not know the history of their own capital.

And another curious thing in connection with the city is this. It has, after a fashion, a Communist history not unlike that which has unrolled itself since the 1917 revolution. It is a fact that about the end of the fifteenth century, and in order to give Moscow power and authority, its dominant princes transported to it and to neighboring cities in their domain—Vladimir, for one, not more than a hundred miles away—no fewer than 18,000 of the richest Novgorod merchant families and themselves, like the Communists of to-day, took over the entire trade of the city. I mentioned this to Kalinin, the Soviet President, and to Tchicherin, the Foreign Minister, but they had never heard of it.

But in the main, my general impression of Moscow, sleighing and walking here and there, was that it was in a comparatively clean and healthy, and even vigorous state. The streets are cobble-stoned, and if the snow has melted are muddy. But between November first and April first, it has not melted; more likely, it has worn away, been powdered and blown heaven knows where, so that more snow has to be hauled (and is) and thrown upon them in order to provide the necessary bedding for the sleighs. During all this long winter season Moscow has a whitey freshness against which the ocher and gray and white buildings outline themselves with an appealing softness, which is only emphasized by the reds, greens, blues, yellows, browns, and glistening gilts of the pineapple-shaped domes of the churches. True, the façades are often mildewed and chipped; the little iron porches so common all over Russia are rusted and the woodwork not generally repainted. And the fine old palaces, museums, houses of once wealthy merchants, are now turned into libraries, art galleries, memorials, hospitals, clinics. And there are no dashing carriages, no splendid motor cars. There is no show, no luxury. You wander here and there, and you will see thousands who are comparatively poorly dressed to ten—at most a hundred —who are well-dressed. And yet, generally speaking, a sense of well-being— none of that haunting sense of poverty or complete defeat that so distresses one in western Europe and America. It is not to be found.

Yet in Moscow there is poverty. There are beggars in the streets now as there were before the proletariat took charge. Plenty of them! But Lord, how picturesque! The multi-colored and voluminous rags of them! I certainly have seen Joseph's coat of many colors, only in these instances so threadbare and dirty. But covering, in the main, people not thin but stout, hence not truly emaciated by want, rather suggesting creatures who at bottom are not as much put upon as you might fear. For indeed their state is not such that they would starve in case you did not give them anything. On the contrary, as you can readily prove for yourself if you wish, they are begging because it is easier to collect an income that way than to go to the government dole agencies and prove that they have no (as we say) "visible means of support"—(What the hang is a "visible support," anyway?)—and so obtain the allotted dole for "down-and-outs"; i.e., fifteen rubles a month and a place to sleep. For that probably involves a return of some sort—a little labor or an effort to find it—whereas begging merely presupposes standing in the streets in the cold and snow, an obligation much less difficult for a Russian than it would be for you, you may be sure.

And there are unemployed. It is claimed that these consist mainly of peasants who have migrated to the towns from the country and office employees who have been discharged as a result of reduction of office staffs in the State and administration departments in connection with the effort to reduce the cost of administration.

But, as I have said, the well-dressed persons, though few, are there also. And while the old palaces and buildings are stained and worn, there are newer things that speak of a brighter day. For the new, if gray and somewhat hygienic, General Post & Telegraph Building is long and high and wide and suggests in all its features the latest details of a Chicago commercial structure (not a skyscraper), and probably is borrowed in spirit from the Great Lake city which Russia so much admires. (If there is one would-be Chicago in Russia, there are nine! Chita, Kharkov, Stalin, Novo-Sibirsk, Baku, Vladikafkaz, Perm, a long company!) Also there is the mighty pile that houses *Izvestia,* the official government's newspaper mouth-piece—the great factory in which the world's news is doctored and sent out sufficiently communized for local consumption. And then many great new warehouses or government wholesale emporiums which house all that is nationally to be had at the moment of hemp, grain, tea, sugar, groceries, hardware, tallow, dry goods, drugs, skins, timber, wool, iron, or the manu-factured products of such things.

Before the revolution, these same bazaars, banks, wholesale houses and what not else were in private hands, and I am told that the Kitai Gorod, or business heart of the city, was as lively a mart as one would wish to see. It had an exchange with twelve hundred brokers—now no more, of course—and the printing office of the Synod of the Greek Orthodox Church, now a pale memory of its former self. Yet to-day, being a Government trading station, the region is lively enough. It covers 121 acres north of the Red Square, one side of which it forms. This *Red Square,* by the way, dates from pre-Bolshevik days—not post. During my struggles for official informa-tion I was constantly running into some part of it, to sit with some Communist chief whose various official rooms were as extensive as those of a hotel. You fancy, perhaps, that these poor Bolsheviks know nothing of business, that there can be no commercial zest unless some one is getting something out of it. Well, dear reader, whether a man can or cannot acquire wealth seems to be neither here nor there when it comes to the functioning of the trader mood. Once a trader, always a trader, money or no money! And so, in the great wholesale houses or centers of the coöpera-tive or the Government enterprises, what a busy and purely commercial sight! New, well-lighted and furnished buildings, with all of those up-to-the-minute devices which you would expect to find in any well-equipped wholesale enterprise—telephones, call bells, speaking tubes, elevators, comp-tometers, cash registers, and the booths and packets, books and safes and what not which go with a lively commercial exchange. And always I was dumbfounded by the stocks on hand, the number of clerks hurrying to and fro, the visiting traders, the groups of conferring officials; the piles of furs, clothes, grains, metals, groceries, spread upon long, well-made tables, about which would be gathered Government buyers and—so odd when you think of it—Government sellers. And as for their facial expres-sions, I personally would never have guessed that these were individuals who were not expecting to make a profit out of their labors. The sight brought home to one the feeling that either the Communist theory could not be all wrong or that in some secret way the non-profit, non-trade idea was being circumvented. For most certainly there is trade, and lots of it.

And a lively interest in it on the part of thousands. Read me that riddle, if you can!

I was likewise astonished by the size of some of the mills in Moscow. But from the fifteenth century on, the villages around Moscow were renowned for the variety of small industries which they carried on. The first large manufactories in cotton and woolen fabrics, china, silk, and glass in Great Russia were established at Moscow in the seventeenth or eighteenth century. After 1830, in consequence of a protective tariff, the manufactories in the province of Moscow increased rapidly in number, and before the war it had become the principal manufacturing city in the empire. To-day it is not so much that, but even now there is much industry, and you encounter belching chimneys and great workingmen's quarters, mostly new, in many parts of the city.

The famous Tverskaya (through which the Czar used to enter the city and which runs, so they say, through to Leningrad) is like the shopping street of a small town. It boasts no high buildings, no brilliant shop windows. Now and then, interiorly, you will be amazed by the color, richness, order and repletion of the stocks offered by some of the Government or coöperative food stores. Gray Molossal caviar; Crimean grapes, sweet as honey and big as plums; pears, apples, plums, oranges, pomegranates, tangerines, figs. And wines, brandies, liquors and vodka. And best of all, the marvelous champagne of the Caucasus, and not nearly as expensive even now as pre-war champagne in America. I heard of famine in Russia (in Germany before going to Russia), but looking in these Moscow stores, as well as in other stores throughout Russia, tended to dispel the idea. There might be undernourishment in some quarters for lack of means, but no real necessity for famine anywhere, unless the Government should prove incompetent or indifferent to its own theories of distribution.

And more, you see long lines of buyers in the stores. And perhaps wonder at this. One explanation is that many persons have two or three jobs. Also you must consider the fact that most of the usual normal expenses are lifted from the shoulders of the worker. He pays very little rent, gets his entertainment free or at reduced prices, can be treated free in a hospital if he is sick, and is insured against nearly every emergency. Therefore, he has money to spend in this fashion if he desires to do so.

Apart from this, and looking at the city in general, you come upon occasional patches of consistent grandeur which scarcely suggests poverty, depression, or indeed anything even remotely connected with the same. For instance, there is the Kremlin (or Kreml, as they call it in Russia)—-a mighty, walled-in block of buildings which until the revolution were occupied by the Boyar aristocracy, but since then house the Communist leaders and their principal officials. But what a world! Above a tall, thick, ruddy wall—on one side facing the Moscow River, on others the Red Square and one of Moscow's parks—bloom such flowers of towers and spires and domes, such princely roofs and cornices as Aladdin himself might have conjured out of his lamp. Indeed, the most Oriental scene in Europe, and a most arresting thing to dream over, leaning against a parapet of one of the Moscow River bridges, in sun or shadow.

To the north of this Kremlin is the Red Square, called so, as I have said, long before the days of Bolsheviks, however appropriate it may seem now. Against its southern border, formed by the north wall of the Kremlin, stands the comparatively humble tomb of Lenin, to which nightly march the faithful, almost a thousand strong, to view his body. Already by the ordinary Russian mind he has been canonized. And I was told by many that his embalmed corpse—quite the same in looks to-day as the day he died—is enmeshed in superstition. So long as he is there, so long as he does not change, Communism is safe and the new Russia will prosper. But—whisper—if he fades or is destroyed, ah, then comes the great, sad change—the end of his kindly dream.

Mysticism? Thy name is Slav.

An old-time rostrum as well as execution block, where princely decrees were read and executions performed, still stands in the center of this square—almost opposite Lenin's tomb. (It is still usable, never fear, and looks ominous enough!) And beyond that, again to the north (the side opposite that of the Kremlin wall), and for almost the entire length of the Square (an oblong, really), the white front of an enormous Government department store, "Goom," literally swarming by day with customers. At the west end is a rather historical museum, with arches underneath for the east and west traffic of the city. But just outside that, a little, gaudy, blue and white and gold shrine, that of the Iberian Virgin, very efficacious for all human ills, and swarming like a bee-hive with mystic Russians crossing themselves, kissing images and Bibles, and mumbling the most reverential of prayers; yet opposite this same shrine again, where all of the mystical worshipers may see and read, if they will, flaring from the wall of the State Finance Department the most daring of all modern announcements: "Religion is the Opiate of the People." If it were left to me, I would alter this to read "Dogmatic Religion is the Opiate of the People."

At the east end of this same Red Square the almost incredible Church of St. Basil (or, as the Russians know it, that of Vassili Blajenoi), pineapple-shaped domes without, gorgeously and yet harmoniously colored, and within lavishly decorated with fretted brass and silver and gold. (Where and when and why should men and women have worked so patiently and intricately, and uselessly, really?) All of the upper part of this church, once a great religious chamber, is now a museum of art. But below are some shrines left intact, and Russians (always the older ones, you will note), smack-smacking with their lips the feet of carved or painted saints, or of Christ or the Virgin, each new pair of lips most unsanitarily laid where but a moment before another pair rested. (Oh, germs! Diseases! Plagues! Contagions!)

But over all, as you look up from the Square, the domes and minarets and towers and spires of the Kremlin—with their flashing double crosses and golden eagles and crescents—of churches and monasteries and shrines built by princes and czars within the Kreml itself, where now are all the irreligious Bolsheviks! And jackdaws! The one flourishing and appropriately temperamental bird of all Russia—as fat, easy, genial and apparently meditative and social as are all Russians. Jackdaws swirling or sitting in rows. Or nudging each other off topmost pinnacles. And below them, their shadows on the ground, trudging Russians. And droshkies or sleighs. And trucks and cars and autos. The new and the old. One could not fail of interest in the Red Square. One can never forget it, really. . . .

Yet Moscow, madly differentiated as it may be in one sense and another, is undeniably a living city, a going concern, as it were. You may feel at times as though life were really topsy-turvy, all askew. For in Moscow it is the sense of tragedy for so many who formerly were here coupled with a form of social relief for those who remain and—who left to themselves might never have been able to achieve it—that gives to the city, and to it more than any other city in Russia, a color and strangeness, which are as fascinating as they are grim. Everything goes. Everything comes. Riches are out. Plethora is out. All those purely material distinctions which so irk or gratify one in this our western world completely swept away. You stare. You will not say that you are bored, for you are not. It is certainly something new, strange, vital, and, for my part, I hope enduring.

MINGLING WITH THE MASSES | LIAM O'FLAHERTY

For five days, comrade Levit accompanied me from morning until night. During that time, I grew extremely fond of him. It was impossible to do otherwise. He was such a delightful fellow. It seemed impossible to deprive him of his good temper. No service seemed too great to demand of him. His enthusiasm for life and his hope for the future, his steadfast belief in the Communist God and his exuberance gave me a fresh grip on reality, which the emptiness of a literary life in Western Europe (where God is dead) had made a faded dream. Yet he bored me to tears. I determined to get rid of him, lest my boredom should make me insolent and unmannerly towards him, who was so kind.

And I was seeing nothing of what I wanted to see, because of the sedulous care with which he convoyed me. He carried me along in such a hurry that I was blind and deaf to my surroundings. I saw churches, theatres, newspaper offices, clubs and crèches which merely bewildered me without teach-

From Liam O'Flaherty, *I Went to Russia* (London, Jonathan Cape, Ltd., 1931).

ing me anything. Even a literary gathering, to which we went, seems to me at this moment nothing more than a prolonged shout.

On the fifth day I escaped. Another comrade and scholar whom I met at the Bureau offered to introduce me to an Englishwoman who had married a prominent Russian official. This comrade also specialized in English literature and as his period almost touched that of comrade Levit there was a certain rivalry between them. Comrade Kashkin was a Slavic Russian. He had a red head and he had fought in the army, where he received a wound which injured his nervous system considerably. For that reason, perhaps, he was more sane than most of his compatriots and not in the least fanatical. Of course he was an ardent Communist but being a highly educated man, belonging to a family that had been civilized before the revolution, his views on life were by no means violent.

Tall and slim, with a freckled face and a subdued voice, it was hard to differentiate between him and an intelligent English schoolboy in manners. But he was exceedingly touchy and could not brook argument, owing, apparently, to his wounds. If one did not argue with him he was very charming; but then it is impossible to live in Russia without argument. Life is so vital there and everything is so new and in such a volcanic state that the simplest discussion becomes an argument to the death.

Indeed, comrade Kashkin disapproved of me; so that we began to argue at once on our way to meet the Englishwoman. When we got on a tramcar, he said to me:

"Have you read much of our new Soviet literature?"

"Not very much," I said. "A little of Pilniak and of Babel and a few other writers whose names I cannot remember."

He shrugged his shoulders and said these writers were not the best.

"Oh!" I cried, eager to please him. "I have read some of a book by a writer called Sholohov in a French translation. It was serialised in *L'Humanité*. I thought it was really first-rate."

Comrade Kashkin got furious at once.

"But why?" he cried irritably. "It is a popular book, but there are others much better. Sholohov is not an intellectual."

"But that's why I like his work," I said. "It's so fresh. It smells of the earth. He knows his art. It's vital and genuine and simple."

"But there is no philosophic depth in it. It's raw."

"But isn't freshness what we want? We have had enough of pretentious philosophies. We want power and natural beauty to regenerate literature. There are skilled craftsmen by the thousand in most European countries, but they are only echoes of what has been written before, critics posing as creative artists."

"You are an anarchist," he cried angrily. "And for that reason you like blood and thunder, raw life."

"Why! Bless my soul," I cried, equally angry, "you speak like the most bourgeois English intellectual. I expected to find a love of life among Soviet literary people, but you are just as bad as Western European intellectuals, who only know of life what they have read of it. That's why I like Sholohov because he seems to me to have lived the life of which he writes, to revel in it and to put it on paper exactly as he found it, without any theories as to how it should be."

"But that's not the point," he cried. "A writer must be disciplined and educated. He must have culture."

"I grant you that it is better if he has culture and it is an axiom that no writer can write anything intelligible or worth while without being disciplined, but nine intellectuals out of ten in Paris, London or Berlin have more culture than Shakespeare, as far as accumulated knowledge of books is concerned. Yet ten thousand of them combined could not write one scene of *Hamlet*. For God's sake don't tell me that what I am beginning to suspect is true."

"What is that?"

"That in Soviet Russia, Communist intellectuals are suffering from a most virulent inferiority complex, which manifests itself in trying to imitate the decadent writers of Western Europe, all the wordy subtlety that has no guts, no blood, no semen."

"You are utterly ridiculous. We are trying to raise the level of civilization, trying to discipline the uncultured writers that are taking to literature, trying to tone down their rawness. . . ."

"Tripe," I cried. "That is the worst form of romanticism. A writer can only express the life he sees around him."

He aggravated me so much, more by his manner than by his ideas, which were probably better than mine, that I almost quarrelled violently with him. For the latter part of the journey we lapsed into an exhausted silence. We arrived at the flat occupied by the English wife of the important Soviet dignitary and I was deeply impressed by its simplicity. It was similar to a Council flat in London. I was still more impressed by the Englishwoman herself. In spite of many years' residence in Soviet Russia she had retained every atom of her British middle-class solidity. It was obvious that she despised Russia and the Russians, was bored with Communism and hankered for London. From her conversation and her attitude towards things, I gathered that she was mildly socialistic and I wondered how she had got herself into her present position. But on consideration, I understood it.

After the World War, a section of the middle-class experienced an aching desire for some religion that would act as an antidote to the depression produced by the war; some vital and virile religion, different from the prevalent Christianity, which has grown unsexed and limp through old age. Those deplorable young men who shirked the war, giving their conscience as an excuse, found in socialism a justification for their lack of courage. Women of no great beauty also found in socialism a justification for forming with working men temporary associations, which they were unable to make among men of their own class, owing to the small numbers of the latter; the majority being slaughtered. But all these middle-class people, both male and female, were not really socialist or revolutionary. They were merely disgruntled and dissatisfied. They remained British and Imperialist to the core, although for the moment the Empire failed to satisfy their needs. To them the Russian Revolution came as a gift from God; but as the Revolution developed they began to see its real nature, that it was not a sentimental attempt to create an earthly paradise of free love and artistic communes, but a savage attempt by enormous masses of peasants to get bread and culture. Revolted by this spectacle, they drew back. Some returned to their Union Jacks. Others joined the British Labour Party and made it respectable. The unfortunate few who had committed themselves irrevocably became bitter.

In conversation with this Englishwoman, my distraught nerves forced me to become as violent in support of the Russians as I had been prone to disparage their efforts in conversation with Kashkin.

"What's the good of it all?" she cried. "This Five Year Plan won't make the world any more interesting. It will just give the Russians motor cars and newspapers and chewing gum, just as people have in America. Their ambition is to create a new America in Russia, only worse. There's nothing new here."

She really terrified me; for although I contradicted everything she said, I felt that she spoke the truth. And although I was trying to persuade myself that I had more in common with the Russian Bolsheviks than with her, my reason told me that I was just as convinced as she was that acquisitive lust rather than idealism was the driving power behind Russia's energy. I left her house in a state of acute depression. I got rid of Kashkin and swore that I was finished with Russian intellectuals. They merely irritated me without teaching me anything of what I wanted to know.

And yet ... what did I want to know? Was there anything to know? Had anything dealing with social relationships been discovered here fundamentally different from what had already been discovered in Europe and America? For another fortnight I wandered about trying to discover it and failed. Nowhere was I able to find a logical attitude towards the universe as one finds in France, the calm judgment and the sound social morality which distinguishes the English, the love of labor and the meticulous exactitude which have made the Germans such unerring craftsmen and designers. Everywhere I found the intellectual wreck of the old Russian grandeur, a nervous, pulsating, worried, unstable mass of human beings, merely held together by terror of the enemies that surrounded them and by the masses that pushed them from the rear, by hunger, by lack of all the necessities of life, by a mystical frenzy which envisaged the conquest of the world.

I had come like a fool to write *Lies About Russia,* foolishly believing that

wise men had gone before me, bringing back true tales of a land where
everything was new. Both those who denounced the Soviets and those who
praised them had come back with tales that everything was new and different. Yet I found everything the same; merely a difference produced by
climate and locality and racial habits.

They tried to persuade me to visit the south, the Ukraine, the Caucasus,
the new cities that were springing up on the Socialist plan, the collective
farms. But I stayed in Moscow, for I am more concerned with spiritual
results than with material causes. Innovations do not begin in the villages,
or in the provinces, where they are certain to meet with greater opposition
than in the capital, to which all the intelligent flock in order to be near
the center of culture. In the capital I must stay, in order to understand the
Soviet mind, in order to understand the lives and the aspirations of the
proletarian masses, upon whom this Revolution is based.

Towards that end, I hid myself from all my intellectual friends and went
among the masses, as the Communists say; but as I did not speak the language of the country, I was severely handicapped. I learned the utter idiocy
of those ladies and gentlemen, who attempted to write books, giving an
exact description of the institutions, the life and the ambitions of countries
as vast as Russia, after a nodding acquaintance; like the foreign gentleman
in *Pickwick Papers*. In a country as completely foreign as Russia, the mind
of the visiting stranger is so confused by the mass of impressions that continually pour in upon it that it is incapable of seeing anything in a normal
light. However, I avoided examining or judging individual things. I sought
to get a general impression of the general life, and in that manner I succeeded in acclimatizing myself to such an extent that I felt comparatively
at home. I felt bored, excited, discontented, eager for change, enthusiastic,
depressed, argumentative, ferocious, bigoted, fanatical, hungry, bitten by
bed bugs, convinced that Europe was preparing war against me, convinced
that a world revolution was imminent, that the Soviets were going to fail,
that the Five Year Plan was going to be a magnificent success, that it would
end in disaster, that socialism was going to be produced in a few years, that
it would never materialize, that there were spies at every street corner, that
I might be taken out at any moment and shot, that I might take out somebody at any moment and shoot him. . . . In a word, I assumed the psychology
of the Russian masses. I went to bed wherever I found myself at three o'clock
in the morning. I slept in old monasteries, in communal lodging houses, in
new flats on the American plan, in rooms of old houses that had once been
clubs, palaces and town houses of the gentry. I met old nuns earning their
living gathering firewood, peeling potatoes in kitchens, begging at street
corners. I met ex-priests that were lousy and degenerate, also begging. I met
couples that were divorced and still lived together owing to the housing
shortage. I met men with two or more wives and women with two or more
husbands. I swam naked in the river with women who wore bathing suits.

I rowed on the river with soldiers, sailors, male and female factory workers. I played the accordion at dances in private rooms and at factory outings. I went on a binge with an ex-prince, who had become a journalist, with a popular Soviet novelist who had been a Cossack, with a Kulak, with cab drivers, with odds and ends of humanity to be met in public houses and at street corners. I stood about kiosks drinking lemonade. I queued up for cigarettes for hours. I hung around the market and mingled with the gypsies, peasants, pick-pockets, speculators. I hung around the hotels at night and mingled with foreign capitalists and engineers and gawky Americans who were making scientific examination for their University theses of the Russian theatre, the Russian school system, the Russian prison system. I picked up girls in the streets, by the same method as in other countries. I kept cab drivers for days at a time, in the same manner as Irishmen used to do in Dublin before the war. I went to the intellectual cinemas, with Russians who shed tears, sang, cheered and shouted "Down with the bourgeois assassins" when Lenin or the other Communist hierarchs were shown on the screen. I went to common cinemas with the masses, where Charles Chaplin, Fatty Arbuckle, cowboys and wild west criminals sent the masses into hysterics with delight and little children kept cheering when the hero rescued the heroine, or threatened to wreck the screen when the villain had the hero in a corner, exactly as they do in the slum cinemas of Dublin, London, New York, Shanghai, Jerusalem or Addis Abbaba. I went to the Circus where the masses roared applause for the acrobats, the sword swallowers and the clowns that delight audiences in the other cities I have mentioned. There they drank light beer and ate buns between the acts, as they do at Collins' or the Holborn Empire in London. I went once to an intellectual theatre and fell asleep during a marvellous play executed by Georgians. I went to a trotting race meeting and lost five races, before I received the information that they were all squared, as in European countries, where racing is not properly controlled. I attended football matches and played football on waste plots with workmen who were enjoying their fifth day holiday. I forgot the day of the week and the day of the month and only stumbled by chance one Sunday into a church where the faithful were hearing Mass in the old style. Another day I visited the atheistic museum, where young people were taught in the new style that Mass was a delusion and a humbug. I frequented another church that had been turned into a library of foreign literature and periodicals, in order to keep in touch with English racing and cricket. Sometimes I had breakfast at four in the afternoon and lunch at three o'clock in the morning. I ate sturgeon, caviare, boeuf Strogonov and borsch. I got drunk on vodka, Napareouli, beer and French brandy. I did physical jerks and Russian dances with bands of workers in the public parks. I went to the Zoo and to a wedding and to a funeral. In other words, I lived completely the life of a knock-about and enjoyed myself and had practically the same experiences as a knock-about in London, Dublin, New York, Jerusalem or Addis Abbaba. I found that humanity in Russia was essentially the same as in any other country, that people had the same wants, the same ambitions, the same virtues and the same vices. The same things and the same types irritated me as at home. I was enthused by the same splendid types, generous, simple, courteous, amusing, courageous, industrious, honest, trustworthy types as one finds at home and in every other country in the world. I found also mean, scavenging, envious scoundrels. I found the same insufferable arrogance in the young.

I found that Moscow and, as a corollary, the whole of Russia was an enlargement of the ship on which I journeyed from London to Leningrad; the same ludicrous evangelistic Communism on the surface and the same greedy, ambitious, admirable human nature beneath. The only difference between the ship and Moscow was that there were fewer cranks, fanatical Jews and useless scoundrels on the ship than in Moscow.

Anything new? Just one, which is not really new, but a recurring phenomenon in man's history: NEW TOOLS APPLIED TO VIRGIN SOIL.

SEEING THE SIGHTS | *E. E. CUMMINGS*

lunch (underground)at circa 2 roubles per head
    fair soup
    sweetly dreadful "macaroni" and unmeat(the latter could not be cut
      either by me or by mentor:when hammered for several minutes it split)
    fearful perfume-beverage
    not quite right dessert
a truly magnificent stink ("they should give clothespins here" says Virgil, nipping his nose)being the one and only redeeming feature of this otherwise merely Very Bad Childs'. "Odear, I must go back to the hotel and take a pill—my stomach isn't what it used to be:afraid I gave you a very bad introduction to Moscow;you shouldn't have been taken here—well just to make up for this,I'll show you Lenin's mausoleum"

Seeing The Sights
    the Slogan Of Slogans
        itself disconcertingly illpresented , occurs near an enticing gate via
        which we're bumped by a most wonderfully refreshing lump of nearly
        comradeless space:on one edge of this lump sits
    L's M
        a rigid pyramidal composition of blocks;an impurely mathematical

game of edges:not quite cruelly a cubic cerebration—equally glamour-
less and emphatic,withal childish . . . perhaps the architectural equivalent for "boo!—I scared you that time!" (hard by are buried martyrs)
the lump ends at Something Fabulous
a frenzy of writhing hues—clusteringly not possible whirls together
grinding into one savage squirtlike ecstasy:a crazed Thinglike dream
solemnly shouting out of timespace,a gesture fatal,acrobatic (goring
tomorrow's lunge with bright beyondness of yesterday)—utterly a Self,
catastrophic;distinct,unearthly and without fear.

The tearing of mere me and this miracle from each other demands effort
on part of failing benevolence("yes,it's impressive—but you should see the
inside , which has been turned into a Revolutionary Museum:really I must
get back to the hotel,please don't desert me now;I wonder if I've been
poisoned—Odear,you can look at that any time:there are so many much
more important things")who increasingly resembles a walking corpse. If
combining the best (I murmur)elements of barberpole and pineapple be
opium , more power to it. We cringes , palm over belly. "Where can I send
a telegram?" I wonder;inconsiderately adding "—to my wife." He starts:
staggers "O yes—of course:a devoted husband . . ." "From the hotel?" I
devotedly persist. "Yes , but the clerk wouldn't know how much to charge—
you'd better go directly to the postoffice just around the corner;there's a
charming woman who speaks French and German and (I think)a little English—ow!—well,we're almost back,thank Heaven!" "Don't be uneasy;I shall
not inform the republic of your heresy" I promise:at which Virgil recovers
sufficiently to gasp "what is that proverb . . . the devil is sick,the devil a monk
—Odear!" "Now you're talking:incidentally,has the proletariat any particular commerce with psychology?" "Psychology? Why,don't you know
Pavlov's work? One of the monumental—" "Or as Pope Watson has it,you
ring a snake and show your bell a child. But what of Our Lord Sigmund
Freud?" "Odear,are you one of those people? You aren't going to analyse
me,are you? Please!"

"charming woman" (50ish)speaks only Russian and German , latter to such
an extent that decide I'll dilate my daily wrestlings with yah nyeh hahchoo.
Purely for practice , lisp in numbers to a grinning comrade at keycounter;
heartened,await lift and further progress. Hereupon occurs a curious
phenomenon:many obviously native citizens are also expecting the elevator
—in fact,there's a small multitude—but when that far from mighty machine
arrives,its deus very rudely excludes a number of worthy compatriots while,
very politely,accepting the mere foreigner myself (who was lurking on the
outskirts and doesn't believe that the last shall be first;just a good democrat).
Sanctuary,not overample,sufficiently sunlit,appears as haven of refuge—but
knock:Sibyl's himself again, wants me to help him call on 2 "young people"

upstairs ... something about having received a note from them,impos-
sibility of their lunching with him;must arrange something. We climb(on
foot,at my request)flights of less and less marble-or-something-or-marble and
exhaustedly arrive before an open door through which the birds have flown.
On foot (by request)we descend to the foyer's cigarettecounter—and vaguely
I observe an adolescent pair of uncouths emanating awkwardly nonhappi-
ness. "You are being signalled" I hint. "Odear,there they are!" (he rushes
forward:instantly parts of the pair begin fallingdown revealing a 3rd uncouth;who's also full of bundles—a livid pigmy with a sharp face,which
upon making my acquaintance almost swallows its cigarette)"we were just
looking for you!" It seems that the pair,pimply American stripling embarrassed in a Russian blouse and his somewhat starved decidedly Radcliffe help-
mate,are on the verge of deserting the Hotel Metropole for a less sumptuous
life. I gather that the livid is assisting. Blouse hasn't enough valuta to patronize "fleet" of Ford taxis outside—the Metropole's modest contribution to
proletarian cause;you,capitalist,pay in advance at the desk—and unattached
taxis are scarcer than hen's teeth and,in short,death is stingless. But Virgil
will have none of that—cheerfully he shoulders bundles(bidding me do
likewise):merrily our quintet attains the sidewalk;blithely the blouse departs
in search of conveyance,gaily his spouse spurns further aid and every cloud
has a silver lining (and the 3rd uncouth bows to the bottom of a ruined
raincoat and waves courtierlike a sweatsoiled sombrero,pronouncing in
Queen's English the word Tomorrow). "They're awfully nice—her husband
teaches English:of course you've read his distinguished father , whom the
Russians consider one of America's great writers although you may not—
that little man helping them is an authority on military tactics" then,beam-
ing upon my greatly perplexed self "three good Cantabrigians should meet
today. Come!"

long gently rising street. A priest passes,motheaten—Virgil gloats "they're
few and far between,now:O not at all,that persecution story is ridiculous
my dear fellow;the point is,anyone who still wants to serve The Lord can
do so,but The Lord's servant must have a useful occupation or starve;people
have awakened to the fact that religion is opium:in a worker's republic
there's no place for parasites ... excuse me." Halting,peeps cautiously into
his shirt;resumes "a false alarm. Yes,religion is inextricably bound up with
the family;and since the safety of the state depends on the abolition of the
family,religion must go. Of course it's hard for some of us who've been
educated according to bourgeois traditions;but if we're intelligent we see
that there's no other way—not that I miss my religion,quite the contrary.
Odear,you really must stay at least six months;there are so many things to
understand,so many thrilling aspects of this new world—" we enter a gloom-
ful dwelling. "I admire Mary more than any girl I've ever met" Virgil states
enthusiastically. "—Mary?" "Yes indeed,a splendid person—notice this

hotel" (as he spoke,a mean reek of rancid food drifted over us)"how I love it! In this hotel I have lived longer than in any other. Yes. I feel about it almost as a wandering mariner feels about his beloved home——not really,of course; my own bourgeois tendencies are pretty well stifled,thank—well,here we are." Corridor pitchdark:glimpse of several buxom nonmen,attired as maids,respectfully who recoil as Virgil gropes toward something . . . knocks. Crack of light—sharp hysterical squeal "you can't come in! You can't!"— tiny door opens—"you mustn't! The room's in such a mess!" and I'm bowing to a worn doll with naked emaciated arms,vast feet,sunken eyes,mop of colourless hair, crazed jumpy laugh,and 2 stockingless laths protruding from ultraabbreviated kiddiefrock.

"Sitdownsitdownsitdownsitdown" the 3rd good Cantabrigian's mangled voice chatters foolishly "can you imagine it,can you imagine what she's done now?the bitch!"

"Mary!" admonishes Virgil,with mock gravity "is that the way to refer to your female progenitor?"

"she is,she is;mother is a bitch—excuse me,I suppose I shouldn't be so frank before a guest . . ."

"what has mother done now?" the benefactor of benefactors inquires with a helpful smile.

"Done? What has she done? She's gotten what she calls pneumonia! That's the latest excuse."

"Perhaps you ought to explain the circumstances" says mentor "I'm sure our guest will be interested."

"Very much" I corroborate.

"Well you see" (twisting her gnarled skinnyness)"I was once a fool—do you understand? No? He doesn't understand!"

"you mean that you got married" the Sibyl slyly interprets.

"Married. Yes. How lovely. I married a man. Nice pretty ceremony. You know. Flowers! Bless you my children and all that sort of nonsense—well,he wasn't a man because he was a beast,a beast!"

"you don't spare your enemies , Mary" our guardian angel comments admiringly.

"Why should I? They don't spare me! Do they? You know me;do they?"

"you're going to win , my dear" encourages the spinner "I'm sure of that."

"I'll win" the doll's voice snapped,to open in a sob "—hun! Yes,I'll win. —Well,ten years ago I was born. Do you know what that means? I became a communist. And I wanted to come to Soviet Russia where a child can grow up to be free;and the beast went to a judge,to the courts of the fair state of Ohio , and the old judge made a great speech giving what he called my Husband the custody of the child—on what grounds? On what grounds do you suppose?—Tell him on what grounds!"

"You tell him" invites benevolence.

"On . . . the . . . grounds . . ." (with a deeply gradual writhe beginning in empty eyes and ending in famished hips)"That A Woman Who Puts Her Political Ideas Before Her Family Is Unfit To Be A Mother. HAHAHAHA HA!"—the sawdust body exploded in paroxysms of coughing ; a snapshot , stuck in mirroredge , slips slightly.

"There is really something unique about the cruelty of what millions call Justice" mentor murmured. A microscopic room quivered with coughing; tranquilly from flimsy wall glared at the smallest bed one fatfaced child . . . "There there,dear Mary:you'll win!"(and coughing subsides).

"So the question was,how to get him here—I asked all my friends,but none of them could manage it—"

"she asked even me" giggles angel,making a wry face "but I somehow couldn't see myself successfully abducting a baby boy from the bosom of his bourgeois family and placing him in the hands of his communist mother in Moscow!—just an old bachelor."

"Bless you,dear friend,for your counsel" the puppet whimpered "if it hadn't been for such encouragement . . . well,finally my mother agreed to do it—My Mother—haha! At the last moment,I got a cable from her,saying my child can't be moved because he's got to have an appendicitis operation! Can you imagine? Can you?—she had one breast cut off for cancer and thought nothing of it;but just because a kid has a scratch on his belly he's got to stay quiet for three weeks! Ugh! —And now she's delayed it a second time,to give herself what she calls A close call . . . Pneumonia! What will that creature do next?"

"you must fight on"cooed benevolence"and you're a great little fighter. I often wonder,Mary,where you got your own fighting spirit."

"Not from her!" the marionette snarled "mother has no strength of character:mother and father never got on since I can remember,but she keeps going back to him—why mother couldn't live without him" words skidding in how much more contempt than a human voice possibly could extrude"—no,really."

"I believe it" said I,seriously.

"Wonderful girl . . . simply extraordinary . . . a perfect trump" Virgil mused "when I think of her I'm almost proud of Cambridge." We turn a corner; embark upon a long muddy treeful boulevard,clogged with overhurrying nonmen and men. "This is one of our main streets,it divides the inner Moscow from the outer—very much like the Ring in Vienna,if you know Vienna . . . lovely tranquil town:but of course I prefer Moscow." "The police were charging when I was in Wien" our hero gently remarks "and the horses were trying not to step on women;and beggars stood just inside cafés, never moving,with holes in their faces for eyes;and it rained a great deal." "Really?" he surveyed me with a mixture of respect and alarm "you were there during the rioting? They smashed the Bristol,didn't they?" "It had been mended when I arrived. O well,I imagine Russia was a most interesting place during the revolution . . ." "You mean that what you've seen so far doesn't interest you?" "I didn't mean that. I did mean,how different something moving is from something won." "O but nothing's really won—that is,of course the revolution's victorious and the future of humanity firmly established,but Russia is still fighting,you know;her triumph can't possibly be complete until the rest of the world comes to its senses,until the proletariat asserts its rights everywhere and capitalism bows its bloody head" (he sighed;adding)"how nice the colour is:do you see that girl with her red scarf? It means she's a young communist . . . there are thousands of fine healthy lassies like her." "Where are we going,if I may ask?" "Why I thought I'd take you to see the president of the Writers' Club:a charming person;you'll like him particularly because he speaks French—not that I don't wish I could speak French well myself;however,I take comfort in the fact that I've really mastered a little Russian,the accent is what bothers me most;but my teachers tell me I'm improving every day(I do hope it isn't mere politeness!)"

An authentic chaos of unhuman smells,a joyous anarchy of noises which are not words,a merciful complexity of illogical shapes and irrational colours,an alive mad intricately free feel of tree and rock,of movingness and earth, welcome my lonely nostrils ears eyes flesh spirit. Wandering carefully among carpenters masons ditchdiggers(and similar comrades disguised as workmen)we walk the plank to a speakeasylike door—and collide with dismally cheerful citizen who promptly reveals himself as personal friend of that prominent Russian-in-Paris novelist whose(by me personally sent)telegram did not scare up a brother in literature. And now I achieve my first bad break;now,asked the prominent's address,I spontaneously reply Don't know but he's always at the Coupole—words better left un-(said John Boyle)return to create amply sorrow when we consider them comfortably defunct
   —nevertheless if not however,am soon speaking with someone whom I immediately liked,someone who perhaps likes me and who certainly enjoys talking French,someone who invites me to a few minutes' conversation quite as if conversation were a perfectly recognized form of derring do;and Virgil,to his eternal credit I record this,shoves me almost brutally at the conversationally inclined comrade ("see you later:be at my room about six; we'll go to Gahlstook—that means Necktie—" and capping the climax "à bientôt!")
   What chiefly interests you?the diminutive president('tis himself,not a picture)quietly asks,asks almost peacefully. A not big untidy room remarkably buntingless(but Lenin's bust listens just outside). Miscellaneous whisper of implements,how unlike generic machine thunder,seeps through Unshutness. —Would you like to see the vast industrial plants by which Russia is trying to get her place in the world? Russia is striving;a whole race,a vast part of earth . . . —I understand:you are interested in the cultural side. More especially drama? Let me know whenever you want to see

a play;I'd be only too delighted to telephone for you,the theatre reserves
your seats gladly—and it will cost you nothing. Tomorrow our great writer,
Gorky,arrives:may I suggest that you visit the club next day and meet him?
Now let me show you our club—as a writer,you're more than welcome here
  (and,astonished,behold—hidden away under ground—positively not depressing rathskeller;nay,an almost ... with several almost lively looking
customers engaged in almost luxurious gastronomics ... and someone
almost who might be an actress,perhaps because herself wears what might
have been (almost and long since)stylish garments,or is it that this comrade
doesn't seem to be exactly carrying the woes of a sinful world upon shoulders precisely which were never made for unpleasure ... and withal an
atmosphere of semitranquility,of notuneasiness,almost of something ap-
proximating that blessedly aesthetic phenomenon;relaxation)
  which bountiful crop of almosts dignifies a not quite terrifying perspective;myself begins-to-begin to almost conjecture that possibly comrade Kem-
min-kz has an impossible place in the impossibly possible USSR. Also,how
sweet(how proudly purely sweet)is the mother of imagination;courtesy
  —Probably that telegram never arrived:I know most of the comrades on
this list of yours and I'm sure they'll do everything they can for you. "Venez
ici déjeuner,c'est le centre des écrivains" our food is good,the beer I can
vouch for. Cigarettes? Of course,over here—

Peacefully returning(proudly,without error)through streetless streets (tranquilly among peopleless people moving)surprise Dante's cicerone in the
very act of consulting his mural theatreschedule. Unpresently present is
faded Interpreter,who very distinctly wears That Elsewhere Look—times
pathetic habit of shifting stance whenever viewed;as if avoiding a well-
aimed blow—probably an erstwhile member of the longlost wellborns;any-
how inwardly ashamed of current occupation (whatever it may be). And
this dodger 'phones Proletcult,where The Necktie's displayed(Virgil must
see The Necktie tonight because he must,because The Necktie won't be
shown again,and finally because Virgil's opus requires liberal documenta-
tion re proletarian histrionics)winning 3 places(the 3rd,I almost understand,
for a distinguished American painter and writer who—luckily for Russia—
happens to be in town). Selah. The distinguished,allowed 15 minutes' freedom,hastens to pump ½baldness anent my not yet arrived worldly goods—
hb promises (Russianly,am beginning to understand)profound action;he will
even interrogate a highly responsible comrade who departed this hotel in
the direction of the outhouseless outhouse at 11 A.M. and is expected back
in something very like ½ an hour,comrade weather permitting ... ("Can you
beat it?"). . . but no sooner am semidesperately upstairs than out respectfully
rushes a not quite cheerfulness,crying Luggage?and pocketing 35 comrade
kopecks almost without a comrade murmur. (Horrors Of Trying To Tip
A Comrade). Acci-or inci-(or both)dentally my poor old suitcase sprung one

noble leak but ("honest thieves")regurgitated nothing;no,not even the means of enjoying singularly painful shave and equally appropriate scrub—therefore, at 6:45 punctually,do I present burnished arms chez Sibyl & Interpreter Inc.

A ponderiferously (And How)YMCA atmosphere,strongly suggesting N (holy image of Ulianov much in evidence)pervades the radiatingly EDuCAtional promenoir replete with sundry and various And How uplifting exhibits(models of bombing planes,tractors,whatnot;around which cluster curiously silent folk,bigeyed patient clumsy beholders,awed childlike beings) ... everywhere a mysterious sense of behaving,of housebrokeness,of watchyour-stepism. No Smoking. Benevolently our delegation graces the 2nd row of a rustic rendezous wriggling with children (including 1 spontaneous and charming and otherwise noteworthy comrade of 8 or 10)for whom The Necktie might well have been composed—for it's all "funnies",slapstick, hocuspocus (example:a bookcase full of ancient tomes and priceless knickknacks receives a good push;whereupon the whole contraption homogeneously disappears to magically become flat wall)and it culminates in 1 suh-wel Universal Cataclysm Finale (with somebody rushing up the aisle and everything and you know what I mean and Tah-de-de-ahhh!)—indeed,circa ⅓ through this hugely long foolery,begin to suspect that all the grownupless grownups in Russia are children...

Item:during the 1st of numberless entr'actes we invade(by special request) an atomic spicandspanness,more than miraculously into which—at the bidding of a flannelshirted necktieless almost jolly comrade manager (?)and a similarly bedecked modestly straightforward comradedirector (?)—are forced delicious tea and luscious sweetmeats. Our hosts (brisk but courteous, efficient but sympathetic,in short:fine fellows both) beg us to partake of the good cheer and with nothing short of incredible patience answer Virgil's innumerable(sic)questions (the numerable answers being recorded in a Harvard Coöperative Society Harvard Square Cambridge Mass notebook). The recorder is adopted,at intermission number3,by an Hebraically extracted Little Girl With A Big Heart,who not unrecently left her native New York with the May Day Unit of radicals,never (she announces)to return (Tah-dede-ahhh!)—viciously almost whose (almost but,alas,not quite sublimated via propaganda)corporeality responds to sundry and various settingupexercises in which members of the cast very frequently indulge:a hungrily dreadful specimen,on the whole—and guzzles 4 cakes to dodger's 1 and seems to know more than is good for any 6 comrades (our hosts' dum & dee faces betray no secrets,but their eyes actually smile when comrade mentor,statisticsward bound,checks comrade Unit's illimitable exposition)

—of this particular proletarian fable the Moral,as explained(a)by dodger to angel (b)by angel to me (c)by Unit to dodger,oddly coincides with my ignorant own interpretation,viz.It's not things that matter,comrade,it's how you make use of things that matters:thus even a necktie,that symbol of bourgeois idiocy,may end as nothing less than a proletarian banner waving from loyal matchlock of Comrade Righto while all Our Boys (and Girls AND HOW)go forth to make the whole world 1 big family. Perhaps—only perhaps—to imagine Life deliberately lifting Itself,by that hypothetical guiltsense which equals Its own bootstraps,out of fatally stupendous unconsciousness into the (how comfortably measurable)tinyness of "humanity"—into a "scientific" infrared-ultraviolet illusion-of-a-future,into an omne-vivum-evivo ABC "reality",into a vicariously infantile Kingdom of Slogan—softly is not to misunderstand the message of Proletcult per(come all ye traumdeutungs!)Necktie.

With an especially dodgeless dodge comrade Interpreter abandons us for comrade streetcar (tactfully thereby allowing comrade Unit unmitigated access to benevolence over the 2 Good Comrades Together or tastes-incommon route). As for I, announce low craving for brightlights—whereupon 2 Good Comrades Together emit mild astonishment and (wrapped in loftier than trivial matters)manoeuvre me several murderful miles to the deathsmelling portals of Hotel Metropole. . .

"well,I suppose you're tired—I'll take the comrade home. . .don't mention it my dear chap! Let's have breakfast in my room tomorrow—I like so much to breakfast in my pyjamas. But not before ten,eh? Just give me a knock. Gahlstook was wonderful,wasn't it;we'll see The West Is Nervous next. Goodnight,tovarich! —O,remember about correspondents,and—something else I wanted to say . . . well,never mind,I can't seem to think;see you tomorrow!"

Away walked one of earth's queerest couples.

SOME CONCLUSIONS BY THE SAME OBSERVERS | EDMUND WILSON

One's first impressions of Russia are likely to be contradictory; but once one begins to get glimpses of what is going on beneath the surface, one becomes aware of an extraordinary heroism.

The effect of this is very sobering. Only idiots gush about the Soviet Union. Only idiots pretend that life there is easy. Whether one runs into a Communist official who is obviously working his head off in an effort to make socialism succeed in the face of inertia at home and hostile pressure abroad; or a professional man or woman of the old bourgeoisie or nobility, who has lost position, property and family, who lives always more or less under suspicion and who may have already done time in a prison or construction camp, yet who still remains loyal to the Revolution; or a member of the Komsomól intoxicating himself with study and work; or a peasant woman applying herself with desperate earnestness to the duties of ticket-taker on a train or a tram; or a doctor or farmer, now old, but deprived of his whole life's achievement, yet still sticking to his former work, in the interests of a future he will never see, of benefits he will never share; or a cultivated and charming young woman grown up amid the anarchy of the Civil Wars and the Spartan early years of the Revolution, with no dancing and no pretty clothes and breaking down her physique and her nerves under the exactions of the Soviet programs—whomever one sees, wherever one turns, one is made to feel the terrible seriousness of what is being done in Russia and the terrible cost it entails.

But it is as foolish, on the other hand, for a foreigner to make an issue of the bad aspects of the dictatorship: the lack of democratic procedure, the suppression of political opposition, the constraint of the official terror. The Russians can always reply that, with all our democratic machinery, we are unable to feed and clothe our people, and that our supposed democratic institutions are illusions to divert our attention from observing that the government and the laws in reality work only one way: to protect the profits of the owning classes. This last is, I believe, not quite true: I feel convinced, since I have been in Russia, that American republican institutions, disastrously as they are often abused, have some permanent and absolute value. I do not believe that they are certain to be destroyed in the course of the transformation of society, any more than our advanced "technique." On the contrary, I think it probable that, like it, they will make easier the transition to socialism. But we shall not be in a position to reprove the Russians till we have put ourselves in a position to show them an American socialism that is free from the Russian defects.

In the meantime, despite these defects, you feel in the Soviet Union that you are living at the moral top of the world, where the light never really goes out, just as you know in the Gulf of Finland, where the summer day never ends, that you are close to the geographical top. The central fact, from which one never can escape, upon which one is always stumbling under all the fluid surface of casualness, frivolity, timidity, evasion and apathy, that is one of the features of Russian life, is the relationship of the Russian people to the tomb under the Kremlin wall. Day after day, rain or shine, the visitors line up for hours in slowly advancing queues that loop back and forth across Red Square, in order to go into the tomb, to step down past the walls of Ural marble, black and gray and sown with flakes of lapis lazuli like bits of blue butterflies' wings, and to stare for a moment at that face, where the soldier with his bayonet stands staring. It is not the face you may have expected if you have been looking at pictures and statues, and it is different even from the death-mask. But, in shrinking, the flesh reveals qualities, fundamental as the fine grain of wood, which are also apparent in this latter. We are used to seeing Lenin represented, as he must usually have been during his waking life, determined, intent, energetic, arguing, explaining, imposing himself; and even in the death-mask we are struck by the aggressive intellect of the boxlike skull which seems always to be tilted forward; here the nose and lips are still rather thick, the eyebrows sharply bristling. The casts of the hands show tapering yet effective and square-tipped fingers. But the head in the tomb, with its high forehead, its straight nose, its pointed beard (which has grown gray on the dead man's cheeks), its sensitive nostrils and eyelids, gives an impression in some ways strangely similar to that one gets from the supposed death-mask of Shakespeare. It is a beautiful face, of exquisite fineness; and—what surely proves its authenticity—it is profoundly aristocratic. Yet if this is an aristocrat, it is an aristocrat who has not specialized as one; and it is a poet who has not specialized as a poet, a scientist who has not specialized as a scientist. Nor is it in the least the face of a saint. Except for the slightly slanting eyes, it seems today hardly even the face of a Russian. For here has humanity bred, independent of all the old disciplines, the scientist whose study is humanity, the poet whose material is not images but the water and salt of human beings—the superior man who has burst out of the classes and claimed all that is superior which man has done for the refinement of mankind as a whole. And here we have come to gaze down at this shriveling shell of flesh, in its last thinness, its fragility and delicacy, before it falls to pieces and loses the mold—this bone and skin that still keeps the stamp of that intellect, that passion, that will, whose emergence has stunned the world almost with more embarrassment at being made to extend its conception of what man, as man alone, can accomplish, than admiration at the achievements of genius. So these countrymen of his are amazed, with their formless and expressionless faces, when they look down on him and know that he was one of them, that he summoned from their sluggish plasm all those triumphs to which life must rise and to which he thought himself but a guidepost.

SOME CONCLUSIONS BY THE SAME OBSERVERS | ANDRE GIDE

The Soviet Union is "in the making"; one cannot say it too often. And to that is due the extraordinary interest of a stay in this immense country which is now in labor; one feels that one is contemplating the parturition of the future.

Good and bad alike are to be found there; I should say rather—the best and the worst. The best was often achieved only by an immense effort. That effort has not always and everywhere achieved what it set out to achieve. Sometimes one is able to think—not yet. Sometimes the worst accompanies and shadows the best; it almost seems as if it were a consequence of the best. And one passes from the brightest light to the darkest shade with a disconcerting abruptness. It often happens that the traveller, according to his own preconceived notions, only grasps one side or the other. It too often happens that the friends of the Soviet Union refuse to see the bad side, or at any rate refuse to admit the bad side; so that, too often what is true about the U.S.S.R. is said with enmity, and what is false with love.

Now my mind is so constructed that its severest criticisms are addressed to those whom I should like always to be able to approve. To confine oneself exclusively to praise is a bad way of proving one's devotion, and I believe I am doing the Soviet Union itself, and the cause that it represents in our eyes, a greater service by speaking without dissimulation or indulgence. It is precisely because of my admiration for the Soviet Union and for the wonders it has already performed, that I am going to criticize— because of what we had expected from it—above all because of what it had allowed us to hope for.

Who shall say what the Soviet Union has been to us? More than a chosen land—an example, a guide. What we have dreamt of, what we have hardly dared to hope, but towards which we were straining all our will and all our strength, was coming into being over there. A land existed where Utopia was in process of becoming reality. Tremendous achievements had already made us exacting. The greatest difficulties appeared to have been overcome, and we entered joyfully and boldly into the sort of engagement this land had contracted in the name of all suffering peoples.

SOME CONCLUSIONS BY THE SAME OBSERVERS | THEODORE DREISER

Even as they talk of the glorious material prosperity that they dream is to come to them, I never met one who spoke of it in purely personal or selfishly possessive terms. On the contrary, it was always a *general* prosperity that was to be, and in which all were to share, plenty for everybody, everybody happy or free to do this and that. And almost as instantly it took the form of leisure to think. If society—not self,—say these Russians, can be supplied by everybody working eight, or seven, or six hours, well and good—then everybody will have more time to do that which he most wishes to do—study, play, think, travel. And if society can supply itself with all that it needs by working only three or four hours a day, then so much the better—more time to do the real and delightful things which have nothing to do with either laborious toil or the hoarding of mere possessions. "Oh," said one old Volga peasant to one of my interpreters, "I shall not live to see it, but my son tells me that no one will have to work more than four or five hours a day after a while, and then every one can study and get a good education." And that, rather than material possessions in the new day, seemed the great point to him.

And truly, talking to the principal statesmen and leaders of Russia as well as many of the industrial workers everywhere, I was persistently impressed by the fact that they also seemed to see this new development in just this way—in terms of general improvement, and always with the goal in view not of luxury but of an intellectual leisure which is to follow upon the acquisition of sufficient material equipment. One could always get ten, twenty, thirty to join in such a discussion anywhere, but never with a dissenting voice from this program of general prosperity and general culture.

And this finally led me to fancy that possibly Russia—and that in the near future, should its present program succeed—is destined to enter upon an intellectual labor which will go farther than has any other thing as yet toward solving the strange mystery of our being here at all.

I wonder.

SOME CONCLUSIONS BY THE SAME OBSERVERS | LIAM O'FLAHERTY

The only thing for a decadent European like myself is to retire and leave them to it. I am convinced that we Europeans have nothing to gain from either Russia or America. We have established our cultures and our civilizations. We can gain nothing by giving them violent shocks. We should hasten our demise. I am still convinced that there is nothing here which gives me as much satisfaction as things to be found in Ireland, England and France. . . .

Indeed as I came away from Duranty's house I felt convinced that religion, be it Bolshevism or Christianity, Mormonism, or Mahomedanism, is the least important thing in life for a normal person. I decided to return at once to Western Europe where life is so pleasant owing to the death of God.

SOME CONCLUSIONS BY THE SAME OBSERVERS | E. E. CUMMINGS

USSR a USSR a night-USSR a nightmare USSR home of the panacea Negation haven of all(in life's name)Death worshippers hopper of hate's Becausemachine(U for un- & S for self S for science and R for -reality)

how it shrivels:how it dwindles withers; how it wilts diminishes wanes,
how it crumbles evaporates collapses disappears—the verily consubstan-
tial cauchemar of premeditated NYET

ABOUT UNIVERSITY EDUCATION

*A WRITER BUILDS with assertions; they are the steel and concrete
of his ideological structure. The truth of this claim would be evident
in a breakdown or outline of almost any essay or book. Indeed, some of the
most important steps in the argument are bound to be those from one
kind of assertion to another. An author frequently begins, for instance, with
definitions, or with assertions based on convention and deduction; then,
having laid the foundation, he shifts to assertions based directly on experience ("facts"). When he has put forth a set of facts, he may move to
generalizations based on those facts. Finally, he is likely to let his case
rest with assertions of the fourth kind discussed in the introduction, those
of ethical import. An imaginary example will clarify the pattern. An
article on "Cultural Cohesion in Chicago's Ethnic Groups" might well
begin with definitions of "cultural cohesion" and "ethnic groups." Having
set straight the sociological* conventions of usage, the author can exhibit
*his facts about, say, the Polish, the Puerto Ricans, the ex-miners from West
Virginia, and so forth, capping these factual assertions with his* opinions
about the effects of cohesion. He may then conclude with one or more
ethical assertions *which to his mind follow from his facts and opinions—*
"Discriminatory renting practices *should be stopped," for example. The
pattern of assertions is the pattern of the article.*

*The four selections in this unit cannot be broken down so neatly into
types of assertion, perhaps because university education is a subject in
which the writers are more deeply and personally involved than the
imaginary sociologist was in Chicago's internal disorders. When an author
is emotionally committed to his hypothesis, his ethical assertions often become inseparably welded to the rest. Questions of good and bad, ought and
must, tend to weigh heavily on the whole structure and to obscure the
factual and conventional base. Still, the main types of assertion appear in
each of the four selections below, and the intricacy of the joints makes
the construction of the whole more worthy of study than a simpler model
would be. In any case, it is useful in judging a piece of writing to know
the proportions which compose it.*

*The writers in this unit are acknowledged authorities in the field of
education. John Henry Newman (1801-1890), besides being a famous cardinal, was at one time a tutor at Oxford and later rector of the new Catholic*

university in Dublin; his book Idea of a University *grew out of lectures given there. Robert Maynard Hutchins (1899-   ) has been one of the most vociferous latter-day critics of John Dewey and his followers in American "progressive" education. Hutchins' vigorous administration as president and later chancellor of the University of Chicago was responsible for instituting many of the educational reforms suggested in* The University of Utopia. *Howard Mumford Jones (1892-   ), professor emeritus at Harvard, is widely known for the vigor and hard-headed liberalism of his interest in American education and public affairs. Alfred North Whitehead (1861-1947), English mathematician and philosopher, proved himself an enlightened admirer and critic of American life during the many years he spent in this country.*

WHAT IS A UNIVERSITY? | *JOHN HENRY NEWMAN*

If I were asked to describe as briefly and popularly as I could, what a University was, I should draw my answer from its ancient designation of a *Studium Generale* or "School of Universal Learning." This description implies the assemblage of strangers from all parts in one spot; *from all parts;* else, how will you find professors and students for every department of knowledge? and *in one spot;* else, how can there be any school at all? Accordingly, in its simple and rudimental form, it is school of knowledge of every kind, consisting of teachers and learners from every quarter. Many things are requisite to complete and satisfy the idea embodied in this description; but such as this a University seems to be in its essence, a place for the communication and circulation of thought, by means of personal intercourse, through a wide extent of country.

There is nothing far-fetched or unreasonable in the idea thus presented to us; and if this be a University, then a University does but contemplate a necessity of our nature, and is but one specimen in a particular medium, out of many which might be adduced in others, of a provision for that necessity. Mutual education, in a large sense of the word, is one of the great and incessant occupations of human society, carried on partly with set purpose, and partly not. One generation forms another; and the existing generation is ever acting and reacting upon itself in the persons of its individual members. Now, in this process, books, I need scarcely say, that is, the *litera scripta,* are one special instrument. It is true; and emphatically so in this age. Considering the prodigious powers of the press, and how they are developed at this time in the never-intermitting issue of periodicals, tracts, pamphlets, works in series, and light literature, we

From *What Is a University?* (1856).

must allow there never was a time which promised fairer for dispensing with every other means of information and instruction. What can we want more, you will say, for the intellectual education of the whole man, and for every man, than so exuberant and diversified and persistent a promulgation of all kinds of knowledge? Why, you will ask, need we go up to knowledge, when knowledge comes down to us? The Sibyl wrote her prophecies upon the leaves of the forest, and wasted them; but here such careless profusion might be prudently indulged, for it can be afforded without loss, in consequence of the almost fabulous fecundity of the instrument which these latter ages have invented. We have sermons in stones, and books in the running brooks; works larger and more comprehensive than those which have gained for ancients an immortality issue forth every morning, and are projected onwards to the ends of the earth at the rate of hundreds of miles a day. Our seats are strewed, our pavements are powdered, with swarms of little tracts; and the very bricks of our city walls preach wisdom, by informing us by their placards where we can at once cheaply purchase it.

I allow all this, and much more; such certainly is our popular education, and its effects are remarkable. Nevertheless, after all, even in this age, whenever men are really serious about getting what, in the language of trade, is called "a good article," when they aim at something precise, something refined, something really luminous, something really large, something choice, they go to another market; they avail themselves, in some shape or other, of the rival method, the ancient method, of oral instruction, of present communication between man and man, of teachers instead of learning, of the personal influence of a master, and the humble initiation of a disciple, and, in consequence, of great centers of pilgrimage and throng, which such a method of education necessarily involves. This, I think, will be found to hold good in all those departments or aspects of society, which possess an interest sufficient to bind men together, or to constitute what is called "a world." It holds in the political world, and in the high world, and in the religious world; and it holds also in the literary and scientific world.

If the actions of men may be taken as any test of their convictions, then we have reason for saying this, viz.: that the province and the inestimable benefit of the *litera scripta* is that of being a record of truth, and an authority of appeal, and an instrument of teaching in the hands of a teacher; but that, if we wish to become exact and fully furnished in any branch of knowledge which is diversified and complicated, we must consult the living man and listen to his living voice. I am not bound to investigate the cause of this, and anything I may say will, I am conscious, be short of its full analysis; perhaps we may suggest, that no books can get through the number of minute questions which it is possible to ask on any extended subject, or can hit upon the very difficulties which are severally felt by each reader in succession. Or again, that no book can convey the special spirit and delicate peculiarities of its subject with that rapidity and certainty which attend on the sympathy of mind with mind, through the eyes, the look, the accent, and the manner, in casual expressions thrown off at the moment, and the unstudied turns of familiar conversation. But I am already dwelling too long on what is but an incidental portion of my main subject. Whatever be the cause, the fact is undeniable. The general principles of any study you may learn by books at home; but the detail, the color, the tone, the air, the life which makes it live in us, you must catch all these from those in whom it lives already. You must imitate the student in French or German, who is not content with his grammar, but goes to Paris or Dresden: you must take example from the young artist, who aspires to visit the great Masters in Florence and in Rome. Till we have discovered some intellectual daguerreotype, which takes off the course of thought, and the form, lineaments, and features of truth, as completely and minutely, as the optical instrument reproduces the sensible object, we must come to the teachers of wisdom to learn wisdom, we must repair to the fountain, and drink there. Portions of it may go from thence to the ends of the earth by means of books; but the fullness is in one place alone. It is in such assemblages and congregations of intellect that books themselves, the masterpieces of human genius, are written, or at least originated.

The principle on which I have been insisting is so obvious, and instances in point are so ready, that I should think it tiresome to proceed with the subject, except that one or two illustrations may serve to explain my own language about it, which may not have done justice to the doctrine which it has been intended to enforce.

For instance, the polished manners and high-bred bearing which are so difficult of attainment, and so strictly personal when attained, which are so much admired in society, from society are acquired. All that goes to constitute a gentleman—the carriage, gait, address, gestures, voice; the ease, the self-possession, the courtesy, the power of conversing, the talent of not offending; the lofty principle, the delicacy of thought, the happiness of expression, the taste and propriety, the generosity and forbearance, the candor and consideration, the openness of hand—these qualities, some of them come by nature, some of them may be found in any rank, some of them are a direct precept of Christianity; but the full assemblage of them, bound up in the unity of an individual character, do we expect they can be learned from books? are they not necessarily acquired, where they are to be found, in high society? The very nature of the case leads us to say so; you cannot fence without an antagonist, nor challenge all comers in disputation before you have supported a thesis; and in like manner, it stands to reason, you cannot learn to converse till you have the world to converse with; you cannot unlearn your natural bashfulness, or awkwardness, or stiffness, or other besetting deformity, till you serve your time in some school of manners. Well, and is it not so in matter of fact? The metropolis, the court, the great houses of the land, are the centers to which at stated times the country comes up, as to shrines of refinement and good taste; and then in due time the country goes back again home, enriched with a portion of the social accomplishments, which those very visits serve to call out and heighten in the gracious dispensers of them. We are unable to conceive how the "gentlemanlike" can otherwise be maintained; and maintained in this way it is.

And now a second instance: and here too I am going to speak without personal experience of the subject I am introducing. I admit I have not been in Parliament, any more than I have figured in the *beau monde;* yet I cannot but think that statesmanship, as well as high breeding, is learned, not by books, but in certain centers of education. If it be not presumption to say so, Parliament puts a clever man *au courant* with politics and affairs of state in a way surprising to himself. A member of the Legislature, if tolerably observant, begins to see things with new eyes, even though his views undergo no change. Words have a meaning now, and ideas a reality, such as they had not before. He hears a vast deal in public speeches and private conversation, which is never put into print. The bearing of measures and events, the action of parties, and the persons of friends and enemies, are brought out to the man who is in the midst of them with a distinctness, which the most diligent perusal of newspapers will fail to impart to them. It is access to the fountain-heads of political wisdom and experience, it is daily intercourse, of one kind or another, with the multitude who go up to them, it is familiarity with business, it is access to the contributions of fact and opinion thrown together by many witnesses from many quarters, which does this for him. However, I need not account for a fact, to which it is sufficient to appeal; that the Houses of Parliament and the atmosphere around them are a sort of University of politics.

As regards the world of science, we find a remarkable instance of the principle which I am illustrating, in the periodical meetings for its advance, which have arisen in the course of the last twenty years, such as the British Association. Such gatherings would to many persons appear at first sight simply preposterous. Above all subjects of study, Science is conveyed, is propagated, by books, or by private teaching; experiments and investigations are conducted in silence; discoveries are made in solitude. What have philosophers to do with festive celebrities, and panegyrical solemnities with mathematical and physical truth? Yet on a closer attention to the subject, it is found that not even scientific thought can dispense with the suggestions, the instruction, the stimulus, the sympathy, the intercourse with mankind on a large scale, which such meetings secure. A fine time of year is chosen, when days are long, skies are bright, the earth smiles, and all nature rejoices; a city or town is taken by turns, of ancient name or modern opulence, where buildings are spacious and hospitality hearty. The novelty of place and circumstance, the excitment of strange, or the refreshment of well-known faces, the majesty of rank or of genius, the amiable charities of men pleased both with themselves and with each other; the elevated spirits, the circulation of thought, the curiosity; the morning sections, the outdoor exercise, the well-furnished, well-earned board, the not ungraceful hilarity, the evening circle; the brilliant lecture, the discussions or collisions or guesses of great men one with another, the narratives of scientific processes, of hopes, disappointments, conflicts, and success, the splendid eulogistic orations; these and the like constituents of the annual celebration, are considered to do something real and substantial for the advance of knowledge which can be done in no other way. Of course they can but be occasional; they answer to the annual Act, or Commencement, or Commemoration of a University, not to its ordinary condition; but they are of a University nature; and I can well believe in their utility. They issue in the promotion of a certain living and, as it were, bodily communication of knowledge from one to another, of a general interchange of ideas, and a comparison and adjustment of science with science, of an enlargement of mind, intellectual and social, of an ardent love of the paritcular study, which may be chosen by each individual and a noble devotion to its interests.

Such meetings, I repeat, are but periodical, and only partially represent the idea of a University. The bustle and whirl which are their usual concomitants, are in ill keeping with the order and gravity of earnest intellectual education. We desiderate means of instruction which involve no interruption of our ordinary habits; nor need we seek it long, for the natural course of things brings it about, while we debate over it. In every great country, the metropolis itself becomes a sort of necessary University, whether we will or no. As the chief city is the seat of the court, of high society, of politics, and of law, so as a matter of course is it the seat of letters also; and at this time, for a long term of years, London and Paris are in fact and in operation Universities, though in Paris its famous University is no more, and in London a University scarcely exists except as a board of administration. The newspapers, magazines, reviews, journals, and periodicals of all kinds, the publishing trade, the libraries, museums, and academies there found, the learned and scientific societies, necessarily invest it with the functions of a University; and that atmosphere of intellect, which in a former age hung over Oxford or Bologna or Salamanca, has, with the change of times, moved away to the center of civil government. Thither come up youths from all parts of the country, the students of Law, medicine, and the fine arts, and the *employés* and *attachés* of literature. There they live, as chance determines; and they are satisfied with their temporary home, for they find in it all that was promised to them there. They have not come in vain, as far as their own object in coming is concerned.

They have not learned any particular religion, but they have learned their own particular profession well. They have, moreover, become acquainted with the habits, manners, and opinions of their place of sojourn, and done their part in maintaining the tradition of them. We cannot then be without virtual Universities; a metropolis is such: the simple question is, whether the education sought and given should be based on principle, formed upon rule, directed to the highest ends, or left to the random succession of masters and schools, one after another, with a melancholy waste of thought and an extreme hazard of truth.

Religious teaching itself affords us an illustration of our subject to a certain point. It does not indeed seat itself merely in centers of the world; this is impossible from the nature of the case. It is intended for the many not the few; its subject matter is truth necessary for us, not truth recondite and rare; but it concurs in the principle of a University so far as this, that its great instrument, or rather organ, has ever been that which nature prescribes in all education, the personal presence of a teacher, or, in theological language, Oral Tradition. It is the living voice, the breathing form, the expressive countenance, which preaches, which catechizes. Truth, a subtle, invisible, manifold spirit, is poured into the mind of the scholar by his eyes and ears, through his affections, imagination, and reason; it is poured into his mind and is sealed up there in perpetuity, by propounding and repeating it, by questioning and requestioning, by correcting and explaining, by progressing and then recurring to first principles, by all those ways which are implied in the word "catechizing." In the first ages, it was a work of long time; months, sometimes years, were devoted to the arduous task of disabusing the mind of the incipient Christian of its pagan errors, and of molding it upon the Christian faith. The Scriptures indeed were at hand for the study of those who could avail themselves of them; but St. Irenaeus does not hesitate to speak of whole races, who had been converted to Christianity, without being able to read them. To be unable to read or write was in those times no evidence of want of learning; the hermits of the desert were, in this sense of the word, illiterate; yet the great St. Anthony, though he knew not letters, was a match in disputation for the learned philosophers who came to try him. Didymus again, the great Alexandrian theologian, was blind. The ancient discipline, called the *Disciplina Arcani,* involved the same principle. The more sacred doctrines of Revelation were not committed to books but passed on by successive tradition. The teaching on Blessed Trinity and the Eucharist appears to have been so handed down for some hundred years; and when at length reduced to writing, it has filled many folios, yet has not been exhausted.

But I have said more than enough in illustration; I end as I began— a University is a place of concourse, whither students come from every quarter for every kind of knowledge. You cannot have the best of every kind everywhere; you must go to some great city or emporium for it. There you have all the choicest productions of nature and art all together, which

you find each in its own separate place elsewhere. All the riches of the
land, and of the earth, are carried up thither; there are the best markets,
and there the best workmen. It is the center of trade, the supreme court
of fashion, the umpire of rival talents, and the standard of things rare and
precious. It is the place for seeing galleries of first-rate pictures, and for
hearing wonderful voices and performers of transcendent skill. It is the
place for great preachers, great orators, great nobles, great statesmen. In the
nature of things, greatness and unity go together; excellence implies a center. And such, for the third or fourth time, is a University; I hope I do
not weary out the reader by repeating it. It is the place to which a thousand
schools make contributions; in which the intellect may safely range and
speculate, sure to find its equal in some antagonist activity, and its judge
in the tribunal of truth. It is a place where inquiry is pushed forward,
and discoveries verified and perfected, and rashness rendered innocuous,
and error exposed, by the collision of mind with mind, and knowledge
with knowledge. It is the place where the professor becomes eloquent, and
is a missionary and a preacher, displaying his science in its most complete
and most winning form, pouring it forth with the zeal of enthusiasm, and
lighting up his own love of it in the breasts of his hearers. It is the place
where the catechist makes good his ground as he goes, treading in the truth
day by day into the ready memory, and wedging and tightening it into the
expanding reason. It is a place which wins the admiration of the young by
its celebrity, kindles the affections of the middle-aged by its beauty, and
rivets the fidelity of the old by its associations. It is a seat of wisdom, a
light of the world, a minister of the faith, an Alma Mater of the rising
generation. It is this and a great deal more, and demands a somewhat
better head and hand than mine to describe it well.

Such is a University in its idea and in its purpose; such in good measure
has it before now been in fact. Shall it ever be again? We are going forward
in the strength of the Cross, under the patronage of the Blessed Virgin,
in the name of St. Patrick, to attempt it.

UNIVERSITIES AND THEIR FUNCTION | ALFRED NORTH WHITEHEAD

The expansion of universities is one marked feature of the social life in
the present age. All countries have shared in this movement, but more especially America, which thereby occupies a position of honor. It is, however,
possible to be overwhelmed even by the gifts of good fortune; and this
growth of universities, in number of institutions, in size, and in internal

From Alfred North Whitehead, *The Aims of Education* (New York, The Macmillan
Company, 1929).

complexity of organization, discloses some danger of destroying the very sources of their usefulness, in the absence of a widespread understanding of the primary functions which universities should perform in the service of a nation. These remarks, as to the necessity for reconsideration of the function of universities, apply to all the more developed countries. They are only more especially applicable to America, because this country has taken the lead in a development which, under wise guidance, may prove to be one of the most fortunate forward steps which civilization has yet taken.

This article will only deal with the most general principles, though the special problems of the various departments in any university are, of course, innumerable. But generalities require illustration, and for this purpose I choose the business school of a university. This choice is dictated by the fact that business schools represent one of the newer developments of university activity. They are also more particularly relevant to the dominant social activities of modern nations, and for that reason are good examples of the way in which the national life should be affected by the activities of its universities. Also at Harvard, where I have the honor to hold office, the new foundation of a business school on a scale amounting to magnificence has just reached its completion.

There is a certain novelty in the provision of such a school of training, on this scale of magnitude, in one of the few leading universities of the world. It marks the culmination of a movement which for many years past has introduced analogous departments throughout American universities. This is a new fact in the university world; and it alone would justify some general reflections upon the purpose of a university education, and upon the proved importance of that purpose for the welfare of the social organism.

The novelty of business schools must not be exaggerated. At no time have universities been restricted to pure abstract learning. The University of Salerno in Italy, the earliest of European universities, was devoted to medicine. In England, at Cambridge, in the year 1316, a college was founded for the special purpose of providing "clerks for the King's service." Universities have trained clergy, medical men, lawyers, engineers. Business is now a highly intellectualized vocation, so it well fits into the series. There is, however, this novelty: the curriculum suitable for a business school, and the various modes of activity of such a school, are still in the experimental stage. Hence the peculiar importance of recurrence to general principles in connection with the molding of these schools. It would, however, be an act of presumption on my part if I were to enter upon any consideration of details, or even upon types of policy affecting the balance of the whole training. Upon such questions I have no special knowledge, and therefore have no word of advice.

II)

The universities are schools of education, and schools of research. But the primary reason for their existence is not to be found either in the mere knowledge conveyed to the students or in the mere opportunities for research afforded to the members of the faculty.

Both these functions could be performed at a cheaper rate, apart from these very expensive institutions. Books are cheap, and the system of apprenticeship is well understood. So far as the mere imparting of information is concerned, no university has had any justification for existence since the popularization of printing in the fifteenth century. Yet the chief impetus to the foundation of universities came after that date, and in more recent times has even increased.

The justification for a university is that it preserves the connection between knowledge and the zest of life, by uniting the young and the old in the imaginative consideration of learning. The university imparts information, but it imparts it imaginatively. At least, this is the function which it should perform for society. A university which fails in this respect has no reason for existence. This atmosphere of excitement, arising from imaginative consideration, transforms knowledge. A fact is no longer a bare fact: it is invested with all its possibilities. It is no longer a burden on the memory: it is energizing as the poet of our dreams, and as the architect of our purposes.

Imagination is not to be divorced from the facts: it is a way of illuminating the facts. It works by eliciting the general principles which apply to the facts, as they exist, and then by an intellectual survey of alternative possibilities which are consistent with those principles. It enables men to construct an intellectual vision of a new world, and it preserves the zest of life by the suggestion of satisfying purposes.

Youth is imaginative, and if the imagination be strengthened by discipline this energy of imagination can in great measure be preserved through life. The tragedy of the world is that those who are imaginative have but slight experience, and those who are experienced have feeble imaginations. Fools act on imagination without knowledge; pedants act on knowledge without imagination. The task of a university is to weld together imagination and experience.

The initial discipline of imagination in its period of youthful vigor requires that there be no responsibility for immediate action. The habit of unbiased thought, whereby the ideal variety of exemplifications is discerned in its derivation from general principles, cannot be acquired when there is the daily task of preserving a concrete organization. You must be free to think rightly and wrongly, and free to appreciate the variousness of the universe undisturbed by its perils.

These reflections upon the general functions of a university can be at once translated in terms of the particular functions of a business school. We need not flinch from the assertion that the main function of such a school is to produce men with a greater zest for business. It is a libel upon human nature to conceive that zest for life is the product of pedestrian purposes directed toward the narrow routine of material comforts. Mankind by its pioneering instinct, and in a hundred other ways, proclaims falsehood of that lie.

In the modern complex social organism, the adventure of life cannot be disjoined from intellectual adventure. Amid simpler circumstances, the pioneer can follow the urge of his instinct, directed toward the scene of his vision from the mountain top. But in the complex organizations of modern business the intellectual adventure of analysis, and of imaginative reconstruction, must precede any successful reorganization. In a simpler world, business relations were simpler, being based on the immediate contact of man with man and on immediate confrontation with all relevant material circumstances. Today business organization requires an imaginative grasp of the psychologies of populations engaged in differing modes of occupation; of populations scattered through cities, through mountains, through plains; of populations on the ocean, and of populations in mines, and of populations in forests. It requires an imaginative grasp of conditions in the tropics, and of conditions in temperate zones. It requires an imaginative grasp of the interlocking interests of great organizations, and of the reactions of the whole complex to any change in one of its elements. It requires an imaginative understanding of laws of political economy, not merely in the abstract, but also with the power to construe them in terms of the particular circumstances of a concrete business. It requires some knowledge of the habits of government, and of the variations of those habits under diverse conditions. It requires an imaginative vision of the binding forces of any human organization, a sympathetic vision of the limits of human nature and of the conditions which evoke loyalty of service. It requires some knowledge of the laws of health, and of the laws of fatigue, and of the conditions for sustained reliability. It requires an imaginative understanding of the social effects of the conditions of factories. It requires a sufficient conception of the rôle of applied science in modern society. It requires that discipline of character which can say "yes" and "no" to other men, not by reason of blind obstinacy, but with firmness derived from a conscious evaluation of relevant alternatives.

The universities have trained the intellectual pioneers of our civilization —the priests, the lawyers, the statesmen, the doctors, the men of science, and the men of letters. They have been the home of those ideals which lead men to confront the confusion of their present times. The Pilgrim Fathers left England to found a state of society according to the ideals of their religious faith; and one of their earlier acts was the foundation of Harvard University in Cambridge, named after that ancient mother of ideals in England, to which so many of them owed their training. The conduct of business now requires intellectual imagination of the same type as that which in former times has mainly passed into those other occupations; and the universities are the organizations which have supplied this type of mentality for the service of the progress of the European races.

In early medieval history the origin of universities was obscure and almost unnoticed. They were a gradual and natural growth. But their existence is the reason for the sustained, rapid progressiveness of European life in so many fields of activity. By their agency the adventure of action met the adventure of thought. It would not have been possible antecedently to have divined that such organizations would have been successful. Even now, amid the imperfections of all things human, it is sometimes difficult to understand how they succeed in their work. Of course there is much failure in the work of universities. But, if we take a broad view of history, their success has been remarkable and almost uniform. The cultural histories of Italy, of France, of Germany, of Holland, of Scotland, of England, of the United States, bear witness to the influence of universities. By "cultural history" I am not chiefly thinking of the lives of scholars; I mean the energizing of the lives of those men who gave to France, to Germany, and to other countries that impress of types of human achievement which, by their addition to the zest of life, form the foundation of our patriotism. We love to be members of society which can do those things.

There is one great difficulty which hampers all the higher types of human endeavor. In modern times this difficulty has even increased in its possibilities for evil. In any large organization the younger men, who are novices, must be set to jobs which consist in carrying out fixed duties in obedience to orders. No president of a large corporation meets his youngest employee at his office door with the offer of the most responsible job which the work of that corporation includes. The young men are set to work at a fixed routine, and only occasionally even see the president as he passes in and out of the building. Such work is a great discipline. It imparts knowledge, and it produces reliability of character; also it is the only work for which the young men, in that novice stage, are fit, and it is the work for which they are hired. There can be no criticism of the custom, but there may be an unfortunate effect—prolonged routine work dulls the imagination.

The result is that qualities essential at a later stage of a career are apt to be stamped out in an earlier stage. This is only an instance of the more general fact, that necessary technical excellence can only be acquired by a training which is apt to damage those energies of mind which should direct the technical skill. This is the key fact in education, and the reason for most of its difficulties.

The way in which a university should function in the preparation for an intellectual career, such as modern business or one of the older professions, is by promoting the imaginative consideration of the various general principles underlying that career. Its students thus pass into their period of technical apprenticeship with their imaginations already practiced in connecting details with general principles. The routine then receives its meaning, and also illuminates the principles which give it that meaning. Hence, instead of a drudgery issuing in a blind rule of thumb, the properly trained man has some hope of obtaining an imagination disciplined by detailed facts and by necessary habits.

Thus the proper function of a university is the imaginative acquisition of knowledge. Apart from this importance of the imagination, there is no reason why business men, and other professional men, should not pick up their facts bit by bit as they want them for particular occasions. A university is imaginative or it is nothing—at least nothing useful.

111)

Imagination is a contagious disease. It cannot be measured by the yard, or weighed by the pound, and then delivered to the students by members of the faculty. It can only be communicated by a faculty whose members themselves wear their learning with imagination. In saying this, I am only repeating one of the oldest of observations. More than two thousand years ago the ancients symbolized learning by a torch passing from hand to hand down the generations. That lighted torch is the imagination of which I speak. The whole art in the organization of a university is the provision of a faculty whose learning is lighted up with imagination. This is the problem of problems in university education; and unless we are careful the recent vast extension of universities in number of students and in variety of activities—of which we are so justly proud—will fail in producing its proper results, by the mishandling of this problem.

The combination of imagination and learning normally requires some leisure, freedom from restraint, freedom from harassing worry, some variety of experiences, and the stimulation of other minds diverse in opinion and diverse in equipment. Also there is required the excitement of curiosity, and the self-confidence derived from pride in the achievements of the surrounding society in procuring the advance of knowledge. Imagination cannot be acquired once and for all, and then kept indefinitely in an ice box to be produced periodically in stated quantities. The learned and imaginative life is a way of living, and is not an article of commerce.

It is in respect to the provision and utilization of these conditions for an efficient faculty that the two functions of education and research meet together in a university. Do you want your teachers to be imaginative? Then encourage them to research. Do you want your researchers to be imaginative? Then bring them into intellectual sympathy with the young at the most eager, imaginative period of life, when intellects are just entering upon their mature discipline. Make your researchers explain themselves to active minds, plastic and with the world before them; make your young students crown their period of intellectual acquisition by some contact with minds gifted with experience of intellectual adventure. Education is discipline for the adventure of life; research is intellectual adventure; and the universities should be homes of adventure shared in common by young and old. For successful education there must always be a certain freshness in the knowledge dealt with. It must either be new in itself or it must be invested with some novelty of application to the new world of new times. Knowledge does not keep any better than fish. You may be dealing with knowledge of the old species, with some old truth; but somehow or other it must come to the students, as it were, just drawn out of the sea and with the freshness of its immediate importance.

It is the function of the scholar to evoke into life wisdom and beauty which, apart from his magic, would remain lost in the past. A progressive society depends upon its inclusion of three groups—scholars, discoverers, inventors. Its progress also depends upon the fact that its educated masses are composed of members each with a tinge of scholarship, a tinge of discovery, and a tinge of invention. I am here using the term "discovery" to mean the progress of knowledge in respect to truths of some high generality, and the term "invention" to mean the progress of knowledge in respect to the application of general truths in particular ways subservient to present needs. It is evident that these three groups merge into each other, and also that men engaged in practical affairs are properly to be called inventors so far as they contribute to the progress of society. But any one individual has his own limitation of function, and his own peculiar needs. What is important for a nation is that there shall be a very close relation between all types of its progressive elements, so that the study may influence the market place, and the market place the study. Universities are the chief agencies for this fusion of progressive activities into an effective instrument of progress. Of course they are not the only agencies, but it is a fact that today the progressive nations are those in which universities flourish.

It must not be supposed that the output of a university in the form of original ideas is solely to be measured by printed papers and books labeled with the names of their authors. Mankind is as individual in its mode of output as in the substance of its thoughts. For some of the most fertile minds composition in writing, or in a form reducible to writing, seems to be an impossibility. In every faculty you will find that some of the more brilliant teachers are not among those who publish. Their originality requires for its expression direct intercourse with their pupils in the form of lectures, or of personal discussion. Such men exercise an immense influence; and yet, after the generation of their pupils has passed away, they sleep among the innumerable unthanked benefactors of humanity. Fortunately, one of them is immortal—Socrates.

Thus it would be the greatest mistake to estimate the value of each member of a faculty by the printed work signed with his name. There is at the present day some tendency to fall into this error; and an emphatic protest is necessary against an attitude on the part of authorities which is damaging to efficiency and unjust to unselfish zeal.

But, when all such allowances have been made, one good test for the general efficiency of a faculty is that as a whole it shall be producing in published form its quota of contributions of thought. Such a quota is to be estimated in weight of thought, and not in number of words.

This survey shows that the management of a university faculty has no analogy to that of a business organization. The public opinion of the faculty, and a common zeal for the purposes of the university, form the only effective safeguards for the high level of university work. The faculty should be a band of scholars, stimulating each other, and freely determining their various activities. You can secure certain formal requirements, that lectures are given at stated times and that instructors and students are in attendance. But the heart of the matter lies beyond all regulation.

The question of justice to the teachers has very little to do with the case. It is perfectly just to hire a man to perform any legal services under any legal conditions as to times and salary. No one need accept the post unless he so desires.

The sole question is, What sort of conditions will produce the type of faculty which will run a successful university? The danger is that it is quite easy to produce a faculty entirely unfit—a faculty of very efficient pedants and dullards. The general public will only detect the difference after the university has stunted the promise of youth for scores of years.

The modern university system in the great democratic countries will only be successful if the ultimate authorities exercise singular restraint, so as to remember that universities cannot be dealt with according to the rules and policies which apply to the familiar business corporations. Business schools are no exception to this law of university life. There is really nothing to add to what the presidents of many American universities have recently said in public on this topic. But whether the effective portion of the general public, in America or other countries, will follow their advice appears to be doubtful. The whole point of a university, on its educational side, is to bring the young under the intellectual influence of a band of imaginative scholars. There can be no escape from proper attention to the conditions which—as experience has shown—will produce such a band.

THE UNIVERSITY OF UTOPIA | ROBERT M. HUTCHINS

Education is the deliberate attempt to form men in terms of an ideal. It is the attempt of a society to produce the type of man that it wants. How does it determine the type of man that it wants? If it does not know the type of man that it wants, how does it judge the educational efforts it makes? It may be said that the type of man a society wants is the product of many historical and psychological factors and that whatever philosophy enters into the formation of its vision of man is simply a rationalization of this largely unconscious product. But, even if this were so, we know that in every society there is some vision of man, his nature and his destiny, elaborated by philosophers living and dead, which interacts with the traditional view of the type of man desired and which amounts to a criticism of the tradition and the practices of the educational system. Education without a philosophy of education, that is, a coherent statement of the aims and possibilities of education, is impossible.

Of course a custodial system is possible without a philosophy of education or any other kind of philosophy. A custodial system may be regarded as the efflorescence of a society's despair that it can make no rational and coherent statement about the type of man that it wants to produce. It therefore decides to leave the matter to chance, providing harmless accommodation and occupation for the young until they reach maturity. This, I should be careful to point out, is an entirely different thing from saying that the kind of man we want is one who can think and act for himself and that therefore we are going to let him learn for himself while the educational system does little more for him than keep him out of harm's way.

Though I do not favor this philosophy of education, I admit that it is one. It is an adaptation of the laissez faire or free-enterprise system to education that approaches that popular at Harvard until the retirement of President Eliot. Vestiges of this philosophy still remain to plague the universities; and some versions of Progressive Education seem to be built on the same premises. The two most obvious disadvantages of it are, first, that it implies that teachers need not know, any more than their pupils, what an education is and, second, that it breaks up the community of learning that might exist among students and deprives them of the assistance of their fellow-students and of the ability to communicate with them during their schooling and with their fellow-men in later life.

A custodial system of that frank and open kind which American education seems bent on developing requires neither philosophy nor educational philosophy. The question is whether the philosophical diversity now rampant in the world leads inevitably to a custodial system. Must we say that because philosophers differ, and some even hold that there is no such thing as philosophy, we cannot have a philosophy of education, and hence not an educational system? I assume that we would like to have an educational system, rather than a custodial one, if we could.

If we are to have a philosophy of education, it has to rest on a rational conception of man and society. It also has to take into account the philosophical diversity characteristic of our time. It has to take account, moreover, of the fact that there is no authority that can decide among competing philosophies. The incredible number of school boards, legislatures, boards of regents, boards of trustees, together with principals, superintendents, presidents, chancellors, and faculties, are all more or less autonomous centers of educational decision. The business of raising ourselves by our own bootstraps into a new and rational world will not be easy.

Let us see what we can learn from Utopia. Utopia is singularly like the United States in that there is no central educational authority. Nevertheless, it has been able to develop a philosophy of education. It has been able to do this in spite of the fact that in Utopia, too, there is philosophical diversity. The Utopians even insist that philosophical diversity is a good thing. They say that it has always existed, even in those periods of history in which there has been a strong religious or political authority that nominally exercised control over the thoughts of men. The Utopians point out that such authorities have never succeeded in suppressing, and have usually not tried to suppress, philosophical diversity. The attempt to suppress such diversity has been a manifestation of modern progress and has appeared only with the totalitarian state.

Of course there are in Utopia no underspecialized institutions. The Utopians have never allowed themselves to be annoyed by such slogans as adjustment to the environment or meeting immediate needs, because they have sharply defined the purpose of their educational system. It is to promote the intellectual development of the people. The reason for the strength of the Utopian family and the Utopian church and the Utopian educational system is that each has its prescribed task. No Utopian, for example, would ever have been guilty of the proposition advanced to me the other day by an eminent bishop, who said that education should be limited to the élite and that the mass of the people should receive such culture as they need from the family and the church. The Utopians think that intellectual development is too important to be left to amateurs; and, since they are devoted to democracy, they do not see how they can maintain and improve their democracy unless every citizen has the chance to become as wise as he can.

The Utopians are sensible people. They have sense enough to know that children at the age of six cannot and should not do the kind of work in school that full-grown men should tackle. The Utopians know that physical and moral development are involved in intellectual development. Their educational system makes provision for the participation of educators in physical and moral development at the proper stages and in the proper ways, but never in such ways as to confuse anybody about who has the responsibility at every stage for intellectual development and who for moral and physical growth.

The Utopians believe that education is a conversation aimed at truth. Their object is to get everybody to take part in this conversation. They therefore start their children off by teaching them the techniques of communication. Those of you who have children may feel that this is a work of supererogation; but the Utopians think there is a great difference between chattering and conversing. The first ten years of the Utopian educational system is devoted primarily to reading, writing, and figuring. Because the Utopians are aware of the axiom that subjects that cannot be understood without experience should not be taught to those who are without experience, they do not bother inexperienced children with what are called the social studies. They want to fill their minds and touch their imaginations with the kind of knowledge suitable to their years. In the first ten years of his education, therefore, the young Utopian studies history, geography, and the greatest literature of the world. It is not supposed that he will understand all the implications of history and literature, but it is believed that he should be introduced to them in childhood and in such a way that he will want to continue to study them all his life. Since no one can understand his own language, or what a language is, by speaking or studying his own, every young Utopian masters a foreign language. And every young Utopian studies science; for this subject the Utopians regard as indispensable to understanding the modern world, and they believe that, as a subject that does not require experience, it is one that children can begin to study very early. In view of the celebrity that Utopians have achieved in the world of art and music, I need hardly add that all of them study these subjects.

By the age of sixteen the young Utopian has studied very few subjects; but he has studied all those appropriate to his time of life. The object has been to get him to go on studying them as long as he lives. The object has also been to fit him to understand any new idea or any new field that presents itself to him. And the great overruling object has been to prepare him to become a member of the republic. Almost all the teaching in Utopia is conducted through discussion. The educational system is a paradigm of the conversation through which a democracy works.

At the age of sixteen, or earlier if he is ready for it, the Utopian passes into the College. Here he continues to study history, geography, literature, science, music, and art, but the emphasis shifts from learning the techniques of communication to obtaining familiarity with the principal views of the world that men have developed and the leading ideas that have animated mankind. The curriculum from the beginning of the elementary school through the College is completely prescribed for all the students. The Utopians do not believe that any civilized man can omit any of the subjects that are included in the course of study. And they do not doubt that the educational profession is better qualified to say what children should study than the children themselves. The Utopians have heard of the American plan, by which a certain number of courses, whatever they are, finally add up to a degree, but the Utopians are, as I have said, a sensible people, and the credit system has never been introduced among them. This is one of the things that makes the country Utopia.

Somewhere between the ages of eighteen and twenty, or whenever he is ready, the Utopian presents himself for examinations that cover the whole of his education up to that point. These examinations, which are constructed by an outside board, reflect what the educational profession of Utopia thinks of as a liberal education, the education appropriate to free men. If the student passes these examinations, he is awarded the degree of Bachelor of Arts. The Utopians have never been confused about the award of this degree at this stage, because the degree has never been debased into a certificate of time served, or credits accumulated, or a license to enter a graduate school, or a qualification for membership in the University Club. It has always stood for liberal education, and this is what the examinations at the end of the College of Utopia stand for, too.

The organization of the University of Utopia I have already roughly described. It is constituted of institutions of about twenty-five professors and two hundred and fifty students each. They are exclusively residential, for the same reason that the centers of adult education in Utopia are residential. Specialized study in Utopia begins only with the University. The University is built on the principle that men who must be intensively trained in the specialties must not lose their liberal education or their ability to communicate with other men or their interest in and capacity to understand ideas in any field of learning. All the major fields of learning are therefore represented in the faculties and among the students of the institutions of which the University of Utopia is composed. Because the Utopians recognize that the tendency of specialization is centrifugal and that every precaution must be taken against this tendency, they require the members of these institutions to live together.

The object of the University of Utopia is the clarification and reinterpretation of basic ideas. All ideas that can seriously pretend to be basic are discussed. The Utopians, because of the character of their liberal education, have little difficulty in assessing the pretensions of various ideas. Those ideas which underlie the learned professions are included. Those occupations which do not rest on any intellectual content or which have none in their own right are necessarily excluded; for how could those interested in them take part in the conversation? Persons who are interested only in the accumulation of data about some subject, even a subject of great importance, like the operations of government, or of the economic system, or of protons or proteins, are, unless they are able to think and communicate about the ideas involved in these phenomena, necessarily excluded, too.

The qualifications of the professors of the University of Utopia are strikingly different from those which prevail in the United States. With us the professor must only be eminent, or give promise of attaining eminence, in his field. In Utopia the professor must be eminent, or give promise of attaining eminence, in his field. This is taken as a matter of course. But unless in addition to meeting this requirement he is also willing and able to receive light from other fields and shed light from his own upon the basic problems that the University is discussing, he cannot be appointed. This conclusion follows remorselessly from the conception of a university that the Utopians entertain.

The students of the University of Utopia are not there because they do not want to go to work, or because they want to move a rung or two up the social ladder, or because they want to learn how to get ahead in some occupation, or because without the civilizing influence of the Dean of Men or the Dean of Women they might turn into juvenile delinquents. The students are there because they have intellectual interests and have shown in the program of liberal education they have passed through that they are capable of developing them. The University is not concerned with the question whether the studies of these students prepare them to carry on some specific activity in later life. Such a question would be incomprehensible to a Utopian. The Utopians have the conviction that intellectual activity and the discussion of the most important theoretical and practical problems is indispensable to a happy life and to the progress, and even the safety, of the state.

The University of Utopia was conceived and established as a center of independent thought. I have said enough to show in what sense it is a center: everybody can and will communicate with everybody else. I have perhaps said enough to suggest in what sense it deals with thought: anything that is not thought can have no place in it. By this I do not mean that the University is opposed to recreation or social life. The program of extracurriculum activities is startling in its range and richness. All I mean is that the University has never confused these activities with the purpose of the institution. One reason for this is, perhaps, that intercollegiate football has never taken root—it has never even been thought of—in Utopia. As I have said, the Utopians are a sensible people.

Since they are sensible, they do not deny the value of the collection of information or data; nor do they deny the importance of technical training in many fields. And they would be the last to say that a society should not organize itself in some way to bring its knowledge and experience to bear on its urgent practical problems. All that the Utopians claim is that such activities, the collection of data, technical training, and the solution of immediate practical problems, cannot be conducted in a university without disrupting, or at least confusing, the institution. Since they regard the University as a highly specialized institution, they do not want it confused. They see confusion as the first step toward underspecialization and disintegration.

The Utopians understand, however, that men engaged in the collection of data, technical training at high levels, and the solution of urgent practical problems have much to gain from association with such men and with such undertakings. This is not because the professors are sensitive to the charge that they live in an ivory tower or have never met a payroll—such absurdities are never heard in Utopia—but because the Utopians recognize that anything worth thinking about has consequences in the practical order and that anything in the practical order may suggest something that is worth thinking about.

The Utopians have therefore surrounded the University with organizations collecting data, giving technical training at high levels, and seeking the solution of urgent practical problems, and the interchange between these groups and the members of the University is very active. Neither side of the exchange is at all confused about what is the University and what is not. Neither side would wish to be the other. Each institution is specialized. These arrangements have worked remarkably well. I have heard that they were modeled after those between the Public Administration Clearing House and the University of Chicago.

I have now shown in what sense the University of Utopia is a center and in what sense it is dedicated to thought. In the next chapter I shall attempt to show in what sense it is independent and is therefore entitled to be called a center of independent thought. But I should say something now about the idea of independence as it affects the students of the University.

As you know, they enter the University between the ages of eighteen and twenty, having sought to obtain the beginnings of a liberal education in the College. Their object in the University is to continue this education, to participate in the discussion that is the University, to understand the reasons for things, and to master the ideas in an important field of learning. The first difference that strikes us in looking at what they do and what the American student does lies in the negligible amount of formal instruction given to them. Twenty years ago, when I asked the chairman of the Economics Department at the University of Chicago why he had such large and frequent classes for graduate students, he replied, "Mr. Hutchins, my students cannot learn anything unless I am in the room." When I asked why he didn't get better students, he said, perhaps correctly, that there weren't any.

In Utopia this problem does not arise, because only those students who are qualified to do independent work and who are interested in doing it are admitted to the University. This is, in fact, one of the two great differences between the College and the University. The College does its work through formal instruction, and there is no specialization. In the University formal instruction is at a minimum, and one of the objects of the institution is to advance knowledge in special fields of learning. The College is in session for thirty-six weeks of the year; the University for only twenty-four. Since the Utopians pay no attention to time served as a criterion of intellectual progress, since, of course, there are no accrediting agencies in Utopia to tell the University that only time served can be such a criterion, and since the credit system has never been heard of, the Utopians have no difficulty in concluding that independent study and reflection should constitute the principal activity of the faculty and students of the University. In Utopia the student seldom attends formal class meetings more than four hours a week, and he is not required to attend those.

The method of instruction is chiefly discussion. The professors in the University of Utopia never lecture, except about work that they have in progress. If that work has reached the stage at which it can be written down, it is written down, distributed among the students, and discussed. No Utopian professor would think of giving a course of lectures more than once. To do so would suggest that he had no work in progress or that he was not making any progress with it.

This brief survey of the organization and operation of the Utopian educational system enables us to see in what sense philosophical diversity is a hazard to education and in what sense it may be a positive advantage. Clearly if the educational system is thought of as a means by which society indoctrinates the young with a certain view of life and the world, then philosophical diversity is fatal and must be eliminated, if necessary, by the most drastic methods. The drastic methods employed by Nazi Germany and those states which have officially embraced Marxism are known to all of us. If the University is thought of as performing, among other things, the task of training the so-called intelligentsia to preserve, interpret, and teach the official philosophy, then of course philosophical diversity cannot be tolerated. Educational systems and universities in countries that have militant official philosophies may be able to cope with industrialization and specialization by some of the methods practiced in Utopia. But they cannot cope with philosophical diversity. They cannot allow it. They have to take the view that the last word has been said, or at least the last important word, and that to permit the addition of another is to promote error and endanger the unity and safety of the state.

At first glance the problems raised by philosophical diversity in countries that are without an official philosophy seem insoluble. If there are many educational philosophies, how can we avoid having many educational systems, which is manifestly absurd? Yet the Utopian experience may suggest to us that it is possible to have one educational philosophy and many philosophies. The Utopian example may show that a country can have one educational system and one educational philosophy in the face of philosophical diversity.

The Utopians have accomplished this feat by making the consideration of philosophical diversity the primary concern of educational philosophy. A glance at the University of Utopia will show how this is done. The University is not a center of propaganda for an official doctrine. Still less is it an institution like many American universities that is not concerned with doctrine at all. It is concerned with all doctrines that can have any reasonable claim to be taken seriously. Its effort is to work toward a definition of the real points of agreement and disagreement among these doctrines, not in the hope of obtaining unanimity, but in the hope of obtaining clarity. The object is not agreement but communication. The Utopians think it would be very boring to agree with one another. They think it helpful and interesting to understand one another. The University of Utopia, like the educational system as a whole, aims to bring together men of different attitudes, backgrounds, interests, temperaments, and philosophies for the purpose of promoting mutual comprehension. The University of Utopia is an understood diversity.

Thus the educational system of Utopia is a paradigm, or prototype, or model of the republic of learning and the world political republic for which the Utopians yearn.

A CURRICULAR PROPOSAL | HOWARD MUMFORD JONES

One difficulty with educational programs is that they are never built for time but are always built for eternity. Each pedagogical reformer, convinced that he has found at last a changeless and enduring way of educating human nature, announces his program as a series of timeless absolutes. Every curriculum has an air of being built upon the impregnable rock of holy scripture; and, since academic institutions are highly conservative, the new curriculum, once alive and vital, when it becomes moribund, either changes slowly or changes not at all. Thus in the British Isles a curriculum for the public schools that had real vitality for the Renaissance lingered spinelessly into the eighteenth and nineteenth centuries, nor could all the wit and wisdom of persons as gifted as Sydney Smith, Thackeray, John Stuart Mill and Thomas Huxley easily effect a change. So in American schools and colleges what has been, by sheer power of endurance, takes on a patina of wisdom and must, in the minds of teachers, forever be. Consider as an example the confused and contradictory arguments for the retention of Greek and Latin in our schools and colleges. Or again, consider how the departmental organization of our college faculties, which has split them into little groups conducting little internecine wars, is regarded by most professors as something absolute and inescapable, whereas, as a matter of history, the departmental system is the creation of the last seventy or eighty years.

I do not have the wisdom to launch another educational reform. The suggestions for a reorientation of college studies which here follow are not absolute and for all time; they are intended as a temporary expedient, one that may conceivably get us through the next fifteen or twenty years. They lack any absolute philosophy like neo-Thomism; and they do not directly offer the student what I regard as the most serious educational demand in

Reprinted by permission of the publishers from Howard Mumford Jones, *Education and World Tragedy*, Cambridge, Mass.: Harvard University Press, Copyright, 1946, by The President and Fellows of Harvard College.

the United States at the moment, namely, a democratic dynamic as vital to the democratic state as the communist dynamic of education seems to be to Russia. The problem of that dynamic is a problem of immense complexity, which only a few philosophers—for example, Ralph Barton Perry— have directly attacked; and to distinguish the merely conventional in our studies from what is lively and useful, to separate the cunning manipulation of democratic phraseology by big business or by demagogues from a really useful democratic philosophy; to attempt here and now a reinterpretation of the seventeenth and eighteenth century postulates of the American state so that these postulates have genuine meaning in our megapolitan, heterogeneous, industrialized society—all this is a prodigious problem, the solution of which would take us far afield and which I do not feel competent to attempt. Moreover, we vaguely feel that if communism is an international force, democracy should be exportable also; but, as this discussion has hinted more than once, "democracy" in the United States cannot be automatically exported to Asia or the Balkans or Africa or, apparently, even to Germany and Italy. The struggles of France to retain political democracy differ so importantly from political behavior in the British Isles or the Scandinavias as to suggest that democracy, unlike communism, is a protean manifestation and should not be confused with congressional elections in Massachusetts or California. All this amounts to a problem of immense magnitude, a problem that requires extended study, a problem that we must solve both nationally and globally. But as we have scarcely begun the explication of this immense and baffling situation, I for one am not prepared here and now to utter any *obiter dicta* on the subject. Solemnly to declare that in the democratic state education should be sympathetic to democracy is to say little enough. I can only claim that the following suggestions for a program, pragmatically conceived, are delivered, I trust, in a spirit of global democracy.

I suggest, then, that American colleges ought to consider some such program as this:

1. Professional or vocational training for all.
2. The study of the theory of science and of the application of scientific discoveries to our technology.
3. The assumptions and workings of representative government, particularly in the United States and in the British Commonwealth of Nations.
4. The study of Russia.
5. The study of the Orient.
6. The study of personal relationships in modern society.

I repeat that this program is intended to get us through the next two or three decades; it is not meant for eternity.

1. *Professional or vocational training for all.*—Perhaps the most persistent illusion of those concerned for liberal education is that it has

nothing to do with vocational or professional training and is contaminated by that training. Thus one finds theorists insisting upon the obsolete distinction descending from a slave-supported society that vocational or professional training is "servile" education. This is regarded as explicitly or implicitly hostile to "liberal" education, and every bit of time and ground that can be gained for "liberal" education from the time and ground of vocational or professional education is hailed with joy as a triumph over a common enemy of inferior intellectual status. The imputation of inferior intellectual status to vocational or professional training is astonishing, in view of the patent fact that medical students, law students, engineering students and other students who know their own minds, work about twice as hard as students in the liberal arts courses. Yet, under present conditions, two years of "general" or "liberal" education are made to precede professional or vocational specialization on the ground that these years furnish a broad foundation for the narrowing vocationalism that is to follow. Except in the artificial world of the college, the human being does not automatically switch from two years of one sort of training to two years of a diametrically opposite sort and at the same time bring to bear upon his new training the well-meant, but unfocussed, education of his first two years. "Broad" the first two years may be, but they are not broadening. This common semantic confusion haunts educational discussion.

In his *Education for Responsible Living* Wallace B. Donham, for twenty-three years dean of the Harvard Business School, reports on his experience with and observation of about 12,000 graduates of five hundred undergraduate colleges and technical schools. In recent years, he tells us, graduates of the liberal arts colleges constituted 50 per cent of students entering that school. Dean Donham makes a powerful plea for the right sort of liberal education. But of the present attitude of liberal arts colleges towards professional and vocational training he says:

> *Their contribution must be powerful enough to balance the convincing demonstration seen all around us that science and scientific training, conceived as narrowly as they conceive themselves, accomplish much in important and obvious but material ways. They must show students the catastrophic consequences of the resulting over-emphasis on material progress. It is too bad that, instead of thoughtful analysis leading to such affirmative demonstration of useful values, the liberal-arts colleges have so generally taken the easy attitude of disclaiming any intent or desire to be useful—truly a pathetic defeatist attitude for the custodians of the highest values. . . .*[1]

> *Many, if not most, college students take part or all of their work as preparation for making a living. Why, so long as this is true, should any college take pride that students who come seeking a general education leave without securing any education which equips them with background habits and skills useful in either living or making a living?*

> *In my observation, the liberal-arts graduate who stops with the A.B. and enters*

[1] Harvard University Press, 1944, p. 25.

active life in many cases faces pathetic problems. Somehow he feels his training ought to prepare him to do a better job in life but, judged by the difficulties of making a real start and the drifting process through which he frequently goes it does not. Some colleges seem to glory in this fact. It is frequently stated that liberal-arts training gives cultural values, trains men for life; not to make a living. But cultural values fly out the window when men can't get and hold jobs, and little self-respect remains if they can't make a living. The gaps now left are too wide even for the ablest men.

Dean Donham is speaking of the men; any one who has year after year seen the bewilderment of graduates of women's colleges (or women graduating from coeducational colleges) which have prepared them neither for domestic life nor for even elementary jobs in our business civilization must join his severe condemnation of an unfocussed "liberal" education. The instinct of the veterans now in colleges, most of whom demand vocational or professional training, is sounder than the theory of academic humanists. "Making a life" is a fine phrase. But you cannot in most cases "make a life" without first making a living. In the midst of a highly competitive society on the profits of whose institutions they live, it seems to me positively immoral for liberal arts colleges elaborately to pretend that their lofty purpose is to avoid soilure and that their graduates are not going to participate in the struggle which is the heart of the capitalist system.

Indeed, I think the claim of the colleges to serious attention would improve if, abandoning an attitude that descends from medieval and Renaissance social patterns, they would insist that no one should be allowed to enter their doors until he gave some reasonable assurance that he proposed to pursue a course of professional or vocational training. It is wonderful how, when the individual establishes such a goal, education comes into focus. The postponement of the necessity for such a decision by two years has left the student wandering aimlessly through freshman and sophomore courses unrelated to each other and meaningless to him, since his understandable attitude is that they are patiently to be endured until he is permitted to begin his real education. But if from the beginning of his college work—indeed, if possible, before beginning that work—the student is faced with the necessity of making an adult choice of occupation, it soon becomes possible for the college to deal with him as an adult. His professional or vocational training will not then be crowded into the last two years of a four-year curriculum, and his "liberal" education will not be administered in the vast and shoreless void of two years of drift; on the contrary, the two can be administered together, the practical necessities of the one will focus the theoretical implications of the other, and the deeper the student plunges into his professional or vocational work, the more clearly will he see the necessity of a governing philosophy. The present order of college work—elementary courses, then advanced courses, then courses in specialization—may, indeed, be logical but it violates every principle of human psychology.

The professional or vocational training desired of the liberal arts college is of two sorts. Many professions—law and medicine are examples—require two years of liberal arts work for admission to professional courses and would gladly see this work better integrated with professional needs. The seven-year curriculum combining work in Harvard College with work in the Harvard Law School indicates that this can be done. Other professions —for example, engineering—demand little of the liberal arts, but would welcome more if that "more" could be made to have meaning for the future engineer. But most liberal arts students who do not look forward to professions like these are, as a matter of fact, attending the liberal arts college for vocational training and will upon graduation launch into the fiercely competitive society that is America. One may regret the fierceness of the competition. One may, as I have done, lament the prepotent influence of technology upon education. But we do not cure a condition by pretending, as liberal arts colleges do, that it does not exist. As Dean Donham acidly remarks: "Now, for most men, liberal education stops on Commencement Day." Liberal education would begin for these same men long before commencement day if the liberal arts colleges, recognizing the vocational aims of the overwhelming majority of their students, would integrate "general education" with vocational training. One would, indeed, suppose that the pathetic belief of professional schools in the liberal arts would be immensely flattering to liberal arts faculties. Even under the programs of reforms we have discussed, these faculties make no attempt to study the nature of the vocational needs of their students but insist that whatever the faculty teaches is a private, mystical and absolute good in itself.

2. *The theory of science and the application of scientific discoveries to our technology.* Professional, vocational, technical or technological training —call it what you will—is unavoidable in a fiercely competitive industrial democracy. The problem is not to deny its necessity but to control and guide its force. The problem is to bring our social engineering up to the maturity of our technological engineering. The soundest element in the programs of general education now being adopted by liberal arts colleges is instruction in science—not in particular sciences, not in the metaphysics of scientific philosophy, but in the ordinary working assumptions of the scientific method; for example, controlled variables, verification, inference, and the like. This is certainly a step in advance of those beginning courses in chemistry, physics, biology or what not usually taught as if the beginner were going to become a professional research worker.

But a course in "general science," a course in the history of science, a course in the postulates of the scientific method will merely increase our technological confusion unless it is joined to something else. That something else is the study of what happens to scientific discoveries when they are practically put to work in our industrial culture. The woeful gap presently existing between the physical and natural scientists and the engineers on the one hand and the economists, sociologists, psychologists and anthropologists on the other hand is the most distressing fissure in our education as it is in our society. That as many persons as possible living in a technological culture should know as much as possible about the working assumptions of the scientist is patent—so patent, it is embarrassing that education has taken this long to make this discovery of the obvious; but that the spread of this information, unless it is positively checked by other, sobering, social forces may merely speed our descent into the maelstrom is also so patent as scarcely to require demonstration. Scientists, many of them, are genuinely distressed at the cultural lag between their work and the imperfections of the social processes which use the results of their labor; yet a movement like Science Search, intended to discover scientific talent in the secondary schools and encourage it to enter research training, merely increases the rapidity of our technological advance without guaranteeing any concomitant social understanding. Economist and sociologist, psychologist and anthropologist must, in my judgment, join the scientist and point out that when science invents the internal combustion engine, vast economic and sociological forces are set to work. It is insufficient to praise research for its own sake. The tremendous (and sometimes tragic) results of research for its own sake, when these results take the form of widespread technological change in modern society, are as basic to an understanding of the modern world as any part of scientific theory. The creation of instructional units of this sort will be a matter of great difficulty, but to keep scientific theory in one compartment and economic and social studies of a technological culture in another compartment is precisely the tragic error of our education and of our culture.

3. *Representative government in the United States and in the British Commonwealth of Nations.* Doubtless there is something to be said for a general history of western institutions or of Europe or of the western world or whatever other formula is advanced in programs of general education. I cannot escape feeling that, however fruitful such instruction may be for philosophers, as an element of common education during the next two decades or so a critical study of the history and function of representative government in this country and in the British Commonwealth of Nations is far more necessary. What are its real strength and weakness? Why does it seem to break down in most of the countries of the earth and why does it not perform more effectively for us? As I have indicated, the fond assumption of western man that British parliamentarianism or the American check-and-balance system is both an absolute good and something for the export trade is one of the dangerous historical illusions of our day. If all undergraduates had time and interest enough, general courses in history might, indeed, throw light upon the problem of the democratic state, but history, to have general meaning, must for most students be focussed upon present problems; and the present problem with us is whether our country can survive under an eighteenth century constitution operative on nine-

teenth century postulates in the "One World" of the twentieth century. If the world during the next few years is going to be split, as it threatens to be, between the communistic and the democratic theories of the state, surely our common studies should be far more realistically focussed upon the workings of the principal democratic states in our tradition. This seems to me so elementary I do not think it requires elaborate explication.

4. *The study of Russia.* The same logic, however, makes the study of Russia—its culture, its government, its economic structure, the character and desires of its myriad peoples—of paramount importance, and it is gratifying to see a slow increase of academic interest in Russian studies. If Russia is to become the chief enemy of the democracies (which God forbid!) we ought to comprehend her; if she is to become the friend and aider of the democracies, all the more reason for the widest spread of sympathetic information about the Russian empire. In the next quarter of a century this empire is going to be of far greater importance to modern man than the empire of the Caesars or of Charlemagne or of Napoleon, now commonly studied in the schools. It is high time the Americans got over their silly attitude toward "communism" and tried to comprehend it. Even sons of members of the National Association of Manufacturers are going to have to understand the workings of the Russian state system.

Of course it takes a certain courage to advocate a sympathetic approach to the Russian problem. Not long ago, when Cornell University founded a school of Russian studies, hysteria swept through the conservative or reactionary New York press. The same educational timidity which in World War I crippled the American war effort by throwing the German language out of the schools on the ground that it was an enemy tongue is, alas! already at work among us, thwarting the spread of elementary information about the Russian state. This vast nation shares with the English-speaking nations the domination of the globe; the average American student knows less about it than he knows about Julius Caesar or Cromwell. We cannot continue indefinitely the policy of ignoring what we fear or dislike. Every consideration—the importance of the Russian theory of economic life, business interest, politics, the life of the arts, the advance of science, gratitude, the solution of the problem of racial tension, geography, diplomacy, the operations of the United Nations charter—demands a primary place in American education for the study and comprehension of the Russian world.

5. *The study of the Orient.* The westward course of the American empire did not halt at the Golden Gate but has gone on to Hawaii, the Philippines, Japan, China, India, and Asia generally. Asia is the problem of the future, a problem we have done as much as any other nation to create and which we must do as much as any other nation to solve. It is at least probable that by sheer force of numbers, if mankind is to survive,

the future of mankind lies with the Asiatics. They are, and they will
remain, numerously the greatest single segment of the human race.
American undergraduates know nothing or next to nothing about the
cultures, the history, the problems and the needs of these myriads with
whom American intercourse is bound constantly to increase. The widespread lack of comprehension of even the simplest postulate of any
Oriental civilization, the profound disruption wrought in the Orient by
crude forcing process of "Occidentalization" hitherto common, the rich
contribution which the Orient has to make to our troubled western world
—these and multiple other considerations demand that if the United
States is a world power in a global universe, its educational system cannot
longer ignore Oriental culture as it has done hitherto except at rarefied
scholarly levels. Chinese universities as a matter of course require the
study of the West; we in our blindness do not think the East worth study.
Yet, together with Russia, it is the most important cultural problem our
technological civilization has to face.

Perhaps the words of Professor Northrop in *The Meeting of East and
West,* may carry conviction if mine do not:

> *The time is here when we must understand the Orient if we would understand
> ourselves, and when we must learn how to combine Oriental and Occidental
> values if further tragedy, bitterness, and bloodshed are not to ensue.*[4]
>
> *These considerations all remind us that neither war nor the peace-time problems
> of our world can be diagnosed as a simple issue between the good and the bad.
> This, to be sure, is the interpretation which each party to the disputes of our time
> puts upon events. But the very number and diversity of conceptions of what the
> good and the divine is give the lie to any such diagnosis, and to the ever present
> proposal that a return to the traditional morality and religion is the cure for our
> ills. All that such proposals accomplish is the return of each person, each religious
> denomination, each political group or nation to its own pet traditional doctrine.
> And since this doctrine (or the sentiments which it has conditioned) varies at
> essential points from person to person, group to group, nation to nation, and
> East to West, this emphasis upon traditional religion and morality generates con-
> flicts and thus intensifies rather than solves our problems. This in fact is the
> basic paradox of our time: our religion, our morality and our "sound" economic
> and political theory tend to destroy the state of affairs they aim to achieve.*
>
> *This condition will expectably increase in complexity and intensity, because
> in addition to continuing conflict between diverse moral, religious, political and
> economic ideologies in the West, there will be a more direct confrontation of
> Occidental cultural values.*
>
> *Nevertheless, to become aware of this complicated, dangerous, and paradox-
> ically confusing situation is to have at hand the clue to the way to meet it.*

At a very high level Professor Northrop's book shows how the conflict of
cultures can be made educationally understandable. What is needed—

[4] The Macmillan Company, 1946. p. 4.

what is desperately needed in our colleges—is a simplification and a generalization of his courageous volume.

6. *The study of personal relationships in modern society.* The elements of general education hitherto suggested may prove difficult in the teaching, but they are at any rate specific. The sixth and last of these elements, highly important though it is, cannot be so specific. I refer to the need of restoring confidence in the relations between man and man.

Perhaps, in a fiercely competitive society, confidence in these relations cannot be wholly restored, but the present corruption of these relations can certainly be checked and the condition improved. The deepest corruption of western life—a corruption revealed by the Nazis only because they exaggerated a tendency everywhere seen in the industrial order—is the profound distrust of personal relationships within that order. The logic of the Nazi state came to be that nobody trusted anybody else. Before we conclude that, by destroying Hitler, we have destroyed the inner weakness of western society, let us ask ourselves how far the sense of insecurity has spread. The common phrases of the day are illuminating. The fear of being double-crossed, the fear of sticking your neck out, the fear of being taken in, the fear, in sum, that your competitor may not play the game according to the rules—these are the fears that seem to haunt our young men and women as they enter the competitive game. One of the most illuminating facts to be observed in this connection is the way many of these younger persons turn to psychology and to anthropology for a more valid explanation of the vagaries of human behavior than is to be found in the official sanctions of that behavior.

The calm good faith of the younger Russian generation in each other and in their culture is in contrast to the uneasiness evident in the American world lest personal relations, business relations, labor relations, or any other of a dozen connections between individual and individual shall prove deceptive. We are each one afraid of being "worked." To repeat Professor Mayo's words: "we have in fact passed beyond that stage of human organization in which effective communication and collaboration were secured by established routines of relationship." Perhaps the most tremendous task before higher education is to seek out means of restoring between human being and human being that calm and confident relationship which our western culture has lost, is losing, and will continue to lose until psychologist and physician, sociologist and anthropologist, by combining their studies, can perhaps restore this simple faith to western man. Professor Mayo rightly charges us with "utter social incompetence." But the beginning of social competence is the trust of man in man; and a wider understanding of the psychology of personal relationships seems to me a more desperate need in our education than polite courses in literature, philosophy and the fine arts. The spirit of scepticism and disillusion which seems to charm many specialists in these latter fields is, however, sorry guarantee for the restoration of confidence; and it may be that nothing short of a renovation of belief in the democratic process will cure our humanists. "Physician, heal thyself" was never more applicable. . . .

A thousand objections immediately arise. "General" or "liberal" education has usually been thought of in formal terms like philosophy, literature, the arts, the sciences, and of right combination among these traditional elements of the college curriculum. The program here outlined as basically desirable says nothing about literature and philosophy and science, except incidentally. How can one be sure that the right balance is maintained? How can one be sure that one is not turning out badly educated men and women unless one demands a certain quantum of literature and philosophy and science?

The tacit assumption of this comment is that existing curricula with their formal requirements of concentration and distribution and their formal logical structures succeed in producing cultivated graduates in the humanistic sense of the word. Attendance upon any alumni gathering is a sufficient practical comment upon this assumption. Aesthetic, literary or philosophical lore is a matter of fact not taught except to a relative minority with any such effectiveness as is professional or vocational training; and however fondly the alumnus may look back upon his dear old college days, it is rather upon an agreeable and harmless utopia than upon the source of a cultural dynamic in his own life. The difficulty with the genteel college is that it remains genteel. "Culture" is something for one's leisure hours, for women, for librarians and for other minority groups. The difficulty is that books read in a vacuum, philosophy taught formally, history as a requirement and science as a required balance to intellectual digestion have a somewhat remote significance for one's later life except to a minority of scholarly or aesthetic temperaments.

Nothing, indeed, more illumines the theoretical approach of the academic mind to the painful problem of values than the question of books, which may here serve as an exposition of why so much college instruction is superficial. To the aesthetic or the bookminded person a classic is a work of stimulating interest, filled with thought about man and the universe, enriched with the patina of history, and beautiful with traditional form and modulated style. What can be more simple and right than, by requiring the young idea to read this work under skillful guidance, to enrich the budding personality through canalizing the wealth of the classic into the personality being shaped by instruction and reading? And the professor of English (and concurrently of any other bookish branch of the curriculum) points with justifiable pride to students of his who have been awakened to literary glories, who have learned to "love books" in college or who have perhaps gone on into the graduate school as a result of this affectionate instruction. All men can, in greater or less degree, profit by the classics. Only—there is the unfortunate unbookish quality of the alumni reunion, from which the professor of English flees and towards which his attitude is one of enforced toleration. Why does not learning to "love books" seem to have more durable effects than it does?

It would require a volume larger than this to explore the truth and error mingled in the theory. Suffice it to say that the meaning of any book lies in its relevance to the reader at the time he reads it. A book of ephemeral value may be extremely cogent and, contrariwise, as college courses in literature frequently show, the great classics may have only a formal, not a living, significance. Indeed, with the vast majority of undergraduates, this formal quality is all that the classics ever possess. In truth, the great classic, product usually of a mature mind which has known the sweat and agony of existence, is remote in actuality from the slight experience, the limited emotional range and the simple intellectual equipment of most college students. The surprising thing in truth is not that the classics too frequently remain inert matter, but that the energy of teachers brings many of them into a real, if fitful, life in the classroom. Unfortunately this life too seldom extends beyond the artifices of course instruction.

All this is not to argue that the classics are not to be taught. It is to say, however, that books have meaning in life or in pedagogy only when, as William James would say, the student faces a real option; and in a world that must either unite or perish, so far as classroom instruction can furnish the semblance of reality, the real options that most students are going to confront are of the sort outlined in the program of general education herein laid down. How far does any book throw light upon the problem of representative (or, if you will, popular) government? What can we learn from the classics of Orient and Occident about living issues East and West? What has Shakespeare or Emerson to tell us about the validity of personal relationships? Curricula do not exist for the sake of books, of philosophy professors, of history texts or even of science; on the contrary, science and the arts exist for the sake of a curriculum relevant to the needs of a society supporting the college. The academic mind is always pretending that "real life" fails in proportion as it does not mirror academic order.

A second objection is that the program demands the study of Russian and of Oriental culture but does not equally demand the study of western culture. This is true. Had we but time and space enough, everything from Cretan civilization to Bikini could be brought to bear upon modern problems. If one supposes that the program here suggested ignores the traditions of western culture (which it does not), I should still defend it on two grounds: first, that the urgency of our times gives priority to the kind of study I have suggested; and second, that in education we must take some things for granted. Surely, unless secondary education is a complete failure, the student has learned enough about the backgrounds of the western world so that he does not feel alien in it. Surely the student intelligent enough to be admitted to college has learned from high school, from newspaper and magazine, from radio and movie at least enough to get along. That "enough" is, I grant, erratic, wrong-headed and ill-organized; and college teachers take perpetual delight in dwelling upon the absurd historical errors and ignorances of the young. But the weakness of the academic mind is the study of perfection; and as between the lamentable incorrectness of undergraduate information about Pericles or the middle ages, Matthew Arnold or Dante, the categorical imperative or solipsism, and the lack of any information whatsoever about the peoples and nations on most of the surface of the globe, for the next twenty years or so I am willing to risk misinformation about Pericles and French classicism in order to gain at least a modicum of information about Russia, the Orient, and other pressing matters. If this be philistinism, make the most of it.

The program here proposed does not concentrate upon the traditions of western history, but neither does it ignore the West. On the contrary, it concentrates upon four highly essential elements in western civilization. Professional, technological or vocational training for skilled or specialized jobs is one of the prime qualities differentiating western culture from traditional Oriental notions of education. If the development of industrial culture has, as it obviously has, led to the curious and disheartening breakdown in the validity of personal relationships, then the study of why these relationships too often fail western man lies at the heart of the western cultural problem. Any catalog of the most characteristic productions of western civilization will certainly include western science and representative government—both are here included, and my proposal to make the assumptions of science clearer to more people goes beyond the claims of traditionalists in that it is proposed also to make clear what happens to a society in which science constantly receives new practical applications. One must not confuse book learning satisfactory in the library with a genuine operational grasp of western culture. And eventually, as I have indicated, I hope that philosophers, educators and psychologists will work out a philosophically based dynamic for democratic society that is not found in any program hitherto set up.

A third objection partially includes the previous two. It arises from the absence of customary terms of academic reference. What about departments? What about degree programs? What place for chemistry or mathematics, foreign language and composition? Is this culture? Is this a liberal education?

I have deliberately avoided all mention of departments and their specialties in connection with this program for a particular reason. Departments are, by and large, one of the two greatest evils in our academic education, the present conduct of graduate schools being the other. Unless and until we abandon the double-entry book-keeping by which in departments we now appoint, promote, pay and subdue our teachers, it really makes no great difference whether we adopt the dogmatic system or fall back upon the traditions of western culture or take over the ideas here suggested, because, in the classic phrase of Al Smith, slice it any way you will, it will still be baloney. We cannot make real education advance, so far as general training is concerned, without overhauling the departmental system.

The present departmental organization of the American college faculty represents, indeed, the inherent contradiction in the aims of that college and may be insoluble. Departments are the products of specialism, which they in turn nourish; specialism is part of the professional or vocational training necessary for survival in capitalist society; and yet specialism, unduly emphasized, is, as traditionalists rightly aver, at war with every sound conception of education or the state. On the other hand, the faculty of the liberal arts and sciences theoretically represents the wholeness of modern knowledge outside the professions; men therefore turn to it for the general training they desiderate. But the college professor cannot serve two masters; he cannot operate simultaneously on the level of "broad" general training and on the level of specialism, inasmuch as his own professional training, his professional loyalty and his professional business are part of the very specialism he is supposed to counteract; and the result is the uneasy compromise of the American college program. The roots of this evil go back to the graduate school, to which I shall by and by turn; here I can only point to the dilemma of all programs of curricular reform.

The situation is difficult and may be insoluble; it is not yet hopeless. Perhaps the most fruitful educational experience coming out of World War II was the discovery that, under stress, departmentalism can be made to curl up and die. In place of the artificial structures of "departments," in surprising degree the creatures of college book-keeping and the bane of administration, there were established during the war what were known as area and language schools. That is to say, the colleges brought to bear upon the interpretation of a given culture—Japan will do for illustration —*any* person and *any* information that were relevant, whether they had to do with economics or dating statues of Buddha or identifying volcanic ash or memorizing verbs. What is here proposed for peace is simply the continuation and amplification of this program. In place of dividing Russia among a dozen hostile departments—Slavic languages, geography, history, economics, fine arts, and the like—we ought to bring to bear upon the interpretation of Russia for general education whatever specialties, whatever disciplines, whatever knowledges illumine the problem. Similarly for other topics—the interpretation of scientific method and the application of science in social terms, the history of representative government, the cultures of the Orient, the problem of personal relationships. I do not see that the problem of personnel organization is greater in peace than it was in war; and as the only alternative to this regrouping of teachers is apparently the continuation of the departmental system, I prefer experimentation. One is told, of course, that it can't be done. The reply is that it has been done, and done successfully. I do not see that the administrative problem is more complicated in peace than in war. I am not utopian enough to think that the evils of academic organization are completely to be remedied; what I do argue is that it is more important for American undergraduates to understand Russia and representative government, science, personal relations and the cultures of the East than it is to perpetuate a scholarly hierarchy. One sadly reflects again, however, that no priesthood is ever reformed by its members.

A fourth objection to the program is that it is too hard. What? Undergraduates to study the Orient? And Russia? And the development of representative government here and abroad, the techniques and application of science, and the problem of relationships in industrial society? Well, I think better of students than objectors do. My uneasiness is not for the student but for the teacher. I am willing to wager that, once the undergraduate discovers the relevancy of the proposed program (or something like it) to the world he lives in, he will bring to it a zeal beyond that he casually lends to conventional college courses and beyond the more active interest an undergraduate minority of a highly literate order brings, it is said, to the study of Great Books. Moreover, the scattered parts of my studies are already present and being pursued in the curriculum—for example, the theory of science and the Brito-American problem of government; all I seek is to bring these scattered parts out from under the departmental system into living wholes for a least the next two decades.

American students are, I think, at least as intelligent as Orientals. I have observed for a good many years that Oriental students manage to familiarize themselves with western culture that is to them at least as difficult as Oriental and Russian cultures seem to be to Americans. I do not see that it is any harder to study the problems proposed than it is to master the scientific and other classics solemnly proposed in the St. John's curriculum, supposing these to be really mastered. The truth is, of course, that the theoretical demands of the conventional college curriculum are high; they are not enforceable because they do not seem to students essential. I hope to make some of these demands essential by giving them reality. Learning and mastery will follow upon interest, precisely as it does in vocational or professional training.

A fifth objection is the vagueness of the plan. Says the objector: You deliberately remove these complicated problems from familiar academic landmarks. You do not say how this general education is to be fused with the professional or vocational training that you regard as necessary or unavoidable. You do not say whether the study of personal relationships is to be a course or a curriculum. You propose to substitute for departmental organization, which is at least in being and familiar, some vague grouping of personnel into staff relationships. Are these units lecture courses, to be taught by sections or recitation affairs? Are you abolishing English composition as a universal requirement? In sum, are not your changes, however excellent in intent, dreamy and impractical in terms of the present American college?

I do not know the workable answer to every question of this order. It is, however, precisely because I do not know the answers to these pragmatical inquiries that I believe answers should be found. I must remind the reader again of Dean Carmichael's shrewd observation that we are carrying forward processes of education on essentially the same basis as that on which our predecessors dealt with them, notwithstanding the fact that the society into which graduates go has undergone marked change. It is not important how academic book-keeping readjusts itself to this six-point program; what is important is that the academic mind shall adjust itself to the atomic world. I hope it is not overly smug to observe that in setting forth educational aims thinkers from Plato to John Dewey have been as specific as they could be about the direction and purpose of education, leaving to others the implementation of their desires. The tentative program of this book is not, to put it mildly, of the order of Plato and Aristotle; it is something designed to get us through the next quarter of a century because the need for adjustment is urgent; but it is no more an objection to this program that it does not offer a blueprint of course credits, salaries, examinations, and other parts of the academic machine than it is an objection to *Emile* that Rousseau did not draw up a lawyer's contract for a teacher and a school.

ABOUT MACHINES AND MEN

TWO CENTURIES AGO, talk about machines was simply talk about machines, without inspiring or unnerving implications. The simple contrivances of those days—spinning wheels, windmills, lathes—were little more than tools used by one man to refine or increase the product of his labor. They did not substantially alter the relationship between man and his environment that had held for many thousands of years before. Assertions about these machines, therefore, were relatively passive, unlikely to explode into larger issues.

But the subject has become charged since 1750. We are all familiar, almost to the point of insensibility, with the changes brought on by machines. Movement, communication, production, warfare, housekeeping, farming, bookkeeping, and dentistry are all thoroughly mechanized. Only switch on a light, and you put into use a system so complex that virtually no one man understands all of it. We confront the world and act upon it, not directly, but by remote control. So statements about machines are, by implication, statements about the condition of human life, and writers about machines, except for the most unremittingly technical, can scarcely ignore such implications.

The first three pieces in this unit, written between 1929 and 1939, explicitly consider machines as influences on the men who build and use them. Stuart Chase (1888—), American popular writer on many subjects, Sherwood Anderson (1876-1941), American novelist, and Friedrich Georg Juenger (1898-   ), German political philosopher, were all acutely conscious of the mechanical revolution that surrounded them and of its human significance, although they were at odds in their attitudes.

In the last twenty-five years the revolution has taken a new leap. Whereas mechanical devices substituted for muscle, digital computers and other new electronic devices assist the sensory organs and the brain. Many of them, in fact, perform prodigies far beyond the capacity of a human brain, and, in so doing, call in question the very uniqueness of man. If a machine can be constructed to simulate (or improve on) the most complex and characteristic sorts of human behavior, what implications does this fact have for our notions of mind, soul, and life? The thought that machines may soon not only reshape human life but actually imitate it lies behind the other three selections in this unit, one by a neurologist (W. Grey Walter, 1910—); one by a specialist in computers (A. M. Turing, 1912-1954); and one by a philosopher (Paul Ziff, 1920—). The first two are British; the third is an American.

SLAVES AND PHILOSOPHERS | *STUART CHASE*

CERTAIN philosophers hold that machinery is enslaving us. I am not a machine tender, but first and last I encounter a good many mechanisms in a day's march, particularly when that day is spent in a city so large and so complicated that it could never have been built by human muscle. Before analyzing the extent of serfdom in others, it might be well to determine how far I am myself a slave.

The first thing that I hear in the morning is a machine—a patented alarm clock. It calls and I obey. But if I do not feel like obeying, I touch its back, and it relapses humbly into silence. Thus we bully each other, with the clock normally leading by a wide margin. (Once, however, I threw a clock out of the window, and it never bullied anyone again.)

I arise and go into the bathroom. Here I take up a second mechanism, and after inserting a piece of leather between its rollers, move it briskly

From *Men and Machines* (New York, The Macmillan Company, 1929), pp. 1-9. Reprinted by permission of the author.

up and down before proceeding to scrape my face with it. I turn various faucets and a mixing valve, and a nickel dial studded with little holes showers me with water. Depending on the season, I may snap on electric lights and an electric heater. Downstairs, if it chances to be either the first or the fifteenth day of the month, I take a can with a very long nose, and oil an electric motor which blows petroleum into my furnace, a motor which runs the washing machine, and a motor which operates my refrigeration engine. Meanwhile an electrical range is cooking my breakfast, and on the table slices of bread are being heated by an electrical toaster which makes a buzzing sound in its vitals, and then suddenly splits open when the toast is browned to a turn. If time allows, I may play a little tune on the piano which stands near the breakfast table, noting the delicate system of levers and hammers upon which the mechanism is based. Before I leave the house, the whine of the vacuum cleaner is already in my ears.

I go to the garage, and by proper and sometimes prolonged manipulations, start explosions in six cylinders of an internal combustion engine. With foot and hand, I put the revolving crank shaft in touch with the rear wheels, and proceed to pilot the whole mechanism to the station, passing or halting before three sets of automatic signal lights as I go. At the station, I cease operating machinery and resign myself to another man's operation of an enormous secondary mover, fed by a third rail from a hydroelectric turbine at Niagara Falls. I cannot glance out of the window without seeing a steamboat on the Hudson River, a steam shovel on the speculative real estate development, a travelling crane on a coal dock, or a file of motor cars on any street. Every so often comes the faint roar and silver glint of an airplane, winging its way above the river.

Arrived at the metropolitan terminal, I buy a package of cigarettes by depositing a coin in a machine which hands me matches and says, "Thank you; it's toasted." I then spend ten minutes walking just three blocks. If I tried to shorten this time appreciably, I should most certainly be killed by a machine. Instead, I look down into an enormous pit where the day before yesterday, according to the best of my recollection, there stood a solid brownstone house. Now it is an inferno of swarming men, horses, trucks, pile drivers, rock drills, steam shovels, clacking pumps, and preparation for erecting a gigantic steel derrick. From across the street comes the deafening rat-tat-too of riveters.

I enter my office building and a machine shoots me vertically towards the roof. I step into a large room, stopping for a moment on the threshold to sort out the various mechanical noises which lend a never-ending orchestral accompaniment to all my working hours in town. The sputter of typewriters; the thud as the carriage is snapped back; the alternate rings and buzzes of the telephone switchboard; the rhythmic thump of the adding machine; the soft grind of a pencil sharpener; the remorseless clack of the addressograph and the mimeograph. During the day I make and receive about twenty calls upon the telephone. I crank an adding machine from time to time. I may operate a typewriter for an hour or so. Meanwhile my eye can seldom stray long from my watch, if the day is to be got through with at all.

To go up or downtown I use one of the three horizontal levels of transporation which the city affords. As a profound melancholia always accompanies a trip on the lowest, I endeavor to use the upper two exclusively. Many of my fellow citizens do the same, particularly since a score of them were killed at Times Square the other day. Killed in the rush hour, like beeves in the Chicago stockyards; except that the packers put no more animals into a pen than can go in.

In the evening I reverse the morning process. At home, I may sit for a few moments beneath a machine which gives off ultra-violet rays, or I may dance to strains of a machine which runs a steel needle over a corrugated rubber disc, and for the governor of whose delicate mechanism we are indebted to James Watt. For days at home, direct contact is limited to running the motor car and making minor repairs upon it; answering the telephone; using, hearing, tinkering with the various household so-called labor savers—particularly the plumbing system.

In the summer, by way of contrast, I may spend weeks in a mountain camp, where the only mechanisms are the motor car, the telephone, and a remarkably temperamental contrivance for pumping water. Year in year out I doubt if my direct contact with machines averages much over two hours a day. When I go to town, the ratio runs considerably higher; when I stay at home, an hour would certainly cover it; in the summer, an hour would be too much.

So far as I am aware, no permanently evil effects befall me by virtue of these two mechanical hours. I suffer from no prolonged monotonies, fatigues or repressions. The worst moments are dodging street traffic and hearing its roar, riding in the subway, changing tires and cleaning out the incinerator. When the telephone becomes unduly obstreperous, I go away and leave it. By far the most fatiguing noise in my office is the scraping of chair legs on the hard composition floor—and chairs I believe antedated Watt. All the depressions that I suffer from direct contact with machinery are certainly compensated for by the helping hand it holds out to me—a calculator for figuring percentages, an oil heater which requires no stoking, a reading lamp which does not have to be trimmed and filled, an elongated radius of travel possibilities, a car for errands, together with the genuine thrill which often comes from controlling its forty horses.

I do not feel like a slave, though of course I may be one all the same. Clocks and watches are hard masters but so they always have been; there is nothing new or ominous about their tyranny. No individual living in a social group is ever free, but I wonder if these two mechanized hours have put more shackles on me than were to be found on the average citizen of Rome two thousand years ago, or of China today—cultures innocent of engines both. As I look about the United States, the most mechanized nation under the sun, I have reason to believe—and later will bring in the statistical proof—that the number of those bound intimately to the rhythm of the machine is a small percentage of the total population, while there are probably more people with contacts remoter than mine than with closer contacts. In other words, I am more mechanized than the majority of my fellow citizens, and, needless to say, far less mechanized than a minority thereof.

Meanwhile an astonishing, not to say disturbing, enlargement has taken place in our several human faculties; an access of power which seems strangely out of place in a race of serfs. Perhaps the best way to indicate it is to sketch a contrast.

One day I came upon an urchin in the middle of the Russian steppe. He watched us change a tire on the first motor car that he had ever seen. We drove him to his village, where all his friends and relatives stood boggle-eyed at our approach. That boy and that village were carrying on substantially as their forebears had done for a thousand years—the timeless rural economy of the spade, the hand loom and the ox. Growing to manhood there, he will in all probability continue to carry on for years to come, despite the commendable exertions of his Government.

He will use his eyes, ears, senses and muscles according to the same biological limitations which the builders of Stonehenge knew—which mankind has always known. His strength will be that of his own back; his sensitiveness that of his own nerves. For heavy loads from time to time a horse or an ox may help him. The power will be that of living organisms, no more.

Suppose that boy is brought to New York. Suppose, as has been the case with many Russians, he develops into a talented scientist. Suppose he becomes, for the moment, a generic figure for the scientist and engineer, familiar with the main aspects of modern technology and capable of operating its mechanical devices.

Suddenly the biological limitations of the peasant youth are banished. He begins to grow in all directions—physical and mental. His eye at the lens of a telescope becomes one million times stronger; his voice before a microphone can be heard ten thousand miles away. His ear picks up the vibrations of a woman's singing in another continent. Although his naked thumb can measure hardly to the thickness of its nail, with an electron tube micrometer he can judge space to one billionth of an inch. An intricate differential equation of the second order may take him weeks to solve, but with the new integrating machine invented by professors of the Massachusetts Institute of Technology, he can have his answer in an hour. Indeed, he can have answers to problems too difficult for any human mind to solve. With his own hand he can write fifty words a minute, but with a rotary press he can, in an equal time, lay down two hundred thousand words.

With his back he can sustain perhaps one thousand pounds and carry half that weight for a short distance. With the electrical controls of a travelling crane he can lift four hundred and thirty tons and carry it as far as the mechanism extends. With his fist he can perhaps knock down a man; with a steam hammer he can crush a three-foot bar of steel as though it were soft clay. He picks up a stone and throws it a few hundred feet at most; he presses a button on a siege gun and throws a ton of metal sixty miles.

His feet at their fleetest will carry him along the ground at close to twenty miles an hour. A racing motor will carry him at two hundred miles an hour, and an airplane, three hundred and thirteen (at last accounts). He can swim about one-thirtieth as fast as a speed boat can take him through the water. He can jump at the best seven yards, but in a glider he can take a jump which covers many miles and lasts all day. In a diver's helmet he can breathe comfortably at the bottom of the sea; in a gas mask he can breathe in a volcano; and if he dies, a pulmotor may bring him back to life.

The peasant in his fields is six feet tall. But this man has swelled into a colossus, straddling continents. With his machines, he sees and hears and lifts and runs as no living organism ever dreamed of doing. He stands enormous, fantastic and alone; outside the laws of living organisms, a control switch in his hand. Power unlimited; sensitiveness unbounded. But one would take no peasant from his village in the certainty of making him happier in New York.

Whether machines for all their power are worth the human price which has been paid for them is still, for the philosophers, an open question.

POWER AND BEAUTY | SHERWOOD ANDERSON

The man, the young mill superintendent, and I, went into the mill. There was a little hallway and we stopped for a moment in there. I had the feeling we were staring at each other.

There would be that question in his head:

What does he want here?

Men and women are coming into factories. They are escorted. Such factories as the huge Ford plant at Detroit make a specialty of escorting people through.

They come in, farmers from their farms, town people, merchants and lawyers. Society women come. They walk through in their soft fluffy dresses.

They are in a world of which they know little and sense less and still they are impressed.

The workmen and the workwomen at the machines stare up at them.

Why, there is a world, a life here, of which those who come thus into the great rooms know nothing. The machines are doing something.

The machines are weaving stockings, they weave cloth, they shape iron. Shoes are shaped in machines.

The visitor sees before him a great machine. Inside the mill all is in order and outside, often, all is disorder. In a certain cotton mill town in the South, at the end of a peculiarly disorderly street, I saw piles of old tin cans along a roadway as I drove down to the mill. There were weed-grown fields and women and men were shuffling aimlessly through the street.

The morning was a dull rainy one. A wife of one of the owners of the mill had taken me there . . .

Inside the mill I saw a Barber-Coleman Spooler Warper.

It was a machine just introduced into that factory, an extension of the thought, of the imagination, of some man, a machine that threw many men out of work.

The factory superintendent at that place told me it cost twenty thousand dollars.

That was more money than I had ever had. The statement did not impress me.

He said that its introduction into the mill did away with the labor of a certain number of hands.

That statement did not at the time impress me much. The machine is pushing men aside. That is going on everywhere. "Let it," I said to myself that morning.

I stood before the machine. It was a mass of moving parts. Its movements were as delicately balanced as the movements of a fine watch.

It was huge. It would have filled to the last inch this room in which I now sit writing of it.

But can I write of it? I cannot say how many parts the machine had, perhaps a thousand, perhaps ten thousand.

It had Herculean legs.

It unwound thread from one sized ball and wound it onto another. The white balls of thread moved about, up and down along hallways of steel. They were moving at unbelievable speed. As the thread wound and unwound, the balls moving thus gayly along steel hallways, dancing there, being playful there, being touched here and there by little steel hands directing their course, so delicately touched . . .

So delicately directed. . . .

Bobbins being loaded with thread . . . I dare say bobbins being loaded with many colored threads . . .

Perhaps some silk, some rayon, some cotton.

I may, for the time, have
stepped outside the province of
this particular machine.

I remember a woman, a mill owner's wife or daughter, tall and delicately gowned, standing near me. I remember two mill girls, one with a mass of yellow hair. No, it was just off yellow, with streaks of gold in it. . . .

Her fingers were doing things rapidly, with precision. I did not understand what she did.

Dancing balls.

Dancing rods.

I remember thinking rebel thoughts, to me new thoughts.

I must have stared at the woman who brought me there and at an alert blue-eyed mill superintendent.

Thinking of artists, striving blunderingly, as I am doing here, to express something.

No accuracy to their movements—if they be writers no words coming from under their flying fingers with such beautiful precision.

There, in that machine, what seemed at first disorder in movement becoming a vast, a beautiful order.

Why, a man goes a little daft.

A thousand, perhaps in the life of such a machine a hundred million, white balls, each containing to the hundredth part of an inch, the same yardage of slender thread . . .

They dancing down steel hallways, every hop, every skip calculated, they landing at little steel doors, never missing . . .

They being touched, handled, directed by fingers of steel.

Never harshly to break thread that I could break easily between my two fingers.

Thread flying, at blinding speed off one spool and onto another.

These handled, something done to these. In this shape, this form, they are serving some obscure purpose . . . in this vast modern passion of goods making.

I am describing this particular machine in a room far away from it, in a quiet room, no technical description of the machine before me, the accuracy of my description mattering nothing

An impression sought, something beautful, something in movement beautiful.

Something in tone beautiful, in sound beautiful.

Why, there is power here. Here is the almost god.

A crazy new grace —

Steel fingers jerking—in movements, calculated, never varied . . .

Great arms moving . . .

Materials touched with such delicacy of touch as I can never know.

I remember standing in that place, that time. I shall never forget that.

I remember thinking of men of my time, thoughtful men, earnest men, who would have destroyed all machines.

I remember there had been such thoughts in me.

I think it must have been the vast order in the mass of steel parts, all in movements, that had caught and held me so.

I, all my life, a lover of artists and their work . . . men working at least toward order.

Thinking — "these men who designed and built this machine may some day be known to be as important in the life swing of mankind, as the man who built the Cathedral of Chartres.

Whispering to myself — "They may be the real artists of our time.

"We in America may be, unknowingly, in one of the great forward-thrusting times of the world."

Thinking also of that woman standing there beside me as I looked at the machine, it in some new way exciting me . . .

A sardonic thought. I am sure I said no rude words to the delicately bodied, delicately gowned rich woman who brought me into that mill.

I thought suddenly, staring hard at her.

"Hell," I remember thinking, "you are a woman delicate and lovely, but you will never find you a lover who will touch that body of yours with the delicacy and strength with which those white balls of cotton are being touched."

Thinking:

"Is blood necessary, is flesh necessary?

"We humans are but little bundles of nerves. Our nerves betray us.

"We think we think.

"In the machine we have made a thing infinitely more nasterful than ourselves."

> It was a moment of pure machine
> worship. I was on my knees before
> the new god, the American god.

Looking up again at that woman standing there.

"You have to wait for hardness in your lover, if you have a lover.

"Here is always hardness.

"Here is always the thing done, accurately and truly.

"No blundering here."

Myself not hysterical, not made hysterical by the wonder of that particular machine . . .

I have felt dimly the same vast order sometimes in the stars, walking at night on some country road.

I have felt it in rivers.

I have felt impotence too. This is not a feeling individual in me. I challenge any painter, song-maker, word-arranger, any poet, to go stand where I stood.

A Barker-Coleman Spooler Warper in a cotton mill will do. It is enough.
Why, if he, the artist, had made that machine . . .
Let him stand as I did, not having made it, never in his whole life having
made anything that moved forward, doing its work, with perfect order . . .
Never having loved perfectly, created perfectly . . .

Let him be a workman at such a machine . . .
The man, the workman, does little but start and stop it.
It works outside him . . .
I, a man, can go blunderingly into blundering other lives.
I can fail in the eyes of others, as I will fail in this book, trying as I am
here to say the unsayable.
I can fail because you who read fail also.
Your whole life is a story of failure.

As for myself, all of my success as a writer has been in telling the story
of failure.
I have told that story and told it well because I know failure.
The machine does not fail.

I ask you men who read to follow me.
Ask yourself . . .
"What will it do to me, as a man, to stand, pulling a lever, let us say,
to a machine that does not fail?
"Can man, being man, actually stand, naked in his inefficiency before
the efficient machine?"

Men, you know it cannot quite be done, not yet in any event.
We know this — impotence comes from the fear of impotence.
In our machine age how can we help fearing?

Why, I was in an American Cotton Mill at night. There was a mill
superintendent with me. I think I ought to tell you, who have not been
in such a mill, either in the daytime or at night, a little of how cotton
from the farms is made into thread and then of how, in the great loom
rooms, it is woven into cloth.
The cotton mill is a complex thing like all modern mills. It has been
built up slowly from small rude beginnings. Here is this cotton, brought
into the mill in its bales. It comes from the fields.
There is a story there too, the story of Southern cotton fields, but it
cannot be told here.
In the mills the machines begin to handle the cotton. They roll and
toss it. Now it has begun to move forward in the mill, a moving snowy mass.
As it moves forward the machines caress it, they stir it—iron fingers
reach softly and tenderly down to it.

The cotton has come into the mill still impregnated with the dust of the fields. There are innumerable little black and brown specks in it. Tiny particles of trash from the fields, bits of the dry brown cotton boll, cling to it, tiny ends of sticks are enmeshed in it.

The cotton gin has removed the seed but there are these particles left. The fibre of the cotton is delicate and short.

Here is a great machine, weighing tons. See the great wheels, the iron arms moving, feel the vibrations in the air now, all the little iron fingers moving. See how delicately the fingers caress the moving mass. They shake it, they comb it, they caress it.

Every movement here is designed to cleanse the cotton, making it always whiter and cleaner, and to lay the delicate fibres of the mass, more and more into parallel lines.

Why, this cotton is already on the road to becoming. It is becoming goods. It moves with roaring speed toward that end.

Long months spent making this cotton in the fields. All the danger of bad weather, boll weevil, drought.

Hope coming, despair . . . a farmer's whole family spending months making a bale of cotton. See how nonchalantly the machines eat it up.

And now it is clean and has begun to emerge from the larger machines in a thin film. You have been in the fields in the early morning and have seen how the dew on the spider webs, spun from weed-top to weed-top, shines and glistens in the morning sun. See how delicate and fragile it is.

But not more delicate or film-like, not more diaphanous than the thin sheet now emerging from yonder huge machine. You may pass your hand under the moving sheet. Look through it and you may see the lines in the palm of your hand.

Yonder great ponderous machine did that. Man made that machine. He made it to do that thing. There is something blind or dead in those of us who do not see and feel the wonder of it.

What delicacy of adjustment, what strength with delicacy! Do you wonder that the little mill girls—half children, some of them—that the women who work in the mills—many of them I have seen with such amazingly delicate and sensitive faces—do you wonder that they are half in love with the machines that they tend, as modern boys are half in love with the automobiles they drive?

But we are in the weaving room now. It is another huge room. The room is a forest of belts. The belts, hundreds of them in this one room, go up to the ceiling as straight as pine trees in a Georgia wood.

They are flying, flying, flying.

In the loom room, visited that night, there might have been fifteen hundred, perhaps even twenty-five hundred looms, all in the one great room. This mill had many thousand spindles. The looms are not so large. They come up to a man's waist.

They clatter and shout. They talk like a million blackbirds in a field. Here, in this room, as everywhere in modern industry, there is something vibrant in the air. The inside of such a room is like the inside of a piano, being played furiously. It is like the inside of an automobile, going at eighty miles an hour.

If I could make you feel this. There is wonder and terror in this room. The night accentuates it.

The whole story of labor in modern industry is a story of nerves. That I have found out. It may be the story of all modern life.

Can man get on top of this? Can man retain the beauty, the wonder, the efficiency of these modern mills and not be destroyed by them?

It is obvious they have destroyed old ideas of government, of the relationship of man to man.

Had I anything in common with the mill superintendent who walked with me that night?

There were the men who made the cotton in the fields and the mill hands in the mill.

They had little or no sense of each other. That is one of the tragedies of modern industrial life.

The workman in the furniture factory has no sense of the lumberman cutting trees in the hills.

The man in the steel mill does not sense the miner. In the South men come from the cotton fields to work in the mills but they lose there, almost at once, the sense of fields.

It is the machine that does it. The machine has become a wall between man and man. One of the striking things about the modern labor world is the loss of a sense of a common interest.

The mill superintendent went smilingly along. His nerves seemed unshaken. I had oddly the feeling, that night in the mill, that he thought me a little silly, and perhaps affected, to be so moved.

THE MACHINE AS CONSUMER | *FRIEDRICH G. JUENGER*

Why does the contemplation of machines give us such pleasure? Because they manifest the fundamental form of man's intelligence, because before our very eyes this constructive and combining intelligence masters and amasses power, because they win a ceaseless triumph over the elements which they beat down, squeeze and forge. Let us enter the workshop, then, to see what goes on.

The impression we gain as we observe technical processes of any sort is

From Friedrich G. Juenger, *The Price of Progress* (Chicago, Henry Regnery Co., 1948).

not at all one of abundance. Where we see abundance and plenty, they give us joy, they are the signs of a fruitfulness which we revere as a life-giving force. Rooting, sprouting, budding, blooming, ripening, and fruition, the exuberance of the motions and forms of life—they strengthen and refresh us. The human body and the human mind possess this power of bestowing strength. Both man and woman have it. But the machine organization gives nothing—it organizes need. The sight of vineyard, orchard, or a blossoming landscape give us cheer, not because they yield profits, but because of the sensation of fertility, abundance, and gratuitous riches. But the industrial scene has lost its fruitfulness; it has become the scene of mechanical production. It is above all a sense of hungriness that overcomes us, particularly in the industrial cities which, in the metaphorical language of technical progress, are the homes of a flourishing industry. The machine gives a hungry impression. And this sensation of a growing, gnawing hunger, a hunger that becomes unbearable, emanates from everything in our entire technical arsenal.

When we enter a factory, be it a cotton mill, a foundry, saw mill, or a powerhouse, everywhere we get the same impression. The consuming, devouring, gluttonous motion racing through time restlessly and insatiably, reveals that never stilled and never to be stilled hunger of the machine. So obvious is this hunger that even the impression of concentrated power which we receive in the centers of heavy industry cannot overcome it. In fact, it is strongest in these centers, because precisely here we find the greatest greed for power. And the rational mind which stands behind the machine and keeps watch over its automatic, mechanical motion—it too is hungry, and hunger follows it everywhere. It cannot shake off hunger, it cannot free itself from it, it cannot be stilled however hard it may try. And how, indeed, should that be possible! This mind itself is consuming, gluttonous; it has no access to riches, and it cannot conjure up abundance. No effort of ingenuity, nor all the inventive power that is brought to bear here can do it. For rationalization only sharpens hunger, and, moreover, it increases consumption. And this growing consumption is a sign not of abundance but of poverty; it is bound up with worry, want, and toil.

It is precisely the methodical, disciplined effort leading to the perfection of the technical processes which destroys all hopes that certain quarters place in this perfection. Progress in its present rapid advance creates an optical illusion, deceiving the observer into seeing things which are not there. Technology can be expected to solve all problems which can be mastered by technical means; but we must expect nothing from it which lies beyond technical possibilities. Even the smallest mechanical process consumes more energy than it produces. How then could the sum of all these processes create abundance?*

* The second main theorem of thermodynamics, the law of entropy, tells us that heat can be converted into work only to a limited extent. Thus, the designer of a machine never gets beyond the degree of efficiency of Carnot's cycle.

There can be no talk of riches produced by technology. What really happens is rather a steady, forever growing, forever greater, consumption. It is a ruthless destruction the like of which the earth has never seen before. For a more and more ruthless destruction of resources is the characteristic of our technology. By this destruction alone it can exist and spread. All theories which overlook this fact are lopsided because they disregard the basic conditions which now govern production and economics.

It characterizes every healthy economy that the substance with which it works is preserved and used sparingly so that consumption and destruction do not overstep the limit beyond which the substance itself would be destroyed, or endangered. Since technology presupposes destruction, since its development indeed depends upon destruction, it cannot be fitted into any healthy economic system; one cannot look at it, in fact, from an economic point of view. The radical consumption of oil, coal and ore cannot be called economy, however rational the methods of drilling and mining. Underlying the strict rationality of technical working methods, we find a way of thinking which cares nothing for the preservation and saving of the substance.

What is euphemistically called production is really consumption. The gigantic technical apparatus, masterpiece of human ingenuity, could not reach perfection if technological thought were to be contained within an economic scheme, if the destructive power of technical progress were to be arrested. But this progress becomes all the more impetuous, the larger the resources at its disposal, and the more energetically it devours them. This is shown by the concentration of men and machines in the great mining centers where the mechanization of work and the organization of man are most advanced. The rationality of technology so impressively displayed here becomes intelligible only when one has understood the conditions on which it depends. Its concomitant is waste, and contempt for all rationality when it comes to exploiting the resources on whose existence technology depends.

Where wastage begins, there begins desolation, and scenes of such desolation can be found even in the early days of our technology, in the era of the steam engine. These scenes are startling by the extraordinary ugliness and the cyclopean power which are characteristic of them. The machine invades the landscape with destruction and transformation, it grows factories and whole manufacturing cities overnight, cities grotesquely hideous, where human misery is glaringly revealed, cities which, like Manchester, represent an entire stage of technology and which have become synonymous with hopeless dreariness. Technology darkens the air with smoke, poisons the water, destroys the plants and animals. It brings about a state in which nature has to be "preserved" from rationalized thinking, in which large tracts of land have to be set apart, fenced off, and placed under a taboo like museum pieces. What all museumlike institutions make evident is that preservation is needed. The extension of protected areas therefore is an indication that destructive processes are at work.

Mining centers in particular are the focal points of organized pillage. The riches of the earth are dug out and consumed. The exploitation of the factory worker (about which socialism is indignant only so long as it is in the opposition) is an inevitable symptom of the universal exploitation to which technology subjects the whole earth from end to end. Man no less than ore deposits belongs to the resources subject to consumption by technology. The ways in which the worker tries to evade this exploitation: associations, labor unions, political parties, are the very methods which tie him forever closer to the progress of technology, to mechanical work and technical organization.

Increasingly, pillage is the reverse side of technology; this must not be overlooked when one speaks of technical progress. True, we have made a technical advance, if by means of artificial fertilizers we succeed in squeezing uninterrupted crops out of our overburdened plough and pasture land. But this advance itself is at the same time the consequence of a lagging behind, a deficiency, for if we did not have the fertilizer we should no longer be able to feed ourselves at all. Technical progress has deprived us of the freedom of nutriment which our ancestors possessed. A machine which trebles the output of a previous model constitutes a technical advance, for it is the result of more rational design. But for this very reason it also possesses a more intense consuming and devouring power. Its hunger is sharper, and it consumes correspondingly more. Thus the whole realm of the machine is full of a restless, devouring power that cannot be satisfied.

Closely linked to this is the rapid wear and tear the machine suffers. That most of our apparatus becomes junk so soon results from design and purpose. Their durability, strength, and usability are lessened, restricted in the very degree to which technology approaches perfection. The consumption which technology brings about extends even to its own apparatus. The repairs and replacements these mechanisms constantly demand represent an immense amount of human labor. And the machine falls quickly into that state of disrepair in which we see it around us everywhere. Technical progress covers the earth not alone with its machines and workshops, but also with technical junk and scrap. All this rusty tin, these twisted girders, these bent and broken machine parts and castaway tools remind the thoughtful observer of the impermanence of the progress he witnesses. Perhaps they keep him from overestimating all this progress and help him understand what really goes on. Wear and tear is a form of consumption; it manifests itself pre-eminently where plundering goes on, and so we find it in particular wherever technology is at work.

If two thousand years hence there should still be archeologists—which is rather unlikely—who were to undertake excavation in, say, Manchester, Essen, or Pittsburgh, they would find but little. They would discover nothing as enduring as Egyptian burial chambers or classic temples. For the stuff with which the factory system works is not *aere perennius* ("more lasting than bronze"—Horace). The earth-spanning power of technology is at the same time of an ephemeral kind—a fact easily overlooked by those engrossed in it. Everywhere it is threatened by decay, given over to decay, and decay follows upon its heels all the more insistently, the faster it marches on towards new triumphs.

The machine does not create new riches. It consumes existing riches through pillage, that is, in a manner which lacks all rationality even though it employs rational methods of work. As technology progresses it devours the resources on which it depends. It contributes to a constant drain, and thereby again and again comes to a point where it is forced to improve its inventory and to rationalize anew its methods of work. Those who deny this, claiming that it is the wealth of new inventions which made the existing apparatus obsolete, are confusing cause and effect. Inventions presuppose a need for improvement; their purpose is the rationalization of work. Nor can the technician legitimately blame the steadily growing deficits of the technical work process, and the recurrent crises and disturbances it causes, upon the political organization, charging that the competing political powers of this earth are burdening industrial production with unjustifiable costs. Such is indeed the case, for the principle of competition is a political and economic rather than a technical one. However, even if the world were one single state, even then the machine would push the process of rationalization to the extreme. The process of rationalization would manifest itself in a free economy no less than in any kind of planned economy which goes hand in hand with technology. When the engineer destroys free economy— that is, the economy in which the businessman rules autonomously—he forces the economy to adopt a plan designed by the engineer.

When economic crises can no longer be overcome by economic means, human hopes turn toward stricter rationalization of technology: the idea of technocracy arises. But first we should examine whether it is not technology itself which brings about such crises. We should examine whether technology is capable of putting our economy in order, and whether such an ordering falls within the scope of its tasks at all. What does "technocracy" mean? If the word has any meaning, it can only be that the technician rules, that he takes over government. But the technician is no statesman; he has no talent for politics. His knowledge is one of technical, functional effects. All technical knowledge is marked by an impersonalism inherently conditioned by the strict factualness of its perceptions. This impersonalism alone is reason enough to doubt whether the technician is capable of taking over and running the affairs of state.

IMITATION OF LIFE | *W. GREY WALTER*

"When we were little . . . we went to school in the sea. The master was an old Turtle—we used to call him Tortoise."
"Why did you call him Tortoise if he wasn't one?" Alice asked.
"We called him Tortoise because he taught us," said the Mock Turtle angrily. "Really you are very dull!"
LEWIS CARROLL, *Alice's Adventures in Wonderland*

In the dark ages before the invention of the electronic vacuum tube there were many legends of living statues and magic pictures. One has only to recall the importance of graven images and holy pictures in many religions to realize how readily living and even divine properties are projected into inanimate objects by hopeful but bewildered men and women. Idolatry, witchcraft and other superstitions are so deeply rooted and widespread that it is possible even the most detached scientific activity may be psychologically equivalent to them; such activity may help to satisfy the desire for power, to assuage the fear of the unknown or to compensate for the flatness of everyday existence.

In any case there is an intense modern interest in machines that imitate life. The great difference between magic and the scientific imitation of life is that where the former is content to copy external appearance, the latter is concerned more with performance and behavior. Except in the comic strips the scientific robot does not look in the least like a living creature, though it may reproduce in great detail some of the complex functions which classical physiologists described as diagnostic of living processes. Some of the simpler of these functions can be duplicated by mechanical contrivances. But it was not until the eletronic age that serious efforts were made to imitate and even to surpass the complex performance of the nervous system.

All the gradations of feeling and action of which we are capable are provided by variations in the frequency of nerve impulses and by the number of nerve cells stimulated. The brain cipher is even simpler than Morse code: it uses only dots, the number of which per second conveys all information. Communication engineers call this system "pulse-frequency modulation." It was "invented" by animals many millions of years ago, and it has advantages over other methods which are only just beginning to be applied. The engineers who have designed our great computing machines adopted this system without realizing that they were copying their own brains. (The popular term electronic brain is not so very fanciful.) In the language of these machines there are only two statements, "yes" and "no," and in their arithmetic only two numbers, 1 and 0. They surpass human capacity mainly in their great speed of action and in their ability to perform many interdependent computations at the same time, *e.g.*, to solve simultaneous differential equations with hundreds of variables.

Magical though these machines may appear to the layman, their resemblance to living creatures is limited to certain details of their design. Above all they are in no sense free as most animals are free; rather they are parasites, depending upon their human hosts for nourishment and stimulation.

In a different category from computing machines are certain devices that have been made to imitate more closely the simpler types of living creatures, including their limitations (which in a computer would be serious faults) as well as their virtues. These less ambitious but perhaps more attractive mechanical creatures have evolved along two main lines. First there are stationary ones—sessile, the biologist would call them—which are rooted in a source of electric power and have very limited freedom. The prototype of these is the "homeostat" made by W. R. Ashby of Gloucester, England. It was created to study the mechanism whereby an animal adapts its total system to preserve its internal stability in spite of violent external changes.

The term "homeostasis" was coined by the Harvard University physiologist Walter B. Cannon to describe the many delicate biological mechanisms which detect slight changes of temperature or chemical state within the body and compensate for them by producing equal and opposite changes. Communication engineers, as Arnold Tustin has shown, rediscovered this important expedient in their grapplings with the problems of circuits and computers. They describe a system in which errors or variations from some desirable state are automatically neutralized as containing "negative or inverse feedback." In an animal most of what is called reflex activity has exactly this property.

In Ashby's homeostat there are a number of electronic circuits similar to the reflex arcs in the spinal cord of an animal. These are so combined with a number of radio tubes and relays that out of many thousands of possible connections the machine will automatically find one that leads to a condition of dynamic internal stability. That is, after several trials and errors the instrument establishes connections which tend to neutralize any change that the experimenter tries to impose from outside. It is a curious fact that although the machine is man-made, the experimenter finds it impossible to tell at any moment exactly what the machine's circuit is without "killing" it and dissecting out the "nervous system"; that is, switching off the current and tracing out the wires to the relays. Nevertheless the homeostat does not behave very like an active animal—it is more like a sleeping creature which when disturbed stirs and finds a comfortable position.

Another branch of electromechanical evolution is represented by the little machines we have made in Bristol. We have given them the mock-biological name *Machina speculatrix*, because they illustrate particularly the exploratory, speculative behavior that is so characteristic of most animals. The machine on which we have chiefly concentrated is a small creature with a smooth shell and a protruding neck carrying a single eye which scans the surroundings for light stimuli; because of its general appearance we call the genus "Testudo," or tortoise. The Adam and Eve of this line are nicknamed Elmer and Elsie, after the initials of the terms describing them—ELectro MEchanical Robots, Light-Sensitive, with Internal and External stability. Instead of the 10,000 million cells of our brains, Elmer and Elsie contain but two functional elements: two miniature radio tubes, two sense organs, one for light and the other for touch, and two effectors or motors, one for crawling and the other for steering. Their power is supplied by a miniature hearing-aid B battery and a miniature six-volt storage battery, which provides both A and C current for the tubes and the current for the motors.

The number of components in the device was deliberately restricted to two in order to discover what degree of complexity of behavior and independence could be achieved with the smallest number of elements connected in a system providing the greatest number of possible interconnections. From the theoretical standpoint two elements equivalent to circuits in the nervous system can exist in six modes; if one is called A and the other B, we can distinguish A, B, A + B, A→B, B→A and A⇌B as possible dynamic forms. To indicate the variety of behavior possible for even so simple a system as this, one need only mention that six elements would be more than enough to form a system which would provide a new pattern every tenth of a second for 280 years — four times the human lifetime of 70 years! It is unlikely that the number of perceptible functional elements in the human brain is anything like the total number of nerve cells; it is more likely to be of the order of 1,000. But even if it were only 10, this number of elements could provide enough variety for a lifetime of experience for all the men who ever lived or will be born if mankind survives a thousand million years.

So a two-element synthetic animal is enough to start with. The strange richness provided by this particular sort of permutation introduces right away one of the aspects of animal behavior—and human psychology—which *M. speculatrix* is designed to illustrate: the uncertainty, randomness, free will or independence so strikingly absent in most well-designed machines. The fact that only a few richly interconnected elements can provide practically infinite modes of existence suggests that there is no logical or experimental necessity to invoke more than *number* to account for our subjective conviction of freedom of will and our objective awareness of personality in our fellow men.

The behavior of Elmer and Elsie is in fact remarkably unpredictable.

The photocell, or "eye," is linked with the steering mechanism. In the absence of an adequate light-stimulus Elmer (or Elsie) explores continuously, and at the same time the motor drives it forward in a crawling motion. The two motions combined give the creature a cycloidal gait, while the photocell "looks" in every direction in turn. This process of scanning and its synchronization with the steering device may be analogous to the mechanism whereby the electrical pulse of the brain known as the alpha rhythm sweeps over the visual brain areas and at the same time releases or blocks impulses destined for the muscles of the body. In both cases the function is primarily one of economy, just as in a television system the scanning of the image permits transmission of hundreds of thousands of point-details on one channel instead of on as many channels.

The effect of this arrangement on Elmer is that in the dark it explores in a very thorough manner a considerable area, remaining alert to the possibility of light and avoiding obstacles that it cannot surmount or push aside. When the photocell sees a light, the resultant signal is amplified by both tubes in the amplifier. If the light is very weak, only a *change* of illumination is transmitted as an effective signal. A slightly stronger signal is amplified without loss of its absolute level. In either case the effect is to halt the steering mechanism so that the machine moves toward the light source or maneuvers so that it can approach the light with the least difficulty. This behavior is of course analogous to the reflex behavior known as "positive tropism," such as is exhibited by a moth flying into a candle. But Elmer does not blunder into the light, for when the brilliance exceeds a certain value—that of a flashlight about six inches away—the signal becomes strong enough to operate a relay in the first tube, which has the reverse effect from the second one. Now the steering mechanism is turned on again at double speed, so the creature abruptly sheers away and seeks a more gentle climate. If there is a single light source, the machine circles around it in a complex path of advance and withdrawal; if there is another light farther away, the machine will visit first one and then the other and will continually stroll back and forth between the two. In this way it neatly solves the dilemma of Buridan's ass, which the scholastic philosophers said would die of starvation between two bundles of hay if it did not possess a transcendental free will.

For Elmer hay is represented, of course, by the electricity it needs to recharge its batteries. Within the hutch where it normally lives is a battery charger and a 20-watt lamp. When the creature's batteries are well charged, it is attracted to this light from afar, but at the threshold the brilliance is great enough to act as a repellent, so the model wanders off for further exploration. When the batteries start to run down, the first effect is to enhance the sensitivity of the amplifier so that the attraction of the light is felt from even farther away. But soon the level of sensitivity falls and then, if the machine is fortunate and finds itself at the entrance to its kennel, it will be attracted right home, for the light no longer seems so dazzling. Once well in, it can make contact with the charger. The moment current flows in the circuit between the charger and the batteries the creature's own nervous system and motors are automatically disconnected; charging continues until the battery voltage has risen to its maximum. Then the internal circuits are automatically reconnected and the little creature, repelled now by the light which before the feast had been so irresistible, circles away for further adventures.

Inevitably in its peripatetic existence *M. speculatrix* encounters many obstacles. These it cannot "see," because it has no vestige of pattern vision, though it will avoid an obstacle that casts a shadow when it is approaching a light. The creature is equipped, however, with a device that enables it to get around obstacles. Its shell is suspended on a single rubber mounting and has sufficient flexibility to move and close a ring contact. This contact converts the two-stage amplifier into a multivibrator. The oscillations so generated rhythmically open and close the relays that control the full power to the motors for steering and crawling. At the same time the amplifier is prevented from transmitting the signals picked up by the photocell. Accordingly when the creature makes contact with an obstacle, whether in its speculative or tropistic mode, all stimuli are ignored and its gait is transformed into a succession of butts, withdrawals and sidesteps until the interference is either pushed aside or circumvented. The oscillations persist for about a second after the obstacle has been left behind; during this short memory of frustration Elmer darts off and gives the danger area a wide berth.

When the models were first made, a small light was connected in the steering-motor circuit to act as an indicator showing when the motor was turned off and on. It was soon found that this light endowed the machines with a new mode of behavior. When the photocell sees the indicator light in a mirror or reflected from a white surface, the model flickers and jigs at its reflection in a manner so specific that were it an animal a biologist would be justified in attributing to it a capacity for self-recognition. The reason for the flicker is that the vision of the light results in the indicator light being switched off, and darkness in turn switches it on again, so an oscillation of the light is set up.

Two creatures of this type meeting face to face are affected in a similar but again distinctive manner. Each, attracted by the light the other carries, extinguishes its own source of attraction, so the two systems become involved in a mutual oscillation, leading finally to a stately retreat. When the encounter is from the side or from behind, each regards the other merely as an obstacle; when both are attracted by the same light, their jostling as they approach the light eliminates the possibility of either reaching its goal. When one machine casually interferes with another while the latter is seriously seeking its charging light, a dog-in-the-manger situation develops which results in the more needy one expiring from exhaustion within sight of succor.

These machines are perhaps the simplest that can be said to resemble animals. Crude though they are, they give an eerie impression of purposefulness, independence and spontaneity. More complex models that we are now constructing have memory circuits in which associations are stored as electric oscillations, so the creatures can learn simple tricks, forget them slowly and relearn more quickly. This compact, plastic and easily accessible form of short-term memory may be very similar to the way in which the brain establishes the simpler and more evanescent conditioned reflexes.

One intriguing effect in these higher forms of synthetic life is that as soon as two receptors and a learning circuit are provided, the possibility of a conflict neurosis immediately appears. In difficult situations the creature sulks or becomes wildly agitated and can be cured only by rest or shock — the two favorite stratagems of the psychiatrist. It appears that it would even be technically feasible to build processes of self-repair and of reproduction into these machines.

Perhaps we flatter ourselves in thinking that man is the pinnacle of an estimable creation. Yet as our imitation of life becomes more faithful our veneration of its marvelous processes will not necessarily become less sincere.

THE FEELINGS OF ROBOTS | PAUL ZIFF

Could a robot have feelings? Some say of course.[1] Some say of course not.[2]

1) I want the right sort of robots. They must be automata and without doubt machines.

I shall assume that they are essentially computing machines, having micro-elements and whatever micro-mechanisms may be necessary for the functioning of these engineering wonders. Furthermore, I shall assume that they are powered by micro-solar batteries: instead of having lunch they will have light.

And if it is clear that our robots are without doubt machines then in all other respects they may be as much like men as you like. They may be the size of men. When clothed and masked they may be virtually indistinguishable from men in practically all respects: in appearance, in move-

From *Analysis,* XIX, 3 (January 1959), pp. 64–68. Reprinted by permission of the author.

[1] Cf. D. M. MacKay, "The Epistemological Problem for Automata", in *Automata Studies* (Princeton: Princeton Univ. Press, 1956), 235–251.

[2] Cf. M. Scriven, "The Mechanical Concept of Mind", *Mind LXII* 246 (1953), 230–240.

ment, in the utterances they utter, and so forth. Thus except for the masks any ordinary man would take them to be ordinary men. Not suspecting they were robots nothing about them would make him suspect.

But unmasked the robots are to be seen in all their metallic lustre. What is in question here is not whether we can blur the line between a man and a machine and so attribute feelings to the machine. The question is whether we can attribute feelings to the machine and so blur the line between a man and a machine.

2) Could robots have feelings? Could they, say, feel tired, or bored?

Ex hypothesi robots are mechanisms, not organisms, not living creatures. There could be a broken-down robot but not a dead one. Only living creatures can literally have feelings.

If I say "She feels tired" one can generally infer that what is in question is (or was or will be in the case of talk about spirits[3]) a living creature. More generally, the linguistic environment ". . . feels tired" is generally open only to expressions that refer to living creatures. Suppose you say "The robot feels tired." The phrase "the robot" refers to a mechanism. Then one can infer that what is in question is not a living creature. But from the utterance of the predicative expression ". . . feels tired" one can infer that what is in question is a living creature. So, if you are speaking literally and you say "The robot feels tired" you imply a contradiction. Consequently one cannot literally predicate ". . . feels tired" of "the robot".

Or again: no robot will ever do everything a man can. And it doesn't matter how robots may be constructed or how complex and varied their movements and operations may be. Robots may calculate but they will not literally reason. Perhaps they will take things but they will not literally borrow them. They may kill but not literally murder. They may voice apologies but they will not literally make any. These are actions that only persons can perform: *ex hypothesi* robots are not persons.

3) "A dead robot" is a metaphor but "a dead battery" is a dead metaphor: if there were a robot around it would put its metaphor to death.

What I don't want to imply I need not imply. An implication can be weakened. The sense of a word can be widened or narrowed or shifted. If one wishes to be understood then one mustn't go too far: that is all. Pointing to one among many paintings, I say "Now *that* one is a *painting.*" Do I mean the others are not? Of course not. Yet the stress on "that" is contrastive. So I say "The robot, that mechanism, not of course a living creature but a machine, it feels tired": you cannot infer that what is in question here is a living creature.

If I say of a person "He feels tired," do you think I am saying that he is a living creature and only that? If I say "The robot feels tired" I am not

[3] I shall henceforth omit the qualification.

saying that what is in question is a living creature, but that doesn't mean that nothing is being said. If I say "The robot feels tired," the predicate "... feels tired" means whatever it usually means except that one cannot infer that what is in question is a living creature. That is the only difference.

And what has been said about "The robot feels tired" could be said equally well about "The robot is conscious," "The robot borrowed my cat," and so forth.

4)   Could robots feel tired? Could a stone feel tired? Could the number 17 feel tired? It is clear that there is no reason to believe that 17 feels tired. But that doesn't prove anything. A man can feel tired and there may be nothing, there need be nothing at all, that shows it. And so with a robot or a stone or the number 17.

Even so, the number 17 could not feel tired. And I say this not because or not simply because there are no reasons to suppose that 17 does feel tired but because there are good reasons not to suppose that 17 feels tired and good reasons not to suppose that 17 ever feels anything at all. Consequently it is necessary to consider whether there are any reasons for supposing that robots feel tired and whether there are good reasons for not supposing that robots ever feel anything at all.

5)   Knowing George and seeing the way he looks I say he feels tired. Knowing Josef and seeing the way he looks I don't say he feels tired. Yet if you don't know either of them then to you George and Josef may look alike.

In one sense they may look alike to me too, but not in another. For George but not Josef will look tired. If you ask me to point out the difference there may be nothing relevant, there need be nothing relevant, to point to. For the relevant difference may be like that between looking at an unframed picture and looking at it framed. Only the frame here is provided by what I know about them: you cannot see what I know.

(Speaking with the robots, one can say that the way things look to me, my present output, will not be the same as yours, the way things look to you, even though at present we may both receive the same input, the same stimuli, and this is because your mechanism was not in the same initial state as mine, owing either to a difference in structure or to a difference in previous inputs.)

If we say of a person that he feels tired, we generally do so not only on the basis of what we see then and there but on the basis of what we have seen elsewhere and on the basis of how what we have seen elsewhere ties in with what we see then and there. And this is only to say that in determining whether or not a person feels tired both observational and theoretic considerations are involved and, as everywhere, are inextricably interwoven.

6) Suppose you and I visit an actor at home. He is rehearsing the role of a grief-stricken man. He ignores our presence as a grief-stricken man might. His performance is impeccable. I know but you do not know that he is an actor and that he is rehearsing a role. You ask "Why is he so miserable?" and I reply "He isn't." "Surely," you say, "he is grief-stricken. Look at him! Show me what leads you to say otherwise!" and of course there may be nothing then and there to show.

So Turing[1] posed the question whether automata could think, be conscious, have feelings, etc., in the following naive way: what test would an automaton fail to pass? MacKay[2] has pointed out that any test for mental or any other attributes to be satisfied by the observable activity of a human being can be passed by automata. And so one is invited to say what would be wrong with a robot's performance.

Nothing need be wrong with either the actor's or a robot's performance. What is wrong is that they are performances.

7) Suppose K is a robot. An ordinary man may see K and not knowing that K is a robot, the ordinary man may say "K feels tired." If I ask him what makes him think so, he may reply "K worked all day digging ditches. Anyway, just look at K: if he doesn't look tired, who does?"

So K looks tired to the ordinary man. That doesn't prove anything. If I know K is a robot, K may not look tired to me. It is not what I see but what I know. Or it is not what I see then and there but what I have seen elsewhere. Where? In a robot psychology laboratory.

8) If I say "The robot feels tired," the predicate ". . . feels tired" means whatever it usually means except that one cannot infer that what is in question is a living creature. That is the only difference.

To speak of something living is to speak of an organism in an environment. The environment is that in which the behavior of the organism takes place. Death is the dissolution of the relation between an organism and its environment. In death I am pluralized, converted from one to many. I become my remains. I merge with my environment.

If we think of robots being put together, we can think of them being taken apart. So in our laboratory we have taken robots apart, we have changed and exchanged their parts, we have changed and exchanged their programs, we have started and stopped them, sometimes in one state, sometimes in another, we have taken away their memories, we have made them seem to remember things that were yet to come, and so on.

And what we find in our laboratory is this: no robot could sensibly be said to feel anything. Why not?

[1] Cf. "Computing Machinery and Intelligence", *Mind LIX* 236 (1950), 433–466.
[2] Cf. "Mentality in Machines", *Arist. Soc. Supp. XXVI* (1952), 61-86.

9) Because there are not psychological truths about robots but only about the human makers of robots. Because the way a robot acts (in a specified context) depends primarily on how we programed it to act. Because we can program a robot to act in any way we want it to act. Because a robot could be programed to act like a tired man when it lifted a feather and not when it lifted a ton. Because a robot couldn't mean what it said any more than a phonograph record could mean what it said. Because we could make a robot say anything we want it to say. Because coveting thy neighbor's robot wife would be like coveting his car and not like coveting his wife. Because robots are replaceable. Because robots have no individuality. Because one can duplicate all the parts and have two virtually identical machines. Because one can exchange all the parts and still have the same machines. Because one can exchange the programs of two machines having the same structure. Because. . . .

Because no robot would act tired. Because a robot could only act like a robot programed to act like a tired man. For suppose some robots are programed to act like a tired man after lifting a feather while some are so programed that they never act like a tired man. Shall we say "It is a queer thing but some robots feel tired almost at once while others never feel tired"? Or suppose some are programed to act like a tired man after lifting something blue but not something green. Shall we say "Some robots feel tired when they lift blue things but not when they lift green things"? And shall we conclude "Some robots find blue things heavier than green things"? Hard work makes a man feel tired: what will make a robot act liked a tired man? Perhaps hard work, or light work, or no work, or anything at all. For it will depend on the whims of the man who makes it (though these whims may be modified by whatever quirks may appear in the robot's electronic nerve network, and there may be unwanted and unforeseen consequences of an ill-conceived program). Shall we say "There's no telling what will make a robot feel tired"? And if a robot acts like a tired man then what? Some robots may be programed to require a rest, others to require more work. Shall we say "This robot feels tired so put it back to work"?

What if all this were someday to be done with and to human beings? What if we were someday to break down the difference between a man and his environment? Then some day we would wake and find that we are robots. But we wouldn't wake to a mechanical paradise or even an automatic hell: for then it might not make sense to talk of human beings having feelings just as it now doesn't make sense to talk of robots having feelings.

A robot would behave like a robot.

Harvard University

THE THOUGHT OF A COMPUTER | A. M. TURING

1. The Imitation Game.

I propose to consider the question, "Can machines think?" This should begin with definitions of the meaning of the terms "machine" and "think." The definitions might be framed so as to reflect so far as possible the normal use of the words, but this attitude is dangerous. If the meaning of the words "machine" and "think" are to be found by examining how they are commonly used it is difficult to escape the conclusion that the meaning and the answer to the question, "Can machines think?" is to be sought in a statistical survey such as a Gallup poll. But this is absurd. Instead of attempting such a definition I shall replace the question by another, which is closely related to it and is expressed in relatively unambiguous words.

The new form of the problem can be described in terms of a game which we call the "imitation game." It is played with three people, a man (A), a woman (B), and an interrogator (C) who may be of either sex. The interrogator stays in a room apart from the other two. The object of the game for the interrogator is to determine which of the other two is the man and which is the woman. He knows them by labels X and Y, and at the end of the game he says either "X is A and Y is B" or "X is B and Y is A." The interrogator is allowed to put questions to A and B thus:

C: Will X please tell me the length of his or her hair?
Now suppose X is actually A, then A must answer. It is A's object in the game to try and cause C to make the wrong identification. His answer might therefore be

"My hair is shingled, and the longest strands are about nine inches long."

In order that tones of voice may not help the interrogator the answers should be written, or better still, typewritten. The ideal arrangement is to have a teleprinter communicating between the two rooms. Alternatively the question and answers can be repeated by an intermediary. The object of the game for the third player (B) is to help the interrogator. The best strategy for her is probably to give truthful answers. She can add such things as "I am the woman, don't listen to him!" to her answers, but it will avail nothing as the man can make similar remarks.

We now ask the question, "What will happen when a machine takes the part of A in this game?" Will the interrogator decide wrongly as often when the game is played like this as he does when the game is played between a man and a woman? These questions replace our original, "Can machines think?"

From "Computing Machinery and Intelligence," *Mind: A Quarterly Review of Psychology and Philosophy LIX* (October, 1950), p. 236.

2. Critique of the New Problem.

As well as asking, "What is the answer to this new form of the question," one may ask, "Is this new question a worthy one to investigate?" This latter question we investigate without further ado, thereby cutting short an infinite regress.

The new problem has the advantage of drawing a fairly sharp line between the physical and the intellectual capacities of a man. No engineer or chemist claims to be able to produce a material which is indistinguishable from the human skin. It is possible that at some time this might be done, but even supposing this invention available we should feel there was little point in trying to make a "thinking machine" more human by dressing it up in such artificial flesh. The form in which we have set the problem reflects this fact in the condition which prevents the interrogator from seeing or touching the other competitors, or hearing their voices. Some other advantages of the proposed criterion may be shown up by specimen questions and answers. Thus:

Q: Please write me a sonnet on the subject of the Forth Bridge.
A: Count me out on this one. I never could write poetry.
Q: Add 34957 to 70764
A: (Pause about 30 seconds and then give as answer) 105621.
Q: Do you play chess?
A: Yes.
Q: I have K at my K1, and no other pieces. You have only K at K6 and R at R1. It is your move. What do you play?
A: (After a pause of 15 seconds) R-R8 mate.

The question and answer method seems to be suitable for introducing almost any one of the fields of human endeavor that we wish to include. We do not wish to penalize the machine for its inability to shine in beauty competitions, nor to penalize a man for losing in a race against an aeroplane. The conditions of our game make these disabilities irrelevant. The "witnesses" can brag, if they consider it advisable, as much as they please about their charms, strength or heroism, but the interrogator cannot demand practical demonstrations.

The game may perhaps be criticized on the ground that the odds are weighted too heavily against the machine. If the man were to try and pretend to be the machine he would clearly make a very poor showing. He would be given away at once by slowness and inaccuracy in arithmetic. May not machines carry out something which ought to be described as thinking but which is very different from what a man does? This objection is a very strong one, but at least we can say that if, nevertheless, a machine can be constructed to play the imitation game satisfactorily, we need not be troubled by this objection.

It might be urged that when playing the "imitation game" the best strategy for the machine may possibly be something other than imitation of the behavior of a man. This may be, but I think it is unlikely that there is any great effect of this kind. In any case there is no intention to investigate here the theory of the game, and it will be assumed that the best strategy is to try to provide answers that would naturally be given by a man.

3.   The Machines concerned in the Game.

The question which we put in § 1 will not be quite definite until we have specified what we mean by the word "machine." It is natural that we should wish to permit every kind of engineering technique to be used in our machines. We also wish to allow the possibility that an engineer or team of engineers may construct a machine which works, but whose manner of operation cannot be satisfactorily described by its constructors because they have applied a method which is largely experimental. Finally, we wish to exclude from the machines men born in the usual manner. It is difficult to frame the definitions so as to satisfy these three conditions. One might for instance insist that the team of engineers should be all of one sex, but this would not really be satisfactory, for it is probably possible to rear a complete individual from a single cell of the skin (say) of a man. To do so would be a feat of biological technique deserving of the very highest praise, but we would not be inclined to regard it as a case of "constructing a thinking machine." This prompts us to abandon the requirement that every kind of technique should be permitted. We are the more ready to do so in view of the fact that the present interest in "thinking machines" has been aroused by a particular kind of machine, usually called an "electronic computer" or "digital computer." Following this suggestion we only permit digital computers to take part in our game.

This restriction appears at first sight to be a very drastic one. I shall attempt to show that it is not so in reality. To do this necessitates a short account of the nature and properties of these computers.

It may also be said that this identification of machines with digital computers, like our criterion for "thinking," will only be unsatisfactory if (contrary to my belief), it turns out that digital computers are unable to give a good showing in the game.

There are already a number of digital computers in working order, and it may be asked, "Why not try the experiment straight away? It would be easy to satisfy the conditions of the game. A number of interrogators could be used, and statistics compiled to show how often the right identification was given." The short answer is that we are not asking whether all digital computers would do well in the game nor whether the computers at present available would do well, but whether there are imaginable computers which would do well. But this is only the short answer. We shall see this question in a different light later. . . .

We may now consider again the point raised at the end of §3. It was suggested tentatively that the question, "Can machines think?" should be replaced by "Are there imaginable digital computers which would do well in the imitation game?" If we wish we can make this superficially more general and ask "Are there discrete state machines which would do well?" But in view of the universality property we see that either of these questions is equivalent to this, "Let us fix our attention on one particular digital computer C. Is it true that by modifying this computer to have an adequate storage, suitably increasing its speed of action, and providing it with an appropriate program, C can be made to play satisfactorily the part of A in the imitation game, the part of B being taken by a man?"

6. Contrary Views on the Main Question.

We may now consider the ground to have been cleared and we are ready to proceed to the debate on our question, "Can machines think?" and the variant of it quoted at the end of the last section. We cannot altogether abandon the original form of the problem, for opinions will differ as to the appropriateness of the substitution and we must at least listen to what has to be said in this connexion.

It will simplify matters for the reader if I explain first my own beliefs in the matter. Consider first the more accurate form of the question. I believe that in about fifty years' time it will be possible to program computers, with a storage capacity of about 10^9, to make them play the imitation game so well that an average interrogator will not have more than 70 per cent. chance of making the right identification after five minutes of questioning. The original question, "Can machines think?" I believe to be too meaningless to deserve discussion. Nevertheless I believe that at the end of the century the use of words and general educated opinion will have altered so much that one will be able to speak of machines thinking without expecting to be contradicted. I believe further that no useful purpose is served by concealing these beliefs. The popular view that scientists proceed inexorably from well-established fact to well-established fact, never being influenced by any unproved conjecture, is quite mistaken. Provided it is made clear which are proved facts and which are conjectures, no harm can result. Conjectures are of great importance since they suggest useful lines of research.

I now proceed to consider opinions opposed to my own.

1) *The Theological Objection.* Thinking is a function of man's immortal soul. God has given an immortal soul to every man and woman, but not to any other animal or to machines. Hence no animal or machine can think.

I am unable to accept any part of this, but will attempt to reply in theological terms. I should find the argument more convincing if animals were classed with men, for there is a greater difference, to my mind, between the typical animate and the inanimate than there is between man and the other animals. The arbitrary character of the orthodox view becomes clearer if we consider how it might appear to a member of some other religious community. How do Christians regard the Moslem view that women have no souls? But let us leave this point aside and return to the main argument. It appears to me that the argument quoted above implies a serious restriction of the omnipotence of the Almighty. It is admitted that there are certain things that He cannot do such as making one equal to two, but should we not believe that He has freedom to confer a soul on an elephant if He sees fit? We might expect that He would only exercise this power in conjunction with a mutation which provided the elephant with an appropriately improved brain to minister to the needs of this soul. An argument of exactly similar form may be made for the case of machines. It may seem different because it is more difficult to "swallow." But this really only means that we think it would be less likely that He would consider the circumstances suitable for conferring a soul. The circumstances in question are discussed in the rest of this paper. In attempting to construct such machines we should not be irreverently usurping His power of creating souls, any more than we are in the procreation of children: rather we are, in either case, instruments of His will providing mansions for the souls that He creates.

However, this is mere speculation. I am not very impressed with theological arguments whatever they may be used to support. Such arguments have often been found unsatisfactory in the past. In the time of Galileo it was argued that the texts, "And the sun stood still . . . and hasted not to go down about a whole day" (Joshua x. 13) and "He laid the foundations of the earth, that it should not move at any time" (Psalm cv. 5) were an adequate refutation of the Copernican theory. With our present knowledge such an argument appears futile. When that knowledge was not available it made a quite different impression.

2) *The "Heads in the Sand" Objection.* "The consequences of machines thinking would be too dreadful. Let us hope and believe that they cannot do so."

This argument is seldom expressed quite so openly as in the form above. But it affects most of us who think about it at all. We like to believe that Man is in some subtle way superior to the rest of creation. It is best if he can be shown to be *necessarily* superior, for then there is no danger of him losing his commanding position. The popularity of the theological argument is clearly connected with this feeling. It is likely to be quite strong in intellectual people, since they value the power of thinking more highly than others, and are more inclined to base their belief in the superiority of Man on this power.

I do not think that this argument is sufficiently substantial to require refutation. Consolation would be more appropriate: perhaps this should be sought in the transmigration of souls.

3) *The Mathematical Objection.* There are a number of results of

mathematical logic which can be used to show that there are limitations to the powers of discrete-state machines. The best known of these results is known as *Gödel's* theorem,[1] and shows that in any sufficiently powerful logical system statements can be formulated which can neither be proved nor disproved within the system, unless possibly the system itself is inconsistent. There are other, in some respects similar, results due to *Church, Kleene, Rosser,* and *Turing.* The latter result is the most convenient to consider, since it refers directly to machines, whereas the others can only be used in a comparatively indirect argument: for instance if Gödel's theorem is to be used we need in addition to have some means of describing logical systems in terms of machines, and machines in terms of logical systems. The result in question refers to a type of machine which is essentially a digital computer with an infinite capacity. It states that there are certain things that such a machine cannot do. If it is rigged up to give answers to questions as in the imitation game, there will be some questions to which it will either give a wrong answer, or fail to give an answer at all however much time is allowed for a reply. There may, of course, be many such questions, and questions which cannot be answered by one machine may be satisfactorily answered by another. We are of course supposing for the present that the questions are of the kind to which an answer "Yes" or "No" is appropriate, rather than questions such as "What do you think of Picasso?" The questions that we know the machines must fail on are of this type, "Consider the machine specified as follows. . . . Will this machine ever answer 'Yes' to any question?" The dots are to be replaced by a description of some machine in a standard form. . . . When the machine described bears a certain comparatively simple relation to the machine which is under interrogation, it can be shown that the answer is either wrong or not forthcoming. This is the mathematical result: it is argued that it proves a disability of machines to which the human intellect is not subject.

The short answer to this argument is that although it is established that there are limitations to the powers of any particular machine, it has only been stated, without any sort of proof, that no such limitations apply to the human intellect. But I do not think this view can be dismissed quite so lightly. Whenever one of these machines is asked the appropriate critical question, and gives a definite answer, we know that this answer must be wrong, and this gives us a certain feeling of superiority. Is this feeling illusory? It is no doubt quite genuine, but I do not think too much importance should be attached to it. We too often give wrong answers to questions ourselves to be justified in being very pleased at such evidence of fallibility on the part of the machines. Further, our superiority can only be felt on such an occasion in relation to the one machine over which we have scored our petty triumph. There would be no question of triumphing simultaneously over *all* machines. In short, then, there might be men cleverer than

---

1 Authors' names in italics refer to the Bibliography.

any given machine, but then again there might be other machines cleverer again, and so on.

Those who hold to the mathematical argument would, I think, mostly be willing to accept the imitation game as a basis for discussion. Those who believe in the two previous objections would probably not be interested in any criteria.

4) *The Argument from Consciousness.* This argument is very well expressed in *Professor Jefferson's* Lister Oration for 1949, from which I quote. "Not until a machine can write a sonnet or compose a concerto because of thoughts and emotions felt, and not by the chance fall of symbols, could we agree that machine equals brain—that is, not only write it but know that it had written it. No mechanism could feel (and not merely artificially signal, an easy contrivance) pleasure at its successes, grief when its valves fuse, be warmed by flattery, be made miserable by its mistakes, be charmed by sex, be angry or depressed when it cannot get what it wants "

This argument appears to be a denial of the validity of our test. According to the most extreme form of this view the only way by which one could be sure that a machine thinks is to *be* the machine and to feel oneself thinking. One could then describe these feelings to the world, but of course no one would be justified in taking any notice. Likewise according to this view the only way to know that a *man* thinks is to be that particular man. It is in fact the solipsist point of view. It may be the most logical view to hold but it makes communication of ideas difficult. A is liable to believe "A thinks but B does not" whilst B believes "B thinks but A does not." Instead of arguing continually over this point it is usual to have the polite convention that everyone thinks.

I am sure that Professor Jefferson does not wish to adopt the extreme and solipsist point of view. Probably he would be quite willing to accept the imitation game as a test. The game (with the player B omitted) is frequently used in practice under the name of *viva voce* to discover whether some one really understands something or has 'learnt it parrot fashion." Let us listen in to a part of such a *viva voce*:

Interrogator: In the first line of your sonnet which reads "Shall I compare thee to a summer's day," would not "a spring day" do as well or better?
Witness: It wouldn't scan.
Interrogator: How about "a winter's day"? That would scan all right.
Witness: Yes, but nobody wants to be compared to a winter's day.
Interrogator: Would you say Mr. Pickwick reminded you of Christmas?
Witness: In a way.
Interrogator: Yet Christmas is a winter's day, and I do not think Mr. Pickwick would mind the comparison.
Witness: I don't think you're serious. By a winter's day one means a typical winter's day, rather than a special one like Christmas.

And so on. What would Professor Jefferson say if the sonnet-writing machine was able to answer like this in the *viva voce?* I do not know whether he would regard the machine as "merely artificially signalling" these answers, but if the answers were as satisfactory and sustained as in the above passage I do not think he would describe it as "an easy contrivance." This phrase is, I think, intended to cover such devices as the inclusion in the machine of a record of someone reading a sonnet, with appropriate switching to turn it on from time to time.

In short then, I think that most of those who support the argument from consciousness could be persuaded to abandon it rather than be forced into the solipsist position. They will then probably be willing to accept our test.

I do not wish to give the impression that I think there is no mystery about consciousness. There is, for instance, something of a paradox connected with any attempt to localize it. But I do not think these mysteries necessarily need to be solved before we can answer the question with which we are concerned in this paper.

5) *Arguments from Various Disabilities.* These arguments take the form, "I grant you that you can make machines do all the things you have mentioned but you will never be able to make one to do X." Numerous features X are suggested in this connection. I offer a selection:

Be kind, resourceful, beautiful, friendly, have initiative, have a sense of humor, tell right from wrong, make mistakes, fall in love, enjoy strawberries and cream, make some one fall in love with it, learn from experience, use words properly, be the subject of its own thought, have as much diversity of behavior as a man, do something really new.

No support is usually offered for these statements. I believe they are mostly founded on the principle of scientific induction. A man has seen thousands of machines in his lifetime. From what he sees of them he draws a number of general conclusions. They are ugly, each is designed for a very limited purpose, when required for a minutely different purpose they are useless, the variety of behavior of any one of them is very small, etc., etc. Naturally he concludes that these are necessary properties of machines in general. Many of these limitations are associated with the very small storage capacity of most machines. (I am assuming that the idea of storage capacity is extended in some way to cover machines other than discrete-state machines. The exact definition does not matter as no mathematical accuracy is claimed in the present discussion.) A few years ago, when very little had been heard of digital computers, it was possible to elicit much incredulity concerning them, if one mentioned their properties without describing their construction. That was presumably due to a similar application of the principle of scientific induction. These applications of the principle are of course largely unconscious. When a burnt child fears the fire and shows that he fears it by avoiding it, I should say that he was applying scientific induction. (I would of course also describe his behavior in many other ways.) The works and customs of mankind do not seem to be very suitable material to which to apply scientific induction. A very large part of space-time must be investigated, if reliable results are to be obtained. Otherwise we may (as most English children do) decide that everybody speaks English, and that it is silly to learn French.

There are, however, special remarks to be made about many of the disabilities that have been mentioned. The inability to enjoy strawberries and cream may have struck the reader as frivolous. Possibly a machine might be made to enjoy this delicious dish, but any attempt to make one do so would be idiotic. What is important about this disability is that it contributes to some of the other disabilities, *e.g.* to the difficulty of the same kind of friendliness occurring between man and machine as between white man and white man, or between black man and black man.

The claim that "machines cannot make mistakes" seems a curious one. One is tempted to retort, "Are they any the worse for that?" But let us adopt a more sympathetic attitude, and try to see what is really meant. I think this criticism can be explained in terms of the imitation game. It is claimed that the interrogator could distinguish the machine from the man simply by setting them a number of problems in arithmetic. The machine would be unmasked because of its deadly accuracy. The reply to this is simple. The machine (programed for playing the game) would not attempt to give the *right* answers to the arithmetic problems. It would deliberately introduce mistakes in a manner calculated to confuse the interrogator. A mechanical fault would probably show itself through an unsuitable decision as to what sort of a mistake to make in the arithmetic. Even this interpretation of the criticism is not sufficiently sympathetic. But we cannot afford the space to go into it much further. It seems to me that this criticism depends on a confusion between two kinds of mistake. We may call them "errors of functioning" and "errors of conclusion." Errors of functioning are due to some mechanical or electrical fault which causes the machine to behave otherwise than it was designed to do. In philosophical discussions one likes to ignore the possibility of such errors; one is therefore discussing "abstract machines." These abstract machines are mathematical fictions rather than physical objects. By definition they are incapable of errors of functioning. In this sense we can truly say that "machines can never make mistakes." Errors of conclusion can only arise when some meaning is attached to the output signals from the machine. The machine might, for instance, type out mathematical equations, or sentences in English. When a false proposition is typed we say that the machine has committed an error of conclusion. There is clearly no reason at all for saying that a machine cannot make this kind of mistake. It might do nothing but type out repeatedly "$o = 1$." To take a less perverse example, it might have some method for drawing conclusions by scientific induction. We must expect such a method to lead occasionally to erroneous results.

The claim that a machine cannot be the subject of its own thought can of course only be answered if it can be shown that the machine has *some* thought with *some* subject matter. Nevertheless, "the subject matter of a machine's operations" does seem to mean something, at least to the people who deal with it. If, for instance, the machine was trying to find a solution of the equation $x^2 - 40x - 11 = 0$ one would be tempted to describe this equation as part of the machine's subject matter at that moment. In this sort of sense a machine undoubtedly can be its own subject matter. It may be used to help in making up its own programs, or to predict the effect of alterations in its own structure. By observing the results of its own behavior it can modify its own programs so as to achieve some purpose more effectively. These are possibilities of the near future, rather than Utopian dreams.

The criticism that a machine cannot have much diversity of behavior is just a way of saying that it cannot have much storage capacity. Until fairly recently a storage capacity of even a thousand digits was very rare.

The criticisms that we are considering here are often disguised forms of the argument from consciousness. Usually if one maintains that a machine *can* do one of these things, and describes the kind of method that the machine could use, one will not make much of an impression. It is thought that the method (whatever it may be, for it must be mechanical) is really rather base. Compare the parenthesis in Jefferson's statement quoted on p. 257.

6) *Lady Lovelace's Objection.* Our most detailed information of Babbage's Analytical Engine comes from a memoir by *Lady Lovelace*. In it she states, "The Analytical Engine has no pretensions to *originate* anything. It can do *whatever we know how to order it* to perform" (her italics). This statement is quoted by *Hartree* (p. 70) who adds: "This does not imply that it may not be possible to construct electronic equipment which will 'think for itself,' or in which, in biological terms, one could set up a conditioned reflex, which would serve as a basis for 'learning.' Whether this is possible in principle or not is a stimulating and exciting question, suggested by some of these recent developments. But it did not seem that the machines constructed or projected at the time had this property."

I am in thorough agreement with Hartree over this. It will be noticed that he does not assert that the machines in question had not got the property, but rather that the evidence available to Lady Lovelace did not encourage her to believe that they had it. It is quite possible that the machines in question had in a sense got this property. For suppose that some discrete-state machine has the property. The Analytical Engine was a universal digital computer, so that, if its storage capacity and speed were adequate, it could by suitable programing be made to mimic the machine in question. Probably this argument did not occur to the Countess or to Babbage. In any case there was no obligation on them to claim all that could be claimed.

This whole question will be considered again under the heading of learning machines.

A variant of Lady Lovelace's objection states that a machine can "never do anything really new." This may be parried for a moment with the saw, "There is nothing new under the sun." Who can be certain the "original work" that he has done was not simply the growth of the seed planted in him by teaching, or the effect of following well-known general principles. A better variant of the objection says that a machine can never "take us by surprise." This statement is a more direct challenge and can be met directly. Machines take me by surprise with great frequency. This is largely because I do not do sufficient calculation to decide what to expect them to do, or rather because, although I do a calculation, I do it in a hurried, slipshod fashion, taking risks. Perhaps I say to myself, "I suppose the voltage here ought to be the same as there: anyway let's assume it is." Naturally I am often wrong, and the result is a surprise for me for by the time the experiment is done these assumptions have been forgotten. These admissions lay me open to lectures on the subject of my vicious ways, but do not throw any doubt on my credibility when I testify to the surprises I experience.

I do not expect this reply to silence my critic. He will probably say that such surprises are due to some creative mental act on my part, and reflect no credit on the machine. This leads us back to the argument from consciousness, and far from the idea of surprise. It is a line of argument we must consider closed, but it is perhaps worth remarking that the appreciation of something as surprising requires as much of a "creative mental act" whether the surprising event originates from a man, a book, a machine or anything else.

The view that machines cannot give rise to surprises is due, I believe, to a fallacy to which philosophers and mathematicians are particularly subject. This is the assumption that as soon as a fact is presented to a mind all consequences of that fact spring into the mind simultaneously with it. It is a very useful assumption under many circumstances, but one too easily forgets that it is false. A natural consequence of doing so is that one then assumes that there is no virtue in the mere working out of consequences from data and general principles.

7) *Argument from Continuity in the Nervous System.* The nervous system is certainly not a discrete-state machine. A small error in the information about the size of a nervous impulse impinging on a neuron, may make a large difference to the size of the outgoing impulse. It may be argued that, this being so, one cannot expect to be able to mimic the behavior of the nervous system with a discrete-state system.

It is true that a discrete-state machine must be different from a continuous machine. But if we adhere to the conditions of the imitation game, the interrogator will not be able to take any advantage of this difference. The situation can be made clearer if we consider some other simpler continuous machine. A differential analyzer will do very well. (A differential analyzer is a certain kind of machine not of the discrete-state type used for some kinds of calculation.) Some of these provide their answers in a typed form, and so are suitable for taking part in the game. It would not be possible for a digital computer to predict exactly what answers the differential analyzer would give to a problem, but it would be quite capable of giving the right sort of answer. For instance, if asked to give the value of π (actually about 3·1416) it would be reasonable to choose at random between the values 3·12, 3·13, 3·14, 3·15, 3·16 with the probabilities of 0·05, 0·15, 0·55, 0·19, 0·06 (say). Under these circumstances it would be very difficult for the interrogator to distinguish the differential analyzer from the digital computer.

8) *The Argument from Informality of Behavior.* It is not possible to produce a set of rules purporting to describe what a man should do in every conceivable set of circumstances. One might for instance have a rule that one is to stop when one sees a red traffic light, and to go if one sees a green one, but what if by some fault both appear together? One may perhaps decide that it is safest to stop. But some further difficulty may well arise from this decision later. To attempt to provide rules of conduct to cover every eventuality, even those arising from traffic lights, appears to be impossible. With all this I agree.

From this it is argued that we cannot be machines. I shall try to reproduce the argument, but I fear I shall hardly do it justice. It seems to run something like this. "If each man had a definite set of rules of conduct by which he regulated his life he would be no better than a machine. But there are no such rules, so men cannot be machines." The undistributed middle is glaring. I do not think the argument is ever put quite like this, but I believe this is the argument used nevertheless. There may however be a certain confusion between "rules of conduct" and "laws of behavior" to cloud the issue. By "rules of conduct" I mean precepts such as "Stop if you see red lights," on which one can act, and of which one can be conscious. By "laws of behavior" I mean laws of nature as applied to a man's body such as "if you pinch him he will squeak." If we substitute "laws of behavior which regulate his life" for "laws of conduct by which he regulates his life" in the argument quoted the undistributed middle is no longer insuperable. For we believe that it is not only true that being regulated by laws of behavior implies being some sort of machine (though not necessarily a discrete-state machine), but that conversely being such a machine implies being regulated by such laws. However, we cannot so easily convince ourselves of the absence of complete laws of behavior as of complete rules of conduct. The only way we know of for finding such laws is scientific observation, and we certainly know of no circumstances under which we could say, "We have searched enough. There are no such laws."

We can demonstrate more forcibly that any such statement would be unjustified. For suppose we could be sure of finding such laws if they existed. Then given a discrete-state machine it should certainly be possible to discover by observation sufficient about it to predict its future behavior, and this within a reasonable time, say a thousand years. But this does not seem to be the case. I have set up on the Manchester computer a small program using only 1000 units of storage, whereby the machine supplied with one sixteen figure number replies with another within two seconds. I would defy anyone to learn from these replies sufficient about the program to be able to predict any replies to untried values.

9) *The Argument from Extra-Sensory Perception.* I assume that the reader is familiar with the idea of extra-sensory perception, and the meaning of the four items of it, *viz.* telepathy, clairvoyance, precognition and psycho-kinesis. These disturbing phenomena seem to deny all our usual scientific ideas. How we should like to discredit them! Unfortunately the statistical evidence, at least for telepathy, is overwhelming. It is very difficult to rearrange one's ideas so as to fit these new facts in. Once one has accepted them it does not seem a very big step to believe in ghosts and bogies. The idea that our bodies move simply according to the known laws of physics, together with some others not yet discovered but somewhat similar, would be one of the first to go.

This argument is to my mind quite a strong one. One can say in reply that many scientific theories seem to remain workable in practice, in spite of clashing with E.S.P.; that in fact one can get along very nicely if one forgets about it. This is rather cold comfort, and one fears that thinking is just the kind of phenomenon where E.S.P. may be especially relevant.

A more specific argument based on E.S.P. might run as follows: "Let us play the imitation game, using as witnesses a man who is good as a telepathic receiver, and a digital computer. The interrogator can ask such questions as 'What suit does the card in my right hand belong to?' The man by telepathy or clairvoyance gives the right answer 130 times out of 400 cards. The machine can only guess at random, and perhaps gets 104 right, so the interrogator makes the right identification." There is an interesting possibility which opens here. Suppose the digital computer contains a random number generator. Then it will be natural to use this to decide what answer to give. But then the random number generator will be subject to the psycho-kinetic powers of the interrogator. Perhaps this psycho-kinesis might cause the machine to guess right more often than would be expected on a probability calculation, so that the interrogator might still be unable to make the right identification. On the other hand, he might be able to guess right without any questioning, by clairvoyance. With E.S.P. anything may happen.

If telepathy is admitted it will be necessary to tighten our test up. The situation could be regarded as analogous to that which would occur if the

interrogator were talking to himself and one of the competitors was listening with his ear to the wall. To put the competitors into a "telepathy-proof
room" would satisfy all requirements.

7. Learning Machines.

The reader will have anticipated that I have no very convincing arguments of a positive nature to support my views. If I had I should not have
taken such pains to point out the fallacies in contrary views. Such evidence
as I have I shall now give.

Let us return for a moment to Lady Lovelace's objection, which stated
that the machine can only do what we tell it to do. One could say that a
man can "inject" an idea into the machine, and that it will respond to a
certain extent and then drop into quiescence, like a piano string struck
by a hammer. Another simile would be an atomic pile of less than critical
size: an injected idea is to correspond to a neutron entering the pile from
without. Each such neutron will cause a certain disturbance which eventually dies away. If, however, the size of the pile is sufficiently increased, the
disturbance caused by such an incoming neutron will very likely go on and
on increasing until the whole pile is destroyed. Is there a corresponding
phenomenon for minds, and is there one for machines? There does seem
to be one for the human mind. The majority of them seem to be "sub-
critical," *i.e.* to correspond in this analogy to piles of sub-critical size. An
idea presented to such a mind will on average give rise to less than one
idea in reply. A smallish proportion are super-critical. An idea presented
to such a mind may give rise to a whole "theory" consisting of secondary,
tertiary and more remote ideas. Animals' minds seem to be very definitely
sub-critical. Adhering to this analogy we ask, "Can a machine be made to
be super-critical?"

The "skin of an onion" analogy is also helpful. In considering the functions of the mind or the brain we find certain operations which we can
explain in purely mechanical terms. This we say does not correspond to
the real mind: it is a sort of skin which we must strip off if we are to find
the real mind. But then in what remains we find a further skin to be
stripped off, and so on. Proceeding in this way do we ever come to the
"real" mind, or do we eventually come to the skin which has nothing in it?
In the latter case the whole mind is mechanical. (It would not be a
discrete-state machine however. We have discussed this.)

These last two paragraphs do not claim to be convincing arguments.
They should rather be described as "recitations tending to produce belief."

The only really satisfactory support that can be given for the view
expressed at the beginning of § 6, will be that provided by waiting for
the end of the century and then doing the experiment described. But what
can we say in the meantime? What steps should be taken now if the experiment is to be successful?

As I have explained, the problem is mainly one of programing. Advances in engineering will have to be made too, but it seems unlikely that these will not be adequate for the requirements. Estimates of the storage capacity of the brain vary from 10^{10} to 10^{15} binary digits. I incline to the lower values and believe that only a very small fraction is used for the higher types of thinking. I should be surprised if more than 10^9 was required for satisfactory playing of the imitation game, at any rate against a blind man. (Note—The capacity of the *Encyclopaedia Britannica,* 11th edition, is 2×10^9.) A storage capacity of 10^7 would be a very practicable possibility even by present techniques. It is probably not necessary to increase the speed of operations of the machines at all. Parts of modern machines which can be regarded as analogues of nerve cells work about a thousand times faster than the latter. This should provide a "margin of safety" which could cover losses of speed arising in many ways. Our problem then is to find out how to program these machines to play the game. At my present rate of working I produce about a thousand digits of program a day, so that about sixty workers, working steadily through the fifty years might accomplish the job, if nothing went into the waste-paper basket. Some more expeditious method seems desirable.

In the process of trying to imitate an adult human mind we are bound to think a good deal about the process which has brought it to the state that it is in. We may notice three components,

(a) The initial state of the mind, say at birth,

(b) The education to which it has been subjected,

(c) Other experience, not to be described as education, to which it has been subjected.

Instead of trying to produce a program to simulate the adult mind, why not rather try to produce one which simulates the child's? If this were then subjected to an appropriate course of education one would obtain the adult brain. Presumably the child-brain is something like a note-book as one buys it from the stationers. Rather little mechanism, and lots of blank sheets. (Mechanism and writing are from our point of view almost synonymous.) Our hope is that there is so little mechanism in the child-brain that something like it can be easily programed. The amount of work in the education we can assume, as a first approximation, to be much the same as for the human child.

We have thus divided our problem into two parts. The child-program and the education process. These two remain very closely connected. We cannot expect to find a good child-machine at the first attempt. One must experiment with teaching one such machine and see how well it learns. One can then try another and see if it is better or worse. There is an obvious connection between this process and evolution, by the identifications

Structure of the child machine = Hereditary material
Changes   "   "   = Mutations
Natural selection   = Judgment of the experimenter

One may hope, however, that this process will be more expeditious than evolution. The survival of the fittest is a slow method for measuring advantages. The experimenter, by the exercise of intelligence, should be able to speed it up. Equally important is the fact that he is not restricted to random mutations. If he can trace a cause for some weakness he can probably think of the kind of mutation which will improve it.

It will not be possible to apply exactly the same teaching process to the machine as to a normal child. It will not, for instance, be provided with legs, so that it could not be asked to go out and fill the coal scuttle. Possibly it might not have eyes. But however well these deficiencies might be overcome by clever engineering, one could not send the creature to school without the other children making excessive fun of it. It must be given some tuition. We need not be too concerned about the legs, eyes, etc. The example of Miss Helen Keller shows that education can take place provided that communication in both directions between teacher and pupil can take place by some means or other.

We normally associate punishments and rewards with the teaching process. Some simple child-machines can be constructed or programed on this sort of principle. The machine has to be so constructed that events which shortly preceded the occurrence of a punishment-signal are unlikely to be repeated, whereas a reward-signal increased the probability of repetition of the events which led up to it. These definitions do not presuppose any feelings on the part of the machine. I have done some experiments with one such child-machine, and succeeded in teaching it a few things, but the teaching method was too unorthodox for the experiment to be considered really successful.

The use of punishments and rewards can at best be a part of the teaching process. Roughly speaking, if the teacher has no other means of communicating to the pupil, the amount of information which can reach him does not exceed the total number of rewards and punishments applied. By the time a child has learnt to repeat "Casabianca" he would probably feel very sore indeed, if the text could only be discovered by a "Twenty Questions" technique, every "NO" taking the form of a blow. It is necessary therefore to have some other "unemotional" channels of communication. If these are available it is possible to teach a machine by punishments and rewards to obey orders given in some language, *e.g.* a symbolic language. These orders are to be transmitted through the "unemotional" channels. The use of this language will diminish greatly the number of punishments and rewards required.

Opinions may vary as to the complexity which is suitable in the child machine. One might try to make it as simple as possible consistently with the general principles. Alternatively one might have a complete system of logical inference "built-in."[1] In the latter case the store would be largely

[1] Or rather "programed in" for our child-machine will be programed in a digital computer. But the logical system will not have to be learnt.

occupied with definitions and propositions. The propositions would have various kinds of status, *e.g.* well-established facts, conjectures, mathematically proved theorems, statements given by an authority, expressions having the logical form of proposition but not belief-value. Certain propositions may be described as "imperatives." The machine should be so constructed that as soon as an imperative is classed as "well-established" the appropriate action automatically takes place. To illustrate this, suppose the teacher says to the machine, "Do your homework now." This may cause "Teacher says 'Do your homework now'" to be included amongst the well-established facts. Another such fact might be, "Everything that teacher says is true." Combining these may eventually lead to the imperative. "Do your homework now," being included amongst the well-established facts, and this, by the construction of the machine, will mean that the homework actually gets started, but the effect is very satisfactory. The processes of inference used by the machine need not be such as would satisfy the most exacting logicians. There might for instance be no hierarchy of types. But this need not mean that type fallacies will occur, any more than we are bound to fall over unfenced cliffs. Suitable imperatives (expressed *within* the systems, not forming part of the rules *of* the system) such as "Do not use a class unless it is a subclass of one which has been mentioned by teacher" can have a similar effect to "Do not go too near the edge."

The imperatives that can be obeyed by a machine that has no limbs are bound to be of a rather intellectual character, as in the example (doing homework) given above. Important amongst such imperatives will be ones which regulate the order in which the rules of the logical system concerned are to be applied. For at each stage when one is using a logical system, there is a very large number of alternative steps, any of which one is permitted to apply, so far as obedience to the rules of the logical system is concerned. These choices make the difference between a brilliant and a footling reasoner, not the difference between a sound and a fallacious one. Propositions leading to imperatives of this kind might be "When Socrates is mentioned, use the syllogism in Barbara" or "If one method has been proved to be quicker than another, do not use the slower method." Some of these may be "given by authority," but others may be produced by the machine itself, *e.g.* by scientific induction.

The idea of a learning machine may appear paradoxical to some readers. How can the rules of operation of the machine change? They should describe completely how the machine will react whatever its history might be, whatever changes it might undergo. The rules are thus quite time-invariant. This is quite true. The explanation of the paradox is that the rules which get changed in the learning process are of a rather less pretentious kind, claiming only an ephemeral validity. The reader may draw a parallel with the Constitution of the United States.

An important feature of a learning machine is that its teacher will often be very largely ignorant of quite what is going on inside, although he may still be able to some extent to predict his pupil's behavior. This should apply most strongly to the later education of a machine arising from a child-machine of well-tried design (or program). This is in clear contrast with normal procedure when using a machine to do computations: one's object is then to have a clear mental picture of the state of the machine at each moment in the computation. This object can only be achieved with a struggle. The view that "the machine can only do what we know how to order it to do,"[1] appears strange in face of this. Most of the programs which we can put into the machine will result in its doing something that we cannot make sense of at all, or which we regard as completely random behavior. Intelligent behavior presumably consists in a departure from the completely disciplined behavior involved in computation, but a rather slight one, which does not give rise to random behavior, or to pointless repetitive loops. Another important result of preparing our machine for its part in the imitation game by a process of teaching and learning is that "human fallibility" is likely to be omitted in a rather natural way, *i.e.* without special "coaching." Processes that are learnt do not produce a hundred per cent. certainty of result; if they did they could not be unlearnt.

It is probably wise to include a random element in a learning machine. A random element is rather useful when we are searching for a solution of some problem. Suppose for instance we wanted to find a number between 50 and 200 which was equal to the square of the sum of its digits, we might start at 51 then try 52 and go on until we got a number that worked. Alternatively we might choose numbers at random until we got a good one. This method has the advantage that it is unnecessary to keep track of the values that have been tried, but the disadvantage that one may try the same one twice, but this is not very important if there are several solutions. The systematic method has the disadvantage that there may be an enormous block without any solutions in the region which has to be investigated first. Now the learning process may be regarded as a search for a form of behavior which will satisfy the teacher (or some other criterion). Since there is probably a very large number of satisfactory solutions the random method seems to be better than the systematic. It should be noticed that it is used in the analogous process of evolution. But there the systematic method is not possible. How could one keep track of the different genetical combinations that had been tried, so as to avoid trying them again?

We may hope that machines will eventually compete with men in all purely intellectual fields. But which are the best ones to start with? Even this is a difficult decision. Many people think that a very abstract activity, like the playing of chess, would be best. It can also be maintained that it it is best to provide the machine with the best sense organs that money

1 Compare Lady Lovelace's statement which does not contain the word "only."

can buy, and then teach it to understand and speak English. This process could follow the normal teaching of a child. Things would be pointed out and named, etc. Again I do not know what the right answer is, but I think both approaches should be tried.

We can only see a short distance ahead, but we can see plenty there that needs to be done.

BIBLIOGRAPHY

Samuel Butler, *Erewhon,* London, 1865. Chapters 23, 24, 25, *The Book of the Machines.*

Alonzo Church, "An Unsolvable Problem of Elementary Number Theory," *American J. of Math.,* 58 (1936), 345-363.

K. Gödel, "Uber formal unentscheidbare Sätze der Principia Mathematica und verwandter Systeme, I" *Monatshefte für Math. und Phys.* (1931), 173-189.

D. R. Hartree, *Calculating Instruments and Machines,* New York, 1949.

S. C. Kleene, "General Recursive Functions of Natural Numbers," *American J. of Math.,* 57 (1935), 153-173 and 219-244.

G. Jefferson, "The Mind of Mechanical Man." Lister Oration for 1949. *British Medical Journal,* I (1949), 1105-1121.

Countess of Lovelace, "Translator's notes to an article on Babbage's Analytical Engine," *Scientific Memoirs* (ed. by R. Taylor), III (1842), 691-731.

Bertrand Russell, *History of Western Philosophy,* London, 1940.

A. M. Turing, "On Computable Numbers, with an Application to the Entscheidungs-problem," *Proc. London Math. Soc.* (2), 42 (1937), 230-265.

ABOUT THE RIGHT OF REVOLUTION

PROBABLY the most important reason for studying implications and assumptions is that only if one is quite conscious of them can one write prose that is fully controlled. Even moderately inept writers know what their words are literally saying. But often beneath the surface sense there is a hidden system of ideas which is to the literal meaning as roots to a tree, or the submerged section of an iceberg to the part above water. These assumptions and implications are likely to reveal logical weaknesses and inconsistencies not evident to the writer; for this reason a truly responsible writer will keep under control not only the facial muscles of his piece, but the less evident tissues as well, lest he be embarrassed by close observation.

But familiarity with assumptions and implications can be a valuable tool in reading as well as writing. To begin with, it enables one to appraise the logical coherence of an essay or book far more clearly than would otherwise be possible. Even more important, the real significance of a piece of writing is often beneath the surface. Assumptions—the unspoken premises of a writer—often involve his most deeply held values, and thus show his relation to other writers and thinkers. Implications, on the other hand, are extensions of the literal meaning. Take, for instance, the following assertion on the subject of this unit: "Since the American people are prosperous, they should not revolt at present." The speaker assumes that poverty is the only justification for revolution. He implies, among other things, that the American people may sometime not be prosperous, that the government is responsible for economic conditions, that the people of Spain, Greece, and India should revolt, and that material comfort is the highest good. Many who would not chafe at the initial assertion would find some of these consequences unpalatable.

The right to revolt is a subject which has received a great amount of attention since the rise of democratic government. The controversy is interesting in itself, and equally interesting for the underlying values it reveals among the disputants. The writers represented here all favor revolution under certain circumstances, but the premises from which they argue differ greatly. John Locke (1632-1704) was one of England's most important philosophers, and an ancestor of American democratic thought. Karl Marx (1818-1883) was the father of modern communism. His collaborator in many works was another German, Friedrich Engels (1820-1895). A milder socialist was George Bernard Shaw (1856-1950), more famous as England's greatest modern dramatist. Harold Laski (1893-1950), British political scientist, was a Marxist, though not at all an uncritical one. Henry David Thoreau (1817-1862), American naturalist and philosopher, stated the con-

cept of rebellion as duty so unequivocally in the essay reprinted below that his work has since become the classic handbook for revolutionaries throughout the world.

OF THE DISSOLUTION OF GOVERNMENT | *JOHN LOCKE*

He that will with any clearness speak of the dissolution of government, ought in the first place to distinguish between the dissolution of the society and the dissolution of the government. That which makes the community, and brings men out of the loose state of nature into one politic society, is the agreement which every one has with the rest to incorporate, and act as one body, and so be one distinct commonwealth. The usual, and almost only way whereby this union is dissolved, is the inroad of foreign force making a conquest upon them: for in that case (not being able to maintain and support themselves, as one entire and independent body) the union belonging to that body which consisted therein, must necessarily cease, and so every one return to the state he was in before, with a liberty to shift for himself, and provide for his own safety, as he thinks fit, in some other society. Whenever the society is dissolved, it is certain the government of that society cannot remain. Thus conquerors' swords often cut up governments by the roots, and mangle societies to pieces, separating the subdued or scattered multitude from the protection of, and dependence on, that society which ought to have preserved them from violence. The world is too well instructed in, and too forward to allow of, this way of dissolving of governments, to need any more to be said of it; and there wants not much argument to prove, that where the society is dissolved, the government cannot remain; that being as impossible, as for the frame of a house to subsist when the materials of it are scattered and dissipated by a whirlwind, or jumbled into a confused heap by an earthquake.

Besides this overturning from without, governments are dissolved from within.

First, When the legislative is altered. Civil society being a state of peace, amongst those who are of it, from whom the state of war is excluded by the umpirage, which they have provided in their legislative, for the ending of all differences that may arise amongst any of them; it is in their legislative, that the members of a commonwealth are united, and combined together into one coherent living body. This is the soul that gives form, life, and unity to the commonwealth: from hence the several members have their mutual influence, sympathy, and connection; and therefore,

From *Of Civil Government* (1685).

when the legislative is broken, or dissolved, dissolution and death follows: for, the essence and union of the society consisting in having one will, the legislative, when once established by the majority, has the declaring, and as it were keeping of that will. The constitution of the legislative is the first and fundamental act of society, whereby provision is made for the continuation of their union, under the direction of persons, and bonds of laws, made by persons authorized thereunto, by the consent and appointment of the people; without which no one man, or number of men, amongst them, can have authority of making laws that shall be binding to the rest. When any one, or more, shall take upon them to make laws, whom the people have not appointed so to do, they make laws without authority, which the people are not therefore bound to obey; by which means they come again to be out of subjection, and may constitute to themselves a new legislative, as they think best, being in full liberty to resist the force of those, who without authority would impose any thing upon them. Every one is at the disposure of his own will, when those who had, by the delegation of the society, the declaring of the public will, are excluded from it, and others usurp the place, who have no such authority or delegation.

This being usually brought about by such in the commonwealth who misuse the power they have, it is hard to consider it aright, and know at whose door to lay it, without knowing the form of government in which it happens. Let us suppose then the legislative placed in the concurrence of three distinct persons.

1. A single hereditary person, having the constant, supreme, executive power, and with it the power of convoking and dissolving the other two, within certain periods of time.

2. An assembly of hereditary nobility.

3. An assembly of representatives chosen pro tempore, by the people. Such a form of government supposed, it is evident.

First, That when such a single person, or prince, sets up his own arbitrary will in place of the laws, which are the will of the society, declared by the legislative, then the legislative is changed: for that being in effect the legislative, whose rules and laws are put in execution, and required to be obeyed; when other laws are set up, and other rules pretended, and enforced, than what the legislative, constituted by society, have enacted, it is plain that the legislative is changed. Whoever introduces new laws, not being thereunto authorized, by the fundamental appointment of the society, or subverts the old; disowns and overturns the power by which they were made, and so sets up a new legislative.

Secondly, When the prince hinders the legislative from assembling in its due time, or from acting freely, pursuant to those ends for which it was constituted, the legislative is altered: for it is not a certain number of men, no, nor their meeting, unless they have also freedom of debating, and leisure of perfecting, what is for the good of the society, wherein the legislative consists; when these are taken away or altered, so as to deprive the society of the due exercise of their power, the legislative is truly altered: for it is not names that constitute governments, but the use and exercise of those powers that were intended to accompany them; so that he, who takes away the freedom, or hinders the acting of the legislative in its due seasons, in effect takes away the legislative, and puts an end to the government.

Thirdly, When, by the arbitrary power of the prince, the electors, or ways of election, are altered, without the consent, and contrary to the common interest of the people, there also the legislative is altered: for, if others than those whom the society hath authorized thereunto, do choose, or in another way than what the society hath prescribed, those chosen are not the legislative appointed by the people.

Fourthly, The delivery also of the people into the subjection of a foreign power, either by the prince, or by the legislative, is certainly a change of the legislative, and so a dissolution of the government: for the end why people entered into society being to be preserved one entire, free, independent society, to be governed by its own laws; this is lost, whenever they are given up into the power of another.

Why, in such a constitution as this, the dissolution of the government in these cases is to be imputed to the prince, is evident; because he, having the force, treasure, and offices of the state to employ, and often persuading himself, or being flattered by others, that as supreme magistrate, he is incapable of control; he alone is in a condition to make great advances toward such changes, under pretense of lawful authority, and has it in his hands to terrify or suppress opposers, as factious, seditious, and enemies to the government: whereas no other part of the legislative, or people, is capable by themselves to attempt any alteration of the legislative, without open and visible rebellion, apt enough to be taken notice of; which, when it prevails, produces effects very little different from foreign conquest. Besides, the prince in such a form of government having the power of dissolving the other parts of the legislative, and thereby rendering them private persons, they can never in opposition to him, or without his concurrence, alter the legislative by a law, his consent being necessary to give any of their decrees that sanction. But yet, so far as the other parts of the legislative any way contribute to any attempt upon the government, and do either promote, or not (what lies in them) hinder such designs; they are guilty, and partake in this, which is certainly the greatest crime men can be guilty of one toward another.

There is one way more whereby such a government may be dissolved, and that is, when he who has the supreme executive power neglects and abandons that charge, so that the laws already made can no longer be put in execution. This is demonstratively to reduce all to anarchy, and so effectually to dissolve the government: for laws not being made for themselves, but to be, by their execution, the bonds of the society, to keep every part of the body politic in its due place and function; when that totally ceases, the government visibly ceases, and the people become a confused multitude, without order or connection. Where there is no longer the administration of justice, for the securing of men's rights, nor any remaining power within the community to direct the force, or provide for the necessities of the public; there certainly is no government left. Where the laws cannot be executed, it is all one as if there were no laws; and a government without laws is, I suppose, a mystery in politics, inconceivable to human capacity, and inconsistent with human society.

In these and the like cases, when the government is dissolved, the people are at liberty to provide for themselves, by erecting a new legislative, differing from the other, by the change of persons, or form, or both, as they shall find it most for their safety and good; for the society can never, by the fault of another, lose the native and original right it has to preserve itself; which can only be done by a settled legislative, and a fair and impartial execution of the laws made by it. But the state of mankind is not so miserable that they are not capable of using this remedy, till it be too late to look for any. To tell people they may provide for themselves, by erecting a new legislative, when by oppression, artifice, or being delivered over to a foreign power, their old one is gone, is only to tell them, they may expect relief when it is too late, and the evil is past cure. This is in effect no more than to bid them first to be slaves, and then to take care of their liberty; and when their chains are on, tell them, they may act like freemen. This, if barely so, is rather mockery than relief; and men can never be secure from tyranny, if there be no means to escape it till they are perfectly under it: and therefore it is, that they have not only a right to get out of it, but to prevent it.

There is, therefore, secondly, another way whereby governments are dissolved, and that is, when the legislative, or the prince, either of them, act contrary to their trust.

First, The legislative acts against the trust reposed in them, when they endeavor to invade the property of the subject, and to make themselves, or any part of the community, masters, or arbitrary disposers of the lives, liberties, or fortunes of the people.

The reason why men enter into society, is the preservation of their property; and the end why they choose and authorize a legislative, is, that there may be laws made, and rules set, as guards and fences to the properties of all the members of the society: to limit the power, and moderate the dominion, of every part and member of the society: for since it can never be supposed to be the will of the society, that the legislative should have a power to destroy that which every one designs to secure by entering into society, and for which the people submitted themselves to legislators of their own making; whenever the legislators endeavor to take away and destroy the property of the people, or to reduce them to slavery under arbitrary power, they put themselves into a state of war with the people, who are thereupon absolved from any farther obedience, and are left to the common refuge, which God hath provided for all men, against force and violence. Whensoever therefore the legislative shall transgress this fundamental rule of society; and either by ambition, fear, folly or corruption, endeavor to grasp themselves, or put into the hands of any other, an absolute power over the lives, liberties, and estates of the people; by this breach of trust they forfeit the power the people had put into their hands for quite contrary ends, and it devolves to the people, who have a right to resume their original liberty, and, by the establishment of a new legislative (such as they shall think fit), provide for their own safety and security, which is the end for which they are in society. What I have said here, concerning the legislative in general, holds true also concerning the supreme executor, who having a double trust put in him, both to have a part in the legislative, and the supreme execution of the law, acts against both, when he goes about to set up his own arbitrary will as the law of the society. He acts also contrary to his trust, when he either employs the force, treasure, and offices of the society to corrupt the representatives, and gain them to his purposes; or openly pre-engages the electors, and prescribes to their choice, such, whom he has, by solicitations, threats, promises, or otherwise, won to his designs: and employs them to bring in such, who have promised beforehand what to vote, and what to enact. Thus to regulate candidates and electors, and new-model the ways of election, what is it but to cut up the government by the roots, and poison the very fountain of public security? for the people having reserved to themselves the choice of their representatives, as the fence to their properties, could do it for no other end, but that they might always be freely chosen, and so chosen, freely act, and advise, as the necessity of the commonwealth, and the public good should, upon examination and mature debate, be judged to require. This, those who give their votes before they hear the debate, and have weighed the reasons on all sides, are not capable of doing. To prepare such an assembly as this, and endeavor to set up the declared abettors of his own will, for the true representatives of the people, and the lawmakers of the society, is certainly as great a breach of trust, and as perfect a declaration of a design to subvert the government, as is possible to be met with. To which if one shall add rewards and punishments visibly employed to the same end, and all the arts of perverted law made use of, to take off and destroy all that stand in the way of such a design, and will not comply and consent to betray the liberties of their country, it will be past doubt what he is doing. What power they ought to have in the society, who thus employ it contrary to the trust that went along with it in its first institution, is easy to determine; and one cannot but see, that he, who has once attempted any such thing as this, cannot any longer be trusted.

To this perhaps it will be said, that the people being ignorant, and always discontented, to lay the foundation of government in the unsteady opinion and uncertain humor of the people, is to expose it to certain ruin; and no government will be able long to subsist, if the people may set up a new legislative, whenever they take offense at the old one. To this I answer, quite the contrary. People are not so easily got out of their old forms as some are apt to suggest. They are hardly to be prevailed with to amend the acknowledged faults in the frame they have been accustomed to. And if there be any original defects, or adventitious ones introduced by time, or corruption: it is not an easy thing to get them changed, even when all the world sees there is an opportunity for it. This slowness and aversion in the people to quit their old constitutions, has in the many revolutions which have been seen in this kingdom, in this and former ages, still kept us to, or, after some interval of fruitless attempts, still brought us back again to, our old legislative of king, lords, and commons: and whatever provocations have made the crown to be taken from some of our princes' heads, they never carried the people so far as to place it in another line.

But it will be said, this hypothesis lays a ferment for frequent rebellion. To which I answer,

First, no more than any other hypothesis: for when the people are made miserable, and find themselves exposed to the ill-usage of arbitrary power, cry up their governors as much as you will, for sons of Jupiter; let them be sacred or divine, descended, or authorized from heaven; give them out from whom or what you please, the same will happen. The people generally ill-treated, and contrary to right, will be ready upon any occasion to ease themselves of a burden that sits heavy upon them. They will wish, and seek for the opportunity, which in the change, weakness, and accidents of human affairs, seldom delays long to offer itself. He must have lived but a little while in the world, who has not seen examples of this in his time; and he must have read very little, who cannot produce examples of it in all sorts of governments in the world.

Secondly, I answer, such revolutions happen not upon every little mismanagement in public affairs. Great mistakes in the ruling part, many wrong and inconvenient laws, and all the slips of human frailty, will be borne by the people without mutiny or murmur. But if a long train of abuses, prevarications and artifices, all tending the same way, make the design visible to the people, and they cannot but feel what they lie under, and see whither they are going; it is not to be wondered, that they should then rouse themselves, and endeavor to put the rule into such hands which may secure to them the ends for which government was at first erected; and without which, ancient names, and specious forms, are so far from being better, that they are much worse, than the state of nature, or pure anarchy; the inconveniences being all as great and as near, but the remedy farther off and more difficult.

Thirdly, I answer, that this doctrine of a power in the people of providing for their safety anew, by a new legislative, when their legislators have acted contrary to their trust, by invading their property, is the best fence against rebellion, and the probablest means to hinder it: for rebellion being an opposition, not to persons, but authority, which is founded only in the constitutions and laws of the government; those, whoever they be, who by force break through, and by force justify their violation of them, are truly and properly rebels: for when men, by entering into society and civil government, have excluded force, and introduced laws for the preservation of property, peace, and unity amongst themselves; those who set up force again in opposition to the laws, do rebellare, that is, bring back again the state of war, and are properly rebels; which they who are in power (by the pretense they have to authority, the temptation of force they have in their hands, and the flattery of those about them) being likeliest to do; the properest way to prevent the evil, is to show them the danger and injustice of it, who are under the greatest temptation to run into it.

In both the forementioned cases, when either the legislative is changed, or the legislators act contrary to the end for which they were constituted, those who are guilty are guilty of rebellion; for if any one by force takes away the established legislative of any society, and the laws by them made pursuant to their trust, he thereby takes away the umpirage, which every one had consented to, for a peaceable decision of all their controversies, and a bar to the state of war amongst them. They who remove, or change the legislative, take away this decisive power, which nobody can have but by the appointment and consent of the people; and so destroying the authority which the people did, and nobody else can set up, and introducing a power which the people hath not authorized, they actually introduce a state of war, which is that of force without authority; and thus, by removing the legislative established by the society (in whose decisions the people acquiesced and united, as to that of their own will), they untie the knot, and expose the people anew to the state of war. And if those, who by force take away the legislative, are rebels, the legislators themselves, as has been shown, can be no less esteemed so; when they, who were set up for the protection and preservation of the people, their liberties and properties, shall by force invade and endeavor to take them away; and so they putting themselves into a state of war with those who made them the protectors and guardians of their peace, are properly, and with the greatest aggravation, rebellantes, rebels.

But if they, who say, "it lays a foundation for rebellion," mean that it may occasion civil wars, or intestine broils, to tell the people they are absolved from obedience when illegal attempts are made upon their liberties or properties, and may oppose the unlawful violence of those who were their magistrates, when they invade their properties contrary to the trust put in them; and that therefore this doctrine is not to be allowed, being so destructive to the peace of the world: they may as well say, upon the same ground, that honest men may not oppose robbers or pirates, because this may occasion disorder or bloodshed. If any mischief come in such cases, it is not to be charged upon him who defends his own right, but on him that invades his neighbor's. If the innocent honest man must quietly quit all he has, for peace sake, to him who will lay violent hands upon it, I desire it may be considered, what a kind of peace there will be in the world, which consists only in violence and rapine; and which is to be maintained only for the benefit of robbers and oppressors. Who would not think it an admirable peace betwixt the mighty and the mean, when the lamb, without resistance, yielded his throat to be torn by the imperious wolf? Polyphemus's den gives us a perfect pattern of such a peace, and such a government, wherein Ulysses and his companions had nothing to do, but quietly to suffer themselves to be devoured. And no doubt Ulysses, who was a prudent man, preached up passive obedience, and exhorted them to a quiet submission, by representing to them of what concernment peace was to mankind, and by showing the inconveniencies might happen, if they should offer to resist Polyphemus, who had now the power over them.

The end of government is the good of mankind: and which is best for mankind, that the people should be always exposed to the boundless will of tyranny; or that the rulers should be sometimes liable to be opposed, when they grow exorbitant in the use of their power, and employ it for the destruction, and not the preservation of the properties of their people?

BOURGEOIS AND PROLETARIANS
KARL MARX and FRIEDRICH ENGELS

The bourgeoisie, historically, has played a most revolutionary part.

The bourgeoisie, wherever it has got the upper hand, has put an end to all feudal, patriarchal, idyllic relations. It has pitilessly torn asunder the motley feudal ties that bound man to his "natural superiors," and has left remaining no other nexus between man and man than naked self-interest, than callous "cash payment." It has drowned the most heavenly ecstasies of religious fervor, of chivalrous enthusiasm, of philistine

From the *Communist Manifesto* (1847).

sentimentalism, in the icy water of egotistical calculation. It has resolved personal worth into exchange value, and in place of the numberless indefeasible chartered freedoms, has set up that single, unconscionable freedom—Free Trade. In one word, for exploitation, veiled by religious and political illusions, it has substituted naked, shameless, direct, brutal exploitation.

The bourgeoisie has stripped of its halo every occupation hitherto honored and looked up to with reverent awe. It has converted the physician, the lawyer, the priest, the poet, the man of science, into its paid wage laborers.

The bourgeoisie has torn away from the family its sentimental veil, and has reduced the family relation to a mere money relation.

The bourgeoisie has disclosed how it came to pass that the brutal display of vigor in the Middle Ages, which reactionaries so much admire, found its fitting complement in the most slothful indolence. It has been the first to show what man's activity can bring about. It has accomplished wonders far surpassing Egyptian pyramids, Roman aqueducts, and Gothic cathedrals; it has conducted expeditions that put in the shade all former exoduses of nations and crusades.

The bourgeoisie cannot exist without constantly revolutionizing the instruments of production, and thereby the relations of production, and with them the whole relations of society. Conservation of the old modes of production in unaltered form was, on the contrary, the first condition of existence for all earlier industrial classes. Constant revolutionizing of production, uninterrupted disturbance of all social conditions, everlasting uncertainty and agitation distinguish the bourgeois epoch from all earlier ones. All fixed, fast-frozen relations, with their train of ancient and venerable prejudices and opinions, are swept away, all new-formed ones become antiquated before they can ossify. All that is solid melts into air, all that is holy is profaned, and man is at last compelled to face with sober senses his real conditions of life and his relations with his kind.

The need of a constantly expanding market for its products chases the bourgeoisie over the whole surface of the globe. It must nestle everywhere, settle everywhere, establish connections everywhere.

The bourgeoisie has through its exploitation of the world market given a cosmopolitan character to production and consumption in every country. To the great chagrin of reactionaries, it has drawn from under the feet of industry the national ground on which it stood. All old-established national industries have been destroyed or are daily being destroyed. They are dislodged by new industries, whose introduction becomes a life and death question for all civilized nations, by industries that no longer work up indigenous raw material, but raw material drawn from the remotest zones; industries whose products are consumed, not only at home, but in every quarter of the globe. In place of the old wants, satisfied by the production of the country, we find new wants, requiring for their satisfaction the products of distant lands and climes. In place of the old local and national seclusion and self-sufficiency, we have intercourse in every direction, universal inter-dependence of nations. And as in material, so also in intellectual production. The intellectual creations of individual nations become common property. National one-sidedness and narrow-mindedness become more and more impossible, and from the numerous national and local literatures there arises a world literature.

The bourgeoisie, by the rapid improvement of all instruments of production, by the immensely facilitated means of communication, draws all, even the most barbarian, nations into civilization. The cheap prices of its commodities are the heavy artillery with which it batters down all Chinese walls, with which it forces the barbarians' intensely obstinate hatred of foreigners to capitulate. It compels all nations, on pain of extinction, to adopt the bourgeois mode of production; it compels them to introduce what it calls civilization into their midst, i.e., to become bourgeois themselves. In one word, it creates a world after its own image.

The bourgeoisie has subjected the country to the rule of the towns. It has created enormous cities, has greatly increased the urban population as compared with the rural, and has thus rescued a considerable part of the population from the idiocy of rural life. Just as it has made the country dependent on the towns, so it has made barbarian and semi-barbarian countries dependent on the civilized ones, nations of peasants on nations of bourgeoisie, the East on the West.

The bourgeoisie keeps more and more doing away with the scattered state of the population, of the means of production, and of property. It has agglomerated population, centralized means of production, and has concentrated property in a few hands. The necessary consequence of this was political centralization. Independent, or but loosely connected provinces, with separate interests, laws, governments and systems of taxation, became lumped together into one nation, with one government, one code of laws, one national class interest, one frontier and one customs tariff.

The bourgeoisie, during its rule of scarce one hundred years, has created more massive and more colossal productive forces than have all preceding generations together. Subjection of nature's forces to man, machinery, application of chemistry to industry and agriculture, steam-navigation, railways, electric telegraphs, cleaning of whole continents for cultivation, canalization of rivers, whole populations conjured out of the ground—what earlier century had even a presentiment that such productive forces slumbered in the lap of social labor?

We see then: the means of production and of exchange, on whose foundation the bourgeoisie built itself up, were generated in feudal society. At a certain stage in the development of these means of production and of exchange, the conditions under which feudal society produced and exchanged, the feudal organization of agriculture and manufacturing industry, in one word, the feudal relations of property, became no longer compatible with the already developed productive forces; they became so many fetters. They had to be burst asunder; they were burst asunder.

Into their place stepped free competition, accompanied by a social and political constitution adapted to it, and by the economical and political sway of the bourgeois class.

A similar movement is going on before our own eyes. Modern bourgeois society with its relations of production, of exchange and of property, a society that has conjured up such gigantic means of productions and of exchange, is like the sorcerer who is no longer able to control the powers of the nether world whom he has called up by his spells. For many a decade past the history of industry and commerce is but the history of the revolt of modern productive forces against modern conditions of production, against the property relations that are conditions for the existence of the bourgeoisie and of its rule. It is enough to mention the commercial crises that by their periodical return put on its trial, each time more threateningly, the existence of the entire bourgeois society. In these crises a great part not only of the existing products, but also of the previously created productive forces, are periodically destroyed. In these crises there breaks out an epidemic that, in all earlier epochs, would have seemed an absurdity—the epidemic of over-production. Society suddenly finds itself put back into a state of momentary barbarism; it appears as if a famine, a universal war of devastation, had cut off the supply of every means of subsistence; industry and commerce seem to be destroyed. And why? Because there is too much civilization, too much means of subsistence, too much industry, too much commerce. The productive forces at the disposal of society no longer tend to further the development of the conditions of bourgeois property; on the contrary, they have become too powerful for these conditions, by which they are fettered, and so soon as they overcome these fetters, they bring disorder into the whole of bourgeois society, endanger the existence of bourgeois property. The conditions of bourgeois society are too narrow to comprise the wealth created by them. And how does the bourgeoisie get over these crises? On the one hand by enforced destruction of a mass of productive forces; on the other, by the conquest of new markets, and by the more thorough exploitation of the old ones. That is to say, by paving the way for more extensive and more destructive crises, and by diminishing the means whereby crises are prevented.

The weapons with which the bourgeoisie felled feudalism to the ground are now turned against the bourgeoisie itself.

But not only has the bourgeoisie forged the weapons that bring death to itself! It has also called into existence the men who are to wield those weapons—the modern working class—the proletarians.

In proportion as the bourgeoisie, i.e., capital, is developed, in the same proportion is the proletariat, the modern working class developed—a class of laborers, who live only so long as they find work, and who find work only so long as their labor increases capital. These laborers, who must sell themselves piecemeal, are a commodity, like every other article of commerce, and are consequently exposed to all the vicissitudes of competition, to all the fluctuations of the market.

Owing to the extensive use of machinery and to division of labor, the work of the proletarians has lost all individual character, and, consequently, all charm for the workman. He becomes an appendage of the machine, and it is only the most simple, most monotonous, and most easily acquired knack that is required of him. Hence, the cost of production of a workman is restricted, almost entirely, to the means of subsistence that he requires for his maintenance, and for the propagation of his race. But the price of a commodity, and therefore also of labor, is equal to its cost of production. In proportion, therefore, as the repulsiveness of the work increases, the wage decreases. Nay more, in proportion as the use of machinery and division of labor increases, in the same proportion the burden of toil also increases, whether by prolongation of the working hours, by increase of the work exacted in a given time, or by increased speed of the machinery, etc.

Modern industry has converted the little workshop of the patriarchal master into the great factory of the industrial capitalist. Masses of laborers, crowded into the factory, are organized like soldiers. As privates of the industrial army they are placed under the command of a perfect hierarchy of officers and sergeants. Not only are they slaves of the bourgeois class, and of the bourgeois state; they are daily and hourly enslaved by the machine, by the overlooker, and above all, by the individual bourgeois manufacturer himself. The more openly his despotism proclaims gain to be its end and aim, the more petty, the more hateful and the more embittering it is.

The less the skill and exertion of strength implied in manual labor, in other words, the more modern industry becomes developed, the more is the labor of men superseded by that of women. Differences of age and sex have no longer any distinctive social validity for the working class. All are instruments of labor, more or less expensive to use, according to their age and sex.

No sooner is the exploitation of the laborer by the manufacturer so far at an end that he receives his wages in cash, than he is sat upon by the other portions of the bourgeoisie, the landlord, the shopkeeper, the pawnbroker, etc.

The lower strata of the middle class—the small tradespeople, shop-keepers, and retired tradesmen generally, the handicraftsmen and peasants —all these sink gradually into the proletariat, partly because their diminutive capital does not suffice for the scale on which modern industry is carried on, and is swamped in the competition with the large capitalists, partly because their specialized skill is rendered worthless by new methods of production. Thus the proletariat is recruited from all classes of the population.

The proletariat goes through various stages of development. With its birth begins its struggle with the bourgeoisie. At first the contest is carried on by the individual laborers, then by the workpeople of a factory, then by the operatives of one trade, in one locality, against the individual bourgeois who directly exploits them. They direct their attacks, not against the bourgeois conditions of production, but against the instruments of production themselves; they destroy imported wares that compete with their labor; they smash to pieces machinery, they set factories ablaze, they seek to restore by force the vanished status of the workman of the Middle Ages.

At this stage the laborers still form an incoherent mass scattered over the whole country, and broken up by their mutual competition. If anywhere they unite to form more compact bodies, this is not yet the consequence of their own active union, but of the union of the bourgeoisie, which class, in order to attain its own political ends, is compelled to set the whole proletariat in motion, and is moreover yet, for a time, able to do so. At this stage, therefore, the proletarians do not fight their enemies, but the enemies of their enemies, the remnants of absolute monarchy, the landowners, the non-industrial bourgeois, the petty bourgeoisie. Thus the whole historical movement is concentrated in the hands of the bourgeoisie; every victory so obtained is a victory for the bourgeoisie.

But with the development of industry the proletariat not only increases in number; it becomes concentrated in greater masses, its strength grows, and it feels that strength more. The various interests and conditions of life within the ranks of the proletariat are more and more equalized, in proportion as machinery obliterates all distinctions of labor and nearly everywhere reduces wages to the same low level. The growing competition among the bourgeois, and the resulting commercial crises, make the wages of the workers ever more fluctuating. The unceasing improvement of machinery, ever more rapidly developing, makes their livelihood more and more precarious; the collisions between individual workmen and individual bourgeois take more and more the character of collisions between two classes. Thereupon the workers begin to form combinations (trade unions) against the bourgeois; they club together in order to keep up the rate of wages; they found permanent associations in order to make provisions beforehand for these occasional revolts. Here and there the contest breaks out into riots.

Now and then the workers are victorious, but only for a time. The real fruit of their battles lies, not in the immediate result, but in the ever-expanding union of the workers. This union is helped on by the improved means of communication that are created by modern industry and that place the workers of different localities in contact with one another. It was just this contact that was needed to centralize the numerous local struggles, all of the same character, into one national struggle between classes. But every class struggle is a political struggle. And that union, to attain which the burghers of the Middle Ages, with their miserable highways, required centuries, the modern proletarians, thanks to railways, achieve in a few years.

This organization of the proletarians into a class, and consequently into a political party, is continually being upset again by the competition between the workers themselves. But it ever rises up again, stronger, firmer, mightier. It compels legislative recognition of particular interests of the workers, by taking advantage of the divisions among the bourgeoisie itself. Thus the ten-hours' bill in England was carried.

Altogether, collisions between the classes of the old society further, in many ways, the course of development of the proletariat. The bourgeoisie finds itself involved in a constant battle. At first with the aristocracy; later on, with those portions of the bourgeoisie itself whose interests have become antagonistic to the progress of industry; at all times, with the bourgeoisie of foreign countries. In all these battles it sees itself compelled to appeal to the proletariat, to ask for its help, and thus, to drag it into the political arena. The bourgeoisie itself, therefore, supplies the proletariat with its own elements of political and general education, in other words, it furnishes the proletariat with weapons for fighting the bourgeoisie.

Further, as we have already seen, entire sections of the ruling classes are, by the advance of industry, precipitated into the proletariat, or are at least threatened in their conditions of existence. These also supply the proletariat with fresh elements of enlightenment and progress.

Finally, in times when the class struggle nears the decisive hour, the process of dissolution going on within the ruling class, in fact within the whole range of old society, assumes such a violent, glaring character that a small section of the ruling class cuts itself adrift, and joins the revolutionary class, the class that holds the future in its hands. Just as, therefore, at an earlier period, a section of the nobility went over to the bourgeoisie, so now a portion of the bourgeoisie goes over to the proletariat, and in particular, a portion of the bourgeois ideologists, who have raised themselves to the level of comprehending theoretically the historical movement as a whole.

Of all the classes that stand face to face with the bourgeoisie today, the proletariat alone is a really revolutionary class. The other classes decay and finally disappear in the face of modern industry; the proletariat is its special and essential product.

The lower middle class: the small manufacturer, the shopkeeper, the artisan, the peasant—all these fight against the bourgeoisie, to save from extinction their existence as fractions of the middle class. They are therefore not revolutionary, but conservative. Nay more, they are reactionary, for they try to roll back the wheel of history. If by chance they are revolutionary, they are so only in view of their impending transfer into the proletariat; they thus defend not their present, but their future interests; they desert their own standpoint to place themselves at that of the proletariat.

The "dangerous class," the social scum, that passively rotting mass thrown off by the lowest layers of old society, may, here and there, be swept into the movement by a proletarian revolution; its conditions of life, however, prepare it far more for the part of a bribed tool of reactionary intrigue.

In the conditions of the proletariat, those of old society at large are already virtually swamped. The proletarian is without property; his relation to his wife and children has no longer anything in common with the bourgeois family relations; modern industrial labor, modern subjection to capital, the same in England as in France, in America as in Germany, has stripped him of every trace of national character. Law, morality, religion, are to him so many bourgeois prejudices, behind which lurk in ambush just as many bourgeois interests.

All the preceding classes that got the upper hand sought to fortify their already acquired status by subjecting society at large to their conditions of appropriation. The proletarians cannot become masters of the productive forces of society, except by abolishing their own previous mode of appropriation, and thereby also every other previous mode of appropriation. They have nothing of their own to secure and to fortify; their mission is to destroy all previous securities for, and insurances of, individual property.

All previous historical movements were movements of minorities, or in the interest of minorities. The proletarian movement is the selfconscious, independent movement of the immense majority, in the interest of the immense majority. The proletariat, the lowest stratum of our present society, cannot stir, cannot raise itself up, without the whole superincumbent strata of official society being sprung into the air.

Though not in substance, yet in form, the struggle of the proletariat with the bourgeoisie is at first a national struggle. The proletariat of each country must, of course, first of all settle matters with its own bourgeoisie.

In depicting the most general phases of the development of the proletariat, we traced the more or less veiled civil war ranging within existing society, up to the point where that war breaks out into open revolution, and where the violent overthrow of the bourgeoisie lays the foundation for the sway of the proletariat.

Hitherto, every form of society has been based, as we have already seen, on the antagonism of oppressing and oppressed classes. But in order to oppress a class, certain conditions must be assured to it under which it can, at least, continue its slavish existence. The serf, in the period of serfdom, raised himself to membership in the commune, just as the petty bourgeois, under the yoke of feudal absolutism, managed to develop into a bourgeois. The modern laborer, on the contrary, instead of rising with the progress of industry, sinks deeper and deeper below the conditions of existence of his own class. He becomes a pauper, and pauperism develops more rapidly than population and wealth. And here it becomes evident that the bourgeoisie is unfit any longer to be the ruling class in society, and to impose its conditions of existence upon society as an overriding law. It is unfit to rule because it is incompetent to assure an existence to its slave within his slavery, because it cannot help letting him sink into such a state that it has to feed him, instead of being fed by him. Society can no longer live under this bourgeoisie, in other words, its existence is no longer compatible with society.

The essential condition for the existence and for the sway of the bourgeois class is the formation and augmentation of capital; the condition for capital is wage labor. Wage labor rests exclusively on competition between the laborers. The advance of industry, whose involuntary promoter is the bourgeoisie, replaces the isolation of the laborers, due to competition, by their revolutionary combination, due to association. The development of modern industry, therefore, cuts from under its feet the very foundation on which the bourgeoisie produces and appropriates products. What the bourgeoisie therefore produces, above all, is its own gravediggers. Its fall and the victory of the proletariat are equally inevitable.

SOCIALIZED EVOLUTION | BERNARD SHAW

Unfortunately the earnest people get drawn off the track of evolution by the illusion of progress. Any Socialist can convince us easily that the difference between Man as he is and Man as he might become, without further evolution, under millennial conditions of nutrition, environment, and training, is enormous. He can shew that inequality and iniquitous distribution of wealth and allotment of labor have arisen through an unscientific economic system, and that Man, faulty as he is, no more intended to establish any such ordered disorder than a moth intends to be burnt when it flies into a candle flame. He can shew that the difference between the grace and strength of the acrobat and the bent back of the rheumatic

From George Bernard Shaw, "The Revolutionist's Handbook," *Man and Superman,* Chaps. 7, 9. Copyright 1903. Reprinted by permission of The Public Trustee and The Society of Authors, London.

field laborer is a difference produced by conditions, not by nature. He can shew that many of the most detestable human vices are not radical, but are mere reactions of our institutions on our very virtues. The Anarchist, the Fabian, the Salvationist, the Vegetarian, the doctor, the lawyer, the parson, the professor of ethics, the gymnast, the soldier, the sportsman, the inventor, the political program-maker, all have some prescription for bettering us; and almost all their remedies are physically possible and aimed at admitted evils. To them the limit of progress is, at worst, the completion of all the suggested reforms and the leveling up of all men to the point attained already by the most highly nourished and cultivated in mind and body.

Here, then, as it seems to them, is an enormous field for the energy of the reformer. Here are many noble goals attainable by many of those paths up the Hill Difficulty along which great spirits love to aspire. Unhappily, the hill will never be climbed by Man as we know him. It need not be denied that if we all struggled bravely to the end of the reformers' paths we should improve the world prodigiously. But there is no more hope in that. If then in the equally plausible assurance that if the sky falls we shall all catch larks. We are not going to tread those paths: we have not sufficient energy. We do not desire the end enough: indeed in most cases we do not effectively desire it at all. Ask any man would he like to be a better man; and he will say yes, most piously. Ask him would he like to have a million of money; and he will say yes, most sincerely. But the pious citizen who would like to be a better man goes on behaving just as he did before. And the tramp who would like the million does not take the trouble to earn ten shillings: multitudes of men and women, all eager to accept a legacy of a million, live and die without having ever possessed five pounds at one time, although beggers have died in rags on mattresses stuffed with gold which they accumulated because they desired it enough to nerve them to get it and keep it. The economists who discovered that demand created supply soon had to limit the proposition to "effective demand," which turned out, in the final analysis, to mean nothing more than supply itself; and this holds good in politics, morals, and all other departments as well: the actual supply is the measure of the effective demand; and the mere aspirations and professions produce nothing. No community has ever yet passed beyond the initial phases in which its pugnacity and fanaticism enabled it to found a nation, and its cupidity to establish and develop a commercial civilization. Even these stages have never been attained by public spirit, but always by intolerant willfullness and brute force. Take the Reform Bill of 1832 as an example of a conflict between two sections of educated Englishmen concerning a political measure which was as obviously necessary and inevitable as any political measure has ever been or is ever likely to be. It was not passed until the gentlemen of Birmingham had made arrangements to cut the throats of the gentlemen of St. James's parish in due military form. It would not have been passed to this day if there had been no force behind it except the logic and public conscience of the Utilitarians. A despotic ruler with as much sense as Queen Elizabeth would have done better than the mob of grown-up Eton boys who governed us then by privilege, and who, since the introduction of practically Manhood Suffrage in 1884, now govern us at the request of proletarian Democracy.

At the present time we have, instead of the Utilitarians, the Fabian Society, with its peaceful, constitutional, moral, economical policy of Socialism, which needs nothing for its bloodless and benevolent realization except that the English people shall understand it and approve of it. But why are the Fabians well spoken of in circles where thirty years ago the word Socialist was understood as equivalent to cut-throat and incendiary? Not because the English have the smallest intention of studying or adopting the Fabian policy, but because they believe that the Fabians, by eliminating the element of intimidation from the Socialist agitation, have drawn the teeth of insurgent poverty and saved the existing order from the only method of attack it really fears. Of course, if the nation adopted the Fabian policy, it would be carried out by brute force exactly as our present property system is. It would become the law; and those who resisted it would be fined, sold up, knocked on the head by policemen, thrown into prison, and in the last resort "executed" just as they are when they break the present law. But as our proprietary class has no fear of that conversion taking place, whereas it does fear sporadic cut-throats and gunpowder plots, and strives with all its might to hide the fact that there is no moral difference whatever between the methods by which it enforces its proprietary rights and the method by which the dynamitard asserts his conception of natural human rights, the Fabian Society is patted on the back just as the Christian Social Union is, whilst the Socialist who says bluntly that a Social revolution can be made only as all other revolutions have been made, by the people who want it killing, coercing, and intimidating the people who don't want it, is denounced as a misleader of the people, and imprisoned with hard labor to shew him how much sincerity there is in the objection of his captors to physical force.

Are we then to repudiate Fabian methods, and return to those of the barricader, or adopt those of the dynamitard and the assassin? On the contrary, we are to recognize that both are fundamentally futile. It seems easy for the dynamitard to say "Have you not just admitted that nothing is ever conceded except to physical force? Did not Gladstone admit that the Irish Church was disestablished, not by the spirit of Liberalism, but by the explosion which wrecked Clerkenwell prison?" Well, we need not foolishly and timidly deny it. Let it be fully granted. Let us grant, further, that all this lies in the nature of things; that the most ardent Socialist, if he owns property, can by no means do otherwise than Conservative proprietors until property is forcibly abolished by the whole nation; nay, that ballots and parliamentary divisions, in spite of their vain ceremony of discussion, differ from battles only as the bloodless surrender of an out-numbered force in the field differs from Waterloo or Trafalgar. I make a present of all these admissions to the Fenian who collects money from thoughtless Irishmen in America to blow up Dublin Castle; to the detective who persuades foolish young workmen to order bombs from the nearest ironmonger and then delivers them up to penal servitude; to our military and naval commanders who believe, not in preaching, but in an ultimatum backed by plenty of lyddite; and, generally, to all whom it may concern. But of what use is it to substitute the way of the reckless and bloodyminded for the way of the cautious and humane? Is England any the better for the wreck of Clerkenwell prison, or Ireland for the disestablishment of the Irish Church? Is there the smallest reason to suppose that the nation which sheepishly let Charles and Laud and Strafford coerce it, gained anything because it afterwards, still more sheepishly, let a few strongminded Puritans, inflamed by the masterpieces of Jewish revolutionary literature, cut off the heads of the three? Suppose the Gunpowder plot had succeeded, and a Fawkes dynasty permanently set on the throne, would it have made any difference to the present state of the nation? The guillotine was used in France up to the limit of human endurance, both on Girondins and Jacobins. Fouquier-Tinville followed Marie Antoinette to the scaffold; and Marie Antoinette might have asked the crowd, just as pointedly as Fouquier did, whether their bread would be any cheaper when her head was off. And what came of it all? The Imperial France of the Rougon Macquart family, and the Republican France of the Panama scandal and the Dreyfus case. Was the difference worth the guillotining of all those unlucky ladies and gentlemen, useless and mischievous as many of them were? Would any sane man guillotine a mouse to bring about such a result? Turn to Republican America. America has no Star Chamber, and no feudal barons. But it has Trusts; and it has millionaires whose factories, fenced in by live electric wires and defended by Pinkerton retainers with magazine rifles, would have made a Radical of Reginald Front de Boeuf. Would Washington or Frank-lin have lifted a finger in the cause of American Independence if they had foreseen its reality?

No: what Caesar, Cromwell and Napoleon could not do with all the physical force and moral prestige of the State in their mighty hands, can-not be done by enthusiastic criminals and lunatics. Even the Jews, who, from Moses to Marx and LaSalle, have inspired all the revolutions, have had to confess that, after all, the dog will return to his vomit and the sow that was washed to her wallowing in the mire; and we may as well make up our minds that Man will return to his idols and his cupidities, in spite of all "movements" and all revolutions, until his nature is changed. Until then, his early successes in building commercial civilizations (and such civilizations, Good Heavens!) are but preliminaries to the inevitable later stage, now threatening us, in which the passions which built the civilization become fatal instead of productive, just as the same qualities which make the lion king in the forest ensure his destruction when he enters a city. Nothing can save society then except the clear head and the wide purpose: war and competition, potent instruments of selection and evolution in one epoch, become ruinous instruments of degeneration in the next. In the breeding of animals and plants, varieties which have arisen by selection through many generations relapse precipitously into the wild type in a generation or two when selection ceases; and in the same way a civilization in which lusty pugnacity and greed have ceased to act as selective agents and have begun to obstruct and destroy, rushes downwards and backwards with a suddenness that enables an observer to see with consternation the upward steps of many centuries retraced in a single lifetime. This has often occurred even within the period covered by history; and in every instance the turning point has been reached long before the attainment, or even the general advocacy on paper, of the leveling-up of the mass to the highest point attainable by the best nourished and cultivated normal individuals.

We must therefore frankly give up the notion that Man as he exists is capable of net progress. There will always be an illusion of progress, because wherever we are conscious of an evil we remedy it, and therefore always seem to ourselves to be progressing, foregetting that most of the evils we see are the effects, finally become acute, of long-unnoticed retrogressions; that our compromising remedies seldom fully recover the lost ground; above all, that on the lines along which we are degenerating, good has become evil in our eyes, and is being undone in the name of progress precisely as evil is undone and replaced by good on the lines along which we are evolving. This is indeed the Illusion of Illusions; for it gives us infallible and appalling assurance that if our political ruin is to come, it will be effected by ardent reformers and supported by enthusiastic patriots as a series of necessary steps in our progress. Let the Reformer, the Progressive, the Meliorist then reconsider himself and his eternal ifs and ans which never become pots and pans. Whilst Man remains what he is, there can be no progress beyond the point already attained and fallen headlong from at every attempt at civilization; and since even that point is but a pinnacle to which a few people cling in giddy terror above an abyss of squalor, mere progress should no longer charm us. . . .

It may be said that though the wild beast breaks out in Man and casts him back momentarily into barbarism under the excitement of war and crime, yet his normal life is higher than the normal life of his forefathers. This view is very acceptable to Englishmen, who always lean sincerely to virtue's side as long as it costs them nothing either in money or in thought. They feel deeply the injustice of foreigners, who allow them no credit for this conditional highmindedness. But there is no reason to suppose that our ancestors were less capable of it than we are. To all such claims for the existence of a progressive moral evolution operating visibly from grand-father to grandson, there is the conclusive reply that a thousand years of such evolution would have produced enormous social changes, of which the historical evidence would be overwhelming. But not Macaulay himself, the most confident of Whig meliorists, can produce any such evidence that will bear cross-examination. Compare our conduct and our codes with those mentioned contemporarily in such ancient scriptures and classics as have come down to us, and you will find no jot of ground for the belief that any moral progress whatever has been made in historic time, in spite of all the romantic attempts of historians to reconstruct the past on that assumption. Within that time it has happened to nations as to private families and individuals that they have flourished and decayed, repented and hardened their hearts, submitted and protested, acted and reacted, oscillated between natural and artificial sanitation (the oldest house in the world, unearthed the other day in Crete, has quite modern sanitary arrangements), and rung a thousand changes on the different scales of income and pressure of population, firmly believing all the time that mankind was advancing by leaps and bounds because men were constantly busy. And the mere chapter of accidents has left a small accumulation of chance discoveries, such as the wheel, the arch, the safety pin, gunpowder, the magnet, the Voltaic pile and so forth: things which, unlike the gospels and philosophic treatises of the sages, can be usefully understood and applied by common men; so that steam locomotion is possible without a nation of Stephensons, although national Christianity is impossible without a nation of Christs. But does any man seriously believe that the *chauffeur* who drives a motor car from Paris to Berlin is a more highly evolved man than the charioteer of Achilles, or that a modern Prime Minister is a more enlightened ruler than Caesar because he rides a tricycle, writes his dispatches by the electric light, and instructs his stockbroker through the telephone?

Enough, then, of this goose-cackle about Progress: Man, as he is, never will nor can add a cubit to his stature by any of its quackeries, political, scientific, educational, religious, or artistic. What is likely to happen when this conviction gets into the minds of the men whose present faith in these illusions is the cement of our social system, can be imagined only by those who know how suddenly a civilization which has long ceased to think (or in the old phrase, to watch and pray) can fall to pieces when the vulgar belief in its hypocrisies and impostures can no longer hold out against its failures and scandals. When religious and ethical formulae become so obsolete that no man of strong mind can believe them, they have also reached the point at which no man of high character will profess them; and from that moment until they are formally disestablished, they stand at the door of every profession and every public office to keep out every able man who is not a sophist or a liar. A nation which revises its parish councils once in three years, but will not revise its articles of religion once in three hundred, even when those articles avowedly began as a political compromise dictated by Mr. Facing-Both-Ways, is a nation that needs remaking.

Our only hope, then, is in evolution. We must replace the man by the superman. It is frightful for the citizen, as the years pass him, to see his own contemporaries so exactly reproduced by the younger generation, that his companions of thirty years ago have their counterparts in every city crowd, where he has to check himself repeatedly in the act of saluting as an old friend some young man to whom he is only an elderly stranger. All hope of advance dies in his bosom as he watches them: he knows that they will do just what their fathers did, and that the few voices which will still, as always before, exhort them to do something else and be something better, might as well spare their breath to cool their porridge (if they can get any). Men like Ruskin and Carlyle will preach to Smith and Brown for the sake of preaching, just as St Francis preached to the birds and St Anthony to the fishes. But Smith and Brown, like the fishes and birds, remain as they are; and poets who plan Utopias and prove that nothing is necessary for their realization but that Man should will them, perceive at last, like Richard Wagner, that the fact to be faced is that Man does not effectively will them. And he never will until he becomes Superman.

And so we arrive at the end of the Socialist's dream of "the socialization of the means of production and exchange," of the Positivist's dream of moralizing the capitalist, and of the ethical professor's, legislator's, educator's dream of putting commandments and codes and lessons and examination marks on a man as harness is put on a horse, ermine on a judge, pipe-clay on a soldier, or a wig on an actor, and pretending that his nature has been changed. The only fundamental and possible Socialism is the socialization of the selective breeding of Man: in other terms, of human evolution. We must eliminate the Yahoo, or his vote will wreck the commonwealth.

THE DANGERS OF OBEDIENCE | *HAROLD LASKI*

Freedom means self-expression, and the secret of freedom is courage. No man ever remains free who acquiesces in what he knows to be wrong. His business as a citizen is to act upon the instructed judgment of his conscience. He may be mistaken; but he ought ceaselessly to be aware that the act he opposes is, after all, no more than the opinion of men who, like himself, are also fallible. The business of government is to satisfy the rational desires of citizens or, at the least, to make possible such satisfaction; and nothing is more likely to prevent the fulfillment of its

From Harold J. Laski, *The Dangers of Obedience and Other Essays* (New York, Harper & Row, Publishers, 1930). Copyright, 1930, by Harold J. Laski.

purpose than silent acquiescence in the prohibition of such desires. Whenever men are silent in the face of a refusal to hear the burden of their experience it is always assumed by powerful interests that they are, in fact, silent because they have nothing to say. Not only does the habit of acquiescence transform the citizen into an inert recipient of orders whom it is difficult to rouse from lethargy; it also persuades a government that it has only to show a bold front to secure acceptance of any commands it chooses to impose. Before attitudes such as these liberty has no chance of survival; for the eternal vigilance which is its necessary price is then wanting.

We cannot, in matters of social constitution, too often insist that there is no finality about our present arrangements. Most of the principles we cherish as fundamental have seemed immoral or monstrous at some time or place. Property, marriage, religion, education, our views upon each of these have changed often enough in the course of history, and they will change again. The business of us who have experience of their operation is to report the burden of that experience; there can be no wise legislation except upon the basis of the widest induction it is open to us to make. For the laws under which we live are someone's induction. They represent a response to someone's interpretation of social needs. If what they do contradicts our experience and our needs, it is simple folly to assume their necessary wisdom and take it for granted that we are wrong. For not only does all new truth somewhere begin in a minority of one; the courage of one man who insists upon social inadequacy heartens others to make articulate their burden of experience as well. It stimulates the sleeping sense of civic obligation. It leads to a sense in those who have been content with passivity, that active-minded obligation may, even though it involve discomfort, not necessarily be dishonorable. Those are always most truly citizens who insist upon bringing back our rulers to a realization of the conditions upon which their power is held.

This, let it be added, is more than ever necessary in the great state. The scale of life today is so vast that individual experience is lost unless it is clamantly articulate about its wants. It is, moreover, a world in which the supporters of conventional morality are anxious at all costs to legislate against the diversities of which they disapprove. These they view as sin; and they seek to clothe the old Calvinist dictatorship in new terminology in order to enjoy the luxury of suppression. The books we are to read, the plays we are to see, the pictures to be exhibited, all these must be molded in the pattern of which they approve. Taboos built on their clamant expression of what they desire never cease to proliferate. And every time they are successful, their appetite grows for power. Mr. Comstock began in a humble way; but he ended by sweeping a continent into his vision. Sir William Joynson-Hicks now pronounces with confidence his judgment upon every subject from the proper closing hours of night clubs to the governmental limits within which the Anglican Church may live a life of its own. Their impudence is the measure of our futility. Their self-expression is purchased by the suppression of ours.

That, indeed, is the invariable nature of power. The law of its being is to hate the process of rational examination. It will not, unless it must, brook criticism of its pronouncements. It assumes the coincidence of its private will with the public good. And it evokes everywhere imitation. Mussolini takes a leaf out of Lenin's book. Italian acquiescence in the suppression of freedom persuades Spain to similar action. The European continent today is scattered with petty tyrannies each one of which has built itself upon the citizen's conviction that he has no alternative save helplessly to obey the commands he receives. All over the world little groups of active-minded men run to the state to urge that some particular convention be made binding upon us all, or to prohibit some particular experiment which, a generation from now, may well become a normal habit of everyday life. And the world runs to meet its chains because the citizen is too afraid to venture out of the little private corner in which he is buried. He does not seem to know that the power to insist upon his freedom lies in his own hands. He is powerless because he is unconscious of his power.

So great is the decline of liberty, by reason of this acquiescence, that the citizen today is notable who protests against injustice. He is not only notable, but even bizarre; we tend to wonder that he has so little to do that he must interfere in public concerns. When Professor Chafee ventured to defend the rights of Americans to freedom of speech there were Harvard alumni anxious for his removal from the university. When Professor Frankfurter expressed his doubts about the guilt of Sacco and Vanzetti powerful interests were not slow to whisper that he must have received a price for his forthrightness. We expect the statesman, the millionaire, the soldier to announce what organization of life is to be imposed; but when the ordinary citizen speaks we are either amazed at his courage or indignant at his intrusion. Yet, after all it is the ordinary citizen who is most likely to be affected by the imposition of other men's experience. The government of today defines with increasing precision the contours of the life he may lead. Unless he is prepared to announce his judgment upon their decision, to concert with others some corporate insistence upon his views, the life permitted him may well become one long frustration of his personal desires.

Nor must we forget the unnecessary pain that results from our unwillingness to engage in public adventure. The indifference of American citizens has meant that Mooney has languished in jail for sixteen years; the indifference of English citizens has meant eighteen grim years of imprisonment for that Oscar Slater whom the Scottish Courts have recently pronounced not guilty of the crime for which he suffered. An unwillingness on our part to confront with frankness the issues of sex means innumerable unhappy lives that might otherwise have been fruitful. Our acquiescence in an eighteenth-century view of freedom of contract enables the American courts to deprive of essential leisure thousands of workingmen who might, otherwise, share in the gain as well as in the toil of living. Our refusal to believe that foreign affairs are our business not less than that of the men who sit in Washington and Westminster may well send the next generation, as it sent the last, to die on the battlefield. Yet, civilization means, above all, an unwillingness to inflict unnecessary pain. Within the ambit of that definition, those of us who heedlessly accept the commands of authority cannot yet claim to be civilized men.

It is said that the individual is powerless; it is merely to embrace one inadequacy for another to seek to pit himself against the state. But that is an exaggeration of the power of authority which it is urgent to deny at the outset. Luther pitted himself against the serried majesty of Rome, and, whatever the price he had to pay, at least he found a larger freedom outside. Francis Place, almost alone, won for English workingmen the right to combine for self-protection against a hostile government and an indifferent House of Commons. Samuel Plimsoll, by a persistent refusal to be silent, won for sailors a protection against maritime disaster which is perhaps their most valuable safeguard. William Lloyd Garrison may have been stoned by Boston mobs, and the good and great may have been shocked by his intransigence; but he lit a flame in the hearts of thousands who later made possible the victory of emancipation. The very nature, indeed, of social organization may give us assurance that our protest need never be single. The injustice we lament, the command we deny, others experience also as lamentable or unjustified. They wait, often enough, for a lead; and when we refuse to act by some inner fear of failure, we leave them to accept defeat. And, by so leaving them, we reinforce the authority of those whose exercise of it appears to us unjust. Our lack of courage makes the next effort of protest more difficult to undertake.

We should, moreover, remember that one thing authority fears to encounter is the insistent conscience of its opponents. Modern governments are doubtless more powerful than at any period in the history of the world; but they are still dependent for that power on their willingness to obey the decent opinion of their subjects. President Masaryk showed in Czechoslovakia what a persistent determination to be free can effect. Arthur Griffiths and Michael Collins showed plainly enough that there is a limit to the coercion a government may employ against men who are conscious of fighting for a great destiny. The woman suffragists in England fought for eight years against a government deaf to the power of rational argument; and their willingness to pay the penalties of illegal conduct rather than acquiesce in their exclusion from effective citizenship was the major factor in the victory of their cause. Those who refused obedience to the Military Service

Acts were able, in the last war, to exemplify the powerlessness of the state. Convinced of the iniquity of war, they claimed the right to be absolved from direct contact with it; and it is important that both in England and America the Quakers should have received express exemption from that contact. That is the tacit admission that where the state conflicts with another group there are occasions when the state will find it wise to forego the claim of paramountcy. And, here again, the real fact involved is that of consent. No state can act in the face of considerable opposition from its citizens, if the latter are deeply and conscientiously moved by the issue in dispute. No American government can hope to enforce Prohibition merely by multiplying the agencies of pressure and penalization; it will succeed only as men are convinced that its objective is worthy of their allegiance. No state will venture in practice to transcend the consciences it encounters in any vital sphere. Acts of authority are always limited by their power to command the moral support of thinking men.

It is important to remember that governments are not always successful, simply because it is urgent to recollect that they are not always right. There is, that is to say, not only no certainty that they will succeed; there is even no certainty that they ought to succeed. The only ground for obedience to the state is where its purpose is morally superior to that of its opponents. The only ground upon which the citizen can give or be asked to give his support for the state is upon the conviction that what it is aiming at is, in each particular action, good. We should not support a given state because the ideal state is patterned upon Utopia. We should not even support a given state because its intentions are sincere. A catalogue of the actions of states undertaken from the highest possible motives could easily be made a list of errors now regarded as monstrous. No sincerity of purpose ever excludes the possibility of conduct for which no excuse can seriously be made. Calvin was completely sincere when he burned Servetus. The Inquisition served the highest motives when it imprisoned Galileo. George III was unquestionably sincere in his opposition to the American colonies and to Catholic Emancipation. In politics, at any rate, it is not only necessary to will what is right, but also to know what it is right to will. It is a nice question whether more harm than good has not been done by governments who have been left unopposed because it has been conjectured that they were doing their best. The most passionate conviction of rightness is never a proof that we are not mistaken.

Nor can it be truly said that governments are usually right because they command the service of experts, while the common man has but a limited knowledge at his command. For it is in the first place essential to realize that, however expert may be the basis of the decision, this does not compensate for an inability to convince the common man of its validity. To override the judgment of the hostile and the doubtful is, in the end, to convince them that the labor of thought is not worth the effort. And it must be remembered that all experts are in matters of social action liable to the gravest defects. They are specialists in a particular theme; and because they are expert therein, they tend to overestimate its importance. No general can ever be entrusted with the function of delimiting strategic frontiers; no admiral could safely be left to draw up a naval program. An expert, moreover, always tends to underestimate the importance of converting people to his point of view. He is so convinced that his principle is right that he rarely considers the price which may have to be paid for its administration, the possibility that its principle might well be lost in the strain of applying it. Only the need to consider the necessity of consent prevents an expert from becoming a tyrant. We wisely leave amateur politicians to control the expert that the latter may learn the limits of public patience.

It is said, again, that to ask the citizen to become a pioneer is to ask him to embark upon adventures doomed, almost inevitably, to fail. A man, it is argued, who can school himself into acquiescence with things as they are will have, on the whole, a not unhappy life; but one who seeks to protest against injustice, or to work for the acceptance of truths rejected by the powers that be, embarks upon a voyage where he can be certain that his ship will be wrecked. The authority of existing interests is so strong that it is folly to rebel against their compulsion. The price of rebellion is martyrdom, and not even martyrdom has any assurance of ultimate reward. Social problems, we are told, must be seen in reasonable proportion. We have our own happiness to achieve; we are not, in any case, our brother's keeper. What profit does a man have who sets himself up for Athanasius? It is rare that his powers are equal to his self-appointed task. He will earn only bitterness and disappointment from effort of which the world is careless or hostile. Those whom he loves will, only too often, pay the price of his sacrifice to his conscience. His spiritual urgency will, to the generality, seem no more than a special form of egotism or stubbornness. Humanity, in history, has always crucified its pioneers.

The plea for inertia is always a powerful one. It enables us to plow our little furrow without an impending sense of contingent disaster. It saves us from the grim need to revise habits it is always dangerous to examine and, sometimes, fatal to destroy. Yet it can be said with certainty that the price of inertia is always, in the long run, the loss of a civic sense in the multitude. Men who insist that some particular injustice is not their responsibility sooner or later become unable to resent any injustice. Tyranny depends upon nothing so much as the lethargy of a people. Autocracy is born above all of the experience that it need not expect active resentment against injustice. This is the inner truth of Thoreau's famous sentence that "under a government which imprisons any unjustly, the true place for a just man is also a prison." For unless he is insistently protestant, his acquiescence in the injustice is assumed. His silence makes him in fact the jailer; and the powers that be rely on him because they know that the inert acceptance he has displayed in the past is a proof that his conscience is dead. The bad employer, the savage justice, the corrupt statesman, these exercise their authority only because they have not been challenged in the past. Let that challenge once be made forthrightly and, where one man has been bold, a thousand are prepared to follow him. And where a thousand are prepared to follow, those whose profession is the doing of wrong think twice before they act. A people attentive to the confines within which power must act have alone the prospect of freedom. The unjust only prevail because they are never guilty of inertia.

It is objected that this is a doctrine of anarchy. If men are to disobey because they disbelieve, there is, it is said, an end of social peace; and in a period of violence it is never justice that triumphs. To argue, therefore, that a man must act upon the dictates of his conscience, to insist that there are times when the law may be rightly disregarded, is to attack the foundations of public well-being. We must approach the state in fear and trembling. We must remember that its habits, its traditions, its purposes are born of the inherited wisdom of the past. Who are we, it is said, with what Burke called "our little stock of reason," to pit our judgment against the immense induction for which it stands?

The argument has the appearance of power; but, in fact, it is wholly void of substance. The present conditions are not just merely because they are the present conditions; they are just to the degree that justice is inherent in them. An American would not condemn Washington for 1776; few Frenchmen would doubt the justice of 1789; fewer Englishmen would deny the common sense of 1688. But Washington and all other revolutionaries have had, at some moment, to make the decision to disobey; and the decision has involved the judgment that their view of the future must be pitted against that for which traditional authority has declared. Obviously enough, we must make our protest proportionate to the event. We need not march out with machine guns because the income-tax inspector has assessed us wrongly. But if the state to which we are reduced is that of the French peasant in 1789, or the Russian peasant in 1917, it is difficult to see why the wisdom of our ancestors should be dignified by the name of wisdom. Social peace need not be invaded for minutiae; but social peace may well be purchased at too high a price. Order may be disturbed; but there are kinds of order which are closely akin to death.

Government is necessary enough in all conscience; but there must be limits to its empire. It is not enough within a social system to proclaim the supreme desirability of peace until we are satisfied with the purposes for which peace is made. And because the individual is so small, the power of government so vast, we may be certain enough that, in general, organized disobedience is always the price of injustice. Men do not revolt until wrong has driven them to revolt. They are not the prey of agitators unless they

THE DANGERS OF OBEDIENCE

have so suffered that the agitator's message transcends for them all other considerations. The danger of anarchy, in a word, is born only when a body of men has come to feel that some wrong imposed upon them has become unendurable.

It is futile, moreover, to argue that there is no longer unendurable wrong. The supreme instance may clothe itself in the humblest garb. It may appear, as with Dreyfus, in the garb of an army officer falsely accused of espionage; or, as with Francisco Ferrer, in the person of a humble school teacher falsely condemned for treason. Our business when we meet such wrong is to challenge it lest authority be victorious over justice. For the price of our freedom is an ultimate courage to resist. We owe no state or church a blind or unreasoning obedience. We owe it only the utmost insight of which our judgment is capable. No state is ever securely founded save in the consciences of its citizens. No state, indeed, has ever a better safeguard against error than respect for those consciences. To treat them as trivial, to regard activity built upon them as moral wrong, is to injure itself far more than it can be injured by them. To know that they have quality of spirit enough to insist upon the lesson inherent for them in their experience of life is already some justification of its effort. To suppress that spirit is to deny its own purpose. Thereby it lends itself not to the enlargement of personality, but to its suppression. That, after all, is the ultimate crime in the historic record.

For no government can, in the long run, ever find an adequate substitute for the individual exercise of active minds. However wide the ambit of its experience, it is never so wide as the totality of civic experience. However well-intentioned, it is always liable, from the necessary limitations of all authority, to error and misjudgment. Its quality, in the end, is never at a higher level than the quality of the humblest of its citizens. Once it post-pones consideration of some judgment he makes, it postpones also the in-crease of its own quality. For to suppress individuality is to diminish it; and the outcome of continuous diminution is the slave-mind. States have perished in history not because they could not conceive great ends, but be-cause their passion for uniformity has deprived them of the instruments necessary to carry out those ends. High purposes in any community require citizens high-minded enough to appreciate them; and men who have been modeled to a pattern are incapable of intellectual stature. Men whose minds have been put in fetters cannot exert that energy of the soul which is the motive power of great achievement.

If all the laws of social organization were as patently reasonable as those of arithmetic, it would not, perhaps, be necessary to plead for toler-ance. But no honesty is possible in matters of social constitution unless we begin by admitting that no faith is really possible in the realm of politics without a large margin of doubt. There is hardly a single certitude in the past which a wider and deeper experience has not rendered untenable.

There is not a single certitude today which will not, to the future, appear meager and inadequate. Implacable hostility by government to diversity of opinion is simply the prevention of rational judgment. Sacco and Vanzetti did not cease to be anarchists because anarchy was penalized; the government of Russia before 1917 did not destroy the Bolshevists by sending them to Siberia. Ideas however foolish, programs however extreme, are always born of some want which their exponents are seeking to satisfy. To penalize the ideas and the programs does not stifle the wants. Either it drives them underground or provokes them into rebellion. A government which encounters bad ideas—even more, a government which provokes rebellion, has, almost always, reason to look into its own conscience. For its business is response to the felt wants of men, and their disobedience to it is the measure of its failure.

This warning was never more needed than in our time. Power tends increasingly to be concentrated in a few hands. A standardized machine-technology degrades the craftsman more and more to a man who fulfills a purely repetitive routine. The press, education, the discipline of political parties remove increasingly from circumference to center the responsibility for thought. In Russia we have the spectacle of a dominant party which seeks to impress a particular creed upon every aspect of the life it controls; and a generation is rapidly coming to manhood there which will have heard of no other. The same is true in only slightly less degree of Italy and of Spain. There government arrogates to itself the character of infallibility and a doctrine born of a particular occasion is made a universal of which doubt is not permitted. Yet it is obvious enough that truth cannot be stabilized in this fashion. Not even Marx exhausted the possibility that new truth may await us in the realm of social ideas.

Russia, Italy, and Spain, indeed, are only extreme instances of an attitude which other states are seeking to enforce less directly and with a subtler power of permeation. Industrial standardization seeks to make men live increasingly within the ambit of patterns it finds most economically serviceable; and the cost of that search is the standardized mind. Like Russian communism, it develops its protective legend. Most American businessmen seriously believe that America has attained the ideal of free competition; all English businessmen with adequate incomes insist that the career is open to the talented. Each sedulously preaches that failure is inherent in the capacity of the individual; and a new Calvinism arises in which poverty is equated with moral fault. This has become very largely the religion of the Western World; and because it is the gospel of the successful man, it is preached in school and newspaper until doubt of its truth seems to the majority like doubt of the multiplication table. At that stage, doubt itself becomes an index either to insanity or bad character. To ask a man in a court of law today if he is a socialist is to suggest to the judge and jury that he is incapable of good citizenship. He must be prepared to accept Leviathan at Leviathan's own estimate if he wishes for the approval of his fellows.

That road lies stagnation, and the consequence of stagnation in ideas is always the decay of freedom. It is extraordinary enough that in the twentieth century it should be necessary to restate the case for freedom. Generation by generation, in religion, politics, science, the arts, men have had manifold experience of the disaster consequent upon suppression of the human spirit. Age by age they have been re-taught that nothing ultimately matters save maintenance of the conditions which make for the emancipation of personality. Our business, if we desire to live a life not utterly devoid of meaning and significance, is to accept nothing which contradicts our basic experience merely because it comes to us from tradition or convention or authority. It may well be that we shall be wrong; but our self-expression is thwarted at the root unless the certainties we are asked to accept coincide with the certainties we experience. That is why the condition of freedom in any state is always a widespread and consistent skepticism of the canons upon which power insists. To doubt is to examine and, with distinguished minds, to examine is to discover. But it is not merely for the value of the new truth that may emerge that we urge the importance of skepticism. The meek do not inherit the earth unless they are prepared to fight for their meekness. Justice does not come to reign unless those who care for its coming are prepared to insist upon its value. Certainly every acquiescence in contradiction of the lesson life has taught us is a deliberate postponement of its opportunity; every acceptance of that against which our soul cries out makes it easier upon another occasion to stifle that cry. We need freedom to be ourselves. But we can be free only as we insist upon freedom. No other person's creed can have validity for us save as it expresses the exigencies of our own life.

Because we share, that is, in a collective experience, we are not effortlessly assured of individual salvation. We do our duty by examination, not by submission, by zeal for truth, not enthusiasm for uniformity. Nothing can ever entitle us, as free spiritual beings, to merge our lives into the common life, to disown our personality, and accept standards which, within ourselves, we know to be worthless. A healthy loyalty is not passive and complacent, but active and critical. If it finds ground for attack, it must occupy that ground. For all obedience that has the right to regard itself as ethical is built upon a conscious agreement with the purpose we encounter. Anything else is a betrayal of ourselves; and when we surrender the truth we see, by that betrayal we betray also the future of civilization. For the triumphs of a free conscience are the landmarks on the road to the ideal.

CIVIL DISOBEDIENCE | *HENRY DAVID THOREAU*

I heartily accept the motto, "That government is best which governs least"; and I should like to see it acted up to more rapidly and systematically. Carried out, it finally amounts to this, which also I believe, "That government is best which governs not at all"; and when men are prepared for it, that will be the kind of government which they will have. Government is at best but an expedient; but most governments are usually, and all governments are sometimes, inexpedient. The objections which have been brought against a standing army, and they are many and weighty, and deserve to prevail, may also at last be brought against a standing government. The standing army is only an arm of the standing government. The government itself, which is only the mode which the people have chosen to execute their will, is equally liable to be abused and perverted before the people can act through it. Witness the present Mexican war, the work of comparatively a few individuals using the standing government as their tool; for, in the outset, the people would not have consented to this measure.

This American government—what is it but a tradition, though a recent one, endeavoring to transmit itself unimpaired to posterity, but each instant losing some of its integrity? It has not the vitality and force of a single living man; for a single man can bend it to his will. It is a sort of wooden gun to the people themselves. But it is not the less necessary for this; for the people must have some complicated machinery or other, and hear its din, to satisfy that idea of government which they have. Governments show thus how successfully men can be imposed on, even impose on themselves, for their own advantage. It is excellent, we must all allow. Yet this government never of itself furthered any enterprise, but by the alacrity with which it got out of its way. *It* does not keep the country free. *It* does not settle the West. *It* does not educate. The character inherent in the American people has done all that has been accomplished; and it would have done somewhat more, if the government had not sometimes got in its way. For government is an expedient by which men would fain succeed in letting one another alone; and, as has been said, when it is most expedient, the governed are most let alone by it. Trade and commerce, if they were not made of India-rubber, would never manage to bounce over the obstacles which legislators are continually putting in their way; and, if one were to judge these men wholly by the effects of their actions and not partly by their intentions, they would deserve to be classed and punished with those mischievous persons who put obstructions on the railroads.

But, to speak practically and as a citizen, unlike those who call them-

From *Resistance to Civil Government* (1849).

selves no-government men, I ask for, not at once no government, but *at once* a better government. Let every man make known what kind of government would command his respect, and that will be one step toward obtaining it.

After all, the practical reason why, when the power is once in the hands of the people, a majority are permitted, and for a long period continue, to rule is not because they are most likely to be in the right, nor because this seems fairest to the minority, but because they are physically the strongest. But a government in which the majority rule in all cases cannot be based on justice, even as far as men understand it. Can there not be a government in which majorities do not virtually decide right and wrong, but conscience? in which majorities decide only those questions to which the rule of expediency is applicable? Must the citizen ever for a moment, or in the least degree, resign his conscience to the legislator? Why has every man a conscience, then? I think that we should be men first, and subjects afterward. It is not desirable to cultivate a respect for the law, so much as for the right. The only obligation which I have a right to assume is to do at any time what I think right. It is truly enough said, that a corporation has no conscience; but a corporation of conscientious men is a corporation *with* a conscience. Law never made men a whit more just; and, by means of their respect for it, even the well-disposed are daily made the agents of injustice. A common and natural result of an undue respect for law is, that you may see a file of soldiers, colonel, captain, corporal, privates, powder-monkeys, and all, marching in admirable order over hill and dale to the wars, against their wills, ay, against their common sense and consciences, which makes it very steep marching indeed, and produces a palpitation of the heart. They have no doubt that it is a damnable business in which they are concerned; they are all peaceably inclined. Now, what are they? Men at all? or small movable forts and magazines, at the service of some unscrupulous man in power? Visit the Navy Yard, and behold a marine, such a man as an American government can make, or such as it can make a man with its black arts—a mere shadow and reminiscence of humanity, a man laid out alive and standing, and already, as one may say, buried under arms with funeral accompaniments, though it may be,

> Not a drum was heard, not a funeral note,
> As his corpse to the rampart we hurried;
> Not a soldier discharged his farewell shot
> O'er the grave where our hero we buried.

The mass of men serve the state thus, not as men mainly, but as machines, with their bodies. They are the standing army, and the militia, jailors, constables, posse comitatus, etc. In most cases there is no free exercise whatever of the judgment or of the moral sense; but they put themselves on a level with wood and earth and stones; and wooden men can perhaps be manufactured that will serve the purpose as well. Such command no more respect than men of straw or a lump of dirt. They have the same sort of worth only as horses and dogs. Yet such as these even are commonly esteemed good citizens. Others—as most legislators, politicians, lawyers, ministers, and office-holders—serve the state chiefly with their heads; and, as they rarely make any moral distinctions, they are as likely to serve the Devil, without *intending* it, as God. A very few, as heroes, patriots, martyrs, reformers in the great sense, and *men,* serve the state with their consciences also, and so necessarily resist it for the most part; and they are commonly treated as enemies by it. A wise man will only be useful as a man, and will not submit to be "clay," and "stop a hole to keep the wind away," but leave that office to his dust at least:

> *I am too high-born to be propertied,*
> *To be a secondary at control,*
> *Or useful serving-man and instrument*
> *To any sovereign state throughout the world.*

He who gives himself entirely to his fellow-men appears to them useless and selfish; but he who gives himself partially to them is pronounced a benefactor and philanthropist.

How does it become a man to behave toward this American government today? I answer, that he cannot without disgrace be associated with it. I cannot for an instant recognize that political organization as *my* government which is the *slave's* government also.

All men recognize the right of revolution; that is, the right to refuse allegiance to, and to resist, the government, when its tyranny or its inefficiency are great and unendurable. But almost all say that such is not the case now. But such was the case, they think, in the Revolution of '75. If one were to tell me that this was a bad government because it taxed certain foreign commodities brought to its ports, it is most probable that I should not make an ado about it, for I can do without them. All machines have their friction; and possibly this does enough good to counterbalance the evil. At any rate, it is a great evil to make a stir about it. But when the friction comes to have its machine, and oppression and robbery are organized, I say, let us not have such a machine any longer. In other words, when a sixth of the population of a nation which has undertaken to be the refuge of liberty are slaves, and a whole country is unjustly overrun and conquered by a foreign army, and subjected to military law, I think that it is not too soon for honest men to rebel and revolutionize. What makes this duty the more urgent is the fact that the country so overrun is not our own, but ours is the invading army. . . .

> *A drab of state, a cloth-o'-silver slut,*
> *To have her train borne up, and her soul trail in the dirt.*

Practically speaking, the opponents to a reform in Massachusetts are not a hundred thousand politicians at the South, but a hundred thousand merchants and farmers here, who are more interested in commerce and agriculture than they are in humanity, and are not prepared to do justice to the slave and to Mexico, *cost what it may.* I quarrel not with far-off foes, but with those who, near at home, cooperate with, and do the bidding of, those far away, and without whom the latter would be harmless. We are accustomed to say, that the mass of men are unprepared; but improvement is slow, because the few are not materially wiser or better than the many. It is not so important that many should be as good as you, as that there be some absolute goodness somewhere; for that will leaven the whole lump. There are thousands who are *in opinion* opposed to slavery and to the war, who yet in effect do nothing to put an end to them; who, esteeming themselves children of Washington and Franklin, sit down with their hands in their pockets, and say that they know not what to do, and do nothing; who even postpone the question of freedom to the question of free-trade, and quietly read the prices-current along with the latest advices from Mexico, after dinner, and, it may be, fall asleep over them both. What is the price-current of an honest man and patriot today? They hesitate, and they regret, and sometimes they petition; but they do nothing in earnest and with effect. They will wait, well disposed, for others to remedy the evil, that they may no longer have it to regret. At most, they give only a cheap vote, and a feeble countenance and God-speed, to the right, as it goes by them. There are nine hundred and ninety-nine patrons of virtue to one virtuous man. But it is easier to deal with the real possessor of a thing than with the temporary guardian of it.

All voting is a sort of gaming, like checkers or backgammon, with a slight moral tinge to it, a playing with right and wrong, with moral questions; and betting naturally accompanies it. The character of the voters is not staked. I cast my vote, perchance, as I think right; but I am not vitally concerned that that right should prevail. I am willing to leave it to the majority. Its obligation, therefore, never exceeds that of expediency. Even voting *for the right* is *doing* nothing for it. It is only expressing to men feebly your desire that it should prevail. A wise man will not leave the right to the mercy of chance, nor wish it to prevail through the power of the majority. There is but little virtue in the action of masses of men. When the majority shall at length vote for the abolition of slavery, it will be because they are indifferent to slavery, or because there is but little slavery left to be abolished by their vote. *They* will then be the only slaves. Only *his* vote can hasten the abolition of slavery who asserts his own freedom by his vote.

I hear of a convention to be held at Baltimore, or elsewhere, for the selection of a candidate for the Presidency, made up chiefly of editors, and men who are politicians by profession; but I think, what is it to any independent, intelligent, and respectable man what decision they may come to?

Shall we not have the advantage of his wisdom and honesty, nevertheless? Can we not count upon some independent votes? Are there not many individuals in the country who do not attend conventions? But no: I find that the respectable man, so called, has immediately drifted from his position, and despairs of his country, when his country has more reason to despair of him. He forthwith adopts one of the candidates thus selected as the only *available* one, thus proving that he is himself *available* for any purposes of the demagogue. His vote is of no more worth than that of any unprincipled foreigner or hireling native, who may have been bought. O for a man who is a *man,* and, as my neighbor says, has a bone in his back which you cannot pass your hand through! Our statistics are at fault: the population has been returned too large. How many *men* are there to a square thousand miles in this country? Hardly one. Does not America offer any inducement for men to settle here? The American has dwindled into an Odd Fellow—one who may be known by the development of his organ of gregariousness, and a manifest lack of intellect and cheerful self-reliance; whose first and chief concern, on coming into the world, is to see that the Almshouses are in good repair; and, before yet he has lawfully donned the virile garb, to collect a fund for the support of the widows and orphans that may be; who, in short, ventures to live only by the aid of the Mutual Insurance company, which has promised to bury him decently.

It is not a man's duty, as a matter of course, to devote himself to the eradication of any, even the most enormous wrong; he may still properly have other concerns to engage him; but it is his duty, at least, to wash his hands of it, and, if he gives it no thought longer, not to give it practically his support. If I devote myself to other pursuits and contemplations, I must first see, at least, that I do not pursue them sitting upon another man's shoulders. I must get off him first, that he may pursue his contemplations too. See what gross inconsistency is tolerated. I have heard some of my townsmen say, "I should like to have them order me out to help put down an insurrection of the slaves, or to march to Mexico—see if I would go"; and yet these very men have each, directly by their allegiance, and so indirectly, at least, by their money, furnished a substitute. The soldier is applauded who refuses to serve in an unjust war by those who do not refuse to sustain the unjust government which makes the war; is applauded by those whose own act and authority he disregards and sets at naught; as if the state were penitent to that degree that it hired one to scourge it while it sinned, but not to that degree that it left off sinning for a moment. Thus, under the name of Order and Civil Government, we are all made at last to pay homage to and support our own meanness. After the first blush of sin comes its indifference; and from immoral it becomes, as it were, *un*moral, and not quite unnecessary to that life which we have made.

The broadest and most prevalent error requires the most disinterested virtue to sustain it. The slight reproach to which the virtue of patriotism is commonly liable, the noble are most likely to incur. Those who, while they disapprove of the character and measures of a government, yield to it their allegiance and support are undoubtedly its most conscientious supporters, and so frequently the most serious obstacles to reform. Some are petitioning the state to dissolve the Union, to disregard the requisitions of the President. Why do they not dissolve it themselves—the union between themselves and the state—and refuse to pay their quota into its treasury? Do not they stand in the same relation to the state that the state does to the Union? And have not the same reasons prevented the state from resisting the Union which have prevented them from resisting the state?

How can a man be satisfied to entertain an opinion merely, and enjoy it? Is there any enjoyment in it, if his opinion is that he is aggrieved? If you are cheated out of a single dollar by your neighbor, you do not rest satisfied with knowing that you are cheated, or with saying that you are cheated, or even with petitioning him to pay you your due; but you take effectual steps at once to obtain the full amount, and see that you are never cheated again. Action from principle, the perception and the performance of right, changes things and relations; it is essentially revolutionary, and does not consist wholly with anything which was. It not only divides states and churches, it divides families; ay, it divides the *individual,* separating the diabolical in him from the divine.

Unjust laws exist: shall we be content to obey them, or shall we endeavor to amend them, and obey them until we have succeeded, or shall we transgress them at once? Men generally, under such a government as this, think that they ought to wait until they have persuaded the majority to alter them. They think that, if they should resist, the remedy would be worse than the evil. But it is the fault of the government itself that the remedy is worse than the evil. *It* makes it worse. Why is it not more apt to anticipate and provide for reform? Why does it not cherish its wise minority? Why does it cry and resist before it is hurt? Why does it not encourage its citizens to be on the alert to point out its faults, and *do* better than it would have them? Why does it always crucify Christ, and excommunicate Copernicus and Luther, and pronounce Washington and Franklin rebels?

One would think, that a deliberate and practical denial of its authority was the only offense never contemplated by government; else, why has it not assigned its definite, its suitable and proportionate penalty? If a man who has no property refuses but once to earn nine shillings for the state, he is put in prison for a period unlimited by any law that I know, and determined only by the discretion of those who placed him there; but if he should steal ninety times nine shillings from the state, he is soon permitted to go at large again.

If the injustice is part of the necessary friction of the machine of government, let it go, let it go: perchance it will wear smooth—certainly the machine will wear out. If the injustice has a spring, or a pulley, or a rope, or a crank, exclusively for itself, then perhaps you may consider whether the remedy will not be worse than the evil; but if it is of such a nature that it requires you to be the agent of injustice to another, then, I say, break the law. Let your life be a counter friction to stop the machine. What I have to do is to see, at any rate, that I do not lend myself to the wrong which I condemn.

As for adopting the ways which the state has provided for remedying the evil, I know not of such ways. They take too much time, and a man's life will be gone. I have other affairs to attend to. I came into this world, not chiefly to make this a good place to live in, but to live in it, be it good or bad. A man has not everything to do, but something; and because he cannot do *everything,* it is not necessary that he should do *something* wrong. It is not my business to be petitioning the Governor or the Legislature any more than it is theirs to petition me; and if they should not hear my petition, what should I do then? But in this case the state has provided no way: its very Constitution is the evil. This may seem to be harsh and stubborn and unconciliatory; but it is to treat with the utmost kindness and consideration the only spirit that can appreciate or deserves it. So is all change for the better, like birth and death, which convulse the body.

I do not hesitate to say, that those who call themselves Abolitionists should at once effectually withdraw their support, both in person and property, from the government of Massachusetts and not wait till they constitute a majority of one, before they suffer the right to prevail through them. I think that it is enough if they have God on their side, without waiting for that other one. Moreover, any man more right than his neighbors constitutes a majority of one already.

I meet this American government, or its representative, the state government, directly, and face to face, once a year—no more—in the person of its tax-gatherer; this is the only mode in which a man situated as I am necessarily meets it; and it then says distinctly, Recognize me; and the simplest, most effectual, and, in the present posture of affairs, the indispensablest mode of treating with it on this head, of expressing your little satisfaction with and love for it, is to deny it then. My civil neighbor, the tax-gatherer, is the very man I have to deal with—for it is, after all, with men and not with parchment that I quarrel—and he has voluntarily chosen to be an agent of the government. How shall he ever know well what he is and does as an officer of the government, or as a man, until he is obliged to consider whether he shall treat me, his neighbor, for whom he has respect, as a neighbor and well-disposed man, or as a maniac and disturber of the peace, and see if he can get over this obstruction to his neighborliness without a ruder and more impetuous thought or speech corresponding with his action. I know this well, that if one thousand, if one hundred, if ten men whom I could name—if ten *honest* men only—ay, if *one* HONEST man, in this State of Massachusetts, *ceasing to hold slaves,* were actually to withdraw from this copartnership, and be locked up in the county jail therefor, it would be the abolition of slavery in America. For it matters not how small the beginning may seem to be: what is once well done is done forever. But we love better to talk about it: that we say is our mission. Reform keeps many scores of newspapers in its service, but not one man. If my esteemed neighbor, the State's ambassador, who will devote his days to the settlement of the question of human rights in the Council Chamber, instead of being threatened with the prisons of Carolina, were to sit down the prisoner of Massachusetts, that State which is so anxious to foist the sin of slavery upon her sister—though at present she can discover only an act of inhospitality to be the ground of a quarrel with her—the Legislature would not wholly waive the subject the following winter.

Under a government which imprisons any unjustly, the true place for a just man is also a prison. The proper place today, the only place which Massachusetts has provided for her freer and less desponding spirits, is in her prisons, to be put out and locked out of the State by her own act, as they have already put themselves out by their principles. It is there that the fugitive slave, and the Mexican prisoner on parole, and the Indian come to plead the wrongs of his race should find them; on that separate, but more free and honorable ground, where the State places those who are not *with* her, but *against* her—the only house in a slave State in which a free man can abide with honor. If any think that their influence would be lost there, and their voices no longer afflict the ear of the State, that they would not be as an enemy within its walls, they do not know by how much truth is stronger than error, nor how much more eloquently and effectively he can combat injustice who has experienced a little in his own person. Cast your whole vote, not a strip of paper merely, but your whole influence. A minority is powerless while it conforms to the majority; it is not even a minority then; but it is irresistible when it clogs by its whole weight. If the alternative is to keep all just men in prison, or give up war and slavery, the State will not hesitate which to choose. If a thousand men were not to pay their tax-bills this year, that would not be a violent and bloody measure, as it would be to pay them, and enable the State to commit violence and shed innocent blood. This is, in fact, the definition of a peaceable revolution, if any such is possible. If the tax-gatherer, or any other public officer, asks me, as one has done, "But what shall I do?" my answer is, "If you really wish to do anything, resign your office." When the subject has refused allegiance, and the officer has resigned his office, then the revolution is accomplished. But even suppose blood should flow. Is there not a sort of blood shed when the conscience is wounded? Through this wound a man's real manhood and immortality flow out, and he bleeds to an everlasting death. I see this blood flowing now.

I have contemplated the imprisonment of the offender, rather than the seizure of his goods—though both will serve the same purpose—because they who assert the purest right, and consequently are most dangerous to a corrupt State, commonly have not spent much time in accumulating property. To such the State renders comparatively small service, and a slight tax is wont to appear exorbitant, particularly if they are obliged to earn it by special labor with their hands. If there were one who lived wholly without the use of money, the State itself would hesitate to demand it of him. But the rich man—not to make any invidious comparison—is always sold to the institution which makes him rich. Absolutely speaking, the more money, the less virtue; for money comes between a man and his objects, and obtains them for him; and it was certainly no great virtue to obtain it. It puts to rest many questions which he would otherwise be taxed to answer; while the only new question which it puts is the hard but superfluous one, how to spend it. Thus his moral ground is taken from under his feet. The opportunities of living are diminished in proportion as what are called the "means" are increased. The best thing a man can do for his culture when he is rich is to endeavor to carry out those schemes which he entertained when he was poor. Christ answered the Herodians according to their condition. "Show me the tribute-money," said he—and one took a penny out of his pocket; if you use money which has the image of Caesar on it and which he has made current and valuable, that is, *if you are men of the State*, and gladly enjoy the advantages of Caesar's government, then pay him back some of his own when he demands it. "Render therefore to Caesar that which is Caesar's, and to God those things which are God's"—leaving them no wiser than before as to which was which; for they did not wish to know. . . .

I have paid no poll-tax for six years. I was put into a jail once on this account, for one night; and, as I stood considering the walls of solid stone, two or three feet thick, the door of wood and iron, a foot thick, and the iron grating which strained the light, I could not help being struck with the foolishness of that institution which treated me as if I were mere flesh and blood and bones, to be locked up. I wondered that it should have concluded at length that this was the best use it could put me to, and had never thought to avail itself of my services in some way. I saw that, if there was a wall of stone between me and my townsmen, there was a still more difficult one to climb or break through before they could get to be as free as I was. I did not for a moment feel confined, and the walls seemed a great waste of stone and mortar. I felt as if I alone of all my townsmen had paid my tax. They plainly did not know how to treat me, but behaved like persons who are underbred. In every threat and in every compliment there was a blunder; for they thought that my chief desire was to stand the other side of that stone wall. I could not but smile to see how industriously they locked the door on my meditations, which followed them out again without let or hindrance, and *they* were really all that was dangerous. As they could not reach me, they had resolved to punish my body; just as boys, if they cannot come at some person against whom they have a spite, will abuse his dog. I saw that the State was half-witted, that it was timid as a lone woman with her silver spoons, and that it did not know its friends from its foes, and I lost all my remaining respect for it, and pitied it.

Thus the State never intentionally confronts a man's sense, intellectual or moral, but only his body, his senses. It is not armed with superior wit or honesty, but with superior physical strength. I was not born to be forced. I will breathe after my own fashion. Let us see who is the strongest. What force has a multitude? They only can force me who obey a higher law than I. They force me to become like themselves. I do not hear of *men* being *forced* to live this way or that by masses of men. What sort of life were that to live? When I meet a government which says to me, "Your money or your life," why should I be in haste to give it my money? It may be in a great strait, and not know what to do: I cannot help that. It must help itself; do as I do. It is not worth the while to snivel about it. I am not responsible for the successful working of the machinery of society. I am not the son of the engineer. I perceive that, when an acorn and a chestnut fall side by side, the one does not remain inert to make way for the other, but both obey their own laws, and spring and grow and flourish as best they can, till one, perchance, overshadows and destroys the other. If a plant cannot live according to its nature, it dies; and so a man. . . .

When I came out of prison—for someone interfered, and paid that tax —I did not perceive that great changes had taken place on the common, such as he observed who went in a youth and emerged a tottering and gray-headed man; and yet a change had to my eyes come over the scene— the town, and State, and country—greater than any that mere time could effect. I saw yet more distinctly the State in which I lived. I saw to what extent the people among whom I lived could be trusted as good neighbors and friends; that their friendship was for summer weather only; that they did not greatly propose to do right; that they were a distinct race from me by their prejudices and superstitions, as the Chinamen and Malays are; that in their sacrifices to humanity they ran no risks, not even to their property; that after all they were not so noble but they treated the thief as he had treated them, and hoped, by a certain outward observance and a few prayers, and by walking in a particular straight though useless path from time to time, to save their souls. This may be to judge my neighbors harshly; for I believe that many of them are not aware that they have such an institution as the jail in their village.

It was formerly the custom in our village, when a poor debtor came out of jail, for his acquaintances to salute him, looking through their fingers, which were crossed to represent the grating of a jail window. "How do ye do?" My neighbors did not thus salute me, but first looked at me, and then at one another, as if I had returned from a long journey. I was put into jail as I was going to the shoemaker's to get a shoe which was mended. When I was let out the next morning, I proceeded to finish my errand, and having put on my mended shoe, joined a huckleberry party, who were impatient to put themselves under my conduct; and in half an hour—for the horse was soon tackled—was in the midst of a huckleberry field, on one of our highest hills, two miles off, and then the State was nowhere to be seen. . . .

I have never declined paying the highway tax, because I am as desirous of being a good neighbor as I am of being a bad subject; and as for supporting schools, I am doing my part to educate my fellow-countrymen now. It is for no particular item in the tax-bill that I refuse to pay it. I simply wish to refuse allegiance to the State, to withdraw and stand aloof from it effectually. I do not care to trace the course of my dollar, if I could, till it buys a man or a musket to shoot with—the dollar is innocent—but I am concerned to trace the effects of my allegiance. In fact, I quietly declare war with the State, after my fashion, though I will still make what use and get what advantage of her I can, as is usual in such cases.

If others pay the tax which is demanded of me, from a sympathy with the State, they do but what they have already done in their own case, or rather they abet injustice to a greater extent than the State requires. If they pay the tax from a mistaken interest in the individual taxed, to save his property, or prevent his going to jail, it is because they have not considered wisely how far they let their private feelings interfere with the public good.

This, then, is my position at present. But one cannot be too much on his guard in such a case, lest his action be biased by obstinacy or an undue regard for the opinions of men. Let him see that he does only what belongs to himself and to the hour.

I think sometimes, Why, this people mean well, they are only ignorant; they would do better if they knew how: why give your neighbors this pain to treat you as they are not inclined to? But I think again, This is no reason why I should do as they do, or permit others to suffer much greater pain of a different kind. Again, I sometimes say to myself, When many millions of men, without heat, without ill will, without personal feeling of any kind, demand of you a few shillings only, without the possibility, such is their constitution, of retracting or altering their present demand, and without the possibility, on your side, of appeal to any other millions, why expose yourself to this overwhelming brute force? You do not resist cold and hunger, the winds and the waves, thus obstinately; you quietly submit to a thousand similar necessities. You do not put your head into the fire. But just in proportion as I regard this as not wholly a brute force, but partly a human force, and consider that I have relations to those millions as to so many millions of men, and not of mere brute or inanimate things, I see that appeal is possible, first and instantaneously, from them to the Maker of them, and, secondly, from them to themselves. But if I put my head deliberately into the fire, there is no appeal to fire or to the Maker of fire, and I have only myself to blame. If I could convince myself that I have any right to be satisfied with men as they are, and to treat them accordingly, and not according, in some respects, to my requisitions and expectations of what they and I ought to be, then, like a good Mussulman and fatalist, I should endeavor to be satisfied with things as they are, and say it is the will of God. And, above all, there is this difference between resisting this and a purely brute or natural force, that I can resist this with some effect; but I cannot expect, like Orpheus, to change the nature of the rocks and trees and beasts.

I do not wish to quarrel with any man or nation. I do not wish to split hairs, to make fine distinctions, or set myself up as better than my neighbors. I seek rather, I may say, even an excuse for conforming to the laws of the land. I am but too ready to conform to them. Indeed, I have reason to suspect myself on this head; and each year, as the tax-gatherer comes round, I find myself disposed to review the acts and position of the general and State governments, and the spirits of the people, to discover a pretext for conformity.

> *We must affect our country as our parents,*
> *And if at any time we alienate*
> *Our love or industry from doing it honor,*
> *We must respect effects and teach the soul*
> *Matter of conscience and religion,*
> *And not desire of rule or benefit.*

I believe that the State will soon be able to take all my work of this sort out of my hands, and then I shall be no better a patriot than my fellow-countrymen. Seen from a lower point of view, the Constitution, with all its faults, is very good; the law and the courts are very respectable; even this State and this American government are, in many respects, very admirable, and rare things, to be thankful for, such as a great many have described them; but seen from a point of view a little higher, they are what I have described them; seen from a higher still, and the highest, who shall say what they are, or that they are worth looking at or thinking of at all?

However, the government does not concern me much, and I shall bestow the fewest possible thoughts on it. It is not many moments that I live under a government, even in this world. If a man is thought-free, fancy-free, imagination-free, that which is *not* never for a long time appearing *to be* to him, unwise rulers or reformers cannot fatally interrupt him.

I know that most men think differently from myself; but those whose lives are by profession devoted to the study of these or kindred subjects content me as little as any. Statesmen and legislators, standing so completely within the institution, never distinctly and nakedly behold it. They speak of moving society, but have no resting-place without it. They may be men of a certain experience and discrimination, and have no doubt invented ingenious and even useful systems, for which we sincerely thank them; but all their wit and usefulness lie within certain not very wide limits. They are wont to forget that the world is not governed by policy and expediency. Webster never goes behind government, and so cannot speak with authority about it. His words are wisdom to those legislators who contemplate no essential reform in the existing government; but for thinkers, and those who legislate for all time, he never once glances at the subject. I know of those whose serene and wise speculations on this theme would soon reveal the limits of his mind's range and hospitality. Yet, compared with the cheap professions of most reformers, and the still cheaper wisdom and eloquence of politicians in general, his are almost the only sensible and valuable words, and we thank Heaven for him. Comparatively, he is always strong, original, and, above all, practical. Still, his quality is not wisdom, but prudence. The lawyer's truth is not Truth, but consistency or a consistent expediency. Truth is always in harmony with herself, and is not concerned chiefly to reveal the justice that may consist with wrong-doing. He well deserves to be called, as he has been called, the Defender of the Constitution. There are really no blows to be given by him but defensive ones. He is not a leader, but a follower. His leaders are the men of '87. "I have never made an effort," he says, "and never propose to make an effort; I have never countenanced an effort, and never mean to countenance an effort, to disturb the arrangement as originally made, by which the various States came into the Union." Still thinking of the sanction which the Constitution gives to slavery, he says, "Because it was a part of the original compact—let it stand." Notwithstanding his special acuteness and ability, he is unable to take a fact out of its merely political relations, and behold it as it lies absolutely to be disposed of by the intellect—what, for instance, it behooves a man to do here in America today with regard to slavery—but ventures, or is driven, to make some such desperate answer as the following while professing to speak absolutely, and as a private man—from which what new and singular code of social duties might be inferred? "The manner," says he, "in which the governments of those States where slavery exists are to regulate it is for their own consideration, under their responsibility to their constituents, to the general laws of propriety, humanity, and justice, and to God. Associations formed elsewhere, springing from a feeling of humanity, or other cause, have nothing whatever to do with it. They have never received any encouragement from me, and they never will."

They who know of no purer sources of truth, who have traced up its stream no higher, stand, and wisely stand, by the Bible and the Constitution, and drink at it there with reverence and humility; but they who behold where it comes trickling into this lake or that pool, gird up their loins once more, and continue their pilgrimage toward its fountainhead.

No man with a genius for legislation has appeared in America. They are rare in the history of the world. There are orators, politicians, and eloquent men, by the thousand; but the speaker has not yet opened his mouth to speak who is capable of settling the much-vexed questions of the day. We love eloquence for its own sake, and not for any truth which it may utter, or any heroism it may inspire. Our legislators have not yet learned the comparative value of free-trade and of freedom, of union, and of rectitude, to a nation. They have no genius or talent for comparatively humble questions of taxation and finance, commerce and manufactures and agriculture. If we were left solely to the wordy wit of legislators in Congress for our guidance, uncorrected by the seasonable experience and the effectual complaints of the people, America would not long retain her rank among the nations. For eighteen hundred years, though perchance I have no right to say it, the New Testament has been written; yet where is the legislator who has wisdom and practical talent enough to avail himself of the light which it sheds on the science of legislation?

The authority of government, even such as I am willing to submit to—for I will cheerfully obey those who know and can do better than I, and in many things even those who neither know nor can do so well—is still an impure one: to be strictly just, it must have the sanction and consent of the governed. It can have no pure right over my person and property but what I concede to it. The progress from an absolute to a limited monarchy, from a limited monarchy to a democracy, is a progress toward a true respect for the individual. Even the Chinese philosopher was wise enough to regard the individual as the basis of the empire. Is a democracy, such as we know it, the last improvement possible in government? Is it not possible to take a step further toward recognizing and organizing the rights of man? There will never be a really free and enlightened State until the State comes to recognize the individual as a higher and independent power, from which all its own power and authority are derived, and treats him accordingly. I please myself with imagining a State at last which can afford to be just to all men, and to treat the individual with respect as a neighbor; which even would not think it inconsistent with its own repose if a few were to live aloof from it, not meddling with it, nor embraced by it, who fulfilled all the duties of neighbors and fellow-men. A State which bore this kind of fruit, and suffered it to drop off as fast as it ripened, would prepare the way for a still more perfect and glorious State, which also I have imagined, but not yet anywhere seen.

* Proving

THE WORD "PROVING" has three common meanings: (1) testing for truth or value ("The exception proves the rule"); (2) finding the answer to one or more possibilities, ("His fears proved groundless"); (3) presenting conclusive evidence for some proposition ("He proved that he was right by opening the box and revealing its contents"). The process of proving, then, is a part both of a writer's inquiry and of his expression, of his attempt to discover and of his attempt to communicate. In the sense of testing, it is a part, as well, of the reader's activity. And if he is led to challenge the writer, it becomes a part of his activity in the sense of demonstrating also. The problem of proof occurs wherever assertions occur, though it takes on various guises according to the context of the assertion: the kind of proof relevant to a poem is very different from that relevant to a historical generalization or to a theory of energy.

Ubiquitous as it is, the problem of proof does not seem intrusive or onerous largely because a great proportion of the assertions by which people live are unquestioned or are accepted on grounds requiring no great effort of mind. A statement may be accepted almost entirely because it has been accepted for a long time ("Women have less artistic talent than men"); or because an "expert" attests to its truth ("Light travels approximately 186,000 miles a second"); or because it is "felt" to be true ("There is a Providence which watches over all"); or, finally, because it is thought to be the valid conclusion to a logical investigation. The grounds of *persistence, authority,* and *intuition* are probably more often invoked than those of logic, and they are certainly necessary to the normal conduct of life. Their weakness is the obvious one that they are unmethodical and therefore rather helpless in the face of challenge. Persistent statements sometimes contradict each other; authorities disagree; and my intuition may not coincide with yours. When conflicts of this kind arise, the thinking man has recourse to logic.

Now logic is nothing but the systematization of thought, the attempt to set a rigorous control over the mind throughout the conduct of a particular inquiry. The formal rules of the various logical systems are devices for keeping the mind on the track, for guarding against errors, and for meeting perplexities. Difficulties, and therefore devices to overcome them, vary from system to system, and the systems themselves have different qualities and therefore different kinds of usefulness. Only a complete book can come close to doing justice to their subtleties, and what is attempted here aims no higher than to present a brief description of the three principal systems and to suggest a few precautions against abuse of them.

Analogy is the simplest of the three methods of proof to be discussed here. At bottom, it is nothing more than a comparison between two things. It argues that if x and y are alike in several ways, they are probably alike in another way or are even identical. Although no specific number of similarities can be named, it is clear that a large number presents a stronger argument than a small number. And it is clear that the similarities cited must have some relevance to the one that is being argued and that they must be real, not merely verbal, similarities. An analogical argument might run like this: it is no more illogical to imprison a debtor than to lock a vagrant dog in the city pound. The argument is weakened, if not entirely defeated, by the simple presentation of a significant dissimilarity: incarcerating a dog will make it neither more nor less able to provide for itself, but doing so to a man will destroy all opportunity for him to pay his debts by working. The fact that peaches and tennis balls are round, firm, and fuzzy on the outside does not argue satisfactorily that both should be classified as fruit. Nor does the fact that both cows and automobiles have horns and glossy coats lead to the conclusion that Chryslers should be supplied with milking machines. The tests of number, relevance, and freedom from significant dissimilarity limit the abuse of analogy. But it is wise to remember, in addition, that exact likenesses are not common in nature, and consequently that analogy is more useful for description, explanation, and persuasion than for formal proof. It is, in fact, a stripped down and less reliable form of the second method of proof, induction.

Induction is today the most widely used procedure of proof, and its pervasiveness speaks best for its usefulness and its success. In simple terms, induction is the development of a generalization from particular instances. It differs from analogy in its independence of comparison; it is like analogy in working from the many to the one and in assuming, at some point in the procedure, that there is sufficient evidence for jumping from the data at hand to a statement about all such data, including those not at hand. Contrary to popular notion, induction does not begin with "facts." Its origin rather is in a question or a doubt raised by observation of some phenomenon. Out of that question or doubt there come one or more tentative answers, or hypotheses. Having selected one of the hypotheses, the investigator proceeds to examine data relevant to it. From his examination— his "proving" of the hypothesis—he gradually reaches a generalization which confirms, alters, or disputes the hypothesis from which he began. Very rarely indeed is he in possession of all possible relevant data. If he were, he might reach a "perfect induction"; since he is not, he must eventually make the *inductive* leap, the jump from the data he has examined to a statement intended to account for all such data. Because he must make that leap, induction—except for "perfect induction"—is never, *as a method,* capable of producing certainty. It may reach truth and often does, or it would not be the method of scientific experiment today, but its methodology limits it to varying degrees of probability.

It is not only at the point of the "leap," however, that the inductive method has a weakness; its susceptibility to abuse and error is great at every step. At the very outset, the investigator meets perplexities in formulating a hypothesis with which to begin his work. If his induction is to be efficient and fruitful, the hypothesis must really provide a possible answer to the problem for which it is proposed; it must be capable of verification; and it must be as simple as the problem allows. (The adjective "simple" in this context refers to the number of different kinds of elements contained in the hypothesis when all its assumptions are included; the fewer the number, the simpler the hypothesis). The adoption of a hypothesis brings with it two particular dangers: the tendency to select evidence which confirms the hypothesis and to ignore evidence which does not, and the tendency to see what is expected or hoped for whether it is there or not. Even if these tendencies are checked, the investigator must guard against, and constantly take into account, the fallibility of human sensory organs. The expression "Do my eyes deceive me, or is that . . . ?" is based on the common knowledge that deceive is precisely what eyes often do. Against the failure of human senses to render accurate accounts, scientists have devised any number of ingenious contrivances for recording and measuring data. Although they reduce the likelihood of error in observation, they introduce the likelihood of another sort of error, that of translation and interpretation. Mechanical and electronic measures render their "observations" in some kind of symbolic code; translating that code and interpreting the significance of the observations remain largely human activities, susceptible, like all things human, to error.

Granting satisfactory control of the stage of hypothesis and of the process of observation and recording of data, the greatest number of difficulties still lie in wait. The data must be studied to discover the relationships from which a generalization is to be drawn. Most of the early "foolproof" methods for controlling this part of the procedure have had their validity punctured or have been shown to have mainly negative value as checks against error rather than as proofs of conclusions. What remains is an insistence on control over the conditions of the investigation or experiment (the method of a single variable), an insistence more practical for a hypothesis about protein than for one about divorce or the stock market. To this is added an insistence on extensive and repeated sampling, on the use of refined means of measurement, on translation of data into varied statistical forms.

As investigators have become more and more sharply aware of the possibilities for error in the inductive process, and more and more ingenious in finding ways to cross-check procedures, they have also come to realize that quantification and reduction to formulas are essential to their work. This realization has had two notable consequences: (1) the attempt to find ways of turning many kinds of data into quantities by separating phenomena into components (in sociology, for instance, the phenomenon of social prejudice into statistical studies of employment, housing populations, membership in organizations, individual attitude-tests, and so on); (2) recognition that for a great part of the analysis of most disciplines the inductive process must remain relatively imprecise in its procedures and largely dependent on the knowledge and perceptiveness of its investigators (a study of a painting by Renoir demands *expertise,* certainly, but neither a poll of reactions to the painting nor an electronic measurement of the thickness of pigment in various parts of the painting is of great value to the expert). Even so, some of the rigorousness of the so-called "scientific method"—the twentieth-century refinement of induction—has rubbed off on all kinds of inquiry and, despite some absurdities, the long-range effect has probably been good.

Deduction is essentially a baring of the implications of a proposition or series of propositions. It begins from accepted premises and "discovers" the necessary consequences of them. The "discovery" it makes according to a plan so constructed as to render error impossible if all conditions are met, as they can be. Mathematics is a deductive system; a musical fugue is, in part, an exercise in deduction. In language, deduction has found its purest practice in the form of proof known as the *syllogism,* a form brought to its ultimate excellence in scholastic theology of the late Middle Ages.

Although the syllogism has for a long time felt, and suffered from, the fire of attack by logicians, it is still an important part of normal rational thought, though seldom expressed in the skeletal form it assumes in analysis. Yet, despite its superficial simplicity of structure, it is actually so intricate a procedure that it is as frequently misused as used correctly. To detail that intricacy here is, for reasons of space, impossible; to attempt an abbreviation would be to encourage the kinds of abuse already so common. In this account we must be content to point out the principal values and hazards of the syllogistic pattern and then to direct the reader to careful study of its mechanics in a textbook of logic.

The principal virtue of the syllogism is that it is a closed system: given the truth of its premises and the validity of its form, it produces a true and logically indisputable conclusion. A simple example shows the neatness of the form and the inexorableness of the development:

All heroes are products of circumstance.   *(major premise)*
John is a hero.   *(minor premise)*
John is a product of circumstance.   *(conclusion)*

The example also suggests the difficulties that beset the syllogizer. To begin with, if he is concerned with truth and not simply with validity (i.e., formal correctness in procedure), he must always be wary about the grounds for his premises. Are they indisputably solid? What is the nature of each premise itself: is it a definition, a generally accepted observation about experience, the result of a prior inductive investigation, the conclusion of another syllogism, a resolution, or simply a hypothesis used in order to initiate inquiry? Where premises are clearly and explicitly stated and where they are not complicated by conditions, they do not offer grave difficulties: most of us are alert enough to give or deny assent to them at the outset of an argument or demonstration. The trouble is that, in ordinary discourse, they often are complicated by conditions and fully as often are not explicit. The conditional premise can be met only by eliminating its conditions and making separate premises of them. Omitted premises must be supplied.

Since the syllogism is fundamentally a system for discovering the implications of statements, its conclusion may be valid even though false; that is, the conclusion may follow logically from the premises and still not be itself a true proposition if one or both of the premises with which the syllogism began is false. A valid conclusion is, then, a statement of what is necessarily true if the premises are true. Opponents of the syllogism have sometimes attacked its usefulness with the following paradox. In order to be valid, a conclusion must be contained in the initial premise, but in order to be useful it must be different from the premise. Since it cannot at the same time be contained in the premise and also be different, it cannot both be valid and useful. A second, and more serious, attack is made by those who say that the truth of an initial premise can be known only if all the conclusions implicit in it are also known to be true. But if the conclusion is already known to be true, the syllogism is obviously useless; and if the truth of the premise depends on the truth of the conclusion being "proved," the syllogism is circular. To both charges one reply is possible: it is not the same to "know" a thing logically as to "know" it psychologically. Therefore a conclusion may be "different" because psychologically unknown and still be "contained" in the premises, just as the major premise may be logically known to be true while the particular instance indicated in the conclusion is not, psychologically speaking, so known. A further reply, however, is needed to the second charge, that of circularity. If all premises were simply enumerations ("*All* heroes are products of circumstance"), the charge would have some weight. But some premises, as noted above, are really resolutions ("Heroes should be men of deliberative nature") or hypotheses ("Heroes may be people of more than ordinary perceptiveness") which are proposed in order that their consequences may be made apparent. Moreover, although syllogisms may be inadequate for proving in the sense of "testing for truth or value," they are clearly useful for proving the sense of "presenting conclusive evidence."

Despite the difficulties about premises and conclusions and the possibilities of error in manipulation of the process, syllogistic reasoning is common in all ordinary discourse. It is common because there is constant need for some machinery for getting from general propositions to particular instances and because a great part of our common and generally accepted knowledge is contained in axioms and aphorisms meant to be inclusive in their application. It is, of course, true that normal discourse ordinarily separates or omits premises in such fashion that the syllogistic pattern is quite disguised; but disguised or not, it underlies nearly all extended argument.

The general conclusion to be drawn from this brief discussion is that, no matter by what method it is sought, propositional truth is hard to come by. Within limits, a high degree of certainty can be achieved; within the confines of a verbal exercise, the certainty can be absolute. But the old problems of relationship between symbol and fact and of the reliability of various modes of knowing make all proving, in the end, a matter of constant alertness and perpetual inconclusiveness. Fortunately, for all practical purposes, the judicious use of analogical, inductive, and deductive procedures provides man with the means to correct much error and to reach steadily toward knowledge.

IS THE WILL FREE?

THE DILEMMA of free-will-or-determinism is an ancient one, but it continues to perplex the philosophers even today. In its earlier forms it generally involved a god, whose power over men's actions was supposedly complete. In later and less religious ages the notion of determinism has been revived by psychologists and social scientists, who have substituted chains of motive, stimulus, drive, environmental conditioning and so forth for the power of a deity. But the problem remains the same. If men's actions are foreordained, then men have no real choice; either they are in the power of fate or they are not. The one solution is damaging to men's egos, and the other either strips their god of power or denies to science the ability to predict their actions. Actually, however, few thinkers other than the strictest Calvinists have accepted either of these simple alternative solutions to the problem. Instead, they have resolved the paradox in many complex ways, salvaging something from both sides. Even so, no one has achieved an answer satisfactory to everyone.

The problems of proof in this argument are one reason for its tenacity.

Until the day when psychologists prove beyond doubt that all human ac-
tions are predictable, the question of free will must be argued theoretically
—that is, deductively. At the same time most theories seem to appeal, for
support, to introspection. They depend partly on psychological coherence
and emotional validity. As a result, most arguments combine logic and
persuasion, as do all the selections in this unit. Two of them, however, are
more or less straightforward rational inquiries. Separated as they are by
fourteen centuries, Boethius (480-524?, Roman philosopher) and Alfred J.
Ayer (1910-   , professor of philosophy at Oxford University) treat of two
different types of determinism, but both are concerned primarily with the
logical force of their arguments. The other two pieces appeal a good deal
more to emotion. The essay by Albert Camus (1913-1960) is philosophical
in outlook, but its persuasive techniques reflect the French writer's principal
occupation as a novelist. Fyodor Dostoevski (1821-1881) does not attack the
free will problem frontally, but deals with it imaginatively through a kind
of parable.

GOD'S FOREKNOWLEDGE AND MAN'S FREE WILL | BOETHIUS

Then said I: "But now I am once more perplexed by a problem yet
more difficult."

"And what is that?" said she; "yet, in truth, I can guess what it is that
troubles you."

"It seems," said I, "too much of a paradox and a contradiction that God
should know all things, and yet there should be free will. For if God foresees everything, and can in no wise be deceived, that which providence
forsees to be about to happen must necessarily come to pass. Wherefore,
if from eternity He foreknows not only what men will do, but also their
designs and purposes, there can be no freedom of the will, seeing that
nothing can be done, nor can any sort of purpose be entertained, save such
as a Divine providence, incapable of being deceived, has perceived beforehand. For if the issues can be turned aside to some other end than that
foreseen by providence, there will not then be any sure foreknowledge of
the future, but uncertain conjecture instead, and to think this of God I
deem impiety.

"Moreover, I do not approve the reasoning by which some think to
solve this puzzle. For they say that it is not because God has foreseen
the coming of an event that *therefore* it is sure to come to pass, but, conversely, because something is about to come to pass, it cannot be hidden
from Divine providence; and accordingly the necessity passes to the op-

From *The Consolation of Philosophy*, trans. by H. R. James (n.d.).

posite side, and it is not that what is foreseen must necessarily come to pass, but that what is about to come to pass must necessarily be foreseen. But this is just as if the matter in debate were, which is cause and which effect—whether foreknowledge of the future cause of the necessity, or the necessity of the future of the foreknowledge. But we need not be at the pains of demonstrating that, whatsoever be the order of the causal sequence, the occurrence of things foreseen is necessary, even though the foreknowledge of future events does not in itself impose upon them the necessity of their occurrence. For example, if a man be seated, the supposition of his being seated is necessarily true; and conversely, if the supposition of his being seated is true, because he is really seated, he must necessarily be sitting. So, in either case, there is some necessity involved— in this latter case, the necessity of the fact; in the former, of the truth of the statement. But in both cases the sitter is not therefore seated because the opinion is true, but rather the opinion is true because antecedently he was sitting as a matter of fact. Thus, though the cause of the truth of the opinion comes from the other side, yet there is a necessity on both sides alike. We can obviously reason similarly in the case of providence and the future. Even if future events are foreseen because they are about to happen, and do not come to pass because they are foreseen, still, all the same, there is a necessity, both that they should be foreseen by God as about to come to pass, and that when they are foreseen they should happen, and this is sufficient for the destruction of free will. However, it is preposterous to speak of the occurrence of events in time as the cause of eternal foreknowledge. And yet if we believe that God foresees future events because they are about to come to pass, what is it but to think that the occurrence of events is the cause of His supreme providence? Further, just as when I *know* that anything is, that thing *necessarily* is, so when I know that anything will be, it will *necessarily* be. It follows, then, that things foreknown come to pass inevitably.

"Lastly, to think of a thing as being in any way other than what it is, is not only not knowledge, but it is false opinion widely different from the truth of knowledge. Consequently, if anything is about to be, and yet its occurrence is not certain and necessary, how can anyone foreknow that it will occur? For just as knowledge itself is free from all admixture of falsity, so any conception drawn from knowledge cannot be other than as it is conceived. For this, indeed, is the cause why knowledge is free from falsehood, because of necessity each thing must correspond exactly with the knowledge which grasps its nature. In what way, then, are we to suppose that God foreknows these uncertainties as about to come to pass? For if He thinks of events which possibly may not happen at all as inevitably destined to come to pass, He is deceived; and this it is not only impious to believe, but even so much as to express in words. If, on the other hand, He sees them in the future as they are in such a sense as to know that they may equally come to pass or not, what sort of foreknowledge is this which comprehends nothing certain nor fixed? What better is this than the absurd vaticination of Teiresias?

> *'Whate'er I say*
> *Shall either come to pass—or not.'*

In that case, too, in what would Divine providence surpass human opinion if it holds for uncertain things the occurrence of which is uncertain, even as men do? But if at that perfectly sure Fountain-head of all things no shadow of uncertainty can possibly be found, then the occurrence of those things which He has surely foreknown as coming is certain. Wherefore there can be no freedom in human actions and designs; but the Divine mind, which foresees all things without possibility of mistake, ties and binds them down to one only issue. But this admission once made, what an upset of human affairs manifestly ensues! Vainly are rewards and punishments proposed for the good and bad, since no free and voluntary motion of the will has deserved either one or the other; nay, the punishment of the wicked and the reward of the righteous, which is now esteemed the perfection of justice, will seem the most flagrant injustice, since men are determined either way not by their own proper volition, but by the necessity of what must surely be. And therefore neither virtue nor vice is anything, but rather good and ill desert are confounded together without distinction. Moreover, seeing that the whole course of events is deduced from providence, and nothing is left free to human design, it comes to pass that our vices also are referred to the Author of all good—a thought than which none more abominable can possibly be conceived. Again, no ground is left for hope or prayer, since how can we hope for blessings, or pray for mercy, when every object of desire depends upon the links of an unalterable chain of causation? Gone, then, is the one means of intercourse between God and man—the communion of hope and prayer—if it be true that we ever earn the inestimable recompense of the Divine favor at the price of a due humility; for this is the one way whereby men seem able to hold communion with God, and are joined to that unapproachable light by the very act of supplication, even before they obtain their petitions. Then, since these things can scarcely be believed to have any efficacy, if the necessity of future events be admitted, what means will there be whereby we may be brought near and cleave to Him who is the supreme Head of all? Wherefore it needs must be that the human race, even as thou didst erstwhile declare in song, parted and dissevered from its Source, should fall to ruin."

> *Why does a strange discordance break*
> *The ordered scheme's fair harmony?*
> *Hath God decreed 'twixt truth and truth*

There may such lasting warfare be,
That truths, each severally plain,
We strive to reconcile in vain?

Or is the discord not in truth,
*   Since truth is self-consistent ever?*
But, close in fleshly wrappings held,
*   The blinded mind of man can never*
Discern—so faint her taper shines—
The subtle chain that all combines?

Ah! then why burns man's restless mind
*   Truth's hidden portals to unclose?*
Knows he already what he seeks?
*   Why toil to seek it, if he knows?*
Yet, haply if he knoweth not,
Why blindly seek he knows not what?

Who for a good he knows not sighs?
*   Who can an unknown end pursue?*
How find? How e'en when haply found
*   Hail that strange form he never knew?*
Or is it that man's inmost soul
Once knew each part and knew the whole?

Now, though by fleshly vapors dimmed,
*   Not all forgot her visions past;*
For while the several parts are lost,
*   To the one whole she cleaveth fast;*
Whence he who yearns the truth to find
Is neither sound of sight nor blind.

For neither does he know in full,
*   Nor is he reft of knowledge quite;*
But, holding still to what is left,
*   He gropes in the uncertain light,*
And by the part that still survives
To win back all he bravely strives.

Then said she: "This debate about providence is an old one, and is vigorously discussed by Cicero in his 'Divination'; thou also hast long and earnestly pondered the problem, yet no one has had diligence and perseverance enough to find a solution. And the reason of this obscurity is that the movement of human reasoning cannot cope with the simplicity of the Divine foreknowledge; for if a conception of its nature could in any wise be framed, no shadow of uncertainty would remain, with a view of

making this at last clear and plain. I will begin by considering the arguments by which thou art swayed. First, I inquire into the reasons why thou
are dissatisfied with the solution proposed, which is to the effect that, seeing the fact of foreknowledge is not thought the cause of the necessity of
future events, foreknowledge is not to be deemed any hindrance to the
freedom of the will. Now, surely the sole ground on which thou arguest
the necessity of the future is that things which are foreknown cannot fail
to come to pass. But if, as thou wert ready to acknowledge just now, the
fact of foreknowlege imposes no necessity on things future, what reason
is there for supposing the results of voluntary action constrained to a fixed
issue? Suppose, for the sake of argument, and to see what follows, we assume
that there is no foreknowledge. Are willed actions, then, tied down to any
necessity in *this* case?"

"Certainly not."

"Let us assume foreknowledge again, but without its involving any
actual necessity; the freedom of the will, I imagine, will remain in complete integrity. But thou wilt say that, even though the foreknowledge is
not the necessity of the future event's occurrence, yet it is a sign that it
will necessarily happen. Granted; but in this case it is plain that, even if
there had been no foreknowledge, the issues would have been inevitably
certain. For a sign only indicates something which is, does not bring to
pass that of which it is the sign. We require to show beforehand that all
things, without exception, happen of necessity in order that a preconception may be a sign of this necessity. Otherwise, if there is no such universal
necessity, neither can any preconception be a sign of a necessity which
exists not. Manifestly, too, a proof established on firm grounds of reason
must be drawn not from signs and loose general arguments, but from suitable and necessary causes. But now can it be that things foreseen should
ever fail to come to pass? Why, this is to suppose us to believe that the
events which providence foresees to be coming were not about to happen,
instead of our supposing that, although they should come to pass, yet
there was no necessity involved in their own nature compelling their
occurrence. Take an illustration that will help to convey by meaning. There
are many thing which we see taking place before our eyes—the movements
of charioteers, for instance, in guiding and turning their cars, and so on.
Now, is any one of these movements compelled by any necessity?

"No; certainly not. There would be no efficacy in skill if all motions
took place perforce."

"Then, things which in taking place are free from any necessity as to
their being in the present must also, before they take place, be about to
happen without necessity. Wherefore there are things which will come to
pass, the occurrence of which is perfectly free from necessity. At all events,
I imagine that no one will deny that things now taking place were about
to come to pass before they were actually happening. Such things, how-

ever much foreknown, are in their occurrence *free*. For even as knowledge of things present imports no necessity into things that are taking place, so foreknowledge of the future imports none into things that are about to come. But this, thou wilt say, is the very point in dispute—whether any foreknowing is possible of things whose occurrence is not necessary. For here there seems to thee a contradiction, and, if they are foreseen, their necessity follows; whereas if there is no necessity, they can by no means be foreknown; and thou thinkest that nothing can be grasped as known unless it is certain, but if things whose occurence is uncertain are foreknown as certain, this is the very mist of opinion, not the truth of knowledge. For to think of things otherwise than as they are, thou believest to be incompatible with the soundness of knowledge.

"Now, the cause of the mistake is this—that men think that all knowledge is cognized purely by the nature and efficacy of the thing known. Whereas the case is the very reverse: all that is known is grasped not conformably to its own efficacy, but rather conformably to the faculty of the knower. An example will make this clear: the roundness of a body is recognized in one way by sight, in another by touch. Sight looks upon it from a distance as a whole by a simultaneous reflection of rays; touch grasps the roundness piecemeal, by contact and attachment to the surface, and by actual movement round the periphery itself. Man himself, likewise, is viewed in one way by Sense, in another by Imagination, in another way, again, by Thought, in another by pure Intelligence. Sense judges figure clothed in material substance, Imagination figure alone without matter. Thought transcends this again, and by its contemplation of universals considers the type itself which is contained in the individual. The eye of Intelligence is yet more exalted; for overpassing the sphere of the universal, it will behold absolute form itself by the pure force of the mind's vision. Wherein the main point to be considered is this: the higher faculty of comprehension embraces the lower, while the lower cannot rise to the higher. For Sense has no efficacy beyond matter, nor can Imagination behold universal ideas, nor Thought embrace pure form; but Intelligence, looking down, as it were, from its higher standpoint in its intuition of form, discriminates also the several elements which underlie it; but it comprehends them in the same way as it comprehends that form itself, which could be cognized by no other than itself. For it cognizes the universal of Thought, the figure of Imagination, and the matter of Sense, without employing Thought, Imagination, or Sense, but surveying all things, so to speak, under the aspect of pure form by a single flash of intuition. Thought also, in considering the universal, embraces images and sense-impressions without resorting to Imagination or Sense. For it is Thought which has thus defined the universal from its conceptual point of view: 'Man is a two-legged animal endowed with reason.' This is indeed a universal notion, yet no one is ignorant that the *thing* is imaginable and presentable to

Sense, because Thought considers it not by Imagination or Sense, but by means of rational conception. Imagination, too, though its faculty of viewing and forming representations is founded upon the sense, nevertheless surveys sense-impressions without calling in Sense, not in the way of Sense-perception, but of Imagination. See'st thou, then, how all things in cognizing use rather their own faculty than the faculty of the things which they cognize? Nor is this strange; for since every judgment is the act of the judge, it is necessary that each should accomplish its task by its own, not by another's power."

> From the Porch's murky depths
>   Comes a doctrine sage,
> That doth liken living mind
>   To a written page;
> Since all knowledge comes through Sense,
> Graven by Experience.
>
> "As," say they, "the pen its marks
>   Curiously doth trace
> On the smooth unsullied white
>   Of the paper's face,
> So do outer things impress
> Images on consciousness."
>
> But if verily the mind
>   Thus all passive lies;
> If no living power within
>   Its own force supplies;
> If it but reflects again,
> Like a glass, things false and vain—
>
> Whence the wondrous faculty
>   That perceives and knows,
> That in one fair ordered scheme
>   Doth the world dispose;
> Grasps each whole that Sense presents,
> Or breaks into elements?
>
> So divides and recombines,
>   And in changeful wise
> Now to low descends, and now
>   To the height doth rise;
> Last in inward swift review
> Strictly sifts the false and true?
>
> Of these ample potencies
>   Fitter cause, I ween,

Were Mind's self than marks impressed
By the outer scene.
Yet the body through the sense
Stirs the soul's intelligence.

When light flashes in the eye,
Or sound strikes the ear,
Mind aroused to due response
Makes the message clear;
And the dumb external signs
With the hidden forms combines.

"Now, although in the case of bodies endowed with sentiency the qualities of external objects affect the sense-organs, and the activity of mind is preceded by a bodily affection which calls forth the mind's action upon itself, and stimulates the forms till that moment lying inactive within, yet, I say, if in these bodies endowed with sentiency the mind is not inscribed by mere passive affection, but of its own efficacy discriminates the impressions furnished to the body, how much more do intelligences free from all bodily affections employ in their discrimination their own mental activities instead of conforming to external objects? So on these principles various modes of cognition belong to distinct and different substances. For to creatures void of motive power—shell-fish and other such creatures which cling to rocks and grow there—belongs Sense alone, void of all other modes of gaining knowledge; to beasts endowed with movement, in whom some capacity of seeking and shunning seems to have arisen, Imagination also. Thought pertains only to the human race, as Intelligence to Divinity alone; hence it follows that that form of knowledge exceeds the rest which of its own nature cognizes not only its proper object, but the objects of the other forms of knowledge also. But what if Sense and Imagination were to gainsay Thought, and declare that universal which Thought deems itself to behold to be nothing? For the object of Sense and Imagination cannot be universal; so that either the judgment of Reason is true and there is no sense-object, or, since they know full well that many objects are presented to Sense and Imagination, the conception of Reason, which looks on that which is perceived by Sense and particular as if it were a something "universal," is empty of content. Suppose, further, that Reason maintains in reply that it does indeed contemplate the object of both Sense and Imagination under the form of universality, while Sense and Imagination cannot aspire to the knowledge of the universal, since their cognizance cannot go beyond bodily figures, and that in the cognition of reality we ought rather to trust the stronger and more perfect faculty of judgment. In a dispute of this sort, should not we, in whom is planted the faculty of reasoning as well as of imagining and perceiving, espouse the cause of reason?

"In like manner is it that human reason thinks that Divine Intelligence cannot see the future except after the fashion in which its own knowledge is obtained. For thy contention is, if events do not appear to involve certain and necessary issues, they cannot be foreseen as certainly about to come to pass. There is, then, no foreknowledge of such events; or, if we can ever bring ourselves to believe that there is, there can be nothing which does not happen of necessity. If, however, we could have some part in the judgment of the Divine mind, even as we participate in Reason, we should think it perfectly just that Human Reason should submit itself to the Divine mind, no less than we judged that Imagination and Sense ought to yield to Reason. Wherefore let us soar, if we can, to the heights of that Supreme Intelligence; for there Reason will see what in itself it cannot look upon; and that is in what way things whose occurrence is not certain may yet be seen in a sure and definite foreknowledge; and that this foreknowledge is not conjecture, but rather knowledge in its supreme simplicity, free of all limits and restriction."

In what divers shapes and fashions do the creatures great and small
Over wide earth's teeming surface skim, or scud, or walk, or crawl!
Some with elongated body sweep the ground, and, as they move,
Trail perforce with writhing belly in the dust a sinuous groove;
Some, on light wing upward soaring, swiftly do the winds divide,
And through heaven's ample spaces in free motion smoothly glide;
These earth's solid surface pressing, with firm paces onward rove,
Ranging through the verdant meadows, crouching in the woodland
  grove.
Great and wondrous is their variance! Yet in all the head low-bent
Dulls the soul and blunts the sense, though their forms be different.
Man alone, erect, aspiring, lifting his forehead to the skies,
And in upright posture steadfast seems earth's baseness to despise.
  If with earth not all besotted, to this parable give ear,
Thou whose gaze is fixed on heaven, who thy face on high dost
  rear:
Lift thy soul, too, heavenward; haply lest it stain its heavenly worth,
And thine eyes alone look upward, while thy mind cleaves to the
  earth!

"Since, then, as we lately proved, everything that is known is cognized not in accordance with its own nature, but in accordance with the nature of the faculty that comprehends it, let us now contemplate, as far as lawful, the character of the Divine essence, that we may be able to understand also the nature of its knowledge.

"God is eternal; in this judgment all rational beings agree. Let us, then, consider what eternity is. For this word carries with it a revelation alike of the Divine nature and of the Divine knowledge. Now, eternity is the possession of endless life whole and perfect at a single moment. What this is becomes more clear and manifest from a comparison with things temporal. For whatever lives in time is a present proceeding from the past to the future, and there is nothing set in time which can embrace the whole space of its life together. Tomorrow's state it grasps not yet, while it has already lost yesterday's; nay, even in the life of today ye live no longer than one brief transitory moment. Whatever, therefore, is subject to the condition of time, although, as Aristotle deemed of the world, it never have either beginning or end, and its life be stretched to the whole extent of time's infinity, it yet is not such as rightly to be thought eternal. For it does not include and embrace the whole space of infinite life at once, but has no present hold on things to come, not yet accomplished. Accordingly, that which includes and possesses the whole fullness of unending life at once, from which nothing future is absent, from which nothing past has escaped, this is rightly called eternal; this must of necessity be ever present to itself in full self-possession, and hold the infinity of movable time in an abiding present. Wherefore they deem not rightly who imagine that on Plato's principles the created world is made co-eternal with the Creator, because they are told that he believed the world to have had no beginning in time, and to be destined never to come to an end. For it is one thing for existence to be endlessly prolonged, which was what Plato ascribed to the world, another for the whole of an endless life to be embraced in the present, which is manifestly a property peculiar to the Divine mind. Nor need God appear earlier in mere duration of time to created things, but only prior in the unique simplicity of His nature. For the infinite progression of things in time copies this immediate existence in the present of the changeless life, and when it cannot succeed in equaling it, declines from movelessness into motion, and falls away from the simplicity of a perpetual present to the infinite duration of the future and the past; and since it cannot possess the whole fullness of its life together, for the very reason that in a manner it never ceases to be, it seems, up to a certain point, to rival that which it cannot complete and express by attaching itself indifferently to any present moment of time, however swift and brief; and since this bears some resemblance to that ever-abiding present, it bestows on everything to which it is assigned the semblance of existence. But since it cannot abide, it hurries along the infinite path of time, and the result has been that it continues by ceaseless movement the life the completeness of which it could not embrace while it stood still. So, if we are minded to give things their right names, we shall follow Plato in saying that God indeed is eternal, but the world everlasting.

"Since, then, every mode of judgment comprehends its objects conformably to its own nature, and since God abides for ever in an eternal present, His knowledge, also transcending all movement of time, dwells in the simplicity of its own changeless present, and, embracing the whole infinite sweep of the past and of the future, contemplates all that falls within its simple cognition as if it were now taking place. And therefore, if thou wilt carefully consider that immediate presentment whereby it discriminates all things, thou wilt more rightly deem it not foreknowledge as of something future, but knowledge of a moment that never passes. For this cause the name chosen to describe it is not prevision, but providence, because, since utterly removed in nature from things mean and trivial, its outlook embraces all things as from some lofty height. Why, then, dost thou insist that the things which are surveyed by the Divine eye are involved in necessity, whereas clearly men impose no necessity on things which they see? Does the act of vision add any necessity to things which thou seest before thy eyes?"

"Assuredly not."

"And yet, if we may without unfitness compare God's present and man's, just as ye see certain things in this your temporary present, so does He see all things in His eternal present. Wherefore this Divine anticipation changes not the natures and properties of things, and it beholds things present before it, just as they will hereafter come to pass in time. Nor does it confound things in its judgment, but in the one mental view distinguishes alike what will come necessarily and what without necessity. For even as ye, when at one and the same time ye see a man walking on the earth and the sun rising in the sky, distinguish between the two, though one glance embraces both, and judge the former voluntary, the latter necessary action: so also the Divine vision in its universal range of view does in no wise confuse the characters of the things which are present to its regard, though future in respect of time. Whence it follows that when it perceives that something will come into existence, and yet is perfectly aware that this is unbound by any necessity, its apprehension is not opinion, but rather knowledge based on truth. And if to this thou sayest that what God sees to be about to come to pass cannot fail to come to pass, and that what cannot fail to come to pass happens of necessity, and wilt tie me down to this word necessity, I will acknowledge that thou affirmest a most solid truth, but one which scarcely anyone can approach to who has not made the Divine his special study. For my answer would be that the same future event is necessary from the standpoint of Divine knowledge, but when considered in its own nature it seems absolutely free and unfettered. So, then, there are two necessities—one simple, as that men are necessarily mortal; the other conditioned, as that, if you know that someone is walking, he must necessarily be walking. For that which is known cannot indeed be otherwise than as it is known to be, and yet this fact by no means carries with it that other simple necessity. For the former necessity is not imposed by the thing's own proper nature, but by the addition of a condition. No necessity compels one who is voluntarily walking to go forward, although it is necessary for him to go forward at the moment of walking. In the same way, then, if Providence sees anything as present, that must necessarily be, though it is bound by no necessity of nature. Now, God views as present those coming events which happen of free will. These, accordingly, from the standpoint of the Divine vision are made necessary conditionally on the Divine cognizance; viewed, however, in themselves, they desist not from the absolute freedom naturally theirs. Accordingly, without doubt, all things will come to pass which God foreknows as about to happen, but of these certain proceed of free will; and though these happen, yet by the fact of their existence they do not lose their proper nature, in virtue of which before they happened it was really possible that they might not have come to pass.

"What difference, then, does the denial of necessity make, since, through their being conditioned by Divine knowledge, they come to pass as if they were in all respects under the compulsion of necessity? This difference, surely, which we saw in the case of the instances I formerly took, the sun's rising and the man's walking; which at the moment of their occurrence could not but be taking place, and yet one of them before it took place was necessarily obliged to be, while the other was not so at all. So likewise the things which to God are present without doubt exist, but some of them come from the necessity of things, others from the power of the agent. Quite rightly, then, have we said that these things are necessary if viewed from the standpoint of the Divine knowledge; but if they are considered in themselves, they are free from the bonds of necessity, even as everything which is accessible to sense, regarded from the standpoint of Thought, is universal, but viewed in its own nature particular. 'But,' thou wilt say, 'if it is in my power to change my purpose, I shall make void providence, since I shall perchance change something which comes within its foreknowledge.' My answer is: Thou canst indeed turn aside thy purpose; but since the truth of providence is ever at hand to see that thou canst, and whether thou dost, and whither thou turnest thyself, thou canst not avoid the Divine foreknowledge, even as thou canst not escape the sight of a present spectator, although of thy free will thou turn thyself to various action. Wilt thou, then, say: 'Shall the Divine knowledge be changed at my discretion, so that, when I will this or that, providence changes its knowledge correspondingly?' "

"Surely not."

"True, for the Divine vision anticipates all that is coming, and transforms and reduces it to the form of its own present knowledge, and varies not, as thou deemest, in its foreknowledge, alternating to this or that, but in a single flash it forestalls and includes thy mutations without altering. And this ever-present comprehension and survey of all things God has received, not from the issue of future events, but from the simplicity of His own nature. Hereby also is resolved the objection which a little while ago gave thee offense—that our doings in the future were spoken of as if supplying the cause of God's knowledge. For this faculty of knowledge, embracing all things in its immediate cognizance, has itself fixed the bounds of all things, yet itself owes nothing to what comes after.

"And all this being so, the freedom of man's will stands unshaken, and laws are not unrighteous, since their rewards and punishments are held forth to wills unbound by any necessity. God, who foreknoweth all things, still looks down from above, and the ever-present eternity of His vision concurs with the future character of all our acts, and dispenseth to the good rewards, to the bad punishments. Our hopes and prayers also are not fixed on God in vain, and when they are rightly directed cannot fail of effect. Therefore, withstand vice, practice virtue, lift up your souls to right hopes, offer humble prayers to Heaven. Great is the necessity of righteousness laid upon you if ye will not hide it from yourselves, seeing that all your actions are done before the eyes of a Judge who seeth all things."

FREEDOM AND NECESSITY | A. J. AYER

When I am said to have done something of my own free will it is implied that I could have acted otherwise; and it is only when it is believed that I could have acted otherwise that I am held to be morally responsible for what I have done. For a man is not thought to be morally responsible for an action that it was not in his power to avoid. But if human behavior is entirely governed by causal laws, it is not clear how any action that is done could ever have been avoided. It may be said of the agent that he would have acted otherwise if the causes of his action had been different, but they being what they were, it seems to follow that he was bound to act as he did. Now it is commonly assumed both that men are capable of acting freely, in the sense that is required to make them morally responsible, and that human behavior is entirely governed by causal laws: and it is the apparent conflict between these two assumptions that gives rise to the philosophical problem of the freedom of the will.

Confronted with this problem, many people will be inclined to agree with Dr. Johnson: "Sir, we *know* our will is free, and *there's* an end on't." But, while this does very well for those who accept Dr. Johnson's premise, it would hardly convince anyone who denied the freedom of the will. Certainly, if we do know that our wills are free, it follows that they are so. But the logical reply to this might be that since our wills are not free, it follows that no one can know that they are: so that if anyone claims, like

From A. J. Ayer, *Philosophical Essays* (New York, St. Martin's Press, Inc.; London, Macmillan & Co., Ltd.; 1954).

Dr. Johnson, to know that they are, he must be mistaken. What is evident, indeed, is that people often believe themselves to be acting freely; and it is to this "feeling" of freedom that some philosophers appeal when they wish, in the supposed interests of morality, to prove that not all human action is causally determined. But if these philosophers are right in their assumption that a man cannot be acting freely if his action is causally determined, then the fact that someone feels free to do, or not to do, a certain action does not prove that he really is so. It may prove that the agent does not himself know what it is that makes him act in one way rather than another: but from the fact that a man is unaware of the causes of his action, it does not follow that no such causes exist.

So much may be allowed to the determinist; but his belief that all human actions are subservient to causal laws still remains to be justified. If, indeed, it is necessary that every event should have a cause, then the rule must apply to human behavior as much as to anything else. But why should it be supposed that every event must have a cause? The contrary is not unthinkable. Nor is the law of universal causation a necessary presupposition of scientific thought. The scientist may try to discover causal laws, and in many cases he succeeds; but sometimes he has to be content with statistical laws, and sometimes he comes upon events which, in the present state of his knowledge, he is not able to subsume under any law at all. In the case of these events he assumes that if he knew more he would be able to discover some law, whether causal or statistical, which would enable him to account for them. And this assumption cannot be disproved. For however far he may have carried his investigation, it is always open to him to carry it further; and it is always conceivable that if he carried it further he would discover the connection which had hitherto escaped him. Nevertheless, it is also conceivable that the events with which he is concerned are not systematically connected with any others: so that the reason why he does not discover the sort of laws that he requires is simply that they do not obtain.

Now in the case of human conduct the search for explanations has not in fact been altogether fruitless. Certain scientific laws have been established; and with the help of these laws we do make a number of successful predictions about the ways in which different people will behave. But these predictions do not always cover every detail. We may be able to predict that in certain circumstances a particular man will be angry, without being able to prescribe the precise form that the expression of his anger will take. We may be reasonably sure that he will shout, but not sure how loud his shout will be, or exactly what words he will use. And it is only a small proportion of human actions that we are able to forecast even so precisely as this. But that, it may be said, is because we have not carried our investigations very far. The science of psychology is still in its infancy and, as it is developed, not only will more human actions be explained, but the explanations will go into greater detail. The ideal of complete explanation may never in fact be attained: but it is theoretically attainable. Well, this may be so: and certainly it is impossible to show a priori that it is not so: but equally it cannot be shown that it is. This will not, however, discourage the scientist who, in the field of human behavior, as elsewhere, will continue to formulate theories and test them by the facts. And in this he is justified. For since he has no reason a priori to admit that there is a limit to what he can discover, the fact that he also cannot be sure that there is no limit does not make it unreasonable for him to devise theories, nor, having devised them to try constantly to improve them.

But now suppose it to be claimed that, so far as men's actions are concerned, there is a limit: and that this limit is set by the fact of human freedom. An obvious objection is that in many cases in which a person feels himself to be free to do, or not to do, a certain action, we are even now able to explain, in causal terms, why it is that he acts as he does. But it might be argued that even if men are sometimes mistaken in believing that they act freely, it does not follow that they are always so mistaken. For it is not always the case that when a man believes that he has acted freely we are in fact able to account for his action in causal terms. A determinist would say that we should be able to account for it if we had more knowledge of the circumstances, and had been able to discover the appropriate natural laws. But until those discoveries have been made, this remains only a pious hope. And may it not be true that, in some cases at least, the reason why we can give no causal explanation is that no causal explanation is available; and that this is because the agent's choice was literally free, as he himself felt it to be?

The answer is that this may indeed be true, inasmuch as it is open to anyone to hold that no explanation is possible until some explanation is actually found. But even so it does not give the moralist what he wants. For he is anxious to show that men are capable of acting freely in order to infer that they can be morally responsible for what they do. But if it is a matter of pure chance that a man should act in one way rather than another, he may be free but he can hardly be responsible. And indeed when a man's actions seem to us quite unpredictable, when, as we say, there is no knowing what he will do, we do not look upon him as a moral agent. We look upon him rather as a lunatic.

To this it may be objected that we are not dealing fairly with the moralist. For when he makes it a condition of my being morally responsible that I should act freely, he does not wish to imply that it is purely a matter of chance that I act as I do. What he wishes to imply is that my actions are the result of my own free choice: and it is because they are the result of my own free choice that I am held to be morally responsible for them.

But now we must ask how it is that I come to make my choice. Either it is an accident that I choose to act as I do or it is not. If it is an accident, then it is merely a matter of chance that I did not choose otherwise; and if it is merely a matter of chance that I did not choose otherwise, it is surely irrational to hold me morally responsible for choosing as I did. But if it is not an accident that I choose to do one thing rather than another, then presumably there is some causal explanation of my choice: and in that case we are led back to determinism.

Again, the objection may be raised that we are not doing justice to the moralist's case. His view is not that it is a matter of chance that I choose to act as I do, but rather that my choice depends upon my character. Nevertheless he holds that I can still be free in the sense that he requires; for it is I who am responsible for my character. But in what way am I responsible for my character? Only, surely, in the sense that there is a causal connection between what I do now and what I have done in the past. It is only this that justifies the statement that I have made myself what I am: and even so this is an over-simplification, since it takes no account of the external influences to which I have been subjected. But, ignoring the external influences, let us assume that it is in fact the case that I have made myself what I am. Then it is still legitimate to ask how it is that I have come to make myself one sort of person rather than another. And if it be answered that it is a matter of my strength of will, we can put the same question in another form by asking how it is that my will has the strength that it has and not some other degree of strength. Once more, either it is an accident or it is not. If it is an accident, then by the same argument as before, I am not morally responsible, and if it is not an accident we are led back to determinism.

Furthermore, to say that my actions proceed from my character or, more colloquially, that I act in character, is to say that my behavior is consistent and to that extent predictable: and since it is, above all, for the actions that I perform in character that I am held to be morally responsible, it looks as if the admission of moral responsibility, so far from being incompatible with determinism, tends rather to presuppose it. But how can this be so if it is a necessary condition of moral responsibility that the person who is held responsible should have acted freely? It seems that if we are to retain this idea of moral responsibility, we must either show that men can be held responsible for actions which they do not do freely, or else find some way of reconciling determinism with the freedom of the will.

It is no doubt with the object of effecting this reconciliation that some philosophers have defined freedom as the consciousness of necessity. And by so doing they are able to say not only that a man can be acting freely when his action is causally determined, but even that his action must be causally determined for it to be possible for him to be acting freely. Nevertheless this definition has the serious disadvantage that it gives to the word "freedom" a meaning quite different from any that it ordinarily bears. It is indeed obvious that if we are allowed to give the word "freedom" any meaning that we please, we can find a meaning that will reconcile it with determinism: but this is no more a solution of our present problem than the fact that the word "horse" could be arbitrarily used to mean what is ordinarily meant by "sparrow" is a proof that horses have wings. For suppose that I am compelled by another person to do something "against my will." In that case, as the word "freedom" is ordinarily used, I should not be said to be acting freely: and the fact that I am fully aware of the constraint to which I am subjected makes no difference to the matter. I do not become free by becoming conscious that I am not. It may, indeed, be possible to show that my being aware that my action is causally determined is not incompatible with my acting freely: but it by no means follows that it is in this that my freedom consists. Moreover, I suspect that one of the reasons why people are inclined to define freedom as the consciousness of necessity is that they think that if one is conscious of necessity one may somehow be able to master it. But this is a fallacy. It is like someone's saying that he wishes he could see into the future, because if he did he would know what calamities lay in wait for him and so would be able to avoid them. But if he avoids the calamities then they don't lie in the future and it is not true that he foresees them. And similarly if I am able to master necessity, in the sense of escaping the operation of a necessary law, then the law in question is not necessary. And if the law is not necessary, then neither my freedom nor anything else can consist in my knowing that it is.

Let it be granted, then, that when we speak of reconciling freedom with determinism we are using the word "freedom" in an ordinary sense. It still remains for us to make this usage clear: and perhaps the best way to make it clear is to show what it is that freedom, in this sense, is contrasted with. Now we began with the assumption that freedom is contrasted with causality: so that a man cannot be said to be acting freely if his action is causally determined. But this assumption has led us into difficulties and I now wish to suggest that it is mistaken. For it is not, I think, causality that freedom is to be contrasted with, but constraint. And while it is true that being constrained to do an action entails being caused to do it, I shall try to show that the converse does not hold. I shall try to show that from the fact that my action is causally determined it does not necessarily follow that I am constrained to do it: and this is equivalent to saying that it does not necessarily follow that I am not free.

If I am constrained, I do not act freely. But in what circumstances can I legitimately be said to be constrained? An obvious instance is the case in which I am compelled by another person to do what he wants. In a case of this sort the compulsion need not be such as to deprive one of the power of choice. It is not required that the other person should have hypnotized me, or that he should make it physically impossible for me to go against his will. It is enough that he should induce me to do what he wants by making it clear to me that, if I do not, he will bring about some situation that I regard as even more undesirable than the consequences of the action that he wishes me to do. Thus, if the man points a pistol at my head I may still choose to disobey him: but this does not prevent its being true that if I do fall in with his wishes he can legitimately be said to have compelled me. And if the circumstances are such that no reasonable person would be expected to choose the other alternative, then the action that I am made to do is not one for which I am held to be morally responsible.

A similar, but still somewhat different, case is that in which another person has obtained an habitual ascendancy over me. Where this is so, there may be no question of my being induced to act as the other person wishes by being confronted with a still more disagreeable alternative: for if I am sufficiently under his influence this special stimulus will not be necessary. Nevertheless I do not act freely, for the reason that I have been deprived of the power of choice. And this means that I have acquired so strong a habit of obedience that I no longer go through any process of deciding whether or not to do what the other person wants. About other matters I may still deliberate; but as regards the fulfillment of this other person's wishes, my own deliberations have ceased to be a causal factor in my behavior. And it is in this sense that I may be said to be constrained. It is not, however, necessary that such constraint should take the form of subservience to another person. A kleptomaniac is not a free agent, in respect of his stealing, because he does not go through any process of deciding whether or not to steal. Or rather, if he does go through such a process, it is irrelevant to his behavior. Whatever he resolved to do, he would steal all the same. And it is this that distinguishes him from the ordinary thief.

But now it may be asked whether there is any essential difference between these cases and those in which the agent is commonly thought to be free. No doubt the ordinary thief does go through a process of deciding whether or not to steal, and no doubt it does affect his behavior. If he resolved to refrain from stealing, he could carry his resolution out. But if it be allowed that his making or not making this resolution is causally determined, then how can he be any more free than the kleptomaniac? It may be true that unlike the kleptomaniac he could refrain from stealing if he chose: but if there is a cause, or set of causes, which necessitate his choosing as he does, how can he be said to have the power of choice? Again, it may be true that no one now compels me to get up and walk across the room: but if my doing so can be causally explained in terms of my history or my environment, or whatever it may be, then how am I any more free than if some other person had compelled me? I do not have the feeling of constraint that I have when a pistol is manifestly pointed at my head; but the chains of causation by which I am bound are no less effective for being invisible.

The answer to this is that the cases I have mentioned as examples of constraint do differ from the others: and they differ just in the ways that I have tried to bring out. If I suffered from a compulsion neurosis, so that I got up and walked across the room, whether I wanted to or not, or if I did so because somebody else compelled me, then I should not be acting freely. But if I do it now, I shall be acting freely, just because these conditions do not obtain; and the fact that my action may nevertheless have a cause is, from this point of view, irrelevant. For it is not when my action has any cause at all, but only when it has a special sort of cause, that it is reckoned not to be free.

But here it may be objected that, even if this distinction corresponds to ordinary usage, it is still very irrational. For why should we distinguish, with regard to a person's freedom, between the operations of one sort of cause and those of another? Do not all causes equally necessitate? And is it not therefore arbitrary to say that a person is free when he is necessitated in one fashion but not when he is necessitated in another?

That all causes equally necessitate is indeed a tautology, if the word "necessitate" is taken merely as equivalent to "cause": but if, as the objection requires, it is taken as equivalent to "constrain" or "compel" then I do not think that this proposition is true. For all that is needed for one event to be the cause of another is that, in the given circumstances, the event which is said to be the effect would not have occurred if it had not been for the occurrence of the event which is said to be the cause, or vice versa, according as causes are interpreted as necessary, or sufficient, conditions: and this fact is usually deducible from some causal law which states that whenever an event of the one kind occurs then, given suitable conditions, an event of the other kind will occur in a certain temporal or spatio-temporal relation to it. In short, there is an invariable concomitance between the two classes of events; but there is no compulsion, in any but a metaphorical sense. Suppose, for example, that a psychoanalyst is able to account for some aspect of my behavior by referring it to some lesion that I suffered in my childhood. In that case, it may be said that my childhood experience, together with certain other events, necessitates my behaving as I do. But all that this involves is that it is found to be true in general that when people have had certain experiences as children, they subsequently behave in certain specifiable ways; and my case is just another instance of this general law. It is in this way indeed that my behavior is explained. But from the fact that my behavior is capable of being explained, in the sense that it can be subsumed under some natural law, it does not follow that I am acting under constraint.

If this is correct, to say that I could have acted otherwise is to say, first, that I should have acted otherwise if I had so chosen; secondly, that my action was voluntary in the sense in which the actions, say, of the kleptomaniac are not; and thirdly, that nobody compelled me to choose as

I did: and these three conditions may very well be fulfilled. When they are fulfilled, I may be said to have acted freely. But this is not to say that it was a matter of chance that I acted as I did, or, in other words, that my action could not be explained. And that my actions should be capable of being explained is all that is required by the postulate of determinism.

If more than this seems to be required it is, I think, because the use of the very word "determinism" is in some degree misleading. For it tends to suggest that one event is somehow in the power of another, whereas the truth is merely that they are factually correlated. And the same applies to the use, in this context, of the word "necessity" and even of the word "cause" itself. Moreover, there are various reasons for this. One is the tendency to confuse causal with logical necessitation, and so to infer mistakenly that the effect is contained in the cause. Another is the uncritical use of a concept of force which is derived from the primitive experiences of pushing and striking. A third is the survival of an animistic conception of causality, in which all causal relationships are modeled on the example of one person's exercising authority over another. As a result we tend to form an imaginative picture of an unhappy effect trying vainly to escape from the clutches of an overmastering cause. But, I repeat, the fact is simply that when an event of one type occurs, an event of another type occurs also, in a certain temporal or spatio-temporal relation to the first. The rest is only metaphor. And it is because of the metaphor, and not because of the fact, that we come to think that there is an antithesis between causality and freedom.

Nevertheless, it may be said, if the postulate of determinism is valid, then the future can be explained in terms of the past: and this means that if one knew enough about the past one would be able to predict the future. But in that case what will happen in the future is already decided. And how then can I be said to be free? What is going to happen is going to happen and nothing that I do can prevent it. If the determinist is right, I am the helpless prisoner of fate.

But what is meant by saying that the future course of events is already decided? If the implication is that some person has arranged it, then the proposition is false. But if all that is meant is that it is possible, in principle, to deduce it from a set of particular facts about the past, together with the appropriate general laws, then, even if this is true, it does not in the least entail that I am the helpless prisoner of fate. It does not even entail that my actions make no difference to the future: for they are causes as well as effects; so that if they were different their consequences would be different also. What it does entail is that my behavior can be predicted: but to say that my behavior can be predicted is not to say that I am acting under constraint. It is indeed true that I cannot escape my destiny if this is taken to mean no more than that I shall do what I shall do. But this is a tautology, just as it is a tautology that what is going to happen is going to happen. And such tautologies as these prove nothing whatsoever about the freedom of the will.

ABSURD FREEDOM | *ALBERT CAMUS*

Now the main thing is done, I hold certain facts from which I cannot separate. What I know, what is certain, what I cannot deny, what I cannot reject—this is what counts. I can negate everything of that part of me that lives on vague nostalgias, except this desire for unity, this longing to solve, this need for clarity and cohesion. I can refute everything in this world surrounding me that offends or enraptures me, except this chaos, this sovereign chance and this divine equivalence which springs from anarchy. I don't know whether this world has a meaning that transcends it. But I know that I do not know that meaning and that it is impossible for me just now to know it. What can a meaning outside my condition mean to me? I can understand only in human terms. What I touch, what resists me—that is what I understand. And these two certainties—my appetite for the absolute and for unity and the impossibility of reducing this world to a rational reasonable principle—I also know that I cannot reconcile them. What other truth can I admit without lying, without bringing in a hope I lack and which means nothing within the limits of my condition?

If I were a tree among trees, a cat among animals, this life would have a meaning, or rather this problem would not arise, for I should belong to this world. I should *be* this world to which I am now opposed by my whole consciousness and my whole insistence upon familiarity. This ridiculous reason is what sets me in opposition to all creation. I cannot cross it out with a stroke of the pen. What I believe to be true I must therefore preserve. What seems to me so obvious, even against me, I must support. And what constitutes the basis of that conflict, of that break between the world and my mind, but the awareness of it? If therefore I want to preserve it, I can through a constant awareness, ever revived, ever alert. This is what, for the moment, I must remember. At this moment the absurd, so obvious and yet so hard to win, returns to a man's life and finds its home there. At this moment, too, the mind can leave the arid, dried-up path of lucid effort. That path now emerges in daily life. It encounters the world of the anonymous impersonal pronoun "one," but henceforth man enters in with his revolt and his lucidity. He has forgotten how to hope. This hell of the present is his Kingdom at last. All problems recover their sharp edge. Abstract evidence retreats before the poetry of forms and colors. Spiritual conflicts become embodied and return to the abject and magnificent shelter of man's heart. None of them is settled. But all are transfigured. Is one going to die, escape by the leap, rebuild a mansion of ideas and forms to one's own

Reprinted from *The Myth of Sisyphus* by Albert Camus, trans. by Justin O'Brien, by permission of Alfred A. Knopf, Inc. Copyright 1955 by Alfred A. Knopf, Inc. The original was first published in 1942.

scale? Is one, on the contrary, going to take up the heart-rending and marvelous wager of the absurd? Let's make a final effort in this regard and draw all our conclusions. The body, affection, creation, action, human nobility will then resume their places in this mad world. At last man will again find there the wine of the absurd and the bread of indifference on which he feeds his greatness.

Let us insist again on the method: it is a matter of persisting. At a certain point on his path the absurd man is tempted. History is not lacking either religions or prophets, even without gods. He is asked to leap. All he can reply is that he doesn't fully understand, that it is not obvious. Indeed, he does not want to do anything but what he fully understands. He is assured that this is the sin of pride, but he does not understand the notion of sin; that perhaps hell is in store, but he has not enough imagination to visualize that strange future; that he is losing immortal life, but that seems to him an idle consideration. An attempt is made to get him to admit his guilt. He feels innocent. To tell the truth, that is all he feels—his irreparable innocence. This is what allows him everything. Hence, what he demands of himself is to live *solely* with what he knows, to accommodate himself to what is, and to bring in nothing that is not certain. He is told that nothing is. But this at least is a certainty. And it is with this that he is concerned: he wants to find out if it is possible to live *without appeal*.

Now I can broach the notion of suicide. It has already been felt what solution might be given. At this point the problem is reversed. It was previously a question of finding out whether or not life had to have a meaning to be lived. It now becomes clear, on the contrary, that it will be lived all the better if it has no meaning. Living an experience, a particular fate, is accepting it fully. Now, no one will live this fate, knowing it to be absurd, unless he does everything to keep before him that absurd brought to light by consciousness. Negating one of the terms of the opposition on which he lives amounts to escaping it. To abolish conscious revolt is to elude the problem. The theme of permanent revolution is thus carried into individual experience. Living is keeping the absurd alive. Keeping it alive is, above all, contemplating it. Unlike Eurydice, the absurd dies only when we turn away from it. One of the only coherent philosophical positions is thus revolt. It is a constant conformation between man and his own obscurity. It is an insistence upon an impossible transparency. It challenges the world anew every second. Just as danger provided man the unique opportunity of seizing awareness, so metaphysical revolt extends awareness to the whole of experience. It is that constant presence of man in his own eyes. It is not aspiration, for it is devoid of hope. That revolt is the certainty of a crushing fate, without the resignation that ought to accompany it.

This is where it is seen to what a degree absurd experience is remote from suicide. It may be thought that suicide follows revolt—but wrongly.

For it does not represent the logical outcome of revolt. It is just the contrary by the consent it presupposes. Suicide, like the leap, is acceptance at its extreme. Everything is over and man returns to his essential history. His future, his unique and dreadful future—he sees and rushes toward it. In its way, suicide settles the absurd. It engulfs the absurd in the same death. But I know that in order to keep alive, the absurd cannot be settled. It escapes suicide to the extent that it is simultaneously awareness and rejection of death. It is, at the extreme limit of the condemned man's last thought, that shoelace that despite everything he sees a few yards away, on the very brink of his dizzying fall. The contrary of suicide, in fact, is the man condemned to death.

That revolt gives life its value. Spread out over the whole length of a life, it restores its majesty to that life. To a man devoid of blinders, there is no finer sight than that of the intelligence at grips with a reality that transcends it. The sight of human pride is unequaled. No disparagement is of any use. That discipline that the mind imposes on itself, that will conjured up out of nothing, that face-to-face struggle have something exceptional about them. To impoverish that reality whose inhumanity constitutes man's majesty is tantamount to impoverishing him himself. I understand then why the doctrines that explain everything to me also debilitate me at the same time. They relieve me of the weight of my own life, and yet I must carry it alone. At this juncture, I cannot conceive that a skeptical metaphysics can be joined to an ethics of renunciation.

Consciousness and revolt, these rejections are the contrary of renunciation. Everything that is indomitable and passionate in a human heart quickens them, on the contrary, with its own life. It is essential to die unreconciled and not of one's own free will. Suicide is a repudiation. The absurd man can only drain everything to the bitter end, and deplete himself. The absurd is his extreme tension, which he maintains constantly by solitary effort, for he knows that in that consciousness and in that day-to-day revolt he gives proof of his only truth, which is defiance. This is a first consequence.

If I remain in that prearranged position which consists in drawing all the conclusions (and nothing else) involved in a newly discovered notion, I am faced with a second paradox. In order to remain faithful to that method, I have nothing to do with the problem of metaphysical liberty. Knowing whether or not man is free doesn't interest me. I can experience only my own freedom. As to it, I can have no general notions, but merely a few clear insights. The problem of "freedom as such" has no meaning. For it is linked in quite a different way with the problem of God. Knowing whether or not man is free involves knowing whether he can have a master. The absurdity peculiar to this problem comes from the fact that the very notion that makes the problem of freedom possible also takes away all its meaning. For in the presence of God there is less a problem of evil.

You know the alternative: either we are not free and God the all-powerful is responsible for evil. Or we are free and responsible but God is not all-powerful. All the scholastic subtleties have neither added anything to nor subtracted anything from the acuteness of this paradox.

This is why I cannot get lost in the glorification or the mere definition of a notion which eludes me and loses its meaning as soon as it goes beyond the frame of reference of my individual experience. I cannot understand what kind of freedom would be given me by a higher being. I have lost the sense of hierarchy. The only conception of freedom I can have is that of the prisoner or the individual in the midst of the State. The only one I know is freedom of thought and action. Now if the absurd cancels all my chances of eternal freedom, it restores and magnifies, on the other hand, my freedom of action. That privation of hope and future means an increase in man's availability.

Before encountering the absurd, the everyday man lives with aims, a concern for the future or for justification (with regard to whom or what is not the question). He weighs his chances, he counts on "someday," his retirement or the labor of his sons. He still thinks that something in his life can be directed. In truth, he acts as if he were free, even if all the facts make a point of contradicting that liberty. But after the absurd, everything is upset. That idea that "I am," my way of acting as if everything has a meaning (even if, on occasion, I said that nothing has)—all that is given the lie in vertiginous fashion by the absurdity of a possible death. Thinking of the future, establishing aims for oneself, having preferences—all this presupposes a belief in freedom, even if one occasionally ascertains that one doesn't feel it. But at that moment I am well aware that that higher liberty, that freedom *to be,* which alone can serve as a basis for a truth, does not exist. Death is there as the only reality. After death the chips are down. I am not even free, either, to perpetuate myself, but a slave, and, above all, a slave without hope of an eternal revolution, without recourse to contempt. And who without revolution and without contempt can remain a slave? What freedom can exist in the fullest sense without assurance of eternity?

But at the same time the absurd man realizes that hitherto he was bound to that postulate of freedom on the illusion of which he was living. In a certain sense, that hampered him. To the extent to which he imagined a purpose to his life, he adapted himself to the demands of a purpose to be achieved and became the slave of his liberty. Thus, I could not act otherwise than as the father (or the engineer or the leader of a nation, or the post-office sub-clerk) that I am preparing to be. I think I can choose to be that rather than something else. I think so unconsciously, to be sure. But at the same time I strengthen my postulate with the beliefs of those around me, with the presumptions of my human environment (others are so sure of being free, and that cheerful mood is so contagious!). However far one may remain from any presumption, moral or social, one is partly influenced by them and even, for the best among them (there are good and bad presumptions), one adapts one's life to them. Thus the absurd man realizes that he was not really free. To speak clearly, to the extent to which I hope, to which I worry about a truth that might be individual to me, about a way of being or creating, to the extent to which I arrange my life and prove thereby that I accept its having a meaning, I create for myself barriers between which I confine my life. I do like so many bureaucrats of the mind and heart who only fill me with disgust and whose only vice, I now see clearly, is to take man's freedom seriously.

The absurd enlightens me on this point: there is no future. Henceforth this is the reason for my inner freedom. I shall use two comparisons here. Mystics, to begin with, find freedom in giving themselves. By losing themselves in their god, by accepting his rules, they become secretly free. In sponstaneously accepted slavery they recover a deeper independence. But what does that freedom mean? It may be said, above all, that they *feel* free with regard to themselves, and not so much free as liberated. Likewise, completely turned toward death (taken here as the most obvious absurdity), the absurd man feels released from everything outside that passionate attention crystallizing in him. He enjoys a freedom with regard to common rules. It can be seen at this point that the initial themes of existential philosophy keep their entire value. The return to consciousness, the escape from everyday sleep represent the first steps of absurd freedom. But it is existential *preaching* that is alluded to, and with it that spiritual leap which basically escapes consciousness. In the same way (this is my second comparison) the slaves of antiquity did not belong to themselves. But they knew that freedom which consists in not feeling responsible. Death, too, has patrician hands which, while crushing, also liberate.

Losing oneself in that bottomless certainty, feeling henceforth sufficiently remote from one's own life to increase it and take a broad view of it—this involves the principle of a liberation. Such new independence has a definite time limit, like any freedom of action. It does not write a check on eternity. But it takes the place of the illusions of *freedom,* which all stopped with death. The divine availability of the condemned man before whom the prison doors open in a certain early dawn, that unbelievable disinterestedness with regard to everything except for the pure flame of life—it is clear that death and the absurd are here the principles of the only reasonable freedom: that which a human heart can experience and live. This is a second consequence. The absurd man thus catches sight of a burning and frigid, transparent and limited universe in which nothing is possible but everything is given, and beyond which all is collapse and nothingness. He can then decide to accept such a universe and draw from it his strength, his refusal to hope, and the unyielding evidence of a life without consolation. . . .

Thus I draw from the absurd three consequences, which are my revolt, my freedom, and my passion. By the mere activity of consciousness I transform into a rule of life what was an invitation to death—and I refuse suicide. I know, to be sure, the dull resonance that vibrates throughout these days. Yet I have but a word to say: that it is necessary. When Nietzsche writes: "It clearly seems that the chief thing in heaven and on earth is to *obey* at length and in a single direction: in the long run there results something for which it is worth the trouble of living on this earth as, for example, virtue, art, music, the dance, reason, the mind—something that transfigures, something delicate, mad, or divine," he elucidates the rule of a really distinguished code of ethics. But he also points the way of the absurd man. Obeying the flame is both the easiest and the hardest thing to do. However, it is good for man to judge himself occasionally. He is alone in being able to do so.

"Prayer," says Alain, "is when night descends over thought." "But the mind must meet the night," reply the mystics and the existentials. Yes, indeed, but not that night that is born under closed eyelids and through the mere will of man—dark, impenetrable night that the mind calls up in order to plunge into it. If it must encounter a night, let it be rather that of despair, which remains lucid—polar night, vigil of the mind, whence will arise perhaps that white and virginal brightness which outlines every object in the light of the intelligence. At that degree, equivalence encounters passionate understanding. Then it is no longer even a question of judging the existential leap. It resumes its place amid the age-old fresco of human attitudes. For the spectator, if he is conscious, that leap is still absurd. In so far as it thinks it solves the paradox, it reinstates it intact. On this score, it is stirring. On this score, everything resumes its place and the absurd world is reborn in all its splendor and diversity.

But it is bad to stop, hard to be satisfied with a single way of seeing, to go without contradiction, perhaps the most subtle of all spiritual forces. The preceding merely defines a way of thinking. But the point is to live.

THE GRAND INQUISITOR | *FYODOR DOSTOEVSKI*

"Even this must have a preface—that is, a literary preface," laughed Ivan, "and I am a poor hand at making one. You see, my action takes place in the sixteenth century, and at that time, as you probably learnt at school, it was customary in poetry to bring down heavenly powers on earth. Not to speak of Dante, in France, clerks, as well as the monks in the monasteries,

From Fyodor Dostoevski, *The Brothers Karamazov,* trans. by Constance Garnett (New York, Modern Library, Inc., 1937).

used to give regular performances in which the Madonna, the saints, the angels, Christ, and God Himself were brought on the stage. In those days it was done in all simplicity. In Victor Hugo's 'Notre Dame de Paris' an edifying and gratuitous spectacle was provided for the people in the Hotel de Ville of Paris in the reign of Louis XI in honor of the birth of the dauphin. It was called *Le bon jugement de la très sainte et gracieuse Vierge Marie,* and she appears herself on the stage and pronounces her *bon jugement.* Similar plays, chiefly from the Old Testament, were occasionally performed in Moscow too, up to the times of Peter the Great. But besides plays there were all sorts of legends and ballads scattered about the world, in which the saints and angels and all the powers of Heaven took part when required. In our monasteries the monks busied themselves with translating, copying, and even composing such poems—and even under the Tatars. There is, for instance, one such poem (of course, from the Greek), 'The Wanderings of Our Lady through Hell,' with descriptions as bold as Dante's. Our Lady visits Hell, and the Archangel Michael leads her through the torments. She sees the sinners and their punishment. There she sees among others one noteworthy set of sinners in a burning lake; some of them sink to the bottom of the lake so that they can't swim out, and 'these God forgets'—an expression of extraordinary depth and force. And so Our Lady, shocked and weeping, falls before the throne of God and begs for mercy for all in Hell—for all she has seen there, indiscriminately. Her conversation with God is immensely interesting. She beseeches Him, she will not desist, and when God points to the hands and feet of her Son, nailed to the Cross, and asks, 'How can I forgive His tormentors?' she bids all the saints, all the martyrs, all the angels and archangels to fall down with her and pray for mercy on all without distinction. It ends by her winning from God a respite of suffering every year from Good Friday till Trinity day, and the sinners at once raise a cry of thankfulness from Hell, chanting, 'Thou art just, O Lord, in this judgment.' Well, my poem would have been of that kind if it had appeared at that time. He comes on the scene in my poem, but He says nothing, only appears and passes on. Fifteen centuries have passed since He promised to come in His glory, fifteen centuries since His prophet wrote, 'Behold, I come quickly'; 'Of that day and that hour knoweth no man, neither the Son, but the Father,' as He Himself predicted on earth. But humanity awaits him with the same faith and with the same love. Oh, with greater faith, for it is fifteen centuries since man has ceased to see signs from Heaven.

> *No signs from Heaven come today*
> *To add to what the heart doth say.*

There was nothing left but faith in what the heart doth say. It is true there were many miracles in those days. There were saints who performed miraculous cures; some holy people, according to their biographies, were visited by the Queen of Heaven herself. But the devil did not slumber, and doubts were already arising among men of the truth of these miracles. And just then there appeared in the north of Germany a terrible new heresy. 'A huge star like to a torch' (that is, to a church) 'fell on the sources of the waters and they became bitter.' These heretics began blasphemously deny- ing miracles. But those who remained faithful were all the more ardent in their faith. The tears of humanity rose up to Him as before, awaited His coming, loved Him, hoped for Him, yearned to suffer and die for Him as before. And so many ages mankind had prayed with faith and fervor, 'O Lord our God, hasten Thy coming,' so many ages called upon Him, that in His infinite mercy He deigned to come down to His servants. Before that day He had come down, He had visited some holy men, martyrs and hermits, as is written in their 'Lives.' Among us, Tyutchev, with absolute faith in the truth of his words, bore witness that

> Bearing the Cross, in slavish dress,
> Weary and worn, the Heavenly King
> Our mother, Russia, came to bless,
> And through our land went wandering.

And that certainly was so, I assure you.

"And behold, He deigned to appear for a moment to the people, to the tortured, suffering people, sunk in iniquity, but loving Him like children. My story is laid in Spain, in Seville, in the most terrible time of the In- quisition, when fires were lighted every day to the glory of God, and 'in the splendid *auto da fé* the wicked heretics were burnt.' Oh, of course, this was not the coming in which He will appear according to His promise at the end of time in all His heavenly glory, and which will be sudden 'as lightning flashing from east to west.' No, He visited His children only for a moment, and there where the flames were crackling round the heretics. In His infinite mercy He came once more among men in that human shape in which He walked among men for three years fifteen centuries ago. He came down to the 'hot pavement' of the southern town in which on the day before almost a hundred heretics had, *ad majorem gloriam Dei,* been burnt by the cardinal, the Grand Inquisitor, in a magnificent *auto da fé,* in the presence of the king, the court, the knights, the cardinals, the most charm- ing ladies of the court, and the whole population of Seville.

"He came softly, unobserved, and yet, strange to say, every one recog- nized Him. That might be one of the best passages in the poem. I mean, why they recognized Him. The people are irresistibly drawn to Him, they surround Him, they flock about Him, follow Him. He moves silently in their midst with a gentle smile of infinite compassion. The sun of love burns in His heart, light and power shine from His eyes, and their radiance, shed on the people, stirs their hearts with responsive love. He holds out His hands to them, blesses them, and a healing virtue comes from contact with Him, even with His garments. An old man in the crowd, blind from childhood, cries out, 'O Lord, heal me and I shall see Thee!' and, as it were, scales fall from his eyes and the blind man sees Him. The crowd weeps and kisses the earth under His feet. Children throw flowers before Him, sing, and cry hosannah. 'It is He—it is He!' all repeat. 'It must be He, it can be no one but Him!' He stops at the steps of the Seville cathedral at the moment when the weeping mourners are bringing in a little open white coffin. In it lies a child of seven, the only daughter of a prominent citizen. The dead child lies hidden in flowers. 'He will raise your child,' the crowd shouts to the weeping mother. The priest, coming to meet the coffin, looks perplexed, and frowns, but the mother of the dead child throws herself at His feet with a wail. 'If it is Thou, raise my child!' she cries, holding out her hands to Him. The procession halts, the coffin is laid on the steps at His feet. He looks with compassion, and His lips once more softly pronounce, 'Maiden, arise!' and the maiden arises. The little girl sits up in the coffin and looks round, smiling with wide-open wondering eyes, holding a bunch of white roses they had put in her hand.

"There are cries, sobs, confusion among the people, and at that moment the cardinal himself, the Grand Inquisitor, passes by the cathedral. He is an old man, almost ninety, tall and erect, with a withered face and sunken eyes, in which there is still a gleam of light. He is not dressed in his gorgeous cardinal's robes, as he was the day before, when he was burning the enemies of the Roman Church—at the moment he was wearing his coarse, old, monk's cassock. At a distance behind him come his gloomy assistants and slaves and the 'holy guard.' He stops at the sight of the crowd and watches it from a distance. He sees everything; he sees them set the coffin down at His feet, sees the child rise up, and his face darkens. He knits his thick gray brows and his eyes gleam with a sinister fire. He holds out his finger and bids the guards take Him. And such is his power, so completely are the people cowed into submission and trembling obedience to him, that the crowd immediately make way for the guards, and in the midst of deathlike silence they lay hands on Him and lead Him away. The crowd instantly bows down to the earth, like one man, before the old inquisitor. He blesses the people in silence and passes on. The guards lead their prisoner to the close, gloomy vaulted prison in the ancient palace of the Holy Inquisition and shut Him in it. The day passes and is followed by the dark, burning 'breathless' night of Seville. The air is 'fragrant with laurel and lemon.' In the pitch darkness the iron door of the prison is suddenly opened and the Grand Inquisitor himself comes in with a light in his hand. He is alone; the door is closed at once behind him. He stands in the doorway and for a minute or two gazes into His face. At last he goes up slowly, sets the light on the table and speaks.

" 'Is it Thou? Thou?' but receiving no answer, he adds at once, 'Don't answer, be silent. What canst Thou say, indeed? I know too well what Thou wouldst say. And Thou hast no right to add anything to what Thou hadst said of old. Why, then, art Thou come to hinder us? For Thou hast come to hinder us, and Thou knowest that. But dost Thou know what will be tomorrow? I know not who Thou art and care not to know whether it is Thou or only a semblance of Him, but tomorrow I shall condemn Thee and burn Thee at the stake as the worst of heretics. And the very people who have today kissed Thy feet, tomorrow at the faintest sign from me will rush to heap up the embers of Thy fire. Knowest Thou that? Yes, maybe Thou knowest it,' he added with thoughtful penetration, never for a moment taking his eyes off the Prisoner."

"I don't quite understand, Ivan. What does it mean?" Alyosha, who had been listening in silence, said with a smile. "Is it simply a wild fantasy, or a mistake on the part of the old man—some impossible *quidproquo*?"

"Take it as the last," said Ivan, laughing, "if you are so corrupted by modern realism and can't stand anything fantastic. If you like it to be a case of mistaken identity, let it be so. It is true," he went on, laughing, "the old man was ninety, and he might well be crazy over his set idea. He might have been struck by the appearance of the Prisoner. It might, in fact, be simply his ravings, the delusion of an old man of ninety, over-excited by the *auto da fé* of a hundred heretics the day before. But does it matter to us after all whether it was a mistake of identity or a wild fantasy? All that matters is that the old man should speak out, should speak openly of what he has thought in silence for ninety years."

"And the Prisoner too is silent? Does He look at him and not say a word?"

"That's inevitable in any case," Ivan laughed again. "The old man has told Him He hasn't the right to add anything to what He has said of old. One may say it is the most fundamental feature of Roman Catholicism, in my opinion at least. 'All has been given by Thee to the Pope,' they say, 'and all, therefore, is still in the Pope's hands, and there is no need for Thee to come now at all. Thou must not meddle for the time, at least.' That's how they speak and write too—the Jesuits, at any rate. I have read it myself in the works of their theologians. 'Hast Thou the right to reveal to us one of the mysteries of that world from which Thou hast come?' my old man asks Him, and answers the question for Him. 'No, Thou hast not; that Thou mayest not add to what has been said of old, and mayest not take from men the freedom which Thou didst exalt when Thou wast on earth. Whatsoever Thou revealest anew will encroach on men's freedom of faith; for it will be manifest as a miracle, and the freedom of their faith was dearer to Thee than anything in those days fifteen hundred years ago. Didst Thou not often say then, "I will make you free"? But now Thou hast seen these "free" men,' the old man adds suddenly, with a pensive smile. 'Yes, we've paid dearly for it,' he goes on, looking sternly at Him, 'but at last we have completed that work in Thy name. For fifteen centuries we have been wrestling with Thy freedom, but now it is ended and over for good. Dost Thou not believe that it's over for good? Thou lookest meekly at me and deignest not even to be wroth with me. But let me tell Thee that now, today, people are more persuaded than ever that they have perfect freedom, yet they have brought their freedom to us and laid it humbly at our feet. But that has been our doing. Was this what Thou didst? Was this Thy freedom?' "

"I don't understand again," Alyosha broke in. "Is he ironical, is he jesting?"

"Not a bit of it! He claims it as a merit for himself and his Church that at last they have vanquished freedom and have done so to make men happy. 'For now' (he is speaking of the Inquistion, of course) 'for the first time it has become possible to think of the happiness of men. Man was created a rebel; and how can rebels be happy? Thou wast warned,' he says to Him. 'Thou hast had no lack of admonitions and warnings, but Thou didst not listen to those warnings; Thou didst reject the only way by which men might be made happy. But, fortunately, departing Thou didst hand on the work to us. Thou hast promised, Thou hast established by Thy word. Thou has given to us the right to bind and to unbind, and now, of course, Thou canst not think of taking it away. Why, then, hast Thou come to hinder us?' "

"And what's the meaning of 'no lack of admonitions and warnings'?" asked Alyosha.

"Why, that's the chief part of what the old man must say.

" 'The wise and dread spirit, the spirit of self-destruction and nonexistence,' the old man goes on, 'the great spirit talked with Thee in the wilderness, and we are told in the books that he "tempted" Thee. Is that so? And could anything truer be said than what he revealed to Thee in three questions and what Thou didst reject, and what in the books is called "the temptation"? And yet if there has ever been on earth a real stupendous miracle, it took place on that day, on the day of the three temptations. The statement of those three questions was itself the miracle. If it were possible to imagine simply for the sake of argument that those three questions of the dread spirit had perished utterly from the books, and that we had to restore them and to invent them anew, and to do so had gathered together all the wise men of the earth—rulers, chief priests, learned men, philosophers, poets—and had set them the task to invent three questions, such as would not only fit the occasion, but express in three words, three human phrases, the whole future history of the world and of humanity—dost Thou believe that all the wisdom of the earth united could have invented anything in depth and force equal to the three questions which were actually put to Thee then by the wise and mighty spirit in the wilderness? From those questions alone, from the miracle of their statement, we can see that we have here to do not with the fleeting human intelligence, but with the absolute and eternal. For in those three questions the whole subsequent history of mankind is, as it were, brought together into one whole, and foretold, and in them are united all the unsolved historical contradictions of human nature. At the time it could not be so clear, since the future was unknown; but now that fifteen hundred years have passed, we see that everything in those three questions was so justly divined and foretold, and has been so truly fulfilled, that nothing can be added to them or taken from them.

" 'Judge Thyself who was right—Thou or he who questioned Thee then? Remember the first question; its meaning, in other words, was this: "Thou wouldst go into the world, and art going with empty hands, with some promise of freedom which men in their simplicity and their natural unruliness cannot even understand, which they fear and dread—for nothing has ever been more insupportable for a man and a human society than freedom. But seest Thou these stones in this parched and barren wilderness? Turn them into bread, and mankind will run after Thee like a flock of sheep, grateful and obedient, though for ever trembling, lest Thou withdraw Thy hand and deny them Thy bread." But Thou wouldst not deprive man of freedom and didst reject the offer, thinking, what is that freedom worth, if obedience is bought with bread? Thou didst reply that man lives not by bread alone. But dost Thou know that for the sake of that earthly bread the spirit of the earth will rise up against Thee and will strive with Thee and overcome Thee, and all will follow him, crying, "Who can compare with this beast? He has given us fire from heaven!" Dost Thou know that the ages will pass, and humanity will proclaim by the lips of their sages that there is no crime, and therefore no sin; there is only hunger? "Feed men, and then ask of them virtue!" that's what they'll write on the banner, which they will raise against Thee, and with which they will destroy Thy temple. Where Thy temple stood will rise a new building; the terrible tower of Babel will be built again, and though, like the one of old, it will not be finished, yet Thou mightest have prevented that new tower and have cut short the sufferings of men for a thousand years; for they will come back to us after a thousand years of agony with their tower. They will seek us again, hidden underground in the catacombs, for we shall be again persecuted and tortured. They will find us and cry to us, "Feed us, for those who have promised us fire from heaven haven't given it!" And then we shall finish building their tower, for he finishes the building who feeds them. And we alone shall feed them in Thy name, declaring falsely that it is in Thy name. Oh, never, never can they feed themselves without us! No science will give them bread so long as they remain free. In the end they will lay their freedom at our feet, and say to us, "Make us your slaves, but feed us." They will understand themselves, at last, that freedom and bread enough for all are inconceivable together, for never, never will they be able to share between them! They will be convinced, too, that they can never be free, for they are weak, vicious, worthless and rebellious. Thou didst promise them the bread of Heaven, but, I repeat again, can it compare with earthly bread in the eyes of the weak, ever sinful and ignoble race of man? And if for the sake of the bread of Heaven thousands and tens of thousands shall follow Thee, what is to become of the millions and tens of thousands of millions of creatures who will not have the strength to forego the earthly bread for the sake of the heavenly? Or dost Thou care only for the tens of thousands of the great and strong, while the millions, numerous as the sands of the sea, who are weak but love Thee, must exist only for the sake of the great and strong? No, we care for the weak too. They are sinful and rebellious, but in the end they too will become obedient. They will marvel at us and look on us as gods, because we are ready to endure the freedom which they have found so dreadful and to rule over them—so awful it will seem to them to be free. But we shall tell them that we are Thy servants, and rule them in Thy name. We shall deceive them again, for we will not let Thee come to us again. That deception will be our suffering, for we shall be forced to lie.

" 'This is the significance of the first question in the wilderness, and this is what Thou hast rejected for the sake of that freedom which Thou hast exalted above everything. Yet in this question lies hid the great secret of this world. Choosing "bread," Thou wouldst have satisfied the universal and everlasting craving of humanity—to find some one to worship. So long as man remains free he strives for nothing so incessantly and so painfully as to find some one to worship. But man seeks to worship what is established beyond dispute, so that all men would agree at once to worship it. For these pitiful creatures are concerned not only to find what one or the other can worship, but to find something that all would believe in and worship; what is essential is that all may be *together* in it. This craving for community of worship is the chief misery of every man individually and of all humanity from the beginning of time. For the sake of common worship they've slain each other with the sword. They have set up gods and challenged one another, "Put away your gods and come and worship ours, or we will kill you and your gods!" And so it will be to the end of the world, even when gods disappear from the earth; they will fall down before idols just the same. Thou didst know, Thou couldst not but have known, this fundamental secret of human nature, but Thou didst reject the one infallible banner which was offered Thee to make all men bow down to Thee alone—the banner of earthly bread; and Thou hast rejected it for the sake of freedom and the bread of Heaven. Behold what Thou didst further. And all again in the name of freedom! I tell Thee that man is tormented by no greater anxiety than to find some one quickly to whom he can hand over that gift of freedom with which the ill-fated creature is born. But only one who can appease their conscience can take over their freedom. In bread there was offered Thee an invincible banner; give bread, and man will worship Thee, for nothing is more certain than bread. But if some one else gains possession of his conscience—oh! then he will cast away Thy bread and follow after him who has ensnared his conscience. In that Thou wast right. For the secret of man's being is not only to live but to have something to live for. Without a stable conception of the object of life, man would not consent to go on living, and would rather destroy himself than remain on earth, though he had bread in abundance. That is true. But what happened? Instead of taking men's freedom from them, Thou didst make it greater than ever! Didst Thou forget that man prefers peace, and even death, to freedom of choice in the knowledge of good and evil? Nothing is more seductive for man than his freedom of conscience, but nothing is a greater cause of suffering. And behold, instead of giving a firm foundation for setting the conscience of man at rest for ever, Thou didst choose all that is exceptional, vague and enigmatic; Thou didst choose what was utterly beyond the strength of men, acting as though Thou didst not love them at all—Thou who didst come to give Thy life for them! Instead of taking possession of men's freedom, Thou didst increase it, and burdened the spiritual kingdom of mankind with its sufferings for ever. Thou didst desire man's free love, that he should follow Thee freely, enticed and taken captive by Thee. In place of the rigid ancient law, man must hereafter with free heart decide for himself what is good and what is evil, having only Thy image before him as his guide. But didst Thou not know he would at last reject even Thy image and Thy truth, if he is weighed down with the fearful burden of free choice? They will cry aloud at last that the truth is not in Thee, for they could not have been left in greater confusion and suffering than Thou hast caused, laying upon them so many cares and unanswerable problems.

" 'So that, in truth, Thou didst Thyself lay the foundation for the destruction of Thy kingdom, and no one is more to blame for it. Yet what was offered Thee? There are three powers, three powers alone, able to conquer and to hold captive for ever the conscience of these impotent rebels for their happiness—those forces are miracle, mystery and authority. Thou hast rejected all three and hast set the example for doing so. When the wise and dread spirit set Thee on the pinnacle of the temple and said to Thee, "If Thou wouldst know whether Thou art the Son of God then cast Thyself down, for it is written: the angels shall hold him up lest he fall and bruise himself, and Thou shalt know then whether Thou art the Son of God and shalt prove then how great is Thy faith in Thy Father." But Thou didst refuse and wouldst not cast Thyself down. Oh! of course, Thou didst proudly and well, like God; but the weak, unruly race of men, are they gods? Oh, Thou didst know then that in taking one step, in making one movement to cast Thyself down, Thou wouldst be tempting God and have lost all Thy faith in Him, and wouldst have been dashed to pieces against that earth which Thou didst come to save. And the wise spirit that tempted Thee would have rejoiced. But I ask again, are there many like Thee? And couldst Thou believe for one moment that men, too, could face such a temptation? Is the nature of men such, that they can reject miracle, and at the great moments of their life, the moments of their deepest, most agonizing spiritual difficulties, cling only to the free verdict of the heart? Oh, Thou didst know that Thy deed would be recorded in books, would be handed down to remote times and the utmost ends of the earth, and Thou didst hope that man, following Thee, would cling to God and not ask for a miracle. But Thou didst not know that when man rejects miracle he rejects God too; for man seeks not so much God as the miraculous. And as man cannot bear to be without the miraculous, he will create new miracles of his own for himself, and will worship deeds of sorcery and witchcraft, though he might be a hundred times over a rebel, heretic and infidel. Thou didst not come down from the Cross when they shouted to Thee, mocking and reviling Thee, "Come down from the cross and we will believe that Thou art He." Thou didst not come down, for again Thou wouldst not enslave man by a miracle, and didst crave faith given freely, not based on miracle. Thou didst crave for free love and not the base raptures of the slave before the might that has overawed him for ever. But Thou didst think too highly of men therein, for they are slaves, of course, though rebellious by nature. Look round and judge; fifteen centuries have passed, look upon them. Whom hast Thou raised up to Thyself? I swear, man is weaker and baser by nature than Thou hast believed him! Can he, can he do what Thou didst? By showing him so much respect, Thou didst, as it were, cease to feel for him, for Thou didst ask far too much from him—Thou who hast loved him more than Thyself! Respecting him less, Thou wouldst have asked less of him. That would have been more like love, for his burden would have been lighter. He is weak and vile. What though he is everywhere now rebelling against our power, and proud of his rebellion? It is the pride of a child and a schoolboy. They are little children rioting and barring out the teacher at school. But their childish delight will end; it will cost them dear. They will cast down temples and drench the earth with blood. But they will see at last, the foolish children, that, though they are rebels, they are impotent rebels, unable to keep up their own rebellion. Bathed in their foolish tears, they will recognize at last that He who created them rebels must have meant to mock at them. They will say this in despair, and their utterance will be a blasphemy which will make them more unhappy still, for man's nature cannot bear blasphemy, and in the end always avenges it on itself. And so unrest, confusion and unhappiness—that is the present lot of man after Thou didst bear so much for their freedom! Thy great prophet tells in vision and in image, that he saw all those who took part in the first resurrection and that there were of each tribe twelve thousand. But if there were so many of them, they must have been not men but gods. They had borne Thy cross, they had endured scores of years in the barren, hungry wilderness, living upon locusts and roots—and Thou mayest indeed point with pride at those children of freedom, of free love, of free and splendid sacrifice for Thy name. But remember that they were only some thousands; and what of the rest? And how are the other weak ones to blame, because they could not endure what the strong have endured? How is the weak soul to blame that it is unable to receive such terrible gifts? Canst Thou have simply come to the elect and for the elect? But if so, it is a mystery and we cannot understand it. And if it is a mystery, we too have a right to preach a mystery, and to teach them that it's not the free judgment of their hearts, not love that matters, but a mystery which they must follow blindly, even against their conscience. So we have done. We have corrected Thy work and have founded it upon *miracle, mystery* and *authority*. And men rejoiced that they were again led like sheep, and that the terrible gift that had brought them such suffering, was, at last, lifted from their hearts. Were we right teaching them this? Speak! Did we not love mankind, so meekly acknowledging their feebleness, lovingly lightening their burden, and permitting their weak nature even sin with our sanction? Why hast Thou come now to hinder us? And why dost Thou look silently and searchingly at me with Thy mild eyes? Be angry. I don't want Thy love, for I love Thee not. And what use is it for me to hide anything from Thee? Don't I know to Whom I am speaking? All that I can say is known to Thee already. And is it for me to conceal from Thee our mystery? Perhaps it is Thy will to hear it from my lips. Listen, then. We are not working with Thee, but with *him*—that is our mystery. It's long—eight centuries—since we have been on *his* side and not on Thine. Just eight centuries ago, we took from him what Thou didst reject with scorn, that last gift he offered Thee, showing Thee all the kingdoms of the earth. We took from him Rome and the sword of Caesar, and proclaimed ourselves sole rulers of the earth, though hitherto we have not been able to complete our work. But whose fault is that? Oh, the work is only beginning, but it has begun. It has long to await completion and the earth has yet much to suffer, but we shall triumph and shall be Caesars, and then we shall plan the universal happiness of man. But Thou mightest have taken even then the sword of Caesar. Why didst Thou reject that last gift? Hadst Thou accepted that last counsel of the mighty spirit, Thou wouldst have accomplished all that man seeks on earth—that is, some one to worship, some one to keep his conscience, and some means of uniting all in one unanimous and harmonious ant-heap, for the craving for universal unity is the third and last anguish of men. Mankind as a whole has always striven to organize a universal state. There have been many great nations with great histories, but the more highly they were developed the more unhappy they were, for they felt more acutely than other people the craving for worldwide union. The great conquerors, Timours and Ghengis-Khans, whirled like hurricanes over the face of the earth striving to subdue its people, and they too were but the unconscious expression of the same craving for universal unity. Hadst Thou taken the world and Caesar's purple, Thou wouldst have founded the universal state and have given universal peace. For who can rule men if not he who holds their conscience and their bread in his hands? We have taken the sword of Caesar, and in taking it, of course, have rejected Thee and followed *him*. Oh, ages are yet to come of the confusion of free thought, of their science and cannibalism. For having begun to build their tower of Babel without us, they will end, of course, with cannibalism. But then the beast will crawl to us and lick our feet and spatter them with tears of blood. And we shall sit upon the beast and raise the cup, and on it will be written, "Mystery." But then, and only then, the reign of peace and happiness will come for men. Thou art proud of Thine elect, but Thou hast only the elect, while we give rest to all. And besides, how many of those elect, those mighty ones who could become elect, have grown weary waiting for Thee, and have transferred and will transfer the powers of their spirit and the warmth of their heart to the other camp, and end by raising their *free* banner against Thee. Thou didst Thyself lift up that banner. But with us all will be happy and will no more rebel nor destroy one another as under Thy freedom. Oh, we shall persuade them that they will only become free when they renounce their freedom to us and submit to us. And shall we be right or shall we be lying? They will be convinced that we are right, for they will remember the horrors of slavery and confusion to which Thy freedom brought them. Freedom, free thought and science, will lead them into such straits and will bring them face to face with such marvels and insoluble mysteries, that some of them, the fierce and rebellious, will destroy themselves, others, rebellious but weak, will destroy one another, while the rest, weak and unhappy, will crawl fawning to our feet and whine to us: "Yes, you were right, you alone possess His mystery, and we come back to you, save us from ourselves!"

" 'Receiving bread from us, they will see clearly that we take the bread made by their hands from them, to give it to them, without any miracle. They will see that we do not change the stones to bread, but in truth they will be more thankful for taking it from our hands than for the bread itself! For they will remember only too well that in old days, without our help, even the bread they made turned to stones in their hands, while since they have come back to us, the very stones have turned to bread in their hands. Too, too well they know the value of complete submission! And until men know that, they will be unhappy. Who is most to blame for their not knowing it, speak? Who scattered the flock and sent it astray on unknown paths? But the flock will come together again and will submit once more, and then it will be once for all. Then we shall give them the quiet humble happiness of weak creatures such as they are by nature. Oh, we shall persuade them at last not to be proud, for Thou didst lift them up and thereby taught them to be proud. We shall show them that they are weak, that they are only pitiful children, but that childlike happiness is the sweetest of all. They will become timid and will look to us and huddle close to us in fear, as chicks to the hen. They will marvel at us and will be awe-stricken before us, and will be proud at our being so powerful and clever, that we have been able to subdue such a turbulent flock of thousands of millions. They will tremble impotently before our wrath, their minds will grow fearful, they will be quick to shed tears like women and children, but they will be just as ready at a sign from us to pass to laughter and rejoicing, to happy mirth and childish song. Yes, we shall set them to work, but in their leisure hours we shall make their life like a child's game, with children's songs and innocent dance. Oh, we shall allow them even sin, they are weak and helpless, and they will love us like children because we allow them to sin. We shall tell them that every sin will be expiated, if it is done with our permission, that we allow them to sin because we love them, and the punishment for these sins we take upon ourselves. And we shall take it upon ourselves, and they will adore us as their saviors who have taken on themselves their sins before God. And they will have no secrets from us. We shall allow or forbid them to live with their wives and mistresses, to have or not to have children—according to whether they have been obedient or disobedient—and they will submit to us gladly and cheerfully. The most painful secrets of their conscience, all, all they will bring to us, and we shall have an answer for all. And they will be glad to believe our answer, for it will save them from the great anxiety and terrible agony they endure at present in making a free decision for themselves. And all will be happy, all the millions of creatures except the hundred thousand who rule over them. For only we, we who guard the mystery, shall be unhappy. There will be thousands of millions of happy babes, and a hundred thousand sufferers who have taken upon themselves the curse of the knowledge of good and evil. Peacefully they will die, peacefully they will expire in Thy name, and beyond the grave they will find nothing but death. But we shall keep the secret, and for their happiness we shall allure them with the reward of heaven and eternity. Though if there were anything in the other world, it certainly would not be for such as they. It is prophesied that Thou wilt come again in victory, Thou wilt come with Thy chosen, the proud and strong, but we will say that they have only saved themselves, but we have saved all. We are told that the harlot who sits upon the beast, and holds in her hands the *mystery,* shall be put to shame, that the weak will rise up again, and will rend her royal purple and will strip naked her loathsome body. But then I will stand up and point out to Thee the thousand millions of happy children who have known no sin. And we who have taken their sins upon us for their happiness will stand up before Thee and say: "Judge us if Thou canst and darest." Know that I fear Thee not. Know that I too have been in the wilderness, I too have lived on roots and locusts, I too prized the freedom with which Thou hast blessed men, and I too was striving to stand among Thy elect, among the strong and powerful, thirsting "to make up the number." But I awakened and would not serve madness. I turned back and jointed the ranks of those *who have corrected Thy work.* I left the proud and went back to the humble, for the happiness of the humble. What I say to Thee will come to pass, and our dominion will be built up. I repeat, tomorrow Thou shalt see that obedient flock who at a sign from me will hasten to heap up the hot cinders about the pile on which I shall burn Thee for coming to hinder us. For if any one has ever deserved our fires, it is Thou. Tomorrow I shall burn Thee. *Dixi.'* "

THE TRADITIONAL OR THE NEW IN ARCHITECTURE?

"SO WHY NOT AT ONCE destroy undesirable things ... make an end of them?"

Frank Lloyd Wright asked this question with specific reference to the bric-a-brac which cluttered up most Victorian homes. But he might well have been speaking for the whole movement in modern architecture, which, if it did not literally wish to tear apart old buildings, saw little to recommend their styles to modern architects, little to make the twentieth century preserve the modes of the past. The controversy which rebels such as Wright stimulated over fifty years ago may seem to have died down: most of the schools of architecture have virtually discarded traditional styles, and even the general public no longer winces at the sight of a house by Frank Lloyd Wright or a structure like the United Nations Building. This surface peacefulness is deceptive, however, if it suggests that the rebels have won an unqualified victory, for a large proportion of actual building today is still imitative. Even the low, ranch-style houses which fill our suburbs are a compromise between traditional design and a modern style which has itself become a cliché, detached from its original surroundings. If this fact suggests that "modern" architecture is a critical success, but a public failure, then the controversy is still a live and meaningful one, and well worth examining.

The examination is troublesome, right from the start. The query of Wright's quoted above sounds reasonable enough except for the word "undesirable," which indicates that the controversy is at bottom one of preference, or taste. Statements such as "the classical style is the greatest style" frequently mean little more than "I prefer the classical style." Writers on architecture naturally support their preferences in numerous ways, in attempting to convince readers that design should take certain directions. They may appeal to natural preferences; that is, they may claim that certain forms are inherently more appealing to human beings than other forms. They may cite the importance of tradition and habit in governing tastes. They may attempt to show that architecture depends upon the materials available and should arise honestly from them. They may set nature up as the proper model of art. And finally, they will almost certainly stress the importance of human needs—physical and emotional—in architecture ("form follows function" has been one battle cry of modern builders). All these "proofs" are valid within certain limits, but they all rest on a base of ethical or esthetic preference.

Therefore these arguments are partly or largely attempts to influence the feelings and tastes of readers, an activity which is not a hopeless one, but does involve skills in expression other than those of logic. The writer must somehow appeal to emotion, since he is dealing with emotionally held convictions. He must attempt to transmit not only his preference, but also some of the intensity with which he feels it. His writing is therefore likely to differ somewhat from formal "proving," in that some of his weapons of argument will be purely persuasive, or emotive. He may lean heavily on rhetorical devices of one sort or another, and buttress his logic with feeling, in order to communicate, in addition to his view, the importance of that view.

Of the seven writers represented here only Le Corbusier (Charles-Edouard Jeanneret, 1887-   ), a Swiss architect who has been one of the leaders of the modern movement, is primarily a practitioner. But the others, as critics and teachers, are quite as much committed to their views, and quite as deeply involved as Le Corbusier in the issues at hand. The main scholarly efforts of Geoffrey Scott (1885-1929) were in another field; he was a prominent British authority on Boswell and Johnson. The other two English writers, however, are both committed to architecture as a profession. W. A. Eden has taught design in the Universities of London and of Liverpool. James M. Richards (1907-   ) is an editor of two architectural periodicals. His collaborator, Elizabeth Mock, has been on the staff of the Museum of Modern Art in New York and has written and edited several books. Sheldon Cheney (1886-   ) is an American drama- and art-critic, as well as a writer on architecture. The third American, Ralph Adams Cram (1863-1942), combined building and teaching. A champion of the Gothic style, he designed the graduate school at Princeton University and other well-known buildings.

THE GOTHIC QUEST | RALPH ADAMS CRAM

It is sometimes acknowledged by those who are seeking for the reason why this country, so brilliant in many ways, should be so barren artistically, that it looks as though we had lost the artistic spirit. This is simply stating the condition in another way. Of course we have lost the artistic spirit, but

From Ralph Adams Cram, *The Gothic Quest* (New York, Baker & Taylor Company, 1907).

why have we lost it, what has been the cause? This is a far more pertinent question, and is one more worthy of consideration. Were the answer to this sought seriously, one or two things would, I think, become apparent. In the first place, we should find that all the art that exists in the world at the present day, all the art, that is, down to the sixteenth century, the art of Egypt, Assyria, India, Japan, the art of every country in Europe, whether created under pagan or Christian influence, all this treasure of wondrous art owes its existence to one motive, one impulse—the passion of worship, the serving of God.

In the second place, we should find that all the Christian art that exists, whether it be architecture, sculpture, painting, music, craftsmanship, owes its life and its glory to one power, the Catholic Church, and we should find also that, although Protestantism has held dominion in Germany, England, Scandinavia, and the United States for several hundred years, it has produced no vital art of any kind; such sporadic instances as have occurred possessing no connection whatever with the dominant form of theology. We should also find that the decadence of art has been almost unbroken since the period called the Reformation. I argue nothing from these facts, I wish only to call attention to them.

In speaking of art in this way, I do not mean that no art whatever has existed in the Christian world since the sixteenth century. That would be grotesque. I only mean that instinctive art, that universal impulse which glorified the humblest kitchen utensil in classical or Medieval or Renaissance times, has disappeared; the instinctive art work of the people is now bad; such art as there is, is the possession of a very few divinely inspired or specially trained men, and if anything good is to be done, application must be made to a "professional artist." Let me call your attention to the fact that for the first time since history began, this thing can be said, the *first* time in thousands of years. Is not this ominous? I think so, and I think also that it is significant.

Now, is it merely a coincidence that this condition should obtain most vigorously in the country which has seen the growth of the most unreligious, materialistic system of life that the century has produced? Is it merely a coincidence that, in the period in the past with which ours has the most in common—the decadence of Rome—we should find what comes nearest to being a downfall of art almost equal to our own?

For myself, I doubt if coincidences occur very frequently. I am disposed to think that there is a close connection between the religious troubles of the sixteenth century and the artistic troubles that followed. In other words, that the substitution of meeting-houses for churches may perhaps lie somewhere near the source of our artistic decadence.

But however this may be, you will not, I am sure, dispute the statement that the era of ugly religious architecture and barren religious art began with the period of the Reformation. The documents in the case prove this.

The enthusiastic reformers in England showed their devotion to God by first burning, plundering, and razing to the ground the monasteries and many of the churches, by dashing into ruin all the statues and carving and the splendid painted glass, and by melting down all the gold and silver vessels, and appropriating all the jewels which had been consecrated to God, and then proceeded to turn the pitiful ruins of once holy and glorious fabrics into whitewashed shells, or to build very terrible structures, square, empty, and forbidding, full of the blind terror of fanatical ignorance and the pharisaic contentment of incorrigible bigotry. And so they have remained until a few years ago, when suddenly rose that most extraordinary cry, "Go to, let us have some High Art." Then the bareness vanished, and that very inartistic man, the architect, plunged in a riot of esthetic debauchery. The whole world was ransacked for motives and schemes, and now in this year of grace there is not a Christian style, or pagan either, that has not been dragged from its grave by this curious resurrection, and made a by-word and a reproach in the sight of men; and yet we have not a real, vital, spontaneous, genuine church in the whole fantastic pageant, not one that says, "I was built in the sweat of the brows of men who loved God, and who brought here of their best that they might do honor to Him with all the beauty and treasure that lay in their hands."

We build churches enough, too many; but how often do they rise, in their outward effect, above the impression of a religious club, or a monument to the wealth of a special parish? Money in plenty is lavished on them, and with a dim idea that by such expenditure a beautiful result will be obtained. But is it? All that glitters is not art. The church may be carved into rivalry with a Japanese ivory ball, it may be painted with all the colors in the paint box, all the patterns in Owen Jones' Grammar of Ornament. Its windows may blaze with intolerable light, it may have a spire taller than the pinnacles of Cologne, and yet it may not possess one breath of art, one line of beauty.

As a matter of fact it mostly does not. Take the ordinary Roman Catholic, Methodist, Baptist structure: can it do otherwise than make the judicious grieve? Its building committee has worn itself out trying to get something that would be "rich and elegant"; its architect has ransacked two hemispheres for inspiration; and the result?—a self-conscious, affected, bizarre monument to the impotence of the age. And here again, for the mental temper, for the spiritual condition which makes this tyranny of the ignorant architect complete, which makes possible a serene contentment in the minds of the public with the grotesque monstrosities we all know, we are justified in looking to the meeting-house builders. Driven by the fancied teachings of a woefully misread and misunderstood Bible, and by the natural reaction from the dominant religious system, weakened and corrupted by the recrudescence of paganism, they ruthlessly stamped out of their souls every vestige of the love of beauty and art, not only the love of the fine arts themselves, but of all beauty of thought, and feeling, and emotion; and as a result they gave to their children lives to which the artistic idea was utterly foreign, lives from which instinctive love of beauty and appreciation thereof had been banished forever.

Now, this is a very serious matter, for the absence of all worship of beauty, of artistic impulse from a people, means far more than that these people will suffer from the loss of one of the ornaments of civilization: it means that their whole mental temper will be changed, that the results will be seen in every domain of life, that the absence of a saving impulse will be felt in the counting-room and stock exchange, as well as in the studio and picture gallery; in the police courts and the reformatory institutions as well as in the churches; in the whole system of living of a nation, not alone in the productions of the painter and the architect. It means that our minds will become narrow, material, unbeautiful; our religion, if it continues, crude, hard, unlovely. It means that we shall flaunt and worship a barren and fictitious civilization from which all elements of real civilization have fled. So high I put art and the influence of beauty and the just love of beauty, and if you want my justification for stating these things in this fashion I must refer you, not to the histories of the past two thousand years, for they are apt not to be historical, but to the *history* of that time.

If we can look on art and the love of beauty in this light, as one of the greatest engines of true civilization in the world, the fact that this age, so far as the United States is concerned, is essentially an age without art, must seem almost the most shocking and ominous fact that we have to confront, and it will also seem that, although the revision of the tariff, and the free coinage of silver, and the income tax are matters of vital importance, there is another that, judged by the standard of actual necessity, becomes in a way the most important and imperative of all, and that is this: how can we change this from an art-less to an art-full age, how can we restore to the people the soul that is gone out of them?

To this question the ordinary reply would be, "By increasing the number and broadening the influence of our schools of art; by multiplying art lectures and strengthening art museums." At the risk of ridicule I am going to confess to a belief that, so far as changing the temper of the time is concerned, or the increasing of the love of art, the worship of beauty, and the production of artistic and beautiful objects, the influence of the accepted agencies is either nothing or of a nature to be deplored. In almost every instance the essence of art and the secret of beauty are utterly ignored, and therefore we confront the phenomenon of the most elaborate system of art education ever evolved, existing simultaneously with the most crudely inartistic conditions that have ever been known. If we are to possess a civilization which is *worth* expressing itself artistically, we must do something besides establish art-lectureships, we must change the conditions of life, the temper of the people; and we must begin by substituting churches for meeting-houses.

For art and true religion are united by the bond of absolute life. Each strives for, each achieves the same end, the realization of the ideal, the idealization of the real. Art trying to express through the mystic and sensuous and spiritual symbolism of color, and form, and light and shade, and musical tone, emotions and impressions otherwise inexpressible; religion striving to voice the same things through the mediumship of art, to sway men's minds and exalt their spiritual consciousness by means of the subtle influence of solemn architecture, splendid color, majestic and sonorous music, stately, wonderful ritual. And each succeeds, or has succeeded in the past, and the reason for the present lamentable failure lies, very largely, I believe, in their separation, in the fact that art has been banished from the Church, the Church from art, until so long a time has passed that each has forgotten the former union. Now our churches here in America have become either bare, ugly meeting-houses, destitute of symbolism either in ritual or ornamentation, or else vulgar and offensive exhibitions of tawdry wealth, striving to purchase for itself the covering of art wherewith to hide its nakedness, failing utterly, only attaining a measure of popular astonishment and gaping admiration; unsatisfactory substitutes indeed for the devotion, and reverence, and awe, which once raised with loving hands mighty temples acceptable to God. Not only this has happened, the direct result of the substitution of the meeting-house for the house of God, but also the destruction of significant and beautiful ceremonial. . . .

Why are churches so almost universally bad as they are now? I think it is, first of all, because during the last two hundred years we have mixed up the functions of a church very seriously, and to the extreme injury of our churches, and of the Church as well.

For sixteen hundred years, from the day of the Apostles until that of Luther, a church had three aspects: first, that of a Tabernacle, an earthly abode of God; second, that of a Sanctuary, a place for the solemnizing of the Church's Sacraments; third, that of a meeting-house. So long as this threefold function was recognized, so long as a church was built in worship, made glorious with all the treasure that might be lavished by devoted hands, so long as it was in very truth a Gate of Heaven where man and the invisible saints and angels met in the awful presence of God—just so long did it remain a true church, the spiritual home of a community. And while this age endured, the church took another aspect, that of a great, silent, irresistible agency for the influencing of the souls of men through the ministry of exalted art. But the moment misguided persons forgot that a church was anything but a meeting-house where any one of an hundred different sets of men, each supremely satisfied with its own trivial version of the teachings of the Bible, might gather to feed its self-satisfaction with the agreeable discourses of its chosen mouthpiece, the moment meeting-houses, with their bare and forbidding walls and their rented pews, their glorified pulpits and insignificant Communion tables, and their atmosphere of a country parlor, open one day in the week, locked on the others—the moment these curious structures took the place of real churches, that moment the dark ages of Christian art began; that moment the world which accepted the new religion was absolved from its allegiance to Christianity, and though strenuous efforts were made to browbeat the nations into terrified subservience, though a more rigid union of Church and state was attempted than had ever been before, the effort was in vain, the legal connection snapped, the spiritual tie was dissolved, and henceforth religion was a thing apart, and, as a result, art vanished in large measure from the daily life of the people.

Now how shall we be saved from the body of this death, for saved we must be if art holds anything of the position I have claimed for it, and if through noble religious architecture may lie in part the way of our deliverance from materialism and skepticism and the ills we are now heir to? In the first place, I should say, we must begin a great movement which can best be called a beginning of the Restoration—for that I am sure is the name by which the next epoch of the world will be known. We must return to the ancient idea of the functions of a church, and the order of their precedence. We must cease looking on the house of God as a Sunday club; we must give as men gave in the fourteenth century; we must give with the spirit with which they gave, for if we give from motives of ostentation, emulation, self-glorification, our work will be as hideous as it is now, and we ourselves shall be deservedly damned. We must build churches which are, first of all, *churches,* and not meeting-houses. We must realize that art is the servant of God, and that its place is in the church rather than in our art museums. We must make our churches all glorious within, with all the pomp and majesty of wonderful art, and if we honestly try to do this, and with an honorable motive, we shall soon have enough good art to do it with. Finally, we must abandon forever our modern theories of church planning. We must go back to medieval times, back to the day when Luther killed all art but music in Germany, when Calvin killed all righteous art in France, and when Henry VIII killed all art of any kind whatever in England, and take up the work where then it was broken off. We must realize that the first desideratum of a church is not that from every seat therein the occupant may be able to see the pulpit without turning his head, but that, so far as man is concerned, it is that he shall be filled with the righteous sense of awe and mystery and devotion. And if this result may be obtained by massive columns and piers, by dim light and narrow, shadowy aisles, by cavernous vaults and soaring arches, then these things we must have, even if some people have to sit behind pillars, and even if we can't see every change in facial expression of the preacher.

For by this course we may be enabled at last to combat the destructive influences of contemporary social and political, artistic and religious conditions, to mitigate in a measure their malign effects on life, and so lay the foundations for the restoration of the noble things that we have rejected, win back the old lamps we have foolishly sold for new. We may cover the land with ateliers and studios, add to the intolerable din the clamor of innumerable "teachers of art," and our labor will be wasted. Only through a new vision of the mystery of life and its duties, only through a restored knowledge of the essentials of this world, can beauty and art be brought back to a people that knows them not. Their return will be the evidence of the victory of the Restoration, showing that the fight is won, and that the reign of materialism is at an end. With the dawn of this new life, art and religion will stand side by side, invincible in union, the fruit of victory, the guaranty of its endurance.

THE ARCHITECTURE OF HUMANISM | GEOFFREY SCOTT

1)

Architecture, simply and immediately perceived, is a combination, revealed through light and shade, of spaces, masses, and of lines. These few elements make the core of architectural experience: an experience which the literary fancy, the historical imagination, the casuistry of conscience and the calculations of science, cannot constitute or determine, though they may encircle and enrich. How great a chaos must ensue when our judgments of architecture are based upon these secondary and encircling interests the previous chapters have suggested, and the present state of architecture might confirm. It remains to be seen how far these central elements—these spaces, masses and lines—can provide a ground for our criticism that is adequate or secure.

The spaces, masses and lines of architecture, as perceived, are appearances. We may infer from them further facts about a building which are not perceived; facts about construction, facts about history or society. But the art of architecture is concerned with their immediate aspect; it is concerned with them as appearances.

And these appearances are related to human functions. Through these spaces we can conceive ourselves to move; these masses are capable, like ourselves, of pressure and resistance; these lines, should we follow or describe them, might be our path and our gesture.

Conceive for a moment a "top-heavy" building or an "ill-proportioned" space. No doubt the degree to which these qualities will be found offensive will vary with the spectator's sensibility to architecture; but

From Geoffrey Scott, *The Architecture of Humanism* (London, Constable & Co., Ltd., 1924).

sooner or later, if the top-heaviness or the disproportion is sufficiently pronounced, every spectator will judge that the building or space is ugly,
and experience a certain discomfort from their presence. So much will be
conceded.

Now what is the cause of this discomfort? It is often suggested that the
top-heavy building and the cramped space are ugly because they suggest
the idea of instability, the idea of collapse, the idea of restriction, and
so forth. But these *ideas* are not in themselves disagreeable. We read the
definition of such words in a dictionary with equanimity, yet the definition, if it is a true one, will have conveyed the idea of restriction or
collapse. Poetry will convey the ideas with vividness. Yet we experience
from it no shadow of discomfort. On the contrary, Hamlet's "cabined,
cribbed, confined" delights us, for the very reason that the idea is vividly
conveyed. Nor does Samson painfully trouble *our* peace, when

> *Those two massie Pillars*
> *With horrible convulsion to and fro*
> *He tugged, he shook, till down they came and drew*
> *The whole roof after them with burst of thunder*
> *Upon the heads of all who sate beneath.*

Clearly, then, our discomfort in the presence of such architecture cannot
spring merely from the idea of restriction or instability.

But neither does it derive from an actual weakness or restriction in
our immediate experience. It is disagreeable to have our movements
thwarted, to lose strength or to collapse; but a room fifty feet square and
seven feet high does not restrict our actual movements, and the sight of
a granite building raised (apparently) on a glass shop-front does not cause
us to collapse.

There is instability—or the appearance of it; but it is in the building.
There is discomfort, but it is in ourselves. What then has occurred? The
conclusion seems evident. The concrete spectacle has done what the mere
idea could not: it has stirred our physical memory. It has awakened in
us, not indeed an actual state of instability or of being overloaded, but
that condition of spirit which in the past has belonged to our actual
experiences of weakness, of thwarted effort or incipient collapse. We have
looked at the building and identified ourselves with its apparent state.
We have transcribed ourselves into terms of architecture.

But the "states" in architecture with which we thus identify ourselves
need not be actual. The actual pressures of a spire are downward; yet
no one speaks of a "sinking" spire. A spire, when well designed, appears
—as common language testifies—to soar. We identify ourselves, not with
its actual downward pressure, but its apparent upward impulse. So, too,
by the same excellent—because unconscious—testimony of speech, arches
"spring," vistas "stretch," domes "swell," Greek temples are "calm," and

baroque façades "restless." The whole of architecture is, in fact, unconsciously invested by us with human movement and human moods. Here,
then, is a principle complementary to the one just stated. *We transcribe
architecture into terms of ourselves.*

This is the humanism of architecture. The tendency to project the image
of our functions into concrete forms is the basis, for architecture, of creative design. The tendency to recognize, in concrete forms, the image of
those functions is the true basis, in its turn, of critical appreciation. . . .

III)

But, how far, it is natural to ask, can such an explanation be carried?
Granting its truth, can we establish its sufficiency? Our pleasure in architectural form seems manifold. Can one such principle explain it? A full
answer to this question is perhaps only to be earned in the long process
of experiment and verification which the actual practice of architecture
entails. How minutely Humanism can enter into the detail of architecture,
how singularly it may govern its main design, could not, in any case,
be demonstrated without a mass of instances and a free use of illustration.
A study of these, drawn from Renaissance architecture, could form the
matter of another volume. But the main divisions of the subject—space,
mass, line and coherence, with their more obvious applications—may here
be singled out.

The principle is perhaps most clearly to be recognized in *line.* Lines of
one sort or another always form a large part of what is visually presented
to us in architecture. Now in most cases, when we bring our attention
to bear on one of these lines, its whole extent is not seen with absolute
simultaneity; we "follow" it with our eye. The mind passes successively
over points in space, and that gives us movement. But when we have
got movement we have got expression. For our own movements are the
simplest, the most instinctive, and the most universal forms of expression
that we know. Identified with ourselves, movement has meaning; and line,
through movement, becomes a gesture, an expressive act. Thus, for example, the curves of a volute are recognized as bold or weak, tense or lax,
powerful, flowing, and so forth. It is by such terms as these, in fact, that
we praise or condemn them. But we must recognize them as having these
qualities by unconscious analogy with our own movements, since it is
only in our own bodies that we know the relation of the line—or movement—to the feeling it denotes.

Movement is most obviously communicated by curved lines; but it is
conveyed also by lines which are straight. No doubt the straight lines
which bound the rectangular forms of architecture, its doors and its
windows, are chiefly realized, not as sensations in themselves, but as definitions of the shapes they enclose. Their chief use is to determine the
position of a patch upon a given surface; and the esthetic value of this

will be considered in a moment. But any emphasis upon vertical lines immediately awakens in us a sense of upward direction, and lines which are spread—horizontal lines—convey suggestions of rest. Thus the architect has already, in the lines of a design, a considerable opportunity. He controls the path of the eye; the path we follow is our movement; movement determines our mood.

But line is not the sole means of affecting our sense of movement. Space, also, controls it. Spaces may be in two dimensions or in three. We may consider the simpler case first. A large part of architectural design consists in the arrangement of forms upon surfaces, that is to say, within spaces. The part which movement here plays will be clear from a common instance. A man who is arranging pictures on a wall will say that one is "crowded" or "lost" in the space it occupies, that it "wants to come" up or down. That is to say, the position of forms upon a surface is realized in terms of our physical consciousness. If a certain patch "wants to come" down, we ourselves, by our unconscious imitation of it, have the sense of a perpetually thwarted instinct of movement. The arrangement of the scheme is imperfectly *humanized*. It may be picturesque, it may be useful, it may be mechanically superior; but it is at variance with our ideal movement. And beauty of disposition in architecture, like beauty of line, arises from our own physical experience of easy movement in space.

But not all movements are pleasant or unpleasant in themselves; the majority of them are indifferent. Nevertheless, a *series* of suggested movements, in themselves indifferent, may awaken in us an expectancy and consequent desire of some further movement; and if the spaces of architecture are so arranged as first to awaken and then falsify this expectation, we have ugliness. For example, if a design be obviously based on symmetry and accustoms us to a rhythm of equal movements—as in the case of a typical eighteenth-century house—and one of the windows were placed out of line and lower than the rest, we should feel discomfort. The offense would lie against our sense of a movement, which, when it reaches that point of a design, is compelled to drop out of step and to dip against its will. Yet the relation of the window to its immediately surrounding forms might not in itself be necessarily ugly.

A converse instance may here be given. Classic design—the style which in Italy culminated in Bramante—aims at authority, dignity, and peace. It does this by conveying at every point a sense of equipoise. The forms are so adjusted amid the surrounding contours as to *cancel all suggested movement:* they are placed, as it were, each at the center of gravity within the space, and our consciousness is thus sustained at a point of rest. But the baroque architects rejected this arrangement. They employed space adjustments which, *taken in isolation,* would be inharmonious. In their church façades, as Wölfflin has pointed out, they quite deliberately congested their forms. The lower windows are jammed between the pilasters on either side; they are placed above the center of gravity; they give the sense of lateral pressure and upward movement. This, taken alone, would leave us perpetually in suspense. But in the upper part of the design our expectancy is satisfied; the upward movement is allowed to disperse itself in greater areas of lateral space, and makes its escape in a final flourish of decorative sculpture; or it is laid to rest by an exaggerated emphasis upon the downward movement of the crowning pediment and on the horizontals of the cornice. Here, therefore, a movement, which in the midst of a Bramantesque design would be destructive and repugnant, is turned to account and made the basis of a more dramatic, but not less satisfying treatment, the motive of which is not peace, but energy.

iv)

But besides spaces which have merely length and breadth—surfaces, that is to say, at which we look—architecture gives us spaces of three dimensions in which we stand. And here is the very center of architectural art. The functions of the arts, at many points, overlap; architecture has much that it holds in common with sculpture, and more that it shares with music. But it has also its peculiar province and a pleasure which is typically its own. It has the monopoly of space. Architecture alone of the Arts can give space its full value. It can surround us with a void of three dimensions; and whatever delight may be derived from that is the gift of architecture alone. Painting can depict space; poetry, like Shelley's, can recall its image; music can give us its analogy; but architecture deals with space directly; it uses space as a material and sets us in the midst.

Criticism has singularly failed to recognize this supremacy in architecture of spatial values. The tradition of criticism is practical. The habits of our mind are fixed on matter. We talk of what occupies our tools and arrests our eyes. Matter is fashioned; space comes. Space is "nothing"—a mere negation of the solid. And thus we come to overlook it.

But though we may overlook it, space affects us and can control our spirit; and a large part of the pleasure we obtain from architecture—a pleasure which seems unaccountable, or for which we do not trouble to account—springs in reality from space. Even from a utilitarian point of view, space is logically our end. To enclose a space is the object of building; when we build we do but detach a convenient quantity of space, seclude it and protect it, and all architecture springs from that necessity. But esthetically space is even more supreme. The architect models in space as a sculptor in clay. He designs his space as a work of art; that is, he attempts through its means to excite a certain mood in those who enter it.

What is his method? Once again his appeal is to Movement Space, in fact, is liberty of movement. That is its value to us, and as such it enters our physical consciousness. We adapt ourselves instinctively to the spaces in which we stand, project ourselves into them, fill them ideally with our movements. Let us take the simplest of instances. When we enter the end of a nave and find ourselves in a long vista of columns, we begin, almost under compulsion, to walk forward: the character of the space demands it. Even if we stand still, the eye is drawn down the perspective, and we, in imagination, follow it. The space has suggested a movement. Once this suggestion has been set up, everything which accords with it will seem to assist us; everything which thwarts it will appear impertinent and ugly. We shall, moreover, require something to close and satisfy the movement—a window, for example, or an altar; and a blank wall, which would be inoffensive as the termination of a symmetrical space, becomes ugly at the end of an emphasized axis, simply because movement without motive and without climax contradicts our physical instincts: it is not humanized.

A symmetrical space, on the other hand, duly proportioned to the body —(for not *all* symmetrical spaces will be beautiful)—invites no movement in any one direction more than another. This gives us equipoise and control; our consciousness returns constantly to the center, and again is drawn from the center equally in all directions. But we possess in ourselves a physical memory of just the movement. For we make it every time we draw breath. Spaces of such a character, therefore, obtain an additional entry to our sense of beauty through this elementary sensation of expansion. Unconscious though the process of breathing habitually is, its vital value is so emphatic that any restriction of the normal function is accompanied by pain, and—beyond a certain point—by a peculiar horror; and the slightest assistance to it—as, for example, is noticed in high air—by delight. The need to expand, felt in all our bodily movements, and most crucially in breathing, is not only profound in every individual, but obviously of infinite antiquity in the race. It is not surprising, then, that it should have become the body's veritable symbol of well-being, and that spaces which satisfy it should appear beautiful, those which offend it ugly.

We cannot, however, lay down fixed proportions of space as architecturally right. Space value in architecture is affected first and foremost, no doubt, by actual dimensions; but it is affected by a hundred considerations besides. It is affected by lighting and the position of shadows: the source of light attracts the eye and sets up an independent suggested movement of its own. It is affected by color: a dark floor and a light roof give a totally different space sensation to that created by a dark roof and a light floor. It is affected by our own expectancy: by the space we have immediately left. It is affected by the character of the predominating lines: an emphasis on verticals, as is well known, gives an illusion of greater height; an emphasis on horizontals gives a sense of greater breadth. It is affected by projections—both in elevation and in plan—which may cut the space and cause us to feel it, not as one, but several. Thus, in a symmetrical domed church it will depend on the relation of the depth of the transepts to their own width, and to that of the span of the dome, whether we experience it as one space or as five; and a boldly projecting cornice may set the upward limit of space-sensation instead of the actually enclosing roof.

Nothing, therefore, will serve the architect but the fullest power to *imagine* the space-value resulting from the complex conditions of each particular case; there are no liberties which he may not sometimes take, and no "fixed ratios" which may not fail him. Architecture is not a machinery but an art; and those theories of architecture which provide ready-made tests for the creation or criticism of design are self-condemned. None the less, in the beauty of every building, space-value, addressing itself to our sense of movement, will play a principal part.

v)

If voids are the necessary medium of movement, solids are the essential instrument of support; and a dependence upon physical firmness and security is not less fundamental to our nature than that instinctive need for expansion which gives value to architectural space. Any unlooked-for failure of *resistance* in tangible objects defeats the vital confidence of the body; and if this were not already obvious, the pervasive physical disquiet which the mildest tremor of earthquake is sufficient to excite, might show how deeply organized in our nature is our reliance upon the elementary stability of mass. Weight, pressure and resistance are part of our habitual body experience, and our unconscious mimetic instinct impels us to identify ourselves with apparent weight, pressure, and resistance exhibited in the forms we see. Every object, by the disposition of the bulk within its contours, carries with it suggestions of weight easily or awkwardly distributed, of pressures within itself and upon the ground, which have found—or failed to find—secure and powerful adjustment. This is true of any block of matter, and the art of sculpture is built upon this fact. But when such blocks are structurally combined, complex suggestions of physical function are involved—greater in number, larger and more obvious in scale. Architecture selects for emphasis those suggestions of pressure and resistance which most clearly answer to, and can most vividly awaken, our own remembrance of physical security and strength. In the unhumanized world of natural forms, this standard of our body is on all hands contradicted. Not only are we surrounded by objects often weak and uncompacted, but also by objects which, being strong, are yet not strong in our own way, and thus incapable of raising in ourselves an echo of their strength. Nature, like the science of the engineer, requires from objects such security and power as shall in fact be necessary to each; but art requires from them a security and power which shall resemble and confirm our own. Architecture, by the value of mass, gives to solid forms this human ade-

quacy, and satisfies a vital instinct in ourselves. It exacts this adequacy
in the detail of its decoration, in the separate elements that go to make its
structure, in the structure itself, and in the total composition. The Salute
at Venice—to take a single instance—possesses the value of mass in all
these particulars. The sweeping movement suggested by the continuous
horizontal curve of the Grand Canal is brought to rest by the static mass
of the church that stands like its gate upon the sea. The lines of the dome
create a sense of massive bulk at rest; of weight that loads, yet does not
seem to crush, the church beneath; as the lantern, in its turn, loads yet does
not crush the dome. The impression of mass immovably at rest is strengthened by the treatment of the sixteen great volutes. These, by disguising
the abrupt division between the dome and church, give to the whole that
unity of bulk which mass requires. Their ingenious pairing makes a perfect transition from the circular plan to the octagonal. Their heaped and
rolling form is like that of a heavy substance that has slidden to its final
and true adjustment. The great statues and pedestals which they support
appear to arrest the outward movement of the volutes, and to pin them
down upon the church. In silhouette the statues serve (like the obelisks
of the lantern) to give a pyramidal contour to the composition, a line
which more than any other gives mass its unity and strength. Save for a
few faults of design in the lower bays, there is hardly an element in
the church which does not proclaim the beauty of mass, and the power
of mass to give essential simplicity and dignity even to the richest and
most fantastic dreams of the baroque.

In architecture, then, the principal conditions of mass are these. In
the first place the effect of the whole must predominate over that of the
parts; the parts must enforce the general character of the whole and help
us to realize its bulk; they must not detach themselves from the mass in
such a way as to detract from its apparent unity. This, for example, is
the ground of the Renaissance insistence upon crowning cornices and
other devices for tying the elements of a building, and forcing it as a single
impression on the eye.

Secondly, the disposition of the whole must conform to our sense of
powerfully adjusted weight. Hence the careful study which the baroque
architects gave to the effect of receding planes, and the influence of upward perspective upon mass. Hence also, obviously, the use of rusticated
bases, battered plinths, pyramidal composition and the subordination of
the Doric to the lighter Ionic and Corinthian Orders.

Finally, it is necessary that the several parts of a building should be
kept in proper "scale." Scale, in any design, is that relation of ornament
(or minor features) to the larger elements, which controls our impression
of its size. In any building three things may be distinguished: the bigness
which it actually has, the bigness which it appears to have, and the feeling
of bigness which it gives. The two last have often been confused, but it is

the feeling of bigness which alone has esthetic value. It is no demerit in a building that it should fail (as St. Peter's is said to fail) to "look its size." For big things are not, as such, more beautiful than small, and the smallest object—a mere gem for example—if it satisfies the three conditions just stated, may convey a feeling of dignity, mass, and largeness. On the other hand, a building which looks big may fail to convey a *feeling* of bigness. No one, for instance, looking at the new Museum at South Kensington, could fail to realize that its dimensions are vast; it looks its size. But the whole does not predominate over the parts, the parts are many and the scale is small. Hence, while we perceive this building to be large, it con-veys a feeling not of largeness, but of smallness multiplied.

Small scale, no less than large, may be employed to emphasize effects of mass, as, for example, when fine moldings are used in combination with large, unbroken surfaces. In transcribing ourselves into such a building we instinctively take its detail as our unit of measurement, and this gives us an increased sense of the grandeur and simplicity of the unbroken mass. Broadly speaking the *quattrocento* architects employed this method, while the baroque architects sought to emphasize mass by the magnitude of the parts themselves. But in both cases the conditions of success were the same: the whole must predominate over the parts, the weight seem powerfully adjusted, the scale be consistently maintained.

vi)

The humanist instinct looks in the world for physical conditions that are related to our own, for movements which are like those we enjoy, for resistances that resemble those that can support us, for a setting where we should be neither lost nor thwarted. It looks, therefore, for certain masses, lines, and spaces, tends to create them and recognize their fitness when created. And, by our instinctive imitation of what we see, their seeming fitness becomes our real delight.

But besides these favorable physical states, our instinct craves for order, since order is the pattern of the human mind. And the pattern of the mind, no less than the body's humor, may be reflected in the concrete world. Order in architecture means the presence of fixed relations in the position, the character and the magnitude of its parts. It enables us to interpret what we see with greater readiness; it renders form intelligible by making it coherent; it satisfies the desire of the mind; it humanizes architecture.

Nevertheless order, or coherence, in architecture stands on a different plane to the values of mass, space, and line; for these, of themselves, give beauty, while order (as was shown in the last chapter) is compatible with ugliness. Yet it is clear that in all the architecture which descends from Greece and Rome, order plays a principal part. What then is its place and function?

Order—a presence of fixed ratios—will not give beauty, nor will a mixture of order and variety, but so much order, merely, and of such a kind, as is necessary for the effects which humanized mass and space and line are at any point intended to convey. Thus, in making the masses, spaces, and lines of architecture respond to our ideal movement and ideal stability, a measure of symmetry and balance are constantly entailed. Not perfect symmetry, necessarily. We in our bodies have a sense of right and left, and instinctively require that architecture should conform to this duality. Without it we could not so smoothly read or interpret architecture in our own terms. Dissymmetry in an object involves an emphasis or inclination to one side or the other in the movement it suggests, and this sometimes may be appropriate to the mood of the design. But, whenever architecture seeks to communicate the pleasure of equipoise and calm, or to impart a sense of forward, unimpeded movement, symmetrical composition and axial planning must result. Symmetry and Balance are forms of Order; but they are beautiful, not because they are orderly, but because they carry with them a movement and stability which are our natural delight. Then, since architecture is a monumental art, surrounding us with an influence never relaxed and not to be escaped, calm and unthwarted movement will here most often be desired. Thus Order, though it cannot ensure beauty, may follow in its wake.

Yet Coherence in architecture, distinct though it is from beauty, has a function of its own. Humanized mass, space, and line are the basis of beauty, but coherence is the basis of style. Mass, space, and line afford the material of individual esthetic pleasures, of beauty isolated and detached. But architecture aims at more than isolated pleasures. It is above all else an art of synthesis. It controls and disciplines the beauty of painting, sculpture, and the minor arts; it austerely orders even the beauty which is its own. It seeks, through style, to give it clarity and scope, and that coherence which the beauty of Nature lacks. Nature, it is true, is for science an intelligible system. But the *groups* which the eye, at any one glance, discovers in Nature are not intelligible. They are understood only by successive acts of attention and elimination; and, even then, we have to supplement what our vision gives us by the memory or imagination of things not actually seen. Thus, Order in Nature bears no relation to *our* act of vision. It is not humanized. It exists, but it continually eludes us. This Order, which in Nature is hidden and implicit, architecture makes patent to the eye. It supplies the perfect correspondence between the act of vision and the act of comprehension. Hence results the law of coherence in architecture; what is simultaneously seen must be simultaneously understood. The eye and the mind must travel together; thought and vision move at one pace and in step. Any breach in continuity, whether of mood or scale, breaks in upon this easy unison and throws us back from the humanized world to the chaotic. The values of mass, space, and line are as infinite as the moods of the spirit, but they are not to be simultaneously achieved, for they are mutually conflicting. Style, through coherence, subordinates beauty to the pattern of the mind, and so selects what it presents that all, at one sole act of thought, is found intelligible, and every part re-echoes, explains, and reinforces the beauty of the whole.

Of all the styles of building that yet have been created, the forms of Greece and Rome, with those of the Renaissance after them, were in this point the most exact and strict. They are by consequence the fittest instruments for giving clarity to sharp ideas, however varied, of function and of scale. Other instruments, doubtless, there will be in the future. For if the scope of classical design could be perpetually enlarged until the eighteenth century, it is not probable that its history is closed. But first we must discard a century of misplaced logic. Architecture must be perceived sensitively but simply; the "theories" of the art have blunted sensitive perception without achieving intellectual force. Architecture that is spacious, massive and coherent, and whose rhythm corresponds to our delight, has flourished most, and most appropriately, at two periods, antiquity and the period of which antiquity became the base—two periods when thought itself was humanistic. The center of that architecture was the human body; its method, to transcribe in stone the body's favorable states; and the moods of the spirit took visible shape along its borders, power and laughter, strength and terror and calm. To have chosen these nobly, and defined them clearly, are the two marks of classic style. Ancient architecture excels in perfect definition. Renaissance architecture in the width and courage of its choice.

THE CLASSICAL IDEA | *W. A. EDEN*

In hewing an axe handle—in hewing an axe handle, the model for it is in our hand.

CHINESE PROVERB

It is now time to return to the statement with which this book began, that it is a commonplace of architectural criticism that the last period in which English architecture showed a uniform and reasonably high level of taste came to an end about a century ago. This, it should be noted, is a statement, not of opinion about early nineteenth-century architecture, but of fact regarding present-day criticism. My reason for repeating it here is that I wish to ask the reader to consider seriously what it means. Is the

From W. A. Eden, *The Process of Architectural Tradition* (London, Macmillan & Co., Ltd., 1942). Reprinted by permission of the author.

fact that most people think that English architecture was better a hundred years ago than it is today merely an interesting, and somewhat unhappy, phenomenon, to be observed in a detached sort of way: or has it some real meaning, here and now, for those who think this way? The great majority of critics and architects talk and build as if the statement were meaningless. For my own part, I think it has very important implications. It means, in fact, that the classical ideal in architecture is as valid today as ever it was: and that in seeking a new style, which, according to their degree of sophistication our architects call modern or contemporary or, with fine presumption, simply architecture, they are pursuing a will-o'-the-wisp. I believe that unless we can understand and follow the classical ideal we shall not achieve, in the twentieth century, an architecture worthy of the name: for, as I understand it, the whole idea of architecture is a classical conception, which it was the glory and the privilege of the ancient Greeks to demonstrate to all who, subsequently, in western Europe, have had eyes to see. Today, unfortunately, such an assertion needs to be supported by argument. My purpose in this chapter is to put forward the arguments by which I myself arrived at this conclusion, and to discuss some of the objections that are constantly being made against it.

To begin with, let me be quite clear about what I mean by the classical ideal. By that phrase I do not mean something vague and mystical, a respectable coat to cover up the skeleton of intended revolution. To me, following the classical ideal means, first and foremost, learning to know and to accept the limitations, not only of circumstances, but, even more important, the limitations of human minds, in general, and of our own, in particular. It means learning, not only to accept these limitations, but to welcome them, and to use them as a means of releasing powerful creative energies in ourselves. Without this willing acceptance of limitations, what I understand as architecture cannot exist: and it is because, throughout the ages, simple country people have shown a tendency to accept limitations, that I suggested, in a previous chapter, that the idea of architecture has, often, received at least a partial expression in the humble buildings of the countryside—in small country churches, and in cottages and farm buildings—at times when the smarter people of the towns have been more concerned to display their own skill and ingenuity in building, than to be architects.

Secondly, since one of the limitations of the human mind is that it is incapable of making something out of nothing; that no man, or generation of men can, out of his or their own mind or minds, produce the forms and ideas which are the essence of civilization; and since it is impossible in the last resort to separate ideas from the language in which they are expressed, following the classical ideal means learning to express our architectural ideas in the language we have inherited from those who have possessed the virtues of full architectural manhood in a supreme degree—that is to say, from the architects of classical Greece and Augustan Rome. Actually it might be possible to argue that our ideas of architecture, being derived from classical antiquity, cannot be other than classical, even when they amount to a negation of the classic: for a negative idea is dependent on the positive idea which it denies. Nevertheless it is enough for the moment if we agree that architects do, at the present time, entertain classical ideas of architecture: and this, it seems to me, is admitted in the common assessment of the merits of early nineteenth-century architecture.

When we admire, shall we say, a fine Regency terrace, we are admiring what we ourselves now see. That, and nothing else, is what we admire. It is a matter of faith with us that what we see is the same as, or similar to, what the builders saw: but we cannot know this because we cannot, literally, see with their eyes. It is therefore nonsense to say of a certain building that it was good in its time. We can say, if we have knowledge of the fact from written records, that it was considered good in its time; or we can say that, bearing in mind the general standard prevailing at the time it was built, it is good for its time; but that it was good in its time, implying that we ourselves have two standards of judgment, one of which we apply to the work of the past and the other to our own work, is scarcely logical. Each of us, if we are whole persons, has but one mind. When we say that we admire a building that was built yesterday, or a hundred or a thousand years ago, it means that there is something in the pattern of our minds that responds to something in the building, here and now. We cannot change our minds according to the date of the building we are looking at, and say, for instance, that Inigo Jones' Banqueting Hall is a good building if it was built in 1619, and if it was really built secretly in the twentieth century, it is a bad building. If we did we should deserve all the practical jokes our irreverent contemporaries might see fit to play on us.

If, therefore, we admire the Banqueting Hall, or the Regency terrace, let us be quite clear in our minds what it is we admire and why we admire it. We admire the forms we see for what they are, and not for their date, nor because they were designed by Jones or Nash, nor yet because of anything we may know about them apart from what they are. This being the case, would it not be reasonable for us to show that we admire them in what we build ourselves? That, indeed, would be in accordance with the way we behave in other matters. If we admire a person, do we not imitate that person in what we admire, so far as it is in our power to do so? There would be no sense in our admiration if we did not: for surely it savors somewhat of hypocrisy, or else of cowardice or laziness, to say that we admire a certain line of conduct, and yet not to follow it when the opportunity presents itself. Indeed Plato suggests that such a course is impossible. "Do you think it in any way possible," asks Socrates, in the

Republic, "that a man should not imitate that with which he lovingly associates?" and the reply is "No, it is impossible." Imitation is the surest means of learning, as we may observe by watching children at play, a little girl loving and scolding her dolls as she herself has been loved and scolded by her mother, or a small boy in his conversations with his toy animals, mercilessly adopting his father's tones of authority

> *As if his whole vocation*
> *Were endless imitation.*

Children are none the less themselves when they are imitating their parents, and the necessity for imitation ends only when the grown man is himself perfect. As Victor Hugo expresses it,

> *Au-dessus de tout homme, et quoiqu'on puisse faire,*
> *Quelqu'un est toujours Dieu, quelqu'un est toujours père,*

and the same idea seems to have been present in Wordsworth's mind when he wrote that

> *. . . Unless above himself he can*
> *Erect himself, how poor a thing is Man!*

It seems to me that the necessity of having an object for our admiration and imitation is no less real in architecture than in life generally.

Nevertheless it is the fashion today to decry all forms of imitation. We are told we must not imitate the work of the past, that it is deceitful to do so, and that those who make a practice of it are escapists. As one who has not been guiltless of following the fashion, or, in other words, of imitating those who were nearest to me, I am not without sympathy for this point of view. It is right that we should be ourselves: but before we can be ourselves we must know ourselves. We should know what to imitate, and why we should imitate it. We should understand that the fact of there being many bad imitations in what we see around is not in itself an argument against all imitation. An imitation is bad when it fails to resemble our idea of the original. It may remind us of the original only to call attention to the fact that it is not the original. We say it does not deceive us, although there is nothing for us to be deceived about, unless it be something extraneous, like the date of a building. A good imitation, on the other hand, conforms with our idea of the original, and that idea, as we have seen, is something that we value for its own sake. If a building we are looking at conforms with an idea of something we value, we are not thereby deceived. On the contrary, we are pleased, unless, let me repeat, it is not the idea of the building that we value, but its date, or the name of the man who designed it. The conclusion we must come to, then, is that a good imitation pleases us: and in this we have the support of Aristotle, according to whom all art is imitation. Nevertheless the mere act of imitating does not make a man an artist.

There are, unfortunately, many who deserve Pope's description of "imitating fools, who of one beauty many blunders make." These are the people who confuse mechanical rules with artistic ideas, who imitate certain things, not because they admire them, but because they have been told by someone in authority that they ought to admire them, and who would just as soon imitate something else provided that they were told to do so by someone whose authority they considered to be still higher. Their imitations are bound to be bad imitations, because they have never seen anything to imitate. They work with scale and dividers, but not with their eyes. To make a good imitation a man must see and admire what he imitates: and he must imitate what he sees and admires, no more and no less. For him it is not a question of what certain rules tell him ought to exist, but of what actually does exist in his imagination. There will then be no question of his pretending to be other than what he is. He will be himself. Even so, we should not forget the case of Sir Max Beerbohn's Happy Hypocrite, who, for love of his mistress, pretended to be the sort of person she could love in return, and eventually grew to be like that person. His saving grace was that he loved.

As for the charge that such an attitude is escapist, perhaps it is true, though the sense in which it is true is surely the opposite of derogatory. It is not a bad thing to escape from bondage of the mind and spirit, and anyone who succeeds in making his escape will find himself in good company outside the prison bars. Most people would hesitate to call the architects of Augustan Rome escapists, in the derogatory sense, for following Greek masters; or Brunelleschi, for modeling his work on that of Ancient Rome: and it is generally agreed that it was to the benefit of English architecture that Inigo Jones, through admiration of Palladio, escaped from the slavery into which his contemporary Jacobeans had fallen. If to be like these is to be an escapist, by all means let us be escapists. For one thing is clear about them all, which is that however much they may have been indebted to the past, each of them was unmistakably himself and of his time. Nobody would mistake the Maison Carrée, at Nîmes, for Greek work, nor the Pazzi Chapel for Roman. In each case the originality of the architect consisted in his success in imitating what he himself saw in the work of the past.

There are many who, seeing the ever-varying character of the work of the past, and without considering how the human imagination works, argue that an architect's business is to "express his own time." They believe that the only way to do this is to cut themselves off as completely as possible from the past, and to look forward, with their eyes thus blinkered, to a future they cannot possibly know. Every teacher in a school of architecture (and, I have no doubt, in other schools as well) has experience of the pupil, who, in his anxiety to be original, avoids the right and obvious solution to a problem because one of his fellows has thought of it first. It seems to me that those who are so desperately anxious to express their own time that they cut themselves off from the past are in a very similar case. For them it may be worth while to emphasize the point made above regarding originality in imitation, by reference to examples nearer home. Let them ask themselves whether they find any difficulty in distinguishing, for instance, Victorian from medieval Gothic, or the Queen Anne style of Norman Shaw and his followers from its prototype in the early eighteenth century; or let them consider the drawings that men of various periods have made of the same buildings—how an eighteenth-century drawing of a medieval building will almost invariably look like a drawing of eighteenth-century Gothic, whilst a nineteenth-century drawing of the same building will in all probability make it look like the work of Street, or Scott, or Butterfield: it should then be abundantly clear that, whether they wish it or not, the men of each succeeding age cannot avoid writing their signatures large over the face of their buildings. Each man sees in the work of the past what he has it in himself to see. This being so, it is surely better that our aim should be to express what is eternal in the spirit of man: and in so doing we shall not fail to express what is best in ourselves and in our time.

So much may be agreed, and yet there may still be some who remain in doubt. They will perhaps argue that, though it is clear that our knowledge is inevitably derived from the past, nevertheless, as we have just seen, the past is various, and speaks to us with an uncertain voice. There are, in the western European tradition, two main divisions which we call respectively Classic and Gothic. There is also the Byzantine tradition of eastern Europe. Furthermore, the European tradition is not the sole tradition on earth. There are the Chinese and the Tibetan traditions, and the various and ancient traditions of India. There have been traditions like those of South and Central America, that have flourished and died out. How, in the face of these facts, can it be claimed that the classical tradition, which has gained acceptance only in a very small section of the globe by a very small number of people, considering all who have lived and died on earth since the creation of man, represents the absolute truth in matters of architecture? Is it not better to accept the implications of Tony Garnier's famous paradox, and say that for the architect everything that is built is classical—"le classique, pour l'architecte, c'est tout ce qui est construit"? Such questions are, indeed, very difficult to answer. One might reply by asking the questioner why he does not speak Chinese, but it is doubtful whether that would get one any farther. He might be one of those who would wish to see the languages of Shakespeare, Molière, Dante and Goethe discarded in favor of Esperanto. I therefore put forward the following argument for what it is worth, knowing full well that it will not convince anyone who is not prepared to be convinced, or who, in other words, does not love the classic.

It seems to me that those who wish to discard the architectural language they can understand because other languages exist, know too much about facts and too little about themselves and about language. Architectural thought, like other modes of thought, does not exist without language. Now let us assume, for the moment, that the architectural language of western Europe is the classical language in all its variety of dialects. If that is so, a European brought up from childhood to understand, if he understands architecture at all, his own classical dialect, is bound to translate whatever he may see into terms of his own language. In other words, he judges the architecture of other civilizations by his own classical standards. . . .

We have now got to a point from which we may profitably embark on a discussion of the technical objections to classicism as a system of "bygone esthetic forms." Briefly the general argument is that life today is so complex, and the needs of the community—the word has largely ousted the more gracious "society"—are so vastly different from anything that has been known before, that the old standards are no longer applicable. Architects who may be asked to design such things as aeroplane hangars, hospitals, railway and motor coach stations, departmental stores, large office blocks, or factories in which thousands of workers may be employed on mass-production processes, are faced with problems for the solution of which there is no known precedent. They have at their disposal, on the other hand, all the resources of modern science, resulting in the production of new materials and the invention of new methods of construction. The possibilities that open before them are boundless. In the application of this new knowledge to their new problems they must necessarily evolve a new esthetic which will completely supersede the old —or, according to the bolder spirits among them, has already superseded it. There is no longer any question of the desirability of retaining the old standards, the argument runs. That is both undesirable and impossible.

Let it be said at once that the problems confronting the architect today are indeed bewildering in their complexity, and that the means to their material solution made available through the progress of scientific discovery are paralyzing in their multiplicity. Should we not therefore beware lest the new esthetic of which we speak were to be simply an expression of our bewilderment and paralysis? The only sane course for a man thus bewildered is to hold on fast to what he already knows. If he lets go of that, the basis of all further thought is destroyed. It is not in the nature of real knowledge to be superseded, any more than it is possible to remove the foundations of a wall when the superstructure has been reached. Any new esthetic knowledge that we may acquire must, therefore, rest on the foundations of the old, without which it cannot exist: and those who have no real knowledge of the old are not the best equipped for making new discoveries. Actually, although there are many signs that ignorance of the old esthetic standards is wide-spread today, there are very few indications of the discovery of anything new: for the discovery of new esthetic truths means the discovery, not of new facts about the material world, but of new truths about the human mind and spirit. We have only to look about us to be convinced of the lack of evidence that men in the twentieth century are possessed of a greater clarity of mind, or of a greater breadth and profundity of spirit, than any that have preceded them.

Perhaps the real crux of the matter rests in a man's attitude to what are called facts. There are some who seem to regard facts as if these, and not architects, were the designers of buildings. Often one hears it said that such and such a particular in a design, even such and such a design as a whole, was dictated by the facts. If that is so, does it not seem to indicate that no such thing as a design—something intended—exists, and that he who should have been the designer is in truth a slave? The real designer knows that facts will not make his design for him; that in any given circumstances the number of facts that can be observed is unlimited; and that his business is to select as the basis of his design those which are relevant to his architectural purpose. The selection he makes must not ignore any other selection made independently of him, as for instance, by his client, in stipulating that certain accommodation is required on a certain site at a certain cost; provided always that these stipulations are not mutually incompatible. Nor must the selection ignore conditions created by other agencies such as cement manufacturers, timber merchants and all those who control the supply of materials; or by trades unions collectively, and their members individually, who control the supply of labor and skill; or by the banks, who control the supply of money; or by local or national government authorities, who control certain aspects of building in the interests of society. Finally, the selection must not run counter to those facts which, whether they are known or not, have existed since the creation of the world as the fixed law of Nature.

All this is simply to say that a design must be possible of execution in a given set of circumstances; which nobody would wish to deny. The question is whether in the circumstances of today there is anything that renders the classical idea impossible of realization. Now if it is true, as I have tried to suggest, that the architectural pattern of the fully developed human mind is, for us western Europeans, a classical pattern, to answer this question in the affirmative is tantamount to saying that architectural thought is today an impossibility. Given the mind as an instrument—

> ... *That ocean where each kind*
> *Does straight its own resemblance find—*

architectural thought may be said to consist in seeing, in the facts relating to any particular problem, a pattern that resembles the pattern of the mind, which is itself a fact of first importance. Needless to say, the facts referred to must be known facts. Some of them are known, as we have just seen, because they are conditions, dictated by circumstances. Others are subject to choice according to architectural principles: and the aim of the architect is to select, from amongst the facts that are to this extent free, just those which, together with the ones that are dictated, make an architectural whole, as he sees an architectural whole. Obviously the greater the number of "free" facts, including facts concerning his own mind and spirit, an architect is able to observe relative to a problem, or in other words, the greater his knowledge, the greater will be his freedom to discover an architectural idea. It may well be that those who would have us believe that classical architecture will not fit the facts of today really meant that it will not fit such facts as they know. The remedy is more knowledge, not the abandonment of classical standards.

Here, possibly, the suggestion will be made that modern science has given men a greater knowledge of the facts of the universe and a greater command over natural resources than they have ever before possessed. If this is so, then it should be easier, and not more difficult, for them to accomplish anything they may wish to do: and if they wish to achieve a classical beauty in their buildings, that should not have become impossible because of their increased knowledge. The fact that renders the classical ideal out of date must therefore be the will of the architect. If scientific discovery has given to the architect in the twentieth century the opportunity to be different from those who have preceded him, he may, of course, choose to be different: but he would surely be wise to remember that this difference binds him to the past from which he differs just as much as if he were to choose the way of imitation. If a man's aim is to be different from something he knows, his actions will be meaningless except by reference to the thing from which he differs. Thus the standard is still that of the tradition in which he has been nurtured. It is possible to think of many recent "progressive" buildings the architectural idea of which would be unintelligible except by reference to a supposed classical standard which they are at pains to deny. Such ideas as the intentional avoidance of an inherent symmetry, or the reliance on concealed counterbalancing weights or anchors to produce the specious thrill of achieving the apparently impossible, and even the prevalent reluctance to finish off a building with that practical and architectural necessity, the cornice, are examples of this negative recognition of classical standards. Surely there is a more direct and simple way of recognizing standards: and simplicity, we are told, is a virtue. . . .

It seems to me that architects at the present time are faced with two alternatives. They can either turn humbly to the past and to Nature to learn there the meaning of the art of architecture, or they can cease to be architects. They can either make themselves and their work fitting channels for the tradition of the knowledge of architecture, or, by refusing to have anything to do with that knowledge, they can be the means of withholding it from generations in the future. There is no necessity for them to choose to hand it on. Architecture serves no practical purpose, and men can exist on earth without it. They can build buildings which may very well serve their material needs, and construct cities which may be marvels of efficiency, and yet be ignorant of architecture, even though they use the word. If a man is ignorant of architecture he cannot by taking thought come to knowledge of it. Only if the idea exists in his mind in the beginning can this knowledge be broadened and deepened until it may perhaps include all that has been known on earth, and—who knows?— may possibly, someday, embrace more: but if it has been well-nigh extinguished in the minds of men, that process of recovery will be painfully slow, and attended by many set-backs. It seems, therefore, that it is for those who know and love architecture, however imperfect their knowledge and however faltering their love may have been in the past, to decide whether their joy in it has been such that they cannot but wish to pass it on. If they decide that it is worth transmitting to others, they may be heartened by the assurance that what they have loved, others will love, and they will seek to devise means to teach them how.

ARCHITECTURE OR REVOLUTION | LE CORBUSIER

Une maison est une machine à habiter.

In every province of industry, new problems have arisen and have been met by the creation of a body of tools capable of dealing with them. We do not appreciate sufficiently the deep chasm between our own epoch and earlier periods; it is admitted that this age has effected a great transformation, but the really useful thing would be to draw up a parallel table of its activities—intellectual, social, economic and industrial—not only in relation to the preceding period at the beginning of the nineteenth century, but to the history of civilizations in general. It would quickly be seen that the tools that man has made for himself, which automatically meet the needs of society, and which till now had undergone only slight modifications in a slow evolution, have been transformed all at once with an amazing rapidity. These tools in the past were always *in man's hands;* today they have been entirely and formidably refashioned and for the time being are out of our grasp. The human animal stands breathless and panting before the tool that he cannot take hold of; progress appears to him as hateful as it is praiseworthy; all is confusion within his mind; he feels

From Le Corbusier, *Towards a New Architecture,* trans. by Frederick Etchells (London. The Architectural Press, Ltd., 1928).

himself to be the slave of a frantic state of things and experiences no sense of liberation or comfort or amelioration. This is a great but critical period, above all of a moral crisis. To pass the crisis we must create the state of mind which can understand what is going on; the human animal must learn to use his tools. When this human animal has put on his new harness and knows the effort that is expected from him, he will see that things have changed: and changed *for the better.*

One more word on the past. Our own epoch, that is to say the last fifty years only, confronts the ten ages that have gone before. During these earlier ages, man ordered his life in conformity with what people call a "natural" system; he took his tasks upon his own shoulders and brought them to a satisfactory conclusion, bearing all the consequences of his own little enterprises: he rose with the sun, went to bed at dusk; he laid down his tools preoccupied with the task in hand and what he would begin on the morrow. He worked at home in a little booth, with his family around him. He lived like a snail in its shell, in a lodging made exactly to his measure; there was nothing to induce him to modify this state of things, which was indeed harmonious enough. The family life unfolded itself in a normal way. The father watched over his children in the cradle and later on in the workshop: effort and gain succeeded one another peacefully within the family order; and in this the family found its profit. Now when this is so, society is stable and likely to endure. That is the story of ten ages of work organized within the family unit; and the story too of every past age up to the middle of the nineteenth century.

But let us observe today the mechanism of the family. Industry has brought us to the mass-produced article; machinery is at work in close collaboration with man; the right man for the right job is coldly selected; laborers, workmen, foremen, engineers, managers, administrators—each in his proper place; and the man who is made of the right stuff to be a manager will not long remain a workman; the higher places are open to all. Specialization ties man to his machine; an absolute precision is demanded of every worker, for the article passed on to the next man cannot be snatched back in order to be corrected and fitted; it must be exact in order that it may play, by that very reason, its part as a detailed unit which will be required to fit automatically into the assembling of the whole. The father no longer teaches his son the various secrets of his little trade; a strange foreman directs severely and precisely the restrained and circumscribed tasks. The worker makes one tiny detail, always the same one, during months of work, perhaps during years of work, perhaps for the rest of his life. He only sees his task reach its finality in the finished work at the moment when it is passed, in its bright and shining purity, into the factory yard to be placed in a delivery-van. The spirit of the worker's booth no longer exists, but certainly there does exist a more collective spirit. If the workman is intelligent he will understand the final end of his labor, and this will fill him with a legitimate pride. When the *Auto* announces that such and such a car has reached 180 miles an hour, the workmen will gather together and tell one another: *"Our* car did that!" There we have a moral factor which is of importance.

The eight hours day! The three "eights" in the factory! The shifts working in relays. This one starting at 10 P.M. and finishing at 6 A.M.; another one ending at 2 P.M. Did our legislators think of that when they granted the eight hours day? What is the man going to do with his freedom from 6 A.M. till 10 P.M.; from 2 P.M. till night? What becomes of the family under these conditions? The lodging is there, you will say, to receive and welcome the human animal, and the worker is sufficiently cultivated to know how to make a healthy use of so many hours of liberty. But this is exactly what is *not* the case; the lodging is hideous, and his mind not sufficiently educated to use all these hours of liberty. We may well say, then: Architecture or demoralization—demoralization and revolution.

Let us examine another point:

There is a formidable industrial activity at present in progress, which is inevitably and constantly at the back of our minds; at every moment either directly, or through the medium of newspapers and reviews, we are presented with objects of an arresting novelty whose why and wherefore engrosses our minds, and fills us with delight and fear. All these objects of modern life create, in the long run, a modern state of mind. Bewilderment seizes us, then, if we bring our eyes to bear on the old and rotting buildings that form our snail-shell, our habitation, which crush us in our daily contact with them—putrid and useless and unproductive. Everywhere can be seen machines which serve to produce something and produce it admirably, in a clean sort of way. The machine that we live in is an old coach full of tuberculosis. There is no real link between our daily activities at the factory, the office or the bank, which are healthy and useful and productive, and our activities in the bosom of the family which are handicapped at every turn. The family is everywhere being killed and men's minds demoralized in servitude to anachronisms.

Every man's mind, being molded by his participation in contemporary events, has consciously or unconsciously formed certain desires; these are inevitably connected with the family, an instinct which is the basis of society. Every man today realizes his need of sun, of warmth, of pure air and clean floors; he has been taught to wear a shiny white collar, and women love fine white linen. Man feels today that he must have intellectual diversion, relaxation for his body, and the physical culture needed to recuperate him after the tension of muscle or brain which his labor—"hard labor"—brings. This mass of desires constitutes in fact a mass of *demands.*

Now our social organization has nothing ready which can answer these **needs.**

Another point: what are the conclusions of the *intellectuals* face to face with the actualities of modern life?

The magnificent flowering of industry in our epoch has created a special class of intellectuals so numerous that it constitutes the really active stratum of society.

In the workshop, in the technical departments, in the learned Societies, in the banks and in the great stores, on newspapers and reviews, there are the engineers, the heads of departments, legal representatives, secretaries, editors, accountants who work out minutely, in accordance with their duty, the formidable things which occupy our attention: there are the men who design our bridges, ships and airplanes, who create our motors and turbines, who direct the workshops and yards, who are engaged in the distribution of capital and in accountancy, who do the purchasing of goods in the colonies or from the factory, who put forth so many articles in the Press on the modern production of so much that is noble and horrible, who record as on a chart the high-temperature curve of a humanity in labor, in perpetual labor, at a crisis—sometimes in delirium. All human material passes through their hands. In the end their observation must lead them to some conclusion. These people have their eyes fixed on the display of goods in the great shops that man has made for himself. The modern age is spread before them, sparkling and radiant . . . on the far side of the barrier! In their own homes, where they live in a precarious ease, since their remuneration bears no real relation to the quality of their work, they find their uncleanly old snail-shell, and they cannot even think of having a family. If they do so there will begin the slow martyrdom that we all know. These people, too, claim their rights to a machine for living in, which shall be in all simplicity a *human* thing.

Both the worker and the intellectual are precluded from following their deepest instincts in regard to the family; each and every day they make use of the brilliant and effective tools that the age has provided, but they are not enabled thereby to use them for themselves. Nothing could be more discouraging or more irritating. Nothing is prepared. We may well say: Architecture or Revolution.

Though modern society does not recompense its intellectuals judiciously, it still tolerates the old arrangements as to property which are a serious barrier in the way of transforming the town or the house. Established property rests on inheritance and its highest aim is a state of inertia, of no change and of maintaining the *status quo.* Although every other sort of human enterprise is subject to the rough warfare of competition, the landlord, ensconced in his property, escapes the common law in a princely fashion: he is a king. On the existing principle of property, it is impossible to establish a constructional program which will hold together. And so the necessary building is not done. But if existing property arrangements were changed, and they are changing, it would be possible to build; there would be an enthusiasm for building, and we should avoid Revolution.

The advent of a new period only occurs after long and quiet preparatory work.

Industry has created its tools.

Business has modified its habits and customs.

Construction has found new means.

Architecture finds itself confronted with new laws.

Industry has created new tools. . . . Such tools are capable of adding to human welfare and of lightening human toil. If these new conditions are set against the past, you have Revolution.

Business has modified its customs: it bears a heavy responsibility today: cost, time, solidity of the work. Engineers in numbers fill its offices, make their calculations, practice the laws of economy to an intensive degree, and seek to harmonize two opposed factors: cheapness and good work. Intelligence lies behind every initiative, bold innovations are demanded. The morality of industry has been transformed: big business is today a healthy and moral organism. If we set this new fact against the past, we have Revolution in method and in the scale of the adventure.

Construction has discovered its methods, methods which in themselves mean a liberation that earlier ages had sought in vain. Everything is possible by calculation and invention, provided that there is at our disposal a sufficiently perfected body of tools, and this does exist. Concrete and steel have entirely transformed the constructional organization hitherto known, and the exactitude with which these materials can be adapted to calculation and theory every day provides encouraging results, both in the success achieved and in their appearance, which recalls natural phenomena and constantly reproduces experiences realized in nature. If we set ourselves against the past, we can then appreciate the fact that new formulas have been found which only need exploitation to bring about (if we are wise enough to break with routine) a genuine liberation from the constraints we have till now been subjected to. There has been Revolution in methods of construction.

Architecture finds itself confronted with new laws. Construction has undergone innovations so great that the old "styles," which still obsess us, can no longer clothe it; the materials employed evade the attentions of the decorative artist. There is so much novelty in the forms and rhythms furnished by these constructional methods, such novelty in arrangement and in the new industrial programs, that we can no longer close our minds to the true and profound laws of architecture which are established on mass, rhythm and proportion: the "styles" no longer exist, they are outside our ken; if they still trouble us, it is as parasites. If we set ourselves against the past, we are forced to the conclusion that the old architectural code, with its mass of rules and regulations evolved during four thousand years, is no longer of any interest; it no longer concerns us: all the values have been revised; there has been revolution in the conception of what Architecture is.

Disturbed by the reactions which play upon him from every quarter, the man of today is conscious, on the one hand, of a new world which is forming itself regularly, logically and clearly, which produces in a straightforward way things which are useful and usable, and on the other hand he finds himself, to his surprise, living in an old and hostile environment. This framework is his lodging; his town, his street, his house or his flat rise up against him useless, hinder him from following the same path in his leisure that he pursues in his work, hinder him from following in his leisure the organic development of his existence, which is to create a family and to live, like every animal on this earth and like all men of all ages, an organized family life. In this way society is helping forward the destruction of the family, while she sees with terror that this will be her ruin.

There reigns a great disagreement between the modern state of mind, which is an admonition to us, and the stifling accumulation of age-long detritus.

The problem is one of adaptation, in which the realities of our life are in question.

Society is filled with a violent desire for something which it may obtain or may not. Everything lies in that: everything depends on the effort made and the attention paid to these alarming symptoms.

Architecture or Revolution.

Revolution can be avoided.

THE PAST AND ITS SLAVES | *SHELDON CHENEY*

Eclecticism is the amiable name given to architectural incompetence in the period 1870-1920. Pickers and choosers from older forms of building, disputers for this or that style within the limits of impotency and imitativeness, tasteful roamers, cultured repeaters of other men's architectural phrases—Eclectics! They were so lost in their worship of pilasters and cornices and acanthus leaves that they never emerged into the fields of creativeness. They studied their heroes and mentors, Palladio and Vignola; they finished off at the Beaux-Arts School in Paris, and added the true French flourish to their adaptations; they usually considered deeply what surface fashion would best become a library or a railroad terminal or a skyscraper; but it never occurred to them, after steel and concrete came in, to approach the building as an organism, to relate structural method to façade designing. Correctness, accuracy, pretty pattern, impeccable copies of stately colonnades and lacy spires and picturesque

From Sheldon Cheney, *The New World Architecture* (New York, David McKay Company, Inc., 1930). Reprinted by permission of the author.

staircases—all was provided in approved museum fashion. And indeed, here in America, in the period of McKim and White and their associates, we had *everything*—except honesty, courage, and creation.

I am speaking now of the time when the *nouveau riche* American architecture of the mid-century and the Centennial era had given way to the Beaux-Arts men and *tasteful* adaption (though I find the French architectural magazines as late as 1900 full of ... junk-jug composition ... as inorganic, restless, showy, and futile as one can imagine). School training, conventional-mindedness, servile catering to imperialistic masters, lack of spiritual insight—these are prime reasons for the lack of creativeness in all the Western world in the period of Eclecticism. There is no reason, I suppose, why we should blame this body of Eclectics more than the eighteenth century men or any others in the long slave-minded period, except that the new principle in construction was there before them, denied by them.

The steel frame for high buildings came into use first in Chicago about 1890. Iron framing had been used in a limited way before that; but in 1891 a twenty-two story skyscraper built on a metal skeleton in Chicago was a world-wonder. Metal framing alone did not make the achievement possible: development of high-speed elevators, and of heating, lighting, and plumbing apparatus on a new scale, was a necessary accompaniment. But it was the invention of steel skeleton construction that afforded the point of departure for the most spectacular builders of modern times. Though obscured by exterior architectural practice through a quarter-century after, here was the revolution in structural engineering that was destined to change world building more than any other development since the invention of the flying buttress.

As we have seen—no understanding of modern architecture is possible until this has been emphasized and re-emphasized—there had been up to this time the three more or less distinctly separated types of building, based on materials and the ways of putting them together: three bases for architectural history. The post-and-lintel system was the simplest: a beam set across from the top of one upright to the top of another, to cover space. On it had been developed the glory that was Greek architecture. Second came the arch system: a method of spanning an opening by spreading the downward push sideways and along curved paths of stone blocks held apart by a keystone (an unscientific explanation, but perhaps expressive if you visualize an isolated arch). The arch and its outgrowth, the vault, made possible Roman architecture; and the Gothic builders found a variation (wherein the arch's thrust was absorbed not by solid masonry walls but by slender piers buttressed for the necessary extra resistance), which permitted the daring achievement of the medieval cathedrals. A third principle in building was introduced with the invention of the truss, for spanning wide spaces: a system in which a network of wooden or metal members in compression or tension came into use where the gap was too great for single beams. This last can hardly be termed a third great determining species of building, since it never gave rise to a style, as the other two did, and it may be used as auxiliary to any other method of construction.

But with the coming of the steel frame, a wholly new sort of engineering came in. Up to its appearance, the masonry at the bottom of a building had to support the weight of all the stories above. This was no great handicap in a church, which was all one great hall, or a fortress or a temple; or in any very low building. But as business exploitation of city land values drove buildings up in the air, as story on story was added, the necessary thickening of the walls at the base, to carry the additional weight above, stole more and more window space. The steel frame, on the other hand, transferred the weight to a few points of support; the problem was so radically solved that the masonry or clay walls could be built from the top story downward if desired; the lowest story (where light was most desired) could be encased with all-glass between the slender steel piers. Here, indeed, was a revolutionary difference out of materials—and a sign that the third great determining method of building in the world's history had arrived.

The second distinctively modern material soon came to aid the fabricators of steel frames: concrete. This was not strictly a new building material—the Romans had used it to a limited degree—but only after 1875 did it assume importance. By 1900 it was displacing a great deal of masonry and wooden building. For the floors of steel-frame structures, for instance, it offered fire-proof construction at low cost. It was merely necessary to construct temporary rough wooden "forms," lay in iron bars, and pour wet concrete to the desired thickness; when the concrete dried the forms could be knocked off and one had in effect a solid stone floor (with a metal heart). Reinforced concrete, or ferroconcrete, found many independent uses, outside connection with the steel frame: entire buildings of nearly twenty stories have been constructed of the material, and poured-concrete unit houses are a favorite form of experiment with Modernist architects. Although it is difficult to rid ourselves of the feeling that important "monumental" buildings must be at least faced with stone, no one who has understood the economy, logic, and adaptability of poured concrete can doubt that a different architecture, large and small, monumental and intimate, will arise out of its potentialities. Its emergence as a determining factor has been less spectacular than that of steel; but already it finds greater world currency and a wider variety of uses.[1]

The use of glass, set in metal, has greatly increased, and measurably

[1] The use of Portland cement, which is mixed with sand and gravel to produce concrete, grew in the United States as follows:

1870	less than 10,000 barrels
1900	approximately 10,000,000 barrel
1928	176,000,000 barrels

aids in trapping sunlight; and there is a very special branch of Modernist effort concerned with the decorative values of glass construction. In the same way, sheet-metal brings its own values, decorative and sanitary and constructive. But after all, it is steel framing and concrete pouring that seem destined to shape the larger forms of the immediate future world architecture.

How a few artist-engineers leapt to meet the challenge of a new principle and new materials constitutes the story of the chapters that follow; it is meet that in the last pages of this present chapter, of historical background, we return to those who spent their lives hiding the new steel core under surface trimmings borrowed from the past. But let us pause to note that Louis Sullivan flung his challenge to the timid, the cultured, and the hypocritical architects as early as 1892, speaking out with a passion and scorn that made him an outcast from the American profession, at the same time establishing him in Europe as a prophet and god of the younger revolting generations. All he asked for, in the final analysis, was *honesty*. He wanted honesty as to both use and materials. Even in the middle nineties he was designing a few skyscrapers in which the exterior walls were frankly a sheath over a frame, not pretending to be masonry piles; and he declared the function, and invented whatever ornament he added. And he kept up his running fire of attack on the Eclectics who went on pasting pilasters and colonnades along the false masonry fronts, who hung useless galvanized iron cornices over the top edges, who so carefully disguised the inward character of the structure.

The Eclectics simply overlooked the significance of the new inventions. They did not recognize that a great change in surface design must come ultimately by virtue of the steel frame or other new material or method—at present, those were matters for the engineer, purely structural matters, and "art" didn't have anything to do with structure.

Nineteenth century architecture in America had begun as Classic revival, had indulged in indiscriminate borrowing—Victorian, Gothic, Chinese, and what not—solidified itself for a time in Romanesque, turned Renaissance, and went out in dual Roman and Beaux-Arts French, the while two or three New-Medievalists shrieked the virtues of the Gothic. Toward the end of the century, quieter counsels prevailed over what had long been a battlefield of the styles; and thenceforth it was decreed that *any* style with a respectable historic lineage might be adopted for any particular job, and the architect remain within the fold of the orthodox and the elect. It was so much better thus—a man need no longer raise a standard on one side or another, strike and defend; instead he had all the past to choose from, respectably. Eclecticism was born, became a new, inclusive God.

Let us see just what this leaning on the past meant—for a whole quarter-century after the steel frame came into use. All decorative façades hung on the steel skeleton were borrowed, all were absolutely unrelated to the life of the time, to industrialism, to democracy. The planning might be true to purpose, the engineering efficient, even daring and soul-stirring; but the architect added façades that lied, that confessed lack of spirit, lack of originality, impotence. The *art* in these buildings was as superficial as that in the old-time painted stage scenery: a veneer, a make-believe, an illusion, a representation. In average work, an almost unbelievable fashion of uselessly heavy, "monumental" masonry was established, with illogical pictorial decoration in stone, weighty false cornices, deep-set windows, etc., etc.

In the outstanding monuments, there was caught occasionally some reflection of nobility or effective proportioning or decorative richness, out of other times. In our "great" American buildings of the decades on either side of 1900—the Boston Public Library, the Pennsylvania Station, the Columbia University Library, the West Point buildings, St. Thomas' on Fifth Avenue, the Yale and Princeton college halls, as well as the early renowned, historic skyscrapers—there are fine surface qualities. Sometimes these go even deeper. But false premises lie under the design of all. Sometimes the outer shell is entirely a disguise, the true building within existing and functioning perfectly behind the pleasant mask; in other cases, the true functioning of the building-organism has been crippled, distorted, in order that architects might erect the stylistically correct façade, with the limited area of windows, the relation of column and cornice, the hollow buttresses, etc., established traditionally by Gothic practice, or Italian Renaissance, or Roman.

All these monuments of the Eclectic age have a common, and not inconsiderable, virtue: they remind one of architecture. The designers in these particular cases chose well; the buildings *reflect* the strong works of eras when some human drive came to architectural expression. Here are echoes of the fine solidity of a Florentine fortress-palace, the nobility of the Pantheon, the gigantic lift of the baths erected by the Emperor Caracalla, the fragmentary grandeur of early Gothic churches. Nor would I want to undermine your enjoyment of these structures; only let us remember that they *are* reminders and echoes, not the real architectural thing. I find pleasing that vague memory of nobility when I am crossing 116th Street, find a momentary repose in gazing across Copley Square, feel a breath of old dreams on Fifth Avenue approaching 53rd Street. These are pleasant museum bits; but there is no living beauty, only vague images transported out of other times.

The architects transferred for our passing enjoyment certain outward forms, because they could not, in the materials, methods, and idiom of their own time, express the fundamental aspirations and powers that had made the originals soul-stirring and "beautiful." These nineteenth century architects were borrowers, servants of other men's minds, imitative professionals. That they were resourceful in their adaptation—some people call it their picking-and-stealing—that they were impeccably trained to maintain correctness, that they had taste, goes without saying. But in the light of the creative new spirit abroad in the world, they were timid, impotent, slave-minded.

Lest we be thought too critical of our own country, let us note that American architecture of the Eclectic era was world-typical. Even as the Classic revival a hundred years ago had brought as intelligent adaptation in the United States as in London or Berlin or Munich or Paris, the culminating nineteenth century Eclectic-materialistic architecture afforded us a sprinkling of monuments comparable to—perhaps more brilliant than—those erected in our "mother countries" across the Atlantic. Railway stations and hotels and universities and country houses were being set out with a lavish hand that gave our architects opportunity to surpass their fellow Eclectics overseas; and in the borrowed envelopes most used one may study on this side of the Atlantic the finest "modern Roman," "modern Collegiate Gothic," and "modern Renaissance villa" existent anywhere. Indeed, long years ago Platt in New York and Polk in California were building Italian houses more lovely than any Italian designer could produce; Cram and Goodhue were doing Gothic and Spanish churches more creatively adapted than any being done in France or Spain; and McKim and White were erecting monuments that cry shame to any erected in Rome within man's memory.

We might profitably pursue this thought about Rome. There are critics who point out that in its most imperialistic decades, the United States swung naturally to the so-appropriate Roman-Imperial architecture. (The Philippines experience and the slight personal experience of the World War have since given Imperialism, except the trade sort, a final set-back in the American group-mind—let Europe and South America believe it or not.) There was the exact duplication in triumphal arch and commemorative tomb, the same spirit behind the showy up-flung railway stations, exposition halls, and libraries, all with their masonry overlays of Roman motives. Need I add that of all the great architectural styles, the Roman is vulgarest, dullest, spiritually emptiest?

But the point we are pursuing at the moment is that Eclecticism made architecture tame and unoriginal *throughout* the European-American world. If you would take London instead of New York as an example, you would find less of brilliant adaptation, though more of passable and uniformly cautious orthodoxy. The fact is that London, center of the dominating imperialistic advance for two centuries and more, is the dullest empire-capital that ever existed. The architectural aspect of the city is drab beyond comparison. The few "monuments" that intrigue one's passing interest—the Houses of Parliament, Wren's churches, parts of Westminster Abbey, Regent Street, the Cenotaph, the Bank—are wholly unrelated in placing, style, spirit, or conception; not one an original British style, hardly two claiming nodding acquaintance as the same sort of Renaissance, the same sort of re-hash. For the rest, London is tamely self-effacing. Few of the strident monstrosities that occasionally happen in Chicago or Brussels or Berlin; but monotonous weakness, bespeaking a total stagnation of the creative faculties. London is occasionally rhetorical in the matter of architecture, but never convincing, never stirring, hardly living. The wastefulness of this moribund building is merely more restrained, the air is more respectfully servile, then elsewhere; it is a different phase of Eclecticism. France suffered less from heterogeneousness than other countries in this era, a thread known as French Renaissance becoming merely weaker and more florid in "Beaux-Arts"—but you may walk from the Classic Madeleine to the Pantheon and see on the way Roman arches, Renaissance railway stations, Baroque churches, Byzantine theaters, Gothic houses. All Europe—and wherever European nations colonized and "brought art" to the natives—is trailed over with this confession of architectural relapse, of spiritual bankruptcy.

That is the architectural background to our study of Modernism: the immediate background to our glimpse of a new world-order and of an appropriate and honest art of building. That is the architectural *status quo* which ninety-nine hundredths of the architects will try to maintain, to the exclusion of the types of building that grow out of the uses and materials of today. That is the mirror, showing how the true art of architecture was betrayed. Again let us remember: as men think, as they plan their lives, as they do, so they practice their arts—weakly, hypocritically, boastfully, materialistically, if those are the ways of the age. As pride, conquest, imperialism, based on social division between weak and strong, on exploitation and civilized savagery, were keywords of the age, so you may see those qualities memorialized, showily, alongside the weaknesses, on your streets, in your proudest public squares, and in your colleges.

Not that there were no *transitional* examples between Eclectic practice and a clean-cut, honest Modernism. No one can draw a line and say, "Here Eclecticism ends, and here the new world architecture begins." The architects might at first torture concrete into a semblance of roughcast stone, or line it out to suggest piled blocks; and they might grain the painting of metal doors to make them look like wood—these were the minor ridiculous sacrifices to the sacredness of the past. And very certainly they did at first, in dressing the skyscraper, build heavily at the base of the building in an effort to suggest that the masonry supported the weight—denying that the load of stone sheath was carried on a metal frame to isolated points of support; they wanted to preserve certain "picturesque" effects of projecting and indented stone courses and of deep-set windows and portals.

But these most illogical of their practices gradually fell away before the ruthless logic of the engineers, before the reasonable demand of owners who wanted economy and who wanted in the lower stories more light than the heavy masonry wall would permit—and before the pursuing mockery and scorn of the little band of architectural rebels led by Louis Sullivan. In the skyscraper the "masonry look" was reluctantly given up. The idea of pasting pilasters and false colonnades and networks of studied arches, pediments, false cornices, decorated entablatures, etc., etc., over the *entire* façade, was eased out of architecture in favor of a different sort of dishonesty which seemed to have at least a catch-hold on architectural precedent. In short, the Eclectics came to that standard mode in which the high building was treated after the manner of a Classic column: base more or less glorified; shaft plain; cap a real flowering of ornament, leading up to a cornice. The tall building was thus divided into three parts, the long middle one lost to the architect with the decorative itch, but the top and bottom parts offering display space for echoes of past architectural glories. But before going into that phase—which is to give place in turn to the Neo-Gothic—let us turn to a few actual examples of early Eclectic skyscraper design. Of the great monuments of the first twenty years, one may note the famous Flatiron Building and the *World* Building in New York as suffering from over-devotion to "the masonry look." Today the huge cornice on the Flatiron Building is alone enough to damn it in all logical eyes. The *World* Building illustrates the attempt to make the stone-work at the base *look* heavy enough to seem organic, as if it were a self-sufficient stone wall of huge building blocks—instead of what it is, a hanging protective screen on a steel frame. You meet the resulting deep window embrasures and cavernous portals, copied from Florentine palaces or Greek temples or Romanesque churches, in a hundred early skyscrapers of New York and Chicago. The same inordinate and unpleasant heaviness marks the *Times* Building—though a section of eight stories somehow escaped into near-modern simplicity—and here one may mark the more direct stealing of motives, particularly in the flowering into Giotto's Tower. It is rather, however, in the Metropolitan Tower that the skyscraper is tortured into a single borrowed stylistic envelope: a St. Mark's Campanile punched full of window-holes. Oftener the disguise was more freely worked out, with mere resting on Classic "elements" or Beaux-Arts idioms: the medium-height Italian palace skyscrapers, or the Singer tower with the Beaux-Arts "bulge."

Since, so far, we have examined the whole question of Eclectic skyscraper-design from the esthetic point of view—seeking the logic or illogic of trying to make a building *look* something it isn't—let us examine now the economic aspect. As a matter of fact, not one of those manipulated buildings escaped sacrifice to the architects' "additions for beauty's sake," in wastefulness of material and labor, and in loss of light (as those of us who at one time or another have had offices, for instance, on the arcade floors of the Metropolitan Tower—the thirty-first, I think, was mine—can testify). The pyramidal top of the Bankers' Trust Building, so long a feature of the downtown New York sky-line, embraced six full stories of blind enclosure, without windows. The Mausoleum in Halicarnassos had no windows, and the top twelve stories of this twentieth century monument were planned as a "creatively adapted" replica of the Tomb—and therefore six floors of space were given over to mausoleum darkness.

This Bankers' Trust Building is in the mode, already mentioned, based on the divisions of a Classic column unit. At this time the orthodox architects were saying to themselves, "We will forget the back and sides of the building, and study the front façade in divisions; we will treat that in the proportions proper to a column with a capital, set on a base." And so there came that nearest approach to a standardized skyscraper: the building with the first four or five stories unified in a designed but not too ornamental "base"; a section of naked honest building for twenty stories or so above, corresponding to the shaft; then a flowering in a sort of classic temple or Renaissance arcade laid over the top stories, for capital. This is the formula of the orthodox men still; driven from considering the whole building as masonry, they pretended that the whole hanging façade was a composition to be divided according to the "laws" of one masonry unit, the column.

The worse examples are with us in a hundred versions, weak and unattractive. (Some photographers, with radical tendencies, seeking truth, have taken malicious pleasure in slighting the carefully studied fronts and picturing the undesigned backs of these buildings, where the engineer's soaring lines and unashamed masses have risen unembarrassed by stylistic overlays; and up to a few years ago, some of us found these records more exciting than those so carefully embalmed by the architects in their trade magazines.) The better examples, however, gave us our least offensive false skyscrapers, occasionally studied *on all four sides*. Among the type examples are the mentioned Bankers' Trust Building, wherein twenty stories of undisguised offices rise between a double base, bearing engaged columns, and a capital of the temple type, with freestanding columns and cornice; and the Municipal Building in New York, with a complete Roman triumphal arch embedded in the false colonnade of the base, sixteen honest stories, and a band of (badly spaced) columns and pilasters at the top. It happens that both these buildings have "show" elements erected above the natural roof: the one the useless pyramid roof referred to, the other a French-pastry sort of agglomeration of temples, minarets, etc. Such afterthoughts are no more trivial and ridiculous in the sound architectural view than was the whole logic of treating a new structural problem in terms of alien ornament and under the theory of ancient building methods, stone on stone.

It is obvious, however, that the sacrifices of light and view, in these three-division buildings, were generally less than where the masking ornamental architecture had been drawn over the entire front.

There was one type of historic ornament that had none of the uglier disadvantages so obvious in Greek, Roman, and Renaissance when applied to the high thin façade. Gothic, the New-Medievalists pointed out, not only emphasized the soaring line; it had been developed in every detail for structures supported by isolated piers. Indeed, the medieval cathedral was the only building in history that showed the slightest analogy to the modern skyscraper: ergo, this was the only decorative idiom that could be logically (?) applied on the front of a thirty- or forty-story building. Admit the basic premise of the Eclectics, that there are no new styles, and we must agree absolutely with these Neo-Gothicists. And certainly the Gothic skyscrapers, whether viewed individually or as units in the Modern City, please the eye as do no other business buildings out of that pre-Modern age. Here if anywhere the Eclectic architects scored a real trimuph. Here is the final reach of the apostles of the past in their effort to hold the machine building of the present to traditional forms. And it is all summed up in the Woolworth Building.

This is the end of history and the beginning of a new time. This is a frankly stylistic envelope taken *in toto* from the past, encasing a steel frame. We have gone now beyond the period when the architect made pretense that the masonry of the lower stories carried the wall-weight above; the walls are frankly light sheaths of terra cotta, with only shallow window-reveals. This is obviously a pier-and-screen system of construction, with weight distributed to a few points of support, through vertical shafts.

And we seldom fail to be stirred by the "lift" of the building. The bulk and the conception of the thing are stupendous. The fundamentals of proportioning and massing are creatively handled, there is surface unity, there is form. From a distance, moreover, where detailed ornament becomes too intricate for the eye to catch, there is no conflict between functional lines and borrowed garment. There, indeed, lies the secret of the architect's success: he chose a style that does not actively belie the structural method, and he set away the more questionable elements to such a height that they blend into shadow and cross-line unobtrusively. In short, failing of creative ability to originate an envelope to match the engineering and proportioning, the designer chose a style originally invented for a similarly vertical method of construction, repressed detail too idiomatic, and cunningly interwove ornamental pattern and engineering fabric. The moment one comes too close for the blurring, then the lying of the ornament becomes apparent: there are even gargoyles at the twenty-seventh story and flying buttresses at the forty-second, and whole rows of offices suffer for light where the main decorative overhang is. To this extent there is compromise—perhaps dishonesty—for the sake of the "picturesque."

Here, then, is where Eclecticism came closest to an acceptable achievement, by the happy circumstances of a past style of ornament being fitted in accent to a new type of structure, and through the architect's understanding of the limits and uses of surface ornament. But nothing that we

can say or do will ever alter the fact that the reason any architect today
borrows a stylistic envelope from the past is because he is not original
enough to create the one truly appropriate to the new era. There is an
element of dishonesty in his approach, in his thinking.

And in the end, reviewing history, and then recalling the examples of
the new world architecture that most please us, it should be clear to us
that honesty is at the heart of the matter. If we have not integrity and
direct dealing, we shall have nothing but further evasions and compromises. There is no use talking about a new art unless one begins where all
creative design must begin, with the capabilities of the medium. If your
purpose is to make concrete seem like something it isn't, or to make
a metal frame support something copied from the days before steel fabri-
cation, then go ahead with your activities but don't call it architecture.
Architecture is the art of building beautifully; and beauty has nothing to
do with shams, with disguise, with overlaid cleverness, with transfers.

During all the quarter-century preceding the Woolworth Building,
there had been a sort of uneasiness in the writings—toward the last, the
apologies—of the Eclectics. It was as if there were a sort of continuous
vague thunder on the horizon; the orthodox, if they stopped to localize it,
probably looked to wherever Louis Sullivan was sitting in his prophetic
chair. Or perhaps it was a music they heard: the hum and drone of
machines—and they knew in their hearts that their architecture had no
relationship to that music.

The architecture of the past, of thirty centuries, had known nothing
of the machine; but somehow, intuitively, the architect of the late nineteenth and early twentieth century must have foreseen that machine-age
thinking would lie at the heart of building design in the time to come—
must have known, even while too servile to acknowledge it.

WHY A "MODERN" ARCHITECTURE? | J. M. RICHARDS and ELIZABETH MOCK

People who do not understand how the design of buildings comes
about criticize modern architecture by saying that after all, architecture
has always had the same function to fulfill, that of sheltering and accom-
modating the various kinds of human activity, so what is all this talk
about a modern architecture for modern people, as though modern people
were a new and different race who did not still get up in the morning and
go to bed at night and go to school and play games in the way they have

From An Introduction to Modern Architecture, by J. M. Richards, revised by
Elizabeth Mock. Copyright 1947 Penguin Books, Ltd., Harmondsworth, Middlesex,
England.

done for centuries? Thereby they suggest that modern architects are only being different in order to be perverse, but they forget that they are looking at people as individuals, whereas, it is people as society that architecture has to cater to. And the needs of society have changed out of all recognition in the last hundred years.

There is only one important respect in which the lives of people as a whole have not changed, that is in the unit on which the organization of their life is based, which is still the biological unit of the family. So the one-family house, at any rate when it is placed by itself, as in the country, is an architectural type that presents no fundamentally new problems. Those of us who happen to live in, say, the kind of eighteenth century house that we described a little while back, do so without noticeable discomfort. It is not so old as to be too primitive in its lighting and sanitation (the latter has probably been modernized, in any case) and it is planned in a rational, straightforward way that allows us to fit into it very comfortably. So near our own requirements are such old houses, in fact, that the best modern houses often bear a remarkable resemblance to them, without ever consciously imitating them. Modern houses do also, of course, differ from eighteenth century houses, but not fundamentally, only in the ways in which the buildings of one century must inevitably differ from those of another—which is a different matter.

When we come to consider other architectural types, however, we find quite a different state of affairs. New problems have been produced by, for instance, the change-over from an agricultural to an industrial economy and by the development of rapid transport. If domestically we remain what we always have been, socially we are without doubt a new race.

The most important of the new needs that modern architecture has to provide for are connected with the growth of cities. There were cities in past centuries, but their population was seldom densely packed. They had more the character of our own market towns, however much more important they may have been in relation to the rest of the country. The large town or city as we know it is entirely a modern conception. It originated when the growing population crowded into new centers to serve the new industries, which resulted in such an increase in land value in the middle of the cities and such a density of population that the traditional forms of housing were no longer practicable. So we got the blocks of apartments and tenements that are so typical of town architecture. And at the same time we got suburbs, as soon as improved transport allowed people who had work to do in the city to live some distance outside it. The increase in the density of population has made the utilization of the available space much more of a problem. This, too, is bound up with transport, not only because the modern city must be most carefully planned with room for motor and other transport, but also because the new suburbs have created fresh problems by cutting off the town from the open country that used to be just outside its doors. These are the problems of planning that have to be dealt with by the new profession that has come into being since they arose: the town-planning profession. As far as individual types of building are concerned these new conditions have produced not only the apartment house, but also railroad stations and garages, airports, power-houses, and industrial plants of many sorts. Equally important is the fact that buildings for purposes that are not themselves new have to answer such changed needs that they are virtually new architectural types: schools have to accommodate a national education system on an entirely new scale, and hospitals must serve modern medical science, while the small, special-ized shop tends to be replaced by the department store and the drive-in supermarket, or shopping center.

Thus architects must go back to first principles in order to solve prob-lems for which history has no precedents. . . .

So, to sum up, the principal reason why a new architecture is coming into existence is that the needs of this age are in nearly every case totally different from the needs of previous ages, and so cannot be satisfied by methods of building that belong to any age but the present. We can satisfy them in the practical sense, by utilizing modern building technique and modern scientific inventions to the full; and we can satisfy them in the esthetic sense, both by being honest craftsmen in our own materials and by taking especial advantage of the opportunities these materials offer of creating effects and qualities in tune with our own times. For example, instead of grafting antique ornaments on to new structures, as is often done today, thereby making them inconvenient and expensive as well as ridiculous, or else constraining the new structures within limits imposed by old ones—clothing a modern steel frame in a mass of masonry, to get the effect of solidity that was quite rightly admired in Classical buildings of solid stone construction, but is entirely false today; instead of either of these timid expedients we can make the most of the precision and machine finish that is so characteristic of modern technique and set out to explore, as our predecessors the Gothic architects so bravely did, the esthetic possibili-ties of lightness and poise. . . .

ARCHITECTURE AND MACHINERY

. . . As there is a popular belief that the modern kind of architecture is functionalist it is necessary to discuss the theory at some length, if only as a way of showing what modern architecture is by explaining one impor-tant thing that it is not.

The confusion arose largely through the theorizing and propaganda about modern architecture that were current during the first quarter of this century. A new architecture was then emerging from the confusion of the nineteenth century. And the most striking difference between the new

architecture and the old was that the former laid stress on the utilitarian
basis of architecture that the latter had largely ignored. Modern architects
took the opportunity provided by all the new materials and methods that
science had made available to rescue architecture from the stagnation of
stylistic revivals. They found it necessary, as we have already described, to
return to first principles, and one among the first principles of architecture
is that it should do the job it has to do as efficiently as possible. It is not
surprising, therefore, that when architects and writers tried to explain to
the world what the new architecture was all about, they should have
stressed this practical side of it as its special virtue. In some instances,
moreover, as in the writings of the famous Swiss architect and propagandist
Le Corbusier, an extreme functionalist attitude was deliberately taken up
as the best way of instilling into the public the importance of being practical first and foremost. His famous pronouncement *"une maison est une
machine à habiter"* served very well as a slogan advertising the simple, but
at that time revolutionary, conception of architecture as primarily a matter
of shelter. His technique of deliberate oversimplification did succeed in
doing a lot to clear away the sentimentalities and prejudices that had come
to form so large a proportion of people's views on architecture. That Le
Corbusier himself, as an architect, never thought of buildings as being
nothing but machines is very clear from the buildings themselves. He is
one of the most brilliant architects of the modern movement, whose buildings are remarkable for their freedom from rule-of-thumb designing. He
never does anything just because it has been done before or because it is
customary, and he therefore fulfills absolutely this ideal of rational design;
but he is also one of the most imaginative architects living. His buildings
are full of a poetic quality that is pure art and very far from being the
product of mechanical thinking.

Le Corbusier also, in his very influential writings about architecture,
was one of the first to illustrate an airplane, an automobile, and a turbine
in a book about architectural design; and this, too, has led people to suppose that modern architects believe that beautiful building can arise automatically from mechanical efficiency.

The difference between these two things, beautiful building and mechanical efficiency, is, of course, the difference between architecture and engineering. It is true that modern architects are influenced by the work of
modern engineers. It is natural that this should be so. For all the new
shapes and materials that made the unexplored possibilities of modern
architecture so exciting arrived in the beginning by way of engineering;
steel was used for bridges with thrilling results before it was used in
architecture, and many architects first saw the beauty of machine products
in the mechanical equipment—the power installations, the kitchen equipment, even the electric light bulbs—that science provided and demanded
that they fit into their buildings, even while the latter were still enslaved

to the ritual of historical styles. The great engineering works that modern science and industry produced had a breath-taking beauty, and it was easy for the architect, confused by contradictory esthetic creeds, to feel that he would ask nothing better than to have designed a building as directly appealing and as moving as this transmission tower or that enormous floating dock, which were primarily utilitarian; and therefore perhaps architecture would do best to follow the same method. But architecture, as the modern architects now appreciate, goes deeper than engineering. The beauty of the new structures that engineering has introduced into the landscape is genuine enough, and one's emotional reaction to them is natural, but this appeal is not really an architectural one. It is the appeal of size, simplicity, clearness, and honesty—in fact of all the qualities that nineteenth century academic architecture lacked. It is the appeal of a new world, inevitably stimulating to people who are becoming conscious that they live surrounded by the leavings of an old one, but it is not the *art* of a new world. One can admire things that possess some of the qualities that modern architecture should have, without taking them for modern architecture itself. One can also learn from them; and the important thing that modern architecture has learned from engineering and machine design —from docks, transmission towers, and airplanes—is first, the technique of using new materials, second, simplicity of line and honesty of expression, and third, the overwhelming grandeur of the fundamental architectural qualities, rhythm, scale, and contrast, which engineering used anonymously and as if by chance. These qualities could instructively be compared with the pettiness of personal mannerism and individual expression that architecture was still wasting so much of its time on. . . .

From machines themselves [the architect] has learned the charm of simplicity and precision. He has learned the value of eliminating everything unnecessary, not so much for reasons of economy as because the process of elimination brings out the essential character of structure. Much of the beauty of a tranmission tower, as of a Gothic spire, lies in its spare economy of means, indicating its designer's complete mastery over the material of which it is constructed. Secondly, machines, as we have seen, have lessened the virtue in elaborate ornament because they have abolished the point of doing something because it is difficult. This does not mean that richness has gone from architecture. Machine-produced shapes and textures lend themselves to infinite complication. The modern equivalent of applied ornament, however, largely lies in the natural qualities of materials themselves; in the grain and surface of beautiful woods, in the sheen of new metal alloys and in the contrasting texture of fabrics; all used with the exactness of finish that machines have introduced into architecture. Indeed, the eventual result of the precision with which machinery works may be an increase in our own awareness of the subtleties produced by precision. Our perceptions in the past have been blunted by the vulgarities of architectural clichés: by the meaningless masses of material hung on to architecture; but the new architecture gives us a chance to develop a more subtle appreciation of proportion and rhythm such as set the standards of eighteenth century taste. One can foresee a new connoisseurship coming into play, developing out of our acceptance of modern architecture's mechanistic basis.

WHAT *IS* THE MEANING OF HOPKINS' "THE WINDHOVER"?

BECAUSE THE language of feeling is so fully exploited in poetry, some critics incline to the view that the meaning of a poem is mainly subjective and that a consensus about meaning is neither possible nor important. It is enough, they argue, that the poem should provide delight or some more profound response: its propositional content does not really matter since its aim is not truth but beauty. The position can be sustained on various grounds, to be sure, yet it seldom satisfies. For any reader of lively intelligence, feeling is not enough. He is curious about the causes of what he feels, perhaps even suspicious of them; he is unwilling to let his response to a poem exist apart from the rest of his intellectual and emotional life and knows he cannot assimilate it without complete understanding.

The impediments to understanding that a particular poem may present are formidable. To begin with, the "argument" is often oblique or deliberately cryptic; it may even seem not to be there at all, and indeed there are poems that can only with a stretch of the imagination be said to contain anything propositional. Above this basic difficulty, poetic language and poetic use of language raise additional barriers to ready understanding. Some of the complication may really be intended as a barrier, a barrier raised to make the reader's access to the poem arduous so that he will summon his intellectual energies to maximum strength as he reads. Most of it, however, is directed at achieving some rhetorical effect, an enhancement—often by concentration—of the argument, to the end that feeling and thought may become equally powerful and actually fused in the poem.

A general argument about objective versus subjective meaning in poetry is not likely to be very fruitful. It is reasonable to assume that a poem does have some fairly definite meaning to the man who writes it: it is clear that a range of meanings must absolutely be excluded from any reading simply because the referential character of specific words in the poem makes them irrelevant. It cannot be denied that good readers do disagree, often radically, about the meaning of a poem. Perhaps, then, the best that can be said for public discussion about the meaning of a poem is that it disposes of the least tenable interpretations and sets in clear light the points at issue in those interpretations that may reasonably be entertained.

The discussion itself is not likely to be conducted in the spirit of that conclusion, however. Because poems do so powerfully affect our feelings, men who write about them care very deeply about what they conceive to be a correct reading. Having set out to propose or defend a position, they inevitably turn to the weapons of argument: definition, enunciation of premises, deduction, dissection of false hypotheses, construction of sound ones, and the like. They may insist that rules of the game limit evidence to what the words of the poem itself will supply, or they may draw freely from other matter (the poet's life and literary output, etymologies, the development of concepts, literary traditions, historical events, known or suspected influences on the poet's thought, and so on). Whatever procedures they adopt, they are likely to be (and why not?) as vigorous and rigorous in pursuit of the truth about a poem as others in like pursuit about foreign policy, economic affairs, or religious doctrine.

The poem under examination in this unit is the one its author most cherished in his own work. Gerard Manley Hopkins (1844-1889) was a poet from his student years to the end of his life, but his poetry was almost unknown until his friend and fellow-poet, Robert Bridges, published Hopkins' collected work posthumously in 1918. The storm of excitement that publication aroused brought to light the sensitive, self-denying creator of a kind of verse radically different from anything then in print. Hopkins was a convert to Catholicism and a Jesuit priest, and his poetry draws on traditional Christian theology though developing the implications of that theology in markedly individual, even eccentric, fashion. It is clear at least that Hopkins was trying to find a mode of expression adequate to convey the intensity of feeling with which he contemplated the immediacy of religious experience.

These essays, except for the collection of letters at the end, are arranged in chronological order because a body of discussion about this poem developed steadily from 1926 on, and later pieces make frequent reference to what has gone before. The opening essay is the work of I. A. Richards (1893-   ), "father" of the leading school of literary criticism in England and the United States since the publication of his Principles of Literary Criticism in 1925. Mr. Richards' most eminent disciple, William Empson (1906-   ), continues to provoke controversy by ingenious speculation about literature, as he did in Seven Types of Ambiguity, his first widely read

*book, from which relevant passages are excerpted here. Marshall McLuhan
(1911-   ) is a professor of English and critic at the University of Toronto;
and Yvor Winters (1900-   ), the same, at Stanford University. The former
is well known for his original and inventive criticism, the latter for his stout
advocacy of rational ground for poetic thought. Geoffrey Grigson (1905-   )
is an English writer equally interested in literature and in nature. Elisabeth
Schneider is Professor of English at Temple University.*

*The exchange of letters with which the unit concludes is interesting
on two scores. It introduces some additional considerations for a reading
of the poem, and it illustrates the most remarkable column of newspaper
correspondence in the English-speaking world. Week after week, in the
pages of the Literary Supplement of the London TIMES, discussions of
this kind appear, usually over a period of several weeks or months but
sometimes continuously over many years. Unlike articles and reviews in
the Supplement, these letters are signed, and it is evident that the correspondents take care to write as though the world were looking on—as,
indeed, a considerable part of it may well be doing.*

THE WINDHOVER | GERARD MANLEY HOPKINS

TO CHRIST OUR LORD

*I caught this morning morning's minion, king-
        dom of daylight's dauphin, dapple-dawn-drawn Falcon, in his
                riding
    Of the rolling level underneath him steady air, and striding
High there, how he rung upon the rein of a wimpling wing
In his ecstasy! then off, off forth on swing,
    As a skate's heel sweeps smooth on a bow-bend: the hurl and
        gliding
    Rebuffed the big wind. My heart in hiding
Stirred for a bird,—the achieve of, the mastery of the thing!*

*Brute beauty and valor and act, oh, air, pride, plume, here
    Buckle! AND the fire that breaks from thee then, a billion
Times told lovelier, more dangerous, O my chevalier!
    No wonder of it: shéer plód makes plough down sillion
Shine, and blue-bleak embers, ah my dear,
        Fall, gall themselves, and gash gold-vermilion.*

GERARD HOPKINS | I. A. RICHARDS

Modern verse is perhaps more often too lucid than too obscure. It passes through the mind (or the mind passes over it) with too little friction and too swiftly for the development of the response. Poets who can compel slow reading have thus an initial advantage. The effort, the heightened attention, may brace the reader, and that peculiar intellectual thrill which celebrates the step-by-step conquest of understanding may irradiate and awaken other mental activities more essential to poetry. It is a good thing to make the light-footed reader work for what he gets. It may make him both more wary and more appreciative of his reward if the "critical point" of value is passed.

These are arguments for some slight obscurity in its own right. No one would pretend that the obscurity may not be excessive. It may be distracting, for example. But what is a distraction in a first reading may be non-existent in a second. We should be clear (both as readers and writers) whether a given poem is to be judged at its first reading or at its nth. The state of intellectual enquiry, the construing interpretative, frame of mind, so much condemned by some critics (through failure perhaps to construe the phrase "simple, sensuous, and passionate") passes away once its task is completed, and the reader is likely to be left with a far securer grasp of the whole poem, including its passional structure, than if no resistance had been encountered.

Few poets illustrate this thesis better than Gerard Hopkins, who may be described, without opposition, as the most obscure of English verse writers. Born in 1844, he became a Jesuit priest in 1868, a more probable fate for him then—he was at Oxford—than now. Before joining the Order he burnt what verses he had already written and "resolved to write no more, as not belonging to my profession, unless it were by the wish of my superiors." For seven years he wrote nothing. Then by good fortune this wish was expressed and Hopkins set to work. "I had long had haunting my ear the echo of a new rhythm which now I realized on paper. . . . However I had to mark the stresses . . . and a great many more oddnesses could not but dismay an editor's eye, so that when I offered it to our magazine . . . they dared not print it." Thenceforward he wrote a good deal, sending his poems in manuscript to Robert Bridges and to Canon Dixon. He died in 1889 leaving a bundle of papers among which were several of his best sonnets. In 1918 the Poet Laureate edited a volume of poems with an introduction and notes of great interest. From this volume comes all our knowledge of his work.

From *The Dial*, LXXXI, 3 (September, 1926).

Possibly their obscurity may explain the fact that these poems are
not yet widely known. But their originality and the audacity of their
experimentation have much to do with the delay. Even their editor found
himself compelled to apologize at length for what he termed "blemishes
in the poet's style." "It is well to be clear that there is no pretence to
reverse the condemnation of these faults, for which the poet has duly
suffered. The extravagances are and will remain what they were ... it may
be assumed that they were not a part of his intention." But too many other
experiments have been made recently, especially in the last eight years,
for this lofty tone and confident assumption to be maintained. The more
the poems are studied, the clearer it becomes that their oddities are always
deliberate. They may be aberrations, they are not blemishes. It is easier
to see this to-day since some of his most daring innovations have been, in
part, attempted independently by later poets.

He uses words always as tools, an attitude towards them which the
purist and grammarian can never understand. He was clear, too, that his
poetry was for the ear, not for the eye, a point that should be noted before
we proceed to The Windhover, which, unless we begin by listening to it,
may *only* bewilder us. To quote from a letter: "Indeed, when, on somebody's returning me the Eurydice, I opened and read some lines, as one
commonly reads, whether prose or verse, with the eyes, so to say, only,
it struck me aghast with a kind of raw nakedness and unmitigated violence
I was unprepared for: but take breath and read it with the ears, as I
always wish to be read, and my verse becomes all right." I have to confess
that The Windhover only became all right for me, in the sense of perfectly clear and explicit, intellectually satisfying as well as emotionally
moving, after many readings and several days of reflection.

The dedication at first sight is puzzling. Hopkins said of this poem that
it was the best thing he ever wrote, which is to me in part the explanation.
It sounds like an echo of the offering made eleven years ago when his early
poems were burnt. For a while I thought that the apostrophe, "O my
chevalier!" (it is perhaps superfluous to mention that this word rhymes
strictly with "here" and has only three syllables), had reference to Christ.
I take it now to refer only to the poet, though the moral ideal, embodied
of course for Hopkins in Christ, is before the mind.

Some further suggestions towards elucidation may save the reader
trouble. If he does not need them I crave his forgiveness. *Kingdom of
daylight's dauphin*—I see (unnecessarily) the falcon as a miniature sun,
flashing so high up. *Rung upon the rein*—a term from the *manège*, ringing
a horse = causing it to circle round one on a long rein. *My heart in hiding*
—as with other good poets I have come to expect that when Hopkins
leaves something which looks at first glance as though it were a concession
to rhyme or a mere pleasing jingle of words, some really important point
is involved. Why in hiding? Hiding from what? Does this link up with

"a billion times told lovelier, more dangerous, O my chevalier!'"? What is the greater danger and what the less? I should say the poet's heart is in hiding from Life, has chosen a safer way, and that the greater danger is the greater exposure to temptation and error than a more adventurous, less sheltered course (sheltered by Faith?) brings with it. Another, equally plausible reading would be this: Renouncing the glamor of the outer life of adventure the poet transfers its qualities of audacity to the inner life. (*Here* is the bosom, the inner consciousness.) The greater danger is that to which the moral hero is exposed. Both readings may be combined, but pages of prose would be required for a paraphrase of the result. The last three lines carry the thought of the achievement possible through renunciation further, and explain, with the image of the ash-covered fire, why the dangers of the inner life are greater. So much for the sense; but the close has a strange, weary, almost exhausted, rhythm, and the word "gall" has an extraordinary force, bringing out painfully the shock with which the sight of the soaring bird has jarred the poet into an unappeased discontent.

AMBIGUITY IN HOPKINS | WILLIAM EMPSON

An example of the seventh type of ambiguity, or at any rate of the last type of this series, as it is the most ambiguous that can be conceived, occurs when the two meanings of the word, the two values of the ambiguity, are the two opposite meanings defined by the context, so that the total effect is to show a fundamental division in the writer's mind. You might think that such a case could never occur and, if it occurred, could not be poetry, but as a matter of fact it is, in one sense or another, very frequent, and admits of many degrees. One might say, clinging to the logical aspect of this series, that the idea of "opposite" is a comparatively late human invention, admits of great variety of interpretation[1] (having been introduced wherever there was an intellectual difficulty), and corresponds to nothing in the real world; that words in poetry, like words in primitive languages (and like, say, the Latin *altus,* high or deep, the English *let,* allow or hinder), often state a pair of opposites without any overt ambiguity; that in such a pair you are only stating, for instance, a scale, which might be extended between any two points, though no two points are in themselves opposites; and that in searching for greater accuracy one might say "2 per cent. white" and mean a very black shade of grey. Or one might admit that the criterion in this last type becomes psychological rather than

[1] $-a \cdot b$ is contrary to a for all values of b.

logical, in that the crucial point of the definition has become the idea of a context, and the total attitude to that context of the individual.

A contradiction of this kind may be meaningless, but can never be a blank; it has at least stated the subject which is under discussion, and has given a sort of intensity to it such as one finds in a gridiron pattern in architecture because it gives prominence neither to the horizontals nor to the verticals, and in a check pattern because neither color is the ground on which the other is placed; it is at once an indecision and a structure, like the symbol of the Cross. Or it may convey an impression of conscious ornamentation such as the Sumerians obtained, in the earliest surviving civilized designs, by putting two beasts in exactly symmetrical attitudes of violence, as in supporting a coat-of-arms, so that whatever tendencies to action are aroused in the alarmed spectator, however he imagines the victim or the huntsman to have been placed, there is just the same claim on his exclusive attention, with a reassuring impossibility, being made on the other side, and he is drawn taut between the two similar impulses into the stasis of appreciation. It may (for the first type) be as faint as the difference of sound heard by the two ears, which, though itself inaudible, decides with unreliable accuracy where the sound is coming from; it may (for the fourth type) be something stronger of the same kind, like the stereoscopic contradictions that imply a dimension.

Opposites, again, are an important element in the Freudian analysis of dreams; and it is evident that the Freudian terminology, particularly the word "condensation," could be employed with profit for the understanding of poetry. Now a Freudian opposite at least marks dissatisfaction; the notion of what you want involves the idea that you have not got it, and this again involves the "opposite defined by your context," which is what you have and cannot avoid. In more serious cases, causing wider emotional reverberation, such as are likely to be reflected in language, in poetry, or in dreams, it marks a center of conflict; the notion of what you want involves the notion that you must not take it, and this again involves the "opposite defined by your context," that you want something different in another part of your mind. Of course, conflict need not be expressed overtly as contradiction, but it is likely that those theories of aesthetics which regard poetry as the resolution of a conflict will find their illustration chiefly in the limited field covered by the seventh type.

The study of Hebrew, by the way, and the existence of English Bibles with alternatives in the margin, may have had influence on the capacity of English for ambiguity; Donne, Herbert, Jonson, and Crashaw, to mention names at random, were all Hebrew scholars, and the flowering of poetry at the end of the sixteenth century corresponded with the first thorough permeation of the English language by the translated texts. This is of interest because Hebrew, having very unreliable tenses, extraordinary idioms, and a strong taste for puns, possesses all the poetical advantages of a thorough primitive disorder.

I invoke primitive languages on the authority of Freud *(Notebooks,* vol. iv. No. 10), and cannot myself pretend to understand their mode of action. The early Egyptians, apparently, wrote the same sign for "young" and "old," showing which was meant by an additional hieroglyphic, not to be pronounced, which may have taken the place of gesture in conversation. They "only gradually learnt to separate the two sides of the antithesis and think of the one without conscious comparison with the other." When a primitive Egyptian saw a baby he at once thought of an old man, and he had to learn not to do this as his language became more civilized. The fact, judging by a dictionary, seems roughly true, and it certainly shows the process of attaching a word to an object as something extraordinary; nobody would do it if his language did not make him; and if one considers the typical propositions which can be applied to a baby, other than those as to its age, the opposite applies less an old man than to a man in the prime of life. Evidently there are two ways in which such a word could be constructed. It may mean, for instance, "no good for soldiers, because of age"; it may have been thought of in connection with some idea which regarded the very young and the very old in the same way. Thus one speaks of the two ends of a stick, though from another point of view one of them must be the beginning. Or it may be important to remember that the notion of age excites conflict in almost all who use it; between recognizing the facts about oneself, and feeling grown-up or feeling still young and strong.

In so far as the opposites are used to resolve or to soften a conflict, so that an aging man is not forced suddenly to find that a new and terrible word will apply to him, or can speak of himself as a young man by an easy and forgivable alteration of tone; to this extent there seems nothing peculiarly primitive about the sentiment, or the delicacy which allows it to be phrased; it has, perhaps, something primitive in its weakness of hold on external truth, and its honesty in voicing desires. And this form of the identity of opposites is not at all what one would expect from other properties of primitive languages; from the African grammars I have already mentioned, which insist on dealing with each case on its own merits; from the vocabulary of the language of Terra del Fuego, which requires a separate noun for each thing that English would name by permuting nouns and adjectives; from the thousand different words in Arabic which describe the different sorts of camel. Indeed, Arabic is a striking case of the mental sophistication required to use a word which covers its own opposite, because, though it possesses many such words, they are of a late origin and were elaborated as a literary grace. The many examples one can find in English (a "restive" horse, for instance, is a horse which is restless because it has been resting for too long) are almost all later developments in the same way. So that I believe myself, though this is only a useful prejudice with which to approach the subject, that though such words appeal to the fundamental habits of the human mind, and are fruit-

ful of irrationality, they are to be expected from a rather sophisticated
state of language and of feeling.

It seems likely, indeed, that words uniting two opposites are seldom
or never actually formed in a language to express the conflict between
them; such words come to exist for more sensible reasons, and may then
be used to express conflict. Thus the Egyptian dictionary has much less
doubt about the identity of "dead white" and "dead black," a case for
which it would be hard to invent a plausible conflict, than about the identity of "young" and "old." One reason is that people much more often
need to mention the noticeable than the usual, so that a word which defines
a scale comes to be narrowed down more and more to its two ends; the
English "temper" is an example of this. Another reason is that of relational
opposites one cannot be known without the other; to know what a ruled
person is you must know whether the ruler is a general or an archbishop.
Thus a word which names both parts of a relation may be more precise
than a word which only names half of it. Another reason is that, in complicated matters, you may know that there are two difficult cases which
ought to be distinguished, but being anxious on the point you find it hard
to remember which is which; to the senses they may be opposite, but they
excite the same feelings. Thus primitive painters make lines parallel when
they know that they are so in fact; but rather less primitive painters make
them meet, equally often, on the horizon and at the eye of the observer.
There was no conflict in their minds between these two ways of making
lines converge; there was only a general anxiety as to the convergence of
lines. In so far, in short, as you know that two things are opposites, you
know a relation which connects them.

This discussion is in some degree otiose because I really do not know
what use the Egyptians made of their extraordinary words, or how "primitive" we should think their use of them if we heard them talking; whereas
I have, at any rate, a rough idea of how the words are being used in the
examples which follow. So that I have really been searching the sources
of the Nile less to explain English verse than to cast upon the reader
something of the awe and horror which were felt by Dante, arriving finally
at the most centric part of earth, of Satan, and of hell.

> Quando noi fummo là, dove la coscia
>   Si volge appunto in sul grosso dell' anche,
> La Duca con fatica e con angoscia
> Volse la testa ov' egli avea le zanche.

We too must now stand upon our heads, and are approaching the secret
places of the Muse.

When a contradiction is stated with an air of conviction it may be
meant to be resolved in either of two ways, corresponding to thought and
feeling, corresponding to knowing and not knowing one's way about the

matter in hand. Grammatical machinery may be assumed which would make the contradiction into two statements; thus "*p and —p*" may mean: "If $a=a_1$, then *p;* if $a=a_2$ then *—p.*" If a_1 and a_2 are very different from one another, so that the two statements are fitted together with an exhilarating ingenuity, then I should put the statement into my sixth type; if a_1 *and* a_2 are very like one another, so that the contradiction draws attention both to the need for and the difficulty of separating them, then I should regard the statement as an ambiguity of the seventh type corresponding to thought and knowing one's way about the matter in hand. But such contradictions are often used, as it were by analogy from this, when the speaker does not know what a_1 and a_2 are; he satisfies two opposite impulses and, as a sort of apology, admits that they contradict, but claims that they are like the soluble contradictions, and can safely be indulged; by admitting the weakness of his thought he seems to have sterilized it, to know better already than any one who might have pointed the contradiction out; he claims the sympathy of his audience in that "we can none of us say more than this," and gains dignity in that even from the poor material of human ignorance he can distill grace of style. One might think that contradictions of this second sort (corresponding to feeling, and not knowing one's way about the matter in hand) must always be foolish, and even if they say anything to one who understands them can quite as justifiably say the opposite to one who does not. But, indeed, human life is so much a matter of juggling with contradictory impulses (Christianworldly, sociable-independent, and suchlike) that one is accustomed to thinking people are probably sensible if they follow first one, then the other, of two such courses; any inconsistency that it seems possible to act upon shows that they are in possession of the right number of principles, and have a fair title to humanity. Thus any contradiction is likely to have some sensible interpretations; and if you think of interpretations which are not sensible, it puts the blame on you.

If "p and —p" could only be resolved in one way into: "If $a=a_1$, then *p;* if $a=a_2$, then *—p,*" it might fairly be called an ambiguity, containing two separate statements under the appearance of one. In most cases the subsidiary uses of language limit very sharply the possible interpretations, and the ambiguity is only of this sensible sort. But it is evident that any degree of complexity of meaning can be extracted by "interpreting" a contradiction; any $_xa_1$ and $_xa_2$ may be selected, that can be attached to some $_xa$ arising out of *p;* and any such pair may then be read the other way round, as "If $_xa=_xa_2$, then *p;* if $_xa=_xa_1$, then *—p.*" The original contradiction has thus been resolved into an indefinite number of contradictions: "If $a=_xa_y$, then *p* and *—p,*" to each of which the same process may again be applied. Since it is the business of the reader to extract the meanings useful to him and ignore the meanings he thinks foolish, it is evident that contradiction is a powerful literary weapon.

Thus the seventh type of ambiguity involves both the anthropological idea of opposite and the psychological idea of context, so that it must be approached warily....

I shall first consider a Sonnet by Gerard Manley Hopkins, *The Windhover, To Christ our Lord,* as a more evident example of the use of poetry to convey an indecision, and its reverberation in the mind.

I am indebted to Mr. Richards for this case; he has already written excellently about it. I have nothing but some grammatical points to add to his analysis, and repeat it here merely because it is so good an example.

Hopkins became a Jesuit, and burnt his early poems on entering the order; there may be some reference to this sacrifice in the *fire* of the Sonnet. Confronted suddenly with the active physical beauty of the bird, he conceives it as the opposite of his patient spiritual renunciation; the statements of the poem appear to insist that his own life is superior, but he cannot decisively judge between them, and holds both with agony in his mind. *My heart in hiding* would seem to imply that the *more dangerous* life is that of the Windhover, but the last three lines insist it is *no wonder* that the life of renunciation should be the more *lovely. Buckle* admits of two tenses and two meanings; "they do buckle here," or "come, and buckle yourself here"; *buckle* like a military belt, for the discipline of heroic action, and *buckle* like a bicycle wheel, "make useless, distorted, and incapable of its natural motion." *Here* may mean "in the case of the bird," or "in the case of the Jesuit"; *then* "when you have become like the bird," or "when you have become like the Jesuit." *Chevalier* personifies either physical or spiritual activity; Christ riding to Jerusalem, or the cavalryman ready for the charge; Pegasus, or the Windhover.

Thus in the first three lines of the sestet we seem to have a clear case of the Freudian use of opposites, where two things thought of as incompatible, but desired intensely by different systems of judgments, are spoken of simultaneously by words applying to both; both desires are thus given a transient and exhausting satisfaction, and the two systems of judgment are forced into open conflict before the reader. Such a process, one might imagine, could pierce to regions that underlie the whole structure of our thought; could tap the energies of the very depths of the mind. At the same time one may doubt whether it is most effective to do it so crudely as in these three lines; this enormous conjunction, standing as it were for the point of friction between the two worlds conceived together, affects one rather like shouting in an actor, and probably to many readers the lines seem so meaningless as to have no effect at all. The last three lines, which profess to come to a single judgment on the matter, convey the conflict more strongly and more beautifully.

The metaphor of the *fire* covered by ash seems most to insist on the beauty the *fire* gains when the ash falls in, when its precarious order is again shattered; perhaps, too, on the pleasure, in that some movement, some risk, even to so determinedly static a prisoner, is still possible. The *gold* that painters have used for the haloes of saints is forced by alliteration to agree with the *gash* and *gall* of their self-tortures; from this precarious triumph we fall again, with *vermilion,* to bleeding.

THE ANALOGICAL MIRRORS | HERBERT MARSHALL McLUHAN

Hopkins is full of pitfalls for the unwary. There is a double difficulty: his Catholic beliefs and experience on one hand; his individual use of the resources of English on the other, to say nothing of his irrelevant theory of prosody. The non-Catholic reader—especially the non-Christian reader —is timid or hostile in the presence of Hopkins' faith and doctrine. He is beset with "mnemonic irrelevance" and stirred to a thousand acts of undemanded vigilance and depreciation which inevitably distort the pattern and texture of the poems.

For the Catholic reader Hopkins has, understandably, a great deal of prestige value. Long accustomed to a defensive position behind a minority culture, English and American Catholics have developed multiple mental squints. Involuntarily their sensibilities have been nourished and ordered by a century or more of an alien literary and artistic activity which, *faute de mieux,* they still approach askance. However, their intellectual distrust in the presence of, say, the emotional chaos of Shelley or Browning has not in the least prevented the assimilation of the vision of those poets. (One might add that it has not in the least prevented them from hailing as "Catholic poetry" the febrile immaturities of Francis Thompson and Joyce Kilmer.)

Thus there was no Catholic magazine which would accept any poem of Hopkins in his lifetime. With Bloomsbury's sudden acclaim of Hopkins as the major poet, however, Catholics were caught off-guard. They hastened to enshrine but not to understand him. Somewhat inconsequentially they have begun to feel at home in the present world of art because "their" poet is a big gun on the literary front. That is the catch. The Catholic reader comes to Hopkins with a mechanism of sensibility which came off the line in 1850. His sensibility has been unmodified by the impact of Baudelaire, Laforgue, Pound or Eliot. Bloomsbury was at least readied for Hopkins by these and *The Seafarer.* But the Catholic assumes his proprietary manner on the strength of doctrinal affinity alone. With equal justification the professors of Anglo-Saxon might have staked out an exclusive claim in Hopkins. Insentience or modesty has prevented them

From *The Kenyon Review,* VI, 3 (Summer, 1944). Reprinted by permission of the author.

so far; or is it simply that they are incapable of seeing that the work of
Hopkins is almost the sole civilized fruit of their brain-starved plodding?

Before there can be any basis for Catholic complacency in the presence
of Hopkins we must explain our tardy recognition of him. Again, if
Catholic doctrine made Hopkins a major poet, why aren't there more
like him? All, I think, that need be said of this peculiarly Catholic pitfall
is that some knowledge (the more the better) of Catholic doctrines and
Scotist philosophy is needed for the full elucidation, though not for the
immediate enjoyment, of Hopkins. Such knowledge, however, will never
reveal his poetic excellence. The Catholic reader has the advantage only
in that he is disposed to give Hopkins a chance. And, of course, he is not
inclined to urp, with Bridges, when Hopkins speaks of the Virgin or the
Trinity. The problem, in short, is much the same as that of reading, say,
Dante or John Donne. The ancillary scholarly effort should, but seldom
does, keep ever sharply focussed the stereoscopic gaze at the work itself.

Before looking at "The Windhover," as our chosen text, let us consider
the crux of Hopkins' sensibility—"inscape." It is the "fineness, proportion
of feature" mastering the recalcitrance of matter which he saw everywhere
in the world. It is the ontological secret

> *It is the forgéd feature finds me; it is the rehearsal*
> *Of own, of abrupt self there so thrusts on, so throngs the ear.*

Hopkins finds this Euclid peering from the chaos of matter alike in the
veins of a violet, the "roped" sides of a mountain, or the bright shoe on
the anvil. (Note the precise yet witty implications of "forged feature"
in this connection.) That Hopkins should take the further step of greeting
Christ at such moments of natural perception should cause even the non-
Catholic reader very little inconvenience, for the poet is making no pan-
theistic claims whatever:

> *Since, tho' he is under the world's splendor and wonder,*
> *His mystery must be instressed, stressed.*

Hopkins is not a nature mystic at all, nor a religious mystic, either, but
an analogist. By stress and instress, by intensity and precision of perception,
by analogical analysis and meditation he achieves all his effects. His is
literally a sacramental view of the world since what of God is there he does
not perceive nor experience but takes on faith. It may sound at first strange
to hear that Hopkins is not a mystic but an analogist. That he does not lay
claim to a perception of natural facts hidden from ordinary men is evident
in every line of description he ever wrote. As for religious experience it
is the same. Nowhere in his work does he draw on an experience which is
beyond the range of any thoughtful and sensitive Catholic who meditates
on his Faith. Let the authoritative statement of Jacques Maritain clarify
this matter at once. He begins a chapter on "Expérience Mystique et
Philosophie" this way:

Nous entendrons ici le mot "expérience mystique," que cela soit convenu une fois pour toutes, non pas en un sens plus ou moins vague (extensible à toutes sortes de faits plus ou moins mystérieux ou préternaturels, ou même à la simple religiosité), mais au sens de connaissance expérimentale des profondeurs de Dieu, ou de passion des choses divines, menant l'âme, par une suite d'états et de transformations, jusqu'à éprouver au fond d'elle-même le toucher de la déité, et à "sentir la vie de Dieu." Les Degrés Du Savoir (Paris, 1935), pp. 489-490.

But there is nothing of this in Hopkins. He deals sensitively with the commonplaces of Catholic dogma in the order of Faith, and he records a vigorous sensuous life in the order of nature. Since for the agnostic no precision is possible in these matters, and all distinctions are nugatory, he will continue to call both Blake and Hopkins "mystical."

Hopkins looks at external nature as a Scripture exactly as Philo Judaeus, St. Paul, and the Church Fathers had done. Their views, which have never ceased to be current, though their prevalence has fluctuated, are summarily expressed by the conventional patristic divine, Jeremy Taylor:

Thus when (God) made the beauteous frame of heaven and earth, he rejoyced in it, and glorified himself, because it was the glasse in which he beheld his wisdom, and Almighty powers . . . For if God is glorified in the Sunne and Moon, in the rare fabric of the honeycombs, in the discipline of Bees, in the œconomy of Pismires, in the little houses of birds, in the curiosity of an eye, God being pleased to delight in those little images and reflexes of himself from those pretty mirrours, which like a crevice in a wall thorow a narrow perspective transmit the species of a vast excellency: much rather shall God be pleased to behold himself in the glasses of our obedience. . . .

Hopkins habitually shifts his gaze from the order and perspectives of nature to the analogous but grander scenery of the moral and intellectual order. And he does this methodically:

> *. . . O the mind, mind has mountains; cliffs of fall*
> *Frightful, sheer, no-man-fathomed.*

Or the book of nature provides parallel passages with the supernatural revelations of Scripture:

> *. . . For Christ plays in ten thousand places,*
> *Lovely in limbs and lovely in eyes not his*
> *To the Father through the features of men's faces.*

As the microcosm of man is a nobler, a more perfect mirror of God's beauty and grandeur, so Christ, as Taylor goes on to say in the same place, "was the image of the Divinity . . . designed from eternal ages to represent as in a double mirrour, not onely the glories of God to himself, but also to all the world; and he glorified God by the instrument of obedience, in which God beheld his own dominion. . . ." Hopkins freely employs these three traditional mirrors (physical, moral, divine) of God's beauty and grandeur, using them sometimes simply ("Pied Beauty"), doubly ("The

Caged Skylark"), or triply ("The Wreck of the Deutschland"). Naturally, these combinations admit of infinite variations since the particulars reflected in each "mirror" can be chosen from a great store.

"The Windhover" exploits all three mirrors of God's grandeur.

> I caught this morning morning's minion, kingdom
>   of daylight's dauphin, dapple-dawn-drawn Falcon, in his riding
>   Of the rolling level underneath him steady air, and striding
> High there, how he rung upon the rein of a wimpling wing
> In his ecstasy! then off, off forth on swing,
>   As a skate's heel sweeps smooth on a bow-bend: the hurl and gliding
>   Rebuffed the big wind. My heart in hiding
> Stirred for a bird,—the achieve of, the mastery of the thing!
> Brute beauty and valor and act, oh, air, pride, plume, here
>   Buckle! AND the fire that breaks from thee, then a billion
> Times told lovelier, more dangerous, O my chevalier!
>   No wonder of it: shéer plód makes plough down sillion
> Shine, and blue-bleak embers, ah my dear,
>   Fall, gall themselves, and gash gold-vermilion.

The bird "literally" mirrors the physical order of sub-rational "valor and act." But, analogously, as "kingdom of daylight's dauphin," it mirrors Christ. As Hopkins transfers his gaze from the first mirror to the second, we see that his own heart is also a hidden mirror (moral obedience) which flashes to God the image not of "brute beauty and valor and act" but a "fire" which is "a billion times told lovelier"—the chevalier image of Christ. We can thus simply, and, I believe for the first time, fully explain the function of "here Buckle!" Rhetorically fire bursts from Hopkins as he looks at the fiery falcon whose action mirrors the mastery of Christ over the world. Now, he says, let us take this mirror (St. Paul's "armor") and buckle it here in my hidden heart, raising the image of Christ in the bird to the image of Christ in the obedience and humility of the heart. Christ's fire will burst on and from the second mirror "a billion times told lovelier" than from the falcon. This is the basic structure of this image. The superstructure of its ambiguity will be shown later on. Hopkins would even seem to have this mirror mechanism in the forefront of his mind as he compares his obedient day-by-day plodding to the homely ploughshare whose polished surface is hidden in the earth ("my heart in hiding") but which imparts a sheen even to the mud and dirt which it turns up. (Compare with this "sheer plod" image "the jading and jar of the cart"—"Deutschland" stanza 27.)

To have seen the dialectic or mechanism of the poem is not, however, to have seen anything of what constitutes its dramatic action. In other words, we have yet to see that it is a poem at all. There is a logical movement which has been indicated. There is also dramatic surprise achieved by a striking peripeteia. This happens when the ecstatic hyperboles of the

THE ANALOGICAL MIRRORS 421

octet are yet rendered trite by the merely homely images of the sestet. Moreover, while the sestet is in a lower key, befitting the change to the theme of humble obedience, it is more intense, fuller of compressed implication. Hopkins has Spiritual humility act out its easy victory over "brute beauty and valor and act." Yet this victory is not won by crushing "brute beauty" but by catching it to the hidden heart which reflects it back to God.

The assonance and alliteration in the first three lines perform just the opposite of their usual functions in Hopkins' verse—the opposite of "gall" and "gash" in the last line, for example. Here, in conjunction with the even phrasing, they convey the delicate poise, the hovering emphasis of the falcon's movements. The falcon is seen as a chevalier, a horseman glorying in the great power under him and the quick response to the rein as he sweeps "forth on swing." (The skate on ice image shifts the point of view only to stress the precision and sharply etched movements of the bird. Compare: "It is the forgèd feature finds me" in "Henry Purcell." "Dapple-dawn-drawn Falcon" also insists upon the etched quality of the scene. The bird is drawn to the light but it is also drawn, etched, against the dawn.)

To a member of a militant order whose founder was a Spanish soldier or chevalier, the feudal character of the opening imagery is quite natural. "Minion," "dauphin," "valour," "plume," and "buckle" alike evoke the world of dedicated knighthood and shining panoply of armor. Thus the mounted chevalier flashing off exploit as he "rung upon the rein" enables Hopkins later to reverse the situation with great dramatic effect in "sheer plod makes plow down sillion shine." The paradox consists in the fact that Hopkins as lowly plowman following a horse flashes off infinitely more exploit than Hopkins the imagined chevalier.

More central still to the dramatic movement of the poem is the way in which the cavalier images of the octet are concentrated in "here Buckle!" Buckling is the traditional gesture of the knight preparing his armor for action. A buckler is the bright shield of defense bearing insignia, flashing defiance. (The relevance of the sense of "buckle" as "collapse" or "crumple" has often been debated in this context. It has been suggested that Hopkins, in shifting his point of view, here means that the sensuous beauty of the world is a feeble prop, that he is making a conventional renunciation of "mortal beauty" as dangerous to the spiritual life. But this is to ignore the dramatic development, to blur it with cliché. It ignores the excited emphasis of "here" at the end of the line and "Buckle!" at the beginning of the next. It is, of course, almost impossible not to accept these suggestions so long as the basic mirror images of his analogist vision are not grasped.) Whichever way one looks at this image the implication of shining brilliance, of enthusiastic gesture, is present. I have already said that "here" means "in the obedient and humble heart," and that "Buckle" means that the "brute beauty" of the bird as mirror of God's grandeur is to be transferred or flashed to the "heart in hiding," just as the burnished surface of the plow in action is hidden in the earth. The high-spirited but obedient heart of a man is a "billion Times" better a mirror of Christ the chevalier than is the mirror of the external world. "AND the fire that breaks from thee then" (note how the eager stress on "AND" serves to flash attention intensely on what follows as being an inevitable result) is ambivalent in suggesting both the fire and ecstasy which the poet has felt as he watched the bird as well as the much greater fire which Christ will flash on him and from him, and which will flame out at the world. The mirror of man's moral life can "give beauty back to God," the beauty of God's world, and in so doing it becomes the mirror in which (by the imitation of Christ) God can flash out more brilliantly. ("Give beauty back," as in a mirror, is also the theme of "The Leaden Echo and the Golden Echo," as the title suggests.)

Once it is seen that the shining armor of the falcon's imitation of Christ's mastery is to be buckled in the hidden heart of the poet it is easy to find other passages in Hopkins which show that this image obsessed him. In the sonnet to St. Alphonsus Rodriguez there is the same running image of military brilliance and valor:

> But be the war within, the brand we wield
> Unseen, the heroic breast not outward-steeled,
> Earth hears no hurtle then from fiercest fray.

The whole sonnet is helpful to an understanding of "Windhover." But there is especial relevance in the second line:

> And those strokes that once gashed flesh on galled shield.

There is here a direct clue to the last lines of our poem.

> No wonder of it: shéer plód makes plough down sillion
> Shine, and blue-bleak embers, ah my dear,
> Fall, gall themselves, and gash gold-vermilion.

"Gall" and "gash" are in both places associated with shield and mirror and flesh—mortified or obedient flesh, of course. The underlying image in these last three lines is that of mortal *clay* transformed. It is made to shine and to fructify by the humble service of the plough (the obedient will). The "blue-bleak" earth provides the transition to the embers covered with clay-like ash. Just as the "fire that breaks from thee then" (after the mirror of mortal beauty has been buckled to the hidden heart) is not a fire produced by any direct action or valor, so the fire that breaks from the "blue-bleak embers" is not the effect of *ethos* but *pathos*, not of action but of suffering or patience. The true "achieve of, the mastery of the thing" from which flashes the most dangerous and daring exploit

> dates from day
> Of his going in Galilee
> Warm-laid grave of a womb-life grey;

here again is the image of the fire in the hidden heart which evokes the "blue-bleak embers," and, which, as some have suggested, leads on to the image of the vermillion side of Christ on the Cross.

One might even suggest that as the ash-covered coals gash gold-vermillion when touched by the poker (spear), so when Hopkins "kissed the rod, Hand rather" ("Carrion Comfort"), he becomes a mirror of Christ, flashing gold-vermillion:

> I kissed the rod,
> Hand rather, my heart lo! lapped strength,
> Stole joy, would laugh, chéer.
>
> Cheer whom though? the hero whose heaven-handling
> flung me, foót tród
> Me? or me that fought him?

The *crucial* ambivalence which Hopkins stresses is owing to the double mirror image which he keeps always in mind. As a mirror of Christ he must imitate both the valor and also the obscure sufferings of Christ. He must overcome and be overcome at the same instant—at every instant. But this complexity does not exist in the mirror of mortal beauty, the "brute beauty and valour and act" which is a simple reflection of Christ's mastery but not of His suffering and love.

Familiarity with Hopkins soon reveals that each of his poems includes all the rest, such is the close-knit character of his sensibility. A relatively small number of themes and images—such is the intensity of his perception —permits him an infinitely varied orchestration. Thus it is really impossible to feel the full impact of "The Windhover" without awareness of the tentacles which its images stretch out into the other poems. To take once more the analogy of "Sheer plod makes plough down sillion Shine," its paradox is brightly illuminated in the poem "That Nature is a Hercalitean Fire." Contemplating his "joyless days, dejection," "flesh-fade, and mortal trash," he reflects that:

> This Jack, joke, poor potsherd, patch, matchwood, immortal diamond,
> Is immortal diamond.

This "Jack, joke" plodding behind the plough makes the trash and mud of earth shine like diamond, "wafting him out of it." And diamond flashing from the silicates of the soil is also, once again, the mirror of Christ in the hidden and humble heart of mortal clay.

Another aspect of this analogy of the plough grinding through the gritty soil is seen in the last line of "Spelt from Sybil's Leaves":

> Where, selfwrung, selfstrung, sheathe—and shelterless, thóughts
> agáinst thoughts in groans grind.

This aspect of the plough and the soil is the more obviously dramatic one— immortal beauty won from the harshest dullest toil, suffering, and discipline.

An inevitable dispersal of attention has accompanied the above elucidation of this poem. But then only an oral reading with all the freedom and flexibility of spoken discussion can really point to the delicate interaction, at each moment of the poem, of all its cumulative vitality of logic, fancy, musical gesture.

"The Windhover" could never have become the richly complex poem it is if Hopkins had not tested and explored all its themes beforehand, in other poems. There is no other poem of comparable length in English, or perhaps in any language, which surpasses its richness and intensity or realized artistic organization. There are two or three sonnets of Shakespeare (for example, "They that have power to hurt" and "The expense of spirit") which might be put with Donne's "At the round earth's" for comparison and contrast with this sonnet. But they are not comparable with the range of the experience and multiplicity of integrated perception which is found in "The Windhover."

THE POETRY OF GERARD MANLEY HOPKINS | YVOR WINTERS

There seems to be some agreement to the effect that Hopkins' commonest method of constructing a poem is to describe a landscape or a part of one and then to provide an application which is usually religious. Arthur Mizener, in an essay devoted very largely to this aspect of Hopkins, writes:

> The basic structure of Hopkins' lyrics is a description followed by a comment, an application. They are, for all their intensity, poems of reflection, in the best sense of the word rhetorical rather than dramatic. Occasionally he indulged in the kind of naked symbolism by which the lion, for instance, becomes God's strength and conducts himself accordingly, without regard for the natural habits of lions. At best this practice made for the fantastic kind of poetry we associate with Crashaw. . . .*

H. M. McLuhan, in an essay in which interpretation is often carried so far from the actual text as to approach pure fantasy, recognizes the same structure, but regards it as an essential property of a certain kind of religious mind:

> Hopkins looks at external nature as a Scripture exactly as Philo Judaeus, St. Paul and the Church Fathers had done. . . . Hopkins habitually shifts his gaze from the order and perspectives of nature to the analogous but grander scenery of the moral and intellectual order. . . . Or the book of nature provides parallel passages with the supernatural revelations of Scripture.†

Reprinted by permission from *The Hudson Review*, Vol. II, No. 1, Spring 1949. Copyright 1949 by The Hudson Review, Inc.

* Arthur Mizener. in *The Kenyon Critics*, p. 103.

† H. M. McLuhan. *Ibid.*, p 19.

McLuhan illustrates these remarks with quotations which I omit. Mizener is perhaps a little apologetic about the method, but is not greatly disturbed by it; McLuhan seems to regard it as a major virtue. Neither appears to discern certain important difficulties inherent in it.

I will try to illustrate certain of these dangers.

> *The world is charged with the grandeur of God.*
> *It will flame out like shining from shook foil;*
> *It gathers to a greatness, like the ooze of oil*
> *Crushed. . . .*

The first line offers a major concept, in impressive phrasing. Instead of developing the concept, as a concept, however, in the manner of a poet of the Renaissance, Hopkins proceeds to illustrate it with two descriptive figures. In the first of these we are confronted with the kind of ambiguity which occurs so often in Hopkins: if we assume that the second line is grammatically correct, then *foil* is a quantitative word and refers to tin-foil or to gold-leaf, or to something of that nature, and we have what amounts, in effect, to an image of a madman (or at least of a remarkably eccentric man) brandishing a metal bouquet; if the foil in question, however, is a fencing foil, then the grammar is defective, for the article is omitted. This particular defect is not an uncommon form of poetic license, especially in Hopkins, and Hopkins takes much greater liberties elsewhere; but the image is indeterminate. In the next image there is a curious inaccuracy of natural description: "crushed" (or spilled) oil does not "gather" to a greatness, it spreads; or if Hopkins is referring to the gathering of oil from the crushing of olives, he is not only incomplete but is again inexact in his grammar. Aside from the difficulties just mentioned, which I suppose will appear trivial to many, but which nevertheless seem to me to introduce an element of shoddiness into the style, both of these figures are almost grotesquely trivial as illustrations of the first line; as so often happens, Hopkins is unable to rise to his occasion, and he relies on violent assertiveness and violent rhythm to carry him over his chasms.

The eighth poem *(The Starlight Night)* devotes the octet to ecstatic description of a natural scene. In the first line of the sestet, we have the interjection:

> *Buy then! bid then!—What?—Prayer, patience, alms, vows.*

Then we have two more lines of description, and in the last three lines a statement to the effect that the universe described is the home of "Christ and his mother and all his hallows." It is a curious poem. The description is sometimes extremely brilliant and is interesting everywhere save in the sestet. Yet the real theme of the poem is to be found in the first line of the sestet, and nothing is done with it. A devotional poet of the Renaissance, dealing with "prayer, patience, alms, vows," would have had a good deal to say of each and of what each meant in terms of daily life and toward

salvation. The reader who wishes to orient himself, might begin by rereading
Ben Jonson's *To Heaven,* John Donne's *Thou hast made me,* Greville's
Down in the depth of mine iniquity, and Herbert's *Church Monuments.*
In no other literary period, I think, save our own, would a poet who was
both a priest and a genuinely devout man have thought that he had dealt
seriously with his love for Christ and his duty toward him by writing an
excited description of a landscape: this kind of thing belongs to the nineteenth and twentieth centuries, to the period of self-expression and the
abnegation of reason. The impressiveness of the landscape described in
this poem provides a more nearly adequate motivation for the feeling
asserted than one can find in many other poems similarly constructed:
Hopkins' method in general is to employ the landscape as the immediate
motive for a feeling which is too great for it, and then to append the
perfunctory moral as a kind of theoretic justification. A few additional
poems in which this formula occurs more or less obviously are the following:
Spring (9), *The Sea and the Skylark* (11), *The Windhover* (12), *Pied Beauty*
(13), *Hurrahing in Harvest* (14), and *Duns Scotus's Oxford* (20). One could
add to this list, but these will serve for illustration; and I shall discuss only
two of these.

   Duns Scotus's Oxford offers an octet devoted to a description of the
Oxford landscape, with especial reference to the mingling of city and
country and the regrettable domination of the city. The sestet then provides
the personal reference:

> *Yet ah! this air I gather and I release*
> *He lived on; these weeds and waters, these walls are what*
> *He haunted who of all men most sways my spirits to peace;*
> *Of realty the rarest veinèd unraveller; a not*
> *Rivalled insight, be rival Italy or Greece;*
> *Who fired France for Mary without spot.*

This is the climax and the point of the poem, yet it is obviously very weak.
We are told that Scotus is the one "who of all men most sways my spirits
to peace;" yet we are not told how he does it nor why. We are told that
he is "of realty the rarest veinèd unraveller; a not/Rivalled insight," yet
these are empty epithets, and the subject of the poem, properly speaking,
is merely mentioned sentimentally and is not defined or developed. It is
as if one should say: "This is a magnificent landscape," or "this is a great
man," or "this is the most beautiful woman I have ever seen." What we
have is a stereotyped assertion, which we are supposed to take seriously,
but which we cannot take seriously for lack of definition and perceptual
evidence. This is not the method of Dante, or of Crashaw, or of Donne, or
of Herbert. These poets discuss the subject and omit or pass lightly over
the incidentals. Hopkins all but ignores the subject and is at his best
in dealing fragmentarily with the incidentals: the "towery city and branchy

between towers," and the like. The incidentals are sometimes, as in this line, charming, but they are minor, and they are not incorporated into a well-organized poem, even a minor one, but are parts, rather, of a disorganized poem which pretends to be more than it is.

The Windhover has been named repeatedly as Hopkins' best poem. Hopkins considered it to be such, and his admirers have followed him in this opinion, and some of them have carried it much farther than Hopkins did. McLuhan, for example, says:

> The Windhover *could never have become the richly complex poem it is if Hopkins had not tested and explored all its themes beforehand, in other poems. There is no other poem of comparable length in English, or perhaps in any language, which surpasses its richness and intensity or realized artistic organization. There are two or three sonnets of Shakespeare . . . which might be put with Donne's "At the round earth's" for comparison and contrast with this sonnet. But they are not comparable with the range of experience and multiplicity of integrated perception which is found in* The Windhover.*

The Windhover begins with the much-discussed description of the bird in flight; if one can keep himself disentangled from perverse theories of scansion while reading it, it is a fine description, but in itself it is merely description, that is, an example of the simplest subject matter available to the poet. As description it can be equalled and even surpassed by a great many passages in Coleridge, Wordsworth, Keats, Hardy, and perhaps others. Hardy's nighthawk, for example, is rendered more clearly and concisely as regards the bird itself; it is free from the pathetic fallacy which occurs in Hopkins' reading of his own ecstasy into an action which for the bird was merely a routine matter of business; and it is not required at any point in the poem to carry a symbolic burden too great for it. I offer Hardy's nighthawk, from the poem entitled *Afterwards*:

> *If it be in the dusk when, like an eyelid's soundless blink,*
> *The dewfall hawk comes crossing the shades to alight*
> *Upon the wind-warped upland thorn. . . .*

The epithet *dewfall* contributes to the sense of the time of day and suggests the soundless and mysterious appearance of the bird: it does this quite as effectively as Hopkins' *dapple-dawn-drawn* achieves its particular ends, more economically, and perhaps with greater originality. The simile in the first line contributes to both of the same effects. Every detail in the description reinforces every other. There is no vaguely excited and actually inefficient description such as Hopkins' *morning's minion, kingdom of daylight's dauphin.*

The unexplained ecstasy which hangs over the octet is supposedly explained in the sestet:

* McLuhan, *Ibid.,* p 27.

> Brute beauty and valour and act, oh, air, pride, plume, here
>   Buckle! AND the fire that breaks from thee then, a billion
> Times told lovelier, more dangerous, O my chevalier!
>   No wonder of it: shéer plód makes plough down sillion
> Shine, and blue-bleak embers, ah my dear,
>   Fall, gall themselves, and gash gold-vermilion.

Before we can discover the degree and kind of success which appear in these lines, however, we must discover the meaning of the words. The first difficulty inheres in the word *buckle;* the second in the identity of the chevalier; and the third in the meaning of the phrase *makes plough down sillion/Shine.*

John Pick, in *Gerard Manley Hopkins, Priest and Poet,** has this to say, after discussing the beauty described in the octet:

> But there is a beauty far, far greater. And the sestet is devoted to a revelation of a beauty beyond this beauty, a beauty which is "a billion times told lovelier, more dangerous" than the purely natural and triumphant flight. And whence comes this achievement which is more than achievement, this mastery which is more than mastery?
>
> It is in the act of "buckling," when the windhover swoops down, when its flight is crumpled, when "brute beauty and valor and act, oh, air, pride, plume" in an act of self-immolation send off a fire far greater than any natural beauty. . . . Nor is this to be wondered at, for this is true even in humble little things— is true of everything: the sheen of common earth shines out when the plough breaks it into furrows; and fire breaks from fire only in the moment of its own destruction. . . . Here is Christ upon the Cross and Hopkins the alter Christus. Beautiful was Christ's public life, but "a billion times told lovelier" was His self-immolation on the Cross, His sacrifice transmuted by the Fire of Love into something far greater than any mere natural beauty. More beautiful than any natural achievement was Hopkins' own humble and plodding continuance of the ethic of redemption through his own mystical self-destruction, his own humble following of Christ to the very Cross of Calvary. And the beauty of Christ and the beauty of the Jesuit to eyes that see more than this world is the beauty of their dying to live.

Pick selects one of several possible meanings for *buckle*: for him the word means to collapse, as if we should say, "The wings of the plane buckled and it crashed." He finds support for his general interpretation in the writings of Loyola, which Hopkins as a Jesuit had studied carefully, and from scattered passages in Hopkins' other writings. But we have no right to suppose that any poem by Hopkins is a gloss on Loyola or on anything else unless there is clear evidence in the text, and there is no such evidence here. The falcon's wings do not buckle, in this sense, when he dives: they are retracted close to the body and are under perfect control; the dive of the falcon is one of the most remarkable physical facts observable in brute nature. Furthermore, the dive is not an act of self-sacrifice, it is an

* Oxford University Press, 1942, p. 71.

attack on the bird's prey. If Pick's interpretation is right, then the poem is badly conceived from start to finish; but it would be unfair to Hopkins to read into his poem a meaning for which the poem offers no evidence and which, once it is there, ruins the poem. Pick apparently takes the expression *O my chevalier!* as being addressed to Christ, but there is no real evidence of this either. Christ is not mentioned in the poem. The poem is dedicated *To Christ our Lord,* but this does not mean that the poem is addressed to Christ. When a man dedicates a novel to a friend, he does not imply that the novel is addressed to his friend or is about him— he is merely offering a gift; since Hopkins regarded this as his best poem, he may merely have offered it to Christ in homage. On the other hand, it is possible that Hopkins meant to imply address in the dedication; there is no way of being sure, but one can at least collate the miscellaneous evidence, which is not greatly in favor of such an interpretation. The difficulty in the second tercet is a minor one, in the sense that it does not affect the interpretation of the poem, but it is troublesome with respect to the particular image. The question is this: does Hopkins mean to say that the sheer plodding of the plowman makes the plow shine as it goes down the furrow, or does he mean to say that the plowed-down earth is made to shine? If the first meaning is correct, then *plough* is a noun and should have an article; if the second meaning is correct, then *plough* is a past participle incorrectly spelled for the sake of euphony. The first of these licenses, though awkward, is common, not only in Hopkins but in other poets; the second would be violent and unlikely in any other poet, but is plausible enough in Hopkins. Pick believes that the earth shines and not the plow, and I agree with him because of the natural detail which is described: the plow does not gain polish in plowing, it loses polish, for a certain amount of earth adheres to it; but the freshly turned earth has a shining surface until the dampness dries or the surface for other reasons begins to crumble. However, the passage has been taken in both ways by various critics.

McLuhan is at least as adventurous as Pick in his departures from the text. He writes:

To a member of a militant order whose founder was a Spanish soldier or chevalier, the feudal character of the opening imagery is quite natural. "Minion," "dauphin," "valor," "plume," and "buckle" alike evoke the world of dedicated knighthood and shining panoply of armor. Thus the mounted chevalier flashing off exploit as he "rung upon the rein" enables Hopkins later to reverse the situation with great dramatic effect in "sheer plod makes plough down sillion Shine." The paradox consists in the fact that Hopkins as lowly plowman following a horse flashes off infinitely more exploit than Hopkins the imagined chevalier.

More central still to the dramatic movement is the way in which the chevalier images of the octet are concentrated in "here Buckle!" Buckling is the traditional gesture of the knight preparing his armor for action. A buckle is the bright shield of defense bearing insignia, flashing defiance. . . . I have already said that "here" *means in the "obedience and humble heart" and that "Buckle" means that the "brute beauty" of the bird as the mirror of God's grandeur is to be transferred or flashed to the "heart in hiding," just as the burnished surface of the plow in action is hidden in the earth. The high-spirited but obedient heart of man is "a billion times" better a mirror of Christ the chevalier than is the mirror of the external world. . . .**

McLuhan supports his interpretation at some length by quoting passages from other poems which suggest the theme which he has here in mind; my objection to his interpretation is simply that he departs too appallingly far from the actual text of the poem in hand. It is worth noting in passing that he agrees with Pick in the meaning of *chevalier,* and that, although he seems here to accept the other meaning of the plow image, he yet accepts both meanings of this latter in the course of his essay.

Miss Ruggles, although she believes that the plow shines rather than the earth, offers a more direct and simple explanation of the other phrases, and she gives us an interpretation which we can find justified, more or less, in the text. She says:

His imagination is caught and lifted as the small spiralling creature, magnificent in his instinctive performance, hovers at the very crux of its mastery, poised almost stationary against the opposing tide of wind.

> *Brute beauty and valor and act, oh, air, pride, plume, here Buckle!*

This is the ultimate assertion, the carrying out of selfhood—

> *AND the fire that breaks from thee then, a billion*
> *Times told lovelier, more dangerous, O my chevalier!*

It is in the act of buckling, when every sinew and chord of the identity thrills, at grips with its appointed function, that the beauty of the self flares brightest.

> *No wonder of it: shéer plód makes plough down sillion*
> *Shine, and blue-bleak embers, ah my dear,*
> *Fall, gall themselves, and gash gold-vermilion.*

The crude plough gleams in the moment of its contact with the resistful soil. Embers, foredoomed to crumble, can glow in this obscure enactment as fiercely as the flame.†

Miss Ruggles interprets the poem in terms of the concept of haecceity, inscape, or selfhood, which so obsesses Hopkins, and so keeps the poem closer to the bird which it apparently describes. For her, *buckle* means to concentrate all one's powers, as when we say: "He buckled to his work." And for her, the chevalier is the bird itself. She is able, also, to support her interpretation through other passages in Hopkins. In terms of her interpretation, we have a conclusion in the second tercet which merely

---

* Op. cit. pp. 22-3.
† *Gerard Manley Hopkins,* by Eleanor Ruggles, W. W. Norton Co., Inc., 1944, p. 156.

points out that two much less impressive actions give off their own fire: the first, the plodding effort of the plowman, which is humble but active; the second, the passive action of the coals when they fall and light up; so that it is no wonder that the striking action of the bird should give off a superior fire.

With this interpretation in mind, we may return to McLuhan for a moment. McLuhan assumes that Hopkins is developing a single chivalric image until he gets to the last tercet and abandons it, but the skate image interrupts this, and even McLuhan makes no effort to translate it into chivalric terms; it is the usual procedure of Hopkins, moreover, to hurl miscellaneous images at his subject from all sides, rather than to develop one of them fully. There is no reason to accept McLuhan's interpretation of *buckle,* therefore, unless it draws the whole poem together, which it fails to do. McLuhan believes that the plowman is figuratively Hopkins, but the poem does not say so; McLuhan says that the figurative plowman "flashes off infinitely more exploit than Hopkins the imagined chevalier," but the poem says that it is no wonder that the bird at the height of his achievement should flash light when a mere plowman can do it in a small way. McLuhan says that "here" means "in the obedient and humble heart," but Hopkins says nothing about obedience and humility, and of his heart he says "my heart in hiding," which on the face of it seems to mean "my heart within me," or "my heart unobserved."

Miss Ruggles takes another step in her interpretation, which brings her closer to Pick and to McLuhan, though still leaves her far behind them. She says:

> The beauty and valor of the winging falcon are Christ's own beauty and valor in an unthinking and finite form. Thus in a sense, the windhover is Christ. Christ is the windhover.

The poem does not say this, and the dedication does not necessarily imply it, but this interpretation would be in line with Hopkins' thought and with his practice in other poems; it would offer, moreover, some explanation of the violent rhapsody of the first tercet. This brings us to the crucial weakness of the poem, however; for if Miss Ruggles is right at this point, as I suspect she is, then the poem falls short of its theme in just about the same fashion as does the poem on Duns Scotus. To describe a bird, however beautifully, and to imply that Christ is like him but greater, is to do very little toward indicating the greatness of Christ.

Let me illustrate this objection with an account of my own experience. For more than thirty years I have bred and exhibited Airedales in a small way, and I have owned some very fine ones. At the present time I own a young dog who seems to me exceptionally beautiful, especially when he is in motion. No less than Hopkins' falcon, he is one of God's little creatures; he is probably a much better specimen of his kind and better adapted to

his peculiar ends, and if one is sufficiently scholarly and sufficiently per-
ceptive, one will be aware of this probability; in addition I am fairly
certain that his moral character is more admirable than that of the bird.
Yet it would never occur to me to write a poem describing his beauty and
then stating that the beauty of Christ was similar but merely greater. To
do so would seem to be ludicrous and perhaps blasphemous as well. Yet
there is no essential difference between my dog and Hopkins' bird; the
bird has the advantage merely of the Romantic and sentimental feeling
attached to birds as symbols of the free and unrestrained spirit, a feeling
derived very largely from Shelley's *Skylark* and from a handful of similar—
and similarly bad—poems of the past century and a half. Hopkins' poem
employs a mechanical and a very easy formula. His image resembles the
image of the anvil in *No worst, there is none,* in which we get the physical
embodiment of the meaning, without the meaning, or with too small a part
of it. To defend this sort of thing with pretentious remarks about the
"sacramental view of nature" is merely foolish, no matter how numerous,
pious, and ancient the precedents which one may be in a position to cite.

Even if we leave Christ out of it and confine the poem to the bird, we
find much the same difficulty in the first tercet: the light that flashes from
the bird when he buckles is "a billion times told lovelier, more dangerous"
than it was before; but the degree and kind of danger are the important
thing, and one is not given them. We are left where we were left with the
"rarest-veinèd unraveller, a not rivalled insight," in *Duns Scotus's Oxford.*

I would like to add one minor suggestion in post-script. I am no great
philologist, myself, but in my casual reading of the more obvious dictionaries
I have observed that the word *buckle,* in Scots and in northern English,
sometimes means *to marry.* In this sense, the word would function as well
as it would in any other sense. I am not aware that Hopkins ever made
a notation of this meaning of the word, though he may have done so; but
we know that Hopkins was inordinately fascinated with folk locutions and
examined them endlessly, and this interest strikes me as being quite as
relevant to the poem as his training in Loyola or his interest in Duns
Scotus's theory of haecceity. What the word actually means in the poem, I
confess I do not know. The reader may proceed from this point as he sees fit.

What should the verdict be on such a poem? As I have shown, the
metrical intentions of the poet are more than uncertain and are probably
unsound; but one can make out fairly well with the rhythm if one simply
reads the poem as it seems to be written. The crucial statement of the poem,
regardless of the interpretation which one accepts, appears to occur in the
second and third lines of the first tercet, yet this statement is merely an
assertion of the importance and of excitement, it is not an explanation and
description. The sestet contains three expressions which have led to various
interpretations and of which no interpretation is certain. As to *buckle,* Pick's
interpretation (like my own as well), has grammar on its side; for if McLuhan

is right, the expression should be *buckle on,* and if Miss Ruggles is right, it is *buckle to,* and each of these calls for an object. But grammar is worth very little as a criterion in dealing with Hopkins; he violates grammar as he sees fit, and the interpreter can seldom call it to witness. He violates grammar as he see fit, mainly to gain results which he considers more valuable than grammar: striking epithets and striking phonic effects. But the phonic effects are frequently over-wrought and badly wrought, and the epithets, when they do not overwhelm the subject with an assortment of ill-adjusted details, are likely to be incomprehensible because of the way in which they have been attained. The first tercet fails to define its subject; the second tercet is more nearly comprehensible, but in itself is not very effective, especially with regard to the embers: the function of the embers in the total theme seems clear enough, at least in Miss Ruggles' terms, but the embers as embers, as "inscape," are described in language which is coarse and imperceptive. The language is violent, and it continues both the tone of strong emotion and the rhythm which seems to have been established, but it offers a poor perception of embers as such. The description of the bird in the octet is impressive in the main, though I believe that it has been overrated. The bird is apparently used to symbolize the perfection of Christ, but the haecceity of the bird and the haecceity of Christ are very different matters indeed, and of the haecceity of Christ we are told precisely nothing in the poem. Unless Christ is symbolized, however, or unless something far greater than the bird is symbolized, then the ecstatic tone of the poem is not justified; and in fact it is not justified if Christ is symbolized, for it could be justified only by an indication of those qualities of Christ which would serve the purpose. The poem is romantic both in its over-wrought emotionalism and in its carelessness. It is not the greatest sonnet ever written, nor even the best poem in Hopkins; it is a poem of real, but minor and imperfect virtues, and that is all.

THE NATURAL IMAGE | GEOFFREY GRIGSON

The discussions about this sonnet were opened in 1926 by the distinguished critic I. A. Richards, yet in no critique, down to the most recent interpretations in this country and America, does any commentator ever seem to have studied, as a watcher of the bird, the one exciting activity upon which the fullness of the poem must hang. No commentator seems to have studied the wing-beating, hovering, gliding, swooping and recovering

From "Gerard Manley Hopkins" in British Council Pamphlet *Writers and Their Work,* No. 59. Published for the British Council and the National Book League. Reprinted by permission of the author.

of the kestrel or windhover, a study which cannot be conducted inside a dictionary, a Cambridge college, or a religious seminary.

There is no great trouble about the activity at least of the first lines. The kestrel, favorite of the morning, drawn forward into prominence by the dappled dawn, rides the air, a knight upon its horse, it hovers into and on the wind; then strides to a new position:

> *and striding*
> *High there, how he rung upon the rein of a wimpling wing.*

He rings ecstatically on the rein of a wimpling wing. This ringing upon the rein—it may not be easy altogether, yet what ingenious technical explanations for it have been advanced! To "ring upon the rein," as of horses reined to the trainer in the riding school—that suggestion was made first of all by I. A. Richards. It doesn't do. It would be no credit to Hopkins, who seldom stretches things so far. To "ring"—it is a technical term of falconry— to rise spirally in flight. Perhaps, but is that required? The kestrel strides to its new position, it does not spiral. After the stride, it must start hovering again, this hawk which is rider and not steed, it must ring again upon the rein of its wing, to keep place in and on the wind, its steed and its environment. But it is not only the rider, the dauphin of daylight's kingdom, the favorite of the morning, it is a hung bell. That it rings on the rein of its wing tells of the bird filling the sky with its own ringing fame (a ringing rhyme runs through the first eight lines), its own report, its own excellence, God's fame, God's excellence; tells also of the tense ringing vibration of the kestrel's typical movement. "*Myself* it speaks and spells," as Hopkins affirmed of each mortal thing in the sonnet *As Kingfishers Catch Fire.* And recall Hopkins declaring that all things are charged with God: all things *give off sparks and take fire* ("the fire that breaks from thee then"), *yield drops and flow, ring and tell of him.*

The hung bell is clinched entirely by that Kingfisher or selving sonnet, which Hopkins wrote some years later; he returned there to the kestrel, its ringing and its swing on the bow bend:

> *As tumbled over rim in roundly wells*
> *Stones ring; like each tucked string tells,* each hung bell's
> *Bow swung finds tongue to fling out broad its name.*

There, too, internally, he uses the same ringing rhyme. But on the rein? It is complex. The wimpling wing, however, is a rein from the bird to the air it rides and controls, and the bird, the rider, is also a bell ringing and jingling upon that moving rein. "Wimpling" is rippling, quick-beating. Yet even this simple word has had its esoteric interpretation: that Hopkins used it (as if he had watched the bird with powerful field-glasses) "because of the way the feathers appear in graceful folds when seen from below." Wimpling is no more than the activity, not absolutely regular but with a variation of speed and beat (the bird misses a beat sometimes), expressed already in the quick-acting words "... daylight's dauphin, dapple-dawn-drawn Falcon," in which the missing of a wing-beat—so close and material are Hopkins's equivalencies between word and object, verse movement and object—is indicated in the pause one has to make after "dawn": "dapple-dawn-drawn Falcon."

There is another crux of meaning later in the sonnet when Hopkins continues

> *Brute beauty and valor and act, oh, air, pride, plume, here Buckle!*

One commentator, happily calling on recollections of his childhood, has suggested that in "buckle" Hopkins was mindful chiefly of buckling as of a bicycle wheel in collision and collapse. Excellent—except that a collapsing cannot fit a context which asks for a quick decisive snapping together, a decisive metallic uniting of beauty, valor, act, air, pride, plume; though, as often or always, other senses or intimations of the word may have been present to Hopkins—a buckling on of armor and "buckling to," for example.

Much more ingenuity than is required has gone to unravelling, or smudging, the rest of the poem and its purpose—that from the conjunctive AND in the tenth line Christ begins to speak to the kestrel, or Hopkins begins to address his own heart; that his "heart in hiding" is in hiding from the kestrel's natural world, lost in the dismality of his vocation. His heart for a while, in fact, was in hiding *from* his vocation, from his proper being, his God, as in a later fragment:

> *Once I turned from thee and hid,*
> *Bound on what thou hadst forbid;*
> *Sow the wind I would; I sinned:*
> *I repent of what I did.*

He was yielding for a while too much to the kestrel's dangerous mortal beauty:

> *To what serves mortal beauty—dangerous; does set danc-*
> *ing blood—the O-seal-that-so feature, flung prouder form*
> *Than Purcell tune lets tread to? See: it does this: keeps warm*
> *Men's wits to the things that are; what good means—where a glance*
> *Master more may than gaze ...*
>
> *What do then? how meet beauty? Merely meet it; own,*
> *Home at heart, heaven's sweet gift; then leave, let that alone.*
> *Yea, wish that though, wish all, God's better beauty, grace.*

Nevertheless, the kestrel was a portion of that dull glory given to God, it was charged with God, giving off sparks and taking fire, ringing and telling of God; it was, though dangerous, heaven's sweet gift.

As for the last three lines, the fire broke from the kestrel, the windhover, the standgale, in the course of, and by dint of, its natural avocation; as in the sheer plod of ploughing, the steel mould-board or breast of the plough becomes shiny from the turned earth down the long strips of land (sillions)[1], and as embers that have become blue-bleak reveal, when their dull surface drops away, the heat and color inside them. He thinks, addressing Christ in "ah my dear," of the sheer plod of his own nine years, as it would soon be, of long preparation; of his own natural avocation since he had chosen to enter the Jesuit Order; of the ascetism of those years. The sheer plod puts a shine upon the plough which is himself; his at times bitter asceticism and exhaustion of mind reduces him to bleak embers which nevertheless gall and gash themselves to gold-vermilion—which are, in fact, the ashes of his other poem *Morning Midday and Evening Sacrifice:*

> *The vault and scope and schooling*
> *And mastery in the mind,*
> *In silk-ash kept from cooling,*
> *And ripest under rind.*

HOPKINS' "THE WINDHOVER" | ELISABETH SCHNEIDER

On "The Windhover" I am disposed to be dogmatic. The poem conveys one direct meaning, and only one in which all the parts of the poem and all the images find a place. Belt buckles and buckles in armor are not part of it; they belong to some other poem, "in another country." Hopkins willingly employed puns when double meaning might be "to one thing wrought" but not when two meanings fractured a poem. The instinct of critics to hover around the word *buckle* is nevertheless sound, for that word is the structural center, the pivot on which the sonnet turns.

Something buckles and something breaks through. Readers who buckle belts neglect the second half of this statement, though Hopkins capitalized the *AND* between the parts. It will not do to take *buckle* as an imperative either, as many writers do, for that leaves *AND* hanging loose and destroys the sentence. It is neither armor nor belt, nor Mr. Empson's bicycle wheel, that buckles or breaks; the pivotal image is of a higher order of magnitude. Deck or bulkheads of a ship buckle before fire breaks through; walls of a building buckle before they crash or burn. In "The Windhover" the whole

From *The Explicator*, XVIII (January, 1960). Reprinted by permission of the author and *The Explicator*.

[1] "Ploughshare" is also intimated in "sheer plod". It must, I think, be the plough that acquires shine, though the mould-board also imparts shine to the furrow. "Plough down sillion" could be a composite noun. However, the context asks for shine self-acquired by an *active* instrument, bird, plough, priest.

material world buckles, "AND the fire" of the spiritual world—or Christ—
"breaks" through. *Buckle* and *break* control the sestet as it subsides from
the climax of spiritual illumination to the everyday imagery of the conclusion.

"The Windhover" is one of several variations on a theme that occupied
Hopkins in 1877. Other sonnets, particularly "The Starlight Night" and
"Spring," display the same pattern of thought: a progression from the concrete beauty of nature described in the octave, to its spiritual meaning or
analogue in the sestet. As is so often true in Hopkins, the plan is simple and
straightforward; only the execution is complex.

"The Windhover" is addressed "To Christ Our Lord," and though Christ
is not mentioned till the tenth line, He is prepared for in the first by epithets
given to the falcon—morning's favorite (minion), "kingdom of daylight's"
crown prince—the Son, not the King or Father. *Dauphin* is more than an
automatic bit of alliteration; it counts for the meaning and for unity. The
falcon is an analogue, however, not a symbol of Christ. Though the power
and beauty of its flight make it prince of the morning scene, it is not more
than a bird, and it is described throughout the octave in the language of
the material world. But the sight of it awakens the poet: "My heart [which
had been] in hiding stirred." Beneath the word *hiding* I hear *hibernating*,
but that may be an accidental personal association; at any rate, the poet's
heart had been stagnant and perhaps reluctant to be moved (cf. *Letters* I,
66). Its awakening preludes the turn of the sonnet.

In the ninth line, the particularities of bird and morning are drained
away, leaving abstractions and universals to represent the power and beauty
in nature. This material world, so abstracted—"brute beauty and valor
and act, oh, air, pride, plume"—"here [at this point, now] buckle[s]," and
as it collapses before the poet's vision, the fire of Christ "breaks" through,
"a billion times" more lovely and more dangerous. Only now does the poet
address Christ directly: "the fire that breaks from thee then...O my
chevalier." The image in Hopkins' mind probably derives from the crackling
of timbers or plates in a fire at sea, a kind of disaster with which his father
was professionally concerned and which from time to time furnished
Hopkins himself, landsman though he was, with a surprising quantity of
imagery. Such an image gives double significance to the epithet *dangerous,*
applied immediately afterwards to Christ. From this point on, tension
relaxes and the pitch drops to a quiet conclusion with the imagery remaining under the shadow of *buckle* and *break.* "No wonder" this transformation
occurs, Hopkins says, when the *breaking open* of the most drab things in
life may reveal brightness within. Mere labor of plowing breaks open the
earth and transforms dull clod into shining furrow ("the near hill glistening
with very bright newly turned sods," he noted in his journal); and "blue-
bleak" coals of an apparently dead fire fall and break apart to show bright
living fire within.

In the outline of its thought, then, "The Windhover" is simple and strict. Its complexities lie, on the one hand, in the elaboration of the visual imagery interwoven with elaborately echoing patterns of sound, and, on the other, in the play between two counterpointed sets of opposites. The first is the opposition of the material and the spiritual which mark the two parts of the sonnet and are expressly brought together by the dauphin-Son parallel and more essentially by the primary theme of the poet's being stirred by one into more intense awareness of the other. The second pair of opposites appear in more shadowy form. The opposition of beauty and terror (or pain), present in so much of Hopkins' writing, runs through the poem without any reconciling of the two, though they are brought together in an uneasy harmony through the idea of power in the "mastery" of the bird and the "lovelier, more dangerous" fire of Christ. These opposites, however, are not evenly balanced in the poem: the terror or pain is no more than an undertone, reflected in one epithet of Christ, in the "gall" and "gash" of the close, possibly in the predatory character as well as the daring of the hawk and in the poet's "hiding" heart. The unresolved suggestions of terror and pain give an edge to the overriding spirit of breathless admiration.

These complexities are enough. Richness of symbolic meaning cannot be had merely by reading into the poem a mechanical, dictionary-flavored ambiguity in *buckle*. For the interpretation of "The Windhover" at least, an inveterate commitment to irony and paradox is apt to defeat itself by producing only disjointed structure and discordant associations that destroy, by neutralizing, the resonance of the poem. Quite a good deal of the resonance of "The Windhover" comes from simplicity of theme, clarity of structure, and directness of movement. This is true even though the final effect is of an extremely complex poem.

AN EXCHANGE OF VIEWS ON "THE WINDHOVER" | *J. G. RITZ, W. EMPSON, and W. H. GARDNER*

(CORRESPONDENCE IN THE TIMES LITERARY SUPPLEMENT)

Times Literary Supplement May 6, 1955

Sir,—Having read a good dozen explanations of the "Windhover," which failed to satisfy me, I beg to offer the following remarks. They may interest those of your readers whom Hopkins captivates and puzzles.

I consider the poem should be read on three different levels, as follows:—

1. "The Windhover."—The octet and the first tercet are wholly devoted to the bird, which *is* a bird of prey. The poet, hidden in some quiet place,

Reprinted by permission of the authors.

watches him as he glides and hovers in the air, and admires his mastery. He then sees the bird swoop down (or he imagines it) and "buckle" or "gather together" his beauty, valor, pride . . . for his sudden fall upon a prey that he will snatch away from the ground. He drops like lightning: "fire" flashes off him, just as "honor flashes off exploit," and this "fell swoop" is for the poet, who is eagerly watching it, even more lovely than the bird's masterly gliding in the air; and it is "more dangerous," since it is a sheer fall and there is a victim. The second tercet justifies the "fire" image. One should not wonder at it. The share and mould-board, as they sink into the soil and tear it open, shine—are on fire, one might say—and grey embers, when some poker stirs them, fall and reveal the fire burning under the "rind" of blue ashes. The unity of the poet's vision and of his images is certain and simply as an artistic poetical picture it can be fully enjoyed.

2. "Christ."—But, of course, the poem is symbolical. The "Kingdom of Daylight's Dauphin" is Christ. The priest-poet, in his quiet retreat in Wales, meditates upon the beauty and mastery of Christ in his Heaven of Glory, hovering over the world. He then turns to Christ's stupendous coming down upon earth. The Son of God "gathered together" the whole majesty of his Godhead, and swooped down like a bird of prey. In this "sweep and hurl" of him to "wring" the hearts of men and snatch them back to heaven, He was "lightning and love." Christ's Incarnation, his lowly life in Galilee, are "lovelier" and "more dangerous" since they imply the redemption of men and their salvation. To be Christ's prey is no small matter for Hopkins; we know his own experience of it, as recorded in the first part of the "Wreck." Now the fire that breaks from Christ's "dark descending" is not to be wondered at if—forgetting for a moment his "too huge Godhead"— we merely consider the life of a Christian.

3. "Christ's imitator."—Whether he takes an active part in ploughing God's fields (priest in parish; missionary; layman) or more passively suffers (like Hopkins) in a bleak "world without event," his efforts or his burning love shine "like shook foil," or gash "gold-vermilion" like Father Francis's "love-scape crucified." The disciple "stresses, instresses" Christ's own "fire." And any Christian can achieve this by imitating, in his own different way, the Windhover and Christ. By gathering together and humbling his own gifts, his spiritual life will become far lovelier and more dangerous than the mere enjoyment of his mortal gifts.

The three levels are evidently intimately linked together in the poet's mind, and should be so in the reader's. The exclamations "O my chevalier!" and "ah my dear" are addressed to the bird, and to Christ, and to the poet's heart. The whole poem is at once one of Hopkins's splendid meditations on Christ's glory and sacrifice as God and Man-God, and one of his deep ponderings over the necessary "stressing and instressing" of the "sake and cipher of suffering Christ" without which it would be impossible for any

Christian (according to the poet), "to bathe in his fall-gold mercies, to breathe in his all-fire glances."

I believe, no doubt with much boldness, that this interpretation of mine answers all the difficulties of the sonnet, while rejecting all far-fetched explanations. Too many critics seem to vie with one another in their quest of subtle niceties. Mr. Grigson's comment on "rung upon the rein" is a perfect example of what I mean. Dr. Richards's is the obvious explanation. And why should Mr. Empson construe so strangely "plough down sillion shine"? True, sillion may shine, but it is the shine of the plough that the poet is considering; and the mould-board looks very much like the fiery wing of a bird!

Finally, the conflict between artist and ascetic, which so many commentators consider as the leading argument of the sonnet, is simply not there. The bird's "achieve" and mastery are admired as those of a creature of God and as a great symbol of Christ. And "buckling" beauty and valor and act . . . is not self-destruction, but self-dedication. It must be remembered that the "Windhover" belongs to Hopkins's "Welsh salad days," not to the terrible years of "No worst there is none."

Lyons   *J. G. Ritz*

Times Literary Supplement May 20, 1955

Sir,—The letter of Mr. Ritz on Hopkins's *Windhover,* in your number of May 6, deserves respect for giving a consistent interpretation of the whole poem; and an interesting one, though I am not convinced by it. Some weeks ago, you, Sir, were mentioning in an editorial the recent letters about the poem, and said that I seemed to have become doubtful. That is not what I meant; I was so sure of the general purport of the poem that I thought it was little affected if one left out, say, the pun on *buckle.* But Mr. Ritz makes the purport quite different, and his argument from the date is rather strong.

I think the poem is about training and about the doubt in Hopkins's mind, expressed with painful force in later sonnets, as to whether the severe Jesuit training had only crippled him. The flight of the bird and the lines made by the ploughman are beautiful with the unconscious grace of an acquired skill; but all that Hopkins has got from his discipline, as far as he can see, is what the Americans call a "slow burn." He none the less exults in the sacrifice. I confess I had not realized that the poem was done in '77, the year of his ordination, whereas all the "terrible sonnets" seem to belong either to '85, when he was sent to Ireland and felt overworked, or '89, the year of his death. However we need not assume that the suspicion was remote in '77; he had been under the training for nine years, burning his youthful poems in '68; and "my heart in hiding" is bound to mean something like it. I can agree that the effect is meant to be less tragic than in the later sonnets.

Mr. Ritz, on the other hand, takes the poem as about gloating over torture. Hopkins must have been "stirred" by the hawk because he saw it, or imagined it, swoop and catch its prey, just as Christ has swooped and mangled Hopkins. The swoop, the act of violence, is what is "lovelier" and "more dangerous" than the masterly gliding (whereas I had assumed that the parallel spiritual achievement was more so than the animal one). The plough has now to be envisaged as both ripping up and searing the flesh of the earth, and what "shines" is this hot weapon. Mr. Ritz expresses surprise at my wanting the new furrows to be what shine, but our two views there merely follow from our basic assumptions. To take "plough down sillion" as a whole scene in movement is not too strained, as grammar, for Hopkins if he wanted it; the trouble is that this mood of contemplation is not wanted by Mr. Ritz, who even has to take a poker, in the last line, to the exhausted fire. I am not sure why he thinks this savage interpretation more suited to the happy "salad days" of Hopkins, but he is well supported by the *Deutschland* of '75—e.g., "the swoon of a heart that the sweep and the hurl of thee trod."

Hopkins must have known, I agree, that the "valour and act" of the bird, the source of its beauty of movement, was killing other creatures; and the idea of the fierceness of God was not strange to him; but if this is the point of the poem why is he so far from saying it? The need for a suggestion of conquest in the bird he does feel, and says merely that it "rebuffed the big wind." The swoop can only be deduced from "Brute beauty and valour, and act, oh, air, pride, plume here/Buckle"; and if we insert this sudden crisis we have next to compare it to rather un-sudden things, the plod of the ploughman and the occasional fall of the embers as the coals that support them burn away. I agree and shall remember that the power to swoop was part of why he felt the bird made a good symbol for Christ; but I do not think it was the center of his mind here, where he is considering the gradual effects of a given course of life. At least, I was sure he was considering that till I was confronted with the date; but then again, it is not an odd theme for the year of his ordination.

The question, I think, has a larger bearing. Christian apologists nowadays, I seem to notice, have become rather defiantly keen on recalling the stark roots of primitive human sacrifice and their place in Christianity, even boasting in print (one is to suppose with a laugh) that the religion provides a more efficient sadistic drug than the forbidden Horror Comics. Hopkins like other mystics was very capable of scolding his God for Cruelty, but I don't think this idea rode his mind all the time; a more impersonal cruelty in the nature of things is what he sighs over in "no wonder of it." I am not sure that he wouldn't have considered Mr. Ritz's interpretation blasphemous, unlike the pun which I proposed on *buckle*.

W. Empson

Times Literary Supplement June 24, 1955

Sir,—Professor J. G. Ritz's statement (May 6) that all previous explanations of the "Windhover" had failed to satisfy him is understandable: our agreement with other critics is at best a "Yes, but —". I feel bound to say, however, that his own valuable exegesis does not differ greatly in its interpretation of the complex symbolism from the one given in Vol. 1 (1944) of my *Gerard Manley Hopkins*, which I know he has read. Professor Ritz says: "I consider the poem should be read on three different levels—*i.e.* in terms of the 'Windhover,' 'Christ,' and 'Christ's Imitator'." I think he is right; and I should like to quote, in support of his view, some extracts from my own critique:

(1) "The poet's emotions — sympathy, admiration, love — were ever aroused by all natural or 'mortal' beauty, but principally by the supreme pattern of 'immortal' beauty—the character of Christ. For this idea the poet had renounced worldly ambition, the fullest life of the senses. . . .

(2) "In the sestet, 'Buckle!' is an imperative, making the whole a plea to Christ." (I admitted that the sonnet *could* be read as a simple nature-poem "to the glory of God"; but such a reading "is like playing the *Appassionata* with one finger. . . .")

(3) "In the sestet Hopkins holds up to a passionate but critical judgment two conflicting sets of values, one represented by the 'Kingdom of daylight's dauphin'—the windhover, the other by the Kingdom of Heaven's 'chevalier'—Christ."

(4) "As the bird co-ordinates all its faculties in graceful flight and dangerous swoop, so the poet asks Christ's help in buckling and enclosing within the belt of the Jesuit rule all his own rich faculties." I pointed out also that "Buckle!" could bear, as overtones, two other relevant meanings, namely:—

(5) "For Hopkins, then, the example of Christ's life linked together three relevant and complementary meanings of 'Buckle!'—buckle within (discipline), buckle to (labor), buckle under (sacrifice). Moreover, the story, implicit throughout the *Letters*, of the poet's own 'imitation of Christ,' is epitomized in the sestet of this sonnet."

(6) "In a direct or straightforward reading, all this (lines 9-11) could be addressed to the kestrel, the 'chevalier' of the air; but, if, as we have decided, the stress is on 'my' (line 11), it is certainly intended for the listening Christ, the perfect example of *spiritual* activity as the bird is a perfect example of *physical* activity. By the same token, the glamor of 'chevalier' is reflected back to the poet himself, who resembles, in opposite ways, both the bird and the Master. By an act of will, the poet has turned from the ruthless freedom and joy of the kestrel to the compassionate servitude of Christ ('O my chevalier'). Hopkins, himself, when free to act, was the curvetting and caracoling knight-errant of poetry; but the King he chose

to serve was He who once rode, slowly and humbly, on an ass. The mental transition from 'chevalier' ... to *soldier of Christ* (the Jesuit priest, or, as I now add, any good Christian) makes the next symbol of humble, useful toil—the plough—both natural and moving. The sequence is: 'The wind-hover flashes a trail of beauty across the morning sky; but the beauty in action, the inspiration, the glory, of Christ (and in a lesser degree of the plodding, inhibited poet-priest) is far, far lovelier. The taut swooping windhover is the terror of the air; but the disciplined life of the spirit is much more dangerous, because it is menaced by, and must itself attack and overcome, a far greater foe—the powers of evil."

I think Professor Ritz will admit that the three-level reading is there, even though we differ on a number of secondary points. He cannot accept the implied (*not* overt) clash between the artist and the ascetic (first perceived by the otherwise erring Dr. I. A. Richards); yet he sees in the poem Hopkins's imitation of "the suffering of Christ," and he must know that by 1877 Hopkins the artist had endured, though willingly, many frustrations. Hopkins was at once the "victim" and the dedicated servant of Christ. Even in his "Welsh salad days" (1874) his necessary abandonment, for a time, of music and Welsh "disappointed me and took an interest away—and at that time I was very bitterly feeling the weariness of life and shed many tears, perhaps not wholly into the breast of God but with some unmanliness in them too, and sighed and panted to Him. ..." Again, in 1876, his great poem "The Wreck of the Deutschland," executed after a seven years' silence with much joy and labor, had been refused by the Jesuit magazine, *The Month*. Already he had felt something of the self-galling, the gash, and the mystical satisfaction of sacrifice, which are so poignantly expressed in the last two lines of the "Windhover." Without the submerged antinomy of what Bridges called "sensualism and asceticism," this sonnet could never have been written; but within the poem itself the artist and the ascetic are triumphantly reconciled and united.

Though I admire Professor Ritz's comparison between the bird swooping and Christ stooping to earth to snatch men back to heaven, I think he oversimplifies by ignoring the common meaning of "Buckle!" which strongly suggests the voluntary self-crippling of the Crucifixion.[1] As I repeated in the Penguin *Hopkins* (p. 135), the poet was always stressing the self-immolation of Christ:

"Christ our Lord ... was doomed to succeed by failure: his plans were baffled, his hopes dashed, and his work was done by being broken off undone.

"In his Passion all this strength was spent, this lissomness crippled, this beauty wrecked, this majesty beaten down."

Anyone who can read these words and still hear no undertones of divine

---

[1] To this Professor Gardner wishes to add:

"I say here 'voluntary self-crippling' because, although the Crucifixion was decreed and executed by men, Christ, being God, could have ordained for Himself a different destiny."

masochism in "Buckle!", "plod," "Fall, gall themselves and gash" is capable of a simplification to which I cannot descend. As I read the sestet I can hold in my mind (both comfortably and uncomfortably) not only the Ritz-Gardner "three levels" but also three meanings of "Buckle!" This may seem "far fetched"; but Hopkins admired "far-fetchedness"—whenever the result was worth the carriage.

Lastly, I cannot take Professor Ritz's poker to stir the embers in Line 13. The poet clearly says that they "fall" and "gall *themselves*," as embers will when the consumed fuel below cannot support the half-consumed above. Yet if the poker is the will of God, or the poet's conscience, it will serve.

University of The Orange Free State   W. H. Gardner
Bloemfontein

DOES THE THEORY OF EVOLUTION HAVE ETHICAL CONSEQUENCES?

ETHICAL DISCUSSIONS are usually grounded in deductive logic. The reason is that moral rules derive from first principles rather than from systematic experiments. Take the example of a mother's admonishment to her small sadistic son: "Don't pull the cat's tail; that's not nice." The moral rule she cites, though she may not know it, is the end product of a syllogism such as this:

> *Unnecessarily cruel actions are bad;*
> *Pulling a cat's tail is an unnecessarily cruel action;*
> *Pulling a cat's tail is bad.*

Certainly the mother's statement is not drawn from an experiment, real or imaginary, with cat's tails a, b, c, . . . n, in which each pulling proved to be bad until the experimenter felt safe in making the inductive leap to "Pulling a cat's tail is bad." Specific moral rules, then, descend deductively from a general first principle. Some, however, might argue that the "first principle" here is not a true first principle, but is itself the result of induction. In other words, the belief that unnecessarily cruel actions are bad comes from long human experience, which has shown that cruel actions frequently do harm to the human race, and never benefit it. But one who reasons in this way does not circumvent first principles, since he is merely setting up as superior a different first principle: "That which harms the human race is bad." Although inductive logic may figure in an ethical dis-

cussion, deductive logic is likely to predominate because ethics grows out of absolutes.

The writers in this section are concerned, at least in part, with the ethical implications of evolution. The question is a difficult one partly because evolution is hard to interpret. Just what is its most important feature, the struggle for survival and supremacy, or the drive toward improvement of the species? And an even greater problem is whether evolution actually has ethical implications. Can mere facts about the world lead to moral rules for men? Does science have anything to say to the ethical philosopher? Does the way things are suggest the way they ought to be? These questions are at the frontier of ethical theory, and all the selections below deal with them either openly or by implication.

The English biologist Thomas H. Huxley (1825-1895) was one of the first, and one of the most important, defenders of Darwinism. His grandson, Julian Huxley (1887-   ) is a prominent geneticist. Earnest Albert Hooton (1887-1954) and George Gaylord Simpson (1902-   ) represent American science; Professor Hooton taught anthropology at Harvard until his death, and Professor Simpson is currently teaching paleontology there. The poet Delmore Schwartz (1913-   ) has taught English and has acted as an editor of the Partisan Review.

EVOLUTION OF ETHICS | *T. H. HUXLEY*

Modern thought is making a fresh start from the base whence Indian and Greek philosophy set out; and, the human wind being very much what it was six-and-twenty centuries ago, there is no ground for wonder if it presents indications of a tendency to move along the old lines to the same results.

We are more than sufficiently familiar with modern pessimism, at least as a speculation; for I cannot call to mind that any of its present votaries have sealed their faith by assuming the rags and the bowl of the mendicant Bhikku, or the wallet of the Cynic. The obstacles placed in the way of sturdy vagrancy by an unphilosophical police have, perhaps, proved too formidable for philosophical consistency. We also know modern speculative optimism, with its perfectibility of the species, reign of peace, and lion and lamb transformation scenes; but one does not hear so much of it as one did forty years ago; indeed, I imagine it is to be met with more commonly at the tables of the healthy and wealthy, than in the congregations of the wise. The majority of us, I apprehend, profess neither pessimism nor optimism. We hold that the world is neither so good, nor so bad, as it conceivably

From *Evolution and Ethics* (1893).

might be; and, as most of us have reason, now and again, to discover that it can be. Those who have failed to experience the joys that make life worth living are, probably, in as small a minority as those who have never known the griefs that rob existence of its savor and turn its richest fruits into mere dust and ashes.

Further, I think I do not err in assuming that, however diverse their views on philosophical and religious matters, most men are agreed that the proportion of good and evil in life may be very sensibly affected by human action. I never heard anybody doubt that the evil may be thus increased, or diminished; and it would seem to follow that good must be similarly susceptible of addition or subtraction. Finally, to my knowledge, nobody professes to doubt that, so far forth as we possess a power of bettering things, it is our paramount duty to use it and to train all our intellect and energy to this supreme service of our kind.

Hence the pressing interest of the question, to what extent modern progress in natural knowledge, and, more especially, the general outcome of that progress in the doctrine of evolution, is competent to help us in the great work of helping one another?

The propounders of what are called the "ethics of evolution," when the "evolution of ethics" would usually better express the object of their specu-lations, adduce a number of more or less interesting facts and more or less sound arguments in favor of the origin of the moral sentiments, in the same way as other natural phenomena, by a process of evolution. I have little doubt, for my own part, that they are on the right track; but as the immoral sentiments have no less been evolved, there is, so far, as much natural sanc-tion for the one as the other. The thief and the murderer follow nature just as much as the philanthropist. Cosmic evolution may teach us how the good and the evil tendencies of man may have come about; but, in itself, it is incompetent to furnish any better reason why what we call good is prefer-able to what we call evil than we had before. Some day, I doubt not, we shall arrive at an understanding of the evolution of the esthetic faculty; but all the understanding in the world will neither increase nor diminish the force of the intuition that this is beautiful and that is ugly.

There is another fallacy which appears to me to pervade the so-called "ethics of evolution." It is the notion that because, on the whole, animals and plants have advanced in perfection of organization by means of the struggle for existence and the consequent "survival of the fittest"; therefore men in society, men as ethical beings, must look to the same process to help them towards perfection. I suspect that this fallacy has arisen out of the unfortunate ambiguity of the phrase "survival of the fittest." "Fittest" has a connotation of "best"; and about "best" there hangs a moral flavor. In cosmic nature, however, what is "fittest" depends upon the conditions. Long since, I ventured to point out that if our hemisphere were to cool again, the survival of the fittest might bring about, in the vegetable kingdom, a population of more and more stunted and humbler and humbler organisms, until the "fittest" that survived might be nothing but lichens, diatoms, and such microscopic organisms as those which give red snow its color; while, if it became hotter, the pleasant valleys of the Thames and Isis might be uninhabitable by any animated beings save those that flourish in a tropical jungle. They, as the fittest, the best adapted to the changed conditions, would survive.

Men in society are undoubtedly subject to the cosmic process. As among other animals, multiplication goes on without cessation, and involves severe competition for the means of support. The struggle for existence tends to eliminate those less fitted to adapt themselves to the circumstances of their existence. The strongest, the most self-assertive, tend to tread down the weaker. But the influence of the cosmic process on the evolution of society is the greater the more rudimentary its civilization. Social progress means a checking of the cosmic process at every step and the substitution for it of another, which may be called the ethical process; the end of which is not the survival of those who may happen to be the fittest, in respect of the whole of the conditions which obtain, but of those who are ethically the best.

As I have already urged, the practice of that which is ethically best— what we call goodness or virtue—involves a course of conduct which, in all respects, is opposed to that which leads to success in the cosmic struggle for existence. In place of ruthless self-assertion it demands self-restraint; in place of thrusting aside, or treading down, all competitors, it requires that the individual shall not merely respect, but shall help his fellows; its influence is directed, not so much to the survival of the fittest, as to the fitting of as many as possible to survive. It repudiates the gladiatorial theory of existence. It demands that each man who enters into the enjoyment of the advantages of a polity shall be mindful of his debt to those who have laboriously constructed it; and shall take heed that no act of his weakens the fabric in which he has been permitted to live. Laws and moral precepts are directed to the end of curbing the cosmic process and reminding the individual of his duty to the community, to the protection and influence of which he owes, if not existence itself, at least the life of something better than a brutal savage.

It is from neglect of these plain considerations that the fanatical individualism of our time attempts to apply the analogy of cosmic nature to society. Once more we have a misapplication of the stoical injunction to follow nature; the duties of the individual to the state are forgotten, and his tendencies to self-assertion are dignified by the name of rights. It is seriously debated whether the members of a community are justified in using their combined strength to constrain one of their number to contribute his share to the maintenance of it; or even to prevent him from doing his best to destroy it. The struggle for existence which has done such admirable work in cosmic nature, must, it appears, be equally beneficent in the ethical sphere. Yet if that which I have insisted upon is true; if the cosmic process has no sort of relation to moral ends; if the imitation of it by man is inconsistent with the first principles of ethics; what becomes of this surprising theory?

Let us understand, once for all, that the ethical progress of society depends, not on imitating the cosmic process, still less in running away from it, but in combating it. It may seem an audacious proposal thus to put the microcosm against the macrocosm and to set man to subdue nature to his higher ends; but I venture to think that the great intellectual difference between the ancient times with which we have been occupied and our day, lies in the solid foundation we have acquired for the hope that such an enterprise may meet with a certain measure of success.

The history of civilization details the steps by which men have succeeded in building up an artificial world within the cosmos. Fragile reed as he may be, man, as Pascal says, is a thinking reed: there lies within him a fund of energy operating intelligently and so far akin to that which pervades the universe, that it is competent to influence and modify the cosmic process. In virtue of his intelligence, the dwarf bends the Titan to his will. In every family, in every polity that has been established, the cosmic process in man has been restrained and otherwise modified by law and custom; in surrounding nature, it has been similarly influenced by the art of the shepherd, the agriculturist, the artisan. As civilization has advanced, so has the extent of this interference increased; until the organized and highly developed sciences and arts of the present day have endowed man with a command over the course of non-human nature greater than that once attributed to the magicians. The most impressive, I might say startling, of these changes have been brought about in the course of the last two centuries; while a right comprehension of the process of life and of the means of influencing its manifestations is only just dawning upon us. We do not yet see our way beyond generalities; and we are befogged by the obtrusion of false analogies and crude anticipations. But Astronomy, Physics, Chemistry, have all had to pass through similar phases, before they reached the stage at which their influence became an important factor in human affairs. Physiology, Psychology, Ethics, Political Science, must submit to the same ordeal. Yet it seems to me irrational to doubt that, at no distant period, they will work as great a revolution in the sphere of practice.

The theory of evolution encourages no millennial anticipations. If, for millions of years, our globe has taken the upward road, yet, some time, the summit will be reached and the downward route will be commenced. The most daring imagination will hardly venture upon the suggestion that the power and the intelligence of man can ever arrest the procession of the great year.

Moreover, the cosmic nature born with us and, to a large extent, necessary for our maintenance, is the outcome of millions of years of severe training, and it would be folly to imagine that a few centuries will suffice to subdue its masterfulness to purely ethical ends. Ethical nature may count upon having to reckon with a tenacious and powerful enemy as long as the world lasts. But, on the other hand, I see no limit to the extent to which intelligence and will, guided by sound principles of investigation, and organized in common effort, may modify the conditions of existence, for a period longer than that now covered by history. And much may be done to change the nature of man himself. The intelligence which has converted the brother of the wolf into the faithful guardian of the flock ought to be able to do something towards curbing the instincts of savagery in civilized men.

But if we may permit ourselves a larger hope of abatement of the essential evil of the world than was possible to those who, in the infancy of exact knowledge, faced the problem of existence more than a score of centuries ago, I deem it an essential condition of the realization of that hope that we should cast aside the notion that the escape from pain and sorrow is the proper object of life.

We have long since emerged from the heroic childhood of our race, when good and evil could be met with the same "frolic welcome"; the attempts to escape from evil, whether Indian or Greek, have ended in flight from the battlefield; it remains to us to throw aside the youthful over-confidence and the no less youthful discouragement of nonage. We are grown men, and must play the man

> strong in will
> To strive, to seek, to find, and not to yield,

cherishing the good that falls in our way, and bearing the evil, in and around us, with stout hearts set on diminishing it. So far, we all may strive in one faith towards one hope:

> It may be that the gulfs will wash us down,
> It may be we shall touch the Happy Isles,
>
> .... but something ere the end,
> Some work of noble note may yet be done.

THE UNIQUENESS OF MAN | JULIAN HUXLEY

Man's opinion of his own position in relation to the rest of the animals has swung pendulum-wise between too great or too little a conceit of himself, fixing now too large a gap between himself and the animals, now too small. The gap, of course, can be diminished or increased at either the animal or the human end. One can, like Descartes, make animals too

From Julian Huxley, *Man Stands Alone* (New York, Harper & Row Publishers, 1939). Copyright, 1939, by Julian S. Huxley.

mechanical, or, like most unsophisticated people, humanize them too much. Or one can work at the human end of the gap, and then either dehumanize one's own kind into an animal species like any other, or superhumanize it into beings a little lower than the angels.

Primitive and savage man, the world over, not only accepts his obvious kinship with animals but also projects into them many of his own attributes. So far as we can judge, he has very little pride in his own humanity. With the advent of settled civilization, economic stratification, and the development of an elaborate religion as the ideological mortar of a now class-ridden society, the pendulum began slowly to swing into the other direction. Animal divinities and various physiological functions such as fertility gradually lost their sacred importance. Gods became anthropomorphic and human psychological qualities pre-eminent. Man saw himself as a being set apart, with the rest of the animal kingdom created to serve his needs and pleasure, with no share in salvation, no position in eternity. In Western civilization this swing of the pendulum reached its limit in developed Christian theology and in the philosophy of Descartes: both alike inserted a qualitative and unbridgeable barrier between all men and any animals.

With Darwin, the reverse swing was started. Man was once again regarded as an animal, but now in the light of science rather than of unsophisticated sensibility. At the outset, the consequences of the changed outlook were not fully explored. The unconscious prejudices and attitudes of an earlier age survived, disguising many of the moral and philosophical implications of the new outlook. But gradually the pendulum reached the furthest point of its swing. What seemed the logical consequences of the Darwinian postulates were faced: man is an animal like any other; accordingly, his views as to the special meaning of human life and human ideals need merit no more consideration in the light of eternity (or of evolution) than those of a bacillus or a tapeworm. Survival is the only criterion of evolutionary success: therefore, all existing organisms are of equal value. The idea of progress is a mere anthropomorphism. Man happens to be the dominant type at the moment, but he might be replaced by the ant or the rat. And so on.

The gap between man and animal was here reduced not by exaggerating the human qualities of animals, but by minimizing the human qualities of men. Of late years, however, a new tendency has become apparent. It may be that this is due mainly to the mere increase of knowledge and the extension of scientific analysis. It may be that it has been determined by social and psychological causes. Disillusionment with *laisser-faire* in the human economic sphere may well have spread to the planetary system of *laisser-faire* that we call natural selection. With the crash of old religious, ethical, and political systems, man's desperate need for some scheme of values and ideals may have prompted a more critical re-examination of his biological position. Whether this be so is a point that I must leave to the social historians. The fact remains that the pendulum is again on the swing, the man-animal gap again broadening. After Darwin, man could no longer avoid considering himself as an animal; but he is beginning to see himself as a very peculiar and in many ways a unique animal. The analysis of man's biological uniqueness is as yet incomplete. This essay is an attempt to review its present position.

The first and most obviously unique characteristic of man is his capacity for conceptual thought; if you prefer objective terms, you will say his employment of true speech, but that is only another way of saying the same thing. True speech involves the use of verbal signs for objects, not merely for feelings. Plenty of animals can express the fact that they are hungry; but none except man can ask for an egg or a banana. And to have words for objects at once implies conceptual thought, since an object is always one of a class. No doubt, children and savages are as unaware of using conceptual thought as Monsieur Jourdain was unaware of speaking in prose; but they cannot avoid it. Words are tools which automatically carve concepts out of experience. The faculty of recognizing objects as members of a class provides the potential basis for the concept: the use of words at once actualizes the potentiality.

This basic human property has had many consequences. The most important was the development of a cumulative tradition. The beginnings of tradition, by which experience is transmitted from one generation to the next, are to be seen in many higher animals. But in no case is the tradition cumulative. Offspring learn from parents, but they learn the same kind and quantity of lessons as they, in turn, impart: the transmission of experience never bridges more than one generation. In man, however, tradition is an independent and potentially permanent activity, capable of indefinite improvement in quality and increase in quantity. It constitutes a new accessory process of heredity in evolution, running side by side with the biological process, a heredity of experience to supplement the universal heredity of living substance.

The existence of a cumulative tradition has as its chief consequence— or if you prefer, its chief objective manifestation—the progressive improvement of human tools and machinery. Many animals employ tools; but they are always crude tools employed in a crude way. Elaborate tools and skilled technique can develop only with the aid of speech and tradition.

In the perspective of evolution, tradition and tools are the characters which have given man his dominant position among organisms. This biological dominance is, at present, another of man's unique properties. In each geological epoch of which we have knowledge there have been types which must be styled biologically dominant: they multiply, they extinguish or reduce competing types, they extend their range, they radiate into new modes of life. Usually at any one time there is one such type—the placental mammals, for instance, in the Cenozoic Epoch; but sometimes there is more than one. The Mesozoic is usually called the Age of Reptiles, but in reality the reptiles were then competing for dominance with the insects: in earlier periods we should be hard put to it to decide whether trilobites, nautiloids, or early fish were *the* dominant type. Today, however, there is general agreement that man is the sole type meriting the title. Since the early Pleistocene, widespread extinction has diminished the previously dominant group of placental mammals, and man has not merely multiplied, but has evolved, extended his range, and increased the variety of his modes of life.

Biology thus reinstates man on a position analogous to that conferred on him as Lord of Creation by theology. There are, however, differences, and differences of some importance for our general outlook. In the biological view, the other animals have not been created to serve man's needs, but man has evolved in such a way that he has been able to eliminate some competing types, to enslave others by domestication, and to modify physical and biological conditions over the larger part of the earth's land area. The theological view was not true in detail or in many of its implications; but it had a solid biological basis.

Speech, tradition, and tools have led to many other unique properties of man. These are, for the most part, obvious and well known, and I propose to leave them aside until I have dealt with some less familiar human characteristics. For the human species, considered as a species, is unique in certain purely biological attributes; and these have not received the attention they deserve, either from the zoological or the sociological standpoint.

In the first place, man is by far the most variable wild species known. Domesticated species like dog, horse, or fowl may rival or exceed him in this particular, but their variability has obvious reasons, and is irrelevant to our inquiry.

In correlation with his wide variability, man has a far wider range than any other animal species, with the possible exception of some of his parasites. Man is also unique as a dominant type. All other dominant types have evolved into many hundreds or thousands of separate species, grouped in numerous genera, families, and larger classificatory groups. The human type has maintained its dominance without splitting: man's variety has been achieved within the limits of a single species.

Finally, man is unique among higher animals in the method of his evolution. Whereas, in general, animal evolution is divergent, human evolution is reticulate. By this is meant that in animals, evolution occurs by the isolation of groups which then become progressively more different in their genetic characteristics, so that the course of evolution can be represented as a divergent radiation of separate lines, some of which become extinct, others continue unbranched, and still other divergently branch again. Whereas in man, after incipient divergence, the branches have come together again, and have generated new diversity from their Mendelian recombinations, this process being repeated until the course of human descent is like a network.

All these biological peculiarities are interconnected. They depend on man's migratory propensities, which themselves arise from his fundamental peculiarities, of speech, social life, and relative independence of environment. They depend again on his capacity, when choosing mates, for neglecting large differences of color and appearance which would almost certainly be more than enough to deter more instinctive and less plastic animals. Thus divergence, though it appears to have gone quite a long way in early human evolution, generating the very distinct white, black, and yellow subspecies and perhaps others, was never permitted to attain its normal culmination. Mutually infertile groups were never produced; man remained a single species. Furthermore, crossing between distinct types, which is a rare and extraordinary phenomenon in other animals, in him became normal and of major importance. According to Mendelian laws, such crosses generate much excess variability by producing new recombinations. Man is thus more variable than other species for two reasons. First, because migration has recaptured for the single interbreeding group divergences of a magnitude that in animals would escape into the isolation of separate species; and secondly, because the resultant crossing has generated recombinations which both quantitatively and qualitatively are on a far bigger scale than is supplied by the internal variability of even the numerically most abundant animal species.

We may contrast this with the state of affairs among ants, the dominant insect group. The ant type is more varied than the human type; but it has achieved this variability by intense divergent evolution. Several thousand species of ants are known, and the number is being added to each year with the increase of biological exploration. Ways of life among ants are divided among different subtypes, each rigidly confined to its own methods. Thus even if ants were capable of accumulating experience, there could exist no single world-wide ant tradition. The fact that the human type comprises but one biological species is a consequence of his capacity for tradition, and also permits his exploitation of that unique capacity to the utmost.

Let us remind ourselves that superposed upon this purely biological or genetic variability is the even greater amount of variability due to differences of upbringing, profession, and personal tastes. The final result is a degree of variation that would be staggering if it were not so familiar. It would be fair to say that, in respect to mind and outlook, individual human beings are separated by differences as profound as those which distinguish the major groups of the animal kingdom. The difference between a somewhat subnormal member of a savage tribe and a Beethoven or a Newton is assuredly comparable in extent with that between a sponge and a higher mammal. Leaving aside such vertical differences, the lateral difference between the mind of, say, a distinguished general or engineer of extrovert type and of an introvert genius in mathematics or religious mysticism is no less than that between an insect and a vertebrate. This enormous range of individual variation in human minds often leads to misunderstanding and even mutual incomprehensibility; but it also provides the necessary basis for fruitful division of labor in human society.

Another biological peculiarity of man is the uniqueness of his evolutionary history. Writers have indulged their speculative fancy by imagining other organisms endowed with speech and conceptual thought—talking rats, rational ants, philosophic dogs, and the like. But closer analysis shows that these fantasies are impossible. A brain capable of conceptual thought could not have been developed elsewhere than in a human body.

The course followed by evolution appears to have been broadly as follows. From a generalized early type, various lines radiate out, exploiting the environment in various ways. Some of these comparatively soon reach a limit to their evolution, at least as regards major alteration. Thereafter they are limited to minor changes such as the formation of new genera and species. Others, on the other hand, are so constructed that they can continue their career, generating new types which are successful in the struggle for existence because of their greater control over the environment and their greater independence of it. Such changes are legitimately called "progressive." The new type repeats the process. It radiates out into a number of lines, each specializing in a particular direction. The great majority of these come up against dead ends and can advance no further: specialization is one-sided progress, and after a longer or shorter time, reaches a biomechanical limit. The horse stock cannot reduce its digits below one; the elephants are near the limits of size for terrestrial animals; feathered flight cannot become aerodynamically more efficient than in existing birds, and so on.

Sometimes all the branches of a given stock have come up against their limit, and then either have become extinct or have persisted without major change. This happened, for instance, to the echinoderms, which with their sea-urchins, star-fish, brittle-stars, sea-lilies, sea-cucumbers, and other types now extinct had pushed the life that was in them into a series of blind alleys: they have not advanced for perhaps a hundred million years, nor have they given rise to other major types.

In other cases, all but one or two of the lines suffer this fate, while the rest repeat the process. All reptilian lines were blind alleys save two—one which was transformed into the birds, and another which became the mammals. Of the bird stock, all lines came to a dead end; of the mammals, all but one—the one which became man.

Evolution is thus seen as an enormous number of blind alleys, with a very occasional path of progress. It is like a maze in which almost all turnings are wrong turnings. The goal of the evolutionary maze, however, is not a central chamber, but a road which will lead definitely onwards.

If now we look back upon the past history of life, we shall see that the avenues of progress have been steadily reduced in number, until by the Pleistocene period, or even earlier, only one was left. Let us remember that we can and must judge early progress in the light of its latest steps. The most recent step has been the acquisition of conceptual thought, which has enabled man to dethrone the non-human mammals from their previous position of dominance. It is biologically obvious that conceptual thought could never have arisen save in an animal, so that all plants, both green and otherwise, are at once eliminated. As regards animals, I need not detail all the early steps in their progressive evolution. Since some degree of bulk helps to confer independence of the forces of nature, it is obvious that the combination of many cells to form a large individual was one necessary step, thus eliminating all single-celled forms from such progress. Similarly, progress is barred to specialized animals with no blood-system, like planarian worms; to internal parasites, like tapeworms; to animals with radial symmetry and consequently no head, like echinoderms.

Of the three highest animal groups—the molluscs, the arthropods, and the vertebrates—the molluscs advanced least far. One condition for the later steps in biological progress was land life. The demands made upon the organism by exposure to air and gravity called forth biological mechanisms, such as limbs, sense-organs, protective skin, and sheltered development, which were necessary foundations for later advance. And the molluscs have never been able to produce efficient terrestrial forms: their culmination is in marine types like squid and octopus.

The arthropods, on the other hand, have scored their greatest successes on land, with the spiders and especially the insects. Yet the fossil record reveals a lack of all advance, even in the most successful types such as ants, for a long time back—certainly during the last thirty million years, probably during the whole of the Tertiary epoch. Even during the shorter of these periods, the mammals were still evolving rapidly, and man's rise is contained in a fraction of this time.

What was it that cut the insects off from progress? The answer appears to lie in their breathing mechanism. The land arthropods have adopted the method of air-tubes or tracheae, branching to microscopic size and conveying gases directly to and from the tissues, instead of using the dual mechanism of lungs and bloodstream. The laws of gaseous diffusion are such that respiration by tracheae is extremely efficient for very small animals, but becomes rapidly less efficient with increase of size, until it ceases to be of use at a bulk below that of a house mouse. It is for this reason that no insect has ever become, by vertebrate standards, even moderately large.

It is for the same reason that no insect has ever become even moderately intelligent. The fixed pathways of instinct, however elaborate, require far fewer nerve-cells than the multiple switchboards that underlie intelligence. It appears to be impossible to build a brain mechanism for flexible behavior with less than a quite large minimum of neurones; and no insect has reached a size to provide this minimum.

Thus only the land vertebrates are left. The reptiles shared biological dominance with the insects in the Mesozoic. But while the insects had reached the end of their blind alley, the reptiles showed themselves capable of further advance. Temperature regulation is a necessary basis for final progress, since without it the rate of bodily function could never be stabilized, and without such stabilization, higher mental processes could never become accurate and dependable.

Two reptilian lines achieved this next step, in the guise of the birds and the mammals. The birds soon, however, came to a dead end, chiefly because their forelimbs were entirely taken up in the specialization for flight. The subhuman mammals made another fundamental advance, in the shape of internal development, permitting the young animal to arrive at a much more advanced stage before it was called upon to face the world. They also (like the birds) developed true family life.

Most mammalian lines, however, cut themselves off from indefinite progress by one-sided evolution, turning their limbs and jaws into specialized and therefore limited instruments. And, for the most part, they relied mainly on the crude sense of smell, which cannot present as differentiated a pattern of detailed knowledge as can sight. Finally, the majority continued to produce their young several at a time, in litters. As J. B. S. Haldane has pointed out, this gives rise to an acute struggle for existence in the prenatal period, a considerable percentage of embryos being aborted or resorbed. Such intra-uterine selection will put a premium upon rapidity of growth and differentiation, since the devil takes the hindmost; and this rapidity of development will tend automatically to be carried on into postnatal growth.

As everyone knows, man is characterized by a rate of development which is abnormally slow as compared with that of any other mammal. The period from birth to the first onset of sexual maturity comprises nearly a quarter of the normal span of his life, instead of an eighth, a tenth or twelfth, as in some other animals. This again is in one sense a unique characteristic of man, although from the evolutionary point of view it represents merely the exaggeration of a tendency which is operative in other Primates. In any case, it is a necessary condition for the evolution and proper utilization of rational thought. If men and women were, like mice, confronted with the problems of adult life and parenthood after a few weeks, or even, like whales, after a couple of years, they could never acquire the skills of body and mind that they now absorb from and contribute to the social heritage of the species.

This slowing (or "foetalization," as Bolk has called it, since it prolongs the foetal characteristics of earlier ancestral forms into postnatal development and even into adult life) has had other important by-products for man. Here I will mention but one—his nakedness. The distribution of hair on man is extremely similar to that on a late foetus of a chimpanzee, and there can be little doubt that it represents an extension of this temporary anthropoid phase into permanence. Hairlessness of body is not a unique biological characteristic of man; but it is unique among terrestrial mammals, save for a few desert creatures, and some others which have compensated for loss of hair by developing a pachydermatous skin. In any case, it has important biological consequences, since it must have encouraged the comparatively defenseless human creatures in their efforts to protect themselves against animal enemies and the elements, and so has been a spur to the improvement of intelligence.

Now, foetalization could never have occurred in a mammal producing many young at a time, since intra-uterine competition would have encouraged the opposing tendency. Thus we may conclude that conceptual thought could develop only in a mammalian stock which normally brings forth but one young at a birth. Such a stock is provided in the primates—lemurs, monkeys, and apes.

The Primates also have another characteristic which was necessary for the ancestor of a rational animal—they are arboreal. It may seem curious that living in trees is a prerequisite of conceptual thought. But Elliot Smith's analysis has abundantly shown that only in an arboreal mammal could the forelimb become a true hand, and sight become dominant over smell. Hands obtain an elaborate tactile pattern of what they handle, eyes an elaborate visual pattern of what they see. The combination of the two kinds of pattern, with the aid of binocular vision, in the higher centers of the brain allowed the Primate to acquire a wholly new richness of knowledge about objects, a wholly new possibility of manipulating them. Tree life laid the foundation both for the fuller definition of objects by conceptual thought and for the fuller control of them by tools and machines.

Higher Primates have yet another pre-requisite of human intelligence —they are all gregarious. Speech, it is obvious, could never have been evolved in a solitary type. And speech is as much the physical basis of conceptual thought as is protoplasm the physical basis of life.

For the passage, however, of the critical point between subhuman and human, between the biological subordination and the biological primacy of intelligence, between a limited and a potentially unlimited tradition—for this it was necessary for the arboreal animal to descend to the ground again. Only in a terrestrial creature could fully erect posture be acquired; and this was essential for the final conversion of the arms from locomotor limbs into manipulative hands. Furthermore, just as land life, ages previously, had demanded and developed a greater variety of response than had been required in the water, so now it did the same in relation to what had been required in the trees. An arboreal animal could never have evolved the skill of the hunting savage, nor ever have proceeded to the domestication of other animals or to agriculture.

We are now in a position to define the uniqueness of human evolution. The essential character of man as a dominant organism is conceptual thought. And conceptual thought could have arisen only in a multicellular animal, an animal with bilateral symmetry, head and blood system, a vertebrate as against a mollusc or an arthropod, a land vertebrate among vertebrates, a mammal among land vertebrates. Finally, it could have arisen only in a mammalian line which was gregarious, which produced one young at a birth instead of several, and which had recently become terrestrial after a long period of arboreal life.

There is only one group of animals which fulfills these conditions—a terrestrial offshoot of the higher Primates. Thus not merely has conceptual thought been evolved only in man: it could not have been evolved except in man. There is but one path of unlimited progress through the evolutionary maze. The course of human evolution is as unique as its result. It is unique not in the trivial sense of being a different course from that of any other organism, but in the profounder sense of being the only path that could have achieved the essential characters of man. Conceptual thought on this planet is inevitably associated with a particular type of Primate body and Primate brain.

A further property of man in which he is unique among higher animals concerns his sexual life. Man is prepared to mate at any time: animals are not. To start with, most animals have a definite breeding season; only during this period are their reproductive organs fully developed and functional. In addition to this, higher animals have one or more sexual cycles within their breeding seasons, and only at one phase of the cycle are they prepared to mate. In general, either a sexual season or a sexual cycle, or both, operates to restrict mating.

In man, however, neither of these factors is at work. There appear to be indications of a breeding season in some primitive peoples like the Eskimo, but even there they are but relics. Similarly, while there still exist physiological differences in sexual desire at different phases of the female sexual cycle, these are purely quantitative, and may readily be over-ridden by psychological factors. Man, to put it briefly, is continuously sexed: animals are discontinuously sexed. If we try to imagine what a human society would be like in which the sexes were interested in each other only during the summer, as in songbirds, or, as in female dogs, experienced sexual desire only once every few months, or even only once in a lifetime, as in ants, we can realize what this peculiarity has meant. In this, as in his slow growth and prolonged period of dependence, man is not abruptly marked off from all other animals, but represents the culmination of a process that can be clearly traced among other Primates. What the biological meaning of this evolutionary trend may be is difficult to understand. One suggestion is that it may be associated with the rise of mind to dominance. The bodily functions, in lower mammals rigidly determined by physiological mechanisms, come gradually under the more plastic control of the brain. But this, for what it is worth, is a mere speculation.

Another of the purely biological characters in which man is unique is his reproductive variability. In a given species of animals, the maximum litter-size may, on occasions, reach perhaps double the minimum, according to circumstances of food and temperature, or even perhaps threefold. But during a period of years, these variations will be largely equalized within a range of perhaps fifty percent either way from the average, and the percentage of wholly infertile adults is very low. In man, on the other hand, the range of positive fertility is enormous—from one to over a dozen, and in exceptional cases to over twenty; and the number of wholly infertile adults is considerable. This fact, in addition to providing a great diversity of patterns of family life, has important bearings on evolution. It means that in the human species differential fertility is more important as a basis for selection than is differential mortality; and it provides the possibility of much more rapid selective change than that found in wild animal species. Such rapidity of evolution would, of course, be effectively realized only if the stocks with large families possessed a markedly different hereditary constitution from those with few children; but the high differential fertility of unskilled workers as against the professional classes in England, or of the French Canadians against the rest of the inhabitants of Canada, demonstrates how rapidly populations may change by this means.

Still another point in which man is biologically unique is the length and relative importance of his period of what we may call "post-maturity." If we consider the female sex, in which the transition from reproductive maturity to nonreproductive post-maturity is more sharply defined than in the male, we find, in the first place, that in animals a comparatively small percentage of the population survives beyond the period of reproduction; in the second place, that such individuals rarely survive long, and so far as known never for a period equal to or greater than the period during which reproduction was possible; and thirdly, that such individuals are rarely of importance in the life of the species. The same is true of the male sex, provided we do not take the incapacity to produce fertile gametes as the criterion of post-maturity, but rather the appearance of signs of age, such as the beginnings of loss of vigor and weight, decreased sexual activity, or graying hair.

It is true that in some social mammals, notably among ruminants and Primates, an old male or old female is frequently found as leader of the herd. Such cases, however, provide the only examples of the special biological utility of post-mature individuals among animals; they are confined to a very small proportion of the population, and it is uncertain to what extent such individuals are post-mature in the sense we have defined. In any event, it is improbable that the period of post-maturity is anywhere near so long as that of maturity. But in civilized man the average expectation of life now includes over ten post-mature years, and about a sixth of the population enjoys a longer post-maturity than maturity. What is more, in all advanced human societies a large proportion of the leaders of the community are always post-mature. All the members of the British War Cabinet are post-mature.

This is truly a remarkable phenomenon. Through the new social mechanisms made possible by speech and tradition, man has been able to utilize for the benefit of the species a period of life which in almost all other creatures is a mere superfluity. We know that the dominance of the old can be over-emphasized; but it is equally obvious that society cannot do without the post-mature. To act on the slogan "Too old at forty"—or even at forty-five—would be to rob man of one of his unique characteristics, whereby he utilizes tradition to the best advantage.

We have now dealt in a broad way with the unique properties of man both from the comparative and the evolutionary point of view. Now we can return to the present and the particular and discuss these properties and their consequences a little more in detail. First, let us remind ourselves that the gap between human and animal thought is much greater than is usually supposed. The tendency to project familiar human qualities into animals is very strong, and colors the ideas of nearly all people who have not special familiarity both with animal behavior and scientific method.

Let us recall a few cases illustrating the unhuman characteristics of animal behavior. Everyone is familiar with the rigidity of instinct in insects. Worker ants emerge from their pupal case equipped not with the instincts to care for ant grubs in general, but solely with those suitable to ant grubs of their own species. They will attempt to care for the grubs of other species, but appear incapable of learning new methods if their instincts kill their foster children. Or again, a worker wasp, without food for a hungry grub, has been known to bite off its charge's tail and present it to its head. But even in the fine flowers of vertebrate evolution, the birds and mammals, behavior, though it may be more plastic than in the insects, is as essentially irrational. Birds, for instance, seem incapable of analyzing unfamiliar situations. For them some element in the situation may act as its dominant symbol, the only stimulus to which they can react. At other times, it is the organization of the situation as a whole which is the stimulus: if the whole is interfered with, analysis fails to dissect out the essential element. A hen meadow-pipit feeds her young when it gapes and squeaks in the nest. But if it has been ejected by a young cuckoo, gaping and squeaking has no effect, and the rightful offspring is neglected and allowed to die, while the usurper in the nest is fed. The pipit normally cares for its own young, but not because it recognizes them as such.

Mammals are no better. A cow deprived of its calf will be quieted by the provision of a crudely stuffed calfskin. Even the Primates are no exception. Female baboons whose offspring have died will continue carrying the corpses until they have not merely putrefied but mummified. This appears to be due not to any profundity of grief, but to a contact stimulus: the mother will react similarly to any moderately small and furry object.

Birds and especially mammals are, of course, capable of a certain degree of analysis, but this is effected, in the main, by means of trial and error through concrete experience. A brain capable of conceptual thought appears to be the necessary basis for speedy and habitual analysis. Without it, the practice of splitting up situations into their components and assigning real degrees of significance to the various elements remains rudimentary and rare, whereas with man, even when habit and trial and error are prevalent, conceptual thought is of major biological importance. The behavior of animals is essentially arbitrary, in that it is fixed within narrow limits. In man it has become relatively free—free at the incoming and outgoing ends alike. His capacity for acquiring knowledge has been largely released from arbitrary symbolism, his capacity for action, from arbitrary canalizations of instinct. He can thus rearrange the patterns of experience and action in a far greater variety, and can escape from the particular into the general.

Thus man is more intelligent than the animals because his brain mechanism is more plastic. This fact also gives him, of course, the opportunity of being more nonsensical and perverse: but its primary effects have been more analytical knowledge and more varied control. The essential fact, from my present standpoint, is that the change has been profound and in an evolutionary sense rapid. Although it has been brought about by the gradual quantitative enlargement of the association areas of the brain, the result has been almost as abrupt as the change (also brought about quantitatively) from solid ice to liquid water. We should remember that the machinery of the change has been an increase in plasticity and potential variety: it is by a natural selection of ideas and actions that the result has been greater rationality instead of greater irrationality.

This increase of flexibility has also had other psychological consequences which rational philosophers are apt to forget: and in some of these, too, man is unique. It has led, for instance, to the fact that man is the only organism normally and inevitably subject to psychological conflict. You can give a dog neurosis, as Pavlov did, by a complicated laboratory experiment: you can find cases of brief emotional conflict in the lives of wild birds and animals. But, for the most part, psychological conflict is shirked by the simple expedient of arranging that now one and now another instinct should dominate the animal's behavior. I remember in Spitsbergen finding the nest of a Red-throated Diver on the shore of an inland pool. The sitting bird was remarkably bold. After leaving the nest for the water, she stayed very close. She did not, however, remain in a state of conflict between fear of intruders and desire to return to her brooding. She would gradually approach as if to land, but eventually fear became dominant, and when a few feet from the shore she suddenly dived, and emerged a good way farther out—only to repeat the process. Here the external circumstances were such as to encourage conflict, but even so what are the most serious features of human conflict were minimized by the outlet of alternate action.

Those who take up bird-watching as a hobby tend at first to be surprised at the way in which a bird will turn, apparently without transition or hesitation, from one activity to another—from fighting to peaceable feeding, from courtship to uninterested preening, from panic flight to unconcern. It represents another aspect of the type of behavior I have just been describing for the Red-throated Diver. In this case, the internal state of the bird changes, presumably owing to some form of physiological fatigue or to a diminution of intensity of a stimulus with time or distance; the type of behavior which had been dominant ceases to have command over the machinery of action, and is replaced by another which just before had been subordinate and latent.

As a matter of fact, the prevention of conflict between opposed modes of action is a very general phenomenon, of obvious biological utility, and it is only the peculiarities of the human mind which have forced its partial abandonment on man. It begins on the purely mechanical level with the nervous machinery controlling our muscles. The main muscles of a limb, for instance, are arranged in two antagonistic sets, the flexors bending and the extensors straightening it. It would obviously be futile to throw both sets into action at the same time, and economical when one set is in action to reduce to the minimum any resistance offered by the other. This has actually been provided for. The nervous connections in the spinal cord are so arranged that when a given muscle receives an impulse to contract, its antagonist receives an impulse causing it to lose some of its tone and thus, by relaxing below its normal level, to offer the least possible resistance to the action of the active muscle.

Sherrington discovered that the same type of mechanism was operative in regard to the groups of muscles involved in whole reflexes. A dog, for instance, cannot very well walk and scratch itself at the same time. To avoid the waste involved in conflict between the walking and the scratching reflex, the spinal cord is constructed in such a way that throwing one reflex into action automatically inhibits the other. In both these cases, the machinery for preventing conflicts of activity resides in the spinal cord. Although the matter has not yet been analyzed physiologically, it would appear that the normal lack of conflict between instincts which we have just been discussing is due to some similar type of nervous mechanism in the brain.

When we reach the human level, there are new complications; for, as we have seen, one of the peculiarities of man is the abandonment of any rigidity of instinct, and the provision of association-mechanisms by which any activity of the mind, whether in the spheres of knowing, feeling, or willing, can be brought into relation with any other. It is through this that man has acquired the possibility of a unified mental life. But, by the same token, the door is opened to the forces of disruption, which may destroy any such unity and even prevent him from enjoying the efficiency of behavior attained by animals. For, as Sherrington has emphasized, the nervous system is like a funnel, with a much larger space for intake than for outflow. The intake cone of the funnel is represented by the receptor nerves, conveying impulses inward to the central nervous system from the sense-organs: the outflow tube is, then, through the effector nerves, conveying impulses outward to the muscles, and there are many more of the former than of the latter. If we like to look at the matter from a rather different standpoint, we may say that, since action can be effected only by muscles (strictly speaking, also by the glands, which are disregarded here for simplicity's sake), and since there are a limited number of muscles in the body, the only way for useful activity to be carried out is for the nervous system to impose a particular pattern of action on them, and for all other competing or opposing patterns to be cut out. Each pattern, when it has seized control of the machinery of action, *should* be in supreme command, like the captain of a ship. Animals are, in many ways, like ships which are commanded by a number of captains in turn, each specializing in one kind of action, and popping up and down between the authority of the bridge and the obscurity of their private cabins according to the business on hand. Man is on the way to achieving permanent unity of command, but the captain has a disconcerting way of dissolving into a wrangling committee.

Even on the new basis, however, mechanisms exist for minimizing conflict. They are what are known by psychologists as suppression and repression. From our point of view, repression is the more interesting. It implies the forcible imprisonment of one of two conflicting impulses in the dungeons of the unconscious mind. The metaphor is, however, imperfect. For the prisoner in the mental dungeon can continue to influence the tyrant above in the daylight of consciousness. In addition to a general neurosis, compulsive thoughts and acts may be thrust upon the personality. Repression may thus be harmful; but it can also be regarded as a biological necessity for dealing with inevitable conflict in the early years of life, before rational judgment and control are possible. Better to have the capacity for more or less unimpeded action, even at the expense of possible neurosis, than an organism constantly inactivated like the ass between the two bundles of hay, balanced in irresolution.

In repression, not only is the defeated impulse banished to the unconscious, but the very process of banishment is itself unconscious. The inhibitory mechanisms concerned in it must have been evolved to counteract the more obvious possibilities of conflict, especially in early life, which arose as by-products of the human type of mind.

In suppression, the banishment is conscious, so that neurosis is not likely to appear. Finally, in rational judgment, neither of the conflicting impulses is relegated to the unconscious, but they are balanced in the light of reason and experience, and control of action is consciously exercised.

I need not pursue the subject further. Here I am only concerned to show that the great biological advantages conferred on man by the unification

of mind have inevitably brought with them certain counterbalancing defects. The freedom of association between all aspects and processes of the
mind has provided the basis for conceptual thought and tradition; but it
has also provided potential antagonists, which in lower organisms were
carefully kept apart, with the opportunity of meeting face to face, and has
thus made some degree of conflict unavoidable.

In rather similar fashion, man's upright posture has brought with it certain consequential disadvantages in regard to the functioning of his internal
organs and his proneness to rupture. Thus man's unique characteristics are
by no means wholly beneficial.

In close correlation with our subjection to conflict is our proneness to
laughter. So characteristic of our species is laughter that man has been defined as the laughing animal. It is true that, like so much else of man's
uniqueness, it has its roots among the animals, where it reveals itself as an
expression of a certain kind of general pleasure—and thus in truth perhaps
more of a smile than a laugh. And in a few animals—ravens, for example—
there are traces of a malicious sense of humor. Laughter in man, however,
is much more than this. There are many theories of laughter, most of them
containing a partial truth. But biologically the important feature of human
laughter seems to lie in its providing a release for conflict, a resolution of
troublesome situations.

This and other functions of laughter can be exaggerated so that it becomes as the crackling of thorns under the pot, and prevents men from
taking anything seriously; but in due proportion its value is very great as
a lubricant against troublesome friction and a lightener of the inevitable
gravity and horror of life, which would otherwise become portentous and
overshadowing. True laughter, like true speech, is a unique possession of
man.

Those of man's unique characteristics which may better be called psychological and social than narrowly biological spring from one or the other of
three characteristics. The first is his capacity for abstract and general
thought: the second is the relative unification of his mental processes, as
against the much more rigid compartmentalization of animal mind and
behavior: the third is the existence of social units, such as tribe, nation,
party, and church, with a continuity of their own, based on organized
tradition and culture.

There are various by-products of the change from pre-human to the
human type of mind which are, of course, also unique biologically. Let us
enumerate a few: pure mathematics; musical gifts; artistic appreciation and
creation; religion; romantic love.

Mathematical ability appears, almost inevitably, as something mysterious.
Yet the attainment of speech, abstraction, and logical thought, bring it into
potential being. It may remain in a very rudimentary state of development;
but even the simplest arithmetical calculations are a manifestation of its
existence. Like any other human activity, it requires proper tools and

machinery. Arabic numerals, algebraic conventions, logarithms, the differential calculus, are such tools: each one unlocks new possibilities of mathematical achievement. But just as there is no essential difference between man's conscious use of a chipped flint as an implement and his design of the most elaborate machine, so there is none between such simple operations as numeration or addition and the comprehensive flights of higher mathematics. Again, some people are by nature more gifted than others in this field; yet no normal human being is unable to perform some mathematical operations. Thus the capacity for mathematics is, as I have said, a by-product of the human type of mind.

We have seen, however, that the human type of mind is distinguished by two somewhat opposed attributes. One is the capacity for abstraction, the other for synthesis. Mathematics is one of the extreme by-products of our capacity for abstraction. Arithmetic abstracts objects of all qualities save their enumerability; the symbol π abstracts in a single Greek letter a complicated relation between the parts of all circles. Art, on the other hand, is an extreme by-product of our capacity for synthesis. In one unique production, the painter can bring together form, color, arrangement, associations of memory, emotion, and idea. Dim adumbrations of art are to be found in a few creatures such as bower-birds; but nothing is found to which the word can rightly be applied until man's mind gave the possibility of freely mingling observations, emotions, memories, and ideas, and subjecting the mixture to deliberate control.

But it is not enough here to enumerate a few special activities. In point of fact, the great majority of man's activities and characteristics are by-products of his primary distinctive characteristics, and therefore, like them, biologically unique.

On the one hand, conversation, organized games, education, sport, paid work, gardening, the theater; on the other, conscience, duty, sin, humiliation, vice, penitence—these are all such unique by-products. The trouble, indeed, is to find any human activities which are not unique. Even the fundamental biological attributes such as eating, sleeping, and mating have been tricked out by man with all kinds of unique frills and peculiarities.

There may be other by-products of man's basic uniqueness which have not yet been exploited. For let us remember that such by-products may remain almost wholly latent until demand stimulates invention and invention facilitates development. It is asserted that there exist human tribes who cannot count above two; certainly some savages stop at ten. Here the mathematical faculty is restricted to numeration, and stops short at a very rudimentary stage of this rudimentary process. Similarly, there are human societies in which art has never been developed beyond the stage of personal decoration. It is probable that during the first half of the Pleistocene period, none of the human race had developed either their mathematical or their artistic potentialities beyond such a rudimentary stage.

It is perfectly possible that today man's so-called supernormal or extra-sensory faculties are in the same case as were his mathematical faculties during the first or second glaciations of the Ice Age—barely more than a potentiality, with no technique for eliciting and developing them, no tradition behind them to give them continuity and intellectual respectability. Even such simple performances as multiplying two three-figure numbers would have appeared entirely magical to early Stone Age men.

Experiments such as those of Rhine and Tyrrell on extra-sensory guessing, experiences like those of Gilbert Murray on thought transference, and the numerous sporadic records of telepathy and clairvoyance suggest that some people at least possess possibilities of knowledge which are not confined within the ordinary channels of sense-perception. Tyrrell's work is particularly interesting in this connection. As a result of an enormous number of trials with apparatus ingeniously designed to exclude all alternative explanation, he finds that those best endowed with this extra-sensory gift can guess right about once in four times when once in five would be expected on chance alone. The results are definite, and significant in the statistical sense, yet the faculty is rudimentary: it does not permit its possessor to guess right all the time or even most of the time—merely to achieve a small rise in the percentage of right guessing. If, however, we could discover in what this faculty really consists, on what mechanism it depends, and by what conditions and agencies it can be influenced, it should be capable of development like any other human faculty. Man may thus be unique in more ways than he now suspects.

So far we have been considering the fact of human uniqueness. It remains to consider man's attitude to these unique qualities of his. Professor Everett, of the University of California, in an interesting paper bearing the same title as this essay, but dealing with the topic from the standpoint of the philosopher and the humanist rather than that of the biologist, has stressed man's fear of his own uniqueness. Man has often not been able to tolerate the feeling that he inhabits an alien world, whose laws do not make sense in the light of his intelligence, and in which the writ of his human values does not run. Faced with the prospect of such intellectual and moral loneliness, he has projected personality into the cosmic scheme. Here he has found a will, there a purpose; here a creative intelligence, and there a divine compassion. At one time, he has deified animals, or personified natural forces. At others, he has created a superhuman pantheon, a single tyrannical world ruler, a subtle and satisfying Trinity in Unity. Philosophers have postulated an Absolute of the same nature as mind.

It is only exceptionally that men have dared to uphold their uniqueness and to be proud of their human superiority to the impersonality and irrationality of the rest of the universe. It is time now, in the light of our knowledge, to be brave and face the fact and the consequences of our uniqueness. That is Dr. Everett's view, as it was also that of T. H. Huxley in his famous Romanes lecture. I agree with them; but I would suggest that the antinomy between man and the universe is not quite so sharp as they have made out. Man represents the culmination of that process of organic evolution which has been proceeding on this planet for over a thousand million years. That process, however wasteful and cruel it may be, and into however many blind alleys it may have been diverted, is also in one aspect progressive. Man has now become the sole representative of life in that progressive aspect and its sole trustee for any progress in the future.

Meanwhile it is true that the appearance of the human type of mind, the latest step in evolutionary progress, has introduced both new methods and new standards. By means of his conscious reason and its chief offspring, science, man has the power of substituting less dilatory, less wasteful, and less cruel methods of effective progressive change than those of natural selection, which alone are available to lower organisms. And by means of his conscious purpose and his set of values, he has the power of substituting new and higher standards for change than those of mere survival and adaptation to immediate circumstances, which alone are inherent in pre-human evolution. To put the matter in another way, progress has hitherto been a rare and fitful by-product of evolution. Man has the possibility of making it the main feature of his own future evolution, and of guiding its course in relation to a deliberate aim.

But he must not be afraid of his uniqueness. There may be other beings in this vast universe endowed with reason, purpose, and aspiration: but we know nothing of them. So far as our knowledge goes, human mind and personality are unique and constitute the highest product yet achieved by the cosmos. Let us not put off our responsibilities onto the shoulders of mythical gods or philosophical absolutes, but shoulder them in the hopefulness of tempered pride. In the perspective of biology, our business in the world is seen to be the imposition of the best and most enduring of our human standards upon ourselves and our planet. The enjoyment of beauty and interest, the achievement of goodness and efficiency, the enhancement of life and its variety—these are the harvest which our human uniqueness should be called upon to yield.

THE SEARCH FOR AN ETHIC | GEORGE GAYLORD SIMPSON

Man is a moral animal. With the exception of a few peculiar beings who are felt to be as surely crippled as if the deformity were physical, all men make judgments of good or bad in ethics and morals. All feel some degree of compulsion to value and promote the good, to condemn and eliminate the bad. It requires no demonstration that a demand for ethical standards is deeply ingrained in human psychology. Like so many human character-

From George Gaylord Simpson, *The Meaning of Evolution* (New Haven, Conn., Yale University Press, 1949).

istics, indeed most of them, this trait is both innate and learned. Its basic mechanism is evidently part of our biological inheritance. The degree of development of this, in the individual and in society, as well as the particular form that it will take are conditioned by learning processes in the family and in the wider aspects of the social structure. Man almost inevitably acquires an ethic and this responds to a deep need in any normal member of the species. The reasons for this need and the immediate elements in its fulfillment are among the most important of subjects for the study of man, but they are, on the whole, outside our present enquiry. It suffices here to recognize the fact that the need does exist.

Through the ages ethical standards responding to this need have been supplied mainly from three closely interrelated sources: introspection, authority, and convention. The basis of acceptance has been intuitive, the feeling of rightness, without objective enquiry into the reasons for this feeling and without possible test as to the truth or falseness of the premises involved. Introspection may produce results so intensely felt and within such an emotional framework that they are considered as having sanction and force from some external, nonmaterial source, that is, they are taken to be inspired and divine in origin. They then become revelations. Such introspective revelations of a gifted few may in time be accepted by many others as valid, just as may also the introspections of philosophers who do not claim to have received revelations. The ethic is then bolstered by authority, the authority of the individual philosopher or of the presumed Inspirer. Second-hand acceptance of revelation or of philosophical introspection is usually as intuitive as were the original introspections. The acceptability of an ethical system has generally corresponded with wishful thinking in the individual, who firmly believes what he enjoys believing, and with some sort of pragmatic validation in society. Conviction that the system is right is confirmed by the feeling that it works. The individual is comforted and made happier by a system that responds to his own wishes (so obscure in origin), and any particular society does operate better by erection of standards automatically, although seldom perfectly, adjusted to that society by the fact that they arise and evolve in it.

The mass of people usually find that their own introspective judgment of right and wrong, the edicts of the authorities accepted by them, and the conventions of their society coincide rather closely. They coincide because their sources are related and because the individuals in society tend to modify them or to ignore their discrepancies so as to produce the illusion, at least, of coincidence. The martyrs who cling to a supposedly revealed ethic that is not accepted by their society and the social rebels whose introspective standards reject convention are relatively few in number—although, of course, new systems which may later become conventional arise among such martyrs and rebels.

In all cases satisfaction with the accepted system of ethics, the feeling

THE SEARCH FOR AN ETHIC

of a filled need and of emotional security, has depended in large measure on conviction that the system is absolute. It is believed to provide standards of right and wrong which are eternally and everywhere valid, for which the individual has no responsibility other than simple acceptance.

The basis for belief in the intuitive systems of ethics with their claims of eternal ubiquitous validity was thoroughly shaken by the discovery that they are, in fact, highly relative. Their validation by intuition and their introspective origin itself were found by the psychologists, largely as a result of the Freudian revolution, to depend on learning and psychological conditioning, mainly in early childhood. They are entirely relative to these processes and their intuitive validation is apparent and equally strong in ethical systems diametrically opposite in tendency. The anthropologists found further that extremely diverse ethical systems exist in different societies, all equally valid as far as pragmatic or other objective tests go, and that they are decidedly relative to social structure and other factors that have nothing to do with their absolute validity.

This demonstration that intuitive ethics are relative and cannot, by their very nature, provide an absolute ethical criterion spurred a search that had, indeed, become widespread even before the demonstration was complete. The attempt was to reach an ethic by a process as little intuitive as possible, to turn to nature, the material cosmos, and to try to deduce standards of conduct from its objective phenomena. The search for a naturalistic ethic was begun long before Darwin, but it was prematurely intensified in the latter part of the nineteenth century with recognition that evolution is a phenomenon of nature which must have ethical bearings. The intensification was premature because the evolutionary process was still insufficiently understood and its possible ethical significance similarly subject to misunderstanding.

The search for a naturalistic ethical system has had as its basis confidence in observation and experiment as leading to discovery of objective truth, or increasing approximation to it, and the conviction that what is ethically right is related in some way to what is materially true. On the negative side, the premise is that there is no necessary relationship between the results of introspection alone and truth or right. These propositions are themselves subjective value judgments and their validity is open to discussion, which it has already received in large measure. A good case can be made out in detail for these convictions, but perhaps their best justification lies in the fact that, even if they had to be taken as articles of faith, they would still be in large measure self-justifying in being fully consistent with our knowledge of nature and of man's place in nature. This seems to me to be sufficiently evident in the preceding and following discussion and at this point I am inclined to abbreviate by simply postulating these principles not as ethics in themselves but as the basis on which a valid ethic must rest. Of course this does not involve endorsement of any particular ethical system erected ostensibly on the same basis, for it will quickly be seen that a majority of these will not stand up when judged on this very basis.

Many of Darwin's immediate followers thought of evolution primarily in terms of struggle, a concept consistent with and based on Darwinian selection, but not carried to such excess by Darwin himself. They evolved what T. H. Huxley called "the gladiatorial theory of existence" and concluded that the evolutionary ethic must be, first, every man for himself, then every tribe, every nation, every class, and so on, for itself in the "struggle for existence." Such tooth-and-claw ethics suited the book of Victorian laissez faire capitalism and also, with only rather superficial remodeling, of its opposing ideology in Marxist socialism. Those who were not suited by this wholly superficial interpretation of an ill-understood natural process found themselves in a serious dilemma. They could not believe that unbounded personal competition, exploitation and dominance of one group by another, class and national warfare, and the other concomitants of a gladiatorial existence were ethically right. But on the other hand they believed that these are the essential features of the evolutionary process. T. H. Huxley concluded that evolution, although it is a fact that must be faced, is ethically bad. Man's problem then becomes not the forwarding of the evolutionary process but its thwarting. Huxley accepted "the essential evil of the world" and only hoped it could be abated by ethical human conduct. He endorsed and accepted the intuitive ethics of his time as non-, in fact anti-, evolutionary and did not even discuss their origin or validity.

The repercussions of this unreal dilemma and of the fallacious tooth-and-claw ethics are still sadly with us. Their influence has been unqualifiedly pernicious. The fact that this widely hailed product of the search was certainly bad has cast a shadow over the whole effort to find a naturalistic ethic, and should certainly make us extremely cautious in our continuance of that search.

The tooth-and-claw ethic was based on the propositions that evolution as a whole has been ethically good and that its process is gladiatorial. T. H. Huxley saw no alternative to tooth-and-claw ethics except the opposite conclusion that evolution as a whole is ethically bad. The dilemma thus set up was unreal on both sides, for it was neither established that the tooth-and-claw ethic is inherent in evolution as a whole nor that what is inherent in evolution as a whole constitutes a fit guide for human life. Aside from details, very basic misapprehensions regarding evolution, as we now know it, were involved. Literal struggle is *not* the essence of natural selection, and natural selection itself is only one of many different factors in evolution. Attention was focused on speciation and the process of speciation was falsely viewed as a competitive struggle between groups of organisms. Furthermore other far more important aspects of evolution were wholly overlooked and the whole course of history viewed in terms of speciation only. There was no reason why speciation, even if it had been correctly understood, should have been taken as *the* basis for an evolutionary ethic. The tooth-and-claw ethic was thoroughly unjustified. Its excesses and its truly unethical conclusions do not follow from the principles of evolution, and this failure need not put an end to the search for an evolutionary ethic.

Herbert Spencer, still under the sway of the gladiatorial theory of evolution current in his day, was among the first to seek to avoid the ferocity of the conclusions that seemed to arise from this theory by proposing one of many varieties of what may be called "life ethics." The postulate is that life is good. Ethical conduct is that which promotes life. Evolution is good, on the whole, because it has promoted life, also on the whole. From determining how evolution has best accomplished this, we can draw guidance as to how we too can promote life. If our conduct does promote life, it will be ethical. Evolution is not over-all a safe guide, but must be viewed selectively. Extinction is a normal part of evolution, but it does not promote life and is therefore ethically wrong. These are some of the conclusions characteristic of the different sorts of life ethics, of which there are many variants now upheld by students of evolution.

Baldly put, the life ethic becomes simply a survival ethic: what best promotes survival is good, what endangers survival is bad. In logical extreme, this becomes only another variant of the old tooth-and-claw ethic. If individual survival is the ultimate good, then it is every man for himself again. (And incidentally, the man who dies for a cause is bad, whether the cause be bad or good; the father who endangers his own life in attempt to rescue his child is bad, and so on.) This extreme is avoided by making group or racial, not individual, survival the goal, but still the ethic is not satisfactory. Of course survival is a condition for any progress or for any continuing medium in which good can exist, but what is basically good, in a moral sense, about survival in itself and what part of the evolutionary process could lead us to take this as an ethical guide? Survival is well assured, we have seen, by arrested evolution, by equilibrium in a static environment. Man himself, who needs the ethic, would never have arisen by such survival. Survival for a longer or shorter time is gained by the most diverse and contradictory means, by progression and by retrogression, by specialization and by adaptability, by parasitism—by such a variety of means that to call them all "good" becomes meaningless and certainly offers no hope of an ethical standard for man. And do not forget that survival is ultimately impossible. All life will cease some day. We may and do hope, surely, that mankind will survive as long as possible, but survival will have no ethical significance except as man be good or bad by other standards than merely existing. Certainly it is "good" to survive, but we fall into a semantic trap if we think that this is an *ethical* good.

By a logical extension, the survival ethic becomes an ethic of satisfaction and harmony. It is "good" to survive, for the individual, for the species, and ultimately for all of life. As Leake has said in a development of this thesis, "Relationships between the individuals and groups in contact with each other to be 'good' must therefore be conducive toward the survival of all concerned." Then the general principle appears that "The probability of survival of individual, or groups of, living things increases with the degree with which they harmoniously adjust themselves to each other and their environment."[1] This is the very opposite of the tooth-and-claw ethic. It is based on a much truer conception of the evolutionary process and of the processes of life in general. It also has the virtue of being congruous with almost any ethic, except the plainly false tooth-and-claw ethic, that can be based on the evolutionary process. That is, almost any other natural-istic system of ethics would agree that behavior consistent with this principle would usually be ethical.

Action on this principle would usually tend to *promote* good, and yet it does not seem to be a basic criterion for judging what *is* good. It still departs from the postulate that survival is "good," and we have noted that this is not necessarily true in an ethical sense. Moreover, this is a purely static concept. It would seem logically to involve a changeless equilibrium, with maximum or complete harmony, as the highest good. If this implica-tion is accepted, then the principle is unrealistic and is not evolutionary, nor surely good. The tooth-and-claw ethic is invalid, but there are teeth and claws in nature. Some organisms must die if others are to live. And evolution involves ceaseless change. Even extinction of races and of whole orders and classes has been a condition of the rise of higher types. The harmonious equilibrium is never reached, and if it had been, man would not now exist. The equilibrium is not achieved with the coming of man, nor is there apparent opportunity for him to attain it.

A further step in the search accepts and emphasizes the dynamic nature of life and of its evolution. Departing, still, from the proposition that life is good, the dynamic inference is that increase in life is good. Whatever tends to increase life is therefore right, and whatever tends to decrease it is wrong—an ethic of increase or of abundance of life. Here again, action under this principle would often or usually be ethical by most other standards of ethics, but reflection raises doubts as to whether the principle is itself ethical, that is, a standard by which right and wrong action may be judged. Its applicability is far narrower than that of the ethic of harmony, which does not contradict it. How many concrete situations can you think of in which you could decide on right and wrong action, as an individual or for a nation or for mankind as a whole, on the basis of consequent increase or decrease in life? Murder becomes bad, to be sure, but most situations which do have ethical bearings elude application of the principle. Other problems, where it does somehow bear, require some other and overriding principle for solution. It is good to plant a crop, but is it good

---

[1] Both quotations are from the following thoughtful and valuable paper: C. D. Leake, "Ethicogenesis" *(Sci. Monthly, 60)* [1945], pp. 245-253.

or bad to harvest it? And is this situation, to which the principle definitely applies although the direction of the application is equivocal, really an ethical one at all? Evidently if the principle is ethical it is severely limited and inadequate as basis for a system of ethics.

Further thought must raise some doubt as to whether the principle would indeed lead to right and to the avoidance of wrong. Which is right and which wrong: an earth so crowded with men that they can barely subsist by laboring all their waking hours and any further increase is cut off by starvation, or an earth moderately populated and with ample provision for all? The alternatives now exist as between, say, parts of China or India and most of the United States. Trend toward maximum population and minimum subsistence is necessarily right and good under the increase ethic. Judgment that it is wrong and bad would be suspect if merely intuitive, but as will appear, this judgment does follow from an ethic more soundly based in the history of life than is the increase ethic.

Various forms of the ethic of increase of life are commonly derived from or supported by the statement that this constitutes a major trend of evolution. This ethic then becomes one of many, sometimes contradictory, possible and proposed ethical systems which depend on the postulate that continuation of the trend, or of a trend, in past evolution is an ethical guide to right conduct and to future good. Such a conclusion follows almost automatically from a finalist view of evolution, especially when this is put on a theistic or otherwise religious basis. If evolution has a goal, if it has all been a progression toward some ultimate and determining end, then we should find out that goal by observations of the facts of evolution and it is reasonable to consider further progress toward the goal as ethically right. This becomes not only reasonable but also obligatory if the goal was set by God. Unfortunately for hopes for so simple a solution of the ethical problem, the basis for this is flatly nonexistent. There is no real evidence whatever that evolution has had a goal, and there is overwhelming evidence that it has not.

Evolution does have trends, many of them, and it has been seen that the most nearly general of these has been toward increase in the total of life on the earth. Hence the increase ethic would seem to be validated if trend ethics were acceptable as valid. But all trend ethics demand the postulate that the trends of evolution or some particular one among these is ethically right and good. There is no evident reason why such a postulate should be accepted. It is, at least, impossible to conclude that *all* evolutionary trends are ipso facto good. They are too diverse and they lead as often to decrease of life and to ultimate extinction as to increase and survival. The problem arises that a choice must be made; it is necessary to decide *which* trends are good. The decision cannot, then, be based on factual observation that a trend has occurred but must involve some other and quite distinct ethical criterion. Any attempt to find a valid trend ethic results merely in a requirement that some other ethic first be found in order to select the right ethical trend. Thus the increase ethic is not validated because it follows a general trend in evolution, but on the contrary, identification of that trend as right depends on prior admission of the validity of the increase ethic—an admission which, as previously shown, is neither forced nor warranted by what is known of the evolutionary process.

There is another group of attempts to derive ethics from aspects of the evolutionary history of life which is often, but not necessarily, supported by the fallacious argument from trend. These proposed systems, which might collectively be called aggregation ethics, see as ethically good the increased aggregation of organic units into higher levels of organization. One form of the argument runs more or less as follows: Evolution has involved a succession of organic levels, with progressive complication and perfection of coordinated structure and function on each level. The protozoans and other one-celled (or noncellular, or cellularly undivided) organisms represent a lowest level. The next level is that of multicellular individuals, metazoans, with increasing differentiation of the cells and their grouping into organs with increasingly specialized functions. There follows another level, the highest, in which metazoan individuals are aggregated into hyperzoan organisms. The hyperzoan or "epi-organism" is society, into which individuals are to merge and be integrated as subordinate parts of a higher whole. It is, in fact, that so-called organic state, considered as having an individuality and life of its own. In such a state individuals or "persons," as some adherents of this view prefer to call them, exist for the state, the good and rights of which are separate from and superior to that of the individuals composing it.

The whole argument and its ethical implications, among which may be support of authoritarian and totalitarian ideologies as biologically and ethically right, are thoroughly erroneous. When the state or any other social structure is called an "organism," the word is being used in a way fundamentally different from its use for a biological organism such as an ameba, a tree, or you. The state is not an individual or a person in anything like the same sense that these organisms are individuals. The parts that compose it retain, and indeed intensify, their organic individuality. Their relationship to the social unit is entirely different from the relationship of cells or organs to a metazoan individual. Calling a state an "organism" and concluding that it is therefore comparable with a metazoan organism is a glaring example of the fallacy of the shifting middle term. Use of the comparison as an analogy provides an interesting descriptive metaphor, but its use in support of an aggregation ethic is a particularly egregious misuse of analogy, confusing it with equivalence and extending it as an interpretive principle far beyond the point to which it is valid even as metaphorical description.

Furthermore, if the fallacious use of "organism" as a shifting term is avoided, it is quite evident that merging of the individual into a higher organic unit is not a common trend in evolution and, specifically, is not at all a trend in human evolution. The trend in human evolution and in many other evolutionary sequences has been, on the contrary, toward greater individualization. The particular type of social organization characteristic of man, as opposed, say, to that in an anthill, has been based on high individualization of its members and has intensified this. It will be necessary to refer again to this fact, and to clarify some of its implications, in the next chapter in connection with what I believe to be a truer conception of the ethical significance of man's place in nature and of his evolution.

These various attempts to find a naturalistic ethic where it is most likely to reside, in the process of evolution, have certainly greatly clarified the issues involved. They have narrowed the field of search and most of them have, at worst, skirted an acceptable solution. At best they have produced partial answers which are indeed ethically good although not achieving a general and firmly based evolutionary ethic. It is now clear that none of the attempts reviewed up to this point can be considered satisfactory. All were seeking a more coherent and realistic basis for ethics than could be found in the older intuitive systems, and in this we must conclude that they were on the right track, but in so doing they have not escaped all the pitfalls of those older systems.

Most of these naturalistic ethics have been attempts, as were intuitive ethics, to find standards of right and wrong with eternal validity for all things from ameba to man. This adherence to an ideal absolutism fails in appreciation of two basic facts of evolution: that change is of its essence and that man represents a new, unique sort of organism subject to a new, distinct sort of evolution in addition to the older sort, which still continues. The need and the search for an ethic are also unique to man and in fact ethics enters into evolution only at this point; ethical judgment arises in the new evolution and is one of its characteristics. There are no ethics but human ethics, and a search that ignores the necessity that ethics be human, relative to man, is bound to fail. Attempts to derive an ethic from evolution as a whole, without particular reference to man, are further examples of the "nothing but" fallacy of the nature of man.

Another basic weakness in not quite all but most of these attempts has been that they involve trying to find out what evolution has been up to, or even what evolution seems to *want*, and then assuming that promotion of this is ethically right. This amounts to placing evolution in the position occupied by God or by His revelation in intuitive ethics. Such naturalistic ethics share with those they attempted to replace a certain evasion of responsibility. They still try to find an external standard, one given without need for choice and without other requirements than discovery and acceptance.

So the enquiry seems to have swung in a circle and to be back rather near where it started. Yet there is a point from which to go on, and the unsatisfactory nature of these attempts does not preclude the possibility of others that can be satisfactory. The point is that an evolutionary ethic *for man* (which is of course the one we, as men, seek, if not the only possible kind) should be based on man's own nature, on his evolutionary position and significance. It cannot be expected to arise *automatically* from the principles of evolution in general, nor yet, indeed, from those of human evolution in particular. It cannot be expected to be absolute, but must be subject to evolution itself and must be the result of responsible and rational *choice* in the full light of such knowledge of man and of life as we have.

MEN OR MORONS? | EARNEST A. HOOTON

OBSOLESCENCE OF NATURAL SELECTION

The obsolescence of natural selection is largely due to humanitarianism and to the efficacy of modern medical science. It is obvious that the most skillful and successful medical practice could have little effect for good or for evil upon the population, as long as it was restricted to those few who could afford the luxury of high fees. When, however, there arose enlightened leaders among men who taught the nobility, not only of casting out devils, but also of healing the sick, making whole the lame, and causing the blind to see, the doctor began to yearn to be the savior of all mankind. This did no harm at all, as long as his miracles were imaginary and his nostrums continued to waft his patients to the Elysian Fields. But when he really began to succeed, Pandora's box was open.

Studies of the individual age composition of ancient and primitive skeletal populations indicate that an increase of longevity is a marked phenomenon of modern civilized life. Statistics of infant mortality show that the constitutional inferiors of today stand a much better chance of surviving to adult years, and of reproducing their kind, than they have presumably enjoyed at any previous time. Again, modern advances in sanitation and in the knowledge of communicable diseases have done much to control the epidemics which periodically have decimated the populations of times past. What are the consequences of such preservation and prolongation of human life?

In the first place the effect must be to increase proportionally that section of the population which is helpless because young, and also that section which is relatively helpless because old. Both increases place additional burdens upon the family and the state. The economically depressed, who seem always the most prolific, have larger numbers of offspring who must be fed, clothed, and educated, and probably more surviving children of inferior bodily and mental endowment. Familial care and earnings must be distributed among a greater number of less fit young. There follows the tendency to dissipate the family resources upon the inferior offspring and to neglect those who are better fitted in individual hereditary endowment to cope with the world. The major portion of parental energy is exerted upon the effort to make the best of bad reproductive jobs. Instead of saving the bacon, we misdirect our hog-raising efforts to the futile task of attempting to make silk purses of the animal's ears. The more active and able-bodied children are left to fend for themselves—an abandonment which for many of them leads to delinquency.

At the other end of the curve we have the increase of the population of advanced age. Let us consider the effect of the continued activity of these elders. It is perhaps most clearly manifested in the modern gerontocracy, or the rule of old men. One of the most constant characteristics of old age is an inability to recognize its own obsolescence and an unwillingness to relinquish its direction of the life of family and state. The dominion of senility in the family increases the conflict between generations, since three instead of two are involved, and must be one of the factors tending toward familial disruption. In the political and economic world, it means that those who have attained the seniority requisite for leadership are likely to be a generation behind their times in thought, relatively impervious to the advance of ideas, and completely unsympathetic with the world of the middle-aged and the juvenile which they dominate.

Add to this the fact that these elderly potentates perform their public functions in a personal aura of corporeal and mental disintegration, being indeed not immortal, but subject not only to ordinary human ailments but also to those of old age. I have said on a previous occasion that it is impossible to estimate, for example, to what extent the miseries of nations may have been enhanced by the vagaries of the enlarged prostates of their senile rulers, or by the climacteric mental disturbances of the latters' wives. If indeed we are to tolerate the sway of those debilitated by age, it would seem necessary at least to make some appraisal of the extent to which their functions are impaired by disease, in order that our entire public policy may not be moribund. For those who retire from active life with the onset of senility, there remains public care in the form of old age pensions and homes for the aged, or alternatively, retirement to the family chimney corner.

Now I am not arguing in favor either of a policy of infanticide or of senicide. I am merely calling attention to the fact that the benevolent and efficient labors of modern medicine are raising new and grave population problems. I may here state what I believe to be the anthropological view of pathology. Man is a made-over and makeshift organism, the end product of many adaptations and unsatisfactory compromises between heredity and environment. Early in the life of the average individual, various working parts of his organism begin to weaken under the attack of infections or through sheer constitutional inferiority, but, in some way or other, functions are partially maintained, and the animal goes limping along through life, aided by the crutches of medical science and sustained by that brutal tenacity of life which seems to be an inheritance from lower evolutionary stages. By some saturnine gift of nature the reproductive system of the human animal continues to function when the nervous system is completely disintegrated, the alimentary and excretory systems thoroughly disorganized, and virtually the entire organism is in a state of morbidity. By superskillful tinkering and patching, life and activity are maintained, and the animal continues to exercise one of its strongest instincts and to produce more and more of worse and worse offspring.

EDUCATION AND ETHICS

The pathway of degressive human evolution, like hell, is paved with good intentions—medical, educational, and ethical. The fallacy of social ethics lies, I think, in the assumption that all human life is inherently good and worthy of preservation, and that by a process of environmental tinkering, fools may be transmuted into sages, criminals into saints, and politicians into statesmen. Surely this conception is nothing but a secularized belief in conversion and personal salvation. The clergyman of yesterday is the unfrocked sociologist of today.

When are we to realize that a great proportion of mankind continues to be as stupid, unteachable, bloodthirsty, predatory, and savage as we are wont to imagine that maligned and regrettably extinct precursor—Neanderthal man? Is it because the precepts of Christianity have not been sufficiently disseminated, or because the blessings of plumbing and mechanical transport have been too narrowly restricted, or because there are still a few persons who lack the degree of Bachelor of Arts? I think it is because no little of the human germ plasm is poisonous slime, and we have not had the intelligence and the courage to attempt to find out anything about human heredity. We have imagined universal education, mutual understanding, and improvement of the social environment to be the ingredients with which we can concoct the human millennium; we have mixed them up and stirred them in, and turned out a horrible mess. There must be something the matter with our basic element—man himself.

It is not yet too late to begin the studies of human inheritance which are essential for man's wise and efficient control of his own evolution. Such studies should begin with genetic researches upon the gross anatomy and general physiology of the human animal, his pathology, his psychology and mental capacity, and should proceed ultimately to his sociability—

or fitness to function in human society. Of course environment is important, but we cannot exercise an intelligent control of environment without a fundamental knowledge of the range of restrictions and hereditary variations.

THE BANNER OF EQUALITY

When Mr. Midshipman Easy was called to account for a serious breach of naval discipline, he replied that it was "all zeal," and when requested to explain why he had flown the silk petticoat of a señorita from the masthead of a prize of war, he stated that "it was the banner of equality and the rights of man." We have adopted this easyish philosophy without its saving grace of humor; we have been plunging zealously ahead under a banner of equality and the rights of man, which turns out to be less significant than the señorita's lingerie.

It might well have been said to Luke: "Thou art the physician, and hast the keys of life and death," for that precisely is the responsibility of the medical profession, of which dental science is not the least important division. In medical science lies the only practicable control of human evolution and of biological progress. Medical science must cease to regard its function as primarily curative and preventive. It must rid itself of the obsession that its chief responsibility is to the individual rather than to society. It must allocate to itself the function of discovering how the human animal may be improved as a biological organism. The future of mankind does not depend upon political or economic theory, nor yet upon measures of social amelioration, but upon the production of better minds in sounder bodies. . . .

THE CHANGING PSYCHOLOGICAL STATUS OF MAN

The survival of the organically unsound and the perpetuation of their constitutional ailments are tolerable only if the lowering of physique is unaccompanied by mental deterioration. Civilized man endeavors to persuade himself that his intelligence improves and his mental health remains unimpaired no matter how enfeebled his body has become. He has tried to believe that mental vigor and high ideals of conduct flourish in an organic environment of pathology and degeneration.

The cumulative tradition of civilization has handed down innumerable inventions and devices for facilitating existence. The individual can maintain life and perpetuate his kind with a minimum of physical effort and with little or no exercise of intelligence. We have become parasites upon the cultural achievements of the past and upon the inventive benefactions of a few creative contemporaries. The stimuli for a full utilization of the hereditary endowment of mental equipment have diminished, since the latter is no longer essential for survival. Loss of function atrophies the intelligence as surely as disuse withers muscles and shrinks bones.

The last century has witnessed in certain advanced nations the appli-

cation of a system of ethics and a practice of sociology which, on the
behavioristic side, may be called humanitarianism and which, in its institutional aspect, is termed democracy. Both theory and practice are the out-
growths of the highest ideals of human conduct. There is little doubt that
the optimum human society is realized under this régime, provided that its
members are possessed individually of high intelligence and are habituated
to a reciprocity of altruistic conduct. However, excessive altruism and
indiscriminate humanitarianism are impracticable because they reduce the
intelligence of the population. The noblest manifestation of human science
is the extension of medical care to all classes of the population. The finest
exemplifications of man's unselfishness are charity toward the weak and
the helpless and forbearance for the wrongdoer. Now it is impossible to
disregard the fact that the preservation of the biologically unfit lowers the
physical level of the population. It is not commonly known, however, that
intelligence declines with organic deterioration, and it is convenient to
deny this psycho-physical parallelism, since its implications are exceedingly unpleasant. I have spent ten cheerless years in studying the relation
of physique to intelligence and to economic and educational status, in the
inmates of American penitentiaries, jails, and insane asylums. Every jot
and tittle of the vast mass of evidence which I have analyzed indicates
that inferior biological status is inextricably associated with diminished
intelligence, and that the combination of the two is mainly responsible for
economic inadequacy and antisocial conduct. Dismiss crime, if you like,
as a pathological by-product of society. Disregard the findings I have stated
without submitting my proof. Deny the logic of the contention that weak
minds are found in weak bodies. Nevertheless, if you will but pause to
survey the state of our society, you must join in my cry, "What must we
do to be saved?"

The howl of the Roman mob, *"Panem et circenses!"* (bread and the
circus) is re-echoing ominously through this nation. However, neither
emotion nor rhetoric will alleviate the situation, and let him who will put
his trust in such sops to Cerberus as bonuses, old age pensions, and legislation for social security. We must either do some biological housecleaning
or delude ourselves with the futile hope that a government of the unfit,
for the unfit, and by the unfit will not perish from the earth.

REMEDIES

Now it seems to me perfectly clear that what we must do, in some way
or other, is to encourage a sit-down reproductive strike of the busy breeders
among the morons, criminals, and social ineffectuals of our population.
Probably compulsory sterilization alone would serve in the case of the
insane and the mentally deficient, but it is very difficult to enforce such
a measure in a democracy, unless it has been preceded by an educational
campaign which has reached all of the teachable and socially minded indi-

viduals of the electorate. Probably the only effective method of obtaining the desired result would be to establish in our secondary schools and colleges courses of applied human biology which would disseminate knowledge of the facts of heredity and of the relation of man's organism to his behavior. Of course science really knows as yet comparatively little about human genetics, and is quite incapable of enunciating directions for breeding geniuses. But it is wholly competent to suggest measures which would prevent the birth of the majority of our imbeciles and morons. The young ought to be brought to an early realization that their success in life and their value to society depend not only upon occupational skill and character, but also upon an undertaking that their reproductive function must be exercised in accordance with their individual capacities and limitations. We must inculcate into the rising generation a code of biological ethics.

The only valid reason for trying to improve the biological status of man is that he be made a better animal—more honest, more unselfish, more decent and considerate in his human relations. I think that a biological purge is the essential prerequisite for a social and a spiritual salvation. Let us temper mercy with justice and dispense charity with intelligence. We must stop trying to cure malignant biological growths with patent sociological nostrums. The emergency demands a surgical operation.

THE HEAVY BEAR | *DELMORE SCHWARTZ*

"the withness of the body"—WHITEHEAD

The heavy bear who goes with me,
A manifold honey to smear his face,
Clumsy and lumbering here and there,
The central ton of every place,
The hungry beating brutish one
In love with candy, anger, and sleep
Crazy factotum, dishevelling all,
Climbs the building, kicks the football,
Boxes his brother in the hate-ridden city.

Breathing at my side, that heavy animal,
That heavy bear who sleeps with me,
Howls in his sleep for a world of sugar,
A sweetness intimate as the water's clasp,

Howls in his sleep because the tight-rope
Trembles and shows the darkness beneath.
—The strutting show-off is terrified,
Dressed in his dress-suit, bulging his pants,
Trembles to think that his quivering meat
Must finally wince to nothing at all.

That inescapable animal walks with me,
Has followed me since the black womb held,
Moves where I move, distorting my gesture,
A caricature, a swollen shadow,
A stupid clown of the spirit's motive,
Perplexes and affronts with his own darkness,
The secret life of belly and bone,
Opaque, too near, my private, yet unknown,
Stretches to embrace the very dear
With whom I would walk without him near,
Touches her grossly, although a word
Would bare my heart and make me clear,
Stumbles, flounders, and strives to be fed
Dragging me with him in his mouthing care,
Amid the hundred million of his kind,
The scrimmage of appetite everywhere.

THE MEANS
AND MODES OF
EXPRESSION

* PART II

* The Writer's Words

THE STORY IS TOLD THAT, after he had been working for some time in his studio while his poet friend Mallarmé stood by, the sculptor and painter Degas turned to the poet and asked, "And now, my friend, how does one make a poem?" Mallarmé answered without hesitation: "Poetry is made with words."

"—and so is prose," he might have added. It is a truism, of course, but it should not for that reason be ignored. Written expression must achieve all it can achieve through manipulation of words, and therefore writers are continually developing or refreshing their sensitivity to the protean nature of words. Although much of that sensitivity is effortlessly and subconsciously acquired, the refinements that distinguish a good writer from a poor one are largely the result of labor. The writer's life is a life of words, whatever else it may incidentally be, and he takes care to know and respect his materials as do good craftsmen of every kind.

With the writer, as with other artists, great art often conceals effort so successfully that the observer knows that he is affected by it but is not at all conscious of the means. Besides being a high tribute to the artist, such a reaction may completely satisfy some observers, at least for the moment. For most, however, and perhaps sooner or later for all, curiosity demands to know *how:* how do lumps of clay or layers of paint or successions of words create this glory? Although it is sometimes claimed that all analysis is a murdering by dissection, the truth seems to be quite different. Those who follow delight by inquiry into the sources of delight find their appreciation heightened and their search rewarded by new kinds of satisfaction. Analysis of the nature and activity of words, then, is not only a respectable discipline in itself but the means to more profound understanding of literature and to a fuller response to its artistry.

Since words are symbolic (that is, representative of something other than themselves), it is natural to begin analysis of them by distinguishing between two discernibly different kinds of representation characteristic of words. The conventional names for these kinds of representation are *denotation* and *connotation.* Denotation is the meaning of a word which identifies it as belonging to a particular class and indicates the characteristics of the class to which it belongs. Every word has one or more denotations whether or not it refers to an object or quality perceivable by the senses. By and large,

485

when we speak of definitions, we have denotative meanings in mind, and it is such meanings that a dictionary will list before it lists any others. Connotation is the meaning (or meanings) of a word which indicates characteristics other than those necessarily a part of the class to which it belongs. "Father" denotes "male begetter of a child"; it connotes age, wisdom, authority, protection, power, and so on. Determining the denotative meaning of a word is not by any means easy, as anyone who works with definitions will attest, but it is much easier than determining the connotative meanings. To begin with, connotations vary from user to user and from hearer to hearer; one man's experience with the class of beings called "father" may be very different from those of another man, and the connotative power, for each, of the word "father" will reflect those experiences. Connotations will vary also with the situation in which the word is used, with the region, with the time. There is, in fact, an uneven but continuing accumulation and attrition of connotative meanings; over a period of a few years circumstances may so alter attitudes toward what is denotatively meant by a word (consider "flivver," or "impressionistic," or "bourgeois") that its connotations also become entirely different from what they were. And over a long period of time connotative meaning may become so strongly associated with a word as to displace its original denotative meaning entirely (as has occurred, for example, to the word "dastard").

Not all words stimulate the growth of connotative meanings although it is almost impossible to find a word completely free of them for everyone. In general, structural words (prepositions and conjunctions) are primarily denotative. Substantive words (nouns, verbs, adjectives, adverbs) are denotative and at the same time in varying degrees connotative. It might be said that substantive words have an "aura," as though the word were live enough to send out rays from its denotative center. For each the aura will, of course, be different not only in radius and brilliance but in temper as well. "New" and "novel" are denotatively alike but connotatively different. "Chickenfeed," "change," and "silver" have almost exactly the same denotation, but the first is unfavorable (*pejorative*) in the associations it calls to mind, the last clearly favorable (*honorific*), and "change" nearly neutral or free of connotation unless reinforced by other words (as in "All I have is some change"). Both "vagrant" and "bum" refer unflatteringly to persons with no visible means of support, but "bum" is today the more intensely pejorative of the two. "Brother" has a greater aura, primarily because of the traditional use of the masculine form for generalization, than has "sister." The point to be made here is that connotation is, in itself, neither good nor bad. Nearly all words are "loaded" or "charged" words, which is to say that, though symbolic in function, words are persuasive in effect. They represent not only what is "out there" but attitudes toward it and situations with which it is, or has been, associated. Since words are, by part of their nature, persuasive, a writer must know them well enough to understand the kind of influence they exert. Although he is a shaper of words, he must recognize that clay cannot be made into a silver pot nor silver into a loaf of bread.

Contemporary writing has been strongly affected by the literary doctrine of the *mot juste,* the exact word, an ideal of precision most strikingly enunciated and practiced by the French novelist Flaubert. Although the doctrine is philosophically suspect (the correspondence between symbol and that which is symbolized, though it be arbitrary, is never more than an approximation or a partial representation), it has had many good effects. Impelled by the search for precise language, writers have come to rely increasingly on verbs instead of adjectives and on "concrete" instead of "abstract" nouns. Now it is not true that abstractions have less persuasive power than words whose referents are more or less directly present to our senses, but it is probably true that the power that abstractions exercise deteriorates more rapidly than that exercised by "concrete" words. A piece of writing full of abstract language may quickly stir us and move us to action yet lose its hold over us in a matter of hours or days. A piece full of concrete detail, whatever its immediate effect, will continue to impress us. It is the work of the psychologist to explain this phenomenon of retention; for our purposes, it is sufficient to point out that the phenomenon accounts for the efficiency of metaphor and for the inefficiency of stock language. Figures of speech either force the concrete and the abstract into conjunction or join concreteness to concreteness; in either case, they intensify the persuasive power of words by calling on a sharply focused and therefore emotionally intensified association. (The failure of a metaphor is always more striking than the failure of a simple adjective for that very reason—the condition for heightened effect is created by the metaphor and then disappointed by the inadequacy of the materials.) Stock language—clichés, jargon, redundancy, cant —are ineffective in writing because they have no power to excite visual impression, associations, or curiosity. They come ready-made to the writer's hand, provoking neither inquiry nor speculation in him, so it is no wonder that they fail to excite or move the reader.

A less desirable effect of the emphasis on precision has been preoccupation with what one group of writers in the early part of this century called the "hard, dry" style. Stripping language down to images, branding the adjective "enemy of the noun" and insisting "Don't tell it, show it!" is a way to reform corrupt practices, but it is only half a way to write. If our thoughts were sheer perception, such a program might be sound, but they are not. The conceptual is also part of our experience. Indeed, it is probably true that there is no percept without a concept, and therefore true that some things can only be told, not shown—and told only through metaphor at that. Since doctrines are more rigorously preached than scrupulously followed, however, and since language itself has exploitable resources too great for confinement in any single doctrine, loss of one kind in expression is generally offset by gain of another. The severity and spareness imposed on literature by current fashion have provoked writers to intensify "wit" in the use of language, and the result is that much contemporary writing is especially rich in allusion and double meanings, deliberately given to ambiguities, and unusually responsive to refined rhetorical devices. To modern ears this kind of linguistic play is generally more attractive than the habit of luxuriating in the surge and flow of words, though the continued popularity of William Faulkner and the meteoric rise of Dylan Thomas are evidence enough that the English language is in no immediate danger of death through austerity.

Whether he selects austerity or luxuriance, the writer has only words with which to do his work, and all that he can do with them is put them in one or another order. All his experiences, his observations, his ideas are locked up until he finds the words and the word order with which to liberate them. The good writer is, like the chatelaine of a castle, preeminently a keeper of keys. The good reader, for that reason, must be as well acquainted as the writer with the rhetorical devices by which meanings are developed and conveyed in literature. A large part of that acquaintanceship comes only with wide, thoughtful, and habitual reading of good prose and poetry, but learning to recognize and appreciate various kinds of rhetorical activity gives a reader the ready means of making the acquaintanceship a rich one.

CONCRETE AND ABSTRACT LANGUAGE: POVERTY

TWO QUITE CONTRARY TENDENCIES in modern writing, one toward abstractness and generalization and the other toward specific and concrete detail, can be traced to a deep-rooted division in our culture. On one hand, specialization requires abstract terminology for efficient and precise operation, and such terminology requires expertly trained users. On the other, the democratic principle of universal education naturally leads to a public language which is concrete and simple enough to be clear to nearly everyone. The distance between the language of the specialist and that of the man in the street is partly one of a particular vocabulary, of course. More importantly, it is a distance created by a difference in habit of mind: a difference between thinking about a particular and localizable thing or incident and thinking about the principle or characteristic by which many things or incidents can be treated as one.

This is not to say that only the specialist uses abstract words, of course, but only to say that he is accustomed to using them carefully and methodically. Nontechnical use of abstractions is inclined to vagueness and, through vagueness, to confusion. It is for that reason that reformers of style (Orwell, for instance, or Ezra Pound) commonly warn against the use of abstractions and urge the superiority of the concrete instance and the specific detail. There are grounds for the intensity of their advocacy, but it must not be allowed to obscure the truth that general and abstract words, properly used, are essential to communication. Without them, all statements must be confined to this *object and to* that *incident, and the forming of principles and concepts must come to an end.*

In practice, of course, there are ways of making abstract and general words become active, even almost personified, in prose; and there are ways of making the concrete and the specific imply or symbolize much more than they actually state. How those devices work becomes readily apparent in the selections below, which are all focused on the problem of poverty.

In point of time, the selections that follow run from the end of the nineteenth century, when poverty and slums were endemic, into the depth of the Great Depression, when whatever progress had been made in the first decades of this century was obliterated with drastic suddenness by the collapse of business economies in nearly all parts of the world. The arrangement here is not chronological, however. The first passage, by James Agee (1909-1955), comes from a book that grew out of an article Agee and a photographer, Walker Evans, were commissioned to prepare for a New York magazine. Their report provides an impressive illustration of the power that can be developed from deliberately dry recital of what has been observed when the observation is that of men who are as passionately interested in value as in fact. The description of depression-ridden Chicago by Edmund Wilson (1895-   ), who writes as a reporter of the social scene, is also highly concrete, but in it detail is humanized, through lurid annals of the poor, and the total effect comes not through a symbolic climax, as in Agee, but through the sheer weight of accumulated scenes. Concreteness does not diminish in the account by George Orwell (1904-1950), but it is supplemented and generalized by a series of abstract words deployed throughout. Secrecy, precariousness, self-pity, boredom, indifference, relief, anxiety: these words are the warp of Orwell's carpet, a reminder that poverty is not a matter of things but of the psychological derangement that accompanies deprivation. A further generalization in his piece derives from the transfer of personal experience into second-person singular, a device that also serves to implicate the reader. What B. O. Flower (1858-1918), socialist editor and humanitarian of the turn of the century, does to implicate his reader is much more elaborate and, though interesting, less successful. In his propagandistic piece from The Arena, *he relies primarily on metaphor and on the cumulative effect of a series of metaphors to make his case. Curiously enough (and quite apart from the fact that his prose is outrageously over-*

extended), the total effect is of abstractness; the passage, one would say, might have been written by anyone with a flair for tropes, whether or not he had any experience of the conditions described.

Direct experience of conditions, of course, is not necessarily expected of a writer unless he claims, or appears, to be writing from it. The soundness of his report derives not from what is seen or heard but from what is known, however the knowledge is acquired. Through Sidney and Beatrice Webb (1859-1947 and 1858-1943) intellectual leaders of British socialism from the 'nineties to the 'thirties, were personally familiar with the poverty of industrial England, their interest is in showing that poverty has its source in economic principles, not in documenting its appearance. Their prose is, for that reason, thoroughly abstract, though occasionally lightened, as here, by sardonic wit. (It is, by the way, quite possible that some of the "leaven" in this passage is from the yeast of George Bernard Shaw, who assisted the Webbs in their writing.)

THE KITCHEN | JAMES AGEE

There is a tin roof on the kitchen. It leaks only when the rain is very heavy and then only along the juncture with the roof of the main house. The difficulty is more with heat. The room is small: very little more than big enough to crowd in the stove and table and chairs: and this slanted lean-to roof is quite low above it, with no ceiling, and half the tin itself visible. The outdoor sunlight alone is in the high nineties during many hours of one day after another for weeks on end; the thin metal roof collects and sends on this heat almost as powerfully as a burning-glass; wood fires are particularly hot and violent and there is scarcely a yard between the stove and one end of the table: between the natural heat, the cumulated and transacted heat driven downward from the roof, and the heat of the stove, the kitchen is such a place at the noon mealtime that, merely entering it, sweat is started in a sheet from the whole surface of the body, and the solar plexus and the throat are clutched into tight kicking knots which relax sufficiently to admit food only after two or three minutes.

This is a lean-to room. The forward wall is the former outside of the house. The hall door is at center of its wall; there is another door just beyond the head of the table, about four feet from the far end of the room, leading into the front room; at center of the rear wall is a window; there is another at center of the side wall. These windows are glassed, thin-rippled and dimpled panes, and are in two parts, but lacking weights, are held open

From James Agee *Let Us Now Praise Famous Men* (Boston, Houghton Mifflin Company, 1941), pp. 177-182.

with stovewood. The stove stands in the corner between them, the "cup-board" stands against the front wall beyond the door to the storeroom, the table along the front wall between that door and the hall, the meal bin and foot basin in the corner made between the rear and hall walls; the wood-box stands along the near side of the stove; under the stove is the dishpan; the coffee-pot and a kettle stand on it, set back; pots are hung on nails along the walls of the stove-corner; lids are stuck between the walls and a two-by-four; one of the skillets stands out nearly level; its handle is stuck through a rift between two boards of the wall and through this rift a small piece of the outdoors is visible. The broom stands in the corner at the foot of the table and above, on nails, hang the round crockery head of the churn, and the dasher. It is pleasantly bright here, with no sunshine, but an almost cool-looking, strong, calm light, of the sort that takes up residence in any piece of glass without glittering in it.

The room is a little small for comfort, and here, as is unnecessary in the other rooms, everything that can be is blocked back hard against the wall. There are no chairs on the wall side of the table, but a long and quite narrow bench, close against the wall, and the table is brought up close against it so that the children have to climb to their places with a fair amount of difficulty: and in spite of this economizing, the table juts out beyond the hall door, the chairs along that side a little more, and when everyone is seated the room is pretty nearly blocked. The chair at the foot is crowded in close, too, for there is just enough room between the hall door and the storeroom door. The stove has to be set well out from the walls of its corner, a couple of feet from each at least, and this leaves just room and no better between the stove and the corner of the table. In spite of all the open air, the kitchen smells powerfully of the cooking, for the walls are saturated with it.

The "cupboard," a carry-all for kitchen implements, china, eating-tools, and the less perishable of the chronic cooking supplies, is never known in the rural south as a cupboard, but always as a safe.[1] The ordinary safe is a tall, dark, flimsy wood cabinet with several shelves, with double doors faced in rusted tin pierced in ventilative patterns of geometry and of radiant flowers, and smelling stuffily yet rather sweetly of hens, butter, and fried pork and of the cheap metals of its forks. I speak of this because the Gudgers' safe veers so wide of the ordinary as to seem comic or even sur-realist in this setting, as a frigidaire might. It is of bright yellow shellacked pine and the doors are white enameled metal in narrow frames, and the door-latches are not buttons shaped like jazz-bows, as in the ordinary nineteenth-century-type safe, but are bright nickel, of the sort used on re-

---

[1] I don't know how this got started, but it seems to me of some interest that farm families, whose most urgent treasures are the food they eat, use for its storage-box the name used among middle-class people for the guardian of money, ledgers, and "valuable papers."

frigerators; and it is more capacious than the old-fashioned safe. There is a metal-lined bin for flour, and there are enameled and labeled cans for SUGAR, COFFEE, SALT, TEA, which look to have come with the house. It is a really good piece of furniture; and has a sort of middle-class, love-nest look to it which connects it to advertisements in women's magazines and to the recipe voices of radio women, so that it is here peculiarly insulting and pathetic; and already it has picked up tenant-kitchen redolences for which it was never intended.

The stove is of baroque rusting iron, with an oven. It is small, and low enough that it must be leaned above at a rather deep angle. A large black iron kettle stands at the back of it; on nails behind it, in its corner, a few dark pots and flat baking-pans are hung, and a heavy black skillet; the skillet is stuck by its handle through a rift in the wall and extends its round hand flat toward the center of the room.

The meal bin is a fifty-pound lard can half full. It is topped off by a sifter, homemade of windowscreen which is broken, and three trapped flies, covered with meal, brain themselves against the lower side.

The broom is of the cheap thirty-to-forty-cent kind and is nearly new, but do not be misled: the old one, still held in limbo because nothing is thrown away, was well used before it was discarded: it has about the sweeping power of a club foot.

The dasher is made deliciously mild and fragrant by milk and butter, and glows as ivory might against the raw wall.

The chairs sit in exact regiment of uneven heights with the charming sobriety of children pretending to be officers or judges.

The table: the lamp

The table is set for dinner.

The yellow and green checked oilcloth is worn thin and through at the corners and along the edges of the table and along the ridged edges of boards in the table surface, and in one or two places, where elbows have rested a great deal, it is rubbed through in a wide hole. In its intact surfaces it shines prettily and bluntly reflects the window and parts of the objects that are on it, for it has been carefully polished with a wet rag, and it shows also the tracings of this rag. Where it has rubbed through, the wood is sour and greasy, and there are bread crumbs in the seams and under the edges of the cloth, which smell of mold, and these odors are so mingled with that of the oilcloth that they are in total the classic odor of a tenant eating-table.

There are two stainless steel knives and forks with neat black handles which would have cost a dime apiece, and against what little we could do about it these are set at our places but by actual usage they belong to the two parents.

Aside from these the forks and knives and spoons are of that very cheap, light, and dull metal which seems to be almost universal among working-class families, and in the more charitable and idealistic kinds of institutions, and which impart to every ounce of food they touch their peculiar taste and stench, which is a little like that of a can which has contained strong fish. The tines of nearly all the forks are bent, then rippled back into approximate order; the knives are saw-edged.

Almost no two of the plates, or cups, or glasses, or saucers, are of the same size or pattern. All of the glasses except one are different sizes and shapes of jelly glass. One of the cups is thin, blue, Woolworth's imitation of willow plate: the handle is gone; two others are thick and white, of the sort used in lunchwagons, but of lower quality, flinty, and a little like sandstone at their brims; one of these is chipped; the fourth is a taller cup of the same sort, with a thready split running its full height. Two of the plates are full dinner size, of the same thick lunchwagon china, another is translucent white of a size between saucer and dinnerplate; another, deep cream-colored, netted with brown cracklings, is pressed with a garland of yellow corn and green leaves. The children eat mainly out of saucers and bowls. The food will be served in part out of pans, and in part out of two wide shallow soup plates and a small thick white platter. At the middle of the table is a mason jar of sorghum, a box of black pepper, and a tall shaker of salt whose top is green, all surrounding the unlighted lamp which stands in the bare daylight in the beauty of a young nude girl.

THE QUARTER | *EDMUND WILSON*

All around the social workers of Hull House there today stretches a sea of misery more appalling even than that which discouraged Miss Addams in the nineties. This winter even those families who had managed to hang on by their savings and earnings have been forced to apply for relief.

A relief worker's cross-section of an industrial suburb shows the sinking of the standard of living. The people here are mostly Poles. Every pressure has been brought to bear on them to induce them to spend their money on motor-cars, radios, overstuffed furniture and other unattractive luxuries; and they are caught now between two worlds, with no way of living comfortably in either. The most urgent problem, however, is how to be sure of living at all.

In one house, a girl of seventeen is interpreter for her mother, in whom the girl's stocky figure has expanded to enormous amorphous bulk, and she changes not only her language but her expression and gestures, her

From *The American Earthquake* (New York, Doubleday & Company, Inc., 1958). Reprinted by permission of the author.

personality, in passing from English to Polish. She had till lately, at $2 a week, been doing all the housework for a real-estate man; but she decided he was imposing on her and quit. She is handsome and evidently high-spirited—Americanized during the whoopee period. Her brother had had a job on the conveyer at a bookbindery; but, due to a mechanical improvement, this job no longer exists: the boy has been laid off, with no prospect of reëmployment. The girl takes us up from the downstairs kitchen, where the family mostly live, and shows you the little-used floor above, which is papered with big blue, pink and magenta blossoms and furnished with all the things that the salesmen of the boom have sold them: a victrola and wadded chairs and couches, spotted with a pattern of oranges, which nobody seems ever to have sat in. On the walls, as in all these houses, exhibited in ornate gold frames, hang Slavic saints and Madonnas, bristling with spiky gold crowns, Byzantine embroidery and Polish inscriptions.

Elsewhere an old man is dying of a tumor, with no heat in the house, on a cold day. His pale bones of arms lie crooked like bent pins; nothing is heard in the house but his gasping. His old wife, her sharp Polish nose sticking out from under a bonnet-like cap, stands beside him, as silent as a ghost. Their granddaughter, who is married and wears well-fitting American street-clothes—an American middle-class woman, but today as badly off as they are—has just been to the relief station for coal.

In another place, a family of five have three small rooms in a basement, and they have sunk below any standard: the father grinningly and glaringly drunk in the middle of the morning, the mother stunned and discouraged by her struggle against poverty and filth. They live around the stove with their small dirty children, in the close sweetish sickish smell of cooking and boiling clothes. Where they sleep on two narrow cots, the bedclothes are old twisted gray rags that have not even been smoothed out flat. They do not know very much English, and they cannot explain to the relief worker what they have done about relief and insurance; they do not understand, themselves. All they know is that they are living in that dirty hole, from which they have not yet been expelled, and where the man, with a little liquor in him, can imagine himself the shrewd and sound father of a family, with the situation well under control. In another basement, however, the young husband has carpentered and painted the big cellar room which, with a tiny bedroom, is all they have, so that it almost resembles a human dwelling. He used to work for the Fruit-Growers' Express, but has been laid off a long time. The stout blond girl to whom he is married has had to be on her feet all day and, from the strain on her heart, has just had a collapse. They do not have any children, but they keep a canary in a cage. The young wife in another household has put kewpie dolls around in an otherwise bare apartment, and has made blue curtains for the cot in which her two children sleep. She and her husband are very fond of one another and very fond of the children. They are the kind of people who do not like to ask for relief, and they have put it off as long as they. could, with the result that, though goodlooking and youthful, they are now pale and thin with undernourishment.

A pink clear-eyed innocent-eyed women, alone in an immaculately kept kitchen, all white oilcloth and green-and-white linoleum and with the latest thing in big gleaming gas-ranges, flushes at the relief worker's questions. She is going to have a baby and has applied for money to pay the midwife. The relief worker offers her a doctor but she is used to having the midwife. An elderly couple from Zürich are living in an apartment equally immaculate, though far less completely equipped, amid blue-and-green chromolithographs of Swiss waterfalls and mountains and lakes. The woman is cooking a few slivers of onions on a tiny coal-stove, which was intended primarily for heat. The husband is out on the railroad tracks picking up pieces of coal in order to keep it going. The woman suddenly begins to cry as she is answering the relief worker's queries, then as suddenly stops. The husband, a little smiling man with Kaiser Wilhelm mustaches, comes back with a few pieces of coal: the railroad detectives have chased him away. He was formerly an industrial chemist and has recently turned his ingenuity to inventing little gambling toys. One of them, he says, he has a fair prospect of selling: you shoot a marble which drops into a hole and knocks up a little tin flap; "Swiss Navy" counts lowest and "America" a hundred per cent. In another place, the bookbinder who has lost his job through a technological improvement has a fellow in the musical field—a young violinist whose profession has been partly abolished by the talkies.

Above the straight criss-cross streets the small houses of brick and gray boards, the newer little two-story Noah's Arks, prick the sharp Roman Catholic spire and the bulbs of the Orthodox Church.

The single men are driven to flophouses. During the last year—September 30, 1931-September 30, 1932—50,000 have registered at the clearing house. Those who are not residents of Chicago are ordered to leave the city: if they got there by paying their fare, they are given a half-fare which will take them home. Others are sent to the asylum, the poorhouse, the veterans' home; referred to the blind pension, the juvenile court. About 500 men a month are disposed of in this way. The Oak Forest poorhouse, called "the Graveyard," has people sleeping in the corridors and turned 19,000 away last year. The rest are directed to the shelters, where they get two meals a day and a bed.

Among the high whitewashed walls of an obsolete furniture factory, the soiled yellow plaster and the scrawled and punctured blackboards of an old public school, the scraped-out offices and pompous paneling of a ghastly old disused courthouse; on the floors befouled with spittle, in the pepperysweetish stink of food cooking, sulphur fumigations, bug exterminators, rank urinals doctored with creosote—ingredients of the general fetor that more or less prominently figure as one goes from floor to floor, from room to room, but all fuse in the predominant odor of stagnant and huddled humanity—these men eat their chicken-feed and slum amid the deafening clanking of trays and dump the slops in g.i. cans; wait for prize-fights or movies of Tarzan (provided to keep them out of the hands of the Communists or from holding meetings themselves) in so-called "recreation halls," on the walls of which they have chalked up "Hoover's Hotel"—big bare chambers smothered with smoke, strewn with newspapers like vacant lots, smeared like the pavements with phlegm. Here they sit in the lecture seats, squat on the steps of the platform, stretch out on the floor on old papers. In one room a great wall-legend reminds them: "The Blood of God Can Make the Vilest Clean," and they get routed to mess through a prayer meeting. When they come back to the recreation hall, they discover that a cheerful waltz has served merely as a bait to draw them to the harangue by an old Cicero policeman who says that he has been saved. They are obliged to send their clothes to be fumigated, and, if they are wet with the winter rain, ruined. They herd into steaming showers, the young men still building some flesh on straight frames, the old with flat chests, skinny arms and round sagging bellies; and they flop at last on the army cots or in the bunks in double tiers, where the windows which are shut to keep out the cold keep in the sour smell—men in slit union suits and holey socks, men tattooed with fancy pictures or the emblems of some service they have left—resting their bunioned feet taken out of flattened shoes or flat arches wound around with adhesive tape—lying with newspapers for pillows, their arms behind their heads or with a sheet pulled over their faces or wrapped up in blankets, rigid on their backs, their skin stretched tight over their jawbones so that these look like the jaws of the dead.

There is a clinic which does what it can to head off the venereal diseases. There is also a great deal of t.b., to which the Negroes have a fatal susceptibility; and in one shelter spinal meningitis got out of hand for a while and broke nine backs on its rack. Another common complaint of the flophouses is the poisoning that results from drinking a dilution of wood alcohol which the inmates buy for fifteen cents a pint, which looks and tastes, as somebody says, like a mixture of benzine, kerosene and milk, and which usually lands them in the infirmary or the psychopathic ward. And yet one man, given his choice between his bottle and admission to the shelter, refused to give up the bottle: he preferred to spend the night in the cold rather than surrender his only support in a life so aimless and hopeless. In the Salvation Army shelter, they will not take in steady drinkers, but the others do the best they can with them. In one, there is a hobbling cripple who comes in drunk every night. "I wouldn't be surprised," says the manager, "if a hearse drove up and a dead man got up and walked out and asked for a flop." One man turned up "lousy as a pet coon—so lousy nobody would go near-um and they put-um in the stable with the horse for the night, and the horse tried to get away. The next morning they gave-um a shower and scrubbed-um with a long-handled brush." But most of the cases in the infirmaries—from exhaustion to bad kidneys and body sores—come down to the same basic disease: starvation.

Razor-slashings and shootings bring in other patients—though the prospect of a day of work a week, with its brief liberation from the shelters, is said to have diminished these. The bad characters are sent to the bull-pens in the basement, where, crowded together, in fetid air, they sleep on hard benches with their coats under their heads. Newcomers for whom there is no room have to be dumped down among them.

Yet Chicago has apparently been particularly efficient in providing and running these shelters. At best, it is not unlike the life of barracks—but without the common work and purpose which give a certain momentum to even a dull campaign. In the shelters, there is nothing to coöperate on and nothing to look forward to, no developments, no chance of success. The old man is ending his life without a home and with no hope of one; the wage-earner who has hitherto been self-dependent now finds himself dropped down among casuals and gradually acquires their attitude; the young man who comes to maturity during the workless period of the depression never learns the habit of work. (There are few actual hoboes here: the hobo can do better by begging or stealing.)

In so far as they are unable to adapt themselves, they must live under a continual oppression of fear or guilt or despair. One sees among them faces that are shocking in their contrast to their environment here: men who look as if they had never had a day's ill health or done a day's careless work in their lives. Now they jump at the opportunity of spending a day a week clearing the rubbish off vacant lots or cleaning the streets underneath the Loop tracks. This is the only thing that stands between them and that complete loss of independence which can obliterate personality itself—which degrades them to the primal dismal undifferentiated city grayness, depriving them even of the glow of life that has formerly set them off from the fog and the pavements and the sodden old newspapers, rubbing them down to nothing, forcing them out of life.

Yet none of these single-men's shelters produce such an impression of horror as the Angelus Building on South Wabash Avenue, where families of homeless Negroes have taken refuge. This neighborhood was once fairly well-to-do; but at the present time, left behind by the city's growth in other directions, it presents a desolation that is worse than the slums. When the snow in the darkening afternoon has come to seem as dingy as the dusk and the sky as cold and tangible as the snow—as if the neutral general medium of the city were condensing in such a way as to make it hard to move and exist—the houses, interminably scattered along the straight miles of the street, monotonous without being uniform, awkward or cheap attempts at various types of respectable architecture in gray limestone, colorless boards or red brick, all seem—whether inhabited or not—equally abandoned now. The windowless slots of one open into a hollow shell: it has been gutted of even its partitions; the Romanesque prongs of another make it look like a blackened pulled tooth; on the brownstone façade of a third, some distance above the ground, is stuck a pretentious doorway, from under which, like a lower jaw, the flight of front steps has been knocked. And, as a suitable climax to this, the Angelus Building looms blackly on the corner of its block: seven stories, thick with dark windows, caged in a dingy mesh of fire-escapes like mattress-springs on a junk-heap, hunched up, hunchback-proportioned, jam-crammed in its dumbness and darkness with miserable wriggling life.

It was built in 1892 and was once the Ozark Hotel, popular at the time of the old World's Fair. In the dim little entrance hall, the smudged and roughened mosaic, the plaster pattern of molding, the fancy black grill of the elevator, most of it broken off, do not recall former splendor—they are abject, mere chips and shreds of the finery of a section now dead, trodden down into the waste where they lie. There is darkness in the hundred cells: the tenants cannot pay for light; and cold: the heating system no longer works. It is a firetrap which has burned several times—the last time several people were burned to death. And, now, since it is not good for anything else, its owner has turned it over to the Negroes, who flock into the tight-packed apartments and get along there as best they can on such money as they collect from the charities.

There are former domestic servants and porters, former mill-hands and stockyard workers; there are prostitutes and hoodlums next door to respectable former laundresses and Baptist preachers. One veteran of the war, once foreman of the Sunkist Pie Company, now lives in cold and darkness with his widowed mother, even the furniture which he had been buying for $285 the outfit and on which he had paid all but the last installment of $50.20, taken away by the furniture company. For light, they burn kerosene lamps, and for warmth, small coal-stoves and charcoal buckets. The water-closets do not flush, and the water stands in the bathtubs.

The children go to play in the dark halls or along the narrow iron galleries of an abysmal central shaft, which, lighted faintly through glass at the top, is foggy and stifling with coal-smoke like a nightmare of jail or Hell. In the silence of this dreadful shaft, sudden breakages and bangs occur—then all is deathly still again. The two top floors have been stripped by fire and by the tenants' tearing things out to burn or sell: apartments have lost their doors and plumbing pipes lie uncovered. These two floors have been condemned and deserted. Relief workers who have visited the Angelus Building have come away so overwhelmed with horror that they have made efforts to have the whole place condemned—to the piteous distress of the occupants, who consider it an all-right-enough place when you've got nowhere else to go. And where to send these sixty-seven Negro families? Brought to America in the holds of slave-ships and afterwards released from their slavery with the chance of improving their lot, they are now being driven back into the black cavern of the Angelus Building, where differing standards of living, won sometimes by the hard work of generations, are all being reduced to zero.

Those who want to keep clear of the jail-like shelters get along as they can in the streets and huddle at night under the Loop or build shacks on empty lots. On whatever waste-places they are permitted to live, the scabby-looking barnacles appear, knocked together from old tar-paper and tin, old car-bodies, old packing boxes, with old stovepipes leaning askew, amid the blackened weeds in the snow and the bones of old rubbish piles. One "Hooverville" on Harrison Street flies a tattered black rag like the flag of despair.

The inhabitants of these wretched settlements chiefly forage from the city dumps, as do many of those whom charity will not help or who for one reason or another will not go to it or for whom the relief they get is inadequate. There is not a garbage-dump in Chicago which is not diligently haunted by the hungry. Last summer in the hot weather, when the smell was sickening and the flies were thick, there were a hundred people a day coming to one of the dumps, falling on the heap of refuse as soon as the truck had pulled out and digging in it with sticks and hands. They would devour all the pulp that was left on the old slices of watermelon and cantelope till the rinds were as thin as paper; and they would take away and wash and cook discarded turnips, onions, and potatoes. Meat is a more difficult matter, but they salvage a good deal of that, too. The best is the butcher's meat which has been frozen and has not spoiled. If they can find only meat that is spoiled, they can sometimes cut out the worst parts, or they scald it and sprinkle it with soda to neutralize the taste and the smell. Fish spoils too quickly, so it is likely to be impossible—though some people have made fish-head soup. Soup has also been made out of chicken claws.

A private incinerator at Thirty-fifth and La Salle Streets which disposes of the garbage from restaurants and hotels, has been regularly visited by people, in groups of as many as twenty at a time, who pounce upon anything that looks edible before it is thrown into the furnace. The women complained to investigators that the men took an unfair advantage by jumping on the truck before it was unloaded; but a code was eventually established which provided that different sets of people should come at different times every day, so that everybody would be given a chance. Another dump at Thirty-first Street and Cicero Avenue has been the center of a Hooverville of three hundred people.

The family of a laid-off dishwasher lived on food from the dump for two years. They had to cook it on the gas of the people downstairs, since their own had been shut off. Their little girl got ptomaine poisoning. Two veterans of the war, who had been expelled from Washington with the bonus army and made their homes in the fireboxes of an old kiln, were dependent on the dump for some time, though a buddy of theirs found he could do better by panhandling at people's doors. One widow with a child of nine, who had formerly made $18 a week in a factory and who has since been living on $4 a week relief and two or three hours' work a day at fifty cents an hour, has tried to get along without garbage but has had to fall back on it frequently during a period of three years. Another widow, who used to do housework and laundry but who was finally left without any work, fed herself and her fourteen-year-old son on garbage. Before she picked up the meat, she would always take off her glasses so that she would not be able to see the maggots; but it sometimes made the boy so sick to look at this offal and smell it that he could not bring himself to eat. He weighed only eighty-two pounds.

Many people in the Hooverville on Cicero Avenue have been poisoned from eating the garbage. One man ate a can of bad crab-meat thrown away by a chain store, and was later found putrefying.

On the endlessly stretching latitude of West Congress Street—lit only on one side at long intervals by livid low-power lamps—along which huge cubes of buildings are infrequently belted by lighted-up floors and where black and blind ranks of trucks stand posted in front of dark factories, some anonymous hand has chalked up on a wall: "VOTE RED. THE PEOPLE ARE GOOFY."

THE TENSIONS OF POVERTY | GEORGE ORWELL

It is altogether curious, your first contact with poverty. You have thought so much about poverty—it is the thing you have feared all your life, the thing you knew would happen to you sooner or later; and it is all so utterly and prosaically different. You thought it would be quite simple; it is extraordinarily complicated. You thought it would be terrible; it is merely squalid and boring. It is the peculiar *lowness* of poverty that you discover first; the shifts that it puts you to, the complicated meanness, the crust-wiping.

You discover, for instance, the secrecy attaching to poverty. At a sudden stroke you have been reduced to an income of six francs a day. But of course you dare not admit it—you have got to pretend that you are living quite as usual. From the start it tangles you in a net of lies, and even with the lies you can hardly manage it. You stop sending clothes to the laundry, and the

laundress catches you in the street and asks you why; you mumble something, and she, thinking you are sending the clothes elsewhere, is your
enemy for life. The tobacconist keeps asking why you have cut down your
smoking. There are letters you want to answer, and cannot, because stamps
are too expensive. And then there are your meals—meals are the worst
difficulty of all. Every day at meal-times you go out, ostensibly to a res-
taurant, and loaf an hour in the Luxembourg Gardens, watching the
pigeons. Afterwards you smuggle your food home in your pockets. Your
food is bread and margarine, or bread and wine, and even the nature of
the food is governed by lies. You have to buy rye bread instead of household
bread, because the rye loaves, though dearer, are round and can be smuggled
in your pockets. This wastes you a franc a day. Sometimes, to keep up appearances, you have to spend sixty centimes on a drink, and go correspondingly short of food. Your linen gets filthy, and you run out of soap and
razor-blades. Your hair wants cutting, and you try to cut it yourself, with
such fearful results that you have to go to the barber after all, and spend
the equivalent of a day's food. All day you are telling lies, and expensive
lies.

You discover the extreme precariousness of your six francs a day. Mean
disasters happen and rob you of food. You have spent your last eighty
centimes on half a litre of milk, and are boiling it over the spirit lamp.
While it boils a bug runs down your forearm; you give the bug a flick with
your nail, and it falls, plop! straight into the milk. There is nothing for it
but to throw the milk away and go foodless.

You go to the baker's to buy a pound of bread, and you wait while the
girl cuts a pound for another customer. She is clumsy, and cuts more than
a pound. *"Pardon, monsieur,"* she says, "I suppose you don't mind paying
two sous extra?" Bread is a franc a pound, and you have exactly a franc.
When you think that you too might be asked to pay two sous extra, and
would have to confess that you could not, you bolt in panic. It is hours
before you dare venture into a baker's shop again.

You go to the greengrocer's to spend a franc on a kilogram of potatoes.
But one of the pieces that make up the franc is a Belgium piece, and the
shopman refuses it. You slink out of the shop, and can never go there again.

You have strayed into a respectable quarter, and you see a prosperous
friend coming. To avoid him you dodge into the nearest café. Once in the
café you must buy something, so you spend your last fifty centimes on a
glass of black coffee with a dead fly in it. One could multiply these disasters
by the hundred. They are part of the process of being hard up.

You discover what it is like to be hungry. With bread and margarine in
your belly, you go out and look into the shop windows. Everywhere there
is food insulting you in huge, wasteful piles; whole dead pigs, baskets of
hot loaves, great yellow blocks of butter, strings of sausages, mountains of
potatoes, vast Gruyère cheeses like grindstones. A snivelling self-pity comes

over you at the sight of so much food. You plan to grab a loaf and run, swallowing it before they catch you; and you refrain, from pure funk.

You discover the boredom which is inseparable from poverty; the times when you have nothing to do and, being underfed, can interest yourself in nothing. For half a day at a time you lie on your bed, feeling like the *jeune squelette* in Baudelaire's poem. Only food could rouse you. You discover that a man who has gone even a week on bread and margarine is not a man any longer, only a belly with a few accessory organs.

This—one could describe it further, but it is all in the same style—is life on six francs a day. Thousands of people in Paris live it—struggling artists and students, prostitutes when their luck is out, out-of-work people of all kinds. It is the suburbs, as it were, of poverty.

I continued in this style for about three weeks. The forty-seven francs were soon gone, and I had to do what I could on thirty-six francs a week from the English lessons. Being inexperienced, I handled the money badly, and sometimes I was a day without food. When this happened I used to sell a few of my clothes, smuggling them out of the hotel in small packets and taking them to a second-hand shop in the Rue de la Montagne St. Gene-viève. The shopman was a red-haired Jew, an extraordinary disagreeable man, who used to fall into furious rages at the sight of a client. From his manner one would have supposed that we had done him some injury by coming to him. *"Merde!"* he used to shout, *"you* here again? What do you think this is? A soup kitchen?" And he paid incredibly low prices. For a hat which I had bought for twenty-five shillings and scarcely worn he gave five francs; for a good pair of shoes, five francs; for shirts, a franc each. He always preferred to exchange rather than buy, and he had a trick of thrusting some useless article into one's hand and then pretending that one had accepted it. Once I saw him take a good overcoat from an old woman, put two white billiard-balls into her hand, and then push her rapidly out of the shop before she could protest. It would have been a pleasure to flatten the Jew's nose, if only one could have afforded it.

These three weeks were squalid and uncomfortable, and evidently there was worse coming, for my rent would be due before long. Nevertheless, things were not a quarter as bad as I had expected. For, when you are approaching poverty, you make one discovery which outweighs some of the others. You discover boredom and mean complications and the beginnings of hunger, but you also discover the great redeeming feature of poverty: the fact that it annihilates the future. Within certain limits, it is actually true that the less money you have, the less you worry. When you have a hundred francs in the world you are liable to the most craven panics. When you have only three francs you are quite indifferent; for three francs will feed you till to-morrow, and you cannot think further than that. You are bored, but you are not afraid. You think vaguely, "I shall be starving in a day or two—shocking, isn't it?" And then the mind wanders to other topics. A bread and margarine diet does, to some extent, provide its own anodyne.

And there is another feeling that is a great consolation in poverty. I believe everyone who has been hard up has experienced it. It is a feeling of relief, almost of pleasure, at knowing yourself at last genuinely down and out. You have talked so often of going to the dogs—and well, here are the dogs, and you have reached them, and you can stand it. It takes off a lot of anxiety.

SOCIETY'S EXILES | B. O. FLOWER

It is difficult to over-estimate the gravity of the problem presented by those compelled to exist in the slums of our popular cities, even when considered from a purely economical point of view. From the midst of this commonwealth of degradation there goes forth a moral contagion, scourging society in all its ramification, coupled with an atmosphere of physical decay —an atmosphere reeking with filth, heavy with foul odors, laden with disease. In time of any contagion the social cellar becomes the hotbed of death, sending forth myriads of fatal germs which permeate the air for miles around, causing thousands to die because society is too short-sighted to understand that the interest of its humblest member is the interest of all. The slums of our cities are the reservoirs of physical and moral death, an enormous expense to the State, a constant menace to society, a reality whose shadow is at once colossal and portentous. In time of social upheavals they will prove magazines of destruction; for while revolution will not originate in them, once let a popular uprising take form and the cellars will reinforce it in a manner more terrible than words can portray. Considered ethically, the problem is even more embarrassing and deplorable; here, as nowhere else in civilized society, thousands of our fellow men are exiled from the enjoyments of civilization, forced into life's lowest strata of existence, branded with that fatal word scum. If they aspire to rise, society shrinks from them; they seem of another world; they are of another world; driven into the darkness of a hopeless existence, viewed much as were lepers in olden times. Over their heads perpetually rests the dread of eviction, of sickness, and of failure to obtain sufficient work to keep life in the forms of their loved ones, making existence a perpetual nightmare, from which death alone brings release. Say not that they do not feel this; I have talked with them; I have seen the agony born of a fear that rests heavy on their souls stamped in their wrinkled faces and peering forth from great pathetic eyes. For them winter has real terror, for they possess neither clothes to keep comfortable the body, nor means with which to properly warm their miserable tenements. Summer is scarcely less frightful in their quarters, with the heat at once stifling, suffocating, almost intolerable; heat which acting on

From *The Arena*, IV, 1 (June 1891).

the myriad germs of disease produces fever, often ending in death, or, what is still more dreaded, chronic invalidism. Starvation, misery, and vice, trinity of despair, haunt their every step. The Golden Rule—the foundation of true civilization, the keynote of human happiness—reaches not their wretched quarters. Placed by society under the ban, life is one long and terrible night. But tragic as is the fate of the present generation, still more appalling is the picture when we contemplate the thousands of little waves of life yearly washed into the cellar of being; fragile, helpless innocents, responsible in no way for their presence or environment, yet condemned to a fate more frightful than the beasts of the field; human beings wandering in the dark, existing in the sewer, ever feeling the crushing weight of the gay world above, which thinks little and cares less for them. Infinitely pathetic is their lot.

The causes that have operated to produce these conditions are numerous and complex, the most apparent being the immense influx of immigration from the crowded centers of the old world; the glamor of city life, which has allured thousands from the country, fascinating them from afar much as the gaudy colors and tinsel before the footlights dazzle the vision of a child; the rapid growth of the saloon, rendered well-nigh impregnable by the wealth of the liquor power; the wonderful labor-saving inventions, which in the hands of greed and avarice, instead of mitigating the burdens of the people, have greatly augmented them, by glutting the market with labor; the opportunities given by the government through grants, special privileges, and protective measures for rapid accumulation of wealth by the few; the power which this wealth has given its possessors over the less fortunate; the spread of that fevered mental condition which subjects all finer feelings and holier aspirations to the acquisition of gold and the gratification of carnal appetites, and which is manifest in such a startling degree in the gambler's world, which to dignify we call the realm of speculation; the desire for vulgar ostentation and luxurious indulgence, in a word the fatal fever for gold which has infested the social atmosphere, and taken possession of hundreds of thousands of our people, chilling their hearts, benumbing their conscience, choking all divine impulses and refined sensibilities; the cowardice and lethargy of the Church, which has grown rich in gold and poor in the possession of moral energy, which no longer dares to denounce the money changers, or alarm those who day by day are anesthetizing their own souls, while adding to the misery of the world. The church has become, to a great extent, subsidized by gold, saying in effect, "I am rich and increased in goods and have need of nothing," apparently ignorant of the fact that she "is wretched, poor, blind, and naked," that she has signally failed in her mission of establishing on earth an ideal brotherhood. Instead of lifting her children into that lofty spiritual realm where each feels the misery of his brother, she has so far surrendered to the mammon of unrighteousness that, without the slightest fear of having their consciences disturbed, men find comfort in her soft-cushioned pews, who are wringing from ten to thirty per cent profit from their fellow men in the wretched tenement districts, or who refuse to pay more than twelve cents a pair for the making of pants, forty-five cents a dozen for flannel shirts, seventy-five cents a dozen for knee pants, and twenty-five cents a dozen for neckties. I refer not to wealthy and fashionable churches, whose ministers do not know and take no steps to find out the misery that is dependent upon the avarice of their parishioners. Then again back of all this is the defective education which has developed all save character in man; education which has trained the brain but shriveled the soul. Last but by no means least is land speculation which has resulted in keeping large tracts of land idle which otherwise would have blossomed with happy homes. To these influences we must add the general ignorance of the people regarding the nature, extent, and growing proportions of the misery and want in the New World which is spreading as an Eastern plague in the filth of an oriental city.

| *THE POVERTY OF THE POOR* | *SIDNEY and*
BEATRICE WEBB |

The outstanding and entirely unexpected result of the capitalist organization of society is the widespread *penury* that it produces in the nation. A whole century of experience, in the most advanced civilizations of Europe and America alike, reveals this widespread penury as the outcome, or at least the invariable concomitant, of the divorce of the mass of the people from the ownership of the instruments of production; and of the aggregation, which has everywhere occurred, of this ownership in a relatively small propertied class. It is of course not suggested that a low standard of livelihood and the imminent peril of starvation is peculiar to capitalism. In more primitive communities, in which the instruments of production are held in common, or are widely distributed among those who gain their livelihood by using them, chronic poverty and recurrent famines have been in the past, and are to-day, by no means uncommon. But in these backward societies the meagerness and insecurity of livelihood is attributable either to man's incapacity to control the forces of nature, as manifested in droughts, floods and diseases; or to the paucity of natural resources, such as the lack of fertile land and minerals, or the severity of the climate; or else to the absence of applied science enabling men to use with efficiency the sources of wealth that exist. But the capitalist organization of industry confronts us with a paradox. The countries in which it has been developed in its

From *The Decay of Capitalist Civilization* (New York, Harcourt, Brace & World, Inc., 1923). Reprinted by permission of Drake, Son and Parton, executors, and the trustees of The Passfield Trust.

most complete form enjoy great natural resources and have made great use of science in turning them to the service of man. Taking these nations as wholes, the aggregate wealth thus produced is relatively enormous. Notwithstanding these favorable conditions, the material circumstances of the people, so far as the bulk of them are concerned and taking all things into account, have scarcely been bettered; they have been, sometimes, under unrestrained capitalism, actually worsened. There is reason to suppose that the England of the yeoman cultivator and the master craftsman, with all its privations and all its drawbacks, yielded to an actual majority of its inhabitants, more food, more serviceable clothing, more light, purer air, pleasanter surroundings, and, be it added, in practice even a greater degree of personal freedom, than did the far more productive England of the first half of the nineteenth century, when the "free enterprise" of the owners and organizers of the instruments of production was at its zenith.

THE RESULTS OF THE INDUSTRIAL REVOLUTION

The tragic process of this worsening of the conditions is described in every account of the industrial revolution, when the enthronement of the capitalist as the unrestrained exploiter of land, machinery and human labor was accompanied by results to the common people more terrible in prolonged agony than those of any war. So far as Great Britain is concerned, the account of what happened between 1760 and 1850 has, during the present generation, become a wearisome platitude of the history text-books, not only of the workman's tutorial class but even of the girls' high school. But if we realize what happened it is difficult to write about it without passion. Relays of young children destroyed in the cotton factories; men and women, boys and girls, weakened and brutalized by promiscuous toil in mines and iron-works; whole families degraded by the indecent occupation of the tenement houses of the crowded slums; constantly recurrent periods of under-employment and unemployment, and consequent hunger and starvation; food adulterated, air poisoned, water contaminated, the sights and sounds of day and night rendered hideous: these are the commonplace incidents of the industrial Britain of the beginning of the nineteenth century, discovered and rediscovered, not by sentimental philanthropists and sensational newspaper reporters, but by departmental inspectors and parliamentary inquiries. It is usually forgotten that essentially similar evils are continuing to-day among the industrial populations in the slums of the great cities in America as well as in Europe to an extent that is positively greater in volume than existed under analogous conditions between 1800 and 1840.

Further, the physical suffering, the accidents and the diseases that have been the concomitants of the capitalist system have not been its biggest evil. It is not in material things only that "the destruction of the poor is their poverty." To the hero on the ice-field or the saint in the desert, the lack of adequate means of subsistence, combined with the utmost hard-

ship, may be compatible with the spiritual exaltation, individual development, and the continuous exercise of personal initiative and enterprise. To
the peasant cultivator and master-craftsman of primitive communities, a
flood, or drought, an epidemic, the murrain or the blight, though it
produces devastation and famine, may create fellowship and stimulate
energy. But what modern industrialism destroyed, generation after generation, in those who succumbed to it, was the soul of the people. There is a
moral miasma as deadly as the physical. Right down to our own day the
dwellers in the slums of the great cities of Europe and America, actually
in increasing numbers as one generation follows another, find themselves
embedded, whether they will it or not, in all the ugliness, the dirt and
the disorder of the mean streets. Breathing, from infancy up, an atmosphere
of morbid alcoholism and sexuality, furtive larceny and unashamed men-
dacity—though here and there a moral genius may survive, saddened but
unscathed—the average man is, mentally as well as physically, poisoned.
The destitution against which the socialist protests is thus a degradation
of character, a spiritual demoralization, a destruction of human personality itself.

THE EVILS NOT INTENDED

In the opening sentence of this chapter we described those appalling
results of capitalism as unexpected. They are, in fact, too bad to have been
intentionally brought about by human beings at any stage of civilization,
much less at a period so full of humanitarian and libertarian sentiment
and of intelligent progressive aspiration as the period extending from
the careers of Voltaire and Rousseau to those of Shelley and Cobden. As
the judge in Ibsen's play remarks, "People don't do such things." That
nevertheless those things were done, and are still in the doing, is explained
by the fact that the first effects of capitalism correspond to certain natural
consequences which have an air of justice and propriety agreeable to the
uninstructed moral sense of mankind, and are accompanied by the breaking
down of restrictions on enterprise the reasonableness of which is apparent
to trained statesmen only. If A becomes poor and B becomes rich, other
things remaining equal, our sense of justice is shocked and our compassion
and indignation aroused. But if simultaneously with the change in relative
income A and his family become repulsively dirty, drunken, and ignorant,
and B becomes attractively well-groomed and invites us to share a delightful
hospitality at the hands of his charmingly dressed wife and daughters;
and if this state of things is clearly and directly traceable to the fact that
A is living recklessly beyond his income and B saving money every year,
nine hundred and ninety-nine men out of a thousand will conclude that
poetic justice demands this very retribution and reward; that A has himself
to thank for his poverty, which is a socially wholesome deterrent from his
vices; and that all can be as prosperous as B if they will follow his example.
And if, in addition, B breaks down a very obvious feudal tyranny, and

wins for all persons like himself the political predominance their apparent virtues seem to deserve, an overwhelming impression of progress and enlightenment will be produced.

It is not until the inequalities have gone so far that they are beyond all reason that people begin to suspect that A's degradation is effect and not cause, and B's prosperity is cause and not effect. When a baby in one street owns a million pounds actually before it is born, and a woman who has worked hard from her eighth year to her eightieth is removed from another to die in the workhouse, eighteenth-century optimism begins to lose confidence. . . .

INEQUALITY OF INCOME

We believe that, apart from the poverty of the poor, so gross a disparity between the income of one citizen and another as is inherent in the present advanced stage of the capitalist organization of industry, is in itself injurious to the commonwealth. The extremes of inequality are known to all men. In every newspaper, capitalist or labor, we find now and again sensational paragraphs drawing attention to the gross disparity in the incomes of selected individuals—between the few shillings or dollars a week of the laboring man or woman, and the hundreds of thousands of pounds or millions of dollars a year credited to the super-capitalists of Great Britain and the United States. But a more significant fact is the inequality in the way in which the national income is shared between one class of society and another.[1] To take, as a leading instance, the United Kingdom at its wealthiest period—the years immediately preceding the Great War. The inhabitants of this country were then producing, in the aggregate, each year, commodities and services priced at a total, in round numbers, of two thousand million pounds, besides drawing a couple of hundred millions of pounds a year from investments in other countries. One-half of this aggregate of commodities and services, out of which the whole people had to live, was taken by the one-ninth of the community which was at that date liable to income tax, comprising, therefore, all the families that had as much as £160 a year income. Nearly one-third of the remaining half (say, three hundred millions sterling) fell to the share of that *nouvelle couche sociale,* the black-coated proletariat of humble clerks and teachers and minor officials, along with the smallest shopkeepers and traders—comprising, with their families, the two-ninths of the population who were not manual working wage-earners, but who nevertheless did not get for their work as

[1] "Inequality" of income may, of course, be understood in several ways (as to which see *Some Aspects of the Inequality of Incomes in Modern Communities* by Hugh Dalton 1920). As to the statistics, see the estimates of various authorities quoted in Fabian Tract No. 5, *Facts for Socialists; Riches and Poverty,* by Sir Leo Chiozza-Money, 1905; *British Incomes and Property,* second edition, 1921, and *Wealth and Taxable Capacity,* 1922, both by Sir Josiah Stamp; and *Changes in the Distribution of Income, 1880-1913,* 1918, and *The Division of the Product of Industry,* 1919, both by A. L. Bowley.

much as £160 a year per family. There remained, out of the aggregate product, for the two-thirds of the population who were manual working wage-earners and their families, somewhere about eight hundred millions, which, after making the necessary deductions for sickness and other spells of unemployment, worked out, for the adult male worker, at an average weekly income throughout the year of something like twenty-five shillings on which to maintain his family. And this glaring inequality in the distribution of the national income was not peculiar to the United Kingdom, or to those particular years. It is characteristic of every capitalist society. The statistics for France, so far as they can be ascertained, were no less extreme in their inequality. Those for the German Empire were apparently much the same. Even in the United States, with all the boundless resources of North America, there stood revealed, so far as the statistics extend, a parallel inequality in the way the national income was shared. To put it another way: in 1890 the total income of that country was so divided that 40 per cent was received as the reward of owning, and 60 per cent as the reward of doing.[1] . . .

THE INEFFICIENT CONSUMPTION OF WEALTH

"For anything I know," wrote the second President of the United States to Jefferson, "this globe may be the Bedlam, *le Bicêtre,* of the universe."[2] The events of the last hundred years almost seem to strengthen the suggestion that, in a universe of transmigrating souls, our particular planet may have been assigned to be the lunatic asylum for the solar system. At least, the way in which the most civilized communities upon our globe consume or use the commodities and services produced by the arduous daily toil of their millions of men and women, appears to be consistent with this hypothesis. We are not referring to the delirium of social lunacy of the four years of the Great War of 1914-18, during which nearly all capitalist governments of the world used up the entire product of the labor of their respective nations, devastated fertile land, burnt innumerable buildings, and deliberately destroyed plant and machinery, in order to kill and maim some thirty millions of the youngest and strongest of their male adults. Let us think, rather, of the normal consumption of the annual product in peace time—a consumption which is taken for granted, and accepted by the well-to-do citizen with the same sort of self-complacency as is the illusion of being God Almighty by the peaceful lunatic.

THE REPORT OF THE COSMIC INSPECTOR

Imagine the report of the Spirit Expert in Scientific Consumption deputed by the government of the ALL GOOD to investigate the progress towards sanity of the inmates of the planetary lunatic asylum. "I cannot

[1] *Americanized Socialism,* by James Mackaye, 1918.
[2] John Adams to Thomas Jefferson, July 16, 1814; in *The Works of John Adams,* by C. E. Adams, 1851-6, Vol. x, p. 101.

agree," he writes, "with my colleague, the Inspector of Scientific Production, that the inhabitants of the Earth are showing any approach to sanity. I need not discuss what is sanity. It will be remembered that we are forbidden, by our instructions, to inquire into the ultimate aims or ideals of the Earthians, seeing that the rightness of ends as distinguished from means has always been a matter of controversy even in the Court Circle of the ALL GOOD. I take as the test of the sanity of individuals or races, sanctioned by the law of the universe, the capacity of selecting the appropriate means to a given end, as verified by the subsequent event. The end or ideal of the Earthians is not in dispute. They are never tired of asserting to each other, with fatuous smiles, that the end they have in view is the health and happiness of the whole community. They admit that, in the earthly state, this depends, in the first place, on the effective application of the necessary commodities and services. My colleague tells me that, in the production of most commodities and of some services, they are showing signs of increasing intelligence in the use of materials and the organization of manual labor and brainwork. In the consumption of wealth they seem to me to be going from bad to worse. Former generations produced less, but what they did produce they seem to me to have consumed more intelligently. Take the three primary necessities of earthly life—food, shelter and clothing. I first made it my business to review the consumption of clothing. In the Idle Quarter, there were a number of women, each of whom prided herself on consuming in the manufacture of her garments the whole year's toil of from one hundred to two hundred garment workers. I overhead one of them say, in a debate on possible economies, that the whole annual product of one worker would barely suffice to supply her 'with a hat and a nightgown.' A younger woman, about to be married, had provided herself, for her exclusive use, of no fewer than seventy-nine nightgowns, besides other garments on which many hundreds of persons had worked for more than a year. In order to consume the toil of one or two hundred persons on the garments of one woman, labor had to be wasted in barbaric decoration, in using materials which would not last long in wear, and in providing separate suits for each occasion (I observed one woman, closely attended by a worker, changing her clothes five times in the day); and, most idiotic of all, in discarding whole wardrobes of garments once or twice a year in order to introduce a new fashion. As Earthians are apparently valued according to their capacity to consume without producing, this inefficient consumption of the garment workers' toil was imitated by women of more limited means, so that the clothing of the whole population reflected the fantastic and unhygienic habits of the wealthy members. Passing from the Idle Quarter to the homes of the garment workers themselves, I found these persons living day and night in the same clothes—ugly, badly fitting, scanty and foul. Their children were attending school in leaky boots; and, in hot weather and cold alike, were wearing rags of the same thickness and texture. The explanation was simple. These makers of garments were each of them restricted, for the whole year, to what could be produced by a single person working for one, two, or three weeks, as against the hundred or two hundred persons working for fifty-two weeks to equip each woman of the Idle Quarter. This example is typical. Hence, as a means to attain the end of the health and happiness of the whole community, the consumption of clothing on Earth cannot but be considered as a symptom of insanity.

"Then as to the shelter which the climate of these parts of the Earth makes essential. The homes in the Idle Quarters are often so large, and contain so many empty rooms, that the constant labor of from five to twenty-five persons is required merely to keep them clean, and to serve the daily needs of the so-called occupiers, who might or might not have wives and children to share them. Meantime, even in the wealthiest cities, 20 per cent of the total population are herded together in one- or two-roomed tene-ments. I actually discovered a number of cases of two or more families working and living in a single room, the resulting indecency and disease being unfit for publication.

"Even in the matter of food—the one absolute necessary for continued existence on Earth, the consumption is madly inefficient. It is noteworthy that the Earthians have now discovered the facts with regard to the con-sumption of food. They know, within a narrow margin, exactly the quantity and quality of food required for healthy, human existence; they know that less than this means starvation and more than this means disease. And yet, if we compare the normal consumption of food-values of the bulk of the inhabitants with the normal consumption of food-values in the Idle Quar-ters, measured in the labor required for their production, we find it ranging in the proportion of something like one to twenty, with the result that the mass of the people, and those who are working hardest, are habitually undernourished, whilst a select few, who are very often absolutely unpro-ductive, are not only wasting food, but are actually making themselves inert and deformed in consuming it."

So far the imaginary report of the Spirit Inspector on Earthian Consump-tion. The mundane economist not merely confirms this criticism but even pushes it further. The present inequality of income conspicuously leads, not only to inefficient consumption, but also to the production of wrong com-modities. The power of commanding from the world just what commodities and services the several owners of the unequal incomes elect to enjoy, vitiates, at a blow, all the assumptions of the earlier economists that pro-duction would, on the whole, be automatically directed to the satisfaction of human needs, *in the order of their urgency*. It gives us the state of things in which a vast amount of labor is lavished on the most futile luxuries, whilst tens of thousands of infants are perishing from lack of milk, innu-merable children are growing up without adequate nurture, millions of men and women find themselves condemned to starved and joyless lives, and the most urgent requirements of the community as a whole—to say nothing of the essentials to the well-being of future generations—remain unprovided for. Under a system of private property in the means of production, the "effective demand" of individuals affords no sort of assurance of the fulfillment of the most indisputable national needs.

FIGURATIVE LANGUAGE:
NO MAN IS AN ISLAND

A LARGE PROPORTION of the words in the English language have their origin, and not very remotely, in physical action. As soon as the word is created, however, its strong physical associations begin to diminish; gradually it may lose its original force so completely that it is adapted to purposes and takes on meanings quite foreign to its original nature. The word "touchdown," for instance, has, by the current rules of the very game for which the word was coined, divested itself of the physical act which suggested it; "handicap" has almost entirely lost its association with its origin; "conjugate" may perhaps call up an image of pupils reciting Latin verbs but certainly not one of their yoking any things together.

Against this tendency of words to lose their vitality, writers constantly devise means of restoring vigor to words and the impact of physical confrontation to their statements. They avoid the overworked expression; they attempt to revive words by using them in unexpected contexts; they pun. Most frequently of all, however, they seek out and exploit the action implicit in the word, or build in a series of words an illustrative action to make their meaning vivid to the senses. Both procedures are essentially metaphorical: the first goes behind the veil of custom which time has thrown over the word and lays bare its original physical sense; the second manipulates words into what are called tropes or figures of speech. Fashions in the use of figurative language change from century to century and vary in frequency and kind according to matter and purpose, but good writing in every age gives testimony to the metaphorical character of language. The erroneous identification of figurative language with "purple prose" stems from ignorance of the fact that a writer has no choice but to write figuratively. According to his sensitivity to language and according to the degree of urgency he feels about putting what he has to say forcefully before his reader, he will make little or much use of the figurative life that is inherent in words. If he is not sensitive, if he is indifferent to the need for vividness, or if he uses current or traditional figures of speech without regard to their physical reference, language will take its revenge. At best, he will sound dull; at worst, he will seem foolish or stupid.

Persuasive writing readily calls forth figures of speech because emotion finds effective outlet in dramatization. The more strongly a subject affects our feelings, the more likely it is to provoke a deliberate use of figurative expression because figurative language is essentially dramatic, or active, in its representation. It alters the nature (personifies and reifies), substitutes part for whole or whole for part (synecdoche) or attribute for object (metonymy), equates the unequal and the unlike (simile and metaphor), and in so doing it both expresses and relieves feeling by imaginative transformations.

War and the threat of war have made the topic of man's inescapable closeness to his fellow man a subject of almost terrifying significance today, but the topic has always been a vital one to civilized men. The manner in which five writers face it is well reflected in the varying metaphorical intensity of the following selections. John Donne (1572-1631) was one of the greatest preachers of the Established Church and a poet of great skill. Thomas Merton (1915-) is a Trappist monk whose several books about the contemplative life have had remarkable success considering the preoccupation of the modern world with motion and material achievement.

Henry Miller (1891-), now a resident of Carmel, California, has spent most of his life abroad, primarily in France, where he was well known among the literati for his audacity, his scorn for convention, and his genuinely impressive skill in fiction. D. H. Lawrence (1885-1930) grew up in the mining town of Nottingham, England, lived for a time on the Continent, and spent the last years of his life in New Mexico. His successive changes of place, like his writing, mirror an unceasing search for a means of freeing healthy instinctual life from what Lawrence believed to be the stultifying and corrosive effects of "civilization." Walt Whitman (1819-1892) was the first American poet to attempt a poetic manner and language at once unorthodox and directly expressive of the American political and social temperament.

MEDITATION; NOW THIS BELL TOLLING SOFTLY FOR ANOTHER, SAYS TO ME: THOU MUST DIE

JOHN DONNE

Perchance he for whom this bell tolls may be so ill, as that he knows not it tolls for him; and perchance I may think myself so much better than I am, as that they who are about me, and see my state, may have caused it to toll for me, and I know not that. The church is Catholic, universal, so are all her actions; all that she does belongs to all. When she baptizes a

From *Devotions upon Emergent Occasions* (1624).

child, that action concerns me; for that child is thereby connected to that body which is my head too, and ingrafted into that body whereof I am a member. And when she buries a man, that action concerns me: all mankind is of one author, and is one volume; when one man dies, one chapter is not torn out of the book, but translated into a better language; and every chapter must be so translated; God employs several translators; some pieces are translated by age, some by sickness, some by war, some by justice; but God's hand is in every translation, and his hand shall bind up all our scattered leaves again for that library where every book shall lie open to one another. As therefore the bell that rings to a sermon calls not upon the preacher only, but upon the congregation to come, so this bell calls us all; but how much more me, who am brought so near the door by this sickness. There was a contention as far as a suit (in which both poetry and dignity, religion and estimation, were mingled), which of the religious orders should ring to prayers first in the morning; and it was determined, that they should ring first that rose earliest. If we understand aright the dignity of this bell that tolls for our evening prayer, we would be glad to make it ours by rising early, in that application, that it might be ours as well as his, whose indeed it is. The bell doth toll for him that thinks it doth; and though it intermit again, yet from that minute that that occasion wrought upon him, he is united to God. Who casts not up his eye to the sun when it rises? but who takes off his eye from a comet when that breaks out? Who bends not his ear to any bell which upon any occasion rings? but who can remove it from that bell which is passing a piece of himself out of this world? No man is an island, entire of itself; every man is a piece of the continent, a part of the main. If a clod be washed away by the sea, Europe is the less, as well as if a promontory were, as well as if a manor of thy friend's or of thine own were: any man's death diminishes me, because I am involved in mankind, and therefore never send to know for whom the bell tolls; it tolls for thee. Neither can we call this a begging of misery, or a borrowing of misery, as though we were not miserable enough of ourselves, but must fetch in more from the next house, in taking upon us the misery of our neighbors. Truly it were an excusable covetousness if we did, for affliction is a treasure, and scarce any man hath enough of it. No man hath affliction enough that is not matured and ripened by it, and made fit for God by that affliction. If a man carry treasure in bullion, or in a wedge of gold, and have none coined into current money, his treasure will not defray him as he travels. Tribulation is treasure in the nature of it, but it is not current money in the use of it, except we get nearer and nearer our home, heaven, by it. Another man may be sick too, and sick to death, and this affliction may lie in his bowels, as gold in a mine, and be of no use to him; but this bell, that tells me of his affliction, digs out and applies that gold to me: if by this consideration of another's danger I take mine own into contemplation, and so secure myself, by making my recourse to my God, who is our only security.

WE ARE ONE MAN | *THOMAS MERTON*

I must look for my identity, somehow, not only in God but in other men.

I will never be able to find myself if I isolate myself from the rest of mankind as if I were a different kind of being.

Some men have perhaps become hermits with the thought that sanctity involved some kind of escape from other men. But the only justification for a life of deliberate solitude is the conviction that it will help you to love not only God but also other men. Otherwise, if you go into the desert merely to get away from crowds of people you dislike, you will not find peace or solitude either: you will only isolate yourself with a tribe of devils.

Go into the desert not to escape other men but in order to find them in God.

There is no true solitude except interior solitude. And interior solitude is not possible for anyone who does not accept his true place in relation to other men. There is no true peace possible for the man who still imagines that some accident of talent or grace or virtue segregates him from other men and places him above them.

God does not give us graces or talents or virtues for ourselves alone. We are members one of another and everything that is given to one member is given for the whole body. I do not wash my feet to make them more beautiful than my face.

The saints love their sanctity not because it separates them from the rest of us and places them above us, but because, on the contrary, it brings them closer to us and in a sense places them below us. Their sanctity is given them in order that they may help us and serve us—for the saints are like doctors and nurses who are better than the sick in the sense that they are healthy and possess arts of healing them, and yet they make themselves the servants of the sick and devote their own health and their art to them.

The saints are glad to be saints, not because their sanctity makes them admirable to others but *because the gift of sainthood makes it possible for them to admire everybody else*. It gives them a vision that can find good in the most terrible criminals. It delivers them from the burden of judging others, condemning other men.

In humility is the greatest freedom. As long as you have to defend the imaginary self that you think is important, you lose your peace of heart. As soon as you compare that shadow with the shadows of other people, you lose all joy, because you have begun to trade in unrealities, and there is no joy in things that do not exist.

As soon as you begin to take yourself seriously and imagine that your virtues are important because they are yours, you become the prisoner of your own vanity and even your best works will blind and deceive you. Then, in order to defend yourself, you will begin to see sins and faults everywhere in the actions of other men. And the more unreasonable importance you attach to yourself and to your own works, the more you will tend to build up your own idea of yourself by condemning other people. Some of the most virtuous men in the world are also the bitterest and most unhappy, because they have unconsciously come to believe that all their happiness depends on their being more virtuous than other men.

When humility delivers a man from attachment to his own works and his own reputation, he discovers that true joy is only possible when we have completely forgotten ourselves. And it is only when we pay no more attention to our own life and our own reputation and our own excellence that we are at last completely free to serve God in perfection for His own sake alone. . . .

The more I become identified with God, the more will I be identified with all the others who are identified with Him. His Love will live in all of us. His Spirit will be our One Life, the Life of all of us and the Life of God. And we shall love one another and God with the same Love with which He loves us and Himself. This Love is a Person, and it is God Himself.

Christ prayed that all men might become One as He was One with His Father, in the Unity of the Holy Spirit. Therefore when you and I become what we are really meant to be, we will discover not only that we love one another perfectly but that we are the same Mystical Person, and that we are both living in Christ and Christ in us, and we are all One Christ.

The ultimate perfection of the contemplative life is not a heaven of separate individuals, each one viewing his own private vision of God: it is a sea of Love which flows through the One Person of all the elect, all the angels and saints, and their contemplation would be incomplete if it were not shared, or if it were shared with fewer souls, or with spirits capable of less vision and less joy.

And I will have more joy in heaven and in the contemplation of God, if you are also there to share it with me; and the more of us there will be to share it the greater will be the joy of all. For contemplation is not ultimately perfect unless it is shared. We do not finally taste the full exultation of God's glory until we share His infinite gift of it by overflowing and transmitting glory all over heaven, and seeing God in all the others, and knowing that He is the Life of all of us and that we are all One in Him.

Even on earth it is the same, but in obscurity. This unity is something we cannot yet realize and enjoy except in the darkness of faith. But even here the more we are alone with God the more we are united with one another; and the silence of contemplation is deep and rich and endless society, not only with God but with men. Yet perhaps for the time being it is better to forget about it, because it might upset our imagination. For if we remembered individuals and thought of them in our contemplation, that would tend to withdraw us from God and therefore from spiritual union with them. We remain more truly with them when we no longer clearly know them. For we are still in transition, waiting to find God in them visibly and clearly. Until then, we find both them and God in one darkness, which is contemplation.

The more we are alone with Him the more we are with one another, in darkness, yet a multitude. And the more we go out to one another in work and activity and communication, according to the will and charity of God, the more we are multiplied in Him and yet we are in solitude.

The more we are alone the more we are together; and the more we are in society, the true society of charity, not of cities and physical mobs, the more we are alone with Him. For in my soul and in your soul I find the same Christ Who is our Life, and He finds Himself in our love, and together we all find Paradise which is the sharing of His Love for His Father in the Person of Their Spirit.

My true personality will be fulfilled in the mystical Person of Christ in this one way above all, that through me, Christ and His Spirit will be able to love you and all men and God the Father in a way that would be possible in no one else.

Love comes out of God and gathers us to God in order to pour itself back into God through all of us and bring us all back to Him on the tide of His own infinite mercy.

So we all become avenues and windows through which God shines back into His own house.

When the Love of God is in me, God is able to love you through me and you are able to love God through me. If my soul were closed to that love, God's love for you and your love for God and God's love for Himself in you and in me, would be denied the particular expression which it finds through me and through no other.

Because God's love is in me it can come to you from a different and special direction that would be closed if He did not live in me, and because His love is in you it can come to me from a quarter from which it would not otherwise come. And because it is in both of us, God has greater glory. His love is expressed in two more ways in which it would not otherwise be expressed: that is, in two more joys that could not exist without Him.

THE WAY OF LIFE | *HENRY MILLER*

There was one thought, however, which bored into me like a gimlet during these sessions with Kronski. It was the notion that every one, no matter how far gone he was, could be saved. Yes, if one had infinite time and infinite patience, it could be done. It began to dawn on me that the healing art was not at all what people imagined it to be, that it was something very simple, too simple, in fact, for the ordinary mind to grasp. To put it in the simple way it came to my mind I would say that it was like this: *everybody becomes a healer the moment he forgets about himself.* The sickness which we see everywhere, the bitterness and disgust which life inspires in so many of us, is only the reflection of the sickness which we carry within us. Prophylactics will never secure us against the world disease, because we bear the world within. No matter how marvelous human beings become the sum total will yield an external world which is painful and imperfect. As long as we live self-consciously we must always fail to cope with the world. It is not necessary to die in order to come at last face to face with reality. Reality is here and now, everywhere, gleaming through every reflection that meets the eye. Prisons and even lunatic asylums are emptied of their inmates when a more vital danger menaces the community. When the enemy approaches the political exile is recalled to share in the defense of his country. At the last ditch it gets dinned into our thick skulls that we are all part and parcel of the same flesh. When our very lives are threatened we begin to live. Even the psychic invalid throws away his crutches in such moments. For him the greatest joy is to realize that there is something more important than himself. All his life he has turned on the spit of his own roasted ego. He made the fire with his own hands. He drips in his own juices. He makes himself a tender morsel for the demons he liberated with his own hands. That is the picture of human life on this planet called the Earth. Everybody is a neurotic, down to the last man and woman. The healer, or the analyst, if you like, is only a super-neurotic. He has put the Indian sign on us. To be cured we must rise from our graves and throw off the cerements of the dead. Nobody can do it for another—it is a private affair which is best done collectively. We must die as egos and be born again in the swarm, not separate and self-hypnotized, but individual and related.

As to salvation and all that... The greatest teachers, the true healers, I would say, have always insisted that they can only point the way. The Buddha went so far as to say: "Believe nothing, no matter where you read

it or who has said it, *not even if I have said it,* unless it agrees with your own reason and your own common sense."

The great ones do not set up offices, charge fees, give lectures, or write books. Wisdom is silent, and the most effective propaganda for truth is the force of personal example. The great ones attract disciples, lesser figures whose mission it is to preach and to teach. These are the gospelers who, unequal to the highest task, spend their lives in converting others. The great ones are indifferent, in the profoundest sense. They don't ask you to believe: they electrify you by their behavior. They are the awakeners. What you do with your petty life is of no concern to them. What you do with your life is only of concern to *you,* they seem to say. In short, their only purpose here on earth is to inspire. And what more can one ask of a human being than that?

To be sick, to be neurotic, if you like, is to ask for guarantees. The neurotic is the flounder that lies on the bed of the river, securely settled in the mud, waiting to be speared. For him death is the only certainty, and the dread of that grim certainty immobilizes him in a living death far more horrible than the one he imagines but knows nothing about.

The way of life is toward fulfillment, however, wherever it may lead. To restore a human being to the current of life means not only to impart self-confidence but an abiding faith in the processes of life. A man who has confidence in himself *must* have confidence in others, confidence in the fitness and rightness of the universe. When a man is thus anchored he ceases to worry about the fitness of things, about the behavior of his fellowmen, about right and wrong, and justice and injustice. If his roots are in the current of life he will float on the surface like a lotus and he will blossom and give forth fruit. He will draw his nourishment from above and below; he will send his roots down deeper and deeper, fearing neither the depths nor the heights. The life that is in him will manifest itself in growth, and growth is an endless, eternal process. He will not be afraid of withering, because decay and death are part of growth. As a seed he began and as a seed he will return. Beginnings and endings are only partial steps in the eternal process. The process is everything . . . the way . . . the Tao.

The way of life! A grand expression. Like saying *Truth.* There is nothing beyond it. It is all.

And so the analyst says, "Adapt yourself!" He does not mean, as some wish to think—adapt yourself to life! *Become an adept!* That is the highest adjustment—to make oneself an adept.

The delicate flowers are the first to perish in a storm; the giant is laid low by a sling-shot. For every height that is gained new and more baffling dangers menace us. The coward is often buried beneath the very wall against which he huddled in fear and anguish. The finest coat of mail can be penetrated by a skillful thrust. The greatest armadas are eventually sunk; Maginot lines are always circumvented. The Trojan horse is always waiting to be trotted out. Where then does security lie? What protection can you invent that has not already been thought of? It is useless to think of security: there is none. The man who looks for security, even in the mind, is like a man who would chop off his limbs in order to have artificial ones which will give him no pain or trouble.

In the insect world is where we see the defense system par excellence. In the gregarious life of the ·animal world we see another kind of defense system. By comparison the human being seems a helpless creature. In the sense that he lives a more exposed life he is. But this ability to expose himself to every risk is precisely his strength. A god would have no recognizable defense whatever. He would be one with life, moving in all dimensions freely.

Fear, hydra-headed fear, which is rampant in all of us, is a hangover from lower forms of life. We are straddling two worlds, the one from which we have just emerged and the one toward which we are heading. That is the deepest meaning of the word human, that we are a link, a bridge, a promise. It is in us that the life process is being carried to fulfillment. We have a tremendous responsibility, and it is the gravity of that which awakens our fears. We know that if we do not move forward, if we do not realize our potential being, we shall relapse, sputter out, and drag the world down with us. We carry Heaven and Hell within us: we are the cosmogonic builders. We have choice—and all creation is our range. For some it is a terrifying prospect. It would be better, think they, if Heaven were above and Hell below—anywhere outside, but not within. But that comfort has been knocked from under us. There are no places to go to, either for reward or punishment. The place is always here and now, in your own person and according to your own fancy. The world is exactly what you picture it to be, always, every instant. It is impossible to shift the scenery about and pretend that you will enjoy another, a different act. The setting is permanent, changing with the mind and heart, not according to the dictates of an invisible stage director. You are the author, director and actor all in one: the drama is always going to be your own life, not someone else's. A beautiful, terrible, ineluctable drama, like a suit made of your own skin. Would you want it otherwise? Could you invent a better drama?

WE NEED ONE ANOTHER | *D. H. LAWRENCE*

We may as well admit it: men and women need one another. We may as well, after all our kicking against the pricks, our revolting and our sulking, give in and be graceful about it. We are all individualists: we are all egoists: we all believe intensely in freedom, our own at all events. We all want to be absolute, and sufficient unto ourselves. And it is a great blow to our self-esteem that we simply *need* another human being. We don't mind airily picking and choosing among women—or among men, if we are a woman. But to have to come down to the nasty, sharp-pointed brass tacks of admitting: My God, I can't live without that obstreperous woman of mine!—this is terribly humiliating to our isolated conceit.

And when I say: "without that woman of mine" I do not mean a mistress, the sexual relation in the French sense. I mean the woman, my relationship to the woman herself. There is hardly a man living who can exist at all cheerfully without a relationship to some particular woman: unless, of course, he makes another man play the role of woman. And the same of woman. There is hardly a woman on earth who can live cheerfully without some intimate relationship to a man; unless she substitutes some other woman for the man.

So there it is. Now for three thousand years men, and women, have been struggling against this fact. In Buddhism, particularly, a man could never possibly attain the supreme Nirvana if he so much as saw a woman out of the corner of his eye. "Alone I did it!" is the proud assertion of the gentleman who attains Nirvana. And "Alone I did it!" says the Christian whose soul is saved. They are the religions of overweening individualism, resulting, of course, in our disastrous modern egoism of the individual. Marriage, which on earth is a sacrament, is dissolved by the decree absolute of death. In heaven there is no giving and taking in marriage. The soul in heaven is supremely individual, absolved from every relationship except that with the Most High. In heaven there is neither marriage nor love, nor friendship nor fatherhood nor motherhood, nor sister nor brother nor cousin: there is just me, in my perfected isolation, placed in perfect relation to the Supreme, the Most High.

When we talk of heaven we talk, really, of that which we would most like to attain, and most like to be here on earth. The condition of heaven is the condition to be longed for, striven for, now.

Now, if I say to a woman, or to a man: "Would you like to be purely free of all human relationships, free from father and mother, brother and sister, husband, lover, friend, or child? free from all these human entanglements, and reduced purely to your own pure self, connected only with the Supreme Power, the Most High?" Then what would the answer be? What is the answer, I ask you? What is your own sincere answer?

I expect, in almost all cases, it is an emphatic "yes." In the past, most men would have said "yes," and most women "no." But today, I think, many men might hesitate, and nearly all women would unhesitatingly say "yes."

Modern men, however, have so nearly achieved this Nirvana-like condition of having no real human relationships at all, that they are beginning to wonder what and where they are. What are you, when you've asserted your grand independence, broken all the ties, or "bonds," and reduced yourself to a "pure" individuality? What are you?

You may imagine you are something very grand, since few individuals even approximate to this independence without falling into deadly egoism and conceit: and emptiness. The real danger is, reduced to your own single merits and cut off from the most vital human contacts, the danger is that you are left just simply next to nothing. Reduce any individual, man or woman, to his elements, or her elements, and what is he? what is she? Extremely little! Take Napoleon, and stick him alone on a miserable island, and what is he?—a peevish, puerile little fellow. Put Mary Stuart in a nasty stone castle of a prison, and she becomes merely a catty little person. Now Napoleon was not a peevish, puerile little fellow, even if he became such when isolated on St. Helena. And Mary Queen of Scots was only a catty little person when she was isolated in Fotheringay or some such hole. This grand isolation, this reducing of ourselves to our very elemental selves, is the greatest fraud of all. It is like plucking the peacock naked of all his feathers to try to get at the real bird. When you've plucked the peacock bare, what have you got? Not the peacock, but the naked corpse of a bird.

And so it is with us and our grand individualism. Reduce any of us to the *mere* individual that we are, and what do we become? Napoleon becomes a peevish, puerile little fellow, Mary Queen of Scots becomes a catty little person, St. Simeon Stylites, stuck up on his pillar, becomes a conceited lunatic, and we, wonderful creatures as we are, become trashy, conceited little modern egoists. The world today is full of silly, impertinent egoists who have broken all the finer human ties, and base their claims to superiority on their own emptiness and nullity. But the empty ones are being found out. Emptiness, which makes a fair noise, deceives for a short time only.

The fact remains that when you cut off a man and isolate him in his own pure and wonderful individuality, you haven't got the man at all, you've only got the dreary fag-end of him. Isolate Napoleon, and he is nothing. Isolate Immanuel Kant, and his grand ideas will still go on tick-tick-ticking inside his head, but unless he could write them down and communicate them, they might as well be the ticking of the death-watch beetle. Take even Buddha himself, if he'd been whisked off to some lonely place and planted cross-legged under a bhô-tree and nobody had even seen him or heard any of his Nirvana talk, then I doubt he would have got much fun out of Nirvana, and he'd have been just a crank. In absolute isolation, I doubt if any individual amounts to much; or if any soul is worth saving, or even having. "And I, if I be lifted up, will draw all men unto me." But if there were no other men to be lifted, the whole show would be a fiasco.

So that everything, even individuality itself, depends on relationship. "God cannot do without me," said an eighteenth-century Frenchman. What he meant was, that if there were no human beings, if Man did not exist, then God, the God of Man, would have no meaning. And it is true. If there were no men and women, Jesus would be meaningless. In the same way,

Napoleon on St. Helena became meaningless, and the French nation lost a great part of its meaning without him in connection with his army and the nation; a great power streamed out of Napoleon, and from the French people there streamed back to him a great responsive power, and therein lay his greatness and theirs. That is, in the relationship. The light shines only when the circuit is completed. The light does not shine with one half of the current. Every light is some sort of completed circuit. And so is every life, if it is going to be a life.

We have our very individuality in relationship. Let us swallow this important and prickly fact. Apart from our connections with other people, we are barely individuals, we amount, all of us, to next to nothing. It is in the living touch between us and other people, other lives, other phenomena that we move and have our being. Strip us of our human contacts and of our contact with the living earth and the sun, and we are almost bladders of emptiness. Our individuality means nothing. A skylark that was alone on an island would be songless and meaningless, his individuality gone, running about like a mouse in the grass. But if there were one female with him, it would lift him singing into the air, and restore him his real individuality.

And so with men and women. It is in relationship to one another that they have their true individuality and their distinct being: in contact, not out of contact. This is sex, if you like. But it is no more sex than sunshine on the grass is sex. It is a living contact, give and take: the great and subtle relationship of men and women, man and woman. In this and through this we become real individuals, without it, without the real contact, we remain more or less nonentities.

But, of course, it is necessary to have the contact alive and unfixed. It is not a question of: Marry the woman and have done with it—that is only one of the stupid recipes for avoiding contact and killing contact. There are many popular dodges for killing every possibility of true contact: like sticking a woman on a pedestal, or the reverse, sticking her beneath notice; or making a "model" housewife of her, or a "'model" mother, or a "model" help-meet. All mere devices for avoiding any contact with her. A woman is not a "model" anything. She is not even a distinct and definite personality. It is time we got rid of these fixed notions. A woman is a living fountain whose spray falls delicately around her, on all that come near. A woman is a strange soft vibration on the air, going forth unknown and unconscious, and seeking a vibration of response. Or else she is a discordant, jarring, painful vibration, going forth and hurting everyone within range. And a man the same. A man, as he lives and moves and has being, is a fountain of life-vibration, quivering and flowing towards someone, something that will receive his outflow and send back an inflow, so that a circuit is completed, and there is a sort of peace. Or else he is a source of irritation, discord, and pain, harming everyone near him.

But while we remain healthy and positive, we seek all the time to come into true human relationship with other human beings. Yet it has to happen, the relationship, almost unconsciously. We can't *deliberately* do much with a human connection, except smash it: and that is usually not difficult. On the positive side we can only most carefully let it take place, without interfering or forcing.

We are laboring under a false conception of ourselves. For centuries, man has been the conquering hero, and woman has been merely the string to his bow, part of his accoutrement. Then woman was allowed to have a soul of her own, a separate soul. So the separating business started, with all the clamor of freedom and independence. Now the freedom and independence have been rather overdone, they lead to an empty nowhere, the rubbish-heap of all our dead feelings and waste illusions.

The conquering hero business is as obsolete as Marshal Hindenburg, and about as effective. The world sees attempts at revival of this stunt, but they are usually silly, in the end. Man is no longer a conquering hero. Neither is he a supreme soul isolated and alone in the universe, facing the unknown in the eternity of death. That stunt is also played out, though the pathetic boys of today keep on insisting on it, especially the pathetic boys who wrap themselves in the egoistic pathos of their sufferings during the late war.

But both stunts are played out, both the conquering hero and the pathetic hero clothed in suffering and facing Eternity in the soul's last isolation. The second stunt is, of course, more popular today, and still dangerous to the self-pitying, played-out specimens of the younger generation. But for all that, it is a dead stunt, finished.

What a man has to do today is to admit, at last, that all these fixed ideas are no good. As a fixed object, even as an individuality or a personality, no human being, man or woman, amounts to much. The great I AM does not apply to human beings, so they may as well leave it alone. As soon as anybody, man or woman, becomes a great I AM, he becomes nothing. Man or woman, each is a flow, a flowing life. And without one another, we can't flow, just as a river cannot flow without banks. A woman is one bank of the river of my life, and the world is the other. Without the two shores, my life would be a marsh. It is the relationship to woman, and to my fellowmen, which makes me myself a river of life.

And it is this, even, that gives me my soul. A man who has never had a vital relationship to any other human being doesn't really have a soul. We cannot feel that Immanuel Kant ever had a soul. A soul is something that forms and fulfils itself in my contacts, my living touch with people I have loved or hated or truly known. I am born with the clue to my soul. The wholeness of my soul I must achieve. And by my soul I mean my wholeness. What we suffer today is the lack of a sense of our own wholeness, or completeness, which is peace. What we lack, what the young lack, is a sense of being whole in themselves. They feel so scrappy, they have no peace. And by peace I don't mean inertia, but the full flowing of life, like a river.

We lack peace because we are not whole. And we are not whole because we have known only a tithe of the vital relationships we might have had. We live in an age which believes in stripping away the relationships. Strip them away, like an onion, till you come to pure, or blank nothingness. Emptiness. That is where most men have come now: to a knowledge of their own complete emptiness. They wanted so badly to be "themselves" that they became nothing at all: or next to nothing.

It is not much fun, being next to nothing. And life ought to be fun, the greatest fun. Not merely "having a good time," in order to "get away from yourself." But real fun in being yourself. Now there are two great relationships possible to human beings: the relationship of man to woman, and the relationship of man to man. As regards both, we are in a hopeless mess.

But the relationship of man to woman is the central fact in actual human life. Next comes the relationship of man to man. And, a long way after, all the other relationships, fatherhood, motherhood, sister, brother, friend.

A young man said to me the other day, rather sneeringly, "I'm afraid I can't believe in the regeneration of England by sex." I said to him: "I'm sure you can't." He was trying to inform me that he was above such trash as sex, and such commonplace as women. He was the usual vitally below par hollow, and egoistic young man, infinitely wrapped up in himself, like a sort of mummy that will crumble if unwrapped.

And what is sex, after all, but the symbol of the relation of man to woman, woman to man? And the relation of man to woman is wide as all life. It consists in infinite different flows between the two beings, different, even apparently contrary. Chastity is part of the flow between man and woman, as to physical passion. And beyond these, an infinite range of subtle communication which we know nothing about. I should say that the relation between any two decently married people changes profoundly every few years, often without their knowing anything about it; though every change causes pain, even if it brings a certain joy. The long course of marriage is a long event of perpetual change in which a man and a woman mutually build up their souls and make themselves whole. It is like rivers flowing on, through new country, always unknown.

But we are so foolish, and fixed by our limited ideas. A man says: "I don't love my wife any more, I no longer want to sleep with her." But why should he always want to sleep with her? How does he know what other subtle and vital interchange is going on between him and her, making them both whole, in this period when he doesn't want to sleep with her? And she, instead of jibbing and saying that all is over and she must find another man and get a divorce—why doesn't she pause, and listen for a new rhythm in her soul, and look for the new movement in the man? With every change, a new being emerges, a new rhythm establishes itself;

we renew our life as we grow older, and there is real peace. Why, oh, why do we want one another to be always the same fixed, like a menu-card that is never changed?

If only we had more sense. But we are held by a few fixed ideas, like sex, money, what a person "ought" to be, and so forth, and we miss the whole of life. Sex is a changing thing, now alive, now quiescent, now fiery, now apparently quite gone, quite gone. But the ordinary man and woman haven't the gumption to take it in all its changes. They demand crass, crude sex-desire, they demand it always, and when it isn't forthcoming, then— smash-bash! smash up the whole show. Divorce! Divorce!

I am so tired of being told that I want mankind to go back to the condition of savages. As if modern city people weren't about the crudest, rawest, most crassly savage monkeys that ever existed, when it comes to the relation of man and woman. All I see in our vaunted civilization is men and women smashing each other emotionally and psychically to bits, and all I ask is that they should pause and consider.

For sex, to me, means the whole of the relationship between man and woman. Now this relationship is far greater than we know. We only know a few crude forms—mistress, wife, mother, sweetheart. The woman is like an idol, or a marionette, always forced to play one role or another: sweetheart, mistress, wife, mother. If only we could break up this fixity, and realize the unseizable quality of real woman: that a woman is a flow, a river of life, quite different from a man's river of life: and that each river must flow in its own way, though without breaking its bounds: and that the relation of man to woman is the flowing of two rivers side by side, sometimes even mingling, then separating again, and travelling on. The relationship is a life-long change and a life-long travelling. And that is sex. At periods, sex-desire itself departs completely. Yet the great flow of the relationship goes on all the same, undying, and this is the flow of living sex, the relation between man and woman, that lasts a lifetime, and of which sex-desire is only one vivid, most vivid, manifestation.

THERE WAS A CHILD WENT FORTH | *WALT WHITMAN*

There was a child went forth every day,
And the first object he look'd upon, that object he became,
And that object became part of him for the day or a certain part of the day,
Or for many years of stretching cycles of years.

The early lilacs became part of this child,
And grass and white and red morning-glories, and white and red clover,
    and the song of the phœbe-bird,

And the Third-month lambs and the sow's pink-faint litter, and the mare's foal and the cow's calf,

And the noisy brood of the barnyard or by the mire of the pondside,

And the fish suspending themselves so curiously below there, and the beautiful curious liquid,

And the water-plants with their graceful flat heads, all became part of him.

The field-sprouts of Fourth-month and Fifth-month became part of him,

Winter-grain sprouts and those of the light-yellow corn, and the esculent roots of the garden,

And the apple-trees cover'd with blossoms and the fruit afterward, and wood-berries, and the commonest weeds by the road,

And the old drunkard staggering home from the outhouse of the tavern whence he had lately risen,

And the schoolmistress that pass'd on her way to the school,

And the friendly boys that pass'd, and the quarrelsome boys,

And the tidy and fresh-cheek'd girls, and the barefoot negro boy and girl,

And all the changes of city and country wherever he went.

And his own parents, he that had father'd him and she that had conceiv'd him in her womb and birth'd him,

They gave this child more of themselves than that,

They gave him afterward every day, they became part of him.

The mother at home quietly placing the dishes on the suppertable,

The mother with mild words, clean her cap and gown, a wholesome odor falling off her person and clothes as she walks by,

The father, strong, self-sufficient, manly, mean, anger'd, unjust,

The blow, the quick loud words, the tight bargain, the crafty lure,

The family usages, the language, the company, the furniture, the yearning and swelling heart,

Affection that will not be gainsay'd, the sense of what is real, the thought if after all it should prove unreal,

The doubts of day-time and the doubts of night-time, the curious whether and how,

Whether that which appears so is so, or is it all flashes and specks?

Men and women crowding fast in the streets, if they are not flashes and specks what are they?

The streets themselves and the façades of houses, and goods in the windows,

Vehicles, teams, the heavy-plank'd wharves, the huge crossing at the ferries,

The village on the highland seen from afar at sunset, the river between,

Shadows, aureola and mist, the light falling on roofs and gables of white or brown two miles off,

The schooner near by sleepily dropping down the tide, the little boat slacktow'd astern,

The hurrying tumbling waves, quick-broken crests, slapping,
The strata of color'd clouds, the long bar of maroon-tint away solitary by
*   itself, the spread of purity it lies motionless in,*
The horizon's edge, the flying sea-crow, the fragrance of salt marsh and
*   shore mud,*
These became part of that child who went forth every day, and who now
*   goes, and will always go forth every day.*

STOCK LANGUAGE, JARGON

CONSIDERING THE PERVASIVE INFLUENCE of citable data about
nearly every aspect of modern life, it is strange that there has been a ten-
dency in some of the most serious writing about that life to use a language
hostile to concreteness. This curious condition may be in part explained as
an attempt to get away from the bareness and anonymity of the factual; it
may be in part a resistance to the reduction of life to quantities or, less
nobly, the desire to avoid the meaning conveyed by data. Whatever the
causes, the style of much analytical and critical writing is abstract, peri-
phrastic, and pompous. The effect of that style is to divorce words from
the reality they are supposed to represent. Modern study in semantics, the
"science of meaning," stems largely from a concern about the consequences
of such a divorcement.
*   Though modern in some of its techniques and formulations, the study*
of meaning is, of course, nothing at all new, and even the specific study of
the kinds of corruption to which language is susceptible goes back at least
as far as the Socratic dialogues. It is hard to say whether the particular
urgency with which the case for analysis of language is made today derives
from an increase in the amount of corruption and in the quickness of its
effects, or whether it may be only the result of a growing awareness that
the flood of words let loose everywhere by newspapers, radio, and television
can ruin crops as well as irrigate them. George Orwell (Eric Blair, 1904-
1950), an English journalist and author of two incisive fictional studies of
communistic society (Animal Farm *and* 1984), *comments in "Politics and*
the English Language" that modern prose is a "mixture of vagueness and
sheer incompetence." His indictment loses some of its particularity when it
is set alongside the similar charges made by critics and scholars of many
earlier periods, but its account of symptoms and consequences, as well as
its prescription for cure, cannot be taken lightly even if they are less specifi-
cally a matter of our times than Orwell thought.
*   The pressure of the circumlocutions, euphemisms, overused metaphors,*

and verbal formulas to which we give the name "stock diction" shows itself not only in the language of politics but in all parts of our life. It is nothing other than the substitution of conventional or palliative expressions for particular and unflinchingly accurate ones, and that is a procedure as common to social clubs as to parliaments. The conscious substitution may, as a matter of fact, sometimes be no more than an indication of good manners; the unconscious substitution is a sure sign of a serious gap between language and thought, a gap as discoverable in one discipline as in another.

Besides Orwell's analysis of the ills of the English language, six other pieces are offered here for study. The first two are practical demonstrations of jargon at work in particular fields. Frank Sullivan (1892-), American humorist, deals with politics, and Theodore Spencer (1902-1949), professor of English at Harvard until his death, attacks some abuses of literary criticism. The next two selections are prose descriptions: one of a lion hunt, by Ernest Hemingway (1898-1961), from one of the novelist's few works of nonfiction; and the other of a fishing expedition, by Tom McNally, outdoor editor of the Chicago Tribune. *The subject matter of both accounts is concrete, and they show that problems of stock diction arise even when few abstract ideas are involved. The last two pieces—poems—express the sense of separation. "Rock Me to Sleep," by Elizabeth Akers Allen (1832-1911), has been one of the most truly popular American poems. "The Return: An Elegy" is the work of Robert Penn Warren (1905-), poet, novelist, and influential critic and teacher, most recently at Yale University.*

POLITICS AND THE ENGLISH LANGUAGE | GEORGE ORWELL

Most people who bother with the matter at all would admit that the English language is in a bad way, but it is generally assumed that we cannot by conscious action do anything about it. Our civilization is decadent and our language—so the argument runs—must inevitably share in the general collapse. It follows that any struggle against the abuse of language is a sentimental archaism, like preferring candles to electric light or hansom cabs to aeroplanes. Underneath this lies the half-conscious belief that language is a natural growth and not an instrument which we shape for our own purposes.

Now, it is clear that the decline of a language must ultimately have political and economic causes: it is not due simply to the bad influence of this or that individual writer. But an effect can become a cause, reinforcing the original cause and producing the same effect in an intensified form, and so on indefinitely. A man may take to drink because he feels himself to be a failure, and then fail all the more completely because he drinks. It is rather the same thing that is happening to the English language. It becomes ugly and inaccurate because our thoughts are foolish, but the slovenliness of our language makes it easier for us to have foolish thoughts. The point is that the process is reversible. Modern English, especially written English, is full of bad habits which spread by imitation and which can be avoided if one is willing to take the necessary trouble. If one gets rid of these habits one can think more clearly, and to think clearly is a necessary first step towards political regeneration: so that the fight against bad English is not frivolous and is not the exclusive concern of professional writers. I will come back to this presently, and I hope that by that time the meaning of what I have said here will have become clearer. Meanwhile, here are five specimens of the English language as it is now habitually written.

These five passages have not been picked out because they are especially bad—I could have quoted far worse if I had chosen—but because they illustrate various of the mental vices from which we now suffer. They are a little below the average, but are fairly representative samples. I number them so that I can refer back to them when necessary:

1) I am not, indeed, sure whether it is not true to say that the Milton who once seemed not unlike a seventeenth-century Shelley had not become, out of an experience even more bitter in each year, more alien [sic] to the founder of that Jesuit sect which nothing could induce him to tolerate.

PROFESSOR HAROLD LASKI (Essay in *Freedom of Expression*).

2) Above all, we cannot play ducks and drakes with a native battery of idioms which prescribes such egregious collocations of vocables as the basic put up with for tolerate or put at a loss for bewilder.

PROFESSOR LANCELOT HOGBEN *(Interglossa).*

3) On the one side we have the free personality: by definition it is not neurotic, for it has neither conflict nor dreams. Its desires, such as they are, are transparent, for they are just what institutional approval keeps in the forefront of consciousness; another institutional pattern would alter their number and intensity; there is little in them that is natural, irreducible, or culturally dangerous. But on the other side, the social bond itself is nothing but the mutual reflection of these self-secure integrities. Recall the definition of love. Is not this the very picture of a small academic? Where is there a place in this hall of mirrors for either personality or fraternity?

Essay on psychology in *Politics* (New York).

4) All the "best people" from the gentlemen's clubs, and all the frantic fascist captains, united in common hatred of Socialism and bestial horror of the rising tide of the mass revolutionary movement, have turned to acts of provocation, to foul incendiarism, to medieval legends of poisoned wells, to legalize their own destruction of proletarian organizations, and rouse the agitated petty-bour-geoisie to chauvinistic fervor on behalf of the fight against the revolutionary way out of the crisis.

Communist pamphlet.

5) *If a new spirit is to be infused into this old country, there is one thorny and contentious reform which must be tackled, and that is the humanization and galvanization of the B.B.C. Timidity here will bespeak canker and atrophy of the soul. The heart of Britain may be sound and of strong beat, for instance, but the British lion's roar at present is like that of Bottom in Shakespeare's* Midsummer Night's Dream—*as gentle as any suckling dove. A virile new Britain cannot continue indefinitely to be traduced in the eyes, or rather ears, of the world by the effete languors of Langham Place, brazenly masquerading as "standard English." When the Voice of Britain is heard at nine o'clock, better far and infinitely less ludicrous to hear aitches honestly dropped than the present priggish, inflated, inhibited, school-ma'amish arch braying of blameless bashful mewing maidens!*

Letter in *Tribune*

Each of these passages has faults of its own, but, quite apart from avoidable ugliness, two qualities are common to all of them. The first is staleness of imagery; the other is lack of precision. The writer either has a meaning and cannot express it, or he inadvertently says something else, or he is almost indifferent as to whether his words mean anything or not. This mixture of vagueness and sheer incompetence is the most marked characteristic of modern English prose, and especially of any kind of political writing. As soon as certain topics are raised, the concrete melts into the abstract and no one seems able to think of turns of speech that are not hackneyed: prose consists less and less of *words* chosen for the sake of their meaning, and more and more of *phrases* tacked together like the sections of a prefabricated hen-house. I list below, with notes and examples, various of the tricks by means of which the work of prose-construction is habitually dodged:

DYING METAPHORS. A newly invented metaphor assists thought by evoking a visual image, while on the other hand a metaphor which is technically "dead" (e.g. *iron resolution*) has in effect reverted to being an ordinary word and can generally be used without loss of vividness. But in between these two classes there is a huge dump of worn-out metaphors which have lost all evocative power and are merely used because they save people the trouble of inventing phrases for themselves. Examples are: *Ring the changes on, take up the cudgels for, toe the line, ride roughshod over, stand shoulder to shoulder with, play into the hands of, no axe to grind, grist to the mill, fishing in troubled waters, on the order of the day, Achilles' heel, swan song, hotbed.* Many of these are used without knowledge of their meaning (what is a "rift," for instance?), and incompatible metaphors are frequently mixed, a sure sign that the writer is not interested in what he is saying. Some metaphors now current have been twisted out of their original meaning without those who use them even being aware of the fact. For example, *toe the line* is sometimes written *tow the line*. Another example is *the hammer and the anvil,* now always used with the implication that the anvil gets the worst of it. In real life it is always the anvil that breaks the hammer, never the other way about: a writer who stopped to think what he was saying would be aware of this, and would avoid perverting the original phrase.

OPERATORS OR VERBAL FALSE LIMBS. These save the trouble of picking out appropriate verbs and nouns, and at the same time pad each sentence with extra syllables which give it an appearance of symmetry. Characteristic phrases are *render inoperative, militate against, make contact with, be subjected to, give rise to, give grounds for, have the effect of, play a leading part (role) in, make itself felt, take effect, exhibit a tendency to, serve the purpose of, etc., etc.* The keynote is the elimination of simple verbs. Instead of being a single word, such as *break, stop, spoil, mend, kill,* a verb becomes a *phrase,* made up of a noun or adjective tacked on to some general-purposes verb such as *prove, serve, form, play, render.* In addition, the passive voice is wherever possible used in preference to the active, and noun constructions are used instead of gerunds (*by examination of* instead of *by examining*). The range of verbs is further cut down by means of the *-ize* and *de-* formations, and the banal statements are given an appearance of profundity by means of the *not un-* formation. Simple conjunctions and prepositions are replaced by such phrases as *with respect to, having regard to, the fact that, by dint of, in view of, in the interests of, on the hypothesis that,* and the ends of sentences are saved by anticlimax by such resounding common-places as *greatly to be desired, cannot be left out of account, a development to be expected in the near future, deserving of serious consideration, brought to a satisfactory conclusion,* and so on and so forth.

PRETENTIOUS DICTION. Words like *phenomenon, element, individual* (as noun), *objective, categorical, effective, virtual, basic, primary, promote, constitute, exhibit, exploit, utilize, eliminate, liquidate,* are used to dress up simple statement and give an air of scientific impartiality to biased judgments. Adjectives like *epoch-making, epic, historic, unforgettable, triumphant, age-old, inevitable, inexorable, veritable,* are used to dignify the sordid processes of international politics, while writing that aims at glorifying war usually takes on an archaic color, its characteristic words being: *realm, throne, chariot, mailed fist, trident, sword, shield, buckler, banner, jackboot, clarion.* Foreign words and expressions such as *cul de sac, ancien régime, deus ex machina, mutatis mutandis, status quo, gleichschaltung, weltanschauung,* are used to give an air of culture and elegance. Except for the useful abbreviations *i.e., e.g.,* and *etc.,* there is no real need for any of the hundreds of foreign phrases now current in English. Bad writers, and especially scientific, political and sociological writers, are nearly always haunted by the notion that Latin or Greek words are grander than Saxon ones, and unnecessary words like *expedite, ameliorate, predict, extraneous, deracinated, clandestine, subaqueous* and hundreds of others constantly gain ground from their Anglo-Saxon opposite numbers.[1] The jargon peculiar to Marxist writing (*hyena, hangman, cannibal, petty bourgeois, these gentry, lackey, flunkey, mad dog, White Guard,* etc.) consists largely of words and phrases translated from Russian, German or French; but the normal way of coining a new word is to use a Latin or Greek root with the appropriate affix and, where necessary, the size formation. It is often easier to make up words of this kind (*deregionalize, impermissible, extramarital, nonfragmentary* and so forth) than to think up the English words that will cover one's meaning. The result, in general, is an increase in slovenliness and vagueness.

MEANINGLESS WORDS. In certain kinds of writing, particularly in art criticism and literary criticism, it is normal to come across long passages which are almost completely lacking in meaning.[2] Words like *romantic, plastic, values, human, dead, sentimental, natural, vitality,* as used in art criticism, are strictly meaningless, in the sense that they not only do not point to any discoverable object, but are hardly ever expected to do so by the reader. When one critic writes, "The outstanding feature of Mr. X's work is its living quality," while another writes, "The immediately striking thing about Mr. X's work is its peculiar deadness," the reader accepts this as a simple difference of opinion. If words like *black* and *white* were involved, instead of the jargon words *dead* and *living,* he would see at once that language was being used in an improper way. Many political words are similarly abused. The word *Fascism* has now no meaning except in so far as it signifies "something not desirable." The words *democracy, socialism, freedom, patriotic, realistic, justice,* have each of them several different meanings which cannot be reconciled with one another. In the case of a word like *democracy,* not only is there no agreed definition, but the attempt to make one is resisted from all sides. It is almost universally felt that when we call a country democratic we are praising it: consequently the defenders of every kind of régime claim that it is a democracy, and fear that they might have to stop using the word if it were tied down to any one meaning. Words of this kind are often used in a consciously dishonest way. That is, the person who uses them has his own private definition, but allows his hearer to think he means something quite different. Statements like *Marshal Pétain was a true patriot, The Soviet Press is the freest in the world, The Catholic Church is opposed to persecution,* are almost always made with

---

[1] An interesting illustration of this is the way in which the English flower names which were in use till very recently are being ousted by Greek ones, *snapdragon* becoming *antirrhinum, forget-me-not* becoming *myosotis,* etc. It is hard to see any practical reason for this change of fashion: it is probably due to an instinctive turning-away from the more homely word and a vague feeling that the Greek word is scientific.

[2] Example: "Comfort's catholicity of perception and image, strangely Whitmanesque in range, almost the exact opposite in aesthetic compulsion, continues to evoke that trembling atmospheric accumulative hinting at a cruel, an inexorably serene timelessness. ... Wrey Gardiner scores by aiming at simple bull's-eyes with precision. Only they are not so simple, and through this contented sadness runs more than the surface bitter-sweet of resignation." (*Poetry Quarterly.*)

intent to deceive. Other words used in variable meanings, in most cases more or less dishonestly, are: *class, totalitarian, science, progressive, reactionary, bourgeois, equality.*

Now that I have made this catalogue of swindles and perversions, let me give another example of the kind of writing that they lead to. This time it must of its nature be an imaginary one. I am going to translate a passage of good English into modern English of the worst sort. Here is a well-known verse from *Ecclesiastes:*

"I returned and saw under the sun, that the race is not to the swift, nor the battle to the strong, neither yet bread to the wise, nor yet riches to men of understanding, nor yet favor to men of skill; but time and chance happeneth to them all."

Here it is in modern English:

"Objective consideration of contemporary phenomena compels the conclusion that success or failure in competitive activities exhibits no tendency to be commensurate with innate capacity, but that a considerable element of the unpredictable must invariably be taken into account."

This is a parody, but not a very gross one. Exhibit (3), above, for instance, contains several patches of the same kind of English. It will be seen that I have not made a full translation. The beginning and ending of the sentence follow the original meaning fairly closely, but in the middle the concrete illustrations—race, battle, bread—dissolve into the vague phrase "success or failure in competitive activities." This had to be so, because no modern writer of the kind I am discussing—no one capable of using phrases like "objective consideration of contemporary phenomena"—would ever tabulate his thoughts in that precise and detailed way. The whole tendency of modern prose is away from concreteness. Now analyze these two sentences a little more closely. The first contains forty-nine words but only sixty syllables, and all its words are those of everyday life. The second contains thirty-eight words of ninety syllables: eighteen of its words are from Latin roots, and one from Greek. The first sentence contains six vivid images, and only one phrase ("time and chance") that could be called vague. The second contains not a single fresh, arresting phrase, and in spite of its ninety syllables it gives only a shortened version of the meaning contained in the first. Yet without a doubt it is the second kind of sentence that is gaining ground in modern English. I do not want to exaggerate. This kind of writing is not yet universal, and outcrops of simplicity will occur here and there in the worst-written page. Still, if you or I were told to write a few lines on the uncertainty of human fortunes, we should probably come much nearer to my imaginary sentence than to the one from *Ecclesiastes.*

As I have tried to show, modern writing at its worst does not consist in picking out words for the sake of their meaning and inventing images in order to make the meaning clearer. It consists in gumming together long strips of words which have already been set in order by someone else, and making the results presentable by sheer humbug. The attraction of this way of writing is that it is easy. It is easier—even quicker, once you have the habit—to say *In my opinion it is not an unjustifiable assumption that* than to say *I think.* If you use ready-made phrases, you not only don't have to hunt about for words; you also don't have to bother with the rhythms of your sentences, since these phrases are generally so arranged as to be more or less euphonious. When you are composing in a hurry—when you are dictating to a stenographer, for instance, or making a public speech—it is natural to fall into a pretentious, Latinized style. Tags like *a consideration which we should do well to bear in mind* or *a conclusion to which all of us would readily assent* will save many a sentence from coming down with a bump. By using stale metaphors, similes and idioms, you save much mental effort, at the cost of leaving your meaning vague, not only for your reader but for yourself. This is the significance of mixed metaphors. The sole aim of a metaphor is to call up a visual image. When these images clash—as in *The Fascist octopus has sung its swan song, the jackboot is thrown into the melting pot*—it can be taken as certain that the writer is not seeing a mental image of the objects he is naming; in other words he is not really thinking. Look again at the examples I gave at the beginning of this essay. Professor Laski (1) uses five negatives in fifty-three words. One of these is superfluous, making nonsense of the whole passage, and in addition there is the slip *alien* for akin, making further nonsense, and several avoidable pieces of clumsiness which increase the general vagueness. Professor Hogben (2) plays ducks and drakes with a battery which is able to write prescriptions, and, while disapproving of the everyday phrase *put up with,* is unwilling to look *egregious* up in the dictionary and see what it means; (3), if one takes an uncharitable attitude towards it, is simply meaningless: probably one could work out its intended meaning by reading the whole of the article in which it occurs. In (4), the writer knows more or less what he wants to say, but an accumulation of stale phrases chokes him like tea leaves blocking a sink. In (5), words and meaning have almost parted company. People who write in this manner usually have a general emotional meaning—they dislike one thing and want to express solidarity with another—but they are not interested in the detail of what they are saying. A scrupulous writer, in every sentence that he writes, will ask himself at least four questions, thus: What am I trying to say? What words will express it? What image or idiom will make it clearer? Is this image fresh enough to have an effect? And he will probably ask himself two more: Could I put it more shortly? Have I said anything that is avoidably ugly? But you are not obliged to go to all this trouble. You can shirk it by simply throwing your mind open and letting the ready-made phrases come crowding in. They will construct your sentences for you—even think your thoughts for you, to a certain extent—and at need they will perform the important service of partially concealing your meaning even from yourself. It is at this point that the special connection between politics and the debasement of language becomes clear.

In our time it is broadly true that political writing is bad writing. Where it is not true, it will generally be found that the writer is some kind of rebel, expressing his private opinions and not a "party line." Orthodoxy, of whatever color, seems to demand a lifeless, imitative style. The political dialects to be found in pamphlets, leading articles, manifestos, White Papers and the speeches of under-secretaries do, of course, vary from party to party, but they are all alike in that one almost never finds in them a fresh, vivid, home-made turn of speech. When one watches some tired hack on the platform mechanically repeating the familiar phrases—*bestial atrocities, iron heel, bloodstained tyranny, free peoples of the world, stand shoulder to shoulder* —one often has a curious feeling that one is not watching a live human being but some kind of dummy: a feeling which suddenly becomes stronger at moments when the light catches the speaker's spectacles and turns them into blank discs which seem to have no eyes behind them. And this is not altogether fanciful. A speaker who uses that kind of phraseology has gone some distance towards turning himself into a machine. The appropriate noises are coming out of his larynx, but his brain is not involved as it would be if he were choosing his words for himself. If the speech he is making is one that he is accustomed to make over and over again, he may be almost unconscious of what he is saying, as one is when one utters the responses in church. And this reduced state of consciousness, if not indispensable, is at any rate favorable to political conformity.

In our time, political speech and writing are largely the defense of the indefensible. Things like the continuance of British rule in India, the Russian purges and deportations, the dropping of the atom bombs on Japan, can indeed be defended, but only by arguments which are too brutal for most people to face, and which do not square with the professed aims of political parties. Thus political language has to consist largely of euphemism, question-begging and sheer cloudy vagueness. Defenseless villages are bombarded from the air, the inhabitants driven out into the countryside, the cattle machine-gunned, the huts set on fire with incendiary bullets: this is called *pacification*. Millions of peasants are robbed of their farms and sent trudging along the roads with no more than they can carry: this is called *transfer of population* or *rectification of frontiers*. People are imprisoned for years without trial, or shot in the back of the neck or sent to die of scurvy in Arctic lumber camps: this is called *elimination of unreliable elements*. Such phraseology is needed if one wants to name things without calling up mental pictures of them. Consider for instance some comfortable English professor defending Russian totalitarianism. He cannot say outright, "I believe in killing off your opponents when you can get good results by doing so." Probably, therefore, he will say something like this:

"While freely conceding that the Soviet régime exhibits certain features which the humanitarian may be inclined to deplore, we must, I think, agree that a certain curtailment of the right to political opposition is an unavoidable concomitant of transitional periods, and that the rigors which the

Russian people have been called upon to undergo have been amply justified in the sphere of concrete achievement."

The inflated style is itself a kind of euphemism. A mass of Latin words falls upon the facts like soft snow, blurring the outlines and covering up all the details. The great enemy of clear language is insincerity. When there is a gap between one's real and one's declared aims, one turns as it were instinctively to long words and exhausted idioms, like a cuttlefish squirting out ink. In our age there is no such thing as "keeping out of politics." All issues are political issues, and politics itself is a mass of lies, evasions, folly, hatred and schizophrenia. When the general atmosphere is bad, language must suffer. I should expect to find—this is a guess which I have not sufficient knowledge to verify—that the German, Russian and Italian languages have all deteriorated in the last ten or fifteen years, as a result of dictatorship.

But if thought corrupts language, language can also corrupt thought. A bad usage can spread by tradition and imitation, even among people who should and do know better. The debased language that I have been discussing is in some ways very convenient. Phrases like *a not unjustifiable assumption, leaves much to be desired, would serve no good purpose, a consideration which we should do well to bear in mind,* are a continuous temptation, a packet of aspirins always at one's elbow. Look back through this essay, and for certain you will find that I have again and again committed the very faults I am protesting against. By this morning's post I have received a pamphlet dealing with conditions in Germany. The author tells me that he "felt impelled" to write it. I open it at random, and here is almost the first sentence that I see: "[The Allies] have an opportunity not only of achieving a radical transformation of Germany's social and political structure in such a way as to avoid a nationalistic reaction in Germany itself, but at the same time of laying the foundations of a co-operative and unified Europe." You see, he "feels impelled" to write—feels, presumably, that he has something new to say—and yet his words, like cavalry horses answering the bugle, group themselves automatically into the familiar dreary pattern. This invasion of one's mind by ready-made phrases *(lay the foundations, achieve a radical transformation)* can only be prevented if one is constantly on guard against them, and every such phrase anesthetizes a portion of one's brain.

I said earlier that the decadence of our language is probably curable. Those who deny this would argue, if they produced an argument at all, that language merely reflects existing social conditions, and that we cannot influence its development by any direct tinkering with words and constructions. So far as the general tone or spirit of a language goes, this may be true, but it is not true in detail. Silly words and expressions have often disappeared, not through any evolutionary process but owing to the conscious action of a minority. Two recent examples were *explore every avenue* and *leave no stone unturned,* which were killed by the jeers of a few journalists. There is a long list of flyblown metaphors which could similarly be got rid of if enough people would interest themselves in the job; and it should also be possible to laugh the *not un-* formation out of existence,[3] to reduce the amount of Latin and Greek in the average sentence, to drive out foreign phrases and strayed scientific words, and, in general, to make pretentiousness unfashionable. But all these are minor points. The defense of the English language implies more than this, and perhaps it is best to start by saying what it does *not* imply.

To begin with it has nothing to do with archaism, with the salvaging of obsolete words and turns of speech, or with the setting up of a "standard English" which must never be departed from. On the contrary, it is especially concerned with the scrapping of every word or idiom which has outworn its usefulness. It has nothing to do with correct grammar and syntax, which are of no importance so long as one makes one's meaning clear, or with the avoidance of Americanisms, or with having what is called a "good prose style." On the other hand it is not concerned with fake simplicity and the attempt to make written English colloquial. Nor does it even imply in every case preferring the Saxon word to the Latin one, though it does imply using the fewest and shortest words that will cover one's meaning. What is above all needed is to let the meaning choose the word, and not the other way about. In prose, the worst thing one can do with words is to surrender to them. When you think of a concrete object, you think wordlessly, and then, if you want to describe the thing you have been visualizing you probably hunt about till you find the exact words that seem to fit it. When you think of something abstract you are more inclined to use words from the start, and unless you make a conscious effort to prevent it, the existing dialect will come rushing in and do the job for you, at the expense of blurring or even changing your meaning. Probably it is better to put off using words as long as possible and get one's meaning as clear as one can through pictures or sensations. Afterwards one can choose—not simply *accept*—the phrases that will best cover the meaning, and then switch round and decide what impression one's words are likely to make on another person. This last effort of the mind cuts out all stale or mixed images, all prefabricated phrases, needless repetitions, and humbug and vagueness generally. But one can often be in doubt about the effect of a word or a phrase, and one needs rules that one can rely on when instinct fails. I think the following rules will cover most cases:

    i)   Never use a metaphor, simile or other figure of speech which you are used to seeing in print.

    ii)   Never use a long word where a short one will do.

    iii)   If it is possible to cut a word out, always cut it out.

---

[3] One can cure oneself of the *not un-* formation by memorizing this sentence: *A not unblack dog was chasing a not unsmall rabbit across a not ungreen field.*

iv)   Never use the passive where you can use the active.

v)   Never use a foreign phrase, a scientific word or a jargon word if you can think of an everyday English equivalent.

vi)   Break any of these rules sooner than say anything outright barbarous.

These rules sound elementary, and so they are, but they demand a deep change of attitude in anyone who has grown used to writing in the style now fashionable. One could keep all of them and still write bad English, but one could not write the kind of stuff that I quoted in those five specimens at the beginning of this article.

I have not here been considering the literary use of language, but merely language as an instrument for expressing and not for concealing or preventing thought. Stuart Chase and others have come near to claiming that all abstract words are meaningless, and have used this as a pretext for advocating a kind of political quietism. Since you don't know what Fascism is, how can you struggle against Fascism? One need not swallow such absurdities as this, but one ought to recognize that the present political chaos is connected with the decay of language, and that one can probably bring about some improvement by starting at the verbal end. If you simplify your English, you are freed from the worst follies of orthodoxy. You cannot speak any of the necessary dialects, and when you make a stupid remark its stupidity will be obvious, even to yourself. Political language—and with variations this is true of all political parties, from Conservatives to Anarchists— is designed to make lies sound truthful and murder respectable, and to give an appearance of solidity to pure wind. One cannot change this all in a moment, but one can at least change one's own habits, and from time to time one can even, if one jeers loudly enough, send some worn-out and useless phrase—some *jackboot, Achilles' heel, hotbed, melting pot, acid test, veritable inferno* or other lump of verbal refuse—into the dustbin where it belongs.

THE CLICHÉ EXPERT TESTIFIES ON POLITICS | *FRANK SULLIVAN*

Q)   Mr. Arbuthnot, I hear you've become a campaign orator.

A)   Fellow American, you have heard correctly. I've been on the stump all fall.

Q)   In that case you ought to be up on your campaign-oratory clichés.

A)   Well, sir, it is not my wont to brag, but I believe I may say with all due modesty that I can point with pride and view with alarm as sententiously and bombastically as any senator who ever thrust one arm in his

From Frank Sullivan, *A Rock in Every Snowball* (Boston, Little, Brown & Company, 1946). Copyright 1946 by Frank Sullivan. Reprinted by permission of the author.

frock coat and with the other called upon high heaven to witness the perfidy of the Other Party.

Q)   Describe your candidate, Mr. Arbuthnot.

A)   My candidate is a man four-square, a true representative of the people, a leader worthy of the trust which has been placed in him, and a standard-bearer who will carry the banner of our ga-reat and ga-lorious party to victory.

Q)   Is he a man of prophetic vision?

A)   He is indeed. He is also a man of sterling character and a champion of the rights of the people.

Q)   What kind of champion?

A)   A stalwart champion.

Q)   What is he close to?

A)   The soil.

Q)   Is his name Jones?

A)   It is not. I have nothing against Mr. Jones personally, but I can't see where he's fitted to be President.

Q)   Why not?

A)   He may be a first-rate businessman, but what does he know about government?

Q)   Then your candidate's name is Brown.

A)   Not at all. I'm a lifelong Democrat and I've always voted the straight Democratic ticket, but this year I'm taking a walk.

Q)   Why?

A)   Because old party lines are disappearing. What this country needs is a *businessman* in the White House.

Q)   Then your man is Jones, after all.

A)   Jones is all right personally, but I don't like the crowd he's tied up with.

Q)   What crowd?

A)   Oh, the public utilities, the Old Guard, and so on. Besides, what does he know about foreign affairs?

Q)   Mr. Arbuthnot, I can't figure out *where* you stand. Let's get back to your campaign-oratory clichés. What kind of questions have you been discussing?

A)   Burning questions. Great, underlying problems.

Q)   What have you arrayed yourself against?

A)   The forces of reaction. There must be no compromise with the forces of reaction.

Q)   And now, Mr. Arbuthnot, may I ask you to characterize these times?

A)   These are troubled times, sir. We are met here today in an hour of grave national crisis.

Q)   What do you, as a campaign orator, propose to do in this grave hour?

A) I shall demand, and denounce, and dedicate, I shall take stock. I shall challenge, pledge, stress, fulfill, indict, exercise, accuse, call upon, affirm, and reaffirm.

Q) Reaffirm what?

A) My undying faith in the principles laid down by the Founding Fathers. And I shall exercise eternal vigilance that our priceless heritage may be safeguarded.

Q) Admirable, Mr. Arbuthnot. And that reminds me: What is it you campaign orators rise above?

A) Narrow partisanship. We must place the welfare of our country above all other considerations, including our desire to win.

Q) Mr. Arbuthnot, how do you campaign orators dedicate yourselves?

A) We dedicate ourselves anew to the task that lies before us.

Q) How does your party approach this task?

A) With a solemn realization of the awful responsibility that rests upon us in this hour of unprecedented national stress.

Q) When our country is—

A) Sore beset by economic ills.

Q) How else do you approach the task?

A) With supreme confidence that our ga-reat party will prove worthy of its ga-lorious tradition.

Q) And if your party failed to approach the task in that spirit, Mr. Arbuthnot, would you say that—

A) It would indeed be recreant to its sacred trust.

Q) Ah. But you feel that it won't be recreant?

A) No, my fellow American, a tha-a-o-u-sand times no! The ga-reat party of Washington, and Jefferson, and Lincoln, and Wilson, and Roosevelt, and Cleveland, and Grant, Garfield, Hayes, and Arthur will not fail our country in this, her hour of need.

Q) Hurrah for Jones!

A) The candidate of Big Business?

Q) Then hurray for Brown!

A) He wants to be a dictator.

Q) Then three rousing cheers for Green!

A) If elected, he couldn't even control his own party.

Q) Then hurray for Smith!

A) Elect him and you'll *never* get rid of him.

Q) I'm afraid there's no pleasing you today, Mr. Arbuthnot. Would you mind telling me who's to blame for our country's hour of need?

A) The Other Party.

Q) What has the Other Party proved?

A) Its utter incapacity to govern. Its record is an unbroken record of failure, of forgotten campaign pledges, of callous disregard for the welfare of the country.

Q) What is the Other Party undermining?

A)   The American way of life. It is spending vast sums of the tax-payers' money.

Q)   For what?

A)   To build up a huge political machine. It has aroused class hatred. Fellow American, in this solemn hour, when the sacred institutions of democracy are challenged on every side and the world is rent by strife, I charge the Other Party with having betrayed the pee-pul of these Yew-nited States.

Q)   What must the pee-pul do?

A)   They must rise in their wrath and elect my candidate.

Q)   Mr. Arbuthnot, perhaps you'll tell us just what kind of leader the hour calls for?

A)   A leader who will lead this country out of the wilderness, elimi-nate waste and extravagance in government, do away with red tape and bureaucratic inefficiency, solve the problem of unemployment, improve living conditions, develop purchasing power, raise the standard of living, provide better housing, and insure national defense by building a navy and air force second to none.

Q)   What about the farmer?

A)   The farmer must have relief.

Q)   What kind of relief?

A)   Farm relief. Labor must have the right to organize. Economy must be the watchword. Mounting deficits must cease; so must these raids on the public treasury. I view with alarm the huge and unwarranted increase in our national debt. Generations yet unborn! Those who would undermine our sacred institutions! Bore from within! Freedom of speech! Monroe Doctrine! I call upon every patriotic American—

Q)   Regardless of race or creed?

A)   Be quiet ... regardless of race or creed, from the snowcapped peaks of the Rockies—

Q)   To the pine-clad shores of Maine?

A)   Shut *up!* . . . to the pine-clad shores of Maine to have faith in the American way of life. Subversive doctrines! Undesirable aliens! Lincoln!

Q)   What kind of Lincoln?

A)   The Immortal Lincoln! The Immortal Washington! The Immor-tal Jefferson! The time for evasions has passed. We must face the facts, put our shoulders to the wheel, put our house in order, meet the challenge of the dictators, carry aloft the torch of liberty, fulfill our high destiny, face the future with confidence, and march forward to victory at the polls in November.

HOW TO CRITICIZE A POEM | *THEODORE SPENCER*

(IN THE MANNER OF CERTAIN CONTEMPORARY CRITICS)

1)

I propose to examine the following poem:

> *Thirty days hath September,*
> *April, June and November,*
> *All the rest have thirty-one,*
> *Excepting February alone,*
> *Which has only eight and a score*
> *Till leap-year gives it one day more.*

2)

The previous critics who have studied this poem, Coleridge among them, have failed to explain what we may describe as its fundamental *dynamic*. This I now propose to do. The first thing to observe is the order in which the names (or verbal constructs) of the months are presented. According to the prose meaning—what I shall henceforth call the prose-*demand*— "September" should not precede, it should follow "April," as a glance at the calendar will show. Indeed "September" should follow not only "April," it should also follow "June" if the prose-demand is to be properly satisfied. The prose order of the first two lines should therefore read: "Thirty days hath April, June, September and November." That is the only sequence consonant with prose logic.

3)

Why, then, we ask ourselves, did the poet violate what educated readers know to be the facts? Was he ignorant of the calendar, believing that September preceded April in the progress of the seasons? It is difficult to imagine that such was the case. We must find another explanation. It is here that the principle of dynamic analysis comes to our aid.

4)

Dynamic analysis proves that the most successful poetry achieves its effect by producing an *expectation* in the reader's mind before his sensibility is fully prepared to receive the full impact of the poem. The reader makes a *proto-response* which preconditions him to the total response toward which his fully equilibrized organs of apperception subconsciously tend. It is the proto-response which the poet has here so sensitively manip-

Theodore Spencer, "How to Criticize a Poem," *New Republic*, December 6, 1943.

ulated. The ordinary reader, trained only to prose-demands, expects the usual order of the months. But the poet's sensibility knows that poetic truth is more immediately effective than the truth of literal chronology. He does not *state* the inevitable sequence; he *prepares* us for it. In his profound analysis of the two varieties of mensual time, he puts the *gentlest* month first. (Notice how the harsh sound of "pt" in "September" is softened by the "e" sound on either side of it.) It is the month in which vegetation first begins to fade, but which does not as yet give us a sense of tragic fatality.

5)

Hence the poet prepares us, dynamically, for what is to follow. By beginning his list of the months *in medias res,* he is enabled to return later to the beginning of the series of contrasts which is the subject of his poem. The analogy to the "Oedipus Rex" of Euripides and the "Iliad" of Dante at once becomes clear. Recent criticism has only too often failed to observe that these works also illustrate the dynamic method by beginning in the middle of things. It is a striking fact, hitherto (I believe) unnoticed, that a Latin poem called the "Aeneid" does much the same thing. We expect the author of that poem to begin with the departure of his hero from Troy, just as we expect the author of our poem to begin with "April." But in neither case is our expectation fulfilled. Cato, the author of the "Aeneid," creates dynamic suspense by beginning with Aeneas in Carthage; our anonymous poet treats his readers' sensibilities in a similar fashion by beginning with "September," and then *going back* to "April" and "June."

6)

But the sensibility of the poet does not stop at this point. Having described what is true of *four* months, he disposes of *seven* more with masterly economy. In a series of pungent constructs his sensibility sums up their inexorable limitations: they *All* (the capitalization should be noted) "have thirty-one." The poet's sensibility communicates a feeling to the sensibility of the reader so that the sensibility of both, with reference to their previous but independent sensibilities, is fused into that momentary communication of sensibility which is the final sensibility that poetry can give both to the sensibility of the poet and the sensibility of the reader. The texture and structure of the poem have erupted into a major reaction. The ambiguity of equilibrium is achieved.

7)

Against these two groups of spatial, temporal and numerical measurements—one consisting of four months, the other of seven—the tragic individual, the sole exception, "February," is dramatically placed. February is "alone," is cut off from communion with his fellows. The tragic note is struck the moment "February" is mentioned. For the initial sound of the word "excepting" is "X," and as that sound strikes the sensibility of the reader's ear a number of associations subconsciously accumulate. We think of the spot, the murderous and lonely spot, which "X" has so frequently marked; we remember the examinations of our childhood where the wrong answers were implacably signaled with "X"; we think of ex-kings and exile, of lonely crossroads and executions, of the inexorable anonymity of those who cannot sign their names. . . .

8)

And yet the poet gives us one ray of hope, though it eventually proves to be illusory. The lonely "February" (notice how the "alone" in line four is echoed by the "only" in line five), the solitary and maladjusted individual who is obviously the hero and crucial figure of the poem, is not condemned to the routine which his fellows, in their different ways, must forever obey. Like Hamlet, he has a capacity for change. He is a symbol of individualism, and the rhythm of the lines which are devoted to him signalize a gayety, however desperate, which immediately wins our sympathy and reverberates profoundly in our sensibility.

9)

But (and this is the illusion to which I have previously referred) in spite of all his variety, his capacity for change, "February" cannot quite accomplish (and in this his tragedy consists) the *quantitative* value of the society in which circumstances have put him. No matter how often he may alternate from twenty-eight to twenty-nine (the poet, with his exquisite sensibility, does not actually *mention* those humiliating numbers), he can never achieve the bourgeois, if anonymous, security of "thirty-one," nor equal the more modest and aristocratic assurance of "thirty." Decade after decade, century after century, millennium after millennium, he is eternally frustrated. The only symbol of change in a changeless society, he is continually beaten down. Once every four years he tries to rise, to achieve the high, if delusive, level of his dreams. But he fails. He is always one day short, and the three years before the recurrence of his next effort are a sad interval in which the remembrance of previous disappointment melts into the futility of hope, only to sink back once more into the frustration of despair. Like Tantalus he is forever stretched upon a wheel.

10)

So far I have been concerned chiefly with the dynamic *analysis* of the poem. Further study should reveal the *synthesis* which can be made on the basis of the analysis which my thesis has tentatively attempted to bring to an emphasis. This, perhaps, the reader with a proper sensibility can achieve for himself.

THE LION | *ERNEST HEMINGWAY*

We were out from under the shade of camp and along the sandy river of a road, driving into the western sun, the bush thick to the edge of the sand, solid as a thicket, the little hills rising above it, and all along the road we passed groups of people making their way to the westward. Some were naked except for a greasy cloth knotted over one shoulder, and carried bows and sealed quivers of arrows. Others carried spears. The wealthy carried umbrellas and wore draped white cloth and their women walked behind them, with their pots and pans. Bundles and loads of skins were scattered along ahead on the heads of other natives. All were traveling away from the famine. And in the heat, my feet out over the side of the car to keep them away from the heat of the engine, hat low over the eyes against the sun, watching the road, the people, and all clearings in the bush for game, we drove to the westward.

Once we saw three lesser kudu cows in an open place of broken bush. Gray, big bellied, long necked, small headed, and with big ears, they moved quickly into the woods and were gone. We left the car and tracked them but there was no bull track.

A little beyond there a flock of guineas quick-legged across the road running steady-headed with the motion of trotters. As I jumped from the car and sprinted after them they rocketed up, their legs tucked close beneath them, heavy-bodied, short wings drumming, cackling, to go over the trees ahead. I dropped two that thumped hard when they fell and as they lay, wings beating, Abdullah cut their heads off so they would be legal eating. He put them in the car where M'Cola sat laughing; his old man's healthy laugh, his making-fun-of-me laugh, his bird-shooting laugh that dated from a streak of raging misses one time that had delighted him. Now when I killed, it was a joke as when we shot a hyena; the funniest joke of all. He laughed always to see the birds tumble and when I missed he roared and shook his head again and again.

"Ask him what the hell he's laughing about?" I asked Pop once.

"At B'wana," M'Cola said, and shook his head, "at the little birds."

"He thinks you're funny," Pop said.

"Goddam it, I am funny. But the hell with him."

"He thinks you're very funny," Pop said. "Now the Memsahib and I would never laugh."

"Shoot them yourself."

"No, you're the bird shot. The self-confessed bird shot," he said.

So bird shooting became this marvelous joke. If I killed, the joke was
on the birds and M'Cola would shake his head and laugh and make his
hands go round and round to show how the bird turned over in the air.
And if I missed, I was the clown of the piece and he would look at me
and shake with laughing. Only the hyenas were funnier.

Highly humorous was the hyena obscenely loping, full belly dragging,
at daylight on the plain, who, shot from the stern, skittered on into speed
to tumble end over end. Mirth provoking was the hyena that stopped out of
range by an alkali lake to look back and, hit in the chest, went over on his
back, his four feet and his full belly in the air. Nothing could be more jolly
than the hyena coming suddenly wedge-headed and stinking out of high
grass by a *donga,* hit at ten yards, who raced his tail in three narrowing,
scampering circles until he died.

It was funny to M'Cola to see a hyena shot at close range. There was
that comic slap of the bullet and the hyena's agitated surprise to find death
inside of him. It was funnier to see a hyena shot at a great distance, in the
heat shimmer of the plain, to see him go over backwards, to see him start
that frantic circle, to see that electric speed that meant that he was racing
the little nickeled death inside him. But the great joke of all, the thing
M'Cola waved his hands across his face about, and turned away and shook
his head and laughed, ashamed even of the hyena; the pinnacle of hyenic
humor, was the hyena, the classic hyena, that hit too far back while running, would circle madly, snapping and tearing at himself until he pulled
his own intestines out, and then stood there, jerking them out and eating
them with relish.

"*Fisi,*" M'Cola would say and shake his head in delighted sorrow at
there being such an awful beast. Fisi, the hyena, hermaphroditic, self-eat-
ing devourer of the dead, trailer of calving cows, ham-stringer, potential
biter-off of your face at night while you slept, sad yowler, camp-follower,
stinking, foul, with jaws that crack the bones the lion leaves, belly dragging, loping away on the brown plain, looking back, mongrel dog-smart in
the face; whack from the little Mannlicher and then the horrid circle starting. "*Fisi,*" M'Cola laughed, ashamed of him, shaking his bald black head.
"*Fisi.* Eats himself. *Fisi.*"

The hyena was a dirty joke but bird shooting was a clean joke. My
whiskey was a clean joke. There were many variations of that joke. Some
we come to later. The Mohammedans and all religions were a joke. A joke
on all the people who had them. Charo, the other gun bearer, was short,
very serious and highly religious. All Ramadan he never swallowed his
saliva until sunset and when the sun was almost down I'd see him watching
nervously. He had a bottle with him of some sort of tea and he would
finger it and watch the sun and I would see M'Cola watching him and pretending not to see. This was not outrightly funny to him. This was something that he could not laugh about openly but that he felt superior to and

wondered at the silliness of it. The Mohammedan religion was very fashion-able and all the higher social grades among the boys were Mohammedans. It was something that gave caste, something to believe in, something fashion-able and god-giving to suffer a little for each year, something that made you superior to other people, something that gave you more complicated habits of eating, something that I understood and M'Cola did not under-stand, nor care about, and he watched Charo watch for the sun to set with that blank look on his face that it put on about all things that he was not a part of. Charo was deadly thirsty and truly devout and the sun set very slowly. I looked at it, red over the trees, nudged him and he grinned. M'Cola offered me the water bottle solemnly. I shook my head and Charo grinned again. M'Cola looked blank. Then the sun was down and Charo had the bottle tilted up, his Adam's apple rising and falling greedily and M'Cola looking at him and then looking away.

In the early days, before we became good friends, he did not trust me at all. When anything came up he went into this blankness. I liked Charo much better then. We understood each other on the question of religion and Charo admired my shooting and always shook hands and smiled when we had killed anything particularly good. This was flattering and pleasing. M'Cola looked on all this early shooting as a series of lucky accidents. We were supposed to shoot. We had not yet shot anything that amounted to anything and he was not really my gun bearer. He was Mr. Jackson Phillip's gun bearer and he had been loaned to me. I meant nothing to him. He did not like me nor dislike me. He was politely contemptuous of Karl. Who he liked was Mama.

The evening we killed the first lion it was dark when we came in sight of camp. The killing of the lion had been confused and unsatisfactory. It was agreed beforehand that P.O.M. should have the first shot but since it was the first lion any of us had ever shot at, and it was very late in the day, really too late to take the lion on, once he was hit we were to make a dogfight of it and any one was free to get him. This was a good plan as it was nearly sundown and if the lion got into cover, wounded, it would be too dark to do anything about it without a mess. I remember seeing the lion looking yellow and heavy-headed and enormous against a scrubby-looking tree in a patch of orchard bush and P.O.M. kneeling to shoot and wanting to tell her to sit down and make sure of him. Then there was the short-barreled explosion of the Mannlicher and the lion was going to the left on a run, a strange, heavy-shouldered, foot-swinging, cat run. I hit him with the Springfield and he went down and spun over and I shot again, too quickly, and threw a cloud of dirt over him. But there he was, stretched out, on his belly, and, with the sun just over the top of the trees, and the grass very green, we walked up on him like a posse, or a gang of Black and Tans, guns ready and cocked, not knowing whether he was stunned or dead. When we were close M'Cola threw a stone at him. It hit him in the flank and from the way it hit you could tell he was a dead animal. I was sure P.O.M. had hit him but there was only one bullet hole, well back, just below the spine and ranging forward to come to the surface under the skin of the chest. You could feel the bullet under the skin and M'Cola made a slit and cut it out. It was a 220-grain solid bullet from the Springfield and it had raked him, going through lungs and heart.

I was so surprised by the way he had rolled over dead from the shot after we had been prepared for a charge, for heroics, and for drama, that I felt more let down than pleased. It was our first lion and we were very ignorant and this was not what we had paid to see. Charo and M'Cola both shook P.O.M.'s hand and then Charo came over and shook hands with me.

"Good shot, B'wana," he said in Swahili. *"Piga m'uzuri."*

"Did you shoot, Karl?" I asked.

"No. I was just going to when you shot."

"You didn't shoot him, Pop?"

"No. You'd have heard it." He opened the breech and took out the two big .450 No. 2's.

"I'm sure I missed him," P.O.M. said.

"I was sure you hit him. I still think you hit him," I said.

"Mama hit," M'Cola said.

"Where?" Charo asked.

"Hit," said M'Cola. "Hit."

"You rolled him over," Pop said to me. "God, he went over like a rabbit."

"I couldn't believe it."

"Mama *piga*," M'Cola said. *"Piga Simba."*

As we saw the camp fire in the dark ahead of us, coming in that night, M'Cola suddenly commenced to shout a stream of high-pitched, rapid, singing words in Wakamba ending in the word *"Simba."* Some one at the camp shouted back one word.

"Mama!" M'Cola shouted. Then another long stream. Then "Mama! Mama!"

Through the dark came all the porters, the cook, the skinner, the boys, and the headman.

"Mama!" M'Cola shouted. "Mama *piga Simba.*"

The boys came dancing, crowding, and beating time and chanting something from down in their chests that started like a cough and sounded like *"Hey la Mama! Hay la Mama! Hey la Mama!"*

The rolling-eyed skinner picked P.O.M. up, the big cook and the boys held her, and the others pressing forward to lift, and if not to lift to touch and hold, they danced and sang through the dark, around the fire and to our tent.

"Hey la Mama! huh! huh! huh! Hay la Mama! huh! huh! huh!" they sang the lion dance with that deep, lion asthmatic cough in it. Then at the tent they put her down and every one, very shyly, shook hands, the boys saying *"m'uzuri, Memsahib,"* and M'Cola and the porters all saying *"m'uzuri,* Mama" with much feeling in the accenting of the word "Mama."

Afterwards in the chairs in front of the fire, sitting with the drinks, Pop said, "You shot it. M'Cola would kill any one who said you didn't."

"You know, I feel as though I did shoot it," P.O.M. said. "I don't believe I'd be able to stand it if I really had shot it. I'd be too proud. Isn't triumph marvelous?"

"Good old Mama," Karl said.

"I believe you did shoot him," I said.

"Oh, let's not go into that," P.O.M. said. "I feel so wonderful about just being supposed to have killed him. You know people never used to carry me on their shoulders much at home."

"No one knows how to behave in America," Pop said. "Most uncivilized."

"We'll carry you in Key West," Karl said. "Poor old Mama."

"Let's not talk about it," P.O.M. said. "I like it too much. Shouldn't I maybe distribute largess?"

"They didn't do it for that," Pop said. "But it is all right to give something to celebrate."

"Oh, I want to give them all a great deal of money," P.O.M. said. "Isn't triumph simply marvelous?"

"Good old Mama," I said. "You killed him."

"No I didn't. Don't lie to me. Just let me enjoy my triumph."

Anyway M'Cola did not trust me for a long time. Until P.O.M.'s license ran out, she was his favorite and we were simply a lot of people who interfered and kept Mama from shooting things. Once her license was out and she was no longer shooting, she dropped back into noncombatant status with him and as we began to hunt kudu and Pop stayed in camp and sent us out alone with the trackers, Karl with Charo and M'Cola and I together, M'Cola dropped Pop visibly in his estimation. It was only temporary of course. He was Pop's man and I believe his working estimations were only from day to day and required an unbroken series of events to have any meaning. But something had happened between us.

THE BONANZA OF NO-NAME POND | TOM McNALLY

"No fisherman ever leaves here without trying our mountain brookies," said Oneida firmly. "We make no exceptions. You can go in the morning with John."

"Well, we have a schedule to meet," I told her, "but if you will kindly twist my arm just a little—"

Actually, I hadn't the slightest desire to leave the fine ranch run by John and Oneida Broderick near Pray, Montana. It's practically on the banks of the Yellowstone River and in some of the most magnificent country nature

Tom McNally, "The Bonanza of No-Name Pond," *Field & Stream,* July, 1956.

ever made to distract a fisherman. But Bill Browning and I were on a fishing tour and had set up a pretty tight schedule. I glanced at him hopefully.

"Look," he said resignedly, "we've spent two days catching rainbows, browns, and brookies, and annoying the Brodericks—Oh, okay. You and John try the mountain trout tomorrow. I'll go along and shoot pictures."

Oneida nodded approvingly. "You'll love this little pond," she said. "It's right up that mountain behind the ranch. Just jumping with fish."

"Rock-and-roll trout, eh?"

"Well," said my hostess, "you roll out a cast and they'll rock you!"

They did. I've still got calluses on the backs of my heels from digging in. It was like this:

John, Bill, and I saddled up early next morning after putting away a ranch breakfast big enough to feed a small Balkan country. Then, while a wrangler stowed our tackle and some cooking gear on a packhorse, I helped John chase down enough live grasshoppers to fill a jar. "They're not full-grown yet," he said apologetically. "Otherwise I'd rope them."

"I have some pretty good flies," I ventured.

"Friend," said John grimly, "those trout up there like *meat*."

Emigrant Peak, in Gallatin National Forest, pushes its gray bulk up to 10,960 feet; it's one of the highest peaks of the Absaroka Range and it starts its climb practically at the back door of the Brodericks' Chico Ranch. The pond is about halfway up the slope and fills a good portion of a tiny valley not far from timberline. To get me to it I had a pinto pony called Shorty; of him, more anon. John was on a beautiful buckskin mare and Bill followed us, taking pictures.

The trail scissored gradually up the slope, which overlooked the broad, golden valley of the Yellowstone River. The river looked like a glittering string of Christmas tinsel as it danced in the sunlight. Ahead and above, the gray-green peak was etched against the sky. The country had the kind of natural grandeur that makes a man feel a little insignificant in the total scheme of things.

Finally, after a two-hour climb, we topped a knoll and there was the pond. Statuesque lodgepole pines lined one bank, and cottonwoods crowded around a cove. The water was black but clear, and quickly I spotted weed beds jutting out from the shores. They were very high-class apartment houses for trout.

But what caught my eye at once was the surface of the pond. The day was still and clear but I'd have sworn that the pond was being pelted by hailstones. I've seen rises before but this really had my mouth gaping. Trout were punching holes in the surface hard and fast, and from the look of things they must have been standing shoulder to shoulder. I almost fell off Shorty in my eagerness to get a fly onto the water.

"Take it easy, friend," grinned Broderick. "Those trout aren't going anywhere."

"Some of 'em are!" I retorted. "Down the mountain with me."

I finally got Shorty lashed to a tree and put my fly outfit together. John was still rigging his gear when I reached the bank and sent a No. 10 Irresistible out onto the water. That's a good fly anywhere and that day on the pond it lived up to its name. Probably those brookies have taken anything that floats, wobbles, or wiggles, but they went silly crazy over the Irresistible.

So did Shorty. Every time I'd cast, he'd shuffle around nervously, paw the ground, and whinny. Maybe, sometime or other, an angler had hung him up with a back cast.

Three trout rose to my first cast. They came out of the water as though they'd taken a running start at the bottom, canting on their caudals and pumping their pectorals. The smallest one got first grab. He took the fly and a few minutes later I eased him up onto the grass, slipped the hook free, and put him back. He swam away indignantly, his vermilion-and-blue markings splashing color like a rainbow.

I rate the brook trout the prettiest fish that swims, and those Emigrant Peak brookies are no exception. They're the most colorful examples of the species I've seen anywhere. And they took so fast that I released half a dozen before John Broderick wet his line. Bill kept busy with the camera, although I knew he was dying to get a little action. The brookies kept chewing on my Irresistible till it lost all semblance of a fly. They took John's crickets, too, but more reluctantly. He got excitement enough for only two or three men.

After a while we rode our saddle horses out into the shoals, to water them and to get a little fishing from horseback, which is a pleasant western custom. My pinto, Shorty, wasn't happy about it. A couple of times I had to bully him to keep him in the water and he'd prance around skittishly whenever I was playing a fish. Once, when I raised a good one that threw a lot of spray, he bolted and tried to take me home. I couldn't give the trout line quickly enough and it broke off. But I couldn't really be sore at Shorty. He toted me up that mountain (and back down again) for one of the best fishing days I've ever had.

I don't know how many brookies John and I caught and released but one of us always had a fish on. Sometimes we played a pair of speckles simultaneously. We'd hook a fish, play it, snake it in, and release it—all without ever leaving the saddle.

Mostly they were one-pounders. "There are plenty of four- and five-pounders in here," John told me. "Trouble is, they don't move nearly as fast as the little fellers, which always get to the lure first. But that fish that Shorty lost for you was a good one—three pounds or better."

Along about noon my aching wrist just couldn't take it any longer; so I called for a recess. We killed four nice trout and got a fire going. Then the three of us sat around the dying embers and shoveled down hunks of delicious red-orange fish. Maybe, somewhere, there is something better than native brook trout, fried crisp and brown, and eaten while mountain air and wood smoke tickle your nose. Maybe—but I'm not going to bother to look for it.

We left our mountain pond reluctantly as day waned. The trout were still kissing the surface. Back at Chico Ranch we took a refreshing plunge in a warm spring. The Brodericks have fixed it up into a sort of indoor swimming pool, with water coming from a natural hot spring. Then we tackled a dinner of western beefsteak and talked about the fishing. John explained that the mountain pond is spring-fed and that in all the years he'd fished it he'd never known it to have a poor season.

"What do you call it?" I asked.

"You name it," John said. "No one here has ever got around to doing it."

"I'll vote for Lake Oneida," I said with a grateful glance toward John's wife.

"You've got an Oneida Lake back East, haven't you?" she countered.

"I've seen a lot of 'fishermen's paradises,'" said Bill dreamily, "but they're bush league compared to this one. Let's just call it Paradise Pond."

ROCK ME TO SLEEP | ELIZABETH AKERS ALLEN

Backward, turn backward, O Time, in your flight,
Make me a child again just for tonight!
Mother, come back from the echoless shore,
Take me again to your heart as of yore;
Kiss from my forehead the furrows of care,
Smooth the few silver threads out of my hair;
Over my slumbers your loving watch keep;—
Rock me to sleep, Mother—rock me to sleep!

Backward, flow backward, O tide of the years!
I am so weary of toil and of tears—
Toil without recompense, tears all in vain—
Take them, and give me my childhood again!
I have grown weary of dust and decay—
Weary of flinging my soul-wealth away;
Weary of sowing for others to reap;—
Rock me to sleep, Mother—rock me to sleep!

Tired of the hollow, the base, the untrue,
Mother, O Mother, my heart calls for you!
Many a summer the grass has grown green,
Blossomed and faded, our faces between:

Yet, with strong yearning and passionate pain,
Long I tonight for your presence again.
Come from the silence so long and so deep;—
Rock me to sleep, Mother—rock me to sleep!

Over my heart, in the days that are flown,
No love like mother-love ever has shone;
No other worship abides and endures—
Faithful, unselfish, and patient like yours:
None like a mother can charm away pain
From the sick soul and the world-weary brain.
Slumber's soft calms o'er my heavy lids creep;—
Rock me to sleep, Mother—rock me to sleep!

Come, let your brown hair, just lighted with gold,
Fall on your shoulders again as of old;
Let it drop over my forehead tonight,
Shading my faint eyes away from the light;
For with its sunny-edged shadows once more
Haply will throng the sweet visions of yore;
Lovingly, softly, its bright billows sweep;—
Rock me to sleep, Mother—rock me to sleep!

Mother, dear Mother, the years have been long
Since I last listened your lullaby song:
Sing, then, and unto my soul it shall seem
Womanhood's years have been only a dream.
Clasped to your heart in a loving embrace,
With your light lashes just sweeping my face,
Never hereafter to wake or to weep;
Rock me to sleep, Mother—rock me to sleep!

THE RETURN: AN ELEGY | *ROBERT PENN WARREN*

The east wind finds the gap bringing rain:
Rain in the pine wind shaking the stiff pine.
Beneath the wind the hollow gorges whine
The pines decline
Slow film of rain creeps down the loam again
Where the blind and nameless bones recline.
   They are conceded to the earth's absolute chemistry

From *Selected Poems, 1923-1943.* Copyright 1944 by Robert Penn Warren.

they burn like faggots in—of damp and dark—
the monstrous bulging flame.
calcium phosphate lust speculation faith treachery
it walked upright with habitation and a name
tell me its name

The pines, black, like combers plunge with spray
Lick the wind's unceasing keel
It is not long till day
The boughs like hairy swine in slaughter squeal
And lurch beneath the thunder's livid heel.
The pines, black, snore what does the wind say?

tell me its name

I have a name: I am not blind.
Eyes, not blind, press to the Pullman pane
Survey the driving dark and silver taunt of rain.
What will I find
What will I find beyond the snoring pine?
O eyes locked blind in death's immaculate design
Shall fix their last distrust in mine

give me the nickels off your eyes
from your hands the violets
let me bless your obsequies
if you possessed conveniently enough three eyes
then I could buy a pack of cigarettes

In gorges where the dead fox lies the fern
Will rankest loop the battened frond and fall
Above the bare and tushèd jaws that turn
Their insolence unto the gracious catafalque and pall.
It will be the season when milkweed blossoms burn.

the old bitch is dead
what have I said!
I have only said what the wind said
wind shakes a bell the hollow head

By dawn, the wind, the blown rain
Will cease their antique concitation.
It is the hour when old ladies cough and wake,
The chair, the table, take their form again
Earth begins the matinal exhalation

does my mother wake

Pines drip without motion
The hairy boughs no longer shake

Shaggy mist, crookbacked, ascends
Round hairy boughs the mist with shaggy fingers bends.
No wind: no rain:
Why do the steady pines complain?
Complain

          the old fox is dead
          what have I said

Locked in the roaring cubicle
Over the mountains through darkness hurled
I race the daylight's westward cycle
Across the groaning rooftree of the world.
The mist is furled.

  a hundred years they took this road
  the lank hunters then men hard-eyed with hope:
  ox breath whitened the chill air: the goad
  fell: here on the western slope
  the hungry people the lost ones took their abode
  here they took their stand:
  alders bloomed on the road to the new land
  here is the house the broken door the shed
  the old fox is dead

The wheels hum hum
The wheels: I come I come
Whirl out of space through time O wheels
Pursue down backward time the ghostly parallels
Pursue past culvert cut fill embankment semaphore
Pursue down gleaming hours that are no more.
The pines, black, snore

    turn backward turn backward o time in your flight
    and make me a child again just for tonight
    good lord he's wet the bed come bring a light

What grief hath the mind distilled?
The heart is unfulfilled
The hoarse pine stilled
I cannot pluck
Out of this land of pine and rock
Of the fallen pine cone
Of red bud their season not yet gone
If I could pluck
(In drouth the lizard will blink on the hot limestone)

    the old fox is dead
    what is said is said
    heaven rest the hoary head

what have I said!
...I have only said what the wind said
honor thy father and mother in the days of thy youth
for time uncoils like the cottonmouth

If I could pluck
Out of the dark that whirled
Over the hoarse pine over the rock
Out of the mist that furled
Could I stretch forth like God the hand and gather
For you my mother
If I could pluck
Against the dry essential of tomorrow
To lay upon the breast that gave me suck
Out of the dark the dark and swollen orchid of this sorrow.

THE ECONOMY OF STYLE I: MAN'S MORTALITY

"ECONOMY" DERIVES from two Greek words meaning "household management." Economy of style may be defined as management of the household of words. Like management of other affairs, this economy may be wise or unwise; and, as either, it may be frugal or luxurious, restrained or flamboyant, direct or elaborately circumlocutory. Occasion may demand one kind of economy or another; a writer's convictions and predilections may lead him to favor this kind of rhetoric and disdain that; and fashion, in writing as in other matters, will in one century find uncouth what in another it thought sober, and praise as elegant in one time what in another it snubs as artificial. Contemporary writers, on the whole, have favored a rather tight-fisted economy, and modern readers tend to be suspicious of the stylist who pours words out abundantly, rather than working with knife-like precision and understatement. But as some of the selections in this unit show, verbal extravagance is as appropriate to certain subjects as a frugal rationing of words.

That criterion of style which we have metaphorically called "economy" is hard to define, but it certainly includes the following more specific gauges: first, the extent of the amount of repetition or of near-repetition, in which a writer attempts to "surround" his meaning by trying one phrase after another; second, the number of things left unsaid, implied, or hinted at, the extent to which the author makes his words do double-duty; third, the amount and richness of imagery, the extent to which the writer seems to luxuriate in the actual process of putting words on paper. It is easy to see that the economy a writer chooses is part of his account of himself, as well as a contributing factor in the relation between writer and reader. For example, the writer who works through varied repetition may reveal himself as passionately concerned with his subject matter; or he may appear a patient schoolmaster, carefully explaining a difficult matter to a willing but not particularly intelligent student. The best economy, therefore, may be described as that which accurately conveys the writer's conviction and personality and sets up a proper relation with the reader. To modify slightly Buffon's famous remark, "Economy is the man himself."

The five selections on death which follow represent quite different senses of literary economy, but, in each, style reveals the man almost as much as statement does. Sir Thomas Browne (1605-1682) was a doctor of medicine and one of the most curiously learned men of his time. The selection from Hydriotaphia—*a speculative essay stimulated by the discovery of ancient burial urns in Norfolk—is characteristic of his writing at its best. Jeremy Taylor (1613-1667), a barber's son who rose to an Anglican bishopric, was author of several works of moral reflection and theology. The selection printed here is from* Holy Dying, *the most often read of those works. Tutor of Edward Gibbon and later the principal figure of a religious community in England, William Law (1686-1761) is significant as a link between English Puritanism and eighteenth-century Methodism. The letters from William James (1824-1910) to two members of his family represent not only that pragmatic philosopher's attitude toward death, but, in some measure, a pervasive change in Western attitudes about most of life's ultimate values. That change is also reflected, though very differently, in William Ernest Hocking's "defense" of death. Like James, Hocking (1873-   ) was a philosopher and a teacher of philosophy at Harvard for most of his adult years.*

MEN AND MONUMENTS | *THOMAS BROWNE*

Now since these dead bones have already out-lasted the living ones of Methuselah, and in a yard underground, and thin walls of clay, out-worn all the strong and specious buildings above it, and quietly rested under the drums and tramplings of three conquests: what prince can promise such diuturnity unto his relics, or might not gladly say,

Sic ego componi versus in ossa velim?

From *Hydriotaphia, Urn-Burial; or a Discourse of the Sepulchral Urns Lately Found in Norfolk* (1658).

Time, which antiquates antiquities, and hath an art to make dust of all things, hath yet spared these minor monuments.

In vain we hope to be known by open and visible conservatories, when to be unknown was the means of their continuation, and obscurity their protection. If they died by violent hands, and were thrust into their urns, these bones become considerable, and some old philosophers would honor them, whose souls they conceived most pure, which were thus snatched from their bodies, and to retain a stronger propension unto them; whereas they weariedly left a languishing corpse, and with faint desires of reunion. If they fell by long and aged decay, yet wrapped up in the bundle of time, they fall into indistinction, and make but one blot with infants. If we begin to die when we live, and long life be but a prolongation of death, our life is a sad composition; we live with death, and die not in a moment. How many pulses made up the life of Methuselah, were work for Archimedes: common counters sum up the life of Moses his man. Our days become considerable, like petty sums, by minute accumulations; where numerous fractions make up but small round numbers; and our days of a span long make not one little finger.

If the nearness of our last necessity brought a nearer conformity into it, there were a happiness in hoary hairs, and no calamity in half-senses. But the long habit of living indisposeth us for dying; when avarice makes us the sport of death, when even David grew politicly cruel, and Solomon could hardly be said to be the wisest of men. But many are too early old, and before the date of age. Adversity stretcheth our days, misery makes Alcmena's nights, and time hath no wings unto it. But the most tedious being is that which can unwish itself, content to be nothing, or never to have been, which was beyond the malcontent of Job, who cursed not the day of his life, but his nativity; content to have so far been as to have a title to future being, although he had lived here but in an hidden state of life, and as it were an abortion.

What song the sirens sang, or what name Achilles assumed when he hid himself among women, though puzzling questions, are not beyond all conjecture. What time the persons of these ossuaries entered the famous nations of the dead, and slept with princes and counselors, might admit a wide solution. But who were the proprietaries of these bones, or what bodies these ashes made up, were a question above antiquarism; not to be resolved by man, nor easily perhaps by spirits, except we consult the provincial guardians, or tutelary observators. Had they made as good provision for their names as they have done for their relics, they had not so grossly erred in the art of perpetuation. But to subsist in bones, and be but pyramidally extant, is a fallacy in duration. Vain ashes which in the oblivion of names, persons, times, and sexes, have found unto themselves a fruitless continuation, and only arise unto late posterity, as emblems of mortal vanities, antidotes against pride, vainglory, and maddening vices. Pagan vainglories, which thought the world might last for ever, had encouragement for ambition; and, finding no Atropos unto the immortality of their names, were never damped with the necessity of oblivion. Even old ambitions had the advantage of ours, in the attempts of their vainglories, who, acting early and before the probable meridian of time, have by this time found great accomplishment of their designs, whereby the ancient heros have already out-lasted their monuments and mechanical preservations. But in this latter scene of time, we cannot expect such mummies unto our memories, when ambition may fear the prophecy of Elias, and Charles the Fifth can never hope to live within two Methuselahs of Hector.

And therefore, restless unquiet for the diuturnity of our memories unto present considerations seems a vanity almost out of date, and superannuated piece of folly. We cannot hope to live so long in our names as some have done in their persons. One face of Janus holds no proportion unto the other. 'Tis too late to be ambitious. The great mutations of the world are acted, or time may be too short for our designs. To extend our memories by monuments, whose death we daily pray for, and whose duration we cannot hope, without injury to our expectations in the advent of the last day, were a contradiction to our beliefs. We whose generations are ordained in this setting part of time are providentially taken off from such imaginations; and, being necessitated to eye the remaining particle of futurity, are naturally constituted unto thoughts of the next world, and cannot excusably decline the consideration of that duration, which maketh pyramids pillars of snow, and all that's past a moment.

Circles and right lines limit and close all bodies, and the mortal right-lined circle must conclude and shut up all. There is no antidote against the opium of time, which temporally considereth all things: our fathers find their graves in our short memories, and sadly tell us how we may be buried in our survivors. Gravestones tell truth scarce forty years. Generations pass while some trees stand, and old families last not three oaks. To be read by bare inscriptions like many in Gruter, to hope for eternity by enigmatical epithets or first letters of our names, to be studied by antiquaries, who we were, and have new names given us like many of the mummies, are cold consolations unto the students of perpetuity, even by everlasting languages.

To be content that times to come should only know there was such a man, not caring whether they knew more of him, was a frigid ambition in Cardan; disparaging his horoscopal inclination and judgment of himself. Who cares to subsist like Hippocrates' patients, or Achilles' horses in Homer, under naked nominations, without deserts and noble acts, which are the balsam of our memories, the *entelechia* and soul of our subsistencies? To be nameless in worthy deeds exceeds an infamous history. The Canaanitish woman lives more happily without a name than Herodias with one. And who had not rather have been the good thief than Pilate?

But the iniquity of oblivion blindly scattereth her poppy, and deals with the memory of men without distinction to merit of perpetuity. Who can but pity the founder of the pyramids? Herostratus lives that burnt the temple of Diana, he is almost lost that built it. Time hath spared the epitaph of Adrian's horse, confounded that of himself. In vain we compute our felicities by the advantage of our good names, since bad have equal durations, and Thersites is like to live as long as Agamemnon. Who knows whether the best of men be known, or whether there be not more remarkable persons forgot than any that stand remembered in the known account of time? Without the favor of the everlasting register, the first man had been as unknown as the last and Methuselah's long life had been his only chronicle.

Oblivion is not to be hired. The greater part must be content to be as though they had not been, to be found in the register of God, not in the record of man. Twenty-seven names make up the first story, and the recorded names ever since contain not one living century. The number of the dead long exceedeth all that shall live. The night of time far surpasseth the day, and who knows when was the equinox? Every hour adds unto that current arithmetic, which scarce stands one moment. And since death must be the Lucina of life, and even Pagans could doubt whether thus to live were to die; since our longest sun sets at right descensions, and makes but winter arches, and therefore it cannot be long before we lie down in darkness, and have our light in ashes; since the brother of death daily haunts us with dying mementos, and time that grows old in itself bids us hope no long duration—diuturnity is a dream and folly of expectation.

Darkness and light divide the course of time, and oblivion shares with memory a great part even of our living beings; we slightly remember our felicities, and the smartest strokes of affliction leave but short smart upon us. Sense endureth no extremities, and sorrows destroy us or themselves. To weep into stones are fables. Afflictions induce callosities; miseries are slippery, or fall like snow upon us, which notwithstanding is no unhappy stupidity. To be ignorant of evils to come, and forgetful of evils past, is a merciful provision in nature, whereby we digest the mixture of our few and evil days, and, our delivered sense not relapsing into cutting remembrances, our sorrows are not kept raw by the edge of repetitions. A great part of antiquity contended their hopes of subsistency with a transmigration of their souls—a good way to continue our memories, while having the advantage of plural successions, they could not but act something remarkable in such variety of beings, and enjoying the fame of their passed selves, make accumulation of glory unto their last durations. Others, rather than be lost in the uncomfortable night of nothing, were content to recede into the common being, and make one particle of the public soul of all things, which was no more than to return into their unknown and divine Original again. Egyptian ingenuity was more unsatisfied, contriving their bodies in sweet consistencies, to attend the return of their souls. But all was vanity, feeding the wind, and folly. The Egyptian mummies, which Cambyses or time hath spared, avarice now consumeth. Mummy is become merchandise, Mizraim cures wounds, and Pharaoh is sold for balsams.

In vain do individuals hope for immortality, or any patent from oblivion, in preservations below the moon; men have been deceived even in their flatteries above the sun, and studied conceits to perpetuate their names in heaven. The various cosmography of that part hath already varied the names of contrived constellations; Nimrod is lost in Orion, and Osiris in the Dog Star. While we look for incorruption in the heavens, we find they are but like the earth—durable in their main bodies, alterable in their parts; whereof, beside comets and new stars, perspectives begin to tell tales, and the spots that wander about the sun, with Phaëton's favor, would make clear conviction.

There is nothing strictly immortal but immortality. Whatever hath no beginning may be confident of no end; all others have a dependent being and within the reach of destruction; which is the peculiar of that necessary Essence that cannot destroy itself; and the highest strain of omnipotency, to be so powerfully constituted as not to suffer even from the power of itself. But the sufficiency of Christian immortality frustrates all earthly glory, and the quality of either state after death makes a folly of posthumous memory. God who can only destroy our soul, and hath assured our resurrection, either of our bodies or names hath directly promised no duration. Wherein there is so much of chance that the boldest expectants have found unhappy frustration; and to hold long subsistence seems but a scape in oblivion. But man is a noble animal, splendid in ashes, and pompous in the grave, solemnizing nativities and deaths with equal luster, nor omitting ceremonies of bravery in the infamy of his nature.

Life is a pure flame, and we live by an invisible sun within us. A small fire sufficeth for life, great flames seemed too little after death, while men vainly affected precious pyres, and to burn like Sardanapalus; but the wisdom of funeral laws found the folly prodigal blazes, and reduced undoing fires unto the rule of sober obsequies, wherein few could be so mean as not to provide wood, pitch, a mourner, and an urn.

Five languages secured not the epitaph of Gordianus. The man of God lives longer without a tomb than any by one, invisibly interred by angels, and adjudged to obscurity, though not without some marks directing human discovery. Enoch and Elias, without either tomb or burial, in an anomalous state of being, are the great examples of perpetuity, in their long and living memory, in strict account being still on this side death, and having a late part yet to act upon this stage of earth. If in the decretory term of the world we shall not all die but be changed, according to received translation, the last day will make but few graves; at least quick resurrections will anticipate lasting sepultures. Some graves will be opened before they be quite closed, and Lazarus be no wonder. When many that feared to die shall groan that they can die but once, the dismal state is the second and living death, when life puts despair on the damned; when men shall wish the coverings of mountains, not of monuments, and annihilations shall be courted.

While some have studied monuments, others have studiously declined them, and some have been so vainly boisterous that they durst not acknowledge their graves; wherein Alaricus seems most subtle, who had a river turned to hide his bones at the bottom. Even Sylla, that thought himself safe in his urn, could not prevent revenging tongues, and stones thrown at his monument. Happy are they whom privacy makes innocent, who deal so with men in this world that they are not afraid to meet them in the next; who, when they die, make no commotion among the dead, and are not touched with that poetical taunt of Isaiah.

Pyramids, arches, obelisks, were but the irregularities of vainglory, and wild enormities of ancient magnanimity. But the most magnanimous resolution rests in the Christian religion, which trampleth upon pride, and sits on the neck of ambition, humbly pursing that infallible perpetuity unto which all others must diminish their diameters, and be poorly seen in angles of contingency.

Pious spirits who passed their days in raptures of futurity made little more of this world than the world that was before it, while they lay obscure in the chaos of preordination, and night of their forebeings. And if any have been so happy as truly to understand Christian annihilation, ecstasies, exolution, liquefaction, transformation, the kiss of the spouse, gustation of God, and ingression into the divine shadow, they have already had an handsome anticipation of heaven; the glory of the world is surely over, and the earth is ashes unto them.

To subsist in lasting monuments, to live in their productions, to exist in their names and predicament of chimeras, was large satisfaction unto old expectations, and made one part of their Elysiums. But all this is nothing in the metaphysics of true belief. To live indeed is to be again ourselves, which being not only an hope, but an evidence in noble believers, 'tis all one to lie in St. Innocent's churchyard, as in the sands of Egypt. Ready to be anything, in the ecstasy of being ever, and as content with six foot as the *moles* of Adrianus.

CONSIDERATIONS OF THE VANITY AND SHORTNESS OF MAN'S LIFE | JEREMY TAYLOR

A man is a bubble, said the Greek proverb; which Lucian represents with advantages and its proper circumstances to this purpose; saying, that all the world is a storm, and men rise up in their several generations, like bubbles

From *The Rule and Exercises of Holy Dying* (1651).

descending *a Jove pluvio,* from God and the dew of heaven, from a tear and drop of man, from nature and providence: and some of these instantly sink into the deluge of their first parent, and are hidden in a sheet of water, having had no other business in the world but to be born that they might be able to die: others float up and down two or three turns, and suddenly disappear, and give their place to others: and they that live longest upon the face of the waters, are in perpetual motion, restless and uneasy; and, being crushed with the great drop of a cloud, sink into flatness and a froth; the change not being great, it being hardly possible it should be more a nothing than it was before. So is every man: he is born in vanity and sin; he comes into the world like morning mushrooms, soon thrusting up their heads into the air, and conversing with their kindred of the same production, and as soon they turn into dust and forgetfulness: some of them without any other interest in the affairs of the world but that they made their parents a little glad, and very sorrowful: others ride longer in the storm; it may be until seven years of vanity be expired, and then peradventure the sun shines hot upon their heads, and they fall into the shades below, into the cover of death and darkness of the grave to hide them. But if the bubble stands the shock of a bigger drop, and outlives the chances of a child, of a careless nurse, of drowning in a pail of water, of being overlaid by a sleepy servant, or such little accidents, then the young man dances like a bubble, empty and gay, and shines like a dove's neck, or the image of a rainbow, which hath no substance, and whose very imagery and colors are fantastical; and so he dances out the gaiety of his youth, and is all the while in a storm, and endures only because he is not knocked on the head by a drop of bigger rain, or crushed by the pressure of a load of indigested meat, or quenched by the disorder of an ill-placed humor: and to preserve a man alive in the midst of so many chances and hostilities, is as great a miracle as to create him; to preserve him from rushing into nothing, and at first to draw him up from nothing, were equally the issues of an almighty power. And therefore the wise men of the world have contended who shall best fit man's condition with words signifying his vanity and short abode. Homer calls a man "a leaf," the smallest, the weakest piece of a short-lived, unsteady plant: Pindar calls him "the dream of a shadow": another, "the dream of the shadow of smoke": but St. James spake by a more excellent spirit, saying, "our life is but a vapor" (James 4:14), *viz.,* drawn from the earth by a celestial influence; made of smoke, or the lighter parts of water, tossed with every wind, moved by the motion of a superior body, without virtue in itself, lifted up on high or left below, according as it pleases the sun its foster-father. But it is lighter yet; it is but "appearing"; a fantastic vapor, an apparition, nothing real: it is not so much as a mist, not the matter of a shower, nor substantial enough to make a cloud; but it is like Cassiopeia's chair, or Pelops' shoulder, or the circles of heaven, φαινομενα, than which you cannot have a word that can signify a verier nothing. And yet the expression is one degree more made diminutive: a "vapor," and "fantastical," or a "mere appearance," and this but for a little while neither; the very dream, the phantasm disappears in a small time, "like the shadow that departeth"; or "like a tale that is told"; or "as a dream when one awaketh." A man is so vain, so unfixed, so perishing a creature, that he cannot long last in the scene of fancy: a man goes off, and is forgotten, like the dream of a distracted person. The sum of all is this: that thou art a man, than whom there is not in the world any greater instance of heights and declensions, of lights and shadows, of misery and folly, of laughter and tears, of groans and death.

And because this consideration is of great usefulness and great necessity to many purposes of wisdom and the spirit, all the succession of time, all the changes in nature, all the varieties of light and darkness, the thousand thousands of accidents in the world, and every contingency to every man, and to every creature, doth preach our funeral sermon, and calls us to look and see how the old sexton Time throws up the earth, and digs a grave where we must lay our sins or our sorrows, and sow our bodies, till they rise again in a fair or in an intolerable eternity. Every revolution which the sun makes about the world, divides between life and death; and death possesses both those portions by the next morrow; and we are dead to all those months which we have already lived, and we shall never live them over again: and still God makes little periods of our age. First we change our world, when we come from the womb to feel the warmth of the sun. Then we sleep and enter into the image of death, in which state we are unconcerned in all the changes of the world: and if our mothers or our nurses die, or a wild boar destroys our vineyards, or our king be sick, we regard it not, but during that state are as disinterested as if our eyes were closed with the clay that weeps in the bowels of the earth. At the end of seven years our teeth fall and die before us, representing a formal prologue to the tragedy; and still every seven years it is odds that we shall finish the last scene: and when nature, or chance, or vice, takes our body in pieces, weakening some parts and loosing others, we taste the grave and the solemnities of our own funerals, first in those parts that ministered to vice, and next in them that served for ornament, and in a short time even they that served for necessity become useless, and entangled like the wheels of a broken clock. Baldness is but a dressing to our funerals, the proper ornament of mourning, and of a person entered very far into the regions and possession of death: and we have more of the same signification; gray hairs, rotten teeth, dim eyes, trembling joints, short breath, stiff limbs, wrinkled skin, short memory, decayed appetite. Every day's necessity calls for a reparation of that portion which death fed on all night, when we lay in his lap, and slept in his outer chambers. The very spirits of a man prey upon the daily portion of bread and flesh, and every meal is a rescue from one death, and lays up for another; and while we think a thought, we die; and the clock strikes, and reckons on our portion of eternity: we form our words with the breath of our nostrils, we have the less to live upon for every word we speak.

Thus nature calls us to meditate of death by those things which are the instruments of acting it: and God by all the variety of his providence makes us see death everywhere, in all variety of circumstances, and dressed up for all the fancies and the expectation of every single person. Nature hath given us one harvest every year, but death hath two, and the spring and the autumn send throngs of men and women to charnel-houses; and all the summer long men are recovering from their evils of the spring, till the dog-days come, and then the Sirian star makes the summer deadly; and the fruits of autumn are laid up for all the year's provision, and the man that gathers them eats and surfeits, and dies and needs them not, and himself is laid up for eternity; and he that escapes till winter only stays for another opportunity which the distempers of that quarter minister to him with great variety. Thus death reigns in all the portions of our time; the autumn with its fruits provides disorders for us, and the winter's cold turns them into sharp diseases, and the spring brings flowers to strew our hearse, and the summers gives green turf and brambles to bind upon our graves. Calentures and surfeit, cold and agues, are the four quarters of the year, and all minister to death; and you can go no whither but you tread upon a dead man's bones.

The wild fellow in Petronius that escaped upon a broken table from the furies of a shipwreck, as he was sunning himself upon the rocky shore espied a man rolled upon his floating bed of waves, ballasted with sand in the folds of his garment, and carried by his civil enemy, the sea, towards the shore to find a grave: and it cast him into some sad thoughts; that peradventure this man's wife in some part of the continent, safe and warm, looks next month for the good man's return; or, it may be, his son knows nothing of the tempest; or his father thinks of that affectionate kiss, which still is warm upon the good old man's cheek, ever since he took a kind farewell; and he weeps with joy to think how blessed he shall be when his beloved boy returns into the circle of his father's arms. These are the thoughts of mortals, this is the end and sum of all their designs: a dark night and an ill guide, a boisterous sea and a broken cable, a hard rock and a rough wind, dashed in pieces the fortune of a whole family, and they that shall weep loudest for the accident are not yet entered into the storm, and yet have suffered shipwreck. Then looking upon the carcass, he knew it, and found it to be the master of the ship, who the day before cast up the accounts of his patrimony and his trade, and named the day when he thought to be at home: see how the man swims who was so angry two days since; his passions are becalmed with the storm, his accounts cast up, his cares at an end, his voyage done, and his gains are the strange events of death, which whether they be good or evil, the men that are alive seldom trouble themselves concerning the interest of the dead.

But seas alone do not break our vessel in pieces: everywhere we may be shipwrecked. A valiant general, when he is to reap the harvest of his crowns and triumphs, fights unprosperously; or falls into a fever with joy and wine, and changes his laurel into cypress, his triumphal chariot to a hearse, dying the night before he was appointed to perish in the drunkenness of his festival joys. It was a sad arrest of the loosenesses and wilder feasts of the French court, when their King Henry the Second was killed really by the sportive image of a fight. And many brides have died under the hands of paranymphs and maidens, dressing them for uneasy joy, the new and undiscerned chains of marriage, according to the saying of Bensirah, the wise Jew, "the bride went into her chamber, and knew not what should befall her there." Some have been paying their vows, and giving thanks for a prosperous return to their own house, and the roof hath descended upon their heads, and turned their loud religion into the deeper silence of a grave. And how many teeming mothers have rejoiced over their swelling wombs, and pleased themselves in becoming the channels of blessing to a family, and the midwife hath quickly bound their heads and feet, and carried them forth to a burial! Or else the birthday of an heir hath seen the coffin of the father brought into the house, and the divided mother hath been forced to travail twice, with a painful birth, and a sadder death.

There is no state, no accident, no circumstance of our life, but it hath been soured by some sad instance of a dying friend: a friendly meeting often ends in some sad mischance, and makes an eternal parting: and when the poet Aeschylus was sitting under the walls of his house, an eagle hovering over his bald head mistook it for a stone, and let fall his oyster, hoping there to break the shell, but pierced the poor man's skull.

Death meets us everywhere, and is procured by every instrument and in all chances, and enters in at many doors; by violence and secret influence, by the aspect of a star and the stink of a mist, by the emissions of a cloud and the meeting of a vapor, by the fall of a chariot and the stumbling at a stone, by a full meal or an empty stomach, by watching at the wine or by watching at prayers, by the sun or the moon, by a heat or a cold, by sleepless nights or sleeping days, by water frozen into the hardness and sharpness of a dagger, or water thawed into the floods of a river, by a hair or a raisin, by violent motion or sitting still, by severity or dissolution, by God's mercy or God's anger; by everything in providence and everything in manners, by everything in nature and everything in chance;

———*eripitur persona, manet res;*

we take pains to heap up things useful to our life, and get our death in the purchase; and the person is snatched away, and the goods remain. And all this is the law and constitution of nature; it is a punishment to our sins, the unalterable event of providence, and the decree of heaven: the chains that confine us to this condition are strong as destiny, and immutable as the eternal laws of God.

I have conversed with some men who rejoiced in the death or calamity of others, and accounted it as a judgment upon them for being on the other side, and against them in the contention: but within the revolution of a few months, the same man met with a more uneasy and unhandsome death: which when I saw, I wept, and was afraid; for I knew that it must be so with all men; for we also shall die, and end our quarrels and contentions by passing to a final sentence.

DEATH AND THE GOOD LIFE | WILLIAM LAW

The best way for any one to know how much he ought to aspire after holiness, is to consider, not how much will make his present life easy, but to ask himself, how much he thinks will make him easy at the hour of death.

Now any man that dares be so serious, as to put this question to himself, will be forced to answer, that at death, every one will wish that he had been as perfect as human nature can be.

Is not this therefore sufficient to put us not only upon wishing, but laboring after all that perfection, which we shall then lament the want of? Is it not excessive folly to be content with such a course of piety as we already know cannot content us, at a time when we shall so want it, as to have nothing else to comfort us? How can we carry a severer condemnation against ourselves, than to believe, that, at the hour of death, we shall want the virtues of the Saints, and wish that we had been amongst the first servants of God, and yet take no methods of arriving at their height of piety, whilst we are alive?

Though this is an absurdity that we can easily pass over at present, whilst the health of our bodies, the passions of our minds, the noise, and hurry, and pleasures, and business of the world, lead us on with eyes that see not, and ears that hear not; yet, at death, it will set itself before us in a dreadful magnitude, it will haunt us like a dismal ghost, and our conscience will never let us take our eyes from it.

We see in worldly matters, what a torment self-condemnation is, and how hardly a man is able to forgive himself, when he has brought himself into any calamity or disgrace, purely by his own folly. The affliction is made doubly tormenting, because he is forced to charge it all upon himself, as his own act and deed, against the nature and reason of things, and contrary to the advice of all his friends.

Now by this we may in some degree guess how terrible the pain of that self-condemnation will be, when a man shall find himself in the miseries of death under the severity of a self-condemning conscience, charging all his distress upon his own folly and madness, against the sense and reason

From *A Serious Call to a Devout and Holy Life* (1728).

of his own mind, against all the doctrines and precepts of religion, and contrary to all the instructions, calls, and warnings, both of God and man.

Penitens was a busy, notable tradesman, and very prosperous in his dealings, but died in the thirty-fifth year of his age.

A little before his death, when the doctors had given him over, some of his neighbors came one evening to see him, at which time he spake thus to them:

I see, my friends, the tender concern you have for me, by the grief that appears in your countenances, and I know the thoughts that you have now about me. You think how melancholy a case it is, to see so young a man, and in such flourishing business, delivered up to death. And perhaps, had I visited any of you in my condition, I should have had the same thoughts of you.

But now, my friends, my thoughts are no more like your thoughts than my condition is like yours.

It is no trouble to me now to think, that I am to die young, or before I have raised an estate.

These things are now sunk into such mere nothings, that I have no name little enough to call them by. For if in a few days or hours, I am to leave this carcass to be buried in the earth, and to find myself either for ever happy in the favor of God, or eternally separated from all light and peace, can any words sufficiently express the littleness of everything else?

Is there any dream like the dream of life, which amuses us with the neglect and disregard of these things? Is there any folly like the folly of our manly state, which is too wise and busy, to be at leisure for these reflections?

When we consider death as a misery, we only think of it as a miserable separation from the enjoyments of this life. We seldom mourn over an old man that dies rich, but we lament the young, that are taken away in the progress of their fortune. You yourselves look upon me with pity, not that I am going unprepared to meet the Judge of quick and dead, but that I am to leave a prosperous trade in the flower of my life.

This is the wisdom of our manly thoughts. And yet what folly of the silliest children is so great as this?

For what is there miserable, or dreadful in death, but the consequences of it? When a man is dead, what does any thing signify to him, but the state he is then in?

Our poor friend Lepidus died, you know, as he was dressing himself for a feast: do you think it is now part of his trouble, that he did not live till that entertainment was over? Feasts, and business, and pleasures, and enjoyments, seem great things to us, whilst we think of nothing else; but as soon as we add death to them, they all sink into an equal littleness; and the soul that is separated from the body no more laments the loss of business, than the losing of a feast.

If I am now going into the joys of God, could there be any reason to grieve, that this happened to me before I was forty years of age? Could it be a sad thing to go to Heaven, before I had made a few more bargains, or stood a little longer behind a counter?

And if I am to go amongst lost spirits, could there be any reason to be content, that this did not happen to me till I was old, and full of riches?

If good Angels were ready to receive my soul, could it be any grief to me, that I was dying upon a poor bed in a garret?

And if God has delivered me up to evil spirits, to be dragged by them to places of torments, could it be any comfort to me, that they found me upon a bed of state?

When you are as near death as I am, you will know that all the different states of life, whether of youth or age, riches or poverty, greatness or meanness, signify no more to you, than whether you die in a poor or stately apartment.

The greatness of those things which follow death makes all that goes before it sink into nothing.

Now that judgment is the next thing that I look for, and everlasting happiness or misery is come so near me, all the enjoyments and prosperities of life seem as vain and insignificant, and to have no more to do with my happiness, than the clothes that I wore before I could speak.

But, my friends, how am I surprised that I have not always had these thoughts? for what is there in the terrors of death, in the vanities of life, or the necessities of piety, but what I might have as easily and fully seen in any part of my life?

What a strange thing is it, that a little health, or the poor business of a shop, should keep us so senseless of these great things, that are coming so fast upon us!

Just as you came in my chamber, I was thinking with myself, what numbers of souls there are now in the world, in my condition at this very time, surprised with a summons to the other world; some taken from their shops and farms, others from their sports and pleasures, these at suits of law, those at gaming tables, some on the road, others at their own firesides, and all seized at an hour when they thought nothing of it; frightened at the approach of death, confounded at the vanity of all their labors, designs, and projects, astonished at the folly of their past lives, and not knowing which way to turn their thoughts, to find any comfort. Their consciences flying in their faces, bringing all their sins to their remembrance, tormenting them with deepest convictions of their own folly, presenting them with the sight of the angry Judge, the worm that never dies, the fire that is never quenched, the gates of hell, the powers of darkness, and the bitter pains of eternal death.

Oh, my friends! bless God that you are not of this number, that you have time and strength to employ yourselves in such works of piety, as may bring you peace at the last.

And take this along with you, that there is nothing but a life of great piety, or a death of great stupidity, that can keep off these apprehensions.

Had I now a thousand worlds, I would give them all for one year more, that I might present unto God one year of such devotion and good works, as I never before so much as intended.

You, perhaps, when you consider that I have lived free from scandal and debauchery, and in the communion of the Church, wonder to see me so full of remorse and self-condemnation at the approach of death.

But, alas! what a poor thing is it, to have lived only free from murder, theft, and adultery, which is all that I can say of myself.

You know, indeed, that I have never been reckoned a sot, but you are, at the same time, witnesses, and have been frequent companions of my intemperance, sensuality, and great indulgence. And if I am now going to a judgment, where nothing will be rewarded but good works, I may well be concerned, that though I am no sot, yet I have no Christian sobriety to plead for me.

It is true, I have lived in the communion of the Church, and generally frequented its worship and service on Sundays, when I was neither too idle, or not otherwise disposed of by my business and pleasures. But, then, my conformity to the public worship has been rather a thing of course, than any real intention of doing that which the service of the Church supposes: had it not been so, I had been oftener at Church, more devout when there, and more fearful of ever neglecting it.

But the thing that now surprises me above all wonders is this, that I never had so much as a general intention of living up to the piety of the Gospel. This never so much as entered into my head or my heart. I never once in my life considered whether I was living as the laws of religion direct, or whether my way of life was such, as would procure me the mercy of God at this hour.

And can it be thought that I have kept the Gospel terms of salvation, without ever so much as intending, in any serious and deliberate manner, either to know them, or keep them? Can it be thought that I have pleased God with such a life as He requires, though I have lived without ever considering what He requires, or how much I have performed? How easy a thing would salvation be, if it could fall into my careless hands, who have never had so much serious thought about it, as about any one common bargain that I have made!

In the business of life I have used prudence and reflection. I have done everything by rules and methods. I have been glad to converse with men of experience and judgment, to find out the reasons why some fail and others succeed in any business. I have taken no step in trade but with great care and caution, considering every advantage or danger that attended it. I have always had my eye upon the main end of business, and have studied all the ways and means of being a gainer by all that I undertook.

But what is the reason that I have brought none of these tempers to religion? What is the reason that I, who have so often talked of the necessity of rules, and methods, and diligence, in worldly business, have all this while never once thought of any rules, or methods, or managements, to carry me on in a life of piety?

Do you think anything can astonish and confound a dying man like this? What pain do you think a man must feel, when his conscience lays all this folly to his charge, when it shall show him how regular, exact, and wise he has been in small matters, that are passed away like a dream, and how stupid and senseless he has lived, without any reflection, without any rules, in things of such eternal moment, as no heart can sufficiently conceive them?

Had I only my frailties and imperfections to lament at this time, I should lie here humbly trusting in the mercies of God. But, alas! how can I call a general disregard, and a thorough neglect of all religious improvement, a frailty or imperfection, when it was as much in my power to have been exact, and careful, and diligent in a course of piety, as in the business of my trade?

I could have called in as many helps, have practiced as many rules, and been taught as many certain methods of holy living, as of thriving in my shop, had I but so intended, and desired it.

Oh, my friends! a careless life, unconcerned and unattentive to the duties of religion, is so without all excuse, so unworthy of the mercy of God, such a shame to the sense and reason of our minds, that I can hardly conceive a greater punishment, than for a man to be thrown into the state that I am in, to reflect upon it.

Penitens was here going on, but had his mouth stopped by a convulsion, which never suffered him to speak any more. He lay convulsed about twelve hours, and then gave up the ghost.

Now if every reader would imagine this Penitens to have been some particular acquaintance or relation of his, and fancy that he saw and heard all that is here described; that he stood by his bedside when his poor friend lay in such distress and agony, lamenting the folly of his past life, it would, in all probability, teach him such wisdom as never entered into his heart before. If to this he should consider how often he himself might have been surprised in the same state of negligence, and made an example to the rest of the world, this double reflection, both upon the distress of his friend, and the goodness of that God, who had preserved him from it, would in all likelihood soften his heart into holy tempers, and make him turn the remainder of his life into a regular course of piety.

This therefore being so useful a meditation, I shall here leave the reader, as I hope, seriously engaged in it.

TWO LETTERS ON DEATH | *WILLIAM JAMES*

BOLTON ST., LONDON, DECEMBER 14, 1882

Darling Old Father—Two letters, one from my Alice last night, and one from Aunt Kate to Harry just now, have somewhat dispelled the mystery in which the telegrams left your condition; and although their news is several days earlier than the telegrams, I am free to suppose that the latter report only an aggravation of the symptoms the letters describe. It is far more agreeable to think of this than of some dreadful unknown and sudden malady.

We have been so long accustomed to the hypothesis of your being taken away from us, especially during the past ten months, that the thought that this may be your last illness conveys no very sudden shock. You are old enough, you've given your message to the world in many ways and will not be forgotten; you are here left alone, and on the other side, let us hope and pray, dear, dear old Mother is waiting for you to join her. If you go, it will not be an inharmonious thing. Only, if you are still in possession of your normal consciousness, I should like to see you once again before we part. I stayed here only in obedience to the last telegram, and am waiting now for Harry—who knows the exact state of my mind, and who will know yours—to telegraph again what I shall do. Meanwhile, my blessed old Father, I scribble this line (which may reach you though I should come too late), just to tell you how full of the tenderest memories and feelings about you my heart has for the last few days been filled. In that mysterious gulf of the past into which the present soon will fall and go back and back, yours is still for me the central figure. All my intellectual life I derive from you; and though we have often seemed at odds in the expression thereof, I'm sure there's a harmony somewhere, and that our strivings will combine. What my debt to you is goes beyond all my power of esti-mating—so early, so penetrating and so constant has been the influence. You need be in no anxiety about your literary remains. I will see them well taken care of, and that your words shall not suffer for being concealed. At Paris I heard that Milsand, whose name you may remember in the "Revue des Deux Mondes" and elsewhere, was an admirer of the "Secret of Swedenborg," and Hodgson told me your last book has deeply impressed him. So will it be; especially, I think, if a collection of *extracts* from your various writings were published, after the manner of the extracts from Carlyle, Ruskin, & Co. I have long thought such a volume would be the best monument to you. As for us; we shall live on each in his way—feeling

From William James, *Letters* (Boston: Little, Brown & Company, 1920). Permission to reprint granted by Paul R. Reynolds & Son, 599 Fifth Avenue, New York 17, N. Y.

somewhat unprotected, old as we are, for the absence of the parental bosoms as a refuge, but holding fast together in that common sacred memory. We will stand by each other and by Alice, try to transmit the torch in our offspring as you did in us, and when the time comes for being gathered in, I pray we may, if not all, some at least, be as ripe as you. As for myself, I know what trouble I've given you at various times through my peculiarities; and as my own boys grow up, I shall learn more and more of the kind of trial you had to overcome in superintending the development of a creature different from yourself, for whom you felt responsible. I say this merely to show how my *sympathy* with you is likely to grow much livelier, rather than to fade—and not for the sake of regrets. As for the other side, and Mother, and our all possibly meeting, I *can't* say anything. More than ever at this moment do I feel that if that *were* true, all would be solved and justified. And it comes strangely over me in bidding you good-bye how a life is but a day and expresses mainly but a single note. It is so much like the act of bidding an ordinary good-night. Good-night, my sacred old Father! If I don't see you again—Farewell! a blessed farewell! Your

WILLIAM

CHOCORUA, N.H., JULY 6, 1891

Dearest Alice,— ... Of course [this medical verdict on your case may mean] as all men know, a finite length of days; and then, good-bye to neurasthenia and neuralgia and headache, and weariness and palpitation and disgust all at one stroke—I should think you would be reconciled to the prospect will all its pluses and minuses! I know you've never cared for life, and to me, now at the age of nearly fifty, life and death seem singularly close together in all of us—and life a mere farce of frustration in all, so far as the realization of the innermost ideals go to which we are made respectively capable of feeling an affinity and responding. Your frustrations are only rather more flagrant than the rule; and you've been saved many forms of self-dissatisfaction and misery which appertain to such a multiplication of responsible relations to different people as I, for instance, have got into. Your fortitude, good spirits and unsentimentality have been simply unexampled in the midst of your physical woes; when you're relieved from your post, just *that* bright note will remain behind, together with the inscrutable and mysterious character of the doom of nervous weakness which has chained you down for all these years. As for that, there's more in it than has ever been told to so-called science. These inhibitions, these split-up selves, all these new facts that are gradually coming to light about our organization, these enlargements of the self in trance, etc., are bringing me to turn for light in the direction of all sorts of despised spiritualistic and unscientific ideas. Father would find in me today a much more receptive listener—all *that* philosophy has got to be brought in. And what a queer

THOUGHTS ON LIFE AND DEATH

contradiction comes to the ordinary scientific argument against immortality (based on body being mind's condition and mind going *out* when body is gone), when one must believe (as now, in these neurotic cases) that some infernality in the body *prevents* really existing parts of the mind from coming to their effective rights at all, suppresses them, and blots them out from participation in this world's experiences, although they are *there* all the time. When that which is *you* passes out of the body, I am sure that there will be an explosion of liberated force and life till then eclipsed and kept down. I can hardly imagine *your* transition without a great oscillation of both "worlds" as they regain their new equilibrium after the change! Everyone will feel the shock, but you yourself will be more surprised than anybody else.

It may seem odd for me to talk to you in this cool way about your end; but, my dear little sister, if one has things present to one's mind, and I know they are present enough to *your* mind, why not speak them out? I am sure you appreciate that best. How many times I have thought, in the past year, when my days were so full of strong and varied impression and activities, of the long unchanging hours in bed which those days stood for with you, and wondered how you bore the slow-paced monotony at all, as you did! You can't tell how I've pitied you. But you *shall* come to your rights ere long. Meanwhile take things gently. Look for the little good in each day as if life were to last a hundred years. Above all things, save yourself from bodily pain, if it can be done. You've had too much of that. Take all the morphia (or other forms of opium if that disagrees) you want, and don't be afraid of becoming an opium-drunkard. What was opium created for except for such times as this? Beg the good Katherine (to whom *our* debt can never be extinguished) to write me a line every week, just to keep the currents flowing, and so farewell until I write again. Your ever loving,

w.j.

THOUGHTS ON DEATH AND LIFE | WILLIAM ERNEST HOCKING

INCREDULITY TOWARD DEATH

Man is the only animal that contemplates death, and also the only animal that shows any sign of doubt of its finality. This does not mean that he doubts it as a future fact. He accepts his own death, with that of others, as inevitable, plans for it, provides for the time when he shall be out of the picture. Yet, not less today than formerly, he confronts this fact with a certain incredulity regarding the scope of its destruction.

From William Ernest Hocking, *Thoughts on Death and Life* (New York, Harper and Row, Publishers, 1937). Copyright, 1937, by William Ernest Hocking.

This incredulity is due partly but not wholly to his wishes. It is first of all a phase of the general suspicion with which all obvious judgments about human destiny come to be regarded: the philosopher who offers the plain and primary facts presented in sensation and perception as also the final facts seems to the plain man the truly credulous person.

And in the special article of death, he has from his own self-consciousness an item which proves nothing, but which intimates a possibility. As a witness of death, now and then the death of a friend, he finds in himself a double response, not a single one: he is defeated in the most signal manner by the physical forces out of which human life emerges—he appreciates this defeat; and it is just then, when the evidence is most complete, that he experiences a vague and hesitant resurgence of confidence. It is as if that defeat were the experience necessary to remind him of something in himself which his every-day self-awareness overlooks, something which at one point breaks through the closed frame of "nature," holds its own in independence of what happens within "nature," and which might conceivably jut out immune beyond the catastrophe of death. In this contradictory eddy of emotion which psychologists well understand—if analogies constitute understanding—the scientific conscience is prone to see perversity. The common man however protests that he is not being led by his emotion; that his emotion is rather a result than a cause; that he has been admitted to a momentary glimpse of objective fact in the structure of things; and that it is this fact which justifies him in ascribing to his wishes in this region a modest evidential value.

So far as wish enters into the situation, it is clear that the wish is not primarily for himself. It takes the form of a demand that someone else, whose death has been witnessed, shall not have perished from the universe. Attachments have been broken off, the emotional habits of life have been thwarted, but the protest is not leveled against this personal pain. It is leveled against the destruction of something admirable. It has little or nothing in common with the demand found by Kant in human conscience, calling for endless time in which this moral self may become perfect! On the contrary, it is a cry that life *has produced* the perfect being, beloved by me, and has thrown it away. I care enough for that appearance to carve it into imperishable stone, yet nature lets the living original perish! It is a protest which moves far beyond personal suffering and expresses outrage at an objective unfitness.

Thus the notion of survival arises far more as a claim of right than as a personal wish. It is based less on the law of individual duty than on the right of affection and on esthetic justice. It is conceived as the obligation of the universe to us before it is our duty to the universe.

The interest in survival has another noteworthy peculiarity. Most desires are desires for specific objects. This desire is not for an object, but for a subject. It contemplates in the first instance, not the satisfaction of any wish, but the continuance of wishing and of the wisher.

In this respect it is like the will to live, which has no definite object of pursuit, but merely drives toward the maintenance of the consciousness of objects-in-general, and is therefore sometimes put down by psychologists as a piece of mythology. But the fact is there: the extraordinary concern which men commonly show in mere being-alive, regardless of whether the actual contents of experience are pleasant or unpleasant. Surgeons now recognize that beside the dread of pain, which anesthesia was invoked to allay, and the further dread of the knife, which anesthesia can partially displace, there is a distinct dread of anesthesia itself, a dread of being put out of the reach of one's aliveness, which in some persons is strong enough to lead them to prefer the undimmed pain of an operation. It is a paradoxical interest in consciousness—a distinction which has its own scientific value.

Is this empty interest irrational? It may seem a vestige of unintelligent animal tenacity-of-life; yet we reflect that unless there are subjects and knowers in the world, there are either no values at all, or else no takers for such values as might be conceived to exist. We might imagine, as among the possible worlds, one particularly hard world in which every particular human wish up to the present moment has been disappointed; yet that world, taken in its entire sweep, need be neither hopeless nor meaningless. But a world devoid of conscious subjects is necessarily a meaningless world. An interest in the survival of conscious subjects, merely in their capacity as necessary conditions for conserving the meaning of things, may well be an instinctive sign of a deeper rationality.

So far, I am concerned merely to point out some of the motives of the belief in survival of death, and to clear our minds of the prevalent but absurd notion that it is based on wishes alone or on wishes essentially selfish.

But we ought also to note that incredulity toward death is only partial; and that notions of survival, reinforced by crowd consciousness and enshrined in the bold assertions of religion, are in most persons only half-sure of themselves, and therefore subject to an alternate Yes and No.

The early men who first conceived survival lost the courage of their affections, and dampened down their idea of the surviving spirit into the melancholy picture of a ghost. And later men, conspiring to preserve intact the perishing memories of the dead, substituted for the flickering medium of remembrance the assumed stabilities of wood, stone, bronze. The physical monument appeared a safer basis of endurance than the mental fact upon its own ground. It is no small part of the pathos of the mortuary customs of all religions—this mute element of doubt which infects the heart of faith, and makes the Christian cemetery a vast invocation of matter to support the hestitant certainties of the immaterial.

The natural attitude toward death remains thus double and antithetical. At one moment we say, Death is an appearance and not an end. At the next, Death is real and final, it is fantastic to think otherwise. No doctrine of survival in any case escapes the universal fact of death, nor the suffering that goes with it: these remain the data of every argument.

POSITIVE MEANINGS OF DEATH

If there is to be any chance of seeing beyond death, we must first be able to see death as it is. And to see death truly, we must recognize what meaning it has both for the race and for the individual who dies.

It is customary to look upon death as unmixed evil, perhaps the severest of evils. Pessimists have taken it as their crowning argument, forgetting that if life is an evil, death which is only the expunging of life must be a good. But if life is a good, as for common consciousness it is, and if in death the self comes to nothing and remains forever nothing for itself, then death must be the major calamity. And if the final state of things gives us the lasting sum of their values, we can hardly avoid the reflection of Tolstoi, that an ultimate annihilation sends its shadow backward and cancels the worth of every present achievement. Religion reflects the universal feeling of the evil of death when it calls it the wages of sin.

But if death is the price of anything, biological death, it is the price not of sin but of love. For if men by way of love are to beget new generations of men continually, the old must pass. The world-room is finite; without perennial death there could be no perennial appearance of childhood. Without childhood, love which is transmission, and whose greatest joy is the handing-on of life, would be choked in its beginnings. Love is the distant acceptance and celebration of one's own transiency. And death, when it comes, should be the glad remembrance and celebration of love.

For the race, death means flexibility in the changes of history. Death renders it unnecessary to be forever educating old men to new ways; for as the old men pass, their rigid formulae pass with them. A suit of armor cast in long pieces—even flexible pieces—is an enemy to agility; but made of tiny flakes or links—even if each one is inflexible—it lends itself to all the supple bending of the body. Were Adam, Noah, Socrates, Confucius still among us, how we would weary of the daily rumor of their views upon the affairs of the moment: would not a certain sense of fair play bring about a conspiracy to ignore them, so that contemporary voices might sound out with due sonority and weight? If there were no natural death, society might well be driven to institute some form of artificial death, such as an honorable ostracism, lest the cumulative weight of great authority hold all new-arriving tongues locked in deference and thwart their arrival at maturity through the exercise of responsible opinion.

It is not merely that the old becomes static—that need not be the case—but they frequently become wise and prudent. And life must progress in part by the imprudence of those who undertake the impossible, not knowing what they do. It is death which insures that the reins shall leave sagacious and experienced hands and come to the unwisdom of youth, with the large probability of new ills but also of a modicum of good otherwise unattainable.

Without death, the inequalities of age alone would become monstrous, and the growing emotional disparity between ancients and beginners insupportable. And so far as there operates in society the rule that to him that hath shall be given, all the geometrically-growing advantages of power and prestige require a natural terminus if they are not to destroy the access of man to man on which society rests. They find this terminus in the democracy of death: a rude mechanical justice, operating without noise, incessantly reduces to common dust all the mounting conquests of personal prowess and distributes their yield to new hands. And if men incline to the opinion that such and such great figure is indispensable, death furnishes the experimental proof that no man is necessary to the race, and so the sanity of the species, always running to the ease and vicarious elevations of hero-worship, is from time to time restored.

Further, the fact that life has a time-limit allows it to have shape and character. Its work can be summed and considered as a whole: it stands for an identifiable something.

Retain Plato in life for two thousand years, growing and producing great works as a Plato must until he parallels the entire history of western thought—for what, then, in our minds could Plato stand, and who could think or write about Plato? Biography is baffled unless a life, limited like a work of art, becomes in some sense the song of its own time, having indeed an epoch of its own, and a limited output into the public treasury. It is with the death of an artist that his work first begins to find its valuation and its historic emplacement.

The vessel which contains a life remains plastic and unfinished, until death—having its whole contents—rounds-in its end; then one can speak of the quality of that life and of the shape of that vessel; and these become the meaning to the world of that personal name. Perhaps we may say that the thing we call "individuality" is not a pre-existing fact but rather a possibility until death finishes the definition. Then alone is this person a complete qualitative fact, distinct from every other.

These considerations among many give death a positive value to the world at large as it witnesses the coming and going of its members. Humanity as a procession is better than humanity as a fixture; and flux, even in the sphere of values, appears to have superiority over the ancient category of substance.

But to the individual who dies, or who is to die—what can death mean to him? It is a matter of course that each individual imbibes the general view of death current in his society: if this current view is resigned to his passing, it becomes him as a man to assume the same attitude; and most men successfully do so, partly because the general view comes to them first and with the vastest possible authority, since all but himself can think of his death as the death of an *other*. But to the dier, his own death is a lonely experience which society, unable to enter, is to this extent disqualified to judge. The partial philosophic reconciliation of the social mind to his own disappearance must, while it alleviates, contribute also an added pang, and emphasize the solitude of the event.

We must note that the belief in one's own death is an acquired and usually a late belief, not at all a native one. The immediate feeling of life touches no limit either of beginning or end: to be alive is to expect that each next moment will be followed by another. Consciousness is not a targeted attention to instantly present data alone; it is also a reaching forward and backward in time, relating what is to what was and to what is coming. And the logic of this character of consciousness is apparent: since it can only exist as time-spinning in this way, a moment which had no next moment would not be a conscious moment. Hence a last moment of consciousness (as well as a first moment) is logically impossible. Neither terminus of life can be experienced; and neither can be realized in imagination. Hence the belief which every mature man acquires that his own death will come, is an intellectual adoption, not an intuitive faith.

This situation explains something of that incredulity which we first remarked, and which continues to attend one's thought of his own death, even if it is banished from the general thought of human destiny. But the common mortality of man must eventually come home to every Socrates. And with the first shock of the deduction, which has the force of a painful discovery, that I, too, shall die, there comes a stern practical consequence—a tendency to curb by farther-reaching purposes and to deal anxiously with time as with an infinitely precious because absolutely limited quantity.

Here one finds the first positive value of his own death. For it is only through this reflection that one realizes the nature of time.

To have endless time to squander on each task leaves one a stranger to the instancy of the moment—its once-onlyness, its *Einmaligkeit!* To perceive that the number of available "nows" is finite and that no "now" recurs is to know what temporal quality is, irreversible, undetainable, inexorable. The "present" assumes an office—it becomes recognized as the invisible portal through which Destiny enters, and silently, under my hands takes on unalterable shapes. I begin to consider a certain time-span as the locus of my life: I become identified with that era; it is, in one sense, a quantum which I own. The future is always the region of possibility; but now that a boundary is drawn at its outer limit, it has the added character of "opportunity," an opportunity which is single and unique. Of this self, there will be no more and no other than what this finite time shall in fact contain. Now for the first time I truly *enter into time;* and this sober arrival, the true date of my human maturity, is a stage of being which, once experienced, I could not willingly forgo.

For human maturity, bringing with it the pervasive reconstruction of all purposes, by the recognition of *limit,* is a notable advance in self-knowledge. Still, such acceptance of death is hardly the same as a reconciliation with death. One continues to think and hope impossible things about prolonging life, or of transposing its unfinished activities to another sphere. But in due time one perceives another aspect of the situation—namely, that living tends to produce the mental conditions for its own closing.

We hear of the biological life-cycle, the maturing and the running-down of the body, the accompanying loss of mental savor and enterprise. We take it for granted that in this decline it is the physical failure which slowly inflicts itself upon the mind, so that death actually begins long before it is consummated, solely because the body has passed its zenith. Why does it not occur to us that there is also a mental life-cycle whereby, even without the aid of the body, a welcome is prepared for death?

Consider this: that living, for a human being, is a series of decisions; and that each decision has the effect of rendering actual what was previously a mere possibility, one among many. Before I decide, my field of possibility has a certain generality and freedom; when I have acted, one possibility is, as we say, "realized," the others are abandoned and thus in effect destroyed. And this one which is realized is pinned down, dated, and entangled with all the circumstances of its particular time and place. So long as I merely wish to eat, I remain free as to what I eat and where; but if I am to continue in existence I must abandon this freedom and come to the actual decision to eat: I must settle on a place and an hour and commit myself to the food then and there available and all its associations. My best foresight is incomplete, so that in choosing I perforce accept much that I have not chosen. In brief, decision must traffic with the facts at hand, and in so doing take *their* color, *their* manner, *their* moment: decision descends into a world of irrelevant particulars, is compromised with a measure of irrationality, and without this cannot touch the ground of concrete existence.

There are persons who keenly feel and resent this stain involved in decision, this acceptance of arbitrary datedness is one's purpose, this descent into irrationality. They are pained by the necessity of decision, scrutinize all their attachments, defer commitment, remain aloof from party-belonging, from institutions, even from friendships, since "friends must descend to meet." But to remain aloof is to die before one begins to live. There is no choice but no immerse oneself in the stream of history, accept one's time-location, breathe-in the contaminations of tradition, become defined as the man of this issue, this party, this emergency.

The mind is at home with its ideas, especially with the ideal possibilites it has built out of the material of imagination; as imaginative, they are "figments"; but as containing the ingredients of value, they claim loyalty as well as desire. But living is a continuous marriage of idea with fact, and like every bridal, on one hand it fulfills one's destiny and on the other limits one's infinitude. Hence it is that mingling with all one's attachments there arises a factor of detachment, a growing tide of criticism of those accidental and irrelevant traits which, accepted with each decision, accumulate as a sediment in self-consciousness. And with this, as the passage of time renders it sensible of its own purport, there arises an impulse to revert to the original wholeness and freedom. One stands less and less under the spell of the excited emphases, the eloquent self-proclaimed importances of the current world, or one adopts the illusion of momentousness in the passing show with a touch of will, as an habitué of the drama. New enterprises attract but fall short of conviction; familiar sayings stir familiar feelings but without dominating the will; a broadening sympathy dilutes the energies of efficiency: the scale of one's values takes its proportion increasingly from moods of serenity, less and less from the enthusiasms and pugnacities of the arena. And death thereby acquires yet a new meaning.

For death begins to mean freedom from the acquired load and burden of the irrational. *This* self, scarred, marked, identified, dated, need not live forever. Coming as a release and as forgiveness for the untruth of the pragmatic personality, death appears with a fitness, a necessity, even a beauty of its own. In this way, living generates in the mind, as well as in the body, a certain willingness to die.

In point of fact, these tempers characteristic of natural age are to some extent always present. For the capacity to regard my particular life as a special object of thought, and so as something separate from the self that judges it—something to be prized but also estimated, criticized and for due cause renounced—this is the special mark of humanity.

I am not altogether free in any action (young or old) so long as I am dominated by an inescapable will to live. Under the spell of that instinct, life appears precious above all things, and no good however great could justify its sacrifice: for when consciousness is gone, there is nothing. As I think of it, I become obsessed by the necessity of living, which means holding to the life I have with a desperate tenacity: and the ordinary risks which men take gladly—the risks of soldier, miner, aviator, traveler, nay, of the common deeds of eating, conversing, losing one's guard in sleep, become forms of madness.

As contrasted with such rational—and craven—fascination with living, the willingness to die appears as a necessary condition of normal life, and a well-considered acceptance of death as a new stage of freedom. The power of suicide—whether the act itself be base or noble, whether it be direct, or the indirect suicide of a Socrates or a Jesus, of men who live too dangerously for natural death—is an exalted power. Property is not mine until I can renounce it.

This type of freedom is peculiarly marked in our own day; and though it disguises itself under the mask of an ironic humor which refuses to take too seriously the only thing of serious import to oneself, it is one sign of the inner greatness of this age. It has been a condition without which the best advances of our science, medicine, technology could hardly have occurred. Tagore, in rebuking the notion that the civilization of the West is "materialistic" as compared with the "spiritual" quality of the Orient, has well recorded this quality underlying our technological advance:

> When the aeroplane rises into the sky, we may marvel at it as the acme of mechanical perfection. But it is more than this: it is a victory of the spirit. For it was not until, in the West, man had overcome the fear of death that he could master the art of flying—the art of the gods!

Through death, then, life becomes a surveyable object, distinct from myself, which I can on occasion and with good will put away. And this may be the beginning of seeing beyond death. But whether this is truth or fancy cannot be judged until we attend to the logical analysis which underlies our ideas of life and death.

THE ECONOMY OF STYLE II: TWO STORIES

ALTHOUGH ALL WRITERS OF QUALITY pay conscious attention to style, to their literary economy, the writer of imaginative literature is particularly concerned to achieve an artful management of words. It is not hard to understand why that is so, for the poet, the novelist, the writer of short stories speaks his truth not directly but through an intermediary—the characters, the plot, the structure, the imagery of his chosen literary form. He deliberately uses illusion to reveal reality, and this indirection makes necessary the subtlest calculation with words. The two modern short stories printed here show clearly how the principles of economy of two authors are related to the effects they chose to create from roughly similar situations. James Joyce (1882-1941) is famous especially for his two novels, Ulysses and Finnegans Wake, as the most daring and the most skilled experimenter in prose fiction of the century. "Clay" comes from a nearly collection of stories about the people of his native Dublin. The American Southerner, Wilbur Daniel Steele (1886-   ), has been a prolific writer of psychological short stories and of novels remarkable for their analysis of character.

CLAY | *JAMES JOYCE*

The matron had given her leave to go out as soon as the women's tea was over and Maria looked forward to her evening out. The kitchen was spick and span: the cook said you could see yourself in the big copper boilers. The fire was nice and bright and on one of the side-tables were four very big barmbracks. These barmbracks seemed uncut; but if you went closer you would see that they had been cut into long thick even slices and were ready to be handed round at tea. Maria had cut them herself.

Maria was a very, very small person indeed but she had a very long nose and a very long chin. She talked a little through her nose, always soothingly: *"Yes, my dear,"* and *"No, my dear,"* She was always sent for when the women quarreled over their tubs and always succeeded in making peace. One day the matron had said to her:

"Maria, you are a veritable peace-maker!"

And the sub-matron and two of the Board ladies had heard the compliment. And Ginger Mooney was always saying what she wouldn't do to the dummy who had charge of the irons if it wasn't for Maria. Everyone was so fond of Maria.

The women would have their tea at six o'clock and she would be able to get away before seven. From Ballsbridge to the Pillar, twenty minutes; from the Pillar to Drumcondra, twenty minutes; and twenty minutes to buy the things. She would be there before eight. She took out her purse with the silver clasps and read again the words *A Present from Belfast*. She was very fond of that purse because Joe had brought it to her five years before when he and Alphy had gone to Belfast on a Whit-Monday trip. In the purse were two half-crowns and some coppers. She would have five shillings clear after paying tram fare. What a nice evening they would have, all the children singing! Only she hoped that Joe wouldn't come in drunk. He was so different when he took any drink.

Often he had wanted her to go and live with them; but she would have felt herself in the way (though Joe's wife was ever so nice with her) and she had become accustomed to the life of the laundry. Joe was a good fellow. She had nursed him and Alphy too; and Joe used often say:

"Mamma is mamma but Maria is my proper mother."

After the break-up at home the boys had got her that position in the *Dublin by Lamplight* laundry, and she liked it. She used to have such a bad opinion of Protestants but now she thought they were very nice people, a little quiet and serious, but still very nice people to live with. Then

From *Dubliners* in *The Portable James Joyce*. Copyright 1946, 1947 by The Viking Press, Inc.

she had her plants in the conservatory and she liked looking after them. She had lovely ferns and wax-plants and, whenever anyone came to visit her, she always gave the visitor one or two slips from her conservatory. There was one thing she didn't like and that was the tracts on the walls; but the matron was such a nice person to deal with, so genteel.

When the cook told her everything was ready she went into the women's room and began to pull the big bell. In a few minutes the women began to come in by twos and threes, wiping their steaming hands in their petticoats and pulling down the sleeves of their blouses over their red steaming arms. They settled down before their huge mugs which the cook and the dummy filled up with hot tea, already mixed with milk and sugar in huge tin cans. Maria superintended the distribution of the barmbrack and saw that every woman got her four slices. There was a great deal of laughing and joking during the meal. Lizzie Fleming said Maria was sure to get the ring and, though Fleming had said that for so many Hallow Eves, Maria had to laugh and say she didn't want any ring or man either; and when she laughed her gray-green eyes sparkled with disappointed shyness and the tip of her nose nearly met the tip of her chin. Then Ginger Mooney lifted up her mug of tea and proposed Maria's health while all the other women clattered with their mugs on the table, and said she was sorry she hadn't a sup of porter to drink it in. And Maria laughed again till the tip of her nose nearly met the tip of her chin and till her minute body nearly shook itself asunder because she knew that Mooney meant well though, of course, she had the notions of a common woman.

But wasn't Maria glad when the women had finished their tea and the cook and the dummy had begun to clear away the tea-things! She went into her little bedroom and, remembering that the next morning was a mass morning, changed the hand of the alarm from seven to six. Then she took off her working skirt and her house-boots and laid her best skirt out on the bed and her tiny dress-boots beside the foot of the bed. She changed her blouse too and, as she stood before the mirror, she thought of how she used to dress for mass on Sunday morning when she was a young girl; and she looked with quaint affection at the diminutive body which she had so often adorned. In spite of its years she found it a nice tidy little body.

When she got outside the streets were shining with rain and she was glad of her old brown waterproof. The tram was full and she had to sit on the little stool at the end of the car, facing all the people, with her toes barely touching the floor. She arranged in her mind all she was going to do and thought how much better it was to be independent and to have your own money in your pocket. She hoped they would have a nice evening. She was sure they would but she could not help thinking what a pity it was Alphy and Joe were not speaking. They were always falling out now but when they were boys together they used to be the best of friends: but such was life.

She got out of her tram at the Pillar and ferreted her way quickly among the crowds. She went into Downes's cake-shop but the shop was so full of people that it was a long time before she could get herself attended to. She bought a dozen of mixed penny cakes, and at last came out of the shop laden with a big bag. Then she thought what else would she buy: she wanted to buy something really nice. They would be sure to have plenty of apples and nuts. It was hard to know what to buy and all she could think of was cake. She decided to buy some plumcake but Downes's plumcake had not enough almond icing on top of it so she went over to a shop in Henry Street. Here she was a long time in suiting herself and the stylish young lady behind the counter, who was evidently a little annoyed by her, asked her was it wedding-cake she wanted to buy. That made Maria blush and smile at the young lady; but the young lady took it all very seriously and finally cut a thick slice of plumcake, parceled it up and said:

"Two-and-four, please."

She thought she would have to stand in the Drumcondra tram because none of the young men seemed to notice her but an elderly gentleman made room for her. He was a stout gentleman and he wore a brown hard hat; he had a square red face and a grayish mustache. Maria thought he was a colonel-looking gentleman and she reflected how much more polite he was than the young men who simply stared straight before them. The gentleman began to chat with her about Hallow Eve and the rainy weather. He supposed the bag was full of good things for the little ones and said it was only right that the youngsters should enjoy themselves while they were young. Maria agreed with him and favored him with demure nods and hems. He was very nice with her, and when she was getting out at the Canal Bridge she thanked him and bowed, and he bowed to her and raised his hat and smiled agreeably; and while she was going up along the terrace, bending her tiny head under the rain, she thought how easy it was to know a gentleman even when he has a drop taken.

Everybody said: "O, here's Maria!" when she came to Joe's house. Joe was there, having come home from business, and all the children had their Sunday dresses on. There were two big girls in from next door and games were going on. Maria gave the bag of cakes to the eldest boy, Alphy, to divide and Mrs. Donnelly said it was too good of her to bring such a big bag of cakes and made all the children say:

"Thanks, Maria."

But Maria said she had brought something special for papa and mamma, something they would be sure to like, and she began to look for her plum-cake. She tried Downes's bag and then in the pockets of her waterproof and then on the hallstand but nowhere could she find it. Then she asked all the children had any of them eaten it—by mistake, of course—but the children all said no and looked as if they did not like to eat cake if they were to be accused of stealing. Everybody had a solution for the mystery and Mrs. Donnelly said it was plain that Maria had left it behind her in the tram.

Maria, remembering how confused the gentleman with the grayish mustache had made her, colored with shame and vexation and disappointment. At the thought of the failure of her little surprise and of the two and four-pence she had thrown away for nothing she nearly cried outright.

But Joe said it didn't matter and made her sit down by the fire. He was very nice with her. He told her all that went on in his office, repeating for her a smart answer which he had made to the manager. Maria did not understand why Joe laughed so much over the answer he had made but she said that the manager must have been a very overbearing person to deal with. Joe said he wasn't so bad when you knew how to take him, that he was a decent sort so long as you didn't rub him the wrong way. Mrs. Donnelly played the piano for the children and they danced and sang. Then the two next-door girls handed round the nuts. Nobody could find the nutcrackers and Joe was nearly getting cross over it and asked how did they expect Maria to crack nuts without a nutcracker. But Maria said she didn't like nuts and that they weren't to bother about her. Then Joe asked would she take a bottle of stout and Mrs. Donnelly said there was port wine too in the house if she would prefer that. Maria said she would rather they didn't ask her to take anything: but Joe insisted.

So Maria let him have his way and they sat by the fire talking over old times and Maria thought she would put in a good word for Alphy. But Joe cried that God might strike him stone dead if ever he spoke a word to his brother again and Maria said she was sorry she had mentioned the matter. Mrs. Donnelly told her husband it was a great shame for him to speak that way of his own flesh and blood but Joe said that Alphy was no brother of his and there was nearly being a row on the head of it. But Joe said he would not lose his temper on account of the night it was and asked his wife to open some more stout. The two next-door girls had arranged some Hallow Eve games and soon everything was merry again. Maria was delighted to see the children so merry and Joe and his wife in such good spirits. The next-door girls put some saucers on the table and then led the children up to the table, blindfold. One got the prayer-book and the other three got the water; and when one of the next-door girls got the ring Mrs. Donnelly shook her finger at the blushing girls as much as to say: *O, I know all about it!* They insisted then on blindfolding Maria and leading her up to the table to see what she would get; and, while they were putting on the bandage, Maria laughed and laughed again till the tip of her nose nearly met the tip of her chin.

They led her up to the table amid laughing and joking and she put her hand out in the air as she was told to do. She moved her hand about here and there in the air and descended on one of the saucers. She felt a soft wet substance with her fingers and was surprised that nobody spoke or took off her bandage. There was a pause for a few seconds; and then a great deal of scuffling and whispering. Somebody said something about the garden, and at last Mrs. Donnelly said something very cross to one of the next-door girls and told her to throw it out at once: that was no play. Maria understood that it was wrong that time and so she had to do it over again: and this time she got the prayer-book.

After that Mrs. Donnelly played Miss McCloud's Reel for the children and Joe made Maria take a glass of wine. Soon they were all quite merry again and Mrs. Donnelly said Maria would enter a convent before the year was out because she got the prayer-book. Maria had never seen Joe so nice to her as he was that night, so full of pleasant talk and reminiscences. She said they were all very good to her.

At last the children grew tired and sleepy and Joe asked Maria would she not sing some little song before she went, one of the old songs. Mrs. Donnelly said: *"Do, please, Maria!"* and so Maria had to get up and stand beside the piano. Mrs. Donnelly bade the children be quiet and listen to Maria's song. Then she played the prelude and said *"Now Maria!"* and Maria, blushing very much, began to sing in a tiny quavering voice. She sang *I Dreamt that I Dwelt,* and when she came to the second verse she sang again:

> *I dreamt that I dwelt in marble halls*
> *With vassals and serfs at my side*
> *And of all who assembled within those walls*
> *That I was the hope and the pride.*
>
> *I had riches too great to count, could boast*
> *Of a high ancestral name,*
> *But I also dreamt, which pleased me most,*
> *That you loved me still the same.*

But no one tried to show her her mistake; and when she had ended her song Joe was very much moved. He said that there was no time like the long ago and no music for him like poor old Balfe, whatever other people might say; and his eyes filled up so much with tears that he could not find what he was looking for and in the end he had to ask his wife to tell him where the corkscrew was.

HOW BEAUTIFUL WITH SHOES | WILBUR DANIEL STEELE

By the time the milking was finished, the sow, which had farrowed the past week, was making such a row that the girl spilled a pint of the warm milk down the trough-lead to quiet the animal before taking the pail to the well-house. Then in the quiet she heard a sound of hoofs on the bridge,

Reprinted from *Harper's Magazine* (1932) by permission of the author.

where the road crossed the creek a hundred yards below the house, and she set the pail down on the ground beside her bare, barn-soiled feet. She picked it up again. She set it down. It was as if she calculated its weight.

That was what she was doing, as a matter of fact, setting off against its pull toward the well-house the pull of that wagon team in the road, with little more of personal will or wish in the matter than has a wooden weather-vane between two currents in the wind. And as with the vane, so with the wooden girl—the added behest of a whip-lash cracking in the distance was enough; leaving the pail at the barn door, she set off in a deliberate, docile beeline through the cow-yard, over the fence, and down in a diagonal across the farm's one tilled field toward the willow brake that walled the road at the dip. And once under way, though her mother came to the kitchen door and called in her high flat voice, "Amarantha, where you goin', Amarantha?" the girl went on apparently unmoved, as though she had been as deaf as the woman in the doorway; indeed, if there was emotion in her it was the purely sensuous one of feeling the clods of the furrows breaking softly between her toes. It was spring time in the mountains.

"Amarantha, why don't you answer me, Amarantha?"

For moments after the girl had disappeared beyond the willows the widow continued to call, unaware through long habit of how absurd it sounded, the name which that strange man her husband had put upon their daughter in one of his moods. Mrs. Doggett had been deaf so long she did not realize that nobody else ever thought of it for the broadfleshed, slow-minded girl, but called her Mary or, even more simply, Mare.

Ruby Herter had stopped his team this side of the bridge, the mules' heads turned into the lane to his father's farm beyond the road. A big-barreled, heavy-limbed fellow with a square, sallow, not unhandsome face, he took out youth in ponderous gestures of masterfulness; it was like him to have cracked his whip above his animals' ears the moment before he pulled them to a halt. When he saw the girl getting over the fence under the willows he tongued the wad of tobacco out of his mouth into his palm, threw it away beyond the road, and drew a sleeve of his jumper across his lips.

"Don't run yourself out o' breath, Mare; I got all night."

"I was comin'." It sounded sullen only because it was matter of fact.

"Well, keep a-comin' and give us a smack." Hunched on the wagon seat, he remained motionless for some time after she had arrived at the hub, and when he stirred it was but to cut a fresh bit of tobacco, as if already he had forgotten why he threw the old one away. Having satisfied his humor, he unbent, climbed down, kissed her passive mouth, and hugged her up to him, roughly and loosely, his hands careless of contours. It was not out of the way; they were used to handling animals, both of them; and it was spring. A slow warmth pervaded the girl, formless, nameless, almost impersonal.

Her betrothed pulled her head back by the braid of her yellow hair. He studied her face, his brows gathered and his chin out.

"Listen, Mare, you wouldn't leave nobody else hug and kiss you, dang you!"

She shook her head, without vehemence or anxiety.

"Who's that?" She hearkened up the road. "Pull your team out," she added, as a Ford came in sight around the bend above the house, driven at speed. "Geddap!" she said to the mules herself.

But the car came to a halt near them, and one of the five men crowded in it called, "Come on, Ruby, climb in. They's a loony loose out o' Dayville Asylum, and they got him trailed over somewheres on Split Ridge and Judge North phoned up to Slosson's store for ever'body come help circle him—come on, hop the runnin'-board!"

Ruby hesitated, an eye on his team.

"Scared, Ruby?" The driver raced his engine. "They say this boy's a killer."

"Mare, take the team in and tell pa." The car was already moving when Ruby jumped in. A moment after it had sounded on the bridge it was out of sight.

"Amarantha, Amarantha, why don't you come, Amarantha?"

Returning from her errand, fifteen minutes later, Mare heard the plaint lifted in the twilight. The sun had dipped behind the back ridge, and though the sky was still bright with day, the dusk began to smoke up out of the plowed field like a ground fog. The girl had returned through it, got the milk, and started toward the well-house before the widow saw her.

"Daughter, seems to me you might!" she expostulated without change of key. "Here's some young man friend o' yourn stopped to say howdy, and I been rackin' my lungs out after you. . . . Put that milk in the cool and come!"

Some young man friend? But there was no good to be got from puzzling. Mare poured the milk in the pan in the dark of the low house over the well, and as she came out, stooping, she saw a figure waiting for her, black in silhouette against the yellowing sky.

"Who are you?" she asked, a native timidity making her sound sulky.

"Amarantha!" the fellow mused. "That poetry." And she knew then that she did not know him.

She walked past, her arms straight down and her eyes front. Strangers always affected her with a kind of muscular terror simply by being strangers. So she gained the kitchen steps, aware by his tread that he followed. There, taking courage at sight of her mother in the doorway, she turned on him, her eyes down at the level of his knees.

"Who are you and what d' y' want?"

He still mused. "Amarantha! Amarantha in Carolina! That makes me happy!"

Mare hazarded one upward look. She saw that he had red hair, brown eyes, and hollows under his cheekbones, and though the green sweater he wore on top of a gray overall was plainly not meant for him, sizes too large as far as girth went, yet he was built so long of limb that his wrists came inches out of the sleeves and made his big hands look even bigger.

Mrs. Doggett complained. "Why don't you introduce us, daughter?"

The girl opened her mouth and closed it again. Her mother, unaware that no sound had come out of it, smiled and nodded evidently taking to the tall, homely fellow and tickled by the way he could not seem to get his eyes off her daughter. But the daughter saw none of it, all her attention centered upon the stranger's hands.

Restless, hard-fleshed, and chap-bitten, they were like a countryman's hands; but the fingers were longer than the ordinary, and slightly spatulate at their ends, and these ends were slowly and continuously at play among themselves.

The girl could not have explained how it came to her to be frightened and at the same time to be calm, for she was inept with words. It was simply that in an animal way she knew animals, knew them in health and ailing, and when they were ailing she knew by instinct, as her father had known, how to move so as not to fret them.

Her mother had gone in to light up; from beside the lampshelf she called back, "If he's aimin' to stay for supper you should've told me, Amarantha, though I guess there's plenty of the side-meat to go 'round, if you'll bring me in a few more turnips and potatoes, though it is late."

At the words the man's cheeks moved in and out. "I'm very hungry," he said.

Mare nodded deliberately. Deliberately, as if her mother could hear her, she said over her shoulder, "I'll go get the potatoes and turnips, ma." While she spoke she was moving, slowly, softly, at first, toward the right of the yard, where the fence gave over into the field. Unluckily her mother spied her through the window.

"Amarantha, where *are* you goin'?"

"I'm goin' to get the potatoes and turnips." She neither raised her voice nor glanced back, but lengthened her stride. "He won't hurt her," she said to herself. "He won't hurt her; it's me, not her," she kept repeating while she got over the fence and down into the shadow that lay more than ever like a fog on the field.

The desire to believe that it actually did hide her, the temptation to break from her rapid but orderly walk grew till she could no longer fight it. She saw the road willows only a dash ahead of her. She ran, her feet floundering among the furrows.

She neither heard nor saw him, but when she realized he was with her she knew he had been with her all the while. She stopped, and he stopped, and so they stood, with the dark open field all around. Glancing sidewise presently, she saw he was no longer looking at her with those strangely importunate brown eyes of his, but had raised them to the crest of the wooded ridge behind her.

By and by, "What does it make you think of?" he asked. And when she made no move to see, "Turn around and look!" he said, and though it was low and almost tender in its tone, she knew enough to turn.

A ray of the sunset hidden in the west struck through the tops of the topmost trees, far and small up there, a thin, bright hem.

"What does it make you think of, Amarantha? . . . Answer!"

"Fire," she made herself say.

"Or blood."

"Or blood, yeh. That's right, or blood." She had heard a Ford going up the road beyond the willows, and her attention was not on what she said.

The man soliloquized. "Fire and blood, both; spare one or the other, and where is beauty, the way the world is? It's an awful thing to have to carry, but Christ had it. Christ came with a sword. I love beauty, Amarantha. . . . I say, I love beauty!"

"Yeh, that's right, I hear." What she heard was the car stopping at the house.

"Not prettiness. Prettiness'll have to go with ugliness, because it's only ugliness trigged up. But beauty!" Now again he was looking at her. "Do you know how beautiful you are, Amarantha, 'Amarantha sweet and fair'?" Of a sudden, reaching behind her, he began to unravel the meshes of her hair-braid, the long, flat-tipped fingers at once impatient and infinitely gentle. " 'Braid no more that shining hair!' "

Flat-faced Mare Doggett tried to see around those glowing eyes so near to hers, but wise in her instinct, did not try too hard. "Yeh," she temporized. "I mean, no, I mean."

"Amarantha, I've come a long, long way for you. Will you come away with me now?"

"Yeh—that is—in a minute I will, mister—yeh . . ."

"Because you want to, Amarantha? Because you love me as I love you? Answer!"

"Yeh—sure uh . . . *Ruby!*"

The man tried to run, but there were six against him, coming up out of the dark that lay in the plowed ground. Mare stood where she was while they knocked him down and got a rope around him; after that she walked back toward the house with Ruby and Older Haskins, her father's cousin.

Ruby wiped his brow and felt of his muscles. "Gees, you're lucky we come, Mare. We're no more'n past the town, when they come hollerin' he'd broke over this way."

When they came to the fence the girl sat on the rail for a moment and rebraided her hair before she went into the house, where they were making her mother smell ammonia.

Lots of cars were coming. Judge North was coming, somebody said. When Mare heard this she went into her bedroom off the kitchen and got her shoes and put them on. They were brand new two-dollar shoes with cloth tops, and she had only begun to break them in last Sunday; she wished afterwards she had put her stockings on too, for they would have eased the seams. Or else that she had put on the old button pair, even though the soles were worn through.

Judge North arrived. He thought first of taking the loony straight through to Dayville that night, but then decided to keep him in the lock-up at the courthouse till morning and make the drive by day. Older Haskins stayed in, gentling Mrs. Doggett, while Ruby went out to help get the man into the Judge's sedan. Now that she had them on, Mare didn't like to take the shoes off till Older went; it might make him feel small, she thought.

Older Haskins had a lot of facts about the loony.

"His name's Humble Jewett," he told them. "They belong back in Breed County, all them Jewetts, and I don't reckon there's none on 'em that's not a mite unbalanced. He went to college though, worked his way, and he taught somethin' 'rother in some academy-school a spell, till he went off his head all of a sudden and took after folks with an axe. I remember it in the paper at the time. They give out one while how the Principal wasn't goin' to live, and there was others—there was a girl he tried to strangle. That was four-five year back."

Ruby came in guffawing. "Know the only thing they can get 'im to say, Mare? Only God thing he'll say is, 'Amarantha, she's goin' with me.' . . . Mare!"

"Yeah, I know."

The cover of the kettle the girl was handling slid off on the stove with a clatter. A sudden sick wave passed over her. She went out to the back, out into the air. It was not till now she knew how frightened she had been.

Ruby went home, but Older Haskins stayed to supper with them, and helped Mare do the dishes afterward; it was nearly nine when he left. The mother was already in bed, and Mare was about to sit down to get those shoes off her wretched feet at last, when she heard the cow carrying on up the barn, lowing and kicking, and next minute the sow was in it with a horning note. It might be a fox passing by to get at the hen-house, or a weasel. Mare forgot her feet, took a broom-handle used in boiling clothes, opened the back door, and stepped out. Blinking the lamplight from her eyes, she peered up toward the outbuildings, and saw the gable end of the barn standing like a red arrow in the dark, and the top of a butternut tree beyond it drawn in skeleton traceries, and just then a cock crowed.

She went to the right corner of the house and saw where the light came from, ruddy above the woods down the valley. Returning into the house, she bent close to her mother's ear and shouted, "Somethin's a-fire down to the town, looks like," then went out again and up to the barn. "Soh! Soh!" she called in to the animals. She climbed up and stood on the top rail of the cow-pen fence, only to find she could not locate the flame even there.

Ten rods behind the buildings a mass of rock mounted higher than their ridgepoles, a chopped-off buttress of the back ridge, covered with oak scrub and wild grapes and blackberries, whose thorny ropes the girl beat away from her skirt with the broom-handle as she scrambled up in the wine-colored dark. Once at the top, and the brush held aside, she could see the tongue-tip of the conflagration half a mile away at the town. And she knew by the bearing of the two church steeples that it was the building where the lock-up was that was burning.

There is a horror in knowing animals trapped in a fire, no matter what the animals.

"Oh, my God!" Mare said.

A car went down the road. Then there was a horse galloping. That would be Older Haskins probably. People were out at Ruby's father's farm; she could hear their voices raised. There must have been another car up from the other way, for lights wheeled and shouts were exchanged in the neighborhood of the bridge. Next thing she knew, Ruby was at the house below, looking for her probably.

He was telling her mother. Mrs. Doggett was not used to him, so he had to shout even louder than Mare had to.

"What y' reckon he done, the hellion! he broke the door and killed Lew Dyke and set the courthouse afire! . . . Where's Mare?"

Her mother would not know. Mare called. "Here, up the rock here."

She had better go down. Ruby would likely break his bones if he tried to climb the rock in the dark, not knowing the way. But the sight of the fire fascinated her simple spirit, the fearful element, more fearful than ever now, with the news. "Yes, I' comin'," she called sulkily, hearing feet in the brush. "You wait; I'm comin'."

When she turned and saw it was Humble Jewett, right behind her among the branches, she opened her mouth to screech. She was not quick enough. Before a sound came out he got one hand over her face and the other arm around her body.

Mare had always thought she was strong, and the loony looked gangling, yet she was so easy for him that he need not hurt her. He made no haste and little noise as he carried her deeper into the undergrowth. Where the hill began to mount it was harder though. Presently he set her on her feet. He let the hand that had been over her mouth slip down to her throat, where the broad-tipped fingers wound, tender as yearning, weightless as caress.

"I was afraid you'd scream before you knew who 'twas, Amarantha. But I didn't want to hurt your lips, dear heart, your lovely, quiet lips."

It was so dark under the trees she could hardly see him, but she felt his breath on her mouth, near to. But then, instead of kissing her, he said, "No! No!" took from her throat an instant the hand that had held her mouth, kissed its palm, and put it back softly against her skin.

She stood stock still. Her mother's voice was to be heard in the distance, strident and meaningless. More cars were on the road. Nearer, around the rock, there were sounds of tramping and thrashing. Ruby fussed and cursed. He shouted, "Mare, dang you, where are you, Mare?" his voice harsh with uneasy anger. Now, if she aimed to do anything, was the time to do it. But there was neither breath nor power in her windpipe. It was as if those yearning fingers had paralyzed the muscles.

"Come!" The arm he put around her shivered against her shoulder blades. It was anger. "I hate killing. It's a dirty, ugly thing. It makes me sick." He gagged, judging by the sound. But then he ground his teeth. "Come away, my love!"

She found herself moving. Once when she broke a branch underfoot with an instinctive awkwardness he chided her. "Quiet, my heart, else they'll hear!" She made herself heavy. He thought she grew tired and bore more of her weight till he was breathing hard.

Men came up the hill. There must have been a dozen spread out, by the angle of their voices as they kept touch. Always Humble Jewett kept caressing Mare's throat with one hand; all she could do was hang back.

"You're tired and you're frightened," he said at last. "Get down here."

There were twigs in the dark, the overhang of a thicket of some sort. He thrust her in under this, and lay beside her on the bed of groundpine. The hand that was not in love with her throat reached across her; she felt the weight of its forearm on her shoulder and its fingers among the strands of her hair, eagerly, but tenderly, busy. Not once did he stop speaking, no louder than breathing, his lips to her ear.

" 'Amarantha sweet and fair—Ah, braid no more that shining hair . . .' "

Mare had never heard of Lovelace, the poet; she thought the loony was just going on, hardly listened, got little sense. But the cadence of it added to the lethargy of all her flesh.

" 'Like a clew of golden thread—Most excellently ravelléd . . .' "

Voices loudened; feet came tramping; a pair went past not two rods away.

" '. . . Do not then wind up the light—In ribbands, and o'ercloud in night . . .' "

The search went on up the woods, men shouting to one another and beating the brush.

" '. . . But shake your head and scatter day!' I've never loved, Amarantha. They've tried me with prettiness, but prettiness is too cheap, yes, it's too cheap."

Mare was cold, and the coldness made her lazy. All she knew was that he talked on.

"But dogwood blowing in the spring isn't cheap. The earth of a field isn't cheap. Lots of times I've laid down and kissed the earth of a field, Amarantha. That's beauty, and a kiss for beauty." His breath moved up her cheek. He trembled violently. "No, no, not yet!" He got to his knees and pulled her by an arm. "We can go now."

They went back down the slope but at an angle, so that when they came to the level they passed two hundred yards to the north of the house, and crossed the road there. More and more, her walking was like sleepwalking, the feet numb in their shoes. Even where he had to let go of her, crossing the creek on stones, she stepped where he stepped with an obtuse docility. The voices of the searchers on the back ridge were small in distance when they began to climb the face of Coward Hill, on the opposite side of the valley.

There is an old farm on top of Coward Hill, big hayfields as flat as tables. It had been half-past nine when Mare stood on the rock above the barn; it was toward midnight when Humble Jewett put aside the last branches of the woods and led her out on the height, and half a moon had risen. And a wind blew there, tossing the withered tops of last year's grasses, and mists ran with the wind, and ragged shadows with the mists, and mares'-tails of clear moonlight among the shadows, so that now the boles of birches on the forest's edge beyond the fences were but opal blurs and now cut alabaster. It struck so cold against the girl's cold flesh, this wind, that another wind of shivers blew through her, and she put her hands over her face and eyes. But the madman stood with his eyes wide open and his mouth open, drinking the moonlight and the wet wind.

His voice, when he spoke at last, was thick in his throat.

"Get down on your knees." He got down on his and pulled her after. "And pray!"

Once in England a poet sang four lines. Four hundred years have forgotten his name, but they have remembered his lines. The daft man knelt upright, his face raised to the wild scud, his long wrists hanging to the dead grass. He began simply:

> " 'O western wind, when wilt thou blow
> That the small rain down can rain?' "

The Adam's-apple was big in his bent throat. As simply he finished.

> " 'Christ, that my love were in my arms
> And I in my bed again!' "

Mare got up and ran. She ran without aim or feeling in the power of the wind. She told herself again that the mists would hide her from him, as she had done at dusk. And again, seeing that he ran at her shoulder, she knew he had been there all the while, making a race of it, flailing the air with his long arms for joy of play in the cloud of spring, throwing his knees high, leaping the moon-blue waves of the brown grass, shaking his bright hair; and her own hair was a weight behind her, lying level on the wind. Once a shape went bounding ahead of them for instants; she did not realize it was a fox till it was gone.

She never thought of stopping; she never thought anything, except once, "Oh, my God, I wish I had my shoes off!" And what would have been the good in stopping or in turning another way, when it was only play? The man's ecstasy magnified his strength. When a snake-fence came at them he took the top rail in flight, like a college hurdler and, seeing the girl hesitate and half turn as if to flee, he would have releaped it without touching a hand. But then she got a loom of buildings, climbed over quickly, before he should jump, and ran along the lane that ran with the fence.

Mare had never been up there, but she knew that the farm and the house belonged to a man named Wyker, a kind of cousin of Rubin Herter's, a violent, bearded old fellow who lived by himself. She could not believe her luck. When she had run half the distance and Jewett had not grabbed her, doubt grabbed her instead. "Oh, my God, go careful!" she told herself. "Go slow!" she implored herself, and stopped running, to walk.

Here was a misgiving the deeper in that it touched her special knowledge. She had never known an animal so far gone that its instincts failed it; a starving rat will scent the trap sooner than a fed one. Yet, after one glance at the house they approached, Jewett paid it no further attention, but walked with his eyes to the right, where the cloud had blown away, and wooded ridges, like black waves rimmed with silver, ran down away toward the Valley of Virginia.

"I've never lived!" In his single cry there were two things, beatitude and pain.

Between the bigness of the falling world and his eyes the flag of her hair blew. He reached out and let it whip between his fingers. Mare was afraid it would break the spell then, and he would stop looking away and look at the house again. So she did something almost incredible; she spoke.

"It's a pretty—I mean a beautiful view down that-away."

"God Almighty beautiful, to take your breath away. I knew I'd never loved, Belovéd—" He caught a foot under the long end of one of the boards that covered the well and went down heavily on his hand and knees. It seemed to make no difference. "But I never knew I'd never lived," he finished in the same tone of strong rapture, quadruped in the grass, while Mare ran for the door and grabbed the latch.

When the latch would not give, she lost what little sense she had. She pounded with her fists. She cried with all her might: "Oh—hey—in there—hey—in there!" Then Jewett came and took her gently between his hands and drew her away, and then, though she was free, she stood in something like an awful embarrassment while he tried shouting.

"Hey! Friend! whoever you are, wake up and let my love and me come in!"

"No!" wailed the girl.

He grew peremptory. "Hey, wake up!" He tried the latch. He passed to full fury in a wink's time; he cursed, he kicked, he beat the door till Mare thought he would break his hands. Withdrawing, he ran at it with his shoulder; it burst at the latch, went slamming in, and left a black emptiness. His anger dissolved in a big laugh. Turning in time to catch her by a wrist, he cried joyously, "Come, my Sweet One!"

"No! No! Please—aw—listen. There ain't nobody there. He ain't to home. It wouldn't be right to go in anybody's house if they wasn't to home, you know that."

His laugh was blither than ever. He caught her high in his arms.

"I'd do the same by his love and him if 'twas my house, I would." At the threshold he paused and thought, "That is, if she was the true love of his heart forever."

The room was the parlor. Moonlight slanted in at the door, and another shaft came through a window and fell across a sofa, its covering dilapidated, showing its wadding in places. The air was sour, but both of them were farmbred.

"Don't, Amarantha!" His words were pleading in her ear. "Don't be so frightened."

He set her down on the sofa. As his hands let go of her they were shaking.

"But look, I'm frightened too." He knelt on the floor before her, reached out his hands, withdrew them. "See, I'm afraid to touch you." He mused, his eyes rounded. "Of all the ugly things there are, fear is the ugliest. And yet, see, it can be the very beautifulest. That's a strange queer thing."

The wind blew in and out of the room, bringing the thin, little bitter sweetness of new April at night. The moonlight that came across Mare's shoulders fell full upon his face, but hers it left dark, ringed by the aureole of her disordered hair.

"Why do you wear a halo, Love?" He thought about it. "Because you're an angel, is that why?" The swift, untempered logic of the mad led him to dismay. His hands came flying to hers, to make sure they were earth; and he touched her breast, her shoulders, and her hair. Peace returned to his eyes as his fingers twined among the strands.

"'Thy hair is a flock of goats that appear from Gilead . . .'" He spoke like a man dreaming. "'Thy temples are like a piece of pomegranate within thy locks.'"

Mare never knew that he could not see her for the moonlight.

"Do you remember, Love?"

She dared not shake her head under his hand. "Yeh, I reckon," she temporized.

"You remember how I sat at your feet, long ago, like this, and made up a song? And all the poets in all the world have never made one to touch it, have they, Love?"

"Ugh-ugh—never."

" '*How beautiful are thy feet with shoes . . .*' Remember?"

"Oh, my God, what's he sayin' now?" she wailed to herself.

" '*How beautiful are thy feet with shoes, O prince's daughter! the joints of thy thighs are like jewels, the work of the hands of a cunning workman.*

Thy navel is like a round goblet, which wanteth not liquor, thy belly is like an heap of wheat set about with lilies. Thy two breasts are like two young roes that are twins.' "

Mare had not been to church since she was a little girl, when her mother's black dress wore out. "No, no!" she wailed under her breath. "You're awful to say such awful things." She might have shouted it; nothing could have shaken the man now, rapt in the immortal, passionate periods of Solomon's song.

" ' . . . *now also thy breasts shall be as clusters of the vine, and the smell of thy nose like apples.*' "

Hotness touched Mare's face for the first time. "Aw, no, don't talk so!"

" '*And the roof of thy mouth like the best wine for my beloved . . . causing the lips of them that are asleep to speak.*' "

He had ended. His expression changed. Ecstasy gave place to anger, love to hate. And Mare felt the change in the weight of the fingers in her hair.

"What do you mean, I mustn't say it like that?" But it was not to her his fury spoke for he answered himself straightway. "Like poetry, Mr. Jewett; I won't have blasphemy around my school."

"Poetry! My God! if that isn't poetry—if that isn't music—" . . . "It's Bible, Jewett. What you're paid to teach here is *literature.*"

"Doctor Ryeworth, you're the blasphemer and you're an ignorant man." . . . "And your Principal. And I won't have you going around reading sacred allegory like earthly love."

"Ryeworth, you're an old man, a dull man, a dirty man, and you'd be better dead."

Jewett's hand had slid down from Mare's head. "Then I went to put my fingers around his throat, so. But my stomach turned, and I didn't do it. I went to my room. I laughed all the way to my room. I sat in my room at my table and I laughed. I laughed all afternoon and long after dark came. And then, about ten, somebody came and stood beside me in my room."

" 'Wherefore dost thou laugh, son?'

"Then I knew who He was, He was Christ.

" 'I was laughing about that dirty, ignorant, crazy old fool, Lord.'

" 'Wherefore dost thou laugh?'

"I didn't laugh any more. He didn't say any more. I kneeled down, bowed my head.

" 'Thy will be done! Where is he, Lord?'

" 'Over at the girls' dormitory, waiting for Blossom Sinckley.'

"Brassy Blossom, dirty Blossom . . ."

It had come so suddenly it was nearly too late. Mare tore at his hands with hers, tried with all her strength to pull her neck away.

"Filthy Blossom! and him an old filthy man, Blossom! and you'll find him in Hell when you reach there, Blossom . . ."

It was more the nearness of his face than the hurt of his hands that gave her power of fright to choke out three words.

"I—ain't—Blossom!"

Light ran in crooked veins. Through the veins she saw his face bewildered. His hands loosened. One fell down and hung; the other he lifted and put over his eyes, took away again and looked at her.

"Amarantha!" His remorse was fearful to see. "What have I done!" His hands returned to hover over the hurts, ravening with pity, grief and tenderness. Tears fell down his cheeks. And with that, damned desire broke its dam.

"Amarantha, my love, my dove, my beautiful love—"

"And I ain't Amarantha neither, I'm Mary! Mary, that's my name!"

She had no notion what she had done. He was like a crystal crucible that a chemist watches, changing hue in a wink with one adeptly added drop; but hers was not the chemist's eye. All she knew was that she felt light and free of him; all she could see of his face as he stood away above the moonlight were the whites of his eyes.

"Mary!" he muttered. A slight paroxysm shook his frame. So in the transparent crucible desire changed its hue. He retreated farther, stood in the dark by some tall piece of furniture. And still she could see the whites of his eyes.

"Mary! Mary Adorable!" A wonder was in him "Mother of God!"

Mare held her breath. She eyed the door, but it was too far. And already he came back to go on his knees before her, his shoulders so bowed and his face so lifted that it must have cracked his neck, she thought; all she could see on the face was pain.

"Mary Mother, I'm sick to my death. I'm so tired."

She had seen a dog like that, one she had loosed from a trap after it had been there three days, its caught leg half gnawed free. Something about the eyes.

"Mary Mother, take me in your arms . . ."

Once again her muscles tightened. But he made no move.

". . . and give me sleep."

No, they were worse than the dog's eyes.

"Sleep, sleep! why won't they let me sleep? Haven't I done it all yet, Mother? Haven't I washed them yet of all their sins? I've drunk the cup that was given me; is there another? They've mocked me and reviled me, broken my brow with thorns and my hands with nails, and I've forgiven them, for they knew not what they did. Can't I go to sleep now, Mother?"

Mare could not have said why, but now she was more frightened than she had ever been. Her hands lay heavy on her knees, side by side, and she could not take them away when he bowed his head and rested his face upon them.

After a moment he said one thing more. "Take me down gently when you take me from the Tree."

Gradually the weight of his body came against her shins, and he slept.

The moon streak that entered by the eastern window crept north across the floor, thinner and thinner; the one that fell through the southern doorway traveled east and grew fat. For a while Mare's feet pained her terribly and her legs too. She dared not move them, though, and by and by they did not hurt so much.

A dozen times, moving her head slowly on her neck, she canvassed the shadows of the room for a weapon. Each time her eyes came back to a heavy earthenware pitcher on a stand some feet to the left of the sofa. It would have had flowers in it when Wyker's wife was alive; probably it had not been moved from its dust-ring since she died. It would be a long grab, perhaps too long; still, it might be done if she had her hands.

To get her hands from under the sleeper's head was the task she set herself. She pulled first one, then the other, infinitesimally. She waited. Again she tugged a very, very little. The order of his breathing was not disturbed. But at the third trial he stirred.

"Gently! gently!" His own muttering waked him more. With some drowsy instinct of possession he threw one hand across her wrists, pinning them together between thumb and fingers. She kept dead quiet, shut her eyes, lengthened her breathing, as if she too slept.

There came a time when what was pretense grew to be a peril; strange as it was, she had to fight to keep her eyes open. She never knew whether or not she really napped. But something changed in the air, and she was wide awake again. The moonlight was fading on the doorsill, and the light that runs before dawn waxed in the window behind her head.

And then she heard a voice in the distance, lifted in maundering song.

It was old man Wyker coming home after a night, and it was plain he had had some whisky.

Now a new terror laid hold of Mare.

"Shut up, you fool you!" she wanted to shout. "Come quiet, quiet!" She might have chanced it now to throw the sleeper away from her and scramble and run, had his powers of strength and quickness not taken her simple imagination utterly in thrall.

Happily the singing stopped. What had occurred was that the farmer had espied the open door and, even befuddled as he was, wanted to know more about it quietly. He was so quiet that Mare began to fear he had gone away. He had the squirrel-hunter's foot, and the first she knew of him was when she looked and saw his head in the doorway, his hard, soiled, whiskery face half up-side-down with craning.

He had been to the town. Between drinks he had wandered in and out of the night's excitement; had even gone a short distance with one search party himself. Now he took in the situation in the room. He used his forefinger. First he held it to his lips. Next he pointed it with a jabbing motion at the sleeper. Then he tapped his own forehead and described wheels. Lastly, with his whole hand, he made pushing gestures, for Mare to wait. Then he vanished as silently as he had appeared.

The minutes dragged. The light in the east strengthened and turned rosy. Once she thought she heard a board creaking in another part of the house, and looked down sharply to see if the loony stirred. All she could see of his face was a temple with freckles on it and the sharp ridge of a cheekbone, but even from so little she knew how deeply and peacefully he slept. The door darkened. Wyker was there again. In one hand he carried something heavy; with the other he beckoned.

"Come jumpin'!" he said out loud.

Mare went jumping, but her cramped legs threw her down half way to the sill; the rest of the distance she rolled and crawled. Just as she tumbled through the door it seemed as if the world had come to an end above her; two barrels of a shotgun discharged into a room make a noise. Afterwards all she could hear in there was something twisting and bumping on the floor-boards. She got up and ran.

Mare's mother had gone to pieces; neighbor women put her to bed when Mare came home. They wanted to put Mare to bed, but she would not let them. She sat on the edge of her bed in her lean-to bedroom off the kitchen, just as she was, her hair down all over her shoulders and her shoes on, and stared away from them, at a place in the wallpaper.

"Yeh, I'll go myself. Lea' me be!"

The women exchanged quick glances, thinned their lips, and left her be. "God knows," was all they would answer to the questionings of those that had not gone in, "but she's gettin' herself to bed."

When the doctor came though he found her sitting just as she had been, still dressed, her hair down on her shoulders and her shoes on.

"What d' y' want?" she muttered and stared at the place in the wall-paper.

How could Doc Paradise say, when he did not know himself?

"I didn't know if you might be—might be feeling very smart, Mary."

"I'm all right. Lea' me be."

It was a heavy responsibility. Doc shouldered it. "No. it's all right," he said to the men in the road. Ruby Herter stood a little apart, chewing sullenly and looking another way. Doc raised his voice to make certain it carried. "Nope, nothing."

Ruby's ears got red, and he clamped his jaws. He knew he ought to go in and see Mare, but he was not going to do it while everybody hung around waiting to see if he would. A mule tied near him reached out and mouthed his sleeve in idle innocence; he wheeled and banged a fist against the side of the animal's head.

"Well, what d' y' aim to do 'bout it?" he challenged its owner.

He looked at the sun then. It was ten in the morning. "Hell, I got work!" he flared, and set off down the road for home. Doc looked at Judge North, and the Judge started after Ruby. But Ruby shook his head angrily. "Lea' me be!" He went on, and the Judge came back.

It got to be eleven and then noon. People began to say, "Like enough she'd be as thankful if the whole neighborhood wasn't camped here." But none went away.

As a matter of fact they were no bother to the girl. She never saw them. The only move she made was to bend her ankles over and rest her feet on edge; her shoes hurt terribly and her feet knew it, though she did not. She sat all the while staring at that one figure in the wallpaper, and she never saw the figure.

Strange as the night had been, this day was stranger. Fright and physical pain are perishable things once they are gone. But while pain merely dulls and telescopes in memory and remains diluted pain, terror looked back upon has nothing of terror left. A gambling chance taken, at no matter what odds, and won was a sure thing since the world's beginning; perils come through safely were never perilous. But what fright does do in restrospect is this—it heightens each sensuous recollection, like a hard, clear lacquer laid on wood, bringing out the color and grain of it vividly.

Last night Mare had lain stupid with fear on groundpine beneath a bush, loud foot-falls and light whispers confused in her ear. Only now, in her room, did she smell the groundpine.

Only now did the conscious part of her brain begin to make words of the whispering.

"Amarantha," she remembered, *"Amarantha sweet and fair."* That

was as far as she could go for the moment, except that the rhyme with
"fair" was "hair." But then a puzzle, held in abeyance, brought other
words. She wondered what "ravel Ed" could mean. *"Most excellently
ravelléd."* It was left to her mother to bring the end.

They gave up trying to keep her mother out at last. The poor woman's
prostration took the form of fussiness.

"Good gracious, daughter, you look a sight. Them new shoes, half
ruined; ain't your feet *dead?* And look at your hair, all tangled like a
wild one!"

She got a comb.

"Be quiet, daughter; what's ailin' you. Don't shake you head!"

" *'But shake your head and scatter day.'* "

"What you say, Amarantha?" Mrs. Doggett held an ear down.

"Go 'way! Lea' me be!"

Her mother was hurt and left. And Mare ran, as she stared at the
wallpaper.

"Christ, that my love were in my arms . . ."

Mare ran. She ran through a wind white with moonlight and wet
with "the small rain." And the wind she ran through, it ran through her,
and made her shiver as she ran. And the man beside her leaped high
over the waves of the dead grasses and gathered the wind in his arms,
and her hair was heavy and his was tossing, and a little fox ran before
them across the top of the world. And the world spread down around in
waves of black and silver, more immense than she had ever known the
world could be, and more beautiful.

"God Almighty beautiful, to take your breath away!"

Mare wondered, and she was not used to wondering. "Is it only
crazy folks ever run like that and talk that way?"

She no longer ran; she walked; for her breath was gone. And there
was some other reason; some other reason. Oh, yes, it was because her
feet were hurting her. So, at last, and round-about, her shoes had made
contact with her brain.

Bending over the side of the bed, she loosened one of them mechanically.
She pulled it half off. But then she looked down at it sharply, and she
pulled it on again.

"How beautiful . . ."

Color overspread her face in a slow wave.

"How beautiful are thy feet with shoes . . ."

"Is it only crazy folks ever say such things?"

"O prince's daughter!"

"Or call you that?"

By and by there was a knock at the door. It opened, and Ruby
Herter came in.

"Hello, Mare old girl!" His face was red. He scowled and kicked

at the floor. "I'd 'a' been over sooner, except we got a mule down sick."
He looked at his dumb betrothed. "Come on, cheer up, forget it! He
won't scare you no more, not that boy, not what's left o' him. What you
lookin' at, sourface? Ain't you glad to see me?"

Mare quit looking at the wallpaper and looked at the floor.

"Yeh," she said.

"That's more like it, babe." He came and sat beside her; reached down
behind her and gave her a spank. "Come on, give us a kiss, babe!" He
wiped his mouth on his jumper sleeve, a good farmer's sleeve, spotted with
milking. He put his hands on her; he was used to handling animals. "Hey,
you, warm up a little, reckon I'm goin' to do all the lovin'?"

"Ruby, lea' me be!"

"What!"

She was up, twisting. He was up, purple.

"What's ailin' of you, Mare? What you bawlin' about?"

"Nothin'—only go 'way!"

She pushed him to the door and through it with all her strength,
and closed it in his face, and stood with her weight against it, crying,
"Go way! Go 'way! Lea' me be!"

COHERENCE

ONE OF THE MOST *general requirements of good prose is that it show
signs of organization. This demand for order is partly in the interest of
economy, for most readers have a limited amount of time and will not
tolerate a writer who scatters thoughts at random, leaving his audience to do
the hard work of arranging. Another reason that organization is requisite to
clear writing is that the processes of the mature mind are orderly, and expository writing is a symbolic account of human thought and observation. The
connections between ideas are often as important to rational inquiry as the
ideas themselves. A final source of the passion for order is undoubtedly the
human esthetic preference for form over disorder. All art is partly an attempt
to give structure to reality, to push back chaos; and the most humble student-
essay has at least this much of art in it. For these reasons, if for no others,
coherence is a virtue in most writing.*

*It is not, however, easy to attain, as the creaking organizational ma-
chinery of much prose will attest. Coherence involves more than a
sprinkling of "therefores" and "neverthelesses," and more than the imposition of a rigid structure, or a division into, say, seventeen neatly numbered
points. These devices frequently do serve as signposts for a genuinely*

logical paper, but they can also be surface paraphernalia, detached from meaning. Besides, the processes of deductive and inductive logic are only one base for building order. Another type of coherence stems from the relationship of cause and effect. Descriptive writing often gains order from concentration on a single subject (a person or a building, for example), from simple chronology, as in accounts of events, or from the natural organization of a process, say the functioning of a steam engine. Many pieces of fiction, as well as of exposition, obtain coherence through a theme, on which the writer plays variations. Occasionally a writer gives his prose coherence by careful repetition of a key phrase or phrases. An even more subtle type of unity is that which comes not from any logical or temporal relationship among the parts, but from singleness of mood or tone. This list by no means exhausts the possibilities, nor does any one method of attaining coherence appear in isolation from the rest: it is impossible to organize well by simple formula. But this brief summary of kinds of coherence may suggest the complexity of the problem, and the necessity that a writer attend to it.

The authors represented here are diverse, as are their subjects. Matthew Arnold (1822-1888) was an English literary and social critic, virtually a prophet in his own time. John Stuart Mill (1806-1873) and Bertrand Russell (1872-   ) represent two schools of British philosophy, utilitarianism and empiricism, respectively. Virginia Woolf (1882-1941) was a distinguished English novelist, Lytton Strachey (1880-1932) an equally distinguished English biographer. August Krogh (1874-1949) was a Danish biologist who taught at the University of Copenhagen, as well as at other European and American universities.

GIBBON | *LYTTON STRACHEY*

Happiness is the word that immediately rises to the mind at the thought of Edward Gibbon: and happiness in its widest connotation—including good fortune as well as enjoyment. Good fortune, indeed, followed him from the cradle to the grave in the most tactful way possible; occasionally it appeared to fail him; but its absence always turned out to be a blessing in disguise. Out of a family of seven he alone had the luck to survive—but only with difficulty; and the maladies of his childhood opened his mind to the pleasures of study and literature. His mother died; but her place was taken by a devoted aunt, whose care brought him through the dangerous years of adolescence to a vigorous manhood. His misadventures at Oxford saved him from becoming a don. His exile to Lausanne, by giving him a command of the French language, initiated him into European culture, and at the same time enabled him to lay the foundations of his scholarship. His father married again; but his stepmother remained childless and became one of his dearest friends. He fell in love; the match was forbidden; and he escaped the dubious joys of domestic life with the future Madame Necker. While he was allowed to travel on the Continent, it seemed doubtful for some time whether his father would have the resources or the generosity to send him over the Alps into Italy. His fate hung in the balance; but at last his father produced the necessary five hundred pounds and, in the autumn of 1764, Rome saw her historian. His father died at exactly the right moment, and left him exactly the right amount of money. At the age of thirty-three Gibbon found himself his own master, with a fortune just sufficient to support him as an English gentleman of leisure and fashion. For ten years he lived in London, a member of Parliament, a placeman, and a diner-out, and during those ten years he produced the first three volumes of his History. After that he lost his place, failed to obtain another, and, finding his income unequal to his expenses, returned to Lausanne, where he took up his residence in the house of a friend, overlooking the Lake of Geneva. It was the final step in his career, and no less fortunate than all the others. In Lausanne he was rich once more, he was famous, he enjoyed a delightful combination of retirement and society. Before another ten years were out he had completed his History; and in ease, dignity, and absolute satisfaction his work in this world was accomplished.

One sees in such a life an epitome of the blessings of the eighteenth century—the wonderful μηδὲν ἄγαν of that most balmy time—the rich fruit ripening slowly on the sun-warmed wall, and coming inevitably to its delicious perfection. It is difficult to imagine, at any other period in history, such a combination of varied qualities, so beautifully balanced—the profound scholar who was also a brilliant man of the world—the votary of cosmopolitan culture, who never for a moment ceased to be a supremely English "character." The ten years of Gibbon's life in London afford an astonishing spectacle of interacting energies. By what strange power did he succeed in producing a masterpiece of enormous erudition and perfect form, while he was leading the gay life of a man about town, spending his evenings at White's or Boodle's or the Club, attending Parliament, oscillating between his house in Bentinck Street, his country cottage at Hampton Court, and his little establishment at Brighton, spending his summers in Bath or Paris, and even, at odd moments, doing a little work at the Board of Trade, to show that his place was not entirely a sinecure? Such a triumph could only have been achieved by the sweet reasonableness of the eighteenth century. "Monsieur Gibbon n'est point mon homme," said Rousseau. Decidedly! The prophet of the coming age of sentiment and romance could have nothing in common with such a nature. It was not that the historian was a mere frigid observer of the golden mean—far from it. He was full of fire and feeling. His youth had been at moments riotous—night after night he had reeled hallooing down St. James's Street. Old age did not diminish the natural warmth of his affections; the beautiful letter—a model of its kind—written on the death of his aunt, in his fiftieth year, is a proof of it. But the fire and the feeling were controlled and co-ordinated. Boswell was a Rousseau-ite, one of the first of the Romantics, an inveterate sentimentalist, and nothing could be more complete than the contrast between his career and Gibbon's. He, too, achieved a glorious triumph; but it was by dint of the sheer force of native genius asserting itself over the extravagance and disorder of an agitated life—a life which, after a desperate struggle, seemed to end at last in darkness and shipwreck. With Gibbon there was never any struggle: everything came naturally to him—learning and dissipation, industry and indolence, affection and skepticism—in the correct proportion; and he enjoyed himself up to the very end.

To complete the picture one must notice another antithesis: the wit, the genius, the massive intellect, were housed in a physical mold that was ridiculous. A little figure, extraordinarily rotund, met the eye, surmounted by a top-heavy head, with a button nose, planted amid a vast expanse of cheek and ear, and chin upon chin rolling downward. Nor was this appearance only; the odd shape reflected something in the inner man. Mr. Gibbon, it was noticed, was always slightly over-dressed; his favorite wear was flowered velvet. He was a little vain, a little pompous; at the first moment one almost laughed; then one forgot everything under the fascination of that even flow of admirably intelligent, exquisitely turned, and most amusing sentences. Among all his other merits this obviously ludicrous egotism took its place. The astonishing creature was able to make a virtue even of absurdity. Without that touch of nature he would have run the risk of being too much of a good thing; as it was there was no such danger; he was preposterous and a human being.

It is not difficult to envisage the character and figure; what seems strange, and remote, and hard to grasp is the connection between this individual and the decline and fall of the Roman Empire. The paradox, indeed, is so complete as to be almost romantic. At a given moment— October 15, 1764—at a given place—the Capitoline Hill, outside the church of Aracoeli—the impact occurred between the serried centuries of Rome and Edward Gibbon. His life, his work, his fame, his place in the history of civilization, followed from that circumstance. The point of his achievement lay precisely in the extreme improbability of it. The utter incongruity of those combining elements produced the masterpiece—the gigantic ruin of Europe through a thousand years, mirrored in the mind of an eighteenth-century English gentleman.

How was the miracle accomplished? Needless to say, Gibbon was a great artist—one of those rare spirits, with whom a vital and penetrating imagination and a supreme capacity for general conceptions express themselves instinctively in an appropriate form. That the question has ever been not only asked but seriously debated, whether History was an art, is certainly one of the curiosities of human ineptitude. What else can it possibly be? It is obvious that History is not a science: it is obvious that History is not the accumulation of facts, but the relation of them. Only the pedantry of incomplete academic persons could have given birth to such a monstrous supposition. Facts relating to the past, when they are collected without art, are compilations; and compilations, no doubt, may be useful; but they are no more History than butter, eggs, salt and herbs are an omelette. That Gibbon was a great artist, therefore, is implied in the statement that he was a great historian; but what is interesting is the particular nature of his artistry. His whole genius was pre-eminently classical; order, lucidity, balance, precision—the great classical qualities—dominate his work; and his History is chiefly remarkable as one of the supreme monuments of Classic Art in European literature.

"L'ordre est ce qu'il y a de plus rare dans les operations de l'esprit." Gibbon's work is a magnificent illustration of the splendid dictum of Fénelon. He brought order out of the enormous chaos of his subject—a truely stupendous achievement! With characteristic good fortune, indeed, the material with which he had to cope was still not too voluminous to be digested by a single extremely competent mind. In the following century even a Gibbon would have collapsed under the accumulated mass of knowledge at his disposal. As it was, by dint of a superb constructive vision, a serene self-confidence, a very acute judgment, and an astonishing facility in the manipulation of material, he was able to dominate the known facts. To dominate, nothing more; anything else would have been foreign to his purpose. He was a classicist; and his object was not comprehension but illumination. He drove a straight, firm road through the vast unexplored forest of Roman history; his readers could follow with easy pleasure along the wonderful way; they might glance, as far as their eyes could reach, into the entangled recesses on either side of them; but they were not invited to stop, or wander, or camp out, or make friends with the natives; they must be content to look and to pass on.

It is clear that Gibbon's central problem was the one of exclusion; how much, and what, was he to leave out? This was largely a question of scale —always one of the major difficulties in literary composition—and it appears from several passages in the Autobiographies that Gibbon paid particular attention to it. Incidentally, it may be observed that the six Autobiographies were not so much excursions in egotism—though no doubt it is true that Gibbon was not without a certain fondness for what he himself called "the most disgusting of the pronouns"—as exercises on the theme

of scale. Every variety of compression and expansion is visible among those
remarkable pages; but apparently, since the manuscripts were left in an
unfinished state, Gibbon still felt, after the sixth attempt, that he had not
discovered the right solution. Even with the scale of the History he was not
altogether satisfied; the chapters on Christianity, he thought, might, with
further labor, have been considerably reduced. But, even more fundamental
than the element of scale, there was something else that, in reality, conditioned the whole treatment of his material, the whole scope and nature
of his History; and that was the style in which it was written. The style
once fixed, everything else followed. Gibbon was well aware of this. He
wrote his first chapter three times over, his second and third twice; then
at last he was satisfied, and after that he wrote on without a hitch. In
particular the problem of exclusion was solved. Gibbon's style is probably
the most exclusive in literature. By its very nature it bars out a great
multitude of human energies. It makes sympathy impossible, it takes no
cognizance of passion, it turns its back upon religion with a withering
smile. But that was just what was wanted. Classic beauty came instead.
By the penetrating influence of style—automatically, inevitably—lucidity,
balance and precision were everywhere introduced; and the miracle of
order was established over the choas of a thousand years.

Of course, the Romantics raised a protest. "Gibbon's style," said Coleridge, "is detestable; but," he added, "it is not the worst thing about him."
Critics of the later nineteenth century were less consistent. They admired
Gibbon for everything except his style, imagining that his History would
have been much improved if it had been written in some other way; they
did not see that, if it had been written in any other way, it would have
ceased to exist; just as St. Paul's would cease to exist if it were rebuilt in
Gothic. Obsessed by the color and movement of romantic prose, they were
blind to the subtlety, the clarity, the continuous strength of Gibbon's writing. Gibbon could turn a bold phrase with the best of them—"the fat slumbers of the Church," for instance—if he wanted to; but he very rarely
wanted to; such effects would have disturbed the easy, close-knit, homo-
geneous surface of his work. His use of words is, in fact, extremely delicate.
When, describing St. Simeon Stylites on his pillar, he speaks of "this last
and lofty station," he succeeds, with the least possible emphasis, merely by
the combination of those two alliterative epithets with that particular substantive, in making the whole affair ridiculous. One can almost see his
shoulders shrug. The nineteenth century found him pompous; they did not
relish the irony beneath the pomp. He produces some of his most delightful
effects by rhythm alone. In the *Vindication*—a work which deserves to be
better known, for it shows us Gibbon, as one sees him nowhere else,
really letting himself go—there is an admirable example of this. "I still
think," he says, in reply to a criticism by Dr. Randolph, "I still think that
an hundred Bishops, with Athanasius at the head, were as competent judges

of the discipline of the fourth century, as even the Lady Margaret's Professor of Divinity in the University of Oxford." Gibbon's irony, no doubt, is the salt of his work; but, like all irony, it is the product of style. It was not for nothing that he read through every year the *Lettres Provinciales of Pascal*. From this point of view it is interesting to compare him with Voltaire. The irony of the great Frenchman was a flashing sword—extreme, virulent, deadly—a terrific instrument of propaganda. Gibbon uses the weapon with far more delicacy; he carves his enemy "as a dish fit for the Gods"; his mocking is aloof, almost indifferent, and perhaps, in the long run, for that very reason, even more effective.

At every period of his life Gibbon is a pleasant thing to contemplate, but perhaps most pleasant of all in the closing weeks of it, during his last visit to England. He had hurried home from Lausanne to join his friend Lord Sheffield, whose wife had died suddenly, and who, he felt, was in need of his company. The journey was no small proof of his affectionate nature; old age was approaching; he was corpulent, gouty, and accustomed to every comfort; and the war of the French Revolution was raging in the districts through which he had to pass. But he did not hesitate, and after skirting the belligerent armies in his chaise, arrived safely in England. After visiting Lord Sheffield he proceeded to Bath, to stay with his stepmother. The amazing little figure, now almost spherical, bowled along the Bath Road in the highest state of exhilaration. "I am always," he told his friend, "so much delighted and improved with this union of ease and motion, that, were not the expense enormous, I would travel every year some hundred miles, more especially in England." Mrs. Gibbon, a very old lady, but still full of vitality, worshiped her stepson, and the two spent ten days together, talking, almost always *tête-à-tête,* for ten hours a day. Then the historian went off to Althorpe, where he spent a happy morning with Lord Spencer, looking at early editions of Cicero. And so back to London. In London a little trouble arose. A protuberance in the lower part of his person, which, owing to years of characteristic *insouciance,* had grown to extraordinary proportions, required attention; an operation was necessary; but it went off well, and there seemed to be no danger. Once more Mr. Gibbon dined out. Once more he was seen, in his accustomed attitude, with advanced forefinger, addressing the company, and rapping his snuff box at the close of each particularly pointed phrase. But illness came on again—nothing very serious. The great man lay in bed discussing how much longer he would live—he was fifty-six—ten years, twelve years, or perhaps twenty. He ate some chicken and drank three glasses of madeira. Life seemed almost as charming as usual. Next morning, getting out of bed for a necessary moment, "Je suis plus adroit," he said with his odd smile to his French valet. Back in bed again, he muttered something more, a little incoherently, lay back among the pillows, dozed, half-woke, dozed again, and became unconscious—for ever.

THE LANGUAGE OF THE BEES | *AUGUST KROGH*

Karl von Frisch, the Austrian naturalist, began working with bees about 40 years ago when he showed that, contrary to prevalent opinion, these insects are not entirely color-blind. From that beginning, he went on to a lifelong study of the other senses of bees and of many lower animals, especially fish. The experiments to be described here were almost all made after the last war in a small private laboratory that von Frisch maintains at Brunnwinkl in the Austrian Alps.

Von Frisch's early experiments showed that bees must possess some means of communication, because when a rich source of food (he used concentrated sugar solution) is found by one bee, the food is soon visited by numerous other bees from the same hive. To find out how they communicated with one another, von Frisch constructed special hives containing only one honeycomb, which could be exposed to view through a glass plate. Watching through the glass, he discovered that bees returning from a rich source of food perform special movements, which he called dancing, on the vertical surface of the honeycomb. Von Frisch early distinguished between two types of dance: the circling dance (*Rundtanz*) and the wagging dance (*Schwänzeltanz*). In the latter a bee runs a certain distance in a straight line, wagging its abdomen very swiftly from side to side, and then makes a turn. Von Frisch concluded from his early experiments that the circling dance meant nectar and the wagging dance pollen, but this turned out to be an erroneous translation as will presently appear.

In any case, the dance excites the bees. Some of them follow the dancer closely, imitating the movements, and then go out in search of the food indicated. They know what kind of food to seek from the odor of the nectar or pollen, some of which sticks to the body of the bee. By means of some ingenious experiments, von Frisch determined that the odor of the nectar collected by bees, as well as that adhering to their bodies, is important. He designed an arrangement for feeding bees odoriferous nectar so that their body surfaces were kept from contact with it. This kind of feeding was perfectly adequate to guide the other bees. In another experiment, nectar having the odor of phlox was fed to bees as they sat on cyclamen flowers. When the bees had only a short distance to fly back to the hive, some of their fellows would go for cyclamen, but in a long flight the cyclamen odor usually was lost completely, and the bees were guided only by the phlox odor.

The vigor of the dance which guides the bees is determined by the

ease with which the nectar is obtained. When the supply of nectar in a certain kind of flower begins to give out, the bees visiting it slow down or stop
their dance. The result of this precisely regulated system of communication
is that the bees form groups just large enough to keep up with the supply
of food furnished by a given kind of flower. Von Frisch proved this by marking with a colored stain a group of bees frequenting a certain feeding
place. The group was fed a sugar solution impregnated with a specific odor.
When the supply of food at this place gave out, the members of the
group sat idle in the hive. At intervals one of them investigated the feeding
place, and if a fresh supply was provided, it would fill itself, dance on
returning and rouse the group. Continued energetic dancing roused other
bees sitting idle and associated them to the group.

But what was the meaning of the circling and wagging dances? Von
Frisch eventually conceived the idea that the type of dance did not
signify the kind of food, as he had first thought, but had something to do
with the distance of the feeding place. This hypothesis led to the following
crucial experiment. He trained two groups of bees from the same hive to
feed at separate places. One group, marked with a blue stain, was taught to
visit a feeding place only a few meters from the hive; the other, marked
red, was fed at a distance of 300 meters. To the experimenter's delight, it
developed that all the blue bees made circling dances; the red, wagging
dances. Then, in a series of steps, von Frisch moved the nearer feeding place
farther and farther from the hive. At a distance between 50 and 100 meters
away, the blue bees switched from a circling dance to wagging. Conversely,
when the red group's food was brought gradually nearer to the hive, the
dance changed from wagging to circling in the 50 to 100 meter range.

Thus it was clear that the dance at least told the bees whether the distance exceeded a certain value. It appeared unlikely, however, that the
information conveyed was actually quite so vague, for bees often feed at
distances up to two miles and presumably need more precise guidance. The
wagging dance was therefore studied more closely. The rate of wagging is
probably significant, but it is too rapid to follow. It was found, however,
that the frequency of turns would give a fairly good indication of the distance. When the feeding place was 100 meters away, the bee made about
10 short turns in 15 seconds. To indicate a distance of 3,000 meters, it
made only three long ones in the same time. A curve plotted from the average of performances by a number of bees shows that the number of turns
varies regularly with the distance, although the correspondence is not very
precise in individual cases.

How accurately do the bees respond to what is told them? Von Frisch
studied this problem with several experiments, of which the following is the
most conclusive. The feeding table was placed in a certain direction and at
four different distances in four trials. At each trial plates containing the
same odor but no food were placed in the three other directions and in

each case at nearly the same distance as the food source. At short distances (about 10 meters) the bees searched almost equally in all directions. But beginning at about 25 meters they evidently had some indication of the right direction, for the plate with food was visited by much larger numbers than the plates at the other points of the compass.

How did the returning bees indicate to the other bees in the hive the direction of the feeding place? A key to the answer was given by the known fact that bees use the sun for orientation during flight. A bee caught far from the hive and liberated after a few minutes will fly straight back. But if it is kept in a dark box for a period, say an hour, it will go astray, because it continues to fly at the same angle to the sun's direction as when it was caught. Von Frisch deduced that the bee dance must signal direction in relation to the position of the sun. Obviously a horizontal direction can not actually be shown on the vertical surface of a honeycomb, but von Frisch discovered that the bees transpose direction and designate the top of the comb as the horizontal position of the sun. When the sun, as seen from the beehive, is just above the feeding place, the straight part of the dance is vertical with the head up. When the feeding place in is the opposite direction, the straight part again is vertical, but with the head down. And when the food is not in line with the sun, the bee shows the horizontal angle between the sun and the feeding place by pointing at the same angle from the vertical on the honeycomb.

This indication of direction changes continuously throughout the day with the changing position of the sun, which is always represented on the vertical. The dance is normally performed in complete darkness within the hive, yet the bees, roused by, following and imitating the dancer, correctly interpret the signals to an accuracy within a few degrees. It can be observed without disturbing the bees in photographic red light, which is invisible to them.

It is a very curious fact, for which no explanation has been found so far, that the position of the sun in the heavens is correctly used by the bees even when it is hidden behind an unbroken layer of clouds, and when in addition the hive is placed in surroundings totally unknown to the bees. This precaution is necessary because in territory that the bees know well they are experts in using landmarks. It appears possible that infrared rays from the sun, penetrating the clouds, may guide the bees. Experiments have shown that bees are not stimulated by heat rays as such, but the possibility cannot be excluded that the eyes of bees could be sensitive to near infrared although insensitive to visible red. This point has not so far been investigated for lack of a suitable light filter. Von Frisch had also undertaken some experiments to determine how the bees would cope with the problem of a mountain ridge or tall building which forced them to make a detour. He found that they would indicate the airline direction from the hive to the feeding place, but would give the distance that they actually had to fly.

Von Frisch tells me that he himself considered some of these results so fantastic that he had to make sure that ordinary bees which had not been experimentally trained could also do the tricks. They could, and moreover they continued to work efficiently on honeycombs removed from the hive. While studying these "wild" bees, von Frisch became curious to see what would happen if the honeycomb was put in a horizontal position instead of the vertical. To his surprise the bees responded by pointing directly toward the feeding place, and they kept on doing this even when the honeycomb was slowly rotated like a turntable. It looked as if the bees had a magnet in them and responded like a compass needle, but experiments showed them to be not the least affected by magnetic force. This method of pointing also takes place under natural conditions, the bees often performing horizontal dances in front of the entrance to the hive.

On the other hand, experiments showed that on the underside of a horizontal surface the bees were unable to indicate any direction, and it turned out that their signals were disturbed when the horizontal surface was placed in the shade. Von Frisch therefore decided to test directly their power of indicating direction on a horizontal surface in the dark. A movable chamber was built to enclose the observer and the observation hive. By photographic red light or even by diffuse white light in a tent, the bees proved unable to indicate any direction on a horizontal surface (although they can work with precision in the dark on a vertical one). They were not restrained from dancing, and the stimulated bees, thoroughly confused, searched for food equally in all directions. The sun can be replaced in these experiments by any artificial light source of sufficient strength. But only if such a light is placed in the direction corresponding to that of the sun at the time, are the bees led toward the feeding place. Placed in any other position, the light will lead them astray.

At this point, some contradictory evidence turned up. On several occasions the bees had proved able to give correct instructions on a horizontal surface even when the sun was not directly visible. Therefore, the experiment was made of removing the north wall of the observation chamber, which allowed the bees to see only the sunless sky. In clear weather this proved sufficient to give them the correct orientation. Indeed, it was eventually found that when light from a blue sky came into the chamber through a tube 40 centimeters long and only 15 centimeters in diameter, this bare glimpse of the sky sufficed to orient the bees toward the sun's position. Light from a cloud, however, was without effect when seen through the tube, and sky light reflected by a mirror was misleading. The most probable explanation is that the bees are able to observe the direction of the polarized light from the sky and thereby infer the sun's position.

When the honeycomb is tipped to an inclination between vertical and horizontal, the bees respond by giving information that combines direct pointing with use of the vertical to indicate the sun's position. This of course results in a deviation from the true course. Analysis of earlier experiments, in which light from the sky complicated the reactions of bees on a vertical honeycomb, showed that the perturbations could all be quantitatively explained on the same basis.

I have tried to give a very condensed account of the principal results which von Frisch has so far obtained. The series of experiments constitutes a most beautiful example of what the human mind can accomplish by tireless effort on a very high level of intelligence. But I would ask you to give some thought also to the mind of the bees. I have no doubt that some will attempt to "explain" the performances of the bees as the result of reflexes and instincts. Such attempts will certainly contribute to our understanding, but for my part I find it difficult to assume that such perfection and flexibility in behavior can be reached without some kind of mental processes— I do not venture to proclaim them as "thoughts"—going on in the small heads of the bees.

THE BEST FORM OF GOVERNMENT | *JOHN STUART MILL*

There is no difficulty in showing that the ideally best form of government is that in which the sovereignty, or supreme controlling power in the last resort, is vested in the entire aggregate of the community, every citizen not only having a voice in the exercise of that ultimate sovereignty, but being, at least occasionally, called on to take an actual part in the government by the personal discharge of some public function, local or general.

To test this proposition, it has to be examined in reference to the two branches into which, as pointed out in the last chapter, the inquiry into the goodness of a government conveniently divides itself, namely, how far it promotes the good management of the affairs of society by means of the existing faculties, moral, intellectual, and active, of its various members, and what is its effect in improving or deteriorating those faculties.

The ideally best form of government, it is scarcely necessary to say, does not mean one which is practicable or eligible in all states of civilization, but the one which, in the circumstances in which it is practicable and eligible, is attended with the greatest amount of beneficial consequences, immediate and prospective. A completely popular government is the only polity which can make out any claim to this character. It is pre-eminent in both the departments between which the excellence of a political Constitution is divided. It is both more favorable to present good government, and promotes a better and higher form of national character than any other polity whatsoever.

From *Considerations on Representative Government* (1861).

Its superiority in reference to present well-being rests upon two principles, of as universal truth and applicability as any general propositions which can be laid down respecting human affairs. The first is, that the rights and interests of every or any person are only secure from being disregarded when the person interested is himself able, and habitually disposed to stand up for them. The second is, that the general prosperity attains a greater height, and is more widely diffused, in proportion to the amount and variety of the personal energies enlisted in promoting it.

Putting these two propositions into a shape more special to their present application—human beings are only secure from evil at the hands of others in proportion as they have the power of being, and are self-*protecting;* and they only achieve a high degree of success in their struggle with Nature in proportion as they are self-dependent, relying on what they themselves can do, either separately or in concert, rather than on what others do for them.

The former proposition—that each is the only safe guardian of his own rights and interests—is one of those elementary maxims of prudence which every person capable of conducting his own affairs implicitly acts upon wherever he himself is interested. Many, indeed, have a great dislike to it as a political doctrine, and are fond of holding it up to obloquy as a doctrine of universal selfishness. To which we may answer, that whenever it ceases to be true that mankind, as a rule, prefer themselves to others, and those nearest to them to those more remote, from that moment Communism is not only practicable, but the only defensible form of society, and will, when that time arrives, be assuredly carried into effect. For my own part, not believing in universal selfishness, I have no difficulty in admitting that Communism would even now be practicable among the *élite* of mankind, and may become so among the rest. But as this opinion is anything but popular with those defenders of existing institutions who find fault with the doctrine of the general predominance of self-interest, I am inclined to think they do in reality believe that most men consider themselves before other people. It is not, however, necessary to affirm even this much in order to support the claim of all to participate in the sovereign power. We need not suppose that when power resides in an exclusive class, that class will knowingly and deliberately sacrifice the other classes to themselves: it suffices that, in the absence of its natural defenders, the interest of the excluded is always in danger of being overlooked; and when looked at, is seen with very different eyes from those of the persons whom it directly concerns. In this country, for example, what are called the working-classes may be considered as excluded from all direct participation in the government. I do not believe that the classes who do participate in it have in general any intention of sacrificing the working classes to themselves. They once had that intention; witness the persevering attempts so long made to keep down wages by law. But in the present day, their ordinary disposition is the very opposite: they willingly make considerable sacrifices, especially of their pecuniary interest, for the benefit of the working classes, and err rather by too lavish and indiscriminating beneficence; nor do I believe that any rulers in history have been actuated by a more sincere desire to do their duty toward the poorer portion of their countrymen. Yet does Parliament or almost any of the members composing it, ever for an instant look at any question with the eyes of a working man? When a subject arises in which the laborers as such have an interest, is it regarded from any point of view but that of the employers of labor? I do not say that the working men's view of these questions is in general nearer to truth than the other, but it is sometimes quite as near; and in any case it ought to be respectfully listened to, instead of being, as it is, not merely turned away from, but ignored. On the question of strikes, for instance, it is doubtful if there is so much as one among the leading members of either House who is not firmly convinced that the reason of the matter is unqualifiedly on the side of the masters, and that the men's view of it is simply absurd. Those who have studied the question know well how far this is from being the case, and in how different, and how infinitely less superficial a manner the point would have to be argued if the classes who strike were able to make themselves heard in Parliament.

It is an inherent condition of human affairs that no intention, however sincere, of protecting the interests of others can make it safe or salutary to tie up their own hands. Still more obviously true is it that by their own hands only can any positive and durable improvement of their circumstances in life be worked out. Through the joint influence of these two principles, all free communities have both been more exempt from social injustice and crime, and have attained more brilliant prosperity than any others, or than they themselves after they lost their freedom. Contrast the free states of the world, while their freedom lasted, with the contemporary subjects of monarchical or oligarchical despotism: the Greek cities with the Persian satrapies; the Italian republics, and the free towns of Flanders and Germany, with the feudal monarchies of Europe; Switzerland, Holland, and England with Austria or ante-revolutionary France. Their superior prosperity was too obvious ever to have been gainsayed; while their superiority in good government and social relations is proved by the prosperity, and is manifest besides in every page of history. If we compare, not one age with another, but the different governments which coexisted in the same age, no amount of disorder which exaggeration itself can pretend to have existed amid the publicity of the free states can be compared for a moment with the contemptuous trampling upon the mass of the people which pervaded the whole life of the monarchical countries, or the disgusting individual tyranny which was of more than daily occurrence under the systems of plunder which they called fiscal arrangements, and in the secrecy of their frightful courts of justice.

It must be acknowledged that the benefits of freedom, so far as they have hitherto been enjoyed, were obtained by the extension of its privileges to a part only of the community, and that a government in which they are extended impartially to all is a desideratum still unrealized. But, though every approach to this has an independent value, and in many cases more than an approach could not, in the existing state of general improvement, be made, the participation of all in these benefits is the ideally perfect conception of free government. In proportion as any, no matter who, are excluded from it, the interests, of the excluded are left without the guaranty accorded to the rest, and they themselves have less scope and encouragement than they might otherwise have to that exertion of their energies for the good of themselves and of the community to which the general prosperity is always proportioned. . . .

From these accumulated considerations, it is evident that the only government which can fully satisfy all the exigencies of the social state is one in which the whole people participate; that any participation, even in the smallest public function, is useful; that the participation should everywhere be as great as the general degree of improvement of the community will allow; and that nothing less can be ultimately desirable than the admission of all to a share in the sovereign power of the state. But since all can not, in a community exceeding a single small town, participate personally in any but some very minor portions of the public business, it follows that the ideal type of a perfect government must be representative.

EMPIRICISM AND DEMOCRACY | BERTRAND RUSSELL

The only philosophy that affords a theoretical justification of democracy, and that accords with democracy in its temper of mind, is empiricism. Locke, who may be regarded, so far as the modern world is concerned, as the founder of empiricism, makes it clear how closely this is connected with his views on liberty and toleration, and with his opposition to absolute monarchy. He is never tired of emphasizing the uncertainty of most of our knowledge, not with a skeptical intention such as Hume's, but with the intention of making men aware that they *may* be mistaken, and that they should take account of this possibility in all their dealings with men of opinions different from their own. He had seen the evils wrought, both by the "enthusiasm" of the sectaries, and by the dogma of the divine right of kings; to both he opposed a piecemeal and patchwork political doctrine, to be tested at each point by its success in practice.

What may be called, in a broad sense, the Liberal theory of politics is a

"Philosophy and Politics" from Bertrand Russell, *Unpopular Essays*. Copyright 1951 by Bertrand Russell. Reprinted by permission of Simon and Schuster, Inc., and of George Allen & Unwin, Ltd.

recurrent product of commerce. The first known example of it was in the
Ionian cities of Asia Minor, which lived by trading with Egypt and Lydia.
When Athens, in the time of Pericles, became commercial, the Athenians
became Liberal. After a long eclipse, Liberal ideas revived in the Lombard
cities of the middle ages, and prevailed in Italy until they were extinguished
by the Spaniards in the sixteenth century. But the Spaniards failed to re-
conquer Holland or to subdue England, and it was these countries that
were the champions of Liberalism and the leaders in commerce in the seventeenth century. In our day the leadership has passed to the United States.

The reasons for the connection of commerce with Liberalism are obvious.
Trade brings men into contact with tribal customs different from their own,
and in so doing destroys the dogmatism of the untraveled. The relation of
buyer and seller is one of negotiation between two parties who are both
free; it is most profitable when the buyer or seller is able to understand the
point of view of the other party. There is, of course, imperialistic commerce,
where men are forced to buy at the point of the sword; but this is not the
kind that generates Liberal philosophies, which have flourished best in
trading cities that have wealth without much military strength. In the
present day, the nearest analogue to the commercial cities of antiquity and
the middle ages is to be found in small countries such as Switzerland,
Holland, and Scandinavia.

The Liberal creed, in practice, is one of live-and-let-live, of toleration
and freedom so far as public order permits, of moderation and absence of
fanaticism in political programs. Even democracy, when it becomes fanatical, as it did among Rousseau's disciples in the French Revolution, ceases
to be Liberal; indeed, a fanatical belief in democracy makes democratic
institutions impossible, as appeared in England under Cromwell and in
France under Robespierre. The genuine Liberal does not say "this is true,"
he says "I am inclined to think that under present circumstances this opinion is probably the best." And it is only in this limited and undogmatic
sense that he will advocate democracy.

What has theoretical philosophy to say that is relevant to the validity
or otherwise of the Liberal outlook?

The essence of the Liberal outlook lies not in *what* opinions are held,
but in *how* they are held: instead of being held dogmatically, they are held
tentatively, and with a consciousness that new evidence may at any moment
lead to their abandonment. This is the way in which opinions are held in
science, as opposed to the way in which they are held in theology. The decisions of the Council of Nicaea are still authoritative, but in science fourth-
century opinions no longer carry any weight. In the U.S.S.R. the dicta of
Marx on dialectical materialism are so unquestioned that they help to
determine the views of geneticists on how to obtain the best breed of wheat,[1]

1 See *The New Genetics in the Soviet Union*, by Hudson and Richens. School of
Agriculture, Cambridge, 1946.

though elsewhere it is thought that experiment is the right way to study such problems. Science is empirical, tentative, and undogmatic; all immutable dogma is unscientific. The scientific outlook, accordingly, is the intellectual counterpart of what is, in the practical sphere, the outlook of Liberalism.

Locke, who first developed in detail the empiricist theory of knowledge, preached also religious toleration, representative institutions, and the limitation of governmental power by the system of checks and balances. Few of his doctrines were new, but he developed them in a weighty manner at just the moment when the English government was prepared to accept them. Like the other men of 1688, he was only reluctantly a rebel, and he disliked anarchy as much as he disliked despotism. Both in intellectual and in practical matters he stood for order without authority; this might be taken as the motto both of science and of Liberalism. It depends, clearly, upon consent or assent. In the intellectual world it involves standards of evidence which, after adequate discussion, will lead to a measure of agreement among experts. In the practical world it involves submission to the majority after all parties have had an opportunity to state their case.

In both respects his moment was a fortunate one. The great controversy between the Ptolemaic and Copernican systems had been decided, and scientific questions could not longer be settled by an appeal to Aristotle. Newton's triumphs seemed to justify boundless scientific optimism.

In the practical world, a century and a half of wars of religion had produced hardly any change in the balance of power as between Protestants and Catholics. Enlightened men had begun to view theological controversies as an absurdity, caricatured in Swift's war between the Big-endians and the Little-endians. The extreme Protestant sects, by relying upon the inner light, had made what professed to be Revelation into an anarchic force. Delightful enterprises, scientific and commercial, invited energetic men to turn aside from barren disputation. Fortunately they accepted the invitation, and two centuries of unexampled progress resulted.

We are now again in an epoch of wars of religion, but a religion is now called an "ideology." At the moment, the Liberal philosophy is felt by many to be too tame and middle-aged: the idealistic young look for something with more bite in it, something which has a definite answer to all their questions, which calls for missionary activity and gives hope of a millennium brought about by conquest. In short, we have been plunging into a renewed age of faith. Unfortunately the atomic bomb is a swifter exterminator than the stake, and cannot safely be allowed so long a run. We must hope that a more rational outlook can be made to prevail, for only through a revival of Liberal tentativeness and tolerance can our world survive.

The empiricist's theory of knowledge—to which, with some reservations, I adhere—is halfway between dogma and skepticism. Almost all knowledge, it holds, is in some degree doubtful, though the doubt, if any, is negligible as regards pure mathematics and facts of present sense-perception. The doubtfulness of what passes for knowledge is a matter of degree; having recently read a book on the Anglo-Saxon invasion of Britain, I am now convinced of the existence of Hengist, but very doubtful about Horsa. Einstein's general theory of relativity is probably broadly speaking true, but when it comes to calculating the circumference of the universe we may be pardoned for expecting later investigations to give a somewhat different result. The modern theory of the atom has pragmatic truth, since it enables us to construct atomic bombs: its consequences are what instrumentalists facetiously call "satisfactory." But it is not improbable that some quite different theory may in time be found to give a better explanation of the observed facts. Scientific theories are accepted as useful hypotheses to suggest further research, and as having some element of truth in virtue of which they are able to colligate existing observations; but no sensible person regards them as immutably perfect.

In the sphere of practical politics, this intellectual attitude has important consequences. In the first place, it is not worth while to inflict a comparatively certain present evil for the sake of a comparatively doubtful future good. If the theology of former times was entirely correct, it was worth while burning a number of people at the stake in order that the survivors might go to heaven, but if it was doubtful whether heretics would go to hell, the argument for persecution was not valid. If it is certain that Marx's eschatology is true, and that as soon as private capitalism has been abolished we shall all be happy ever after, then it is right to pursue this end by means of dictatorships, concentration camps, and world wars; but if the end is doubtful or the means not sure to achieve it, present misery becomes an irresistible argument against such drastic methods. If it were certain that without Jews the world would be a paradise, there could be no valid objection to Auschwitz; but if it is more probable that the world resulting from such methods would be a hell, we can allow free play to our natural humanitarian revulsion against cruelty.

Since, broadly speaking, the distant consequences of actions are more uncertain than the immediate consequences, it is seldom justifiable to embark on any policy on the ground that, though harmful in the present, it will be beneficial in the long run. This principle, like all others held by empiricists, must not be held absolutely; there are cases where the future consequences of one policy are fairly certain and very unpleasant, while the present consequences of the other, though not agreeable, are easily endurable. This applies, for instance, to saving food for the winter, investing capital in machinery, and so on. But even in such cases uncertainty should not be lost sight of. During a boom there is much investment that turns out to have been unprofitable, and modern economists recognize that the habit of investing rather than consuming may easily be carried too far.

It is commonly urged that, in a war between Liberals and fanatics, the fanatics are sure to win, owing to their more unshakable belief in the righteousness of their cause. This belief dies hard, although all history, including that of the last few years, is against it. Fanatics have failed, over and over again, because they have attempted the impossible, or because, even when what they aimed at was possible, they were too unscientific to adopt the right means; they have failed also because they roused the hostility of those whom they wished to coerce. In every important war since 1700 the more democratic side has been victorious. This is partly because democracy and empiricism (which are intimately interconnected) do not demand a distortion of facts in the interests of theory. Russia and Canada, which have somewhat similar climatic conditions, are both interested in obtaining better breeds of wheat; in Canada this aim is pursued experimentally, in Russia by interpreting the Marxist Scriptures.

Systems of dogma without empirical foundation, such as those of scholastic theology, Marxism, and fascism, have the advantage of producing a great degree of social coherence among their disciples. But they have the disadvantage of involving persecution of valuable sections of the population. Spain was ruined by the expulsion of the Jews and Moors; France suffered by the emigration of Huguenots after the Revocation of the Edict of Nantes; Germany would probably have been first in the field with the atomic bomb but for Hitler's hatred of Jews. And, to repeat, dogmatic systems have the two further disadvantages of involving false beliefs on practically important matters of fact, and of rousing violent hostility in those who do not share the fanaticism in question. For these various reasons, it is not to be expected that, in the long run, nations addicted to a dogmatic philosophy will have the advantage over those of a more empirical temper. Nor is it true that dogma is necessary for social coherence when social coherence is called for; no nation could have shown more of it than the British showed in 1940.

Empiricism, finally, is to be commended not only on the ground of its greater truth, but also on ethical grounds. Dogma demands authority, rather than intelligent thought, as the source of opinion; it requires persecution of heretics and hostility to unbelievers; it asks of its disciples that they should inhibit natural kindliness in favor of systematic hatred. Since argument is not recognized as a means of arriving at truth, adherents of rival dogmas have no method except war by means of which to reach a decision. And war, in our scientific age, means, sooner or later, universal death.

I conclude that, in our day as in the time of Locke, empiricist Liberalism (which is not incompatible with *democratic* socialism) is the only philosophy that can be adopted by a man who, on the one hand, demands some scientific evidence for his beliefs, and, on the other hand, desires human happiness more than the prevalence of this or that party or creed. Our confused and difficult world needs various things if it is to escape disaster, and among these one of the most necessary is that, in the nations which still uphold Liberal beliefs, these beliefs should be wholehearted and profound, not apologetic towards dogmatisms of the right and of the left, but deeply persuaded of the value of liberty, scientific freedom, and mutual forbearance. For without these beliefs life on our politically divided but technically unified planet will hardly continue to be possible.

SWEETNESS AND LIGHT | *MATTHEW ARNOLD*

The disparagers of culture make its motive curiosity; sometimes, indeed, they make its motive mere exclusiveness and vanity. The culture which is supposed to plume itself on a smattering of Greek and Latin is a culture which is begotten by nothing so intellectual as curiosity; it is valued either out of sheer vanity and ignorance or else as an engine of social and class distinction, separating its holder, like a badge or title, from other people who have not got it. No serious man would call this *culture,* or attach any value to it, as culture, at all. To find the real ground for the very differing estimate which serious people will set upon culture, we must find some motive for culture in the terms of which may lie a real ambiguity; and such a motive the word *curiosity* gives us.

I have before now pointed out that we English do not, like the foreigners, use this word in a good sense as well as in a bad sense. With us the word is always used in a somewhat disapproving sense. A liberal and intelligent eagerness about the things of the mind may be meant by a foreigner when he speaks of curiosity, but with us the word always conveys a certain notion of frivolous and unedifying activity. In the *Quarterly Review,* some little time ago, was an estimate of the celebrated French critic, M. Sainte-Beuve, and a very inadequate estimate it in my judgment was. And its inadequacy consisted chiefly in this: that in our English way it left out of sight the double sense really involved in the word *curiosity,* thinking enough was said to stamp M. Sainte-Beuve with blame if it was said that he was impelled in his operations as a critic by curiosity, and omitting either to perceive that M. Sainte-Beuve himself, and many other people with him, would consider that this was praiseworthy and not blameworthy, or to point out why it ought really to be accounted worthy of blame and not of praise. For as there is a curiosity about intellectual matters which is futile, and merely a disease, so there is certainly a curiosity—a desire after the things of the mind simply for their own sake and for the pleasure of seeing them as they are—which is, in an intelligent being, natural and laudable. Nay, and the very desire to see things as they are, implies a balance and regulation of mind which is not

From *Culture and Anarchy* (1869).

often attained without fruitful effort, and which is the very opposite of the blind and diseased impulse of mind which is what we mean to blame when we blame curiosity. Montesquieu says: "The first motive which ought to impel us to study is the desire to augment the excellence of our nature, and to render an intelligent being yet more intelligent." This is the true ground to assign for the genuine scientific passion, however manifested, and for culture, viewed simply as a fruit of this passion; and it is a worthy ground, even though we let the term *curiosity* stand to describe it.

But there is of culture another view, in which not solely the scientific passion, the sheer desire to see things as they are, natural and proper in an intelligent being, appears as the ground of it. There is a view in which all the love of our neighbor, the impulses toward action, help, and beneficence, the desire for removing human error, clearing human confusion, and diminishing human misery, the noble aspiration to leave the world better and happier than we found it—motives eminently such as are called social— come in as part of the grounds of culture, and the main and pre-eminent part. Culture is then properly described not as having its origin in curiosity, but as having its origin in the love of perfection; it is *a study of perfection*. It moves by the force, not merely or primarily of the scientific passion for pure knowledge, but also of the moral and social passion for doing good. As, in the first view of it, we took for its worthy motto Montesquieu's words: "To render an intelligent being yet more intelligent!" so, in the second view of it, there is no better motto which it can have than these words of Bishop Wilson: "To make reason and the will of God prevail!"

Only, whereas the passion for doing good is apt to be overhasty in determining what reason and the will of God say, because its turn is for acting rather than thinking and it wants to be beginning to act; and whereas it is apt to take its own conceptions, which proceed from its own state of development and share in all the imperfections and immaturities of this, for a basis of action; what distinguishes culture is, that it is possessed by the scientific passion as well as by the passion of doing good; that it demands worthy notions of reason and the will of God, and does not readily suffer its own crude conceptions to substitute themselves for them. And knowing that no action or institution can be salutary and stable which is not based on reason and the will of God, it is not so bent on acting and instituting, even with the great aim of diminishing human error and misery ever before its thoughts, but that it can remember that acting and instituting are of little use, unless we know how and what we ought to act and to institute.

This culture is more interesting and more far-reaching than that other, which is founded solely on the scientific passion for knowing. But it needs times of faith and ardor, times when the intellectual horizon is opening and widening all round us, to flourish in. And is not the close and bounded intellectual horizon within which we have long lived and moved now lifting up, and are not new lights finding free passage to shine in upon us? For a long time there was no passage for them to make their way in upon us, and then it was of no use to think of adapting the world's action to them. Where was the hope of making reason and the will of God prevail among people who had a routine which they had christened reason and the will of God, in which they were inextricably bound, and beyond which they had no power of looking? But now the iron force of adhesion to the old routine—social, political, religious—has wonderfully yielded; the iron force of exclusion of all which is new has wonderfully yielded. The danger now is, not that people should obstinately refuse to allow anything but their old routine to pass for reason and the will of God, but either that they should allow some novelty or other to pass for these too easily, or else that they should underrate the importance of them altogether, and think it enough to follow action for its own sake, without troubling themselves to make reason and the will of God prevail therein. Now, then, is the moment for culture to be of service, culture which believes in making reason and the will of God prevail, believes in perfection, is the study and pursuit of perfection, and is no longer debarred, by a rigid invincible exclusion of whatever is new, from getting acceptance for its ideas, simply because they are new.

The moment this view of culture is seized, the moment it is regarded not solely as the endeavor to see things as they are, to draw towards a knowledge of the universal order which seems to be intended and aimed at in the world, and which it is a man's happiness to go along with or his misery to go counter to—to learn, in short, the will of God—the moment, I say, culture is considered not merely as the endeavor to *see* and learn this, but as the endeavor, also, to make it *prevail,* the moral, social, and beneficent character of culture becomes manifest. The mere endeavor to see and learn the truth for our own personal satisfaction is indeed a commencement for making it prevail, a preparing the way for this, which always serves this, and is wrongly, therefore, stamped with blame absolutely in itself and not only in its caricature and degeneration. But perhaps it has got stamped with blame, and disparaged with the dubious title of curiosity, because in comparison with this wider endeavor of such great and plain utility it looks selfish, petty, and unprofitable.

And religion, the greatest and most important of the efforts by which the human race has manifested its impulse to perfect itself—religion, that voice of the deepest human experience—does not only enjoin and sanction the aim which is the great aim of culture, the aim of setting ourselves to ascertain what perfection is and to make it prevail; but also, in determining generally in what human perfection consists, religion comes to a conclusion identical with that which culture—culture seeking the determination of this question through *all* the voices of human experience which have been heard upon it, of art, science, poetry, philosophy, history, as well as of religion, in order to give a greater fullness and certainty to its solution

—likewise reaches. Religion says: *The Kingdom of God is within you;* and culture, in like manner, places human perfection in an *internal* condition, in the growth and predominance of our humanity proper, as distinguished from our animality. It places it in the ever-increasing efficacy and in the general harmonious expansion of those gifts of thought and feeling, which make the peculiar dignity, wealth, and happiness of human nature. As I have said on a former occasion; "It is in making endless additions to itself, in the endless expansion of its powers, in endless growth in wisdom and beauty, that the spirit of the human race finds its ideal. To reach this ideal, culture is an indispensable aid, and that is the true value of culture." Not a having and a resting, but a growing and a becoming, is the character of perfection as culture conceives it; and here, too, it coincides with religion.

And because men are all members of one great whole, and the sympathy which is in human nature will not allow one member to be indifferent to the rest or to have a perfect welfare independent of the rest, the expansion of our humanity, to suit the idea of perfection which culture forms, must be a *general* expansion. Perfection, as culture conceives it, is not possible while the individual remains isolated. The individual is required, under pain of being stunned and enfeebled in his own development if he disobeys, to carry others along with him in his march towards perfection, to be continually doing all he can to enlarge and increase the volume of the human stream sweeping thitherward. And, here, once more, culture lays on us the same obligation as religion, which says, as Bishop Wilson has admirably put it, that "to promote the kingdom of God is to increase and hasten one's own happiness."

But, finally, perfection—as culture from a thorough disinterested study of human nature and human experience learns to conceive it—is a harmonious expansion of *all* the powers which make the beauty and worth of human nature, and is not consistent with the over-development of any one power at the expense of the rest. Here culture goes beyond religion as religion is generally conceived by us. . . .

The pursuit of perfection . . . is the pursuit of sweetness and light. He who works for sweetness and light, works to make reason and the will of God prevail. He who works for machinery, he who works for hatred, works only for confusion. Culture looks beyond machinery, culture hates hatred; culture has one great passion, the passion for sweetness and light. It has one even yet greater!—the passion for making them *prevail*. It is not satisfied till we *all* come to a perfect man; it knows that the sweetness and light of the few must be imperfect until the raw and unkindled masses of humanity are touched with sweetness and light. If I have not shrunk from saying that we must work for sweetness and light, so neither have I shrunk from saying that we must have a broad basis, must have sweetness and light for as many as possible. Again and again I have insisted how those are the happy moments of humanity, how those are the marking epochs of a people's life, how those are the flowering times for literature and art and all the creative power of genius, when there is a *national* glow of life and thought, when the whole of society is in the fullest measure permeated by thought, sensible to beauty, intelligent and alive. Only it must be *real* thought and *real* beauty; *real* sweetness and *real* light. Plenty of people will try to give the masses, as they call them, an intellectual food prepared and adapted in the way they think proper for the actual condition of the masses. The ordinary popular literature is an example of this way of working on the masses. Plenty of people will try to indoctrinate the masses with the set of ideas and judgments constituting the creed of their own profession or party. Our religious and political organizations give an example of this way of working on the masses. I condemn neither way; but culture works differently. It does not try to teach down to the level of inferior classes; it does not try to win them for this or that sect of its own, with ready-made judgments and watchwords. It seeks to do away with classes; to make the best that has been thought and known in the world current everywhere; to make all men live in an atmosphere of sweetness and light, where they may use ideas, as it uses them itself, freely—nourished, and not bound by them.

This is the *social idea;* and the men of culture are the true apostles of equality. The great men of culture are those who have had a passion for diffusing, for making prevail, for carrying from one end of society to the other, the best knowledge, the best ideas of their time; who have labored to divest knowledge of all that was harsh, uncouth, difficult, abstract, professional, exclusive; to humanize it, to make it efficient outside the clique of the cultivated and learned, yet still remaining the *best* knowledge and thought of the time, and a true source, therefore, of sweetness and light. Such a man was Abelard in the Middle Ages, in spite of all his imperfections; and thence the boundless emotion and enthusiam which Abelard excited. Such were Lessing and Herder in Germany, at the end of the last century; and their services to Germany were in this way inestimably precious. Generations will pass, and literary monuments will accumulate, and works far more perfect that the works of Lessing and Herder will be produced in Germany; and yet the names of these two men will fill a German with reverence and enthusiasm such as the names of the most gifted masters will hardly awaken. And why? Because they *humanized* knowledge; because they broadened the basis of life and intelligence; because they worked powerfully to diffuse sweetness and light, to make reason and the will of God prevail. With Saint Augustine they said: "Let us not leave Thee alone to make in the secret of thy knowledge, as thou didst before the creation of the firmament, the division of light from darkness; let the children of thy spirit placed in their firmament, make their light shine upon the earth, mark the division of night and day, and announce the revolution of the times; for the old order is passed, and the new arises; the night is

spent, the day is come forth; and thou shalt crown the year with thy blessing, when thou shalt send forth laborers into thy harvest sown by other
hands than theirs; when thou shalt send forth new laborers to new seed
times, whereof the harvest shall be not yet."

THE SUN AND THE FISH | *VIRGINIA WOOLF*

It is an amusing game, especially for a dark winter's morning. One says
to the eye Athens; Segesta; Queen Victoria; and one waits, as submissively
as possible, to see what will happen next. And perhaps nothing happens,
and perhaps a great many things happen, but not the things one might expect. The old lady in horn spectacles—the late Queen—is vivid enough; but
somehow she has allied herself with a soldier in Picadilly who is stooping
to pick up a coin; with a yellow camel who is swaying through an archway
in Kensington Gardens; with a kitchen chair and a distinguished old gentleman waving his hat. Dropped years ago into the mind, she has become
stuck about with all sorts of alien matter. When one says Queen Victoria,
one draws up the most heterogeneous collection of objects, which it will
take a week at least to sort. On the other hand, one may say to oneself
Mont Blanc at dawn, the Taj Mahal in the moonlight; and the mind remains a blank. For a sight will only survive in the queer pool in which we
deposit our memories if it has the good luck to ally itself with some other
emotion by which it is preserved. Sights marry, incongruously, morganati-
cally (like the Queen and the Camel), and so keep each other alive. Mont
Blanc, the Taj Mahal, sights which we traveled and toiled to see, fade and
perish and disappear because they failed to find the right mate. On our
deathbeds we shall see nothing more majestic than a cat on a wall or an
old woman in a sun-bonnet.

So, on this dark winter's morning, when the real world has faded, let us
see what the eye can do for us. Show me the eclipse, we say to the eye; let
us see that strange spectacle again. And we see at once—but the mind's eye
is only by courtesy an eye; it is a nerve which hears and smells, which
transmits heat and cold, which is attached to the brain and rouses the mind
to discriminate and speculate—it is only for brevity's sake that we say that
we "see" at once a railway station at night. A crowd is gathered at a barrier; but how curious a crowd! Mackintoshes are slung over their arms; in
their hands they carry little cases. They have a provisional, extemporized
look. They have that moving and disturbing unity which comes from the
consciousness that they (but here it would be more proper to say "we")

have a purpose in common. Never was there a stranger purpose than that which brought us together that June night in Euston Railway Station. We were come to see the dawn. Trains like ours were starting all over England at that very moment to see the dawn. All noses were pointing north. When for a moment we halted in the depths of the country, there were the pale yellow lights of motor cars also pointing north. There was no sleep, no fixity in England that night. All were on the roads; all were traveling north. All were thinking of the dawn. As the night wore on, the sky, which was the object of so many million thoughts, assumed greater substance and prominence than usual. The consciousness of the whitish soft canopy above us increased in weight as the hours passed. When in chill early morning we were turned out on a Yorkshire roadside, our senses had orientated themselves differently from usual. We were no longer in the same relation to people, houses, and trees; we were related to the whole world. We had come, not to lodge in the bedroom of an inn; we were come for a few hours of disembodied intercourse with the sky.

Everything was very pale. The river was pale and the fields, brimming with grasses and tasseled flowers which should have been red, had no color in them, but lay there whispering and waving round colorless farmhouses. Now the farmhouse door would open, and out would step to join the procession the farmer and his family in their Sunday clothes, neat, dark and silent as if they were going up hill to church; or sometimes women merely leant on the window sills of the upper rooms watching the procession pass with amused contempt, it appeared—they have come such hundreds of miles, and for what? they seemed to say—in complete silence. We had an odd sense of keeping an appointment with an actor of such vast proportions that he would come silently and be everywhere.

By the time we were at the meeting place, on a high fell where the hills stretched their limbs out over the flowing brown moorland below, we had put on too—though we were cold and with our feet stood in red bog water were likely to be still colder, though some of us were squatted on mackintoshes among cups and plates, eating, and others were fantastically accoutered and none were at their best—still we had put on a certain dignity. Rather, perhaps, we had put off the little badges and signs of individuality. We were strung out against the sky in outline and had the look of statues standing prominent on the ridge of the world. We were very, very old; we were men and women of the primeval world come to salute the dawn. So the worshipers at Stonehenge must have looked among tussocks of grass and boulders of rock. Suddenly, from the motor car of some Yorkshire squire, there bounded four large, lean, red dogs, hounds of the ancient world, hunting dogs, they seemed, leaping with their noses close to the ground on the track of boar or deer. Meanwhile, the sun was rising. A cloud glowed as a white shade glows when the light is slowly turned up behind it. Golden wedge-shaped streamers fell from it and marked the trees in the valley green and the villages blue-brown. In the sky behind us there swam white islands in pale blue lakes. The sky was open and free there, but in front of us a soft snowbank had massed itself. Yet, as we looked, we saw it proving worn and thin in patches. The gold momentarily increased, melting the whiteness to a fiery gauze, and this grew frailer and frailer till, for one instant, we saw the sun in full splendor. Then there was a pause, a moment of suspense, like that which precedes a race. The starter held his watch in his hand, counting the seconds. Now they were off.

The sun had to race through the clouds and to reach the goal, which was a thin transparency to the right, before the sacred seconds were up. He started. The clouds flung every obstacle in his way. They clung, they impeded. He dashed through them. He could be felt, flashing and flying when he was invisible. His speed was tremendous. Here he was out and bright; now he was under and lost. But always one felt him flying and thrusting through the murk to his goal. For one second he emerged and showed himself to us through our glasses, a hollowed sun, a crescent sun. Finally, he went under for his last effort. Now he was completely blotted out. The moments passed. Watches were held in hand after hand. The sacred twenty-four seconds were begun. Unless he could win through before the last one was over, he was lost. Still one felt him tearing and racing behind the clouds to win free; but the clouds held him. They spread; they thickened; they slackened; they muffled his speed. Of the twenty-four seconds only five remained, and still he was obscured. And, as the fatal seconds passed, and we realized that the sun was being defeated, had now, indeed, lost the race, all the color began to go from the moor. The blue turned to purple; the white became livid as at the approach of a violent but windless storm. Pink faces went green, and it became colder than ever. This was the defeat of the sun, then, and this was all, so we thought, turning in disappointment from the dull cloud blanket in front of us to the moors behind. They were livid, they were purple; but suddenly one became aware that something more was about to happen; something unexpected, awful, unavoidable. The shadow growing darker and darker over the moor was like the heeling over of a boat, which, instead of righting itself at the critical moment, turns a little further and then a little further on its side; and suddenly capsizes. So the light turned and heeled over and went out. This was the end. The flesh and blood of the world was dead; only the skeleton was left. It hung beneath us, a frail shell; brown; dead; withered. Then, with some trifling movement, this profound obeisance of the light, this stooping down and abasement of all splendor was over. Lightly, on the other side of the world, up it rose; it sprang up as if the one movement, after a second's tremendous pause, completed the other, and the light which had died here rose again elsewhere. Never was there such a sense of rejuvenescence and recovery. All the convalescences and respites of life seemed rolled into one. Yet, at first, so light and frail and strange the color was, sprinkled rainbow-like in a hoop of color, that it seemed as if the earth could never live decked out in such frail tints. It hung beneath us, like a cage, like a hoop, like a globe of glass. It might be blown out; it might be stove in. But steadily and surely our relief broadened and our confidence established itself as the great paint-brush washed in woods dark on the valley, and massed hills blue above them. The world became more and more solid; it became populous; it became a place where in infinite number of farmhouses, of villages, of railway lines have lodgment; until the whole fabric of civilization was modeled and molded. But still the memory endured that the earth we stand on is made of color; color can be blown out; and then we stand on a dead leaf; and we who tread the earth securely now have seen it dead.

But the eye has not done with us yet. In pursuit of some logic of its own, which we cannot follow immediately, it now presents us with a picture, or generalized impression rather, of London on a hot summer day, when, to judge, by the sense of concussion and confusion, the London season is at its height. It takes us a moment to realize, first, the fact that we are in some public gardens, next, from the asphalt and paper bags thrown about, that they must be the Zoological Gardens, and then without further preparation we are presented with a complete and perfect effigy of two lizards. After destruction, calm; after ruin, steadfastness—that, perhaps, is the logic of the eye at any rate. One lizard is mounted immobile on the back of another, with only the twinkle of a gold eyelid or the suction of a green flank to show that they are the living flesh, and not made of bronze. All human passion seems furtive and feverish beside this still rapture. Time seems to have stopped and we are in the presence of immortality. The tumult of the world has fallen from us like a crumbling cloud. Tanks cut in the level blackness enclose squares of immortality, worlds of settled sunshine, where there is neither rain nor cloud. There the inhabitants perform forever evolutions whose intricacy, because it has no reason, seems the more sublime. Blue and silver armies, keeping a perfect distance for all their arrowlike quickness, shoot first this way, then that. The discipline is perfect, the control absolute; reason there is none. The most majestic of human evolutions seems feeble and fluctuating compared with theirs. Each of these worlds too, which measures perhaps four feet by five, is as perfect in its order as in its method. For forests, they have half a dozen bamboo canes; for mountains, sandhills; in the curves and crinkles of a sea-shell lie for them all adventure, all romance. The rise of a bubble, negligible elsewhere, is here an event of the highest importance. The silver bead bores its way up a spiral staircase through the water to burst against the sheet of glass, which seems laid flat across the top. Nothing exists needlessly. The fish themselves seem to have been shaped deliberately and slipped into the world only to be themselves. They neither work nor weep. In their shape is their reason. For what other purpose except the sufficient one of perfect existence can they have been thus made, some so round, some so thin, some with radiating fins upon their backs, others lined with red electric light, others undulating like white pancakes on a frying pan, some armored in blue mail, some given prodigious claws, some outrageously fringed with huge whiskers? More care has been spent upon half a dozen fish than upon all the races of men. Under our tweed and silk is nothing but a monotony of pink nakedness. Poets are not transparent to the backbone as these fish are. Bankers have no claws. Kings and Queens themselves have neither ruffs nor frills. In short, if we were to be turned naked into an aquarium—but enough. The eye shuts now. It has shown us a dead world and an immortal fish.

RHYTHM

RHYTHM IS GENERALLY SUPPOSED to be the medium of the poet and the musician, yet books have been written on the principles of prose rhythm, and obviously, since prose does have accents and pauses, it must indeed have rhythm, irregular though it be. Because the problems in this sphere are mainly esthetic, they have less place than many others in an expository writing course and, in fact, pleasant prose rhythms are a matter more of instinct than of reasoning. True, a few principles, mainly negative, can be taught. For example, it is well to avoid extended use of poetic meters: a dactylic hexameter in a paper on the two-party system would probably sound like a misplaced scrap from a Gilbert and Sullivan patter song, and a long series of words each requiring a pause for full and correct pronunciation is certain to stop the forward movement of the prose and divert attention from its ideas. In general, prose rhythm should be as inconspicuous as possible. Beyond a few rules such as these, however, there is little to be said.

On the other hand, there is a less formal kind of rhythm which is exceedingly important even in the expository essay. It might be called rhythm of ideas. Just as the ear is tuned to beats and pauses, the mind, eye, and ear together are tuned to length of phrase, clause, sentence—of all the units of ordinary prose. By attention to the lengths of these units and to their similarities and differences, the writer can achieve significant effects which are esthetically valuable, as well as expressive of thought. For instance, an idea-rhythm which was popular especially in the eighteenth century and is still common today (sometimes with unfortunate effects, as in some political oratory) is that involving prominent use of parallel structure. This orderly grouping of ideas in balanced, equal units tends to give prose a ring of formality, and of grace as well, if it is competently handled. Similar to this rhythm in its complexity, but less systematic, is one in which the units, especially the sentences, are extended to great length, and in which the writer frequently interrupts his main line of thought with short interjections, qualifications, interpolations, and so forth. This style allows the writer to gather all the loose ends as he goes along, and to deliver up his ideas to the reader in their full complexity. The twentieth century has tended to turn away from such idea-rhythms, possibly because they tend to be pompous and confusing in unskilled hands. One sort of thing the rebels have done is to destroy the delicate weighting of units, the hierarchy of ideas, and to substitute the practice of tying thoughts together consecutively, with little stress and with little indication of logical relationship. The running rhythm which results has appeared particularly in fiction, but also in the expository prose of such writers as Ernest Hemingway and Gertrude Stein. Another line the revolt has taken is the discarding of long units altogether in favor of a truncated and aphoristic style. The advantage of this clipped manner is that it does away with all ornament, and leaves the bones of writing bare, sometimes impressively so. Finally, most characteristic of modern prose is a "natural" idea-rhythm, one having units of various lengths, seemingly arranged at random. This style can seem to be (or really be) quite artless, but impressive effects are possible within it. For example, a short sentence after two or three long ones can forcefully wind up a paragraph, or bring home an idea. There are many more varieties of idea-rhythm, and the possibilities they offer for effective emphasis are both great and, in comparison with the rhythms of poetry, relatively unexploited. Rhythm, in this sense is a vital part of good prose.

Four of the selections in this unit are by novelists. Henry James (1843-1916) was an American who spent most of his creative life in England. David H. Lawrence (1885-1930) was a critic and poet, as well as a novelist. His fellow Englishman, Edward Morgan Forster (1879-   ), is the author of Passage to India *and* Howards End. *The American novelist Thomas Wolfe (1900-1938) died prematurely, but not before he had written several long novels, among them* Of Time and the River *and* Look Homeward Angel. *George M. Young (1882-1959) was a notable English historian and essayist.*

ART FOR ART'S SAKE | *E. M. FORSTER*

I believe in art for art's sake. It is an unfashionable belief, and some of my statements must be of the nature of an apology. Fifty years ago I should have faced you with more confidence. A writer or a speaker who chose "Art for Art's Sake" for his theme fifty years ago could be sure of being in the swim, and could feel so confident of success that he sometimes dressed himself in esthetic costumes suitable to the occasion—in an

From *Two Cheers for Democracy* by E. M. Forster, copyright 1951, by E. M. Forster. Reprinted by permission of Harcourt, Brace & World, Inc. and of Edward Arnold & Co.

embroidered dressing-gown, perhaps, or a blue velvet suit with a Lord Fauntleroy collar; or a toga, or a kimono, and carried a poppy or a lily or a long peacock's feather in his medieval hand. Times have changed. Not thus can I present either myself or my theme today. My aim rather is to ask you quietly to reconsider for a few minutes a phrase which has been much misused and much abused, but which has, I believe, great importance for us—has, indeed, eternal importance.

Now we can easily dismiss those peacock's feathers and other affectations—they are but trifles—but I want also to dismiss a more dangerous heresy, namely the silly idea that only art matters, an idea which has somehow got mixed up with the idea of art for art's sake, and has helped to discredit it. Many things, besides art, matter. It is merely one of the things that matter, and high though the claims are that I make for it, I want to keep them in proportion. No one can spend his or her life entirely in the creation or the appreciation of masterpieces. Man lives, and ought to live, in a complex world, full of conflicting claims, and if we simplified them down into the esthetic he would be sterilized. Art for art's sake does not mean that only art matters, and I would also like to rule out such phrases as "The Life of Art," "Living for Art," and "Art's High Mission." They confuse and mislead.

What does the phrase mean? Instead of generalizing, let us take a specific instance—Shakespeare's *Macbeth,* for example, and pronounce the words, "*Macbeth* for *Macbeth's* sake" What does that mean? Well, the play has several aspects—it is educational, it teaches us something about legendary Scotland, something about Jacobean England, and a good deal about human nature and its perils. We can study its origins, and study and enjoy its dramatic technique and the music of its diction. All that is true. But *Macbeth* is furthermore a world of its own, created by Shakespeare and existing in virtue of its own poetry. It is in this aspect *Macbeth* for *Macbeth's* sake, and that is what I intend by the phrase "art for art's sake." A work of art—whatever else it may be—is a self-contained entity, with a life of its own imposed on it by its creator. It has internal order. It may have external form. That is how we recognize it.

Take for another example that picture of Seurat's which I saw two years ago in Chicago—"*La Grande Jatte.*" Here again there is much to study and to enjoy: the pointillism, the charming face of the seated girl, the nineteenth-century Parisian Sunday sunlight, the sense of motion in immobility. But here again there is something more; "*La Grande Jatte*" forms a world of its own, created by Seurat and existing by virtue of its own poetry: "*La Grande Jatte*" *pour* "*La Grande Jatte*": *L'art pour l'art.* Like *Macbeth* it has internal order and internal life.

It is to the conception of order that I would now turn. This is important to my argument, and I want to make a digression, and glance at order in daily life, before I come to order in art.

In the world of daily life, the world which we perforce inhabit, there is much talk about order, particularly from statesmen and politicians. They tend, however, to confuse order with orders, just as they confuse creation with regulations. Order, I suggest, is something evolved from within, not something imposed from without; it is an internal stability, a vital harmony, and in the social and political category it has never existed except for the convenience of historians. Viewed realistically, the past is really a series of disorders, succeeding one another by discoverable laws, no doubt, and certainly marked by an increasing growth of human interference, but disorders all the same. So that, speaking as a writer, what I hope for today is a disorder which will be more favorable to artists than is the present one, and which will provide them with fuller inspirations and better material conditions. It will not last—nothing lasts—but there have been some advantageous disorders in the past—for instance, in ancient Athens, in Renaissance Italy, eighteenth-century France, periods in China and Persia—and we may do something to accelerate the next one. But let us not again fix our hearts where true joys are not to be found. We were promised a new order after the first world war through the League of Nations. It did not come, nor have I faith in present promises, by whomsoever endorsed. The implacable offensive of Science forbids. We cannot reach social and political stability for the reason that we continue to make scientific discoveries and to apply them, and thus to destroy the arrangements which were based on more elementary discoveries. If Science would discover rather than apply—if, in other words, men were more interested in knowledge than in power—mankind would be in a far safer position, the stability statesmen talk about would be a possibility, there could be a new order based on vital harmony, and the earthly millennium might approach. But Science shows no signs of doing this: she gave us the internal combustion engine, and before we had digested and assimilated it with terrible pains into our social system, she harnessed the atom, and destroyed any new order that seemed to be evolving. How can man get into harmony with his surroundings when he is constantly altering them? The future of our race is, in this direction, more unpleasant than we care to admit, and it has sometimes seemed to be that its best chance lies through apathy, uninventiveness, and inertia. Universal exhaustion might promote that Change of Heart which is at present so briskly recommended from a thousand pulpits. Universal exhaustion would certainly be a new experience. The human race has never undergone it, and is still too perky to admit that it may be coming and might result in a sprouting of new growth through the decay.

I must not pursue these speculations any further—they lead me too far from my terms of reference and maybe from yours. But I do want to emphasize that order in daily life and in history, order in the social and political category, is unattainable under our present psychology.

Where is it attainable? Not in the astronomical category, where it was for many years enthroned. The heavens and the earth have become terribly alike since Einstein. No longer can we find a reassuring contrast to chaos in the night sky and look up with George Meredith to the stars, the army of unalterable law, or listen for the music of the spheres. Order is not there. In the entire universe there seem to be only two possibilities for it. The first of them—which again lies outside my terms of reference— is the divine order, the mystic harmony, which according to all religions is available for those who can contemplate it. We must admit its possibility, on the evidence of the adepts, and we must believe them when they say that it is attained, if attainable, by prayer. "O thou who changest not, abide with me," said one of its poets. *"Ordina questo amor, o tu che m'ami,"* said another: "Set love in order, thou who lovest me." The existence of a divine order, though it cannot be tested, has never been disproved.

The second possibility for order lies in the esthetic category, which is my subject here: the order which an artist can create in his own work, and to that we must now return. A work of art, we are all agreed, is a unique product. But why? It is unique not because it is clever or noble or beautiful or enlightened or original or sincere or idealistic or useful or educational—it may embody any of those qualities—but because it is the only material object in the universe which may possess internal harmony. All the others have been pressed into shape from outside, and when their mold is removed they collapse. The work of art stands up by itself, and nothing else does. It achieves something which has often been promised by society, but always delusively. Ancient Athens made a mess—but the *Antigone* stands up. Renaissance Rome made a mess—but the ceiling of the Sistine got painted. James I made a mess—but there was *Macbeth*. Louis XIV—but there was Phèdre. Art for art's sake? I should just think so, and more so than ever at the present time. It is the one orderly product which our muddling race has produced. It is the cry of a thousand sentinels, the echo from a thousand labyrinths; it is the lighthouse which cannot be hidden: *c'est le meilleur témoignage que nous puissions donner de notre dignité. Antigone* for *Antigone's* sake, *Macbeth* for *Macbeth's*, *"La Grande Jatte" pour "La Grande Jatte."*

If this line of argument is correct, it follows that the artist will tend to be an outsider in the society to which he has been born, and that the nineteenth-century conception of him as a Bohemian was not inaccurate. The conception erred in three particulars: it postulated an economic system where art could be a full-time job, it introduced the fallacy that only art matters, and it overstressed idiosyncrasy and waywardness—the peacock-feather aspect—rather than order. But it is a truer conception than the one which prevails in official circles on my side of the Atlantic—I don't know about yours: the conception which treats the artist as if he were a particularly bright government advertiser and encourages him to be friendly and matey with his fellow citizens, and not to give himself airs.

Estimable is mateyness, and the man who achieves it gives many a pleasant little drink to himself and to others. But it has no traceable connection with the creative impulse, and probably acts as an inhibition on it. The artist who is seduced by mateyness may stop himself from doing the one thing which he, and he alone, can do—the making of something out of words or sounds or paint or clay or marble or steel or film which has internal harmony and presents order to a permanently disarranged planet. This seems worth doing, even at the risk of being called uppish by journalists. I have in mind an article which was published some years ago in the London *Times,* an article called "The Eclipse of the Highbrow," in which the "Average Man" was exalted, and all contemporary literature was censured if it did not toe the line, the precise position of the line being naturally known to the writer of the article. Sir Kenneth Clark, who was at that time director of our National Gallery, commented on this pernicious doctrine in a letter which cannot be too often quoted. "The poet and the artist," wrote Clark, "are important precisely because they are not average men; because in sensibility, intelligence, and power of invention they far exceed the average." These memorable words, and particularly the words "power of invention," are the Bohemian's passport. Furnished with it, he slinks about society, saluted now by a brickbat and now by a penny, and accepting either of them with equanimity. He does not consider too anxiously what his relations with society may be, for he is aware of something more important than that—namely the invitation to invent, to create order, and he believes he will be better placed for doing this if he attempts detachment. So round and round he slouches, with his hat pulled over his eyes, and maybe with a louse in his beard, and—if he really wants one—with a peacock's feather in his hand.

If our present society should disintegrate—and who dare prophesy that it won't?—this old-fashioned and démodé figure will become clearer: the Bohemian, the outsider, the parasite, the rat—one of those figures which have at present no function either in a warring or a peaceful world. It may not be dignified to be a rat, but many of the ships are sinking, which is not dignified either—the officials did not build them properly. Myself, I would sooner be a swimming rat than a sinking ship—at all events I can look around me for a little longer—and I remember how one of us, a rat with particularly bright eyes called Shelley, squeaked out, "Poets are the unacknowledged legislators of the world," before he vanished into the waters of the Mediterranean.

What laws did Shelley propose to pass? None. The legislation of the artist is never formulated at the time, though it is sometimes discerned by future generations. He legislates through creating. And he creates through his sensitiveness and his power to impose form. Without form the sensitiveness vanishes. And form is as important today, when the human race is trying to ride the whirlwind, as it ever was in those less agitating days of the past, when the earth seemed solid, and the stars fixed, and the discoveries of science were made slowly, slowly. Form is not tradition. It alters from generation to generation. Artists always seek a new technique, and will continue to do so as long as their work excites them. But form of some kind is imperative. It is the surface crust of the internal harmony, it is the outward evidence of order.

My remarks about society may have seemed too pessimistic, but I believe that society can only represent a fragment of the human spirit, and that another fragment can only get expressed through art. And I wanted to take this opportunity, this vantage ground, to assert not only the existence of art, but its pertinacity. Looking back into the past, it seems to me that that is all there has ever been: vantage grounds of discussion and creation, little vantage grounds in the changing chaos, where bubbles have been blown and webs spun, and the desire to create order has found temporary gratification, and the sentinels have managed to utter their challenges, and the huntsmen, though lost individually, have heard each other's calls through the impenetrable wood, and the lighthouses have never ceased sweeping the thankless seas. In this pertinacity there seems to me, as I grow older, something more and more profound, something which does in fact concern people who do not care about art at all.

In conclusion, let me summarize the various categories that have laid claim to the possession of Order.

1) The social and political category. Claim disallowed on the evidence of history and of our own experience. If man altered psychologically, order here might be attainable; not otherwise.

2) The astronomical category. Claim allowed up to the present century, but now disallowed on the evidence of the physicists.

3) The religious category. Claim allowed on the evidence of the mystics.

4) The esthetic category. Claim allowed on the evidence of various works of art, and on the evidence of our own creative impulses, however weak these may be, or however imperfectly they may function. Works of art, in my opinion, are the only objects in the material universe to possess internal order, and that is why, though I don't believe that only art matters, I do believe in Art for Art's Sake.

THE DREAM | *THOMAS WOLFE*

In all the dreams and visions that now swarmed across his sleep, dreams and visions which can only be described as haunted fatally by the sense of time—his mind seemed to exercise the same complete control it ever had shown in all the operations of its conscious memory. He slept, and knew he slept, and saw the whole vast structure of the sleeping world about him as he slept; he dreamed, and knew he dreamed, and like a sorcerer, drew upward at his will, out of dark deeps and blue immensities of sleep, the strange, dark fish of his imagining.

Sometimes they came with elvish flakings of a hoary light, sometimes they came like magic and the promise of immortal joy, they came with victory and singing and a shout of triumph in his blood, and again he felt the strange and deathless joy of voyages: he was a passenger upon great ships again, he walked the broad, scrubbed decks exultantly, and smelled the hot, tarred roofs of powerful and ugly piers, he smelled the spermy sea-wrack of the harbor once again, the tastes of oil, the sharp, acrid and exultant smoke from busy little tugs, the odor of old, worn plankings, drenched with sunlight, and the thousand strange compacted spices of the laden piers. Again he felt the gold and sapphire loveliness of a Saturday in May, and drank the glory of the earth into his heart, and heard in lucent and lyrical air the heavy shattering "baugh" of the great ship's whistle, as it spoke gloriously, of springtime, new lands and departure. Again he saw ten thousand faces, touched with their strange admixture of sorrow and joy, swarm past the openings of the pier, and again he saw the flashing tides that girdled the city, whitened around the prows of a hundred boats, and gleaming with a million iridescent points of light. Again the great walled cliff, the crowded isle, the fabulous spires and ramparts of the city, as delicate as the hues of light that flashed around them, slid away from him, and one by one, the great ships, with the proud sweep of their breasts of white, their opulent storied superstructure, their music of power and speed, fell into line at noon on Saturday. And now, like bridled horses held in rein, with princely chafe and curvetings, they breach the mighty harbor, nose the narrows, circle slowly to brief pauses at the pilot's boat, and then, like racers set loose from the barriers, they are sent away, their engines tremble to a mighty stroke, the ships are given to the sea, to solitude, and to their proper glory once more.

And again he walked the decks, he walked the decks alone, and saw the glittering sea-flung city melt within his sight, and watched the sandy edges of the land fade away, and felt the incredible gold and sapphire glory of the day, the sparkle of dancing waters, and smelled salt, sea-borne air again, and saw upon the decks the joyful and exultant faces of the passengers, their looks of wonder, hope, and speculation, as they looked into the faces of strange men and women, now by the miracle of the voyage and chance isled with them in the loneliness of water, upon the glorious prison of a ship. And again he saw the faces of the lovely women, and saw the lights of love and passion in their eyes, and again he felt the plangent and depthless undulance, the unforgettable feeling of the fathomless might of the sea beneath a ship; a wild cry was torn from his throat, and a thousand unutterable feelings of the voyage, of white coasts and sparkling harbors and the creaking, eerie cries of gulls, of the dear, green dwelling of the earth again, and of strange, golden cities, potent wines, delicious foods, of women, love, and amber thighs spread amorously in ripe golden hay, of discovery and new land, welled up in him like deathless song and certitude.

But just as these visions of delight and joy thronged upward through the deep marine of sleep, so, by the same fiat, the same calm order of an imperial will, the visions of a depthless shame, a faceless abomination of horror, and indefinable and impalpable corruption, returned to haunt his brain with their sentences of inexpiable guilt and ruin: under their evil spell he lay tranced upon his bed in a hypnosis of acquiescent horror, in a willing suspension of all his forces of resistance, like some creature held captive before the hypnotic rhythm of a reptile's head, the dull, envenomed fascination of its eye.

He moved on ceaselessly across a naked and accursed landscape and beneath a naked and accursed sky, an exile in the center of a planetary vacancy that, like his guilt and shame, had neither place among things living nor among things dead, in which there was neither vengeance of lightning, nor mercy or burial, in which there was neither shade nor shelter, curve nor bend, nor hill, nor tree, nor hollow, in which—earth, air, sky, and limitless horizon—there was only one vast naked eye, inscrutable and accusing, from which there was no escape, and which bathed his naked soul in its fathomless depths of shame.

And then the vision faded, and suddenly, with the bridgeless immediacy of a dream, he found himself within the narrow canyon of a street, pacing interminably along on endless pavements where there was neither face nor footfall save his own, nor eye, nor window, nor any door that he might enter.

He thought he was walking through the harsh and endless continuity of one of those brownstone streets of which most of the city was constructed fifty years ago, and of which great broken lengths and fragments still remain. These streets, even if visited by some one in his waking hours, by some stranger in the fullness of health and sanity, and under the living and practical light of noon or, more particularly, by some man stunned with drink, who came there at some desolate and empty hour of night, might have a kind of cataleptic horror, a visionary unreality, as if some great maniac of architecture had conceived and shaped the first, harsh, ugly pattern of brown angularity, and then repeated it, without a change, into an infinity of illimitable repetition, with the mad and measureless insistence of an idiot monotony.

And forever he walked the street, under the brown and fatal light that fell upon him. He walked the street, and looked for a house there that was his own, for a door he knew that he must enter, for some one who was

waiting for him in the house, and for the merciful dark wall and door
that would hide and shelter him from the immense and naked eye of
shame that peered upon him constantly. Forever he walked the street
and searched the bleak, untelling façades for the house he knew and had
forgotten, forever he prowled along before the endless and unchanging
façades of the street, and he never found it, and at length he became
aware of a vast sibilant whispering, of an immense conspiracy of subdued
and obscene laughter, and of the mockery of a thousand evil eyes, that
peered in silence from these bleak façades, and that he could never find
or see; and forever he walked the streets alone, and heard the immense
and secret whisperings and laughter, and was bathed in the bottomless
depths of a wordless shame, and could never find the house he had lost,
the door he had forgotten.

GOVERNMENT AND FAMILY IN THE VICTORIAN AGE | G. M. YOUNG

When I think of old people I remember, people whose first memories
were rich with stories of how Nelson stood and how Nelson fell; who saw
the prentices marching with marrow-bones and cleavers through the streets
of the City in 1821,[1] and heard the great bell of St. Paul's tolling in
1901; of the next generation, whose span covered the last stagecoach and
the first airplane, who had sat waiting for news from Lucknow and
Sebastopol, and lived to listen for the guns defending London; when I
consider their assured morality, their confident acceptance of the social
order, their ready undertaking of its obligations; I have a sense of solidity,
tenacity, and uniformity, which all the time I know to be in large part an
illusion of distance, and I shall have failed of my purpose if I have not
made it clear that the very word "Victorian" may be used to mask a
fallacy and a misconception.

I was born when the Queen had still nearly nineteen years to reign;
I saw her twice, Gladstone once; I well remember the death of Newman
and Tennyson, and my earliest recollection of the Abbey brings back the
flowers fresh on Browning's grave. But if I place myself in 1900, and then
look forward for thirty-six years, and backward for as many, I feel doubt-

From G. M. Young, *Victorian England, Portrait of an Age* (London, Oxford University
Press, 1953).

[1] As I have never seen their song in print, I may as well set it down, as it was told
me by one who had heard it:

> May Scotland's thistle never grow,
> May Ireland's shamrock never blow,
> May the Rose of England still decay,
> Till the Queen of England's gained the day.

ful whether the changes made in the earlier time were not greater than anything I have seen since. I am speaking of changes in men's minds, and I cannot in my own time observe anything of greater consequence than the dethronement of ancient faith by natural science and historical criticism, and the transition from oligarchic to democratic representation. Yet the generation whose memories went back yet another thirty-six years had seen and felt changes surely as great: the political revolution of 1830, the economic and social revolution produced by the railway and the steamship, the founding of the great Dominions. I read constantly that the Victorians did this and the Victorians believed that; as if they had all lived within the sound of the towncrier's bell, and at all times behaved, and thought, and worshiped with the disciplined unanimity of a city state on a holy day. I ask myself, Who are these Victorians? By what mark are we to know them? What creed, what doctrine, what institution was there among them which was not at some time or other debated or assailed?

I can think of two only: Representative Institutions and the Family.[2] I am speaking of sincere debate and earnest assault, of doubts widely felt, and grounded on the belief that there is a better way: and for the ordering of public and private life that age could imagine none better. I know that at times its fancy, flushed perhaps by Carlyle, would stray towards some simpler, more heroic mode of government; and that it was not very willing, could readily find reasons for not being willing, to extend the best mode of government to lesser breeds without the law. But, within the pale of civilized humanity, it had no doubts that Representative Institutions, if they were safeguarded from corruption, and if they were dominated by men with a high sense of the common good, afforded the only sure guarantee of public improvement or even stability. They were preservative, they were educative; they reconciled rulers and ruled, the cohesion of society with the rights and aspirations of its members; and the natural shortcomings of all representative bodies, vacillation, short views, slowness in action, were a price worth paying for their inestimable advantages. If, indeed, upon these there were induced faction and deliberate obstruction, then the future took a greyer color. An age of great cities, Bagehot once said, requires strong Government. An age of great armaments and swift decisive movements by land and sea, required a corresponding rapidity and certainty of authority. Eyes turned anxiously and admiringly toward Germany, her precision and thoroughness, the intelligence with which she was mapping out her future, the energy with which her government provided for the health and good order of her towns.

Really, the elements of strong government were here all the time, if we knew how to use them. The Benthamites had seen, long ago, where the secret lay; and if, as we are told, the ghost of Bentham sometimes

[2] If any one chooses to substitute "monogamic idealism about sex," he may.

walks in Gower Street, it must have danced on the night when Ritchie's
Local Government Bill was carried in 1888. That measure might be
quoted in proof of Lord Salisbury's paradox. No one had agitated for it;
few were greatly interested in it; it was brought out of the departmental
pigeon-hole where Dilke had left it, was accepted with almost universal
approval, and may, without much exaggeration, be said to have transformed the tissue of English existence. Ritchie left the School Boards
and the Guardians to be absorbed later. When the transfer of power was
complete, the entire range of ordinary life, from birth, or even before
birth, to burial, had been brought within the ambit of public interest and
observation. In the middle, like a Tudor gateway worked into a modern
building, remains the joint control of the Justices and County Council
over the constabulary. Otherwise, the whole system, now so comprehensive and searching, is nothing but the logical evolution of the Benthamite
formula—local representation controlled by central experience, public zeal
guided by professional knowledge.

The other vital article of the common Victorian faith is less easy to
analyze. The Family may be regarded as of Divine institution, as a Divine
appointment for the comfort and education of mankind. Or it may be
thought of as a mode of social organization, based on certain primary
facts, the natural attraction of the sexes and the long infancy of the human creature, and affording on the whole, with all its defects, the most
satisfactory provision for that education and comfort. A very cursory observation of human affairs is, indeed, enough to show that the attraction
may be as transient as it is powerful; that relations within the family may
be both painful and oppressive; and that, while the cessation of affection
between the spouses is likely to make itself quickly felt, disaffection between parents and children may smoulder unseen to the mischief of both.
To the religious man or woman, boy or girl, the trouble will appear as a
cross to be borne, an infirmity or even a sin to be overcome: to others,
as a misfortune to be endured as long as possible and then, if possible,
thrown off.

The increasing secularism of English thought might have been expected to compel a more critical attitude to the family than in fact we
find. Sexual ethic had attracted to itself so great a body of romantic
sentiment: it was so closely associated, and even identified, with virtue
in general, with the elevated, the praiseworthy, the respectable life,
that the faintest note of dissidence might attract a disproportionate volume of suspicion and censure. Examples crowd on one's memory. I will
mention only one. In 1873, on the death of Mill, a public memorial was
proposed. The story of his youthful Malthusian activities was revived, and
Mr. Gladstone ostentatiously withdrew his support.

I do not believe that we are at a sufficient distance from the Victorian age to judge with perfect fairness its prevalent philosophy in a matter where only the utmost vigilance can prevent our thought from being at once clouded and colored with, often unconscious, emotion. I have already indicated that I believe to be two vital elements in the analysis; physical recoil, exaggerating the ordinary asceticism of religion, and the necessary dependence of the women as a body in society, on the men. To these must be added the tighter domestic discipline that came from the management of large families: a discipline not yet enlightened—or distracted —by the psychological explorations which may perhaps, in the long run, prove to be the decisive achievement of our age. To go further would, in an Essay of this brevity, be to go too far. I will only record my belief— and I think I remember enough, and have read and thought enough to give my belief some weight—that the preoccupation, social or personal, with one emotion and its manifestations was mischievous; that it produced much falsehood and much injustice, much suffering and much cruelty; but that, on the other hand, in the circumstances of the age, the instinct of the age was sound in regarding romantic love as the right starting-point for the family, and family life, administered with sympathy and intelligence, as the right training ground for the generations in their succession:

sic fortis Etruria crevit,
scilicet et facta est rerum pulcherrima Roma.

The incidents and circumstances, too, of this life: its durable furniture and stated hours; its evening reading and weekly church-going; its long-prepared and long-remembered holidays; its appointed visits from and to the hierarchy of grandparents, uncles, aunts, and cousins; a life which did not differ in essentials whether the holiday was spent at Balmoral or Broadstairs; gave to those who were within it a certain standing with themselves, and a cheerful confidence in the face of novelty, which is perhaps the clue to the Victorian paradox—the rushing swiftness of its intellectual advance, and the tranquil evolution of its social and moral ideals. The advance was in all directions outwards, from a stable and fortified center. Of certain reformers of his own day, Morris tartly remarked that their aim was to turn the working classes into middle classes. Of Victorian reform as a whole the aim was the steady diffusion of culture and comfort downwards and outwards in widening circles. This was the ideal which Mill bequeathed to his disciples, and the better mind of the later nineteenth century was still guided, if no longer dominated, by the thought of Mill; and it could best be pictured to the imagination as such a way of life as the middle classes had fashioned for themselves in their families.

BENJAMIN FRANKLIN | D. H. LAWRENCE

The Perfectibility of Man! Ah heaven, what a dreary theme! The perfectibility of the Ford car! The perfectibility of the Ford car! The perfectibility of which man! I am many men. Which of them are you going to perfect? I am not a mechanical contrivance.

Education! Which of the various me's do you propose to educate, and which do you propose to suppress?

Anyhow I defy you. I defy you, oh society, to educate me or to suppress me, according to your dummy standards.

The ideal man! And which is he, if you please? Benjamin Franklin or Abraham Lincoln? The ideal man! Roosevelt or Porfirio Diaz?

There are other men in me, besides this patient ass who sits here in a tweed jacket. What am I doing, playing the patient ass in a tweed jacket? Who am I talking to? Who are you, at the other end of this patience?

Who are you? How many selves have you? And which of these selves do you want to be?

Is Yale College going to educate the self that is in the dark of you, or Harvard College?

The ideal self! Oh, but I have a strange and fugitive self shut out and howling like a wolf or a coyote under the ideal windows. See his red eyes in the dark? This is the self who is coming into his own.

The perfectibility of man, dear God! When every man as long as he remains alive is in himself a multitude of conflicting men. Which of these do you choose to perfect, at the expense of every other?

Old Daddy Franklin will tell you. He'll rig him up for you, the pattern American. Oh, Franklin was the first downright American. He knew what he was about, the sharp little man. He set up the first dummy American.

At the beginning of his career, this cunning little Benjamin drew up for himself a creed that should "satisfy the professors of every religion, but shock none."

Now wasn't that a real American thing to do?

"That there is One God, who made all things."

(But Benjamin made Him.)

"That He governs the world by His Providence."

(Benjamin knowing all about Providence.)

"That He ought to be worshiped with adoration, prayer, and thanks-giving."

(Which cost nothing.)

"But—" But me no buts, Benjamin, saith the Lord.

"But that the most acceptable service of God is doing good to men."

(God having no choice in the matter.)

"That the soul is immortal."

(You'll see why, in the next clause.)

"And that God will certainly reward virtue and punish vice, either here or hereafter."

Now if Mr. Andrew Carnegie, or any other millionaire, had wished to invent a God to suit his ends, he could not have done better. Benjamin did it for him in the eighteenth century. God is the supreme servant of men who want to get on, to *produce*. Providence. The provider. The heavenly storekeeper. The everlasting Wanamaker.

And this is all the God the grandsons of the Pilgrim Fathers had left. Aloft on a pillar of dollars.

"That the soul is immortal."

The trite way Benjamin says it!

But man has a soul, though you can't locate it either in his purse or his pocketbook or his heart or his stomach or his head. The *wholeness* of a man is his soul. Not merely that nice comfortable bit which Benjamin marks out.

It's a queer thing, is a man's soul. It is the whole of him. Which means it is the unknown him, as well as the known. It seems to me just funny, professors and Benjamins fixing the functions of the soul. Why the soul of man is a vast forest, and all Benjamin intended was a neat back garden. And we've all got to fit in to his kitchen garden scheme of things. Hail Columbia!

The soul of man is a dark forest. The Hercynian Wood that scared the Romans so, and out of which came the white-skinned hordes of the next civilization.

Who knows what will come out of the soul of man? The soul of man is a dark vast forest, with wild life in it. Think of Benjamin fencing it off!

Oh, but Benjamin fenced a little tract that he called the soul of man, and proceeded to get it into cultivation. Providence, forsooth! And they think that bit of barbed wire is going to keep us in pound forever? More fools them.

This is Benjamin's barbed wire fence. He made himself a list of virtues, which he trotted inside like a grey nag in a paddock.

1) TEMPERANCE • Eat not to fullness; drink not to elevation.
2) SILENCE • Speak not but what may benefit others or yourself;

avoid trifling conversation.

3) ORDER • Let all your things have their places; let each part of your business have its time.

4) RESOLUTION • Resolve to perform what you ought; perform without fail what you resolve.

5) FRUGALITY • Make no expense but to do good to others or yourself—i.e., waste nothing.

6) INDUSTRY • Lose no time, be always employed in something useful; cut off all unnecessary action.

7) SINCERITY • Use no hurtful deceit; think innocently and justly, and, if you speak, speak accordingly.

8) JUSTICE • Wrong none by doing injuries, or omitting the benefits that are your duty.

9) MODERATION • Avoid extremes, forbear resenting injuries as much as you think they deserve.

10) CLEANLINESS • Tolerate no uncleanliness in body, clothes, or habitation.

11) TRANQUILLITY • Be not disturbed at trifles, or at accidents common or unavoidable.

12) CHASTITY • Rarely use venery but for health and offspring, never to dullness, weakness, or the injury of your own or another's peace or reputation.

13) HUMILITY • Imitate Jesus and Socrates.

A Quaker friend told Franklin that he, Benjamin, was generally considered proud, so Benjamin put in the Humility touch as an afterthought. The amusing part is the sort of humility it displays. "Imitate Jesus and Socrates," and mind you don't outshine either of these two. One can just imagine Socrates and Alcibiades roaring in their cups over Philadelphian Benjamin, and Jesus looking at him a little puzzled, and murmuring: "Aren't you wise in your own conceit, Ben?"

"Henceforth be masterless," retorts Ben. "Be ye each one his own master unto himself, and don't let even the Lord put his spoke in." "Each man his own master" is but a puffing up of masterlessness.

Well, the first of Americans practiced this enticing list with assiduity, setting a national example. He had the virtues in columns, and gave himself good and bad marks according as he thought his behavior deserved. Pity these conduct charts are lost to us. He only remarks that Order was his stumbling block. He could not learn to be neat and tidy.

Isn't it nice to have nothing worse to confess?

He was a little model, was Benjamin. Doctor Franklin. Snuff-colored little man! Immortal soul and all!

The immortal soul part was a sort of cheap insurance policy.

Benjamin had no concern, really, with the immortal soul. He was too busy with social man.

1) He swept and lighted the streets of young Philadelphia.
2) He invented electrical appliances.
3) He was the center of a moralizing club in Philadelphia, and he wrote the moral humorisms of Poor Richard.
4) He was a member of all the important councils of Philadelphia, and then of the American colonies.
5) He won the cause of American Independence at the French Court, and was the economic father of the United States.

Now what more can you want of a man? And yet he is *infra dig*, even in Philadelphia.

I admire him. I admire his sturdy courage first of all, then his sagacity, then his glimpsing into the thunders of electricity, then his common-sense humor. All the qualities of a great man, and never more than a great citizen. Middle-sized, sturdy, snuff-colored Doctor Franklin, one of the soundest citizens that ever trod or "used venery."

I do not like him.

And, by the way, I always thought books of Venery were about hunting deer.

There is a certain earnest naïveté about him. Like a child. And like a little old man. He has again become as a little child, always as wise as his grandfather, or wiser.

Perhaps, as I say, the most complete citizen that ever "used venery."

Printer, philosopher, scientist, author and patriot, impeccable husband and citizen, why isn't he an archetype?

Pioneer, Oh Pioneers! Benjamin was one of the greatest pioneers of the United States. Yet we just can't do with him.

What's wrong with him then? Or what's wrong with us?

I can remember, when I was a little boy, my father used to buy a scrubby yearly almanack with the sun and moon and stars on the cover. And it used to prophesy bloodshed and famine. But also crammed in corners it had little anecdotes and humorisms, with a moral tag. And I used to have my little priggish laugh at the woman who counted her chickens before they were hatched, and so forth, and I was convinced that honesty was the best policy, also a little priggishly. The author of these bits was Poor Richard, and Poor Richard was Benjamin Franklin, writing in Philadelphia well over a hundred years before.

And probably I haven't got over those Poor Richard tags yet. I rankle still with them. They are thorns in young flesh.

Because although I still believe that honesty is the best policy, I dislike policy altogether; though it is just as well not to count your chickens before they are hatched, it's still more hateful to count them with gloating when they *are* hatched. It has taken me many years and countless smarts to get out of that barbed wire moral enclosure that Poor Richard rigged up. Here am I now in tatters and scratched to ribbons, sitting in

the middle of Benjamin's America looking at the barbed wire, and the fat
sheep crawling under the fence to get fat outside and the watchdogs
yelling at the gate lest by chance anyone should get out by the proper
exit. Oh America! Oh Benjamin! And I just utter a long loud curse against
Benjamin and the American corral.

Moral America! Most moral Benjamin. Sound, satisfied Ben!

He had to go to the frontiers of his State to settle some disturbance
among the Indians. On this occasion he writes:

> We found that they had made a great bonfire in the middle of the square; they
> were all drunk, men and women quarreling and fighting. Their dark-colored bodies,
> half naked, seen only by the gloomy light of the bonfire, running after and beating
> one another with fire-brands, accompanied by their horrid yellings, formed a scene
> the most resembling our ideas of hell that could well be imagined. There was no
> appeasing the tumult, and we retired to our lodging. At midnight a number of
> them came thundering at our door, demanding more rum, of which we took no
> notice.
>
> The next day, sensible they had misbehaved in giving us that disturbance, they
> sent three of their counselors to make their apology. The orator acknowledged the
> fault, but laid it upon the rum, and then endeavored to excuse the rum by saying:
> "The Great Spirit, who made all things, made everything for some use; and what-
> ever he designed anything for, that use it should always be put to. Now, when
> he had made rum, he said: 'Let this be for the Indians to get drunk with.' And it
> must be so."
>
> And, indeed, if it be the design of Providence to extirpate these savages in order
> to make room for the cultivators of the earth, it seems not improbable that rum
> may be the appointed means. It has already annihilated all the tribes who formerly
> inhabited all the seacoast....

This from the good doctor, with such suave complacency is a little
disenchanting. Almost too good to be true.

But there you are! The barbed wire fence. "Extirpate these savages
in order to make room for the cultivators of the earth." Oh, Benjamin
Franklin! He even "used venery" as a cultivator of seed.

Cultivate the earth, ye gods! The Indians did that, as much as they
needed. And they left off there. Who built Chicago? Who cultivated the
earth until it spawned Pittsburgh, Pa.?

The moral issue! Just look at it! Cultivation included. If it's a mere
choice of Kultur or cultivation, I give it up.

Which brings us right back to our question, what's wrong with Benjamin, that we can't stand him? Or else, what's wrong with us, that we
find fault with such a paragon?

Man is a moral animal. All right. I am a moral animal. And I'm going
to remain such. I'm not going to be turned into a virtuous little automaton
as Benjamin would have me. "This is good, that is bad. Turn the little
handle and let the good tap flow," saith Benjamin and all America with

him. "But first all extirpate those savages who are always turning on the bad tap."

I am a moral animal. But I am not a moral machine. I don't work with a little set of handles or levers. The Temperance-silence-order-resolution-frugality-industry-sincerity-justice-moderation-cleanliness-tranquility-chastity-humility keyboard is not going to get me going. I'm really not just an automatic piano with a moral Benjamin getting tunes out of me.

Here's my creed, against Benjamin's. This is what I believe:

"That I am I."

"That my soul is a dark forest."

"That my known self will never be more than a little clearing in the forest."

"That gods, strange gods, come forth from the forest into the clearing of my known self, and then go back."

"That I must have the courage to let them come and go."

"That I will never let mankind put anything over me, but that I will try always to recognize and submit to the gods in me and the gods in other men and women."

There is my creed. He who runs may read. He who prefers to crawl, or to go by gasoline, can call it rot.

Then for a "list." It is rather fun to play at Benjamin.

1) TEMPERANCE • Eat and carouse with Bacchus, or munch dry bread with Jesus, but don't sit down without one of the gods.

2) SILENCE • Be still when you have nothing to say; when genuine passion moves you, say what you've got to say, and say it hot.

3) ORDER • Know that you are responsible to the gods inside you and to the men in whom the gods are manifest. Recognize your superiors and your inferiors, according to the gods. This is the root of all order.

4) RESOLUTION • Resolve to abide by your own deepest promptings and to sacrifice the smaller thing to the greater. Kill when you must, and be killed the same: the *must* coming from the gods inside you, or from the men in whom you recognize the Holy Ghost.

5) FRUGALITY • Demand nothing; accept what you see fit. Don't waste your pride or squander your emotion.

6) INDUSTRY • Lose no time with ideals; serve the Holy Ghost; never serve mankind.

7) SINCERITY • To be sincere is to remember that I am I, and that the other man is not me.

8) JUSTICE • The only justice is to follow the sincere intuition of the soul, angry or gentle. Anger is just, and pity is just, but judgment is never just.

9) MODERATION • Beware of absolutes. There are many gods.

10) CLEANLINESS • Don't be too clean. It impoverishes the blood.

11) TRANQUILLITY • The soul has many motions, many gods come
and go. Try to find your deepest issue, in every confusion, and
abide by that. Obey the man in whom you recognize the Holy
Ghost; command when your honor comes to command.

12) CHASTITY • Never "use" venery at all. Follow your passional
impulse, if it be answered in the other being; but never have any
motive in mind, neither off-spring nor health nor even pleasure,
nor even service. Only know that "venery" is of the great gods.
An offering-up of yourself to the very great gods, the dark ones,
and nothing else.

13) HUMILITY • See all men and women according to the Holy
Ghost that is within them. Never yield before the barren.

There's my list. I have been trying dimly to realize it for a long time,
and only America and old Benjamin have at last goaded me into trying
to formulate it.

And now I, at least, know why I can't stand Benjamin. He tries to
take away my wholeness and my dark forest, my freedom. For how can
any man be free, without an illimitable background? and Benjamin tries
to shove me into a barbed-wire paddock and make me grow potatoes or
Chicagoes.

And how can I be free, without gods that come and go? But Benjamin
won't let anything exist except my useful fellow-men, and I'm sick of
them; as for his Godhead, his Providence, He is Head of nothing except
a vast heavenly store that keeps every imaginable line of goods, from vic-
trolas to cat-o-nine tails.

And how can any man be free without a soul of his own, that he believes in and won't sell at any price? But Benjamin doesn't let me have a
soul of my own. He says I am nothing but a servant of mankind—galley-
slave I call it—and if I don't get my wages here below—that is, if Mr.
Pierpont Morgan or Mr. Nosey Hebrew or the grand United States Government, the great US, US or SOMEOFUS, manages to scoop in my bit along with
their lump—why, never mind, I shall get my wages HEREAFTER.

Oh Benjamin! Oh Binjum! You do NOT suck me in any longer.

And why oh why should the snuff-colored little trap have wanted to
take us all in? Why did he do it?

Out of sheer human cussedness, in the first place. We do all like to
get things inside a barbed-wire corral. Especially our fellow-men. We love
to round them up inside the barbed-wire enclosure of FREEDOM, and
make 'em work. *"Work, you free jewel,* WORK*!"* shouts the liberator, cracking
his whip. Benjamin, I will not work. I do not choose to be a free democrat.
I am absolutely a servant of my own Holy Ghost.

Sheer cussedness! But there was as well the salt of a subtler purpose.

Benjamin was just in his eyeholes—to use an English vulgarism meaning he was just delighted—when he was at Paris judiciously milking money out of the French monarchy for the overthrow of all monarchy. If you want to ride your horse to somewhere you must put a bit in his mouth. And Benjamin wanted to ride his horse so that it would upset the whole apple-cart of the old masters. He wanted the whole European apple-cart upset. So he had to put a strong bit in the mouth of his ass.

"Henceforth be masterless."

That is, he had to break-in the human ass completely, so that much more might be broken, in the long run. For the moment it was the British Government that had to have a hole knocked in it. The first real hole it ever had: the breach of the American rebellion.

Benjamin, in his sagacity, knew that the breaking of the old world was a long process. In the depths of his own under-consciousness he hated England, he hated Europe, he hated the whole corpus of the European being. He wanted to be American. But you can't change your nature and mode of consciousness like changing your shoes. It is a gradual shedding. Years must go by, and centuries must elapse before you have finished. Like a son escaping from the domination of his parents. The escape is not just one rupture. It is a long and half-secret process.

So with the American. He was a European when he first went over the Atlantic. He is in the main a recreant European still. From Benjamin Franklin to Woodrow Wilson may be a long stride, but it is a stride along the same road. There is no new road. The same old road, become dreary and futile. Theoretic and materialistic.

Why then did Benjamin set up this dummy of a perfect citizen as a pattern to America? Of course he did it in perfect good faith, as far as he knew. He thought it simply was the true ideal. But what we *think* we do is not very important. We never really know what we are doing. Either we are materialistic instruments, like Benjamin or we move in the gesture of creation, from our deepest self, usually unconscious. We are only the actors, we are never wholly the authors of our own deeds or works. IT is the author, the unknown inside us or outside us. The best we can do it to try to hold ourselves in unison with the deeps which are inside us. And the worst we can do is to try to have things our own way, when we run counter to IT, and in the long run get our knuckles rapped for our presumption.

So Benjamin contriving money out of the Court of France. He was contriving the first steps of the overthrow of all Europe, France included. You can never have a new thing without breaking an old. Europe happens to be the old thing. America, unless the people in America assert themselves too much in opposition to the inner gods, should be the new thing. The new thing is the death of the old. But you can't cut the throat of an epoch. You've got to steal the life from it through several centuries.

And Benjamin worked for this both directly and indirectly. Directly, at the Court of France, making a small but very dangerous hole in the side of England, through which hole Europe has by now almost bled to death. And indirectly in Philadelphia, setting up this unlovely, snuff-colored little ideal, or automaton, of a pattern American. The pattern American, this dry, moral utilitarian little democrat, has done more to ruin the old Europe than any Russian nihilist. He has done it by slow attrition, like a son who has stayed at home and obeyed his parents, all the while silently hating their authority, and silently, in his soul, destroying not only their authority but their whole existence. For the American spiritually stayed at home in Europe. The spiritual home of America was and still is Europe. This is the galling bondage, in spite of several billions of heaped-up gold. Your heaps of gold are only so many muck-heaps, America, and will remain so till you become a reality to yourselves.

All this Americanizing and mechanizing has been for the purpose of overthrowing the past. And now look at America, tangled in her own barbed wire, and mastered by her own machines. Absolutely got down by her own barbed wire of shalt-nots, and shut up fast in her own "productive" machines like millions of squirrels running in millions of cages. It is just a farce.

Now is your chance, Europe. Now let Hell loose and get your own back, and paddle your own canoe on a new sea, while clever America lies on her muck-heaps of gold, strangled in her own barbed-wire of shalt-not ideals and shalt-not moralisms. While she goes out to work like millions of squirrels in millions of cages. Production!

Let Hell loose, and get your own back, Europe!

CHARLESTON | HENRY JAMES

Charleston early in the morning, on my driving from the station, was, it had to be admitted, no very finished picture, but at least, already, it was different—ever so different in aspect and "feeling," and above all for intimation and suggestion, from any passage of the American scene as yet deciphered; and such became on the spot one's appetite for local color that one was fairly grateful to a friend who, by having promised to arrive from the interior of the State the night before, gave one a pretext for seeking him up and down. My quest, for the moment, proved vain; but the intimations and suggestions, while I proceeded from door to door in the sweet blank freshness of the day, of the climate, of the streets, began to swarm at such a rate that I had the sense of gathering my harvest

From Henry James, *The American Scene* (New York, Harper & Row, Publishers, 1907). Copyright, 1907, by Harper & Row, Publishers. Copyright 1935, by Henry James.

with almost too eager a thrift. It was like standing steeped at the bookstall itself in the volume picked up and opened—though I may add that when I had presently retreated upon the hotel, to which I should in the first instance have addressed myself, it was quite, for a turning of pages, as if I had gone on with the "set." Thus, before breakfast, I entered upon my brief residence with the right vibrations already determined and unable really to say which of a couple of contacts just enjoyed would have most ministered to them. I had roused, guilelessly, through an easy misunderstanding, two more or less sleeping households; but if I had still missed my clew to my friend I had yet put myself into possession of much of whatever else I had wanted. What had I most wanted, I could easily ask myself, but some small inkling (a mere specimen-scrap would do) of the sense, as I have to keep forever calling my wanton synthesis, of "the South before the War"?—an air-bubble only to be blown, in any case, through some odd fragment of a pipe. My pair of early Charleston impressions were thus a pair of thin prismatic bubbles—which could have floated before me moreover but for a few seconds, collapsing even while I stood there.

Prismatically, none the less, they had shown me the "old" South; in one case by the mere magic of the manner in which a small, scared, starved person of color, of very light color, an elderly mulattress in an improvised wrapper, just barely held open for me a door through which I felt I might have looked straight and far back into the past. The past, that of the vanished order, was hanging on there behind her—as much of it as the scant place would accommodate; and she knew this, and that I had so quickly guessed it; which led her, in fine, before I could see more, and that I might not sound the secret of shy misfortune, of faded pretension, to shut the door in my face. So it seemed to me, had I been confronted, in Italy, under quite such a morning air and light, quite the same touch of a tepid, odorous medium, with the ancient sallow crones who guard the locked portals and the fallen pride of provincial *palazzini*. That was all, in the one instance; there had been no more of it than of the little flare of a struck match—which lasted long enough, however, to light the sedative cigarette, smoked and thrown away, that renews itself forever between the picture-seeker's lips. The small historic whiff I had momentarily inhaled required the correction, I should add, of the sweeter breath of my commentary. Fresh altogether was the air behind the garden wall that next gave way to my pursuit; there being a thrill, for that matter, in the fact that here at last again, if nowhere else over the land, rose the real walls that alone make real gardens and that admit to the same by real doors. Close such a door behind you, and you are at once *within* —a local relation, a possibility of retreat, in favor of which the custom of the North has so completely ceased to discriminate. One sacrificed the North, with its mere hard conceit of virtuously meeting exhibition—

much as if a house were just metallic machine, number so-and-so in a catalogue—one sacrificed it on the spot to this finer feeling for the enclosure.

That had really sufficed, no doubt, for my second initiation; since I remember withdrawing, after my fruitless question, as on the completion of a mystic process. Initiation into *what* I perhaps couldn't have said; only, at the most, into the knowledge that what such Southern walls generally shut in proves exactly what one would have wished. I was to see this loose quantity afterwards in greater profusion; but for the moment the effect was as right as that of privacy for the habit of the siesta. The details escape me, or rather I tenderly withhold them. For the siesta there—what would it have been most like but some deep doze, or call it frankly some final sleep, of the idea of "success"? And how could one better have described the privacy, with the mild street shut off and with the deep gallery, where resignation might sit in the shade or swing without motion in a hammock, shut in, than as some dim dream that things were still as they had been—still pleasant behind garden walls— before the great folly? I was to find myself liking, in the South and in the most monstrous fashion, it appeared, those aspects in which the consequences of the great folly were, for extent and gravity, still traceable; I was cold-bloodedly to prefer them, that is, to the aspects, occasionally to be met, from which the traces had been removed. And this, I need hardly say, from a point of view having so little in common with the vindictive as to be quite directly opposed to it. For what in the world was one candidly to do? It is the manner of the purged and renovated, the disconnected element, anywhere, after great trials, to express itself in forms comparatively vulgar, whereas those parts of the organism that, having been through the fire, still have kept the scorches and scars, resemble for tone, for color and value, the products of the potter's oven; when the potter, I mean, or when, in other words, history, has been the right great artist. They at least are not cheerful rawnesses—they have been baked beautiful and hard.

I even tried, I fear, when once installed there, to look at my hotel in that light; availing myself, to this end, of its appearance of "dating," with its fine old neo-classic front and of a certain romantic grandeur of scale, the scale positively of "Latin" construction, in my vast saloon-like apartment, which opened to a high colonnade. The great canopied and curtained bed was really in the grand manner, and the ghost of a rococo tradition, the tradition of the transatlantic South, memory of other lands, glimmered generally in the decoration. When once I had—though almost exclusively under the charm of these particular faded graces, I admit— again privately protested that the place might have been a "palace," my peace was made with Charleston: I was ripe for the last platitude of appreciation.

* The Writer's Identity

IN A LITTLE BOOK about the writing of fiction, Thomas Wolfe observed that all novels are autobiographical. In the sense that no man can write about what he has not in some way known, the statement is true: a novel—indeed, any creative work—must be an expression of experience. In another sense, it is fully as true to say that art is never "true to life," that it always distorts, selects, and rearranges, that not even if the artist could would he be content to render exactly what he has experienced. The writer, like every other artist, is always engaged primarily in the effort to control the experiences which he wishes to use; if they prove refractory, and he pretends to let them lead him where they will, he is simply playing for time, waiting for his chance to move back into the driver's seat.

Now there are drivers and drivers. Some hold the reins slack and appear to keep only one eye open; others sit nervously alert and grip reins and whip as firmly as though they were charioteers careening around a curve of the Circus Maximus. No matter what the posture or stance, the writer is doing two things in these situations: he is gauging very carefully the amount and kind of control he must exercise, and he is playing a role. This role-playing is something all writers engage in part of the time, doing and saying what they conceive the character they represent would do or say. They become the stern father, the dutiful son, the injured victim, the gay young thing, the incorruptible seeker of truth—the list is endless. And for as long as they play the role—an hour, a week, or many years—they make, half-consciously, certain choices of language, clothing, gesture, and manner; these they discard or alter as they move from role to role. Although such role-playing is common in everyone's life, hypocrisy is almost universally detested in our culture. Since a charge of hypocrisy assumes that there is one self for each person, a self which is violated by the action condemned as hypocritical, it may seem paradoxical that role-playing is so characteristic a part of our lives. One reason for it, however, is certainly not unflattering: like the writer, the average man faces constantly the problem of identity. The question "Who am I?" is perhaps the hardest of all questions to answer both because "I" am too complex for definition at any moment and because, if "I" could be defined at a moment, "I" would not be the same in the moment that followed. There is merit in the old saw about the number of persons involved in a conversation between John and Peter, for John *is* at the same time John-as-he-sees-himself, John-as-Peter-sees-him, John-as-John-thinks-Peter-sees-him, John-as-he-is-seen-by-others, John-as-he-conceives-himself-to-be-seen-by-others, and so on. Most of us get along, fortunately for our efficiency, without constant concern about our protean character; but occasionally we surprise ourselves by our own actions or are surprised to discover that we are by reputation quite other than what we conceive ourselves to be.

Knowing the ambiguity of any answer to the question of identity, the writer makes a deliberate effort to establish his identity in every piece he writes. In this one he may be the interested observer; in another, severe and uncompromising judge; in a third, hero or victim. He may be young or old, wise or naïve, gentle or irascible, inconstant or as reliable as granite. However concealed, he is never absent, and through the disguises he dons and the parts he plays he gradually makes apparent, to himself and his reader, his own complex identity. As unlike as are *Bleak House, David Copperfield,* and *Hard Times,* the reader knows that one identity dominates all three. No matter how diverse an author's works, there is always an identifiable someone whose shadow moves behind the words; that someone is the author's discovered self. The double motive for all art—inquiry and expression—works here as elsewhere: searching for a means of expression leads to discovery of what must be expressed, and searching for what is to be expressed suggests the means for expression. The writer's deliberate assumption of a role is, then, at once a part of his inquiry and a means to its expression.

Quite commonly the author avoids making his identity directly known to the reader. He does not declaim and strut upon the stage but manages the cues, the lights, the scenery, and the curtain, all from the wings. Even when he makes a bold appearance, he is like the ghost of Hamlet's father rather than like the perturbed prince himself: the reader is more than half convinced that the terrible figure and the dreadful voice are illusions, not real identities at all. Nonetheless, the writer's presence makes itself felt in all good writing, and the reader who fails to sense that presence misses complete literary experience. Learning to sense it is, in large measure, a matter of learning how to detect the *tone* of a piece and how to understand the *perspective* in which the author presents his material.

Tone has been defined by one astute reader (Professor Reuben Brower, in *Fields of Light*) as "1) the implied social relationship of the speaker to his auditor and 2) the manner he adopts in addressing his auditor." The definition assumes that a writer consciously or unconsciously has a reader in mind as he writes and that he addresses himself not to thin air but to that reader or group of readers, real or imaginary. If he writes, like Stendhal, for the "happy few," he shuts his ears to the demands of the unhappy many knowing the few to be of his kind, he treats them as equals, tells all without condescension, is frankly cynical and frankly sentimental, respects thei code and expects their understanding. If he is revealing mysteries to the uninitiated, he speaks in the voice of authority, assured and unequivocal, though perhaps kindly. The reader must learn to pick up, just as the writer learns to provide, those cues which characterize his role. Sometimes the cues are obvious—a particular kind of idiom, a defining vocabulary, or a revealing set of habits (redundancy, exaggeration, epigrammatic terseness, and the like); more often, they are less easily detectable. A form of address, an unpredictable choice of word, a peculiar turn of phrase—by such small means an author makes himself "known" to his reader. Often an author will produce his major effect in a piece of writing by shifting tone, by stepping from one role to another; always it is the tone he adopts that governs or directs his choice of language, his syntax, his stylistic economy. Steady reading develops a reader's inner ear; the habit of watching for the distinctive clues to tone develops the ability to recognize, and name, what the ear has detected.

There is a second, and rather more common, sense in which a reader uses the word "tone" about a piece of writing. In this sense, he refers to the emotional temper, to what might also be called the "mood" of a passage. Used in that way, "tone" is still a matter of the emotional attitude of the writer, but of the emotional attitude toward his subject, not toward his reader. The subject stirs him to indignation, to melancholy, to pity, to nostalgia—and, being thus stirred, he shapes his material in the heat of his feeling. His means remain much the same as those used in developing his "role," but the devices are less concealed, and often not concealed at all.

In addition to the inescapable relationships of author to reader and to material which make their appearance in tone, there is another relationship of great importance. The writer may or may not make a conscious selection of tone; that is to say, he may or may not be fully conscious of his relationship to his material and to his reader. The better craftsman he is, the stronger his awareness will be, and only such awareness makes possible the detailed revision and rewriting to which most authors subject their work. Still, the tone may in one sense seem to come "naturally" to the author, to be the inevitably right tone for that matter and for that use of it. It is not quite the same with the other relationship, the relationship to which the name *perspective* may be given.

Perspective is the author's conscious and deliberate choice of a position from which he wants his reader to view his material. The simplest perspective is that in which the author invites the reader to stand beside him and confront the material directly. In such a direct confrontation, the writer appears to be doing no more than gesturing toward the matter which both he and the reader have in view. It is well to remember, however, that even a gesture is persuasive in that it calls attention to one thing and does not call attention to another. If the writer does no more than announce and explain his subject, he has nonetheless already become

critic and commentator by the mere fact that he has chosen this rather than
that subject and this rather than that category of explanation. All the same,
direct confrontation avoids deliberate distortion of material; its persuasive-
ness is the result of focus and, of course, the result as well of tone, which
operates here as elsewhere. Its peculiar characteristic is an almost physical
sense of nearness or distance, either in time or in space, as though writer
and reader had stooped over to examine with care the detail of an object
or were gazing with detachment down the long corridor of time at the
almost inexplicable actions of puppet people awkwardly strutting out their
days before a painted panorama. Distant events, viewed from so great a
distance that their causes, purposes, and rationale are unknown, often become meaningless or ridiculous: at its limit, then, this backing away from
an object may produce irony and satire.

When direct confrontation is carried so far, a degree of distortion has
already been introduced. Some aspects of the object or event in view are
systematically reduced in importance or in size so that other aspects may
be emphasized. This is substantially what occurs in the process of understatement (*meiosis*) and overstatement (*hyperbole*), but in such processes
the results are quite different from those produced by irony and satire. When
a writer carefully dilates something insignificant, he may aim to intensify
paltriness rather than to make insignificance seem important. When he
minimizes, or slurs over, something of importance—particularly something
almost too horrible or too tragic for words—he may aim to magnify, not
to depreciate, significance. Understatement and overstatement seem to produce their effects by disappointing expectation.

Other oblique approaches have more elaborate mechanisms. Parody,
for instance, is a compound of mockery and of appreciation. The parodist
is ostensibly concerned only to hold something up to ridicule. His means
is imitation, and the imitation must be competent enough in form and in
content to come very close to the real thing; at the same time it must
cautiously exaggerate those characteristics of the original which are its
most distinctive properties. No one can write a competent parody without
being sensitive to the virtues as well as to the eccentricities (or, from the
point of view of the parodist, the "failures") of the piece to be parodied.
Gross distortion turns parody into burlesque; the limitation of parody to
formal matters turns it into pastiche; limitation to content, into satire.
Genuine parody is criticism of a high order for the reason that it is possible only to the critic who is refined enough to duplicate the form, as
well as to analyze the significance, of the original. The perspective is
achieved by putting a microscope before the reader's eyes.

Satire is both less subtle and more serious than parody. Generally, it
seeks reform and, perhaps because it is so strongly motivated by social and
moral purpose, it often sacrifices detail for large effect. The satirist does
not allow his reader to look upon the usual appearance of the object at all;

instead, he has him peer into a distorting mirror in which he will see the lineaments of the object so contorted that the object itself is momentarily unfamiliar. The satirist is convinced that things are not what they seem, and he uses his skill at distortion to divulge the reality beneath the appearance. He does not so much alter the object he deals with as displace its parts, so that what is hidden or obscure becomes unexpectedly prominent, and not only prominent but obviously discordant with the conventional appearance of the object.

Satire is a public art. By comparison with it, irony is private and exclusive and for that reason a favorite tool of writers who choose to deal with delicate or dangerous material. Now irony of situation, usually through a reversal of circumstances, is common to good and bad writing alike, from the cheap irony in a gratuitous "twist" ending of a story by O. Henry to the tragic irony of the reversal in a Greek drama. But irony of statement is less easily exploited. To begin with, it assumes a rapport between writer and reader that is almost perfect, for the words actually used when the irony is created may or may not carry a hint of their self-negation. Frequently, a reader perceives an irony because the writer has already made his disposition so well known that the reader recognizes the particular statement to be a contradiction of the writer as he has come to know him. More commonly, however, it is an author's apparently unruffled acceptance of what is outrageous or vile that makes a reader recognize the thrust and bite of irony. The game is an elaborate one because, on the surface of the matter, it seems foolish for a writer to say what he does not believe for the purpose of having those who know him well enough to judge recognize that he means something different from what he says. Irony may be choice for the reason that it relies upon this intimate relationship between reader and writer and, by implication, upon the shutting out of a larger public. Whatever the reason, this boldest and most downright of distortions generally turns out to be the least readily perceived and the most devastating, once its activity is discovered.

All discussion of rhetoric assumes a high degree of conscious artistry, so high a degree that the uninitiated are likely to suspect that rhetoric is a consideration peculiar to critics rather than to artists themselves. In this suspicion they are often confirmed by the statements of writers, painters, and other creative artists. Yet, even were there not ample evidence in the form of reams of worksheets representing preparatory stages of great works, the suspicion would hang upon the question-begging word "conscious." Whether a writer labels effects as he tries them is not important; if he tries one, then another, and finally achieves the effect he is seeking, he is consciously manipulating rhetorical devices. The casual reader, of course, cares little about the labor that makes a work of art possible, but casual reading is less than works of art deserve. They yield their full power only to those who know enough to appreciate their achievement; and, while knowledge of rhetoric is not by any means the only—or the most important—kind of knowing for a reader, it is one kind and important enough to warrant a student's thoughtful attention.

TONE: CHILDREN AND THEIR ELDERS

THE WORD "TONE," as it refers to written language, is a metaphor. It comes, of course, from tone of voice. Because there are no conventions of notation in English by which a writer can indicate loudness or softness or high pitch or gruffness, the metaphor cannot be taken literally. But tone in writing, like tone of voice, has to do with the indicating of emotional attitude, since the way a speaker or writer feels will determine the manner of his speaking or writing. Tone, then, expresses a writer's attitude, either toward his material, toward his audience, or toward both. Thus, an advocate of federal aid to schools may display anger about the mediocre quality of American education, or he may be enraged at his audience for its indifference to the situation. The distinction is important since one characteristic of good writing is careful control of emotion and if the writer is not sure in what direction to point his guns, he can hardly fire accurately. But the two main dangers which attend the use of written tone are inappropriateness and inconsistency. The former is easy to avoid in its extremes—few would use a jocular tone in relating the death of a friend. But borderline questions are more difficult: is it best to be plaintive or stern in an editorial on speeding violations? The danger of inconsistency involves similar problems of taste. A writer may shift his tone in the course of an essay, but he must make certain that the emotional leap is not too great for his reader to make and that the new tone grows organically out of the old rather than grating against it.

Tone is created most obviously through the kinds of words used. To an extent, the feelings of joy, pique, incredulity, distress, and so forth all have vocabularies of their own. But more subtly, tone comes from the ways in which a writer combines words. The length of the units, for example, can make the difference between curtness and expansiveness. And within long sentences, use of mainly subordinate constructions may create formality of tone, and use of a chain of coordinate clauses, something akin to casualness. Word patterns are also important—repetition of phrases, or even of constructions, for example. Finally, a writer may govern tone by the way he deals with the conventions of grammar. This is not merely to say that an essay which fractures all the rules is likely to sound casual. A writer may choose to depart from convention to create urgency of tone, or flippancy, or mere excitement. The intricacies of tone are far too complicated to deal with here, but the foregoing discussion may at least suggest how important it is for a writer to consider the emotional implications, as well as the substance, of what he says.

All of the following selections deal with the relationship between children and their parents or guardians, a relationship so intimate that tone is of first importance. The brief selection by E. E. Cummings (1894-1962) is a very early reminiscence which the author later incorporated into one of his lectures as Charles Eliot Norton Professor at Harvard in 1953. John Stuart Mill (1806-1873), foremost logician of the nineteenth-century scientific movement, brought his habitual rigor of analysis to his autobiography; the effect such rigor has on tone in the passage presented here is quite remarkable. Edmund Gosse (1849-1928), English literary historian and critic, here treats his relationship with his father at a critical stage of its development. An entirely different kind of relationship is recorded by James Agee (1909-1955), novelist and script-writer for moving pictures and television, in a warm account of family life in a southern town forty years ago. The next selection, by novelist Mary McCarthy (1912-   ), introduces a new condition of relationship that is immediately reflected in the tone; in it an orphan describes her foster parents, relatives who are culturally alien to her.

The first selection in the unit is somewhat different from the others in its substance, but it captures magnificently a particular tone appropriate to the relationship between parent and child. It is a translation by William Prescott (1796-1859), the first American historian to make extensive studies of the culture of Mexico and of South America. The document itself dates from the period known in Europe as the Middle Ages, a period in which the Aztec culture was at its height.

ADVICE OF AN AZTEC MOTHER TO HER DAUGHTER | *ANONYMOUS*

My beloved daughter, very dear little dove, you have already heard and attended to the words which your father has told you. They are precious words, and such as are rarely spoken or listened to, and which have proceeded from the bowels and heart in which they were treasured up; and your beloved father well knows that you are his daughter, begotten of him, are his blood, and his flesh; and God our Lord knows that it is so. Although you are a woman, and are *the image of your father,* what more can I say to you than has already been said? What more can you hear than what you have heard from your lord and father? who has fully told you what it is

Trans. by William H. Prescott, as an appendix to his *History of the Conquest of Mexico* (1843).

becoming for you to do and to avoid; nor is there anything remaining, which concerns you, that he has not touched upon. Nevertheless, that I may do toward you my whole duty, I will say to you some few words.

The first thing that I earnestly charge upon you is, that you observe and do not forget what your father has now told you, since it is all very precious; and persons of his condition rarely publish such things; for they are the words which belong to the noble and wise—valuable as rich jewels. See, then, that you take them and lay them up in your heart, and write them in your bowels. If God gives you life, with these same words will you teach your sons and daughters, if God shall give you them.

The second thing that I desire to say to you is, that I love you much, that you are my dear daughter. Remember that nine months I bore you in my womb, that you were born and brought up in my arms. I placed you in your cradle, and in my lap, and with my milk I nursed you. This I tell you, in order that you may know that I and your father are the source of your being; it is we who now instruct you. See that you receive our words, and treasure them in your breast.

Take care that your garments are such as are decent and proper; and observe that you do not adorn yourself with much finery, since this is a mark of vanity and of folly. As little becoming is it, that your dress should be very mean, dirty, or ragged; since rags are a mark of the low, and of those who are held in contempt. Let your clothes be becoming and neat, that you may neither appear fantastic nor mean. When you speak, do not hurry your words from uneasiness, but speak deliberately and calmly. Do not raise your voice very high, nor speak very low, but in a moderate tone. Neither mince, when you speak, nor when you salute, nor speak through your nose; but let your words be proper, of a good sound, and your voice gentle. Do not be nice in the choice of your words. In walking, my daughter, see that you behave becomingly, neither going with haste, nor too slowly; since it is an evidence of being puffed up, to walk too slowly, and walking hastily causes a vicious habit of restlessness and instability. Therefore neither walk very fast, nor very slow; yet, when it shall be necessary to go with haste, do so—in this use your discretion. And when you may be obliged to jump over a pool of water, do it with decency, that you may neither appear clumsy nor light. When you are in the street, do not carry your head much inclined, or your body bent; nor as little go with your head very much raised; since it is a mark of ill breeding; walk erect, and with your head slightly inclined. Do not have your mouth covered, or your face, from shame, nor go looking like a near-sighted person, nor, on your way, make fantastic movements with your feet. Walk through the street quietly, and with propriety. Another thing that you must attend to, my daugher, is, that when you are in the street you do not go looking hither and thither, nor turning your head to look at this and that; walk neither looking at the skies nor on the ground. Do not look upon those whom you meet with the eyes of an offended person, nor have the appearance of being uneasy; but of one who looks upon all with a serene countenance; doing this, you will give no one occasion of being offended with you. Show a becoming countenance; that you may neither appear morose, nor, on the other hand, too complaisant. See, my daughter, that you give yourself no concern about the words you may hear, in going through the street, nor pay any regard to them, let those who come and go say what they will. Take care that you neither answer nor speak, but act as if you neither heard nor understood them; since, doing in this manner, no one will be able to say with truth that you have said anything amiss. See, likewise, my daughter, that you never paint your face, or stain it or your lips with colors, in order to appear well; since this is a mark of vile and unchaste women. Paints and coloring are things which bad women use—the immodest, who have lost all shame and even sense, who are like fools and drunkards, and are called *rameras* [prostitutes]. But, that your husband may not dislike you, adorn yourself, wash yourself, and cleanse your clothes; and let this be done with moderation; since if every day you wash yourself and your clothes it will be said of you that you are over-nice—too delicate; they will call you *tapepetzon tinemaxoch*.

My daughter, this is the course you are to take; since in this manner the ancestors from whom you spring brought us up. Those noble and venerable dames, your grandmothers, told us not so many things as I have told you— they said but few words, and spoke thus: "Listen, my daughters; in this world it is necessary to live with much prudence and circumspection. Hear this allegory, which I shall now tell you, and preserve it, and take from it a warning and example for living aright. Here, in this world, we travel by a very narrow, steep, and dangerous road, which is as a lofty mountain ridge, on whose top passes a narrow path; on either side is a great gulf without bottom; and if you deviate from the path you will fall into it. There is need, therefore, of much discretion in pursuing the road." My tenderly loved daughter, my little dove, keep this illustration in your heart, and see that you do not forget it—it will be to you as a lamp and a beacon so long as you shall live in this world.

Only one thing remains to be said, and I have done. If God shall give you life, if you shall continue some years upon the earth, see that you guard yourself carefully, that no stain come upon you; should you forfeit your chastity and afterwards be asked in marriage and should marry anyone, you will never be fortunate, nor have true love—he will always remember that you were not a virgin, and this will be the cause of great affliction and distress; you will never be at peace, for your husband will always be suspicious of you. O my dearly beloved daughter, if you shall live upon the earth, see that not more than one man approaches you; and observe what I now shall tell you, as a strict command. When it shall please God that you receive a husband, and you are placed under his authority, be free from arrogance, see that you do not neglect him, nor allow your heart to be in opposition to him. Be not disrespectful to him. Beware that in no time or place you commit the treason against him called adultery. See that you give no favor to another; since this, my dear and much-loved daughter, is to fall into a pit without bottom, from which there will be no escape. According to the custom of the world, if it shall be known, for this crime they will kill you, they will throw you into the street, for an example to all the people, where your head will be crushed and dragged upon the ground. Of these says a proverb, "You will be stoned and dragged upon the earth, and others will take warning at your death." From this will arise a stain and dishonor upon our ancestors, the nobles and senators from whom we are descended. You will tarnish their illustrious fame, and their glory, by the filthiness and impurity of your sin. You will, likewise, lose your reputation, your nobility, and honor of birth; your name will be forgotten and abhorred. Of you will it be said that you were buried in the dust of your sins. And remember, my daughter, that, though no man shall see you, nor your husband ever know what happens, *God, who is in every place, sees you,* will be angry with you, and will also excite the indignation of the people against you, and will be avenged upon you as he shall see fit. By his command, you shall either be maimed, or struck blind, or your body will wither, or you will come to extreme poverty, for daring to injure your husband. Or perhaps he will give you to death, and put you under his feet, sending you to the place of torment. Our Lord is compassionate; but, if you commit treason against your husband, God, who is in every place, shall take vengeance on your sin, and will permit you to have neither contentment, nor repose, nor a peaceful life; and he will excite your husband to be always unkind toward you, and always to speak to you with anger. My dear daughter, whom I tenderly love, see that you live in the world in peace, tranquillity, and contentment, all the days that you shall live. See that you disgrace not yourself, that you stain not your honor, nor pollute the luster and fame of your ancestors. See that you honor me and your father, and reflect glory on us by your good life. May God prosper you, my first-born, and may you come to God, who is in every place.

ABOUT MY FATHER | E. E. CUMMINGS

I wot not how to answer your query about my father. He was a New Hampshire man, 6 foot 2, a crack shot & a famous fly-fisherman & a firstrate sailor (his sloop was named The Actress) & a woodsman who could find his way through forests primeval without a compass & a canoeist who'd still-

paddle you up to a deer without ruffling the surface of a pond & an orni-
thologist & taxidermist & (when he gave up hunting) an expert photographer (the best I've ever seen) & an actor who portrayed Julius Caesar in
Sanders Theatre & a painter (both in oils & watercolors) & a better carpenter
than any professional & an architect who designed his own houses before
building them & (when he liked) a plumber who just for the fun of it
installed all his own waterworks & (while at Harvard) a teacher with small
use for professors—by whom (Royce, Lanman, Taussig, etc.) we were
literally surrounded (but not defeated)—& later (at Doctor Hale's socalled
South Congregational really Unitarian church) a preacher who announced,
during the last war, that the Gott Mit Uns boys were in error since the only
thing which mattered was for man to be on God's side (& one beautiful
Sunday in Spring remarked from the pulpit that he couldn't understand
why anyone had come to hear him on such a day) & horribly shocked his
pewholders by crying "the Kingdom of Heaven is no spiritual roofgarden:
it's inside you" & my father had the first telephone in Cambridge & (long
before any Model T Ford) he piloted an Orient Buckboard with Friction
Drive produced by the Waltham watch company & my father sent me to a
certain public school because its principal was a gentle immense coalblack
negress & when he became a diplomat (for World Peace) he gave me &
my friends a tremendous party up in a tree at Sceaux Robinson & my father
was a servant of the people who fought Boston's biggest & crookedest politician fiercely all day & a few evenings later sat down with him cheerfully at
the Rotary Club & my father's voice was so magnificent that he was called
on to impersonate God speaking from Beacon Hill (he was heard all over
the common) & my father gave me Plato's metaphor of the cave with my
mother's milk.

MY FATHER'S RELIGIOUS AND MORAL TEACHINGS | JOHN STUART MILL

I was brought up from the first without any religious belief, in the
ordinary acceptation of the term. My father, educated in the creed of Scotch
Presbyterianism, had by his own studies and reflections been early led to
reject not only the belief in Revelation, but the foundations of what is
commonly called Natural Religion, I have heard him say, that the turning
point of his mind on the subject was reading Butler's Analogy. That work,
of which he always continued to speak with respect, kept him, as he said,
for some considerable time, a believer in the divine authority of Christianity; by proving to him, that whatever are the difficulties in believing that
the Old and New Testaments proceed from, or record the acts of, a perfectly

From the *Autobiography* (1873).

wise and good being, the same and still greater difficulties stand in the way of the belief, that a being of such a character can have been the Maker of the universe. He considered Butler's argument as conclusive against the only opponents for whom it was intended. Those who admit an omnipotent as well as perfectly just and benevolent maker and ruler of such a world as this, can say little against Christianity but what can, with at least equal force, be retorted against themselves. Finding, therefore, no halting place in Deism, he remained in a state of perplexity, until, doubtless after many struggles, he yielded to the conviction, that, concerning the origin of things nothing whatever can be known. This is the only correct statement of his opinion; for dogmatic atheism he looked upon as absurd; as most of those, whom the world has considered Atheists, have always done. These particulars are important, because they show that my father's rejection of all that is called religious belief, was not, as many might suppose, primarily a matter of logic and evidence: the grounds of it were moral, still more than intellectual. He found it impossible to believe that a world so full of evil was the work of an Author combining infinite power with perfect goodness and righteousness. His intellect spurned the subtleties by which men attempt to blind themselves to this open contradiction. The Sabaean, or Manichaean theory of a Good and an Evil Principle, struggling against each other for the government of the universe, he would not have equally condemned; and I have heard him express surprise, that no one revived it in our time. He would have regarded it as a mere hypothesis; but he would have ascribed to it no depraving influence. As it was, his aversion to religion, in the sense usually attached to the term, was of the same kind with that of Lucretius: he regarded it with the feelings due not to a mere mental delusion, but to a great moral evil. He looked upon it as the greatest enemy of morality: first, by setting up fictitious excellences—belief in creeds, devotional feelings, and ceremonies, not connected with the good of human-kind—and causing these to be accepted as substitutes for genuine virtues: but above all, by radically vitiating the standard of morals; making it consist in doing the will of a being, on whom it lavishes indeed all the phrases of adulation, but whom in sober truth it depicts as eminently hateful. I have a hundred times heard him say, that all ages and nations have represented their gods as wicked, in a constantly increasing progression, that mankind have gone on adding trait after trait till they reached the most perfect conception of wickedness which the human mind can devise, and have called this God, and prostrated themselves before it. This *ne plus ultra* of wickedness he considered to be embodied in what is commonly presented to mankind as the creed of Christianity. Think (he used to say) of a being who would make a Hell—who would create the human race with the infallible foreknowledge, and therefore with the intention, that the great majority of them were to be consigned to horrible and everlasting torment. The time, I believe, is drawing near when this dreadful conception of an object of worship will be no longer identified with Christianity; and when all persons, with any sense of moral good and evil, will look upon it with the same indignation with which my father regarded it. My father was as well aware as any one that Christians do not, in general, undergo the demoralizing consequences which seem inherent in such a creed, in the manner or to the extent which might have been expected from it. The same slovenliness of thought, and subjection of the reason to fears, wishes, and affections, which enable them to accept a theory involving a contradiction in terms, prevents them from perceiving the logical consequences of the theory. Such is the facility with which mankind believe at one and the same time things inconsistent with one another, and so few are those who draw from what they receive as truths, any consequences, but those recommended to them by their feelings, that multitudes have held the undoubting belief in an Omnipotent Author of Hell, and have nevertheless identified that being with the best conception they were able to form of perfect goodness. Their worship was not paid to the demon which such a Being as they imagined would really be, but to their own ideal of excellence. The evil is, that such a belief keeps the ideal wretchedly low; and opposes the most obstinate resistance to all thought which has a tendency to raise it higher. Believers shrink from every train of ideas which would lead the mind to a clear conception and an elevated standard of excellence, because they feel (even when they do not distinctly see) that such a standard would conflict with many of the dispensations of nature, and with much of what they are accustomed to consider as the Christian creed. And thus morality continues a matter of blind tradition, with no consistent principle, nor even any consistent feeling, to guide it.

It would have been wholly inconsistent with my father's idea of duty, to allow me to acquire impressions contrary to his convictions and feelings respecting religion: and he impressed upon me from the first, that the manner in which the world came into existence was a subject on which nothing was known: that the question, "Who made me?" cannot be answered, because we have no experience or authentic information from which to answer it; and that any answer only throws the difficulty a step further back, since the question immediately presents itself, "Who made God?" He, at the same time, took care that I should be acquainted with what had been thought by mankind on these impenetrable problems. I have mentioned at how early an age he made me a reader of ecclesiastical history; and he taught me to take the strongest interest in the Reformation, as the great and decisive contest against priestly tyranny for liberty of thought.

I am thus one of the very few examples, in this country, of one who has, not thrown off religious belief, but never had it: I grew up in a negative state with regard to it. I looked upon the modern exactly as I did upon the ancient religion, as something which in no way concerned me. . . .

My father's moral convictions, wholly dissevered from religion, were very

much of the character of those of the Greek philosophers; and were delivered with the force and decision which characterized all that came from
him. Even at the very early age at which I read with him the Memorabilia
of Xenophon, I imbibed from that work and from his comments a deep
respect for the character of Socrates; who stood in my mind as a model of
ideal excellence: and I well remember how my father at that time impressed
upon me the lesson of the "Choice of Hercules." At a somewhat later period
the lofty moral standard exhibited in the writings of Plato operated upon
me with great force. My father's moral inculcations were at all times mainly
those of the "Socratici viri"; justice, temperance (to which he gave a very
extended application), veracity, perseverance, readiness to encounter pain
and especially labor; regard for the public good; estimation of persons
according to their merits, and of things according to their intrinsic usefulness; a life of exertion in contradiction to one of self-indulgent ease and
sloth. These and other moralities he conveyed in brief sentences, uttered
as occasion arose, of grave exhortation, or stern reprobation and contempt.

But though direct moral teaching does much, indirect does more; and
the effect my father produced on my character, did not depend solely on
what he said or did with that direct object, but also, and still more, on
what manner of man he was.

In his views of life he partook of the character of the Stoic, the Epicurean, and the Cynic, not in the modern but the ancient sense of the word.
In his personal qualities the Stoic predominated. His standard of morals
was Epicurean, inasmuch as it was utilitarian, taking as the exclusive test
of right and wrong, the tendency of actions to produce pleasure or pain.
But he had (and this was the Cynic element) scarcely any belief in pleasure;
at least in his later years, of which alone, on this point, I can speak confidently. He was not insensible to pleasures; but he deemed very few of them
worth the price which, at least in the present state of society, must be paid
for them. The greater number of miscarriages in life, he considered to be
attributable to the overvaluing of pleasures. Accordingly, temperance, in
the large sense intended by the Greek philosophers—stopping short at the
point of moderation in all indulgences—was with him, as with them, almost
the central point of educational precept. His inculcations of this virtue fill
a large place in my childish remembrances. He thought human life a poor
thing at best, after the freshness of youth and of unsatisfied curiosity had
gone by. This was a topic on which he did not often speak, especially, it
may be supposed, in the presence of young persons: but when he did, it was
with an air of settled and profound conviction. He would sometimes say,
that if life were made what it might be, by good government and good education, it would be worth having: but he never spoke with anything like
enthusiasm even of that possibility. He never varied in rating intellectual
enjoyments above all others, even in value as pleasures, independently of
their ulterior benefits. The pleasures of the benevolent affections he placed

high in the scale; and used to say, that he had never known a happy old man, except those who were able to live over again in the pleasures of the young. For passionate emotions of all sorts, and for everything which has been said or written in exaltation of them, he professed the greatest contempt. He regarded them as a form of madness. "The intense" was with him a bye-word of scornful disapprobation. He regarded as an aberration of the moral standard of modern times, compared with that of the ancients, the great stress upon feeling. Feelings, as such, he considered to be no proper subjects of praise or blame. Right and wrong, good and bad, he regarded as qualities solely of conduct—of acts and omissions; there being no feeling which may not lead, and does not frequently lead, either to good or to bad actions: conscience itself, the very desire to act right, often leading people to act wrong. Consistently carrying out the doctrine, that the object of praise and blame should be the discouragement of wrong conduct and the encouragement of right, he refused to let his praise or blame be influenced by the motive of the agent. He blamed as severely what he thought a bad action, when the motive was a feeling of duty, as if the agents had been consciously evil doers. He would not have accepted as a plea in mitigation for inquisitors, that they sincerely believed burning heretics to be an obligation of conscience. But though he did not allow honesty of purpose to soften his disapprobation of actions, it had its full effect on his estimation of characters. No one prized conscientiousness and rectitude of intention more highly, or was more incapable of valuing any person in whom he did not feel assurance of it. But he disliked people quite as much for any other deficiency, provided he thought it equally likely to make them act ill. He disliked, for instance, a fanatic in any bad cause, as much or more than one who adopted the same cause from self-interest, because he thought him even more likely to be practically mischievous. And thus, his aversion to many intellectual errors, or what he regarded as such, partook, in a certain sense, of the character of a moral feeling. All this is merely saying that he, in a degree once common, but now very unusual, threw his feelings into his opinions; which truly it is difficult to understand how any one who possesses much of both, can fail to do. None but those who do not care about opinions, will confound this with intolerance. Those, who having opinions which they hold to be immensely important, and their contraries to be prodigiously hurtful, have any deep regard for the general good, will necessarily dislike, as a class and in the abstract, those who think wrong what they think right, and right what they think wrong: though they need not therefore be, nor was my father, insensible to good qualities in an opponent, nor governed in their estimation of individuals by one general presumption, instead of by the whole of their character. I grant that an earnest person, being no more infallible than other men, is liable to dislike people on account of opinions which do not merit dislike; but if he neither himself does them any ill office, nor connives at its being done by others, he is not intolerant: and the forbearance which flows from a conscientious sense of the importance to mankind of the equal freedom of all opinions, is the only tolerance which is commendable, or, to the highest moral order of minds, possible.

It will be admitted, that a man of the opinions, and the character, above described, was likely to leave a strong moral impression on any mind principally formed by him, and that his moral teaching was not likely to err on the side of laxity or indulgence. The element which was chiefly deficient in his moral relation to his children was that of tenderness. I do not believe that this deficiency lay in his own nature. I believe him to have had much more feeling than he habitually showed, and much greater capacities of feeling than were ever developed. He resembled most Englishmen in being ashamed of the signs of feeling, and by the absence of demonstration, starving the feelings themselves. If we consider further that he was in the trying position of sole teacher, and add to this that his temper was constitutionally irritable, it is impossible not to feel true pity for a father who did, and strove to do, so much for his children, who would have so valued their affection, yet who must have been constantly feeling that fear of him was drying it up at its source. This was no longer the case later in life, and with his younger children. They loved him tenderly: and if I cannot say so much of myself, I was always loyally devoted to him. As regards my own education, I hesitate to pronounce whether I was more a loser or gainer by his severity. It was not such as to prevent me from having a happy childhood. And I do not believe that boys can be induced to apply themselves with vigor, and what is so much more difficult, perseverance, to dry and irksome studies, by the sole force of persuasion and soft words. Much must be done, and much must be learnt, by children, for which rigid discipline, and known liability to punishment, are indispensable as means. It is, no doubt, a very laudable effort, in modern teaching, to render as much as possible of what the young are required to learn, easy and interesting to them. But when this principle is pushed to the length of not requiring them to learn anything *but* what has been made easy and interesting, one of the chief objects of education is sacrificed. I rejoice in the decline of the old brutal and tyrannical system of teaching, which, however, did succeed in enforcing habits of application; but the new, as it seems to me, is training up a race of men who will be incapable of doing anything which is disagreeable to them. I do not, then, believe that fear, as an element in education, can be dispensed with; but I am sure that it ought not to be the main element; and when it predominates so much as to preclude love and confidence on the part of the child to those who should be the unreservedly trusted advisers of after years, and perhaps to seal up the fountains of frank and spontaneous communicativeness in the child's nature, it is an evil for which a large abatement must be made from the benefits, moral and intellectual, which may flow from any other part of the education.

MY FATHER'S FALL FROM OMNIPOTENCE | *EDMUND GOSSE*

In the course of this, my sixth year, there happened a series of minute and soundless incidents which, elementary as they may seem when told, were second in real importance to none in my mental history. The recollection of them confirms me in the opinion that certain leading features in each human soul are inherent to it, and cannot be accounted for by suggestion or training. In my own case, I was most carefully withdrawn, like Princess Blanchefleur in her marble fortress, from every outside influence whatever, yet to me the instinctive life came as unexpectedly as her lover came to her in the basket of roses. What came to me was the consciousness of self, as a force and as a companion, and it came as the result of one or two shocks, which I will relate.

In consequence of hearing so much about an Omniscient God, as being of supernatural wisdom and penetration who was always with us, who made, in fact, a fourth in our company, I had come to think of Him, not without awe, but with absolute confidence. My Father and Mother, in their serene discipline of me, never argued with one another, never even differed; their wills seemed absolutely one. My Mother always deferred to my Father, and in his absence spoke of him to me, as if he were all-wise. I confused him in some sense with God; at all events I believed that my Father knew everything and saw everything. One morning in my sixth year, my Mother and I were alone in the morning-room, when my Father came in and announced some fact to us. I was standing on the rug, gazing at him, and when he made this statement, I remember turning quickly, in embarrassment, and looking into the fire. The shock to me was that of a thunderbolt, for what my Father had said *was not true*. My Mother and I, who had been present at the trifling incident, were aware that it had not happened exactly as it had been reported to him. My Mother gently told him so, and he accepted the correction. Nothing could possibly have been more trifling to my parents, but to me it meant an epoch. Here was the appalling discovery, never suspected before, that my Father was not as God, and did not know everything. The shock was not caused by any suspicion that he was not telling the truth, as it appeared to him, but by the awful proof that he was not, as I had supposed, omniscient.

This experience was followed by another, which confirmed the first, but carried me a great deal further. In our little back-garden, my Father had built up a rockery for ferns and mosses, and from the water-supply of the house he had drawn a leaden pipe so that it pierced upwards through the rockery and produced, when a tap was turned, a pretty silvery parasol of water. The pipe was exposed somewhere near the foot of the rockery. One day, two workmen, who were doing some repairs, left their tools during the dinner-hour in the back-garden, and as I was marching about I suddenly thought that to see whether one of these tools could make a hole in the pipe would be attractive. It did make such a hole, quite easily, and then the matter escaped my mind. But a day or two afterwards, when my Father came in to dinner, he was very angry. He had turned the tap, and, instead of the fountain arching at the summit, there had been a rush of water through a hole at the foot. The rockery was absolutely ruined.

Of course I realized in a moment what I had done, and I sat frozen with alarm, waiting to be denounced. But my Mother remarked on the visit of the plumbers two or three days before, and my Father instantly took up the suggestion. No doubt that was it; the mischievous fellows had thought it amusing to stab the pipe and spoil the fountain. No suspicion fell on me; no question was asked of me. I sat there, turned to stone within, but outwardly sympathetic, and with unchecked appetite.

We attribute, I believe, too many moral ideas to little children. It is obvious that in this tremendous juncture, I ought to have been urged forward by good instincts, or held back by naughty ones. But I am sure that the fear which I experienced for a short time, and which so unexpectedly melted away, was a purely physical one. It had nothing to do with the emotions of a contrite heart. As to the destruction of the fountain, I was sorry about that, for my own sake, since I admired the skipping water extremely, and had no idea that I was spoiling its display. But the emotions which now thronged within me, and which led me with an almost unwise alacrity, to seek solitude in the back-garden, were not moral at all, they were intellectual. I was not ashamed of having successfully—and so surprisingly— deceived my parents by my crafty silence; I looked upon that as a providential escape, and dismissed all further thought of it. I had other things to think of.

In the first place, the theory that my Father was omniscient or infallible was now dead and buried. He probably knew very little; in this case he had not known a fact of such importance that if you did not know that, it could hardly matter what you knew. My Father, as a deity, as a natural force of immense prestige, fell in my eyes to a human level. In future, his statements about things in general need not be accepted implicitly. But of all the thoughts which rushed upon my savage and undeveloped little brain at this crisis, the most curious was that I had found a companion and a confidant in myself. There was a secret in this world and it belonged to me and to a somebody who lived in the same body with me. There were two of us, and we could talk with one another. It is difficult to define impressions so rudimentary, but it is certain that it was in this dual form that the sense of my individuality now suddenly descended upon me, and it is equally certain that it was a great solace to me to find a sympathizer in my own breast.

A TIN BUTTERFLY | MARY McCARTHY

We both had enviable possessions and did not have them. In the closet in my bedroom, high on the top shelf, beyond my reach even standing on a chair, was a stack of cardboard doll boxes, containing wonderful French dolls, dressed by my Seattle grandmother in silks, laces, and satins, with crepe-de-Chine underwear and shoes with high heels. These and other things were sent us every year at Christmastime, but my aunt had decreed that they were all too good for us, so they remained in their boxes and wrappers, *verboten*, except on the rare afternoon, perhaps once in a twelvemonth or so, when a relation or a friend of the family would come through from the West, and then down would come the dolls, out would come the baseball gloves and catchers' masks and the watches and the shiny cars and the doll houses, and we would be set to playing with these things on the floor of the living room while the visitor tenderly looked on. As soon as the visitor left, bearing a good report of our household, the dolls and watches and cars would be whisked away, to come out again for the next emergency. If we had been clever, we would have refused this bait and paraded our misery, but we were too simple to do anything but seize the moment and play out a whole year's playtime in this gala hour and a half. Such techniques, of course, are common in concentration camps and penal institutions, where the same sound calculation of human nature is made. The prisoners snatch at their holiday; they trust their guards and the motto *"Carpe diem"* more than they do the strangers who have come to make the inspection. Like all people who have been mistreated, we were wary of being taken in; we felt uneasy about these visitors—Protestants from Seattle—who might be much worse than our uncle and aunt. The latter's faults, at any rate, we knew. Moreover, we had been subjected to propaganda: we had been threatened with the Seattle faction, time and again, by our uncle, who used to jeer and say to us, *"They'd* make you toe the chalk line."

The basis, I think, of my aunt's program for us was in truth totalitarian: she was idealistically bent on destroying our privacy. She imagined herself as enlightened in comparison with our parents, and a super-ideal of health, cleanliness, and discipline softened in her own eyes the measures she applied to attain it. A nature not unkindly was warped by bureaucratic zeal and by her subservience to her husband, whose masterful autocratic hand cut through our nonsense like a cleaver. The fact that our way of life resembled that of an orphan asylum was not a mere coincidence; Aunt Margaret strove purposefully toward a corporate goal. Like most heads of institutions, she longed for the eyes of Argus. To the best of her ability, she saw to it that nothing was hidden from her. Even her health measures had this purpose. The aperients we were continually dosed with guaranteed that our daily processes were open to her inspection, and the monthly medical checkup assured her, by means of stethoscope and searchlight and tongue depressor, that nothing was happening inside us to which she was not privy. Our letters to Seattle were written under her eye, and she scrutinized our homework sharply, though her arithmetic, spelling, and grammar were all very imperfect. We prayed, under supervision, for a prescribed list of people. And if we were forbidden companions, candy, most toys, pocket money, sports, reading, entertainment, the aim was not to make us suffer but to achieve efficiency. It was simpler to interdict other children than to inspect all the children with whom we might want to play. From the standpoint of efficiency, our lives, in order to be open, had to be empty; the books we might perhaps read, the toys we might play with figured in my aunt's mind, no doubt, as what the housewife calls "dust catchers"—around these distractions, dirt might accumulate. The inmost folds of consciousness, like the belly button, were regarded by her as unsanitary. Thus, in her spiritual outlook, my aunt was an early functionalist.

Like all systems, my aunt's was, of course, imperfect. Forbidden to read, we told stories, and if we were kept apart, we told them to ourselves in bed. We made romances out of our schoolbooks, even out of the dictionary, and read digests of novels in the *Book of Knowledge* at school. My uncle's partiality for my youngest brother was a weakness in him, as was my aunt Mary's partiality for me. She was supposed to keep me in her room, sewing on squares of cheap cotton, making handkerchiefs with big, crude, ugly hems, and ripping them out and making them over again, but though she had no feeling for art or visual beauty (she would not even teach me to darn, which is an art, or to do embroidery, as the nuns did later on, in the convent), she liked to talk of the old days in Chicago and to read sensational religious fiction in a magazine called the *Extension,* which sometimes she let me take to my room, with a caution against being caught. And on the Sunday walks that my uncle headed, at the end of an interminable streetcar ride, during which my bigger brothers had to scrunch down to pass for under six, there were occasions on which he took us (in military order) along a wooded path, high above the Mississippi River, and we saw late-spring harebells and, once, a coral-pink snake. In Minnehaha Park, a favorite resort, we were allowed to play on the swings and to examine the other children riding on the ponies or on a little scenic railway. Uncle Myers always bought himself a box of Cracker Jack, which we watched him eat and delve into, to find the little favor at the bottom—a ritual we deeply envied, for, though we sometimes had popcorn at home (Myers enjoyed popping it) and even, once or twice, homemade popcorn balls with molasses, we had never had more than a taste of this commercial Cracker Jack, with peanuts in it, which seemed to us the more valuable because *he* valued it and would often come home eating a box he had bought at a ball game. But one Sunday, Uncle Myers, in full, midsummer mood, wearing his new pedometer, bought my brother Sheridan a whole box for himself.

Naturally, we envied Sheridan—the only blond among us, with fair red-gold curls, while the rest of us were all pronounced brunets, with thick black brows and lashes—as we watched him, the lucky one, munch the sticky stuff and fish out a painted tin butterfly with a little pin on it at the bottom. My brothers clamored around him, but I was too proud to show my feelings. Sheridan was then about six years old, and this butterfly immediately became his most cherished possession—indeed, one of the few he had. He carried it about the house with him all the next week, clutched in his hand or pinned to his shirt, and my two other brothers followed him, begging him to be allowed to play with it, which slightly disgusted me, at the age of ten, for I knew that I was too sophisticated to care for tin butterflies and I felt in this whole affair the instigation of my uncle. He was relishing my brothers' performance and saw to it, strictly, that Sheridan clung to his rights in the butterfly and did not permit anybody to touch it. The point about this painted tin butterfly was not its intrinsic value; it was the fact that it was virtually the only toy in the house that had not been, so to speak, socialized, but belonged privately to one individual. Our other playthings— a broken-down wooden swing, an old wagon, a dirty sandbox, and perhaps a fire engine or so and some defaced blocks and twisted second-hand train tracks in the attic—were held by us all in common, the velocipedes we had brought with us from Seattle having long ago foundered, and the skipping rope, the jacks, the few marbles, and the pair of rusty roller skates that were given us being decreed to be the property of all. Hence, for a full week this butterfly excited passionate emotions, from which I held myself stubbornly apart, refusing even to notice it, until one afternoon, at about four o'clock, while I was doing my weekly chore of dusting the woodwork, my white-haired aunt Mary hurried softly into my room and, closing the door behind her, asked whether I had seen Sheridan's butterfly.

The topic wearied me so much that I scarcely lifted my head, answering no, shortly, and going on with my dusting. But Aunt Mary was gently persistent: Did I know that he had lost it? Would I help her look for it? This project did not appeal to me but in response to some faint agitation in her manner, something almost pleading, I put down my dustcloth and helped her. We went all over the house, raising carpets, looking behind curtains, in the kitchen cupboards, in the Victrola, everywhere but in the den, which was closed, and in my aunt's and uncle's bedroom. Somehow—I do not know why—I did not expect to find the butterfly, partly, I imagine, because I was indifferent to it and partly out of the fatalism that all children have toward lost objects, regarding them as irretrievable, vanished into the flux of things. At any rate I was right: we did not find it and I went back to my dusting, vindicated. Why should *I* have to look for Sheridan's stupid butterfly, which he ought to have taken better care of? "Myers is upset," said Aunt Mary, still hovering, uneasy and diffident, in the doorway. I made a slight face, and she went out, plaintive, remonstrant, and sighing, in her pale, high necked, tight-buttoned dress.

It did not occur to me that I was suspected of stealing this toy, even when Aunt Margaret, five minutes later, burst into my room and ordered me to come and look for Sheridan's butterfly. I protested that I had already done so, but she paid my objections no heed and seized me roughly by the arm. "Then do it again, Miss, and mind that you find it." Her voice was rather hoarse and her whole furrowed iron-gray aspect somewhat tense and disarrayed, yet I had the impression that she was not angry with me but with something in outer reality—what one would now call fate or contingency. When I had searched again, lackadaisically, and again found nothing, she joined in with vigor, turning everything upside down. We even went into the den, where Myers was sitting, and searched all around him, while he watched us with an ironical expression, filling his pipe from a Bull Durham sack. We found nothing, and Aunt Margaret led me upstairs to my room, which I ransacked while she stood and watched me. All at once, when we had finished with my bureau drawers and my closet, she appeared to give up. She sighed and bit her lips. The door cautiously opened and Aunt Mary came in. The two sisters looked at each other and at me. Margaret shrugged her shoulders. "She hasn't got it, I do believe," she said.

She regarded me then with a certain relaxing of her thick wrinkles, and her heavy-skinned hand, with its wedding ring, came down on my shoulder. "Uncle Myers thinks you took it," she said in a rusty whisper, like a spy or a scout. The consciousness of my own innocence, combined with a sense of being let into the confederacy of the two sisters, filled me with excitement and self-importance. "But I didn't, Aunt Margaret," I began proclaiming, making the most of my moment. "What would I want with his silly old butterfly?" The two sisters exchanged a look. "That's what I said, Margaret!" exclaimed old Aunt Mary sententiously. Aunt Margaret frowned; she adjusted a bone hairpin in the coiled rings of her unbecoming coiffure. "Mary Therese," she said to me, solemnly, "if you know anything about the butterfly, if one of your brothers took it, tell me now. If we don't find it, I'm afraid Uncle Myers will have to punish you." "He *can't* punish me, Aunt Margaret," I insisted, full of righteousness. "Not if I didn't do it and *you* don't think I did it." I looked up at her, stagily trustful, resting gingerly on this solidarity that had suddenly appeared between us. Aunt Mary's pale old eyes watered. "You mustn't let Myers punish her, Margaret, if you don't think she's done wrong." They both glanced up at the Murillo Madonna that was hanging on my stained wall. Intelligence passed between them and I was sure that, thanks to our Holy Mother, Aunt Margaret would save me. "Go along, Mary Therese," she said hoarsely. "Get yourself ready for dinner. And don't you say a word of this to your uncle when you come downstairs."

When I went down to dinner, I was exultant, but I tried to hide it. Throughout the meal, everyone was restrained; Herdie was in the dumps about his butterfly, and Preston and Kevin were silent, casting covert looks at me. My brothers, apparently, were wondering how I had avoided punishment, as the eldest, if for no other reason. Aunt Margaret was rather flushed, which improved her appearance slightly. Uncle Myers had a cunning look, as though events would prove him right. He patted Sheridan's golden head from time to time and urged him to eat. After dinner, the boys filed into the den behind Uncle Myers, and I helped Aunt Margaret clear the table. We did not have to do the dishes, for at this time there was a "girl" in the kitchen. As we were lifting the white tablecloth and the silence pad, we found the butterfly—pinned to the silence pad, right by my place.

My hash was settled then, though I did not know it. I did not catch the significance of its being found at *my* place. To Margaret, however, this was grimly conclusive. She had been too "easy," said her expression; once again Myers had been right. Myers went through the formality of interrogating each of the boys in turn ("No, sir," "No, sir," "No, sir") and even, at my insistence, of calling in the Swedish girl from the kitchen. Nobody knew how the butterfly had got there. It had not been there before dinner, when the girl set the table. My judges therefore concluded that I had had it hidden on my person and had slipped it under the tablecloth at dinner, when nobody was looking. This unanimous verdict maddened me, at first simply as an indication of stupidity—how could they be so dense as to imagine that I would hide it by my own place, where it was sure to be discovered? I did not really believe that I was going to be punished on such ridiculous evidence, yet even I could form no theory of how the butterfly had come there. My first base impulse to accuse the maid was scoffed out of my head by reason. What would a grownup want with a silly six-year-old's toy? And the very unfairness of the condemnation that rested on me made me reluctant to transfer it to one of my brothers. I kept supposing that the truth somehow would out, but the interrogation suddenly ended and every eye avoided mine.

Aunt Mary's dragging step went up the stairs, the boys were ordered to bed, and then, in the lavatory, the whipping began. Myers beat me with the strop, until his lazy arm tired; whipping is hard work for a fat man, out of condition, with a screaming, kicking, wriggling ten-year-old in his grasp. He went out and heaved himself, panting, into his favorite chair and I presumed that the whipping was over. But Aunt Margaret took his place, striking harder than he, with a hairbrush, in a businesslike, joyless way, repeating, "Say you did it, Mary Therese, say you did it." As the blows fell and I did not give in, this formula took on an intercessory note, like a prayer. It was clear to me that she was begging me to surrender and give Myers his satisfaction, for my own sake, so that the whipping could stop. When I finally cried out "All right!" she dropped the hairbrush with a sigh of relief; a new doubt of my guilt must have been visiting her, and my confession set everything square. She led me in to my uncle, and we both stood facing him, as Aunt Margaret, with a firm but not ungentle hand on my shoulder, whispered, "Just tell him, 'Uncle Myers, I did it,' and you can go to bed." But the sight of him, sprawling in his leather chair, complacently waiting for this, was too much for me. The words froze on my tongue. I could not utter them to *him*. Aunt Margaret urged me on, reproachfully, as though I were breaking our compact, but as I looked straight at him and assessed his ugly nature, I burst into yells. "I didn't! I didn't!" I gasped, between screams. Uncle Myers shot a vindictive look at his wife, as though he well understood that there had been collusion between us. He ordered me back to the dark lavatory and symbolically rolled up his sleeve. He laid on the strop decisively, but this time I was beside myself, and when Aunt Margaret hurried in and tried to reason with me, I could only answer with wild cries as Uncle Myers, gasping also, put the strop back on its hook. "You take her," he articulated, but Aunt Margaret's hairbrush this time was perfunctory, after the first few angry blows that punished me for having disobeyed her. Myers did not take up the strop again; the whipping ended, whether from fear of the neighbors or of Aunt Mary's frail presence upstairs or sudden guilty terror, I do not know; perhaps simply because it was past my bedtime.

I finally limped up to bed, with a crazy sense of inner victory, like a saint's, for I had not recanted, despite all they had done or could do to me. It did not occur to me that I had been unchristian in refusing to answer a plea from Aunt Margaret's heart and conscience. Indeed, I rejoiced in the knowledge that I had *made* her continue to beat me long after she must have known that I was innocent; this was her punishment for her condonation of Myers. The next morning, when I opened my eyes on the Murillo Madonna and the Baby Stuart, my feeling of triumph abated; I was afraid of what I had done. But throughout that day and the next, they did not touch me. I walked on air, incredulously and, no doubt, somewhat pompously, seeing myself as a figure from legend: my strength was *as* the strength of ten because my *heart* was pure! Afterward, I was beaten, in the normal routine way, but the question of the butterfly was closed forever in that house.

In my mind, there was, and still is, a connection between the butterfly and our rescue, by our Protestant grandfather, which took place the following year, in the fall or early winter. Already defeated, in their own view, or having ceased to care what became of us, our guardians, for the first time, permitted two of us, my brother Kevin and me, to be alone with this strict, kindly lawyer, as we walked the two blocks between our house and our grandfather McCarthy's. In the course of our walk, between the walls of an early snow, we told Grandpa Preston everything, overcoming our fears and fixing our minds on the dolls, the baseball gloves, and the watches. Yet, as it happened, curiously enough, albeit with a certain aptness, it was not the tale of the butterfly or the other atrocities that chiefly impressed him as he followed our narration with precise legal eyes but the fact that I was not wearing my glasses. I was being punished for breaking them in a fall on the school playground by having to go without; and I could not see why my account of this should make him flush up with anger—to me it was a great relief to be free of those disfiguring things. But he shifted his long, lantern jaw and, settling our hands in his, went straight as a writ up my grandfather McCarthy's front walk. Hence it was on a question of health that this good American's alarms finally alighted; the rest of what we poured out to him he either did not believe or feared to think of, lest he have to deal with the problem of evil.

On health grounds, then, we were separated from Uncle Myers, who disappeared back into Elkhart with his wife and Aunt Mary. My brothers were sent off to the sisters in a Catholic boarding school, with the exception of Sheridan, whom Myers was permitted to bear away with him, like a golden trophy. Sheridan's stay, however, was of short duration. Very soon, Aunt Mary died, followed by Aunt Margaret, followed by Uncle Myers; within five years, still in the prime of life, they were all gone, one, two, three, like ninepins. For me, a new life began, under a happier star. Within a few weeks after my Protestant grandfather's visit, I was sitting in a compartment with him on the train, watching the Missouri River go westward to its source, wearing my white-gold wrist watch and a garish new red hat, a highly nervous child, fanatical against Protestants, who, I explained to Grandpa Preston, all deserved to be burned at the stake. In the dining car, I ordered greedily, lamb chops, pancakes, sausages, and then sat, unable to eat them. "Her eyes," observed the waiter, "are bigger than her stomach."

Six or seven years later, on one of my trips east to college, I stopped in Minneapolis to see my brothers, who were all together now, under the roof of a new and more indulgent guardian, my uncle Louis, the handsomest and youngest of the McCarthy uncles. All the old people were dead; my grandmother McCarthy, but recently passed away, had left a fund to erect a chapel in her name in Texas, a state with which she had no known connection. Sitting in the twilight of my uncle Louis' screened porch, we sought a common ground for our reunion and found it in Uncle Myers.

It was then that my brother Preston told me that on the famous night of the butterfly, he had seen Uncle Myers steal ino the dining room from the den and lift the tablecloth, with the tin butterfly in his hand.

KNOXVILLE: SUMMER OF 1915 | *JAMES AGEE*

We are talking now of summer evenings in Knoxville, Tennessee in the time that I lived there so successfully disguised to myself as a child. It was a little bit mixed sort of block, fairly solidly lower middle class, with one or two juts apiece on either side of that. The houses corresponded: middle-sized gracefully fretted wood houses built in the late nineties and early nineteen hundreds, with small front and side and more spacious back yards, and trees in the yards, and porches. These were soft-wooded trees, poplars, tulip trees, cottonwoods. There were fences around one or two of the houses, but mainly the yards ran into each other with only now and then a low hedge that wasn't doing very well. There were few good friends among the grown people, and they were not poor enough for the other sort of intimate acquaintance, but everyone nodded and spoke, and even might talk short times, trivially, and at the two extremes of the general or the particular, and ordinarily nextdoor neighbors talked quite a bit when they happened to run into each other, and never paid calls. The men were mostly small businessmen, one or two very modestly executives, one or two worked with their hands, most of them clerical, and most of them between thirty and forty-five.

But it is of these evenings, I speak.

Supper was at six and was over by half past. There was still daylight, shining softly and with a tarnish, like the lining of a shell; and the carbon lamps lifted at the corners were on in the light, and locusts were started, and fireflies were out, and a few frogs were flopping in the dewy grass, by the time the fathers and the children came out. The children ran out first hell bent and yelling those names by which they were known; then the fathers sank out leisurely in crossed suspenders, their collars removed and their necks looking tall and shy. The mothers stayed back in the kitchen washing and drying, putting things away, recrossing their traceless footsteps like the lifetime journeys of bees, measuring out the dry cocoa for breakfast. When they came out they had taken off their aprons and their skirts were dampened and they sat in rockers on their porches quietly.

It is not of the games children play in the evening that I want to speak now, it is of a contemporaneous atmosphere that has little to do with them: that of the fathers of families, each in his space of lawn, his shirt fish-

like pale in the unnatural light and his face nearly anonymous, hosing his
lawn. The hoses were attached at spigots that stood out of the brick foundations of the houses. The nozzles were variously set but usually so there was a
long sweet stream of spray, the nozzle wet in the hand, the water trickling
the right forearm and the peeled-back cuff, and the water whishing out a
long loose and low-curved cone, and so gentle a sound. First an insane
noise of violence in the nozzle, then the still irregular sound of adjustment,
then the smoothing into steadiness and a pitch as accurately tuned to the
size and style of stream as any violin. So many qualities of sound out of
one hose: so many choral differences out of those several hoses that were
in earshot. Out of any one hose, the almost dead silence of the release,
and the short still arch of the separate big drops, silent as a held breath,
and the only noise the flattering noise on leaves and the slapped grass
at the fall of each big drop. That, and the intense hiss with the intense
stream; that, and that same intensity not growing less but growing more
quiet and delicate with the turn of the nozzle, up to that extreme tender
whisper when the water was just a wide bell of film. Chiefly, though, the
hoses were set much alike, in a compromise between distance and tenderness of spray (and quite surely a sense of art behind this compromise, and
a quiet, deep joy, too real to recognize itself) and the sounds therefore
were pitched much alike; pointed by the snorting start of a new hose; decorated by some man playful with the nozzle; left empty like God by the
sparrow's fall, when any single one of them desists: and all, though near
alike, of various pitch; and in this unison. These sweet pale streamings in
the light lift out their pallors and their voices all together, mothers hushing
their children, the hushing unnaturally prolonged, the men gentle and
silent and each snail-like withdrawn into the quietude of what the single
is doing, the urination of huge children stood loosely military against an
invisible wall, and gently happy and peaceful, tasting the mean goodness
of their living like the last of their suppers in their mouths; while the
locusts carry on this noise of hoses on their much higher and sharper key.
The noise of the locust is dry, and it seems not to be rasped or vibrated
but urged from him as if through a small orifice by a breath that can never
give out. Also there is never one locust but an illusion of at least a thousand.
The noise of each locust is pitched in some classic locust range out of
which none of them varies more than two full tones: and yet you seem to
hear each locust discrete from all the rest, and there is a long, slow, pulse
in their noise, like the scarcely defined arch of a long and high set bridge.
They are all around in every tree, so that the noise seems to come from
nowhere and everywhere at once, from the whole shell heaven, shivering
in your flesh and teasing your eardrums, the boldest of all the sounds of
night. And yet it is habitual to summer nights, and is of the great order
of noises, like the noises of the sea and of the blood her precocious grand-
child, which you realize you are hearing only when you catch yourself
listening. Meantime from low in the dark, just outside the swaying horizons

of the hoses, conveying always grass in the damp of dew and its strong green-black smear of smell, the regular yet spaced noises of the crickets, each a sweet cold silver noise three-noted, like the slipping each time of three matched links of a small chain.

But the men by now, one by one, have silenced their hoses and drained and coiled them. Now only two, and now only one, is left, and you see only ghostlike shirt with the sleeve garters, and sober mystery of his mild face like the lifted face of large cattle inquiring of your presence in a pitch-dark pool of meadow; and now he too is gone; and it has become that time of evening when people sit on their porches, rocking gently and talking gently and watching the street and the standing up into their sphere of possession of the trees, of birds' hung havens, hangars. People go by; things go by. A horse, drawing a buggy, breaking his hollow iron music on the asphalt: a loud auto: a quiet auto: people in pairs, not in a hurry, scuffling, switching their weight of estival body, talking casually, the taste hovering over them of vanilla, strawberry, pasteboard, and starched milk, the image upon them of lovers and horsemen, squared with clowns in hueless amber. A streetcar raising its iron moan; stopping; belling and starting, stertorous; rousing and raising again its iron increasing moan and swimming its gold windows and straw seats on past and past and past, the bleak spark crackling and cursing above it like a small malignant spirit set to dog its tracks; the iron whine rises on rising speed; still risen, faints; halts; the faint stinging bell; rises again, still fainter; fainting, lifting, lifts, faints foregone: forgotten. Now is the night one blue dew.

*Now is the night one blue dew, my father has drained, he has coiled the
    hose.*
Low on the length of lawns, a frailing of fire who breathes.
*Content, silver, like peeps of light, each cricket makes his comment over
    and over in the drowned grass.*
A cold toad thumpily founders.
*Within the edges of damp shadows of side yards are hovering children
    nearly sick with joy of fear, who watch the unguarding of a telephone
    pole.*
*Around white carbon corner lamps bugs of all sizes are lifted elliptic, solar
    systems. Big hardshells bruise themselves, assailant: he is fallen on his
    back, legs squiggling.*
*Parents on porches: rock and rock. From damp strings morning glories hang
    their ancient faces.*
*The dry and exalted noise of the locusts from all the air at once enchants
    my eardrums.*

On the rough wet grass of the back yard my father and mother have spread quilts. We all lie there, my mother, my father, my uncle, my aunt, and I too am lying there. First we were sitting up, then one of us lay down, and then we all lay down, on our stomachs, or on our sides, or on our backs, and they have kept on talking. They are not talking much, and the talk is quiet, of nothing in particular, of nothing at all in particular, of nothing at all. The stars are wide and alive, they seem each like a smile of great sweetness, and they seem very clear. All my people are larger bodies than mine, quiet, with voices gentle and meaningless like the voices of sleeping birds. One is an artist, he is living at home. One is a musician, she is living at home. One is my mother who is good to me. One is my father who is good to me. By some chance, here they are, all on this earth; and who shall ever tell the sorrow of being on this earth, lying, on quilts, on the grass, in a summer evening, among the sounds of the night. May God bless my people, my uncle, my aunt, my mother, my good father, oh, remember them kindly in their time of trouble; and in the hour of their taking away.

After a little I am taken in and put to bed. Sleep, soft smiling, draws me unto her: and those receive me, who quietly treat me, as one familiar and well-beloved in that home: but will not, oh, will not, not now, not ever; but will not ever tell me who I am.

DISTANCE: JOAN OF ARC

THE QUESTION OF IDENTITY is one which writers most frequently solve by speaking as themselves. Rather than assume a role such as that of the bored cynic, or a mask such as that of irony, they choose a direct, undisguised approach. But a writer does not sidestep the problem of identity by determining to be himself; he must still decide what he himself is like. The difficulty is not trivial: since writing is in some degree a formal expression of personality, it does not allow the hemming and hawing and qualifications with which people may make clear their feelings in speech; neither does it allow gesture or facial expression. As a result, a sentence which a writer dashes off casually may echo from the paper with an altogether alien ring. Another barrier in the path of honest expression is that often the writer may not even know accurately his emotional state. If he does not, writing may be for him a process of discovery—of trying a word, a phrase, or a feeling on for size, accepting, rejecting, or modifying it, and gradually arriving at a faithful revelation of identity.

The two main questions the writer must answer when he writes in his own character are how he feels and to what extent he is involved in or detached from his subject. The first question concerns tone, which is treated in another section of this book. The second concerns a quality which we may call distance. The difference between tone and distance, roughly, is the difference between kind of emotion and degree of emotion.

A writer is distant from his subject to the extent that he treats it as a purely academic problem, one not involving him personally. A psychologist writing on the ability of rats to run mazes may preserve a considerable amount of detachment, but if he is defending a theory on which he has spent years of research, he will probably show his stake in it by writing at a "shorter" distance. A refugee whose family has been killed by the Nazis will certainly write with more feeling about the persecutions than will an American student of mob psychology and prejudice. This much is clear; but distance involves more than measured quantities of a given emotion. A writer may show great distance from his material by being flippant or by being coldly detached. He may be sadly or passionately or enthusiastically involved. He may constrain profound emotion within a tight jacket of discipline, hinting at, but not expressing, his commitment. Given this complexity, the management of distance is one of the most taxing problems that a writer faces. It is also one of the most important, for even untrained readers are often highly sensitive to effusiveness, frigidity, and what lies between.

Joan of Arc is a good test case. That extraordinary girl inspired in her own day, and has inspired since, writing which displays every shade and every degree of feeling. Even among those directly concerned with her trial, in 1431, the range is apparent. The court recorder preserved, as one in his position must, almost total impersonality. Pierre Maurice, canon of Rouen, in his admonition to Joan, and the University of Paris, in its letter to the Pope and the Emperor, are far less detached, although they speak in official roles. Writing forty years after the trial, the historian Thomas Basin (1412-1491) allows more than a little emotion to color his dignified narrative. And if anything, the passing of the centuries has intensified, rather than dulled, the power Joan exercises over human imagination. The English essayist Thomas De Quincey (1785-1859), the American humorist Samuel L. Clemens (1835-1910), and the Irish-English dramatist George Bernard Shaw (1856-1950) are but three of the many famous writers who have turned to Joan—with varying degrees of immediacy, but always with fascination.

RECORDS OF THE TRIAL

FEBRUARY 24TH. THIRD SESSION

On the following Saturday, February 24th, we the said bishop repaired to the same room in the castle of Rouen where Jeanne appeared in judgment before us in the presence of many reverend fathers, doctors and

From *The Trial of Jeanne D'Arc,* trans. by W. P. Barrett (New York, Gotham House, 1932.

masters, namely: Gilles, abbot of Ste. Trinité de Fécamp; Pierre, prior of Longueville-Giffard; Jean de Châtillon, Erard Emengart, Jean Beaupère, Jacques de Touraine, Nicolas Midi, Jean de Nibat, Jacques Guesdon, Maurice du Quesnay, Jean Le Fèvre, Guillaume Le Boucher, Pierre Houdenc, Pierre Maurice, Richard Prati, Jean Charpentier, Gérard Feuillet, and Denis de Sabrevois, doctors of sacred theology; Nicolas de Jumièges, Guillaume de Ste. Catherine, Guillaume de Cormeilles, abbots; Jean Garin, doctor of canon law and Raoul Roussel, doctor of canon and civil law; Nicolas Couppequesne, William Haiton, Thomas de Courcelles, Jean Le Maistre, Nicolas Loiseleur, Raoul Le Sauvage, Guillaume de Baudribosc, Nicolas Lemire, Richard Le Gagneux, Jean Duval, Guillaume Le Maistre, and Guillaume l'Ermite, bachelors of sacred theology; the abbots of St. Ouen, of St. Georges, and of Préaux; the priors of St. Lô and of Sigy; also Robert Le Barbier, Denis Gastinel, and Jean Le Doulx, bachelors of canon and civil law; Nicholas de Venderès, Jean Pinchon, Jean de la Fontaine, Aubert Morel, Jean Duchemin, Jean Colombel, Laurent Du Busc, Raoul Auguy, Richard des Saulx, bachelors of canon law; André Marguerie, Jean Alespée, Geoffroy du Crotary, Gilles Deschamps, Nicolas Maulin, Pierre Carel, Bureau de Cormeilles, licentiates in civil law; Robert Morellet, and Jean Le Roy, canons of the cathedral of Rouen, and Nicolas de Foville.

We first of all required the aforementioned Jeanne to speak the simple and absolute truth on the questions put to her, and to make no reservation to her oath; and we thrice admonished her to do this. The said Jeanne answered: "Give me leave to speak" and then said: "By my faith, you could ask things such as I would not answer." She said also: "Perhaps I shall not answer you truly in many things that you ask me, concerning the revelations; for perhaps you would constrain me to tell things I have sworn not to utter, and so I should be perjured, and you would not want that." And she added, "I tell you, take good heed of what you say, that you are my judge, for you assume a great responsibility, and over-burden me." She said also that she thought it should be enough to have twice taken the oath.

Moreover, asked if she would swear, simply and absolutely, she answered: "You may well do without it! I have sworn enough, twice"; adding that all the clergy of Rouen and Paris could not condemn her, but by law. She said that of her coming to France she would willingly speak the truth, but not the whole truth; and a week would not be enough for that.

But we, the aforementioned bishop, told her to take the advice of the assessors, whether or not she should swear. To that she replied that of her coming she would willingly speak the truth, and not otherwise; and that we must not speak of it to her any more.

We said that she lay herself open to suspicion if she would not swear to speak the truth. She replied in the same way as before. Again we required her to swear, precisely and absolutely. Then she answered that she would willingly say what she knew, but not all. She said also that she came from God, and that there is nothing for her to do here, and asked to be sent back to God, from whom she came.

Required and admonished to swear, under pain of being charged with what was imputed to her, she answered: "Continue."

A last time we required her to swear, and urgently admonished her to speak the truth in matters concerning the trial, telling her she exposed herself to great danger by her refusal. Then she answered: "I am ready to swear to speak the truth of what I know concerning the trial." And in this manner she took the oath.

Then, at our order, she was questioned by the distinguished doctor Jean Beaupère above-mentioned, who first asked her when she had last taken food and drink. She answered that since yesterday noon she had not taken either.

Asked when she had heard the voice come to her, she answered: "I heard it yesterday and to-day."

Asked at what hour yesterday she had heard this voice, she answered that she had heard it three times: once in the morning, once at vespers, and once when the *Ave Maria* was rung in the evening. And often she heard it more frequently than she said.

Asked what she was doing yesterday morning when the voice came to her, she said she was sleeping and the voice awakened her.

Asked if the voice woke her by touching her on the arm, she answered that it was without touching her.

Asked if the voice was actually in the room, she said she did not know, but it was in the castle.

Asked if she did not thank it and kneel down, she answered that she thanked it, but she was sitting on the bed, and she put her hands together; and this was after she asked counsel of it. Whereupon the voice told her to answer boldly.

Asked what the voice had said when she was awakened, she answered that she asked the voice to counsel her in her replies, telling the voice to beseech therein the counsel of Our Lord. And the voice told her to answer boldly and God would comfort her.

Asked if it had not spoken certain words to her before she questioned it, she replied that the voice spoke certain words, but she did not understand them all. However, when she awakened from her sleep, the voice told her to answer boldly.

Then she said to us, the aforementioned bishop: "You say that you are my judge; take good heed of what you do, because, in truth, I am sent by God, and you put yourself in great peril," in French 'en grant dangier.'

Asked if the voice sometimes varied in its counsel, she answered that she had never found it utter two contrary opinions. She said also that that night she had heard it tell her to answer boldly.

Asked whether the voice had forbidden her to answer everything she was asked, she said: "I will not answer you that. I have revelations concerning the king which I shall not tell you."

Asked if the voice had forbidden her to tell of the revelations, she answered: "I have not been advised upon that. Give me a fortnight and I will answer you." And as she had again asked for a delay in her reply, she said: "If the voice forbade me, what would you say?"

Asked again if that had been forbidden her [by the voice], she replied: "Believe me, it was not men who forbade me." She said that she would not answer that day; and that she does not know if she ought to reply, or not, until it has been revealed to her. She said she firmly believes, as firmly as she believes in the Christian faith and that the Lord redeemed us from the pains of hell, that this voice comes from God, and by His command.

Asked whether this voice, which she says appears to her, comes as an angel, or directly from God, or whether it is the voice of one of the saints, she answered: "This voice comes from God; I believe I do not tell you everything about it; and I am more afraid of failing the voices by saying what is displeasing to them, than of answering you. For this question, I beseech you to grant me a delay."

Asked if she believes it displeasing to God to speak the truth, she answered: "My voices told me to say certain things to the king, and not to you." She saw that that night the voice told her many things for the good of the king, which she wished he might know forthwith, even if she had to go without wine till Easter! For, as she said, he would eat the more happily for it.

Asked if she could not so influence the voice that it would obey her and take news to her king: she answered she did not know whether the voice would obey her, unless it were God's will, and God consented thereto. "And if it please God," she said, "He will be able to send revelations to the king; and with this I shall be well pleased."

Asked why this voice no longer speaks with the king, as it did when Jeanne was in his presence, she answered that she did not know, if it were not the will of God. And she added that but for the will of God she could do nothing.

Asked if her counsel revealed to her that she should escape from prison, she answered: "Must I tell you that?"

Asked whether that night the voice had not counseled and advised her upon what she should reply, she said that if the voice revealed such things she did not understand them.

Asked whether, on the two last days that she heard the voices, she had seen a light, she answered that the light comes in the name of the voice.

Asked if she saw anything else with the voices, she answered: "I will not tell you everything: I have not leave, nor does my oath touch on that. This voice is good and worthy; and I am not bound to answer you." She asked that the points on which she did not straightway answer should be given her in writing.

Asked whether the voice, of which she asked counsel, had sight and eyes, she answered: "You will not learn that yet"; and said that there was a saying among little children, "Men are sometimes hanged for telling the truth."

Asked if she knows she is in God's grace, she answered: "If I am not, may God put me there; and if I am, may God so keep me. I should be the saddest creature in the world if I knew I were not in His grace." She added, if she were in a state of sin, she did not think that the voice would come to her; and she wished every one could hear the voice as well as she did. She thought she was about thirteen when the voice came to her for the first time.

Asked whether in her youth she had played in the fields with the other children, she answered that she certainly went sometimes, but she did not know at what age.

Asked if the people of Domrémy sided with the Burgundians or the other party, she answered that she only knew one Burgundian; and that she would have been quite willing for him to have his head cut off, that is if it had pleased God.

Asked if at Maxey the people were Burgundians or enemies of the Burgundians, she answered they were Burgundians.

Asked if the voice told her in her youth to hate the Burgundians, she answered that since she had known that the voices were for the king of France, she did not like the Burgundians. She said the Burgundians will have war unless they do as they ought; she knows it from her voice.

Asked if it was revealed to her in her early years that the English should come to France, she answered that the English were already in France when the voices began to come to her.

Asked if she was ever with the children who fought for her party, she answered no, as far as she remembered; but she sometimes saw certain children from Domrémy, who had fought against those from Maxey, re- turning wounded and bleeding.

Asked whether in her youth she had any great intention of defeating the Burgundians, she answered that she had a great desire and will for her king to have his kingdom.

Asked if she had wanted to be a man when it was necessary for her to come to France, she said she had answered elsewhere.

Asked if she took the animals to the fields, she said that she had answered elsewhere; and that since she had grown up, and had reached understanding, she did not generally look after the beasts, but helped to take them to the meadows and to a castle called the Island, for fear of the soldiers; but she does not recall whether or not she tended them in her youth.

Then she was questioned about a certain tree growing near her village. To which she answered that, fairly near Domrémy, there was a certain tree called the Ladies' Tree, and others called it the Fairies' Tree; and near by is a fountain. And she has heard that people sick of the fever drink of this fountain and seek its water to restore their health; that, she has seen herself; but she does not know whether they are cured or not. She said she has heard that the sick, when they can rise, go to the tree and walk about it. It is a big tree, a beech, from which they get the fair May, in French *le beau may;* and it belongs, it is said, to Pierre de Bourlemont, knight. She said sometimes she would go playing with the other young girls, making garlands for Our Lady of Domrémy there; and often she had heard the old folk say (not those of her family) that the fairies frequented it. And she heard a certain Jeanne, the wife of mayor Aubery of Domrémy, her godmother, say that she had seen the fairies; but she herself doesn't know whether it is true or not. As far as she knew, she said, she never saw the fairies at the tree. Asked if she saw them elsewhere, she does not know at all. She had seen the young girls putting garlands on the branches of the tree, and she herself sometimes hung them there with the other girls; sometimes they took them away, and sometimes they left them there.

She said that since she learned that she must come to France, she had taken as little part as possible in games or dancing; and did not know whether she had danced near the tree since she had grown to understanding. Although on occasions she may well have danced there with the children, she more often sang than danced. There is also a wood, called the oak-wood, in French *le Bois-chesnu,* which can be seen from her father's door; not more than half a league away. She does not know, nor has she ever heard, that the fairies repair there; but she has heard from her brother that in the country around it is said she received her message at the tree; but she says she did not, and she told him quite the contrary. Further, she says, when she came to the king, several people asked her if there were not in her part of the country a wood called the oak-wood; for there was a prophecy which said that out of this wood would come a maid who should work miracles; but Jeanne said that she put no faith in that.

Asked if she wanted a woman's dress, she answered: "Give me one. I will take it and go: otherwise I will not have it, and am content with this, since it pleases God that I wear it."

Whereupon we put an end to all interrogation for this day, and assigned for the next session the following Tuesday, so that at the same hour and in the same place the whole convocation should assemble and proceed to the subsequent interrogations.

AN ADMONITION | *PIERRE MAURICE*

"Jeanne, dearest friend, it is now time, near the end of your trial to think well over all that has been said. Although you have four times already, by the lord bishop of Beauvais, by the lord vicar of the Inquisitor, by other doctors sent to you on their behalf, been most diligently admonished for the honor and reverence of God, for the faith and law of Jesus Christ, for the tranquillity of their consciences, and the alleviation of the scandal you have caused, to the salvation of your body and soul; although you have been shown the perils to which you expose your body and soul if you do not reform yourself and your sayings and correct them by submitting your acts and your words to the Church, and by accepting her judgment, nevertheless up till now you have not wished to listen.

"Now although many of your judges would have been satisfied with the evidence collected against you, in their anxiety for the salvation of your body and soul they have submitted your sayings for examination to the University of Paris, the light of all knowledge and the extirpator of errors. When the lord judges received the deliberations of the University they decided that you should to this end be once more admonished, warned of your errors, scandals and other crimes, and that we should beg, exhort and advise you by the bowels of Our Lord Jesus Christ who suffered cruel death for the redemption of mankind, to correct your words and submit them to the judgment of the Church, as every loyal Christian is bound and obliged to do. Do not permit yourself to be separated from Our Lord Jesus Christ who created you to be a partaker in His glory; do not choose the way of eternal damnation with the enemies of God who daily endeavor to disturb men, counterfeiting often the likeness of Christ, His angels and His saints, who they profess and affirm themselves to be, as is shown more fully in the lives of the Fathers and in the Scriptures. Therefore if such apparitions have appeared to you, do not believe them: more than that, put away the belief or imagination you had in such things, and believe rather in the words and opinions of the University of Paris and other doctors who, being well acquainted with the law of God and the Holy Scriptures, have concluded that no faith should be given to such apparitions or in any extraordinary apparition or forbidden novelty which is not supported by Holy Scripture or sign or miracle, none of which you have.

"You have believed these apparitions lightly, instead of turning to God in devout prayer to grant you certainty; and you have not consulted prelates or learned ecclesiastics to enlighten yourself: although, considering your

From *The Trial of Jeanne D'Arc,* trans. by W. P. Barrett (New York, Gotham House, 1932).

condition and the simplicity of your knowledge, you ought to have done so. Take this example: suppose your king had appointed you to defend a fortress, forbidding you to let any one enter. Would you not refuse to admit whoever claimed to come in his name but brought no letters or authentic sign? Likewise Our Lord Jesus Christ, when He ascended into Heaven, committed the government of His Church to the apostle St. Peter and his successors, forbidding them to receive in the future those who claimed to come in His name but brought no other token than their own words. So you should not have put faith in those which you say came to you, nor ought we to believe in you, since God commands the contrary.

"First, Jeanne, you should consider this: if when you were in your king's domain, a soldier or other person born in his realm or fealty, had arisen and said, 'I will not obey the king or submit to any of his officers,' would you not have said this man should be condemned? What shall you say of yourself, who, brought up in the faith of Christ by the sacrament of baptism, have become the daughter of the Church and the spouse of Christ, if you do not obey Christ's officers, that is to say, the prelates of the Church? What judgment shall you deliver upon yourself? Cease, I pray you, from uttering these things if you love your Creator, your precious spouse and your salvation; obey the Church and submit to its judgment; know that if you do not, if you persevere in this error, your soul will be condemned to eternal punishment and perpetual torture, and I do not doubt that your body will come to perdition.

"Let not human pride and empty shame, which perhaps constrain you, hold you back because you fear that if you do as I advise you will lose the great honors which you have known. For the honor of God and the salvation of your body and soul must come first: you will lose all if you do not as I say, for you will separate yourself from the Church and from the faith you swore in the holy sacrament of baptism, you cut the authority of Our Lord from the Church which is nevertheless led, ruled and governed by His spirit and authority. For He said to the prelates of the Church: 'He that heareth you heareth Me, he that despiseth you despiseth Me.' Therefore if you will not submit to the Church you separate yourself in fact, and if you will not submit to her you refuse to submit to God, and you err in respect of this article: *Unam Sanctam Ecclesiam*. What the Church is, and her authority, has been sufficiently explained to you already in former admonitions.

"Therefore, in view of all these things, on behalf of your judges the lord bishop of Beauvais and the lord vicar of the Inquisitor, I admonish, beg and exhort you by the pity you have for the passion of your Creator, by the love you bear for the salvation of your body and soul, correct and amend these errors, return to the way of truth, by obedience to the Church and submission in all things to her judgment and decision. By so doing you will save your soul and redeem, as I hope, your body from death; but if you do not, if you persist, know that your soul will be overwhelmed in damnation and I fear the destruction of your body. From these ills may Our Lord preserve you!"

A LETTER TO THE POPE | from THE UNIVERSITY OF PARIS

"We believe, most Holy Father, that vigilant endeavors to prevent the contamination of the Holy Church by the poison of the errors of false prophets and evil men, are the more necessary since the end of the world appears to be at hand. For the doctor of the nations latterly announced these dangerous times to come, when men will no longer hold to sound beliefs: for they will turn away from the truth, and be converted to fables. The gospel also said: 'There will arise false Christs and false prophets, and shall show great signs and wonders, insomuch that, if it were possible, they shall deceive the very elect.' So when we see new prophets arise who boast of receiving revelations from God and the blessed of the triumphant land, when we see them announce to men the future and things passing the keenness of human thoughts, daring to accomplish new and unwonted acts, then it is fitting to our pastoral solicitude to set all our energies to prevent them from overwhelming the people, too eager to believe new things, by these strange doctrines, before the spirits which they claim to come from God have been confirmed. It would indeed be easy for these crafty and dangerous sowers of deceitful inventions to infect the Catholic people, if every one, without the approbation and consent of our Holy Mother Church, were free to invent supernatural revelations at his own pleasure, and could usurp the authority of God, and His saints. Therefore, most Holy Father, the watchful diligence lately shown by the reverend father in Christ, the lord bishop of Beauvais and the vicar of the lord Inquisitor of Heretical Error, appointed by the apostolic Holy See to the kingdom of France, for the protection of the Christian religion, seems to us most commendable. For these have been at pains to examine carefully a certain woman, captured in the limits of the diocese of Beauvais, wearing the costume and armor of a man, accused judicially before them of falsely inventing divine revelations, of grave crimes against the orthodox faith: and they showed the whole truth of her actions.

"And after they had acquainted us with the course of the trial and asked us to give them our opinion on certain articles affirmed by her, so that it should not be said that silence has covered up that which was done for the exaltation of the orthodox faith, we resolved to inform your Highness

From *The Trial of Jeanne D'Arc*, trans. by W. P. Barrett (New York, Gotham House, 1932).

of what we received. As we were instructed by the said lord judges, this woman, calling herself Jeanne *the Maid,* of her own accord, in her trial, confessed many points which, weighed by the diligent examination of many prelates, maturely considered by the doctors and other men learned in canon and civil law, submitted to the decision and judgment of our University, proved she should be held superstitious, a prophetess, a caller up of demons, idolatrous, blasphemous towards God and the Saints, schismatic and in every way erring in the faith of Jesus Christ. Full of affliction and sorrow for the soul of this miserable sinner caught in the pernicious snares of so many crimes, her judges, by frequent warnings and charitable exhortations, set all their efforts to draw her back from the path of her error and to effect her subjugation to the judgment of our Holy Mother Church. But the spirit of wickedness had so completely filled her heart that for a long time she rejected our salutary monitions with a hardened heart, refused to submit to any living man, of whatever dignity, or to the holy Council General, and recognized no other judge than God. At last it came to pass that the persevering labor of the said judges slightly diminished her great presumption: listening to their sound counsels, she denied and verbally abjured her errors, in the presence of a great multitude of people; she subscribed to and signed with her own hand a formula of abjuration and recantation. But hardly had a few days passed, when this wretched woman fell back into her former foolishness, and adhered once more to the errors which she had denied. Therefore the said judges condemned her, in their final decree, as a relapsed heretic, and gave her over to the judgment of the secular power. Now, when this woman learned that the destruction of her body was near, she confessed before all with many lamentations that she had been mocked and deceived by these spirits which she said had appeared visibly before her; and repenting *in articulo mortis,* she asked pardon of all: and so quitted this life. Wherefore it was clearly recognized by all how dangerous it was, how fearful, to give too light credence to the modern inventions which have for some time past been scattered in this most Christian kingdom, not by this woman only, but by many others also; and all the faithful of the Christian religion must be warned by such a sad example not to act so hastily after their own desires, but to listen to the teachings of the Church and the instruction of the prelates rather than the fables of superstitious women. For if we are at last through our own faults arrived at the point where witches falsely prophesying in God's name but without His authority, are better received by the frivolous people than pastors and doctors of the Church to whom Christ formerly said, 'Go ye and teach the nations,' the end is come, religion will perish, faith is in decay, the Church is trampled underfoot and the iniquity of Satan dominates the whole world. Which may Jesus Christ prevent, and under the happy direction of your Beatitude, keep His flock from stain and contamination."

THE SAVIOR | *THOMAS BASIN*

Now Compiègne, on the river Oise, had for a long time lain under siege by the English and the Burgundians, and Joan the Maid along with a sizable body of French soldiery made her way there. And there, on a particular day [23 May, 1430: ed.] occurred this grievous incident: as, along with a large number of soldiers, she was making a sortie against the enemy, she was captured by a Burgundian and sold by him for a sum of gold to the English, who very much desired her downfall and death. This event delighted the English who time after time had been defeated and put to rout simply through dread of her name. They took her to Rouen where Prince Henry was sitting with his council and entourage. There, having discussed at length what should be done with her, they reached a decision to put her under heavy guard in a crude prison of the citadel of Rouen and then to bring her before Pierre Couchon, one of the principal advisers of the English king and bishop of Beauvais (since she had been captured within the boundaries of his diocese), on a charge having to do with matters of faith.

Numerous deliberations on the matter followed; then, over a period of months, in varying kinds of sessions, before members of the Inquisition, before professors of theology and of divine and human law brought from Paris for this specific purpose, she was repeatedly interrogated. The questions posed, and the answers she made to each, were recorded with scrupulous care by notaries and edited into public notices. And almost everywhere there was astonishment at the wisdom and pertinence with which the little peasant had answered questions of faith and dogma that would have proved difficult even for learned men. The assessors, relentless and partisan promoters of the English cause, had no interest other than in so managing affairs that, caught by subtle and ambiguous questions, Joan might be tricked into making herself liable to a charge of heresy. But they could find nothing substantive or significant on that account from any of her statements or replies.

She had always been pious, worshipping as often as she could in churches and in oratories consecrated to God: so testified those who knew her life and habits before she came into the presence of the King, and so testified as well those who knew her after she had lived among soldiers. Indeed when she was at home, tending flocks in the field, and heard the church bells ring in honor of the Virgin or at the moment of elevation of the Body and Blood of Christ in the mass, she always knelt to pray with deep and fervent devotion.

From *Histoire de Charles VII*, I (Paris, Société d'Edition "Les Belles Lettres" 1933) trans. by H. C. M.

Moreover, she swore that she had consecrated her own body to God. And, despite the fact that she had lived for months in the midst of soldiers and of dissolute and lawless men, no one felt warranted in making the least suggestion that she had broken her vow. As a matter of fact, during the time of her imprisonment by the English, women examined her to determine whether or not she was still a virgin: without qualification they reported her untouched. She herself accounted for the male garb she wore simply by saying that God had ordered her to put on armor lest the men with whom she would be obliged to live day and night during military campaigns might be stirred to lust, something she could scarcely have avoided had she retained women's dress. But obviously, whatever the evidence of virtue she displayed, she could not hope to justify herself in the eyes of those who held her prisoner since they desired and sought nothing so single-mindedly as her deposition and death. For the English were unanimous in believing and saying that they would never defeat the French and wrest a victory from them so long as the Maid, whom they looked on as a witch and sorceress, remained alive. And how could her innocence prevail, what indeed could it do in her behalf, caught as she was in the hands of so many maddened enemies and calumniators as the English were and beset by so many others zealous in making representation to the tribunal and of so many more who, by every means and through every effort, sought only a way to destroy her?

In the matter of the visitations by saints to which she testified, she held stubbornly to a single declaration of them as fact; held to it until, already worn out by prolonged and repeated interrogation, weakened and disheartened by the squalor and bad food of her long imprisonment—she was guarded day and night, both inside and outside her cell, by English soldiers—and (it is said) promised her freedom if she did as her judges asked, she denied for a moment that the visitations of which she had spoken were real ones or in any way a divine revelation. And it is claimed that she was induced to abjure, before those sitting on the tribunal, all those things that followed from her earlier claims. But a few days after that, when no moderating of the cruelty of her imprisonment occurred, word spread that she had been maltreated in order to provoke denial of the truth of her visions and revelations and that once more the saints had appeared to her in prison, reproaching her severely for her weakness. . . .

The report was made known to the judges, and Joan, once more on public trial, was condemned for having abjured heresy and then relapsed, and she was turned over to the secular authority.

At once the executioners took charge of her, supported by the English army then present in force at Rouen with their prince Henry. Then, in the presence of a vast throng of onlookers, drawn not only from the city but from the countryside surrounding and even from neighboring towns (for many were attracted to Rouen for this affair as though to a public spectacle), the same Joan, calling incessantly on God and on the Glorious

Mother of Our Lord Jesus Christ, was burned and consumed by the flames. Afterward they gathered all the ashes that the fire had left, those remaining from the wood and those from her flesh and bones, and threw them from a bridge into the Seine, perhaps out of superstition, perhaps to guarantee that nothing appertaining to her might be kept and prized as a relic. Thus ended the brief life of Joan.

The reader of this account may expect from us a comment on the deeds of this Maid whose fame in her own time was great throughout France. Even if we are not so bold as to insist that her visions and revelations came from God (having ourselves no personal knowledge of the signs of her special mission which, it is said, she revealed to Charles), we can boldly say that, as regards the trial itself, of which we examined the documents when Normandy came into its own again as part of the kingdom of Charles after the defeat of the English, it is far from apparent that she could legitimately have been convicted of having fallen into an error of dogma contrary to the truth of catholic doctrine or that she made any avowal that would stand in law. And thus both the accusation of heresy and that of relapse clearly lack substance. Besides, one could on several heads consider disallowable a trial begun and carried out before the very enemies whom she had freely denounced, above all a trial in which she was refused counsel though she was inexperienced in such affairs, as will be readily apparent to those who have opportunity to locate and time to read the memoir we prepared at the request of King Charles when he sought our advice in the matter. Once the English had been driven out of Normandy, the same Charles did in fact require many prelates of his realm and others versed in human and divine law to examine carefully and discuss together the aforementioned trial. Having done so, they presented several memoranda to the King which were then made available to, and thoroughly studied by, judges whom the Holy See appointed to bring the whole matter to a clear and final judgment. These judges concurred with the memoranda mentioned above, and the sentence pronounced against her under English authority was vacated and revoked.

Now some may be surprised that, if Joan was truly sent by God, she should have been captured and put to death. Yet how can anyone reasonably feel surprise at that, seeing that Our Lord, saint of saints and savior of us all, and the holy prophets and apostles sent by God to lead men to Truth and teach them about salvation, divine law, and the will of God—that all these were also subjected to various torments and trials and finished their mortal existence in the triumph of martyrdom? Do we not read in the Old Testament, moreover, that the people of Israel destroyed the Canaanites at God's command and did battle against idolators and other enemies, yet later—either because of their sins or because of the sins of some among them—were overwhelmed by their enemies, defeated and made to grovel in the dust? For "who knows the designs of the Lord? Who has given counsel to Him?" (Rom. XI, 34)

Now we do not hold the view that, simply for having departed this vain life in the manner we have described, the merits of Joan are to be compared with those of saints or holy martyrs. But we do not hesitate to believe (nor do we find these beliefs incompatible) that Joan was indeed sent by God to save the realm and the people of France from the English; to chasten equally the pride of the French and of the English; to insure that no man come to trust in the flesh (Jeremiah XVII, 5) and fail to glory in God rather than in his own self and his own power. We contend that God allowed her to be taken by the enemy and put to torture because the king or the people of France, unmindful of the many benefits that God miraculously provided through his intermediary, not only did not give thanks to God for the assistance they had received from him but even attributed the victories they had been vouchsafed not to the grace of God but to their own merits and strength (merits which, in truth, were either negligible or tainted, for they were people of deeply corrupted habit). We suggest also the possibility that God permitted her to be sacrificed for some other reason, a just one most assuredly (since God knows no injustice), but a reason hidden from us, his protection at times being given to those of no deserts and then withdrawn from those who show themselves unworthy through ingratitude For it often happens that what divine mercy accords unasked it withdraws without notice.

That God should make use of women, armed or unarmed, as his inter- mediaries to bring to his people the sweetness of salvation and of victory over their enemies, history attests in the accounts of Deborah, Judith and Esther as reported in Holy Scriptures.

This, then, is the story of Joan, called the Maid. As to her mission, her visions, and the revelations she claimed to have received, we leave every man to make up his own mind, corresponding to our way of thinking or differently, as depends upon his intelligence and his understanding.

THE GENTLE GIRL | *THOMAS DE QUINCEY*

What is to be thought of *her*? What is to be thought of the poor shep- herd girl from the hills and forests of Lorraine, that—like the Hebrew shepherd boy from the hills and forests of Judaea—rose suddenly out of the quiet, out of the safety, out of the religious inspiration, rooted in deep pastoral solitudes, to a station in the van of armies, and to the more perilous station at the right hand of kings? The Hebrew boy inaugurated his patri- otic mission by an *act*, by a victorious *act,* such as no man could deny. But so did the girl of Lorraine, if we read her story as it was read by those who

From *Joan of Arc* (1847).

saw her nearest. Adverse armies bore witness to the boy as no pretender; but so they did to the gentle girl. Judged by the voices of all who saw them *from a station of good-will,* both were found true and loyal to any promises involved in their first acts. Enemies it was that made the difference between their subsequent fortunes. The boy rose to a splendor and a noonday prosperity, both personal and public, that rang through the records of his people, and became a by-word amongst his posterity for a thousand years, until the sceptre was departing from Judah. The poor, forsaken girl, on the contrary, drank not herself from that cup of rest which she had secured for France. She never sang together with the songs that rose in her native Domrémy, as echoes to the departing steps of invaders. She mingled not in the festal dances at Vaucouleurs which celebrated in rapture the redemption of France. No! for her voice was then silent: no! for her feet were dust. Pure, innocent, noble-hearted girl! whom, from earliest youth, ever I believed in as full of truth and self-sacrifice, this was amongst the strongest pledges for *thy* truth, that never once—no, not for a moment of weakness—didst thou revel in the vision of coronets and honor from man. Coronets for thee! O no! Honors, if they come when all is over, are for those that share thy blood. Daughter of Domrémy, when the gratitude of thy king shall awaken, thou wilt be sleeping the sleep of the dead. Call her, King of France, but she will not hear thee! Cite her by thy apparitors to come and receive a robe of honor, but she will be found *en contumace.* When the thunders of universal France, as even yet may happen, shall proclaim the grandeur of the poor shepherd girl that gave up all for her country, thy ear, young shepherd girl, will have been deaf for five centuries. To suffer and to do, that was thy portion in this life; that was thy destiny; and not for a moment was it hidden from thyself. Life, thou saidst, is short: and the sleep which is in the grave is long! Let me use that life, so transitory, for the glory of those heavenly dreams destined to comfort the sleep which is so long. This pure creature—pure from every suspicion of even a visionary self-interest, even as she was pure in senses more obvious— never once did this holy child, as regarded herself, relax from her belief in the darkness that was travelling to meet her. She might not prefigure the very manner of her death; she saw not in vision, perhaps, the aerial altitude of the fiery scaffold, the spectators without end on every road pouring into Rouen as to a coronation, the surging smoke, the volleying flames, the hostile faces all around, the pitying eye that lurked but here and there, until nature and imperishable truth broke loose from artificial restraints,— these might not be apparent through the mists of the hurrying future. But the voice that called her to death, *that* she heard for ever.

Great was the throne of France even in those days, and great was he that sat upon it: but well Joanna knew that not the throne, nor he that sat upon it, was for *her;* but, on the contrary, that she was for *them;* not she by them, but they by her, should rise from the dust. Gorgeous were the lilies of France, and for centuries had the privilege to spread their beauty over land and sea, until, in another century, the wrath of God and man combined to wither them; but well Joanna knew, early at Domrémy she had read that bitter truth, that the lilies of France would decorate no garland for *her*. Flower nor bud, bell nor blossom, would ever bloom for *her*. . . .

On Easter Sunday, when the trial had been long proceeding, the poor girl fell so ill as to cause a belief that she had been poisoned. It was not poison. Nobody had any interest in hastening a death so certain. M. Michelet, whose sympathies with all feelings are so quick, that one would gladly see them always as justly directed, reads the case most truly. Joanna had a twofold malady. She was visited by a paroxysm of the complaint called *home-sickness;* the cruel nature of her imprisonment, and its length, could not but point her solitary thoughts, in darkness and in chains (for chained she was), to Domrémy. And the season, which was the most heavenly period of the spring, added stings to this yearning. That was one of her maladies— *nostalgia,* as medicine calls it; the other was weariness and exhaustion from daily combats with malice. She saw that everybody hated her, and thirsted for her blood; nay, many kind-hearted creatures that would have pitied her profoundly, as regarded all political charges, had their natural feelings warped by the belief that she had dealings with fiendish powers. She knew she was to die; that was *not* the misery: the misery was, that this consummation could not be reached without so much intermediate strife, as if she were contending for some chance (where chance was none) of happiness, or were dreaming for a moment of escaping the inevitable. Why, then, *did* she contend? Knowing that she would reap nothing from answering her persecutors, why did she not retire by silence from the superfluous contest? It was because her quick and eager loyalty to truth would not suffer her to see it darkened by frauds, which *she* could expose, but others, even of candid listeners, perhaps could not; it was through that imperishable grandeur of soul, which taught her to submit meekly and without a struggle to her punishment, but taught her *not* to submit—no, not for a moment—to calumny as to facts, or to misconstruction as to motives. Besides, there were secretaries all around the court taking down her words. That was meant for no good to *her*. But the end does not always correspond to the meaning. And Joanna might say to herself—these words that will be used against me to-morrow and the next day, perhaps in some nobler generation may rise again for my justification. Yes, Joanna, they *are* rising even now in Paris, and for more than justification. . . .

Bishop of Beauvais! thy victim died in fire upon a scaffold—thou upon a down bed. But for the departing minutes of life, both are oftentimes alike. At the farewell crisis, when the gates of death are opening, and flesh is resting from its struggles, oftentimes the tortured and torturer have the same truce from carnal torment; both sink together into sleep; together both, sometimes, kindle into dreams. When the mortal mists were gathering fast upon you two, bishop and shepherd girl—when the pavilions of life were closing up their shadowy curtains about you—let us try, through the gigantic glooms, to decipher the flying features of your separate visions.

The shepherd girl that had delivered France—she, from her dungeon, she, from her baiting at the stake, she, from her duel with fire, as she entered her last dream—saw Domrémy, saw the fountain of Domrémy, saw the pomp of forests in which her childhood had wandered. That Easter festival, which man had denied to her languishing heart—that resurrection of spring-time, which the darkness of dungeons had intercepted from *her,* hungering after the glorious liberty of forests—were by God given back into her hands, as jewels that had been stolen from her by robbers. With those, perhaps (for the minutes of dreams can stretch into ages), was given back to her by God the bliss of childhood. By special privilege, for *her* might be created, in this farewell dream, a second childhood, innocent as the first; but not, like *that,* sad with the gloom of a fearful mission in the rear. The mission had now been fulfilled. The storm was weathered, the skirts even of that mighty storm were drawing off. The blood that she was to reckon for had been exacted; the tears that she was to shed in secret had been paid to the last. The hatred to herself in all eyes had been faced steadily, had been suffered, had been survived. And in her last fight upon the scaffold she had tri-umphed gloriously; victoriously she had tasted the stings of death. For all, except this comfort from her farewell dreams, she had died—died, amidst the tears of ten thousand enemies—died, amidst the drums and trumpets of armies—died, amidst peals redoubling upon peals, volleys upon volleys, from the saluting clarions of martyrs.

Bishop of Beauvais! because the guilt-burdened man is in dreams haunted and waylaid by the most frightful of his crimes, and because upon that fluctuating mirror—rising (like the mocking mirrors of *mirage* in Arabian deserts) from the fens of death—most of all are reflected the sweet countenances which the man has laid in ruins; therefore I know, bishop, that you also, entering your final dream, saw Domrémy. That fountain, of which the witnesses spoke so much, showed itself to your eyes in pure morn-ing dews: but neither dews, nor the holy dawn, could cleanse away the bright spots of innocent blood upon its surface. By the fountain, bishop, you saw a woman seated, that hid her face. But as *you* draw near, the woman raises her wasted features. Would Domrémy know them again for the fea-tures of her child? Ah, but *you* know them, bishop, well! Oh, mercy! what a groan was *that* which the servants, waiting outside the bishop's dream at his bedside, heard from his laboring heart, as at this moment he turned away from the fountain and the woman, seeking rest in the forests afar off. Yet not *so* to escape the woman, whom once again he must behold before he dies. In the forests to which he prays for pity, will he find a respite? What a tumult, what a gathering of feet is there! In glades, where only wild deer should run, armies and nations are assembling; towering in the fluctuating crowd are phantoms that belong to departed hours. There is the great English Prince, Regent of France. There is my Lord of Winchester, the princely cardinal, that died and made no sign. There is the Bishop of Beauvais, clinging to the shelter of thickets. What building is that which hands so rapid are raising? Is it a martyr's scaffold? Will they burn the child of Domrémy a second time? No: it is a tribunal that rises to the clouds; and two nations stand around it, waiting for a trial. Shall my Lord of Beauvais sit again upon the judgment-seat, and again number the hours for the innocent? Ah! no: he is the prisoner at the bar. Already all is waiting: the mighty audience is gathered, the Court is hurrying to their seats, the witnesses are arrayed, the trumpets are sounding, the judge is taking his place. Oh! but this is sudden. My lord, have you no counsel? "Counsel I have none: in heaven above, or on earth beneath, counsellor there is none now that would take a brief from *me:* all are silent." Is it, indeed, come to this? Alas the time is short, the tumult is wondrous, the crowd stretches away into infinity, but yet I will search in it for somebody to take your brief: I know of somebody that will be your counsel. Who is this that cometh from Domrémy? Who is she in bloody coronation robes from Rheims? Who is she that cometh with blackened flesh from walking the furnaces of Rouen? This is she, the shepherd girl, counsellor that had none for herself, whom I choose, bishop, for yours. She it is, I engage, that shall take my lord's brief. She it is, bishop, that would plead for you: yes, bishop, SHE—when heaven and earth are silent.

THE PARAGON | SAMUEL L. CLEMENS

To ARRIVE at a just estimate of a renowned man's character one must judge it by the standards of his time, not ours. Judged by the standards of one century, the noblest characters of an earlier one lose much of their luster; judged by the standards of to-day, there is probably no illustrious man of four or five centuries ago whose character could meet the test at all points. But the character of Joan of Arc is unique. It can be measured by the standards of all times without misgiving or apprehension as to the result. Judged by any of them, judged by all of them, it is still flawless, it is still ideally perfect; it still occupies the loftiest place possible to human attainment, a loftier one than has been reached by any other mere mortal.

When we reflect that her century was the brutalest, the wickedest, the rottenest in history since the darkest ages, we are lost in wonder at the miracle of such a product from such a soil. The contrast between her and

From "Translator's Preface," *Personal Recollections of Joan of Arc* (1896).

her century is the contrast between day and night. She was truthful when lying was the common speech of men; she was honest when honesty was become a lost virtue; she was a keeper of promises when the keeping of a promise was expected of no one; she gave her great mind to great thoughts and great purposes when other great minds wasted themselves upon pretty fancies or upon poor ambitions; she was modest, and fine, and delicate when to be loud and coarse might be said to be universal; she was full of pity when a merciless cruelty was the rule; she was steadfast when stability was unknown, and honorable in an age which had forgotten what honor was; she was a rock of convictions in a time when men believed in nothing and scoffed at all things; she was unfailingly true in an age that was false to the core; she maintained her personal dignity unimpaired in an age of fawnings and servilities; she was of a dauntless courage when hope and courage had perished in the hearts of her nation; she was spotlessly pure in mind and body when society in the highest places was foul in both—she was all these things in an age when crime was the common business of lords and princes, and when the highest personages in Christendom were able to astonish even that infamous era and make it stand aghast at the spectacle of their atrocious lives black with unimaginable treacheries, butcheries, and bestialities.

She was perhaps the only entirely unselfish person whose name has a place in profane history. No vestige or suggestion of self-seeking can be found in any word or deed of hers. When she had rescued her King from his vagabondage, and set his crown upon his head, she was offered rewards and honors, but she refused them all, and would take nothing. All she would take for herself—if the King would grant it—was leave to go back to her village home, and tend her sheep again, and feel her mother's arms about her, and be her housemaid and helper. The selfishness of this unspoiled general of victorious armies, companion of princes, and idol of an applauding and grateful nation, reached but that far and no farther.

The work wrought by Joan of Arc may fairly be regarded as ranking any recorded in history, when one considers the conditions under which it was undertaken, the obstacles in the way, and the means at her disposal. Caesar carried conquest far, but he did it with the trained and confident veterans of Rome, and was a trained soldier himself; and Napoleon swept away the disciplined armies of Europe, but he also was a trained soldier, and he began his work with patriot battalions inflamed and inspired by the miracle-working new breath of Liberty breathed upon them by the Revolution—eager young apprentices to the splendid trade of war, not old and broken men-at-arms, despairing survivors of an age-long accumulation of monotonous defeats; but Joan of Arc, a mere child in years, ignorant, unlettered, a poor village girl unknown and without influence, found a great nation lying in chains, helpless and hopeless under an alien domination, its treasury bankrupt, its soldiers disheartened and dispersed, all spirit torpid, all courage dead in the hearts of the people through long years of foreign and domestic outrage and oppression, their King cowed, resigned to its fate, and preparing to fly the country; and she laid her hand upon this nation, this corpse, and it rose and followed her. She led it from victory to victory, she turned back the tide of the Hundred Years' War, she fatally crippled the English power, and died with the earned title of DELIVERER OF FRANCE, which she bears to this day.

And for all reward, the French King, whom she had crowned, stood supine and indifferent, while French priests took the noble child, the most innocent, the most lovely, the most adorable the ages have produced, and burned her alive at the stake.

THE MARTYR | *GEORGE BERNARD SHAW*

JOAN THE ORIGINAL AND PRESUMPTUOUS

JOAN OF ARC, a village girl from the Vosges, was born about 1412; burnt for heresy, witchcraft, and sorcery in 1431; rehabilitated after a fashion in 1456; designated Venerable in 1904; declared Blessed in 1908; and finally canonized in 1920. She is the most notable Warrior Saint in the Christian calendar, and the queerest fish among the eccentric worthies of the Middle Ages. Though a professed and most pious Catholic, and the projector of a Crusade against the Husites, she was in fact one of the first Protestant martyrs. She was also one of the first apostles of Nationalism, and the first French practitioner of Napoleonic realism in warfare as distinguished from the sporting ransom-gambling chivalry of her time. She was the pioneer of rational dressing for women, and, like Queen Christina of Sweden two centuries later, to say nothing of the Chevalier D'Eon and innumerable obscure heroines who have disguised themselves as men to serve as soldiers and sailors, she refused to accept the specific woman's lot, and dressed and fought and lived as men did.

As she contrived to assert herself in all these ways with such force that she was famous throughout western Europe before she was out of her teens (indeed she never got out of them), it is hardly surprising that she was judicially burnt, ostensibly for a number of capital crimes which we no longer punish as such, but essentially for what we call unwomanly and insufferable presumption. At eighteen Joan's pretensions were beyond those of the proudest Pope or the haughtiest emperor. She claimed to be the ambassador and plenipotentiary of God, and to be, in effect, a member of the Church Triumphant whilst still in the flesh on earth. She patronized her own king, and summoned the English king to repentance and obedi-

From the "Preface" to *Saint Joan*. Reprinted by arrangement with The Public Trustee and The Society of Authors.

ence to her commands. She lectured, talked down, and overruled statesmen and prelates. She poohpoohed the plans of generals, leading their troops to victory on plans of her own. She had an unbounded and quite unconcealed contempt for official opinion, judgment, and authority, and for War Office tactics and strategy. Had she been a sage and monarch in whom the most venerable hierarchy and the most illustrious dynasty converged, her pretensions and proceedings would have been as trying to the official mind as the pretensions of Caesar were to Cassius. As her actual condition was pure upstart, there were only two opinions about her. One was that she was miraculous: the other that she was unbearable.

JOAN AND SOCRATES

If Joan had been malicious, selfish, cowardly or stupid, she would have been one of the most odious persons known to history instead of one of the most attractive. If she had been old enough to know the effect she was producing on the men whom she humiliated by being right when they were wrong, and had learned to flatter and manage them, she might have lived as long as Queen Elizabeth. But she was too young and rustical and inexperienced to have any such arts. When she was thwarted by men whom she thought fools, she made no secret of her opinion of them or her impatience with their folly; and she was naïve enough to expect them to be obliged to her for setting them right and keeping them out of mischief. Now it is always hard for superior wits to understand the fury roused by their exposures of the stupidities of comparative dullards. Even Socrates, for all his age and experience, did not defend himself at his trial like a man who understood the long accumulated fury that had burst on him, and was clamoring for his death. His accuser, if born 2300 years later, might have been picked out of any first class carriage on a suburban railway during the evening or morning rush from or to the City; for he had really nothing to say except that he and his like could not endure being shewn up as idiots every time Socrates opened his mouth. Socrates, unconscious of this, was paralyzed by his sense that somehow he was missing the point of the attack. He petered out after he had established the fact that he was an old soldier and a man of honorable life, and that his accuser was a silly snob. He had no suspicion of the extent to which his mental superiority had roused fear and hatred against him in the hearts of men towards whom he was conscious of nothing but good will and good service.

CONTRAST WITH NAPOLEON

If Socrates was as innocent as this at the age of seventy, it may be imagined how innocent Joan was at the age of seventeen. Now Socrates was a man of argument, operating slowly and peacefully on men's minds, whereas Joan was a woman of action, operating with impetuous violence on their bodies. That, no doubt, is why the contemporaries of Socrates endured him so long, and why Joan was destroyed before she was fully grown. But both of them combined terrifying ability with a frankness, personal modesty, and benevolence which made the furious dislike to which they fell victims absolutely unreasonable, and therefore inapprehensible by themselves. Napoleon, also possessed of terrifying ability, but neither frank nor disinterested, had no illusions as to the nature of his popularity. When he was asked how the world would take his death, he said it would give a gasp of relief. But it is not so easy for mental giants who neither hate nor intend to injure their fellows to realize that nevertheless their fellows hate mental giants and would like to destroy them, not only enviously because the juxtaposition of a superior wounds their vanity, but quite humbly and honestly because it frightens them. Fear will drive men to any extreme; and the fear inspired by a superior being is a mystery which cannot be reasoned away. Being immeasurable it is unbearable when there is no presumption or guarantee of its benevolence and moral responsibility: in other words, when it has no official status. The legal and conventional superiority of Herod and Pilate, and of Annas and Caiphas, inspires fear; but the fear, being a reasonable fear of measurable and avoidable consequences which seem salutary and protective, is bearable; whilst the strange superiority of Christ and the fear it inspires elicit a shriek of Crucify Him from all who cannot divine its benevolence. Socrates has to drink the hemlock, Christ to hang on the cross, and Joan to burn at the stake, whilst Napoleon, though he ends in St. Helena, at least dies in his bed there; and many terrifying but quite comprehensible official scoundrels die natural deaths in all the glory of the kingdoms of this world, proving that it is far more dangerous to be a saint than to be a conqueror. Those who have been both, like Mahomet and Joan, have found that it is the conqueror who must save the saint, and that defeat and capture mean martyrdom. Joan was burnt without a hand lifted on her own side to save her. The comrades she had led to victory and the enemies she had disgraced and defeated, the French king she had crowned and the English king whose crown she had kicked into the Loire, were equally glad to be rid of her.

Was Joan innocent or guilty?

As this result could have been produced by a crapulous inferiority as well as by a sublime superiority, the question which of the two was operative in Joan's case has to be faced. It was decided against her by her contemporaries after a very careful and conscientious trial; and the reversal of the verdict twenty-five years later, in form a rehabilitation of Joan, was really only a confirmation of the validity of the coronation of Charles VII. It is the more impressive reversal by a unanimous Posterity, culminating in her canonization, that has quashed the original proceedings, and put her judges on their trial, which, so far, has been much more unfair than their trial of her. Nevertheless the rehabilitation of 1456, corrupt job as it was, really did produce evidence enough to satisfy all reasonable critics that Joan was not a common termagant, not a harlot, not a witch, not a blasphemer, no more an idolator than the Pope himself, and not ill conducted in any sense apart from her soldiering, her wearing of men's clothes, and her audacity, but on the contrary good-humored, an intact virgin, very pious, very temperate (we should call her meal of bread soaked in the common wine which is the drinking water of France ascetic), very kindly, and, though a brave and hardy soldier, unable to endure loose language or licentious conduct. She went to the stake without a stain on her character except the overweening presumption, the superbity as they called it, that led her thither. It would therefore be waste of time now to prove that the Joan of the first part of the Elizabethan chronicle play of Henry VI (supposed to have been tinkered by Shakespear) grossly libels her in its concluding scenes in deference to Jingo patriotism. The mud that was thrown at her has dropped off by this time so completely that there is no need for any modern writer to wash up after it. What is far more difficult to get rid of is the mud that is being thrown at her judges, and the whitewash which disfigures her beyond recognition. When Jingo scurrility had done its worst to her, sectarian scurrility (in this case Protestant scurrility) used her stake to beat the Roman Catholic Church and the Inquisition. The easiest way to make these institutions the villains of a melodrama was to make The Maid its heroine. That melodrama may be dismissed as rubbish. Joan got a far fairer trial from the Church and the Inquisition than any prisoner of her type and in her situation gets nowadays in any official secular court; and the decision was strictly according to law. And she was not a melodramatic heroine: that is, a physically beautiful lovelorn parasite on an equally beautiful hero, but a genius and a saint, about as completely the opposite of a melodramatic heroine as it is possible for a human being to be.

Let us be clear about the meaning of the terms. A genius is a person who, seeing farther and probing deeper than other people, has a different set of ethical valuations from theirs, and has energy enough to give effect to this extra vision and its valuations in whatever manner best suits his or her specific talents. A saint is one who having practiced heroic virtues, and enjoyed revelations or powers of the order which The Church classes technically as supernatural, is eligible for canonization. If a historian is an Anti-Feminist, and does not believe women to be capable of genius in the traditional masculine departments, he will never make anything of Joan, whose genius was turned to practical account mainly in soldiering and politics. If he is Rationalist enough to deny that saints exist, and to hold that new ideas cannot come otherwise than by conscious ratiocination, he will never catch Joan's likeness. Her ideal biographer must be free from nineteenth century prejudices and biases; must understand the Middle Ages, the Roman Catholic Church, and the Holy Roman Empire much more intimately than our Whig historians have ever understood them; and must be capable of throwing off sex partialities and their romance, and regarding woman as the female of the human species, and not as a different kind of animal with specific charms and specific imbecilities.

JOAN'S GOOD LOOKS

To put the last point roughly, any book about Joan which begins by describing her as a beauty may be at once classed as a romance. Not one of Joan's comrades, in village, court, or camp, even when they were straining themselves to please the king by praising her, ever claimed that she was pretty. All the men who alluded to the matter declared most emphatically that she was unattractive sexually to a degree that seemed to them miraculous, considering that she was in the bloom of youth, and neither ugly, awkward, deformed, nor unpleasant in her person. The evident truth is that like most women of her hardy managing type she seemed neutral in the conflict of sex because men were too much afraid of her to fall in love with her. She herself was not sexless: in spite of the virginity she had vowed up to a point, and preserved to her death, she never excluded the possibility of marriage for herself. But marriage, with its preliminary of the attraction, pursuit, and capture of a husband, was not her business: she had something else to do. Byron's formula, "Man's love is of man's life a thing apart: 'tis woman's whole existence" did not apply to her any more than to George Washington or any other masculine worker on the heroic scale. Had she lived in our time, picture postcards might have been sold of her as a general: they would not have been sold of her as a sultana. Nevertheless there is one reason for crediting her with a very remarkable face. A sculptor of her time in Orleans made a statue of a helmeted young woman with a face that is unique in art in point of being evidently not an ideal face but a portrait, and yet so uncommon as to be unlike any real woman one has ever seen. It is surmised that Joan served unconsciously as the sculptor's model. There is no proof of this; but those extraordinarily spaced eyes raise so powerfully the question "If this woman be not Joan, who is she?" that I dispense with further evidence, and challenge those who disagree with me to prove a negative. It is a wonderful face, but quite neutral from the point of view of the operatic beauty fancier.

Such a fancier may perhaps be finally chilled by the prosaic fact that Joan was the defendant in a suit for breach of promise of marriage, and that she conducted her own case and won it.

JOAN'S SOCIAL POSITION

By class Joan was the daughter of a working farmer who was one of the headmen of his village, and transacted its feudal business for it with the neighboring squires and their lawyers. When the castle in which the villagers were entitled to take refuge from raids became derelict, he organized a combination of half a dozen farmers to obtain possession of it so as to occupy it when there was any danger of invasion. As a child, Joan could please herself at times with being the young lady of this castle. Her mother and brothers were able to follow and share her fortune at court without making themselves notably ridiculous. These facts leave us no excuse for the popular romance that turns every heroine into either a princess or a beggarmaid. In the somewhat similar case of Shakespear a whole inverted pyramid of wasted research has been based on the assumption that he was an illiterate laborer, in the face of the plainest evidence that his father was a man of business, and at one time a very prosperous one, married to a woman of some social pretensions. There is the same tendency to drive Joan into the position of a hired shepherd girl, though a hired shepherd girl in Domrémy would have deferred to her as the young lady of the farm.

The difference between Joan's case and Shakespear's is that Shakespear was not illiterate. He had been to school, and knew as much Latin and Greek as most university passmen retain: that is, for practical purposes, none at all. Joan was absolutely illiterate. "I do not know A from B" she said. But many princesses at that time and for long after might have said the same. Marie Antoinette, for instance, at Joan's age could not spell her own name correctly. But this does not mean that Joan was an ignorant person, or that she suffered from the diffidence and sense of social disadvantage now felt by people who cannot read or write. If she could not write letters, she could and did dictate them and attach full and indeed excessive importance to them. When she was called a shepherd lass to her face she very warmly resented it, and challenged any woman to compete with her in the household arts of the mistresses of well furnished houses. She understood the political and military situation in France much better than most of our newspaper fed university women-graduates understand the corresponding situation of their own country today. Her first convert was the neighboring commandant at Vaucouleurs; and she converted him by telling him about the defeat of the Dauphin's troops at the Battle of Herrings so long before he had official news of it that he concluded she must have had a divine revelation. This knowledge of and interest in public affairs was nothing extraordinary among farmers in a warswept countryside. Politicians came to the door too often sword in hand to be disregarded: Joan's people could not afford to be ignorant of what was going on in the feudal world. They were not rich; and Joan worked on the farm as her father did, driving the sheep to pasture and so forth; but there is no evidence or suggestion of sordid poverty, and no reason to believe that Joan had to work as a hired servant works, or indeed to work at all when she preferred to go to confession, or dawdle about waiting for visions and listening to the church bells to hear voices in them. In short, much more of a young lady, and even of an intellectual, than most of the daughters of our petty bourgeoisie.

JOAN'S VOICES AND VISIONS

Joan's voices and visions have played many tricks with her reputation. They have been held to prove that she was mad, that she was a liar and impostor, that she was a sorceress (she was burnt for this), and finally that

she was a saint. They do not prove any of these things; but the variety
of the conclusions reached show how little our matter-of-fact historians
know about other people's minds, or even about their own. There are people
in the world whose imagination is so vivid that when they have an idea it
comes to them as an audible voice, sometimes uttered by a visible figure.
Criminal lunatic asylums are occupied largely by murderers who have
obeyed voices. Thus a woman may hear voices telling her that she must
cut her husband's throat and strangle her child as they lie asleep; and she
may feel obliged to do what she is told. By a medico-legal superstition it
is held in our courts that criminals whose temptations present themselves
under these illusions are not responsible for their actions, and must be
treated as insane. But the seers of visions and the hearers of revelations are
not always criminals. The inspirations and intuitions and unconsciously
reasoned conclusions of genius sometimes assume similar illusions. Socrates,
Luther, Swedenborg, Blake saw visions and heard voices just as Saint Francis
and Saint Joan did. If Newton's imagination had been of the same vividly
dramatic kind he might have seen the ghost of Pythagoras walk into the
orchard and explain why the apples were falling. Such an illusion would
have invalidated neither the theory of gravitation nor Newton's general
sanity. What is more, the visionary method of making the discovery would
not be a whit more miraculous than the normal method. The test of sanity
is not the normality of the method but the reasonableness of the discovery.
If Newton had been informed by Pythagoras that the moon was made of
green cheese, then Newton would have been locked up. Gravitation, being
a reasoned hypothesis which fitted remarkably well into the Copernican
version of the observed physical facts of the universe, established Newton's
reputation for extraordinary intelligence, and would have done so no matter how fantastically he had arrived at it. Yet his theory of gravitation is
not so impressive a mental feat as his astounding chronology, which establishes him as the king of mental conjurors, but a Bedlamite king whose
authority no one now accepts. On the subject of the eleventh horn of the
beast seen by the prophet Daniel he was more fantastic than Joan, because
his imagination was not dramatic but mathematical and therefore extraordinarily susceptible to numbers: indeed if all his works were lost except his
chronology we should say that he was as mad as a hatter. As it is, who dares
diagnose Newton as a madman?

In the same way Joan must be judged a sane woman in spite of her
voices because they never gave her any advice that might not have come to
her from her mother wit exactly as gravitation came to Newton. We can all
see now, especially since the late war threw so many of our women into
military life, that Joan's campaigning could not have been carried on in
petticoats. This was not only because she did a man's work, but because
it was morally necessary that sex should be left out of the question as
between her and her comrades-in-arms. She gave this reason herself when

she was pressed on the subject; and the fact that this entirely reasonable necessity came to her imagination first as an order from God delivered through the mouth of Saint Catherine does not prove that she was mad. The soundness of the order proves that she was unusually sane; but its form proves that her dramatic imagination played tricks with her senses. Her policy was also quite sound: nobody disputes that the relief of Orleans, followed up by the coronation at Rheims of the Dauphin as a counterblow to the suspicions then current of his legitimacy and consequently of his title, were military and political masterstrokes that saved France. They might have been planned by Napoleon or any other illusionproof genius. They came to Joan as an instruction from her Counsel, as she called her visionary saints; but she was none the less an able leader of men for imagining her ideas in this way.

THE EVOLUTIONARY APPETITE

What then is the modern view of Joan's voices and visions and messages from God? The nineteenth century said that they were delusions, but that as she was a pretty girl, and had been abominably ill-treated and finally done to death by a superstitious rabble of medieval priests hounded on by a corrupt political bishop, it must be assumed that she was the innocent dupe of these delusions. The twentieth century finds this explanation too vapidly commonplace, and demands something more mystic. I think the twentieth century is right, because an explanation which amounts to Joan being mentally defective instead of, as she obviously was, mentally excessive, will not wash. I cannot believe, nor, if I could, could I expect all my readers to believe, as Joan did, that three ocularly visible well dressed persons, named respectively Saint Catherine, Saint Margaret, and Saint Michael, came down from heaven and gave her certain instructions with which they were charged by God for her. Not that such a belief would be more improbable or fantastic than some modern beliefs which we all swallow; but there are fashions and family habits in belief, and it happens that, my fashion being Victorian and my family habit Protestant, I find myself unable to attach any such objective validity to the form of Joan's visions.

But that there are forces at work which use individuals for purposes far transcending the purpose of keeping these individuals alive and prosperous and respectable and safe and happy in the middle station in life, which is all any good bourgeois can reasonably require, is established by the fact that men will, in the pursuit of knowledge and of social readjustments for which they will not be a penny the better, and are indeed often many pence the worse, face poverty, infamy, exile, imprisonment, dreadful hardship, and death. Even the selfish pursuit of personal power does not nerve men to the efforts and sacrifices which are eagerly made in pursuit of extensions of our power over nature, though these extensions may not touch the personal life of the seeker at any point. There is no more mystery about this

appetite for knowledge and power than about the appetite for food: both
are known as facts and as facts only, the difference between them being that
the appetite for food is necessary to the life of the hungry man and is therefore a personal appetite, whereas the other is an appetite for evolution, and
therefore a superpersonal need.

The diverse manners in which our imaginations dramatize the approach
of the superpersonal forces is a problem for the psychologist, not for the
historian. Only, the historian must understand that visionaries are neither
impostors nor lunatics. It is one thing to say that the figure Joan recognized
as St Catherine was not really St Catherine, but the dramatization by
Joan's imagination of that pressure upon her of the driving force that is
behind evolution which I have just called the evolutionary appetite. It
is quite another to class her visions with the vision of two moons seen by
a drunken person, or with Brocken specters, echoes and the like. Saint
Catherine's instructions were far too cogent for that; and the simplest
French peasant who believes in apparitions of celestial personages to
favored mortals is nearer to the scientific truth about Joan than the Rationalist and Materialist historians and essayists who feel obliged to set
down a girl who saw saints and heard them talking to her as either crazy
or mendacious. If Joan was mad, all Christendom was mad too; for people
who believe devoutly in the existence of celestial personages are every
whit as mad in that sense as the people who think they see them. Luther,
when he threw his inkhorn at the devil, was no more mad than any other
Augustinian monk: he had a more vivid imagination, and had perhaps
eaten and slept less: that was all. . . .

JOAN SUMMED UP

We may accept and admire Joan, then, as a sane and shrewd country
girl of extraordinary strength of mind and hardihood of body. Everything
she did was thoroughly calculated; and though the process was so rapid
that she was hardly conscious of it, and ascribed it all to her voices, she was
a woman of policy and not of blind impulse. In war she was as much a
realist as Napoleon: she had his eye for artillery and his knowledge of
what it could do. She did not expect besieged cities to fall Jerichowise
at the sound of her trumpet, but, like Wellington, adapted her methods
of attack to the peculiarities of the defense; and she anticipated the
Napoleonic calculation that if you only hold on long enough the other
fellow will give in: for example, her final triumph at Orleans was achieved
after her commander Dunois had sounded the retreat at the end of a
day's fighting without a decision. She was never for a moment what so
many romancers and playwrights have pretended: a romantic young lady.
She was a thorough daughter of the soil in her peasantlike matter-of-fact-
ness and doggedness, and her acceptance of great lords and kings and
prelates as such without idolatry or snobbery, seeing at a glance how

much they were individually good for. She had the respectable country-woman's sense of the value of public decency, and would not tolerate foul language and neglect of religious observances, nor allow disreputable women to hang about her soldiers. She had one pious ejaculation *"En nom Dé!"* and one meaningless oath *"Par mon martin";* and this much swearing she allowed to the incorrigibly blasphemous La Hire equally with herself. The value of this prudery was so great in restoring the self-respect of the badly demoralized army that, like most of her policy, it justified itself as soundly calculated. She talked to and dealt with people of all classes, from laborers to kings, without embarrassment or affectation, and got them to do what she wanted when they were not afraid or corrupt. She could coax and she could hustle, her tongue having a soft side and a sharp edge. She was very capable: a born boss.

JOAN'S IMMATURITY AND IGNORANCE

All this, however, must be taken with one heavy qualification. She was only a girl in her teens. If we could think of her as a managing woman of fifty we should seize her type at once; for we have plenty of managing women among us of that age who illustrate perfectly the sort of person she would have become had she lived. But she, being only a lass when all is said, lacked their knowledge of men's vanities and of the weight and proportion of social forces. She knew nothing of iron hands in velvet gloves: she just used her fists. She thought political changes much easier than they are, and, like Mahomet in his innocence of any world but the tribal world, wrote letters to kings calling on them to make millennial rearrangements. Consequently it was only in the enterprises that were really simple and compassable by swift physical force, like the coronation and the Orleans campaign, that she was successful.

Her want of academic education disabled her when she had to deal with such elaborately artificial structures as the great ecclesiastical and social institutions of the Middle Ages. She had a horror of heretics without suspecting that she was herself a heresiarch, one of the precursors of a schism that rent Europe in two, and cost centuries of bloodshed that is not yet staunched. She objected to foreigners on the sensible ground that they were not in their proper place in France; but she had no notion of how this brought her into conflict with Catholicism and Feudalism, both essentially international. She worked by commonsense; and where scholarship was the only clue to institutions she was in the dark and broke her shins against them, all the more rudely because of her enormous self-confidence, which made her the least cautious of human beings in civil affairs.

This combination of inept youth and academic ignorance with great natural capacity, push, courage, devotion, originality and oddity, fully accounts for all the facts in Joan's career, and makes her a credible historical and human phenomenon; but it clashes most discordantly both with the idolatrous romance that has grown up round her, and the belittling scepticism that reacts against that romance.

EMPHASIS: IN PLAGUE TIME

UNTIL THE END of the seventeenth century life in Europe was under a periodic menace unfamiliar to us today, the bubonic plague. About once every generation this devastating sickness came mysteriously from the East, via the European port cities, and spread inland, killing most of those whom it infected. Its effects on history were enormous, although most historians have paid relatively little attention to it until recently, perhaps because it was such a continuous menace compared to more unusual cataclysms. But if later authorities have underemphasized the plague, those who lived through one or more of its appearances have done it justice. They saw the visitations not as primary influences in the making of history, but as intense personal and social crises. Such a terrible attack as the Black Death of 1348-1350 (which destroyed over one-third of Europe's population) left virtually no family intact and scarred the European mind for centuries afterward with a sense of the immediacy and horror of death.

The problems of reporting such an event are obvious. The eyewitness must describe an event inherently freighted with emotion and terribly vivid for him, to a presumably uninitiated reader. He needs to express somehow the extreme horror of the thing, to cajole, persuade, or wrench the reader into understanding and sharing the original experience, to make the fleshless statistics take life. In order to do this, he may be tempted to overstate, to squeeze dry his stock of language. But by using words commensurate with the violence of his feelings, or even more extreme, he may alienate the reader, or arouse incredulity, for merely to pile up superlatives is not necessarily to convince. So the plague chronicler may choose the opposite course: he may attempt to strip his language of emotion and merely report the facts, or even to understate, that is, use words less emotionally pregnant than the events they express. Understatement, at its best, leaves the subject matter to do its own work on the reader, language serving only as a vehicle not as a bludgeon. But the danger of this method is that it may never overcome the reader's inertia. Neither way, then, is categorically better, both may be used with extreme effectiveness.

The six pieces in this section represent varied compromises between heavy and light emphasis, and no one selection is uniform throughout in emotional stress. Too, the problems confronting the writers differ greatly

*Two of the accounts, those of Thucydides (471?-?400 B.C., Greek historian)
and Henry Knighton (fl. 1363, obscure English annalist) are straightforward
chronicles of actual plagues. A third, that from the* Decameron *of Giovanni
Boccaccio (1313-1375, Italian raconteur), is based on actual observation,
although it is the introduction to a work of fiction. Samuel Pepys (1633-
1703), the great English diarist, reports a real plague, but writes for no
audience but himself. The plague of 1665 is also Daniel Defoe's (1660-
1731) subject, but the author of* Robinson Crusoe *was not an eyewitness, as
he claims to have been. He pieced together his vivid but imaginary description from written and traditional tales. The plague in Oran, subject of
French novelist Albert Camus (1913-1960) is wholly fictitious. Finally,
Thomas Nashe (1567-1601), who was an Elizabethan poet, novelist and
dramatist, deals with entirely different problems of expression, since his
medium is verse. Though these approaches are various, it is fruitful to compare the writers' handling of emphasis.*

THE PLAGUE OF ATHENS | *THUCYDIDES*

Such was the funeral that took place during this winter, with which
the first year of the war came to an end. In the first days of summer the
Lacedaemonians and their allies, with two-thirds of their forces as before,
invaded Attica, under the command of Archidamus, son of Zeuxidamus,
king of Lacedaemon, and sat down and laid waste the country. Not many
days after their arrival in Attica the plague first began to show itself among
the Athenians. It was said that it had broken out in many places previously
in the neighborhood of Lemnos and elsewhere; but a pestilence of such
extent and mortality was nowhere remembered. Neither were the physicians at first of any service, ignorant as they were of the proper way to
treat it, but they died themselves the most thickly, as they visited the sick
most often; nor did any human art succeed any better. Supplications in
the temples, divinations, and so forth were found equally futile, till the
overwhelming nature of the disaster at last put a stop to them altogether.

It first began, it is said, in the parts of Ethiopia above Egypt, and
thence descended into Egypt and Libya and into most of the king's country.
Suddenly falling upon Athens, it first attacked the population in Piraeus—
which was the occasion of their saying that the Peloponnesians had poisoned the reservoirs, there being as yet no wells there—and afterwards
appeared in the upper city, when the deaths became much more frequent.

From the book *The History of the Peloponnesian War* by Thucydides, trans. by
Richard Crawley. Everyman's Library Edition. Reprinted by permission of the publishers,
E. P. Dutton & Co., Inc., and J. M. Dent & Sons, Ltd.

All speculation as to its origin and its causes, if causes can be found adequate to produce so great a disturbance, I leave to other writers, whether lay or professional; for myself, I shall simply set down its nature, and explain the symptoms by which perhaps it may be recognized by the student, if it should ever break out again. This I can the better do, as I had the disease myself, and watched its operation in the case of others.

That year then is admitted to have been otherwise unprecedentedly free from sickness; and such few cases as occurred, all determined in this. As a rule, however, there was no ostensible cause; but people in good health were all of a sudden attacked by violent heats in the head, and redness and inflammation in the eyes, the inward parts, such as the throat or tongue, becoming bloody and emitting an unnatural and fetid breath. These symptoms were followed by sneezing and hoarseness, after which the pain soon reached the chest, and produced a hard cough. When it fixed in the stomach, it upset it; and discharges of bile of every kind named by physicians ensued, accompanied by very great distress. In most cases also an ineffectual retching followed, producing violent spasms, which in some cases ceased soon after, in others much later. Externally the body was not very hot to the touch, nor pale in its appearance, but reddish, livid, and breaking out into small pustules and ulcers. But internally it burned so that the patient could not bear to have on him clothing or linen even of the very lightest description; or indeed to be otherwise than stark naked. What they would have liked best would have been to throw themselves into cold water; as indeed was done by some of the neglected sick, who plunged into the rain-tanks in their agonies of unquenchable thirst; though it made no difference whether they drank little or much. Besides this, the miserable feeling of not being able to rest or sleep never ceased to torment them. The body meanwhile did not waste away so long as the distemper was at its height, but held out to a marvel against its ravages; so that when they succumbed, as in most cases, on the seventh or eighth day to the internal inflammation, they had still some strength in them. But if they passed this stage, and the disease descended further into the bowels, inducing a violent ulceration there accompanied by severe diarrhea, this brought on a weakness which was generally fatal. For the disorder first settled in the head, ran its course from thence through the whole of the body, and even where it did not prove mortal, it still left its mark on the extremities; for it settled in the privy parts, the fingers and the toes, and many escaped with the loss of these, some too with that of their eyes. Others again were seized with an entire loss of memory on their first recovery, and did not know either themselves or their friends.

But while the nature of the distemper was such as to baffle all description, and its attacks almost too grievous for human nature to endure, it was still in the following circumstance that its difference from all ordinary disorders was most clearly shown. All the birds and beasts that prey upon human bodies, either abstained from touching them (though there were many lying unburied), or died after tasting them. In proof of this, it was noticed that birds of this kind actually disappeared; they were not about the bodies, or indeed to be seen at all. But of course the effects which I have mentioned could best be studied in a domestic animal like the dog.

Such then, if we pass over the varieties of particular cases, which were many and peculiar, were the general features of the distemper. Meanwhile the town enjoyed an immunity from all the ordinary disorders; or if any case occurred, it ended in this. Some died in neglect, others in the midst of every attention. No remedy was found that could be used as a specific; for what did good in one case, did harm in another. Strong and weak constitutions proved equally incapable of resistance, all alike being swept away, although dieted with the utmost precaution. By far the most terrible feature in the malady was the dejection which ensued when anyone felt himself sickening, for the despair into which they instantly fell took away their power of resistance, and left them a much easier prey to the disorder; besides which, there was the awful spectacle of men dying like sheep, through having caught the infection in nursing each other. This caused the greatest mortality. On the one hand, if they were afraid to visit each other, they perished from neglect; indeed many houses were emptied of their inmates for want of a nurse: on the other, if they ventured to do so, death was the consequence. This was especially the case with such as made any pretensions to goodness: honor made them unsparing of themselves in their attendance in their friends' houses, where even the members of the family were at last worn out by the moans of the dying, and succumbed to the force of the disaster. Yet it was with those who had recovered from the disease that the sick and dying found most compassion. These knew what it was from experience, and had now no fear for themselves; for the same man was never attacked twice—never at least fatally. And such persons not only received the congratulations of others, but themselves also, in the elation of the moment, half entertained the vain hope that they were for the future safe from any disease whatsoever.

An aggravation of the existing calamity was the influx from the country into the city, and this was especially felt by the new arrivals. As there were no houses to receive them, they had to be lodged at the hot season of the year in stifling cabins, where the mortality ranged without restraint. The bodies of dying men lay one upon another, and half-dead creatures reeled about the streets and gathered round all the fountains in their longing for water. The sacred places also in which they had quartered themselves were full of corpses of persons that had died there, just as they were; for as the disaster passed all bounds, men, not knowing what was to become of them, became utterly careless of everything, whether sacred or profane. All the burial rites before in use were entirely upset, and they buried the bodies as best they could. Many from want of the proper appliances, through so many of their friends having died already, had recourse to the most shameless sepultures: sometimes getting the start of those who had raised a pile, they threw their own dead body upon the stranger's pyre and ignited it; sometimes they tossed the corpse which they were carrying on the top of another that was burning, and so went off.

Nor was this the only form of lawless extravagance which owed its origin to the plague. Men now coolly ventured on what they had formerly done in a corner, and not just as they pleased, seeing the rapid transitions produced by persons in prosperity suddenly dying and those who before had nothing succeeding to their property. So they resolved to spend quickly and enjoy themselves, regarding their lives and riches as alike things of a day. Perseverance in what men called honor was popular with none, it was so uncertain whether they would be spared to attain the object; but it was settled that present enjoyment, and all that contributed to it, was both honorable and useful. Fear of gods or law of man there was none to restrain them. As for the first, they judged it to be just the same whether they worshiped them or not, as they saw all alike perishing; and for the last, no one expected to live to be brought to trial for his offenses, but each felt that a far severer sentence had been already passed upon them all and hung ever over their heads, and before this fell it was only reasonable to enjoy life a little.

Such was the nature of the calamity, and heavily did it weigh on the Athenians; death raging within the city and devastation without.

THE IMPACT OF THE BLACK DEATH | *HENRY KNIGHTON*

In this year [1348] and in the following one there was a general mortality of men throughout the whole world. It first began in India, then in Tharsis, then it came to the Saracens, and finally to the Christians and Jews, so that in the space of one year, from Easter to Easter, as the rumor spread in the Roman curia, there had died, as if by sudden death, in those remote regions eight thousand legions, besides the Christians. The king of Tharsis, seeing such a sudden and unheard-of slaughter of his people began a journey to Avignon with a great multitude of his nobles, to propose to the pope that he would become a Christian and be baptized by him, thinking that he might thus mitigate the vengeance of God upon his people because of their wicked unbelief. Then, when he had journeyed for twenty days, he heard that the pestilence had struck among the Christians, just as among other peoples. So, turning in his tracks, he traveled no

From *The Portable Medieval Reader*, trans. by Mary Martin McLaughlin. Copyright 1949 by the Viking Press, Inc.

farther but hastened to return home. The Christians, pursuing these people from behind, slew about seven thousand of them.

There died in Avignon in one day one thousand three hundred and twelve persons, according to a count made for the pope, and, another day, four hundred persons and more. Three hundred and fifty-eight of the Friars Preachers in the region of Provence died during Lent. At Montpellier, there remained out of a hundred and forty friars only seven. There were left at Magdalena only seven friars out of a hundred and sixty, and yet enough. At Marseilles, of a hundred and fifty Friars Minor, there remained only one who could tell the others; that was well, indeed. Of the Carmelites, more than a hundred and sixty-six had died at Avignon before the citizens found out what had happened. For they believed that one had killed another. There was not one of the English Hermits left in Avignon.

At this same time the pestilence became prevalent in England, beginning in the autumn in certain places. It spread throughout the land, ending in the same season of the following year. At the same time many cities in Corinth and Achaia were overturned, and the earth swallowed them. Castles and fortresses were broken, laid low, and swallowed up. Mountains in Cyprus were leveled into one, so that the flow of the rivers was impeded, and many cities were submerged and villages destroyed. Similarly, when a certain friar was preaching at Naples, the whole city was destroyed by an earthquake. Suddenly, the earth was opened up, as if a stone had been thrown into the water, and everyone died along with the preaching friar, except for one friar who, fleeing, escaped into a garden outside the city. All of these things were done by an earthquake. . . .

Then that most grievous pestilence penetrated the coastal regions [of England] by way of Southampton, and came to Bristol, and people died as if the whole strength of the city were seized by sudden death. For there were few who lay in their beds more than three days or two and a half days; then that savage death snatched them about the second day. In Leicester, in the little parish of St. Leonard, more than three hundred and eighty died; in the parish of the Holy Cross, more than four hundred, and in the parish of St. Margaret in Leicester, more than seven hundred. And so in each parish, they died in great numbers. Then the bishop of Lincoln sent through the whole diocese, and gave the general power to each and every priest, both regular and secular, to hear confessions and to absolve, by the full and entire power of the bishop, except only in the case of debt. And they might absolve in that case if satisfaction could be made by the person while he lived, or from his property after his death. Likewise, the pope granted full remission of all sins, to be absolved completely, to anyone who was in danger of death, and he granted this power to last until the following Easter. And everyone was allowed to choose his confessor as he pleased.

During this same year, there was a great mortality of sheep everywhere in the kingdom; in one place and in one pasture, more than five thousand sheep died and became so putrefied that neither beast nor bird wanted to touch them. And the price of everything was cheap, because of the fear of death; there were very few who took any care for their wealth, or for anything else. For a man could buy a horse for half a mark, which before was worth forty shillings, a large fat ox for four shillings, a cow for twelve pence, a heifer for sixpence, a large fat sheep for four pence, a sheep for threepence, a lamb for two pence, a fat pig for five pence, a stone of wool for nine pence. And the sheep and cattle wandered about through the fields and among the crops, and there was no one to go after them or to collect them. They perished in countless numbers everywhere, in secluded ditches and hedges, for lack of watching, since there was such a lack of serfs and servants, that no one knew what he should do. For there is no memory of a mortality so severe and so savage from the time of Vortigern, king of the Britons, in whose time, as Bede says, the living did not suffice to bury the dead. In the following autumn, one could not hire a reaper at a lower wage than eight pence with food, or a mower at less than twelve pence with food. Because of this, much grain rotted in the fields for lack of harvesting, but in the year of the plague, as was said above, among other things there was so great an abundance of all kinds of grain that no one seemed to have concerned himself about it.

The Scots, hearing of the cruel pestilence in England, suspected that this had come upon the English by the avenging hand of God, and when they wished to swear an oath, they swore this one, as the vulgar rumor reached the ears of the English, "be the foul deth of Engelond." And so the Scots, believing that the horrible vengeance of God had fallen on the English, came together in the forest of Selkirk to plan an invasion of the whole kingdom of England. But savage mortality supervened, and the sudden and frightful cruelty of death struck the Scots. In a short time, about five thousand died; the rest, indeed, both sick and well, prepared to return home, but the English, pursuing them, caught up with them, and slew a great many of them.

Master Thomas Bradwardine was consecrated archbishop of Canterbury by the pope, and when he returned to England, came to London. In less than two days he was dead. He was famous above all other clerks in Christendom, in theology especially, but also in other liberal studies. At this same time there was so great a lack of priests everywhere that many widowed churches had no divine services, no masses, matins, vespers, sacraments, and sacramentals. One could hardly hire a chaplain to minister to any church for less than ten pounds or ten marks, and whereas, before the pestilence, when there were plenty of priests, one could hire a chaplain for five or four marks or for two marks, with board, there was scarcely anyone at this time who wanted to accept a position for twenty pounds or twenty marks. But within a short time a very great multitude whose wives had died of the plague rushed into holy orders. Of these many were illiterate, and, it seemed, simply laymen who knew nothing except how to read to some extent. The hides of cattle went up from a low price to twelve pence, and for shoes the price went to ten, twelve, fourteen pence; for a pair of leggings, to three and four shillings.

Meanwhile, the king ordered that in every county of the kingdom, reapers and other laborers should not receive more than they were accustomed to receive, under the penalty provided in the statute, and he renewed the statute from this time. The laborers, however, were so arrogant and hostile that they did not heed the king's command, but if anyone wished to hire them, he had to pay them what they wanted, and either lose his fruits and crops or satisfy the arrogant and greedy desire of the laborers as they wished. When it was made known to the king that they had not obeyed his mandate, and had paid higher wages to the laborers, he imposed heavy fines on the abbots, the priors, the great lords and the lesser ones, and on others both greater and lesser in the kingdom. From certain ones he took a hundred shillings, from some, forty shillings, from others, twenty shillings, and from each according to what he could pay. And he took from each ploughland in the whole kingdom twenty shillings, and not one-fifteenth less than this. Then the king had many laborers arrested, and put them in prison. Many such hid themselves and ran away to the forests and woods for a while, and those who were captured were heavily fined. And the greater number swore that they would not take daily wages above those set by ancient custom, and so they were freed from prison. It was done in like manner concerning other artisans in towns and villages. . . .

After the aforesaid pestilence, many buildings, both large and small, in all cities, towns, and villages had collapsed, and had completely fallen to the ground in the absence of inhabitants. Likewise, many small villages and hamlets were completely deserted; there was not one house left in them, but all those who had lived in them were dead. It is likely that many such hamlets will never again be inhabited. In the following summer [1350], there was so great a lack of servants to do anything that, as one believed, there had hardly been so great a dearth in past times. For all the beasts and cattle that a man possessed wandered about without a shepherd, and everything a man had was without a caretaker. And so all necessities became so dear that anything that in the past had been worth a penny was now worth four or five pence. Moreover, both the magnates of the kingdom and the other lesser lords who had tenants, remitted something from the rents, lest the tenants should leave, because of the lack of servants and the dearth of things. Some remitted half the rent, some more and others less, some remitted it for two years, some for three, and others for one year, according as they were able to come to an agreement with their tenants. Similarly, those who received day-work from their tenants throughout the year, as is usual from serfs, had to release them and to remit such services. They either had to excuse them entirely or had to fix them in a laxer manner at a small rent, lest very great and irreparable damage be done to the buildings, and the land everywhere remain completely uncultivated. And all foodstuffs and all necessities became exceedingly dear.

THE BLACK DEATH IN FLORENCE | GIOVANNI BOCCACCIO

In the year 1348 after the fruitful incarnation of the Son of God, that most beautiful of Italian cities, noble Florence, was attacked by deadly plague. It started in the East either through the influence of the heavenly bodies or because God's just anger with our wicked deeds sent it as a punishment to mortal men; and in a few years killed an innumerable quantity of people. Ceaselessly passing from place to place, it extended its miserable length over the West. Against this plague all human wisdom and foresight were vain. Orders had been given to cleanse the city of filth, the entry of any sick person was forbidden, much advice was given for keeping healthy; at the same time humble supplications were made to God by pious persons in processions and otherwise. And yet, in the beginning of the spring of the year mentioned, its horrible results began to appear, and in a miraculous manner. The symptoms were not the same as in the East, where a gush of blood from the nose was the plain sign of inevitable death; but it began both in men and women with certain swellings in the groin or under the armpit. They grew to the size of a small apple or an egg, more or less, and were vulgarly called tumors. In a short space of time these tumors spread from the two parts named all over the body. Soon after this the symptoms changed and black or purple spots appeared on the arms or thighs or any other part of the body, sometimes a few large ones, sometimes many little ones. These spots were a certain sign of death, just as the original tumor had been and still remained.

No doctor's advice, no medicine could overcome or alleviate this disease. An enormous number of ignorant men and women set up as doctors in addition to those who were trained. Either the disease was such that no treatment was possible or the doctors were so ignorant that they did not know what caused it, and consequently could not administer the proper remedy. In any case very few recovered; most people died within about three days of the appearance of the tumors described above, most of them without any fever or other symptoms.

The violence of this disease was such that the sick communicated it

From Giovanni Boccaccio, *The Decameron*, trans. by Richard Aldington (New York, Doubleday & Company, Inc., 1930). Reprinted by permission of the translator and of Rosica Colin, London.

to the healthy who came near them, just as a fire catches anything dry or oily near it. And it even went further. To speak to or go near the sick brought infection and a common death to the living; and moreover, to touch the clothes or anything else the sick had touched or worn gave the disease to the person touching.

What I am about to tell now is a marvelous thing to hear; and if I and others had not seen it with our own eyes I would not dare to write it, however much I was willing to believe and whatever the good faith of the person from whom I hear it. So violent was the malignancy of this plague that it was communicated, not only from one man to another, but from the garments of a sick or dead man to animals of another species, which caught the disease in that way and very quickly died of it. One day among other occasions I saw with my own eyes (as I said just now) the rags left lying in the street of a poor man who had died of the plague; two pigs came along and, as their habit is, turned the clothes over with their snouts and then munched at them, with the result that they both fell dead almost at once on the rags, as if they had been poisoned.

From these and similar or greater occurrences, such fear and fanciful notions took possession of the living that almost all of them adopted the same cruel policy, which was entirely to avoid the sick and everything belonging to them. By so doing, each one thought he would secure his own safety.

Some thought that moderate living and the avoidance of all superfluity would preserve them from the epidemic. They formed small communities, living entirely separate from everybody else. They shut themselves up in houses where there were no sick, eating the finest food and drinking the best wine very temperately, avoiding all excess, allowing no news or discussion of death and sickness, and passing the time in music and such-like pleasures. Others thought just the opposite. They thought the sure cure for the plague was to drink and be merry, to go about singing and amusing themselves, satisfying every appetite they could, laughing and jesting at what happened. They put their words into practice, spent day and night going from tavern to tavern, drinking immoderately; or went into other people's houses, doing only those things which pleased them. This they could easily do because everyone felt doomed and had abandoned his property, so that most houses became common property and any stranger who went in made use of them as if he had owned them. And with all this bestial behavior, they avoided the sick as much as possible.

In this suffering and misery of our city, the authority of human and divine laws almost disappeared, for, like other men, the ministers and the executors of the laws were all dead or sick or shut up with their families, so that no duties were carried out. Every man was therefore able to do as he pleased.

Many others adopted a course of life midway between the two just described. They did not restrict their victuals so much as the former, nor allow themselves to be drunken and dissolute like the latter, but satisfied their appetites moderately. They did not shut themselves up, but went about, carrying flowers or scented herbs or perfumes in their hands, in the belief that it was an excellent thing to comfort the brain with such odors; for the whole air was infected with the smell of dead bodies, of sick persons and medicines.

Others again held a still more cruel opinion, which they thought would keep them safe. They said that the only medicine against the plague-stricken was to go right away from them. Men and women, convinced of this and caring about nothing but themselves, abandoned their own city, their own houses, their dwellings, their relatives, their property, and went abroad or at least to the country round Florence, as if God's wrath in punishing men's wickedness with this plague would not follow them but strike only those who remained within the walls of the city, or as if they thought nobody in the city would remain alive and that its last hour had come.

Not everyone who adopted any of these various opinions died, nor did all escape. Some when they were still healthy had set the example of avoiding the sick, and, falling ill themselves, died untended.

One citizen avoided another, hardly any neighbor troubled about others, relatives never or hardly ever visited each other. Moreover, such terror was struck into the hearts of men and women by this calamity, that brother abandoned brother, and the uncle his nephew, and the sister her brother, and very often the wife her husband. What is even worse and nearly incredible is that fathers and mothers refused to see and tend their children, as if they had not been theirs.

Thus, a multitude of sick men and women were left without any care except from the charity of friends (but these were few), or the greed of servants, though not many of these could be had even for high wages. Moreover, most of them were coarse-minded men and women, who did little more than bring the sick what they asked for or watch over them when they were dying. And very often these servants lost their lives and their earnings. Since the sick were thus abandoned by neighbors, relatives and friends, while servants were scarce, a habit sprang up which had never been heard of before. Beautiful and noble women, when they fell sick, did not scruple to take a young or old manservant, whoever he might be, and with no sort of shame, expose every part of their bodies to these men as if they had been women, for they were compelled by the necessity of their sickness to do so. This, perhaps, was a cause of looser morals in those women who survived.

In this way many people died who might have been saved if they had been looked after. Owing to the lack of attendants for the sick and the violence of the plague, such a multitude of people in the city died

day and night that it was stupefying to hear of, let alone to see. From
sheer necessity, then, several ancient customs were quite altered among
the survivors.

The custom had been (as we still see it today) that women relatives
and neighbors should gather at the house of the deceased, and there
lament with the family. At the same time the men would gather at the
door with the male neighbors and other citizens. Then came the clergy,
few or many according to the dead person's rank; the coffin was placed
on the shoulders of his friends and carried with funeral pomp of lighted
candles and dirges to the church which the deceased had chosen before
dying. But as the fury of the plague increased, this custom wholly or
nearly disappeared, and new customs arose. Thus, people died, not only
without having a number of women near them, but without a single witness. Very few indeed were honored with the piteous laments and bitter
tears of their relatives, who, on the contrary, spent their time in mirth,
feasting and jesting. Even the women abandoned womanly pity and adopted
this custom for their own safety. Few were they whose bodies were accompanied to church by more than ten or a dozen neighbors. Nor were these
grave and honorable citizens but grave-diggers from the lowest of the
people who got themselves called sextons, and performed the task for
money. They took up the bier and hurried it off, not to the church chosen
by the deceased but to the church nearest, preceded by four or six of
the clergy with few candles and often none at all. With the aid of the grave-
diggers, the clergy huddled the bodies away in any grave they could find,
without giving themselves the trouble of a long or solemn burial service.

The plight of the lower and most of the middle classes was even more
pitiful to behold. Most of them remained in their houses, either through
poverty or in hopes of safety, and fell sick by thousands. Since they received
no care and attention, almost all of them died. Many ended their lives
in the streets both at night and during the day; and many others who died
in their houses were only known to be dead because the neighbors smelled
their decaying bodies. Dead bodies filled every corner. Most of them were
treated in the same manner by the survivors, who were more concerned
to get rid of their rotting bodies than moved by charity towards the dead.
With the aid of porters, if they could get them, they carried the bodies
out of the houses and laid them at the doors, where every morning quantities of the dead might be seen. They then were laid on biers or, as these
were often lacking, on tables.

Often a single bier carried two or three bodies, and it happened frequently that a husband and wife, two or three brothers, or father and son
were taken off on the same bier. It frequently happened that two priests,
each carrying a cross, would go out followed by three or four biers carried by porters; and where the priests thought there was one person to
bury, there would be six or eight, and often, even more. Nor were these

dead honored by tears and lighted candles and mourners, for things had reached such a pass that people cared no more for dead men than we care for dead goats. Thus it plainly appeared that what the wise had not learned to endure with patience through the few calamities of ordinary life, became a matter of indifference even to the most ignorant people through the greatness of this misfortune.

Such was the multitude of corpses brought to the churches every day and almost every hour that there was not enough consecrated ground to give them burial, especially since they wanted to bury each person in the family grave, according to the old custom. Although the cemeteries were full they were forced to dig huge trenches, where they buried the bodies by hundreds. Here they stowed them away like bales in the hold of a ship and covered them with a little earth, until the whole trench was full.

Not to pry any further into all the details of the miseries which afflicted our city, I shall add that the surrounding country was spared nothing of what befell Florence. The villages on a smaller scale were like the city; in the fields and isolated farms the poor wretched peasants and their families were without doctors and any assistance, and perished in the highways, in their fields and houses, night and day, more like beasts than men. Just as the townsmen became dissolute and indifferent to their work and property, so the peasants, when they saw that death was upon them, entirely neglected the future fruits of their past labors both from the earth and from cattle, and thought only of enjoying what they had. Thus it happened that cows, asses, sheep, goats, pigs, fowls and even dogs, those faithful companions of man, left the farms and wandered at their will through the fields, where the wheat crops stood abandoned, unreaped and ungarnered. Many of these animals seemed endowed with reason, for, after they had pastured all day, they returned to the farms for the night of their own free will, without being driven.

Returning from the country to the city, it may be said that such was the cruelty of Heaven, and perhaps in part of men, that between March and July more than one hundred thousand persons died within the walls of Florence, what between the violence of the plague and the abandonment in which the sick were left by the cowardice of the healthy. And before the plague it was not thought that the whole city held so many people.

Oh, what great palaces, how many fair houses and noble dwellings, once filled with attendants and nobles and ladies, were emptied to the meanest servant! How many famous names and vast possessions and renowned estates were left without an heir! How many gallant men and fair ladies and hand-some youths, whom Galen, Hippocrates and Aesculapius themselves would have said were in perfect health, at noon dined with their relatives and friends, and at night supped with their ancestors in the next world!

IN PLAGUE TIME | *THOMAS NASHE*

Adieu, farewell earth's bliss,
This world uncertain is;
Fond are life's lustful joys,
Death proves them all but toys,
None from his darts can fly.
I am sick, I must die.
     Lord, have mercy on us!

Rich men, trust not in wealth,
Gold cannot buy you health;
Physic himself must fade,
All things to end are made,
The plague full swift goes by
I am sick, I must die.
     Lord, have mercy on us!

Beauty is but a flower
Which wrinkles will devour:
Brightness falls from the air,
Queens have died young and fair,
Dust hath closed Helen's eye.
I am sick, I must die.
     Lord, have mercy on us!

Strength stoops unto the grave,
Worms feed on Hector brave,
Swords may not fight with fate.
Earth still holds ope her gate;
Come! come! the bells do cry.
I am sick, I must die.
     Lord, have mercy on us!

Wit with his wantonness
Tasteth death's bitterness;
Hell's executioner
Hath no ears for to hear
What vain art can reply.
I am sick, I must die.
     Lord, have mercy on us!

Haste, therefore, each degree,
To welcome destiny.

> Heaven is our heritage,
> Earth but a player's stage;
> Mount we unto the sky.
> I am sick, I must die.
> Lord, have mercy on us!

DIARY IN A PLAGUE YEAR | SAMUEL PEPYS

[1665, MAY] 24TH To the Coffee-house, where all the news is of the Dutch being gone out, and of the plague growing upon us in this town; and of remedies against it: some saying one thing, and some another. . . .

[JUNE] 7TH . . . The hottest day that ever I felt in my life. This day, much against my will, I did in Drury Lane see two or three houses marked with a red cross upon the doors, and "Lord have mercy upon us!" writ there; which was a sad sight to me, being the first of that kind that, to my remembrance, I ever saw. It put me into an ill conception of myself and my smell, so that I was forced to buy some roll-tobacco to smell to and chaw, which took away the apprehension. . . .

10TH In the evening home to supper; and there, to my great trouble, hear that the plague is come into the City, though it hath, these three or four weeks since its beginning, been wholly out of the City; but where should it begin but in my good friend and neighbor's, Dr. Burnett, in Fenchurch Street: which, in both points, troubles me mightily. . . .

[JULY] 13TH By water, at night late, to Sir G. Carteret's but, there being no oars to carry me, I was fain to call a skuller that had a gentleman already in it, and he proved a man of love to music, and he and I sung together the way down with great pleasure. Above 700 died of the plague this week. . . .

26TH . . . The Duke of Monmouth is the most skittish leaping gallant that ever I saw, always in action, vaulting, or leaping, or clambering. Sad news of the death of so many in the parish of the plague, forty last night. The bell always going. To the Exchange, where I went up and sat talking with my beauty, Mrs. Batelier, a great while, who is indeed one of the finest women I ever saw in my life. . . .

[AUGUST] 15TH It was dark before I could get home, and so land at Church-yard stairs, where, to my great trouble, I met a dead corpse of the plague, in the narrow alley, just bringing down a little pair of stairs. But I thank God I was not much disturbed at it. However, I shall beware of being late abroad again.

16TH To the Exchange, where I have not been a great while. But, Lord!

From the *Diary* which was first transcribed into English from Pepys' private shorthand by Reverend J. Smith in 1825.

how sad a sight it is to see the streets empty of people, and very few upon the 'Change! Jealous of every door that one sees shut up, lest it should be the plague; and about us two shops in three, if not more, generally shut up. This day, I had the ill news from Dagenhams, that my poor Lord of Hinchingbroke his indisposition is turned to the smallpox. Poor gentleman! that he should be come from France so soon to fall sick, and of that disease too, when he should be gone to see a fine lady, his mistress! I am most heartily sorry for it. . . .

22ND Up, and being importuned by my wife and her two maids, which are both good wenches, for me to buy a necklace of pearl for her, and I promising to give her one of £60 in two years at furthest, and less if she pleases me in her painting. I went away, and walked to Greenwich, in my way seeing a coffin with a dead body therein, dead of the plague, lying in an open close belonging to Coome farme, which was carried out last night, and the parish have not appointed any body to bury it; but only set a watch there all day and night, that nobody should go thither or come thence: this disease making us more cruel to one another than we are to dogs. Walked to Redriffe, troubled to go through the little lane where the plague is, but did, and took water and home, where all well. . . .

31ST Up: and, after putting several things in order to my removal to Woolrich; the plague having a great increase this week, beyond all expectation, of almost 2,000 making the general Bill 7,000 odd 100; and the plague above 6,000. Thus this month ends with great sadness upon the public, through the greatness of the plague everywhere through the kingdom almost. Every day sadder and sadder news of its increase. In the City died this week 7,496, and of them 6,102 of the plague. But it is feared that the true number of the dead this week is near 10,000; partly from the poor that cannot be taken notice of, through the greatness of the number, and partly from the Quakers and others that will not have any bell ring for them. Our fleet gone out to find the Dutch, we having about 100 sail in our fleet, and in them the Sovereign one; so that it is a better fleet than the former with which the Duke was. All our fear is, that the Dutch should be got in before them; which would be a very great sorrow to the public, and to me particularly, for my Lord Sandwich's sake: a great deal of money being spent, and the kingdom not in a condition to spare, nor a parliament, without much difficulty to meet, to give more. And to that; to have it said, what hath been done by our late fleets? As to myself, I am very well, only in fear of the plague, and as much of an ague, by being forced to go early and late to Woolrich, and my family to lie there continually. My late gettings have been very great, to my great content, and am likely to have yet a few more profitable jobs in a little while; for which Tangier and Sir W. Warren I am wholly obliged to. . . .

[OCTOBER] 7TH Did business, though not much, at the office, because of the horrible crowd and lamentable moan of the poor seamen, that lie starving in the streets for lack of money, which do trouble and perplex me to the heart; and more at noon, when we were to go through them, for then above a whole hundred of them followed us; some cursing, some swearing, and some praying to us. A letter come this afternoon from the Duke of Albemarle, signifying the Dutch to be in sight, with 80 sail, yesterday morning, off Solebay, coming right into the bay. God knows what they will and may do to us, we having no force abroad able to oppose them, but to be sacrificed to them. At night come two wagons from Rochester, with more goods from Captain Cocke; and in housing them come two of the Custom-house, and did seize them: but I showed them my *Transire*. However, after some angry words, we locked them up, and sealed up the key, and did give it to the constable to keep till Monday and so parted. But, Lord! to think how the poor constable come to me in the dark, going home; "Sir," says he, "I have the key, and, if you would have me do any service for you, send for me betimes tomorrow morning, and I will do what you would have me." Whether the fellow do this out of kindness or knavery, I cannot tell; but it is pretty to observe. Talking with him in the high way, come close by the bearers with a dead corpse of the plague; but, Lord! to see what custom is, that I am come almost to think nothing of it.

JOURNAL OF THE PLAGUE YEAR | *DANIEL DEFOE*

... The locking up the doors of people's houses, and setting a watchman there night and day to prevent their stirring out or any coming to them, when perhaps the sound people in the family might have escaped if they had been removed from the sick, looked very hard and cruel; and many people perished in these miserable confinements which, 'tis reasonable to believe, would not have been distempered if they had had liberty, though the plague was in the house; at which the people were very clamorous and uneasy at first, and several violences were committed and injuries offered to the men who were set to watch the houses so shut up; also several people broke out by force in many places, as I shall observe by-and-by. But it was a public good that justified the private mischief, and there was no obtaining the least mitigation by any application to magistrates or government at that time, at least not that I heard of. This put the people upon all manner of stratagem in order, if possible, to get out; and it would fill a little volume to set down the arts used by the people of such houses to shut the eyes of the watchmen who were employed, to deceive them, and to escape or break out from them, in which frequent scuffles and some mischief happened. . . .

As these were prisons without bars and bolts, which our common prisons

From *A Journal of the Plague Year* (1722).

are furnished with, so the people let themselves down out of their windows, even in the face of the watchman, bringing swords or pistols in their hands, and threatening the poor wretch to shoot him if he stirred or called for help.

In other cases, some had gardens, and walls or pales, between them and their neighbors, or yards and back-houses; and these, by friendship and entreaties, would get leave to get over those walls or pales, and so go out at their neighbors doors; or, by giving money to their servants, get them to let them through in the night; so that, in short, the shutting up of houses was in no wise to be depended upon. Neither did it answer the end at all, serving more to make the people desperate, and drive them to such extremities as that they would break out at all adventures.

And that which was still worse, those that did thus break out spread the infection farther by their wandering about with the distemper upon them, in their desperate circumstances, than they would otherwise have done; for whoever considers all the particulars in such cases must acknowledge, and we cannot doubt but the severity of those confinements made many people desperate, and made them run out of their houses at all hazards, and with the plague visibly upon them, not knowing either whither to go or what to do, or, indeed, what they did; and many that did so were driven to dreadful exigencies and extremities, and perished in the streets or fields for mere want, or dropped down by the raging violence of the fever upon them. Others wandered into the country, and went forward any way, as their desperation guided them, not knowing whither they went or would go, till faint and tired, and not getting any relief, the houses and villages on the road refusing to admit them to lodge, whether infected or no, they have perished by the roadside, or gotten into barns and died there, none daring to come to them or relieve them, though perhaps not infected, for nobody would believe them.

On the other hand, when the plague at first seized a family, that is to say, when any one body of the family had gone out and unwarily or otherwise catched the distemper and brought it home, it was certainly known by the family before it was known to the officers, who, as you will see by the order, were appointed to examine into the circumstances of all sick persons when they heard of their being sick.

In this interval, between their being taken sick and the examiners coming, the master of the house had leisure and liberty to remove himself or all his family, if he knew whither to go, and many did so. But the great disaster was, that many did thus after they were really infected themselves, and so carried the disease into the houses of those who were so hospitable as to receive them, which, it must be confessed, was very cruel and ungrateful.

And this was, in part, the reason of the general notion, or scandal rather, which went about of the temper of people infected, namely, that they did not take the least care or make any scruple of infecting others, though I cannot say but there might be some truth in it too, but not so general as was reported. What natural reason could be given for so wicked a thing at a time when they might conclude themselves just going to appear at the bar of Divine Justice I know not. I am very well satisfied that it cannot be reconciled to religion and principle any more than it can be to generosity and humanity, but I may speak of that again.

I am speaking now of people made desperate by the apprehensions of their being shut up, and their breaking out by stratagem or force, either before or after they were shut up, whose misery was not lessened when they were out, but sadly increased. On the other hand, many that thus got away had retreats to go to and other houses, where they locked themselves up and kept hid till the plague was over; and many families, foreseeing the approach of the distemper, laid up stores of provisions sufficient for their whole families, and shut themselves up, and that so entirely that they were neither seen or heard of till the infection was quite ceased, and then came abroad sound and well. I might recollect several such as these, and give you the particulars of their management; for, doubtless, it was the most effectual secure step that could be taken for such whose circumstances would not admit them to remove, or who had not retreats abroad proper for the case; for, in being thus shut up, they were as if they had been a hundred miles off. Nor do I remember that any one of those families miscarried. Among these several Dutch merchants were particularly remarkable, who kept their houses like little garrisons besieged, suffering none to go in or out or come near them, particularly one in a court in Throgmorton Street, whose house looked into Draper's Garden.

But I come back to the case of families infected, and shut up by the magistrates. The misery of those families is not to be expressed; and it was generally in such houses that we heard the most dismal shrieks and outcries of the poor people, terrified and even frighted to death by the sight of the condition of their dearest relations, and by the terror of being imprisoned as they were.

I remember, and while I am writing this story I think I hear the very sound of it, a certain lady had an only daughter, a young maiden about nineteen years old, and who was possessed of a very considerable fortune. They were only lodgers in the house where they were. The young woman, her mother, and the maid had been abroad on some occasion, I do not remember what, for the house was not shut up; but about two hours after they came home the young lady complained she was not well; in a quarter of an hour more she vomited and had a violent pain in her head. "Pray God," says her mother, in a terrible fright, "my child has not the distemper!" The pain in her head increasing, her mother ordered the bed to be warmed, and resolved to put her to bed, and prepared to give her things to sweat, which was the ordinary remedy to be taken when the first apprehensions of the distemper began.

While the bed was airing the mother undressed the young woman, and just as she was laid down in the bed, she, looking upon her body with a candle, immediately discovered the fatal tokens on the inside of her thighs. Her mother, not being able to contain herself, threw down her candle and screeched out in such a frightful manner that it was enough to place horror upon the stoutest heart in the world; nor was it one scream or one cry, but the fright having seized her spirits, she fainted first, then recovered, then ran all over the house, up the stairs and down the stairs, like one distracted, and indeed really was distracted, and continued screeching and crying out for several hours void of all sense, or, at least, government of her senses, and, as I was told, never came thoroughly to herself again. As to the young maiden, she was a dead corpse from that moment, for the gangrene which occasions the spots had spread [over] her whole body, and she died in less than two hours. But still the mother continued crying out, not knowing anything more of her child, several hours after she was dead. It is so long ago that I am not certain, but I think the mother never recovered, but died in two or three weeks after.

This was an extraordinary case, and I am therefore the more particular in it, because I came so much to the knowledge of it; but there were innumerable such-like cases, and it was seldom that the weekly bill came in but there were two or three put in frighted; that is, that may well be called frighted to death. But besides those who were so frighted as to die upon the spot, there were great numbers frighted to other extremes, some out of their memory, and some out of their understanding. But I return to the shutting up of houses.

As several people, I say, got out of their houses by stratagem after they were shut up, so others got out by bribing the watchmen, and giving them money to let them go privately out in the night. I must confess I thought it at that time the most innocent corruption or bribery that any man could be guilty of, and therefore could not but pity the poor men, and think it was hard when three of those watchmen were publicly whipped through the streets for suffering people to go out of houses shut up. . . .

I went all the first part of the time freely about the streets, though not so freely as to run myself into apparent danger, except when they dug the great pit in the churchyard of our parish of Aldgate. A terrible pit it was, and I could not resist my curiosity to go and see it. As near as I may judge, it was about forty feet in length, and about fifteen or sixteen feet broad, and, at the time I first looked at it, about nine feet deep; but it was said they dug it near twenty feet deep afterwards in one part of it, till they could go no deeper for the water; for they had, it seems, dug several large pits before this. For though the plague was long a-coming to our parish, yet, when it did come, there was no parish in or about London where it raged with such violence as in the two parishes of Aldgate and Whitechapel.

I say they had dug several pits in another ground, when the distemper began to spread in our parish, and especially when the dead-carts began to go about, which was not, in our parish, till the beginning of August. Into these pits they had put perhaps fifty or sixty bodies each; then they made larger holes, wherein they buried all that the cart brought in a week, which, by the middle to the end of August, came to from 200 to 400 a week; and they could not well dig them larger, because of the order of the magistrates confining them to leave no bodies within six feet of the surface; and the water coming on at about seventeen or eighteen feet, they could not well, I say, put more in one pit. But now, at the beginning of September, the plague raging in a dreadful manner, and the number of burials in our parish increasing to more than was ever buried in any parish about London of no larger extent, they ordered this dreadful gulf to be dug, for such it was rather than a pit.

They had supposed this pit would have supplied them for a month or more when they dug it, and some blamed the churchwardens for suffering such a frightful thing, telling them they were making preparations to bury the whole parish, and the like; but time made it appear the churchwardens knew the condition of the parish better than they did, for the pit being finished the 4th of September, I think, they began to bury in it the 6th, and by the 20th, which was just two weeks, they had thrown into it 1114 bodies, when they were obliged to fill it up, the bodies being then come to lie within six feet of the surface. I doubt not but there may be some ancient persons alive in the parish who can justify the fact of this, and are able to show even in what place of the churchyard the pit lay better than I can. The mark of it also was many years to be seen in the churchyard on the surface, lying in length parallel with the passage which goes by the west wall of the churchyard out of Houndsditch, and turns east again into Whitechapel, coming out near the Three Nuns' Inn.

It was about the 10th of September that my curiosity led, or rather drove, me to go and see this pit again, when there had been near 400 people buried in it; and I was not content to see it in the day-time, as I had done before, for then there would have been nothing to have been seen but the loose earth; for all the bodies that were thrown in were immediately covered with earth by those they called the buriers, which at other times were called bearers; but I resolved to go in the night and see some of them thrown in.

There was a strict order to prevent people coming to those pits, and that was only to prevent infection. But after some time that order was more necessary, for people that were infected and near their end, and delirious also, would run to those pits, wrapt in blankets or rugs, and throw themselves in, and, as they said, bury themselves. I cannot say that the officers suffered any willingly to lie there; but I have heard that in a great pit in Finsbury, in the parish of Cripplegate, it lying open then to the fields, for it was not then walled about, [some] came and threw themselves in, and expired there, before they came to bury others, and found them there, before they threw any earth upon them; and that when they came to bury others, and found them there, they were quite dead, though not cold.

This may serve a little to describe the dreadful condition of that day, though it is impossible to say anything that is able to give a true idea of it to those who did not see it, other than this, that it was indeed very, very, very dreadful, and such as no tongue can express.

THE PLAGUE OF ORAN | *ALBERT CAMUS*

There was darkness also in men's hearts, and the true facts were as little calculated to reassure our townsfolk as the wild stories going round about the burials. The narrator cannot help talking about these burials, and a word of excuse is here in place. For he is well aware of the reproach that might be made him in this respect; his justification is that funerals were taking place throughout this period and, in a way, he was compelled, as indeed everybody was compelled, to give heed to them. In any case it should not be assumed that he has a morbid taste for such ceremonies; quite the contrary, he much prefers the society of the living and to give a concrete illustration—sea-bathing. But the bathing-beaches were out of bounds and the company of the living ran a risk, increasing as the days went by, of being perforce converted into the company of the dead. That was, indeed, self-evident. True, one could always refuse to face this disagreeable fact, shut one's eyes to it, or thrust it out of mind, but there is a terrible cogency in the self-evident; ultimately it breaks down all defenses. How, for instance, continue to ignore the funerals on the day when somebody you loved needed one?

Actually the most striking feature of our funerals was their speed. Formalities had been whittled down, and, generally speaking, all elaborate ceremonial suppressed. The plague victim died away from his family and the customary vigil beside the dead body was forbidden, with the result that a person dying in the evening spent the night alone, and those who died in the daytime were promptly buried. Needless to say, the family was notified, but in most cases, since the deceased had lived with them, its members were in quarantine and thus immobilized. When, however, the deceased had not lived with his family, they were asked to attend at a fixed time; after, that is to say, the body had been washed and put in the coffin and when the journey to the cemetery was about to begin.

Let us suppose that these formalities were taking place at the auxiliary hospital of which Dr. Rieux was in charge. This converted school had an exit at the back of the main building. A large storeroom giving on the corridor contained the coffins. On arrival, the family found a coffin already nailed up in the corridor. Then came the most important part of the business: the signing of official forms by the head of the family. Next the coffin was loaded on a motor-vehicle—a real hearse or a large converted ambulance. The mourners stepped into one of the few taxis still allowed to ply and the vehicles drove hell-for-leather to the cemetery by a route avoiding the center of the town. There was a halt at the gate, where police officers applied a rubber stamp to the official exit permit, without which it was impossible for our citizens to have what they called a last resting-place. The policeman stood back and the cars drew up near a plot of ground where a number of graves stood open, waiting for inmates. A priest came to meet the mourners, since church services at funerals were now prohibited. To an accompaniment of prayers the coffin was dragged from the hearse, roped up, and carried to the graveside; the ropes were slipped and it came heavily to rest at the bottom of the grave. No sooner had the priest begun to sprinkle holy water than the first sod rebounded from the lid. The ambulance had already left and was being sprayed with disinfectant, and while spadefuls of clay thudded more and more dully on the rising layer of earth, the family were bundling into the taxi. A quarter of an hour later they were back at home.

The whole process was put through with the maximum of speed and the minimum of risk. It cannot be denied that, anyhow in the early days, the natural feelings of the family were somewhat outraged by these lightning funerals. But obviously in time of plague such sentiments can't be taken into account, and all was sacrificed to efficiency. And though, to start with, the morale of the population was shaken by this summary procedure—for the desire to have a "proper funeral" is more widespread than is generally believed—as time went on, fortunately enough, the food problem became more urgent and the thoughts of our townsfolk were diverted to more instant needs. So much energy was expended on filling up forms, hunting round for supplies, and lining up that people had no time to think of the manner in which others were dying around them and they themselves would die one day. Thus the growing complications of our everyday life, which might have been an affliction, proved to be a blessing in disguise. Indeed, had not the epidemic, as already mentioned, spread its ravages, all would have been for the best.

For then coffins became scarcer; also there was a shortage of winding-sheets, and of space in the cemetery. Something had to be done about this, and one obvious step, justified by its practical convenience, was to combine funerals and, when necessary, multiply the trips between the hospital and the burial-place. At one moment the stock of coffins in Rieux's hospital was reduced to five. Once filled, all five were loaded together in the ambulance. At the cemetery they were emptied out and the iron-gray corpses put on stretchers and deposited in a shed reserved for that purpose, to wait their turn. Meanwhile the empty coffins, after being sprayed with antiseptic fluid, were rushed back to the hospital, and the process was repeated as often as necessary. This system worked excellently and won the approval of the Prefect. He even told Rieux that it was really a great improvement on the death-carts driven by Negroes of which one reads in accounts of former visitations of this sort.

"Yes," Rieux said, "And though the burials are much the same, we keep careful records of them. That, you will agree, is progress."

Successful, however, as the system proved itself in practice, there was something so distasteful in the last rites as now performed that the Prefect felt constrained to forbid relations of the deceased being present at the actual interment. They were allowed to come only as far as the cemetery gates, and even that was not authorized officially. For things had somewhat changed as regards the last stage of the ceremony. In a patch of open ground dotted with lentiscus trees at the far end of the cemetery, two big pits had been dug. One was reserved for the men, the other for the women. Thus, in this respect, the authorities still gave thought to propriety and it was only later that, by the force of things, this last remnant of decorum went by the board, and men and women were flung into the death-pits indiscriminately. Happily, this ultimate indignity synchronized with the plague's last ravages.

In the period we are now concerned with, the separation of the sexes was still in force and the authorities set great store by it. At the bottom of each pit a deep layer of quicklime steamed and seethed. On the lips of the pit a low ridge of quicklime threw up bubbles that burst in the air above it. When the ambulance had finished its trips, the stretchers were carried to the pits in Indian file. The naked, somewhat contorted bodies were slid off into the pit almost side by side, then covered with a layer of quicklime and another of earth, the latter only a few inches deep, so as to leave space for subsequent consignments. On the following day the next of kin were asked to sign the register of burials, which showed the distinction that can be made between men and, for example, dogs; men's deaths are checked and entered up.

Obviously all these activities called for a considerable staff, and Rieux was often on the brink of a shortage. Many of the gravediggers, stretcher-bearers, and the like, public servants to begin with, and later volunteers, died of plague. However stringent the precautions, sooner or later contagion did its work. Still, when all is said and done, the really amazing thing is that, so long as the epidemic lasted, there was never any lack of men for these duties. The critical moment came just before the outbreak touched high-water mark, and the doctor had good reason for feeling anxious. There was then a real shortage of man power both for the higher posts and for the rough work, as Rieux called it. But, paradoxically enough, once the whole town was in the grip of the disease, its very prevalence tended to make things easier, since the disorganization of the town's economic life threw a great number of persons out of work. Few of the workers thus made available were qualified for administrative posts, but the recruiting of men for the "rough work" became much easier. From now on, indeeed, poverty showed itself a stronger stimulus than fear, especially as, owing to its risks, such work was highly paid. The sanitary authorities always had a waiting-list of applicants for work; whenever there was a vacancy the men at the top of the list were notified, and unless they too had laid off work for good, they never failed to appear when summoned. Thus the Prefect, who had always been reluctant to employ the prisoners in the jail, whether short-term men or lifers, was able to avoid recourse to this distasteful measure. As long, he said, as there were unemployed, we could afford to wait.

Thus until the end of August our fellow citizens could be conveyed to their last resting-place, if not under very decorous conditions, at least in a manner orderly enough for the authorities to feel that they were doing their duty by the dead and the bereaved. However, we may here anticipate a little and describe the pass to which we came in the final phase. From August onwards the plague mortality was and continued such as far to exceed the capacity of our small cemetery. Such expedients as knocking down walls and letting the dead encroach on neighboring land proved inadequate; some new method had to be evolved without delay. The first step taken was to bury the dead by night, which obviously permitted a more summary procedure. The bodies were piled into ambulances in larger and larger numbers. And the few belated wayfarers who, in defiance of the regulations, were abroad in the outlying districts after curfew hour, or whose duties took them there, often saw the long white ambulances hurtling past, making the nightbound streets reverberate with the dull clangor of their bells. The corpses were tipped pell-mell into the pits and had hardly settled into place when spadefuls of quicklime began to sear their faces and the earth covered them indistinctively, in holes dug steadily deeper as time went on.

Shortly afterwards, however, it became necessary to find new space and to strike out in a new direction. By a special urgency measure the denizens of grants in perpetuity were evicted from the graves and the exhumed remains dispatched to the crematorium. And soon the plague victims likewise had to go to a fiery end. This meant that the old crematorium east of the town, outside the gates, had to be utilized. Accordingly the east-gate sentry post was moved farther out. Then a municipal employee had an idea that greatly helped the harassed authorities; he advised them to employ the streetcar line running along the coastal road, which was now unused. So the interiors of streetcars and trailers were adapted to this new purpose, and a branch line was laid down to the crematorium, which thus became a terminus.

During all the late summer and throughout the autumn there could

daily be seen moving along the road skirting the cliffs above the sea
a strange procession of passengerless streeetcars swaying against the sky-
line. The residents in this area soon learned what was going on. And
though the cliffs were patrolled day and night, little groups of people
contrived to thread their way unseen between the rocks and would toss
flowers into the open trailers as the cars went by. And in the warm darkness of the summer nights the cars could be heard clanking on their way,
laden with flowers and corpses.

During the first few days an oily, foul-smelling cloud of smoke hung
low upon the eastern districts of the town. These effluvia, all the doctors
agreed, though unpleasant, were not in the least harmful. However, the
residents of this part of the town threatened to migrate in a body, convinced that germs were raining down on them from the sky, with the
result that an elaborate apparatus for diverting the smoke had to be installed to appease them. Thereafter only when a strong wind was blowing
did a faint, sickly odor coming from the east remind them that they
were living under a new order and that the plague fires were taking their
nightly toll.

Such were the consequences of the epidemic at its culminating point.
Happily it grew no worse, for otherwise, it may well be believed, the re-
sourcefulness of our administration, the competence of our officials, not to
mention the burning-capacity of our crematorium, would have proved
unequal to their tasks. Rieux knew that desperate solutions had been
mooted, such as throwing the corpses into the sea, and a picture had risen
before him of hideous jetsam lolling in the shallows under the cliffs. He
knew, too, that if there was another rise in the death-rate, no organization,
however efficient, could stand up to it; that men would die in heaps, and
corpses rot in the street, whatever the authorities might do, and the town
would see in public squares the dying embrace the living in the frenzies
of an all too comprehensible hatred or some crazy hope.

Such were the sights and apprehensions that kept alive in our towns-
people their feeling of exile and separation. In this connection the
narrator is well aware how regrettable is his inability to record at this
point something of a really spectacular order—some heroic feat or memorable deed like those that thrill us in the chronicles of the past. The truth
is that nothing is less sensational than pestilence, and by reason of their
very duration great misfortunes are monotonous. In the memories of those
who lived through them, the grim days of plague do not stand out like
vivid flames, ravenous and inextinguishable, beaconing a troubled sky, but
rather like the slow, deliberate progress of some monstrous thing crushing
out all upon its path.

No, the real plague had nothing in common with the grandiose
imaginings that had haunted Rieux's mind at its outbreak. It was, above

all, a shrewd, unflagging adversary; skilled organizer, doing his work thoroughly and well. That, it may be said in passing, is why, so as not to play false to the facts, and, still more, so as not to play false to himself, the narrator has aimed at objectivity. He has made hardly any changes for the sake of artistic effect, except those elementary adjustments needed to present his narrative in a more or less coherent form. And in deference to this scruple he is constrained to admit that, though the chief source of distress, the deepest as well as the most widespread, was separation—and it is his duty to say more about it as it existed in the later stages of the plague—it cannot be denied that even this distress was coming to lose something of its poignancy.

Was it that our fellow citizens, even those who had felt the parting from their loved ones most keenly, were getting used to doing without them? To assume this would fall somewhat short of the truth. It would be more correct to say that they were wasting away emotionally as well as physically. At the beginning of the plague they had a vivid recollection of the absent ones and bitterly felt their loss. But though they could clearly recall the face, the smile and voice of the beloved, and this or that occasion when (as they now saw in retrospect) they had been supremely happy, they had trouble in picturing what he or she might be doing at the moment when they conjured up these memories, in a setting so hopelessly remote. In short, at these moments memory played its part, but their imagination failed them. During the second phase of the plague their memory failed them, too. Not that they had forgotten the face itself, but— what came to the same thing—it had lost fleshly substance and they no longer saw it in memory's mirror.

Thus, while during the first weeks they were apt to complain that only shadows remained to them of what their love had been and meant, they now came to learn that even shadows can waste away, losing the faint hues of life that memory may give. And by the end of their long sundering they had also lost the power of imagining the intimacy that once was theirs or understanding what it can be to live with someone whose life is wrapped up in yours.

In this respect they had adapted themselves to the very condition of the plague, all the more potent for its mediocrity. None of us was capable any longer of an exalted emotion; all had trite, monotonous feelings. "It's high time it stopped," people would say, because in time of calamity the obvious thing is to desire its end, and in fact they wanted it to end. But when making such remarks, we felt none of the passionate yearning or fierce resentment of the early phase; we merely voiced one of the few clear ideas that lingered in the twilight of our minds. The furious revolt of the first weeks had given place to a vast despondency, not to be taken for resignation, though it was none the less a sort of passive and provisional acquiescence.

Our fellow citizens had fallen into line, adapted themselves, as people say, to the situation, because there was no way of doing otherwise. Naturally they retained the attitudes of sadness and suffering, but they had ceased to feel their string. Indeed, to some, Dr. Rieux among them, this precisely was the most disheartening thing: that the habit of despair is worse than despair itself. Hitherto those who were parted had not been utterly unhappy; there was always a gleam of hope in the night of their distress; but that gleam had now died out. You could see them at street corners, in cafés or friends' houses, listless, indifferent, and looking so bored that, because of them, the whole town seemed like a railway waiting-room. Those who had jobs went about them at the exact tempo of the plague, with dreary perserverance. Everyone was modest. For the first time exiles from those they loved had no reluctance to talk freely about them, using the same words as everybody else, and regarding their deprivation from the same angle as that from which they viewed the latest statistics of the epidemic. This change was striking since until now they had jealously withheld their personal grief from the common stock of suffering; now they accepted its inclusion. Without memories, without hope, they lived for the moment only. Indeed, the here and now had come to mean everything to them. For there is no denying that the plague had gradually killed off in all of us the faculty not of love only but even of friendship. Naturally enough, since love asks something of the future, and nothing was left us but a series of present moments.

However, this account of our predicament gives only the broad lines. Thus, while it is true that all who were parted came ultimately to this state, we must add that all did not attain it simultaneously; moreover, once this utter apathy had fallen on them, there were still flashes of lucidity, broken lights of memory that rekindled in the exiles a younger, keener sensibility. This happened when, for instance, they fell to making plans implying that the plague had ended. Or when, quite unexpectedly, by some kindly chance, they felt a twinge of jealousy, none the less acute for its objectlessness. Others, again, had sudden accesses of energy and shook off their languor on certain days of the week—for obvious reasons, on Sundays and Saturday afternoons, because these had been devoted to certain ritual pleasures in the days when the loved ones were still accessible. Sometimes the mood of melancholy that descended on them with the nightfall acted as a sort of warning, not always fulfilled, however, that old memories were floating up to the surface. That evening hour which for believers is the time to look into their consciences is hardest of all hours on the prisoner or exile who has nothing to look into but the void. For a moment it held them in suspense; then they sank back into their lethargy, the prison door had closed on them once again.

Obviously all this meant giving up what was most personal in their lives. Whereas in the early days of the plague they had been struck by the host of small details that, while meaning absolutely nothing to others, meant so much to them personally, and thus had realized, perhaps for the first time, the uniqueness of each man's life; now, on the other hand, they took an interest only in what interested everyone else, they had only general ideas, and even their tenderest affections now seemed abstract, items of the common stock. So completely were they dominated by the plague that sometimes the one thing they aspired to was the long sleep it brought, and they caught themselves thinking: "A good thing if I get plague and have done with it!" But really they were asleep already; this whole period was for them no more than a long night's slumber. The town was peopled with sleepwalkers, whose trance was broken only on the rare occasions when at night their wounds, to all appearance closed, suddenly reopened. Then, waking with a start, they would run their fingers over the wounds with a sort of absent-minded curiosity, twisting their lips, and in a flash their grief blazed up again, and abruptly there rose before them the mournful visage of their love. In the morning they harked back to normal conditions—in other words, the plague.

What impression, it may be asked, did these exiles of the plague make on the observer? The answer is simple; they made none. Or, to put it differently, they looked like everybody else, nondescript. They shared in the torpor of the town and in its puerile agitations. They lost every trace of a critical spirit, while gaining an air of *sang-froid*. You could see, for instance, even the most intelligent among them making a show like all the rest of studying the newspapers or listening to the radio, in the hope apparently of finding some reason to believe the plague would shortly end. They seemed to derive fantastic hopes or equally exaggerated fears from reading the lines that some journalist had scribbled at random, yawning with boredom at his desk. Meanwhile they drank their beer, nursed their sick, idled, or doped themselves with work, filed documents in offices, or played the phonograph at home, without betraying any difference from the rest of us. In other words, they had ceased to choose for themselves; plague had leveled out discrimination. This could be seen by the way nobody troubled about the quality of the clothes or food he bought. Everything was taken as it came.

And, finally, it was worth noting that those who were parted ceased to enjoy the curious privilege that had been theirs at the outset. They had lost love's egoism and the benefit they derived from it. Now, at least, the position was clear; this calamity was everybody's business. What with the gunshots echoing at the gates, the punctual thuds of rubber stamps marking the rhythm of lives and deaths, the files and fires, the panics and formalities, all alike were pledged to an ugly but recorded death, and, amidst noxious fumes and the muted clang of ambulances, all of us ate the same sour bread of exile, unconsciously waiting for the same reunion, the same miracle of peace regained. No doubt our love persisted, but in practice it served nothing; it was an inert mass within us, sterile as crime or a life sentence. It had declined on a patience that led nowhere, a dogged expectation. Viewed from this angle, the attitude of some of our fellow citizens resembled that of the long queues one saw outside the food-shops. There was the same resignation, the same long-sufferance, inexhaustible and without illusions. The only difference was that the mental state of the food-seekers would need to be raised to a vastly higher power to make it comparable with the gnawing pain of separation, since this latter came from a hunger fierce to the point of insatiability.

In any case, if the reader would have a correct idea of the mood of these exiles, we must conjure up once more those dreary evenings sifting down through a haze of dust and golden light upon the treeless streets filled with teeming crowds of men and women. For, characteristically, the sound that rose toward the terraces still bathed in the last glow of daylight, now that the noises of vehicles and motors—the sole voice of cities in ordinary times—had ceased, was but one vast rumor of low voices and incessant footfalls, the drumming of innumerable soles timed to the eerie whistling of the plague in the sultry air above, the sound of a huge concourse of people marking time, a never ending, stifling drone that, gradually swelling, filled the town from end to end, and evening after evening gave its truest, mournfulest expression to the blind endurance that had ousted love from all our hearts.

SATIRE: AGGRESSIVENESS AND WAR

THE IDEA OF SATIRE is not quite so crisp and clear as our ideas of irony, parody, burlesque, and other devices of criticism. For one thing, satire sometimes includes these other genres; it is certainly a broader one than they. In spite of uncertain boundaries, however, the general shape of satire is clear: it works by drawing an unfavorable picture of its object. And it has two main ways of doing so. One is by attacking the object of criticism directly, pointing out its faults, perhaps exaggerating them, certainly pouring verbal acid on them. This type, "invective satire," is of ancient origin, and has flourished in this century with such writers as H. L. Mencken. We omit specimens of invective satire from this section primarily because it does not involve oblique perspective, or esthetic "distance," but is the direct expression of a writer's rage. The second method of satire is subtler; it demands that the writer put on a mask and disguise his anger. Instead of hurling invective, he imitates those whose foibles he wishes to attack, or he describes them through the eyes of a naïve observer; either way he pretends to be someone else. By assuming a pose, he encourages his readers to be amused at, scornful of, or outraged over the object of satire. Most modern satirists have found this method more successful than trying to gain the reader's sympathy by applying directly the epithets of abuse.

The selections in this unit are about human aggressiveness and war.

Most people are against War, but in favor of particular wars; others are against wars, too, but take them for granted as a deplorable but unavoidable condition of human life. The satirist must combat both of these attitudes by painting the horrors of war, or by exposing the irrationality of war, or by pointing out the triviality of man's squabbles, compared with the atrocious bloodshed which accompanies them—one way or another the satirist must shake the reader loose from complacency. To do so, Jonathan Swift (1667-1745) works through the narration of his famous character Gulliver, who in the selection below is in a land where the rational governing creatures are a superior race of horses called Houyhnhnms, who have as beasts of burden the Yahoos, a revolting species of manlike animals. Samuel Clemens (1835-1910) also attacks the aggressiveness of men by employing a naïve narrator and a superhuman critic of human actions. American novelist John Dos Passos (1896-   ) works more directly, by drawing a composite picture of man's death in war. Finally, humorist James Thurber (1894-1961) achieves more satiric distance than any of the other writers by using the actions of animals as a vehicle for caustic criticism of human beings.

GULLIVER EXPLAINS WARFARE TO THE HOUYHNHNMS | *JONATHAN SWIFT*

THE AUTHOR, AT HIS MASTER'S COMMAND, INFORMS HIM OF THE STATE OF ENGLAND. THE CAUSES OF WAR AMONG THE PRINCES OF EUROPE.

The reader may please to observe, that the following extract of many conversations I had with my master, contains a summary of the most material points which were discoursed at several times for above two years; his Honor often desiring fuller satisfaction as I farther improved in the Houyhnhnm tongue. I laid before him, as well as I could, the whole state of Europe; I discoursed of trade and manufactures, of arts and sciences; and the answers I gave to all the questions he made, as they arose upon several subjects, were a fund of conversation not to be exhausted. But I shall here only set down the substance of what passed between us concerning my own country, reducing it into order as well as I can, without any regard to time or other circumstances, while I strictly adhere to truth. My only concern is that I shall hardly be able to do justice to my master's arguments and expressions, which must needs suffer by my want of capacity, as well as by a translation into our barbarous English.

In obedience therefore to his Honor's commands, I related to him the Revolution under the Prince of Orange; the long war with France entered

From *Gulliver's Travels*, Pt. IV, Chap. 5 (1726).

into by the said prince, and renewed by his successor the present Queen, wherein the greatest powers of Christendom were engaged, and which still continued: I computed at his request that about a million of Yahoos might have been killed in the whole progress of it, and perhaps a hundred or more cities taken, and thrice as many ships burnt or sunk.

He asked me what were the usual causes or motives that made one country go to war with another. I answered they were innumerable, but I should only mention a few of the chief. Sometimes the ambition of princes, who never think they have land or people enough to govern; sometimes the corruption of ministers, who engage their master in a war in order to stifle or divert the clamor of the subjects against their evil administration. Difference in opinions hath cost many millions of lives: for instance, whether flesh be bread, or bread be flesh; whether the juice of a certain berry be blood or wine; whether whistling be a vice or a virtue; whether it be better to kiss a post, or throw it into the fire; what is the best color for a coat, whether black, white, red, or gray; and whether it should be long or short, narrow or wide, dirty or clean; with many more. Neither are any wars so furious and bloody, or of so long continuance, as those occasioned by difference in opinion, especially if it be in things indifferent.

Sometimes the quarrel between two princes is to decide which of them shall dispossess a third of his dominions, where neither of them pretend to any right. Sometimes one prince quarreleth with another, for fear the other should quarrel with him. Sometimes a war is entered upon, because the enemy is too strong, and sometimes because he is too weak. Sometimes our neighbors want the things which we have, or have the things we want; and we both fight, till they take ours or give us theirs. It is a very justifiable cause of a war to invade a country after the people have been wasted by famine, destroyed by pestilence, or embroiled by factions among themselves. It is justifiable to enter into war against our nearest ally, when one of his towns lies convenient for us, or a territory of land, that would render our dominions round and complete. If a prince sends forces into a nation where the people are poor and ignorant, he may lawfully put half of them to death, and make slaves of the rest, in order to civilize and reduce them from their barbarous way of living. It is a very kingly, honorable, and frequent practice, when one prince desires the assistance of another to secure him against an invasion, that the assistant, when he hath driven out the invader, should seize on the dominions himself, and kill, imprison or banish the prince he came to relieve. Alliance by blood or marriage is a frequent cause of war between princes; and the nearer the kindred is, the greater is their disposition to quarrel: poor nations are hungry, and rich nations are proud; and pride and hunger will ever be at variance. For these reasons, the trade of a soldier is held the most honorable of all others; because a soldier is a Yahoo hired to kill in cold blood as many of his own species, who have never offended him, as possibly he can.

There is likewise a kind of beggarly princes in Europe, not able to make war by themselves, who hire out their troops to richer nations, for so much a day to each man; of which they keep three fourths to themselves, and it is the best part of their maintenance; such are those in Germany and other northern parts of Europe.

What you have told me (said my master), upon the subject of war, does indeed discover most admirably the effects of that reason you pretend to: however, it is happy that the shame is greater than the danger; and that nature hath left you utterly uncapable of doing much mischief.

For your mouths lying flat with your faces, you can hardly bite each other to any purpose, unless by consent. Then as to the claws upon your feet before and behind, they are so short and tender, that one of our Yahoos would drive a dozen of yours before him. And therefore in recounting the numbers of those who have been killed in battle, I cannot but think that you have *said the thing which is not.*

I could not forbear shaking my head and smiling a little at his ignorance. And being no stranger to the art of war, I gave him a description of cannons, culverins, muskets, carabines, pistols, bullets, powder, swords, bayonets, battles, sieges, retreats, attacks, undermines, countermines, bombardments, sea fights; ships sunk with a thousand men, twenty thousand killed on each side; dying groans, limbs flying in the air, smoke, noise, confusion, trampling to death under horses' feet; flight, pursuit, victory; fields strewed with carcasses left for food to dogs, and wolves, and birds of prey; plundering, stripping, ravishing, burning, and destroying. And to set forth the valor of my own dear countrymen, I assured him that I had seen them blow up a hundred enemies at once in a siege, and as many in a ship, and beheld the dead bodies come down in pieces from the clouds, to the great diversion of the spectators.

I was going on to more particulars, when my master commanded me silence. He said whoever understood the nature of Yahoos might easily believe it possible for so vile an animal to be capable of every action I had named, if their strength and cunning equaled their malice. But as my discourse had increased his abhorrence of the whole species, so he found it gave him a disturbance in his mind, to which he was wholly a stranger before. He thought his ears being used to such abominable words, might by degrees admit them with less detestation. That although he hated the Yahoos of this country, yet he no more blamed them for their odious qualities, than he did a *gnnayh* (a bird of prey) for its cruelty, or a sharp stone for cutting his hoof. But when a creature pretending to reason could be capable of such enormities, he dreaded lest the corruption of that faculty might be worse than brutality itself. He seemed therefore confident, that instead of reason, we were only possessed of some quality fitted to increase our natural vices; as the reflection from a troubled stream returns the image of an ill-shapen body, not only larger but more distorted.

A LESSON FROM SATAN | *SAMUEL L. CLEMENS*

It was wonderful, the mastery Satan had over time and distance. For him they did not exist. He called them human inventions, and said they were artificialities. We often went to the most distant parts of the globe with him, and stayed weeks and months, and yet were gone only a fraction of a second, as a rule. You could prove it by the clock. One day when our people were in such awful distress because the witch commission were afraid to proceed against the astrologer and Father Peter's household, or against any, indeed, but the poor and the friendless, they lost patience and took to witch-hunting on their own score, and began to chase a born lady who was known to have the habit of curing people by devilish arts, such as bathing them, washing them, and nourishing them instead of bleeding them and purging them through the ministrations of a barber-surgeon in the proper way. She came flying down, with the howling and cursing mob after her, and tried to take refuge in houses, but the doors were shut in her face. They chased her more than half an hour, we following to see it, and at last she was exhausted and fell, and they caught her. They dragged her to a tree and threw a rope over the limb, and began to make a noose in it, some holding her, meantime, and she crying and begging, and her young daughter looking on and weeping, but afraid to say or do anything.

They hanged the lady, and I threw a stone at her, although in my heart I was sorry for her; but all were throwing stones and each was watching his neighbor, and if I had not done as the others did it would have been noticed and spoken of. Satan burst out laughing.

All that were near by turned upon him, astonished and not pleased. It was an ill time to laugh, for his free and scoffing ways and his supernatural music had brought him under suspicion all over the town and turned many privately against him. The big blacksmith called attention to him now, raising his voice so that all should hear, and said:

"What are you laughing at? Answer! Moreover, please explain to the company why you threw no stone."

"Are you sure I did not throw a stone?"

"Yes. You needn't try to get out of it; I had my eye on you."

"And I—I noticed you!" shouted two others.

"Three witnesses," said Satan: "Mueller, the blacksmith; Klein, the butcher's man; Pfeiffer, the weaver's journeyman. Three very ordinary liars. Are there any more?"

From Mark Twain (Samuel L. Clemens), *The Mysterious Stranger* (New York, Harper & Row, Publishers, 1916). Copyright, 1916, by Mark Twain. Copyright, 1944, by Clara Clemens Gabrilowitsch.

"Never mind whether there are others or not, and never mind about what you consider us—three's enough to settle your matter for you. You'll prove that you threw a stone, or it shall go hard with you."

"That's so!" shouted the crowd, and surged up as closely as they could to the center of interest.

"And first you will answer that other question," cried the blacksmith, pleased with himself for being mouthpiece to the public and hero of the occasion. "What are you laughing at?"

Satan smiled and answered, pleasantly: "To see three cowards stoning a dying lady when they were so near death themselves."

You could see the superstitious crowd shrink and catch their breath, under the sudden shock. The blacksmith, with a show of bravado, said:

"Pooh! What do you know about it?"

"I? Everything. By profession I am a fortune-teller, and I read the hands of you three—and some others—when you lifted them to stone the woman. One of you will die tomorrow week; another of you will die tonight; the third has but five minutes to live—and yonder is the clock!"

It made a sensation. The faces of the crowd blanched, and turned mechanically toward the clock. The butcher and the weaver seemed smitten with an illness, but the blacksmith braced up and said, with spirit:

"It is not long to wait for prediction number one. If it fails, young master, you will not live a whole minute after, I promise you that."

No one said anything; all watched the clock in a deep stillness which was impressive. When four and a half minutes were gone the blacksmith gave a sudden gasp and clapped his hands upon his heart, saying, "Give me breath! Give me room!" and began to sink down. The crowd surged back, no one offering to support him, and he fell lumbering to the ground and was dead. The people stared at him, then at Satan, then at one another; and their lips moved, but no words came. Then Satan said:

"Three saw that I threw no stone. Perhaps there are others; let them speak."

It struck a kind of panic into them, and, although no one answered him, many began to violently accuse one another, saying, "You said he didn't throw," and getting for reply, "It is a lie, and I will make you eat it!" And so in a moment they were in a raging and noisy turmoil, and beating and banging one another; and in the midst was the only indifferent one—the dead lady hanging from her rope, her troubles forgotten, her spirit at peace.

So we walked away, and I was not at ease, but was saying to myself, "He told them he was laughing at them, but it was a lie—he was laughing at me."

That made him laugh again, and he said, "Yes, I was laughing at you, because, in fear of what others might report about you, you stoned the woman when your heart revolted at the act—but I was laughing at the others, too."

"Why?"

"Because their case was yours."

"How is that?"

"Well, there were sixty-eight people there, and sixty-two of them had no more desire to throw a stone than you had."

"Satan!"

"Oh, it's true. I know your race. It is made up of sheep. It is governed by minorities, seldom or never by majorities. It suppresses its feelings and its beliefs and follows the handful that makes the most noise. Sometimes the noisy handful is right, sometimes wrong; but no matter, the crowd follows it. The vast majority of the race, whether savage or civilized, are secretly kind-hearted and shrink from inflicting pain, but in the presence of the aggressive and pitiless minority they don't dare to assert themselves. Think of it! One kind-hearted creature spies upon another, and sees to it that he loyally helps in iniquities which revolt both of them. Speaking as an expert, I know that ninety-nine out of a hundred of your race were strongly against the killing of witches when that foolishness was first agitated by a handful of pious lunatics in the long ago. And I know that even today, after ages of transmitted prejudice and silly teaching, only one person in twenty puts any real heart into the harrying of a witch. And yet apparently everybody hates witches and wants them killed. Some day a handful will rise up on the other side and make the most noise—perhaps even a single daring man with a big voice and a determined front will do it—and in a week all the sheep will wheel and follow him, and witch-hunting will come to a sudden end.

"Monarchies, aristocracies, and religions are all based upon that large defect in your race—the individual's distrust of his neighbor, and his desire, for safety's or comfort's sake, to stand well in his neighbor's eye. These institutions will always remain, and always flourish, and always oppress you, affront you, and degrade you, because you will always be and remain slaves of minorities. There was never a country where the majority of the people were in their secret hearts loyal to any of these institutions."

I did not like to hear our race called sheep, and said I did not think they were.

"Still, it is true, lamb," said Satan. "Look at you in war—what mutton you are, and how ridiculous!"

"In war? How?"

"There has never been a just one, never an honorable one—on the part of the instigator of the war. I can see a million years ahead, and this rule will never change in so many as half a dozen instances. The loud little handful—as usual—will shout for the war. The pulpit will—warily and cautiously—object—at first; the great, big, dull bulk of the nation will rub its sleepy eyes and try to make out why there should be a war, and will say, earnestly and indignantly, 'It is unjust and dishonorable, and there is no necessity for it.' Then the handful will shout louder. A few fair men on the other side will argue and reason against the war with speech and pen, and at first will have a hearing and be applauded; but it will not last long; those others will out-shout them, and presently the anti-war audiences will thin out and lose popularity. Before long you will see this curious thing: the speakers stoned from the platform, and free speech strangled by hordes of furious men who in their secret hearts are still at one with those stoned speakers—as earlier—but do not dare to say so. And now the whole nation—pulpit and all—will take up the war-cry, and shout itself hoarse, and mob any honest man who ventures to open his mouth; and presently such mouths will cease to open. Next the statesmen will invent cheap lies, putting the blame upon the nation that is attacked, and every man will be glad of those conscience-soothing falsities, and will diligently study them, and refuse to examine any refutations of them; and thus he will by and by convince himself that the war is just, and will thank God for the better sleep he enjoys after this process of grotesque self-deception."

THE BODY OF AN AMERICAN | *JOHN DOS PASSOS*

Whereasthe Congressoftheunitedstates byaconcurrentresolution adoptedon the4thdayofmarch lastauthorizedthe Secretaryofwarto cause to be brought to theunitedstatesthe body of an American who wasamemberoftheamericanexpeditionaryforceineuropewho losthislifeduringtheworldwarandwhoseidentityhasnotbeenestablishedfor burialinthememorialamphitheatreofthenationalcemeteryatarlingtonvirginia

In the tarpaper morgue at Châlons-sur-Marne in the reek of chloride of lime and the dead, they picked out the pine box that held all that was left of

enie menie minie moe plenty other pine boxes stacked up there containing what they'd scraped up of Richard Roe

and other person or persons unknown. Only one can go. How did they pick John Doe?

Make sure he ain't a dinge, boys,

make sure he ain't a guinea or a kike,

how can you tell a guy's a hundredpercent when all you've got's a gunnysack full of bones, bronze buttons stamped with the screaming eagle and a pair of roll puttees?

. . . and the gagging chloride and the puky dirtstench of the yearold dead . . .

The day withal was too meaningful and tragic for applause. Silence, tears, songs and prayer, muffled drums and soft music were the instrumentalities today of national approbation.

John Doe was born (thudding din of blood in love into the shuddering soar of a man and a woman alone indeed together lurching into

and ninemonths sick drowse waking into scared agony and the pain and blood and mess of birth). John Doe was born

and raised in Brooklyn, in Memphis, near the lakefront in Cleveland, Ohio, in the stench of the stockyards in Chi, on Beacon Hill, in an old brick house in Alexandria, Virgina, on Telegraph Hill, in a halftimbered Tudor cottage in Portland, the city of roses,

in the Lying-In Hospital old Morgan endowed on Stuyvesant Square,

across the railroad tracks, out near the country club, in a shack cabin tenement apartmenthouse exclusive residential suburb;

scion of one of the best families in the social register, won first prize in the baby parade at Coronado Beach, was marbles champion of the Little Rock grammarschools, crack basketballplayer at the Booneville High, quarterback at the State Reformatory, having saved the sheriff's kid from drowning in the Little Missouri River was invited to Washington to be photographed shaking hands with the President on the White House steps;—

though this was a time of mourning, such an assemblage necessarily has about it a touch of color. In the boxes are seen the court uniforms of foreign diplomats, the gold braid of our own and foreign fleets and armies, the black of the conventional morning dress of American statesmen, the varicolored furs and outdoor wrapping garments of mothers and sisters come to mourn, the drab and blue of soldiers and sailors, the glitter of musical instruments and the white and black of a vested choir

—busboy harvestiff hogcaller boyscout champeen cornshucker of Western Kansas bellhop at the United States Hotel at Saratoga Springs officeboy callboy fruiter telephone-lineman longshoreman lumberjack plumber's helper,

worked for an exterminating company in Union City, filled pipes in an opium joint in Trenton, New Jersey.

Y.M.C.A. secretary, express agent, truckdriver, fordmechanic, sold books in Denver, Colorado: Madam would you be willing to help a young man work his way through college?

President Harding, with a reverence seemingly more significant because of his high temporal station, concluded his speech:

We are met today to pay the impersonal tribute;

the name of him whose body lies before us took flight with his imperishable soul . . .

as a typical soldier of this representative democracy he fought and died believing in the indisputable justice of his country's cause . . .

by raising his right hand and asking the thousands within the sound of his voice to join in the prayer:

Our Father which art in heaven hallowed be thy name . . .

Naked he went into the army;

they weighed you, measured you, looked for flat feet, squeezed your penis to see if you had clap, looked up your anus to see if you had piles, counted your teeth, made you cough, listened to your heart and lungs, made you read the letters on the card, charted your urine and your intelligence,

gave you a service record for a future (imperishable soul)

and an identification tag stamped with your serial number to hang around your neck, issued O.D. regulation equipment, a condiment can and a copy of the articles of war.

Atten'SHUN suck in your gut you c——r wipe that smile off your face eyes right wattja tink dis is a choirch-social? For-war-D'ARCH.

John Doe

and Richard Roe and other person or persons unknown

drilled, hiked, manual of arms, ate slum, learned to salute, to soldier, to loaf in the latrines, forbidden to smoke on deck, overseas guard duty, forty men and eight horses, shortarm inspection and the ping of shrapnel and the shrill bullets combining the air and the sorehead woodpeckers the machineguns mud cooties gasmasks and the itch.

Say feller tell me how I can get back to my outfit.

John Doe had a head.

for twentyodd years intensely the nerves of the eyes the ears the palate the tongue the fingers the toes the armpits, the nerves warmfeeling under the skin charged the coiled brain with hurt sweet warm cold mine must don't sayings print headlines:

Thou shalt not the multiplication table long division, Now is the time for all good men knocks but once at a young man's door, It's a great life if Ish gebibbel, The first five years'll be the Safety First, Suppose a Hun tried to rape your my country right or wrong, Catch 'em young What he don't know won't treat 'em rough, Tell 'em nothin', He got what was coming to him he got his, This is a white man's country, Kick the bucket, Gone west, If you don't like it you can croaked him

Say buddy can't you tell me how I can get back to my outfit?

Can't help jumpin' when them things go off, give me the trots them things do. I lost my identification tag swimmin' in the Marne, roughousin' with a guy while we was waitin' to be deloused, in bed with a girl named

Jeanne (Love moving picture wet French postcard dream began with saltpeter in the coffee and ended at the propho station);—

Say soldier for chrissake can't you tell me how I can get back to my outfit?

John Doe
heart pumped blood:
alive thudding silence of blood in your ears
down in the clearing in the Oregon forest where the punkins were punkincolor pouring into the blood through the eyes and the fallcolored trees and the bronze hoopers were hopping through the dry grass, where tiny striped snails hung on the underside of the blades and the flies hummed, wasps droned, bumblebees buzzed, and the woods smelt of wine and mushrooms and apples, homey smell of fall pouring into the blood,

and I dropped the tin hat and the sweaty pack and lay flat with the dogday sun licking my throat and adamsapple and the tight skin over the breastbone.

The shell had his number on it.

The blood ran into the ground.

The service record dropped out of the filing cabinet when the quarter-master sergeant got blotto that time they had to pack up and leave the billets in a hurry.

The identification tag was in the bottom of the Marne.

The blood ran into the ground, the brains oozed out of the cracked skull and were licked up by the trenchrats, the belly swelled and raised a generation of bluebottle flies,

and the incorruptible skeleton,

and the scraps of dried viscera and skin bundled in khaki

they took to Châlons-sur-Marne

and laid it out neat in a pine coffin

and took it home to God's Country on a battleship

and buried it in a sarcophagus in the Memorial Amphitheater in the Arlington National Cemetery

and draped the Old Glory over it

and the bugler played taps

and Mr. Harding prayed to God and the diplomats and the generals and the admirals and the brasshats and the politicians and the handsomely dressed ladies out of the society column of the *Washington Post* stood up solemn

and thought how beautiful sad Old Glory God's Country it was to have the bugler play taps and the three volleys made their ears ring.

Where his chest ought to have been they pinned

the Congressional Medal, the D.S.C., the Médaille Militaire, the Belgian Croix de Guerre, the Italian gold medal, the Vitutea Militara sent by

Queen Marie of Rumania, the Czechoslovak War Cross, the Virtuti Militari of the Poles, a wreath sent by Hamilton Fish, Jr., of New York, and a little wampum presented by a deputation of Arizona redskins in warpaint and feathers. All the Washingtonians brought flowers.

Woodrow Wilson brought a bouquet of poppies.

THREE FABLES OF OUR TIME | *JAMES THURBER*

1) THE BIRDS AND THE FOXES

Once upon a time there was a bird sanctuary in which hundreds of Baltimore orioles lived together happily. The refuge consisted of a forest entirely surrounded by a high wire fence. When it was put up, a pack of foxes who lived nearby protested that it was an arbitrary and unnatural boundary. However, they did nothing about it at the time because they were interested in civilizing the geese and ducks on the neighboring farms. When all the geese and ducks had been civilized, and there was nothing else left to eat, the foxes once more turned their attention to the bird sanctuary. Their leader announced that there had once been foxes in the sanctuary but that they had been driven out. He proclaimed that Baltimore orioles belonged in Baltimore. He said, furthermore, that the orioles in the sanctuary were a continuous menace to the peace of the world. The other animals cautioned the foxes not to disturb the birds in their sanctuary.

So the foxes attacked the sanctuary one night and tore down the fence that surrounded it. The orioles rushed out and were instantly killed and eaten by the foxes.

The next day the leader of the foxes, a fox from whom God was receiving daily guidance, got upon the rostrum and addressed the other foxes. His message was simple and sublime. "You see before you," he said, "another Lincoln. We have liberated all those birds!"

Moral: Government of the orioles, by the foxes, and for the foxes, must perish from the earth.

2) THE RABBITS WHO CAUSED ALL THE TROUBLE

Within the memory of the youngest child there was a family of rabbits who lived near a pack of wolves. The wolves announced that they did not like the way the rabbits were living. (The wolves were crazy

"The Birds and the Foxes" and "The Rabbits Who Caused All the Trouble" from *Fables for Our Time* (New York, Harper & Row, Publishers, 1940); "The Tiger Who Would Be King" from *Further Fables for Our Time* (New York, Simon and Schuster, Inc., 1956). Reprinted by permission. Copyright 1939, 1956, The New Yorker Magazine, Inc.

about the way they themselves were living, because it was the only way to live.) One night several wolves were killed in an earthquake and this was blamed on the rabbits, for it is well known that rabbits pound on the ground with their hind legs and cause earthquakes. On another night one of the wolves was killed by a bolt of lightning and this was also blamed on the rabbits, for it is well known that lettuce-eaters cause lightning. The wolves threatened to civilize the rabbits if they didn't behave, and the rabbits decided to run away to a desert island. But the other animals, who lived at a great distance, shamed them, saying, "You must stay where you are and be brave. This is no world for escapists. If the wolves attack you, we will come to your aid, in all probability." So the rabbits continued to live near the wolves and one day there was a terrible flood which drowned a great many wolves. This was blamed on the rabbits, for it is well known that carrot-nibblers with long ears cause floods. The wolves descended on the rabbits, for their own good, and imprisoned them in a dark cave, for their own protection.

When nothing was heard about the rabbits for some weeks, the other animals demanded to know what had happened to them. The wolves replied that the rabbits had been eaten and since they had been eaten the affair was a purely internal matter. But the other animals warned that they might possibly unite against the wolves unless some reason was given for the destruction of the rabbits. So the wolves gave them one. "They were trying to escape," said the wolves, "and, as you know, this is no world for escapists."

Moral: Run, don't walk, to the nearest desert island.

3)   THE TIGER WHO WOULD BE KING

One morning the tiger woke up in the jungle and told his mate that he was king of beasts.

"Leo, the lion, is king of beasts," she said.

"We need a change," said the tiger. "The creatures are crying for a change."

The tigress listened but she could hear no crying, except that of her cubs.

"I'll be king of beasts by the time the moon rises," said the tiger. "It will be a yellow moon with black stripes, on my honor."

"Oh, sure," said the tigress as she went to look after her young, one of whom, a male, very like his father, had got an imaginary thorn in his paw.

The tiger prowled through the jungle till he came to the lion's den. "Come out," he roared, "and greet the king of beasts! The king is dead, long live the king!"

Inside the den, the lioness woke her mate. "The king is here to see you," she said.

"What king?" he inquired, sleepily.

"The king of beasts," she said.

"I am the king of beasts," roared Leo, and he charged out of the den to defend his crown against the pretender.

It was a terrible fight, and it lasted until the setting of the sun. All the animals of the jungle joined in, some taking the side of the tiger and others the side of the lion. Every creature from the aardvark to the zebra took part in the struggle to overthrow the lion or to repulse the tiger, and some did not know which they were fighting for, and some fought for both, and some fought whoever was nearest, and some fought for the sake of fighting.

"What are we fighting for?" someone asked the aardvark.

"The old order," said the aardvark.

"What are we dying for?" someone asked the zebra.

"The new order," said the zebra.

When the moon rose, fevered and gibbous, it shone upon a jungle in which nothing stirred except a macaw and a cockatoo, screaming in horror. All the beasts were dead except the tiger, and his days were numbered and his time was ticking away. He was monarch of all he surveyed, but it didn't seem to mean anything.

Moral: You can't very well be king of beasts if there aren't any.

PARODY I: THE JAMESIAN MANNER

ONE WAY OF CRITICIZING *the style or manner of an author or poet is methodically to list his faults, to appeal to reason and common sense. This method is the one commonly used in book reviews. Some critics, however, choose to attack by mimicking: the result is parody. Of course, a parodist will not mock successfully by mere slavish copying; he must select the more notable flaws or idiosyncrasies of his model and bring them out, warp them, make them ludicrous. Consider, as an object of parody, the formal address of Milton's Satan to his camp of rebellious angels: "Thrones, Dominations, Princedoms, Virtues, Powers." To write*

> *Thrones, regal Powers, famed Principalities,*
> *Exalted Noblemen . . .*

is only to imitate badly, whereas the following lines achieve parody of at least one Miltonic trait

> *O heavenly Presences, deific Ones,*
> *Ethereal Essences ineffable,*
> *Vague Entities, most incorporeal Things . . .*

Parody, then, criticizes artistic mannerisms by a mocking exaggeration.

"The Mote in the Middle Distance" parodies the plot, characterization,

and style of Henry James's The Beast in the Jungle, *from which we have included a chapter. The basic situation of the novel is as follows: Marcher is obsessed by the belief that his life will be distinguished from all others by a notable and possibly tragic experience; he therefore resists personal attachments (such as marriage with May Bartram), and spends his time waiting for the great thing to happen. His tragedy, ironically, turns out to be that nothing whatever happens to him—his life is uniquely barren. And its barrenness is directly the result of his having waited for an experience which would be worthy of him while he steadily showed himself to be unworthy of the experience repeatedly offered to him—the love of a sensitive and loyal woman.*

Henry James (1843-1916), brother of the psychologist William James, was an American-born novelist, who spent most of his adult life in England. Sir Max Beerbohm (1872-1956) was an English writer and caricaturist.

THE BEAST IN THE JUNGLE | *HENRY JAMES*

Then it was that, one afternoon, while the spring of the year was young and new she met all in her own way his frankest betrayal of these alarms. He had gone in late to see her, but evening hadn't settled and she was presented to him in that long fresh light of waning April days which affects us often with a sadness sharper than the grayest hours of autumn. The week had been warm, the spring was supposed to have begun early, and May Bartram sat, for the first time in the year, without a fire; a fact that, to Marcher's sense, gave the scene of which she formed part a smooth and ultimate look, an air of knowing, in its immaculate order and cold meaningless cheer, that it would never see a fire again. Her own aspect—he could scarce have said why—intensified this note. Almost as white as wax, with the marks and signs in her face as numerous and as fine as if they had been etched by a needle, with soft white draperies relieved by a faded green scarf on the delicate tone of which the years had further refined, she was the picture of a serene and exquisite but impenetrable sphinx, whose head, or indeed all whose person, might have been powdered with silver. She was a sphinx, yet with her white petals and green fronds she might have been a lily too— only an artificial lily, wonderfully imitated and constantly kept, without dust or stain, though not exempt from a slight droop and a complexity of faint creases, under some clear glass bell. The perfection of household care, of high polish and finish, always reigned in her rooms, but they now looked most as if everything had been wound up, tucked up, put away, so that she might sit with folded hands and with nothing more to do. She was "out of it," to Marcher's vision; her work was over; she communicated with him as across some gulf or from some island of rest that she had already reached, and it made him feel strangely abandoned. Was it—or rather wasn't it— that if for so long she had been watching with him the answer to their question must have swum into her ken and taken on its name, so that her occupation was verily gone? He had as much as charged her with this in saying to her, many months before, that she even then knew something she was keeping from him. It was a point he had never since ventured to press, vaguely fearing as he did that it might become a difference, perhaps a disagreement, between them. He had in this later time turned nervous, which was what he in all the other years had never been; and the oddity was that his nervousness should have waited till he had begun to doubt, should have held off so long as he was sure. There was something, it seemed to him, that the wrong word would bring down on his head, something that would so at least ease off his tension. But he wanted not to speak the wrong word; that would make everything ugly. He wanted the knowledge he lacked to drop on him, if drop it could, by its own august weight. If she was to forsake him it was surely for her to take leave. This was why he didn't directly ask her again what she knew; but it was also why, approaching the matter from another side, he said to her in the course of his visit: "What do you regard as the very worst that at this time of day *can* happen to me?"

He had asked her that in the past often enough; they had, with the odd irregular rhythm of their intensities and avoidances, exchanged ideas about it and then had seen the ideas washed away by cool intervals, washed like figures traced in sea-sand. It had ever been the mark of their talk that the oldest allusions in it required but a little dismissal and reaction to come out again, sounding for the hour as new. She could thus at present meet his enquiry quite freshly and patiently. "Oh yes, I've repeatedly thought, only it always seemed to me of old that I couldn't quite make up my mind. I thought of dreadful things, between which it was difficult to choose; and so must you have done."

"Rather! I feel now as if I had scarce done anything else. I appear to myself to have spent my life in thinking of nothing *but* dreadful things. A great many of them I've at different times named to you, but there were others I couldn't name."

"They were too, too dreadful?"

"Too, too dreadful—some of them."

She looked at him a minute, and there came to him as he met it an inconsequent sense that her eyes, when one got their full clearness, were still as beautiful as they had been in youth, only beautiful with a strange cold light—a light that somehow was a part of the effect, if it wasn't rather a part of the cause, of the pale hard sweetness of the season and the hour. "And yet," she said at last, "there are horrors we've mentioned."

It deepened the strangeness to see her, as such a figure in such a picture, talk of "horrors," but she was to do in a few minutes something stranger yet—though even of this he was to take the full measure but afterwards—and the note of it already trembled. It was, for the matter of that, one of the signs that her eyes were having again the high flicker of their prime. He had to admit, however, what she said. "Oh yes, there were times when we did go far." He caught himself in the act of speaking as if it all were over. Well, he wished it were; and the consummation depended for him clearly more and more on his friend.

But she had now a soft smile. "Oh far—!"

It was oddly ironic. "Do you mean you're prepared to go further?"

She was frail and ancient and charming as she continued to look at him, yet it was rather as if she had lost the thread. "Do you consider that we went far?"

"Why I thought it the point you were just making—that we *had* looked most things in the face."

"Including each other?" She still smiled. "But you're quite right. We've had together great imaginations, often great fears; but some of them have been unspoken."

"Then the worst—we haven't faced that. I *could* face it, I believe, if I knew what you think it. I feel," he explained, "as if I had lost my power to conceive such things." And he wondered if he looked as blank as he sounded. "It's spent."

"Then why do you assume," she asked, "that mine isn't?"

"Because you've given me signs to the contrary. It isn't a question for you of conceiving, imagining, comparing. It isn't a question now of choosing." At last he came out with it. "You know something I don't. You've shown me that before."

These last words had affected her, he made out in a moment, exceedingly, and she spoke with firmness. "I've shown you, my dear, nothing."

He shook his head. "You can't hide it."

"Oh, oh!" May Bartram sounded over what she couldn't hide. It was almost a smothered groan.

"You admitted it months ago, when I spoke of it to you as of something you were afraid I should find out. Your answer was that I couldn't, that I wouldn't, and I don't pretend I have. But you had something therefore in mind, and I now see how it must have been, how it still is, the possibility that, of all possibilities, has settled itself for you as the worst. This," he went on, "is why I appeal to you. I'm only afraid of ignorance today—I'm not afraid of knowledge." And then as for a while she said nothing: "What makes me sure is that I see in your face and feel here, in this air and amid these appearances, that you're out of it. You've done. You've had your experience. You leave me to my fate."

Well, she listened, motionless and white in her chair, as on a decision to be made, so that her manner was fairly an avowal, though still, with a small fine inner stiffness, an imperfect surrender. "It *would* be the worst," she finally let herself say. "I mean the thing I've never said."

It hushed him a moment. "More monstrous than all the monstrosities we've named?"

"More monstrous. Isn't that what you sufficiently express," she asked, "in calling it the worst?"

Marcher thought. "Assuredly—if you mean, as I do, something that includes all the loss and all the shame that are thinkable."

"It would if it *should* happen," said May Bartram. "What we're speaking of, remember, is only my idea."

"It's your belief," Marcher returned. "That's enough for me. I feel your beliefs are right. Therefore if, having this one, you give me no more light on it, you abandon me."

"No, no!" she repeated. "I'm with you—don't you see?—still." And as to make it more vivid to him she rose from her chair—a movement she seldom risked in these days—and showed herself, all draped and all soft, in her fairness and slimness. "I haven't forsaken you."

It was really, in its effort against weakness, a generous assurance, and had the success of the impulse not, happily, been great, it would have touched him to pain more than to pleasure. But the cold charm in her eyes had spread, as she hovered before him, to all the rest of her person, so that it was for the minute almost a recovery of youth. He couldn't pity her for that; he could only take her as she showed—as capable even yet of helping him. It was as if, at the same time, her light might at any instant go out; wherefore he must make the most of it. There passed before him with intensity the three or four things he wanted most to know; but the question that came of itself to his lips really covered the others. "Then tell me if I shall consciously suffer."

She promptly shook her head. "Never!"

It confirmed the authority he imputed to her, and it produced on him an extraordinary effect. "Well, what's better than that? Do you call that the worst?"

"You think nothing is better?" she asked.

She seemed to mean something so special that he again sharply wondered, though still with the dawn of a prospect of relief. "Why not, if one doesn't *know*?" After which, as their eyes, over his question, met in a silence, the dawn deepened and something to his purpose came prodigiously out of her very face. His own, as he took it in, suddenly flushed to the forehead, and he gasped with the force of a perception to which, on the instant, everything fitted. The sound of his gasp filled the air; then he became articulate. "I see—if I don't suffer!"

In her own look, however, was doubt. "You see what?"

"Why what you mean—what you've always meant."

She again shook her head. "What I mean isn't what I've always meant. It's different."

"It's something new?"

She hung back from it a little. "Something new. It's not what you think. I see what you think."

His divination drew breath then; only her correction might be wrong. "It isn't that I *am* a blockhead?" he asked between faintness and grimness. "It isn't that it's all a mistake?"

"A mistake?' she pityingly echoed. *That* possibility, for her, he saw, would be monstrous; and if she guaranteed him the immunity from pain it would accordingly not be what she had in mind. "Oh no," she declared; "it's nothing of that sort. You've been right."

Yet he couldn't help asking himself if she weren't, thus pressed, speaking but to save him. It seemed to him he should be most in a hole if his history should prove all a platitude. "Are you telling me the truth, so that I shan't have been a bigger idiot than I can bear to know? I *haven't* lived with a vain imagination, in the most besotted illusion? I haven't waited but to see the door shut in my face?"

She shook her head again. "However the case stands *that* isn't the truth. Whatever the reality, it *is* a reality. The door isn't shut. The door's open," said May Bartram.

"Then something's to come?"

She waited once again, always with her cold sweet eyes on him. "It's never too late." She had, with her gliding step, diminished the distance between them, and she stood nearer to him, close to him, a minute, as if still charged with the unspoken. Her movement might have been for some finer emphasis of what she was at once hesitating and deciding to say. He had been standing by the chimney-piece, fireless and sparely adorned, a small perfect old French clock and two morsels of rosy Dresden constituting all its furniture; and her hand grasped the shelf while she kept him waiting, grasped it a little as for support and encouragement. She only kept him waiting, however; that is he only waited. It had become suddenly, from her movement and attitude, beautiful and vivid to him that she had something more to give him; her wasted face delicately shone with it—it glittered almost as with the white luster of silver in her expression. She was right, incontestably, for what he saw in her face was the truth, and strangely, without consequence, while their talk of it as dreadful was still in the air, she appeared to present it as inordinately soft. This, prompting bewilderment, made him but gape the more gratefully for her revelation, so that they continued for some minutes silent, her face shining at him, her contact imponderably pressing, and his stare all kind but all expectant. The end, none the less, was that what he had expected failed to come to him. Something else took place instead, which seemed to consist at first in the mere closing of her eyes. She gave way at the same instant to a slow fine shudder, and though he remained staring—though he stared in fact but the harder—turned off and regained her chair. It was the end of what she had been intending, but it left him thinking only of that.

"Well, you don't say—?"

She had touched in her passage a bell near the chimney and had sunk back strangely pale. "I'm afraid I'm too ill."

"Too ill to tell me?" It sprang up sharp to him, and almost to his lips, the fear she might die without giving him light. He checked himself in time from so expressing his question, but she answered as if she had heard the words.

"Don't you know—now?"

" 'Now'—?" She had spoken as if some difference had been made within the moment. But her maid, quickly obedient to her bell, was already with them. "I know nothing." And he was afterwards to say to himself that he must have spoken with odious impatience, such an impatience as to show, that, supremely disconcerted, he washed his hands of the whole question.

"Oh!" said May Bartram.

"Are you in pain?" he asked as the woman went to her.

"No," said May Bartram.

Her maid, who had put an arm round her as if to take her to her room, fixed on him eyes that appealingly contradicted her; in spite of which, however, he showed once more his mystification. "What then has happened?"

She was once more, with her companion's help, on her feet, and, feeling withdrawal imposed on him, he had blankly found his hat and gloves and had reached the door. Yet he waited for her answer. "What *was* to," she said.

THE MOTE IN THE MIDDLE DISTANCE | *MAX BEERBOHM*

It was with the sense of a, for him, very memorable something that he peered now into the immediate future, and tried, not without compunction, to take that period up where he had, prospectively, left it. But just where the deuce *had* he left it? The consciousness of dubiety was, for our friend, not, this morning, quite yet clean-cut enough to outline the figures on what she had called his "horizon," between which and himself the twilight was indeed of a quality somewhat intimidating. He had run up, in the course of time, against a good number of "teasers"; and the function of teasing them back—of, as it were, giving them, every now and then, "what for"—was in

From the book *A Christmas Garland* by Max Beerbohm. Dutton Paperback Series. Reprinted by permission of the publishers, E. P. Dutton & Co., Inc., and William Heinemann, Ltd.

him so much a habit that he would have been at a loss had there been, on the face of it, nothing to lose. Oh, he always had offered rewards, of course—had ever so liberally pasted the windows of his soul with staring appeals, minuted descriptions, promises that knew no bounds. But the actual recovery of the article—the business of drawing and crossing the cheque, blotched though this were with tears of joy—had blankly appeared to him rather in the light of a sacrilege, casting, he sometimes felt, a palpable chill on the fervor of the next quest. It was just this fervor that was threatened as, raising himself on his elbow, he stared at the foot of his bed. That his eyes refused to rest there for more than the fraction of an instant, may be taken—*was,* even then, taken by Keith Tantalus—as a hint of his recollection that after all the phenomenon wasn't to be singular. Thus the exact repetition, at the foot of Eva's bed, of the shape pendulous at the foot of *his* was hardly enough to account for the fixity with which he envisaged it, and for which he was to find, some years later, a motive in the (as it turned out) hardly generous fear that Eva had already made the great investigation "on her own." Her very regular breathing presently reassured him that, if she *had* peeped into "her" stocking, she must have done so in sleep. Whether he should wake her now, or wait for their nurse to wake them both in due course, was a problem presently solved by a new development. It was plain that his sister was now watching him between her eyelashes. He had half expected that. She really was—he had often told her that she really was—magnificent; and her magnificence was never more obvious than in the pause that elapsed before she all of a sudden remarked "They so very indubitably *are,* you know!"

It occurred to him as befitting Eva's remoteness, which was a part of Eva's magnificence, that her voice emerged somewhat muffled by the bedclothes. She was ever, indeed, the most telephonic of her sex. In talking to Eva you always had, as it were, your lips to the receiver. If you didn't try to meet her fine eyes, it was that you simply couldn't hope to: there were too many dark, too many buzzing and bewildering and all frankly not negotiable leagues in between. Snatches of other voices seemed often to intertrude themselves in the parley; and your loyal effort not to overhear these was complicated by your fear of missing what Eva might be twittering. "Oh, you certainly haven't, my dear, the trick of propinquity!" was a trust she had once parried by saying that, in that case, *he* hadn't—to which his unspoken rejoinder that she had caught her tone from the peevish young women at the Central seemed to him (if not perhaps in the last, certainly in the last but one, analysis) to lack finality. With Eva, he had found, it was always safest to "ring off." It was with a certain sense of his rashness in the matter, therefore, that he now, with an air of feverishly "holding the line," said "Oh, as to that!"

Had *she,* he presently asked himself, "rung off"? It was characteristic of our friend—was indeed "him all over"—that his fear of what she was going to say was as nothing to his fear of what she might be going to leave unsaid. He had, in his converse with her, been never so conscious as now of the intervening leagues; they had never so insistently beaten the drum of his ear; and he caught himself in the act of awfully computing, with a certain statistical passion, the distance between Rome and Boston. He had never been able to decide which of these points he was psychically the nearer to at the moment when Eva, replying "Well, one does, anyhow, leave a margin for the pretext, you know!" made him, for the first time in his life, wonder whether she were not more magnificent than even he had even given her credit for being. Perhaps it was to test this theory, or perhaps merely to gain time, that he now raised himself to his knees, and, leaning with outstretched arm towards the foot of his bed, made as though to touch the stocking which Santa Claus had, overnight, left dangling there. His posture, as he stared obliquely at Eva, with a sort of beaming defiance, recalled to him something seen in an "illustration." This reminiscence, however—if such it was, save in the scarred, the poor dear old woebegone and so very beguilingly *not* refractive mirror of the moment— took a peculiar twist from Eva's behavior. She had, with startling suddenness, sat bolt upright, and looked to him as if she were overhearing some tragedy at the other end of the wire, where, in the nature of things, she was unable to arrest it. The gaze she fixed on her extravagant kinsman was of a kind to make him wonder how he contrived to remain, as he beautifully did, rigid. His prop was possibly the reflection that flashed on him that, if *she* abounded in attenuations, well, hang it all, so did *he!* It was simply a difference of plane. Readjust the "values," as painters say, and there you were! He was to feel that he was only too crudely "there" when, leaning further forward, he laid a chubby forefinger on the stocking, causing that receptacle to rock ponderously to and fro. This effect was more expected than the tears which started to Eva's eyes, and the intensity with which "Don't you," she exclaimed, "see?"

"The mote in the middle distance?" he asked. "Did you ever, my dear, know me to see anything else? I tell you it blocks out everything. It's a cathedral, it's a herd of elephants, it's the whole habitable globe. Oh, it's, believe me, of an obsessiveness!" But his sense of the one thing it *didn't* block out from his purview enabled him to launch at Eva a speculation as to just how far Santa Claus had, for the particular occasion, gone. The gauge, for both of them, of this seasonable distance seemed almost blatantly suspended in the silhouettes of the two stockings. Over and above the basis of (presumably) sweetmeats in the toes and heels, certain extrusions stood for a very plenary fulfillment of desire. And, since Eva *had* set her heart on a doll of ample proportions and practicable eyelids—*had* asked that most admirable of her sex, their mother, for it with not less directness than he himself had put into his demand for a sword and helmet— her coyness now struck Keith as lying near to, at indeed a hardly measurable distance from, the border-line of his patience. If she didn't *want* the doll, why the deuce had she made such a point of getting it? He was perhaps on the verge of putting this question to her, when, waving her hand to include both stockings, she said "Of course, my dear, you *do* see. There they are, and you know I know you know we wouldn't, either of us, dip a finger into them." With a vibrancy of tone that seemed to bring her voice quite close to him, "One doesn't," she added, "violate the shrine—pick the pearl from the shell!"

Even had the answering question "Doesn't one just?" which for an instant hovered on the tip of his tongue, been uttered, it could not have obscured for Keith the change which her magnificence had wrought in him. Something, perhaps, of the bigotry of the convert was already discernible in the way that, averting his eyes, he said "One doesn't even peer." As to whether, in the years that have elapsed since he said this either of our friends (now adult) has, in fact, "peered," is a question which, whenever I call to the house, I am tempted to put to one or other of them. But any regret I may feel in my invariable failure to "come up to the scratch" of yielding to this temptation is balanced, for me, by my impression— my sometimes all but throned and anointed certainty—that the answer, if vouchsafed, would be in the negative.

PARODY II: THE EPIC ENCOUNTER

WE HAVE INCLUDED chapters from Tom Jones, *masterpiece of English novelist Henry Fielding (1707-1754), under the heading of parody, because Fielding here mimics some of the mannerisms of Homer's* Iliad. *Properly speaking, however, the selection belongs to a genre called "mock heroic," so named because it involves applying ancient heroic conventions and stylistic elevation to subject matter inappropriately base. This type of satire is a double-edged sword, which cuts both at the triviality or lowness of its subject and at the artificiality and hypocrisy of the style when used by modern writers to whom it is not native. And needless to say, the mock heroic aims at sheer fun, in addition to its more serious satiric purposes.*

FROM THE ILIAD | *HOMER*

Achilles' wrath, to Greece the direful spring
Of woes unnumber'd, heav'nly Goddess, sing!
That wrath which hurl'd to Pluto's gloomy reign
The souls of mighty chiefs untimely slain;
Whose limbs unbury'd on the naked shore,
Devouring dogs and hungry vultures tore:
Since great Achilles and Atrides strove,
Such was the sov'reign doom, and such the will of Jove!
   Declare, O Muse! in what ill-fated hour
Sprung the fierce strife, from what offended pow'r?
Latona's son a dire contagion spread,
And heap'd the camp with mountains of the dead;
The king of men his rev'rend priest defy'd,
And for the king's offence the people dy'd.

FROM BOOK I

   Thus pray'd Tydides, and Minerva heard;
His nerves confirm'd, his languid spirits cheer'd;
He feels each limb with wonted vigor light;
His beating bosom claim'd the promis'd fight.
Be bold (she cry'd) in ev'ry combat shine,
War be thy province, thy protection mine;
Rush to the fight, and ev'ry foe control;
Wake each paternal virtue in thy soul;
Strength swells thy boiling breast, infus'd by me,
And all thy godlike father breathes in thee!
Yet more, from mortal mists I purge thy eyes,
And set to view the warring Deities.
These see thou shun, thro' all th' embattled plain,
Nor rashly strive where human force is vain.
If Venus mingle in the martial band,
Her shalt thou wound: so Pallas gives command.
Vast was his wealth, and these the only heirs
Of all his labors, and a life of cares.
Cold death o'ertakes them in their blooming years,
And leaves the father unavailing tears:
To strangers now descends his heavy store,
The race forgotten, and the name no more.
   Two sons of Priam in one chariot ride,

Trans. by Alexander Pope (1715-1720).

Glitt'ring in arms, and combat side by side.
As when the lordly lion seeks his food
Where grazing heifers range the lonely wood,
He leaps amidst them with a furious bound,
Bends their strong necks, and tears them to the ground:
So from their feats the brother-chiefs are torn,
Their steeds and chariot to the navy borne.

FROM BOOK **V**

Tydides first, of all the Grecian force,
Oe'r the broad ditch impell'd his foaming horse,
Pierced the deep ranks, their strongest battle tore,
And dyed his javelin red with Trojan gore.
Young Agelaüs (Phradmon was his sire)
With flying coursers shunn'd his dreadful ire;
Struck through the back, the Phrygian fell oppress'd;
The dart drove on, and issued at his breast:
Headlong he quits the car: his arms resound;
His ponderous buckler thunders on the ground.
Forth rush a tide of Greeks, the passage freed;
The Atridae first, the Ajaces next succeed:
Meriones, like Mars in arms renown'd,
And godlike Idomen, now passed the mound;
Evaemon's son next issues to the foe,
And last young Teucer with his bended bow.
Secure behind the Telamonian shield
The skillful archer wide survey'd the field,
With every shaft some hostile victim slew,
Then close beneath the sevenfold orb withdrew:
The conscious infant so, when fear alarms,
Retires for safety to the mother's arms.
Thus Ajax guards his brother in the field,
Moves as he moves, and turns the shining shield.
Who first by Teucer's mortal arrows bled?
Orsilochus; then fell Ornemus dead:
The godlike Lycophon next press'd the plain,
With Chromius, Daetor, Ophelestes slain;
Bold Hamopäon breathless sunk to ground;
The bloody pile great Melanippus crown'd.
Heaps fell on heaps, sad trophies of his art,
A Trojan ghost attending every dart.

FROM BOOK **VIII**

MOLLY'S BATTLE | HENRY FIELDING

Her mother first perceived the alteration in the shape of Molly; and in order to hide it from her neighbors, she foolishly clothed her in that sack which Sophia had sent her; though, indeed, that young lady had little apprehension that the poor woman would have been weak enough to let any of her daughters wear it in that form.

Molly was charmed with the first opportunity she ever had of showing her beauty to advantage; for though she could very well bear to contemplate herself in the glass, even when dressed in rags, and though she had in that dress conquered the heart of Jones, and perhaps of some others, yet she thought the addition of finery would much improve her charms and extend her conquests.

Molly, therefore, having dressed herself out in this sack, with a new laced cap, and some other ornaments which Tom had given her, repairs to church with her fan in her hand the very next Sunday. The great are deceived if they imagine they have appropriated ambition and vanity to themselves. These noble qualities flourish as notably in a country church and churchyard as in the drawing-room or in the closet. Schemes have indeed been laid in the vestry which would hardly disgrace the conclave. Here is a ministry, and here is an opposition. Here are plots and circumventions, parties and factions, equal to those which are to be found in courts.

Nor are the women here less practiced in the highest feminine arts than their fair superiors in quality and fortune. Here are prudes and coquettes. Here are dressing and ogling, falsehood, envy, malice, scandal; in short, everything which is common to the most splendid assembly or politest circle. Let those of high life, therefore, no longer despise the ignorance of their inferiors, nor the vulgar any longer rail at the vices of their betters.

Molly had seated herself some time before she was known by her neighbors. And then a whisper ran through the whole congregation, "Who is she?" but when she was discovered, such sneering, giggling, tittering, and laughing ensued among the women, that Mr. Allworthy was obliged to exert his authority to preserve any decency among them. . . .

Mr. Western had an estate in this parish; and as his house stood at little greater distance from this church than from his own, he very often came to Divine service here; and both he and the charming Sophia happened to be present at this time.

Sophia was much pleased with the beauty of the girl, whom she pitied for her simplicity in having dressed herself in that manner, as she saw the

From the *History of Tom Jones, a Foundling,* Bk. IV, Chaps. 7 and 8 (1749).

envy which it had occasioned among her equals. She no sooner came home than she sent for the gamekeeper, and ordered him to bring his daughter to her, saying she would provide for her in the family, and might possibly place the girl about her own person, when her own maid, who was now going away, had left her.

Poor Seagrim was thunderstruck at this; for he was no stranger to the fault in the shape of his daughter. He answered, in a stammering voice, "That he was afraid Molly would be too awkward to wait on her ladyship, as she had never been at service."—"No matter for that," says Sophia; "she will soon improve. I am pleased with the girl, and am resolved to try her."

Black George now repaired to his wife, on whose prudent counsel he depended to extricate him out of this dilemma; but when he came thither he found his house in some confusion. So great envy had this sack occasioned, that when Mr. Allworthy and the other gentry were gone from church, the rage, which had hitherto been confined, burst into an uproar; and, having vented itself at first in *opprobrious* words, laughs, hisses, and gestures, betook itself at last to certain missile weapons; which, though from their plastic nature they threatened neither the loss of life nor of limb, were, however, sufficiently dreadful to a well-dressed lady. Molly had too much spirit to bear this treatment tamely. Having therefore—but hold, as we are diffident of our own abilities, let us here invite a superior power to our assistance.

Ye Muses, then, whoever ye are, who love to sing battles, and principally thou who whilom didst recount the slaughter in those fields where Hudibras and Trulla fought, if thou wert not starved with thy friend Butler, assist me on this great occasion. All things are not in the power of all.

As a vast herd of cows in a rich farmer's yard, if, while they are milked, they hear their calves at a distance, lamenting the robbery which is then committing, roar and bellow, so roared forth the Somersetshire mob an hallaloo, made up of almost as many squalls, screams, and other different sounds as there were persons, or indeed passions among them: some were inspired by rage, others alarmed by fear, and others had nothing in their heads but the love of fun; but chiefly Envy, the sister of Satan, and his constant companion, rushed among the crowd, and blew up the fury of the women, who no sooner came up to Molly than they pelted her with dirt and rubbish.

Molly, having endeavored in vain to make a handsome retreat, faced about; and laying hold of ragged Bess, who advanced in the front of the enemy, she at one blow felled her to the ground. The whole army of the enemy (though near a hundred in number), seeing the fate of their general, gave back many paces, and retired behind a new-dug grave; for the church-yard was the field of battle, where there was to be a funeral that very evening. Molly pursued her victory, and catching up a skull which lay on the side of the grave, discharged it with such fury, that having hit a tailor on the head, the two skulls sent equally forth a hollow sound at their meeting, and the tailor took presently measure of his length on the ground, where the skulls lay side by side, and it was doubtful which was the more valuable of the two. Molly then taking a thigh-bone in her hand, fell in among the flying ranks, and dealing her blows with great liberality on either side, overthrew the carcass of many a mighty hero and heroine.

Recount, O Muse, the names of those who fell on this fatal day. First, Jemmy Tweedle felt on his hinder head the direful bone. Him the pleasant banks of sweetly-winded Stour had nourished, where he first learnt the vocal art, with which, wandering up and down at wakes and fairs, he cheeered the rural nymphs and swains when upon the green they interweaved the sprightly dance; while he himself stood fiddling and jumping to his own music. How little now avails his fiddle! He thumps the verdant floor with his carcass. Next, old Echepole, the sowgelder, received a blow in his forehead from our Amazonian heroine, and immediately fell to the ground. He was a swinging fat fellow, and fell with almost as much noise as a house. His tobacco-box dropped at the same time from his pocket, which Molly took up as lawful spoils. Then Kate of the Mill tumbled unfortunately over a tombstone, which catching hold of her ungartered stocking inverted the order of nature, and gave her heels the superiority to her head. Betty Pippin, with young Roger her lover, fell both to the ground; where, oh, perverse fate! she salutes the earth, and he the sky. Tom Freckle, the smith's son, was the next victim to her rage. He was an ingenious workman, and made excellent pattens; nay, the very patten with which he was knocked down was his own workmanship. Had he been at that time singing psalms in the church he would have avoided a broken head. Miss Crow, the daughter of a farmer; John Giddish, himself a farmer; Nan Slouch, Esther Codling, Will Spray, Tom Bennet; the three Misses Potter, whose father keeps the sign of the Red Lion; Betty Chambermaid, Jack Ostler, and many others of inferior note, lay rolling among the graves.

Not that the strenuous arm of Molly reached all these; for many of them in their flight overthrew each other.

But now Fortune, fearing she had acted out of character, and had inclined too long to the same side, especially as it was the right side, hastily turned about: for now Goody Brown—whom Zekiel Brown caressed in his arms; nor he alone, but half the parish besides; so famous was she in the fields of Venus, nor indeed less in those of Mars. The trophies of both these her husband always bore about on his head and face; for if ever human head did by its horns display the amorous glories of a wife, Zekiel's did! nor did his well-scratched face less denote her talents (or rather talons) of a different kind.

No longer bore this Amazon the shameful flight of her party. She stopped short, and, calling aloud to all who fled, spoke as follows: "Ye Somersetshire men, or rather ye Somersetshire women, are ye not ashamed thus to fly

from a single woman? But if no other will oppose her, I myself and Joan
Top here will have the honor of the victory." Having thus said, she flew
at Molly Seagrim, and easily wrenched the thighbone from her hand, at
the same time clawing off her cap from her head. Then laying hold of the
hair of Molly with her left hand, she attacked her so furiously in the face
with the right, that the blood soon began to trickle from her nose. Molly
was not idle this while. She soon removed the clout from the head of Goody
Brown, and then fastening on her hair with one hand, with the other she
caused another bloody stream to issue forth from the nostrils of the enemy.

When each of the combatants had borne off sufficient spoils of hair from
the head of her antagonist, the next rage was against the garments. In this
attack they exerted so much violence, that in a very few minutes they were
both naked to the middle.

It is lucky for the women that the seat of fisticuff war is not the same
with them as among men; but though they may seem a little to deviate
from their sex when they go forth to battle, yet I have observed they never
so far forget as to assail the bosoms of each other, where a few blows would
be fatal to most of them. This, I know, some derive from their being of
a more bloody inclination than the males. On which account they apply
to the nose, as to the part whence blood may most easily be drawn; but this
seems a far-fetched as well as ill-natured supposition.

Goody Brown had great advantage of Molly in this particular; for the
former had indeed no breasts, her bosom (if it may be so called), as well
in color as in many other properties, exactly resembling an ancient piece
of parchment, upon which any one might have drummed a considerable
while without doing her any great damage.

Molly, beside her present unhappy condition, was differently formed in
those parts, and might, perhaps, have tempted the envy of Brown to give
her a fatal blow, had not the lucky arrival of Tom Jones at this instant
put an immediate end to the bloody scene.

IRONY: THE DEMISE OF CHRISTIANITY

*IRONY IS NOT so much a literary form as a manner, a way of disposing
words within a literary form. Satire, for instance, may be and usually is
full of ironic thrusts; sober history (like Gibbon's* Decline and Fall) *may be
barbed with irony; even judicial documents such as Justice Wolsey's now
famous judgment on the legal propriety of admitting James Joyce's novel,*
Ulysses, *to general circulation in the United States, may join wit and
trenchant observation by an ironic phrase. Yet, despite its use in nearly
all forms of literature, irony is hard to define and hard to separate decisively*

from other kinds of wit. The Greek root for the word means "to hide, to cover up," and that is indeed the one reliable characteristic of the device: it hides, or covers up what it means, generally by saying the opposite of what it means. But lies do that also: the difference is that the intent of a lie is to deceive, the intent of irony to undeceive. Irony stems, then, from the conviction that some proposition generally held to be true or some kind of behavior generally held to be good is in fact the very reverse of true or good. Perhaps because he doubts the likelihood that a direct attack on falseness or evil will be successful, the ironist pretends to espouse what he detests and then, by excessive admiration or the adducing of spurious attributes, to bring it into ridicule.

Some irony is so subtle that only extensive acquaintance with an author's work allows a reader to be sure of what is ironic, what straight-forward. Most irony, however, reveals its true colors before it has gone far primarily because the force of indignation which is commonly behind it produces enough distortion so that the reader, even if he is not of the writer's mind on the subject, comes to realize that irony is at work. Because it is so commonly the vehicle of vehemence, irony seldom provokes light-hearted laughter. The greatest ironists, as a matter of fact, have been men of almost savage contempt for hypocrisy in every form, for stupidity coupled with arrogance, for pretension, self-indulgence, and superciliousness. And contempt is less likely to produce laughter than to produce a snarl.

Jonathan Swift (1667-1745) is unquestionably the greatest master of irony in English. An Irishman, a clergyman of the Established Chruch and dean of St. Patrick's Cathedral in Dublin, Swift wrote violent satires throughout his career, first against specific abuses, and as he grew older (in Gulliver's Travels) against all human folly, corruptness, and persistence in evil, Clive Staples Lewis (1898-   ), a Cambridge professor, has created in The Screwtape Letters the fictitious correspondence between a senior devil and his missionary in England, a twentieth-century parallel to Swift's Argument. The notable differences between the two ironic pieces tell much about the differences between the controversial atmosphere of the rationalist eighteenth century and the atmosphere of laissez-aller which dominates religious attitudes in our own time. Both are good examples of irony devoted to uncovering the comfortably hidden seaminess of human action and thought. The concluding piece is a selection from the Decline and Fall of the Roman Empire, a masterpiece of historical writing by Edward Gibbon (1737-1794). He uses irony in a different manner from the others. Instead of relying on situation for effect, he develops the contradiction between statement and intention through an undercurrent so sly that it is sometimes impossible to tell when tongue is in cheek and when it is not.

AN ARGUMENT AGAINST THE ABOLISHMENT OF CHRISTIANITY | JONATHAN SWIFT

I am very sensible what a weakness and presumption it is, to reason against the general humor and disposition of the world. I remember it was with great justice, and a due regard to the freedom both of the public and the press, forbidden upon several penalties to write, or discourse, or lay wagers against the Union, even before it was confirmed by parliament, because that was looked upon as a design, to oppose the current of the people, which, besides the folly of it, is a manifest breach of the fundamental law that makes this majority of opinion the voice of God. In like manner, and for the very same reasons, it may perhaps be neither safe nor prudent to argue against the abolishing of Christianity, at a juncture when all parties appear so unanimously determined upon the point, as we cannot but allow from their actions, their discourses, and their writings. However, I know not how, whether from the affection of singularity, or the perverseness of human nature, but so it unhappily falls out, that I cannot be entirely of this opinion. Nay, though I were sure an order were issued for my immediate prosecution by the attorney-general, I should still confess that in the present posture of our affairs at home or abroad, I do not yet see the absolute necessity of extirpating the Christian religion from among us.

This perhaps may appear too great a paradox even for our wise and paradoxical age to endure; therefore I shall handle it with all tenderness, and with the utmost deference to that great and profound majority which is of another sentiment.

And yet the curious may please to observe how much the genius of a nation is liable to alter in half an age: I have heard it affirmed for certain by some very old people that the contrary opinion was even in their memories as much in vogue as the other is now; and that a project for the abolishing of Christianity would then have appeared as singular, and been thought as absurd, as it would be at this time to write or discourse in its defense.

Therefore I freely own that all appearances are against me. The system of the Gospel, after the fate of other systems, is generally antiquated and exploded; and the mass or body of the common people, among whom it seems to have had its latest credit, are now grown as much ashamed of it as their betters; opinions, like fashions, always descending from those of quality to the middle sort, and thence to the vulgar, where at length they are dropped and vanish.

From *An Argument to Prove That the Abolishment of Christianity in England May Be Attended with Some Inconveniences* . . . (1708).

But here I would not be mistaken, and must therefore be so bold as to borrow a distinction from the writers on the other side, when they make a difference between nominal and real Trinitarians. I hope no reader imagines me so weak to stand up in the defense of real Christianity, such as used in primitive times (if we may believe the authors of those ages) to have an influence upon men's belief and actions: to offer at the restoring of that would indeed be a wild project; it would be to dig up foundations; to destroy at one blow all the wit, and half the learning of the kingdom; to break the entire frame and constitution of things; to ruin trade, extinguish arts and sciences with the professors of them; in short, to turn our courts, exchanges, and shops into deserts; and would be full as absurd as the proposal of Horace, where he advises the Romans all in a body to leave their city and seek a new seat in some remote part of the world, by way of cure for the corruption of their manners.

Therefore I think this caution was in itself *altogether* unnecessary (which I have inserted only to prevent all possibility of caviling), since every candid reader will easily understand my discourse to be intended only in defense of nominal Christianity, the other having been for some time wholly laid aside by general consent as utterly inconsistent with our present schemes of wealth and power.

But why we should therefore cast off the name and title of Christians, although the general opinion and resolution be so violent for it, I confess I cannot (with submission) apprehend the consequence necessary. However, since the undertakers propose such wonderful advantages to the nation by this project, and advance many plausible objections against the system of Christianity, I shall briefly consider the strength of both, fairly allow them their greatest weight, and offer such answers as I think most reasonable. After which I will beg leave to show what inconveniences may possibly happen by such an innovation, in the present posture of our affairs.

First, One great advantage proposed by the abolishing of Christianity is, that it would very much enlarge and establish liberty of conscience, that great bulwark of our nation, and of the protestant religion, which is still too much limited by priestcraft, notwithstanding all the good intentions of the legislature, as we have lately found by a severe instance. For it is confidently reported, that two young gentlemen of real hopes, bright wit, and profound judgment, who upon a thorough examination of causes and effects, and by the mere force of natural abilities, without the least tincture of learning, having made a discovery, that there was no God, and generously communicating their thoughts for the good of the public, were some time ago, by an unparalleled severity, and upon I know not what obsolete law, broke for blasphemy. And as it hath been wisely observed, if persecution once begins, no man alive knows how far it may reach, or where it will end.

In answer to all which, with deference to wiser judgments, I think this rather shows the necessity of a nominal religion among us. Great wits love to be free with the highest objects: and if they cannot be allowed a God to revile or renounce, they will speak evil of dignities, abuse the government, and reflect upon the ministry; which I am sure few will deny to be of much more pernicious consequence, according to the saying of Tiberius, *Deorum offensa diis curae*. As to the particular fact related, I think it is not fair to argue from one instance, perhaps another cannot be produced; yet (to the comfort of all those who may be apprehensive of persecution) blasphemy we know is freely spoken a million of times in every coffee-house and tavern, or wherever else good company meet. It must be allowed indeed, that to break an English freeborn officer only for blasphemy, was, to speak the gentlest of such an action, a very high strain of absolute power. Little can be said in excuse for the general; perhaps he was afraid it might give offense to the allies among whom, for aught we know, it may be the custom of the country to believe in a God. But if he argued, as some have done, upon a mistaken principle, that an officer who is guilty of speaking blasphemy, may some time or other proceed so far as to raise a mutiny, the consequence is by no means to be admitted; for, surely the commander of an English army is likely to be but ill obeyed, whose soldiers fear and reverence him as little as they do a Deity.

It is further objected against the gospel system, that it obliges men to the belief of things too difficult for free-thinkers, and such who have shaken off the prejudices that usually cling to a confined education. To which I answer, that men should be cautious, how they raise objections which reflect upon the wisdom of the nation. Is not everybody freely allowed to believe whatever he pleases, and to publish his belief to the world whenever he thinks fit, especially if it serves to strengthen the party which is in the right? Would any indifferent foreigner, who should read the trumpery lately written by Asgil, Tindal, Toland, Coward, and forty more, imagine the Gospel to be our rule of faith, and confirmed by parliaments? Does any man either believe, or say he believes, or desire to have it thought that he says he believes one syllable of the matter? And is any man worse received upon that score, or does he find his want of nominal faith a disadvantage to him in the pursuit of any civil or military employment? What if there be an old dormant statute or two against him are they not now obsolete, to a degree, that Empson and Dudley themselves if they were now alive, would find it impossible to put them in execution?

It is likewise urged that there are by computation in this kingdom above ten thousand parsons, whose revenues, added to those of my lords the bishops, would suffice to maintain at least two hundred young gentlemen of wit and pleasure, and free-thinking, enemies to priestcraft, narrow principles, pedantry, and prejudices; who might be an ornament to the Court and Town: And then, again, so great a number of able-bodied divines might be a recruit to our fleet and armies. This indeed appears to be a consideration of some weight: but then, on the other side, several things deserve to be considered likewise: as, first, whether it may not be thought necessary that in certain tracts of country, like what we call parishes, there shall be one man at least of abilities to read and write. Then it seems a wrong computation, that the revenues of the Church throughout this island would be large enough to maintain two hundred young gentlemen, or even half that number, after the present refined way of living; that is, to allow each of them such a rent, as in the modern form of speech, would make them easy. But still there is in this project a greater mischief behind; and we ought to beware of the woman's folly, who killed the hen that every morning laid her a golden egg. For, pray what would become of the race of men in the next age, if we had nothing to trust to beside the scrofulous, consumptive productions, furnished by our men of wit and pleasure, when, having squandered away their vigor, health and estate, they are forced by some disagreeable marriage to piece up their broken fortunes, and entail rottenness and politeness on their posterity? Now, here are ten thousand persons reduced by the wise regulations of Henry the Eighth, to the necessity of a low diet and moderate exercise, who are the only great restorers of our breed, without which the nation would in an age or two become one great hospital.

Another advantage proposed by the abolishing of Christianity is the clear gain of one day in seven, which is now entirely lost, and consequently the kingdom one seventh less considerable in trade, business, and pleasure; besides the loss to the public of so many stately structures now in the hands of the clergy, which might be converted into playhouses, exchanges, market-houses, common dormitories, and other public edifices.

I hope I shall be forgiven a hard word, if I call this a perfect *cavil*. I readily own there hath been an old custom time out of mind, for people to assemble in the churches every Sunday, and that shops are still frequently shut, in order, as it is conceived, to preserve the memory of that ancient practice, but how this can prove a hindrance to business or pleasure, is hard to imagine. What if the men of pleasure are forced, one day in the week, to game at home instead of the chocolate-house? Are not the taverns and coffee-houses open? Can there be a more convenient reason for taking a dose of physics? Are fewer claps got upon Sundays than other days? Is not that the chief day for traders to sum up the accounts of the week, and for lawyers to prepare their briefs? But I would fain know how it can be pretended that the churches are misapplied? Where are more appointments and rendezvous of gallantry? Where more care to appear in the foremost box with greater advantage of dress? Where more meetings for business? Where more bargains driven of all sorts? And where so many conveniences or incitements to sleep?

There is one advantage greater than any of the foregoing, proposed by the abolishing of Christianity: that it will utterly extinguish parties among us, by removing those factious distinctions of High and Low Church, of Whig and Tory, Presbyterian and Church of England, which are now so many mutual clogs upon public proceedings, and are apt to prefer the gratifying themselves, or depressing their adversaries, before the most important interest of the state.

I confess, if it were certain that so great an advantage would redound to the nation by this expedient, I would submit and be silent: but will any man say, that if the words *whoring, drinking, cheating, lying, stealing,* were by act of parliament ejected out of the English tongue and dictionaries, we should all awake next morning chaste and temperate, honest and just, and lovers of truth? Is this a fair consequence? Or, if the physicians would forbid us to pronounce the words *pox, gout, rheumatism* and *stone,* would that expedient serve like so many talismans to destroy the diseases themselves? Are party and faction rooted in men's hearts no deeper than phrases borrowed from religion, or founded upon no firmer principles? And is our language so poor that we cannot find other terms to express them? Are *envy, pride, avarice,* and *ambition* such ill nomenclators, that they cannot furnish appellations for their owners? Will not *heydukes* and *mamalukes, mandarins* and *patshaws,* or any other words formed at pleasure, serve to distinguish those who are in the ministry from others who would be in it if they could? What, for instance, is easier than to vary the form of speech, and instead of the word *church,* make it a question in politics, whether the Monument be in danger? Because religion was nearest at hand to furnish a few convenient phrases, is our invention so barren we can find no other? Suppose, for argument sake, that the Tories favored Margarita, the Whigs Mrs. Tofts, and the Trimmers Valentini, would not *Margaritians, Toftians* and *Valentinians* be very tolerable marks of distinction? The *Prasini* and *Veniti,* two most virulent factions in Italy, began (if I remember right) by a distinction of colors in ribbons, which we might do with as good a grace about the dignity of the blue and the green, and would serve as properly to divide the Court, the Parliament, and the Kingdom between them, as any terms of art whatsoever borrowed from religion. And therefore I think there is little force in this objection against Christianity, or prospect of so great an advantage as is proposed in the abolishing of it.

'Tis again objected, as a very absurd ridiculous custom, that a set of men should be suffered, much less employed and hired, to bawl one day in seven against the lawfulness of those methods most in use toward the pursuit of greatness, riches and pleasure, which are the constant practice of all men alive on the other six. But this objection is, I think, a little unworthy so refined an age as ours. Let us argue this matter calmly: I appeal to the breast of any polite freethinker, whether in the pursuit of gratifying a predominant passion he hath not always felt a wonderful incitement, by reflecting it was a thing forbidden: and therefore we see, in order to culti-vate this taste, the wisdom of the nation hath taken special care that the ladies should be furnished with prohibited silks, and the men with pro-hibited wine. And indeed, it were to be wished that some other prohibi-tions were promoted, in order to improve the pleasures of the town; which, for want of such expedients begin already, as I am told, to flag and grow languid, giving way daily to cruel inroads from the spleen.

'Tis likewise proposed as a great advantage to the public that if we once discard the system of the Gospel, all religion will of course be ban-ished for ever; and consequently, along with it, those grievous prejudices of education, which under the names of *virtue, conscience, honor, justice,* and the like, are so apt to disturb the peace of human minds, and the notions whereof are so hard to be eradicated by right reason or freethink-ing, sometimes during the whole course of our lives. Here first I observe how difficult it is to get rid of a phrase which the world is once grown fond of, though the occasion that first produced it be entirely taken away. For several years past, if a man had but an ill-favored nose, the deep-thinkers of the age would some way or other contrive to impute the cause to the prejudice of his education. From this fountain were said to be derived all our foolish notions of justice, piety, love of our country, all our opinions of God, or a future state, Heaven, Hell, and the like; and there might for-merly perhaps have been some pretense for this charge. But so effectual care hath been since taken to remove those prejudices, by an entire change in the methods of education, that (with honor I mention it to our polite innovators) the young gentlemen who are now on the scene, seem to have not the least tincture of those infusions, or string of those weeds; and, by consequence, the reason for abolishing nominal Christianity upon that pretext, is wholly ceased.

For the rest, it may perhaps admit a controversy, whether the banish-ing of all notions of religion whatsoever, would be convenient for the vul-gar. Not that I am in the least of opinion with those who hold religion to have been the invention of politicians, to keep the lower part of the world in awe by the fear of invisible powers; unless mankind were then very different from what it is now: For I look upon the mass or body of our people here in England to be as freethinkers, that is to say, as staunch unbelievers, as any of the highest rank. But I conceive some scattered notions about a superior power to be of singular use for the common people, as furnishing excellent materials to keep children quiet when they grow peevish, and providing topics of amusement in a tedious winter-night.

Lastly, 'tis proposed as a singular advantage, that the abolishing of Christianity will very much contribute to the uniting of Protestants, by en-larging the terms of communion so as to take in all sorts of dissenters, who are now shut out of the pale upon account of a few ceremonies which all sides confess to be things indifferent: that this alone will effectually answer the great ends of a scheme for comprehension, by opening a large noble gate, at which all bodies may enter; whereas the chaffering with dissenters, and dodging about this or t'other ceremony, is but like opening a few wickets, and leaving them at jar, by which no more than one can get in at a time, and that, not without stooping, and sideling, and squeezing his body.

To all this I anwer that there is one darling inclination of mankind, which usually affects to be a retainer to religion, though she be neither its parent, its godmother, or its friend; I mean the spirit of opposition, that lived long before Christianity, and can easily subsist without it. Let us, for instance, examine wherein the opposition of sectaries among us consists, we shall find Christianity to have no share in it at all. Does the Gospel anywhere prescribe a starched, squeezed countenance, a stiff, formal gait, a singularity of manners and habit, or any affected modes of speech different from the reasonable part of mankind? Yet, if Christianity did lend its name to stand in the gap, and to employ or divert these humors, they must of necessity be spent in contraventions to the laws of the land, and disturbance of the public peace. There is a portion of enthusiasm assigned to every nation, which, if it hath not proper objects to work on, will burst out, and set all into a flame. If the quiet of a state can be bought by only flinging men a few ceremonies to devour, it is a purchase no wise man would refuse. Let the mastiffs amuse themselves about a sheep's skin stuffed with hay, provided it will keep them from worrying the flock. The institution of convents abroad seems in one point a strain of great wisdom, there being few irregularities in human passions, which may not have recourse to vent themselves in some of those orders, which are so many retreats for the speculative, the melancholy, the proud, the silent, the politic and the morose, to spend themselves, and evaporate the noxious particles; for each of whom we in this island are forced to provide a several sect of religion, to keep them quiet: and whenever Christianity shall be abolished, the legislature must find some other expedient to employ and entertain them. For what imports it how large a gate you open, if there will be always left a number who place a pride and a merit in not coming in?

Having thus considered the most important objections against Christianity and the chief advantages proposed by the abolishing thereof, I shall now with equal difference and submission to wiser judgments as before, proceed to mention a few inconveniences that may happen, if the Gospel should be repealed; which perhaps the projectors may not have sufficiently considered.

And first, I am very sensible how much the gentlemen of wit and pleasure are apt to murmur, and be choked at the sight of so many draggled-tail parsons, that happen to fall in their way, and offend their eyes; but at the same time, these wise reformers do not consider what an advantage and felicity it is, for great wits to be always provided with objects of scorn and contempt, in order to exercise and improve their talents, and divert their spleen from falling on each other or on themselves; especially when all this may be done without the least imaginable danger to their persons.

And to urge another argument of a parallel nature: if Christianity were once abolished, how could the freethinkers, the strong reasoners, and the men of profound learning, be able to find another subject so calculated in all points whereon to display their abilities? What wonderful productions of wit should we be deprived of, from those whose genius by continual practice hath been wholly turned upon raillery and invectives against religion, and would therefore never be able to shine or distinguish themselves upon any other subject! We are daily complaining of the great decline of wit among us, and would we take away the greatest, perhaps the only, topic we have left? Who would ever have suspected Asgil for a wit, or Toland for a philosopher, if the inexhaustible stock of Christianity had not been at hand to provide them with materials? What other subject, through all art or nature, could have produced Tindal for a profound author, or furnished him with readers? It is the wise choice of the subject that alone adorns and distinguishes the writer. For, had a hundred such pens as these been employed on the side of religion, they would have immediately sunk into silence and oblivion.

Nor do I think it wholly groundless, or my fears altogether imaginary, that the abolishing of Christianity may perhaps bring the Church into danger, or at least put the senate to the trouble of another securing vote. I desire I may not be mistaken: I am far from presuming to affirm or think that the Church is in danger at present, or as things now stand; but we know not how soon it may be so when the Christian religion is repealed. As plausible as this project seems, there may a dangerous design lurk under it: Nothing can be more notorious, than that the Atheists, Deists, Socinians, Antitrinitarians, and other subdivisions of freethinkers, are persons of little zeal for the present ecclesiastical establishment: Their declared opinion is for repealing the Sacramental Test: they are very different with regard to ceremonies; nor do they hold the *jus divinum* of Episcopacy. Therefore this may be intended as one politic step toward altering the constitution of the Church established, and setting up Presbytery in the stead, which I leave to be further considered by those at the helm.

In the last place, I think nothing can be more plain, than that by this expedient, we shall run into the evil we chiefly pretend to avoid; and that the abolishment of the Christian religion will be the readiest course we can take to introduce popery. And I am the more inclined to this opinion, because we know it has been the constant practice of the Jesuits to send over emissaries with instructions to personate themselves members of the several prevailing sects among us. So it is recorded, that they have at sundry times appeared in the guise of Presbyterians, Anabaptists, Independents and Quakers, according as any of these were most in credit; so, since the fashion hath been taken up of exploding religion, the popish missionaries have not been wanting to mix with the freethinkers; among whom, Toland the great oracle of the Antichristians is an Irish priest, the son of an Irish priest; and the most learned and ingenious author of a book called "The *Rights* of the Christian Church," was in a proper juncture reconciled to the Romish faith, whose true son, as appears by a hundred passages in his treatise, he still continues. Perhaps I could add some others to the number; but the fact is beyond dispute, and the reasoning they proceed by is right: for, supposing Christianity to be extinguished, the people will never be at ease till they find out some other method of worship; which will as infallibly produce superstition, as this will end in popery.

And therefore, if notwithstanding all I have said, it still be thought necessary to have a bill brought in for repealing Christianity, I would humbly offer an amendment; that instead of the word, Christianity, may be put religion in general; which I conceive will much better answer all the good ends proposed by the projectors of it. For, as long as we leave in being a God and his providence, with all the necessary consequences which curious and inquisitive men will be apt to draw from such premises, we do not strike at the root of the evil, though we should ever so effectually annihilate the present scheme of the Gospel: for of what use is freedom of thought, if it will not produce freedom of action, which is the sole end, how remote soever in appearance, of all objections against Christianity? And, therefore, the freethinkers consider it as a sort of edifice, wherein all the parts have such a mutual dependence on each other, that if you happen to pull out one single nail, the whole fabric must fall to the ground. This was happily expressed by him who had heard of a text brought for proof of the Trinity, which in an ancient manuscript was differently read; he thereupon immediately took the hint, and by a sudden deduction of a long *sorites,* most logically concluded; "Why, if it be as you say, I may safely whore and drink on, and defy the parson." From which, and many the like instances easy to be produced, I think nothing can be more manifest than that the quarrel is not against any particular points of hard digestion in the Christian system, but against religion in general; which, by laying restraints on human nature, is supposed the great enemy to the freedom of thought and action.

Upon the whole, if it shall still be thought for the benefit of Church and States, that Christainity be abolished, I conceive, however, it may be more convenient to defer the execution to a time of peace, and not venture in this conjuncture to disoblige our allies, who, as it falls out, are all Christians, and many of them, by the prejudices of their education, so bigoted, as to place a sort of pride in the appellation. If upon being rejected by them, we are to trust an alliance with the Turk, we shall find ourselves much deceived: for, as he is too remote, and generally engaged in war with the Persian emperor, so his people would be more scandalized at our infidelity, than our Christian neighbors. For they are not only strict servers of religious worship, but what is worse, believe a God; which is more than required of us even while we preserve the name of Christians.

To conclude: Whatever some may think of the great advantages to trade by this favorite scheme, I do very much apprehend, that in six months time after the act is passed for the extirpation of the Gospel, the Bank, and East-India Stock, may fall at least one *per cent*. And since that is fifty times more than ever the wisdom of our age thought fit to venture for the preservation of Christianity, there is no reason we should be at so great a loss, merely for the sake of destroying it.

LETTERS FROM HELL
C. S. LEWIS

LETTER II

My dear Wormwood,

I note with grave displeasure that your patient has become a Christian. Do not indulge the hope that you will escape the usual penalties; indeed, in your better moments, I trust you would hardly even wish to do so. In the meantime we must make the best of the situation. There is no need to despair; hundreds of these adult converts have been reclaimed after a brief sojourn in the Enemy's camp and are now with us. All the *habits* of the patient, both mental and bodily, are still in our favor.

One of our great allies at present is the Church itself. Do not misunderstand me. I do not mean the Church as we see her spread out through all time and space and rooted in eternity, terrible as an army with banners. That, I confess, is a spectacle which makes our boldest tempters uneasy. But fortunately it is quite invisible to these humans. All your patient sees is the half-finished, sham Gothic erection on the new building estate. When he goes inside, he sees the local grocer with rather an oily expression on his face bustling up to offer him one shiny little book containing a liturgy which neither of them understands, and one shabby little book containing corrupt texts of a number of religious lyrics, mostly bad, and in very small print. When he gets to his pew and looks round him he sees just that selection of his neighbors whom he has hitherto avoided. You want to lean pretty heavily on those neighbors. Make his mind flit to and fro between an expression like "the body of Christ" and the actual faces in the next pew. It matters very little, of course, what kind of people that

From C. S. Lewis, *The Screwtape Letters* (London, Geoffrey Bles, Ltd., 1942; New York The Macmillan Company, 1944).

next pew really contains. You may know one of them to be a great warrior on the Enemy's side. No matter. Your patient, thanks to Our Father below, is a fool. Provided that any of those neighbors sing out of tune, or have boots that squeak, or double chins, or odd clothes, the patient will quite easily believe that their religion must therefore be somehow ridiculous. At his present stage, you see, he has an idea of "Christians" in his mind which he supposes to be spiritual but which, in fact, is largely pictorial. His mind is full of togas and sandals and armor and bare legs and the mere fact that the other people in church wear modern clothes is a real—though of course an unconscious—difficulty to him. Never let it come to the surface; never let him ask what he expected them to look like. Keep everything hazy in his mind now, and you will have all eternity wherein to amuse yourself by producing in him the peculiar kind of clarity which Hell affords.

Work hard, then, on the disappointment or anticlimax which is certainly coming to the patient during his first few weeks as a churchman. The Enemy allows this disappointment to occur on the threshold of every human endeavor. It occurs when the boy who has been enchanted in the nursery by *Stories from the Odyssey* buckles down to really learning Greek. It occurs when lovers have got married and begin the real task of learning to live together. In every department of life it marks the transition from dreaming aspiration to laborious doing. The Enemy takes this risk because He has a curious fantasy of making all these disgusting little human vermin into what He calls His "free" lovers and servants—"sons" is the word He uses, with His inveterate love of degrading the whole spiritual world by unnatural liaisons with the two-legged animals. Desiring their freedom, He therefore refuses to carry them, by their mere affections and habits, to any of the goals which He sets before them: He leaves them to "do it on their own." And there lies our opportunity. But also, remember, there lies our danger. If once they get through this initial dryness successfully, they become much less dependent on emotion and therefore much harder to tempt.

I have been writing hitherto on the assumption that the people in the next pew afford no *rational* ground for disappointment. Of course if they do—if the patient knows that the woman with the absurd hat is a fanatical bridgeplayer or the man with squeaky boots a miser and an extortioner—then your task is so much the easier. All you then have to do is to keep out of his mind the question "If I, being what I am, can consider that I am in some sense a Christian, why should the different vices of those people in the next pew prove that their religion is mere hypocrisy and convention?" You may ask whether it is possible to keep such an obvious thought from occurring even to a human mind. It is, Wormwood, it is! Handle him properly and it simply won't come into his head. He has not been anything like long enough with the Enemy to have any real humility yet. What he says, even on his knees, about his own sinfulness is all parrot talk. At bottom, he still believes he has run up a very favorable credit-balance in the Enemy's ledger by allowing himself to be converted, and thinks that he is showing great humility and condescension in going to church with these "smug," commonplace neighbors at all. Keep him in that state of mind as long as you can.

Your affectionate uncle
Screwtape

LETTER XXIII

My dear Wormwood,

Through this girl and her disgusting family the patient is now getting to know more Christians every day, and very intelligent Christians too. For a long time it will be quite impossible to *remove* spirituality from his life. Very well then; we must *corrupt* it. No doubt you have often practiced transforming yourself into an angel of light as a parade-ground exercise. Now is the time to do it in the face of the Enemy. The World and the Flesh have failed us; a third Power remains. And success of this third kind is the most glorious of all. A spoiled saint, a Pharisee, an inquisitor, or a magician, makes better sport in Hell than a mere common tyrant or debauchee.

Looking round your patient's new friends I find that the best point of attack would be the border-line between theology and politics. Several of his new friends are very much alive to the social implications of their religion. That, in itself, is a bad thing; but good can be made out of it.

You will find that a good many Christian-political writers think that Christianity began going wrong, and departing from the doctrine of its Founder, at a very early stage. Now this idea must be used by us to encourage once again the conception of a "historical Jesus" to be found by clearing away later "accretions and perversions" and then to be contrasted with the whole Christian tradition. In the last generation we promoted the construction of such a "historical Jesus" on liberal and humanitarian lines; we are now putting forward a new "historical Jesus" on Marxian, catastrophic, and revolutionary lines. The advantages of these constructions, which we intend to change every thirty years or so, are manifold. In the first place they all tend to direct men's devotion to something which does not exist, for each "historical Jesus" is unhistorical. The documents say what they say and cannot be added to; each new "historical Jesus" therefore has to be got out of them by suppression at one point and exaggeration at another, and by that sort of guessing (*brilliant* is the adjective we teach humans to apply to it) on which no one would risk ten shillings in ordinary life, but which is enough to produce a crop of new Napoleons, new Shakespeares, and new Swifts, in every publisher's autumn list. In the second place, all such constructions place the importance of their Historical Jesus in some peculiar theory He is supposed to have promulgated. He has to be a "great man" in the modern sense of the word—one standing at the terminus of some centrifugal and unbalanced line of thought—a crank vending a panacea. We thus distract men's minds from Who He is, and what He did. We first make Him solely a teacher, and then conceal the very substantial agreement between His teachings and those of all other great moral teachers. For humans must not be allowed to notice that all great moralists are sent by the Enemy not to inform men but to remind them, to restate the primeval moral platitudes against our continual concealment of them. We make the Sophists: He raises up a Socrates to answer them. Our third aim is, by these constructions, to destroy the devotional life. For the real presence of the Enemy, otherwise experienced by men in prayer and sacrament, we substitute a merely probable, remote, shadowy, and uncouth figure, one who spoke a strange language and died a long time ago. Such an object cannot in fact be worshiped. Instead of the Creator adored by its creature, you soon have merely a leader acclaimed by a partisan, and finally a distinguished character approved by a judicious historian. And fourthly, besides being unhistorical in the Jesus it depicts, religion of this kind is false to history in another sense. No nation, and few individuals, are really brought into the Enemy's camp by the historical study of the biography of Jesus, simply as biography. Indeed materials for a full biography have been withheld from men. The earliest converts were converted by a single historical fact (the Resurrection) and a single theological doctrine (the Redemption) operating on a sense of sin which they already had—and sin, not against some new fancy-dress law produced as a novelty by a "great man," but against the old, platitudinous, universal moral law which they had been taught by their nurses and mothers. The "Gospels" come later and were written not to make Christians but to edify Christians already made.

The "Historical Jesus" then, however dangerous he may seem to be to us at some particular point, is always to be encouraged. About the general connection between Christianity and politics, our position is more delicate. Certainly we do not want men to allow their Christianity to flow over into their political life, for the establishment of anything like a really just society would be a major disaster. On the other hand we do want, and want very much, to make men treat Christianity as a means; preferably, of course, as a means to their own advancement, but, failing that, as a means to anything—even to social justice. The thing to do is to get a man at first to value social justice as a thing which the Enemy demands, and then work him on to the stage at which he values Christianity because it may produce social justice. For the Enemy will not be used as a convenience. Men or nations who think they can revive the Faith in order to make a good society might just as well think they can use the stairs of Heaven as a short cut to the nearest chemist's shop. Fortunately it is quite easy to coax humans round this little corner. Only today I have found a passage in a Christian writer where he recommends his own version of Christianity on the ground that "only such a faith can outlast the death of old cultures and the birth of new civilizations." You see the little rift? "Believe this, not because it is true, but for some other reason." That's the game,

Your affectionate uncle
Screwtape

LETTER XXV

My dear Wormwood,

The real trouble about the set your patient is living in is that it is *merely* Christian. They all have individual interests, of course, but the bond remains mere Christianity. What we want, if men become Christians at all, is to keep them in the state of mind I call "Christianity And." You know—Christianity and the Crisis, Christianity and the New Psychology, Christianity and the New Order, Christianity and Faith Healing, Christianity and Psychical Research, Christianity and Vegetarianism, Christianity and Spelling Reform. If they must be Christians let them at least be Christians with a difference. Substitute for the faith itself some Fashion with a Christian coloring. Work on their horror of the Same Old Thing.

The horror of the Same Old Thing is one of the most valuable passions we have produced in the human heart—an endless source of heresies in religion, folly in counsel, infidelity and marriage, and inconstancy in friendship. The humans live in time, and experience reality successively. To experience much of it, therefore, they must experience many different things; in other words, they must experience change. And since they need change, the Enemy (being a hedonist at heart) has made change pleasurable to them, just as He has made eating pleasurable. But since He does not wish them to make change, any more than eating, an end in itself, He has balanced the love of change in them by a love of permanence. He has contrived to gratify both tastes together in the very world He has made, by that union of change and permanence which we call Rhythm. He gives them the seasons, each season different yet every year the same, so that spring is always felt as a novelty yet always as the recurrence of an immemorial theme. He gives them in His Church a spiritual year; they change from a fast to a feast, but it is the same feast as before.

Now just as we pick out and exaggerate the pleasure of eating to produce gluttony, so we pick out this natural pleasantness of change and twist it into a demand for absolute novelty. This demand is entirely our workmanship. If we neglect our duty, men will be not only contented but transported by the mixed novelty and familiarity of snowdrops *this* January, sunrise *this* morning, plum pudding *this* Christmas. Children, until we have taught them better, will be perfectly happy with a seasonal round of games in which conkers succeed hopscotch as regularly as autumn follows summer. Only by our incessant efforts is the demand for infinite, or un-rhythmical, change kept up.

This demand is valuable in various ways. In the first place it diminishes pleasure while increasing desire. The pleasure of novelty is by its very nature more subject than any other to the law of diminishing returns. And continued novelty costs money, so that the desire for it spells avarice or unhappiness or both. And again, the more rapacious this desire, the sooner it must eat up all the innocent sources of pleasure and pass on to those the Enemy forbids. Thus by inflaming the horror of the Same Old Thing we have recently made the Arts, for example, less dangerous to us than perhaps, they have ever been, "low-brow" and "high-brow" artists alike being now daily drawn into fresh, and still fresh, excesses of lasciviousness, unreason, cruelty, and pride. Finally, the desire for novelty is indispensable if we are to produce Fashions or Vogues.

The use of Fashions in thought is to distract the attention of men from their real dangers. We direct the fashionable outcry of each generation against those vices of which it is least in danger and fix its approval on the virtue nearest to that vice which we are trying to make endemic. The game is to have them all running about with fire extinguishers whenever there is a flood, and all crowding to that side of the boat which is already nearly gunwale under. Thus we make it fashionable to expose the dangers of enthusiasm at the very moment when they are all really becoming worldly and lukewarm; a century later, when we are really making them all Byronic and drunk with emotion, the fashionable outcry is directed against the dangers of the mere "understanding." Cruel ages are put on their guard against Sentimentality, feckless and idle ones against Respectability, lech-erous ones against Puritanism; and whenever all men are really hastening to be slaves or tyrants we make Liberalism the prime bogey.

But the greatest triumph of all is to elevate this horror of the Same Old Thing into a philosophy so that nonsense in the intellect may rein-force corruption in the will. It is here that the general Evolutionary or Historical character of modern European thought (partly our work) comes in so useful. The Enemy loves platitudes. Of a proposed course of action He wants men, so far as I can see, to ask very simple questions; is it righteous? is it prudent? is it possible? Now if we can keep men asking "Is it in accordance with the general movement of our time? Is it progressive or reactionary? Is this the way that History is going?" they will neglect the relevant questions. And the questions they *do* ask are, of course, unanswer-able; for they do not know the future, and what the future will be depends very largely on just those choices which they now invoke the future to help them to make. As a result, while their minds are buzzing in this vacuum, we have the better chance to slip in and bend them to the action *we* have decided on. And great work has already been done. Once they knew that some changes were for the better, and others for the worse, and others again indifferent. We have largely removed this knowledge. For the descriptive adjective "unchanged' we have substituted the emotional adjective "stagnant." We have trained them to think of the Future as a promised land which favored heroes attain—not as something which everyone reaches at the rate of sixty minutes an hour, whatever he does, whoever he is.

Your affectionate uncle
Screwtape

THE PROGRESS OF THE CHRISTIAN RELIGION | *EDWARD GIBBON*

Importance of the Inquiry. A candid but rational inquiry into the progress and establishment of Christianity may be considered as a very essential part of the history of the Roman empire. While that great body was invaded by open violence, or undermined by slow decay, a pure and humble religion gently insinuated itself into the minds of men, grew up in silence and obscurity, derived new vigor from opposition, and finally erected the triumphant banner of the Cross on the ruins of the Capitol. Nor was the influence of Christianity confined to the period or to the limits of the Roman empire. After a revolution of thirteen or fourteen centuries, that religion is still professed by the nations of Europe, the most distinguished portion of human kind in arts and learning as well as in arms. By the industry and zeal of the Europeans it has been widely diffused to the most distant shores of Asia and Africa; and by the means of their colonies has been firmly established from Canada to Chile, in a world unknown to the ancients.

Its Difficulties. But this inquiry, however useful or entertaining, is attended with two peculiar difficulties. The scanty and suspicious materials of ecclesiastical history seldom enable us to dispel the dark cloud that hangs over the first age of the Church. The great law of impartiality too often obliges us to reveal the imperfections of the uninspired teachers and believers of the Gospel; and, to a careless observer, *their* faults may seem to cast a shade on the faith which they professed. But the scandal of the pious Christian and the fallacious triumph of the Infidel should cease as soon as they recollect not only *by whom,* but likewise *to whom,* the Divine Revelation was given. The theologian may indulge the pleasing task of describing Religion as she descended from heaven arrayed in her native purity. A more melancholy duty is imposed on the historian. He must discover the inevitable mixture of error and corruption which she contracted in a long residence upon earth, among a weak and degenerate race of beings.

From *Decline and Fall of the Roman Empire,* Chap. 15 (1776).

Five Causes of the Growth of Christianity. Our curiosity is naturally prompted to inquire by what means the Christian faith obtained so remarkable a victory over the established religions of the earth. To this inquiry an obvious but satisfactory answer may be returned—that it was owing to the convincing evidence of the doctrine itself and to the ruling providence of its great Author. But as truth and reason seldom find so favorable a reception in the world, and as the wisdom of Providence frequently condescends to use the passions of the human heart and the general circumstances of mankind as instruments to execute its purpose, we may still be permitted, though with becoming submission, to ask, not indeed what were the first, but what were the secondary causes of the rapid growth of the Christian Church. It will perhaps appear that it was most effectually favored and assisted by the five following causes:

I.   The inflexible (and, if we may use the expression, the intolerant) zeal of the Christians, derived, it is true, from the Jewish religion, but purified from the narrow and unsocial spirit which, instead of inviting, had deterred the Gentile from embracing the law of Moses. II. The doctrine of a future life, improved by every additional circumstance which could give weight and efficacy to that important truth. III. The miraculous powers ascribed to the primitive Church. IV. The pure and austere morals of the Christians. V. The union and discipline of the Christian republic, which gradually formed an independent and increasing state in the heart of the Roman empire....

II.   The Second Cause: The Doctrine of the Immortality of the Soul among the Philosophers.   The writings of Cicero represent in the most lively colors the ignorance, the errors, and the uncertainty of the ancient philosophers with regard to the immortality of the soul. When they are desirous of arming their disciples against the fear of death, they inculcate, as an obvious though melancholy position, that the fatal stroke of our dissolution releases us from the calamities of life, and that those can no longer suffer who no longer exist. Yet there were a few sages of Greece and Rome who had conceived a more exalted, and in some respects a juster, idea of human nature, though it must be confessed that in the sublime inquiry their reason had been often guided by their imagination, and that their imagination had been prompted by their vanity. When they viewed with complacency the extent of their own mental powers, when they exercised the various faculties of memory, of fancy, and of judgment in the most profound speculations or the most important labors, and when they reflected on the desire of fame, which transported them into future ages, far beyond the bounds of death and of the grave, they were unwilling to confound themselves with the beasts of the field, or to suppose that a being for whose dignity they entertained the most sincere admiration could be limited to a spot of earth and to a few years of duration. With this favorable prepossession, they summoned to their aid the science, or rather the language, of Metaphysics. They soon discovered that, as none of the properties of matter will apply to the operations of the mind, the human soul must consequently be a substance distinct from the body—pure, simple, and spiritual, incapable of dissolution, and susceptible of a much higher degree of virtue and happiness after the release from its corporeal prison. From these specious and noble principles the philosophers who trod in the footsteps of Plato deduced a very unjustifiable conclusion, since they asserted not only the future immortality, but the past eternity of the human soul, which they were too apt to consider as a portion of the infinite and self-existing spirit which pervades and sustains the universe. A doctrine thus removed beyond the senses and the experience of mankind might serve to amuse the leisure of a philosophic mind, or, in the silence of solitude, it might sometimes impart a ray of comfort to desponding virtue; but the faint impression which had been received in the schools was soon obliterated by the commerce and business of active life. We are sufficiently acquainted with the eminent persons who flourished in the age of Cicero and of the first Caesars—with their actions, their characters, and their motives—to be assured that their conduct in this life was never regulated by any serious conviction of the rewards or punishments of a future state. At the bar and in the senate of Rome the ablest orators were not apprehensive of giving offense to their hearers by exposing that doctrine as an idle and extravagant opinion, which was rejected with contempt by every man of a liberal education and understanding. . . .

When the promise of eternal happiness was proposed to mankind on condition of adopting the faith and of observing the precepts of the Gospel, it is no wonder that so advantageous an offer should have been accepted by great numbers of every religion, of every rank, and of every province in the Roman empire. The ancient Christians were animated by a contempt for their present existence, and by a just confidence of immortality, of which the doubtful and imperfect faith of modern ages cannot give us any adequate notion. In the primitive Church the influence of truth was very powerfully strengthened by an opinion which, however it may deserve respect for its usefulness and antiquity, has not been found agreeable to experience. It was universally believed that the end of the world, and the kingdom of heaven, were at hand. The near approach of this wonderful event had been predicted by the apostles; the tradition of it was preserved by their earliest disciples; and those who understood in their literal sense the discourses of Christ himself were obliged to expect the second and glorious coming of the Son of Man in the clouds, before that generation was totally extinguished which had beheld his humble condition upon earth, and which might still be witness of the calamities of the Jews under Vespasian or Hadrian. The revolution of seventeen centuries has instructed us not to press too closely the mysterious language of prophecy and revelation; but as long as, for wise purposes, this error was permitted to subsist in the Church, it was productive of the most salutary effects on the faith and practice of Christians, who lived in the awful expectation of that moment when the globe itself, and all the various races of mankind, should tremble at the appearance of their divine Judge.

Doctrine of the Millennium. The ancient and popular doctrine of the millennium was intimately connected with the second coming of Christ. As the works of the creation had been finished in six days, their duration, in their present state, according to a tradition which was attributed to the prophet Elijah, was fixed to six thousand years. By the same analogy it was inferred that this long period of labor and contention, which was now almost elapsed, would be succeeded by a joyful Sabbath of a thousand years; and that Christ, with the triumphant band of the saints, and the elect who had escaped death, or who had been miraculously revived, would reign upon earth till the time appointed for the last and general resurrection. So pleasing was this hope to the mind of believers, that the *New Jerusalem,* the seat of this blissful kingdom, was quickly adorned with all the gayest colors of the imagination. A felicity consisting only of pure and spiritual pleasure would have appeared too refined for its inhabitants, who were still supposed to possess their human nature and senses. A garden of Eden, with the amusements of the pastoral life, was no longer suited to the advanced state of society which prevailed under the Roman empire. A city was therefore erected of gold and precious stones, and a supernatural plenty of corn and wine was bestowed on the adjacent territory; in the free enjoyment of whose spontaneous productions the happy and benevolent people was never to be restrained by any jealous laws of exclusive property. The assurance of such a millennium was carefully inculcated by a succession of fathers from Justin Martyr and Irenaeus, who conversed with the immediate disciples of the apostles, down to Lactantius, who was preceptor to the son of Constantine. Though it might not be universally received, it appears to have been the reigning sentiment of the orthodox believers; and it seems so well adapted to the desires and apprehensions of mankind that it must have contributed in a very considerable degree to the progress of the Christian faith. But when the edifice of the Church was almost completed, the temporary support was laid aside. The doctrine of Christ's reign upon earth was at first treated as a profound allegory; was considered by degrees as a doubtful and useless opinion; and was at length rejected as the absurd invention of heresy and fanaticism. A mysterious prophecy, which still forms a part of the sacred canon, but which was thought to favor the exploded sentiment, has very narrowly escaped the proscription of the Church.

Conflagration of Rome and of the World. Whilst the happiness and glory of a temporal reign were promised to the disciples of Christ, the most dreadful calamities were denounced against an unbelieving world. The edification of the New Jerusalem was to advance by equal steps with the destruction of the mystic Babylon; and as long as the emperors who reigned before Constantine persisted in the profession of idolatry, the epithet of Babylon was applied to the city and to the empire of Rome. A regular series was prepared of all the moral and physical evils which can afflict a flourishing nation: intestine discord, and the invasion of the fiercest barbarians from the unknown regions of the North; pestilence and famine, comets and eclipses, earthquakes and inundations. All these were only so many preparatory and alarming signs of the great catastrophe of Rome, when the country of the Scipios and Caesars should be consumed by a flame from heaven, and the City of the Seven Hills, with her palaces, her temples, and her triumphal arches, should be buried in a vast lake of fire and brimstone. It might, however, afford some consolation to Roman vanity that the period of their empire would be that of the world itself; which, as it had once perished by the element of water, was destined to experience a second and a speedy destruction from the element of fire. In the opinion of a general conflagration, the faith of the Christian very happily coincided with the tradition of the East, the philosophy of the Stoics, and the analogy of nature; and even the country which, from religious motives, had been chosen for the origin and principal scene of the conflagration was the best adapted for that purpose by natural and physical causes—by its deep caverns, beds of sulphur, and numerous volcanoes, of which those of Aetna, of Vesuvius, and of Lipari exhibit a very imperfect representation. The calmest and most intrepid skeptic could not refuse to acknowledge that the destruction of the present system of the world by fire was in itself extremely probable. The Christian, who founded his belief much less on the fallacious arguments of reason than on the authority of tradition and the interpretation of Scripture, expected it with terror and confidence as a certain and approaching event; and, as his mind was perpetually filled with the solemn idea, he considered every disaster that happened to the empire as an infallible symptom of an expiring world.

The Pagans Devoted to Eternal Punishment.   The condemnation of the wisest and most virtuous of the pagans on account of their ignorance or disbelief of the divine truth seems to offend the reason and the humanity of the present age. But the primitive Church, whose faith was of a much firmer consistence, delivered over, without hesitation, to eternal torture the far greater part of the human species. A charitable hope might perhaps be indulged in favor of Socrates, or some other sages of antiquity who had consulted the light of reason before that of the Gospel had arisen. But it was unanimously affirmed that those who, since the birth or the death of Christ, had obstinately persisted in the worship of the demons, neither deserved nor could expect a pardon from the irritated justice of the Deity. These rigid sentiments, which had been unknown to the ancient world, appear to have infused a spirit of bitterness into a system of love and harmony. The ties of blood and friendship were frequently torn asunder by the difference of religious faith; and the Christians who, in this world, found themselves oppressed by the power of the pagans, were sometimes seduced by resentment and spiritual pride to delight in the prospect of their future triumph. "You are fond of spectacles," exclaims the stern Tertullian; "expect the greatest of all spectacles—the last and eternal judgment of the universe. How shall I admire, how laugh, how rejoice, how exalt, when I behold so many proud monarchs and fancied gods groaning in the lowest abyss of darkness; so many magistrates, who persecuted the name of the Lord, liquefying in fiercer fires than they ever kindled against the Christians; so many sage philosophers blushing in red-hot flames with their deluded scholars; so many celebrated poets trembling before the tribunal, not of Minos, but of Christ; so many tragedians, more tuneful in the expression of their own sufferings; so many dancers—" But the humanity of the reader will permit me to draw a veil over the rest of this infernal description which the zealous African pursues in a long variety of affected and unfeeling witticisms.

Were Often Converted by Their Fears. Doubtless there were many among the primitive Christians of a temper more suitable to the meekness and charity of their profession. There were many who felt a sincere compassion for the danger of their friends and countrymen, and who exerted the most benevolent zeal to save them from the impending destruction. The careless polytheist, assailed by new and unexpected terrors, against which neither his priests nor his philosophers could afford him any certain protection, was very frequently terrified and subdued by the menace of eternal tortures. His fears might assist the progress of his faith and reason; and, if he could once persuade himself to suspect that the Christian religion might possibly be true, it became an easy task to convince him that it was the safest and most prudent party that he could possibly embrace.

III. The Third Cause: Miraculous Powers of the Primitive Church. The supernatural gifts which even in this life were ascribed to the Christians above the rest of mankind must have conduced to their own comfort, and very frequently to the conviction of infidels. Besides the occasional prodigies which might sometimes be effected by the immediate interposition of the Deity when He suspended the laws of nature for the service of religion, the Christian Church, from the time of the apostles and their first disciples, has claimed an uninterrupted succession of miraculous powers; the gift of tongues, of vision, and of prophecy; the power of expelling demons, of healing the sick, and of raising the dead. The knowledge of foreign languages was frequently communicated to the contemporaries of Irenaeus, though Irenaeus himself was left to struggle with the difficulties of a barbarous dialect whilst he preached the Gospel to the natives of Gaul. The divine inspiration, whether it was conveyed in the form of a waking or of a sleeping vision, is described as a favor very liberally bestowed on all ranks of the faithful, on women as on elders, on boys as well as upon bishops. When their devout minds were sufficiently prepared by a course of prayer, of fasting, and of vigils, to receive the extraordinary impulse, they were transported out of their senses, and delivered in ecstasy what was inspired, being mere organs of the Holy Spirit, just as a pipe or flute is of him who blows into it. We may add that the design of these visions was, for the most part, either to disclose the future history or to guide the present administration of the Church. The expulsion of the demons from the bodies of those unhappy persons whom they had been permitted to torment was considered as a signal though ordinary triumph of religion, and is repeatedly alleged by the apologists as the most convincing evidence of the truth of Christianity. The awful ceremony was usually performed in a public manner, and in the presence of a great number of spectators; the patient was relieved by the power or the skill of the exorcist, and the vanquished demon was heard to confess that he was one of the fabled gods of antiquity who had impiously usurped the adoration of mankind. But the miraculous cure of diseases of the most inveterate or even preternatural kind can no longer occasion any surprise when we recollect that in the days of Irenaeus, about the end of the second century, the resurrection of the dead was very far from being esteemed an uncommon event; that the miracle was frequently performed on necessary occasions by great fasting and the joint supplication of the Church of the place; and that the persons thus restored to their prayers had lived afterwards among them many years. At such a period, when faith could boast of so many wonderful victories over death, it seems difficult to account for the skepticism of those philosophers who still rejected and derided the doctrine of the resurrection. A noble Grecian had rested on this important ground the whole controversy, and promised Theophilus, Bishop of Antioch, that if he could be gratified with the sight of a single person who had been actually raised from the dead, he would immediately embrace the Christian religion. It is somewhat remarkable that the prelate of the first Eastern Church, however anxious for the conversion of his friend, thought proper to decline this fair and reasonable challenge.

Their Truth Contested. The miracles of the primitive Church, after obtaining the sanction of ages, have been lately attacked in a very free and ingenious inquiry, which, though it has met with the most favorable reception for the public, appears to have excited a general scandal among the divines of our own as well as of the other Protestant churches of Europe. Our different sentiments on this subject will be much less influenced by any particular arguments than by our habits of study and reflection, and, above all, by the degree of the evidence which we have accustomed ourselves to require for the proof of a miraculous event. The duty of an historian does not call upon him to interpose his private judgment in this nice and important controversy; but he ought not to dissemble the difficulty of adopting such a theory as may reconcile the interest of religion with that of reason, of making a proper application of that theory, and of defining with precision the limits of that happy period, exempt from error and from deceit, to which we might be disposed to extend the gift of supernatural powers. From the first of the fathers to the last of the popes, a succession of bishops, of saints, of martyrs, and of miracles is continued without interruption; and the progress of superstition was so gradual, and almost imperceptible, that we know not in what particular link we should break the chain of tradition. Every age bears testimony to the wonderful events by which it was distinguished, and its testimony appears no less weighty and respectable than that of the preceding generation, till we are insensibly led on to accuse our own inconsistency if, in the eighth or in the twelfth century, we deny to the venerable Bede or to the holy Bernard the same degree of confidence which, in the second century, we had so liberally granted to Justin or to Irenaeus. If the truth of any of those miracles is appreciated by their apparent use and propriety, every age had unbelievers to convince, heretics to confute, and idolatrous nations to convert; and sufficient motives might always be produced to justify the interposition of Heaven. And yet, since every friend to revelation is persuaded of the reality, and every reasonable man is convinced of the cessation, of miraculous powers, it is evident that there must have been *some period* in which they were either suddenly or gradually withdrawn from the Christian Church. Whatever era is chosen for that purpose, the death of the apostles, the conversion of the Roman empire, or the extinction of the Arian heresy, the insensibility of the Christians who lived at that time will equally afford a just matter of surprise. They still supported their pretensions after they had lost their power. Credulity performed the office of faith; fanaticism was permitted to assume the language of inspiration, and the effects of accident or contrivance were ascribed to supernatural causes. The recent experience of genuine miracles should have instructed the Christian world in the ways of providence, and habituated their eye (if we may use a very inadequate expression) to the style of the Divine Artist. Should the most skillful painter of modern Italy presume to decorate his feeble imitations with the name of Raphael or of Correggio, the insolent fraud would be soon discovered and indignantly rejected.

Use of the Primitive Miracles. Whatever opinion may be entertained of the miracles of the primitive Church since the time of the apostles, this unresisting softness of temper, so conspicuous among the believers of the second and third centuries, proved of some accidental benefit to the cause of truth and religion. In modern times, a latent and even involuntary skepticism adheres to the most pious dispositions. Their admission of supernatural truths is much less an active consent than a cold and passive acquiescence. Accustomed long since to observe and to respect the invariable order of nature, our reason, or at least our imagination, is not sufficiently prepared to sustain the visible action of the Deity. But in the first ages of Christianity the situation of mankind was extremely different. The most curious, or the most credulous, among the pagans were often persuaded to enter into a society which asserted an actual claim of miraculous powers. The primitive Christians perpetually trod on mystic ground, and their minds were exercised by the habits of believing the most extraordinary events. They felt, or they fancied, that on every side they were incessantly assaulted by demons, comforted by visions, instructed by prophecy, and surprisingly delivered from danger, sickness, and from death itself, by the supplications of the Church. The real or imaginary prodigies of which they so frequently conceived themselves to be the objects, the instruments, or the spectators, very happily disposed them to adopt with the same ease, but with far greater justice, the authentic wonders of the evangelic history; and thus miracles that exceeded not the measure of their own experience inspired them with the most lively assurance of mysteries which were acknowledged to surpass the limits of their understanding. It is this deep impression of supernatural truths which has been so much celebrated under the name of faith—a state of mind described as the surest pledge of the divine favor and of future felicity, and recommended as the first or perhaps the only merit of a Christian. According to the more rigid doctors, the moral virtues, which may be equally practiced by infidels, are destitute of any value or efficacy in the work of our justification.

IV. The Fourth Cause: Virtues of the First Christians. But the primitive Christian demonstrated his faith by his virtues; and it was very justly supposed that the divine persuasion which enlightened or subdued the understanding must at the same time purify the heart and direct the actions of the believer. The first apologists of Christianity who justify the innocence of their brethren, and the writers of a later period who celebrate the sanctity of their ancestors, display, in the most lively colors, the reformation of manners which was introduced into the world by the preaching of the Gospel. As it is my intention to remark only such human causes as were permitted to second the influence of revelation, I shall slightly mention two motives which might naturally render the lives of the primitive Christians much purer and more austere than those of their pagan contemporaries or their degenerate successors—repentance for their past sins, and the laudable desire of supporting the reputation of the society in which they were engaged.

Effects of Their Repentance. It is a very ancient reproach, suggested by the ignorance or the malice of infidelity, that the Christians allured into their party the most atrocious criminals, who, as soon as they were touched by a sense of remorse, were easily persuaded to wash away, in the water of baptism, the guilt of their past conduct, for which the temples of the gods refused to grant them any expiation. But this reproach, when it is cleared from misrepresentation, contributes as much to the honor as it did to the increase of the Church. The friends of Christianity may acknowledge without a blush that many of the most eminent saints had been before their baptism the most abandoned sinners. Those persons who in the world had followed, though in an imperfect manner, the dictates of benevolence and propriety, derived such a calm satisfaction from the opinion of their own rectitude as rendered them much less susceptible of the sudden emotions of shame, of grief, and of terror, which have given birth to so many wonderful conversions. After the example of their Divine Master, the missionaries of the Gospel disdained not the society of men, and especially of women, oppressed by the consciousness, and very often by the effects, of their vices. As they emerged from sin and superstition to the glorious hope of immortality, they resolved to devote themselves to a life, not only of virtue, but of penitence. The desire of perfection became the ruling passion of their soul; and it is well known that, while reason embraces a cold mediocrity, our passions hurry us with rapid violence over the space which lies between the most opposite extremes.

Care of Their Reputation. When the new converts had been enrolled in the number of the faithful, and were admitted to the sacraments of the Church, they found themselves restrained from relapsing into their past disorders by another consideration of a less spiritual but of a very innocent and respectable nature. Any particular society that has departed from the great body of the nation, or the religion to which it belonged, immediately becomes the object of universal as well as invidious observation. In proportion to the smallness of its numbers, the character of the society may be affected by the virtue and vices of the persons who compose it; and every member is engaged to watch with the most vigilant attention over his own behavior, and over that of his brethren, since, as he must expect to incur a part of the common disgrace, he may hope to enjoy a share of the common reputation. When the Christians of Bithynia were brought before the tribunal of the younger Pliny, they assured the proconsul that, far from being engaged in any unlawful conspiracy, they were bound by a solemn obligation to abstain from the commission of those crimes which disturb the private or public peace of society, from theft, robbery, adultery, perjury, and fraud. Near a century afterwards, Tertullian with an honest pride could boast that very few Christians had suffered by the hand of the executioner, except on account of their religion. Their serious and sequestered life, averse to the gay luxury of the age, inured them to chastity, temperance, economy, and all the sober and domestic virtues. As the greater number were of some trade or profession, it was incumbent on them, by the strictest integrity and the fairest dealing, to remove the suspicions which the profane are too apt to conceive against the appearance of sanctity. The contempt of the world exercised them in the habits of humility, meekness, and patience. The more they were persecuted, the more closely they adhered to each other. Their mutual charity and unsuspecting confidence have been remarked by infidels, and were too often abused by perfidious friends.

Morality of the Fathers. It is a very honorable circumstance for the morals of the primitive Christians that even their faults, or rather errors, were derived from an excess of virtue. The bishops and doctors of the Church, whose evidence attests, and whose authority might influence, the professions, the principles, and even the practice of their contemporaries, had studied the Scriptures with less skill than devotion; and they often received in the most literal sense those rigid precepts of Christ and the apostles to which the prudence of succeeding commentators has applied a looser and more figurative mode of interpretation. Ambitious to exalt the perfection of the Gospel above the wisdom of philosophy, the zealous fathers have carried the duties of self-mortification, of purity, and of patience to a height which it is scarcely possible to attain, and much less to preserve, in our present state of weakness and corruption. A doctrine so extraordinary and so sublime must inevitably command the veneration of the people; but it was ill calculated to obtain the suffrage of those worldly philosophers who, in the conduct of this transitory life, consult only the feelings of nature and the interest of society.

Principles of Human Nature. There are two very natural propensities which we may distinguish in the most virtuous and liberal dispositions, the love of pleasure and the love of action. If the former is refined by art and learning, improved by the charms of social intercourse, and corrected by a just regard to economy, to health, and to reputation, it is productive of the greatest part of the happiness of private life. The love of action is a principle of a much stronger and more doubtful nature. It often leads to anger, to ambition, and to revenge; but when it is guided by the sense of propriety and benevolence, it becomes the parent of every virtue; and if those virtues are accompanied with equal abilities, a family, a state, or an empire may be indebted for its safety and prosperity to the undaunted courage of a single man. To the love of pleasure we may therefore ascribe most of the agreeable, to the love of action we may attribute most of the useful and respectable, qualifications. The character in which both the one and the other should be united and harmonized would seem to constitute the most perfect idea of human nature. The insensible and inactive disposition, which should be supposed alike destitute of both, would be rejected, by the common consent of mankind, as utterly incapable of procuring any happiness to the individual or any public benefit to the world. But it was not in *this* world that the primitive Christians were desirous of making themselves either agreeable or useful.

The Primitive Christians Condemn Pleasure and Luxury. The acquisition of knowledge, the exercise of our reason or fancy, and the cheerful flow of unguarded conversation may employ the leisure of a liberal mind. Such amusements, however, were rejected with abhorrence, or admitted with the utmost caution by the severity of the fathers, who despised all knowledge that was not useful to salvation, and who considered all levity of discourse as a criminal abuse of the gift of speech. In our present state of existence the body is so inseparably connected with the soul that it seems to be our interest to taste, with innocence and moderation, the enjoyments of which that faithful companion is susceptible. Very different was the reasoning of our devout predecessors: vainly aspiring to imitate the perfection of angels, they disdained, or they affected to disdain, every earthly and corporeal delight. Some of our senses, indeed, are necessary for our preservation, others for our subsistence, and others again for our information; and thus far it was impossible to reject the use of them. The first sensation of pleasure was marked as the first moment of their abuse. The unfeeling candidate for heaven was instructed, not only to resist the grosser allurements of the taste or smell, but even to shut his ears against the profane harmony of sounds, and to view with indifference the most finished productions of human art. Gay apparel, magnificent houses, and elegant furniture were supposed to unite the double guilt of pride and of sensuality. A simple and mortified appearance was more suitable to the Christian, who was certain of his sins and doubtful of his salvation. In their censures of luxury the fathers are extremely minute and circumstantial; and among the various articles which excite their pious indignation we may enumerate false hair, garments of any color except white, instruments of music, vases of gold or silver, downy pillows (as Jacob reposed his head on a stone), white bread, foreign wines, public salutations, the use of warm baths, and the practice of shaving the beard, which, according to the expression of Tertullian, is a lie against our own faces and an impious attempt to improve the works of the Creator. When Christianity was introduced among the rich and the polite, the observation of these singular laws was left, as it would be at present, to the few who were ambitious of superior sanctity. But it is always easy as well as agreeable for the inferior ranks of mankind to claim a merit from the contempt of that pomp and pleasure which fortune has placed beyond their reach. The virtue of the primitive Christians, like that of the first Romans, was very frequently guarded by poverty and ignorance. . . .

V. The Fifth Cause: The Christians Active in the Government of the Church. But the human character, however it may be exalted or depressed by a temporary enthusiasm, will return by degrees to its proper and natural level, and will resume those passions that seem the most adapted to its present condition. The Primitive Christians were dead to the business and pleasures of the world; but their love of action, which could never be entirely extinguished, soon revived, and found a new occupation in the government of the Church. A separate society, which attacked the established religion of the empire, was obliged to adopt some form of internal policy, and to appoint a sufficient number of ministers, entrusted not only with the spiritual functions, but even with the temporal direction of the Christian commonwealth. . . .

The Dignity of Episcopal Government. The well-tempered mixture of liberality and rigor, the judicious dispensation of rewards and punishments, according to the maxims of policy as well as justice, constituted the *human* strength of the Church. The bishops, whose paternal care extended itself to the government of both worlds, were sensible of the importance of these prerogatives; and, covering their ambition with the fair pretense of the love of order, they were jealous of any rival in the exercise of a discipline so necessary to prevent the desertion of those troops which had enlisted themselves under the banner of the Cross, and whose numbers every day became more considerable. From the imperious declamations of Cyprian, we should naturally conclude that the doctrines of excommunication and penance formed the most essential part of religion; and that it was much less dangerous for the disciples of Christ to neglect the observance of the moral duties than to despise the censures and authority of their bishops. Sometimes we might imagine that we were listening to the voice of Moses when he commanded the earth to open and to swallow up, in consuming flames, the rebellious race which refused obedience to the priesthood of Aaron; and we should sometimes suppose that we heard a Roman consul asserting the majesty of the republic, and declaring his inflexible resolution to enforce the rigor of the laws. "If such irregularities are suffered with impunity" (it is thus that the Bishop of Carthage chides the lenity of his colleague)—"if such irregularities are suffered, there is an end of EPISCOPAL VIGOR; an end of the sublime and divine power of governing the Church; an end of Christianity itself." Cyprian had renounced those temporal honors which it is probable he would never have obtained; but the acquisition of such absolute command over the consciences and understanding of a congregation, however obscure or despised by the world, is more truly grateful to the pride of the human heart than the possession of the most despotic power imposed by arms and conquest on a reluctant people.

Recapitulation of the Five Causes. In the course of this important, though perhaps tedious inquiry, I have attempted to display the secondary causes which so efficaciously assisted the truth of the Christian religion. If among these causes we have discovered any artificial ornaments, any accidental circumstances, or any mixture of error and passion, it cannot appear surprising that mankind should be the most sensibly affected by such motives as were suited to their imperfect nature. It was by the aid of these causes—exclusive zeal, the immediate expectation of another world, the claim of miracles, the practice of rigid virtue, and the constitution of the primitive Church—that Christianity spread itself with so much success in the Roman empire. To the first of these the Christians were indebted for their invincible valor, which disdained to capitulate with the enemy whom they were resolved to vanquish. The three succeeding causes supplied their valor with the most formidable arms. The last of these causes united their courage, directed their arms, and gave their efforts that irresistible weight which even a small band of well-trained and intrepid volunteers has so often possessed over an undisciplined multitude ignorant of the subject and careless of the event of the war.

Weakness of Polytheism.   In the various religions of polytheism, some wandering fanatics of Egypt and Syria, who addressed themselves to the credulous superstition of the populace, were perhaps the only order of priests that derived their whole support and credit from their sacerdotal profession, and were very deeply affected by a personal concern for the safety or prosperity of their tutelar deities. The ministers of polytheism, both in Rome and in the provinces, were, for the most part, men of a noble birth and of an affluent fortune, who received, as an honorable distinction, the care of a celebrated temple or of a public sacrifice, exhibited (very frequently at their own expense) the sacred games, and with cold indifference performed the ancient rites according to the laws and fashion of their country. As they were engaged in the ordinary occupations of life, their zeal and devotion were seldom animated by a sense of interest, or by the habits of an ecclesiastical character. Confined to their respective temples and cities, they remained without any connection of discipline or government; and whilst they acknowledged the supreme jurisdiction of the senate, of the college of pontiffs, and of the emperor, those civil magistrates contented themselves with the easy task of maintaining in peace and dignity the general worship of mankind. We have already seen how various, how loose, and how uncertain were the religious sentiments of polytheists. They were abandoned, almost without control, to the natural workings of a superstitious fancy. The accidental circumstances of their life and situation determined the object, as well as the degree, of their devotion; and as long as their adoration was successively prostituted to a thousand deities, it was scarcely possible that their hearts could be susceptible of a very sincere or lively passion for any of them.

The Skepticism of the Pagan World Proved Favorable to the New Religion.   When Christianity appeared in the world, even these faint and imperfect impressions had lost much of their original power. Human reason, which by its unassisted strength is incapable of perceiving the mysteries of faith, had already obtained an easy triumph over the folly of paganism; and when Tertullian and Lactantius employ their labors in exposing its falsehood and extravagance, they are obliged to transcribe the eloquence of Cicero or the wit of Lucian. The contagion of these skeptical writings had been diffused far beyond the number of their readers. The fashion of incredulity was communicated from the philosopher to the man of pleasure or business, from the noble to the plebeian, and from the master to the menial slave who waited at his table, and who eagerly listened to the freedom of his conversation. On public occasions the philosophic part of mankind affected to treat with respect and decency the religious institutions of their country, but their secret contempt penetrated through the thin and awkward disguise; and even the people, when they discovered that their deities were rejected and derided by those whose rank or understanding they were accustomed to reverence, were filled with doubts and apprehensions concerning the truth of those doctrines to which they had yielded the most implicit belief. The decline of ancient prejudice exposed a very numerous portion of humankind to the danger of a painful and comfortless situation. A state of skepticism and suspense may amuse a few inquisitive minds. But the practice of superstition is so congenial to the multitude that, if they are forcibly awakened, they still regret the loss of their pleasing vision. Their love of the marvelous and supernatural, their curiosity with regard to future events, and their strong propensity to extend their hopes and fears beyond the limits of the visible world, were the principal causes which favored the establishment of polytheism. So urgent on the vulgar is the necessity of believing, that the fall of any system of mythology will most probably be succeeded by the introduction of some other mode of superstition. Some deities of a more recent and fashionable cast might soon have occupied the deserted temples of Jupiter and Apollo, if, in the decisive moment, the wisdom of Providence had not interposed a genuine revelation fitted to inspire the most rational esteem and conviction, whilst, at the same time, it was adorned with all that could attract the curiosity, the wonder, and the veneration of the people. In their actual disposition, as many were almost disengaged from their artificial prejudices, but equally susceptible and desirous of a devout attachment, an object much less deserving would have been sufficient to fill the vacant place in their hearts and to gratify the uncertain eagerness of their passions. Those who are inclined to pursue this reflection, instead of viewing with astonishment the rapid progress of Christianity, will perhaps be surprised that its success was not still more rapid and still more universal. . . .

General Proportion of Christians and Pagans. From [a] survey of the progress of Christianity, it may perhaps seem probable that the number of its proselytes has been excessively magnified by fear, on the one side, and by devotion on the other. According to the irreproachable testimony of Origen, the proportion of the faithful was very inconsiderable when compared with the multitude of an unbelieving world; but, as we are left without any distinct information, it is impossible to determine, and it is difficult even to conjecture, the real numbers of the primitive Christians. The most favorable calculation, however, that can be deduced from the examples of Antioch and of Rome will not permit us to imagine that more than a twentieth part of the subjects of the empire had enlisted themselves under the banner of the Cross before the important conversion of Constantine. But their habits of faith, of zeal, and of union seemed to multiply their numbers; and the same causes which contributed to their future increase served to render their actual strength more apparent and more formidable.

Whether the First Christians Were Mean and Ignorant. Such is the constitution of civil society that, whilst a few persons are distinguished by

riches, by honors, and by knowledge, the body of the people is condemned
to obscurity, ignorance, and poverty. The Christian religion, which addressed itself to the whole human race, must consequently collect a far
greater number of proselytes from the lower than from the superior ranks
of life. This innocent and natural circumstance has been improved into a
very odious imputation, which seems to be less strenuously denied by the
apologists than it is urged by the adversaries of the faith; that the new sect
of Christians was almost entirely composed of the dregs of the populace,
of peasants and mechanics, of boys and women, of beggars and slaves, the
last of whom might sometimes introduce the missionaries into the rich and
noble families to which they belonged. These obscure teachers (such was
the charge of malice and infidelity) are as mute in public as they are loqua-
cious and dogmatical in private. Whilst they cautiously avoid the dangerous
encounter of philosophers, they mingle with the rude and illiterate crowd,
and insinuate themselves into those minds whom their age, their sex, or
their education has the best disposed to receive the impression of superstitious terrors.

Some Exceptions with Regard to Learning. This unfavorable picture,
though not devoid of a faint resemblance, betrays, by its dark coloring and
distorted features, the pencil of an enemy. As the humble faith of Christ
diffused itself through the world, it was embraced by several persons who
derived some consequence from the advantages of nature or fortune.
Aristides, who presented an eloquent apology to the Emperor Hadrian, was
an Athenian philosopher. Justin Martyr had sought divine knowledge in
the schools of Zeno, of Aristotle, of Pythagoras, and of Plato, before he
fortunately was accosted by the old man, or rather the angel, who turned
his attention to the study of the Jewish prophets. Clemens of Alexandria
had acquired much various reading in the Greek, and Tertullian in the
Latin language. Julius Africanus and Origen possessed a very considerable
share of the learning of their times; and although the style of Cyprian is
very different from that of Lactantius, we might also discover that both
those writers had been public teachers of rhetoric. Even the study of philosophy was at length introduced among the Christians, but it was not
always productive of the most salutary effects; knowledge was as often the
parent of heresy as of devotion, and the description which was designed
for the followers of Artemon may, with equal propriety, be applied to the
various sects that resisted the successors of the apostles: "They presume to
alter the Holy Scriptures, to abandon the ancient rule of faith, and to form
their opinions according to the subtle precepts of logic. The science of the
Church is neglected for the study of geometry, and they lose sight of heaven
while they are employed in measuring the earth. Euclid is perpetually in
their hands. Aristotle and Theophrastus are the objects of their admiration;
and they express an uncommon reverence for the works of Galen. Their
errors are derived from the abuse of the arts and sciences of the infidels,

and they corrupt the simplicity of the Gospel by the refinements of human reason."

With Regard to Rank and Fortune. Nor can it be affirmed with truth that the advantages of birth and fortune were always separated from the profession of Christianity. Several Roman citizens were brought before the tribunal of Pliny, and he soon discovered that a great number of persons of *every order* of men in Bithynia had deserted the religion of their ancestors. His unsuspected testimony may, in this instance, obtain more credit than the bold challenge of Tertullian, when he addresses himself to the fears as well as to the humanity of the Proconsul of Africa by assuring him that if he persists in his cruel intentions he must decimate Carthage, and that he will find among the guilty many persons of his own rank, senators and matrons of noblest extraction, and the friends or relations of his most intimate friends. It appears, however, that about forty years afterwards the Emperor Valerian was persuaded of the truth of this assertion, since in one of his rescripts he evidently supposes that senators, Roman knights, and ladies of quality were engaged in the Christian sect. The Church still continued to increase its outward splendor as it lost its internal purity; and, in the reign of Diocletian, the palace, the courts of justice, and even the army, concealed a multitude of Christians who endeavored to reconcile the interests of the present with those of a future life.

Christianity Most Favorably Received by the Poor and Simple. And yet these exceptions are either too few in number or too recent in time entirely to remove the imputation of ignorance and obscurity which has been so arrogantly cast on the first proselytes of Christianity. Instead of employing in our defense the fictions of later ages, it will be more prudent to convert the occasion of scandal into a subject of edification. Our serious thoughts will suggest to us that the apostles themselves were chosen by Providence among the fishermen of Galilee; and that the lower we depress the temporal condition of the first Christians, the more reason we shall find to admire their merit and success. It is incumbent on us diligently to remember that the kingdom of heaven was promised to the poor in spirit, and that minds afflicted by calamity and the contempt of mankind cheerfully listen to the divine promise of future happiness; while, on the contrary, the fortunate are satisfied with the possession of this world, and the wise abuse in doubt and dispute their vain superiority of reason and knowledge.

Rejected by Some Eminent Men of the First and Second Centuries. We stand in need of such reflections to comfort us for the loss of some illustrious characters, which in our eyes might have seemed the most worthy of the heavenly present. The names of Seneca, of the elder and the younger Pliny, of Tacitus, of Plutarch, of Galen, of the slave Epictetus, and of the Emperor Marcus Antoninus adorn the age in which they flourished, and exalt the dignity of human nature. They filled with glory their respective stations, either in active or contemplative life; their excellent understandings were improved by study philosophy had purified their minds from the prejudices of the popular superstition; and their days were spent in the pursuit of truth and the practice of virtue. Yet all these sages (it is no less an object of surprise than of concern) overlooked or rejected the perfection of the Christian system. Their language or their silence equally discovers their contempt for the growing sect which in their time had diffused itself over the Roman empire. Those among them who condescend to mention the Christians consider them only as obstinate and perverse enthusiasts, who exacted an implicit submission to their mysterious doctrines, without being able to produce a single argument that could engage the attention of men of sense and learning.

Their Neglect of Prophecy. It is at least doubtful whether any of these philosophers perused the apologies which the primitive Christians repeatedly published in behalf of themselves and of their religion; but it is much to be lamented that such a cause was not defended by abler advocates. They expose with superfluous wit and eloquence the extravagance of polytheism. They interest our compassion by displaying the innocence and sufferings of their injured brethren. But when they would demonstrate the divine origin of Christianity, they insist much more strongly on the predictions which announced than on the miracles which accompanied the appearance of the Messiah. Their favorite argument might serve to edify a Christian or to convert a Jew, since both the one and the other acknowledge the authority of those prophecies, and both are obliged, with devout reverence, to search for their sense and their accomplishment. But this mode of persuasion loses much of its weight and influence when it is addressed to those who neither understand nor respect the Mosaic dispensation and the prophetic style. In the unskillful hands of Justin and of the succeeding apologists, the sublime meaning of the Hebrew oracles evaporates in distant types, affected conceits, and cold allegories; and even their authenticity was rendered suspicious to an unenlightened Gentile by the mixture of pious forgeries which, under the names of Orpheus, Hermes, and the Sibyls, were obtruded on him as of equal value with the genuine inspirations of Heaven. The adoption of fraud and sophistry in the defense of revelation too often reminds us of the injudicious conduct of those poets who load their *invulnerable* heroes with a useless weight of cumbersome and brittle armor.

And of Miracles. But how shall we excuse the supine inattention of the pagan and philosophic world to those evidences which were presented by the hand of Omnipotence, not to their reason, but to their senses? During the age of Christ, of his apostles, and of their first disciples, the doctrine which they preached was confirmed by innumerable prodigies. The lame walked, the blind saw, the sick were healed, the dead were raised, demons were expelled, and the laws of nature were frequently suspended for the benefit of the Church. But the sages of Greece and Rome turned aside from the awful spectacle, and, pursuing the ordinary occupations of life and study, appeared unconscious of any alterations in the moral or physical government of the world. Under the reign of Tiberius, the whole earth, or at least a celebrated province of the Roman empire, was involved in a preternatural darkness of three hours. Even this miraculous event, which ought to have excited the wonder, the curiosity, and the devotion of mankind, passed without notice in an age of science and history. It happened during the lifetime of Seneca and the elder Pliny, who must have experienced the immediate effects, or received the earliest intelligence, of the prodigy. Each of these philosophers, in a laborious work, has recorded all the great phenomena of nature—earthquakes, meteors, comets, and eclipses—which his indefatigable curiosity could collect. Both the one and the other have omitted to mention the greatest phenomenon to which the mortal eye has been witness since the creation of the globe. A distinct chapter of Pliny is designed for eclipses of an extraordinary nature and unusual duration; but he contents himself with describing the singular defect of light which followed the murder of Caesar, when, during the greatest part of a year, the orb of the sun appeared pale and without splendor. This season of obscurity, which cannot surely be compared with the preternatural darkness of the Passion, had been already celebrated by most of the poets and historians of that memorable age.

INDEX